ALL NEW MERRILL PHYSICAL SCIENCE

MERRILL PHYSICAL SCIENCE

REACHES STUDENTS THROUGH

REAL LIFE APPLICATIONS!

An Educational Program from
GLENCOE

Students experience the principles of physical science each and every day. The simple act of walking involves gravity, which holds them to Earth, friction between the soles of their shoes and ground, which enables them to overcome inertia, accelerate forward, make turns, and even stop. The all new **Merrill Physical Science** makes students aware that everything they see, hear, touch, and smell involves physical science principles.

The **Merrill Physical Science** comprehensive learning and teaching program makes the study of physical science an **active learning experience.** Your students will learn through:

- **Solid concept development,** thematically structured to focus on the principle ideas of physical science.
- **Hands-on activities** that actively involve students in the subject matter.
- **Strong skill development** which leads to success in science and the real world.
- **Fascinating, real-world applications** that will make the study of physical science come alive in your classroom.

As for teacher's classroom support, the new **Merrill Physical Science** provides a wealth of resource materials in the **Teacher Wraparound Edition** and **Teacher Resource Package.** Teaching suggestions, background information, reinforcement activities, and extension activities are just a few of the valuable tools we provide to help enrich your program and reduce your preparation time.

STUDENTS LEARN TO APPLY...
THEN APPLY TO LEARN MORE!

The all new **Merrill Physical Science** takes learning one step further. Our program offers a variety of thought-provoking, hands-on activities that do wonders to enhance understanding. Once your students read how physical science principles relate to daily life, they are encouraged to apply what they have learned through relevant hands-on activities, making observations, and asking questions. Students will achieve maximum understanding and build important skills needed to become responsible decision makers and critical thinkers in our society.

Two full-page **Activity** features, in each chapter, give your students opportunities to learn by doing. Each encourages the use of scientific methods of investigation.

ACTIVITY 15-2
Boiling Points of Solutions

Problem: How is boiling point affected by the addition of a solute?

Materials

- 400 mL distilled water
- thermometer
- ring stand
- 12 g table salt, NaCl
- laboratory burner
- 250-mL beaker

Procedure

1. Copy the data table and use it to record your observations.
2. Bring 100 mL of distilled water in a 250-mL beaker to a gentle boil. Record the temperature.
3. Dissolve 12 g of NaCl in 100 mL of distilled water. Bring this solution to a gentle boil and record its boiling point. **CAUTION:** Always keep the thermometer away from the flame.
4. Repeat Step 2, using 24 g of NaCl.
5. Repeat Step 2 again, using 36 g of NaCl.
6. Plot your results on a graph that shows boiling point on the vertical axis and g of NaCl on the horizontal axis.

Data and Observations

Grams of NaCl Solute	Boiling Point (°C)
0	
12	
24	
36	

Analyze

1. What difference is there between the boiling point of a pure solvent and a solution?
2. Instead of doubling the amount of NaCl in Step 4, what would have been the effect of doubling the amount of water?
3. What would be the result of using tap water instead of distilled water?

Conclude and Apply

4. In cooking, why would adding salt to water cause some foods to cook faster?
5. If you continued to add more salt, would your graph would continue in the same pattern or level off? Explain your prediction.

398 SOLUTIONS

The clothes you wear can make you feel warmer or cooler. They affect the amount of thermal energy that reaches and leaves your body. How else can the movement of thermal energy be affected?

FIND OUT!

Do this simple activity to find out how you can affect the movement of thermal energy.

Turn on a lamp with a bare light bulb. *Being careful not to touch the bulb,* put your hand near it. Do you feel warm from the bulb? How is thermal energy getting to your hand? What happens if you move your hand nearer to the bulb or farther away? What happens if you put a book between your hand and the lamp? Suppose you use only a piece of paper instead of a whole book. Find some other things that you can put between your hand and the light bulb. Do some seem to block heat better than others? Feel the objects after they've been near the light bulb. Do some feel warmer than others? How can you explain the differences?

Gearing Up
Previewing this Chapter
Use this outline to help you focus on important ideas in this chapter.

Section 6-1 Moving Thermal Energy
- Conduction
- Convection
- Radiation
- Reducing Movement of Thermal Energy

Section 6-2 Heating Systems
- Conventional Heating Systems
- Solar Heating

Section 6-3 Science and Society
Thermal Pollution
- Not So Hot!

Section 6-4 Using Heat to Do Work
- Heat Engines
- Heat Movers

Previewing Science Skills
- In the Skill Builders, you will use variables, constants, and controls, make and use tables, and map concepts.
- In the Activities, you will observe, collect and organize data, sequence, analyze, and infer.
- In the MINI-Lab, you will observe and hypothesize.

What's next?

You have discovered that you can exert some control over the movement of thermal energy. Now you will learn about how thermal energy moves and how that movement can be put to useful purposes.

133

132

MINI-Lab
How can a graph help you observe change?

Place a thermometer in a plastic foam cup of hot water. Measure and record the temperature every 30 seconds for 5 minutes. Make a line graph of the changing temperature showing time on the x-axis and temperature on the y-axis. Repeat the experiment, starting with freshly heated water. This time, cover the cup with a plastic lid. Plot the curve on the same grid as before. List all the information this graph tells you about the two cups.

Chapter Openers offer fun, interesting ways to get your students excited about the upcoming lesson.
- A unique **Find Out** activity entices students to make observations and raise questions about upcoming content.
- **Gearing Up** previews key concepts and skills.
- **What's Next** provides an intriguing transition into the chapter's main ideas.

Mini-Labs are quick hands-on activities that give your students additional opportunities to practice important process skills. Great for in-class instruction or take-home exercises.

The Packet of Mystery Crystals

When a new video cassette recorder (VCR) was delivered to Peter's home, he was eager to start using it to tape programs. So he asked for and got the job of unpacking the VCR. When he lifted the instrument from the carton, a small flat packet fell out. A label on the packet read "Contains silica gel. Do not eat."

Peter was curious about the contents of the packet, so he looked up "silica gel" in a reference book. There he read that silica gel is the anhydrous form of silica, a mineral that consists mainly of silicon(IV) oxide, SiO_2.

Think Critically: What would silica gel do if water molecules were in the air? Why was the packet of silica gel placed in the carton with the VCR?

SECTION REVIEW

1. Name the following: NaI, FeI_2, K_2SO_4, NH_4Br.
2. Write formulas for compounds composed of (a) lithium and sulfur, (b) calcium and the acetate ion, and (c) barium and oxygen.
3. Write formulas for the following: (a) the anhydrous form of $CoCl_2 \cdot 6H_2O$ and (b) calcium sulfate dihydrate.
4. **Apply:** The label on a package of plant food lists potassium nitrate as one ingredient. What is the formula for this compound?

Skill Builder — ☐ Using Variables, Constants, and Controls

Design an experiment to distinguish between crystals that are hydrates and those that are not. Include crystals of iron(II) chloride, copper(I) nitrate, and crystals of sucrose. If you need help, refer to Using Variables, Constants, and Controls in the **Skill Handbook** on page 682.

Problem Solving features are real-life stories about kids. A critical thinking question engages the student in solving an everyday problem linked to the chapter content.

Flex Your Brain blends critical thinking and problem solving. Students use a step-by-step method to explore a topic while they learn to develop good problem solving skills.

---

at the screw, you'll see that the threads form a tiny "ramp" that runs around the screw from its tip to near its top.

Imagine you're driving a screw into a board. As you turn the screw, the threads seem to "pull" the screw into the wood. The wood slides through the wood. Actually, the plane slides through the wood.

A **wedge** is an inclined plane with one or two sloping sides. Chisels, knives, and axe blades are examples of wedges. A typical inclined plane, such as a ramp, stays in one place while materials move along its surface. With a wedge, the material remains in one place while the wedge moves through it.

Figure 7-11. The blade of the axe and the threads of the screw are special types of inclined planes.

While reading about the six types of simple machines, perhaps you've noticed that they are all variations of two basic machines—the lever and the inclined plane. As you go about your daily activities, look for examples of each type of simple machine. See if you can tell how each makes work easier.

SECTION REVIEW

1. Give one example of each kind of simple machine. Use examples different from the ones in the text.
2. Explain why the six kinds of simple machines are really variations on just two basic machines.
3. **Apply:** When would the friction of an inclined plane be useful?

Skill Builder — ☐ Making and Using Tables

Organize information about the six kinds of simple machines into a table. Include the type of machine, an example of each type, and a brief description of how it works. You may include other information if you wish. If you need help, refer to Making and Using Tables in the **Skill Handbook** on page 686.

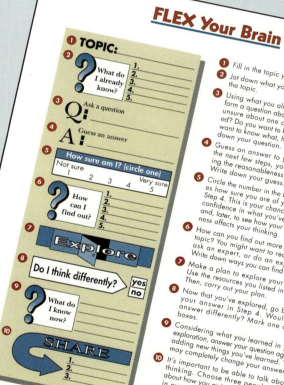

FLEX Your Brain

① TOPIC:

② ❓ What do I already know?
1.
2.
3.
4.
5.

③ Q: Ask a question

④ A: Guess an answer

⑤ How sure am I? (circle one)
Not sure 1 2 3 4 5 Very sure

⑥ ❓ How can I find out?
1.
2.
3.
4.
5.

⑦ Explore

⑧ Do I think differently? yes / no

⑨ ❓ What do I know now?

⑩ SHARE
1.
2.
3.

① Fill in the topic your teacher gives you.

② Jot down what you already know about the topic.

③ Using what you already know (Step 2), form a question about the topic. Are you unsure about one of the items you listed? Do you want to know more? Do you want to know what, how, or why? Write down your question.

④ Guess an answer to your question. In the next few steps, you will be exploring the reasonableness of your answer. Write down your guess.

⑤ Circle the number in the box that matches how sure you are of your answer in Step 4. This is your chance to rate your confidence in what you've done so far and, later, to see how your level of sureness affects your thinking.

⑥ How can you find out more about your topic? You might want to read a book, ask an expert, or do an experiment. Write down ways you can find out more.

⑦ Make a plan to explore your answer. Use the resources you listed in Step 6. Then, carry out your plan.

⑧ Now that you've explored, go back to your answer in Step 4. Would you answer differently? Mark one of the boxes.

⑨ Considering what you learned in your exploration, answer your question again, adding new things you've learned. You may completely change your answer.

⑩ It's important to be able to talk about thinking. Choose three people to tell about how you arrived at your response in every step. For example, don't just read what you wrote down in Step 2. Try to share how you thought of those things.

A **Skill Builder,** at the end of each section, challenges students to use basic process skills. The activity also directs the students to the **Skill Handbook,** located at the back of the text, for a step-by-step overview on how to accomplish that particular skill.

To recognize and prevent pollution. To understand machinery. To become a broadcast engineer or computer programmer. The all new **Merrill Physical Science** contains a variety of special features to give students an appreciation of physical science and the variety of ways it impacts people and places around the world. Everyday applications are what make physical science real. And they are what make the all new **Merrill Physical Science** more enriching than any other physical science program currently available.

EcoTip

Instead of using poisonous chemical sprays, chase away insect pests by planting chrysanthemums near your doorways or in your garden.

Ecotips enhance students' environmental awareness by suggesting simple changes in their own behavior that can have positive effects on the environment.

Two **Careers** are featured in every unit to expose students to the interesting and wide range of career choices available for those with a knowledge of science.

UNIT 1
GLOBAL CONNECTIONS

Physical Science Basics
In this unit, you studied the nature of science and physical science methods. Now find out how the nature and methods of physical science are connected to other subjects and places around the world.

CHEMISTRY
BURNING A DIAMOND
Paris, France
In 1772, Antoine Lavoisier placed a diamond in a closed vessel and focused sunlight on it with a magnifying glass. When it grew hot enough, the diamond disappeared and carbon dioxide appeared in the vessel. Lavoisier concluded that a diamond was made of carbon and was thus chemically related to coal. How did Lavoisier's experiment use the scientific method?

ART
ZAPPING ARTWORK CLEAN
Venice, Italy
How do you clean corrosion from ancient statues without destroying them? John Asmus zaps them with a laser. The laser quickly vaporizes the black crust of calcium sulfate caused by air pollution without harming the marble underneath. His lasers have also been used to clean tapestries and remove coffee stains from ancient parchment. Find out about other methods used to clean artwork.

PHYSICS
ROBOT CLEANUP CREW
Cambridge, Massachusetts
Two robots small enough to crawl through a 15-centimeter duct have been designed. They can go into a nuclear generator to inspect machinery and pick up nuclear litter. What problem will these robots help solve in nuclear power plants?

GEOGRAPHY
THE SLIDING ROOF
Washington, D.C.
The National Cathedral was built to be like the cathedrals in England, including its lead roof. When the National Cathedral was only a few years old, it was discovered that the lead roof was flowing downward, a problem not encountered in England. What did the geographic location, particularly the latitude of Washington, have to do with the

HISTORY
HOW BIG IS EARTH?
Alexandria, Egypt
Around 240 B.C., Eratosthenes found a way to measure the circumference of Earth. He used the positions of the sun at summer solstice at Alexandria and Syrene and the distance between the two cities to calculate a circumference equal to 40 000 kilometers. Find out how accurate he was.

53

SCIENCE & ART

Earthships: Environmental Architecture

The passage that follows describes a house design that solves a number of environmental problems.

Architecture is the art and profession of designing buildings. Architecture is one of the oldest art forms and dates from prehistoric times. It has been said that a society's architecture reflects the values and ideals of its people.

In that context, environmental architecture reflects the growing concern of people for the future of planet Earth with its fragile ecology and disappearing resources. Architect Michael Reynolds' concern for the environment led him to design houses he calls "Earthships."

Reynolds' earthships help solve a number of environmental problems simultaneously. First, they use discarded tires as building materials. The Environmental Protection Agency says that tires are discarded at a rate of 240 million per year in the United States. The interior and exterior walls of the earthships are constructed of tires filled with dirt and laid like concrete blocks. The walls are then covered with a coat of plaster or adobe.

Using tires provides a house with walls that are about one meter thick and gives it a very large mass. Because of this "thermal mass," the house utilizes little or no energy for cooling and heating. The base of the house is built below the frost line, meaning that the temperature of the walls will stay

at approximately the temperature of Earth below that point — about 15°C. If a house gets no sun at all, but has this amount of mass, it will never get below 15°C.

Earthships in the Southwest have been built in the mountains where temperatures reach −34° in winter and +38° in summer. These houses are able to maintain a temperature that varies only a few degrees year round with no energy used for heating or cooling. Asked if earthships would work anywhere in the country, Reynolds said yes—even if you put them where there is no sun and you are heating with gas, you will reduce your heating costs by 90 percent.

Some earthships also generate their own electricity with solar panels mounted on the roof. They also are able to grow food year round in the greenhouse that Reynolds incorporated in the earthship design. Even the design of the plumbing system was given environmental consideration. "Black water" from toilets goes into a septic system, but "gray water" from sinks, bathtubs, and the washing machine goes into holding tanks to be used in greenhouse irrigation.

Reynolds stresses that earthships are easy and comparatively inexpensive to build. But more importantly, he said, these are buildings that take care of people. That is why he calls them earthships.

In Your Own Words
► Would you like to live in an earthship? Write an essay explaining why or why not.

669

Global Connections, at the end of every unit, relate the concepts studied in the unit to other subjects and events around the world. Each vignette raises important questions for further study in such areas as history, oceanography, astronomy, and biology.

The natural world has inspired artists, authors, sculptors, and musicians to express their creativity. **Science and Literature** and **Science and Art** features promote students' appreciation of the value and importance of science to the humanities.

STRATEGIES AND RESOURCES
ARE RIGHT AT YOUR FINGERTIPS

*As a teacher, you will thoroughly enjoy all the valuable information **Merrill Physical Science** provides in our **Teacher Wraparound Edition.** Everything is well organized, highly visible and positioned, at the point of instruction, to give you the most teaching value.*

The **Three-Step Teaching Cycle** includes **Motivate, Teach,** and **Close.** It provides various strategies for developing your individual lesson plans plus highlights optional activities and program resources for enhancing your presentation.

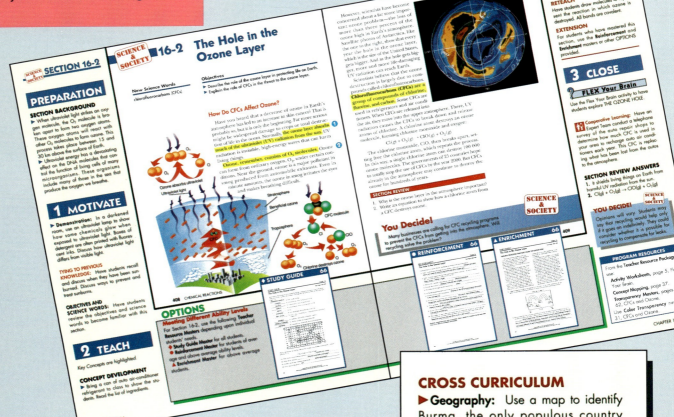

Preceding each chapter is a two-page **Planning Guide** which gives you quick access to chapter content, features, activities, skill exercises, and all other program components.

CROSS CURRICULUM

▶ **Geography:** Use a map to identify Burma, the only populous country besides the United States that does not use the metric system.

Cross Curriculum strategies provide unique ways to connect physical science to other sciences and other disciplines such as math, reading, writing, fine arts, and health.

Student masters, designed to help you address different learning abilities, are shown in reduced form in the bottom margins. They include **Study Guide** worksheets, a great review for those students who need a little extra help; **Reinforcement** worksheets, ideal for enhancing student understanding of key concepts; and **Enrichment** worksheets, the best way to challenge your above average students.

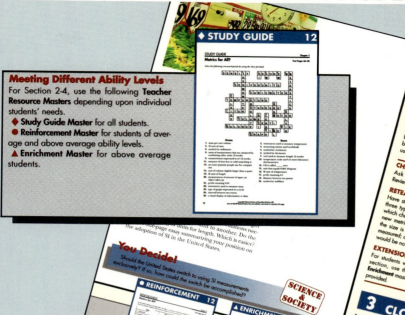

Multicultural Awareness puts students in touch with a medley of events and people from around the world and their contributions to the advancement of physical science.

Multicultural Awareness

Pickling, a process of food preservation that depends upon the chemical process of fermentation and the prohibition of bacterial growth in a highly acidic solution, is found in the cuisine of many cultures. Have students research different pickling processes and prepare lists of how and what products are pickled in different cultures. You may want to enlist the aid of the cafeteria director to assemble pickled foods from various cultures for a tasting.

For Your Gifted and Talented Students and **For Your Mainstream Students** provide activity-based suggestions that reinforce chapter content. These features stimulate critical thinking, and/or tie together current material with previous chapter content.

OPTIONS

For Your Gifted Students

▶ Have students research the speeds of light and sound in different media, make a bar graph for each, and make a hypothesis about how the density of matter affects both light and sound.

▶ Have students determine the ratio of the speed of light and the speed of sound in air at a specific temperature.

For Your Mainstreamed Students

▶ Have students make a crossword puzzle or word search from the key science words found at the end of the chapter. Clues for the puzzle can be definitions or descriptions of those words found in the chapter. Students could also make flash cards. On one side they can place the word and on the other side the definition. They can quiz each other using the cards.

▶ Special effort should be made to have mainstreamed students perform or assist in Activity 17-2. Some students could carry out their own titrations of vinegar, lemon juice, and orange juice to compare the acidity with that of carbonated beverages. Mainstreamed students might like to perform the suggested extension of this activity in which they compare the acidity of different brands and types of beverages.

A FULL RANGE OF SUPPORT MATERIALS

When you purchase the **Merrill Physical Science** program, you'll get everything you have come to expect in support materials plus a whole lot more! Not only do you receive a **Teacher Classroom Resources** that contains 13 exciting theme booklets, you have the opportunity to purchase a variety of additional resources sure to motivate your students and further enliven their learning experience.

Teacher Resource Guide contains a program planning guide, lab design and equipment, safety instruction, a media worksheet, and a Flex Your Brain worksheet in one convenient booklet.

Activity Worksheets include worksheets for every Mini-Lab and full-page Activity in the chapters.

Study Guide Worksheets are tailored to the needs of students who need a little extra help. They reinforce understanding of the topics and vocabulary found in each chapter.

Reinforcement Worksheets provide a variety of interesting activities to help students of average ability levels retain the important points in every chapter.

Enrichment Worksheets challenge your students of above average ability to design, interpret, and research scientific topics based on the text in each lesson.

Critical Thinking/Problem Solving helps your students develop important critical thinking and problem solving skills as they work through additional problems related to chapter topics.

Concept Mapping masters reinforce learning by having students complete a concept map for each chapter.

Cross-Curriculum Connections are interdisciplinary worksheets. They emphasize learning by doing and provide valuable insight into the connection physical science has with other disciplines.

Science And Society worksheets encourage further involvement with Science and Society lessons in the student text.

Technology masters explore recent developments in science and technology or explain how familiar machines, tools, or systems work.

Transparency Masters include blackline reproductions and student worksheets for each of the program's full-color transparencies.

Chapter Review masters are two-page review worksheets consisting of 25 questions for each chapter. Ideal for test preparation, alternative test, and vocabulary review.

Chapter Test Masters provide comprehensive tests for each chapter.

ADDITIONAL RESOURCES GIVE YOU CONVENIENT WAYS TO PROMOTE GREATER UNDERSTANDING

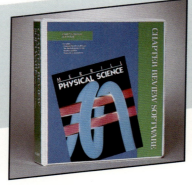

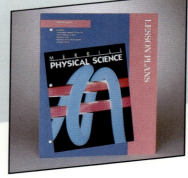

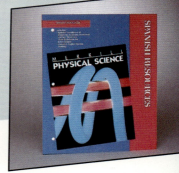

Lab Partner is a spreadsheet program that allows you and your students to record, collect, and graph data from laboratory activities. A user guide is also available to assist students through the programs.

Chapter Review Software presents chapter-end review questions in random order and provides feedback, for incorrectly answered questions, by noting the textbook page where the answer is found.

Lesson Plan Book is a complete lesson planning resource for teachers. It is a correlation of lessons, objectives, features, and program resources.

Spanish Resources provides Spanish translations of chapter objectives, glossary terms, and definitions. Ideal for bilingual classrooms.

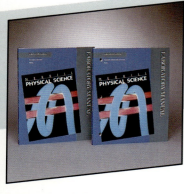

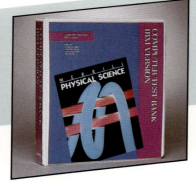

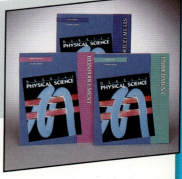

Laboratory Manual contains at least 2 hands-on laboratory activities for each chapter. Students get more chances to acquire scientific knowledge while you get more opportunities to reinforce and apply chapter concepts. A **Teacher Edition** provides suggestions for alternate materials, teaching tips, sample data, and answers to all student questions.

Computer Test Bank Package, available in Apple and IBM versions, provides a convenient tool for creating your own chapter test. The software allows you to add your own problems or edit the existing questions.

Color Transparency Package includes 50 full-color transparencies, some with overlays, in a three-ring binder with a resource book of blackline masters and student worksheets for each transparency. Excellent for direct instruction, reteaching, and review.

Study Guide, Reinforcement, and Enrichment workbooks provide activities for every ability level.

Videodisc Correlation Booklet uses a bar code reader to correlate the colorful diagrams, movie clips, and thousands of photographs, found in Optical Data's Videodiscs, with the pages in *Merrill Physical Science.* This booklet is available from your Glencoe representative. Videodiscs are available direct from Optical Data:

Physical Science Videodiscs
Optical Data Corporation
30 Technology Drive
P.O. Box 4919
Warren, NJ 07060

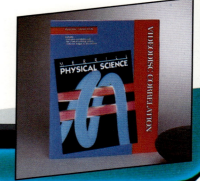

EDUCATION THROUGH APPLICATION...
THAT'S THE MERRILL
PHYSICAL SCIENCE DIFFERENCE

Student Edition	0-675-16776-0
Teacher Wraparound Edition	0-675-16777-9
Teacher Classroom Resources	
Activity Worksheets	0-675-16488-5
Chapter and Unit Tests	0-675-16498-2
Chapter Review	0-675-16497-4
Concept Mapping	0-675-16493-1
Critical Thinking/ Problem Solving	0-675-16492-3
Cross-Curriculum Connections	0-675-16494-X
Enrichment Worksheets	0-675-16491-5
Reinforcement Worksheets	0-675-16490-7
Science and Society	0-675-16495-8
Study Guide Worksheets	0-675-16489-3
Teacher Resource Guide	0-675-16784-1
Technology	0-675-16499-0
Transparency Masters	0-675-16496-6
Study Guide SE	0-675-16780-9
Reinforcement SE	0-675-16781-7
Enrichment SE	0-675-16796-5
Laboratory Manual SE	0-675-16778-7
Laboratory Manual TE	0-675-16779-5
Color Transparency Package	0-675-16785-X
Spanish Resources	0-675-16782-5
Lesson Plan Book	0-675-16804-X
Computer Test Bank (Apple)	0-675-16787-6
Computer Test Bank (IBM)	0-675-16789-2
Chapter Review Software (Apple)	0-675-16788-4
Chapter Review Software (IBM)	0-675-16790-6
Lab Partner Software Package (Apple)	0-675-02487-0
Lab Partner Software Package (IBM)	0-675-17271-3
Videodisc Correlation Booklet	0-675-16805-8

Optical Data Videodiscs:
Order Direct from
**Optical Data Corporation
30 Technology Drive
P.O. Box 4919
Warren, NJ 07060**

For more information contact your nearest regional office or call 1-800-334-7344.

1. Northeast Region
GLENCOE
17 Riverside Drive
Nashua, NH 03062
603-880-4701

2. Mid-Atlantic Region
GLENCOE
5 Terri Lane
Suite 5
Burlington, NJ 08016

3. Atlantic-Southeast Region
GLENCOE
Brookside Park
One Harbison Way, Suite 101
Columbia, SC 29212
803-732-2365

4. Southeast Region
GLENCOE
6510 Jimmy Carter Boulevard
Norcross, GA 30071
404-446-7493

5. Mid-America Region
GLENCOE
4635 Hilton Corporate Drive
Columbus, OH 43232
614-759-6600

6. Mid-Continent Region
GLENCOE
846 East Algonquin Road
Schaumburg, IL 60173
708-397-8448

7. Southwest Region
GLENCOE
320 Westway Place, Suite 550
Arlington, TX 76018
817-784-2100

8. Western Region
GLENCOE
610 East 42nd Street, #102
Boise, ID 83714
208-378-4002
Includes Alaska

9. California Region
GLENCOE
15319 Chatsworth Street
P. O. Box 9609
Mission Hills, CA 91346
818-898-1391

Canada
Maxwell Macmillan Ca
1200 Eglinton Avenue
Suite 200
Don Mills, Ontario M3
Telephone: 416-449-6
Telex: 069.59372
Telefax: 416-449-006

Overseas and Hawai
Macmillan/McGraw-H
International
866 Third Avenue
New York, NY 10022-
Telephone: 212-702-
Telex: 225925 MACM
Telefax: 212-605-937

**Glencoe Catholic
School Region**
GLENCOE
25 Crescent Street, 1
Stamford, CT 06906
203-964-9109

GLENCOE

MacMillan/McGraw-Hill
936 Eastwind Drive
Westerville, OH 43081

M E R R I L L

PHYSICAL SCIENCE

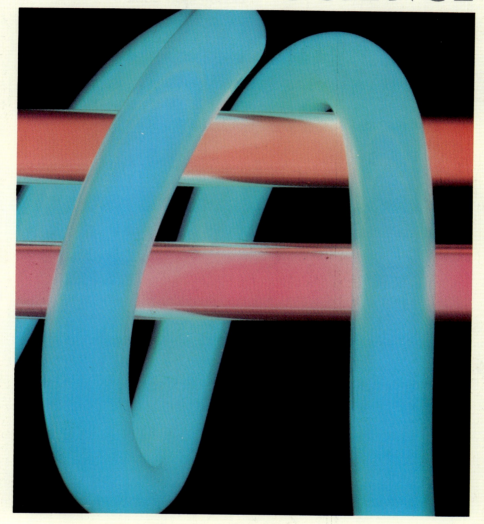

TEACHER WRAPAROUND EDITION

GLENCOE
Macmillan/McGraw-Hill

Lake Forest, Illinois   Columbus, Ohio   Mission Hills, California   Peoria, Illinois

MERRILL PHYSICAL SCIENCE

Student Edition
Teacher Wraparound Edition
Teacher Resource Package
Study Guide Student Edition
Reinforcement Student Edition
Enrichment Student Edition

Transparency Package
Laboratory Manual
Laboratory Manual, Teacher Annotated Edition
Spanish Resources
Chapter Review Software
Computer Test Bank
Videodisc Correlation
Lesson Plan Book

AUTHORS

Marilyn Thompson
Richard G. Smith
Jack T. Ballinger

Copyright 1993, by the Glencoe Division of Macmillan/McGraw-Hill Publishing Company.
Previously copyrighted by Merrill Publishing Company. All rights reserved. No part of this
book may be reproduced in any form electronic or mechanical, including photocopy,
recording, or any information storage retrieval system, without permission in writing from
the publisher.

Send all inquiries:
GLENCOE DIVISION
Macmillan/McGraw-Hill
936 Eastwind Drive
Westerville, Ohio 43081

ISBN 0-675-16776-0 (Student's Edition)
ISBN 0-675-16777-9 (Teacher's Edition)

Printed in the United States of America

2 3 4 5 6 7 8 9–VH–99 98 97 96 95 94 93 92

Table of Contents

Merrill Physical Science
Goals and Philosophy

Merrill Physical Science is designed to help students with a wide range of backgrounds and abilities to learn physical science.

Over the last several years there has been significant dialogue about reforming the science curriculum. Catalysts for the reform movement are the many recent reports that rank American students at or near the bottom in math and science performance when compared to other developed nations. Of the numerous reform-oriented proposals Project 2061: Science for All Americans (sponsored by AAAS) and Scope, Sequence, and Coordination (sponsored by National Science Teacher's Association) have attained national prominence.

These two projects suggest sweeping changes in what, when, and how science is taught. In response to the science curriculum reform movement, *Merrill Physical Science* presents solid, accurate content, a thematic orientation, hands-on activities that employ scientific thinking, science process skills methods of inquiry emphasis, and integration of science concepts across the curriculum.

Themes

The themes of science are broad, unifying ideas that integrate the major concepts of many disciplines. They are an important part of any teaching strategy because they help students see the importance of truly understanding concepts rather than simply memorizing isolated facts. Themes help students see connections between physical science and other science courses.

Merrill Physical Science is a study of matter and energy. The approach of this text emphasizes everyday applications of physical laws. As students progress through the course, they soon realize that most of the technological advances they have taken for granted are merely applications of basic physical science principles.

Several unifying themes pervade *Merrill Physical Science.* These themes serve as a conceptual framework for a physical science course and provide a rationale for the sequence of topics in the text. Major themes in the text are

- energy
- stability
- patterns of change
- scale and structure
- systems and interactions

Integration of Science Concepts Across the Curriculum

Because no subject or skill can be taught in isolation and subject areas naturally interweave and overlap, *Merrill Physical Science* connects science learning to many other disciplines.

Each of the seven units closes with a two-page Global Connections feature. Students see geographic connections to the content of the unit as well as five examples of connections to other disciplines. Each example with its geographic connection to physical science ends with an extension activity to engage students in the other disciplines. These features have a strong multicultural perspective.

Science and Literature and Science and Art features help students understand the value and importance of science to the arts. Science and Math, Science and Reading, and Science and Writing integrate physical science with those subjects. Ecotips relate chapter concepts to the environment; many Did You Know features offer historical connections.

Learning Science naturally develops interactive, cooperative group skills as students work in teams to complete activities. The implementation of cooperative learning in *Merrill Physical Science* is discussed on pages 26T to 29T.

Text Features

Chapter Opener

Each chapter opens with a striking full-page photograph illustrating a concept introduced in the chapter. The chapter introductory paragraph establishes a relationship between the photo and the chapter. **FIND OUT,** an inquiry activity, is featured at each chapter's beginning. Designed to give students an opportunity to make observations and raise questions about upcoming chapter content, these brief activities require few materials. **FIND OUT** provides a hands-on introduction to the chapter content. **Gearing Up,** an outline of the chapter sections, assists students in previewing the chapter and focusing on its most important ideas. **What's Next** leads students into the body of the chapter.

Teaching Sections

Each chapter is divided into three to five sections, with student objectives listed at the beginning of each. When appropriate, major sections are divided into subsections, making it easier for students to organize material and giving them better insight into the hierarchy of topics. **Objectives** provide the framework for the review questions, chapter review, review worksheets (in the *Teacher Resource Package*), and chapter tests. At the beginning of each section, **New Science Words** for that section are listed to help students preview the vocabulary words they will learn in that section.

Narrative Features

Presenting concepts in a comfortable, conversational style, this text is user friendly. Concepts are personalized and made relevant to students' lives with the use of familiar examples and analogies. To match the developmental and conceptual needs of the middle or junior high student, concepts are presented in logical order moving from the concrete to the abstract.

Special Text Features

Science and Society

Each chapter has a **Science and Society** section that shows the impact of society on current societal issues and problems. The impact of technology on the environment and economics is included, and some sections are controversial, but all provide facts on both sides of the issue discussed. Concluding each of these lessons is a **You Decide** feature that provides students an opportunity to practice critical thinking and problem-solving skills as they formulate opinions on the issue discussed.

Flex Your Brain

Flex Your Brain is a self-directed activity students use while investigating content areas. **Flex Your Brain** occurs as a one-page activity in Chapter 1 accompanying a text section discussing critical thinking and problem solving. The Teacher Resource Guide of the *Teacher Resource Package* provides a master with spaces for students to write their responses.

Flex Your Brain is a tool for developing problem-solving and critical thinking skills. It provides students with an opportunity to explore a topic in an organized, self-checking way and to discover how they arrived at their responses during each step of their investigation. It helps students to think about their own thinking and learn about thinking from their peers.

Technology

Technology features show "real-life" applications of the science concepts. Some topics are high-tech; some are low, but all are of high interest to students. A color photograph helps students visualize the application. *Think Critically* at the end of the feature provides for student involvement in real-life applications of science principles.

Problem Solving

Problem Solving features are stories about kids who are confronting a problem linked to the chapter content. The feature's real-life application question engages students in the solving of the problem.

Activities

Activities provide students with opportunities to learn by doing and to actively engage in learning concepts by using the scientific method. Each chapter has two full-page laboratory activities that can each be done in one laboratory period. Each **Activity** includes a problem statement, materials list, step-by-step procedures, and questions to help students review their observations, form hypotheses, draw conclusions, and apply what they've learned. The accompanying color illustrations either show the steps of the procedure or are used by the students in the **Activity.** Additional information about lab safety and equipment and supplies can be found in this Teacher Guide. A worksheet for each activity for recording data and answering questions is available in the Activities Worksheets book of the *Teacher Resource Package.*

Margin Features

MINI-Labs provide students with another opportunity to practice science process skills while using the scientific method. Observing scientific phenomena engages students in science content. **MINI-Labs** are hands-on activities that students can complete in a short amount of time. Required materials are easily accessible. A worksheet for reporting results and conclusions is in the Activities Worksheets component of the *Teacher Resource Package.*

Science and Reading, Science and Writing, Science and Math are features that provide problems or projects that require reading, writing, or math calculations to further explore the science concept discussed on the text page.

Did You Know? features present students with interesting facts related to the content being developed; they occur at least once per chapter. As students react with an "I didn't know that!" feeling, they experience the wonder of science and their curiosity is excited.

EcoTips relate to the content of each chapter. **EcoTips** suggest small changes in students' lifestyles that will have positive effects on the environment. **EcoTips** extend the environmental theme of the book, make the text relevant to students' lives, and increase their sense that their actions have an effect in the world.

Student notes are blue margin questions about main ideas; they serve as a study guide for students.

Example Problems

Each new type of problem or equation is introduced with an **Example Problem** to provide students and teachers with completely worked models. A step-by-step problem-solving procedure is provided for calculation, formula, and equation problems. Immediately following **Example Problems** are **Practice Problems,** which afford students opportunities to practice and apply the steps of the preceding example. These exercises are designed to provide immediate reinforcement and feedback whenever new quantitative concepts are presented.

Section and Chapter End

Following each numbered section are three to five **Section Review** questions, including an **Apply** question that demands a higher level of thinking to answer. One question correlates to each objective for the section. Answers to these questions are provided in the margin of the *Teacher Wraparound Edition.*

The three-page chapter-end material begins with a **Summary** that concisely reviews the major concepts and principles of the chapter. Each summary statement is numbered to correspond to a section objective.

- **Key Science Words** list the chapter's vocabulary terms in order of occurrence.
- **Understanding Vocabulary** is an exercise in matching definitions to key terms.
- **Checking Concepts** provides multiple choice recall questions.
- **Understanding Concepts** provides sentence completion exercises.
- **Think and Write Critically** provides higher level thinking questions.
- **Apply** questions require application of chapter concepts.
- **More Skill Builders** require students to use process skills as they answer content-related questions.
- **Projects** provide ideas for researching, creating, or investigating topics based on chapter concepts.

Answers to all chapter end questions are provided in the margin of the *Teacher Wraparound Edition.*

Unit Introductions and Closures

What's Happening Here? photographs and text combine for an inquiry strategy to introduce each unit. A two-page full-color photo picturing a dramatic scene, a puzzling situation, or an intriguing relationship and a smaller photo connected to it opens each unit. The text will connect the photos with each other and with the upcoming concepts of the unit. The *Teacher Wraparound Edition* provides more background on the relationships set up in the photographs and inquiry questions to engage students in unit topics.

The units close with four-page features that include **Global Connections, Careers, Readings,** and **Science and Literature** or **Science and Art. Global Connections** features a two-page world map with topics from five or six places that relate to the chapter content. Each topic is also related to another discipline and each engages the student in the topic with an extension activity. These features provide a strong multicultural perspective.

In the **Careers,** students see real-world applications of science knowledge acquired in the unit. Because one career in each unit requires a college degree and the other does not, students can see the range of careers available for people with a science background. **Readings** provides three or four books or magazine articles related to the unit content.

Closing each unit is a **Science and Literature** or **Science and Art** feature that connects science concepts to literature or art and promotes understanding of the value and importance of science to the humanities. Included may be fiction or nonfiction book excerpts, paintings, sculpture, photos, or music related to the unit. Students are actively engaged at the close of the feature as they respond to application or critical thinking questions.

Skill Reinforcement

Skills are reinforced throughout *Merrill Physical Science.* Each section ends with a **Skill Builder** feature that challenges students to practice basic process skills on a specific science concept. The skill to be learned or practiced is explained in the **Skill Handbook,** a fourteen-page illustrated reference in the back of the student text. Specific examples are used to guide students through the steps of acquiring skills. **More Skill Builders** in the **Chapter Review** material also reference the **Skill Handbook.**

Appendices

There are three appendices that may be used to expand student learning or application of concepts. **Appendix A** shows SI units and English/Metric conversions. It provides tables for quick reference to SI base units, derived units, and common SI prefixes. **Appendix B** includes procedures students should practice to ensure lab safety. A chart of safety symbols that are used throughout the text activities alerts students to possible laboratory hazards. **Appendix C,** the Periodic Table, is available for reference throughout the course.

Glossary and Index

The **Glossary** provides students with a quick reference to key terms and their pronunciations within the text. Page references are provided for all New Science Words from each chapter so students can easily locate the page on which a word is defined. Because it is complete and cross-referenced, the **Index** allows text material to be found quickly and easily.

Features of the Teacher Wraparound Edition

The *Teacher Wraparound Edition* is designed to make teaching **Merrill Physical Science** as easy as possible. Two pages of planning charts precede every chapter. The Chapter Planning Guide lists the objectives, activities, and chapter features for every section. Also correlated to each section is all material in the *Teacher Resource Package* and other components, including the *Laboratory Manual* and *Color Transparency Package*. The equipment and materials required for the chapter's Activities and MINI-Labs are listed; commercially available software and audiovisuals such as films, filmstrips, and slide sets are also referenced.

The majority of the teacher material is conveniently placed in the margin right next to the student page. At the beginning of each chapter, a **Theme Development** section describes how one or all of the themes of the book are incorporated into the chapter. A **Chapter Overview** lists and describes the material in the sections of the chapter; **Chapter Vocabulary** lists boldface terms as they will occur in the chapter.

Introducing the Chapter and **FIND OUT** provide suggestions for an inquiry approach to starting the chapter. **Gearing Up** helps direct students in previewing the Chapter and **What's Next** helps make the connection between the FIND OUT inquiry activity and the topics to follow. Each lesson, or section, starts with **PREPARATION** containing **Section Background** and **Preplanning** sections. **MOTIVATE** follows; it contains several ideas to grab students' interest in the coming section. It can include **Demonstrations, Tying to Previous Knowledge,** and **Objectives and Science Words** all correlated to the section.

TEACH sections include a multitude of teaching suggestions for **Concept Development** and **Check for Understanding** ideas, which may include a **MINI Quiz.** MINI Quizzes are three to five recall questions to use in assessing students' mastery of the material. The answers are provided in the margin and are also keyed by numbers in blue circles next to the place where they occur in the student text. **Reteach** and **Extension** ideas provide alternate ways for teachers to present a particular concept. **Teacher F.Y.I.** includes interesting extensions or applications of the science content. **Revealing Misconceptions** provides suggestions for eliciting and/or correcting student misconceptions. **Cross Curriculum** strategies connect physical science with another science or other subject areas. **Flex Your Brain** and **Cooperative Learning** strategies appear whenever applicable throughout the chapter. Answers to and teaching strategies for Problem Solving, Technology, Science and Reading, Science and Math, Science and Writing occur next to the student page feature.

CLOSE sections consist of two or three ideas for bringing closure to a lesson. The closure activity summarizes the section, bridges to the next lesson, or provides an application of the lesson.

Information for teaching each **Activity** and **MINI-Lab** is included in the margins where these activities occur. Time needed to complete each Activity, objectives, process skills, teaching suggestions, troubleshooting ideas, alternate materials, and answers to questions are included for each.

OPTIONS material, located directly below the page on which it is to be used, includes strategies **For Your Gifted Students** that are activity-based as are strategies **For Your Mainstreamed Students,** which are suggestions for students who are physically or emotionally challenged in some way or for those with learning disabilities.

Inquiry Questions are suggested critical-thinking questions that teachers may use for stimulating class discussions. Possible student responses are in italic type. Suggestions for **Enrichment** activities or articles to read will further students' content knowledge of the content covered or of tangential concepts. **Program Resources** contain references to other instructional materials coordinated to the section.

Major concepts are highlighted in yellow on the reduced student pages, and blue circles point out locations on the student pages of answers to MINI Quiz questions.

Misconceptions

How do students learn science? Decades ago, many educators believed students were empty vessels into which one could pour the pure wisdom gained by humans over centuries. Now, we understand that students come to science class with firmly-held beliefs about how the world works. Students themselves have formed these views of the world and found them to be consistent with everyday life.

Students interpret lectures, books, and even demonstrations and experiments in the light of this world-view. Since what we say in class is interpreted by the student in light of his or her own world view, a student may internalize an idea in a form completely different from what we intend. Each student's adoption of a false perspective becomes a misconception.

Refer to the problem-solving concept map on page 13T. Notice the interactive arrow between misconceptions and critical thinking. Misconceptions may result from a student not using appropriate critical thinking skills. For example, a student may jump to a conclusion, disregarding inconsistencies that may or may not be apparent. Misconceptions may interfere with a student's effectively applying critical thinking skills. A false premise that a student may incorporate while otherwise using sound critical thinking processes may lead to wrong conclusions and new misconceptions.

Misconceptions are complicated by increased vocabulary without conceptual understanding. Students attempt to explain concepts by using words that they really don't understand. Questions may be concisely and satisfactorily answered, however, students' lack of understanding lays the groundwork for misconceptions.

Strategies to treat misconceptions include

- using free recall, word association, structured questioning, and recognition to elicit background knowledge and misconceptions.
- using concept mapping.
- clarifying and interviewing.
- modeling questioning techniques.
- using Activities and MINI-Labs.
- collecting a chapter's misconceptions for review use at its conclusion.
- using Merrill's Flex Your Brain activity (see page 19T).

In the **Merrill Physical Science** *Teacher Wraparound Edition,* "Misconceptions" suggests strategies for eliciting misconceptions about specific content in the student edition. "Tying to Previous Knowledge" strategies will also prove useful in identifying and treating misconceptions.

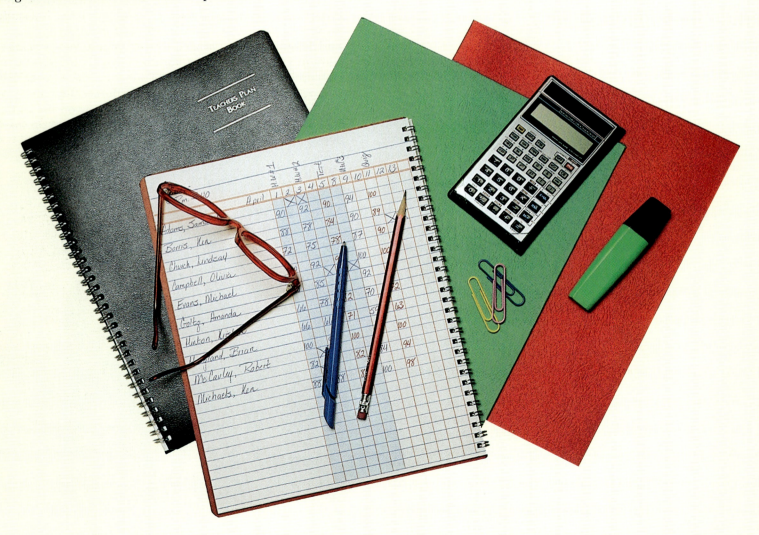

Supplementary Materials

Teacher Resource Package

The *Teacher Resource Package* for **Merrill Physical Science** provides background information and comprehensive teaching material to aid in the effective teaching of physical science. The following worksheet masters are provided: Activity, MINI-Lab, Study Guide, Reinforcement, Enrichment, Critical Thinking/Problem Solving, Concept Mapping, Cross-Curricular Connections, Science and Society, Transparency, Technology, Chapter Review, Chapter Test, and Unit Test.

For each section, three worksheets for students of different ability levels are provided. The **Study Guide** worksheets are suitable for all students; they are closely tied to the text and require recall of text content. **Reinforcement** worksheets are for students of average and above average ability; a variety of formats are used to reinforce each text lesson. **Enrichment** worksheets are tailored for students with above average ability; a wide range of formats allows students to design, interpret, research, and create based on the text of each lesson. The three types of worksheets are also available in consumable books—Study Guide, Reinforcement, and Enrichment.

For every text **Activity** and **MINI-Lab** there is a worksheet that reproduces the complete text for the Activity or MINI-Lab, provides charts for data collection, and illustrates the procedures.

Critical Thinking/Problem Solving worksheets consist of a reading selection related to a chapter topic and questions that help to develop critical thinking skills while applying important concepts learned in the classroom to new situations.

Concept Mapping masters challenge students to construct a visual representation of relationships among particular chapter concepts. This booklet is developmental in its approach; early concept maps are nearly complete; later ones provide only a skeleton and linking words.

Cross-Curricular Connections masters are interdisciplinary worksheets that relate science to other disciplines. There is one worksheet per chapter; the emphasis is on "doing" the related discipline whenever possible.

Science and Society worksheets show the impact of science on current societal issues and problems. There is one worksheet for each chapter; each ends with a question requiring students to draw conclusions and/or make decisions.

Transparency Masters are blackline versions of the 50 color transparencies. For each transparency there is a student worksheet and a teacher guide with instructions.

Chapter Review masters are two-page review worksheets consisting of 25 questions for each chapter. They can be used to prepare for tests, as alternate tests, and as vocabulary review. **Chapter and Unit Test** masters test the concepts of each chapter.

Technology masters explain how something works and/or integrate the sciences. The topics are tied to the student text.

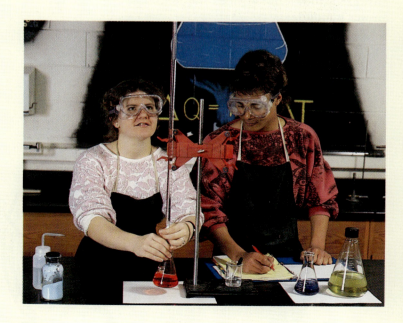

Laboratory Program

The *Laboratory Manual* is a learning-through-doing program of activities. Based on the philosophy that scientific knowledge is acquired through individual activity and experimentation, the manual consists of many, varied laboratory activities designed to reinforce concepts presented in **Merrill Physical Science.** Laboratory investigations for each student edition chapter require students to work through a problem by observing, analyzing, and drawing. Some of the chemistry labs are microlabs, which involve using less than a milliliter of reactants, to make your lab program more efficient and cost effective. The *Laboratory Manual, Teacher Edition* consists of the student edition pages with teacher answers on reduced pages in the back. The reduced pages include suggestions for alternate materials, teaching tips, sample data, and answers to all student questions.

Transparency Package

The **Color Transparency Package** contains 50 full-color transparencies, as well as a book containing a blackline version of each transparency, a student worksheet, and instructions for using the transparencies. The book is also part of the **Teacher Resource Package.** The color transparencies and book are conveniently packaged in a 3-ring binder.

Computer Software

Two types of software have been created to correlate with the **Merrill Physical Science** program.

The *Chapter Review Software* provides chapter-end review questions for student use. Based on the review questions found in the textbook at the end of the chapter, the software presents questions in random order. Feedback for incorrectly-answered questions provides the textbook page where the answer is found.

The *Computer Test Bank* provides the teacher with a tool to design a test from a bank of questions. Features include selection of sections to be tested, number of questions for each section, total number of questions on a test, inclusion or exclusion of specific questions, and multiple test forms.

Lesson Plan Book

The **Lesson Plan Booklet** contains complete lesson plans for every lesson in the Student Text. Also included are references to all program components of **Merrill Physical Science.**

Spanish Resources

The **Spanish Resources** book provides Spanish translations of objectives, summary statements, and key terms and their definitions for every chapter. Also included is a complete English/Spanish glossary to **Merrill Physical Science.**

Videodisc Correlation

The **Videodisc Correlation** book contains the complete correlation with bar codes of OPTICAL DATA'S Videodisc images to the content of **Merrill Physical Science.**

Thinking in Science

What *are* thinking skills? How are thinking skills developed? We educators know that learning involves a crucial awareness followed by an evaluation and judgment.

Throughout the *Merrill Physical Science* program are experiences that help students develop, practice, and apply thinking process skills. The process skills are carefully introduced and developed through the use of higher level divergent questions, controlled experiments, problem-solving activities, critical thinking questions, and creative activities. The Flex Your Brain critical thinking matrix introduced in Chapter 1 provides a method for self-directed problem solving that can be used throughout the course.

Shown below is a concept map that explains the relationships of the thinking skills developed and reinforced in *Merrill Physical Science* and the ways they are incorporated in the text.

Thinking extends and refines knowledge and can lead to problem solving. As our concept map shows, effective problem solving relies on the integration of three types of thinking. The first, critical thinking, is characterized by
- a search for clarity and accuracy.
- open-mindedness.
- taking and defending a position.
- sensitivity to others' knowledge and feelings.

The next type of thinking, creative thinking, is characterized by
- engaging in tasks when answers are not apparent.
- pushing the limits of one's knowledge and abilities.
- generating and following one's own standard of evaluation.
- generating new ways of viewing situations.

The third type of thinking, self-regulated thinking, consists of
- planning.
- sensitivity to feedback.
- using available resources.
- awareness and evaluation of the effectiveness of one's own thinking.

Critical, creative, and self-regulated thinking skills contribute to successful problem solving. These skills help one to evaluate accuracy and worth, to construct logical arguments, and, finally, to determine truth. The developmental goal of the *Merrill Physical Science* skill strand is to help you produce discriminating, disciplined, questioning problem solvers.

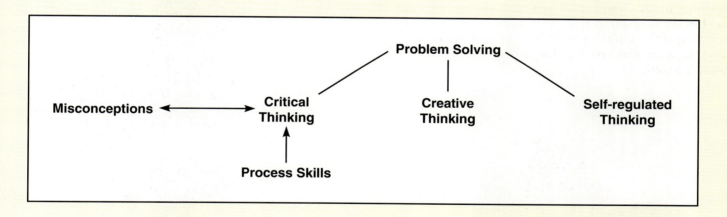

Developing and Applying Thinking Skills

Merrill Physical Science provides a wide range of experiences that help students develop and apply thinking process skills. **Apply** questions that require higher level, divergent thinking appear in every Section Review. Problem-Solving features ask students to solve real-life problems. **Think Critically** questions provide students an opportunity to reflect on issues related to technology.

Critical thinking skills developed in the text include
- observing and inferring
- comparing and contrasting
- recognizing cause and effect
- defining operationally
- formulating models

Refer again to the Thinking in Science concept map on page 13T. It shows diagrammatically that the process skills help develop and reinforce critical thinking.

The fourteen-page illustrated **Skill Handbook** includes specific examples to guide students through the steps of acquiring skills. As students complete each section, a **Skill Builder** gives them a chance to reinforce the concepts just learned as they practice a particular skill explained in the handbook.

FIND OUT inquiry activities that open each chapter allow students to start generating questions about the concepts to come, make observations as they do "hands-on" work, and share prior knowledge about the chapter content. Student misconceptions often surface during this activity.

Activities and MINI-Labs provide the "learn by doing" experiences necessary for acquiring safe, efficient laboratory techniques, learning and applying the scientific method, and practicing all of the thinking skills.

The Activities and MINI-Labs are designed to help you provide an engaging, diverse, active program for learning and practicing process skills.

The MINI-Labs provide short, quick hands-on experiences that require a minimum of equipment. You might make students responsible for their organization and execution. Also, you might use MINI-Labs as demonstrations.

Activities in *Merrill Physical Science* provide students experiences that develop and reinforce or restructure concepts as well as develop the ability to use process skills. The format is structured to guide students to make discoveries using a scientific method. Science process skills such as observing, classifying, hypothesizing, measuring, interpreting data, analyzing, and concluding are learned and reinforced as they do the Activities.

Process skills developed and reinforced in the text are

- Organizing Information
    - classifying
    - sequencing
    - outlining

- Thinking Critically
    - observing and inferring
    - comparing and contrasting
    - recognizing cause and effect
    - defining operationally
    - formulating models

- Experimentation Skills
    - measuring in SI
    - hypothesizing
    - using variables, constants and controls
    - collecting and organizing data
    - interpreting data
    - experimenting
    - analyzing

- Graphic Organizers
    - concept mapping
    - making and using tables
    - making and using graphs
    - interpreting scientific illustrations

- Others
    - communicating
    - using numbers

A chart showing chapter-by-chapter development of skills is on page 16T. Several features to aid teachers in skills assessment have been built into *Merrill Physical Science*. **Think and Write Critically, Apply,** and **More Skill Builders** sections of the Chapter Review material ask students questions that relate the chapter material to the skill from that chapter, as well as to skills learned in previous chapters. Questions relating to the skill developed in the chapter are included in each of the chapter tests found in the **Teacher Resource Package.**

Questioning Strategies that Support Critical Thinking

The following categories of questions and examples can help you devise critical thinking strategies for handling class discussion.

Clarifying Questions
- What is the main issue?
- How does this relate to our discussion?
- Can you summarize in your own words?

Questioning Assumptions
- Are you taking this for granted?
- Is this always the case?
- Why do you think this assumption is correct?

Questioning Reasons and Evidence
- Give an example.
- What reasons do you have to doubt the evidence?
- How did you come to that conclusion?
- How could we find out whether that is true?
- How does this apply in this case?

Questioning Viewpoints or Perspectives
- How do you think other groups or types of people would respond? Why?
- If you disagreed what would you say?
- Give an alternative.

Probing Implications and Consequences
- If that happened, what else might happen and why?
- How might that affect the situation?
- Given the situation, would that always happen?
- If this is the case, then what else must be true?

Questioning the Question
- Why is this important?
- What other questions can we ask?
- Why do we need to know this?

Legend: ● Activity (green) ● SKILL BUILDER/More SKILL BUILDERS (red)

Chapters	Using Numbers	Communicating	Interpreting Scientific Illustrations	Making & Using Graphs	Making & Using Tables	Concept Mapping	Analyzing	Experimenting	Interpreting Data	Collecting & Organizing Data	Using Variables, Constants, and Controls	Hypothesizing	Measuring in SI	Formulating Models	Defining Operationally	Recognizing Cause & Effect	Comparing & Contrasting	Observing & Inferring	Outlining	Classifying	Sequencing
1		●	●			●						●	●				●	● ●	●		
2		●		●		●				●		●	● ●	●			●	●			●
3	●	●		●	●	●	●					●	● ●				●	●			●
4			●	●	●	●			● ●			●		●		●	●	● ●			
5	●					●			● ●			●	●				●	● ●			●
6				●		●	●			●	●	●				●	●	● ●			●
7	●	●	●	●		●			●							●	●	● ●		●	
8				●	●	●							● ●			●	●	● ●			
9						●			●					●		●	●	● ●			
10	●			●	●	●			●			●	●	●			●	●		●	
11			●	●	●	●					●	●	●				●	● ●		●	
12			●	●	●	●							●			●	●	● ●		●	
13			●	●		●						●	● ●	●		●	●	● ●			
14						●			●				●			●	●	● ●			
15	●			●	●	●						●	●			●	●	● ●			
16						●							●	●	●	●	● ●	● ●	●	●	
17					●	●						●	●	●		●	●	● ●			
18	●		●	●	●	●			●			●	● ●	●		●	●	● ●			
19					●	●		●	●			●	●			●	●	● ●	● ●	●	
20					●	●			●			●	● ●			●	●	● ●	●	●	
21		●	●	●	●	●		●	● ●		●	●		●			●	●			
22						●			●			●	● ●			● ●	●	● ●			
23		●	● ●	●	●	●		●	●			●	●		●	● ●	● ●	●		●	
24			●	●	●	●		●	●			●	●			● ●	●	● ●			
25		●				●	●						●				●	●		●	

Concept Maps

Concept maps are visual representations of relationships among particular concepts. In science they make abstract information more concrete and useful, improve retention of information, and show students that thought has shape. Concept maps can be generated by individual students, small groups, or an entire class. *Merrill Physical Science* develops and reinforces three types of graphic organizers—the **network tree, events chain,** and **cycle concept map** that are most applicable to studying science. Examples of the three types and their applications are shown below.

Students can learn how to construct each of these types of concept maps by reading pages 684 and 685 of the Skill Handbook. They will practice this skill throughout the course.

Network Tree

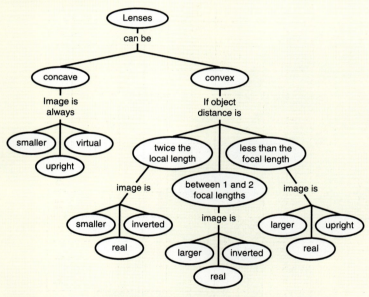

Applications: shows causal information, a hierarchy, and branching procedures.

Events Chain

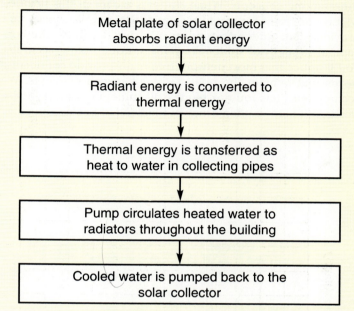

Applications: describes the stages of process, the steps in a linear procedure, a sequence of events

Cycle

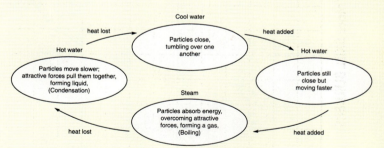

Applications: shows how a series of events interacts to produce a set of results again and again.

The section-ending Skill Builders and the More Skill Builders section of Chapter Reviews in early chapters direct students to make a specific type of concept map and in most cases concept terms to be used are provided. Later, in a developmental approach, students are given general guidelines. For example, concept terms to be used may be provided and students are required to select the appropriate model to apply or vice-versa. Finally students may be asked to provide both the terms and type of concept map to explain relationships among concepts. When students are given this flexibility, it is important for you to recognize that sample answers are provided, but student responses may vary. Look for the conceptual strength of student responses, not absolute accuracy. You'll notice that most network tree maps provide connecting words that explain the relationships between concepts. We recommend that you not require all students to supply these words, but many students may be challenged by this aspect.

More Skill Builders in the Chapter Reviews that ask students to make a concept map usually provide the concept map format and the specific concept terms to use. This will ensure you more consistent student responses, making grading easier, than when students are asked to make more determinations about their concept maps.

The Concept Mapping book of the *Teacher Resource Package,* too, provides a developmental approach for students to practice concept mapping.

As a teaching strategy, generating concept maps can be used to preview a chapter's content by visually relating the concepts to be learned and allowing the students to read with purpose. Using concept maps for previewing is especially useful when there are many new key science terms for students to learn. As a review strategy, constructing concept maps reinforces main ideas and clarifies their relationships. Construction of concept maps using cooperative learning strategies as described on pages 26T-29T of this Teacher Guide will allow students to practice both interpersonal and process skills.

Flex Your Brain

A key element in the coverage of problem solving and critical thinking skills in *Merrill Physical Science* is a critical thinking matrix called **Flex Your Brain.**

Flex Your Brain is a self-directed activity intended to assist students in developing critical thinking skills while investigating content areas.

Flex Your Brain provides students with an opportunity to explore a topic in an organized, self-checking way and then identify how they arrived at their responses during each step of their investigation. The activity incorporates many of the skills of critical thinking. It helps students to think about their own thinking and learn about thinking from their peers.

In a step-by-step way, Flex Your Brain asks students to:

(1) focus on a single topic;
(2) consider their prior knowledge of the topic;
(3) pose questions regarding the topic;
(4) hypothesize answers to their questions;
(5) evaluate their confidence in their answer;
(6) identify ways to investigate the topic to prove, disprove, or amend their responses;
(7) follow through with their investigation;
(8) evaluate their responses to their questions, checking for their own misconceptions or lack of understanding;
(9) rewrite their question responses, incorporating new knowledge gained; and
(10) review and share the thinking processes that they used during the activity.

Where is FLEX YOUR BRAIN found?

In Chapter 1, page 14, of the student text is an introduction to the topics of critical thinking and problem solving. Flex Your Brain accompanies the text section as a one-page activity in Chapter 1. Brief student instructions are given, along with the matrix itself. A two-page version of Flex Your Brain appears as a worksheet in the Teacher Resource Guide of the *Teacher Resource Package.* This version provides spaces for students to write in their responses.

In the *Teacher Wraparound Edition,* suggested topics are given in each chapter for the use of Flex Your Brain. You can either refer students to Chapter 1 for the procedure or photocopy the worksheet master from the Teacher Resource Guide.

Use of Flex Your Brain is certainly not restricted to those topics suggested in the *Teacher Wraparound Edition.* Feel free to use it for practice in critical thinking about any concept or topic.

Using FLEX YOUR BRAIN

Flex Your Brain can be used as a whole-class activity or in cooperative groups, but is primarily designed to be used by individual students within the class. There are three basic steps.

1. Teachers assign a class topic to be investigated using Flex Your Brain.
2. Students use Flex Your Brain to guide them in their individual explorations of the topic.
3. After students have completed their explorations, teachers guide them in a discussion of their experiences with Flex Your Brain, bridging content and thinking processes.

Flex your Brain can be used at many different points in the lesson plan.

▶**Introduction:** Ideal for introducing a topic, Flex Your Brain elicits students' prior knowledge and identifies misconceptions, enabling the teacher to formulate plans specific to student needs.

▶**Development:** Flex Your Brain leads students to find out more about a topic on their own, and develops their research skills while increasing their knowledge. Students actually pose their own questions to explore, making their investigations relevant to their personal interests and concerns.

▶**Review and Extension:** Flex Your Brain allows teachers to check student understanding while allowing students to explore aspects of the topic that go beyond the material presented in class.

FLEX YOUR BRAIN
Annotated Directions

To assist teachers in using Flex Your Brain, an annotated version of the directions appearing on the student page is given below.

1. **Fill in the topic your teacher gives you.**

   Focus students by providing a topic that you need to introduce, develop, or review. Topics should be fairly broad and stated in only a few words; for example, "frog life cycle" or "weathering." Later, when students are familiar with Flex Your Brain, you may want students to select the topic.

2. **Jot down what you already know about the topic. If you know more than five things, write them on another sheet of paper.**

   As a class or cooperative group, this could be a brainstorming process. Otherwise, students should recall individually what they know about the topic. Set a reasonable time limit for this step.

   As you track student progress through this step, look for evidence of misconceptions. Encourage students to draw knowledge from their own experiences as well as from academic sources.

3. **Using what you already know (Step 2), form a question about the topic. Are you unsure about one of the items listed? Do you want to know more about anything? Do you want to know what, how, or why? Write down your question.**

   Students can pose their own questions about the topic and pursue their answers independently; or as a class or group, they can generate several questions. Groups may choose one of these questions to investigate, or the entire class can select one question for all to research.

4. **Guess an answer to your question. In the next few steps, you will be exploring the reasonableness of your answer. Write down your guess.**

   The significance of this step is to get students to think, not just know the right answer. Based on what they already know about the topic, students should form hypotheses about their questions in Step 3. The correctness of their answers at this point is not as important as the means by which they arrive at them.

   Guessing is not a poor means to arrive at an answer if students first consider the facts they know about the topic. Still, students may hesitate to write down answers that they aren't sure of. Encourage students to provide a "best guess."

5. **Circle the number in the box that matches how sure you are of your answer in Step 4. This is your chance to rate your confidence in what you've done so far and, later, to see how your level of sureness affects your thinking.**

   Students should evaluate their feelings at this point and begin to recognize the extent to which they are confident of their answers. Self-evaluation is critical to successful problem solving. This step becomes especially important when students review their thinking process in Step 10. Make sure students know that emotions and intuition are important aspects of problem solving.

6. **How can you find out more about your topic? You might want to read a book, ask an expert, or do an experiment. Write down ways you can find out more.**

   The first time through this activity, you may want to have the class brainstorm ways to explore topics. Discuss the usefulness and appropriateness of the different means of investigation.

   Evaluating the appropriateness of sources is an important skill to emphasize at this step. Encourage students to gain knowledge from the world at large, not just from expert sources. Be sure to bring out in your discussion that checking with a friend may be appropriate in some situations, but not in others.

7. **Make a plan to explore your answer. Use the resources you listed in Step 6. Then, carry out your plan.**

   Students should use at least three resources before drawing conclusions. Encourage them to consider and use resources that might provide different perspectives on the topic in question.

   Experimenting should be encouraged as a means of exploration. Review the scientific method when introducing this step and emphasize the science process skills.

8. **Now that you've explored, go back to your answer in Step 4. Would you answer differently? Mark one of the boxes.**

   Students should consider whether they want to change their original answers. If their original answers require modifying in any way, they should mark the "yes" box.

   At this step, students should begin to recognize their original misconceptions regarding the topic.

9. **Considering what you learned in your exploration, answer your question again. You may want to add new things you've learned or completely change your answer.**

   If students' original answers were correct, request that they restate their answers incorporating new knowledge gained from their explorations. Otherwise, students should correct or modify their answers as needed.

   This step leads students to draw conclusions. Help students to recognize how even a wrong answer in Step 4 contributed to the new answer by giving them a basis for exploration. Wrong answers are an important part of the scientific process.

10. **It's important to be able to talk about thinking. Choose three people to tell about how you arrived at your response in every step. For example, don't just read what you wrote in Step 2. Try to share how you thought of those things.**

    The process of sharing ensures that students will reflect on what they have done. Encourage students to review each preceding step to determine how they arrived at their responses. Make sure students know that this is not an easy task and that they may struggle to put their process into words.

Verbalizing is important. When students put their own process into their own words, meaningful, internalized learning occurs. Discourage students from ridiculing other students during the sharing process.

The primary goal of Flex Your Brain is to improve students' ability to think effectively. Until their thought processes are somehow made clear to them, this will never occur. Step 10 achieves this by engaging students in metacognition, or the process of thinking about thinking.

Metacognition makes the process of thinking conscious and thus allows the process to be examined and improved. It is important to emphasize the importance of sharing and give adequate time to complete this step.

FLEX YOUR BRAIN is flexible.

Flex Your Brain was designed to be flexible in approaching critical thinking and problem solving. These directions are suggestions for one possible use of Flex Your Brain, but certainly not the only use. Teachers should feel free to adapt the activity to best suit their own needs and the needs of the diverse classes and students they teach.

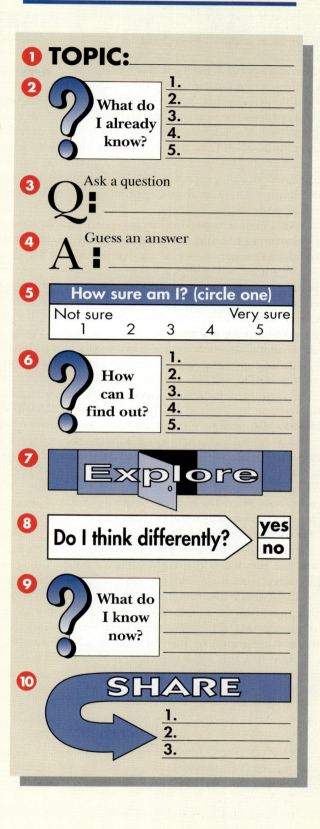

FLEX Your Brain

1 **TOPIC:** _____

2 **?** What do I already know?
1. _____
2. _____
3. _____
4. _____
5. _____

3 Q: Ask a question _____

4 A: Guess an answer _____

5 How sure am I? (circle one)
Not sure				Very sure
1	2	3	4	5

6 **?** How can I find out?
1. _____
2. _____
3. _____
4. _____
5. _____

7 Explore

8 Do I think differently? yes / no

9 **?** What do I know now? _____

10 SHARE
1. _____
2. _____
3. _____

Planning the Course

Merrill Physical Science provides a flexibility in the selection of topics and content that allows for adapting the text to the needs of individual students and classes. In this regard, the teacher is in the best position to decide what topics are to be presented, the pace at which the content is covered, and what material should be given the most emphasis. To assist the teacher in planning the course, a planning guide has been provided. The purpose of this guide is to aid the teacher in developing a course that will offer the best possible program for students.

Merrill Physical Science may be used in a full-year course or two semesters covering the text activities and chapter-end materials. It is assumed that a year-long course in physical science will entail 180 periods of approximately 45 minutes each. In the planning guide, each chapter is listed along with the number of class sessions recommended for teaching the chapter. Within each chapter certain sections will require major emphasis for the material to be developed adequately. These sections are so designated in the planning guide. Use the planning guide to gauge the amount of time you will spend on each topic.

Through the selection of specific units, chapters, and sections that conform to the local course of study, *Merrill Physical Science* also may be used in a one-semester course. There are two additional alternatives to one-semester courses. One alternative is a course in basic physics. The second alternative is a course in chemistry. The PH (physics) and CH (chemistry) columns in the planning guide list the number of class sessions suggested for the study of the chapter sections in each of the one-semester alternatives.

Please remember that the planning guide is provided as an aid in planning the best course for your students. You should use the planning guide in relation to the interests and ability levels of the classes you teach, the materials available for activities, and the time available for teaching. You may decide to extend the scope and time devoted to certain topics through the use of enrichment activities and supplementary materials presented in the Teacher Resource Guide. The planning guide will assist you in developing and following a schedule that will enable you to complete your goals for the school year or semester.

Planning Guide

	CLASS SESSIONS			
Chapter	Full-Year Course	Semester Science	Semester PH	CH
1	5	2	3	5
2	9	5	6	9
3	7	4	7	
4	7	4	7	
5	7	4	7	
6	7	3	5	
7	7	3	5	
8	10	4	8	6
9	7	4		7
10	9	5		9
11	9	5		8
12	8	4		8
13	8	3		6
14	3	2		3
15	7	4		7
16	8	4		8
17	9	5		9
18	6	4	6	
19	6	4	6	
20	6	3	6	
21	8	4	8	
22	9	4	8	
23	5	3	4	
24	7	3	4	5
25	6			
TOTALS	180	90	90	90

Teaching Cycle

The *Merrill Physical Science* Teacher Wraparound Edition delivers the collective teaching experience of its authors, consultants, and reviewers. By furnishing you with an effective teaching model, this book saves you preparation time and energy. You, in turn, are free to spend that time and energy on your most important responsibility—your students.

As a professional, you will be pleased to find that this program provides you with readily available activities that will engage your students for the entire class period. Each major section of every chapter may be considered an individual lesson that includes a preparation section followed by a comprehensive three-part teaching cycle that, when utilized consistently, will result in better cognitive transfer for your students.

Each chapter begins with a section called **Theme Development** that describes how one or all of the themes of the book are incorporated into the chapter. Following Theme Development is a **Chapter Overview** that lists and describes the material in each of the sections of the chapter. The **Chapter Vocabulary** is then listed for you in the order in which the words occur in the chapter.

Each chapter opens with a **FIND OUT** activity that helps you focus the students' attention on the chapter and get them into the material immediately. Everything you will need to help the students complete the **FIND OUT** is given alongside the student page. Any advanced preparation and materials needed are listed for you. A **Cooperative Learning** strategy is suggested and teaching tips are given to help you conduct the activity smoothly.

In the **OPTIONS** section of the chapter opener, activity-based strategies are given to help you with any gifted or mainstreamed students you may have in your class.

PREPARATION

Preparation is an extremely important part of teaching any lesson. The **PREPARATION** section contains **SECTION BACKGROUND** which will provide you with science content that is relevant to the section. Also provided for you in **PRE-PLANNING** is a list of things you may wish to do to prepare for the section in advance. The **PREPARATION** section will give you the foundation for keeping your lesson instructionally sound.

1 MOTIVATE

The first step to teaching any lesson is to motivate the students. Several **Motivate** ideas are provided for each section. The ideas may include demonstrations, cooperative learning techniques, audiovisuals, brainstorming, or other ideas that help motivate and focus the class so the lesson can begin. You may pick one of the motivate ideas listed or alternate them among your classes according to student need. One unique way to get students interested in the section content is by using the FLEX YOUR BRAIN activity. This activity will give students confidence to begin learning section content by helping them find out what they already know and don't know about a certain topic.

Another important way to help motivate students is by connecting the current lesson with previous lessons or to common knowledge possessed by most students. The **Tying to Previous Knowledge** section helps you do this. Research has shown that connecting ideas provides for greater concept retention among students.

2 TEACH

The primary aim of the *Merrill Physical Science* Teacher Wraparound Edition is to give you the tools to accomplish the task of getting concepts of physical science across to your students. Many teaching suggestions are given to you under a series of clearly defined headings. Each section contains, under the **CONCEPT DEVELOPMENT** heading, ways for you to develop the content of the section. This may include a series of questions for you to ask students followed by possible student responses. These questions are a tool for you to use to develop the concepts in the section. Demonstration ideas also appear in Concept Development when they can help you develop student interest in the concepts to be taught.

To help you monitor and adjust your teaching to what students are learning a **CHECK FOR UNDERSTANDING** idea is provided for you in each section where it seems the most appropriate. For students who are having trouble, a **RETEACH** suggestion immediately follows the CHECK FOR UNDERSTANDING hint. The RETEACH tip is a way to teach the same concepts or facts differently to adjust to students' individual learning styles. For those students in the class who do not need additional help understanding the lesson, there are suggestions for **ENRICHMENT** to allow these students to go on while others are reviewing the section. These ENRICHMENT ideas are provided for you in the **OPTIONS** boxes at the bottom of the *Teacher Wraparound Edition* pages.

The **TEACH** step of the *Teacher Wraparound Edition* provides many other strategies to help you teach the content of the section. In each section you will find a way to connect physical science to another discipline in the **CROSS CURRICULUM** teaching tip. A **MINI QUIZ** is provided for you to use in assessing students' mastery of the material. These can also be used as CHECK FOR UNDERSTANDING activities. An annotation key is provided with each of these to help you refer students to the page on which the answer is found.

Many times students have misconceptions about a particular concept you are teaching. The **REVEALING MISCONCEPTIONS** teaching tip suggests questions you may ask to elicit student misconceptions about section content or provides you with a possible misconception held by students and a method of correcting that misconception.

There are **TEACHER F.Y.I.** tips that give you additional information to help you teach the section. These may be everyday applications or connections to other disciplines. Answers are given in the margin to any text questions to be answered by students. Also, for your convenience we have highlighted the key concepts.

COOPERATIVE LEARNING suggestions are given in various locations of the *Teacher Wraparound Edition*. They are found in the FIND OUT activities, in the lab activities and when appropriate within the Teach section. In each COOPERATIVE LEARNING tip, a specific cooperative grouping strategy is given to help you make the most of these activities.

You are also provided with information needed to teach each of the special features of the student edition such as; **MINI-Labs, Science and..., TECHNOLOGY, PROBLEM SOLVING, and ACTIVITIES.**

And There's More

Our special *Teacher Wraparound Edition* has been designed to provide you with the most meaningful teacher information in the most convenient way. At the bottom of most pages is an OPTIONS Box containing a variety of items. The OPTIONS Box on the Chapter Opener pages provides you with ideas to help you teach the Gifted students and the Mainstreamed students in your class. Both of these groups pose a challenge to any teacher and these tips are designed to help you teach the content of the chapter to these exceptional students.

Every classroom contains students with a variety of different ability levels. The OPTIONS box on the first two pages of each section shows you reduced copies of pages in the *Teacher Resource Package* to help you deal with all of the different ability levels. The Study Guide Master can be used by all students to review the basic content of the section. For the average students, the Reinforcement Master will allow them to go beyond the basic concepts of the chapter while reinforcing them. The Enrichment Master will provide those students who quickly master section content with an additional challenge to explore the ideas in the section more fully.

On the pages in the chapter, the OPTIONS Boxes provide you with Inquiry Questions and additional Enrichment activities to use with all students. The Inquiry Questions are suggested questions you may ask that require critical thinking on the part of the students. The questions relate specifically to the content of the page on which they are located.

With the materials present in the TEACH step of the teacher edition your efficiency and productivity as a teacher will increase. The TEACH section brings together the major elements that form a sound teaching approach.

3 CLOSE

Closing the lesson is the last but one of the most important steps of teaching any lesson. This step is the complement in many ways to the MOTIVATE step. While the motivate step helps students become involved in the lesson, the close step helps students bring things together in their minds to make sense of what went on in the lesson. The *Merrill Physical Science Teacher Wraparound Edition* gives you a variety of ways to provide effective closure to a lesson. The close options are activities that summarize the section, bridge to the next lesson, or provide an application of the lesson.

As you review the *Merrill Physical Science Teacher Wraparound Edition*, you will discover that you and your students are considered very important. With the enormous number of teaching strategies provided by the teacher edition, you should be able to accomplish the goals of your curriculum. The materials allow adaptability and flexibility so that student needs, and curricular needs, can be met.

Cooperative Learning

What is Cooperative Learning?

In cooperative learning, students work together in small groups to learn academic material and interpersonal skills. Group members are responsible for the *group* accomplishing an assigned task as well as for learning the material themselves. When compared to competitive or individual learning situations in which students either work against each other or alone, cooperative learning fosters academic, personal, and social success for all students. Recent research shows that cooperative learning results in

- development of positive attitudes toward science.
- choosing to take more science courses as electives.
- positive attitudes toward science carrying over to positive attitudes toward school.
- lower drop-out rates for at-risk students.
- building respect for others regardless of race, ethnic origin, or sex.
- increased awareness of diverse perspectives.
- increased capability for problem solving in sciences.
- increased realization of potential for girls in science classes.
- development of kindness, sensitivity, and tolerance.

What is the Teacher's Role in Cooperative Learning?

Before teaching the lesson, the teacher must decide the academic task and interpersonal skills students will learn or practice in groups. Students can learn most any academic objective in cooperative groups.

The teacher should also specify what interpersonal behaviors are necessary for a group to work cooperatively. When first starting out, it is wise to list and discuss with students basic interpersonal skills needed for people to work together. Basic interpersonal skills you might discuss include being responsible for your own actions, staying on task, listening while others are speaking, and respecting other people and their ideas. Students can learn and practice other interpersonal skills such as using quiet voices, encouraging other group members to participate, summarizing, checking for understanding, disagreeing constructively, reaching a group consensus, and criticizing ideas rather than people.

Cooperative groups usually contain from two to six students. If students are not experienced working in groups, start with small groups. You might consider grouping students in pairs and then joining pairs later to form groups of four or even six.

Generally, it is best to assign students to heterogeneous groups. Be certain that each heterogeneous group contains a mixture of abilities, genders, and ethnicity. The use of heterogeneous groups exposes students to ideas different from their own and helps them learn how to work with persons different from themselves.

Students may also be randomly assigned to groups, or they can be allowed to select their own groups. Consider using random grouping to let students get acquainted at the beginning of the year or for students to learn to work with all students in the class. As a general rule, it is not good to allow students to choose groups until students have experience with cooperative learning. Have student-selected groups work together when students have interests in common.

Initially, cooperative learning groups should only work together for a day or two. After the students are more experienced, they can do group work effectively for longer periods of time. Some teachers change groups every week, while others keep groups of students together during the study of a unit or chapter. Regardless of the duration you choose, it is important to keep groups together long enough for each group to experience success and to change groups often enough that students have the opportunity to work with others.

You can structure the learning task to promote the participation of each group member by the arrangement of your classroom and the provision of materials. Limiting the materials needed to accomplish the assigned task forces students to share them. Also, consider assigning students roles that contribute to accomplishing the group task. Student roles should be rotated so each group member has the opportunity to perform each role.

Finally, you must decide on how you will evaluate the learning task and how well the students worked together in learning groups. Since students are responsible for themselves and other group members learning the material, you can evaluate group performance during a lesson by frequently asking questions to group members picked at random. Other forms of group evaluation include having each group take a quiz together or having all students write and choosing one student's paper at random to grade. Individual learning can be assessed by traditional tests and quizzes.

To assess the learning of interpersonal skills, you can observe their use during the lesson. Or, you or a group member could tally the use of a specific interpersonal skill. Groups can assess themselves by rating themselves on a scale from one to ten; they then list ways group members used interpersonal skills and ways to improve group performance.

Teaching the Lesson

Explain the day's lesson before students start group work. Do so by writing the following headings on the chalkboard or a transparency and discussing each.

▶**Academic Task:** Prepare students for the academic task by teaching any material they might need to know and by giving specific instructions for the task.

▶**Criteria for Success:** Instruct students that they are responsible for their own learning as well as the learning of other members of the group. Explain the sharing of materials and assuming of roles. Explain your criteria for evaluating group and individual learning.

▶**Interpersonal Skills:** Specify the interpersonal skills students will be working on, and list what behaviors look and sound like. Explain how you will evaluate interpersonal skills.

▶**Group Formation:** Divide the class into groups. Assign roles or divide materials.

▶**Provide Assistance with the Academic Task:** Make certain each student can see and hear all other group members. When students are having trouble with the task, answer questions, clarify the assignment, reteach, or provide background as needed. When answering questions, make certain that no students in the group can answer the question before you reply.

▶**Monitor Student Behavior:** Spend most of your time monitoring the functioning of groups. Praise group cooperation and good use of interpersonal skills.

▶**Intervene to Teach Interpersonal Skills:** Whenever possible, allow groups to work out their own problems. When groups are having problems, ask group members to figure out how the group can function more effectively. Record your observations of the use of interpersonal skills; share your observations with the groups.

▶**Provide Closure to the Lesson:** Reinforce student learning by having groups share their products or summarize the assignment. Answer any questions about the lesson.

▶**Evaluate Group and Individual Learning:** Use the criteria discussed before the lesson began to evaluate and give feedback on how well the academic task was mastered by the groups. Assess individual learning by your traditional method.

▶**Assess How Well Groups Functioned:** Have students analyze how well their groups functioned and how well they used interpersonal skills. Groups can list what they did well and what they could do to improve. Have groups share their analysis with the class, and summarize the analyses of the whole class.

Using Cooperative Learning in Merrill Physical Science

In *Merrill Physical Science* Teacher Wraparound Edition, Activities, MINI-Labs, Find Outs, and Chapter Reviews contain specific suggestions for Cooperative Learning. In addition, cooperative learning groups can be used with section reviews and problem solving, concept mapping, and skill builder features. The following cooperative learning strategies are referenced in the *Teacher Wraparound Edition*.

Paired Partners

Assign each student a partner, and ask a question or present a problem for them to solve. Each student composes an answer or solution; the pair then shares answers with each other. If partners disagree, they explain and discuss the issues until they agree. When both agree and can explain the answer, partners raise their hands to signify both agree and can explain the answer. After determining if groups have the correct answer, some teachers use thumbs up to indicate "correct" and thumbs down to indicate "incorrect." Students can also write their answers on the chalkboard or on response cards. Paired Partners can be used for problem solving, concept mapping, and Skill Builder features.

Expert Teams

Form students into groups of two to six. Give each group member a different part of an assignment to study and master. Send group members with the same part of the assignment from the different teams to work together to become experts on their parts. Bring the experts back to their original groups. Each group member teaches his or her part of the assignment to other members of the original group until everyone has mastered all the material. Expert Teams can be used for section and chapter reviews.

Study Buddies

Study Buddies work together to help one another study for tests or to create concept maps. Group students in fours. After a chapter is completed, give students one class period to work in groups to master the material in the Chapter Review before giving the end of chapter test. If you wish, Study Buddies can be divided into Expert Teams to study and then teach the material. To have Study Buddies create concept maps, give each group member a different colored pen. Group members pass the concept map around the table adding to the map on each pass with their colored pens.

Numbered Heads Together

Form groups of three to five and have students number off. Then, ask a question or give an assignment. Have students in each group either agree on an answer or, for higher level thinking skills, name an example, make a prediction, or state an application. When students have agreed on an answer, call a number at random. Students with that number raise their hands and wait to be called on. Select one student to provide an answer. Determine if other students with that number have the correct answer by indicating thumbs up or down or by having them write their responses on index cards or on the chalkboard. Numbered Heads Together can be used for section and chapter reviews, problem solving, concept mapping, and Skill Builders.

Problem Solving Team

Form groups of four students, and assign roles. The reader reads the problem; the clarifier restates it; the solver suggests answers. If the group agrees on answers, the recorder writes the answers on a paper that all members sign. Review the answers and discuss the problem by calling on any group member. Use thumbs up or down, write responses on response cards or the chalkboard to determine if all groups have the same answers. This strategy can be used for problem solving and Skill Builder features.

Science Investigation

Science Investigation group members work together to perform hands-on science investigations. The Science Investigation strategy is used for Activities, MINI-Labs, and FIND OUT features. In Science Investigation, each group member has a different role and duties to perform for the investigation. Some roles are working roles to accomplish the investigation, while others are interpersonal skill roles that help the group function effectively. Following are possible roles for Science Investigation groups.

Working Roles

Reader: reads the activity directions out loud

Materials Handler: obtains, dispenses, and returns all materials

Safety Officer: informs group of safety precautions; ensures group handles equipment safely

Recorder: records data collected during the activity; writes answers to activity questions; has all group members sign data collection and answer sheets

Reporter: reports data collected and answers to activity questions

Timekeeper: keeps group on task; and manages the group's time

Calculator: performs activity calculations and measurements

Interpersonal Skill Roles

Monitor: ensures each group member participates and encourages participation

Praiser: compliments group members on fulfilling their assigned tasks; compliments group members on use of interpersonal skills

Checker: checks on learning of group members; ensures each group member can summarize the results of the activity and answer activity questions.

Applications

The following chart provides strategies for applying cooperative learning during **Merrill Physical Science** activities.

Merrill Physical Science features	Applicable Cooperative Learning Strategies
Find Out	Science Investigation, Paired Partners, Numbered Heads Together
Concept Mapping	Study Buddies, Paired Partners, Numbered Heads Together
Problem Solving	Problem Solving Teams, Paired Partners, Numbered Heads Together
Skill Builder	Problem Solving Team, Paired Partners, Numbered Heads Together
Section Review	Study Buddies, Expert Teams, Paired Partners, Numbered Heads Together
Chapter Review	Study Buddies, Expert Teams, Paired Partners, Numbered Heads Together
MINI-Lab	Science Investigation, Paired Partners, Numbered Heads Together
Activity	Science Investigation, Paired Partners, Numbered Heads Together

Resources

Adams, D.M., and M.E. Hamm. *Cooperative Learning, Critical Thinking, and Collaboration Across the Curriculum.* Springfield, IL: Charles C. Thomas Publisher, 1990.

Association for Supervision and Curriculum Development. *Educational Leadership,* Volume 47, Number 4, December, 1989-January, 1990.

Foot, H.C., M.J. Morgan, and R.H. Shute. *Children Helping Children.* New York: John Wiley & Sons, 1990.

Johnson, D.W., and R.T. Johnson. *Learning Together and Alone: Cooperative, Competitive, and Individualistic Learning.* Englewood Cliffs, NJ: Prentice-Hall, 1987.

Johnson, D.W., and R.T. Johnson., E.J. Holubec, and P. Roy. *Circles of Learning: Cooperation in the Classroom.* Alexandria, VA: Association for Supervision and Curriculum Development, 1984.

Kagan, S. *Cooperative Learning: Resources for Teachers.* Riverside, CA: University of California, 1988.

Shlomo, S. *Cooperative Learning Theory and Research.* Westport, CT: Praeger, 1990.

Slavin, R. *Cooperative Learning Theory, Research, and Practice.* Englewood Cliffs, NJ: Prentice Hall, 1990.

Slavin, R. *Using Student Team Learning.* Baltimore, MD: The John Hopkins Team Learning Project, 1986.

Meeting Individual Needs

	DESCRIPTION	SOURCES OF HELP/INFORMATION
Learning Disabled	All learning disabled students have an academic problem in one or more areas, such as academic learning, language, perception, social-emotional adjustment, memory, or attention.	*Journal of Learning Disabilities* *Learning Disability Quarterly*
Behaviorally Disordered	Children with behavior disorders deviate from standards or expectations of behavior and impair the functioning of others and themselves. These children may also be gifted or learning disabled.	*Exceptional Children* *Journal of Special Education*
Physically Challenged	Children who are physically disabled fall into two categories—those with orthopedic impairments and those with other health impairments. Orthopedically impaired children have the use of one or more limbs severely restricted, so the use of wheelchairs, crutches, or braces may be necessary. Children with other health impairments may require the use of respirators or have other medical equipment.	Batshaw, M.L. and M.Y. Perset. *Children with Handicaps: A Medical Primer*. Baltimore: Paul H. Brooks, 1981. Hale, G. (Ed.). *The Source Book for the Disabled*. NY: Holt, Rinehart & Winston, 1982. *Teaching Exceptional Children*
Visually Impaired	Children who are visually disabled have partial or total loss of sight. Individuals with visual impairments are not significantly different from their sighted peers in ability range or personality. However, blindness may affect cognitive, motor, and social development, especially if early intervention is lacking.	*Journal of Visual Impairment and Blindness* *Education of Visually Handicapped* American Foundation for the Blind
Hearing Impaired	Children who are hearing impaired have partial or total loss of hearing. Individuals with hearing impairments are not significantly different from their hearing peers in ability range or personality. However, the chronic condition of deafness may affect cognitive, motor, and social development if early intervention is lacking. Speech development also is often affected.	*American Annals of the Deaf* *Journal of Speech and Hearing Research* *Sign Language Studies*
Limited English Proficiency	Multicultural and/or bilingual children often speak English as a second language or not at all. Customs and behavior of people in the majority culture may be confusing for some of these students. Cultural values may inhibit some of these students from full participation.	*Teaching English as a Second Language Reporter* R.L. Jones, ed., *Mainstreaming and the Minority Child*. Reston, VA: Council for Exceptional Children, 1976.
Gifted	Although no formal definition exists, these students can be described as having above average ability, task commitment, and creativity. Gifted students rank in the top 5% of their class. They usually finish work more quickly than other students, and are capable of divergent thinking.	*Journal for the Education of the Gifted* *Gifted Child Quarterly* *Gifted Creative/Talented*

TIPS FOR INSTRUCTION

1. Provide support and structure; clearly specify rules, assignments, and duties.
2. Establish situations that lead to success.
3. Practice skills frequently—use games and drills to help maintain student interest.
4. Allow students to record answers on tape and allow extra time to complete tests and assignments.
5. Provide outlines or tape lecture material.
6. Pair students with peer helpers, and provide classtime for pair interaction.

---

1. Provide a clearly structured environment with regard to scheduling, rules, room arrangement, and safety.
2. Clearly outline objectives and how you will help students obtain objectives. Seek input from them about their strengths, weaknesses, and goals.
3. Reinforce appropriate behavior and model it for students.
4. Do not expect immediate success. Instead, work for long term improvement.
5. Balance individual needs with group requirements.

---

1. Openly discuss with student any uncertainties you have about when to offer aid.
2. Ask parents or therapists and students what special devices or procedures are needed, and if any special safety precautions need to be taken.
3. Allow physically disabled students to do everything their peers do, including participating in field trips, special events, and projects.
4. Help nondisabled students and adults understand physically disabled students.

---

1. As with all students, help the student become independent. Some assignments may need to be modified.
2. Teach classmates how to serve as guides.
3. Limit unnecessary noise in the classroom.
4. Encourage students to use their sense of touch. Provide tactile models whenever possible.
5. Describe people and events as they occur in the classroom.
6. Provide taped lectures and reading assignments.
7. Team the student with a sighted peer for laboratory work.

---

1. Seat students where they can see your lip movements easily, and avoid visual distractions.
2. Avoid standing with your back to the window or light source.
3. Using an overhead projector allows you to maintain eyecontact while writing.
4. Seat students where they can see speakers.
5. Write all assignments on the board, or hand out written instructions.
6. If the student has a manual interpreter, allow both student and interpreter to select the most favorable seating arrangements.

---

1. Remember students' ability to speak English does not reflect their academic ability.
2. Try to incorporate the student's cultural experience into your instruction. The help of a bilingual aide may be effective.
3. Include information about different cultures in your curriculum to aid students' self-image—avoid cultural stereotypes.
4. Encourage students to share their cultures in the classroom.

---

1. Make arrangements for students to take selected subjects early and to work on independent projects.
2. Let students express themselves in art forms such as drawing, creative writing, or acting.
3. Make public services available through a catalog of resources, such as agencies providing free and inexpensive materials, community services and programs, and people in the community with specific expertise.
4. Ask "what if" questions to develop high-level thinking skills; establish an environment safe for risk taking.
5. Emphasize concepts, theories, ideas, relationships, and generalizations.

Performance Objectives

Books on science education list many valid reasons for teaching science. These reasons range from general to more specific goals. A general goal might be to help students acquire habits of critical thinking. A specific goal might be to teach these students the definition of an element and a compound. How do you know if you are accomplishing these goals in your teaching? Herein lies the value of performance objectives—the behaviors that you, the teacher, can observe and which indicate that students are achieving the goals of science education.

In many cases, several types of behaviors will indicate that the students are achieving the objectives. For example, how do you determine that the students are acquiring habits of critical thinking? Some student behaviors you might observe include:

1. asking related questions.
2. gathering data or offering evidence that supports their answers.
3. questioning or expressing doubt about the hypotheses posed by others.

Other behaviors will indicate if students are learning other things. These behaviors can be written as performance objectives to aid you in assessing student accomplishment. A good performance objective is written in three parts:

1. the condition,
2. the performance or criterion, and
3. the criterion measure.

The condition tells what causes, stimulates, or motivates the student to perform the behaviors, or under what circumstances those behaviors will be performed. The performance or criterion tells exactly what behavior you are looking for. A good performance objective would avoid using such terms as *know about, appreciate,* or *sense the relationship between.* The criterion measure tells how many of the students have achieved the objective, or to what degree of accuracy or level of performance the behavior should be performed for you to know the students have actually achieved the objective.

In other words, a good performance objective uses verbs that express some type of observable action. Here are some examples of action verbs that describe observable behaviors: states orally, identifies, watches, matches, lists, states, distinguishes, manipulates, hypothesizes, measures, constructs.

Performance objectives are related to the four broad goals of science education:

Attitudes: To develop students' attitudes of curiosity and involvement with occurrences in their environment; to develop an appreciation for the contributions of science; and to recognize the value of solving problems in a scientific manner.

Processes: To develop those intellectual processes of inquiry by which scientific problems and occurrences are explained, predicted, and/or controlled.

Knowledge: To develop knowledge of facts, terminology, concepts, generalizations, and principles that help students confront and interpret occurrences in their environment.

Skills: To develop students' abilities to handle, construct, and manipulate materials and equipment in a productive and safe manner; and to develop the ability to measure, organize, and communicate scientific information.

Performance objectives are listed for students at the beginning of each section of *Merrill Physical Science.* Review questions located at the end of each major text section and the chapter review questions test students' mastery of the objectives. The Chapter Review and Chapter Tests of the *Teacher Resource Package* are correlated with the section objectives.

Laboratory Safety

Safety is of prime importance in every classroom. However, the need for safety is even greater when science is taught. Outlined below are some considerations on laboratory safety that are intended primarily for teachers and administrators.

The activities in **Merrill Physical Science** are designed to minimize dangers in the laboratory. Even so, there are no guarantees against accidents. However, careful planning and preparation as well as being aware of hazards can keep accidents to a minimum. Numerous books and pamphlets are available on laboratory safety with detailed instructions on preventing accidents. However, much of what they present can be summarized in the phrase, *Be prepared!* Know the rules and what common violations occur. Know the Safety Symbols used in this book (see p. 34T). Know where emergency equipment is stored and how to use it. Practice good laboratory housekeeping and management by observing these guidelines.

Classroom/Laboratory

1. Store chemicals properly.
   a. Separate chemicals by reaction type.
   b. Label all chemical containers. Include purchase date, special precautions, and expiration date.
   c. Discard chemicals when outdated, according to appropriate disposal methods.
   d. Do not store chemicals above eye level.
   e. Wood shelving is preferable to metal. All shelving should be firmly attached to walls. Anti-roll lips should be placed on all shelves.
   f. Store only those chemicals that you plan to use.
   g. Flammable and toxic chemicals require special storage containers.
2. Store equipment properly.
   a. Clean and dry all equipment before storing.
   b. Protect electronic equipment and microscopes from dust, humidity, and extreme temperatures.
   c. Label and organize equipment so that it is accessible.
3. Provide adequate workspace.
4. Provide adequate room ventilation.
5. Post safety and evacuation guidelines.
6. Be sure safety equipment is accessible and works.
7. Provide containers for disposing of chemicals, waste products, and biological specimens. Disposal methods must meet local guidelines.
8. Use hot plates whenever possible as a heat source. If burners are used, a central shut-off valve for the gas supply should be available to the teacher. Never use open flames when a flammable solvent is in the same room.

First Day of Class/Labs (with students)

1. Distribute and discuss safety rules, safety symbols, first aid guidelines, and safety contract found in the Teacher Resource Guide. Have students refer to Appendix B on pages 673 and 674, to review safety symbols and guidelines.
2. Review safe use of equipment and chemicals.
3. Review use and location of safety equipment.
4. Discuss safe disposal of materials and laboratory cleanup policy.
5. Discuss proper laboratory attitude and conduct.
6. Document students' understanding of above points.
   a. Have students sign the safety contract and return it.
   b. Administer the safety assessment found in the *Teacher Resource Package*. Reteach those points that students do not understand.

Before Each Investigation

1. Perform each investigation yourself before assigning it.
2. Arrange the lab in such a way that equipment and supplies are clearly labeled and easily accessible.
3. Have available only equipment and supplies needed to complete the assigned investigation.
4. Review the procedure with students, emphasizing any caution statements or safety symbols that appear.
5. Be sure all students know proper procedures to follow if an accident should occur.

During the Investigation

1. Make sure the lab is clean and free of clutter.
2. Insist that students wear goggles and aprons.
3. Never allow a student to work alone in the lab.
4. Never allow students to use a cutting device with more than one edge.
5. Students should not point the open end of a heated test tube toward anyone.
6. Remove broken glassware or frayed cords from use. Also clean up any spills immediately. Dilute solutions with water before removing.
7. Be sure all glassware that is to be heated is of a heat-treated type that will not shatter.
8. Remind students that hot glassware looks cool.
9. Prohibit eating and drinking in the lab.

After the Investigation

1. Be sure that the lab is clean.
2. Be certain that students have returned all equipment and disposed of broken glassware and chemicals properly.
3. Be sure all hot plates and electrical connections are off.
4. Insist that each student wash his or her hands when lab work is completed.

The **Merrill Physical Science** program uses safety symbols to alert you and your students to possible laboratory dangers. These symbols are explained on the following page. Be sure your students understand each symbol before they begin an investigation or skill.

Safety Symbols

DISPOSAL ALERT	This symbol appears when care must be taken to dispose of materials properly.	**ANIMAL SAFETY**	This symbol appears whenever live animals are studied and the safety of the animals and the students must be ensured.
BIOLOGICAL HAZARD	This symbol appears when there is danger involving bacteria, fungi, or protists.	**RADIOACTIVE SAFETY**	This symbol appears when radioactive materials are used.
OPEN FLAME ALERT	This symbol appears when use of an open flame could cause a fire or an explosion.	**CLOTHING PROTECTION SAFETY**	This symbol appears when substances used could stain or burn clothing.
THERMAL SAFETY	This symbol appears as a reminder to use caution when handling hot objects.	**FIRE SAFETY**	This symbol appears when care should be taken around open flames.
SHARP OBJECT SAFETY	This symbol appears when a danger of cuts or punctures caused by the use of sharp objects exists.	**EXPLOSION SAFETY**	This symbol appears when the misuse of chemicals could cause an explosion.
FUME SAFETY	This symbol appears when chemicals or chemical reactions could cause dangerous fumes.	**EYE SAFETY**	This symbol appears when a danger to the eyes exists. Safety goggles should be worn when this symbol appears.
ELECTRICAL SAFETY	This symbol appears when care should be taken when using electrical equipment.	**POISON SAFETY**	This symbol appears when poisonous substances are used.
PLANT SAFETY	This symbol appears when poisonous plants or plants with thorns are handled.	**CHEMICAL SAFETY**	This symbol appears when chemicals used can cause burns or are poisonous if absorbed through the skin.

Chemical Storage and Disposal

General Guidelines

Be sure to store all chemicals properly. The following are guidelines commonly used. Your school, city, county, or state may have additional requirements for handling chemicals. It is the responsibility of each teacher to become informed as to what rules or guidelines are in effect in his or her area.

1. Separate chemicals by reaction type. Strong acids should be stored together. Likewise, strong bases should be stored together and should be separated from acids. Oxidants should be stored away from easily oxidized materials and so on.
2. Be sure all chemicals are stored in labeled containers indicating contents, concentration, source, date purchased (or prepared), any precautions for handling and storage, and expiration date.
3. Dispose of any outdated or waste chemicals properly according to accepted disposal procedures.
4. Do not store chemicals above eye level.
5. Wood shelving is preferable to metal. All shelving should be firmly attached to all walls and have anti-roll edges.
6. Store only those chemicals that you plan to use.
7. Hazardous chemicals require special storage containers and conditions. Be sure to know what those chemicals are and the accepted practices for your area. Some substances must even be stored outside the building.
8. When working with chemicals or preparing solutions, observe the same general safety precautions that you would expect from students. These include wearing an apron and goggles. Wear gloves and use the fume hood when necessary. Students will want to do as you do whether they admit it or not.
9. If you are a new teacher in a particular laboratory, it is your responsibility to survey the chemicals stored there and to be sure they are stored properly or disposed of. Consult the rules and laws in your area concerning what chemicals can be kept in your classroom. For disposal, consult up-to-date disposal information from the state and federal governments.

Disposal of Chemicals

Local, state, and federal laws regulate the proper disposal of chemicals. These laws should be consulted before chemical disposal is attempted. Although most substances encountered in high school courses can be flushed down the drain with plenty of water, it is not safe to assume that is always true. It is recommended that teachers who use chemicals consult the following books from the National Research Council.

Prudent Practices for Handling Hazardous Chemicals in Laboratories, Washington, DC: National Academy Press, 1981.

Prudent Practices for Disposal of Chemicals from Laboratories, Washington, DC: National Academy Press, 1983.

These books are useful and still in print, although they are several years old. Current laws in your area would, of course, supersede the information in these books.

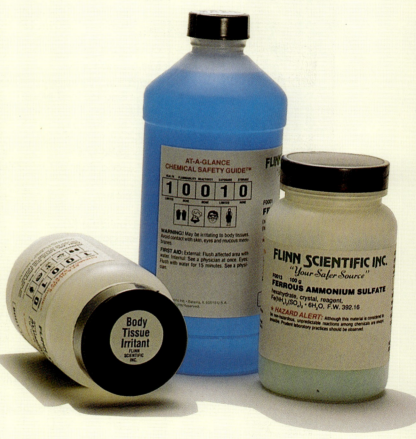

Physical Science Materials List

NONCONSUMABLES			
ITEM	**ACTIVITY**	**MINI LAB**	**FIND OUT**
Aluminum foil,	9-1, 22-2 25-1	144, 548 646	
heavy duty	14-2		
pieces (2)		523	
strips		567	
Apron	8-1, 15-1		
Balance	2-2, 3-2 5-2, 7-2 15-1	40, 177 405, 646	425
Ball, soccer			189
Balloons,			83
medium, round (2)	8-2		
Battery, 6-volt (4)	22-2, 23-1 22-1		
6 or 9 volt	21-2		
Beaker,	3-2, 14-2		267
beakers, 100-mL (7)	25-1	383, 646	
beakers, 250-mL (5)	6-1, 15-2 21-1	7	
beakers, small			299
Biology textbook			351
Board, approximately 100 cm	7-1	66	
long inclined plane		177	
Books,	7-1		157
box full (5+)			109
Bottle,		405	
soda pop			457
soda pop, plastic, 2-liter		210	
Bowl, plastic		520	
Box, plastic	19-2		
Brick,	7-1		
building (2)	4-2		
Burner, gas	11-2, 15-1, 15-2	301	299
or hot plate			327
Calculator, pocket-sized		609	
Candle		646	
Car			643
Cardboard,		646	
thick, (22 cm × 28 cm)			
marked with rectangles	17-1		
Cards		412	
Cellophane, sheets, different colors	19-1		
Charcoal, briquettes crushed into powder (1 or 2)			379
Clamp, utility		577	
Clay, green, balls (6)		631	
modeling	19-2, 25-1		
white, balls (6)		631	
Cloth, or yarn; small piece	6-2		
cotton		548	
Coat hangers, wire		144	
Coins, (3)	7-2		
Compass, magnetic	22-1		

NONCONSUMABLES

ITEM	ACTIVITY	MINI LAB	FIND OUT
Conductivity tester		428	
Construction supplies, misc.	25-2		
Container, plastic, 1 quart	2-2		
Copper foil	9-1		
Corks (10)	4-1		
Cups,			
foam	3-2, 5-2	42, 490	
foam, with lid		118	
measuring	2-2, 14-2		
paper	8-1, 22-1		219
paper or foam			379
Diffraction grating	19-1		
Diode,	23-1		
light emitting,			
different colors(2)	23-1		
Dish, per group (1)			403
Dosimeter		631	
Dowels, pencil sized (2)	7-1		
Dropper,	8-1	201, 210	
medicine (4)	17-1, 17-2	405	403
pipette	13-1		
Dynamics carts (2)	4-2		
Egg carton, modified	11-1		
Evaporating dish, small	9-2		
(2)	14-1		
Extension cord			133
Filter paper			425
Film, undeveloped, or photo-			
graphic film badge		621	
Flask, 250-mL	6-2		
Forceps	25-1		
Freezer bag, plastic, containing			
tagged items	9-1		
Funnel, plastic	22-1		425
Gauge, air pressure			189
Glove, heat proof	8-2		
Glue		144	
Goggles, safety	8-1, 8-2		
	9-2, 11-2		
	12-1, 15-1		
	18-1, 25-1		
Graduated cylinder,	2-2, 5-2,	40	
	8-1, 13-1,		
	15-1, 16-1,		
	16-2, 17-1,		
	17-2		
10-cm3	9-2		
Granite, piece of	9-1		379
Gravel, fine			219
Greeting card, musical			595
Hair curlers, set	5-2		
Hammer	14-2		
Hand lens	9-2		
Heat lamp, or portable hair dryer			425
Hot plate, electric	2-2, 9-2		
	16-2		
Inflation needle			189
Iron wire, thin pieces of,			
such as hairpins		301	
Jars, small, or beakers		428	619
Knife	22-2		
Lamp, with bare bulb			133

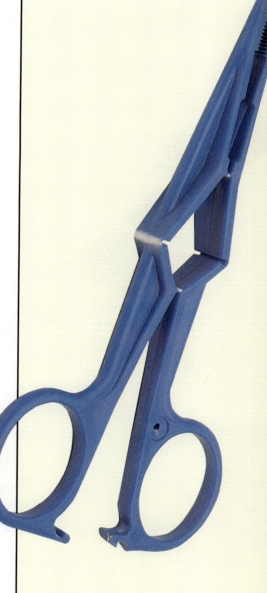

ITEM	ACTIVITY	MINI LAB	FIND OUT
NONCONSUMABLES			
LEDs, different colors (2)	23-1		
Lid, with straw hole	2-2		
Light, fluorescent		490	
incandescent		490	
low voltage	22-2		
with base	19-1, 19-2	523	
	20-1		
with socket (3)	21-2		
Magnet,		577	
disk (12)	23-2		
small		603	
Magnetic board, 20 cm × 27 cm	10-1		
Magnet wire, 22 ga	22-1		
32 ga	22-1		
Marble chips			425
Marbles,	11-1	66	
or other small, uniformly			
shaped objects			619
Markers	10-1	412	
Mass, 20-g		73	
Masses		87	
Matches,	6-2	631	
large wooden	12-1		
Metersticks,	3-1, 4-1	66, 73	
	4-2, 8-2	177	59
	22-1		
(2)	5-1		
Microscope			643
Milliammeter		567	
Mirrors, plane (2)	20-1		
Munchie ingredients	2-2		
Nail,	22-1		
large	22-2		
Needle		523, 577	
Newspaper	3-2		
Note cards	13-2		
Nut, and bolt	12-2		
Nuts, bolts, washers; various			
small			241
Objects, metal		466	
small		520	
with flat, hard surfaces	20-2		
Pads, heavy		476	
Paper,			573
cardstock, thin strip and			
sheets (2)	23-2		
graph	5-2		
poster, large sheet	25-2		
selection of strips	3-2		
sheet, 22 cm × 28 cm	7-2		
sheets of various types,			
weights, sizes	3-1		
tissue			545
typing, 22 cm × 28 cm,			
marked with rectangles	17-1		
white, plain,		73, 287	327
circles, 4-cm wide	10-1		
Paper clips	3-1, 13-2		299
	14-2, 20-1		
	22-2		
(6)	21-2		
Paper towel	14-2		403

NONCONSUMABLES

ITEM	ACTIVITY	MINI LAB	FIND OUT
Pencils,		40, 257	573
colored	19-1		
round (2)	19-2		157
Penny, copper	14-1		
darkened (2)			403
Pens,		257	
felt-tip	4-1		
colored, set of	25-2		
marking	8-2, 12-2		
Pinch clamps (2)	6-2		
Pipe, plastic	18-2		
Plaster of paris	14-2		
Plastic food wrap	25-1	490, 520	403
		548	
Polarizing filters (2)	20-2		
Polystyrene sheets	12-2		
Poster board		144	
Power supply, AC, low voltage	22-2, 23-1		
Protractor	20-1		
Pulley	7-1		
Punch, paper		548	
Pump, inflation			189
Radio		476	
Resistor, 10 ohm	23-1		
Ring stand,	14-1, 15-2	577, 646	
(2)	1-1		
and ring	3-2, 5-1		
	7-1, 21-1		
Rubber bands, (4)	18-2, 25-1		
large (2)		87	
long	4-2		
Rubber magnetic strips,			
0.5-cm piece (1) and			
2-cm pieces (24)	10-1		
Rubber tubing, 1 m	21-1		
pieces, (3)	6-2		
Rulers,			157, 351, 545
metric	1-1, 7-2		
	18-2, 23-2		
Sand	3-2, 16-2	118	219, 379
Sand paper,	22-1		
coarse		73	
Scissors	1-1, 2-1		
	3-2, 17-1		
	21-2		
Slides, microscope			643
Slinky, small	18-1		
Soda straw,	22-1	7	
cut to length of nail	22-2		
Solder, piece of	9-1		
Spatula, laboratory	16-2		
Splint, wooden	16-1, 16-2		
Spoons, metal			511
Stapler	3-1		
Steel wool			267
Stick or dowel, slightly more			
than 2 m long	4-1		
wooden	8-1		
Stirring rod, (3)	6-1	383	
glass		287	

NONCONSUMABLES

ITEM	ACTIVITY	MINI LAB	FIND OUT
Stopper, 2-hole	15-1		
2-hole rubber, medium	5-1		
2-hole rubber with glass			
tubing	6-2		
Stopwatches	3-1, 18-1	66	
or clock	21-1		
or timer with second hand		177	
String	1-1, 2-1,	144, 466	
	3-1, 3-2		
	4-1, 5-1		
	7-1, 8-2		
Support rod, 30-cm	5-1		
Support rod clamp, right angle	5-1		
Syringe, large, plastic	6-2		
"T," glass or plastic	6-2		
Table, large surface		257	
Tablespoon, measuring	2-2		
Tape,	22-1	577	
masking	2-1, 3-2		133
	4-2, 5-1		
	20-1		
transparent	3-1, 20-1		
	21-2, 23-2		
or rubber bands		567	
Teaspoon, measuring	2-2		
Test tubes, (7)	11-2, 16-1		327
	17-1, 17-2		
large	12-1, 15-1		
medium-sized (3)	16-2		
same size (2)			267
and stopper	13-1		
Test-tube holders, wire	11-2, 15-1,		
	16-1, 16-2		
Thermometers	5-2, 6-1	42, 118	
	8-2, 15-1	490, 646	
	15-2		
Thread, 1 m		577	
Thumbtacks (10)	4-1		
Timer, with second hand	17-1		
Tongs	6-1, 8-2	301	299, 643
	14-1		
Toothpicks		330	241
Toy, car, windup		177	
electric, with battery		567	
truck, small		87	
TV set		603	
Twist ties (2)	25-1		
Weights, identical (3)	1-1		
small	1-1		
Wires, copper, bare, 16 ga	22-1		
hook-up	23-1		
insulated, 32 ga	22-2		
with small alligator			
clips (3)		567	

CONSUMABLES

ITEM	ACTIVITY	MINI LAB	FIND OUT
Bread, white			327
Candy-coated chocolates, (2 red, 3 green)	10-2		
Candy-coated peanuts, (4 red, 3 green)	10-2		
Carbonated beverage, colorless	17-2		
Gumdrops, of one color		330	
Hot dog		144	
Ice, crushed	11-2		
Ice cubes, colored	6-1		
Orange juice		428	
Raisins		330	
Salt	6-1, 9-1 11-2, 15-2	403	
Spaghetti, thin, pieces (6)	12-2		
Sugar,	11-2		
cubes (4)		383	
Sugar water	9-1		

CHEMICAL SUPPLIES

ITEM	ACTIVITY	MINI LAB	FIND OUT
Acetic acid, dilute	17-1		
Baking soda	9-1, 9-2		
Beta radiation, source		631	
Bleach, liquid laundry, 5% sodium hypochlorite	12-1		
Borax solution, 4%	8-1		
Calcium carbonate tablets, crushed, (10 g)			219
Cleaner, containing ammonia		428	
Cobalt(II) chloride (0.5 g)	12-1		
solution, dilute		287	
Copper, small piece	16-1		
Copper(II) sulfate			299
Detergent, dishwashing		7	
Food coloring	8-1		
Ethyl alcohol	13-1		
Graphite, powdered	12-2		
Hydrochloric acid,			
1M	9-2		
dilute	16-1, 17-1		
Hydrogen peroxide solution, 3%	16-2		
Iron(III) chloride solution, dilute, FeCl3		405	
Magnesium, small piece	16-1		
Manganese dioxide	16-2		
Nitric acid, dilute	14-1		
Petroleum jelly			643
Phenolphthalein indicator, 1%	17-2, 25-1		
pH paper	17-1		
Polyvinyl alcohol (PVA), 4% solution	8-1		
Potassium bromide	15-1		
Potassium permanganate (0.01M)	13-1		
Radioactive source, weak		621	
Rubbing alcohol		201	
Soap		405	
Sodium chloride			299
Sodium hydroxide solution, (6M)	13-1, 14-1	405	
dilute	17-2		
4 pellets	25-1		
Solids, selection, includes iron and pure nickel		577	
Strontium chloride			299
Vinegar			403
Water			
distilled	15-1, 15-2		299
Zinc, 30 mesh			
small piece	16-1		

Preparation of Solutions

The following text gives some general hints on solution preparation and some safety tips to keep in mind.

For best results, the preparation of each solution is tailored to the requirements of the Activity, Mini-Lab, or Find Out activity in which it is used. Directions for preparing needed solutions are given in the margin of the *Teacher Wraparound Edition* adjacent to each activity. It is not recommended that solutions be made far in advance. Rather, they should be prepared fresh as needed.

Unless otherwise specified, solutions are prepared by adding the solid to a small amount of water and then diluting with water to the volume listed. Use distilled water for the preparation of solutions. For example, to make a $0.1M$ solution of aluminum sulfate, dissolve 34.2 g of $Al_2(SO_4)_3$ in a small amount of distilled water and dilute to a liter with water. If you use a hydrate that is different from the one specified in a particular preparation, you will need to adjust the amount of the hydrate to obtain the required concentration.

It is most important to use safe laboratory techniques when handling all chemicals. Many substances may appear harmless but are, in fact, toxic, corrosive, or very reactive. Always check the hazard information on the reagent bottle. If in doubt, check with the manufacturer or with Flinn Scientific Inc., (312) 879-6900. Chemicals should never be ingested. Be sure to use proper techniques to smell solutions or other reagents. Always wear safety goggles and an apron. The following general cautions should be used.

1. *Liquid and/or vapor poisonous/corrosive. Use in the fume hood.*

acetic acid	hydrochloric acid
ammonium hydroxide	nitric acid

2. *Poisonous and corrosive to eyes, lungs, and skin.*

acids	limewater	iron(III) chloride
bases	silver nitrate	potassium permanganate
iodine		

3. *Poisonous if swallowed, inhaled, or absorbed through the skin.*

acetic acid, glacial	copper compounds
barium chloride	lead compounds
chromium compounds	lithium compounds
cobalt(II) chloride	silver compounds

4. *Always add acids to water, never the reverse.*

5. *When sulfuric acid and sodium hydroxide are added to water, a large amount of thermal energy is released. Sodium metal reacts violently with water. Use extra care if handling any of these substances.*

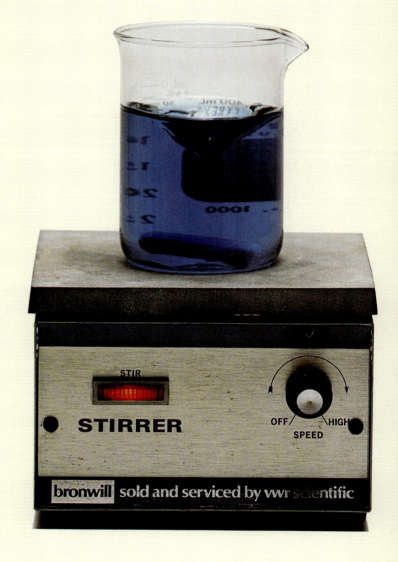

Supplier Addresses

EQUIPMENT SUPPLIERS

Central Scientific Company
11222 Melrose Avenue
Franklin Park, IL 60131

Edmund Scientific Company
103 Gloucester Pike
Barrington, NJ 08007

Fisher Scientific Company
4901 W. LeMoyne Avenue
Chicago, IL 60615

Flinn Scientific Inc.
P.O. Box 219
Batavia, IL 60510

LaPine Scientific Company
13636 Western Avenue
Blue Island, IL 60406-0780

McKilligan Supply Corporation
435 Main Street
Johnson City, NY 13790

Nasco
901 Janesville Avenue
Fort Atkinson, WI 53538

Sargent-Welch Scientific Co.
7300 N. Linder Avenue
Skokie, IL 60077

Sargent-Welch Scientific of
    Canada, Ltd.
285 Garyray Drive
Weston, Ontario,
Canada M9L 1P3

Science Kit and Boreal Labs
777 E. Park Drive
Tonawanda, NY 14150

Turtox/Cambosco
8200 S. Hoyne Avenue
Chicago, IL 60620

Ward's Natural Science
    Establishment, Inc.
5100 W. Henrietta Road
Rochester, NY 14692

AUDIOVISUAL DISTRIBUTORS

Agency for Instructional
    Technology (AIT)
Box A
Bloomington, IN 47402

Aims Media
9710 Desoto Avenue
Chatsworth, CA 91311-4409

BFA Educational Media
468 Park Avenue S.
New York, NY 10016

Center for the Humanities
Box 1000
90 S. Bedford Road
Communications Park
Mount Kisco, NY 10549

Churchill Films
12210 Nebraska Avenue
Los Angeles, CA 90025

Coronet/MTI Film and Video
Distributors of LCA
108 Wilmot Road
Deerfield, IL 60015

CRM Films
2233 Faraday Avenue
Suite F
Carlsbad, CA 92008

Educational Materials and
    Equipment Co. (EME)
P.O. Box 2805
Danbury, CT 06813-2805

Encyclopedia Britannica
    Educational Corp. (EBEC)
310 S. Michigan Avenue
Chicago, IL 60604

Focus Media, Inc.
839 Stewart Avenue
P.O. Box 865
Garden City, NY 11530

Handel Film Corporation
8730 Sunset Blvd.
West Hollywood, CA 90069

Hawkill Associates, Inc.
125 E. Gilman Street
Madison, WI 53703

Image Entertainment
9333 Oso Avenue
Chatsworth, CA 91311

JCE: Software
Department of Chemistry
University of Wisconsin,
    Madison
1101 University Avenue
Madison, WI 53706

Journal Films, Inc.
930 Pitner Avenue
Evanston, IL 60202

Learning Arts
Box 179
Wichita, KS 67201

Macmillan/McGraw-Hill
    School Division
4635 Hilton Corporate Drive
Columbus, OH 43232

Modern Talking Picture Service
5000 Park Street N.
Saint Petersburg, FL 33709

National Geographic Society
    Educational Services
17th and "M" Streets, NW
Washington, DC 20036

PBS Video
1320 Braddock Place
Alexandria, VA 22314-1698

Science Software Systems
11890 W. Pico Blvd.
Los Angeles, CA 90064

Singer Media Corporation
3164 Tyler Avenue
Anaheim, CA 92801

Society for Visual
    Education Inc. (SVE)
Dept. VM
1345 Diversey Parkway
Chicago, IL 60614-1299

Time-Life Videos
Time and Life Building
Avenue of the Americas
New York, NY 10020

SOFTWARE DISTRIBUTORS

Agency for Instructional
    Technology, (AIT)
Box A
Bloomington, IN 47402-0120

American Chemical Society
    Computer Courses
1155 16th Street NW
Washington, DC 20036

Bergwall Productions, Inc.
106 Charles Lindbergh Blvd.
Uniondale, NY 11553

Carolina Biological Supply Co.
2700 York Road
Burlington, NC 27215

(Classroom Consortia Media
    Inc.) Gemstar
P.O. Box 050228
Staten Island, NY 10305

COMPress
P.O. Box 102
Wentworth, NH 03282

Cross Educational Software
P.O. Box 1536
504 E. Kentucky Avenue
Ruston, LA 71270

Educational Materials and
    Equipment Company (EME)
P.O. Box 2805
Danbury, CT 06813-2805

Educational Courseware
3 Nappa Lane
Westport, CT 06880

Focus Media, Inc.
839 Stewart Avenue
P.O. Box 865
Garden City, NY 11530

IBM Educational Systems
    Department PC
4111 Northside Parkway
Atlanta, GA 30327

J and S Software
135 Haven Avenue
Port Washington, NY 11050

Merlan Scientific, Ltd.
247 Armstrong Avenue
Georgetown, Ontario,
Canada L7G 4X6

Micro-ED, Inc.
P.O. Box 24750
Edina, MN 55424

Microphys
1737 W. Second Street
Brooklyn, NY 11223

Minnesota Educational
    Computing Corporation (MECC)
3490 Lexington Avenue N.
Saint Paul, MN 55126

Muse Software
P.O. Box 283
Monrovia, MD 21770

Queue, Inc.
562 Boston Avenue
Bridgeport, CT 06610

Scott, Foresman, and Company
1900 E. Lake Avenue
Glenview, IL 60025

Sunburst Communications
39 Washington Avenue
Pleasantville, NY 10570

Wm. K. Bradford Publishing Co.
310 School Street
Acton, MA 01720

Ventura Educational Systems
3440 Brokenhill Street
Newbury Park, CA 91320

We want your opinions!

We at Merrill Publishing feel that with this edition of **Merrill Physical Science,** we have produced a quality textbook program—but the final proof of that rests with you, the teachers who have had the opportunity to put our materials to use in your classrooms. That's why we would appreciate it if you would take the time to respond to any part of this questionaire that is appropriate for you. In doing so, you will be letting us know how good a job we've done and where we can work to improve.

Please note: (1) you need not have used all of the program components to respond to this questionnaire; and (2) we encourage you to give us your honest and most candid opinions.

Student Text

Excellent				Poor	
5	4	3	2	1	Organization
5	4	3	2	1	Narrative sytle
5	4	3	2	1	Readability
5	4	3	2	1	Visual impact
5	4	3	2	1	Usable Table of Contents
5	4	3	2	1	Accuracy of content
5	4	3	2	1	Coverage of science principles
5	4	3	2	1	Reduced number of bold-face terms
5	4	3	2	1	Skill builder questions
5	4	3	2	1	Skill Handbook
5	4	3	2	1	Mini Labs Activities
5	4	3	2	1	Problem Solving features
5	4	3	2	1	Technology features
5	4	3	2	1	Science & Society Sections
5	4	3	2	1	Glossary and Index
5	4	3	2	1	Appendices
5	4	3	2	1	Global Connections features
5	4	3	2	1	Unit End features

Teacher Edition

Excellent				Poor	
5	4	3	2	1	Teachability
5	4	3	2	1	Planning charts
5	4	3	2	1	Organization of teaching cycle
5	4	3	2	1	Performance objectives

Supplements

5	4	3	2	1	Teacher Resource Package
5	4	3	2	1	Laboratory Manual
5	4	3	2	1	Color Transparency Package
5	4	3	2	1	Test Bank
5	4	3	2	1	Chapter Review Software

School Information

1. What is the grade level of the students you teach?   6   7   8   9
2. Total number of students in that grade?   1-50   51-100   101-200   200+
3. Average class size?   25 or less   26-30   31-40   41 or more
4. Total school enrollment?   1-200   201-500   501-1000   1000+
5. Ability level of your average class?   Basic   Average   Advanced
6. How appropriate is this text for your class?   Too easy   On level   Too difficult
7. How many years have you used this text?   1   2   3   4   5

Fold

Please feel free to include additional comments on a separate sheet.

Name _____   Date _____

School _____

Street _____

City _____   State _____   Zip _____

Fold

BUSINESS REPLY MAIL
FIRST CLASS PERMIT NO 284 COLUMBUS OHIO

POSTAGE WILL BE PAID BY ADDRESSEE

GLENCOE

SCIENCE PRODUCT MANAGER

PO BOX 508

COLUMBUS OHIO 43272-6174

NO POSTAGE
NECESSARY
IF MAILED
IN THE
UNITED STATES

MERRILL
PHYSICAL SCIENCE

GLENCOE
Macmillan/McGraw-Hill

Lake Forest, Illinois   Columbus, Ohio   Mission Hills, California   Peoria, Illinois

A GLENCOE PROGRAM

MERRILL PHYSICAL SCIENCE

Student Edition
Teacher Wraparound Edition
Teacher Resource Package
Study Guide, Student Edition
Reinforcement, Student Edition
Enrichment, Student Edition
Transparency Package

Laboratory Manual
Laboratory Manual,
    Teacher Annotated Edition
Spanish Resources
Chapter Review Software
Computer Test Bank
Videodisc Correlation

REVIEWERS

Richard A. Boolootian, Ph.D.
Director of Science Curriculum
Mirman School
Los Angeles, California

Theodore L. Boydston, III
Science Coordinator
Dade County Public Schools Region V
Miami, Florida

Robert C. Cambric
Science Dept. Chairperson
St. Francis Academy
Joliet, Illinois

Stephen A. Clark
Chemistry and Physics Teacher
Elbert County Comprehensive High School
Elberton, Georgia

Billie R. Easley
Science Dept. Head
Thackerville High School
Thackerville, Oklahoma

Elder Harrison, Jr.
Instructor
Chicago Public Schools
Chicago, Illinois

Mathew Keller
Physical Science and Chemistry Teacher
Rancho Cotate High School
Rohnert Park, California

Lillie B. Kelly
Science Dept. Chairperson
Shades Mountain Christian School
Birmingham, Alabama

Sr. Mary Ita O'Donnell
Science Dept. Chairperson
St. Joseph High School
Brooklyn, New York

Sandra McMillen Pace
Science Dept. Chairperson
Southeast High School
Macon, Georgia

Dominic Salinas
Assistant Principal
Parkway High School
Bossier City, Louisiana

Cover Photograph: Neon Tubes by Jim Osborn

Send all inquiries to:
GLENCOE DIVISION
Macmillan/McGraw-Hill
936 Eastwind Drive
Westerville, OH 43081

ISBN 0-675-16776-0

Printed in the United States of America.

1 2 3 4 5 6 7 8 9 -VH- 99 98 97 96 95 94 93 92 91

AUTHORS

Richard G. Smith has been teaching chemistry at the high school level for 25 years. He received a regional outstanding teacher award from the American Chemical Society and has participated in NSF summer institutes in chemistry. Mr. Smith graduated Phi Beta Kappa with a B.S. degree in Education from Ohio University and earned his M.A.T. in Chemistry from Indiana University. He is a member of the American Chemical Society and the National Science Teachers Association as well as other national professional organizations.

Jack T. Ballinger is a chemistry professor at St. Louis Community College in St. Louis, Missouri, where he has taught for 21 years. He received his B.S. degree in chemistry at Eastern Illinois University and his M.S. degree in organic chemistry at Southern Illinois University. He is a member of the American Chemical Society, the St. Louis Society of Analysts, and the National Education Association.

Marilyn Thompson teaches physics, chemistry, and physical science at Center Senior High School in Kansas City, Missouri. Ms. Thompson holds a B.A. degree in chemistry with an emphasis in physics and education from Carleton College, Northfield, Minnesota. She is a member of the American Association of Physics Teachers and the National Science Teachers Association.

CONSULTANTS

Senior Consultant, Physics:
John D. McGervey
Professor of Physics
Case Western Reserve University
Cleveland, Ohio

Physics:
Patrick Hamill, Ph.D.
Professor of Physics
San Jose State University
San Jose, California

Chemistry:
Robert C. Smoot, M.S.
Chemistry Teacher and Rollins Fellow in Science
McDonogh School
McDonogh, Maryland

Reading:
Barbara Pettegrew, Ph.D.
Director of Reading/Study Center
Assistant Professor of Education
Otterbein College
Westerville, Ohio

Safety:
Robert Tatz, Ph.D.
Instructional Lab Supervisor
Department of Chemistry
The Ohio State University
Columbus, Ohio

Special Features:
Stephen C. Blume
Elementary Science Specialist
St. Tammany Public School System
Slidell, Louisiana

Charles McLaughlin
Coordinator of Science Education
St. Joseph Public Schools
St. Joseph, Missouri

John R. Grube
High School Science Coordinator (former)
Eastside Union High School District
San Jose, California

Gifted and Mainstreamed:
Barbara Murdock
Elementary Consultant For Instruction
Gahanna–Jefferson Public Schools
Gahanna, Ohio

Judy Ratzenberger
Middle School Science Instructor
Gahanna Middle School West
Gahanna, Ohio

CONTENTS

UNIT 3 THE NATURE OF MATTER 186

UNIT 4 KINDS OF SUBSTANCES 296

UNIT 5 INTERACTIONS OF MATTER   376

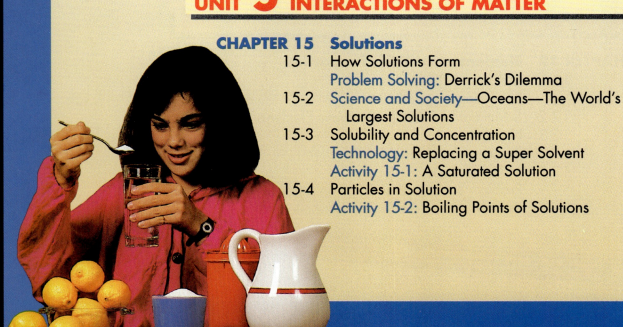

UNIT 6 WAVES, LIGHT, AND SOUND   454

UNIT 7   ELECTRICITY & ENERGY RESOURCES   542

14

6 **C** Carbon 12.011
14 **Si** Silicon 28.0855
32 **Ge** Germanium 72.59
50 **Sn** Tin 118.710
82 **Pb** Lead 207.2

ACTIVITIES

MINI-Labs

PROBLEM SOLVING

TECHNOLOGY

SKILL BUILDERS

ORGANIZING INFORMATION
Sequencing: 32, 131, 155, 217, 265, 509, 533, 665

Outlining: 17, 74, 107, 181, 423, 491, 509, 537, 661

THINKING CRITICALLY
Observing and Inferring: 8, 77, 81, 107, 217, 235, 291, 325, 367, 412, 423, 449, 481, 505, 509, 537, 549, 632, 641

Comparing and Contrasting: 27, 51, 89, 116, 131, 239, 265, 291, 325, 349, 371, 385, 401, 433, 449, 462, 581, 593, 611, 617, 623, 647

Recognizing Cause and Effect: 107, 155, 161, 217, 239, 325, 349, 371, 407, 423, 449, 478, 516, 537, 593, 617, 665

EXPERIMENTATION SKILLS
Measuring in SI: 51, 81, 131, 181, 214, 371, 401

Hypothesizing: 27, 51, 131, 207, 291, 349, 401, 415, 481, 525, 537, 563, 577, 593

Using Variables, Constants, and Controls: 27, 140, 155, 239, 288, 571

Interpreting Data: 107, 127, 155, 217, 239, 265, 371, 401, 423, 445, 449, 571

GRAPHIC ORGANIZERS
Concept Mapping: 23, 27, 41, 63, 103, 121, 131, 151, 155, 178, 203, 224, 246, 265, 280, 291, 321, 325, 345, 358, 371, 397, 419, 423, 436, 470, 496, 509, 521, 537, 568, 571, 587, 593, 605, 635, 641, 652

Making and Using Tables: 81, 94, 145, 170, 196, 239, 253, 265, 272, 325, 401, 449, 481, 509, 558, 617, 641, 665

Making and Using Graphs: 45, 51, 67, 81, 107, 181, 217, 262, 314, 333, 349, 393, 481, 571, 641

Interpreting Scientific Illustrations: 27, 181, 291, 307, 336, 349, 481, 601, 617, 628

GLOBAL CONNECTIONS

CAREERS

SCIENCE AND LITERATURE/ART

USING MERRILL PHYSICAL SCIENCE

Physical Science is an everyday experience. It's a subject you're familiar with because every part of your day is based upon physical science principles…the simple act of walking involves gravity, which holds you to Earth, friction between the soles of your shoes and the ground, which allows you to overcome inertia, accelerate forward, make turns, and even stop. Depending on temperature, the morning drizzle may have left a puddle or an icy spot for you to cross. What you see, hear, touch, and smell along your walk all involve physical science principles. **Merrill Physical Science** will help you understand science principles and recognize their applications to everyday life.

a quick tour of your textbook

What's happening here? Have you ever considered what allows gum to be stretched? Each unit begins with thought-provoking photographs that will make you wonder. The unit introduction then explains what is happening in the photographs and how the two relate to each other and to the content of the unit. What allows gum to be stretched? Read the opener to Unit 4 to find out.

It's clearly organized to get you started and keep you going.

As you begin each new chapter, use the **Gearing Up** to preview what topics are covered and how they are organized. You will also preview the skills you will use in this chapter.

After you've performed the **FIND OUT** activity and previewed the chapter, you're ready to further explore the topics ahead. Read **What's next** to see what's ahead.

Chapters are organized into three to five numbered sections. The **Objectives** at the beginning of the numbered section tell you what major topics you'll be covering and what you should expect to learn about them. The **New Science Words** are also listed in the order in which they appear in the section.

Experience science by observing, experimenting, and asking questions.

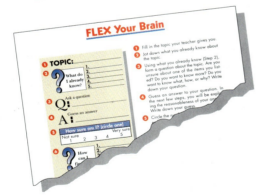

MINI-Lab

What energy changes take place during evapoartion?

Use a dropper to place five drops of rubbing alcohol on the back of your hand. Wait for two minutes. What sensations did you feel? What change of state did you observe? Is energy entering or leaving your hand? Where does the energy for this process come from?

FLEX Your Brain

Flex Your Brain is a unique activity you can use to sharpen your critical thinking skills. Starting from what you already know about a science topic, you will apply a simple ten-step procedure to extend your knowledge about the topic from a perspective that interests you.

Science is more than words in a book. The two Activities and the MINI-Labs in each chapter give you the chance to further explore and investigate the science topics covered in your textbook.

In the **Activities,** you'll use household items and laboratory equipment as you follow the easy, step-by-step procedure. At the end of each Activity are questions that ask you to analyze what you've done.

Most **MINI-Labs** are designed so you can do them on your own or with friends outside of the science classroom using materials you find around the house. Doing a MINI-Lab is an easy and fun way to further your knowledge about the topics you're studying.

Each **Problem Solving** feature gives you a chance to solve a real world problem or understand a science principle.

PROBLEM SOLVING

Ivan's Isotopes

After carrying out many medical tests, the doctor found a tumor in Ivan's thyroid gland. The doctor decided to treat the tumor with iodine-131, an isotope of iodine. Ivan asked her how the treatment would work. She explained that atoms of some isotopes, like iodine-131, are unstable. One of these atoms has too many neutrons for the number of protons. The nucleus in an unstable isotope rearranges itself spontaneously, resulting in the release of energy called radiation.

The thyroid gland absorbs iodine because the gland needs iodine to function properly. The doctor told Ivan the tumor cells in his thyroid are more sensitive to radiation than the healthy thyroid cells. A controlled dose of radiation from the iodine-131 would kill the tumor cells but would not affect the healthy cells.

Think Critically: Why is iodine-131 unstable? Why is the number of neutrons in an atom important in the field of medicine?

Explore news-making issues, concerns about the environment, and how science shapes your world through technology.

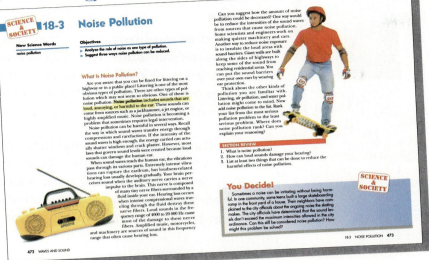

The impact of science on society directly affects you. In the **Science and Society** section in each chapter, you'll learn about an issue that's affecting the world around you. The topics you'll read about are controversial, and you'll explore them from several sides. Then, you'll have a chance to express your opinion in the You Decide feature that follows.

In the **Technology** feature in each chapter, you'll read about recent discoveries, newly developed instruments, and applications of technology that have shaped our world and furthered our knowledge.

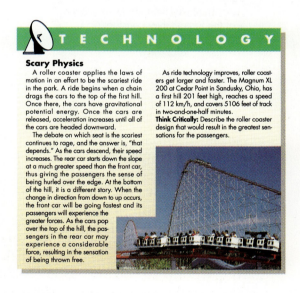

T E C H N O L O G Y

Scary Physics

A roller coaster applies the laws of motion in an effort to be the scariest ride in the park. A ride begins when a chain drags the cars to the top of the first hill. Once there, the cars have gravitational potential energy. Once the cars are released, acceleration increases until all of the cars are headed downward.

The debate on which seat is the scariest continues to rage, and the answer is, "that depends." As the cars descend, their speed increases. The rear car starts down the slope at a much greater speed than the front car, thus giving the passengers the sense of being hurled over the edge. At the bottom of the hill, it is a different story. When the change in direction from down to up occurs, the front car will be going fastest and its passengers will experience the greater forces. As the cars pop over the top of the hill, the passengers in the rear car may experience a considerable force, resulting in the sensation of being thrown free.

As ride technology improves, roller coasters get larger and faster. The Magnum XL 200 at Cedar Point in Sandusky, Ohio, has a first hill 201 feet high, reaches a speed of 112 km/h, and covers 5106 feet of track in two-and-one-half minutes.

Think Critically: Describe the roller coaster design that would result in the greatest sensations for the passengers.

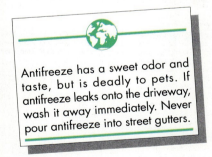

Antifreeze has a sweet odor and taste, but is deadly to pets. If antifreeze leaks onto the driveway, wash it away immediately. Never pour antifreeze into street gutters.

Each **EcoTip** suggests a simple step you can take to help improve the environment. EcoTips explain how you can get involved in making Earth a better place to live.

Discover that you can apply what you've learned as you answer questions and practice your science skills.

At the end of each section are several Section Review questions that help you test your knowledge. The last question challenges you to think critically and **Apply** what you've learned.

The **Skill Builder** feature lets you sharpen your science skills using only paper and pencil. If you need help with these skills, refer to the **Skill Handbook** at the back of the book. Here, you can find complete information about each type of skill covered in the Skill Builders.

Science and READING

Before a runner is given credit for a record in track, officials carefully analyze the conditions under which the event was held. What are some of the factors they consider?

Science is related to every other subject you study. The **Science And** features challenge you to solve math problems, read literature excerpts, and to write about topics you're studying as you make the connections between science and other disciplines.

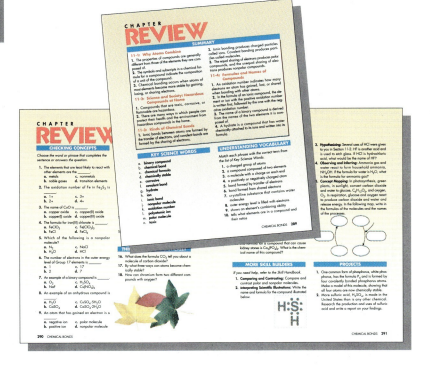

The **Chapter Review** starts with a summary so you can review the major concepts from each section. Then, you'll apply your knowledge and practice thinking skills as you answer the questions that follow.

Discover how physical science topics relate to people and places all over the world.

Global Connections help you to see how physical science is related to other sciences as well as social studies, history and health.

Also at the end of each unit you will find two **Careers** that relate to the material in the unit you just read. What jobs may be related to waves, light, and sound? Read the careers at the end of Unit 6 to find out.

What do physical science and literature have in common? A lot, as you'll discover when you read the unit close to Unit 1. Each unit is closed with a reading from literature or an example of art that makes a connection with physical science.

In Unit 1, students are introduced to the role of problem solving as an activity of science. The identification of problems and strategies to solve them are related to the scientific method and experimental design. Students then briefly explore the content of physical science. The unit closes with a discussion of the importance of measurements in science, the SI system of measurements, and graphing as a useful means of displaying and interpreting data.

CONTENTS

ADVANCE PREPARATION

Audiovisuals
▶ Show the film *What is Science?* Coronet/MTI Films.
▶ Show the video *Newton: The Mind that Found the Future*, LCA.
▶ Show videos from *Conversations with Great Scientists* Video Series, Focus.
▶ Show the film *School Lab Safety,* Handel Film Corporation.

Field Trips and Speakers
▶ Arrange for a speaker from your local dental or medical association to visit your class.
▶ Arrange a field trip to an elementary school classroom.

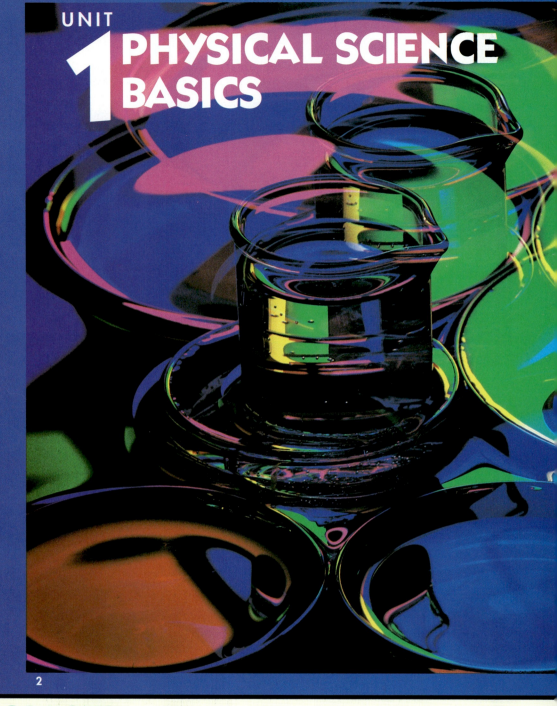

UNIT

1 PHYSICAL SCIENCE BASICS

2

OPTIONS

Cross Curriculum
▶ Have students keep logs of types of measurements, measuring instruments, and units of measurements used in other classes.
▶ Have students keep logs of types of problems that arise in other classes and strategies used to solve them. Have the students compare and contrast these strategies to those presented in the unit.

Science at Home
▶ Have students keep logs of the types of measurements, measuring instruments, and units of measurement that they use at home or that they observe being used in various occupations. Have students present their finding to the class.

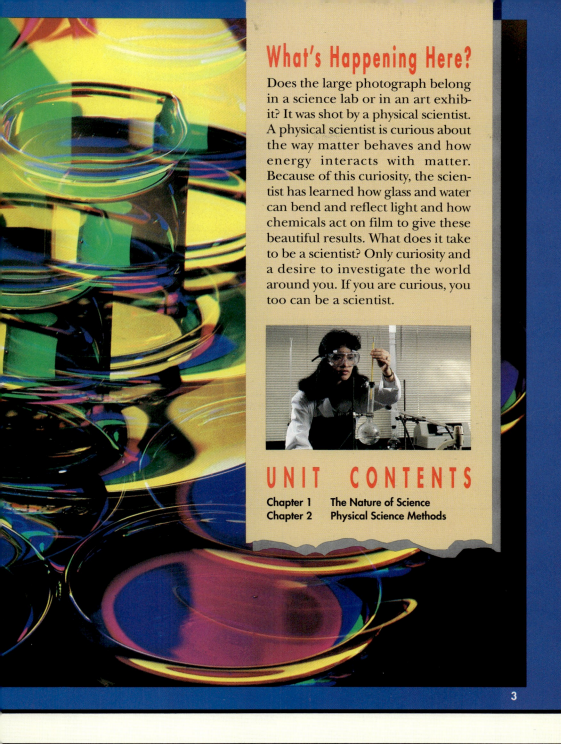

What's Happening Here?

Does the large photograph belong in a science lab or in an art exhibit? It was shot by a physical scientist. A physical scientist is curious about the way matter behaves and how energy interacts with matter. Because of this curiosity, the scientist has learned how glass and water can bend and reflect light and how chemicals act on film to give these beautiful results. What does it take to be a scientist? Only curiosity and a desire to investigate the world around you. If you are curious, you too can be a scientist.

UNIT CONTENTS

Multicultural Awareness

Have interested students research the contributions of various cultures to inventions and technological achievements in astronomy and navigation that illustrate systematic and accurate observations and measurements.

Inquiry Questions

Use the following questions to focus a discussion of observations and physical science.
▶ **What are the names of the laboratory glasswares shown in the photograph?** *Beaker, Petri dish*
▶ **What observations and measurements do you think the student is making? What question do you think the student may be trying to answer?** *Accept all reasonable answers.*

INTRODUCING THE UNIT

What's Happening Here?
▶ Have students look at the photos and read the text. Ask them to tell you what's happening here. Point out to students that in this unit they will be studying the relationship between problem solving and physical science. They will also learn how curiosity, careful observations, hunches, and accurate measurements are used to solve problems.
▶ **Background:** The photograph consists of four images of the same subject each taken with a different colored flash of light. The flashes were provided by a strobe light with colored filters. The images were recorded by a multiple-image camera that has four apertures, allowing four independent images to be recorded on the film.
▶ Students may be interested in knowing that the photograph was taken by a former professional scientist with a doctoral degree in chemistry who integrated his training as a physical scientist and his interests in photography to become a full-time, professional photographer.

Previewing the Chapters
▶ Name and locate a margin feature in the unit that tells what the inventor of dynamite did with his fortune (Did You Know? page 23); is an activity about bubbles you can do by yourself (MINI-Lab, page 7); outlines Chapter 2 (Gearing Up, page 29); lists kelvin as a section vocabulary word (New Science Words, page 34); tells you how much water is used in a typical home (EcoTip, page 45); and suggests researching physical science and careers (Science and Reading, page 8).

Tying to Previous Knowledge
▶ Have students brainstorm lists of different types of measuring devices and units they have used. Urge them to think of situations, such as buying shoes, clothing, and groceries, in which consumers purchase materials that have been premeasured or sized and packaged.
▶ Use the questions in the OPTIONS box below to discuss science and observations.

The Nature of Science

CHAPTER SECTION	OBJECTIVES	ACTIVITIES
1-1 Physical Science and You (1 day)	1. **Compare** and **contrast** "pure" science and technology. 2. **Define** physical science. 3. **Discuss** some of the topics covered in physical science.	**MINI-Lab:** *How can patterns help explain complicated systems?* p. 7
1-2 Problem Solving (2 days)	1. **Distinguish** between problems and exercises. 2. **Evaluate** approaches for solving problems. 3. **Compare** and **contrast** hypothesis, theory, and scientific law.	
1-3 Problems? What Problems? Science & Society (1 day)	1. **Describe** some of the environmental issues presently being studied by scientists. 2. **Examine** how scientific controversies arise.	
1-4 Exploring Science (2 days)	1. **Appreciate** the importance of following guidelines in doing experiments. 2. **Define** independent variable and dependent variable. 3. **Understand** laboratory safety rules.	**Activity 1-1:** *Identifying and Controlling Variables,* p. 24
Chapter Review		

ACTIVITY MATERIALS

FIND OUT	ACTIVITIES	MINI-LABS
Page 5 none	**1-1 Identifying and Controlling Variables, p. 24** string, 1.5 m 3 identical weights 1 smaller weight metric ruler 2 ring stands scissors	**How can patterns help explain complicated systems? p. 7** 250-mL beaker water dishwashing detergent soda straw

CHAPTER FEATURES	TEACHER RESOURCE PACKAGE	OTHER RESOURCES
Skill Builder: *Observing and Inferring,* p. 8	**Ability Level Worksheets** ◆ **Study Guide,** p. 5 ● **Reinforcement,** p. 5 ▲ **Enrichment,** p. 5 **MINI-Lab Worksheet,** p. 11	
Technology: *Driving Smart,* p. 13 **Skill Builder:** *Outlining,* p. 17	**Ability Level Worksheets** ◆ **Study Guide,** p. 6 ● **Reinforcement,** p. 6 ▲ **Enrichment,** p. 6 **Critical Thinking/Problem Solving,** p. 7 **Transparency Masters,** pp. 1, 2	**Color Transparency 1,** Flex Your Brain
You Decide! p. 19	**Ability Level Worksheets** ◆ **Study Guide,** p. 7 ● **Reinforcement,** p. 7 ▲ **Enrichment,** p. 7 **Concept Mapping,** pp. 7, 8	
Problem Solving: *Lauren's Experiment,* p. 22 **Skill Builder:** *Concept Mapping,* p. 23	**Ability Level Worksheets** ◆ **Study Guide,** p. 8 ● **Reinforcement,** p. 8 ▲ **Enrichment,** p. 8 **Activity Worksheet,** pp. 7, 8 **Cross-Curricular Connections,** p. 5 **Science and Society,** p. 5 **Transparency Masters,** pp. 3, 4	**Color Transparency 2,** Safety Symbols **Lab Manual 1,** No Need to Count Your Pennies
Summary Think & Write Critically Key Science Words Apply Understanding Vocabulary More Skill Builders Checking Concepts Projects Understanding Concepts	**Chapter Review,** pp. 5, 6 **Chapter Test,** pp. 5-8	**Chapter Review Software** **Test Bank**

◆ **Basic**   ● **Average**   ▲ **Advanced**

ADDITIONAL MATERIALS

SOFTWARE	AUDIOVISUAL	BOOKS/MAGAZINES
Discovery Lab, MECC. *Black Box,* EME. *Thinking and Learning,* EME. *The Lortep Project,* Queue. *Discovering the Scientific Method: Snigs...Flirks...Blorgs,* Focus.	*What is Science,* film, Coronet/MTI Films. *Newton: The Mind That Found the Future,* video, LCA. *Conversations with Great Scientists,* video, Focus. *School Lab Safety,* film, Handel Film Corp.	Arons, Arnold. *The Various Language: An Inquiry Approach to the Physical Sciences.* New York: Oxford University Press, 1977. Resnick, Robert. *Fundamentals of Physics,* 2nd ed. New York: John Wiley and Sons, 1987. Kuntz, Margy. *Adventures in Physical Science.* Fearon Teaching Aids, 1987.

THEME DEVELOPMENT: This chapter presents the scientific method as an example of problem solving. The systematic approach to identifying, formulating, and solving problems should be used to link the sections within the chapter.

CHAPTER OVERVIEW

▶ **Section 1-1:** In this section the relationship between science and technology is discussed. The scope of topics studied in the physical sciences is presented.

▶ **Section 1-2:** This section continues the theme of problem solving by discussing what a problem is. Four problem-solving strategies are presented and developed.

▶ **Section 1-3: Science and Society:** Three topics—the greenhouse effect, depletion of the ozone layer, and acid rain—are used as examples to discuss how to define and solve environmental problems.

▶ **Section 1-4:** This section discusses experimentation by introducing the concepts of experimental controls and variables. Five steps that aid in organizing a scientific experiment are outlined. The section concludes with a discussion of the importance of safety in the science classroom.

CHAPTER VOCABULARY

technology	ozone layer
physical science	experiment
model	control
critical thinking	constant
observation	independent
hypothesis	variable
theory	dependent
scientific law	variable
greenhouse	
effect	

C H A P T E R

1 The Nature of Science

4

OPTIONS

For Your Gifted Students

Have students develop cartoon characters that can be used throughout the year. Ask students to pick a concept that is illustrated in the text, such as lab safety. They can use the cartoon characters to illustrate the points in a humorous way. This cartoon strip can help record their year in science.

Isn't it frustrating when something doesn't work the way you'd like it to? Sometimes that feeling of frustration can lead to ideas for improvements or new inventions.

FIND OUT!

Do this exercise to explore some ways of solving problems.

Working with a partner, think of something in your school that doesn't work as well as it could. You may choose a device, like a pencil sharpener or window shade, or a system, such as the cafeteria line or the grading process.

Without showing each other your work, you and your partner each make a list of ways you could improve the device or system you chose. Then write down the steps you would go through to make these improvements.

Now show each other your lists. How are they different? Why do you think you and your partner came up with different approaches to the same problem? Would your answers have been different if you had worked together? Is there any way to find out whether one approach would work better?

Gearing Up
Previewing the Chapter
Use this outline to help you focus on important ideas in the chapter.

Section 1-1   Physical Science and You
▶ Applying Science
▶ Physical Science

Section 1-2   Problem Solving
▶ What Is a Problem?
▶ Problem-Solving Strategies
▶ Critical Thinking
▶ Problem Solving in Science

Section 1-3   Science and Society
Problems? What Problems?
▶ Research or Action?

Section 1-4   Exploring Science
▶ Experimentation
▶ Safety

Previewing Science Skills
▶ In the **Skill Builders,** you will observe and infer, outline, and make a concept map.
▶ In the **Activity,** you will observe, predict, and control variables.
▶ In the **MINI-Lab,** you will observe and infer.

What's next?

You have identified a problem and attempted to work out a solution to the problem. Now find out how your approach to problem solving compares with the approach used by scientists.

5

INTRODUCING THE CHAPTER
Use the Find Out activity to introduce students to the importance of problem solving as a major activity in science.

FIND OUT!
Cooperative Learning: Have Paired Partners share solutions and determine a single course of action. Allow students to discuss how the "two brains are better than one" approach clarified or enriched their individual thinking about solving the problem. Take time to discuss cooperative learning in general.

Teaching Tips
▶ Emphasize that a long cafeteria line is a "problem," but the problem that must be tackled by the students is determining the *method* to reduce the cafeteria line.
▶ Point out that "Why are hand-thrown pizzas always round?" is a question. The problem is how to find a method to answer the question.
▶ To avoid "quick-fix" solutions, have students consider if their improvements have any deleterious or detrimental short-term or long-term effects.

Gearing Up
Have students study the Gearing Up feature to familiarize themselves with the chapter. Discuss the relationships of the topics in the outline.

What's Next?
Before beginning the first section, make sure students understand the connection between the Find Out activity and the topics to follow.

For Your Mainstreamed Students
Have students make a chart showing the major safety rules that should be followed while conducting a lab. Their charts should illustrate the rules and be displayed all year in the classroom.

Physical Science and You

PREPARATION

SECTION BACKGROUND
▶ Science and technology are sometime classified as R&D, research and development. Advances in one depend upon the other.

PREPLANNING
▶ Obtain a pair of toddler's sneakers with laces and a pair with Velcro fasteners for the Motivation activity; dishwashing detergent and straws for the Mini-Lab.

1 MOTIVATE

▶ Show students a pair of children's old tie-sneakers and a pair with Velcro fasteners. Have students compare them and conjecture on the problems that were solved by the new fasteners.
▶ Have students bring in examples of packaging that show technological improvements such as twist-off bottles, tab-open cans, twist-tie and self-sealing food storage bags, and plastic foam containers. Have them compare the benefits and possible drawbacks of such new products.

TYING TO PREVIOUS
KNOWLEDGE: Have students discuss their understanding of the term *high tech.* Point out that in this section, they will learn more about this term.

OBJECTIVE AND
SCIENCE WORDS: Have students review the objectives and science words to become familiar with this section.

New Science Words

technology
physical science

Objectives

▶ Compare and contrast "pure" science and technology.
▶ Define *physical science.*
▶ Discuss some of the topics covered in physical science.

Applying Science

How are scientific discoveries made? Do scientists, with a specific goal in mind, conduct experiments until they reach that goal? The answer is "Sometimes, but not always." Read the brief true accounts that follow.

A scientist forgot to rinse out a flask. It was later discovered that a coating left on the inside of the flask kept the flask from shattering when dropped. This discovery led to the invention of safety glass, similar to that used in automobile windshields.

While studying data from a radio telescope, an astronomy student noticed that a particular star seemed to be emitting short, regular pulses of energy. Her observation led to the discovery of pulsars, stars that are as massive as the sun, but are only the size of a large mountain.

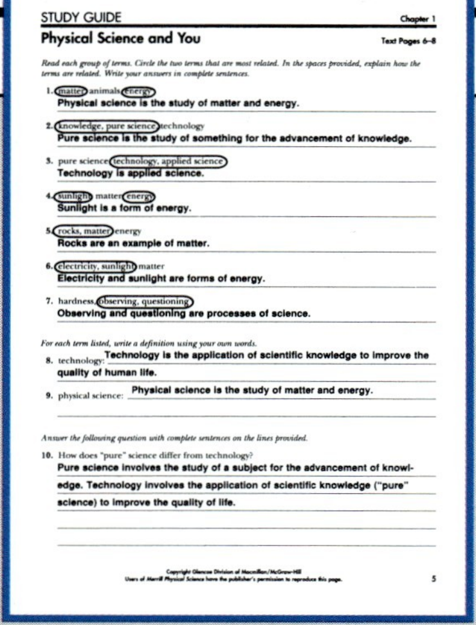

As these accounts show, the path to scientific discovery is not always a direct one. But the processes of science are always the same—observing, questioning, exploring, and seeking answers. Scientists are always trying to understand the world around them—from processes in their own bodies to reactions in the laboratory; from the burning of paper to the explosion of a star.

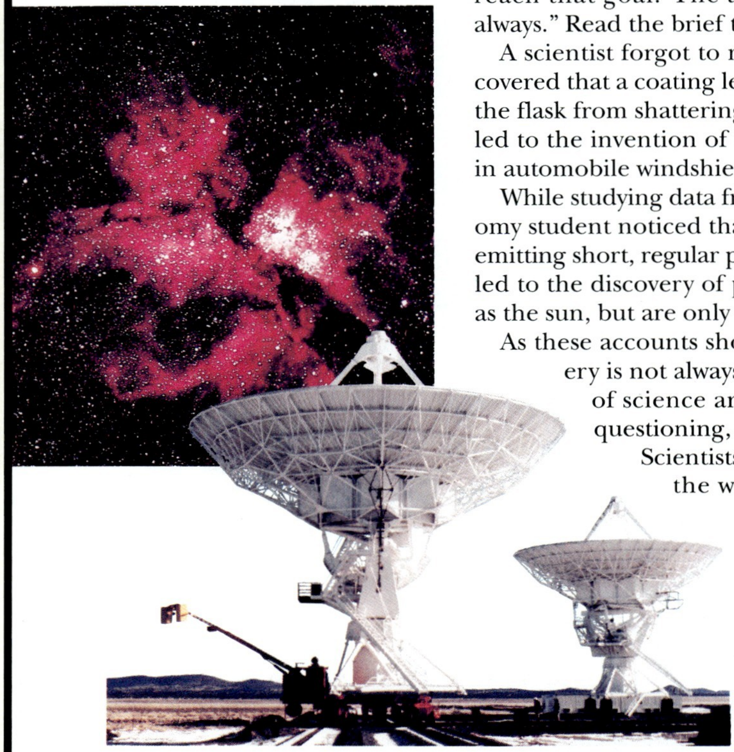

Figure 1-1. Scientists seek to learn more about Earth by studying the stars.

6 THE NATURE OF SCIENCE

OPTIONS

Meeting Different Ability Levels
For Section 1-1, use the following **Teacher Resource Masters** depending upon individual students' needs.
◆ **Study Guide Master** for all students.
● **Reinforcement Master** for students of average and above average ability levels.
▲ **Enrichment Master** for above average students.
Additional Teacher Resource Package masters are listed in the OPTIONS box throughout the section. The additional masters are appropriate for all students.

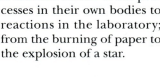

In their search for knowledge, scientists often make surprising discoveries. Not every discovery will have common, everyday applications. For example, the discovery of pulsars did not lead to the development of any consumer products. However, it did open up a whole new field of investigation. Scientists have learned about how matter behaves under the special condition that exists inside the very dense stars. Someday this information may help them to learn more about matter here on Earth.

Other scientific discoveries, such as the shatterproof glass flask, lead directly to practical and useful everyday applications. The application of scientific knowledge to improve the quality of human life is called **technology.**

There is no sharp boundary between science and technology. Scientific discoveries lead to technological inventions. Inventions, in turn, may lead to further discoveries. Science includes both "pure" science, for the advancement of knowledge, and "applied" science, or technology.

Figure 1-2. By applying their scientific knowledge, scientists and engineers develop products that make our lives easier.

Physical Science

Physical science is the study of matter and energy. Everything in the universe is either matter or energy. Plants and animals, rocks and clouds, eggs and elephants are all examples of matter. And lightning, thunder, heat, and sunlight are all examples of energy.

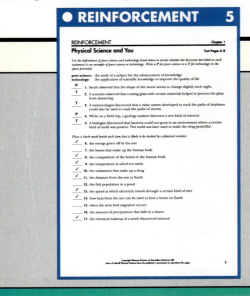

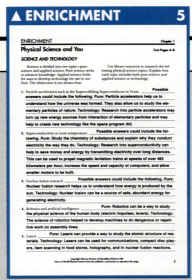

What is technology?

2 TEACH

Key Concepts are highlighted.

CONCEPT DEVELOPMENT

▶ Ask students to discuss their attitudes about science and technology by asking them which is more important. Most students are pragmatic and will choose technology. Keep this prejudice in mind as you discuss the importance and interrelationships of both.

CROSS CURRICULUM

▶ **Language Arts:** Have students use a dictionary to look up the words *science* and *technology.* Students should find that the words come from the Latin root *sciens* (having knowledge) and the Greek roots *techne* (craft or skill) and *logia* (study of), respectively. Have students comment on how the meanings of the words reflect their roots.

8 CHAPTER 1

CHECK FOR UNDERSTANDING

Ask questions 1-2 and the **Apply** Question in the Section Review.

RETEACH

Demonstration: Collect some plant burrs and show how they adhere to clothing. Have students use hand lenses or stereo-microscopes to observe plant burrs. Compare pieces of Velcro to these burrs. Point out that making the structures of Velcro mimic that of burrs is an example of both biological science and physical science; fashioning Velcro into a closure is technology.

EXTENSION

For students who have mastered this section, use the **Reinforcement** and **Enrichment** masters or other OPTIONS provided.

Science and READING

In a whole class you should have a real cross section of chosen careers. These can be used through the year as a given subject is studied.

3 CLOSE

▶ Invite a dentist to your class to discuss technological advances in dentistry.

SECTION REVIEW ANSWERS

1. Science is a study solely for the advance of knowledge. Technology is the application of scientific knowledge to improve the quality of life. The study of the electrical nature of matter is science, whereas the development of an electric generator is technology.

2. Physical science is the study of matter and energy.

3. Apply: Student responses will vary. Examples: (1) What causes tides? (2) How fast does sound travel in air? (3) Why are fuses used in an electrical circuit?

Skill Builder

Articles collected by students will vary. Make sure that students correctly identify the content as a scientific discovery or as a technological development.

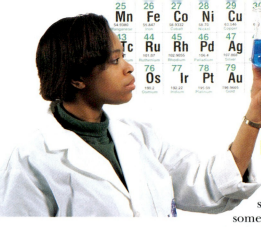

Figure 1-3. In the laboratory, scientists test their own ideas and check the work of other scientists.

Science and READING

Look through the table of contents for this book to find out what subjects a physical scientist studies. Then find a book in the library that lists such careers, such as The Occupational Outlook Handbook. Select a career that relates to physical science and describe it in a brief oral report to your class.

Physical science deals with the composition and properties of matter. Composition has to do with what matter is made up of. Properties have to do with what matter is like and how it behaves. You're already familiar with some properties of different kinds of matter. You know that rocks are hard, wax melts at low temperatures, and sugar tastes sweet. Hardness, melting point, and taste are some of the properties of matter.

In physical science, you'll learn how matter and energy are related. You'll discover how energy is transferred through matter, as when the sound from a stereo reaches your ears. You'll find out how refrigerators stay cold and why a down jacket keeps you warm.

As you learn about electricity, sound, heat, and light, you'll discover how energy is used to do work. In the study of force and motion, you'll learn why acorns fall to Earth while satellites remain in orbit.

As you study physical science, be on the lookout for patterns. Observe how things and ideas are organized into systems, and how different parts of a system interact. Your observations are bound to lead you to ask questions. The rest of this chapter will help you find out how to go about answering those questions.

SECTION REVIEW

1. What is the difference between science and technology? Give an example of each.
2. Define *physical science*.
3. **Apply:** Pose three questions that you think could be answered by the activities of physical science.

Skill Builder ☑ **Observing and Inferring**

Bring in a newspaper or magazine article related to physical science. Summarize the article and explain whether it deals with a scientific discovery or a technological development. If you need help, refer to Observing and Inferring in the **Skill Handbook** on page 678.

OPTIONS

INQUIRY QUESTIONS

▶ **Why do meteorologists use physical science to study thunderstorms?** *Meteorologists use physical science to study thunderstorms because the storms involve clouds, which are matter, and lightning and thunder, which are energy.*

▶ **What does the term R&D mean?** *research and development* **What does the term have to do with science and technology?** *The research can be thought of as pure science and the development as technology.*

ENRICHMENT

▶ Have interested students research the technological advances in common objects, such as pens, clocks, radios, televisions, and cameras, in the last 50 years. Have them share their findings with the class.

Problem Solving

Objectives

▶ Distinguish between problems and exercises.
▶ Evaluate approaches for solving problems.
▶ Compare and contrast hypothesis, theory, and scientific law.

What Is a Problem?

How can astronauts be kept safe and healthy on long space missions? Is Earth's climate warming up? What's the best way to make recorded music sound like the real thing? Each of these questions suggests a problem that can be approached scientifically. They are considered problems because their solutions are not obvious. Some crucial information is missing.

==Solving a problem involves finding missing information, but sometimes it's not clear at first what kind of information is needed.== For example, to find out whether the temperature of Earth's troposphere is increasing, where should temperature readings be made? Many weather stations throughout the world are in or near cities, but temperatures in cities generally are higher than temperatures in unpopulated areas. Scientists must decide whether temperature readings from cities should be included in their data. They also must decide how many years back they should go. Should they check temperatures starting at 1950? 1900? or even further back? As you can see, there are a lot of "problems" in deciding how to go about solving a problem.

New Science Words

model
critical thinking
observation
hypothesis
theory
scientific law

What do all problems have in common?

Figure 1-4. Infrared satellite images provide valuable information about temperatures at Earth's surface.

PREPARATION

SECTION BACKGROUND

▶ Problem solving is an important skill. The techniques used are the same as those used to develop and test hypotheses by scientific experimentation.
▶ A scientific law is a description of how two physical quantities that describe a phenomenon are related. A theory is a series of assumptions that unifies a large number of different and seemingly unrelated phenomena. A theory must comply with past and present appropriate observations and scientific laws as well as predict new hypotheses.

1 MOTIVATE

▶ Have students determine the answers to the following questions. **What is the value of four dimes?** *$0.40* **What is the minimum number of coins that total that value?** *3 (a quarter, a dime, and a nickel)* Have students discuss which of the two questions presented a greater challenge and explain the procedures they used to solve each question.
▶ Develop a set of elementary math exercises, such as addition or subtraction problems, and have students do them. Then ask a volunteer to perform a few knee-bends or jumping-jacks. Discuss why they are both called exercises.

TYING TO PREVIOUS KNOWLEDGE: Have students recall how they solved the problem of finding different classrooms when they first started school in this building. Point out that they will learn other methods of problem solving in this section.

OBJECTIVES AND SCIENCE WORDS: Have students review the objectives and science words to become familiar with this section.

Key Concepts are highlighted.

CONCEPT DEVELOPMENT

Cooperative Learning: Using a Numbered Heads Together strategy, have each team of students select a sport, board game, or video game and explain how it poses a problem to be solved. Have teams discuss how the various game moves can be used as strategies to solve the problem posed by the game.

CROSS CURRICULUM

▶ **Earth Science:** The *troposphere* is the lowest layer of the atmosphere and extends from the surface of Earth to an altitude of about 10-16 km.

Figure 1-5. Thomas Edison was an inventor who perfected the technique of applying scientific discoveries to develop and improve hundreds of products.

Figure 1-6. Maps and street signs can help a stranger find an address.

Solving problems always involves uncertainty. So, it's not surprising that scientists sometimes make false starts or end up on dead-end paths before they arrive at solutions. Solving problems sometimes involves trial-and-error and the ability to learn from mistakes. For example, in the process of inventing the light bulb, Thomas Edison tried more than 100 materials before he found one that would work as the filament of the bulb.

A problem for one person may not be a problem for someone else. For a stranger, finding a certain building downtown is a problem that requires using a map and reading street signs. For someone who passes the building on the way to work every day, finding the building is not a problem.

There's a difference between a problem and an exercise. In an exercise, the steps required to find the solution are usually obvious. ❶ For example, finding the average weight of five classmates is an exercise if you know how to calculate averages. If you don't know how to find averages, you are faced with a problem.

Problem-Solving Strategies

Before you can solve a problem, you need to understand exactly what the problem is. That may sound obvious, but people often have trouble solving problems because they don't know where to start. Sometimes that's because they haven't defined the problem clearly enough.

10 THE NATURE OF SCIENCE

OPTIONS

Meeting Different Ability Levels

For Section 1-2, use the following **Teacher Resource Masters** depending upon individual students' needs.

◆ **Study Guide Master** for all students.

● **Reinforcement Master** for students of average and above average ability levels.

▲ **Enrichment Master** for above average students.

Additional Teacher Resource Package masters are listed in the OPTIONS box throughout the section. The additional masters are appropriate for all students.

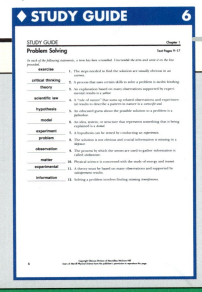

Suppose a friend asks you to help fix a broken bicycle. How will you proceed? Maybe you'll look over the bike and ask your friend a lot of questions. Is something wrong with a tire? Is there a problem with the gears? Does the bicycle rattle? Your questions and observations will help you pinpoint the specific problem. You'll progress from knowing only that the bicycle is broken to knowing, for example, that the gears don't shift properly. The more precisely you can define the problem, the less time you'll waste looking for solutions.

Once you've defined the problem, there's no single "right" way to start looking for answers. The important thing is to be systematic. Proceed in logical steps from what you know to what you don't know. Keep track of your steps, so that if something doesn't work, you can move on to something else instead of trying the same thing over again.

Here are some ways to try solving problems:

• Use what you know about the problem to predict a solution and try it. ❷ If your effort fails, think about why it didn't work. Then make another prediction and try that. Keep eliminating possibilities until you find the one that works. You've probably used this method to search for something you've lost. You think about when you last saw the item, and where you've been since then. This helps you to direct your search. Then you consider where you may have left the item, and you look there. If you don't find it, you look in the next logical place.

What is the first step in solving a problem?

CONCEPT DEVELOPMENT
► Continue the discussion of exercises begun in the Motivation by having students identify differences between solving problems and completing exercise problems. Point out that some tasks that at first require problem solving skills, such as riding a bike, roller-skating, and tying shoelaces, eventually become a learned skill.

● REINFORCEMENT   6

▲ ENRICHMENT   6

11

REINFORCEMENT   Chapter 1
Problem Solving   Text Pages 9–17

Complete the following.

1. How does a problem differ from an exercise? In an exercise, the steps required to find a solution usually are obvious. In a problem, the steps needed to find a solution may not be obvious.

Identify the sense you would use to make each of the following observations.

sight   2. the distance between two points
hearing   3. the loudness of a stereo system
taste   4. the saltiness of a stew
sight   5. the number of students in a classroom
touch   6. determining whether bathwater was too hot or too cold
taste or smell 7. determining whether milk in a container has soured
taste   8. the spiciness of a dinner

Identify the sense that each object listed is designed to help.

hearing   9. hearing aid
sight   10. microscope
touch   11. thermometer
sight   12. ruler
hearing   13. stereo headphones
sight   14. telescope
hearing   15. stethoscope

Place the following terms in logical order by writing the numbers 1 through 4 in the space provided.

3   16. theory
4   17. scientific law
2   18. hypothesis
1   19. problem
20. What is an experiment? a test of a hypothesis

6   Copyright Glencoe Division of Macmillan/McGraw-Hill
        Users of Merrill Physical Science have the publisher's permission to reproduce this page.

ENRICHMENT   Chapter 1
Problem Solving   Text Pages 9–17

SOLVING A MEASUREMENT PROBLEM

One type of problem solving that we often encounter is determining the size of something. When this type of problem occurs, we do not always have the appropriate measuring tools available. For example, you may be out shopping and need to know if a large box will fit in the trunk of your parents' car. If you could find the dimensions of the box and the trunk, you could determine if the box will fit before you spend time and energy lifting the box up to the trunk.

In this activity you will use paper clips as your measuring device. You will find the height and width of your textbook with a large paper clip. Then you will use this information and other data to find the height and length of your textbook using a small paper clip.

Procedure

1. Measure the height and width of the figure below using a large paper clip. Record these values in the table.

2. Measure the height and width of the figure using the small paper clip. Record these values in the table.
3. Measure the height and width of your textbook using the large paper clip. Record these values in the table.
4. Predict the height and width of your textbook in small paper clips. Record your prediction in the table.

Data	Large paper clip	Sample data Small paper clip
Figure height	1	1.5
Figure width	3.5	5.2
Textbook height	5.2	7.8
Textbook width	3.8	5.7

Analyze and Conclude

1. How can you find the height and width of your textbook in small paper clips, without measuring it with a small paper clip? Multiply the measurement in large paper clips by 1.5. Example: 5.2 × 1.5 = 7.8

2. Measure your textbook with a small paper clip and record your measurements in the table. Compare your prediction with the actual measurements. Answers will vary.

6   Copyright Glencoe Division of Macmillan/McGraw-Hill
        Users of Merrill Physical Science have the publisher's permission to reproduce this page.

CROSS CURRICULUM

▶ **Mathematics:** Point out that patterns can be used to solve sequence problems. Have students discuss patterns in the following sequences and predict the missing integer.

0, 1, 2, 3, 4, ... (5)
0, 1, 4, 9, 16, ... (25)
0, 1, 1, 2, 3, 5, 8, ... (13)

▶ **Earth Science:** Have students identify and discuss patterns that occur in the earth sciences. These patterns may include crystal structures or cycles, such as days, lunar months, years, tides, and phases of the moon. Ask students how these patterns can be used to identify materials or predict events.

▶ **Life Science:** Have students discuss patterns of change, such as life cycles, that take place in living organisms.

What is a model?

• Look for patterns that will help you make predictions about the problem. Suppose you occasionally break out in a rash. If you pay attention to what you eat, touch, and wear every day, you may find a pattern that helps you discover what's causing the rash. Putting information into a table or graph or making a drawing sometimes can help you find patterns.

• Develop a model. When your problem deals with something complicated or difficult to see, it may help to develop a model. A **model** is an idea, system, or structure that represents whatever you're trying to explain. The model is never exactly like the thing being explained, but it is similar enough to allow comparisons.

To find out how the shape of an airplane can affect performance, scientists and engineers make model airplanes of different shapes. These models are based on theories that describe how moving air behaves. They then test the different models under various conditions to find out which shape works best. They might also create different computer models, which are programs that predict the outcomes of different designs under various conditions.

Figure 1-7. The wind tunnel is used to test the effects of wind on the airplane model.

OPTIONS

ENRICHMENT

▶ Have interested students research the life and inventions of Thomas Edison and present their findings to the class.

▶ Arrange to have students visit an elementary school classroom to observe how small children use problem-solving skills.

▶ Have interested students research the tangram, an ancient Chinese design puzzle, and demonstrate several of its solutions to the class with a poster.

TECHNOLOGY

Driving Smart

The time spent sitting in traffic is expected to increase fourfold by the year 2000. In an effort to improve safety and traffic flow, scientists and engineers are working on systems that use traffic monitoring, navigation equipment, and radio links. Early efforts are directed at helping motorists avoid traffic jams. Traffic sensors embedded in the road transmit data about traffic volume and speed to a central computer. This computer analyzes the data to predict the locations of traffic jams. This information is then transmitted by radio to an onboard computer in an individual car. The location of pending traffic jams and possible alternate routes are then projected on the car's video screen to help the driver choose the best route.

Another line of research involves vision-enhancement systems originally developed for the military. These systems could be linked to vehicle control to provide automatic speed control and emergency braking. Improvement of the sensory apparatus of a car would enable more vehicles to travel closer together, safely, at high speeds.

Think Critically: What problems exist with a system that provides drivers alternate routes around a traffic jam?

• Break the problem down into smaller, simpler problems. Sometimes it's hard to see what needs to be done when the problem is complicated. Look for ways to solve it step-by-step. ❷

If one problem-solving approach doesn't work, try another. As you search for solutions, keep thinking about what you first knew about the problem and what you've learned about from each problem-solving attempt. When you find a solution, think again about the problem and ask yourself if your solution makes sense.

TECHNOLOGY

CONCEPT DEVELOPMENT

▶ Discuss inductive and deductive reasoning aspects in determining why the chili discussed in the text tasted bland. In the process of inductive reasoning, one generalizes from many experiences. Having eaten many bowls of chili, one can generalize on the attributes of chili, such as (a personal choice of) color, texture, and taste. Having made many bowls of chili, one can generalize on the methods of making it, such as cooking time and temperature. Having reached a general idea of what "good" chili is, *both* from making and eating a lot of it, one can evaluate a particular batch.

▶ From generalizing about the cooking times and temperatures of many batches of chili, one can eliminate these as factors in making this batch bland, unless it was uncooked or burned. This elimination is an example of deductive reasoning, or evaluating from a generalization.

Critical Thinking

What is critical thinking?

Imagine that you have just made a batch of chili, and it just doesn't taste right. It tastes bland. What could have gone wrong? Did you follow the recipe? Did you cook it at the right temperature for the proper length of time? After thinking about it, you decide that you may have left out an essential ingredient—chili powder. How did you arrive at this conclusion? Without being aware of it, you probably used some aspect of critical thinking.

Critical thinking is a process that uses certain skills to solve a problem. Let's see how you may have used critical thinking to solve the "great chili problem." First you identified the problem—the bland taste—by mentally comparing the taste of your chili with that of other batches of chili you've eaten. Next you may have separated important information from unimportant information by deciding that the temperature and cooking time of the chili had little to do with its flavor. Finally, you examined your assumption that you had followed the recipe correctly. This seemed like the best bet. You looked at the recipe again and concluded that you had left out the chili powder.

You probably went one step further and analyzed your conclusion. You asked if leaving the chili powder out would make the chili bland. If the answer was "yes," then you may have solved the problem.

"Flex Your Brain," as seen on the next page, is an activity that can be used throughout this book. This activity will help you to think about and examine your thinking. "Flex Your Brain" is a way to keep your thinking on track when you are investigating a topic. Each activity takes you through a series of steps, starting with what you already know and believe, and leading to new conclusions and awareness. Then, it encourages you to review and discuss the steps you took.

The "Flex Your Brain" activities, and other features of this book, are designed to help you improve your critical thinking skills. You'll become a better problem solver, and your next batch of chili will taste great.

OPTIONS

ENRICHMENT

▶ Have students interview their parents to see how they use problem solving in their lives.

FLEX Your Brain

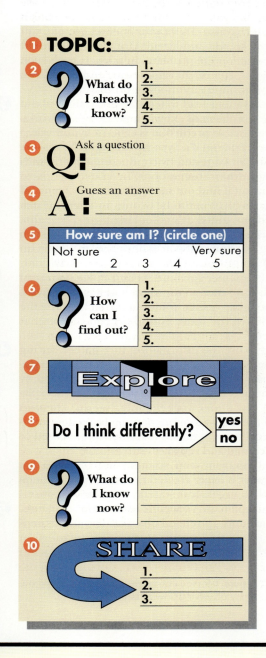

1. **TOPIC:** _____

2. **?** **What do I already know?**
   1. _____
   2. _____
   3. _____
   4. _____
   5. _____

3. Ask a question
   Q: _____

4. Guess an answer
   A: _____

5. **How sure am I? (circle one)**

Not sure				Very sure
1	2	3	4	5

6. **?** **How can I find out?**
   1. _____
   2. _____
   3. _____
   4. _____
   5. _____

7. **Explore**

8. **Do I think differently?** [yes] [no]

9. **?** **What do I know now?** _____

10. **SHARE**
    1. _____
    2. _____
    3. _____

---

1. Fill in the topic your teacher gives you.

2. Jot down what you already know about the topic.

3. Using what you already know (Step 2), form a question about the topic. Are you unsure about one of the items you listed? Do you want to know more? Do you want to know what, how, or why? Write down your question.

4. Guess an answer to your question. In the next few steps, you will be exploring the reasonableness of your answer. Write down your guess.

5. Circle the number in the box that matches how sure you are of your answer in Step 4. This is your chance to rate your confidence in what you've done so far and, later, to see how your level of sureness affects your thinking.

6. How can you find out more about your topic? You might want to read a book, ask an expert, or do an experiment. Write down ways you can find out more.

7. Make a plan to explore your answer. Use the resources you listed in Step 6. Then, carry out your plan.

8. Now that you've explored, go back to your answer in Step 4. Would you answer differently? Mark one of the boxes.

9. Considering what you learned in your exploration, answer your question again, adding new things you've learned. You may completely change your answer.

10. It's important to be able to talk about thinking. Choose three people to tell about how you arrived at your response in every step. For example, don't just read what you wrote down in Step 2. Try to share how you thought of those things.

1-2 PROBLEM SOLVING **15**

CONCEPT DEVELOPMENT

▶ To acquaint students with this strategy, divide the class into small groups and have them explore a topic using the Flex Your Brain worksheet. Students should have some familiarity with the topic chosen. Possible topics might include cacti, volcanoes, and robots, or topics from a list the class brainstorms. See pages 20T-23T for a more detailed description of the Flex Your Brain process.

TEACHER F.Y.I.

▶ A reproducible version of the Flex Your Brain activity with space for students to write in their responses can be found in the **Activity Worksheets** booklet in the Teacher Resource Package. See the Program Resources box below.

PROGRAM RESOURCES

From the **Teacher Resource Package** use:

Transparency Masters, pages 1-2, Flex Your Brain.

Activity Worksheets, page 5, Flex Your Brain.

Use **Color Transparency** number 1, Flex Your Brain.

► Students often fail to conceptualize the difference between a scientific law and a theory. Use the following demonstration to initiate a discussion of the two.

► **Demonstration:** Fill one beaker with 1 L of hot water and the other with 1 L of cold water. Have students feel each. Ask the students to predict what the mixture of the two would feel like. Pour the hot and cold water into a 2-L beaker and have students verify their predictions by feeling the temperature of the mixture. Ask them why they were so sure of their predictions. Most will discuss past experience and make a rudimentary statement of heat flowing from hot to cold materials. Inform them that they were making their predictions based on scientific law. Point out that a scientific law describes what will happen. Ask them why the mixture became warm. Point out that a law doesn't explain why—that is the function of a theory. Tell the students that the "why" will be discussed in later chapters.

Figure 1-8. Observations of the simple cocklebur led to the idea for the "zipperless" fastener.

What is a hypothesis?

Problem Solving in Science

The steps to solving a scientific problem are similar to those you use to solve any problem. The first step is observation. **Observation** is the process of using your senses to gather information. To fix your friend's bicycle, you examined the bicycle and listened for clues that would help you zero in on the problem. In science, tools such as microscopes, rulers, thermometers, and clocks can help make your observations more precise.

Good observations lead to testable predictions about how to solve a problem or explain how something works. In science, a testable prediction is called a **hypothesis.** ③

How do you find out if a hypothesis is right? You test it. A hypothesis can be tested by conducting experiments and making further observations. In a later section of this chapter, you'll find out more about experiments. If one hypothesis turns out to be wrong, another one can be proposed and tested. It's never possible to prove that a hypothesis is absolutely right. However, you can keep ruling out different possibilities until you settle on one you think is most likely to be right. It may take many experiments and many different kinds of data to thoroughly test a hypothesis. The more results you obtain that support the hypothesis, the more confident you can be that it's correct.

Scientists use the information they gather during experimentation to form a theory. A **theory** is an explanation based on many observations supported by experimental results. A theory is the most logical explanation of why things work the way they do. Theories may lead the way to more experiments. As new information is collected, a theory may need to be revised or discarded and replaced with another theory. ④

Over many years, scientists have observed that matter is never created nor destroyed in chemical changes. It is stated as the law of conservation of mass. A **scientific law** is a "rule of nature" that sums up related observations and experimental results to describe a pattern in nature. Generally, laws predict what ⑤

Figure 1-9. You can learn something about gravity by observing how different objects fall.

OPTIONS

INQUIRY QUESTIONS

► **What is an inference?** *An inference is a judgment or statement based on past experience.* **Which of the following statements are inferences and which are observations? a. The sun rose this morning. b. The sun rises in the morning. c. Good chili must have beans. d. This chili contains beans. e. This light bulb doesn't light. f. The light bulb is burned out because it doesn't light.** *Inferences: b, c, and f; observations: a, d, and e*

Figure 1-10. A simple event, such as the falling of an apple, inspired Isaac Newton to investigate gravity. This study eventually led to the development of an entirely new field of physics.

will happen in a given situation, but don't explain why. Theories may serve as explanations of laws. Like theories, laws may be changed or discarded if new observations show them to be incorrect.

Whether you're puzzling over a physical science mystery in the classroom or just trying to figure out where you left your homework, you can use what you've learned about problem solving to lead you to a solution.

SECTION REVIEW

1. Explain the difference between an exercise and a problem. Give an example of each.
2. Compare and contrast these terms: *hypothesis, theory, scientific law.*
3. **Apply:** Develop a model to describe how you decide what to wear to school every day. Could someone who doesn't know you use the model to predict what you'll wear tomorrow?

☑ Outlining

Think of a problem you solved or tried to solve recently. Outline the steps you followed in searching for the solution. If you need help, refer to Outlining in the **Skill Handbook** on page 677.

Skill Builder

Ask questions 1-2 and the **Apply** question in the Section Review.

RETEACH
Cooperative Learning: Using a Numbered Heads Together strategy, have each team of students propose a method of teaching a group of small children a task by using one or more of the problem-solving methods described in the text.

EXTENSION
For students who have mastered this section, use the **Reinforcement** and **Enrichment** masters or other OPTIONS provided.

3 CLOSE

▶ Write several traffic regulations pertaining to bicycles on the chalkboard. Have students discuss how these regulations allow car drivers, bike riders, and pedestrians to make probable predictions about what will happen at an intersection. Compare these regulations to scientific laws.

SECTION REVIEW ANSWERS
1. With an exercise, the method for reaching the solution is known; solving a crossword puzzle. With a problem the method of solution must be developed; fixing a flat tire.
2. A hypothesis is an educated guess, based on the best available knowledge. A theory is an explanation based on observations supported by test results. A scientific law is a rule of nature that sums up related observations and experimental results.
3. Apply: Student responses will vary, but could include such considerations as weather conditions, school dress codes, and current fashion trends. A stranger should be able to use a well-conceived model to make fairly accurate predictions.

Skill Builder
Student responses should outline the steps followed in solving a problem.

PREPARATION

SECTION BACKGROUND

▶ The greenhouse effect, ozone depletion, and acid rain are results of physical processes that take place in the atmosphere. The extents and effects of these processes are debated.

1 MOTIVATE

▶ Ask students to describe the environment of a greenhouse. Discuss similar environments, such as solariums, that demonstrate solar energy being absorbed and converted to heat.
▶ Have students check the labels of aerosols that contain statements advertising that the products contain no chlorofluorocarbons.

TYING TO PREVIOUS KNOWLEDGE:
Have students recall the distinctive smell of ozone in the air that occurs after an electrical storm. Point out that ozone blocks ultraviolet radiation from the sun which is responsible for sunburn and various human and animal cancers.

OBJECTIVES AND SCIENCE WORDS:
Have students review the objectives and science words to become familiar with this section.

2 TEACH

Key Concepts are highlighted.

CONCEPT DEVELOPMENT

▶ Only 40 nations signed the 1987 Montreal Protocol which called for a 50 percent reduction in the production of CFCs by 1999. However, in 1989 they were joined by sixty other nations and all agreed to accelerate the Montreal Protocol and eliminate the production of all CFCs by the year 2000.

SCIENCE & SOCIETY   **1-3**

Problems? What Problems?

New Science Words

greenhouse effect
ozone layer

Objectives

▶ Describe some of the environmental issues presently being studied by scientists.
▶ Examine how scientific controversies arise.

Research or Action?

Is Earth's environment changing? You may have heard a lot about such problems as global warming, ozone depletion, and acid rain. But did you know that scientists disagree about the extent of these problems and what should be done about them?

Back in 1957, a scientist first raised concerns about the **greenhouse effect—the gradual heating up of Earth's troposphere brought on by the increase in the carbon dioxide present in the atmosphere.** This increase could be caused by the burning of fossil fuels, such as oil, coal, and gasoline.

What is the greenhouse effect?

In the 1970s, scientists began to worry about damage to the ozone layer. The **ozone layer is a part of the atmosphere that protects life on Earth from the damaging effects of ultraviolet radiation from the sun.** Scientists suggested that continued use of chlorofluorocarbons (KLOR uh floor uh kar bunz) (CFCs), chemicals used in refrigerators and air conditioners and in manufacturing plastic foam products, would destroy the ozone layer.

Around the same time, other scientists warned that sulfur dioxide and nitrogen oxides released when fossil fuels burn were making rain, snow, and other forms of precipitation very acidic. This precipitation, called acid rain, was harmful to trees, crops, and aquatic life.

18   THE NATURE OF SCIENCE

OPTIONS

Meeting Different Ability Levels

For Section 1-3, use the following **Teacher Resource Masters** depending upon individual students' needs.
◆ **Study Guide Master** for all students.
● **Reinforcement Master** for students of average and above average ability levels.
▲ **Enrichment Master** for above average students.

◆ STUDY GUIDE   7

STUDY GUIDE   Chapter 1
Problems? What Problems?   Text Pages 18–19

Determine whether the italicized term makes each statement true or false. If the statement is true, write the word "true" in the space provided. If the statement is false, write in the blank the term that makes the statement true.

greenhouse effect	1. The gradual heating up of Earth's troposphere is called the *ozone layer.*
true	2. The chemicals used in refrigerators that are helping to destroy the ozone layer are called *chlorofluorocarbons.*
carbon dioxide	3. The greenhouse effect is caused by an increase in the amount of *oxygen* in the air.
global warming	4. The greenhouse effect is also called *acid rain.*
true	5. Acidic precipitation that falls to Earth is called *acid rain.*
ozone layer	6. The part of the atmosphere that protects Earth from the damaging effects of ultraviolet radiation is the *troposphere.*
true	7. Scientists believe that increased carbon dioxide levels could be caused by the burning of *fossil fuels.*
CFCs	8. Chlorofluorocarbons are also called *ozone.*
fossil fuels	9. Oil, coal, and natural gas are examples of *chlorofluorocarbons.*
true	10. *Sulfur dioxide* is one of the gases responsible for acid rain.
true	11. Acid rain is believed to be harmful to *plants.*
true	12. Not all scientists *agree* that acid rain, the greenhouse effect, and the depletion of the ozone layer are serious environmental problems.

Copyright Glencoe Division of Macmillan/McGraw-Hill
Users of Merrill Physical Science have the publisher's permission to reproduce this page.   7

Since these predictions were made, scientists have gathered data by taking measurements, creating models, doing experiments, and using other problem-solving techniques. Some scientists say their data show that the problems are serious and need immediate action. Others say the data are flawed and that more research is needed before drastic action is taken to solve problems that could be minor. Just about everyone agrees that changes that are taking place in the atmosphere today may have harmful effects far beyond what is presently suspected. At the very least, we must reduce those activities that continue to add acids and carbon dioxide to the atmosphere.

Figure 1-11. The trees in this forest show the effects of acid rain.

SECTION REVIEW

1. Think of a topic on which you think more scientific research needs to be done. How would you decide what kind of research should be done next?
2. Does it ever make sense to start trying to solve a problem before you've learned everything you can about it?

You Decide!

If you were a scientist studying the greenhouse effect, ozone depletion, or acid rain, how would you decide when enough research had been done and when action should be taken? How would you know what action to take? Who should make these decisions, scientists doing the research, government, or the public? Would your answers be the same if you were considering a smaller scientific problem that would not affect the health of a whole planet and its inhabitants?

● **REINFORCEMENT** 7

▲ **ENRICHMENT** 7

19

CONCEPT DEVELOPMENT
▶ Ozone depletion takes place when a chlorofluorocarbon, such as CCl_2F_2, is decomposed by ultraviolet radiation and free chlorine reacts with ozone.
$$Cl + O_3 \rightarrow ClO \text{ and } O_2$$

CHECK FOR UNDERSTANDING
Ask questions 1-2 in the Section Review.

RETEACH
 FLEX Your Brain

Have students use the Flex Your Brain activity to explore GREENHOUSE EFFECT, OZONE DEPLETION, or ACID RAIN.

EXTENSION
For students who have mastered this section, use the **Reinforcement** and **Enrichment** masters or other OPTIONS provided.

3 CLOSE

Cooperative Learning: Have Problem Solving teams devise models from which to collect data to demonstrate the greenhouse effect.

SECTION REVIEW ANSWERS
1. Responses will vary. An example topic is gasoline alternatives. Its research is needed due to depletion of gasoline supplies.
2. No; you should always learn as much about a problem as possible before attempting to find a solution.

YOU DECIDE!
Student responses will vary, but should indicate that the amount of information available, the critical nature of the problem, and the need for a speedy solution will play a part in any decision about when action should be taken.

PROGRAM RESOURCES
From the **Teacher Resource Package** use:
Concept Mapping, pages 7-8.

PREPARATION

SECTION BACKGROUND

▶ Galileo is credited with establishing the scientific method, in which explanations of phenomena are verified by controlled observations.

1 MOTIVATE

▶ Have students discuss the following situation. The coach heard Jeff and Juan bragging that each could hit a ball harder than the other. Coach asks you to set up and referee a contest between Jeff and Juan. What would you do to make sure the contest is fair?

TYING TO PREVIOUS KNOWLEDGE: Have students recall the meaning of term *hypothesis*. Point out that in this section they will learn a standard method that is used to confirm a hypothesis.

OBJECTIVES AND SCIENCE WORDS: Have students review the objectives and science words to become familiar with this section.

1-4 Exploring Science

New Science Words

experiment
control
constant
independent variable
dependent variable

Objectives

▶ Appreciate the importance of following guidelines in doing experiments.
▶ Define *independent variable* and *dependent variable*.
▶ Understand laboratory safety rules.

Experimentation

You've learned that ==problem solving in science involves making observations, forming a hypothesis, and testing the hypothesis with experiments.== Now you'll learn just how to conduct an experiment.

An **experiment** ==is an organized procedure for testing a hypothesis.== When scientists conduct experiments, they usually are seeking new information. Classroom experiments often demonstrate and verify information that already is known but may be new to you.

When doing an experiment, it is important to follow certain guidelines to reduce the chance of reaching wrong conclusions. Suppose you want to know whether storing microwave popcorn in a freezer will make it pop better. You store a package of popcorn in the freezer for a day or two, pop the corn, and count the unpopped kernels.

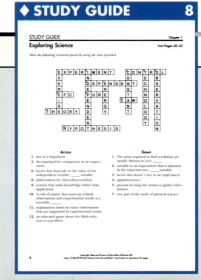

Could you draw a meaningful conclusion from this "experiment?" No, because you don't have anything to compare your results with. Maybe you'd get the same number of unpopped kernels with corn stored at room temperature. But you don't know, because you didn't test any unfrozen popcorn.

==To draw a conclusion, you need a control—a standard for comparison. In an experiment, a **control** shows that your result is related to the condition you're testing and not to some other condition.==

To find out if storing popcorn in the freezer makes a difference, you need to test popcorn stored at room temperature, as a control. All other conditions should be the

---

OPTIONS

Meeting Different Ability Levels

For Section 1-4, use the following **Teacher Resource Masters** depending upon individual students' needs.

◆ **Study Guide Master** for all students.
● **Reinforcement Master** for students of average and above average ability levels.
▲ **Enrichment Master** for above average students.

Additional Teacher Resource Package masters are listed in the OPTIONS box throughout the section. The additional masters are appropriate for all students.

◆ **STUDY GUIDE** 8

STUDY GUIDE   Chapter 1
Exploring Science   Text Pages 20–24

Solve the following crossword puzzle by using the clues provided.

Across
1. test of a hypothesis
3. the standard for comparison in an experiment
6. factor that depends on the value of the independent variable; _____ variable
8. abbreviation for chlorofluorocarbon
9. science that seeks knowledge rather than application
10. A rule of nature that sums up related observations and experimental results is a scientific _____.
11. explanation based on many related observations that are supported by experimental results
12. an educated guess about the likely solution to a problem

Down
1. The steps required to find a solution are usually obvious in a(n) _____.
2. variable in an experiment that is adjusted by the experimenter; _____ variable
5. factor that doesn't vary in an experiment
6. applied science
4. process of using the senses to gather information
7. one part of the study of physical science

same for both batches of popcorn. The popcorn should be the same brand, equally fresh, stored for the same period of time, and popped in the same microwave oven, at the same power, for the same length of time. Only one condition, the place of storage, should differ between the two batches. All of the other factors are constants. A **constant** is a factor that doesn't vary in an experiment.

Can you be confident in conclusions based on the results of popping just one bag of popcorn stored each way? What if one of the bags happened to be defective? To be sure of your conclusions, you should repeat the experiment several times with different bags of popcorn, storing half of each bag in the freezer and half at room temperature.

If your experiment shows that storing microwave popcorn in the freezer makes it pop better, you may want to do another experiment to find out if the length of time the popcorn is stored makes a difference. You could store different batches of popcorn for different lengths of time. Length of time stored would be the **independent variable,** the factor adjusted by the experimenter. The measure of popping success—the number of unpopped kernels—would be the dependent variable. A **dependent variable** depends on the value of the independent variable. What factors would be constants?

Keeping an orderly procedure for an experiment will help you to draw conclusions and decide what to do next in your investigation. It will also allow others to duplicate your investigation. Although scientists agree that there is no one way to solve a problem, their scientific methods often include the following steps:

Determine the problem. What do you want to find out?
Make a hypothesis. What prediction do you want to test?
Test your hypothesis. What steps can you take to reach a conclusion about your hypothesis? What measurements should you record?
Analyze the results. What happens during your experiment?
Draw conclusions. Do your observations and data suggest that your hypothesis is correct? If not, do you think your hypothesis is wrong, or do you need to change your experimental procedure?

EcoTip

Design an experiment to test for smog outside your house. HINT: Rubber bands left outside in a very polluted area will break easily in a few weeks.

What are dependent and independent variables?

Figure 1-12. Keeping accurate records is an important part of scientific experimentation.

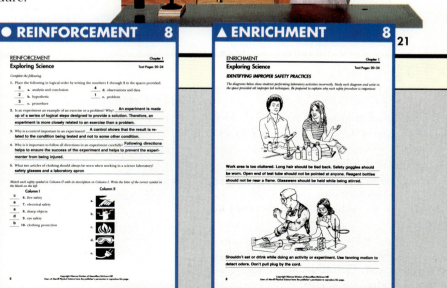

● REINFORCEMENT 8

REINFORCEMENT   Chapter 1
Exploring Science   Text Pages 20–24

Complete the following.

1. Place the following in logical order by writing the numbers 1 through 5 in the spaces provided.
   5 a. analysis and conclusion   4 d. observations and data
   2 b. hypothesis   1 e. problem
   3 c. procedure

2. Is an experiment an example of an exercise or a problem? Why? **An experiment is made up of a series of logical steps designed to provide a solution. Therefore, an experiment is more closely related to an exercise than a problem.**

3. Why is a control important in an experiment? **A control shows that the result is related to the condition being tested and not to some other condition.**

4. Why is it important to follow all directions in an experiment carefully? **Following directions helps to ensure the success of the experiment and helps to prevent the experimenter from being injured.**

5. What two articles of clothing should always be worn when working in a science laboratory? **safety glasses and a laboratory apron**

Match each safety symbol in Column II with its description in Column I. Write the letter of the correct symbol in the blank on the left.
        Column I   Column II
   c 6. fire safety   A.
   e 7. electrical safety   B.
   a 8. sharp objects   C.
   d 9. eye safety   D.
   b 10. clothing protection E.

Copyright Glencoe Division of Macmillan/McGraw-Hill
Users of Merrill Physical Science have the publisher's permission to reproduce this page.
8

▲ ENRICHMENT 8

ENRICHMENT   Chapter 1
Exploring Science   Text Pages 20–24

IDENTIFYING IMPROPER SAFETY PRACTICES

The diagrams below show students performing laboratory activities incorrectly. Study each diagram and write in the space provided all improper lab techniques. Be prepared to explain why each safety procedure is important.

Work area is too cluttered. Long hair should be tied back. Safety goggles should be worn. Open end of test tube should not be pointed at anyone. Reagent bottles should not be near a flame. Glassware should be held while being stirred.

Shouldn't eat or drink while doing an activity or experiment. Use fanning motion to detect odors. Don't pull plug by the cord.

Copyright Glencoe Division of Macmillan/McGraw-Hill
Users of Merrill Physical Science have the publisher's permission to reproduce this page.
8

21

Key Concepts are highlighted.

CONCEPT DEVELOPMENT

▶ Discuss operational definitions. Have students discuss what criteria they would use to demonstrate and verify that frozen microwave popcorn "pops better." Have students discuss the criterion offered in the text and generate new criteria, such as the size of popped kernels, time needed to pop the corn, taste, color, and texture. Discuss how agreement on how to evaluate the hypothesis is important.

▶ Point out that experiments are conducted to confirm a hypothesis or to confirm a *null* hypothesis, that is, the hypothesis that the independent variable in the experiment does not affect the dependent variable.

Cooperative Learning: Have students generate a list of factors, such as temperature, moisture, and sunlight, that might be factors when rubber bands are used to test for smog as described in the EcoTip. Assign factors to individual Problem Solving teams and have them generate hypotheses and devise experiments to eliminate these factors.

STUDENT TEXT QUESTION

▶ Page 21, paragraph 3: **What factors would be constants?** *The constants are the same as before with the addition of similar storage conditions.*

CROSS CURRICULUM

▶ **Language Arts:** Have students look up the word *experiment* in a dictionary. Students should find that it is related to the Greek root *experiri* (to try). Have students explain how the meaning of the word reflects its root.

PROBLEM SOLVING

To operate the tape player, the carbon dry cells cost 16.2 cents per hour and the alkaline dry cells cost 12.6 cents per hour. The alkaline dry cells are the better buy, even though their initial cost is more than that of the carbon dry cells.

Critical Thinking: Lauren solved the problem by stating a hypothesis; testing the hypothesis by comparing the efficiency of the two types of dry cells while keeping all other factors constant; collecting and analyzing data; and drawing a conclusion.

PROGRAM RESOURCES

From the **Teacher Resource Package** use:

Use **Laboratory Manual,** No Need to Count Your Pennies.

Safety

When working in the physical science laboratory, you'll handle glass, hot objects, sharp objects, and chemicals. A few rules will help you carry out experiments and activities safely.

PROBLEM SOLVING

Lauren's Experiment

Lauren walked for about 40 minutes every morning before school. During her walk, she used headphones to listen to a tape player attached to her belt.

Lauren found that she had to replace the carbon dry cell batteries in the tape player about every two and one-half weeks. So, she decided to conduct an experiment to find out whether alkaline dry cells, which cost more, would be less expensive to use than carbon dry cells. She hypothesized that, over a period of time, using alkaline dry cells would save her money.

She purchased two alkaline dry cells for $2.04 and two carbon dry cells for $1.38. She tested the dry cells on her morning walks, keeping track of the amount of time the tape player was in operation using each pair of dry cells. To keep the test fair, she played the same tape and kept the volume of the player constant throughout the experiment.

Two alkaline dry cells lasted 16 hours and 15 minutes, whereas two carbon dry cells lasted only eight and one-half hours. Lauren then divided the cost of the dry cells by the number of hours to determine which dry cells were less expensive to use. Which dry cells were the better buy?

Think Critically: What problem-solving methods did Lauren use in the experiment?

OPTIONS

INQUIRY QUESTIONS

▶ **What good is knowing that a null hypothesis is true?** *It eliminates the need to keep the null independent variable constant in any future experiments.*

▶ **What are placebos and how are they used in experiments?** *Placebos are materials that are known to have no medical effects on humans. They are used as controls in the experimental testing of medicines and drugs. Because they have no effects they are given to one group of people in place of the experimental medications given to another group.*

ENRICHMENT

▶ Have students research safety icons used in the construction industry, on medicines and household goods, in buildings, and along streets and highways. Have students draw samples of the icons and quiz the class on their meanings.

First, know what you're supposed to do before you begin. Read and follow all directions carefully and pay attention to any cautions.

Dress appropriately to reduce the chance of accidents. Avoid clothing with large, floppy sleeves. Remove dangling jewelry, such as chains and bracelets, and tie back or cover long hair.

Think about what you're doing. Handle glass carefully, and don't touch hot objects with your bare hands. To be on the safe side, treat all equipment as if it were hot. Wear safety glasses and a protective apron.

Be sure you understand the safety symbols explained in Appendix B on page 674. They will be used throughout the textbook to alert you to possible laboratory dangers.

Learn the proper way to clean up spills and clean them up immediately.

Your workspace should contain only those materials you need for your experiment. Keep books and other objects out of the way. Arrange your equipment so that you won't have to reach over burners or across equipment that could be knocked over.

Watch closely when your teacher demonstrates how to handle equipment, how to dispose of materials, and any other safety practices.

Make sure you know the location and proper operation of safety equipment, such as fire extinguishers.

Did You Know?

Alfred Nobel, the man who left his fortune to fund the Nobel Prizes, was the inventor of dynamite.

SECTION REVIEW

1. What is the function of a control in an experiment?
2. You are doing an experiment to find out how the temperature of water affects the rate at which sugar dissolves. What factors should remain constant? What factors will vary?
3. **Apply:** Design an experiment to determine the fastest route from your home to school.

☑ Concept Mapping

Arrange these steps in organizing a scientific experiment to make an events chain concept map: *draw conclusions, make a hypothesis, determine the problem, analyze the results, test your hypothesis.* If you need help, refer to Concept Mapping in the **Skill Handbook** on pages 684 and 685.

Skill Builder

Skill Builder

Initiating Event

```
Determine the problem.
        ↓
Make a hypothesis.
        ↓
Test your hypothesis.
        ↓
Analyze the results.
        ↓
Draw conclusions.
```

CROSS CURRICULUM

▶ **Art:** Safety symbols are icons—images that convey information. Have students design an icon to alert students to the laboratory safety hazards of long hair, clothing with floppy sleeves, or jewelry.

CHECK FOR UNDERSTANDING

Ask questions 1-2 and the **Apply** question in the Section Review.

RETEACH

👥 **Cooperative Learning:** Using a Numbered Heads Together strategy, divide the class into teams. Give each team a large index card on which to write a problem for an experiment. Have teams exchange their cards. Each team now generates a hypothesis for the question they now hold and writes it on the card. Again, they exchange the cards. Ask each team to devise an experiment based on the question and hypothesis on the card that it now has.

EXTENSION

For students who have mastered this section, use the **Reinforcement** and **Enrichment** masters or other OPTIONS provided.

3 CLOSE

▶ Have students review the microwave popcorn experiments discussed in the text and identify the instruments they would use to measure the controls, constants, and variables mentioned in the text.

SECTION REVIEW ANSWERS

1. A control is used as a basis for comparing data collected during an experiment.
2. Constants: quantity of water, quantity of sugar; variable: temperature of water
3. Apply: Student responses will vary, but should include at least one constant—mode of transportation—and one variable—routes taken.

ACTIVITY 1-1
30 minutes

OBJECTIVE: **Identify** and **manipulate** variables in a controlled experiment.

PROCESS SKILLS applied in this activity:
▶ **Observing** in Procedure Steps 4 and 5.
▶ **Predicting** in Procedure Step 7.
▶ **Controlling variables** in Procedure Step 6.

COOPERATIVE LEARNING
Divide the class into Science Investigation teams of three.

TEACHING THE ACTIVITY
Troubleshooting: Advise students to securely tie the weights. Use twine that is heavy enough to untie easily.
▶ Objects in the 20- to 5-gram range are suitable for weights. The smaller weight should be about half the mass of the heavier weights.
▶ When one weight swings, its motion is transferred to the other weight and then back again. The pattern is obvious and changes in the pattern are easily recognized. Adding a third weight produces a much more complex pattern.
▶ Focus the lesson on investigating cause and effect by controlling variables.

PROGRAM RESOURCES
From the **Teacher Resource Package** use:
Transparency Masters, pages 3-4, Safety Symbols.
Activity Worksheets, pages 7-8, Activity 1-1: Identifying and Controlling Variables.
Use **Color Transparency** number 2, Safety Symbols.

ACTIVITY 1-1
Identifying and Controlling Variables

Problem: *How do variables help solve problems?*

Materials
- string, 1.5 meters
- identical weights (3)
- smaller weight (1)
- metric ruler
- ring stands (2)
- scissors
- stopwatch

CAUTION: *Refer to page 674 in Appendix B for an explanation of safety symbols.*

Procedure
1. Cut the string into one 60-cm length and three 30-cm lengths.
2. Tie one 30-cm string to each of the identical weights.
3. Tie the long string between the two ring stands and attach the short strings as shown. Use knots that can be easily untied.
4. Swing one of the weights and observe what happens to the other weight. Measure distances and times as precisely as possible. Record this information.
5. Make a list of variables, such as length of string and amount of weight, that may affect the movements of the weights.
6. Adjust the identified variables one at a time. Measure and record the response of the swinging weights.
7. When all variables have been tested, predict the effect of adding a third string and weight. Test your prediction.

Analyze
1. How do the two swinging weights affect each other?
2. What variables did you identify?
3. Which variable has the greatest effect and which has the least?

Conclude and Apply
4. Why is it important to change only one variable at a time?
5. Is adding the third weight the same as one variable or is it more than one? Explain.

ANSWERS TO QUESTIONS
1. Energy is transferred through the horizontal string. When one weight loses all of its energy to the other, it stops moving.
2. Variables include: the distance between the weights, the length of the string, differences in the lengths of the string, and differences in the weights.
3. Unequal string length has the greatest effect. Distance between weights has the least effect.

4. to identify the response for which the variable is responsible
5. The third weight can transfer energy to either one or two weights. Also, it changes the tension of the horizontal string. Adding this weight introduces at least three variables.

SUMMARY

1-1: Physical Science and You

1. Science includes both "pure" science, which is study for the purpose of advancing human knowledge, and technology, which is applying science to improve the quality of human life.
2. Physical science is the study of matter and energy.
3. Some physical science topics include the composition of matter, the types of energy, and the interactions of matter and energy.

1-2: Problem Solving

1. A problem and an exercise both involve finding missing information. With an exercise, the method for finding the information is known. With a problem, the method must be developed as the solution is sought.
2. In solving a problem, a systematic series of steps should be followed, always leading from known information to unknown information.
3. A hypothesis is an testable prediction. A theory is an explanation based on many observations supported by experimental rsults. A scientific law describes a pattern in nature.

1-3: Science and Society: Problems? What Problems?

1. Some environmental issues being studied by scientists include global warming, ozone depletion, and acid rain.
2. Different interpretations of the same observations often lead to different conclusions.

1-4: Exploring Science

1. In conducting a scientific experiment, certain guidelines should be followed to ensure that the purpose of the experiment is met and the results of the experiment are valid.
2. All experiments involve certain variables. An independent variable is determined by the experimenter. A dependent variable depends on the value of the independent variable.
3. Certain safety rules and procedures must be followed in the science laboratory at all times.

KEY SCIENCE WORDS

a. constant
b. control
c. critical thinking
d. dependent variable
e. experiment
f. greenhouse effect
g. hypothesis
h. independent variable
i. model
j. observation
k. ozone layer
l. physical science
m. scientific law
n. technology
o. theory

UNDERSTANDING VOCABULARY

Match each phrase with the correct term from the list of Key Science Words.

1. the study of matter
2. applying science to improve quality of life
3. an idea, system, or structure that can be used to solve a problem
4. a testable prediction
5. the use of human senses to gather information
6. an organized method of testing a hypothesis
7. describes but doesn't explain a pattern in nature
8. a factor that doesn't change in an experiment
9. caused by increased amounts of carbon dioxide gas in Earth's atmosphere
10. factor in an experiment that is adjusted by the experimenter

---

SUMMARY

Have students read the summary statements to review the major concepts of the chapter.

UNDERSTANDING VOCABULARY

1. l	6. e
2. n	7. m
3. i	8. a
4. g	9. f
5. j	10. h

OPTIONS

ASSESSMENT

To assess student understanding of material in this chapter, use the resources listed.

COOPERATIVE LEARNING

Consider using cooperative learning in the THINK AND WRITE CRITICALLY, APPLY, and MORE SKILL BUILDERS sections of the Chapter Review.

PROGRAM RESOURCES

From the **Teacher Resource Package** use:

Cross-Curricular Connections, page 5, Using Analogies to Develop Thinking Skills.

Science and Society, page 5, Consumer Product Testing.

Chapter Review, pages 5-6.

Chapter and Unit Tests, pages 5-8, Chapter Test.

CHECKING CONCEPTS

1. b	6. c
2. c	7. d
3. a	8. b
4. b	9. b
5. d	10. a

UNDERSTANDING CONCEPTS

11. Technology
12. carbon dioxide
13. experiment
14. constant
15. Critical thinking

THINK AND WRITE CRITICALLY

16. With an exercise, you know exactly what you are trying to solve and the method to use to reach the solution. Solving a crossword puzzle is an example of an exercise. A problem involves a great deal of uncertainty. A problem is often not well defined, and the best method for solving it is not known. A crossword puzzle would be a problem if the clues were not numbered.

17. A hypothesis, a theory, and a scientific law are similar in that they all deal with using information to answer a question or solve a problem. A hypothesis is an educated guess based on the best information available. A theory is an explanation that has been tested and supported by results. A scientific law is a statement that describes a pattern in nature.

18. A written record of observations and data allows another person to duplicate the experiment exactly and to compare the results with those of the original experiment.

19. Student responses may vary, but should include four of the safety precautions included in the chapter.

20. Student responses may vary, but will probably include one of the three issues discussed in this chapter—global warming, ozone depletion, or acid rain.

CHECKING CONCEPTS

Choose the word or phrase that completes the sentence or answers the question.

1. Study of science for the sole purpose of advancing our knowledge is called _____ science.
   a. experimental   c. theoretical
   b. pure   d. technological

2. Physical science would involve the study of all of the following except _____.
   a. the melting point of wax
   b. the composition of wax
   c. the behavior of bees producing wax
   d. energy released by burning wax

3. A(n) _____ is used as a standard for comparison in an experiment.
   a. control   c. independent variable
   b. theory   d. constant

4. A _____ is an explanation supported by experimental results.
   a. conclusion   c. scientific law
   b. theory   d. model

5. It is believed that chlorofluorocarbons are responsible for _____.
   a. the greenhouse effect
   b. acid rain
   c. global warming
   d. ozone depletion

6. Which of these is not a safety rule to be followed in the laboratory?
   a. follow all directions carefully
   b. clean up all spills immediately
   c. wear rubber-soled shoes at all times
   d. know the location of the fire extinguisher

7. The _____ shields Earth from the damaging effects of ultraviolet radiation.
   a. troposphere   c. nitrogen oxide
   b. carbon dioxide   d. ozone

8. The _____ describes the steps followed in conducting an experiment.
   a. problem   c. conclusion
   b. procedure   d. data

9. A scientific _____ is sometimes called a "rule of nature."
   a. theory   c. model
   b. law   d. hypothesis

10. Which is the final step in an experiment?
   a. reach a conclusion
   b. state the problem
   c. set up a procedure
   d. record data

UNDERSTANDING CONCEPTS

Complete each sentence.

11. _____ is the application of scientific knowledge to improve the quality of life.

12. The greenhouse effect is produced by increased amounts of _____ present in the atmosphere.

13. A(n) _____ is an organized procedure for testing a hypothesis.

14. In an experiment involving popcorn, the brand name would be a _____.

15. _____ is a process that uses certain skills to solve a problem.

THINK AND WRITE CRITICALLY

16. Why is it usually easier to find the solution to an exercise than it is to find the solution to a problem? Include examples in your answer.

17. Describe how a hypothesis, a theory, and a scientific law are related.

18. Discuss the importance of recording all observations and data when conducting a science experiment.
19. Describe four safety precautions to be followed in the science laboratory.
20. Describe one current environmental issue that is controversial and explain why scientists disagree on the issue.

APPLY

21. In a study of the sun, what questions might a pure scientist ask? What questions might an applied scientist ask? How might the two sets of questions be related?
22. What aspects of the following items would a physical scientist be interested in?
    a. an electric guitar **b.** a piece of coal
23. Which problem-solving approach would you use to solve the following problems? Explain your choice in each case.
    a. solving a complex word problem in math
    b. figuring out a secret code
    c. predicting how a skyscraper would be affected by an earthquake
24. Design an experiment to determine how the temperature of water affects the time it takes sugar to dissolve in it. Identify the variables, constants, and control, if any.
25. Explain this statement: Scientists often learn as much from an incorrect hypothesis as they do from one that is correct.

MORE SKILL BUILDERS

If you need help, refer to the Skill Handbook.

1. **Comparing and Contrasting:** Compare and contrast the methods used to complete an exercise and to solve a problem.

2. **Hypothesizing:** Propose a hypothesis to explain why a balloon filled with air weighs more than a deflated balloon.

3. **Interpreting Scientific Illustrations:** The following are safety symbols used in two different experiments. Using Table B-2 on page 674 in Appendix B, describe the safety precautions that should be taken in each experiment.

a.
b.

4. **Using Variables, Constants, and Controls:** Do some objects fall faster than others? Design an experiment to find out. State your hypothesis and describe your procedure for testing it. Identify your controls, constants, and variables.

PROJECTS

1. Make a poster illustrating laboratory safety techniques.
2. Make a scrapbook of recent newspaper or magazine articles dealing with the scientific debate surrounding the greenhouse effect, the ozone layer, and/or acid rain. Read the articles carefully and include at the end of your scrapbook a short essay explaining your position on the problem.

4. **Using Variables, Constants, and Controls:** Students should describe an experiment in which they measure the time it takes for objects having different physical characteristics (mass, shape, size) to fall the same distance. The distance will be constant. Variables will consist of the differences in the objects tested.

APPLY

21. A pure scientist might ask about the sun's size, composition, age, temperature, movements, and methods of energy production. An applied scientist might ask how the sun's energy can be harnessed for use on Earth.
22. Student responses may vary. Examples could include the following:
    a. how the length and thickness of the strings or the shape, composition, and structure of the guitar body affect the sound.
    b. the chemical composition of the coal, its hardness and color, how hot it must be before it burns.
23. **a.** Word Problem: Break it down into simpler problems.
    b. Code: Look for patterns.
    c. Predicting: Create and study models.
24. Constants: volume of water, mass of sugar
    Control: water at same temperature
    Independent variable: water temperature
    Dependent variable: time required for sugar to dissolve
25. A scientist is able to eliminate an incorrect hypothesis as a possible solution to a problem.

MORE SKILL BUILDERS

1. **Comparing and Contrasting:** The methods used to solve a problem are developed as the solution to the problem is sought. The methods used to complete an exercise have already been tested and are found to produce the desired results.
2. **Hypothesizing:** Student responses may vary, but should include the idea that the inflated balloon contains something that the deflated balloon does not—air—and it has weight.
3. **Interpreting Scientific Illustrations:**
   a. The first symbol indicates an open flame; the second indicates safety goggles should be worn; the third indicates that the chemicals used are poisonous; the fourth that the chemicals are caustic to the skin.
   b. The first symbol indicates a possible electric hazard; the second symbol indicates that the equipment being used is quite hot; the third symbol indicates that goggles should be worn; the fourth symbol indicates that the chemicals used are potentially explosive.

CHAPTER 2 Physical Science Methods

CHAPTER SECTION	OBJECTIVES	ACTIVITIES
2-1 Standards of Measurement (2 days)	1. **Define** standard of measurement. 2. **Recognize** the need for standards of measurement. 3. **Name** the prefixes used in SI and tell what multiple of ten each represents.	**Activity 2-1:** *Scales of Measurement,* p. 33
2-2 Using SI Units (2 days)	1. **Identify** SI units and symbols for length, volume, mass, density, time, and temperature. 2. **Define** derived unit. 3. **Demonstrate** an ability to convert related SI units.	**MINI-Lab:** *What is the density of a pencil?* p. 40
2-3 Graphing (1 day)	1. **Identify** three types of graphs and explain the correct use of each type. 2. **Distinguish** between dependent and independent variables. 3. **Interpret** graphs.	**MINI-Lab:** *How can a graph help you observe change?* p. 42
2-4 Metrics for All? Science & Society (1 day)	1. **Analyze** the benefits and drawbacks of universal use of the SI system. 2. **Give examples** of SI units used in the United States.	**Activity 2-2:** *Metric Munchies,* p. 48
Chapter Review		

ACTIVITY MATERIALS

FIND OUT	ACTIVITIES		MINI-LABS	
Page 29 classroom objects	**2-1 Scales of Measurement, p. 33** string 1 m long scissors masking tape	**2-2 Metric Munchies, p. 48** balance 100-mL graduated cylinder munchie ingredients measuring cup measuring teaspoon measuring tablespoon 1 quart plastic container hot plate	**What is the density of a pencil? p. 40** balance pencil 100-mL graduated cylinder	**How can a graph help you observe change? p. 42** thermometer plastic foam cup lid with straw hole

CHAPTER FEATURES		TEACHER RESOURCE PACKAGE	OTHER RESOURCES
Problem Solving: *Nonstandard Measurement Units,* p. 32 **Skill Builder:** *Sequencing,* p. 32		**Ability Level Worksheets** ◆ **Study Guide,** p. 9 ● **Reinforcement,** p. 9 ▲ **Enrichment,** p. 9 **Activity Worksheet,** pp. 13, 14 **Transparency Masters,** pp. 5, 6	**Color Transparency 3,** SI Units and Prefixes
Technology: *Space Spheres,* p. 37 **Skill Builder:** *Concept Mapping,* p. 41		**Ability Level Worksheets** ◆ **Study Guide,** p. 10 ● **Reinforcement,** p. 10 ▲ **Enrichment,** p. 10 **MINI-Lab Worksheet,** p. 19 **Concept Mapping,** pp. 9, 10 **Cross-Curricular Connections,** p. 6 **Technology,** pp. 7, 8	**Lab Manual 2,** Relationships **Lab Manual 3,** Viscosity
Skill Builder: *Making and Using Graphs,* p. 45		**Ability Level Worksheets** ◆ **Study Guide,** p. 11 ● **Reinforcement,** p. 11 ▲ **Enrichment,** p. 11 **MINI-Lab Worksheet,** p. 20 **Critical Thinking/Problem Solving,** p. 8 **Science and Society,** p. 6 **Transparency Masters,** pp. 7, 8	**Color Transparency 4,** Types of Graphs
You Decide! p. 47		**Ability Level Worksheets** ◆ **Study Guide,** p. 12 ● **Reinforcement,** p. 12 ▲ **Enrichment,** p. 12 **Activity Worksheet,** pp. 15, 16	
Summary Key Science Words Understanding Vocabulary Checking Concepts Understanding Concepts	Think & Write Critically Apply More Skill Builders Projects	**Chapter Review,** pp. 7, 8 **Chapter Test,** pp. 9–12 **Unit Test,** pp. 13, 14	**Chapter Review Software** **Test Bank**

◆ **Basic**   ● **Average**   ▲ **Advanced**

ADDITIONAL MATERIALS		
SOFTWARE	**AUDIOVISUAL**	**BOOKS/MAGAZINES**
SI/Metric Literacy, EME. *Measurements: Length, Mass, and Volume,* Focus. *The Metric System,* Queue. *The Great Metrics Knowledge Race,* Queue.	*Why does a helium balloon rise?,* film, EME. *Mass and Density: Investigating Matter,* laserdisc, AIMS Media.	Lamon, William E. *Metric System of Measurement: A Handbook for Teachers.* Portland, OR: Continuing Ed. Pr., 1981.

THEME DEVELOPMENT: This chapter introduces the SI system of measurements and graphing as two methods of gaining and interpreting information. In developing the SI system, stress how base units are related to each other and how the same set of prefixes is used for all units.

CHAPTER OVERVIEW

▶ **Section 2-1:** This section introduces the SI system as a standardized decimal system of measurements that is used ostensibly by the scientific community and by most countries.

▶ **Section 2-2:** The SI prefixes and base units for length, mass, time, and temperature are introduced in this section. The relationships among length, volume, mass, and density are discussed.

▶ **Section 2-3:** Three types of graphs and their specific uses are presented as ways of displaying information.

▶ **Section 2-4:** Science and Society: Students are asked to evaluate the impact of converting the United States to the SI system.

CHAPTER VOCABULARY

standard	kilogram
SI	density
meter	time
volume	second
derived units	kelvin
liter	graph
mass	

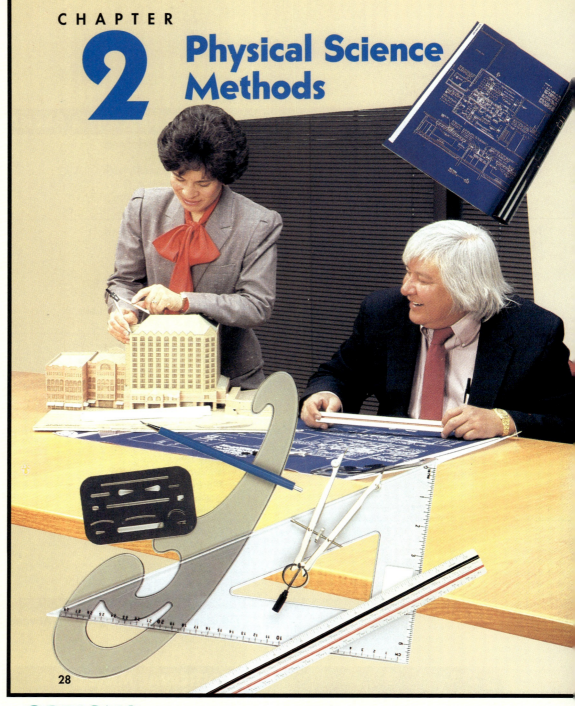

CHAPTER

2 Physical Science Methods

28

OPTIONS

For Your Gifted Students

▶ Have students research the standardization of currency. When did it occur? Why? They can compare the need for standard units of measurement discussed in the chapter to the need for standard currency.

▶ Students can use centimeter-graph paper to draw a scaled floor plan of their classroom, home, or school.

Look around your classroom. In order to build the room and produce all the things inside it, such as the desks, chairs, shelves, and chalkboards, many measurements had to be made. Think about some of the things that were measured and the tools used to measure them.

FIND OUT!

Do this simple activity to find out how measurements are made.

Imagine that measuring tools have not been invented. Pick something in your classroom to use as a tool for measuring length. It can be an object from your desk; a hand, foot, or arm; or anything else that can easily be used.

Working with a partner, measure a distance in the room with your measuring device. Now have your partner measure the same distance, first using his or her own measuring device, then using yours. Which measurements can you compare? How similar are they? How could you improve your measuring devices?

Gearing Up

Previewing the Chapter

Use this outline to help you focus on important ideas in this chapter.

Previewing Science Skills

► In the **Skill Builders**, you will sequence, make a concept map, and make and use graphs.
► In the **Activities**, you will observe, collect and organize data, and measure in SI.
► In the **MINI-Labs**, you will measure in SI, make inferences, and make and use graphs.

What's next?

Now that you have compared measurements made with your own measuring devices, find out what a measurement standard is. Once you know why standards are so important in making measurements, learn to use the system of measurement that is used by scientists throughout the world.

29

INTRODUCING THE CHAPTER
Use the Find Out activity to introduce students to the inherent difficulties of measuring without standardized units.

FIND OUT!
Materials: ordinary classroom objects
Cooperative Learning: Select a measuring device at random from the class discussion and assign Problem Solving teams to devise ways of using the device to measure the length of a paper clip and the length of the school building; and the diameter of the wire in a paper clip and the diameter of a tree.
Teaching Tips
► Have all the students measure at least two common objects, such as the length of the chalk tray and the width of a student desk, for comparisons.
► Students should discuss the measurements they made. Focus the discussion on the conceptualization of the unit, the measuring device and its relationship to the unit, how the device is used in making the measurement, and the value of the measurement.
► Have the students discuss the limitations of the measurements they made.

Gearing Up
Have students study the Gearing Up section to familiarize themselves with the chapter. Discuss the relationships of the topics in the outline.

What's Next?
Before beginning the first section, make sure students understand the connection between the Find Out activity and the topics to follow.

For Your Mainstreamed Students

► Using a paper clip as a unit of measure for 1 gram, have students use a balance to weigh several items (pencil, tennis ball, crayon, etc.).
► Have students estimate the Celsius temperature for the classroom, normal body temperature, a summer day at the beach, and a winter day skiing. Compare with classmates and discuss.

► Ask students to take a look at the family automobile. How many metric measurements are used? Are metric tools required for repair?

SECTION BACKGROUND
▶ Science has progressed because of its reliance on quantitative observations. The SI system is used by the scientific community to collect and communicate these observations.

1 MOTIVATE

Cooperative Learning: Using the Numbered Heads Together strategy, have students suggest solutions to the following paradox: A pound of feathers will balance a pound of gold, but an ounce of feathers will not balance an ounce of gold. Lead students to realize that there are two standard ounces: the avoirdupois ounce, of which 16 constitute a pound; and the troy ounce, of which 12 constitute a pound.

▶ Have students recall standard sizes of products such as batteries (AAA, AA, B, C, D) clothing sizes (10, 12, 14, 16; S, M, L, XL), and light bulbs (75 W, 100 W). Ask them why these products must be standardized and conjecture how manufacturers make sure their products meet these standards.

TYING TO PREVIOUS KNOWLEDGE:
Have students recall the relationships among pennies, dimes, and dollars. Point out that their knowledge of the relationships being based upon ten will be important in their understanding of the metric system studied in this section.

OBJECTIVES AND SCIENCE WORDS:
Have students review the objectives and science words to become familiar with this section.

2-1 Standards of Measurement

New Science Words	Objectives
standard SI	▶ Define standard of measurement. ▶ Recognize the need for standards of measurement. ▶ Name the prefixes used in SI and tell what multiple of ten each represents.

Units and Standards

How wide is your desk? At what temperature does ice cream start to melt? How fast does sugar dissolve? In order to answer any of these questions, some measurement must be made.

Measuring is an important skill. It is especially important in science. In order for a measurement to be useful, a measurement standard must be used. A **standard** is an exact quantity that people agree to use for comparison. When all measurements are made using the same standard, the measurements can be compared to each other.

Suppose you and a friend want to make some measurements to find out if a desk will fit through a doorway. You have no ruler, so you decide to use your hands as measuring tools. Using the width of his or her hands, your friend measures the doorway and says it is 8 "hands" wide. Using the width of your hands, you measure the desk and find it is 7-3/4 "hands" wide. Will the desk fit through the doorway? You can't be sure. What if your hands are wider than your friend's hands? Then the distance equal to 7-3/4 of your hands might be greater than the distance equal to 8 of your friends hands.

What mistake did you make? Even though you both used your hands to measure, you didn't check to see if your hands were the same width as your friend's hands. In other words, you didn't use a measurement standard, so you can't compare measurements.

30 PHYSICAL SCIENCE METHODS

OPTIONS

Meeting Different Ability Levels
For Section 2-1, use the following **Teacher Resource Masters** depending upon individual students' needs.
◆ **Study Guide Master** for all students.
● **Reinforcement Master** for students of average and above average ability levels.
▲ **Enrichment Master** for above average students.
Additional Teacher Resource Package masters are listed in the OPTIONS box throughout the section. The additional masters are appropriate for all students.

◆ STUDY GUIDE   9

STUDY GUIDE   Chapter 2
Standards of Measurement   Text Pages 30–33

Some prefixes used in SI are listed in the table below. Use the information in the table to answer questions 1–5.

SI Prefix	Meaning
kilo-	thousand (1000)
hecto-	hundred (100)
deka-	ten (10)
deci-	tenth (0.10)
centi-	hundredth (0.01)
milli-	thousandth (0.001)

1. How many meters are in one kilometer? _____ 1000 m
2. What part of a liter is one milliliter? _____ 0.001 m or one thousandth meter
3. How many grams are in two dekagrams? _____ 20 g
4. If one gram of water has a volume of one milliliter, what would the mass of one liter of water be in kilograms? _____ one kilogram
5. What part of a meter is a decimeter? _____ 0.10 m or one tenth meter

In the blank at the left, write the term that correctly completes each statement. Choose from the terms listed below.

metric   SI   standard
ten   prefixes   tenth

standard   6. An exact quantity that people agree to use for comparison is a _____.
SI   7. The system of measurement used worldwide in science is _____.
ten   8. SI is based on units of _____.
metric   9. The first system of measurement that was based on units of ten was the _____ system.
prefixes   10. In SI, _____ are used with the names of the base unit to indicate the multiple of ten that is being used with the base unit.
tenth   11. The prefix deci- means _____.

International System of Units

Suppose the label on a ball of string indicates that the length of the string in the ball is "150." Can you tell how much string is in the ball? No. It could be 150 feet, 150 meters, or 150 of some unit you've never heard of. In order for a measurement to make sense, it must include a number and a unit.

Your family probably buys lumber by the foot, milk by the quart, and potatoes by the pound. These measurement units are part of the English system of measurement, which is most commonly used in the United States. Most other nations use a system of measurement based on multiples of ten. The first such system of measurement, called the metric system, was devised by a group of scientists in the late 1700s. The system was based on a set of standards established and agreed to by the scientists.

In 1960 an improved version of the metric system was devised. Known as the International System of Units, this system is often abbreviated SI, from the French *Le Système Internationale d'Unités*. **SI is the standard system of measurement used worldwide. All SI standards are universally accepted and understood throughout the scientific community.**

In SI, each type of measurement has a base unit, such as the meter, which is the base unit of length. In the next section, you will learn the units used to measure length, mass, time, temperature, volume, and density.

The system is easy to use because it is based on multiples of ten. Prefixes are used with the names of the base units to indicate what multiple of ten should be used with the base unit. For example, the prefix *kilo-* means 1000. So a *kilometer* is 1000 meters. The most frequently used prefixes are shown in Table 2-1. Based on information from the table, how long is a centimeter?

What system of measurement is used in the U.S.?

Figure 2-1. The standard kilogram mass, composed of a platinum-iridium alloy, is kept at the International Bureau of Weights and Measures in Sevres, France.

Table 2-1

IMPORTANT SI PREFIXES		
Prefixes	**Symbol**	**Multiplying factor**
kilo-	k	1000
deci-	d	0.1
centi-	c	0.01
milli-	m	0.001
micro-	μ	0.000 001
nano-	n	0.000 000 001

2 TEACH

Key Concepts are highlighted.

CONCEPT DEVELOPMENT
► Make sure students understand that the term *exact quantity* indicates that people have agreed how to define, reproduce, and use the quantity.

CROSS CURRICULUM
► **Social Studies:** Have students compare and contrast standards used for government and standards used for measurements.

MINI QUIZ
Use the Mini Quiz to check students' recall of chapter content.

1 A standard is an exact quantity that people agree to use for _____ . *comparison*

2 _____ is the standard system of measurements used worldwide. *SI*

3 SI is easy to use because it is based on multiples of _____ . *ten*

CHECK FOR UNDERSTANDING
Ask questions 1-2 and the **Apply** Question in the Section Review.

RETEACH
Write the terms *decade, century,* and *millennium* on the chalkboard and have students identify them as 10-, 100-, and 1000-year periods. Ask the students to use the metric prefixes to define a year in terms of a decade (decidecade), century (centicentury), and millennium (millimillennium). Ask students to interpret the meaning of the *i* in the three metric prefixes.

EXTENSION
For students who have mastered this section, use the **Reinforcement** and **Enrichment** masters or other OPTIONS provided.

STUDENT TEXT QUESTION
► Page 31, paragraph 5: **Based on information from the table, how long is a centimeter?** *A centimeter is one-hundredth of a meter long.*

PROBLEM SOLVING

The students measuring with string had a measurement standard, whereas those measuring in cubits did not.

Think Critically: Measurement standards are necessary in order that different measurements of the same quantity can be compared.

3 CLOSE

▶ Have students identify several Olympic track and swimming events such as the 100-m dash and the 200-m free-style. Ask them to explain why these events are measured in SI units.

SECTION REVIEW ANSWERS

1. Student responses may vary, but should include the ideas that SI is based on ten and that the same prefixes are used for all measurements. Students may also indicate that most nations use this system.

2. 0.1 meter = one decimeter; 1000 meters = one kilometer

3. Apply: Student responses will vary. Accept all reasonable responses.

Skill Builder

kilogram, gram, decigram, centigram, milligram

PROGRAM RESOURCES

From the **Teacher Resource Package** use:

Transparency Masters, pages 5-6, SI Units and Prefixes.

Use **Color Transparency** number 3, SI Units and Prefixes.

PROBLEM SOLVING

Nonstandard Measurement Units

As the students in Mr. Craig's science class entered the classroom, everyone noticed a long strip of tape on the chalkboard. Mr. Craig informed the students that they would be measuring the length of the tape.

The students were divided up into two teams. One team was to measure the length of the tape in cubits, the distance from the elbow to the end of the middle finger. The other team was given a piece of wood and a ball of string. Each student was to cut a piece of string exactly as long as the piece of wood, and then use the string to measure the tape.

Although the students in each group made their measurements carefully, each student using cubits came up with a different number of units for the length of the tape. The students using pieces of string all came up with the same number of units.

Why were the measurements in cubits all different, but those made with string all the same?

Think Critically: Why is it important to use a system of measurement based on standard units?

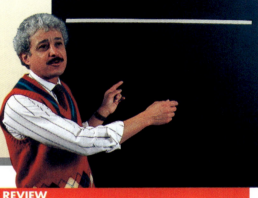

SECTION REVIEW

1. What are some advantages of using the International System of measurement over the English system of measurement?
2. In SI, the base unit of length is the meter. What would you call 0.1 meter? 1000 meters?
3. **Apply:** Make a list of measuring tools you have used in the past month. For each example, tell what units you used to make your measurements.

Skill Builder

☑ **Sequencing**

Using the data in Table 2-1, arrange the following units in order, from largest to smallest: centigram, gram, milligram, kilogram, decigram. If you need help, refer to Sequencing in the **Skill Handbook** on page 676.

OPTIONS

INQUIRY QUESTIONS

▶ What specialized units are used to measure the size of printing type? *point or pica* the weight of gems? *carat* the height of horses? *hand* nautical speed? *knot* the diameter of wire? *mil (1/1000 inch)* speed of playing music? *m.m. (metronome marking)* an amount of wood? *cord* corrective lenses? *diopter* small concentrations? *ppm (parts per million)* recording speeds? *RPM (revolutions per minute)* cross-stitch fabric? *threads per inch* loudness? *bel*

▶ The price of gasoline is 112-9/10 cents. How many millidollars is that? *1129 millidollars* Where else is the value of something estimated in millidollars? *The tax rate of real estate is expressed as millidollars per dollar of valuation.*

ACTIVITY 2-1
Scales of Measurement

Problem: *Can you invent your own system of measurement?*

Materials
- string 1 m long
- scissors
- masking tape

Procedure
1. Cut your piece of string to match the length, width, or height of some object in the room.
2. Cut a narrow strip of masking tape and fasten it to one end of the string. Mark the tape "0."
3. Cut a second strip of tape and fasten it to the other end of the string. Mark this strip "1."
4. Fold the string in half and use tape to mark the halfway point "1/2."
5. Fold the string again and mark the "1/4" positions. Repeat again for the "1/8" positions.
6. Cut a second piece of string the same length as the first. Devise a way to divide the string into 1/3, 1/6, and 1/12 segments.
7. Repeat Step 6 to divide a third piece of string into 1/5 and 1/10 segments.
8. Select two objects in the room to measure, one larger than the string and one smaller.
9. Have each team member use one of the strings to measure both objects. Record all measurements on a data sheet.

Data and Observations Sample Data

String*	Object measured	Object length
1/8	book	4/8
1/8	table	3 3/8
1/12	book	6/12
1/12	table	3 5/12
1/10	book	5/10
1/10	table	3 4/10

*Object used to determine length of string: _____ width of desk

Analyze
1. Which of the three scales is most likely to provide the most accurate measurement of a small object? Why?
2. Which of the three scales is easiest to record in decimal numbers?
3. Which scale is easiest to make and which is easiest to use?

Conclude and Apply
4. To understand measurements made by another team, why is it important to know what object matched the length of their string?
5. How is it possible for different numbers to represent the same length?

ACTIVITY 2-1
30 minutes

OBJECTIVE: **Design** a scale of measurement and use it to **measure** the length of objects.

PROCESS SKILLS applied in this activity:
▶ **Measuring** in Procedure Step 8.
▶ **Formulating Models** in Procedure Steps 1-7.
▶ **Collecting and Organizing Data** in Procedure Step 9.

COOPERATIVE LEARNING
Divide the class into Science Investigation teams.

TEACHING THE ACTIVITY
Troubleshooting: Use fairly heavy twine to make handling easy. Do not expect a high amount of accuracy.
▶ Do not make metersticks or any other measuring device available.
▶ Encourage students to measure room dimensions, tables, or counters.
▶ Give as little initial instruction as possible. As a follow-up let students share problems and suggest solutions.

PROGRAM RESOURCES
From the **Teacher Resource Package** use:

Activity Worksheets, pages 13-14, Activity 2-1: Scales of Measurement.

ANSWERS TO QUESTIONS
1. The 1/12 scale is most likely to measure small objects accurately because the measurement marks are closer together.
Exception: The student may have invented a way to further subdivide one of the other scales.
2. The 1/10 scale is easiest to record in decimal numbers.
3. The 1/8 scale is probably the easiest to make, because it involves repeated divisions by two. The 1/10 scale is probably easiest to use, because it matches the base ten number system.

4. The object used as the standard for preparing the scale allows the numbers to represent a known size.
5. If the numbers are based on different standards, they could be unlike but measure the same length.

2-2 **Using SI Units**

SECTION BACKGROUND

▶ The SI system consists of seven base units. In this section four base units, those that measure length, mass, time, and temperature, are introduced. These units are necessary to describe motion and energy, the subjects of the next six chapters.

PREPLANNING

▶ To prepare for the Mini-Lab, obtain several 100-mL graduated cylinders.

1 MOTIVATE

▶ Have students approximate the dimensions or volumes of common objects around the classroom. Ask them to explain how they could determine whose approximations were the most correct. Discuss the similarities in the processes of approximating (mentally comparing the object to another object which represents a standard unit) and measuring (physically comparing an object to standard units on a measuring instrument).

▶ **Demonstration:** Using three identical opaque plastic bottles, fill one with sand, the second with water, and leave the third empty. Stopper each. Have students close their eyes as you rearrange the bottles. After they have opened their eyes, ask if they can determine the contents of each bottle by sight. Now pass the bottles around the classroom and have students determine their contents without opening the bottles. Ask how they made their determinations.

2-2 Using SI Units

New Science Words

meter
volume
derived units
liter
mass
kilogram
density
time
second
kelvin

Objectives

▶ Identify SI units and symbols for length, volume, mass, density, time, and temperature.
▶ Define *derived unit.*
▶ Demonstrate an ability to convert related SI units.

SI Units and Symbols

Every type of measurement in SI has a base unit and a symbol for that unit. These names and symbols are shown in Table 2-2.

Table 2-2

SI BASE UNITS		
Measurement	**Unit**	**Symbol**
Length	Meter	m
Mass	Kilogram	kg
Time	Second	s
Electric current	Ampere	A
Temperature	Kelvin	K
Amount of substance	Mole	mol
Intensity of light	Candela	cd

What is the SI unit of length?

Length

The word *length* is used in many different ways. For example, the length of a novel is the number of pages it contains. The length of a movie is the number of hours and minutes it runs. In scientific measurement, length is the distance between two points. That distance may be the diameter of a period on this page or the distance from Earth to the moon. The SI unit of length is the **meter** (m). A baseball bat is about 1 meter long. Metric rulers and metersticks are used to measure length.

OPTIONS

Meeting Different Ability Levels

For Section 2-2, use the following **Teacher Resource Masters** depending upon individual students' needs.

◆ **Study Guide Master** for all students.
● **Reinforcement Master** for students of average and above average ability levels.
▲ **Enrichment Master** for above average students.

Additional Teacher Resource Package masters are listed in the OPTIONS box throughout the section. The additional masters are appropriate for all students.

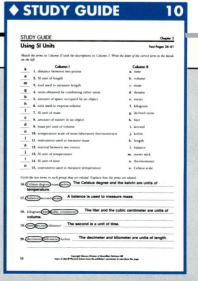

Figure 2-2. A metric ruler is used to measure the length of small objects, such as a pencil.

Recall that measurement in SI is based on multiples of ten. The prefix *deci-* means 1/10, so a decimeter is one-tenth of a meter. Similarly, a centimeter (cm) is one-hundredth of a meter. The diameter of a shirt button is about 1 cm.

$$100 \text{ cm} = 10 \text{ dm} = 1 \text{ m}$$

How many centimeters are in 1 decimeter?

Centimeters can be divided into smaller units called millimeters (mm). A millimeter is 1/1000 of a meter. One tooth along the edge of a postage stamp is about 1 mm long.

The size of the unit you select to make a measurement will depend on the size of the item being measured. For example, you would probably use the centimeter to measure the length of your pencil and the meter to measure the length of your classroom. What unit would you use to measure the distance from your home to school? You would probably want to use a unit larger than a meter. The kilometer (km), which is 1000 meters, is used to measure long distances. One kilometer is about ten football fields long.

Suppose you know the length of something in meters and want to change, or *convert,* the measurement to centimeters. Because 1 m = 100 cm, you can convert from

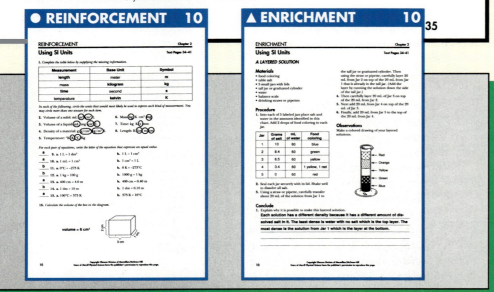
TYING TO PREVIOUS KNOWLEDGE: Have students associate familiar metric units with products or uses such as milligrams (vitamin pills), watt (light bulb), megahertz or kilohertz (radio station frequencies), millimeter (camera film), liter (pop bottles), and volt (batteries). Point out that these units are associated with the metric system of measurements which students will be learning more about in this section.

OBJECTIVES AND SCIENCE WORDS: Have students review the objectives and science words to become familiar with this section.

STUDENT TEXT QUESTION
▶ Page 35, paragraph 2: **How many centimeters are in 1 decimeter?** *There are 10 cm in 1 dm.*

2 TEACH

Key Concepts are highlighted.

CONCEPT DEVELOPMENT
▶ Distribute metric rulers and have students identify the millimeter, centimeter, and decimeter markings on the ruler. Have them measure common objects. As they are measuring, have each of them choose an object that best represents a centimeter. Allow them to make estimations and use their rulers to check their estimations.

CONCEPT DEVELOPMENT

▶ Review the Example and Practice Problems using the factor label method.

$$1.98 \; \cancel{m} \times \frac{100 \text{ cm}}{1 \; \cancel{m}}$$
$$= (1.98 \times 100) \text{ cm} = 198 \text{ cm}$$

$$253.8 \; \cancel{km} \times \frac{1000 \; \cancel{m}}{1 \; \cancel{km}} \times \frac{100 \text{ cm}}{1 \; \cancel{m}}$$
$$= (253.8 \times 1000 \times 100) \text{ cm}$$
$$= 2 \; 538 \; 000 \text{ cm}$$

$$75 \; \cancel{cm} \times \frac{1 \text{ dm}}{10 \; \cancel{cm}} = (75 \div 10) \text{ dm}$$
$$= 7.5 \text{ dm}$$

$$75 \; \cancel{cm} \times \frac{1 \text{ m}}{100 \; \cancel{cm}} = (75 \div 100) \text{ m}$$
$$= 0.75 \text{ m}$$

▶ In SI measurements that have values greater than 9999 or less than 0.999, groups of three integers to the left and to the right of the decimal point are separated by spaces, not commas, because a comma is used to represent the decimal point in some European countries. Thus 12345.6789 cm is expressed 12 345.678 9 cm.

TEACHER F.Y.I.

▶ There are prefixes that represent 10 and 100, namely *deka-* and *hecto-*. However, they are rarely used.

REVEALING MISCONCEPTIONS

▶ Students may believe that the SI system is more precise than the English system because it is used by scientists. Point out that both systems can yield equally precise measurements. For instance, a micrometer used by machinists can measure the diameters of bolts to the nearest 0.0001 inch. Scientists use SI because it is *easier to use* than the English system.

PRACTICE PROBLEM ANSWERS

1.   1 km = 100 000 cm
    253.8 km = 2 538 000 cm
2.   1 cm = 0.1 dm
    75 cm = 7.5 dm
    1 cm = 0.01 m
    75 cm = 0.75 m

---

meters to centimeters simply by multiplying by 100. Because SI is based on multiples of ten, any unit can be converted to a related unit by multiplying or dividing it by the appropriate multiple of ten.

If you follow these "rules," conversion will be easy:

- When converting from larger to smaller units, multiply—move the decimal to the right.
- When converting from smaller to larger units, divide—move the decimal to the left.
- Move the decimal point as many places as there are zeros in the multiple of ten you are using.

For example, to convert 532 cm to meters, you divide because you're converting from smaller (cm) to larger (m) units. Because 100 cm = 1 m, move the decimal point two places to the left. So, 532 cm = 5.32 m.

Another way to convert units is to multiply by one. For example, 1 meter = 100 centimeters. Therefore,

$$\frac{1 \text{ meter}}{100 \text{ centimeters}} = \frac{100 \text{ centimeters}}{100 \text{ centimeters}} = 1$$

To convert 532 cm to meters, write

$$532 \text{ cm} \times \frac{1 \text{ m}}{100 \text{ cm}} = \frac{532 \text{ m}}{100} = 5.32 \text{ m}$$

The cm label is cancelled, because it appears in both the numerator and the denominator.

EXAMPLE PROBLEM

Problem Statement: How many centimeters are in 1.98 meters?

Known Information: 1 m = 100 cm
Strategy Hint: Think about which way you should move the decimal point. When converting from larger to smaller units, multiply. Because 1 m = 100 cm; move the decimal two places to the right.

Solution: 1.98 m = 198 cm

PRACTICE PROBLEMS

Strategy Hint: First change kilometers to meters; then change meters to centimeters.

1. How many centimeters are in 253.8 kilometers?

Strategy Hint: Remember the meanings of the prefixes.

2. A bookshelf is 75 cm wide. How many dm is this? How many m would this be?

OPTIONS

INQUIRY QUESTIONS

▶ **How many millimeters are there in 2.5 meters?** *2500 millimeters*

▶ **How many meters are there in 650 millimeters?** *0.65 meter*

▶ **How many centimeters are there in 0.464 meter?** *46.4 centimeters*

▶ **A vitamin capsule contains 200 milligrams of vitamin C. How many capsules could be made from 1.0 kilogram of vitamin C? Hint: Convert 1.0 kilogram to milligrams.** *1.0 kilogram = 1000 grams = 1 000 000 milligrams. Therefore, 1 000 000 milligrams × 1 capsule/200 milligrams = 5000 capsules.*

▶ **How many square centimeters are there in a square meter?** *One m^2 is 1 m × 1 m = 100 cm × 100 cm = 10 000 cm^2.*

▶ **What is the area of a rectangular tabletop that measures 150 centimeters by 200 centimeters?** *30 000 cm^2* **What is the area of the table in square meters?** *30 000 cm^2 =*

$$30 \; 000 \; cm^2 \times \frac{1 \; m^2}{10 \; 000 \; cm^2} = 3m^2$$

TECHNOLOGY

Space Spheres

The space shuttle *Challenger* served as the manufacturing site for one of the latest reference materials produced by the National Bureau of Standards. The reference material is a polystyrene sphere that measures 10 micrometers across. The head of a pin could hold 18 000 of these spheres. The spheres will be packaged in a 5-mL vial containing about 30 million spheres in water. These spheres can be used as a reference for manufacturers and researchers who need to calibrate instruments to check particle size in products such as cosmetics, paint pigments, flour, toner used in photocopiers, and so on. The spheres can also be used to improve microscopic measurements made in areas such as medicine and electronics.

The *Challenger* was chosen as the manufacturing site because of its gravity-free environment. Spheres produced by conventional processes on Earth tend to float or sink during their formation. This results in spheres with a variation in diameter that is too great for use as a standard. The reduced gravity of space allows the production of spheres that are very uniform in size and shape.

Think Critically: Name some products that you use or encounter daily that had to be calibrated to ensure their proper operation.

As you move ahead in this section, you will learn about several different types of measurements. Keep in mind that the conversion "rules" you have used here can be used with any base unit in SI, because the system is based on multiples of ten. The prefixes remain the same, no matter what base unit you may be using.

Volume

The amount of space occupied by an object is called its **volume.** If you wanted to know the volume of a solid object, such as a building brick, you would measure its length, width, and height, and multiply the three figures together. For the brick, your measurements would be in centimeters, and the volume would be expressed in cubic centimeters (cm^3). For a larger object, such as a truck, your measurements would be in meters and the volume in cubic meters (m^3).

Think Critically: Student responses will vary, but should contain only items made up of extremely small particles, such as baby talcum and graphite lubricant. Accept all reasonable responses.

CONCEPT DEVELOPMENT

▶ Discuss the uncertainty in measurements that come from (a) measuring with an improper instrument, such as a warped or chipped meterstick; (b) using and reading the instrument incorrectly, such as not holding a meterstick parallel to the dimension of the object being measured; and (c) recording the measurement improperly.

▶ **Demonstration:** Have students use metersticks to measure the sizes of their waists or heads, or the circumference of a round wastebasket or a tree. Have them repeat the measurements with a metric tape measure. Ask them to explain why the measurements made with the tape measure are more accurate.

INQUIRY QUESTIONS

▶How many centimeters are there in a decimeter? *10 cm* How many cubic centimeters are there in a cubic decimeter? *1000 cm³* A cubic decimeter is the same as a liter. How many cubic centimeters are there in a liter? *1000 cm³*

▶A bottle of orange juice contains 1.2 liters. How many cubic centimeters is this? *1200 cm³* How many glasses of 200 cm³ each can be filled with this bottle of juice? *six*

▶A medical procedure requires a solution containing 2 milligrams of antibiotic dissolved in 5 cubic centimeters of sterile salt solution. If you have a bottle containing 650 cm³ of sterile salt solution, how many 5-cm³ doses could be prepared from the bottle? *130 doses of 5 cm³ each* How much antibiotic would you have to dissolve in the bottle to get the correct solution? *260 milligrams*

▶ In science, the *accuracy* of a measurement is an indication of how well the value of a measurement represents the measure of the object being made. A measurement is accurate if its value compares well to the values of other measurements made of the object by other people or by using different instruments.

▶ *Precision* indicates how well the instrument is calibrated; that is, how well its smallest measurement unit is marked. For instance, a metal ruler that has markings indicating millimeters is more precise than a plastic ruler that has only centimeter markings.

▶ The following diagrams indicate that measurements should have both accuracy and precision.

not precise/
not accurate

precise/
not accurate

precise/
accurate

CONCEPT DEVELOPMENT

▶ Review the Example Problem using the factor-label method.

$$538 \text{ cm}^3 \times \frac{1 \text{ mL}}{1 \text{ cm}^3} \times \frac{1 \text{ L}}{1000 \text{ mL}}$$

$$= (538 \div 1000) \text{ L} = 0.538 \text{ L}$$

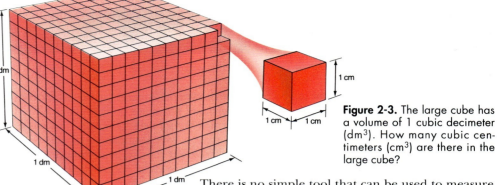

Figure 2-3. The large cube has a volume of 1 cubic decimeter (dm^3). How many cubic centimeters (cm^3) are there in the large cube?

What is a derived unit?

There is no simple tool that can be used to measure the volume of an object directly. Volume units are obtained by combining other SI units. Units obtained this way are called **derived units.**

How do you measure the volume of a liquid? A liquid has no "sides" to measure. In measuring a liquid's volume, you indicate the capacity of a container that holds that amount of liquid. Liquid volumes are sometimes expressed in cubic centimeters, as in doses of medicine. The most common units for expressing liquid volumes are liters and milliliters. A **liter** occupies the same volume as a cubic decimeter (dm^3). That is, a liter is the same volume as a cube that is 1 dm (10 cm) on each side. A liter is slightly larger than a quart of milk. The liter is not an SI unit, but it is used with that system.

One liter (L) is equal to 1000 milliliters (mL). A cubic decimeter (dm^3) is equal to 1000 cubic centimeters (cm^3). So, because 1 L = 1 dm^3, 1 mL = 1 cm^3.

Suppose you wanted to convert a measurement in liters to cubic centimeters. The same "rules" you used for converting length can be used for any SI unit.

EXAMPLE PROBLEM

Problem Statement: How many liters of gasoline are in 538 cm^3?

Known Information:
Strategy Hint: 1 L = 1000 cm^3.
Change cm^3 to mL.

1 cm^3 = 1 mL
1 L = 1000 mL; therefore, 1 L = 1000 cm^3.
Because you are converting from smaller to larger units, you divide. Move the decimal point three places to the left.

Solution: 538 cm^3 = 0.538 L

OPTIONS

INQUIRY QUESTIONS

▶ **What is the curved surface of a liquid contained in a graduated cylinder called?** *meniscus*

▶ **What is the mass of the sun?** *about 2 000 000 000 000 000 000 000 000 000 000 kg (about two million-trillion-trillion kg)*

▶ **A commercial brand of low-sodium table salt (crystals of sodium chloride) advertises 50% less sodium per teaspoon than regular table salt. The label indicates that 100 g of this product and 100 g of regular table salt contain the same amount of sodium. How** *can this be? The volume of the sodium chloride crystals in this product is twice as large as the volume of the sodium chloride crystals in regular table salt.*

To measure volume in the laboratory, you will use a slender glass container called a graduated cylinder. The volumes are marked on a scale along the cylinder, as shown in Figure 2-4.

Mass

A table tennis ball and a golf ball have about the same volume. But if you pick them up, you notice a difference. The golf ball has more mass. **Mass is the amount of matter in an object. The SI unit of mass is the kilogram (kg).** For measuring objects of small mass, the gram (g) is used. How many grams are there in 1 kilogram?

In the laboratory, mass is measured with a balance. There are several different types of balances, but they all operate on the same principle. You use something of known mass to balance something else of unknown mass.

Figure 2-4. To read the volume of a liquid, look along the bottom of the curved surface of the liquid.

Figure 2-5. Although the two balls are about the same size, the ball on the left has more mass.

Density

If you were to take a cube of polished aluminum and a cube of silver the same size, they would look quite similar. And they would have the same volume. But the cube of silver would have more mass. The mass and volume of an object can be used to find the density of the material it is made of. **Density is the mass per unit volume of a material.**

Like volume, density is a derived unit. You can find the density of an object by dividing its mass by its volume. For example, the density of an object having a

Did You Know?

The mass of the Milky Way galaxy is more than 100 million times that of the sun.

2-2   USING SI UNITS   **39**

CHECK FOR UNDERSTANDING

Ask questions 1-2 and the **Apply** Question in the Section Review.

RETEACH

Use the following diagram to illustrate the mechanics of converting decimal units.

```
k– - - [h–] - [dk–] - (base) - - d– - - -c– - - -m–
|        |       |       |         |       |      |
k– - - [h–] - [dk–] - (base) - - d– - - -c– - - -m–
```

To convert a measurement from one unit to another, locate the original unit of the measurement on the top line and draw an arrow from it to the desired unit on the bottom line. The direction and size of the arrow indicate the direction and number of decimal places needed to convert the measurement. For example, to convert 3.46 m to centimeters, locate *m* on the top line and draw an arrow to *cm* on the bottom line.

```
km - [hm] - [dkm] - - m - - -dm - - -cm - - -mm
|       |        |       |        |       |      |
km - [hm] - [dkm] - - m - - -dm - - -cm - - -mm
```

To convert, move the decimal point *two* places to the *right*. Thus, 3.46 m = 346 cm.
To express 350 g as kilograms, locate *g* on the top line and connect it by an arrow to *kg* on the line below.

```
kg - [hg] - [dkg] - - g - - - dg - - - cg - - - mg
|       |        |       |        |       |      |
kg - [hg] - [dkg] - - g - - - dg - - - cg - - - mg
```

The diagram indicates that the decimal point must be moved *three* places to the *left*. Thus, 350 g = 0.350 kg.

Table 2-3

DENSITIES OF SOME MATERIALS			
Material	**Density (g/cm³)**	**Material**	**Density (g/cm³)**
Hydrogen	0.000 09	Quartz	2.6
Oxygen	0.0013	Aluminum	2.7
Cork	0.24	Iron	7.9
Water	1.0	Copper	8.9
Glue	1.27	Lead	11.3
Sugar	1.6	Mercury	13.6
Table salt	2.2	Gold	19.3

mass of 10 g and a volume of 2 cm³ is 5 g/cm³. This value is expressed as 5 grams per cubic centimeter. Notice that both the mass and volume units are used to express density.

Sometimes the density of an object can help you to identify the material it's made of. Table 2-3 lists the densities of some familiar materials.

Time and Temperature

When working in the laboratory, it is often necessary to keep track of how long it takes for something to happen, or whether something heats up or cools down. These measurements involve time and temperature.

Time is the interval between two events. The SI unit for time is the **second.** In the laboratory, you will use a stopwatch or a clock with a second hand to measure time.

Figure 2-6. The stopwatch (left) and the atomic clock (above) both measure the same thing—time.

OPTIONS

ENRICHMENT

▶Have students research supercooling and its role in superconductivity.
▶Interested students can research the difference between mass and weight.
▶Have students devise a way to measure the thickness of a postage stamp or its mass.

You will learn the scientific meaning of temperature in a later chapter. For now you can think of temperature as a measure of how "hot" or how "cold" something is. The temperature of a material is measured with thermometer that has a scale marked on it.

Figure 2-7. A Celsius Thermometer

For most scientific work, temperature is measured on the Celsius (C) scale. On this scale, the freezing point of water is zero degrees (0°C), and the boiling point of water is one hundred degrees (100°C). Between these points, the scale is divided into 100 equal divisions. Each one represents 1 Celsius degree. On the Celsius scale, normal human body temperature is 37°C and a comfortable room temperature is 25°C.

The SI unit of temperature is the **kelvin** (K). Zero on the Kelvin scale (0 K) is the coldest possible temperature. This temperature is also known as absolute zero. On the Celsius scale, 0 K is approximately −273°C. That is 273 degrees below the freezing point of water—very cold indeed!

Most laboratory thermometers are marked only with the Celsius scale. Because the divisions on the two scales are the same size, the Kelvin temperature can be found by adding 273 to the Celsius reading. So, on the Kelvin scale, water freezes at 273 K and boils at 373 K. Notice that degree signs are not used with the Kelvin scale.

Science and MATH

You probably know how much you weigh in pounds. Find your mass in kilograms. HINT: 1 pound has a mass of 0.454 kg.

SECTION REVIEW

1. Make the following conversions.
   a. 100 cm to meters
   b. 2.3 dm³ to liters
   c. 27°C to K
2. Explain why density is a derived unit.
3. **Apply:** How many examples of the use of SI units can you find? Observe road signs and outside thermometers and check labels of products in your home.

☑ Concept Mapping

Make a network tree concept map to show the SI base units used to measure length, mass, time, and temperature. If you need help, refer to Concept Mapping in the **Skill Handbook** on pages 684 and 685.

Skill Builder

For students who have mast section, use the **Reinforcement** and **Enrichment** masters or other OPTIONS provided.

CROSS CURRICULUM

▶ **History:** The Celsius and Kelvin temperature scales were named in honor of Anders Celsius and William Thomson, Lord Kelvin, two scientists who made many contributions to the study of heat.

Science and MATH

To find your mass, multiply your weight expressed in pounds by the factor 0.454 kg/1 lb. For example,

$$70 \text{ lb} \times \frac{0.454 \text{ kg}}{1 \text{ lb}} = (70 \times 0.454) \text{ kg}$$
$$= 32 \text{ kg}$$

3 CLOSE

Cooperative Learning: Use the following demonstration and the Numbered Heads Together strategy to have students explain how SI mass units are related to SI volume units for water.

▶ **Demonstration:** Fill a 10-mL graduated cylinder with water and place it on one pan of a balanced double-pan balance. On the other pan, place an empty, identical 10-mL graduate and a 10-g mass.

SECTION REVIEW ANSWERS

1. a. 1 cm = 0.01 m; 100 cm = 1 m
   b. 1 dm³ = 1 L; 2.3 dm³ = 2.3 L
   c. 27°C + 273 = 300 K
2. Density units are obtained by combining other SI units.
3. **Apply:** Student responses will vary.

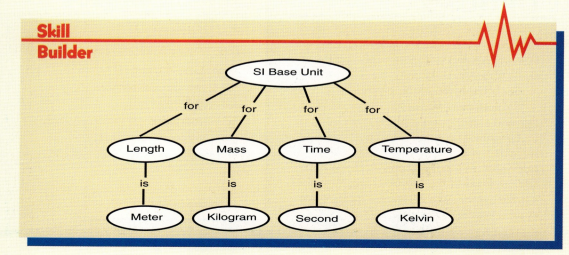

Skill Builder

2-3 Graphing

PREPARATION

SECTION BACKGROUND

▶ Graphs are important means of displaying information to be compared. Line graphs are the most important type of graph in science because they can be analyzed to provide equations that relate the information being displayed.

MINI-Lab

Materials: plastic foam cup, lid with straw hole, thermometer

Teaching Tips

▶ Use the activity to teach students to read the Celsius thermometer.

▶ Have students insert the thermometer through the straw hole in the lid.

Answer to Question: The graph will show that the rate of temperature reduction is most rapid when the temperature is highest. It will also show that adding a lid significantly reduces the rate at which temperature decreases.

1 MOTIVATE

Cooperative Learning: Assign students to cut graphs from newspapers and magazines and bring them to class. Using the Numbered Heads Together strategy, have each group devise a classification system for the graphs.

▶ **Demonstration:** Stick 10 birthday cake candles in holders in a long piece of plastic foam. Light the second candle and let it burn for only 5 seconds. Light the remaining candles in turn, letting the third candle burn for 10 seconds, the fourth for 15 seconds, etc. Remove the candles from the holders, clip their wicks, and place them side by side, bases aligned, on an overhead projector. Ask students to discuss what the silhouette displays.

New Science Words

graph

Objectives

▶ Identify three types of graphs and explain the correct use of each type.
▶ Distinguish between dependent and independent variables.
▶ Interpret graphs.

Using Graphs

What happens when heat is applied to an ice cube? Did you answer, "The ice cube melts"? Most people would. However, suppose this were a scientific investigation. You would measure and record mass, temperature, temperature changes, changes in state, and the time intervals involved. At the end of the investigation, you would describe the procedure and results in both words and numbers.

Often it is helpful to be able to show what happens during the course of an investigation. This can be done with a graph. A **graph** is a visual display of information or data. A graph of the ice cube investigation would look something like Figure 2-8.

Graphs are not only used in science. They are useful for displaying information in business, sports, and many everyday situations. Different kinds of graphs are appropriate for displaying different types of information. It is important to use the correct kind of graph for the data you are presenting.

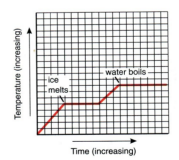

MINI-Lab

How can a graph help you observe change?

Place a thermometer in a plastic foam cup of hot water. Measure and record the temperature every 30 seconds for 5 minutes. Make a line graph of the changing temperature showing time on the x-axis and temperature on the y-axis. Repeat the experiment, starting with freshly heated water. This time, cover the cup with a plastic lid. Plot the curve on the same grid as before. List all the information this graph tells you about the two cups.

Figure 2-8. The graph shows what happens when water is heated over a period of time.

OPTIONS

Meeting Different Ability Levels

For Section 2-3, use the following **Teacher Resource Masters** depending upon individual students' needs.

◆ **Study Guide Master** for all students.
● **Reinforcement Master** for students of average and above average ability levels.
▲ **Enrichment Master** for above average students.

Additional Teacher Resource Package masters are listed in the OPTIONS box throughout the section. The additional masters are appropriate for all students.

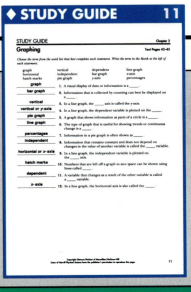

◆ **STUDY GUIDE** 11

Three of the most commonly used kinds of graphs are line graphs, bar graphs, and pie graphs. The section on Making and Using Graphs, on page 687 in the **Skill Handbook,** is a step-by-step guide to constructing each of these kinds of graphs. Study this material when you have finished reading this section.

Line Graphs

Line graphs are used to show trends or continuous change. Suppose you want to show how the temperature of a room changes after you switch on the heat one chilly morning. Taking temperature readings in the room every five minutes, you might collect information that looks like that shown in Table 2-4. If you look closely at the data, you can see how temperatures changed over time. But the relationship is easier to see in the graphs shown in Figure 2-9. Both graphs show that temperature increased for the first 60 minutes, then stayed constant. Do the graphs tell you anything about what made the temperature change?

In this example, two things are changing, or varying—time and temperature. Time is the independent variable. Its value does not depend on changes in the value of the other variable, temperature. Temperature is the dependent variable. Its value depends on changes in the time. ①
In a line graph, the dependent variable always is plotted on the vertical *y*-axis, and the independent variable is plotted on the horizontal *x*-axis.

Both graphs in Figure 2-9 show the same information. Notice, however, that the temperature scales along the vertical axes are different. In the graph on the left, each square represents 5°C. What does each square represent in the graph on the right? The hatch marks on the

Table 2-4

ROOM TEMPERATURE	
Time (minutes after turning on heat)	Temperature (°C)
0	16
5	17
10	19
15	20
20	20
25	20

Figure 2-9. Two Graphs of the Same Room Temperature Data

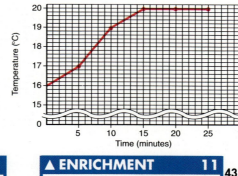

43

TYING TO PREVIOUS KNOWLEDGE: Have students recall that one way of displaying a lot of information is in a table. Point out that in this section, they will learn another method of displaying information.

OBJECTIVES AND SCIENCE WORDS: Have students review the objectives and science words to become familiar with this section.

STUDENT TEXT QUESTIONS
▶Page 43, paragraph 2: **Do the graphs tell you anything about what made the temperature change?** *No; the graphs do not give any information about the cause of the temperature changes.*
▶Page 43, paragraph 4: **What does each square represent in the graph on the right?** *One square represents 1°C.*

2 TEACH

Key Concepts are highlighted.

CONCEPT DEVELOPMENT
▶Make sure students can read graphs by citing various times from the graph shown in Figure 2-8 and having students respond with the appropriate temperatures.
▶Have students discuss why the graphs of the Mini-Lab slant in the opposite direction of the graphs shown in Figures 2-8 and 2-9.
▶Ask students to discuss what assumptions they are making when they connect two data points by a line. Are they sure about all or any of the points on the line? Point out that the values at the beginning and end of the interval were measured. However, those in-between were not. The students are assuming that the line would represent the measurement.

PROGRAM RESOURCES
From the **Teacher Resource Package** use:

Activity Worksheets, page 20, Mini-Lab: How can a graph help you observe a change?

▶ **Language Arts:** Have students write paragraphs describing how ice melts by using Figure 2-8. Allow students to share their paragraphs with the class.

▶ **Social Studies:** Have students identify graphs in their social studies textbooks. Have a volunteer cite a page in the text. Instruct the class to turn to this page and follow along as the volunteer describes what the graph represents. Allow time for several students to respond.

MINI QUIZ

Use the Mini Quiz to check students' recall of chapter content.

1 In a line graph, the _____ variable is plotted on the vertical, *y*-axis. *dependent*

2 _____ graphs are useful for showing information collected by counting. *Bar*

3 The "slices" of a pie graph usually are represented as _____ of the total. *percentages*

vertical axis between the 0 and the 15 mean that numbers between 0 and 15 have been left out to save space. Compare the two graphs in Figure 2-9. Which graph shows a bigger temperature change over the same time period? Be careful! The two graphs show exactly the same information, but because there is more space between the numbers on the vertical axis in the graph on the right, the change looks larger.

Bar Graphs

A bar graph is useful for showing information collected by counting. For example, suppose you measured the temperature in every classroom in your school and organized your data in a table like Table 2-5. You could show these data in a bar graph like the one shown in Figure 2-10. The height of each bar corresponds to the number of rooms at a particular temperature.

In a line graph, adjacent points are connected with a straight or curving line. In a bar graph, the bars are not connected. Do you see why? If the bars corresponding to 20°C and 21°C were connected, for example, the graph would suggest that a number of rooms had temperatures between 20°C and 21°C, when actually, no rooms had such temperatures.

Table 2-5

TEMPERATURE OF CLASSROOMS	
Temperature (°C)	Number of Classrooms
16	1
17	3
18	3
19	2
20	3
21	5
22	5
23	3

Figure 2-10. A typical bar graph shows comparisons, but does not indicate trends.

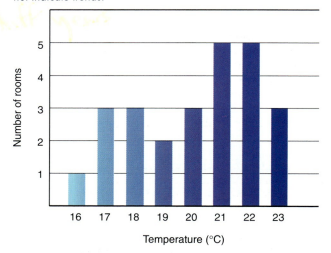

OPTIONS

INQUIRY QUESTIONS

▶ **What would the graph shown in Figure 2-8 display if the time axis were reversed?** *It would show what happens to a small amount of water as it freezes.*

▶ **What do you think the flat line in the graph on Figure 2-8 indicates?** *the time interval during which the ice is turning from a solid into a liquid at 0°C*

▶ **What *time* is displayed in the graphs shown in Figure 2-9?** *the time that has gone by since the heater was turned on*

▶ **What does the amount of tilt of a part of a line graph indicate?** *the amount by which the dependent variable changes as the independent variable changes*

Pie Graphs

A pie graph is used to show how some fixed quantity is broken down into parts. The circular "pie" represents the total, and the "slices" represent the parts. The slices usually are represented as percentages of the total.

Figure 2-11 shows how a pie graph could be used to show the percentage of buildings in a neighborhood using each of a number of fuels in their heating systems. You can see at a glance that more buildings use gas heat than any other kind of system. What else does the graph tell you?

When you use graphs, think carefully about the conclusions you can draw from them. Can you infer cause and effect from looking at a graph? How might the scale of the graph affect your conclusions? Is any information missing or improperly connected?

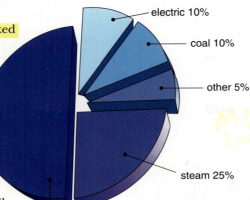

Figure 2-11. A pie graph shows the different parts of a whole quantity.

electric 10%
coal 10%
other 5%
steam 25%
Gas 50%

SECTION REVIEW

1. Your class does an experiment to show how the volume of a gas changes with changes in temperature. You are asked to make a line graph of the results. What are the dependent and independent variables?
2. Explain why points are connected in a line graph, but not in a bar graph.
3. **Apply:** Suppose you take a survey to find out how 150 adults in your neighborhood get to work. Your survey shows that 75 ride the bus; 45 drive their own cars; 15 carpool; 9 walk, ride bikes, or ride motorcycles; and the rest use different methods on different days. What kind of graph would be best for displaying your results at a neighborhood meeting?

EcoTip

The following percentages show water usage in a typical U.S. home: Toilet flushing, 33%; laundry, 26%; bathing, 20%; dishwashing, 3%; miscellaneous, 18%.

☑ Making and Using Graphs

Find a graph in a newspaper or magazine. Tell what kind of graph you found and write an explanation of what the graph shows. If you need help, refer to Making and Using Graphs in the **Skill Handbook** on page 687.

Skill Builder

Ask questions 1-2 and the **Apply** Question in the Section Review.

RETEACH

From the second part of the Motivation activity, tape the candles to a clear piece of acetate on top of the overhead projector. Using the silhouette, trace a line representing the height of the unburned candle. Ask a volunteer to carefully measure the difference in height between this line and each of the burned candles using a clear metric ruler. Have students make a table of the data and graph the results. Ask them to interpret the meaning of the graph.

EXTENSION

For students who have mastered this section, use the **Reinforcement** and **Enrichment** masters or other OPTIONS provided.

3 CLOSE

▶Have students display the information in the EcoTip as a pie graph.

SECTION REVIEW ANSWERS

1. Independent variable is temperature; dependent variable is volume.
2. Line graphs show trends, and the spaces between measured points have meaning. Bar graphs show information collected by counting, and the spaces between bars do not represent any information.
3. **Apply:** This information would best be represented by a pie graph.

Skill Builder

Student responses will vary according to the graph they select. Accept all reasonable responses.

ENRICHMENT

▶Have interested students research how to write equations for straight-line graphs.

PROGRAM RESOURCES

From the **Teacher Resource Package** use:

Transparency Masters, pages 7-8, Types of Graphs.

Critical Thinking/Problem Solving, page 8, Sports Performance.

Science and Society, page 6, The Move to Metric.

Use **Color Transparency** number 4, Types of Graphs.

 **2-4 Metrics for All?**

PREPARATION

SECTION BACKGROUND
▶ In 1971, the General Conference of Weights and Measures, which represents over 45 countries including the United States, established the seven base units of the SI system. These are shown on Table 2-2, page 34.
▶ Other units in the SI system are defined by adding prefixes to these base units or by combining base units.

1 MOTIVATE

▶ Have students poll adults and teenagers to see how they agree or disagree with adopting the SI (metric) system as the standard system of measurement. Combine the data and have students graph the results of the poll.
▶ Have students identify products that are now packaged with both metric and English units.

TYING TO PREVIOUS
KNOWLEDGE: Have students recall SI measurements that they are familiar with. Point out that these measurements are also familiar to citizens of most countries of the world.

OBJECTIVES AND
SCIENCE WORDS: Have students review the objectives and science words to become familiar with this section.

2 TEACH

Key Concepts are highlighted.

CONCEPT DEVELOPMENT
▶ Inform students that the Metric Conversion Act of 1975 outlined a method by which the voluntary metrification of the United States would take place. Lack of funding and public interest have hampered the project.

Objectives
▶ Analyze the benefits and drawbacks of universal use of the SI system.
▶ Give examples of SI units used in the United States.

Metrics in the United States

In the United States, athletes compete on courses that are measured in meters, medicine is sold in milligrams and milliliters, and many automobile parts are measured in SI units. But carpenters still buy lumber measured in feet and inches, farmers measure their land in acres and their crops in bushels, fabric is sold by the yard, and highway signs give distances in miles and speed limits in miles per hour.

For nearly 100 years, advocates of the metric system have argued for widespread adoption of the system in the United States. But opponents have argued just as vigorously against it.

Representatives of industry say such a changeover would require them to replace or convert their machinery—a costly process. But people in favor of the change point out that machinery is often replaced anyway, and the cost would be a one-time expense that would produce lasting benefits. Switching to SI units would make trade easier with other countries, most of which use the SI system. And because SI is based on multiples of ten, it makes calculations and conversions much easier. Using the system might reduce calculation errors and save time.

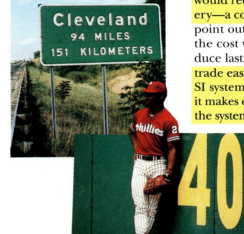

46 PHYSICAL SCIENCE METHODS

OPTIONS

Meeting Different Ability Levels
For Section 2-4, use the following **Teacher Resource Masters** depending upon individual students' needs.
◆ **Study Guide Master** for all students.
● **Reinforcement Master** for students of average and above average ability levels.
▲ **Enrichment Master** for above average students.

Many citizens resist the switch to SI units because they have grown up using such units as feet, pounds, and gallons, and they feel more comfortable continuing to use them. However, most people do not really know very much about these units, especially how units relate to one another. For example, do you know how many cubic inches there are in a fluid ounce? Do you know how many ounces there are in a pound, or how many inches are in a mile? For that matter, do you know that there are two different kinds of miles—the nautical mile and the statute mile? How many feet are in each? How many yards? How many square feet make up an acre?

These are just a few of the questions that arise in using our present system. Look up the information needed to answer them. Then think about how easy such measurement conversions would be in a system like SI.

SECTION REVIEW

1. Write a list of different units used to measure length in the United States. Then show the calculations necessary to convert from one unit to another. Do the same thing using SI units for length. Which is easier?
2. Write a one-page essay summarizing your position on the adoption of SI in the United States.

You Decide!

Should the United States switch to using SI measurements exclusively? If so, how could the switch be accomplished?

SCIENCE & SOCIETY

47

STUDENT TEXT QUESTIONS

▶Page 47, paragraph 1: **How many feet are in each?** *A nautical mile is equal to 6067 feet; a statue mile is equal to 5280 feet.* **How many yards?** *2025.3 yards and 1760 yards, respectively* **How many square feet make up an acre?** *There are 43 560 square feet in 1 acre.*

CROSS CURRICULUM

▶**Geography:** Use a map to identify Burma, the only populous country besides the United States that does not use the metric system.

CHECK FOR UNDERSTANDING

Ask questions 1-2 in the Section Review.

RETEACH

Have students classify examples using three types of conversions: HARD—which changes the size of a product to new metric dimensions; SOFT—where the size is not affected, only how it is measured; and NONE—in which there would be no conversion.

EXTENSION

For students who have mastered this section, use the **Reinforcement** and **Enrichment** masters or other OPTIONS provided.

3 CLOSE

▶Ask students to consider how the conversion to the metric system will be affected by the United States becoming less industrialized and a more technological nation.

SECTION REVIEW ANSWERS

1. Student responses should include inch, foot, yard, and mile. Students should conclude that converting in SI is easier than in the English system.

2. Student essays should give reasons for either support or rejection of SI adoption in the United States.

YOU DECIDE!

SCIENCE & SOCIETY

Answers will vary from total conversion mandated by the government to individual choice.

ACTIVITY 2-2
40 minutes

OBJECTIVE: **Compare** advantages and disadvantages of converting from English to metric measure.

PROCESS SKILLS applied in this activity:
▶**Measuring** in Procedure Steps 2 and 3.
▶**Observing** in Procedure Step 7.

👥 COOPERATIVE LEARNING
Divide the class into Science Investigation teams with one ingredient assigned to each team. All teams must share data and may share in the experimental product.

TEACHING THE ACTIVITY
Troubleshooting: To cook the Munchies you will need a large saucepan, a large spoon for mixing, a hot plate or burner, a small spoon, and a roll of waxed paper. Allow ample room for students to view the preparation.
▶Provide each team with an assigned ingredient and the appropriate measuring equipment.
▶Prepare a master ingredient list on the overhead or the chalkboard.
▶Have students put the first five ingredients into the pot. Heat slowly to a boil, then boil for four minutes while mixing constantly. Remove from heat and add the rest of the ingredients. Immediately portion onto wax paper using the small spoon. You should have enough for a class set.
▶A class discussion is recommended prior to completing Conclude and Apply.

PROGRAM RESOURCES
From the **Teacher Resource Package** use:

Activity Worksheets, pages 15-16, Activity 2-2: Metric Munchies.

ACTIVITY 2-2
Metric Munchies

Problem: *What is involved in converting from English to metric measure?*

Materials
- balance
- graduated cylinder, 100-mL
- munchie ingredients
- measuring cup
- measuring teaspoon
- measuring tablespoon
- plastic container, 1 quart
- hot plate

Procedure
1. Copy the data table and the list of munchie ingredients.
2. Use the English measuring cup or spoon to measure out the proper amount of munchie ingredient assigned to your team.
3. Use the balance or graduated cylinder to determine the metric value of the measured ingredient. Convert solid measure to grams. Convert liquid measure to milliliters.
4. Write the metric equivalent in your data table. Also write it on the metric ingredients list posted in the classroom.
5. Copy the completed list of metric measures.
6. At the direction of the teacher, place your ingredient in the cooking pot.
7. Watch how the teacher cooks the munchies and write cooking instructions.

Data and Observations   Sample Data

Ingredient	Object measured	Metric
Margarine	1/4 pound	114 g
Sugar	2 cups	432 g
Cocoa	6 tablespoons	39 g
Milk	1/2 cup	118 mL
Rolled oats	3 cups	258 g
Vanilla	1 teaspoon	5 mL
Nuts	1/2 cup	52 g

Analyze
1. The volume ratio of sugar to oatmeal is 2 to 3. What is their mass ratio?
2. Which recipe, English or metric, requires the use of the most measuring devices?
3. Which kind of measure tends to be more accurate, volume or mass?

Conclude and Apply
4. English measured recipes tend to use whole numbers and simple fractions. How could you simplify the metric recipe?
5. How would kitchen equipment change if all recipes were metric?
6. What benefits and problems can you see in changing all recipes to metric?

ANSWERS TO QUESTIONS
1. roughly 2 to 1
2. The English recipe requires at least three. Metric could be done with two.
3. mass
4. Round numbers off to the nearest 5 or 10.
5. A gram scale and volume measure in milliliters would be added.
6. Measuring by mass may simplify some procedures. Conversion from volume to mass is difficult due to density variation.

CHAPTER
REVIEW

SUMMARY

2-1: Standards of Measurement

1. A standard of measurement is an exact quantity that people agree to use as a basis of comparison.

2. When a standard of measurement is established, all measurements are compared to the same exact quantity—the standard. Therefore, all measurements can be compared with one another.

3. In SI, prefixes are used to make the base units larger or smaller by multiples of ten. The most common prefixes and their values are: *kilo-* 1000, *deci-* 0.1, *centi-* 0.01, *milli-* 0.001, *micro-* 0.000 001, and *nano-* 0.000 000 001.

2-2: Using SI Units

1. The most commonly used units in SI and their symbols include: length—meter, m; volume—cubic decimeter, dm³; mass—kilogram, kg; density—grams per cubic centimeter, g/cm³; time—second, s; and temperature—kelvin, K. Liter and degree Celsius are also commonly used for volume and temperature, respectively.

2. A derived unit is one that is obtained by combining other SI units. Volume and density units are derived units.

3. Any SI unit can be converted to any other related SI unit by multiplying or dividing by the appropriate multiple of ten.

2-3: Graphing

1. Different kinds of graphs are appropriate for displaying different types of information. Three commonly used types of graphs are line graphs, bar graphs, and pie graphs.

2. In a line graph, the independent variable is always plotted on the horizontal *x*-axis; the dependent variable is always plotted on the vertical *y*-axis.

3. Many different kinds of data can be interpreted from graphs.

2-4: Science and Society: Metrics for All?

1. There are many benefits and drawbacks to the adoption of the SI system.

2. SI units are already in wide use on consumer goods and distance signs throughout the United States.

KEY SCIENCE WORDS

a. **density**
b. **derived units**
c. **graph**
d. **kelvin**
e. **kilogram**
f. **liter**
g. **mass**
h. **meter**
i. **second**
j. **SI**
k. **standard**
l. **time**
m. **volume**

UNDERSTANDING VOCABULARY

Match each phrase with the correct term from the list of Key Science Terms.

1. the modern version of the metric system
2. the amount of space occupied by an object
3. an agreed-upon quantity to be used for comparison
4. the amount of matter in an object
5. obtained by combining other SI units
6. a visual display of data
7. the SI unit of mass
8. the SI unit of length
9. a metric unit of volume
10. mass per unit volume

CHAPTER
REVIEW

SUMMARY

Have students read the summary statements to review the major concepts of the chapter.

UNDERSTANDING VOCABULARY

1. j
2. m
3. k
4. g
5. b
6. c
7. e
8. h
9. f
10. a

OPTIONS

ASSESSMENT

To assess student understanding of material in this chapter, use the resources listed.

👫 COOPERATIVE LEARNING

Consider using cooperative learning in the THINK AND WRITE CRITICALLY, APPLY, and MORE SKILL BUILDERS sections of the Chapter Review.

PROGRAM RESOURCES

From the **Teacher Resource Package** use:

Chapter Review, pages 7-8.

Chapter and Unit Tests, pages 9-12, Chapter Test.

Chapter and Unit Tests, pages 13-14, Unit Test.

CHAPTER
REVIEW

CHECKING CONCEPTS

1.	c	**6.**	a
2.	b	**7.**	c
3.	a	**8.**	b
4.	d	**9.**	b
5.	d	**10.**	d

UNDERSTANDING CONCEPTS

11. graduated cylinder
12. volume
13. divide
14. 273
15. kilometer

THINK AND WRITE CRITICALLY

16. SI measurements are used in science classes because they are used throughout the world and allow scientists to compare measurements.

17. Conversions between two different units of length can be made by multiplying or dividing by the proper multiple of ten. All SI measurements, including volume and mass, can be converted in this way.

18. Line graphs consist of data plotted on a grid within a set of axes. Line graphs are best used to show a continuous change in data that involves two variables.
Bar graphs consist of a pair of axes and a series of bars. Bar graphs are best used to show data collected by counting.
Pie graphs consist of a circle divided into segments. Pie graphs are best used to show the different parts that make up a whole quantity.

19. A line graph; time would be the independent variable and temperature would be the dependent variable.

20. Advantages: SI measurements are based on multiples of ten and the same prefixes are used for all types of measurement, thus making conversion easy; people in most nations measure in SI units. Disadvantages: Conversion would involve considerable expense; people are reluctant to change from a system they are familiar with.

CHECKING CONCEPTS

Choose the word or phrase that completes the sentence or answers the question.

1. A meaningful measurement must have _____.
  a. a number only
  b. a unit only
  c. a number and a unit
  d. a prefix and a unit

2. The _____ is an example of an SI unit.
  a. foot   **c.** pound
  b. second   **d.** gallon

3. The system of measurement used by scientists around the world is the _____.
  a. SI   **c.** English system
  b. Standard system   **d.** Kelvin system

4. SI is based on _____.
  a. inches   **c.** English units
  b. multiples of five   **d.** multiples of ten

5. The SI prefix that means 1/1000 is _____.
  a. *kilo-*   **c.** *cent-*
  b. *nano-*   **d.** *milli-*

6. The symbol for deciliter is _____.
  a. dL   **c.** dkL
  b. dcL   **d.** Ld

7. The symbol for _____ is µg.
  a. nanogram   **c.** microgram
  b. kilogram   **d.** milligram

8. _____ is the distance between two points.
  a. Volume   **c.** Mass
  b. Length   **d.** Density

9. Which of the following is *not* a derived unit?
  a. liter   **c.** cubic centimeter
  b. meter   **d.** grams per milliliter

10. 1000 mL is equal to all of the following except _____.
  a. 1 L   **c.** 1 dm^3
  b. 100 cL   **d.** 1 cm^3

UNDERSTANDING CONCEPTS

Complete each sentence.

11. A(n) _____ is used to measure the volume of a liquid.

12. The _____ of a block can be found by multiplying its length × width × height.

13. To convert from milligrams to grams, _____ by 1000.

14. Water freezes at _____ kelvin.

15. The SI unit used to measure distance between two cities would be the _____.

THINK AND WRITE CRITICALLY

16. Why are SI measurements used in science classes?

17. Explain how to convert from one length measurement in the SI system to another. Can volume and mass measurements be converted in the same way? Why or why not?

18. Describe three different types of graphs and the types of data best displayed by each.

19. Suppose you set a glass of water in direct sunlight for two hours and measured its temperature every ten minutes. What type of graph would you use to display your data? What would the dependent variable be? the independent variable?

20. What are some advantages and disadvantages of adopting the SI system for use in the United States?

APPLY

21. Make the following conversions.
  a. 1500 mL to liters
  b. 2 km to centimeters
  c. 5.8 dg to milligrams
  d. 22° C to kelvin

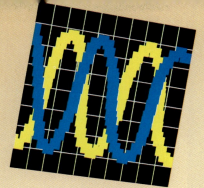

22. If you were able to travel back in time to the Middle Ages, you would find that different kingdoms had different standards of measurement, and that these standards were often based on such things as the length of the king's or queen's arm. What arguments would you use to convince people of the need for a true system of standard measurements?

23. List the SI units of length you would use to express the following. Refer to Table 2-1 on page 31.
  a. the diameter of an atom
  b. the width of your classroom
  c. the width of a pencil lead
  d. the length of a sheet of paper
  e. the distance to the moon

24. Determine the density of each of the following objects.
  a. mass = 15 g, volume = 2 cm^3
  b. mass = 200 g, volume = 80 mL
  c. mass = 1.8 kg, volume = 0.2 L

25. Suppose you want to study the motion of a go-cart for a period of one minute. To do this, you measure the distance it travels every five seconds for the 60-second period. What kind of graph would you use to display your data? What would the dependent and independent variables be?

MORE SKILL BUILDERS

If you need help, refer to the Skill Handbook.

1. Comparing and Contrasting: Compare and contrast the SI system of measurement and the system now used in the United States. Be sure to discuss the base units in each system and how conversions are made in each system.

2. Hypothesizing: A metal sphere is found to have a density of 5.2 g/cm^3 at 25°C and a density of 5.1 g/cm^3 at 50°C. Propose a

hypothesis to explain this observation. How could you easily test your hypothesis?

3. Measuring in SI: Determine the mass, volume, and density of your textbook, a container of milk, and an air-filled balloon. Make your measurements in SI units using the appropriate measuring tool and the quickest, most accurate method possible.

4. Making and Using Graphs: Using the data in Table 2-3 on page 40, graph the densities of the following materials: water, sugar, salt, iron, copper, lead, and gold. Use the proper type of graph and let each unit on your graph represent 0.5 g/cm^3. Then, answer the following questions:
  a. Why did you choose this type of graph to display this data?
  b. What would be the mass of 5 cm^3 of sugar?
  c. If you had a 1-g sample of each material shown in the graph, which sample would have the greatest volume?
  d. How could your graph be made more accurate?

PROJECTS

1. Devise your own system of measurements. What will be the standard for each type of measurement in your system? How will conversions between units be made?

2. Find the metric equivalent of such things as your weight in pounds, a gallon of milk, and the distance to your school in miles.

a. A bar graph was chosen because the data consist of discrete bits of information that do not involve variables and do not make up a whole quantity.
b.
$$\text{mass} = \text{density} \times \text{volume}$$
$$\text{mass of sugar} = 1.6 \text{ g/cm}^3 \times 5 \text{ cm}^3$$
$$= 8 \text{ g}$$
c. water
d. The graph could be made more accurate by using units smaller than 0.5 g/cm^3.

APPLY

21. a. 1.5 L
  b. 200 000 cm
  c. 580 mg
  d. 295 K

22. Student responses should include importance of being able to compare measurements.

23. a. nanometer, nm
  b. meter, m
  c. millimeter, mm
  d. centimeter, cm
  e. kilometer, km

24. a. 7.5 g/cm^3
  b. 2.5 g/mL
  c. 9 kg/L

25. A line graph; time in seconds would be the independent variable and distance would be the dependent variable.

MORE SKILL BUILDERS

1. Comparing and Contrasting: Students should name and compare the base units of measurement of length, mass, volume, temperature, and time for the two systems. The fact that SI measurements are based on multiples of ten should be contrasted with the lack of any consistent or logical base in our system. The ease of converting in SI should be contrasted with the difficulty in our system.

2. Hypothesizing: Hypothesis: the metal expands when heated. The hypothesis can be tested by measuring the mass and volume of the ball at the two temperatures.

3. Measuring in SI: Student answers will vary. Make sure that students used the correct methods to make the required measurements.

4. Making and Using Graphs:

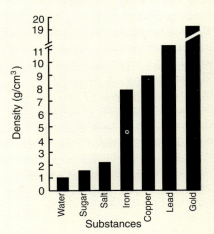

Objective

In this unit ending feature, the unit topic "Physical Science Basics" is extended into other disciplines. Students will see how the basics of physical science are used in events occurring around the planet.

Motivate

Cooperative Learning: Assign one Connection to each group of students. Using the Expert Teams strategy, have each group research to find out more about the geographic location of the Connection—its climate, culture, flora and fauna, and ecological issues.

Teaching Tips

▶ Tell students to keep in mind the connection between problem solving and the scientific methods while they are reading this feature.

▶ Ask students to identify the problem in each Connection and discuss possible ways that scientists could have found solutions to the problems.

Wrap-Up

Conclude this lesson by presenting students with a problem, such as which freezes faster—cold, warm, or hot water? Then have them devise a method to solve the problem.

PHYSICS

Background: Both robots have miniature video cameras that tilt and rotate. This gives the technician operating the robots a clear view. One of the robots is able to pull itself upright after leaving the ducts and then climb up to inspect the reactor.

Discussion: Discuss other places where similar robots might prove useful. Ask students to describe the kinds of movements a robot would need to make in each situation.

Answer to Question: They allow inspection and cleanup to be done in areas unsafe for human workers.

Extension: Ask students to design a robot for a particular job and label its parts and functions.

Physical Science Basics

In this unit, you studied the nature of science and physical science methods. Now find out how the nature and methods of physical science are connected to other subjects and places around the world.

PHYSICS

ROBOT CLEANUP CREW
Cambridge, Massachusetts
Two robots small enough to crawl through a 15-centimeter duct have been designed. They can go into a nuclear generator to inspect machinery and pick up nuclear litter. What problem will these robots help solve in nuclear power plants?

GEOGRAPHY

THE SLIDING ROOF
Washington, D.C.
The National Cathedral was built to be like the cathedrals in England, including its lead roof. When the National Cathedral was only a few years old, it was discovered that the lead roof was flowing downward, a problem not encountered in England. What did the geographic location, particularly the latitude of Washington, have to do with the problem?

120° 60°

60°

52

GEOGRAPHY

Background: Pure lead is soft enough to cut with a fingernail. At about 80°C, the lead would be malleable enough to begin to flow. The roof was remade with a less malleable alloy of 94% lead and 6% antimony.

Discussion: Discuss how geographic location must be taken into account when building.

Answer to Question: When the summer sun in Washington, DC, heated the roof of the cathedral, it got hot enough for the lead to start flowing under its own weight. In England, which is farther north, summer days are not as hot.

Extension: Have students research the properties of lead.

BURNING A DIAMOND
Paris, France

In 1772, Antoine Lavoisier placed a diamond in a closed vessel and focused sunlight on it with a magnifying glass. When it grew hot enough, the diamond disappeared and carbon dioxide appeared in the vessel. Lavoisier concluded that a diamond was made of carbon and was thus chemically related to coal. How did Lavoisier's experiment use the scientific method?

ART

ZAPPING ARTWORK CLEAN
Venice, Italy

How do you clean corrosion from ancient statues without destroying them? John Asmus zaps them with a laser. The laser quickly vaporizes the black crust of calcium sulfate caused by air pollution without harming the marble underneath. His lasers have also been used to clean tapestries and remove coffee stains from ancient parchment. Find out about other methods used to clean artwork.

HISTORY

HOW BIG IS EARTH?
Alexandria, Egypt

Around 240 B.C., Eratosthenes found a way to measure the circumference of Earth. He used the positions of the sun at summer solstice at Alexandria and Syrene and the distance between the two cities to calculate a circumference equal to 40 000 kilometers. Find out how accurate he was.

0°

53

HISTORY

Background: Eratosthenes used as a unit the Greek *stadion*. The Romans reckoned 8 stadia to their mile of 1000 double paces. The Roman mile is equivalent to about 1665 English yards.

Discussion: Tell students that most people of his time thought Eratosthenes' figure was too high. Discuss why people might have preferred to believe Earth was smaller.

Answer to Question: Present measurements give the circumference of Earth as 24 846 miles (39 977 kilometers).

Extension: Have students research ancient units of measurement.

CHEMISTRY

Background: Lavoisier had earlier proved that combustion came about through the combination of a substance with some portion of the air.

Discussion: Lavoisier is considered the father of modern chemistry. He was the first scientist to combine experimentation and observation with measurement. Discuss with students the importance of measurement in science.

Answer to Question: Lavoisier identified the problem, gathered experimental data, and made a conclusion.

Extension: Have students prepare a report on the work of Lavoisier.

ART

Background: Asmus was in Venice in 1972 to make laser holograms of art treasures threatened by tides and air pollution when he first used a laser to clean a statue.

Discussion: When Asmus was trying to get funding for projects, the National Endowment for the Arts told him "this is science" and the National Science Foundation told him "this is art." Ask students to discuss this contradiction.

Answer to Question: Other ways involve mechanical methods, such as using a scalpel, or chemical methods, such as dissolving the black crust with solvents.

Extension: Have students research the life-size terra cotta army found in the tomb of Chinese Emperor Qin Shi-huang and plans to restore it.

SURVEYOR

Background: About one third of all surveyors work for federal, state, or local governments. Others work for utility companies, gas and oil companies, or construction, engineering, and architectural firms.

Related Career	Education
Drafter	technical school
Cartographer	college degree
Machinist	high school
Instrument maker	technical school

Career Issue: Laser technology replaces the surveyor's transit and the instrument worker. Using a laser requires additional training on the part of the survey crew and also is more expensive, but lasers are extremely accurate.

What do you think? Lead students in a discussion of their attitudes about using lasers for surveying. Do they think the increased expense and loss of a job on the team is worth the increase in accuracy?

QUALITY-CONTROL INSPECTOR

Background: Although most inspectors work for private industries, they must be knowledgeable about federal and state laws that govern the manufacturing of the products they inspect.

Related Career	Education
Food-processing technician	technical school
Pharmaceutical technician	technical school
Paper pulp tester	high school
Automotive parts inspector	high school

Career Issue: Many companies are working to get all employees, not just quality-control inspectors, involved in quality control. Some people think this would eliminate the need for inspectors.

What do you think? Lead students in a discussion of their own attitudes toward quality control in the manufacture of products.

SURVEYOR

Before any construction project can begin, a *surveyor* must establish land boundaries, collect information from maps, charts, or plats, and measure or locate elevations and land contours.

Surveyors work in parties ranging from 3 to 6 people, consisting of a party chief and assistants. An instrument worker sets up the transit and takes gradings. A rod worker holds a graduated rod that measures elevations. The chain workers work in pairs to measure distances between surveying points.

If you're interested in becoming a surveyor, you should enjoy outdoor work, have good eyesight, and be in good physical condition. You should also enjoy teamwork. High school classes in science, mathematics, and drafting would be helpful.

Technical and community colleges offer 1-, 2-, or 3-year programs in surveying. All states require surveyors to be licensed or registered.

For Additional Information
Contact American Congress on Surveying and Mapping, 210 Little Falls Street, Falls Church, Virginia 22046.

UNIT READINGS

▶ Aaseng, Mathan. *Better Mousetraps: Product Improvements That Led to Success.* Minneapolis, MN: Lerner Publications Co., 1990.
▶ Holzinger, Philip R. *The House of Science.* New York, NY: John Wiley & Sons, 1990.

54

QUALITY-CONTROL INSPECTOR

Quality-control inspectors oversee a production process to ensure that the quality of a given product meets certain minimum standards. The products they inspect include things as varied as automobiles, chemicals, clothing, pharmaceuticals, food products, computers, and electronics.

If you're interested in becoming a quality-control inspector, you should like the practical aspects of science and mathematics, especially laboratory work. You must pay close attention to details, and your work must be accurate.

Most quality-control inspectors have a college degree with an emphasis on science. An inspector in the food industry, for example, should have a degree in food science or biology, while an inspector in the chemical or pharmaceutical industry should have a degree in chemistry.

For Additional Information
Contact American Society for Quality Control, 310 West Wisconsin Avenue, Milwaukee, Wisconsin 53203.

UNIT READINGS

Background
▶ *Better Mousetraps: Product Improvements That Led to Success* focuses on people who have taken a product and improved or adapted it.
▶ "Science in the Service of Art" describes how physical science technology is used to restore artworks and to verify their value.
▶ *The House of Science* asks students to visualize science as a series of connected rooms. The "house" has rooms for chemistry, physics, biology, geology, and so on.

More Readings
1. Ansley, David. "Have Laser, Will Travel." *Discover.* December, 1990, pp. 44-48. This article presents a detailed description of laser technology in art restoration.
2. Crump, Donald J., ed. *Frontiers of Science.* Washington, DC: National Geographic Society, 1982. Scientists explain how advances may bring changes.

Asimov on Physics

by Isaac Asimov

The passage that follows is a brief history of the development of the common thermometer.

ne applicable physical characteristic, which must have been casually observed by countless people, is the fact that substances expand when warmed and contract when cooled. The first of all those countless people, however, who tried to make use of this fact to measure temperature was the Italian physicist Galileo Galilei. In 1603 he inverted a tube of heated air into a bowl of water. As the air cooled to room temperature, it contracted and drew the water up into the tube. Now Galileo was ready. The water level kept on changing as room temperature changed, being pushed down when it warmed and expanded the trapped air, and being pulled up when it cooled and contracted the trapped air. Galileo had a thermometer (which, in Greek, means "heat measure"). The only trouble was that the basin of water was open to the air and air pressure kept changing. That also shoved the water level up and down, independently of temperature, and skewed the results.

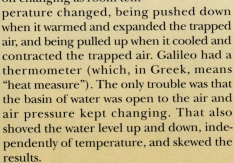

By 1654, the Grand Duke of Tuscany, Ferdinand II, evolved a thermometer that was independent of air pressure. It contained a liquid sealed into a tube, and the contraction and expansion of the liquid itself was used as an indication of temperature change. The volume change in liquids is much smaller than in gases, but by using a sizable reservoir of liquid which was filled so that further expansion could only take place up a very narrow tube, the rise and fall within that tube, for even tiny volume changes, was considerable.

This was the first reasonably accurate thermometer, and was also one of the few occasions on which the nobility contributed to scientific advance.

In 1701, Isaac Newton suggested that the thermometer be thrust into melting ice and that the liquid level so obtained be marked as 0, while the level attained at body temperature be marked off as 12, and the interval divided into twelve equal parts.

In Your Own Words

▶ The measurement of temperature is a fairly recent idea—less than 400 years old. Write an essay on how your life might be different if thermometers had never been invented.

55

Classics

▶ Asimov, Isaac. *Asimov's Biographical Encyclopedia of Science and Technology.* New York, NY: Doubleday & Co., 1982. Traces the history of science through the careers of people.

▶ Berger, Melvin. *Mad Scientists in Fact and Fiction.* New York, NY: Watts, 1980. Discusses real and fictional scientists who have formed unusual theories.

Source: Isaac Asimov. *Asimov on Physics.* New York, NY: Doubleday & Co., 1976.

Biography: Isaac Asimov was born in Russia in 1920. When he was 3 years old, his family moved to New York City. He taught biochemistry at Boston University from 1949 to 1958, then left to become a full-time writer. Asimov has written more than 400 books, mostly nonfiction emphasizing science and technology. He is, however, best known as an author of science fiction.

TEACHING STRATEGY

Have students read through the passage by Isaac Asimov. Then have them respond to the discussion questions below.

Discussion Questions

1. **From the passage given here, what does Asimov think about Newton's temperature scale and the fact that Newton was English?** *He states that a 12-degree scale was a logical choice for Newton, because he was English, and the English seem to have a fondness for things in multiples of 12.*

2. **What is Asimov's opinion of the contributions of European nobility to science?** *He does not think they contributed much at all. He states that the Grand Duke of Tuscany's invention of the first reasonably accurate thermometer was one of "the few occasions on which the nobility contributed to scientific advance."*

Other Works

▶ Other books by Isaac Asimov include: *Asimov's New Guide to Science.* New York, NY: Doubleday & Co., 1984. *X Stands for Unknown.* New York, NY: Doubleday & Co., 1984.

In Unit 2, students are introduced to kinematics, the study of the description of motion, and dynamics, the study of the causes of motion. Newton's three laws of motion are introduced to encapsulate the relationship between motion and force. From forces, students then move on to the concept of energy, the various types of energy, and the law of conservation of energy.

CONTENTS

ADVANCE PREPARATION

Activities
▶ **Activity 7-1, page 162, and Activity 4-2, page 104,** require building bricks for each activity group.
▶ **Activity 5-2, page 128,** requires a set of heated hair curlers.

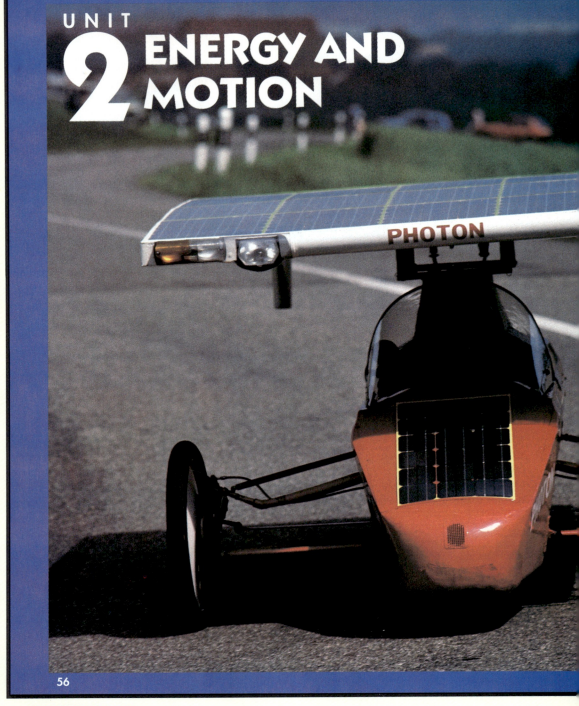

U N I T

2 ENERGY AND MOTION

56

OPTIONS

Cross Curriculum
▶ Have students keep logs of how terms, such as *force, energy, work, power,* and *efficiency* are used in other classes. At the end of the unit, have students compare and contrast the usages of the words in these classes and in science class.
▶ Have students note how motion is described in words, music, and pictures in various classes.

Science at Home
▶ Have students monitor TV and newspaper articles on sports events and collect verbs and adjectives used to describe the action.
▶ Have students monitor TV and newspapers to find measurements of motion. Have them categorize the types of motion and the units used to measure motion.

What's Happening Here?

Would you like to have a car that never needs gas? If so, then the car in this picture—built by students competing in the National Collegiate Solar Car Race—is the car for you. It runs on sunshine, or solar energy. Do you run on solar energy? The vegetables and grains that give you energy couldn't grow without the sun. So, in a way, you run on sunshine, too. How is energy changed into motion? Is heat a form of energy? In Unit 2, you'll learn more about energy and motion.

UNIT CONTENTS

57

INTRODUCING THE CHAPTER

What's Happening Here?

▶ Have students look at the photos and read the text. Ask them to tell you what's happening here, Point out to students that in this unit they will be studying motion, force, and energy and the relationships among them.

▶ **Background:** The photograph shows a solar-powered car participating in the Tour de Sol, a 210-mile race from Montpelier, Vermont to Cambridge, Massachusetts. The race, sponsored by the Massachusetts Institute of Technology, encourages the development of solar-powered cars for limited-distance commuting. The race which started on May 25, 1989, with five entries, was won five days later by a car entered by the University of Alabama. The cost of the winning car was $3000.

Previewing the Chapters

▶ Have students use photographs to list the sports, entertainment, and recreational activities that will be discussed in the unit. Ballet (pages 74 and 111); baseball (pages 70 and 71); bicycling, (page 174); bowling (page 103); diving (page 75); downhill sledding (page 116); drag car racing (page 65); frisbee throwing (page 88); isometric exercises (page 87); pool (page 101); roller coaster riding (page 93); sailing (page 166); sky-diving (page 89); soap-box car racing (page 82); swimming (pages 99 and 132); swinging (pages 92 and 114); track (page 61); tug-of-war (page 71); weight training (page 108)

Tying to Previous Knowledge

▶ Have students brainstorm for words that describe different types of motion, such as *swirling, tumbling, gliding*. Have them associate these words with the photographs in the unit.

▶ Use the **inquiry questions** in the OPTIONS box below to investigate motion with students.

Multicultural Awareness

Have interested students research ways in which motion in the natural world has been artistically portrayed and interpreted by various cultures. Have students focus their attention on performing arts, such as ceremonial and ritual dancing and chants; visual arts, such as prints, petroglyphs, carvings, and pottery; and in language arts, such as poetry.

Inquiry Questions

Use the following questions to focus a discussion of motion and energy.

▶ **Which is moving faster, the car or the sprinter? What evidence do you have for your answer?** *Accept all reasonable answers. Clues should come from photo: blurriness of photo background or of car/sprinters; distance each moved in photo; dust from car; type of race*

▶ **Why do you think the car has a streamlined shape?** *Accept all reasonable answers. To reduce "wind force" [air resistance].*

3 Moving Objects

CHAPTER SECTION	OBJECTIVES	ACTIVITIES
3-1 Describing Motion (2 days)	1. **Describe** speed as a rate. 2. **Perform calculations** involving speed, time, and distance. 3. **Interpret** distance-time graphs.	**Activity 3-1:** *Measuring Speed,* p. 64
3-2 Velocity and Acceleration (1 day)	1. **Compare** and **contrast** speed, velocity, and acceleration. 2. **Calculate** acceleration.	**MINI-Lab:** *Does greater velocity require greater acceleration?* p. 66
3-3 Crashing to Save Lives Science & Society (1 day)	1. **Evaluate** the effects of wearing seat belts during a car crash. 2. **Form an opinion** about whether laws should make people wear seat belts.	
3-4 Force and Motion (2 days)	1. **Recognize** different kinds of forces. 2. **Identify** cause and effect relationships between force and changes in velocity. 3. **Give examples** of the effects of inertia. 4. **State** Newton's first law of motion.	**MINI-Lab:** *Is friction a force?* p. 73
3-5 Effects of Gravity (2 days)	1. **Give examples** of the effects of gravity. 2. **Examine** how gravitational force is related to mass and distance. 3. **Distinguish** between mass and weight.	**Activity 3-2:** *Balancing Forces Against Gravity,* p. 78
Chapter Review		

ACTIVITY MATERIALS

FIND OUT	ACTIVITIES		MINI-LABS	
Page 59 metersticks	**3-1 Measuring Speed, p. 64** stopwatch or watch with second hand meterstick string paper sheets of various types, weights, and sizes transparent tape paper clips and stapler	**3-2 Balancing Forces Against Gravity, p. 78** selection of paper strips scissors masking tape plastic foam cup string 250 mL sand beaker balance ring stand and rin sheets of newspaper	**Does greater velocity require greater acceleration? p. 66** stopwatches metersticks marbles 1/4 inch hardboard (10cm x 50cm to 100 cm)	**Is friction a force? p. 73** 1 sheet plain, white paper 20-g mass 1 sheet coarse sandpaper meterstick

CHAPTER FEATURES	TEACHER RESOURCE PACKAGE	OTHER RESOURCES
Skill Builder: *Concept Mapping, p. 63*	**Ability Level Worksheets** ◆ **Study Guide**, p. 13 ● **Reinforcement**, p. 13 ▲ **Enrichment**, p. 13 **Critical Thinking/Problem Solving,** p. 9 **Activity Worksheet,** pp. 22, 23 **Transparency Master,** pp. 9, 10	**Color Transparency 5,** Distance-time Graph
Skill Builder: *Making and Using Graphs, p. 67*	**Ability Level Worksheets** ◆ **Study Guide**, p. 14 ● **Reinforcement**, p. 14 ▲ **Enrichment**, p. 14 **MINI-Lab Worksheet,** p. 28	**Lab Manual 4,** Speed and Acceleration
You Decide! p. 69	**Ability Level Worksheets** ◆ **Study Guide**, p. 15 ● **Reinforcement**, p. 15 ▲ **Enrichment**, p. 15	
Technology: *Inertia Sponges, p. 72* **Skill Builder:** *Outlining, p. 74*	**Ability Level Worksheets** ◆ **Study Guide**, p. 16 ● **Reinforcement**, p. 16 ▲ **Enrichment**, p. 16 **Cross-Curricular Connections,** p. 7 **Science and Society,** p. 7 **MINI-Lab Worksheet,** p. 29 **Transparency Master,** pp. 11, 12	**Color Transparency 6,** Newton's First Law **Lab Manual 5,** Projectile Motion
Problem Solving: *An Experiment for the Shuttle,* p. 76 **Skill Builder:** *Observing and Inferring, p. 77*	**Ability Level Worksheets** ◆ **Study Guide**, p. 17 ● **Reinforcement**, p. 17 ▲ **Enrichment**, p. 17 **Concept Mapping,** pp. 11, 12 **Activity Worksheet,** pp. 24, 25	
Summary Think & Write Critically Key Science Words Apply Understanding Vocabulary More Skill Builders Checking Concepts Projects Understanding Concepts	**Chapter Review,** pp. 9, 10 **Chapter Test,** pp. 20-23	**Chapter Review Software** **Test Bank**

◆ **Basic**   ● **Average**   ▲ **Advanced**

ADDITIONAL MATERIALS

SOFTWARE	AUDIOVISUAL	BOOKS/MAGAZINES
Motion and Energy: Physical Science Simulations, Focus. *Motion: A Microcomputer Based Lab,* Queue. *Fall Guy: Investigations of Falling Objects,* Queue. *Investigating Gravitational Force,* IBM.	*Attraction of Gravity,* film, BFA. *Black Holes of Gravity,* film, Time-Life Films. *Mr. Wizard's World: Inertia,* video, Gravity, Macmillan/McGraw-Hill School Division.	Brehmer, Steven. "Driving Home the Laws of Motion," *The Science Teacher,* Dec. 1981, pp. 14-15. Lightman, Alan P. et al. *Problem Book in Relativity and Gravitation.* Princeton, NJ: Princeton University Press, 1975.

THEME DEVELOPMENT: A theme that emerges in this chapter is that objects can undergo patterns of changes in their positions when forces act upon them. A net force acting on an object can be inferred from changes in its motion.

CHAPTER OVERVIEW

▶ **Section 3-1:** This section introduces the concept of an object's speed as the rate of change in its position. Instantaneous speed, constant speed, average speed, and distance-time graphs are discussed.

▶ **Section 3-2:** Velocity and speed are compared. The concept of acceleration is introduced as a rate of uniform change in velocity.

▶ **Section 3-3:** **Science and Society:** This section describes how seat belts reduce the effects of car crashes and asks students to form an opinion on the mandatory use of seat belts.

▶ **Section 3-4:** The concept of force and the property of inertia are described, followed by a discussion of Newton's first law of motion.

▶ **Section 3-5:** The concept of an object's weight is developed. The operation of scales is explained.

CHAPTER VOCABULARY

speed	balanced
instantaneous	forces
speed	net force
constant speed	inertia
average speed	friction
velocity	gravity
acceleration	weight
force	

58

OPTIONS

For Your Gifted Students

▶ Have students use a spring scale attached to a block of wood to explore how friction impedes motion. They will pull the wood over a rough surface such as sandpaper, and record the force needed. Have students think of ways to reduce friction, thus reducing the force needed to move the wood. (For example, apply soap, water, a row of pencils, or other materials between the block and the sandpaper to see if the amount of friction is reduced.)

Every day people and things move around you—cars go by, your classmates mill about in the halls, leaves blow in the wind. You know these things are moving because you see the motion. Now think about motion that you don't see. A magician makes an object seem to disappear by distracting the people in the audience so that they don't see where the object goes. If you don't see motion, how can you tell something has moved?

FIND OUT!

Do the following activity to find out if you can detect movement without seeing motion.

Close your eyes while a classmate moves something in the classroom. Now open your eyes and see if you can tell what was moved. Be aware of the clues you're using. Are you using only your eyes, or are other senses helping? If you figure out what was moved, can you tell how far it moved? How do you know?

Gearing Up

Previewing the Chapter

Use this outline to help you focus on important ideas in this chapter.

Previewing Science Skills

▶ In the Skill Builders, you will make a concept map, graph, outline, and observe and infer.
▶ In the Activities, you will observe, collect and organize data, and infer.
▶ In the MINI-Labs, you will observe and infer and make and use graphs.

What's next?

You can tell that something has moved without actually seeing the motion. Now you will learn about how and why things move and how different forces affect motion.

59

INTRODUCING THE CHAPTER

Use the Find Out activity to introduce students to the notion that an object's motion can be inferred from a change in its position. Inform the students that they will be learning more about motion as they read the chapter.

FIND OUT!

Materials: metersticks

Cooperative Learning: Use the Numbered Heads Together strategy to group students into threes. Have one student shut his or her eyes while a second student moves an object. The third student should record the responses of the first student. Then have the students rotate roles.

Teaching Tips

▶ Seat a volunteer in front of the class. Have the volunteer move the chair away from the students and sit in it while their eyes are closed. After the students open their eyes and discover that the volunteer has moved, have them determine if the volunteer moved away from them or if they moved away from the volunteer. Ask the students if the volunteer moved relative to the chair.

▶ If students measure how far an object has moved, they will likely measure the distance in a straight line. Ask them if the object could have followed any other path to arrive at its resting position. Ask them if they can determine the true path the object followed.

Gearing Up

Have students study the Gearing Up feature to familiarize themselves with the chapter. Discuss the relationships of the topics in the outline.

What's Next?

Before beginning the first section, make sure students understand the connection between the Find Out activity and the topics to follow.

For Your Mainstreamed Students

▶ Roll a marble through a toilet paper tube that is raised 1 cm at one end. Measure the distance the marble rolls. Place different types of material at the bottom end of the tube. Ask students to predict the distance the marble will roll. Test the predictions.

PREPARATION

SECTION BACKGROUND

▶ The back and forth motion of a tuning fork is oscillatory motion, a type of periodic motion.

▶ Since an object's motion can be considered as a change in its position, the term *position* must be described. An object's position at any moment is given relative to or measured from some arbitrary reference point which may be stationary or considered stationary.

▶ Average speed is *defined* by the equation

$$v = d/t$$

where *d* represents the distance *measured along the path* which the object moved and *t* represents the time during which the object moved.

▶ The *slope* at any point on a distance-time graph is equivalent to the instantaneous speed of the object at that time and location. If a segment of a graph is a straight line, the speed is constant and the value of the slope of the line also represents the average velocity during the time interval.

PREPLANNING

▶ To prepare for Activity 3-1, obtain construction paper and oak tag.

▶ Obtain a small rubber ball, string, a thumbtack, and several wind-up or battery-operated toy cars.

1 MOTIVATE

▶ **Demonstration:** (1) Roll a rubber ball across a desk. (2) Drop it onto the desk and catch it on the rebound. (3) Attach a piece of string to the ball with a thumbtack and swing the ball back and forth. Ask volunteers to demonstrate other types of motion using the ball. Discuss similarities and differences in these motions.

3-1 Describing Motion

New Science Words

speed
instantaneous speed
constant speed
average speed

Objectives

▶ Describe speed as a rate.
▶ Perform calculations involving speed, time, and distance.
▶ Interpret distance-time graphs.

Speed

When something moves, it changes position. It travels from one place to another, if only for an instant. Look at the tuning fork. Its prongs are vibrating—they are moving. You may not be able to see their motion, but the sound they produce tells you they are moving. If asked to describe the motion of a tuning fork, you would probably say something like "back-and-forth." How would you describe the motion of a rubber ball bouncing along a sidewalk?

You don't always have to see something move to know that motion has taken place. For example, suppose you look out a window and see a mail truck parked next to a mailbox. One minute later, you look out again and see the same truck parked down the street from the mailbox. Although you didn't observe the motion, you know the truck moved. How do you know? Its position relative to the mailbox has changed.

Motion can be described as a change in position. To  know if the position of something has changed, you need a reference point. In the case of the mail truck, the mailbox was a reference point. You can also use the reference point to get a rough idea of how far the truck moved. But there's one thing you don't know. You don't know how *fast* the truck moved in reaching its new position.

Descriptions of motion often include speed—how "fast" something moves. If you think of motion as a change in position, then speed is an expression of how much time it takes for that change in position to occur. Any change over time is called a rate. **Speed,** then, is the rate of change in position. Speed can also be described as simply a rate of motion.

There are different "kinds" of speed. The speedometer in a car shows instantaneous speed. **Instantaneous**

Figure 3-1. Although the tuning fork does not move from one place to another, the prongs of the fork are in motion.

EcoTip

When you have to go somewhere, move your muscles. Walk, bike, or skate to the store or to a friend's house instead of riding in a car or bus. It's good for you and for the environment.

OPTIONS

Meeting Different Ability Levels

For Section 3-1, use the following **Teacher Resource Masters** depending upon individual students' needs.

◆ **Study Guide Master** for all students.

● **Reinforcement Master** for students of average and above average ability levels.

▲ **Enrichment Master** for above average students.

Additional Teacher Resource Package masters are listed in the OPTIONS box throughout the section. The additional masters are appropriate for all students.

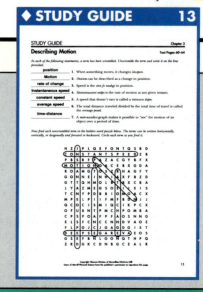

◆ **STUDY GUIDE** 13

STUDY GUIDE   Chapter 3
Describing Motion   Text Pages 60–64

In each of the following statements, a term has been scrambled. Unscramble the term and write it on the line provided.

position	1. When something moves, it changes *isopton.*
Motion	2. *Otoinm* can be described as a change in position.
rate of change	3. Speed is the *etra fo nachge* in position.
instantaneous speed	4. *Sttnaoaunesi sedps* is the rate of motion at any given instant.
constant speed	5. A speed that doesn't vary is called a *tnstaocn dsepe.*
average speed	6. The total distance traveled divided by the total time of travel is called *the average peesd.*
time-distance	7. A *mait-nasidtce* graph makes it possible to "see" the motion of an object over a period of time.

Now find each unscrambled term in the hidden word puzzle below. The terms can be written horizontally, vertically, or diagonally and forward or backward. Circle each term as you find it.

speed is the rate of motion at any given instant. At the moment the picture in Figure 3-2 was taken, the car was traveling at a speed of 80 km/h. On a highway, a car may travel at the same speed for a fairly long period of time. A speed that does not vary is called a **constant speed.**

Much of the time, the speeds you deal with are not constant. Think about riding your bicycle for a distance of 5 kilometers. As you start out, your speed increases from 0 km/h to, say, 30 km/h. You slow down to 18 km/h as you pedal up a steep hill and speed up to 45 km/h going down the other side of the hill. You stop for a red light, speed up again, and move at a constant speed for a while. As you near the end of the trip, you slow down and then stop. Checking your watch, you find that the trip took 15 minutes, or one-quarter of an hour. How would you express your speed on such a trip? Would you use your fastest speed, your slowest speed, or some speed in-between the two?

In cases where rate of motion varies a great deal, such as this bicycle trip, the best way to describe speed is to use average speed. **Average speed** is total distance traveled divided by total time of travel. On the trip just described, your average speed was 5 kilometers divided by 1/4 hour, or 20 km/h.

Calculating Speed

How could you find out who is the fastest runner in your school? One way would be to get all the students together to run in a giant race. However, this isn't very practical. A better way would be to have each student run a certain distance and to time each runner. The runner with the shortest time is the fastest student. In other words, if you know the distance and time, you can calculate speed. Knowing these values, you can use this equation:

$$v = \frac{d}{t}$$

Figure 3-2. The speedometer of a car shows how fast the car is moving at any given instant.

Did You Know?

In the finals of the 100-m dash of the 1988 Olympics, Ben Johnson and Carl Lewis each reached a peak speed of 43.37 km/h during one 10-m stretch.

Find avg speed of splits of a race, then total avg speed.

Marble race activity

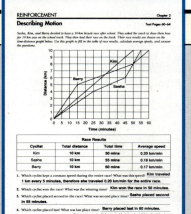

61

TYING TO PREVIOUS KNOWLEDGE: Ask students to recall that the units marked on a speedometer of a bike or car are miles per hour and kilometers per hour. Have them recall that the quantities which make up these units were introduced in Chapter 2. Have them name the quantities, and identify the instruments and metric units that can be used to measure them.

OBJECTIVES AND SCIENCE WORDS: Have students review the objectives and science words to become familiar with this section.

2 TEACH

Key Concepts are highlighted.

CONCEPT DEVELOPMENT

▶ Ask students to describe other types of periodic motion, such as the motion of a bee's wing or the post in a cassette recorder.

▶ Students may have difficulty with the term *relative* used in describing an object's position. Explain that the term means "dependent upon" or "connected to."

▶ Ask each student to secretly choose a classmate and write a description of his or her position in the classroom. Have students exchange and read descriptions to see if they can identify the persons chosen. Discuss common characteristics of those descriptions that lead to the correct identifications of individuals.

▶ To refresh students' memories about the concept of rate, have them measure their breathing rates. Discuss other time rates, such as heart rate (pulse), liquid flow rates, growth rates, and banking rates. Discuss the units that describe these rates and point out similarities in the units.

CONCEPT DEVELOPMENT

▶Show students that time units really do emerge from the equation

$$t = d/v$$

That is,

$$m \div \frac{m}{s} = m \times \frac{s}{m} = s$$

Make sure that the students realize that the vertical axis in Figure 3-3 represents the distance each swimmer has swum from the beginning of the workout and the horizontal axis represents the time that has elapsed since the start of the workout.

REVEALING MISCONCEPTIONS

▶Students often interpret the height of the graph as its slope. Point out that the steepness of the line of a distance-time graph indicates the average speed; the height of the line indicates the distance the object has traveled.

CROSS CURRICULUM

▶**Math:** Photocopy a picture of a speedometer calibrated in metric and English units from a newspaper or magazine car advertisement. Distribute copies and have students determine if a speed of 1 mi/h is faster or slower than 1 km/h. Allow students to defend their answers.

PRACTICE PROBLEM ANSWERS
1. 9.37 m/s

PRACTICE PROBLEM ANSWERS
1. 21.9 s

CHECK FOR UNDERSTANDING

Use the Mini Quiz to check for understanding.

MINI QUIZ

Use the Mini Quiz to check students' recall of chapter content.

① **What is motion?** *a change in position*

② **What two quantities do you need to know to calculate average speed?** *distance and time*

③ **What does a flat line on a segment of distance-time graph tell you about the average speed for that time period?** *no change in distance occurs therefore average speed is zero*

EXAMPLE PROBLEM: Calculating Speed

Problem Statement:	Your neighbor says she can skate at a speed of 1 m/s. To see if you can skate faster, you have her time you as you skate as fast as you can for 100 m. Your time is 67 s. Who skates faster?
Known Information: Strategy Hint: Remember that speed is a rate.	distance, d = 100 m time, t = 67 s
Unknown Information:	speed, v
Equation to Use:	$v = \dfrac{d}{t}$
Solution:	$v = \dfrac{100 \text{ m}}{67 \text{ s}} = 1.5 \text{ m/s}$

You skate faster than your neighbor.

PRACTICE PROBLEM

Strategy Hint: What units will your answer be given in?

1. Florence Griffith Joyner set a world record by running 200 m in 21.34 s. What was her speed?

EXAMPLE PROBLEM: Calculating Time from Speed

Problem Statement:	Sound travels at a speed of 330 m/s. If a firecracker explodes 3630 m away from you, how long does it take for the sound of the explosion to reach you?
Known Information: Strategy Hint: Rearrange equation to solve for time.	velocity, v = 330 m/s distance, d = 3630 m
Unknown Information:	time, t
Equation to Use:	$v = \dfrac{d}{t}$ Rearranged becomes: $t = \dfrac{d}{v}$
Solution:	$t = \dfrac{d}{v} = \dfrac{3630 \text{ m}}{330 \text{ m/s}} = 11 \text{ s}$

It takes 11 seconds for the sound of the explosion to reach you.

PRACTICE PROBLEM

Strategy Hint: Rearrange the equation.

1. The world's fastest passenger elevator operates at a speed of about 10 m/s. If the 60th floor is 219 m above the first floor, how long does it take the elevator to go from the first floor to the 60th floor?

OPTIONS

ENRICHMENT

▶Have students find out how the speedometer on a bike or a car works.

▶Have students investigate the speeds at which various organisms such as ants, wasps, turtles, horses, leopards, ostriches, and falcons move. Ask them to present the information as a bar graph on a poster.

PROGRAM RESOURCES

From the **Teacher Resource Package** use:
Critical Thinking/Problem Solving, page 9, Radar Detectors and Speeding.

Transparency Masters, pages 9-10, Distance-Time Graph.

Use **Color Transparency** number 5, Distance-Time Graph.

Graphing Speed

A distance-time graph makes it possible to "see" the motion of an object over a period of time. For example, the graphs in Figure 3-3 show how two swimmers performed during a 30-minute workout. The smooth, red line represents the motion of a swimmer who swam at a constant speed during the entire workout. She swam 800 m during each 10-minute period. Her speed was constant at 80 m/min.

The blue line represents the motion of a second swimmer, who did not swim at a constant speed. She covered 400 m during the first 10 minutes of her workout. Then she rested for the next 10 minutes. During this time, her speed was 0 m/min. The steepness of the graph over the next 10 minutes shows that she swam faster than before. During this period she covered 800 m. How much distance did she cover during the workout? What was her average speed for the 30-minute period?

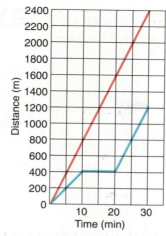

Figure 3-3. Distance-time graphs like the one shown here make it possible to visualize motion over a period of time.

SECTION REVIEW

1. What units would you use to describe the speed of a car? Would you use different units to give the speeds of runners in a neighborhood race? Explain your answer.
2. In a skateboarding marathon, the winner covered 435 km in 36.75 h. What was the winner's average speed?
3. **Apply:** Make a graph of distance versus time for a 2-hour car trip. During the first 30 minutes the car covered 50 km. During the next 30 minutes the car was stopped. An additional 50 km was covered during the final 60 minutes of the trip. Note the three graph segments. Which graph segment slopes the most? Which one does not slope? What was the car's average speed?

☑ Concept Mapping

Make a network tree concept map that shows and defines the three kinds of speed described in this section. If you need help, refer to Concept Mapping in the **Skill Handbook** on pages 684 and 685.

Skill Builder

RETEACH

Have students calculate the average speed of a wind-up or battery-operated toy car. They can use metersticks and a wall clock to measure the distance and time.

EXTENSION

For students who have mastered this section, use the **Reinforcement** and **Enrichment** masters or other OPTIONS provided.

STUDENT TEXT QUESTION

▶ Page 63, paragraph 2: **How much distance did she cover during the workout?** *1200 m* **What was her average speed for the 30-minute period?** *The second swimmer's average speed was 40 m/min.*

3 CLOSE

▶ Repeat the Demonstration described in the Motivation section of this section. Have students identify the situations in which the ball appeared to move with constant speed.

▶ Ask questions 1-2 and the **Apply** Question in the Section Review.

SECTION REVIEW ANSWERS

1. km/h; yes, m/s; the neighborhood race would involve short distances and short periods of time
2. 11.8 km/h
3. **Apply:** Graph segment of the first 30 minutes slopes the most; the segment for the next 30 minutes doesn't slope; the average speed is 50 km/h.

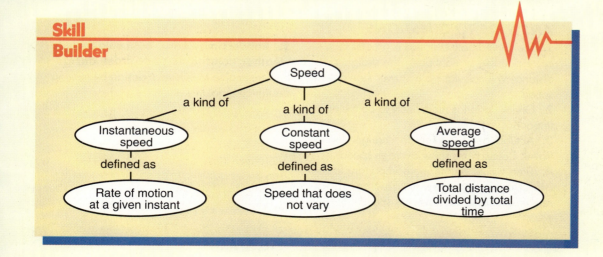

Skill Builder

ACTIVITY 3-1
35 minutes

OBJECTIVE: Examine a variety of variables included in the measurement of speed.

PROCESS SKILLS applied in this activity:
▶ **Communicating** in Procedure Step 2.
▶ **Measuring** in Procedure Step 3.
▶ **Using Numbers** in Procedure Step 4.
▶ **Controlling Variables** in Procedure Step 5.

👥 COOPERATIVE LEARNING

The class must invent rules for the contest: flight distance, manner of launch, assignment of judges, etc. Use the Science Investigation strategy to divide the class into small teams (3 or 4). Each team designs and tests a glider to compete against other teams.

TEACHING THE ACTIVITY

Alternate Materials: Supply a variety of papers: tissue paper, wrapping paper, etc. Encourage creativity.
Troubleshooting: Competition must be based on calculated speed; not side-to-side flight. Use the inventing of rules to explore variables affecting speed measurement, such as curved paths and average speed.

PROGRAM RESOURCES
From the **Teacher Resource Package** use:

Activity Worksheets, pages 22-23, Activity 3-1: Measuring Speed.

ACTIVITY 3-1
Measuring Speed

Problem: *How slow can you make a glider fly?*

Materials
- stopwatch or timer with second hand
- metric tape measure or meterstick
- string
- paper sheets of various types, weights, and sizes
- transparent tape
- paper clips and stapler

Procedure
1. Design a paper glider. Construct your glider using the materials provided.
2. Test fly the glider following all rules that have been established by the class.
3. Measure the distance of flight in centimeters and time of flight in seconds. Record this data in a table like the one shown here.
4. Calculate the speed of the glider.
5. Make any adjustments in the glider to achieve the slowest possible speed. If necessary, redesign the glider.
6. Repeat Steps 2, 3, and 4.
7. When you are satisfied with your design, fly the glider, record the measurements, and calculate the speed. Compare your results with those of other teams.

Data and Observations Sample Data

	Distance (cm)	Time (s)	Speed (cm/s)
Test 1	520	3.5	149
Test 2	280	3.1	90
Final	430	4.2	102

Analyze
1. If your glider travels a curved path, which distance measurement will give the slowest speed calculation—along the curved path or along a straight line between the starting point and landing point? Explain your reasoning.
2. Which is more important in glider speed—how hard you throw the glider or the design of the glider?

Conclude and Apply
3. When calculating the speed of your glider, did you find its fastest speed, slowest speed, or average speed?
4. In designing a slow glider, which should you try for, long distance or long time?
5. What factors affected the flight of your glider? Which of these factors were you able to control or influence, and by what means?

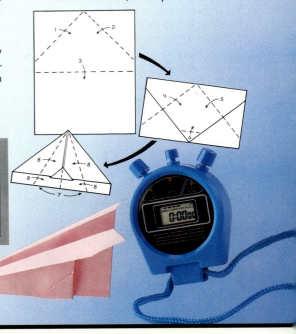

ANSWERS TO QUESTIONS
1. The curved path distance is greater than a corresponding straight path. The straight path distance will calculate to a slower than actual speed.
2. Glider design is more likely to be the most important variable.
3. Actual speed is likely to change during travel. Calculations show *average* speed.
4. Time would be the more important factor affecting speed. The longer the glider remains in flight, the slower its speed.
5. Answers may vary, but could include weather conditions and glider design. Student is able to influence design by making design changes.

Velocity and Acceleration

Objectives

▶ Compare and contrast speed, velocity, and acceleration.
▶ Calculate acceleration.

New Science Words

velocity
acceleration

Velocity and Speed

① You turn on the radio and hear the tail-end of a news story about a swarm of killer bees. The swarm, moving at a speed of 60 km/h, has just left a town 60 kilometers north of your location. Should you be worried? What should you do? Unfortunately, you don't have enough information. Knowing the speed of the swarm isn't much help. Speed only describes how fast something is moving. You also need to know the direction the swarm is moving. In other words, you need to know the velocity of the swarm. **Velocity** describes both speed and direction.

Picture a motorcycle racing down the highway at 100 km/h. It passes another motorcycle going 100 km/h in the opposite direction. The speeds of the motorcycles are the same, but their velocities are different because the motorcycles are not moving in the same direction.

You learned earlier that speed isn't always constant. Like speed, velocity may also change. Unlike speed, the velocity of an object can change, even if the speed of the object remains constant! How can this be? Read on and you'll find out.

Acceleration

At the starting line of a drag strip, a driver sits, idling the dragster's engine. With the starting signal, the driver presses the gas pedal to the floor. The car leaps for-

OPTIONS

INQUIRY QUESTIONS

▶ **How would you convert a car's speedometer to a velocity meter?** *Attach a compass to the speedometer panel so that speed and direction could be read simultaneously.*

▶ Using information found in the first paragraph of this section, draw the possible locations from the town after one hour of flight. **What velocity of the swarm should make you [the reader] worried?** *60 km/h, south* **What velocity will put the swarm farthest from the reader in one hour?** *60 km/h, north*

PREPARATION

SECTION BACKGROUND

▶ Velocity and acceleration are both rates of motion. Velocity is the rate of change in position. That is, it describes how far something moves in each time interval. Acceleration is the rate of change in velocity. Acceleration indicates how much something changes speed or direction during each time interval.

▶ The slope of a velocity-time graph represents acceleration.

PREPLANNING

▶ Obtain boards and marbles for the Mini-Lab. Remind students who have digital wristwatches with automatic stopwatches to wear them the day of the activity.

▶ Obtain several wind-up or battery-operated toy cars.

1 MOTIVATE

▶ **Demonstration:** Place a wind-up or battery-operated toy car on the floor and release it. Have students observe its motion. Repeat the demonstration with the car moving in the opposite direction. Make sure students understand that the average speed in both demonstrations was the same. Ask them if speed indicates "how fast" and/or "where" something is going. Have them explain how they would describe where something is going.

TYING TO PREVIOUS KNOWLEDGE: Have a student explain the meaning of the phrase "stepping on the gas." Relate the function of the accelerator and the motion of a car. Tell students they will learn more about motion caused by "stepping on the gas."

SCIENCE WORDS: Have students review the objectives and science words to become familiar with this section.

2 TEACH

Key Concepts are highlighted.

CONCEPT DEVELOPMENT

▶ Point out that *velocity* describes the speed of an object in a given direction. Usually the direction is given using compass points. Ask students to give other ways of describing direction, such as uphill, downhill, right, and left.

▶ Discuss several units of acceleration, such as km/h/s, used to express a car's acceleration. Another unit, m/s/s, is used to express the acceleration of a falling object. In each case have students identify the units in which the *change in velocity* is described and the units in which the change in time is expressed.

MINI-Lab

Materials: stopwatches, meter-sticks, marbles, 1/4 inch hardboard (10 cm by 50 cm to 100 cm)

▶ Arrange students in small groups.

▶ Show the students how to use their data to make velocity-time graphs. Be sure to point out that the slope of the graph indicates acceleration.

▶ **Answer:** The rate of acceleration does not significantly change when the ramp is at the same angle, but the velocity increases with time as the marble accelerates.

CROSS CURRICULUM

▶ **Math:** Have students show that the equation $v = at$ yields units of velocity.

PROGRAM RESOURCES

From the **Teacher Resource Package** use:

Activity Worksheets, page 28, Mini-Lab: Does greater velocity require greater acceleration?

Use **Laboratory Manual,** Speed and Acceleration.

MINI-Lab

Does greater velocity require greater acceleration?

Make a ramp by propping a board on a textbook. Let a marble roll down the ramp and across a hard, flat surface. Make two time measurements: travel time of the marble down the ramp and travel time of the marble across the flat surface for a distance of 1 m from the bottom of the ramp. Calculate the marble's velocity across the flat surface. Change the starting point of the marble on the ramp and repeat the procedure. Does acceleration change? Does velocity change?

---

ward and builds up speed, moving faster and faster until it crosses the finish line. Then the driver releases a drag chute, and the car rapidly slows down and comes to a stop. All the while the car gains speed, it is accelerating. Strange as it may seem, the car is also accelerating as it slows down! How is this possible?

② **Acceleration** is the rate of change of velocity. Keep in mind that velocity includes both speed and direction. If the direction of motion stays the same, as with the dragster, then acceleration is just the rate of change in speed. Because "slowing down" is a change in speed, the dragster is accelerating as it slows down. If the acceleration is opposite in direction to the velocity, then the speed decreases.

Because velocity includes both speed and direction, if *either* value changes, velocity will change. For example, if a car goes around a curve, its direction changes. So even if its speed remains constant, the velocity of the car changes. In other words, acceleration occurs.

The size of an acceleration depends on both the change in velocity and the time interval. The *time interval* is the amount of time that passed while the change in velocity was taking place. If the change in velocity is large, the acceleration will be large. Acceleration will also be large if the change in velocity occurs in a small time interval.

To calculate acceleration, divide the change in velocity by the time interval. To find the *change in velocity,* subtract the initial velocity (starting velocity) from the final velocity.

$$a = \frac{v_f - v_i}{t} = \frac{\Delta v}{t}$$

The symbol Δ is the Greek letter *delta* and stands for "change in."

When an object is slowing down, its final velocity will be less than its initial velocity. Thus, the acceleration will have a negative value. When calculating acceleration, be sure to include all proper units and algebraic signs. The unit for velocity is meters/second (m/s) and the unit for **③** time is seconds (s). Thus, the unit for acceleration is

$$\frac{meters/second}{second}.$$

This unit is usually written as m/s² and is read as "meters per second square" or "meters per second per second."

66 MOVING OBJECTS

OPTIONS

Meeting Different Ability Levels

For Section 3-2, use the following **Teacher Resource Masters** depending upon individual students' needs.

◆ **Study Guide Master** for all students.

● **Reinforcement Master** for students of average and above average ability levels.

▲ **Enrichment Master** for above average students.

Additional Teacher Resource Package masters are listed in the OPTIONS box throughout the section. The additional masters are appropriate for all students.

EXAMPLE PROBLEM: Calculating Acceleration

Problem Statement:	The velocity of a dragster changes from 0 m/s at the starting line to 60 m/s when it crosses the finish line 10 seconds later. Calculate the car's average acceleration.
Known Information:	initial velocity, v_i, = 0 m/s
<u>Strategy Hint:</u> Figure velocity change by subtracting initial velocity from final velocity.	final velocity, v_f, = 60 m/s
	time interval, t, = 10 s
Unknown Information:	Acceleration, a
Equation to Use:	$a = \dfrac{v_f - v_i}{t}$
Solution:	$a = \dfrac{v_f - v_i}{t} = \dfrac{60 \text{ m/s} - 0 \text{ m/s}}{10 \text{ s}} = 6 \text{ m/s}^2$

PRACTICE PROBLEM

<u>Strategy Hint:</u> Find the change in velocity by subtracting initial velocity from final velocity.

1. At the top of its highest hill, a roller coaster's velocity is 10 m/s. Plunging downward, it gains speed, reaching a velocity of 32 m/s just before it gets to the bottom three seconds later. What is the roller coaster's acceleration?

SECTION REVIEW

1. A jet plane is flying east at 880 km/h. In the air above it, another plane is traveling north at 880 km/h. Do the two planes have the same velocity? Are their speeds the same? Explain your answer.
2. Near the end of a daily swim, a swimmer pushes himself to swim faster. His speed gradually increases from 1.1 m/s to 1.3 m/s during the last 20 s of his workout. What is his acceleration during this interval?
3. **Apply:** Describe three different ways to change your velocity when you're riding a bicycle.

☑ Making and Using Graphs

Decide which kind of graph—a line graph, a bar graph, or a pie graph—you should use to show how velocity changes over time. Explain your choice. Show how you would set up the graph. If you need help, refer to Making and Using Graphs in the **Skill Handbook** on page 687.

Skill Builder

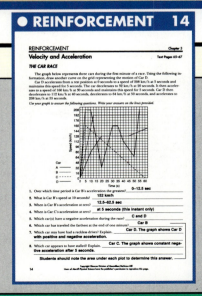
● **REINFORCEMENT 14**

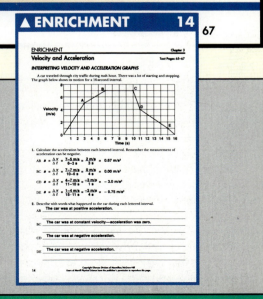
▲ **ENRICHMENT 14**

67

PRACTICE PROBLEM ANSWERS
7.3 m/s²

MINI QUIZ

Use the Mini Quiz to check students' recall of chapter content.

❶ **What is velocity?** *both speed and direction*
❷ **What is acceleration?** *rate of change of velocity*
❸ **What is the unit of acceleration?** *m/s²*

CHECK FOR UNDERSTANDING

Have students state how speed and velocity differ.

RETEACH

Have volunteers demonstrate two different walking velocities in the same direction, two different walking velocities with the same speed, and an accelerated walk.

EXTENSION

For students who have mastered this section, use the **Reinforcement** and **Enrichment** masters or other OPTIONS provided.

3 CLOSE

▶ Repeat the Demonstration found in the Motivation of Section 3-1.
▶ Ask questions 1-2 and the **Apply** Question in the Section Review.

SECTION REVIEW ANSWERS

1. No, they are traveling in different directions; the speeds are the same; they will travel the same distance in the same amount of time.
2. 0.01 m/s²
3. **Apply:** Answers may include: apply brakes, pedal faster, change directions, etc. Accept all reasonable responses.

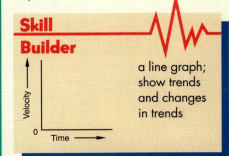
Skill Builder

a line graph; show trends and changes in trends

PREPARATION

SECTION BACKGROUND

▶ Inertia is the tendency of an object to resist any change in its motion. It accounts for unbelted car passengers crashing into windshields and backs of seats. This concept will be developed in Section 3-4.

PREPLANNING

▶ Obtain a skateboard, a long ramp, a small piece of clay, several rubber bands, a plastic foam cup, some cotton, paper towels, and two (raw or) hard-boiled eggs.

1 MOTIVATE

▶ Have students discuss commercials that advocate seat belt use.

TYING TO PREVIOUS KNOWLEDGE:
Recall the meaning of a negative acceleration, or deceleration, from Section 3-2. You will see the tremendous negative accelerations involved in car or bike crashes.

OBJECTIVES AND SCIENCE WORDS:
Have students review the objectives and science words to become familiar with this section.

2 TEACH

Key Concepts are highlighted.

CONCEPT DEVELOPMENT

▶ Be sure students realize that the unbelted passenger has a shorter stopping time than the car and therefore has a greater deceleration. Wearing seat belts increases the stopping time and reduces the deceleration.

 **3-3 Crashing to Save Lives**

Objectives

▶ Evaluate the effects of wearing seat belts during a car crash.
▶ Form an opinion about whether laws should make people wear seat belts.

Studying Crashes

How would you like to develop and perfect something that could save thousands of lives every year and keep hundreds of thousands of other people from being hurt? That's what scientists are trying to do with experiments called crash tests. In crash tests, researchers put lifelike dummies in cars, then crash the cars into each other or into concrete walls. Sometimes the dummies are placed on a sledlike device that runs on tracks. As cameras and other instruments record the process, the sled accelerates, then stops suddenly.

By studying the results of crash tests and real car collisions, scientists have learned what happens to people in accidents and how some injuries and deaths can be prevented.

OPTIONS

Meeting Different Ability Levels

For Section 3-3, use the following **Teacher Resource Masters** depending upon individual students' needs.

◆ **Study Guide Master** for all students.
● **Reinforcement Master** for students of average and above average ability levels.
▲ **Enrichment Master** for above average students.

Additional Teacher Resource Package masters are listed in the OPTIONS box throughout the section. The additional masters are appropriate for all students.

◆ **STUDY GUIDE** 15

STUDY GUIDE   Chapter 3
Crashing to Save Lives   Text Pages 68–69

Listed below are statements that either agree with the textbook or don't agree with the textbook. If the statement does agree, place a (✓) to the left of the statement. If the statement doesn't agree, rewrite it so it will agree with the textbook. Underline the words you change.

✓ 1. Researchers put lifelike dummies in cars for crash tests.

___ 2. When a car traveling about 50 km/h collides head-on with something solid, the car begins to expand and speed up. **When a car traveling about 50 km/h collides head-on with something solid, the car begins to crumple and slow down.**

___ 3. Within 0.1 second after a car crash, the car stops; but because of gravity, any passenger not wearing a seat belt continues to move forward at the same speed the car was traveling. **Within 0.1 second after a car crash, the car stops but because of inertia, any passenger not wearing a seat belt continues to move forward at the same speed the car was traveling.**

✓ 4. By studying the results of crash tests and real car collisions, scientists have learned what happens to people in auto accidents.

✓ 5. A person in a car wearing a seat belt becomes "part" of the car.

___ 6. The force needed to slow a person down from 50 km/h to zero in 1 second is equal to 2 times that person's height. **The force needed to slow a person down from 50 km/h to zero in 1 second is equal to 14 times that person's weight.**

___ 7. A seat belt not only holds a person in place, but it also helps deflect and concentrate some of the force of the crash. **A seat belt not only holds a person in place, but it also helps absorb and spread out some of the force of the crash.**

Copyright Glencoe Division of Macmillan/McGraw-Hill
Users of Merrill Physical Science have the publisher's permission to reproduce this page.   15

When a car traveling about 50 km/h collides head-on with something solid, the car begins to crumple and slow down. Within 0.1 second after the crash, the car stops. Any passenger not wearing a seat belt continues to move forward at the same speed the car was traveling.

Within 0.02 second (one-fiftieth of a second) after the car stops, the unbelted person slams into the windshield, dashboard, or steering wheel with great force. Back-seat passengers slam into the backs of the seats in front of them at a speed of 50 km/h. That's as much as the speed you would reach while falling from a three-story building.

A person wearing a seat belt becomes "part" of the car. When the car slows down, the person also slows down. The force needed to slow a person down from 50 km/h to zero in 0.1 seconds is equal to 14 times that person's weight. The belt not only holds the person in place, it also "gives", reducing the force and spreading out the force so that it's not all concentrated on one part of the body.

SECTION REVIEW

1. Describe what happens to a person who's not wearing a seat belt during a car crash.
2. Describe how seat belts protect passengers and drivers during accidents.

You Decide!

Safety experts say that about half the people who die in car crashes would survive if they wore seat belts. Most states have passed laws that require drivers and front-seat passengers to wear seat belts. But some people resent the laws. They think everyone should be free to decide whether or not to use seat belts. Some people feel the same way about laws that require motorcycle riders to wear helmets. Should laws require people to wear seat belts? What about motorcycle helmets?

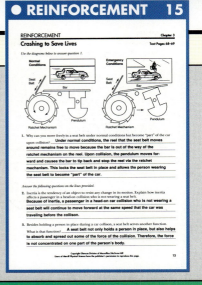

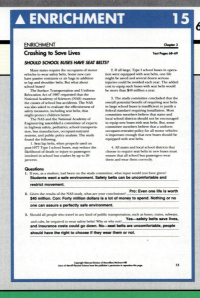

69

CONCEPT DEVELOPMENT

▶**Demonstration:** Attach a hard-boiled egg to the middle of a skateboard with a small bit of clay. Position the skateboard about 2 m from the wall and thrust it toward the wall. Securely attach another hard-boiled egg to the skateboard with several rubber bands and repeat the demonstration. Have students compare the effects of the crash on the eggs in both demonstrations.

CHECK FOR UNDERSTANDING

Ask questions 1-2 in the Section Review.

RETEACH

Construct a crash helmet for a hard-boiled egg from a small, plastic foam cup filled with cotton. Repeat the Demonstration described above.

EXTENSION

For students who have mastered this section, use the **Reinforcement** and **Enrichment** masters or other OPTIONS provided.

3 CLOSE

FLEX Your Brain

Use the Flex Your Brain activity to have students explore REQUIRING SEAT BELTS IN SCHOOL BUSES.

PROGRAM RESOURCES

From the **Teacher Resource Package** use:

Activity Worksheets, page 5, Flex Your Brain.

SECTION REVIEW ANSWERS

1. A person not wearing a seat belt in a crash will continue to move forward after the car comes to a sudden stop, and will collide with the inside of the car.

2. The belt causes the wearer to stop with the car.

YOU DECIDE!

Answers will vary; students should support their answers.

New Science Words

force
balanced forces
net force
inertia
friction

Objectives

▶ Recognize different kinds of forces.
▶ Identify cause and effect relationships between force and changes in velocity.
▶ Give examples of the effects of inertia.
▶ State Newton's first law of motion.

Figure 3-4. The force exerted by the bat sends the ball flying. How does the force exerted by the ball affect the motion of the bat?

What Is a Force?

Push a door open. Stretch a rubber band. Squeeze a piece of clay. Shove a book across a table. In each case, you are applying a force. A **force** is a push or a pull one body exerts on another. Sometimes the effects of a force are obvious, as when a moving car crashes into a stationary object, such as a tree. Other forces aren't as noticeable. Can you feel the force the floor exerts on your feet?

List all the forces you might exert or encounter in a typical day. Think about pushing, pulling, stretching, squeezing, bending, and falling.

Effects of Forces on Objects

In the examples you thought of, what happened to the objects that had forces exerted on them? If an object was moving, did the force change the object's velocity? Think of a speeding baseball meeting the force of a swinging bat. The ball's velocity certainly changes when the bat hits the ball.

Force does not always change velocity. Think about a game of tug-of-war with your dog. You plant your feet firmly and push against the ground. This force enables you to pull on one end of a rope. If your dog on the other end pulls just as hard as you do, the rope doesn't move. The forces acting on the rope balance each other. Forces that are equal in size and opposite in direction are called **balanced forces.**

Now what happens if your feet hit a slippery spot on the ground? Your feet slip and you can't exert as much force on the rope. The forces acting on the rope become

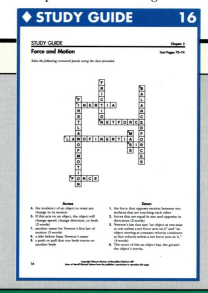

◆ STUDY GUIDE 16

STUDY GUIDE
Force and Motion

unbalanced, and there is a net force. A **net force** on an object always changes the velocity of the object. So, when your dog on the other end exerts more force on the rope than you do, the rope (and you) will accelerate in the direction of greater force.

You should keep in mind that velocity involves both speed and direction. If a net force acts on an object, the object will change speed, change direction, or both. In the tug-of-war, the net force causes both speed and direction to change.

Inertia and Mass

Picture a hockey puck sliding across the ice. Its velocity hardly changes until it hits something, such as the wall, net, or another stick. The velocity of the puck is constant, and its acceleration is zero until it hits something that alters its speed or direction.

The sliding puck demonstrates the property of inertia. **Inertia** (ihn UR shuh) is the tendency of an object to resist any change in its motion. If an object is moving, it tends to keep moving at the same speed and in the same direction unless a force acts on it. In other words, the velocity of the object remains constant unless a force changes it. If an object is at rest, it tends to remain at rest. Its velocity remains equal to zero unless a force makes it move. 2

Would you expect that a bowling ball would have the same inertia as a table tennis ball? Why would there be a difference? The more mass an object has, the greater its inertia. Recall that mass is the amount of matter in an object, and a bowling ball certainly contains more matter than a table tennis ball. So the bowling ball would have greater inertia than the table tennis ball.

Science and READING

Before a runner is given credit for a record in track, officials carefully analyze the conditions under which the event was held. What are some of the factors they consider?

71

TYING TO PREVIOUS KNOWLEDGE: Have students describe the motion of passengers in a car crash described in Section 3-3. Tell them that in this section the causes of such motion will be discussed.

OBJECTIVES AND SCIENCE WORDS: Have students review the objectives and science words to become familiar with this section.

2 TEACH

Key Concepts are highlighted.

CONCEPT DEVELOPMENT

- Have students classify the forces on their lists into pulls or pushes. From the lists have volunteers sketch situations on the chalkboard. Have them label what was being pulled or pushed and what was doing the pulling or pushing.
- This is a good opportunity to have students begin visualizing forces as arrows. Sketch two arrows representing the force needed to lift a book and a TV. Explain that the length of the arrow indicates the size of the force. A long arrow means a bigger force than a smaller arrow. The direction of the arrow indicates the direction of the push or pull. Encourage volunteers to try to sketch arrows to represent the forces in their lists.
- After discussing balanced forces and net forces, have students sketch the forces involved in the tug-of-war described on pages 70 and 71 when there were balanced forces acting on the rope and when there was a net force acting on the rope.

● REINFORCEMENT 16

REINFORCEMENT — Chapter 3

Force and Motion — Text Pages 70–74

Listed below are answers. Write a question for each answer. The first one has been done as an example.

1. push or pull — What is a force?
2. net force — **What kind of force always changes the velocity of an object?**
3. balanced forces — **What kind of forces are equal in size and opposite in directions?**
4. friction — **What is the force that opposes motion between surfaces that touch each other?**
5. inertia — **What is the tendency of an object to resist any change in its motion?**
6. Newton's first law of motion — **What law says that an object at a constant velocity keeps moving at that velocity unless a net force acts on it?**

Study the diagram below. Then answer the following questions by circling the letter that best answers each question.

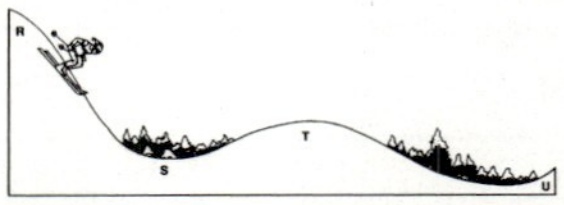

7. A person skis downhill from point *R* to point *U*. The speed of the skier increases in going from point *R* to point *S* because
   a. only balanced forces act on the skier. (b.) an unbalanced force acts on the skier. c. only inside forces act on the skier. d. no forces act on the skier.
8. The skier is able to coast between points *S* and *T* even though it is uphill because of
   a. gravity. b. centripetal force. c. cohesive force. (d.) inertia.
9. The force that opposes motion between the skier's skis and the surface of the snow is
   a. net b. balanced. (c.) friction. d. inertia.

16

▲ ENRICHMENT 16

ENRICHMENT — Chapter 3

Force and Motion — Text Pages 70–74

APPLYING NEWTON'S FIRST LAW OF MOTION: WHICH STRING WILL BREAK?

Tie a piece of heavy cord around the middle of your science textbook. Find two pieces of lighter weight string. Tie one piece to the center of the cord on the front (top) of the book. Tie the other piece to the bottom (back) of the book, as shown in the figure. Have one of your classmates hold the book securely at the top of the string while you pull very *slowly* but firmly on the bottom string. Describe what happens. **The top string breaks.**

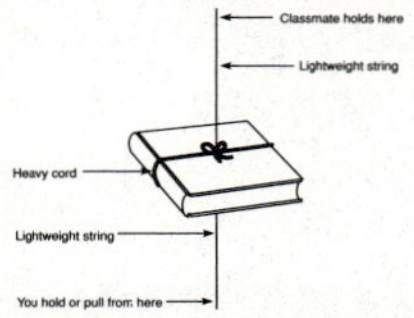

Tie another piece of lightweight string to replace the one that broke. Have one of your classmates hold the string firmly again at the top. This time, however, you pull very *fast* and very hard on the bottom string. Describe what happens. **This time the bottom string breaks.**

Explain your observations.
Pulling down slowly on the bottom string requires the top string to support all the weight of the book as well as the force of your pulling on the bottom string. However, when you pull fast and hard on the bottom string, the force of your pull on the string below the book is not great enough to overcome the book's inertia, so the string below the book breaks. When you pull hard and fast, the book doesn't move. No force is exerted on the top string.

16

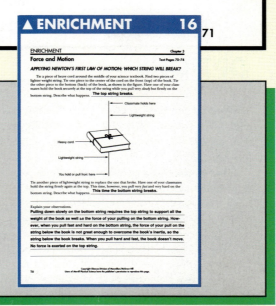

▶ Have students describe two ways to determine which of two skateboards has more inertia.

▶ Have students make a class list of highway design and traffic features that exist to accommodate inertia (e.g., banked curves, reduced speed limits for curves, guard rails, etc.).

TECHNOLOGY

For more information on air bags in automobiles, see "Air Bags vs. Seat Belts: Why You Should Care" by Henry, Ed, and Sherri Miller, *Changing Times,* March 1988, pp. 67-70.

Think Critically: An air bag offers little or no protection against a side impact, second impact, or rollover, or if the passengers aren't using seat belts.

TEACHER F.Y.I.

▶ The general study of motion in physics is called *mechanics.* Mechanics is further subdivided into two areas of study. *Kinematics* is the study of the relationships among the quantities which describe motion, such as position, time, velocity, and acceleration. The equations of average speed and acceleration are examples of kinematic equations. *Dynamics* is the quantitative study of the causes of motion.

TECHNOLOGY

Inertia Sponges

Seat belts are designed to reduce the effect of inertia in a crash by holding the passengers in place. However, in a high-speed crash, belts provide limited protection to the head and upper body. These parts of the body can be protected by air bags, which provide an instantaneous cushion for the head and upper body at the time of impact.

Air bags are designed to be used in addition to seat belts. An air-bag system consists of one or more crash sensors, an ignitor and gas generator, and an inflatable nylon bag. The nylon bag for the driver is stored in the steering wheel, and the bag for the front-seat passenger is inside the dashboard. If a car hits something with sufficient force (speeds in excess of from 15 to 20 kilometers per hour), impact sensors trigger the flow of electric current to an ignitor. The ignitor causes a chemical reaction to occur, producing harmless nitrogen gas. The nitro-gen gas pushes the air bag from its storage compartment just in time to absorb the inertia of the occupants. The bag then immediately deflates so that it will not interfere with the driver.

Think Critically: Under what crash conditions would an air bag offer little or no protection?

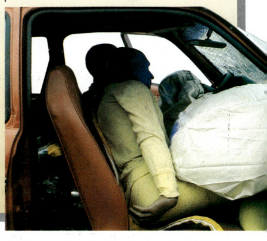

You wouldn't change the velocity of a bowling ball very much by swatting it with a paddle, but you could easily change the velocity of a table tennis ball. Because of its greater inertia, a much greater force would be needed to change the velocity of the bowling ball.

Newton's First Law

Forces change the motion of an object in very specific ways—so specific that Sir Isaac Newton (1642 - 1727) was able to state laws to describe the effects of forces. *Newton's first law of motion* says that an object moving at a constant velocity keeps moving at that velocity unless a net force acts on it. If an object is at rest, it stays at rest unless a net force acts on it. Does this sound familiar? It

OPTIONS

INQUIRY QUESTIONS

▶ **What evidence do you have that there is a change in velocity of a ball when you hit it with a bat?** *The speed and direction of the ball both change.*

▶ **What evidence do you have that there is a change in velocity of the bat when you hit a ball?** *The bat slows down a little. You can also feel the change in the motion of the bat.*

PROGRAM RESOURCES

From the **Teacher Resource Package** use:

Cross Curricular Connections, page 7, Reading Maps.

Science and Society, page 7, Is 65 mph Safe?

is the same as the earlier discussion of inertia. Thus, you'll understand why this law is sometimes called the *law of inertia.* You've probably seen—and felt—this law at work without even knowing it.

Suppose you're pushing a wheelbarrow full of leaves across your yard. Your rake is resting on top of the load. The wheel hits a rock and the wheelbarrow stops suddenly. What would happen to the rake? The rake would probably continue forward and fly out of the wheelbarrow. Why would this happen? No one would have pushed the rake. No net forward force would have acted on it. But because of inertia, the rake would keep moving forward at the same speed. If it wasn't for the rake hitting the ground, it would have kept moving until some other force stopped it.

Friction

You've just learned that ==inertia causes an object that is moving at constant velocity to keep moving at that velocity unless a net force acts on it.== But you know that if you shove a book across a long table, it seems to slow down and stop by itself. You don't see any force acting on the book. Why does it stop?

There is a force between the surfaces of the book and the table. The force is friction. ==**Friction** is the force that opposes motion between two surfaces that are touching each other.== Would you expect more friction between an

Figure 3-5. When the wheelbarrow strikes a rock, it stops suddenly. The rake keeps moving forward at its original speed because of its inertia.

MINI-Lab
Is friction a force?
Place a sheet of plain white paper on a flat surface. Set a 20-g mass on the paper about 7 cm from one end of the paper. Grip the edge of the other end of the paper and give it a quick, smooth yank. What happens to the 20-g mass? Replace the paper with a sheet of coarse sandpaper, rough side up, and repeat the procedure. What happens to the 20-g mass now? How do you account for the different results? Use Newton's first law to explain your observations.

CONCEPT DEVELOPMENT
▶ Ask students what they think the term *constant velocity* means in Newton's first law. Help students realize that constant velocity means that both the speed and the direction of motion remain the same.
▶ **Demonstration:** Put a handful of dried beans into one of two empty glass soda bottles. Place one end of a 3 cm × 30 cm strip of very smooth bond paper over the mouth of the bottle containing the beans. Carefully invert it onto the mouth of the second bottle so it balances. Hold the opposite end of the paper strip tightly between your thumb and index finger and allow the strip to sag slightly. With the edge of your free hand, strike the middle of the paper strip with a quick downward blow. The strip will be pulled from between the bottles, allowing the beans to fall. The bottles shouldn't move. Discuss the effects of inertia in this demonstration.
▶ Discuss situations where friction is not desirable. Ask students to describe ways to reduce friction.

CROSS CURRICULUM
▶ Health: Have students list methods used around the house and in school to reduce the possibility of people injuring themselves by slipping and falling.

MINI-Lab
▶ **Materials:** 1 sheet plain white paper, 20-g mass, 1 sheet coarse sandpaper
▶ The sheets of paper and sandpaper should be about equal in size. Use course grade sandpaper.
▶ **Answer:** The 20-g mass stays in the same place when the paper is yanked from under it, and moves with the sandpaper when it is yanked from under it.
▶ **Answer:** Students should recognize the effects of friction on the mass. They should realize that the net force of the sandpaper is greater than that of the plain paper due to friction.
▶ **Results:** The 20-g mass tended to remain at rest due to the force of inertia, until the force of friction overcame the inertia.

INQUIRY QUESTIONS
▶ **Does an object at rest have a constant velocity?** *Yes, its speed of 0 m/s is constant and it isn't changing direction.*
▶ **Does a net force of zero mean that there may be balanced forces acting on an object?** *Yes.*
▶ **Why do football players wear more equipment than basketball players?** *Football is a contact sport in which people exert forces on each other to stop motion very quickly, which may produce injuries. In basketball people do not exert forces on each other.*

PROGRAM RESOURCES
From the **Teacher Resource Package** use:
Activity Worksheets, page 29, Mini-Lab: Is friction a force?
Transparency Masters, pages 11-12, Newton's First Law.
Use **Color Transparency** number 6, Newton's First Law.
Use **Laboratory Manual,** Projectile Motion.

RETEACH

Tie a piece of string around a book and suspend it. Cut the string. Point out that before the string was cut, the book was at rest, indicating that there were balanced forces acting on it. After the string was cut, it accelerated, indicating there was a net force acting on it.

EXTENSION

For students who have mastered this section, use the **Reinforcement** and **Enrichment** masters or other OPTIONS provided.

3 CLOSE

▶ Have students explain why some people may feel they are falling forward when they step off an escalator.
▶ Ask questions 1-2 and the **Apply** Question in the Section Review.

SECTION REVIEW ANSWERS

1. The rosin increases the friction between the dancer's shoes and the floor, thus reducing chances of the dancer slipping. Friction.

2. The jet airplane; inertia is related to mass, not speed.

3. Apply: Answers will vary. Some possible answers are catching a football, sliding into a base, diving from a diving board. Accept all reasonable responses.

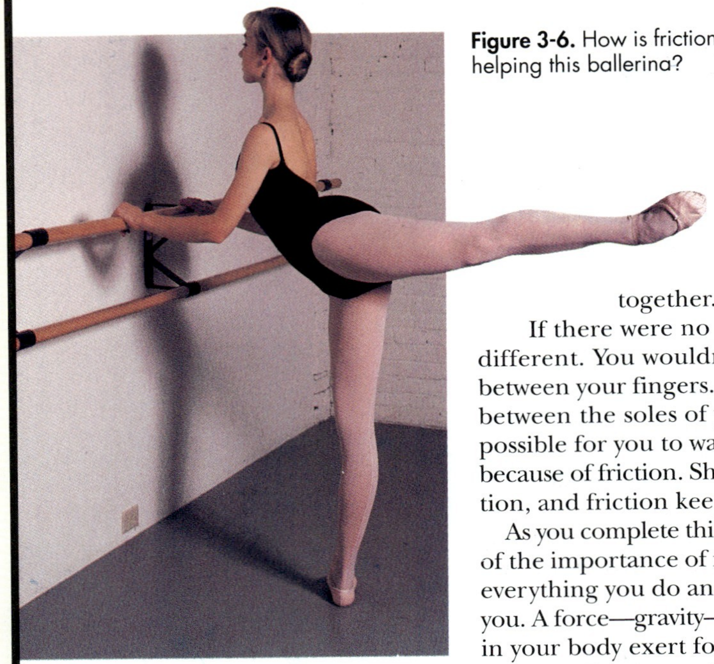

Figure 3-6. How is friction helping this ballerina?

oily floor and a slick, leather shoe sole or between a rough sidewalk and the bottom of a tennis shoe? The amount of friction that exists between two surfaces depends on two factors—the kinds of surfaces and the force pressing the surfaces together.

If there were no friction, your life would be much different. You wouldn't be able to walk or hold things between your fingers. Your shoes would fall off. Friction between the soles of your shoes and the floor makes it possible for you to walk. You can hold with your fingers because of friction. Shoelaces remain tied because of friction, and friction keeps your shoes on your feet.

As you complete this section, you should be more aware of the importance of force and motion. They are part of everything you do and everything that happens around you. A force—gravity—keeps you on the ground. Muscles in your body exert forces that move your arms and legs and eyes. Friction makes it possible for you to walk and to turn the pages of this book. And these are but a few examples of how force and motion affect your life.

SECTION REVIEW

1. Before dancing on a smooth wooden floor, ballet dancers sometimes put a sticky powder called rosin on their shoe soles. Why? What force are they taking advantage of?
2. Explain which has greater inertia, a speeding car or a jet airplane sitting on a runway.
3. **Apply:** Think of and describe three examples from sports in which a force changes the velocity of an object or a person.

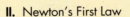

Skill Builder   ☑ **Outlining**

In an outline, organize all of the information you have learned relating to inertia and Newton's first law of motion. If you need help, refer to Outlining in the **Skill Handbook** on page 677.

Skill Builder

I. Inertia
  1. The tendency of an object to resist any change in motion
    a. proportional to mass
    b. proportional to force needed to overcome it

II. Newton's First Law
  1. An object moving at a constant velocity keeps moving at that velocity unless a net force acts upon it.
    a. The force needed to change an object's velocity depends on its inertia.

Effects of Gravity

3-5

Objectives
▶ Give examples of the effects of gravity.
▶ Examine how gravitational force is related to mass and distance.
▶ Distinguish between mass and weight.

New Science Words
gravity
weight

Gravitational Force

An Olympic diver is poised high above the water on a diving platform. The diver bounces up in the air and then hurtles toward the water. Did you ever wonder why the diver plunges downward instead of flying off into space? Probably not. Seeing objects "fall" is a very common experience. You may not have thought about it, but you've been watching the force of gravity at work.

Every object in the universe exerts a force on every other object, and that force is **gravity.** Often, the force is too slight to notice. For example, there's a gravitational force of attraction between your hand and your notebook, but when you let go of your notebook, it doesn't stay in your hand. The force is too small.

The amount of gravitational force between objects depends on two things: their masses and the distance between them. The masses of your hand and your notebook are quite small, so the force of attraction between them is weak. The mass of the Earth is very large, so its gravitational force is strong.

The amount of Earth's gravity acting on an orbiting satellite depends on its distance from Earth. The closer it is to Earth, the stronger the pull of gravity. The farther away it is, the less effect gravity has on it. How would this affect the satellite's velocity?

Weight

The measure of the force of gravity on an object is the object's weight. The term weight is most often used in reference to the gravitational force between Earth and a body

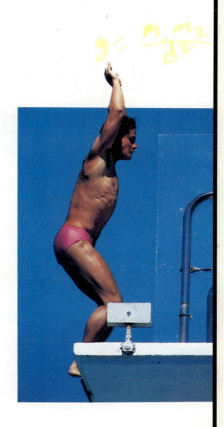

$$g = \frac{m_1 m_2}{d^2}$$

OPTIONS

INQUIRY QUESTIONS
▶ **Why is the word** *weightless* **often used to describe astronauts in outer space, but never the word** *massless***?** *Astronauts in outer space are weightless because there is no measurable gravitational force on them there. However, all objects (including astronauts) have mass.*
▶ **What would a 40-N backpack weigh on the moon?** *About 7-N*
▶ **What is the weight of Earth relative to you?** *The value of your weight.*

PROGRAM RESOURCES
From the **Teacher Resource Package** use:
Concept Mapping, page 11.

PREPARATION

SECTION BACKGROUND
▶ Newton was the first to describe the gravitational force between two objects quantitatively. The force is directly proportional to the product of the two masses and inversely proportional to the square of the distance between their centers. This indicates that if the distance between two objects is doubled, the force between them will fall to one-quarter of the value it was before the objects were moved.

PREPLANNING
▶ Borrow a plumb line or make one by using a heavy fishing sinker or washer as a plumb bob tied to a long piece of string.

1 MOTIVATE

Cooperative Learning: Assign Problem Solving teams to devise a way of determining the direction "up" by using only long pieces of strings and their science books. After discussing the results, demonstrate how a plumb line is used to determine verticality. Lead students to realize that "up" is the opposite direction of the pull on the book or plumb bob.

TYING TO PREVIOUS KNOWLEDGE:
Have the students recall balanced and net forces from Section 3-4. If you had students do the Cooperative Learning activity in the Motivation section, ask them to determine if the plumb bob had balanced forces or a net force acting on it. Tell them that they will learn more about one of the balanced forces in this section.

OBJECTIVES AND SCIENCE WORDS:
Have students review the objectives and science words to become familiar with this section.

Key Concepts are highlighted.

CONCEPT DEVELOPMENT

▶ The satellite must travel faster the closer it is to Earth to overcome the greater force of gravity.

▶ Discuss the concept of free-fall. Inertia causes the satellite to move in a straight line, but Earth's gravity causes it to "fall" away from that line. The same effects would be felt in a falling elevator; you would feel weightless.

▶ Discuss the difference between mass and weight. Point out that an object has mass in and by itself. However, there must be *another* object for it to have weight.

PROBLEM SOLVING

Its mass would stay the same.
Think Critically: The astronauts' masses could change if they ate more or less than normal, or if their activity patterns changed.

CROSS CURRICULUM

▶ **Earth Science:** Have students research how gravitational forces of the moon and sun affect tides.

CHECK FOR UNDERSTANDING

Use the Mini Quiz to check for understanding.

MINI QUIZ

Use the Mini Quiz to check students' recall of chapter content.

1 **What is the force of gravity?** *the force that every object exerts on another object*

2 **What is weight?** *the measure of the force of gravity on an object*

3 **Weight is measured in what units?** *newtons*

4 **What instrument is used to measure weight?** *a scale*

PROBLEM SOLVING

An Experiment for the Shuttle

NASA was having a competition to select several student experiments for scientists to conduct while the shuttle orbited Earth. Ellen decided to enter an experiment about how the time spent on a shuttle flight would affect the masses of the astronauts. The mass of each astronaut would be determined before and after the mission. During the flight, the astronauts would have to list the foods they ate and the liquids they drank and the masses of each. Ellen's experiment required that the masses of the food and liquid packets be measured and labeled to the nearest 0.01 gram.

How would the mass of any material on Earth compare with its mass during the shuttle mission?

Think Critically: What factors could cause changes in the astronauts' masses?

at Earth's surface. Weight isn't the same as mass, but the two are related. Recall from Chapter 2 that mass is the amount of matter in an object. The greater an object's mass, the stronger the gravitational force on it. In other words, the more mass an object has, the more it weighs.

Mass is measured in grams (g) and kilograms (kg).
3 Weight, which is a force, is measured in units called newtons (N). A kilogram of mass on Earth's surface weighs 9.8 N. On Earth, a tape cassette weighs about 0.5 N, a backpack full of books weighs about 40 N, you probably weigh 450 to 500 N, and a wide-bodied jumbo jet weighs about 3.4 million N.

The gravitational force an object exerts on other objects is related to its mass. Earth exerts a stronger gravitational force than the moon, because Earth has more mass. Because of the moon's weaker gravitational force, a person weighing about 480 N on Earth would weigh only about 80 N on the moon. Does this mean that the person would have less mass on the moon than on Earth? No. Unlike weight, mass doesn't change with changes in gravity. Because mass remains constant, the person would have the same inertia on the moon as on Earth.

76 MOVING OBJECTS

OPTIONS

Meeting Different Ability Levels

For Section 3-5, use the following **Teacher Resource Masters** depending upon individual students' needs.

◆ **Study Guide Master** for all students.

● **Reinforcement Master** for students of average and above average ability levels.

▲ **Enrichment Master** for above average students.

Additional Teacher Resource Package masters are listed in the OPTIONS box throughout the section. The additional masters are appropriate for all students.

◆ **STUDY GUIDE** 17

STUDY GUIDE   Chapter 3
Effects of Gravity   Text Pages 75-78

In the blank at the left, write the letter of the term that correctly completes each statement.

b   1. Every object in the universe exerts a force on every other object. This force is called____.
        a. friction   b. gravity

a   2. The measure of the force of gravity on an object is the object's ____.
        a. weight   b. inertia

b   3. The amount of gravitational force between two objects depends on their ____.
        a. color and density   b. mass and distance

b   4. Weight is measured in units called ____.
        a. Newtons   b. seconds

a   5. The greater an object's ____, the stronger the gravitational force on it.
        a. mass   b. velocity

b   6. Mass is measured in units called ____.
        a. meters and kilometers   b. grams and kilograms

b   7. A scale uses the principle of ____ to measure how much something weighs.
        a. acceleration   b. balanced forces

b   8. Earth exerts a stronger gravitational force than the moon because ____ has more mass.
        a. the moon   b. Earth

b   9. The masses of your hand and your notebook are quite small, so the force of attraction between them is ____.
        a. strong   b. weak

b   10. An object transported from the surface of Earth to the surface of the moon has its weight ____.
        a. increased   b. decreased

a   11. ____ doesn't change with changes in gravity.
        a. Mass   b. Weight

a   12. The ____ mass an object has, the more that object weighs.
        a. more   b. less

b   13. On Earth gravity exerts a(n) ____ force on your body.
        a. upward   b. downward

Copyright Glencoe Division of Macmillan/McGraw-Hill
Users of Merrill Physical Science have the publisher's permission to reproduce this page.   17

Measuring Forces

④ **Scales use the principle of balanced forces to measure how much something weighs.** To see how the principle works, hang a rubber band from a hook or a nail. Then attach something heavy to the lower end of the rubber band and see how much the band stretches. If you attach something even heavier, will the band stretch more? It will, because the length of the rubber band is a measure of the force on it. The band stretches until it is exerting an upward force equal to the weight of the object hung on it.

A scale works something like the rubber band. When you step on a bathroom scale, the force of your body stretches a spring inside the scale. The stretched spring pulls on levers, as shown in Figure 3-7, until the upward force of the scale equals the downward force of your weight. The dial on the scale, which is marked off in units of weight, moves as the spring stretches. When the spring stops moving, the number showing on the dial indicates your weight.

Gravity, like friction, is a force we tend to take for granted, even though it affects everything we do. Try to imagine living on a planet where the force of gravity was only half as great as Earth's. How would your life be different?

Figure 3-7. When you step on a bathroom scale, the downward force of gravity—your weight— is balanced by the upward force exerted by the spring.

SECTION REVIEW

1. Arriving on a newly discovered, Earth-sized planet, you find that you weigh one-third as much as on Earth. Is the planet's mass greater or less than Earth's?
2. Why don't you feel the gravitational force between your hand and a pencil?
3. **Apply:** Use Newton's first law and the concept of gravity to explain how a satellite orbits Earth.

☑ Observing and Inferring

Select three objects in the room and, without touching them, try to guess which weighs the most. What clues help you to make your guesses? How can you tell if you guessed right? If you need help, refer to Observing and Inferring in the **Skill Handbook** on page 678.

Skill Builder

RETEACH

Have students find the mass and weight of a book. Ask them to explain which measurement would change on the moon.

EXTENSION

For students who have mastered this section, use the **Reinforcement** and **Enrichment** masters or other OPTIONS provided.

3 CLOSE

▶ Invite a representative from the city or county Department of Weights and Measures to discuss the department's responsibilities and to demonstrate procedures used to validate commercial scales.

▶ Ask questions 1-2 and the **Apply** Question in the Section Review.

▶ Ask students what they feel in Question 2 of the Section Review. They feel the gravitational attraction between the pencil and Earth

SECTION REVIEW ANSWERS

1. The mass is less.
2. Gravitational force is related to mass; the masses are small and the gravitational forces weak.
3. Apply: Inertia makes the satellite move in a straight line. Gravity acts upon it to pull it toward Earth. As a result it orbits Earth.

Skill Builder

Students might infer that the bigger an object is, the more it will weigh. They might also consider the density of the object. They can find out by weighing each object.

● REINFORCEMENT 17

REINFORCEMENT   Chapter 3
Effects of Gravity   Text Pages 75-78

Write answers to the following questions on the blank lines provided.

1. What is gravity? __Gravity is a force that every object in the universe exerts on__ __every other object.__

2. What are two things that the amount of gravitational force between two objects depends on? __their masses and the distance between them__

3. Why does Earth exert a stronger gravitational force than the moon? __Earth has more mass__ __than the moon.__

4. If an object weighs 40 N on Earth would it weigh more than 40 N on the moon? Explain your answer. __No. The moon exerts a smaller gravitational force than Earth. Weight is__ __the measure of the force of gravity on an object, therefore an object that weighs__ __40 N on Earth would weigh less than 40 N on the moon.__

5. If an object has a mass of 26 g on Earth, would its mass be less than 26 g on the moon? Explain your answer. __No. Unlike weight, mass doesn't change with changes in gravity.__

Circle the picture in each set below that shows the greater gravitational force between the two objects.

▲ ENRICHMENT 17

ENRICHMENT   Chapter 3
Effects of Gravity   Text Pages 75-78

EFFECTS OF MICROGRAVITY

Read the following report adapted from NASA Educational Briefs. Answer the questions that follow.

The tendency of a spacecraft to remain in motion in a straight path away from Earth helps it to overcome the pull of Earth's gravity. The spacecraft approaches a state of freefall, where all objects in the craft are "weightless." However, the gases venting from the craft and the small pull exerted by the thin atmosphere at that altitude create very small forces, called microgravity, on objects.

A microgravity environment causes a variety of changes to humans. People in space seem to have smaller eyes because their faces become puffy. They have rosy cheeks and enlarged veins in their foreheads and necks. They may even be taller than they are on Earth because of reduced weight on their spines. Their leg muscles shrink. They need to move in a slight crouch with heads and arms forward.

Many of these effects of microgravity are the result of a shift in body fluids from the lower to upper parts of the body. So much fluid goes to the head that the brain thinks

the body has too much water. This may result in increased production of urine.

Long periods in a microgravity environment tend to shrink the heart and decrease production of red blood cells. Production of white blood cells is increased, and the rate of bone tissue formation is reduced. Important minerals such as calcium, phosphorus, potassium, and nitrogen are dissolved out of the bones and muscles and enter the body fluids. These fluids then leave the body as urine.

Most of these effects of microgravity seem to level off in space and even reverse after return to Earth. A good exercise program and diet can decrease the negative effects of microgravity.

Exercise on a treadmill seems to allow body fluids to flow throughout the body and not concentrate in the brain. Exercise also allows muscles to be used that normally wouldn't be used in a microgravity environment. A special diet replaces fluid, minerals, and electrolytes lost due to increased urine output.

1. What special nutritional, packaging, and serving requirements must be considered for astronauts' food? __Materials must be designed so that they do not float freely. Body__ __function and nutritional requirements change in space. The nutritional content__ __of the food must meet these changing requirements.__

2. What physical capabilities would you have on the Columbia shuttle but not on Earth? __You would have the capabilities to lift heavy objects and float freely.__

3. Why do our bodies need minerals like potassium, phosphorus, and calcium? __These minerals__ __are used by muscles and bones and must be replaced.__

4. In what ways are our bodily functions and construction designed to enable us to live on Earth? What does this tell us about future long-distance space travel? __Our bodies work best in an__ __environment where the right amount of gravity is present. In space, physiologi-__ __cal adjustments cause the body to act differently. Special exercise and diet must__ __be arranged during space flights to counteract these effects.__

ACTIVITY 3-2
35 minutes

OBJECTIVE: Apply knowledge of gravitational force to the investigation of a physical property.

PROCESS SKILLS applied in this activity:
► **Measuring** in Procedure Step 4.
► **Using Numbers** in Procedure Step 6.
► **Experimenting** in Conclude and Apply Questions 3 and 4.

👥 COOPERATIVE LEARNING
Use the Science Investigation strategy and divide class into teams of three students. Provide each team with a different type of paper to start. Conclude lab by having teams share data and observations.

TEACHING THE ACTIVITY

Troubleshooting: Prior to class, prepare and label paper strips and put handles on cups.
► If sand is poured too rapidly, the paper may give way suddenly and cause spills.
► When paper starts to tear it will continue without significant addition of force.
► The acceleration of gravity number could be rounded off to 10 to make math easier.
► Students should be allowed to practice on two or three paper strips.
► Teams can be expected to measure strength of two or three types of paper each.

PROGRAM RESOURCES
From the **Teacher Resource Package** use:

Activity Worksheets, pages 24-25, Activity 3-2: Balancing Forces Against Gravity.

ACTIVITY 3-2
Balancing Forces Against Gravity

Problem: *How can gravity be used to test the strength of a material?*

Materials
- selection of paper strips
- scissors
- masking tape
- plastic cup
- string
- sand, 250 mL
- beaker
- balance
- ring stand and ring

Procedure
1. Prepare a data table with the headings "sample," "mass of sand," and "weight of sand."
2. Place the ring stand as shown. Select a paper strip and record its identity in the data table. Cut the strip as shown. Tape one side of the strip to the ring and tape the other side to the handle of the cup as shown.
3. *Slowly* pour sand into the cup. When the paper strip *begins* to tear, stop pouring.
4. Use the balance to measure the combined mass of the cup and sand. Record this measurement and return the sand to its container.
5. Repeat Steps 3, 4, and 5 using different paper strips.
6. Using the formula below, calculate the weights of the cup and sand for each paper strip tested. Record these weights.

$$\text{Weight} = \frac{\text{mass of sample in g}}{1000 \text{ g/kg}} \times 9.80 \text{ N/kg}$$

Data and Observations   Sample Data

Sample	Mass of Sand (g)	Weight of Sand (N)
a	85	0.83
b	44	0.43
c	82	0.80

Analyze
1. The ability of a material to resist tearing is called shear strength. What did this investigation show about the shear strengths of different types of paper?
2. Why would it be incorrect to refer to shear strength in grams or kilograms?

Conclude and Apply
3. This investigation tests the shear strength of each paper sample in one direction only. How could you find out if the shear strength of a type of paper depends on the direction in which the paper is torn?
4. Would this investigation work as well if water were used in place of sand?
5. Why is gravity a good choice of force to use for measuring the strength of different materials?

ANSWERS TO QUESTIONS
1. Each kind of paper has its own shear strength. (Some are several times stronger than others.)
2. Kilogram is a mass measurement. Shear strength is resistance to force.
3. Using samples of the same papers, repeat the investigation, tearing the papers at an angle of 90° to the direction tested the first time.
4. Anything that adds weight will work.
5. Gravity is a uniform force. The experiment is repeatable anywhere on Earth.

SUMMARY

3-1: Describing Motion
1. Motion is a change in position of a body. Speed is the rate at which a body changes position.
2. Average speed, which is the ratio of distance traveled to travel time, describes the motion of a body, even if its speed is not constant.
3. A distance-time graph is a visual representation of the motion of an object throughout a travel period.

3-2: Velocity and Acceleration
1. Velocity describes the speed and direction of a moving body. A change in velocity may be a change in speed, direction, or both.
2. Acceleration is the rate of change in the velocity. It is calculated by dividing change in velocity by the time interval involved.

3-3: Science and Society: Crashing to Save Lives
1. Researchers conduct crash tests on automobiles. Crash test results are used to design safer vehicles and safety devices for occupants.
2. Some people believe that seat belts should be required by law, others don't. Seat belts have been proven to save lives.

3-4: Force and Motion
1. A force is a push or a pull one body exerts on another body. Balanced forces acting on a body do not change the motion of the body. Unbalanced forces result in a net force, which always changes the motion of a body.
2. Inertia is the tendency of a body to resist any change in its motion.
3. Friction is a force that opposes motion between two surfaces that are touching.
4. Newton's first law says that the motion of an object will not change unless a net force acts on the object.

3-5: Effects of Gravity
1. Gravity is the force of attraction that exists between any two bodies in the universe.
2. Weight is a measure of the force of gravity between two objects. The term *weight* is most often used in reference to the gravitational force between Earth and a body at Earth's surface.
3. A force can be measured by determining the change it produces in a material, such as a rubber band or a steel spring.

KEY SCIENCE WORDS

a. **acceleration**
b. **average speed**
c. **balanced forces**
d. **constant speed**
e. **force**
f. **friction**
g. **gravity**
h. **inertia**
i. **instantaneous speed**
j. **net force**
k. **speed**
l. **velocity**
m. **weight**

UNDERSTANDING VOCABULARY

Match each phrase with the correct term from the list of Key Science Words.

1. rate of change in position
2. speed that does not change
3. rate of change in velocity
4. a push or pull exerted on an object
5. type of force that changes the motion of an object
6. tendency of an object to resist change in motion
7. a force that opposes motion between surfaces
8. force exerted by every object in the universe on every other object
9. measure of the force of gravity on an object
10. rate of motion at a given point in time

MOVING OBJECTS **79**

SUMMARY

Have students read the summary statements to review the major concepts of the chapter.

UNDERSTANDING VOCABULARY

1. k
2. d
3. a
4. e
5. j
6. h
7. f
8. g
9. m
10. i

OPTIONS

ASSESSMENT

To assess student understanding of material in this chapter, use the resources listed.

COOPERATIVE LEARNING
Consider using cooperative learning in the THINK AND WRITE CRITICALLY, APPLY, and MORE SKILL BUILDERS sections of the Chapter Review.

PROGRAM RESOURCES

From the **Teacher Resource Package** use:
Chapter Review, pages 9-10.
Chapter and Unit Tests, pages 20-23, Chapter Test.

CHECKING CONCEPTS

1. a	6. a
2. b	7. b
3. b	8. c
4. b	9. b
5. d	10. d

UNDERSTANDING CONCEPTS

11. force
12. weight
13. instantaneous
14. inertia
15. Balanced

THINK AND WRITE CRITICALLY

16. An object has moved if its position relative to a reference point has changed. To calculate its speed, you would need to know the distance it moved and the amount of time it took to move that distance. To determine its velocity, you need to know the direction in which it traveled.

17. Any change in the speed and/or direction of a moving object is accelerated motion. So, if the car changes direction by turning a corner, the car is accelerating, even if its speed does not change.

18. Friction is a net force because it acts on a body to change its motion. Friction is usually not balanced because no other force is present to off-set it.

19. Weight is a measure of the force of gravity on a body. The more mass a body has, the more it will weigh. Mass and weight differ in that the mass of a body never changes due to its position. The weight of a body is not constant; it varies with location. The weight of a body depends upon the distance of the body from Earth.

20. Inertia resists any change in motion. Because of its inertia, a body at rest tends to remain at rest, and a body in motion tends to keep moving in a straight line at a constant velocity.

CHAPTER
REVIEW

CHECKING CONCEPTS

Choose the word or phrase that completes the sentence or answers the question.

1. The best way to describe the rate of motion of an object that changes speed several times is to calculate the object's _____.
   a. average speed   c. instantaneous speed
   b. constant speed   d. variable speed

2. Which of the following is a force?
   a. inertia   c. acceleration
   b. friction   d. velocity

3. The unit for _____ is m/s^2.
   a. weight   c. inertia
   b. acceleration   d. gravity

4. Which of the following is not used in calculating acceleration?
   a. initial velocity   c. time interval
   b. average speed   d. final velocity

5. A body accelerates if it _____.
   a. speeds up   c. changes direction
   b. slows down   d. all of these

6. The gravitational force between two objects depends on their _____.
   a. masses   c. shapes
   b. velocities   d. volume

7. _____ opposes motion.
   a. Inertia   c. Gravity
   b. Friction   d. A net force

8. The weight of an object is directly related to its _____.
   a. volume   c. mass
   b. velocity   d. shape

9. Compared to an object of small mass, an object of large mass has _____.
   a. less inertia   c. less weight
   b. more inertia   d. greater acceleration

10. If the velocity of an object is constant, its acceleration is _____.
    a. positive   c. increasing
    b. negative   d. zero

UNDERSTANDING CONCEPTS

Complete each sentence.

11. The SI unit for _____ is the newton.
12. Your _____ on the moon would be less than it is on Earth.
13. The speedometer on a car indicates _____ speed.
14. Newton's first law is called the law of _____.
15. _____ forces acting on an object do not cause any change in its motion.

THINK AND WRITE CRITICALLY

16. How can you tell an object has moved if you do not see its motion? What information would you need to calculate the object's speed? Its velocity?
17. Explain how it is possible for an automobile traveling at constant speed to be accelerating.
18. Explain why friction is a net force.
19. How are mass and weight similar? How are they different?
20. Describe some common effects of inertia.

APPLY

21. Explain why an object can lose weight without losing mass, but it cannot lose mass without losing weight.
22. A cyclist must travel 800 kilometers. How many days will the trip take if the cyclist travels at an average speed of 16 km/h?
23. At 1:00 PM, a satellite's velocity is 30 000 m/s. At 1:01 PM, its velocity is 15 000 m/s. What is the satellite's acceleration during this time interval?
24. A cyclist leaves home and rides due east for a distance of 45 kilometers. She returns home on the same bike path. If the entire trip takes 4 hours, what is her average speed?

APPLY

21. An object can lose weight simply by changing location—by moving farther from Earth. The mass of the object is not affected. The only way an object can lose mass is for some matter to be removed from it. When this happens, the object also loses weight, because weight depends on mass.

22. Known information: distance = 800 km; speed = 16 km/h
Unknown information: Time in days
Formula to use: $t = d/v$
Solution: t = 800 km/16 km/h
            = 50 h
            = 2 days, 2 hours

23. Known information:
v_i = 30 000 m/s; v_f = 15 000 m/s
time interval = 1 minute or 60 s
Unknown information: acceleration
Formula to use: $a = v_f - v_i/t$
Solution:
   a = (15 000 m/s – 30 000 m/s)/60s
      = –250 m/s^2

24. Known information:
distance = 90 km; time = 4 h
Unknown information: average speed
Formula to use: $v = d/t$
Solution: v = 90 km/4 h = 22.5 km/h

25. The return trip of the cyclist in Question 24 took 30 minutes longer than her trip east. What was her velocity in each direction?

MORE SKILL BUILDERS

If you need help, refer to the Skill Handbook.

1. **Measuring in SI:** Which of the following represents the greatest speed: 20 m/s, 200 cm/s, or 0.2 km/s? HINT: Express all three in meters/second and then compare them.

2. **Observing and Inferring:** A car sits motionless on a hill. What two major forces are acting on the car? Are the forces balanced or unbalanced? Explain how you inferred your answers.

3. **Making and Using Tables:** The four cars shown in the table were traveling at the same speed and the brakes were applied in all four cars at the same instant.

Car	Mass	Stopping Distance
A	1000 kg	80 m
B	1250 kg	100 m
C	1500 kg	120 m
D	2000 kg	160 m

From the data in the table, what is the relationship between the mass of a car and its stopping distance? How do you account for this relationship?

4. **Making and Using Graphs:** The following data were obtained for two runners.

SALLY		ALONZO	
Distance	Time	Distance	Time
2 m	1 s	1 m	1 s
4 m	2 s	2 m	2 s
6 m	3 s	2 m	3 s
8 m	4 s	4 m	4 s

Make a distance-time graph that shows the motion of both runners. What is the average speed of each runner? What is the instantaneous speed of each runner 1 second after they start? Which runner stops briefly? During what time interval do Sally and Alonzo run at the same speed?

5. **Making and Using Graphs:** Study this acceleration graph.

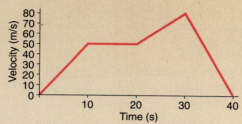

What is the acceleration of the object between 0 seconds and 10 seconds? Between 30 and 40 seconds? When is the object not accelerating? What is its speed during that interval? During what interval does the object have negative acceleration?

PROJECTS

1. Look up the mass of the sun, Earth's moon, and each planet in the solar system. Make a poster to share this information with your classmates. Include some information about conditions on each of the bodies. Speculate what your weight might be on each of the planets if they were the same size as Earth. Discuss how conditions might affect the motion of objects on and near the surface of each planet.

2. Write a letter to your state representative explaining your position on whether or not there should be a law requiring the use of safety belts in cars. Be sure to use scientific facts to support your position.

---

5. **Making and Using Graphs:** acceleration between 0 s and 10 s =

$$a = \frac{v_2 - v_i}{t} = \frac{50 \text{ m/s} - 0 \text{ m/s}}{10 \text{ s}} = \frac{50 \text{ m/s}}{10 \text{ s}}$$
$$= 5 \text{ m/s}^2$$

acceleration between 30 s and 40 s =

$$a = \frac{v_2 - v_i}{t} = \frac{0 \text{ m/s} - 80 \text{ m/s}}{10 \text{ s}} = \frac{-80 \text{ m/s}}{10 \text{ s}}$$
$$= -8 \text{ m/s}^2$$

The object is not accelerating between 10 s and 20 s. Its velocity is constant at 50 m/s. The object has negative acceleration between 30 s and 40 s.

---

25. trip west – 2.25 h; trip east – 1.75 h
v = 45 km/1.75 h = 30 km/h east
v = 45 km/2.25 h = 20 km/h west

MORE SKILL BUILDERS

1. **Measuring in SI:** In meters/second, the three speeds are: 20 m/s, 2 m/s, and 200 m/s. The third speed— 0.2 km/s—represents the greatest speed.

2. **Observing and Inferring:** The two major forces acting on the car are gravity and friction. Gravity tends to pull the car down the hill, friction of the hand brake tends to prevent the car from rolling down the hill. Since the car is at rest, there is no net force acting on it. Thus, the logical inference is that the force tending to pull the car down the hill is exactly balanced by the force of friction.

3. **Making and Using Tables:** The greater the mass of the car, the greater its stopping distance. The greater the mass of the car, the greater its inertia, and therefore, the more difficult it will be to change the motion of the car and bring it to rest. Assuming equal braking force is applied to each car, the most massive car, D, will take the greatest amount of time to come to rest, and will therefore travel the greatest distance.

4. **Making and Using Graphs:**

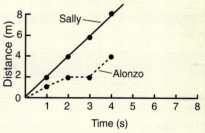

Average speed:
Sally, 8 m/4 s = 2 m/s
Alonzo, 4 m/4 s = 1 m/s
Instantaneous speed:
Sally, 2 m/1 s = 2 m/s
Alonzo, 1 m/1 s = 1 m/s
Alonzo stops briefly after 2 seconds for a 1-s period. Between 3 and 4 seconds the two runners have the same speed, 2 m/s. This can be seen by noting the identical slopes of the graphs during this interval, or it can be calculated by noting the distance traveled by each runner during that period.

4 Acceleration and Momentum

CHAPTER SECTION	OBJECTIVES	ACTIVITIES
4-1 Accelerated Motion (1 day)	**1. Explain** how force, mass, and acceleration are related. **2. Compare** the rates at which different objects fall. **3. Observe** the effects of air resistance.	**MINI-Lab:** *How does mass affect acceleration due to gravity?* p. 87
4-2 Projectile and Circular Motion (2 days)	**1. Explain** why things that are thrown or shot follow a curved path. **2. Compare** motion in a straight line with circular motion. **3. Define** weightlessness.	**Activity 4-1:** *Trajectories,* p. 95
4-3 To Boldly—and Safely—Go Science & Society (1 day)	**1. Analyze** the advantages and disadvantages of exposing astronauts to weightlessness. **2. Draw conclusions** about the safety of space travel.	
4-4 Action and Reaction (2 days)	**1. Analyze** action and reaction forces. **2. Calculate** momentum. **3. Explain** conservation and momentum.	**Activity 4-2:** *Momentum,* p. 104
Chapter Review		

ACTIVITY MATERIALS			
FIND OUT	**ACTIVITIES**		**MINI-LABS**
Page 83 balloons	**4-1 Trajectories, p. 95** stick or dowel, slightly more than 2 m long meterstick string or thread 10 corks 10 thumbtacks felt-tip pen	**4-2 Momentum, p. 104** 2 dynamic carts long rubber band 2 building bricks meterstick masking tape	**How does mass affect acceleration due to gravity? p. 87** small toy truck masses 2 large rubber bands

CHAPTER FEATURES	TEACHER RESOURCE PACKAGE	OTHER RESOURCES
Skill Builder: *Comparing and Contrasting*, p. 89	**Ability Level Worksheets** ◆ **Study Guide,** p. 18 ● **Reinforcement,** p. 18 ▲ **Enrichment,** p. 18 **MINI-Lab Worksheet,** p. 37	
Technology: *Scary Physics*, p. 93 **Skill Builder:** *Making and Using Tables*, p. 94	**Ability Level Worksheets** ◆ **Study Guide,** p. 19 ● **Reinforcement,** p. 19 ▲ **Enrichment,** p. 19 **Activity Worksheet,** pp. 31, 32 **Concept Mapping,** pp. 13, 14 **Transparency Masters,** pp. 13, 14	**Color Transparency 7,** Motion of a Projectile
You Decide! p. 97	**Ability Level Worksheets** ◆ **Study Guide,** p. 20 ● **Reinforcement,** p. 20 ▲ **Enrichment,** p. 20	
Problem Solving: *The Icy Challenge*, p. 102 **Skill Builder:** *Concept Mapping*, p. 103	**Ability Level Worksheets** ◆ **Study Guide,** p. 21 ● **Reinforcement,** p. 21 ▲ **Enrichment,** p. 21 **Activity Worksheet,** pp. 33, 34 **Critical Thinking/Problem Solving,** p. 10 **Cross-Curricular Connections,** p. 8 **Science and Society,** p. 8 **Transparency Masters,** pp. 15, 16	**Color Transparency 8,** Newton's Third Law **Lab Manual 6,** Conservation of Momentum **Lab Manual 7,** Velocity and Momentum
Summary Think & Write Critically Key Science Words Apply Understanding Vocabulary More Skill Builders Checking Concepts Projects Understanding Concepts	**Chapter Review,** pp. 11, 12 **Chapter Test,** pp. 24–27	**Chapter Review Software** **Test Bank**

◆ **Basic**   ● **Average**   ▲ **Advanced**

ADDITIONAL MATERIALS

SOFTWARE	AUDIOVISUAL	BOOKS/MAGAZINES
Physics—Free Fall, Educational Courseware. *Newton's Laws*, J&S Software. *Sir Isaac Newton's Games*, Sunburst.	*Projectile Motion*, film, EME. *Mr. Wizard's World: Action and Reaction*, video, Macmillan/McGraw-Hill School Division. *Let's Move It: Newton's Laws of Motion*, video, Focus. *Newton's Laws of Motion: Demonstrations of Mass, Force, and Momentum*, laserdisc, AIMS Media.	Morecki, A. *Biomechanics of Motion.* New York: Springer-Verlag Inc., 1981. Radetsky, Peter, "The Man Who Mastered Motion" *Science 86*, May, 1986, pp. 52-60.

THEME DEVELOPMENT: The theme of patterns of change is continued in this chapter. Newton established his three laws of motion by considering common patterns of changes in all motion. These laws can be used to analyze and predict changes in the motion of objects. The importance of having only three laws to explain the motion of almost all objects should be stressed in each section.

CHAPTER OVERVIEW

▶ **Section 4-1:** This section develops Newton's second law of motion. Falling objects and the effects of air resistance on their motion are discussed.

▶ **Section 4-2:** Concepts of projectile motion and circular motion are developed in this section. Centripetal acceleration and force are introduced and weightlessness is discussed.

▶ **Section 4-3: Science and Society:** The effects of long periods of weightlessness on astronauts are presented. Students are asked to weigh the advantages and disadvantages of sending humans on long space voyages.

▶ **Section 4-4:** Newton's third law of motion is presented with a discussion of momentum and the law of conservation of momentum.

CHAPTER VOCABULARY

Newton's second law of motion
air resistance
terminal velocity
projectile
centripetal acceleration
conservation of momentum
centripetal force
isometric exercise
Newton's third law of motion
momentum

CHAPTER

4 Acceleration and Momentum

82

OPTIONS

⚡ For Your Gifted Students

▶ Have students test the effect of air pressure on a projectile. They can make a projectile by taping a straw to an inflated balloon and feeding fishing line through the straw. Have the students string the line across the room. After the projectile has traveled across the string, students should measure the distance covered. Air pressure should remain constant as other variables are introduced. Have students add a notecard to the front of the projectile. They can vary the shape of the card, hypothesizing the effect of the design on the speed and distance covered.

The force of gravity acts on this sky diver, causing him to accelerate toward Earth. A second force acting on the diver allows him to change speed and direction as he falls. What do you think this second force is?

FIND OUT!

Do this activity to find out what determines how a balloon moves.

Drop an uninflated balloon from shoulder level. What does it do? Now, blow up the balloon, but don't tie it closed. Again, hold the balloon at shoulder level and let it go. What happens to it? Does it fall to the ground right away?

Next, blow up the balloon, tie it closed, and drop it from shoulder level. How is its motion different from its motion in the first two trials? If you keep batting the balloon with your hand, can you keep it from touching the floor?

Gearing Up

Previewing the Chapter

Use this outline to help you focus on important ideas in this chapter.

Section 4-1   Accelerated Motion
► Newton's Second Law
► Falling Objects
► Terminal Velocity

Section 4-2   Projectile and Circular Motion
► Projectiles
► Moving in Circles
► Weightlessness in Orbit

Section 4-3   Science and Society
To Boldly—and Safely—Go
► Effects of Weightlessness

Section 4-4   Action and Reaction
► Newton's Third Law
► Rocket Propulsion
► Momentum

Previewing Science Skills

► In the Skill Builders, you will design an experiment, make and use tables, and make a concept map
► In the Activities, you will observe, collect and organize data, and analyze.
► In the MINI-Lab, you will construct models, observe and infer, and hypothesize.

What's next?

Now that you know that conditions can cause the motion of an object to vary, find out what some of those conditions are. You can also learn how outside forces can affect the motion of an object.

83

INTRODUCING THE CHAPTER

Use the Find Out activity to introduce students to the motion of falling objects. Tell them that they will learn how objects fall and what all falling objects have in common as they read this chapter.

FIND OUT!

Preparation: Obtain one balloon for each student.
Materials: balloons
Cooperative Learning: Assign Problem Solving teams to investigate if the shape of an inflated and tied off balloon affects the way if falls.
Teaching Tips
► You may wish to do this activity out of doors or in a hallway to allow students to observe the motions of the balloons more easily.
► Have students carefully note the changes in motion when (1) a falling balloon is tapped upward, (2) a falling balloon is tapped downward, (3) a falling balloon is tapped sideways, (4) a rising balloon is tapped upward, (5) a rising balloon is tapped downward, (6) a rising balloon is tapped sideways, (7) a balloon resting in one hand is tapped sideways.
► Allow students to discuss their observations and then compare and contrast the above changes.

Gearing Up

Have students study the Gearing Up feature to familiarize themselves with the chapter. Discuss the relationships of the topics in the outline.

What's Next?

Before beginning the first section, make sure students understand the connection between the Find Out activity and the topics to follow.

PREPARATION

SECTION BACKGROUND

▶ Newton's first law describes the motion of an object on which there were either no forces or balanced forces acting in the direction of its motion. Newton's second law describes the *effect* on an object's motion while there is a net force acting on it. In metric units, the unit of force is a newton and is defined as the force necessary to produce an acceleration of one meter per second per second on an object with a mass of one kilogram. That is, $1 \text{ N} = 1 \text{ kg} \cdot \text{m/s}^2$.

▶ Because of gravitational attraction, an object near Earth's surface falls with an acceleration of about 9.8 m/s^2 in a vacuum. However, the observed acceleration of an object is usually less because of the effects of air resistance.

PREPLANNING

▶ Obtain a Ping Pong ball for the motivation demonstration; a soccer ball, a golf ball, and two flexible plastic rulers for the Reteach demonstration on page 85; 7 metal washers and fishing tackle for the demonstration on page 87; a large bottle of liquid dishwashing soap or shampoo and a marble for the demonstration on page 89.

1 MOTIVATE

▶ **Demonstration:** Make a slingshot using a rubber band and two fingers. Use it to accelerate a Ping Pong ball across a table top. Ask students to hypothesize how the change in motion of the Ping Pong ball would be affected by the stretch of the rubber band or how it would be affected if a stiffer, thicker rubber band were used.

TYING TO PREVIOUS
KNOWLEDGE: Have students recall the weight of a kilogram on Earth's surface from Section 3-5. Tell them that they will learn why this is so in this section.

New Science Words

Newton's second law of motion
air resistance
terminal velocity

Objectives

▶ Explain how force, mass, and acceleration are related.
▶ Compare the rates at which different objects fall.
▶ Observe the effects of air resistance.

Newton's Second Law

With Newton's first law, you learned how to describe the motion of a speeding sports car or a stationary hockey puck. You also learned that the motion of an object will not change unless a net force acts on it, such as the brakes of a car or a fast-moving hockey stick. As you read on in this chapter, you will find out some of the reasons why things move the ways they do.

Suppose you are a passenger in a car stalled on the tracks at a railroad crossing. It is threatening to rain at any minute, and you want to push the car off the tracks before you get soaked. Would you rather be riding in a compact car or a stretch limousine? Would you rather

Figure 4-1. The two men want to get the car off the tracks as quickly as possible. What two factors will determine how fast they can push the car?

OPTIONS

Meeting Different Ability Levels

For Section 4-1, use the following **Teacher Resource Masters** depending upon individual students' needs.

◆ **Study Guide Master** for all students.

● **Reinforcement Master** for students of average and above average ability levels.

▲ **Enrichment Master** for above average students.

Additional Teacher Resource Package masters are listed in the OPTIONS box throughout the section. The additional masters are appropriate for all students.

◆ **STUDY GUIDE** 18

STUDY GUIDE   Chapter 4
Accelerated Motion   Text Pages 84–89

Solve the puzzle below by writing the term in the diagram that best completes each statement. You will find an other term spelled vertically in the black box.

1.   M A S S
2.   S E C O N D
3.   B A L A N C E D
4.   N E W T O N
5.   F A L L I N G
6.   W E I G H T
7.   L A R G E R
8.   A I R R E S I S T A N C E
9.   G R A V I T Y
10.   M O T I O N
11.   F O R C E
12.   T E R M I N A L

1. Force equals _____ times acceleration.
2. Newton's _____ law of motion states that a net force acting on an object causes the object to accelerate in the direction of the force.
3. The law of inertia states that when the forces acting upon an object are _____, the motion of the object will not change.
4. The unit of force is the _____.
5. Gravity causes _____ objects to accelerate.
6. The force of gravity upon the mass of an object is the object's _____.
7. The _____ the force acting on an object, the greater the acceleration of the object.
8. The force air exerts on a moving object is _____. (2 words)
9. Weight is a measure of the force of _____.
10. Any change in an object's position is _____.
11. In the equation $F = m \times a$, F stands for _____.
12. The highest velocity reached by a falling object is its _____ velocity.

Fill in the blank below with the term in the black box.

Force equals ____acceleration____ times mass.

18   Copyright Glencoe Division of Macmillan/McGraw-Hill

the driver be about as strong as you or a weightlifting champion?

From experience, you know that mass, force, and acceleration are somehow related. You may not realize it, but in arriving at your answers to the questions, you used Newton's second law of motion. 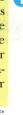 **Newton's second law of motion** says that a net force acting on an object causes the object to accelerate in the direction of the force. The acceleration of the object is affected by two factors—the size of the force and the mass of the object. The larger the force acting on an object, the greater the acceleration of the object. The larger an object's mass, the greater the force needed to give it the same acceleration.

Think about the stalled car on the tracks. To get the greatest acceleration across the tracks, you'd want to push the smallest mass while exerting the greatest force. So, you'd want to push the compact car, and you'd want the weightlifter to help you exert the strongest force.

Newton's second law can be expressed in equation form as:

$$force = mass \times acceleration$$
$$F = ma$$

Mass is expressed in kilograms and acceleration in m/s^2. Thus, force is expressed in $kg \cdot m/s^2$.

You learned in Chapter 3 that one newton is the standard unit for measuring force. The equation for force can be used to define a newton. A newton is the amount of force needed to give a sample of matter having a mass of 1 kg an acceleration of $1 \ m/s^2$. In other words, $1 \ N = 1 \ kg \cdot m/s^2$.

EXAMPLE PROBLEM: Calculating Force

Problem Statement:

How much force is needed to accelerate a 70-kg rider and the 200-kg motorcycle the rider is on at 4 m/s^2?

Known Information:

Strategy Hint: Remember to combine the masses of the rider and motorcycle.

mass, $m = 70 \ kg + 200 \ kg = 270 \ kg$
acceleration, $a = 4 \ m/s^2$

Unknown Information:

force (F)

Equation to Use:

$F = m \times a$

Solution:

$F = m \times a = 270 \ kg \times 4 \ m/s^2$
$= 1080 \ kg \cdot m/s^2 = 1080 \ N$

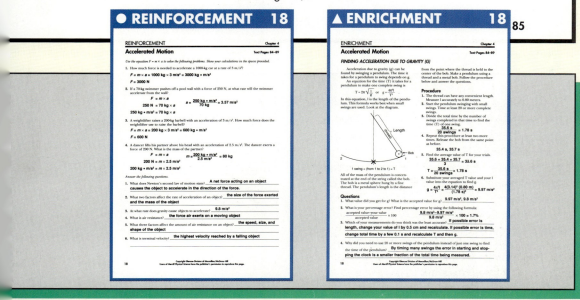

85

2 TEACH

Key Concepts are highlighted.

CONCEPT DEVELOPMENT

▶ Discuss the motivation demonstration using Newton's second law. Have students explain the motion of the dragster's car mentioned on pages 65 and 66 using this law.

CHECK FOR UNDERSTANDING

Use the Mini Quiz to check for understanding.

MINI QUIZ

Use the Mini Quiz to check students' recall of chapter content.

1. **State Newton's second law of motion in words and as an equation.** *A net force acting on an object will cause the object to accelerate in the direction of the force; F = ma.*

2. **Define one newton of force.** *the amount of force needed to give a mass of 1 kg an acceleration of 1 m/s²*

RETEACH

Demonstration: Show how mass affects acceleration with a constant force. Place a flexed ruler next to a golf ball and release the ruler. Have students observe the motion of the ball. Show how force affects acceleration with constant mass. Place a flexed ruler next to a golf ball and release it. Repeat the demonstration by using two flexed rulers taped together. Have students compare the accelerations and the forces.

EXTENSION

For students who have mastered this section, use the **Reinforcement** and **Enrichment** masters or other OPTIONS provided.

PRACTICE PROBLEM ANSWERS

1. $F = m \times a$
   $= (1000 \text{ kg} + 160 \text{ kg}) \times 3 \text{ m/s}^2$
   $= 3480 \text{ N}$

2. $F = m \times a$
   $a = \dfrac{F}{m}$

   $kg = \dfrac{300 \text{ N}}{63 \text{ kg}} = \dfrac{300 \text{ kg} \cdot \text{m/s}^2}{63 \text{ kg}}$
   $= 4.76 \text{ m/s}^2$

CONCEPT DEVELOPMENT

▶ Make sure students realize that a falling object doesn't fall *fast*, it continually falls *faster*. Have students think of the difference in the feelings they would have in their hands catching a flower pot that fell from a first-floor balcony and one that fell from a twelfth-floor balcony.

▶ The acceleration of gravity varies with location on Earth's surface. Its value increases slightly with latitude (because of Earth's rotation) and decreases with altitude. However, the variation is only about 0.3 percent at the most—hardly a motivation to move to lose weight.

▶ The table below illustrates the relationship between the time during which an object falls, its final speed, and the distance it has fallen from rest.

Time (s)	Final Speed (m/s)	Distance (m)
0.1	1	0.05
0.5	5	0.3
1.0	10	5
2.0	20	20
3.0	30	45

PRACTICE PROBLEMS

Strategy Hint: What units combine to make a newton?

Strategy Hint: Rearrange the equation.

1. It takes a force of 3000 N to accelerate an empty 1000-kg car at 3 m/s². If a 160-kg wrestler is inside the car, how much force will be needed to produce the same acceleration?

2. A 63-kg skater pushes off from a wall with a force of 300 N. What is the skater's acceleration?

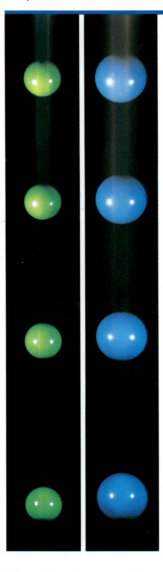

Falling Objects

You may find this hard to believe, but if you dropped a bowling ball and a marble from a bridge at the same time, they'd both splash into the water at almost the same instant. (As you read further, you'll find out why they don't hit the water at exactly the same instant.) As the two objects fall through the air, their accelerations would be just about the same. Would you have expected the bowling ball to hit the water sooner because it has more mass? Think about that. It's true that the force of gravity would be greater on the bowling ball because of its larger mass. But the larger mass also gives the bowling ball more inertia, so more force is needed to change its velocity. The marble has a much smaller mass than the bowling ball, but its inertia also is much less. Figure 4-2 shows the motion of two balls frozen by high-speed photography. The blue ball is more massive than the green one, but you can see that they fall at the same rate.

Near Earth's surface, gravity causes all falling objects to accelerate at a rate of 9.8 m/s². Does this number 9.8 seem familiar? When you studied the relationship between mass and weight, you learned that any sample of matter having a mass of one kilogram weighs 9.8 newtons on Earth. Now you'll find out why.

The weight of an object is the force of gravity acting on its mass. Any force can be calculated using the equation $F = m \times a$. Because weight is a force, we can substitute W for F and write $W = m \times a$. If acceleration due to gravity is 9.8 m/s², then $W = m \times 9.8 \text{ m/s}^2$. So a mass of 1 kg weighs 9.8 kg · m/s², or 9.8 newtons. You could calculate your weight in newtons if you knew your mass. For example, a person with a mass of 50 kg would have a weight of 490 newtons.

Figure 4-2. As the photograph shows, the rate of acceleration of a falling body is not affected by the mass of the body.

OPTIONS

INQUIRY QUESTIONS

▶ What is the difference in the forces on a bat used to hit a home run and to bunt a baseball? How does the baseball react in each situation? How can you explain this phenomenon in terms of Newton's second law of motion? *The force of the bat on the ball is less in a bunt than in a hit. Thus, the ball undergoes less of an acceleration and it moves away at a slower speed than a ball which is hit.*

Acceleration due to gravity (*g*) is the same for all objects, regardless of mass. This means that if no force other than gravity is present, all samples of matter fall at the same rate—9.8 m/s². Think about that for a minute. Does a leaf fall as fast as an acorn? Does a feather fall as fast as a penny?

Suppose you took two identical sheets of paper, crumpled one into a tight ball, and dropped both sheets from a balcony at the same time? What would happen? If your answer is that the crumpled ball of paper would fall faster than the flat sheet of paper, you are correct. But this behavior does not agree with what you've just learned about falling objects near Earth's surface. How can this disagreement be explained?

Figure 4-3. Some force other than gravity must affect the flat sheet of paper, causing it to fall more slowly than the crumpled sheet of paper.

MINI-Lab

How does mass affect acceleration due to gravity?

With a small toy truck, some masses, and two large rubber bands, you can make a model of the force of gravity. Attach one rubber band to the truck and pull the truck back until the rubber band is fully stretched. Release the truck and let the force of the rubber band accelerate the truck across the table top. Now place masses in the truck to double its mass. Stretch the rubber band the same distance as before and release the truck. What happens to the acceleration of the truck? Double the force by attaching a second rubber band beside the first one. Repeat the procedure. What do the rubber bands represent in this model? Why did you add a second rubber band?

CONCEPT DEVELOPMENT

▶ **Demonstration:** Securely attach a metal washer at each of the following positions along a 2.0-m length of fishing line: 0 cm, 5 cm, 20 cm, 80 cm, 125 cm, and 180 cm. Drop a washer into a metal trash can to focus the students' attention. Now hold the string at the 2-m end as high as possible over a metal waste can or a metal cake pan. Have students discuss what they would hear if the string of washers fell at a constant speed. (An increasing interval between the clicks of the washers striking the metal can.) Release the string. Have students discuss why the regular interval between clicks indicated that the string of washers had a constant acceleration. (The constant time interval between the washers striking the can indicated that successive washers were striking the can at higher speeds. They had to fall greater distances in the same time interval because of their location on the string. The increasing velocity supports the notion of a constant acceleration.)

TEACHER F.Y.I.

▶ The relationship between the distance an object falls from rest and the time that it has fallen, is given by the equation $d = 1/2 \, gt^2$, where *g* represents the value of the acceleration of gravity. The equation indicates that an object that has fallen for 2 seconds will fall 4 times as far as one that has fallen only one second.

MINI-Lab

Materials: small toy truck, 2 long rubber bands, assorted masses

Teaching Tips

▶ Once the rubber band is stretched, it should be allowed to do all the pulling. The amount of stretching should be the same each time.

Answers to Questions

▶ There is less acceleration when you double the mass of the truck.

▶ The rubber bands represent force.

▶ A second rubber band was added to increase the force.

INQUIRY QUESTIONS

▶ A force of 10 N is needed to produce an acceleration of 2.0 m/s² on a 3.0-kg wooden block sliding across a table. **What is the force of friction acting on the sliding block? What is its direction?** *The net force on the block is 6 N, 3 kg × 2 m/s². The difference between the 10 N acting on the block and the net force of 6 N, must be the force of friction. Thus, the force of friction is 4 N. It is acting in the direction opposite the direction in which the block is moving.*

PROGRAM RESOURCES

From the **Teacher Resource Package** use:

Activity Worksheets, page 37, Mini-Lab: How does mass affect acceleration due to gravity?

Figure 4-4. The Frisbee is designed to use air resistance to help it soar and maneuver as it moves through the air.

Gravity accelerates all samples of matter at the same rate. So, the only explanation for the behavior of the two sheets of paper is that some force is at work in addition to gravity. Anything that moves in Earth's atmosphere is affected by air resistance. **Air resistance** is the force air exerts on a moving object. This force acts in the opposite direction to that in which the object is moving. In the case of a falling object, air resistance pushes up as gravity pulls down.

The amount of air resistance on an object depends on the speed, size, and shape of the object. The larger the

Figure 4-5. The snowflakes (left) and the hailstones (right) are both solid forms of water. Yet, because of differences in shape and size, snowflakes tend to drift and blow through the air, while hailstones fall straight to the ground.

88   ACCELERATION AND MOMENTUM

object, the greater the amount of air resistance on it. This is why feathers, leaves, and sheets of paper fall more slowly than acorns, pennies, and crumpled balls of paper. Now think back to the example of the bowling ball and marble dropped from a bridge. Recall that they don't fall at exactly the same rate. Which do you think hits the water first?

Terminal Velocity

As an object falls, air resistance gradually increases until it equals the pull of gravity. When this happens, the two forces are balanced. According to the law of inertia, when the forces acting on an object are balanced, the motion of the object will not change. So, the falling object will stop accelerating. It will continue to fall, but at a constant, final velocity. This **terminal velocity** is the highest velocity reached by a falling object.

Think about all of the things you now know about moving objects. You always knew that a leaf fell more slowly than an acorn. But now you know why. And you will learn more about moving things as you continue reading this chapter.

Figure 4-6. Air resistance acts on the parachute, allowing the parachutist to fall at a terminal velocity that is slow enough to allow a safe landing.

SECTION REVIEW

1. A weightlifter raises a 440-kg barbell with an acceleration of 2 m/s². How much force does the weightlifter exert on the barbell?
2. A flower pot falls from the balcony of a 12th-floor apartment. It smashes on the ground 2.5 s later. How fast is it moving just before it hits?
3. **Apply:** Use what you have learned about falling objects, air resistance, and terminal velocity to explain why a person can parachute safely to Earth from a high-flying airplane.

☑ **Comparing and Contrasting**

Find the masses of an uninflated balloon and a balloon filled with air. Drop the two balloons from the same height at the same time and compare and contrast the rates at which they fall. If you need help, refer to Comparing and Contrasting in the **Skill Handbook** on page 679.

Skill Builder

Ask questions 1 and 2 and the **Apply** Question in the Section Review.

RETEACH
Have students measure the distance either of the two balls shown in Figure 4-2 fell between each flash. Make a bar graph showing distance fallen versus flash number. Ask them to explain how this graph supports the idea that the balls are accelerating downward.

EXTENSION
For students who have mastered this section, use the **Reinforcement** and **Enrichment** masters or other OPTIONS provided.

3 CLOSE

▶ Invite members of a local skydiving organization to talk to the students about the preparation and training necessary for skydiving.

SECTION REVIEW ANSWERS
1. Note: The upward acceleration must be added to the acceleration due to gravity, which is already acting.
$F = m \times a$
$= 440$ kg $\times$ (9.8 m/s² + 2 m/s²)
$= 5200$ N
2. $a = \dfrac{v_f - v_i}{t}$ Note: $v_i = 0$
$v_f = a \times t = 9.8$ m/s̸² $\times$ 2.5 s̸
$= 24.5$ m/s
3. **Apply:** Because of the large size and shape of an open parachute, air resistance exerts a large force on it. This force, which acts opposite to the force of gravity, makes the terminal velocity of the parachute slow enough to permit a safe landing on Earth.

Skill Builder
Students should set up an experiment where they can measure the speed at which several different objects fall. Distance should be measured in meters and time in seconds.

INQUIRY QUESTIONS:
▶ Some small insects can fall hundreds of meters and walk away unharmed after hitting the ground. **Can you explain this phenomenon in terms of air resistance and terminal velocity?** *If the insect has a low weight and a relatively large surface area, then air resistance can overcome the force of gravity before the insect reaches a high rate of acceleration. This is its terminal velocity—the highest velocity the falling insect will reach. The insect is falling slowly enough when it lands that it won't be harmed.*

PREPARATION

SECTION BACKGROUND

▶ The motion of a projectile can be explained by considering its vertical and horizontal motions independently. At any instant during its motion, the projectile has a vertical acceleration downward because of its weight and, therefore, a continuously increasing downward velocity. However, since there are no horizontal forces acting on the moving projectile (assuming air resistance is negligible), it has a constant horizontal velocity. The constant horizontal speed and constantly increasing speed downward cause the projectile to follow a curved path called a parabola.

PREPLANNING

▶ Obtain a flexible plastic ruler, a rubber ball, a plastic ruler with a central groove or a tube from a roll of paper towels, and two large matched marbles or ball bearings for demonstrations.

▶ For Activity 4-1, obtain a 2-m dowel or stick, 10 small corks, and 10 thumbtacks for each activity group.

1 MOTIVATE

▶ **Demonstration:** Place a rubber ball at the edge of a table. Gently strike the ball with a slightly flexed plastic ruler so that it falls off the table. Repeat the demonstration flexing the ruler more each time you repeat the demonstration. Have students describe the shape of the curve that the ball makes and ask them when they have seen similar curves.

▶ Have students describe what they would see in a weightless situation such as in an orbiting satellite.

New Science Words

projectile
centripetal acceleration
centripetal force

Objectives

▶ Explain why things that are thrown or shot follow a curved path.
▶ Compare motion in a straight line with circular motion.
▶ Define weightlessness.

Figure 4-7. The fireworks in this photograph illustrate the curved path followed by a projectile.

Projectiles

Have you noticed anything about the moving objects described in this unit so far? Nearly all have been moving in a straight line. But that's not the only kind of motion you know about. Skateboarders wheel around in circles, cars go around hairpin curves, and rockets shoot into the air and curve back to Earth. How do the laws of motion account for these kinds of motion?

If you've ever played darts, thrown a ball, or shot an arrow from a bow, you have probably noticed that the dart, ball, or arrow didn't travel in a straight line. It started off straight, but then curved downward. That's why dart players and archers learn to aim above the targets they're trying to hit.

Anything that's thrown or shot through the air is called a **projectile.** Because of Earth's gravitational pull and their own inertia, projectiles follow a curved path. ❶

Here's why. When you throw a ball, the force from your hand makes the ball move forward. Suppose that it gives the ball *horizontal motion*, that is, motion parallel to Earth's surface. Once you let go of the ball, no other force moves it forward, so it doesn't accelerate in the horizontal direction. Its horizontal velocity is constant. ❷

When you let go of the ball, something else happens as well. Gravity starts pulling it downward, giving it *vertical motion*, or motion perpendicular to Earth's surface. Gravity makes the ball accelerate downward. Now the ball has constant horizontal velocity, but increasing vertical

OPTIONS

Meeting Different Ability Levels

For Section 4-2, use the following **Teacher Resource Masters** depending upon individual students' needs.
◆ **Study Guide Master** for all students.
● **Reinforcement Master** for students of average and above average ability levels.
▲ **Enrichment Master** for above average students.
Additional Teacher Resource Package masters are listed in the OPTIONS box throughout the section. The additional masters are appropriate for all students.

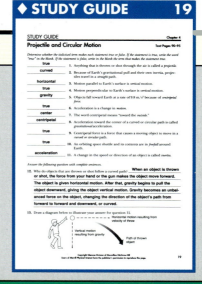

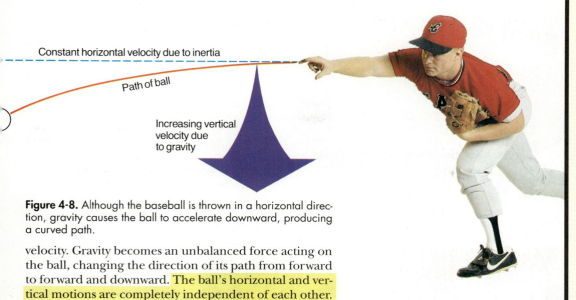

Constant horizontal velocity due to inertia

Path of ball

Increasing vertical velocity due to gravity

Figure 4-8. Although the baseball is thrown in a horizontal direction, gravity causes the ball to accelerate downward, producing a curved path.

velocity. Gravity becomes an unbalanced force acting on the ball, changing the direction of its path from forward to forward and downward. The ball's horizontal and vertical motions are completely independent of each other.

If you throw a ball horizontally from shoulder height, will it take longer to hit the ground than a ball you simply drop from the same height? Surprisingly, the answer is no. Both will hit the ground at the same time. If you have a hard time believing this, Figure 4-9 may help. The two balls have the same acceleration due to gravity, 9.8 m/s² downward.

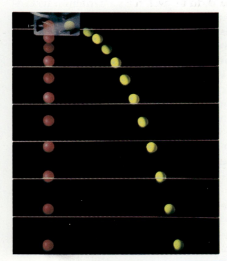

Figure 4-9. The two balls in the photograph were released at the same time. Although one ball has horizontal velocity, gravity causes both balls to accelerate downward at the same rate.

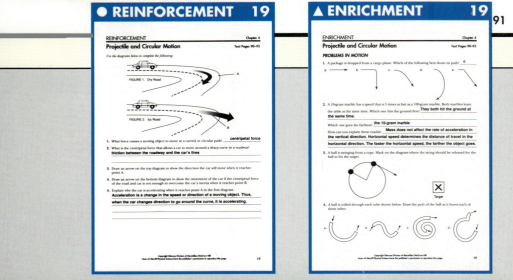

TYING TO PREVIOUS KNOWLEDGE: Have students recall the explanation of the motion of a hockey puck using Newton's first law from Section 3-4 and the motion of a falling ball described in the previous section. Tell them that this lesson will build upon their knowledge to help them explain the motion of an arrow and a pop fly to center field.

OBJECTIVES AND SCIENCE WORDS: Have students review the objectives and science words to become familiar with this section.

2 TEACH

Key Concepts are highlighted.

CONCEPT DEVELOPMENT

▶ **Demonstration:** Rest a marble or steel ball bearing at the edge of a table. Make a ramp from a plastic ruler or from half of a cardboard tube from a roll of paper towels. Place a second ball in the raised end of the ramp so that as the second ball reaches the end of the ramp, it will strike the first ball and both will fall onto the floor. Have the students observe that both balls hit the floor almost simultaneously.

REVEALING MISCONCEPTIONS

▶ Ask students to draw the forces on a ball *immediately after* it is hit by a bat, and have them explain their drawings. Many students will describe three forces: the weight of the ball downward, air resistance opposite to the motion of the ball, and a force causing the ball to continue moving horizontally due to the bat. Point out that the force causing the object to move opposite the bat existed only when the ball was in contact with the bat. Only two forces are acting on the ball.

CONCEPT DEVELOPMENT

▶ Make sure students realize that as an object moves in a circle, the *change* in its direction of motion is always toward the center of the circle while the direction of its motion is always perpendicular to the radius of the circle.

▶ To help students understand the difference, have them visualize moving a very heavy brick along a big circle. Each time they move the brick, they must slide it forward just a little and then twist it a bit so it fits along the circle. The twist, which represents the change in direction of the brick, is always toward the center of the circle. The brick itself is always aligned along the circle itself, which means it is always perpendicular to the radius of the circle.

▶ Students may be familiar with the term *centrifugal force*. Point out that this force appears to be acting outward on an object when viewed by someone moving in a circle with the object. Have students think of sunglasses sliding across the dashboard away from the driver as the car makes a sharp left turn. In reality, the apparent motion away from the center is due to a lack of a sufficiently large centripetal force keeping the object moving in a circle.

CROSS CURRICULUM

▶ **Language Arts:** Have students look up *centripetal* in a dictionary. Students should find that it comes from the Latin roots, *centri* (center) and *petere* (to go seek). Ask a volunteer to explain how the word reflects the meaning of its roots.

Figure 4-10. The chains exert centripetal force on the swings, causing the swings to accelerate toward the center of the ride.

EcoTip

The faster a car goes, the faster it burns fuel. Every day in the United States, cars traveling over the speed limit waste hundreds of liters of gasoline. Encourage drivers you ride with to obey speed limits.

Moving in Circles

Recall that acceleration is a change in velocity. That change may be a change in speed, a change in direction, or both. Now picture a bicycle moving at a constant speed along the westbound straight-away of an oval track. Because its speed is constant in a straight line, the bicycle is not accelerating. However, when the bicycle enters a curve, even if its speed does not change it is accelerating, because its direction is changing.

While the bicycle was moving on the straightaway, its velocity was toward the west. As it entered the curve, it accelerated because the direction of its velocity changed. The change in the direction of the velocity was toward the center of the curve. Acceleration toward the center of a curved or circular path is called **centripetal** (sen TRIHP uh tuhl) **acceleration.** The word *centripetal* means "toward the center."

In order for the bicycle to be accelerating, some unbalanced force must be acting on it in a direction toward the center of the curve. That force is a centripetal force. **Centripetal force** is a force that causes a moving object to move in a curved or circular path.

When a car rounds a sharp curve on a highway, the centripetal force is the friction between the tires and the road surface. But if the road is icy or wet, and the tires lose their grip, the centripetal force may not be enough to overcome the car's inertia. Then, the car would not follow the curve in the road, but would shoot off in a straight line in the direction it was traveling from the spot where it lost traction.

Weightlessness in Orbit

Maybe you've seen pictures of astronauts floating inside the space shuttle, with various pieces of equipment suspended in midair beside them. The astronauts and their belongings are experiencing weightlessness.

OPTIONS

INQUIRY QUESTIONS

▶ Suppose the flower pot mentioned in question 2 of the Section Review on page 89 is thrown sideways with a speed of 1 m/s from the same balcony. **How far from the side of the building will the pot crash?** *2.5 m*

PROGRAM RESOURCES

From the **Teacher Resource Package** use:

Transparency Masters, pages 13-14, Motion of a Projectile.

Concept Mapping, pages 13-14.

Use **Color Transparency** number 7, Motion of a Projectile.

TECHNOLOGY

Scary Physics

A roller coaster applies the laws of motion in an effort to be the scariest ride in the park. A ride begins when a chain drags the cars to the top of the first hill. Once there, the cars have gravitational potential energy. Once the cars are released, acceleration increases until all of the cars are headed downward.

The debate on which seat is the scariest continues to rage, and the answer is, "that depends." As the cars descend, their speed increases. The rear car starts down the slope at a much greater speed than the front car, thus giving the passengers the sense of being hurled over the edge. At the bottom of the hill, it is a different story. When the change in direction from down to up occurs, the front car will be going fastest and its passengers will experience the greater forces. As the cars pop over the top of the hill, the passengers in the rear car may experience a considerable force, resulting in the sensation of being thrown free.

As ride technology improves, roller coasters get larger and faster. The Magnum XL 200 at Cedar Point in Sandusky, Ohio, has a first hill 201 feet high, reaches a speed of 112 km/h, and covers 5106 feet of track in two-and-one-half minutes.

Think Critically: Describe the roller coaster design that would result in the greatest sensations for the passengers.

But to be truly weightless, the astronauts would have to be free from the effects of gravity. Orbiting 400 km above Earth, the shuttle and everything inside it still respond to those effects. In fact, gravity keeps the shuttle in orbit.

So what does it really mean to say that something is weightless in orbit? Think about how the weight of an object is measured. When you place an object on a scale, gravity causes the object to push down on the scale. In turn, the scale "pushes back" on the object with the same force. The dial on the scale measures the amount of upward force needed to offset gravity.

Did You Know?

The pull of gravity differs from place to place on Earth. In the U.S., gravity is greatest in Minot, North Dakota, and smallest in Key West, Florida.

ENRICHMENT

▶ Have students research applications of centripetal force to explain how the spin cycle of a washing machine damp-dries clothing.

TECHNOLOGY

Walker, Jearl. "Thinking about physics while scared to death (on a falling roller coaster)." *Scientific American*, Oct. 1983, pp. 162-169.

▶ Have the students share their scariest roller coaster ride. Have them explain which seat they chose and why.

▶ Diagram a roller coaster ride on the chalkboard. Explain the energetics of the ride on the initial hill, the valley, and the crest of the next hill.

Think Critically: The first hill should be high, the slope should be steep, and the remainder of the ride should be low so that most of the energy remains kinetic.

CONCEPT DEVELOPMENT

▶ **Demonstration:** Place a small hole in the bottom of a foam plastic cup. While holding the hole shut, fill the cup with colored water. Hold the cup as high as you can and drop it into a bucket placed directly beneath it on the floor. Have students observe that no water ran from the cup as it fell because both the cup and water were in free-fall.

▶ Point out that weightlessness can be explained by two factors: the lack of a gravitational force (such as in outer space) or the lack of a means of detecting the effect of a gravitational force, as in free-fall.

MINI QUIZ

Use the Mini Quiz to check students' recall of chapter content.

1 **What is a projectile?** *anything thrown or shot through the air*

2 **What is vertical motion and what is horizontal motion?** *Horizontal motion is parallel to Earth's surface and vertical motion is perpendicular to Earth's surface.*

3 **What is centripetal acceleration?** *acceleration toward the center of a curved or circular path*

RETEACH

Have students place tracing paper over Figure 4-2 and mark the vertical positions of one of the falling balls. Then have them imagine that the ball was also moving sideways with a constant speed. Have them change their drawing to account for this. Ask them to describe the curve showing the motion of the ball.

EXTENSION

For students who have mastered this section, use the **Reinforcement** and **Enrichment** masters or other OPTIONS provided.

3 CLOSE

▶ Ask students to identify the force that causes the centripetal acceleration of the moon.

SECTION REVIEW ANSWERS

1. Refer to Figure 4-8 in the student text. Student diagram should show the dart being launched on a slightly upward path, so that the downward curve of the dart caused by gravity brings the dart to the target bull's-eye.
2. The string provides the centripetal force that keeps the yo-yo moving in a circular path. If the string breaks, the yo-yo will fly off in a straight line in the direction it was moving when the string broke.
3. Apply: No; mass is independent of gravity.

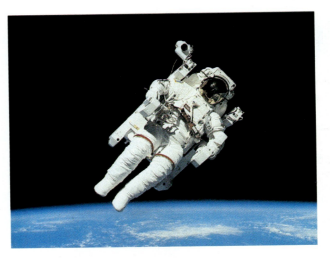

Figure 4-11. The space shuttle and everything in it are in free-fall around Earth, thus producing apparent weightlessness.

What is free-fall?

Now suppose that the scale is falling, being pulled downward by gravity at the same rate as the object being weighed. The scale couldn't push back on the object, so its dial would read zero. The object would seem to be weightless. This is what is happening in a space shuttle orbiting Earth. The shuttle and everything in it, including the astronauts, are all "falling" toward Earth at exactly the same rate of acceleration. When an object is influenced only by gravity, it is said to be falling freely, or in free-fall. An orbiting space shuttle and all its contents are in free-fall around Earth.

SECTION REVIEW

1. Use a diagram similar to Figure 4-8 to show why a dart player has to aim above the target to hit the bull's-eye. In your diagram, show the forces acting on the dart, the dart's path, and the two kinds of motion involved.
2. A child is swinging a yo-yo in a circle around her head. What provides the force to keep the yo-yo going in a circle? What is the force called? What happens if the string breaks?
3. **Apply:** Does the mass of an astronaut change when he or she becomes weightless in orbit?

Skill Builder ☑ Making and Using Tables

Make a table showing important characteristics of three kinds of motion mentioned in this section: projectile motion, circular motion, and free-fall. Table headings should include: Kind of Motion, Shape of Path, and Laws or Forces Involved. You may add other headings. If you need help, refer to Making and Using Tables in the **Skill Handbook** on page 686.

Skill Builder

Tables should be set up as shown at right. Accept any correct data students include to complete the table.

Important Characteristics of Three Kinds of Motion		
Kind of Motion	Shape of Path	Laws or Forces
Projectile		
Circular		
Free-fall		

ACTIVITY 4-1
Trajectories

Problem: *What pathway will a thrown object follow?*

Materials
- stick or dowel, slightly more than 2 m long
- meterstick
- string or thread
- corks (10)
- thumbtacks (10)
- felt-tip pen

Procedure
1. Using a felt-tip pen, place marks at 20-cm intervals along the length of the stick as shown. Number the marks 0 through 10.
2. Obtain 10 corks. Use thumbtacks to attach a length of string to each cork.
3. Tie one cork to each numbered position along the stick. For each position, adjust the length of the string to match the length shown on the drawing.
4. While the stick is held in a horizontal position, try to throw a small object, such as an eraser, exactly 2 meters along the length of the stick. Observe the path followed by the object.

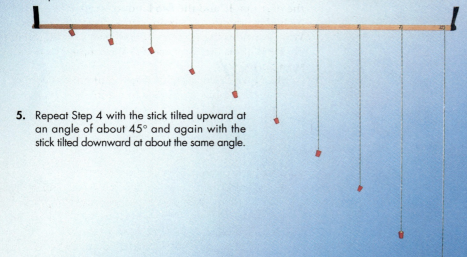

5. Repeat Step 4 with the stick tilted upward at an angle of about 45° and again with the stick tilted downward at about the same angle.

Analyze
1. Describe the path followed by the thrown object. What forces acted on the object to cause it to follow this path?
2. Describe the path followed by the object when it was thrown along the length of the stick when it was tilted upward and when it was tilted downward.
3. In this model, the distance between each string represents the speed of the moving object. What do the lengths of the strings represent?

Conclude and Apply
4. How could you use this model to determine the upward angle at which a thrown object would travel the greatest distance?
5. If you are aiming a rifle at a target, where would you aim in order to hit the bull's-eye? How would your aim at a distance of 100 meters be different from your aim at a distance of 50 meters? 200 meters?

ACTIVITY 4-1
30 minutes

OBJECTIVE: Construct and **use a model** to predict the trajectory of a thrown object.

PROCESS SKILLS applied in this activity:
► **Formulating Models** in Procedure Steps 1-4.
► **Predicting** in Conclude and Apply Question 4.
► **Interpreting** in Analyze Question 3.

COOPERATIVE LEARNING
The class can be divided into four or more teams. Each team can construct a device by dividing the work among team members.

TEACHING THE ACTIVITY
► **Troubleshooting:** String can be taped so it hangs from the lower edge of the stick. The best measurement of length should be from the lower edge to the center of the cork.
► The distances listed are rounded off to the nearest centimeter. The throw speed is assumed to be 3 m/sec. The time of travel from one cork to the next is 0.05 sec. The calculation of fall distance is based on
$$d = 1/2\, gt^2.$$
► Horizontal and vertical components of speed can be shown by the model if the class is ready for that concept.

ANSWERS TO QUESTIONS
1. The path curved downward; gravity.
2. Upward—the path is more horizontal, downward—the path curves down.
3. The string length is the fall of the object due to gravity.
4. Draw a horizontal line from the "zero" end of the stick. Tilt the stick until a cork touches the line at the greatest distance.
5. You would aim above the target. The greater the distance to the target, the higher you must aim.

PROGRAM RESOURCES

From the **Teacher Resource Package** use:
Activity Worksheets, pages 31-32, Activity 4-1: Trajectories.

PREPARATION

SECTION BACKGROUND

► Isometric exercise is a method of strengthening muscles by having them exert forces repetitively against the force exerted by groups of muscles or bones.

1 MOTIVATE

► Ask students to explain why leg weights are sometimes worn by athletes in training.

TYING TO PREVIOUS KNOWLEDGE: Have students recall the two situations that lead to weightlessness mentioned in Sections 3-4 and 4-1. Tell them that in this section they will learn more about the effects of weightlessness.

OBJECTIVES AND SCIENCE WORDS: Have students review the objectives and science words to become familiar with this section.

2 TEACH

Key Concepts are highlighted.

CONCEPT DEVELOPMENT

► One concept is to build a large doughnut-shaped ring called a torus. If the torus is set spinning in outer space, the centripetal force on someone standing on the outer wall of the torus would cause a feeling similar to standing on the floor on Earth. One torus has been proposed that would have a radius of about 500 m and rotate about 5 revolutions per minute.

CROSS CURRICULUM

► **Physical Education:** Have students research several *isometric* exercises and demonstrate them to the class.

 **4-3** **To Boldly—and Safely—Go**

New Science Words

isometric exercises

Objectives

► Analyze the advantages and disadvantages of exposing astronauts to weightlessness.
► Draw conclusions about the safety of space travel.

Effects of Weightlessness

If you could be the first person to set foot on Mars, would you go? What if you knew the trip might be bad for your health? It takes about nine months for a spacecraft to travel from Earth to Mars. No one is sure how astronauts' bodies might react to such long exposure to weightlessness.

When Russian cosmonauts experienced weightlessness for more than 200 consecutive days, they had health problems. Their experiences and other experiments show that long periods of weightlessness weaken the heart and bones. After being in space for nine

96   ACCELERATION AND MOMENTUM

OPTIONS

Meeting Different Ability Levels

For Section 4-3, use the following **Teacher Resource Masters** depending upon individual students' needs.

◆ **Study Guide Master** for all students.
● **Reinforcement Master** for students of average and above average ability levels.
▲ **Enrichment Master** for above average students.

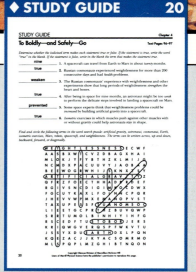

months, an astronaut might be too weak to perform the delicate steps involved in landing a spacecraft on Mars.

Some space experts say the problems could be prevented by building artificial gravity into the spacecraft. A special exercise program might help, too. Some exercises, like jogging, wouldn't be as effective on Mars as on Earth. But **isometric exercises,** in which muscles push against other muscles, with or without gravity, could help astronauts stay in shape.

Other space experts argue that it's better not to send people to Mars at all. These experts claim that robots loaded with sensors, instruments, and arms for gathering samples could do the job just as well as humans, if not better.

But could robots explore the planet as thoroughly as humans? And should humans have to miss out on the adventure?

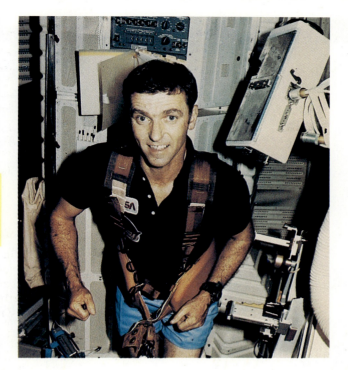

What are isometric exercises?

SECTION REVIEW

1. Why do you think scientists don't know as much as they'd like to know about the effects of prolonged weightlessness on astronauts?
2. Do space mission planners need to consider the effects of weightlessness on anything besides astronauts? Explain your answer.

You Decide!

You are a space agency official planning a mission to Mars. You can send instruments to be operated by astronauts or robots. What would be your choice, and how would you make the decision? Now suppose you're an astronaut. Would you volunteer for the Mars mission?

 SCIENCE & SOCIETY

CHECK FOR UNDERSTANDING

Have students explain why a hand-grip exerciser would be good exercise equipment to have on a space flight.

RETEACH

Draw balanced forces on a compressed hand-grip exerciser. Have students identify the forces being exerted by the person exercising. Have students indicate which forces would not exist without gravity.

EXTENSION

For students who have mastered this section, use the **Reinforcement** and **Enrichment** masters or other OPTIONS provided.

3 CLOSE

▶ Ask questions 1-2 in the Section Review.

? FLEX Your Brain

Use the Flex Your Brain Activity to have students explore SAFETY OF SPACE TRAVEL.

SECTION REVIEW ANSWERS

1. Scientists have not observed humans under weightless conditions over prolonged periods because simulated weightlessness doesn't compare exactly with actual weightlessness and animal responses in weightlessness experiments may differ from human responses.

2. They would have to consider the effects of weightlessness on plants and animals and design ways to overcome weightlessness to perform daily activities.

YOU DECIDE!

Answers will vary. Students should support their opinions with logical statements and assumptions.

PROGRAM RESOURCES

From the **Teacher Resource Package** use:

Activity Worksheets, page 5, Flex Your Brain.

PREPARATION

SECTION BACKGROUND

▶ Newton's third law states that forces arise in pairs; that is, if one body exerts a force on a second body, the second body exerts an equal and opposite force on the first body. The forces are sometimes called action-reaction pairs.

▶ The momentum of an object is equal to the product of its mass and its instantaneous velocity. The momentum of a system is the sum of all the momentum (momenta) of the parts of the system.

▶ The law of conservation of momentum states that if there is no external, net force acting on an object or a system, the momentum of the object or system remains the same. Conversely, the value in the change of momentum of an object or system is equal to the product of the external force and the time interval during which the force acts.

PREPLANNING

▶ Obtain three large, identical rubber bands, several wire ties from plastic food storage bags, and a small weight for the motivation demonstration; a bathroom scale, preferably metric, for the demonstration on page 99.

PROGRAM RESOURCES

From the **Teacher Resource Package** use:

Transparency Masters, pages 15-16, Newton's Third Law.

Use **Color Transparency** number 8, Newton's Third Law.

New Science Words

Newton's third law of motion
momentum
law of conservation of momentum

Objectives

▶ Analyze action and reaction forces.
▶ Calculate momentum.
▶ Explain conservation of momentum.

Newton's Third Law

A boy blows up a balloon for his sister. He lets the balloon go and it darts away on a zigzag course, making her giggle. A young soldier, firing a rifle for the first time, is startled by the backward "kick" of the rifle. A man leaping from a boat toward land falls in the water when the boat scoots away from the shore. As different as these examples of motion may seem, they all illustrate one point: forces always act in pairs, called action-reaction pairs.

① **Newton's third law of motion** describes action-reaction pairs this way: When one object exerts a force on a second object, the second one exerts a force on the first that is equal in size and opposite in direction. A less formal way of saying the same thing is "to every action there is an equal and opposite reaction."

Let's look at the examples of action-reaction pairs described earlier. The balloon exerts force on the air inside, causing the air to rush out of the neck of the balloon. The air exerts an equal force on the balloon, but in the opposite direction. This reaction force causes the balloon to dart away from the escaping air.

When a soldier fires a rifle, the hot gases from the exploding gunpowder exert a force on the bullet, sending it speeding out of the barrel of the gun. The bullet exerts an equal and opposite force on the trapped gases, causing the rifle to "kick" backward.

In the third example, when the man leaps from the boat, the boat exerts a force on his feet, moving him forward. His feet exert an equal and opposite force on the boat, sending it backward.

State Newton's third law of motion.

98 ACCELERATION AND MOMENTUM

OPTIONS

Meeting Different Ability Levels

For Section 4-4, use the following **Teacher Resource Masters** depending upon individual students' needs.

◆ **Study Guide Master** for all students.

● **Reinforcement Master** for students of average and above average ability levels.

▲ **Enrichment Master** for above average students.

Additional Teacher Resource Package masters are listed in the OPTIONS box throughout the section. The additional masters are appropriate for all students.

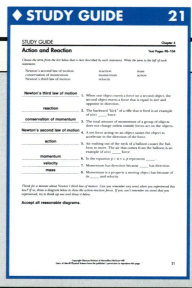

Figure 4-12. As the swimmer's hands and feet push against the water, the water pushes back, moving the swimmer forward.

Figure 4-13. The action of passing the basketball forward will propel the player backward.

Newton's third law can be used to explain how a swimmer moves through the water. With each stroke, the swimmer's arm exerts a force on the water. The water pushes back on the swimmer with an equal force in the opposite direction. But if the forces are equal, how can the swimmer move forward? It's possible because the forces are acting on different things. The "action" force acts on the water; the "reaction" force acts on the swimmer. The swimmer, having less mass than the pool full of water, accelerates more than the water.

A very important point to keep in mind when dealing with ==Newton's third law is that action-reaction forces always act on *different* objects. Thus, even though the forces may be equal, they are not balanced.== In the case of the swimmer, one force acts on the swimmer. Thus, a net force, or unbalanced force, acts on the swimmer, and a change in motion can take place.

Compare the example of the swimmer with that of two teams in a tug-of-war contest. Both teams exert force on the ground with their feet. This force is transferred to the rope. Thus, all of the forces exerted in the contest act on the *same* object—the rope. So, if both teams exert equal forces in opposite directions, the forces *on the rope* will be balanced, and no change in motion will take place. Only when one team exerts a greater force than

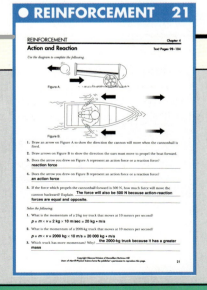

99

▶ **Demonstration:** Have a student measure the lengths of the three rubber bands. Suspend a weight from one rubber band and have a student measure its new length. Remove and link an identical rubber band to the first with a wire tie from a plastic food storage bag. Ask students to predict by how much each rubber band will elongate if you suspend a weight from the second rubber band. Demonstrate the elongation of each rubber band and have a student measure the length of each rubber band. Have students compare the elongations with the elongation of the single rubber band. Link a third rubber band to the chain in a similar fashion and repeat the questioning and the demonstration. Ask students to summarize their observations.

👥 **Cooperative Learning:** Have Problem Solving teams determine if the shape of an inflated balloon "rocket" affects its motion.

TYING TO PREVIOUS KNOWLEDGE: Have students recall the motion of the untied inflated balloon from the Find Out activity on page 83. Point out that the cause of the motion is much like that which causes a rocket to move. Tell students they will learn more about rocket propulsion in this chapter.

OBJECTIVES AND SCIENCE WORDS: Have students review the objectives and science words to become familiar with this section.

Key Concepts are highlighted.

CONCEPT DEVELOPMENT

▶ Have students draw arrows representing action-reaction pairs in each situation described on pages 98 and 99. Make sure students identify each force, the source of the forces, and the object on which the force is acting.

▶ **Demonstration:** Have a student stand on a bathroom scale and another report the scale reading to the class. While bracing the scale with your foot, instruct the first student to carefully jump off the scale while the student observes any changes to the scale reading when the first student jumps. Have the student report the observation to the class. Discuss the sudden increase in the scale reading as the student jumped in terms of Newton's third law. Point out that the new value was the sum of her weight and the force she pushed down on the scale while beginning to jump. The force that the scale exerted upward on the student was equal to this new value but opposite in direction. The difference between the weight of the student and this upward force that the scale exerted on the student resulted in a net upward force on the student. The net force caused the student to accelerate upward, off the scale, as described by Newton's second law.

Science and MATH

The bigger the mass of the club the greater the momentum. Also the longer the shaft the greater the swing arc, the greater the velocity it can develop, and the greater the momentum. The # 1 wood (driver) is the biggest and longest, produces the most momentum, and also has the least loft, so the ball will go lower and farther when hit by it. It is followed by the 5 wood, 5 iron, and 9 iron.

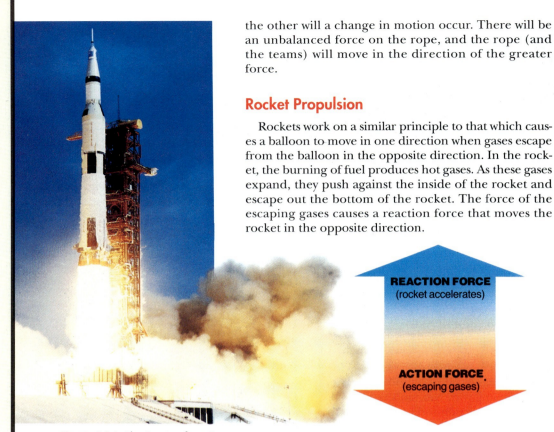

Figure 4-14. The "action force" of the expanding gases rushing out of the rocket results in a "reaction force" being exerted on the rocket, sending the rocket in the opposite direction.

Science and MATH

Compare different golf clubs—for example, a #1 wood, a #5 wood, a #9 iron, and a #5 iron—with regard to the momentum each can give to a golf ball. Explain how each club is different.

the other will a change in motion occur. There will be an unbalanced force on the rope, and the rope (and the teams) will move in the direction of the greater force.

Rocket Propulsion

Rockets work on a similar principle to that which causes a balloon to move in one direction when gases escape from the balloon in the opposite direction. In the rocket, the burning of fuel produces hot gases. As these gases expand, they push against the inside of the rocket and escape out the bottom of the rocket. The force of the escaping gases causes a reaction force that moves the rocket in the opposite direction.

REACTION FORCE
(rocket accelerates)

ACTION FORCE
(escaping gases)

Momentum

If a toy truck rolls toward you, you can easily stop it with your hand. However, such a tactic would not work with a full-sized truck, even if it were moving at the same speed as the toy truck. It takes more force to stop the full-sized truck because it has more momentum (moh MENT um) than the toy truck has. **Momentum** is a property a moving object has due to its mass and velocity. Momentum can be calculated with this equation, in which p represents momentum: ❷

$$momentum = mass \times velocity$$
$$p = m \times v$$

The unit for momentum is kg • m/s. Notice that momentum has a direction, because velocity has a direction. ❸

OPTIONS

INQUIRY QUESTIONS

▶ A 70-kg girl jumps off a bathroom scale with an upward acceleration of 0.5 m/s². **What is the reading of the scale as she was jumping?** *Her weight 70 kg × 9.8 m/s² + 70 kg × 0.5 m/s² = 720 N.*
▶ **During your dive into a swimming pool, how big a force are you exerting on Earth?** *your weight* **Why doesn't the Earth fall up to you?** *Its mass is so great, about 6 × 10²⁴ kg, that the gravitational force you exert on it produces a negligible acceleration.*

▶ **Explain why you feel an outward force on your hand by the string when you spin a yo-yo above your head.** *You feel an outward force of the string on your hand because you are causing an inward force on the string and the string exerts an equal and opposite force on you.*

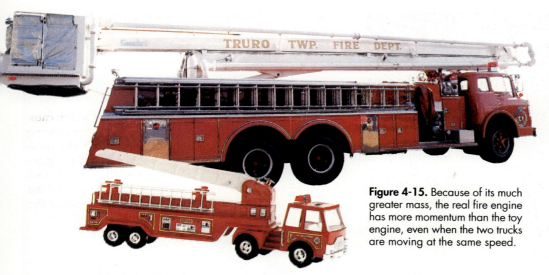

Figure 4-15. Because of its much greater mass, the real fire engine has more momentum than the toy engine, even when the two trucks are moving at the same speed.

The two trucks described on the previous page may have the same velocity, but the full-sized truck has more momentum because of its greater mass. A speeding bullet can have a large momentum because of its high velocity, even though its mass is small. A lumbering elephant may have a low velocity, but because of its large mass it has a large momentum. The momentum of an object doesn't change unless its mass or velocity, or both, change. But momentum can be transferred from one object to another. Think about what happens when a ball rolling across a pool table hits another ball that is standing still. At first, the rolling ball has momentum, the motionless ball does not. When they collide, the ball that was at rest starts moving. It gains

Figure 4-16. Before the balls collide, the moving ball has all the momentum (left). After the balls collide, all of the balls have momentum (right). The total momentum of the balls is the same in both photographs.

▶ The action force is Stewart throwing the shoe; the reaction force is the shoe exerting an opposite force on Stewart.

Think Critically: When Stewart threw the shoe away from the edge of the pond, the effect was Stewart's moving in the opposite direction toward the edge. Since the pond was slippery, momentum was conserved.

CONCEPT DEVELOPMENT

▶ Discuss shooting a rubber dart gun in terms of conservation of momentum. Make sure students realize that the total momentum was zero both before and after the dart was fired. Since the dart had forward momentum, the gun had to recoil with an equal momentum in the opposite direction; because the gun had more mass than the dart, its speed was slower than that of the dart.

CROSS CURRICULUM

▶ **Social Studies:** Have students research the history of rocketry.

STUDENT TEXT QUESTION

Page 102, paragraph 2: **What outside force makes that happen?** *The outside force acting on the pool balls is friction.*

MINI QUIZ

Use the Mini Quiz to check students' recall of chapter content.

1. **How do the sizes and the directions of the forces in action-reaction pairs compare?** *equal in size and opposite in direction*
2. **What two measurements are needed to calculate the momentum of an object?** *mass and velocity*
3. **What is the unit of momentum?** *kg • m/s*

The Icy Challenge

The winter had been very cold, and the ice on the local pond was thick and smooth—just right for ice hockey. One day Stewart and his friends were walking across the pond, carrying their skates and hockey equipment. A few meters from the edge of the pond, Stewart slipped and fell and landed on his back.

After making sure he wasn't hurt, Stewart's friends challenged him to make it to land without turning over or standing up. Stewart tried pushing against the ice with his hands and feet, but the ice was so slippery that he didn't move. Then he had a brainstorm. He took one of his skates and threw it as hard as he could toward the center of the pond. Stewart continued to throw pieces of his hockey equipment toward the center of the pond until he found himself at the pond's edge.

Think Critically: Describe the forces involved in the throwing of the equipment. Explain what motions took place and why they occurred.

EcoTip

Get in motion! Weed gardens by hand or by hoe instead of using harmful chemicals. You and your garden will benefit from the exercise.

momentum. The first ball slows down and loses momentum. If you were to measure the total momentum of the two balls before and after the collision, it would be the same. The momentum the second ball gains is equal to the momentum that the first ball loses. Total momentum is conserved—it doesn't change.

The **law of conservation of momentum** states that the total amount of momentum of a group of objects does not change unless outside forces act on the objects. After the collision, the balls on the pool table eventually slow down and stop rolling. What outside force makes that happen?

OPTIONS

INQUIRY QUESTIONS

▶ In a circus, a 50-kg clown is shot out of a cannon at 20 m/s. **What is the recoil speed of the cannon if it has a mass of 250 kg?** *The momentum of the clown is 50 kg × 20 m/s = 1000 kg • m/s. Because momentum is conserved, the cannon must have an equal momentum in the opposite direction. The cannon recoils with a speed of 4 m/s because 250 kg × 4 m/s = 1000 kg • m/s.*

PROGRAM RESOURCES

From the **Teacher Resource Package** use:

Critical Thinking/Problem Solving, page 10, Tires and Hazardous Weather Conditions.

Cross-Curricular Connections, page 8, A 17th Century Timer.

Science and Society, page 8, Bicycle Helmets.

Use **Laboratory Manual,** Conservation of Momentum and Velocity and Momentum.

With Newton's third law and conservation of momentum, you can explain all sorts of motion that may seem complicated at first. Bouncing on a trampoline, knocking down bowling pins with a ball, and tackling a football player are a few examples. Think about how you would explain these and other examples of motion that you think of.

SECTION REVIEW

1. After rowing to within a few feet of shore, a boater stands up in the boat and tries to jump to land. Instead, he lands in the water. Explain why he took the unexpected dip.
2. Compare the momentum of a 50-kg dolphin swimming 16.4 m/s with the momentum of a 6300-kg elephant walking 0.11 m/s.
3. **Apply:** Some choreographers assign larger dancers to parts with slow, graceful movements, saving the parts that require quick starts and stops for smaller dancers. Does this plan make sense?

☑ Concept Mapping

Skill Builder

Use the words provided to make two events chains. The chains should show what happens to two pool balls when the rolling ball (Ball One) hits the resting ball (Ball Two). Phrases to use: *gains momentum; rests; rolls more slowly or stops; hits Ball Two; rolls; loses momentum; is hit by Ball One; starts rolling.* If you need help, refer to Concept Mapping in the **Skill Handbook** on pages 684 and 685.

Ask questions 1-2 and the **Apply** Question in the Section Review.

RETEACH
Have students bring in action photographs of various sporting events and identify action-reaction pairs and net forces. Have students explain their choices to the class.

EXTENSION
For students who have mastered this section, use the **Reinforcement** and **Enrichment** masters or other OPTIONS provided.

3 CLOSE

▶ Have students explain the results of the motivation demonstration in terms of Newton's third law.

SECTION REVIEW ANSWERS
1. In reaction to the force of the boater's foot pushing against the boat, the boat moves in the direction of the force (away from land). This causes the boater to land in the water.
2. Dolphin's momentum: 50 kg × 16.4 m/s = 820 kg • m/s; Elephant's momentum: 6300 kg × 0.11 m/s = 693 kg • m/s. The dolphin has greater momentum.
3. Apply: Yes; a large dancer moving quickly would have more momentum than a smaller dancer moving at the same speed. Because of his or her greater momentum, it would be more difficult for a larger dancer to quickly change speed or direction.

Skill Builder

You may wish to provide students with the map forms and initial entries as shown.

Ball 1	Ball 2
Rolls	Rests
Hits ball 2	Hit by ball
Loses momentum	Gains momentum
Rolls more slowly	Starts rolling

ACTIVITY 4-2
30 minutes

OBJECTIVE: Compare the role of mass and velocity in the momentum of an object.

PROCESS SKILLS applied in this activity:
▶ **Observing** in Procedure Steps 5, 6, and 7.
▶ **Controlling Variables** in Procedure Steps 6 and 7.
▶ **Defining Operationally** in Analyze Questions 2 and 3 and Conclude and Apply Question 6.

👥 COOPERATIVE LEARNING
The ideal group size is three. But it may be necessary to work in larger teams if lab space and equipment are limited.

TEACHING THE ACTIVITY
Troubleshooting: The lab set-up requires about 2 meters of counter or table space.
▶ Keep extra rubber bands handy. If the extra long type is not available, link together several shorter ones.
▶ Lighter carts than those pictured can be used but may not survive the collisions.
▶ If appropriate, the lab can lead to a discussion of momentum within a stationary or a moving frame of reference. (What is the momentum of the carts if this lab were conducted inside a moving railroad car?)

ACTIVITY 4-2
Momentum

Problem: *How are mass and momentum related?*

Materials
- dynamics carts (2)
- long rubber band
- building bricks (2)
- meterstick
- masking tape

Procedure
1. Prepare a data table like the one shown.
2. Attach a long rubber band to the two dynamics carts. Move the carts apart until the rubber band is taut but not stretched.
3. Place a piece of tape on the table to mark the halfway point between the two carts. Lay the meterstick on the table with the 50-cm mark beside the piece of tape.
4. Pull the carts apart until the ends of the rubber band line up with the ends of the meterstick.
5. Release both carts at the same time so that they gain the same momentum. Observe and record the point along the meterstick where the carts collide. Also observe where the carts stop after the collision.
6. Place a brick on cart A and repeat Steps 4 and 5.
7. Add a second brick to cart A and repeat Steps 4 and 5.

Analyze
1. How can you tell from the data which cart was moving faster?
2. How can both carts have the same momentum if they are traveling at different speeds?
3. How does the addition of mass to one cart affect the location of the collision point? How does it affect what happens to the carts after the collision?

Conclude and Apply
4. If one cart were released slightly before the other, how would the momentum of the two carts be affected?
5. If one cart has more momentum than the other, what happens when the carts collide?
6. Suppose momentum is said to be negative (–) in one direction and positive in the opposite direction. If two carts having the same amount of momentum are traveling in opposite directions, what is the total momentum of the two-cart system?

Sample Data

Data and Observations

	Collision Point	Distance Traveled		Location after Collision	
		Cart A	Cart B	Cart A	Cart B
Trial 1	50 cm	50 cm	50 cm	20 cm	80 cm
Trial 2	40 cm	40 cm	60 cm	15 cm	77 cm
Trial 3	20 cm	20 cm	80 cm	12 cm	68 cm

104 ACCELERATION AND MOMENTUM

ANSWERS TO QUESTIONS
1. Because both carts traveled for the same period of time, the cart that traveled farther had the higher average velocity.
2. The faster cart has a lower mass.
3. The collision point will be closer to the origin of cart A. Cart A will move less distance from the collision than cart B.
4. The cart released first will gain the greatest momentum.
5. If the cart with the greatest momentum also has the greatest mass, it will continue to move forward.
6. The sum of the total momentum is zero.

PROGRAM RESOURCES
From the **Teacher Resource Package** use:
Activity Worksheets, pages 33-34, Activity 4-2: Momentum.

SUMMARY

4-1: Accelerated Motion

1. According to Newton's second law, a net force acting on an object causes the object to accelerate in the direction of the force. The size of the acceleration depends on the strength of the force and the mass of the object.

2. Near Earth's surface, gravity causes falling objects to accelerate at a rate of 9.8 m/s^2. All objects accelerate at this rate, regardless of mass.

3. Air resistance acts in the opposite direction to that in which the object is moving.

4-2: Projectile and Circular Motion

1. Objects that are thrown or shot through the air are called projectiles. All projectiles have both horizontal and vertical velocities. The horizontal velocity is constant; the vertical velocity, which is affected by gravity, is accelerated.

2. When an object moves along a circular path, it is accelerated toward the center of the circle.

3. When an object is influenced only by gravity, it is said to be in free-fall. Objects in free-fall are weightless. To be truly weightless, an object would have to be free from gravity.

4-3: Science and Society: To Boldly— and Safely—Go

1. Health problems have resulted from long exposure to weightlessness. Experimentation has shown that some of the problems can be prevented.

2. Space experts argue whether or not robots could explore planets as well as humans without endangering astronauts.

4-4: Action and Reaction

1. Forces always act in pairs. The forces in an action-reaction pair are always equal in size and opposite in direction.

2. All moving objects have momentum. The momentum of an object is the product of its mass and velocity.

3. The total momentum of a set of objects is conserved unless a net force acts on the set.

KEY SCIENCE WORDS

a. **air resistance**
b. **centripetal acceleration**
c. **centripetal force**
d. **isometric exercises**
e. **law of conservation of momentum**
f. **momentum**
g. **Newton's second law of motion**
h. **Newton's third law of motion**
i. **projectile**
j. **terminal velocity**

UNDERSTANDING VOCABULARY

Match each phrase with the correct term from the list of Key Science Words.

1. deals with action-reaction forces
2. force that opposes the motion of a falling object near Earth's surface.
3. an object that is thrown through the air
4. acceleration toward the center of a circle
5. product of an object's mass and velocity
6. describes the effect of a net force on an object
7. exerting muscles against muscles
8. causes circular motion
9. achieved when acceleration due to gravity is balanced by air resistance
10. unchanging nature of the total momentum of a set of objects

ACCELERATION AND MOMENTUM   **105**

CHAPTER
REVIEW

SUMMARY

Have students read the summary statements to review the major concepts of the chapter.

UNDERSTANDING VOCABULARY

1. h   **6.** g
2. a   **7.** d
3. i   **8.** c
4. b   **9.** j
5. f   **10.** e

OPTIONS

ASSESSMENT

To assess students understanding of material in this chapter use the resources listed.

COOPERATIVE LEARNING

Consider using cooperative learning in the THINK AND WRITE CRITICALLY, APPLY, and MORE SKILL BUILDERS sections of the Chapter Review.

PROGRAM RESOURCES

From the **Teacher Resource Package** use:
Chapter Review, pages 11-12.
Chapter and Unit Tests, pages 24-27, Chapter Test.

CHAPTER
REVIEW

CHECKING CONCEPTS

1. b		**6.** c	
2. d		**7.** a	
3. b		**8.** d	
4. c		**9.** b	
5. d		**10.** a	

UNDERSTANDING CONCEPTS

11. Centripetal

12. gravity

13. third

14. Momentum

15. isometric

THINK AND WRITE CRITICALLY

16. The weight of an object is the force of gravity acting on its mass. Therefore, the greater the mass of an object, the greater the force of gravity that acts on it and the greater its weight. $m_1 m_2$

17. The rate at which gravity causes a falling object to accelerate is independent of the mass of the object. Although the force of gravity acting on a large mass at the same distance from Earth is greater than for a small mass, the greater inertia of the larger mass requires more force be exerted on it to change its motion.

18. In order for two forces to be balanced, they must act on the same object. The forces in an action-reaction pair act on different objects; therefore, they cannot be balanced.

19. Although the spaceship is kept from flying off into space by Earth's gravity, the spaceship and everything in it are in free-fall around Earth. This condition produces the impression of weightlessness because there is no "upward" force to act against gravity. Because the spaceship does not exert any force against the astronauts, the astronauts feel weightless.

20. A ball rolling across a table has no net force acting on it to cause it to change its direction of motion. Once the ball rolls off the edge of the table, gravity is the only force acting on it and the ball becomes a projectile. Because the ball has a constant horizontal velocity and a constant vertical acceleration downward, the path of the ball is curved.

CHAPTER
REVIEW

CHECKING CONCEPTS

Choose the word or phrase that completes the sentence or answers the question.

1. A net force acting on a moving object causes the object to _____.
- **a.** fall
- **b.** accelerate
- **c.** stop
- **d.** curve

2. _____ is the effect of gravity on an object.
- **a.** Mass
- **b.** Momentum
- **c.** Centripetal force
- **d.** Weight

3. Which of these opposes acceleration due to gravity?
- **a.** momentum
- **b.** air resistance
- **c.** reaction force
- **d.** terminal velocity

4. According to Newton's second law, _____ equals mass times acceleration.
- **a.** gravity
- **b.** momentum
- **c.** force
- **d.** weight

5. What force causes a leaf to fall more slowly than a penny?
- **a.** gravity
- **b.** momentum
- **c.** inertia
- **d.** air resistance

6. Which illustrates Newton's third law?
- **a.** projectile motion
- **b.** circular motion
- **c.** rocket propulsion
- **d.** centripetal force

7. The _____ velocity of a projectile is considered to be constant.
- **a.** horizontal
- **b.** circular
- **c.** accelerated
- **d.** vertical

8. An object in free-fall is _____.
- **a.** moving horizontally
- **b.** moving vertically
- **c.** motionless
- **d.** weightless

9. _____ is reached when air resistance and acceleration due to gravity are equal.
- **a.** Negative acceleration
- **b.** Terminal velocity
- **c.** Centripetal acceleration
- **d.** Weightlessness

10. Which of the following does not affect the amount of air resistance that acts on an object?
- **a.** mass
- **b.** size
- **c.** shape
- **d.** speed

UNDERSTANDING CONCEPTS

Complete each sentence.

11. _____ force causes a moving object to move in a curved or circular path.

12. The vertical acceleration of a projectile is caused by _____.

13. The kick of a rifle illustrates Newton's _____ law.

14. _____ is a property a moving object has due to its mass and velocity.

15. In _____ exercises, muscles push against other muscles.

THINK AND WRITE CRITICALLY

16. On Earth, why does an object of large mass weigh more than an object of smaller mass?

17. Explain why gravity does not cause a falling object of large mass to accelerate at a faster rate than a falling object of smaller mass.

18. If the forces in an action-reaction pair are equal in size and opposite in direction, why aren't they balanced forces?

19. A spaceship orbiting Earth is held in its orbit by Earth's gravity. Yet, astronauts in the spaceship are said to be weightless. Explain.

20. Explain why a marble moves in a straight line as it rolls across the table, but follows a curved path once it rolls off the table.

21. What force is exerted by a 1000-kg car accelerating at a rate of 50 m/s²?

22. The motion of a 12-kg object is opposed by a 30-N force of friction. At what rate does friction slow the object down?

23. You are asked to design a winding mountain road. What force must you try to increase in designing this road? How might you do this?

24. A 5-kg object with a velocity of 6 m/s strikes the motionless 10-kg ball. The object stops moving as a result of the collision. What is the velocity of the ball after the collision?

25. The moon has no atmosphere and its gravity is about one-sixth as strong as that of Earth. Considering these factors, how would the motions of objects near the moon be different than the same motions near Earth?

MORE SKILL BUILDERS

If you need help, refer to the Skill Handbook.

1. **Interpreting Data:** The table contains data about four objects dropped to the ground from the same height at the same time.

Object	A	B	C	D
Mass	5.0 g	5.0 g	30.0 g	35.0 g
Time of Fall	2.0 s	1.0 s	0.5 s	1.5 s

a. Which object falls fastest? slowest?
b. On which object is the force of gravity greatest?
c. Is air resistance stronger on A or B?
d. Which object is probably largest? Explain your reasoning.

2. **Observing and Inferring:** A girl weighing 360 N gets on a motionless elevator at the ground floor. She steps onto a scale and remains on the scale while the elevator slowly accelerates up to the 120th floor. During that time, the readings on the scale range from a high of 365 N to a low of 355 N. Infer what the reading was on the ground floor, on the way up, stopping, and stopped on the 120th floor. Why do these readings change?

3. **Recognizing Cause and Effect:** When using a high-pressure hose, why is it necessary for firefighters to grip the hose strongly and plant their feet firmly?

4. **Making and Using Graphs:** Construct a time-distance graph of the following data for a ball thrown into the air at an angle to the ground.

Height	0	25	40	45	40	25	0
Time	0	1	2	3	4	5	6

Use the graph to answer the following:
a. Does the ball accelerate vertically? How do you know?
b. When is the ball's vertical velocity zero?
c. If the ball has a horizontal velocity of 40 m/s, how far will it travel before it hits the ground?

PROJECTS

1. Make a poster diagram of a rocket engine showing how it works. If possible, build a model rocket. Share the results of the project with your classmates. Use Newton's third law to explain why a rocket lifts off.

2. Research the positive and negative aspects of prolonged space flight. Write an essay stating your position on this topic. Read your essay aloud and have a class debate.

---

21. $F = m \times a$
$= 1000 \text{ kg} \times 50 \text{ m/s}$
$= 50\,000 \text{ N}$

22. $F = m \times a$
$a = \dfrac{F}{m}$
$= \dfrac{30 \text{ N}}{12 \text{ kg}} = \dfrac{30 \text{ kg} \bullet \text{m/s}^2}{12 \text{ kg}}$
$= 2.5 \text{ m/s}^2$

23. The centripetal force acting on any cars moving along the road must be made as large as possible to keep the cars moving in a curved path around the mountain. This force is affected by the force of friction between the road surface and the tires and by the shape of the curves. Therefore, you could use a slightly rougher material for the road surface, to increase friction, and you could avoid making sharp curves. The road surface could also be angled upward in the outside parts of the curves.

24. Momentum must be conserved, so the momentum of the ball must be the same as that of the object that started it in motion.

Momentum of object:

$p = m \times v$
$= 5 \text{ kg} \times 6 \text{ m/s} = 30 \text{ kg} \bullet \text{m/s}$

Velocity of ball:

$v = \dfrac{p}{m} = \dfrac{30 \text{ kg} \bullet \text{m/s}}{10 \text{ kg}} = 3 \text{ m/s}$

25. Because of the moon's smaller force of gravity, the rate of acceleration of a falling object due to gravity would be smaller on the moon than on Earth. However, there would be no air resistance to slow a falling object near the moon, so there would be no terminal velocity. A falling object would continue to accelerate at the same rate until it struck the moon's surface.

The low reading occurs as the elevator slows at the top. The scale must exert a force less than the girl's weight to produce a net downward force, slowing her to a stop. Any time the elevator is not accelerating (stopped or moving at constant velocity) the scale must produce a force equal to the girl's weight.

3. **Recognizing Cause and Effect:** The force of the water may knock them down (Newton's third law).

4. **Graphing:**
a. Yes; the time-distance graph for the ball's vertical motion is curved, indicating that the motion is accelerated.
b. The vertical velocity of the ball is zero at $t = 3$ seconds.

c. $v = \dfrac{d}{t}$ $d = v \times t$
$= 40 \text{ m/s} \times 6 \text{ s} = 240 \text{ m}$

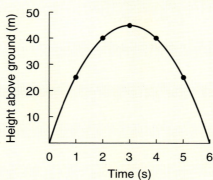

MORE SKILL BUILDERS

1. **Interpreting Data:**
a. Object C falls fastest, object A most slowly.
b. object D   c. object A
d. object D, because it has more mass

2. **Observing and Inferring:** The high reading occurs as the elevator begins its upward motion. The scale must exert a greater upward force than the weight of the girl to produce a net upward force.

5 Energy

CHAPTER SECTION	OBJECTIVES	ACTIVITIES
5-1 Energy and Work (2 days)	1. **Distinguish** between kinetic and potential energy. 2. **Recognize** that energy can change from one form to another with no loss of energy. 3. **Compare** the scientific meaning of *work* with its everyday meaning.	**Activity 5-1:** *Conversion of Energy,* p. 117
5-2 Temperature and Heat (2 days)	1. **Recognize** the difference between the motion of an object and the motion of the particles that make up the object. 2. **Contrast** heat and temperature. 3. **Explain** what determines the thermal energy of a sample of matter.	**MINI-Lab:** *Can you "create" energy?* p. 118
5-3 Energy from the Oceans and Earth Science & Society (1 day)	1. **Explain** why ocean waters and subsurface rock may represent possible new sources of thermal energy. 2. **Discuss** the benefits and drawbacks of proceeding with research and development of these new energy sources.	
5-4 Measuring Thermal Energy (2 days)	1. **Define** *specific heat.* 2. **Calculate** changes in thermal energy.	**Activity 5-2:** *Specific Heat,* p. 128
Chapter Review		

ACTIVITY MATERIALS

FIND OUT	ACTIVITIES		MINI-LABS
Page 109 box full of books (more than 4)	**5-1 Conversion of Energy, p. 117** ring stand and ring support rod clamp, right angle 30 cm support rod 2 metersticks rubber stopper, 2-hole, medium 100 cm string masking tape	**5-2 Specific Heat, p. 128** set of hair curlers 2 Celsius thermometers plastic foam cup graph paper balance graduated cylinder	**Can you "create" energy? p. 118** sand plastic foam cup with lid Celsius thermometer

CHAPTER FEATURES	TEACHER RESOURCE PACKAGE	OTHER RESOURCES
Skill Builder: *Comparing and Contrasting*, p. 116	**Ability Level Worksheets** ◆ **Study Guide**, p. 22 ● **Reinforcement**, p. 22 ▲ **Enrichment**, p. 22 **Activity Worksheet**, pp. 39, 40 **Cross-Curricular Connections**, p. 9 **Science and Society**, p. 9 **Transparency Master**, pp. 17, 18	**Color Transparency 9**, Kinetic and Potential Energy **Lab Manual 8**, The Energy of a Pendulum **Lab Manual 9**, Work and Power
Problem Solving: *A Cold Cup of Tea and a Warm Soft Drink*, p. 120 **Skill Builder:** *Concept Mapping*, p. 121	**Ability Level Worksheets** ◆ **Study Guide**, p. 23 ● **Reinforcement**, p. 23 ▲ **Enrichment**, p. 23 **MINI-Lab Worksheet**, p. 45 **Transparency Masters**, pp. 19, 20	**Color Transparency 10**, Cool and Hot Matter
You Decide! p. 123	**Ability Level Worksheets** ◆ **Study Guide**, p. 24 ● **Reinforcement**, p. 24 ▲ **Enrichment**, p. 24 **Critical Thinking/Problem Solving**, p. 11	
Technology: *Infrared Weather Eyes*, p. 125 **Skill Builder:** *Interpreting Data*, p. 127	**Ability Level Worksheets** ◆ **Study Guide**, p. 25 ● **Reinforcement**, p. 25 ▲ **Enrichment**, p. 25 **Activity Worksheet**, pp. 41, 42 **Concept Mapping**, pp. 15, 16	**Lab Manual 10**, Heat Transfer
Summary Think & Write Critically Key Science Words Apply Understanding Vocabulary More Skill Builders Checking Concepts Projects Understanding Concepts	**Chapter Review**, pp. 13, 14 **Chapter Test**, pp. 28-31	**Chapter Review Software** **Test Bank**

◆ **Basic**   ● **Average**   ▲ **Advanced**

ADDITIONAL MATERIALS		
SOFTWARE	**AUDIOVISUAL**	**BOOKS/MAGAZINES**
Energy, Focus. *Motion and Energy: Physical Science Simulations*, Focus. *Investigating Conservation of Energy*, IBM.	*Investigations in Science: Energy and Motion*, filmstrips with cassettes, BFA. *Energy*, film, Hawkhill. *Heat and Temperature—Molecular Energy*, film, Science Software. *The Forms of Energy*, video, Focus.	Gordon, Douglas. *Energy*. North Pomfret, VT: Trafalgar Square/ Davis & Charles Inc., 1984. Steffens, Henry J. *James Prescott Joule and the Concept of Energy*. Canton, MA: Watson Pub. Int., 1979.

THEME DEVELOPMENT: The theme of this chapter is energy and its use in describing how matter behaves. The notion that energy is the ability to cause a change is introduced and should be emphasized in each section. Mechanical energy of a macroscopic object is discussed and is used to introduce the concept of thermal energy at the microscopic level.

CHAPTER OVERVIEW

▶ **Section 5-1:** Kinetic and potential energies are discussed qualitatively in this section. Work is introduced as the means of transferring energy through motion. The mechanical energy of a pendulum is used to introduce the law of conservation of energy.

▶ **Section 5-2:** This section presents the relationship between the temperature of a material and the average kinetic energy of its particles. The difference between thermal energy and heat is discussed.

▶ **Section 5-3: Science and Society:** Possible energy resources from the oceans and Earth are presented. Students are asked to analyze the economic and environmental factors of research projects involving these energy resources.

▶ **Section 5-4:** Specific heat is introduced as a means of measuring changes in thermal energy.

CHAPTER VOCABULARY

energy	temperature
kinetic energy	thermal
potential energy	energy
work	heat
mechanical energy	magma
law of conservation	specific heat
of energy	

CHAPTER

5 Energy

108

OPTIONS

For Your Gifted Students

Have the students make a liquid thermometer. They should devise a way to make their own temperature scale and compare it with the Fahrenheit, Celsius, and Kelvin scales. Have students come up with a formula to convert their scales to one of the scales mentioned.
(See "For Your Mainstreamed Students" for directions on making a liquid thermometer.)

How many ways do you use your own energy every day? Do some kinds of work take more effort than others? Is all exertion work?

FIND OUT!

Do this activity to get started thinking about energy and work.

Standing, hold your arms out in front of you at waist level, with your hands together, palms up. Have a classmate stack two books on your hands. Raise the books to about shoulder level, then lower them. Now try raising them overhead. Are you working harder than you did when you raised them to shoulder level? Lower the books again. Have your classmate put two more books on the pile, so you're holding four books. Try to raise them to shoulder level. Are you using more force than when you were holding only two books?

Hold the four books at shoulder level until your arms get tired. Are you exerting force? Do you think you're doing work?

Now fill a box of books and try pushing it along the floor. Can you push it farther if a classmate helps?

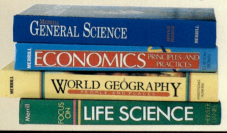

Gearing Up
Previewing the Chapter
Use this outline to help you focus on important ideas in this chapter.

Section 5-1   Energy and Work
► Kinetic and Potential Energy
► Work
► Conservation of Energy
Section 5-2   Temperature and Heat
► Temperature
► Thermal Energy
► Heat
Section 5-3   Science and Society
Energy from the Oceans and Earth
► Exploring New Energy Resources
Section 5-4   Measuring Thermal Energy
► Specific Heat
► Using Specific Heat

Previewing Science Skills
► In the **Skill Builders,** you will compare and contrast, make a concept map, and interpret data.
► In the **Activities,** you will measure in SI, observe and infer, collect and interpret data, and hypothesize.
► In the **MINI-Lab,** you will measure in SI, observe and infer, and hypothesize.

What's next?

You have seen that sometimes things move when you exert force, sometimes they don't. Now find out why this is so. As you move through this chapter, you will learn what energy is and how it's related to work. You will learn to recognize when work is done and when it isn't. And, finally, you will find out some things about heat and temperature that may surprise you, especially if you've always thought they meant the same thing.

Use the Find Out activity to introduce students to the concept of work and energy. Tell them that they will learn more about these concepts and how they are related in this chapter.

FIND OUT!
Preparation: If you wish to do this activity quantitatively, obtain sets of similar books and measure the weight of a book or calculate its weight from its mass measurement.
Materials: four books per pair of students

Cooperative Learning: Assign Problem Solving Teams to conduct this activity quantitatively. Have students measure the weight of the books or calculate the weight from mass measurements of the books. Have the team use the measurements from this activity to calculate work as an enrichment for Section 5-1.
Teaching Tips
► CAUTION: *Students with health problems should limit their participation in this activity.*
► Have students raise or lower the books each time at a slow, constant speed.
► During this activity, ask students to state when they are doing work and when the work is increased.

Gearing Up
Have students study the Gearing Up feature to familiarize themselves with the chapter. Discuss the relationships of the topics in the outline.

What's Next?
Before beginning the first section, make sure students understand the connection between the Find Out activity and the topics to follow.

For Your Mainstreamed Students
Students can make a liquid thermometer by filling a milk carton with colored water. Make a hole at the center top of the carton. Insert a plastic straw in the hole and seal it in place. Fill the straw part way with colored water. Record the daily increase or decrease in the water level of the straw. Chart the rise and fall of the thermometer.

PREPARATION

SECTION BACKGROUND

▶ Energy is defined operationally as the ability of an object or phenomenon to cause a change. You know a moving baseball has energy because you can see and feel the change in motion of your hand as you catch it. Light is energy because it causes pigments in photographic film and in the retina of the eye to change.

▶ An object can be described as having kinetic energy, which is a measure of its motion, and potential energy, which is a measure of its position or condition. The mechanical energy of an object is the sum of its kinetic and potential energies.

PREPLANNING

▶ Obtain a roll of waxed paper for the Motivation demonstration; a small weight and wood block for the Close demonstration.

1 MOTIVATE

▶ **Demonstration:** Attach a 1.0-m piece of waxed paper to several books with thumbtacks to form a track as shown below.

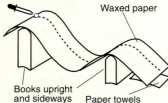

Waxed paper

Books upright and sideways   Paper towels

Using a medicine dropper, place a drop of water at the top of the ramp. Have students observe its motion. Repeat the demonstration several times, each time altering the shape of the ramp. Before releasing the drop, have students predict its motion. After demonstrating the motion, allow students to explain their reasoning in making their predictions.

▶ Have students discuss where changes of motion occur during a roller coaster ride.

5-1   Energy and Work

New Science Words

energy
kinetic energy
potential energy
work
mechanical energy
law of conservation of energy

Objectives

▶ Distinguish between kinetic and potential energy.
▶ Recognize that energy can change from one form to another with no loss of energy.
▶ Compare the scientific meaning of work with its everyday meaning.

Kinetic and Potential Energy

Have you seen any examples of energy in action today? Unless you stayed in bed all day with the covers over your head, the answer to the question is "yes." Just about everything you see or do involves energy.

Energy is a bit mysterious. You can't feel it or smell it. In most cases, you can't even see it. Light is one form of energy you can see. Light doesn't seem to do much, but without it, you wouldn't be able to see anything else. You can't see electricity, but you can see its effects in a glowing light bulb and you can feel its effects in the coils of a toaster. You can't see the energy in milk, but you can see and feel its effects when your muscles move.

Scientists have a problem defining energy, because they don't know exactly what it is. However, they can measure it. The basic unit of energy is the joule (JEWL), named for British scientist James Prescott Joule. You'll learn more about this unit later in this chapter.

Traditionally, energy has been defined as the ability to do work—to cause something to move. But this definition doesn't go far enough. As all of the examples above show, energy involves change. This close association with change offers a more precise and useful definition: **Energy is the ability to cause change. Any sample of matter has energy if it can produce a change in itself or in its surroundings. Energy comes in many forms. Some of these forms include radiant, electrical, chemical, thermal, and nuclear energy.**

Figure 5-1. A healthful diet, such as the well-balanced breakfast shown here, provides the body with "fuel." Energy stored in food is converted to energy that the body can use.

110   ENERGY

OPTIONS

Meeting Different Ability Levels

For Section 5-1, use the following **Teacher Resource Masters** depending upon individual students' needs.

◆ **Study Guide Master** for all students.

● **Reinforcement Master** for students of average and above average ability levels.

▲ **Enrichment Master** for above average students.

Additional Teacher Resource Package masters are listed in the OPTIONS box throughout the section. The additional masters are appropriate for all students.

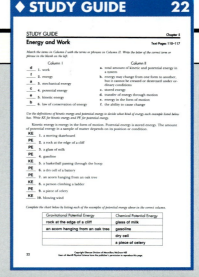

◆ **STUDY GUIDE**   **22**

STUDY GUIDE   Chapter 5
Energy and Work   Text Pages 110–117

Match the items in Column I with the terms or phrases in Column II. Write the letter of the correct term or phrase in the blank on the left.

	Column I		Column II
d	1. work	a.	total amount of kinetic and potential energy in a system
f	2. energy	b.	energy may change from one form to another, but it cannot be created or destroyed under ordinary conditions
a	3. mechanical energy	c.	stored energy
c	4. potential energy	d.	transfer of energy through motion
e	5. kinetic energy	e.	energy in the form of motion
b	6. law of conservation of energy	f.	the ability to cause change

Use the definitions of kinetic energy and potential energy to decide what kind of energy each example listed below has. Write KE for kinetic energy and PE for potential energy.

Kinetic energy is energy in the form of motion. Potential energy is stored energy. The amount of potential energy in a sample of matter depends on its position or condition.

KE	1. a moving skateboard
PE	2. a rock at the edge of a cliff
PE	3. a glass of milk
PE	4. gasoline
KE	5. a basketball passing through the hoop
PE	6. a dry cell of a battery
PE	7. an acorn hanging from an oak tree
KE	8. a person climbing a ladder
PE	9. a piece of celery
KE	10. blowing wind

Complete the chart below by listing each of the examples of potential energy above in the correct column.

Gravitational Potential Energy	Chemical Potential Energy
rock at the edge of a cliff	glass of milk
an acorn hanging from an oak tree	gasoline
	dry cell
	a piece of celery

22

Usually when you think of energy, you think of action—of some motion taking place. Motion-related energy is called kinetic energy. **Kinetic energy** is energy in the form of motion. A spinning motorcycle wheel, a leaping ballet dancer, and a flying Frisbee all have kinetic energy. How much? That depends on the mass and velocity of the moving object.

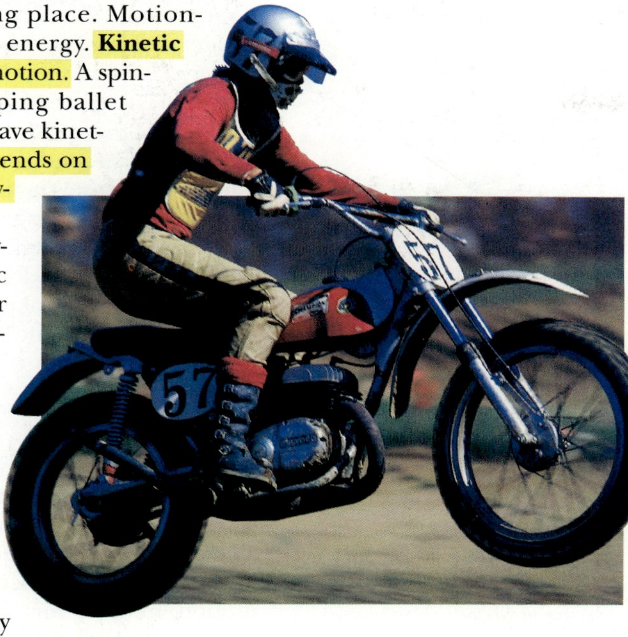

The greater the mass of a moving object, the more kinetic energy it has. Similarly, the greater its velocity, the more kinetic energy it has. A truck traveling at 100 km/h has more kinetic energy than a motorcycle traveling at the same speed. However, the motorcycle has more kinetic energy than an identical motorcycle moving at 80 km/h.

Energy doesn't have to involve motion. Even motionless, any sample of matter may have stored energy that gives it the potential to cause change if certain conditions are met. **Potential energy** is stored energy. The amount of potential energy a sample of matter has depends on its position or condition.

A flowerpot sitting on a second-floor windowsill has potential energy due to its position. If something knocks it off the windowsill, gravity will cause it to fall toward the ground. As it falls, its potential energy will change to kinetic energy.

Figure 5-2. This motorcycle is converting energy stored in gasoline into kinetic energy.

Figure 5-3. The kinetic energy of each vehicle is different because kinetic energy depends on mass and velocity.

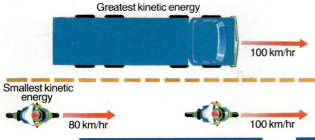

Greatest kinetic energy

100 km/hr

Smallest kinetic energy

80 km/hr   100 km/hr

● **REINFORCEMENT** 22   ▲ **ENRICHMENT** 22   111

TYING TO PREVIOUS KNOWLEDGE: Have students recall the conservation of momentum law from Section 4-4 and give examples. Allow them to explain the concept of conservation. Tell them that in this section they will learn about another conservation law, that of energy.

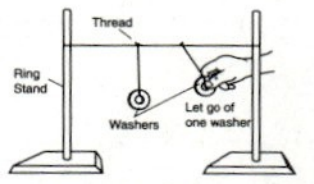

OBJECTIVES AND SCIENCE WORDS: Have students review the objectives and science words to become familiar with this section.

2 TEACH

Key Concepts are highlighted.

CONCEPT DEVELOPMENT

▶ Have students describe what they see and hear when a bowling ball strikes pins. Ask them to explain by using the operational definition of energy how these observations indicate that the moving bowling ball has energy. Have them explain why the breeze from an electric fan indicates that the spinning fan blades have energy. Ask them how they would determine if a coiled spring has energy.

▶ As new forms of energy are introduced, have students identify situations that illustrate how each form is indeed energy by using the operational definition of energy.

MINI QUIZ

Use the Mini Quiz to check students' recall of chapter content.

❶ **What is energy?** *the ability to cause change*

❷ **What is the unit of energy?** *joule*

❸ **What is potential energy?** *stored energy*

❹ **What is kinetic energy?** *energy in the form of motion*

PROGRAM RESOURCES

From the **Teacher Resource Package** use:

Cross-Curricular Connections, page 9, Food Energy.

Transparency Masters, pages 17-18, Kinetic and Potential Energy.

Use **Color Transparency** number 9, Kinetic and Potential Energy.

Figure 5-4. The spring in the wound condition has potential energy that can be used to make the toy move. In the enlarged view, the unwound spring has neither potential nor kinetic energy.

Potential energy due to height above Earth's surface is sometimes called gravitational potential energy. The greater the height, the greater the potential energy. A flowerpot sitting on a fifth-floor windowsill has more potential energy than one sitting on a lower windowsill.

Think of the spring in a wind-up toy. The tension in the spring is its condition. As the spring is wound, it gains potential energy. When the spring is released, the spring unwinds and makes the toy move. The potential energy of the spring is changed to kinetic energy of the toy.

The energy stored in foods, fuels, and dry cells are examples of chemical potential energy. These and other forms of potential energy will be discussed in later chapters of this book.

Work

To most people, the word *work* means something they do to earn money. Work can be anything from filling fast-food orders, loading trucks, or teaching, to lying around all day testing mattresses. The scientific meaning of work is more specific. **Work is the transfer of energy through motion. In order for work to take place, a force must be exerted through a distance.** ⑤

Figure 5-5. Work is done on the books when they are being lifted, but no work is done on them when they are being held or carried horizontally.

In which case would you do more work—lifting a pack of gum from the floor to waist level or lifting a pile of books through the same distance? Would more work be done if you lifted the books from the floor to your waist or if you raised them all the way over your head? Common sense tells you that the amount of work done depends on two things: the amount of force exerted and the distance over which the force is applied.

When a force acts over a distance, the work done can be calculated as

$$\text{Work} = \text{force} \times \text{distance}$$
$$W = F \times d$$

Work, like energy, is measured in joules. One joule is equal to a newton-meter (N • m), which is the amount of work done when a force of one newton acts through a distance of one meter.

Science and WRITING

Spend a few minutes observing the different forms of energy around you. List all the different forms and describe events that result from one form of energy changing to another.

EXAMPLE PROBLEM: Calculating Work

Problem Statement:

A student's full backpack weighs 10 N. She lifts it from the floor to a shelf 1.5 m high. How much work is done on the pack full of books?

Known Information:
Strategy Hint: Remember that weight is a measure of the force of gravity on an object.

force, F = 10 N
distance, d = 1.5 m

Unknown Information:

Work (W)

Equation to Use:

$$W = F \times d$$
$$= 10\ \text{N} \times 1.5\ \text{m}$$
$$= 15\ \text{N} \bullet \text{m}$$

Solution:

$$= 15\ \text{J}$$

PRACTICE PROBLEMS

Strategy Hint: The joule is a derived unit. What other units make it up?

Strategy Hint: Work requires a force to be exerted over a distance.

1. A carpenter lifts a 45-kg beam 1.2 m. How much work is done on the beam?

2. A dancer lifts a 400-N ballerina overhead a distance of 1.4 m and holds her there for several seconds. How much work is done on the ballerina?

CONCEPT DEVELOPMENT

▶ **Demonstration:** Using two thumb tacks, attach opposite ends of a long stretched, rubber band to a board forming a sling shot. Carefully use the sling shot to propel a small toy car along the board. Have students relate the kinetic energy of the car to the elastic potential energy of the rubber band.

▶ Have students realize that the relationship between a joule of energy and a joule of work comes from the definition: *work is the transfer of energy through motion.* When one joule of work is done on an object, one joule of energy has been transferred to the object.

▶ Point out that work can have a negative value. If friction acts on a moving object, the direction of the force is opposite the direction of motion; the work is negative.

TEACHER F.Y.I.

▶ The joule is equivalent to a newton-meter. If fundamental metric units are substituted for a newton, a newton-meter becomes
$$\text{kg} \bullet \text{m/s}^2 \times \text{m} = \text{kg} \bullet \text{m}^2/\text{s}^2$$
Likewise, if fundamental metric units are substituted in the equations for potential energy and kinetic energy, identical units emerge.
$$\text{kg} \times \text{m/s}^2 \times \text{m} = \text{kg} \bullet \text{m}^2/\text{s}^2$$
and
$$\text{kg} \times (\text{m/s})^2 = \text{kg} \bullet \text{m}^2/\text{s}^2$$

PRACTICE PROBLEM ANSWERS

1. $W = F \times d$
$$= (45\ \text{kg} \times 9.8\ \text{N/kg}) \times 1.2\ \text{m}$$
$$= 441\ \text{N} \times 1.2\ \text{m}$$
$$= 529.2\ \text{J}$$
2. $W = F \times d$
$$= 400\ \text{N} \times 1.4\ \text{m}$$
$$= 560\ \text{J}$$

PROGRAM RESOURCES

From the **Teacher Resource Package** use:
Science and Society, page 9, Energy Efficient Engines.
Use **Laboratory Manual,** Work and Power.

▶ It is often difficult for students to understand why they feel tired holding books if they are not doing any work. Point out that in describing work, it is important to identify on what the work is being done. When holding books, the students are not doing work *on their books*. They are doing work *on their muscles*. Discuss that thousands of fibrils which make up muscle tissue can be pictured as small, coiled springs. When a muscle is contracted, these fibrils are constantly contracting, and relaxing. In contracting, work is being done on the fibrils. The students feel tired because they are doing work on their muscles.

TEACHER F.Y.I.

▶ Energy can be considered as a convenient number to describe an object or situation much like an accountant uses numbers in bookkeeping to describe incomes, expenditures, and bankruptcy. The conservation of energy means that the number which describes the amount of energy does not change.

Name two factors to keep in mind when deciding when work is being done.

There are two factors to keep in mind when deciding when work is being done: something has to move, and the motion must be in the direction of the applied force. If you pick up a pile of books from the floor, work is done on the books. They move upward, in the direction of the applied force. If you hold the books in your arms, no work is done. Some upward force is still being applied (to keep the books from falling), but no movement is taking place. Even if you carry the books across the floor at a constant speed, no work is done on the books. The force being applied to the books is still upward, but your motion across the floor is sideward, or horizontal.

Conservation of Energy

Have you ever ridden on the swings in a playground? Try to remember what it was like swinging back and forth, high and low. Now think about the energy changes involved in such a ride.

The ride starts with a push to start you moving—to give you some kinetic energy. As the swing rises, kinetic energy changes to potential energy of position. At the top of each swing, potential energy is greatest. Then, as the swing moves downward, potential energy changes to kinetic energy. At the bottom of each swing, kinetic energy is greatest, and potential energy is at its minimum.

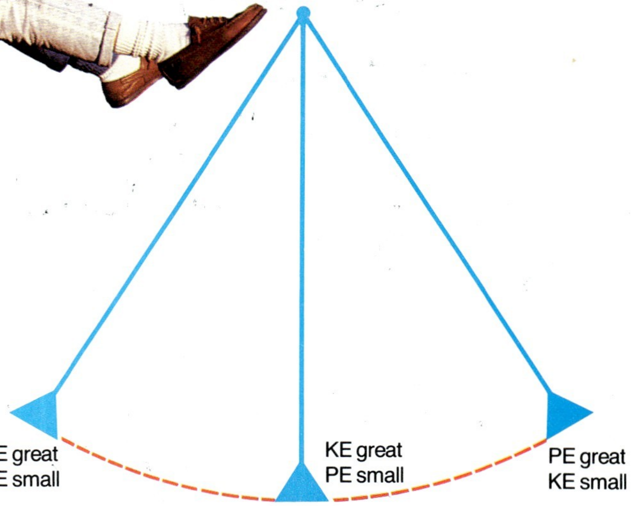

Figure 5-6. The diagram shows the energy conversions that take place in a moving swing.

PE great KE small

KE great PE small

PE great KE small

OPTIONS

INQUIRY QUESTIONS

▶ The kinetic energy of a hockey puck is 20 J as it moves from ice onto the cement surrounding the rink. By how much is its energy decreased if it stops on the cement? *20 J*

▶ If the cement causes the frictional force of 10 N on the puck, how far does it slide? *$-10 N 2 d = -20 N \cdot m = -20 J; d = 2.0 m$*

▶ What happens to this energy? *It is converted into heat.*

PROGRAM RESOURCES

Use **Laboratory Manual**, The Energy of a Pendulum.

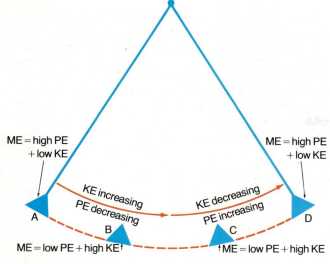

ME = high PE + low KE

ME = high PE + low KE

KE increasing
PE decreasing

KE decreasing
PE increasing

A

B

C

D

ME = low PE + high KE↑

↑ME = low PE + high KE

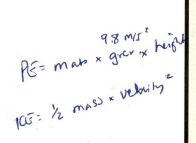

$PE = mass \times grav \times height$

$KE = \frac{1}{2} mass \times velocity^2$

Figure 5-7. The mechanical energy (K.E. + P.E.) of a moving swing is always the same.

As the swing continues to move back and forth, energy is converted from kinetic to potential to kinetic, over and over again. At any point along its path, the swing will have both potential energy and kinetic energy. Taken together, potential and kinetic energy of the swing make up its mechanical energy. **Mechanical energy** is the total amount of kinetic and potential energy in a system. ⑦

Scientists have learned that in any given situation, energy may change from one form to another, but the total amount of energy remains constant. In other words, energy is conserved. This fact is recognized as a law of nature. According to the **law of conservation of energy,** energy may change form but it cannot be created or destroyed under ordinary conditions.

Suppose the law of conservation of energy is applied to the swing. Would you expect the swing to continue moving back and forth forever? You know this doesn't happen. The swing slows down and comes to a stop. Where does the energy go?

If you think about it, friction and air resistance are constantly acting on the swing and rider. These unbalanced forces cause some of the mechanical energy of the swing to change to thermal energy—heat. With every pass of the swing, the temperatures of the swing, the rider, and the air around them go up a little bit. So the mechanical energy of the swing isn't lost, it is converted to thermal energy. Thermal energy is discussed in the next section.

Did You Know?

A person on a bicycle converts chemical energy into kinetic energy ten times more efficiently than does a seagull in flight.

CONCEPT DEVELOPMENT

▶ **Demonstration:** Clamp each end of a 1-m length of plastic tubing to a ring stand. Adjust the clamps so that both ends of the tubing are the same height above the table forming a shallow, U-shaped ramp. Hold a marble slightly above one end of the tubing and ask students to predict the height that the marble will reach on the opposite side. Have a student mark the predicted positions on the tube using a felt tipped marker. Release the marble and have students observe the height it reaches. Rearrange the tubing to form various shaped ramps and discuss the motion of the marble, stressing the conservation of mechanical energy.

▶ Point out that the conservation of mechanical energy is independent of time. That is, the value of the mechanical energy is constant and does not change from moment to moment. For example, even though the potential and kinetic energies are constantly changing for a swinging pendulum, their sum is constant.

MINI QUIZ

Use the Mini Quiz to check students' recall of chapter content.

⑤ **What is work?** *the transfer of energy through motion*
⑥ **What unit measures work?** *joule*
⑦ **What is mechanical energy?** *the total of kinetic and potential energy in a system*

INQUIRY QUESTIONS

▶ **Why is the first hill of a roller coaster ride the highest?** *The total mechanical energy of the ride is due to the potential energy of the roller coaster at the top of this hill. Because this hill is the highest, the gravitational energy is a maximum and, thus, its total mechanical energy is a maximum. If a later hill was higher, the mechanical energy needed would exceed this maximum and the coaster could not reach the top.*

▶ **Where will this roller coaster be moving fastest: immediately after it comes down the first hill, above ground level, at ground level, or in a valley below ground level?** *The roller coaster will be moving fastest below ground level since its kinetic energy will be a maximum because its gravitational energy will be a minimum.*

Ask questions 1-2 and the **Apply** Question in the Section Review.

RETEACH
Repeat the demonstration on page 113. This time, securely attach the car to the rubber band with a wire tie. Pull back on the rubber band indicating that you are doing work on the system. Release the rubber band, and discuss how the mechanical energy is conserved as the car oscillates. As the oscillations decrease, discuss how friction is doing work on the system.

EXTENSION
For students who have mastered this section, use the **Reinforcement** and **Enrichment** masters or other OPTIONS provided.

3 CLOSE

▶ **Demonstration:** Construct a small pendulum using a small weight and a piece of string. Have students describe how mechanical energy is conserved as it swings back and forth.

SECTION REVIEW ANSWERS
1. As the ball is tossed up to you, kinetic energy is changing to gravitational potential energy. When you drop the ball, the potential energy is changing to kinetic energy. When the ball hits the floor and bounces upward, kinetic energy is again changing to potential energy. The potential energy becomes less with each bounce. When the ball stops bouncing, its energy has been transformed into heat, sound, etc.

2. $W = F \times d$

$F = \dfrac{W}{d} = \dfrac{1470\,J}{20\,m}$

$= 73.5\,N$

3. Apply: In reality, it is not energy but the fuels that are burned to supply our energy that are in short supply. By driving more slowly and using less electricity, we are conserving the supplies of fuel.

Figure 5-8. As the sled moves down the hill, what energy changes are taking place? Is any work being done on the sled?

The next time you hear someone talking about *energy* or *work*, think about the scientific meanings of those words. Ask yourself what kind of energy is being discussed and whether the work involves a force being applied over a distance.

SECTION REVIEW

1. Imagine you're standing on a stepladder and someone tosses a basketball up to you. When you drop the ball, it bounces several times. The first bounce will be highest, and each bounce after that will be lower and lower until the ball stops bouncing. Describe the energy changes that take place, starting with the ball being tossed to you.
2. To win a prize on a game show, a contestant pushed a bowling ball a distance of 20 m using just his nose. The amount of work done was 1470 J. How much force did the person exert on the ball?
3. **Apply:** In recent years a lot of discussion has focused on the need to save energy by driving more efficient cars and using less electricity. If the law of conservation of energy is true, and the total amount of energy always stays the same, why are people worried about energy conservation?

Skill Builder ☑ **Comparing and Contrasting**

Compare and contrast the everyday meaning of *work* with the scientific definition of that term. Give examples of work in the everyday sense that would not be considered work in the scientific sense. If you need help, refer to Comparing and Contrasting in the **Skill Handbook** on page 679.

116 ENERGY

Skill Builder
The everyday meaning of work would include any time effort was given. The scientific meaning of work would require a force being exerted through a distance. Examples of work in the everyday sense that would not meet scientific meaning are: Jim worked hard in reading his English assignment, or Jennifer worked in holding the garage door open.

ACTIVITY 5-1
Conversion of Energy

Problem: *What happens to the energy of a pendulum?*

Materials
- ring stand and ring
- support rod clamp, right angle
- support rod, 30 cm
- metersticks (2)
- rubber stopper, 2-hole, medium
- string (100 cm)
- masking tape

Procedure
1. Prepare a data table like the one shown.
2. Set up the apparatus as shown.
3. Use masking tape to mark the center of the stopper. Use this line to measure heights above the tabletop.
4. Move the stopper away from the cross arm. Measure the height of the stopper above the table. Record this measurement.
5. Release the stopper and let it swing. Observe carefully and measure the height the stopper reaches at the opposite end of its swing. Record this measurement.
6. Repeat Steps 4 and 5 several times, each time starting the stopper at a greater height.

Data and Observations Sample Data

Trial	Starting Height	Ending Height
1	20.0 cm	19.0 cm
2	30.0 cm	28.0 cm

Analyze
1. For a single swing, is the ending height of the stopper exactly the same as its starting height? Explain why or why not.
2. What happens when the starting height is higher than the cross arm?

3. What is the highest ending point that the stopper will reach? What happens if the starting point is higher than that point?

Conclude and Apply
4. At what point along a single swing does the stopper have the greatest kinetic energy? the least kinetic energy?
5. At what point does the stopper have the greatest potential energy? the least potential energy?
6. Under what conditions can the cross arm prevent the stopper from returning to its maximum potential energy?
7. When are the potential energy and the kinetic energy of the stopper both zero at the same time?

OBJECTIVE: Compare the exchange of potential and kinetic energies.

PROCESS SKILLS applied in this activity:
▶ **Measuring** in Procedure Steps 3 and 4.
▶ **Observing** in Analyze Questions 1, 2, and 3.
▶ **Interpreting** in Conclude and Apply Questions 1, 2, and 3.

COOPERATIVE LEARNING
Use the Science Investigation team strategy in groups of four. Teams should be encouraged to share ideas with other teams.

TEACHING THE ACTIVITY
Troubleshooting: Remind students that a change in the height of the weight affects the pendulum's P.E. and a change in velocity its K.E.
▶ Any equipment arrangement that will result in the pendulum string wrapping around the cross arm will work.
▶ Variation in the placement of the cross arm may result in a more interesting follow-up discussion.

PROGRAM RESOURCES
From the **Teacher Resource Package** use:

Activity Worksheets, pages 39-40, Activity 5-1: Conversion of Energy.

ANSWERS TO QUESTIONS
1. Air friction slows the stopper down so it cannot quite reach the starting height.
2. The stopper continues to wrap the string around the cross bar until it stops and falls. If it is going fast enough, it will wrap all the string.
3. The highest point depends on where the string hits the cross bar. If the starting point is higher, the stopper will wrap all the string around the cross bar.
4. The highest K.E. is at the bottom of the swing. The lowest is at the top.

5. The highest P.E. is at the top of the swing. The lowest is at the bottom.
6. if the cross arm keeps the stopper from reaching its starting height
7. K.E. and P.E. are both zero when the stopper comes to rest at the lowest point. All its energy of motion has converted to heat.

PREPARATION

SECTION BACKGROUND

▶ The average kinetic energy of particles in a material is directly related to the absolute temperature of the material.

▶ By comparing the temperatures of two samples of a material, one can compare the average kinetic energy of the particles in the two samples.

▶ The thermal energy of a material is the total kinetic and potential energies of all of its particles and therefore, depends upon the amount of material present.

▶ Heat is the thermal energy transferred between objects because of a difference in their temperatures.

1 MOTIVATE

▶ Have students rub their hands together and then touch their cheeks. Ask them to explain if work is being done on their hands. Have them observe how the work changes the mechanical energy of their hands. Ask them if they can use a sense other than sight to detect other energy changes in their hands.

Cooperative Learning: Have Problem Solving Teams devise several ways of detecting if equal amounts of water in two identical containers are at different temperatures.

TYING TO PREVIOUS KNOWLEDGE: Have students recall the operational definition of *energy* from Section 4-1. Have them list and discuss situations which indicate that heat is a kind of energy. Tell them they will be learning more about heat in this section.

OBJECTIVES AND SCIENCE WORDS: Have students review the objectives and science words to become familiar with this section.

5-2 Temperature and Heat

New Science Words

temperature
thermal energy
heat

Objectives

▶ Recognize the difference between the motion of an object and the motion of the particles that make up the object.
▶ Contrast heat and temperature.
▶ Explain what determines the thermal energy of a sample of matter.

Temperature

What do you know about temperature? When the air temperature outside is high, you probably describe the weather as "hot." Ice cream, which has a low temperature, feels "cold." The words *hot* and *cold* are commonly used to describe the temperature of a material. Although not very scientific, these terms can be useful. Just about everyone understands that "hot" indicates high temperature and "cold" indicates low temperature.

Most people, when they think of temperature, automatically think of heat also. This association makes sense, because heat and temperature are related. But, they are not the same. To understand the relationship between temperature and heat, you need to know about matter.

All matter is made up of particles so small that you can't see them, even with an ordinary microscope. The particles that make up any sample of matter are constantly moving, even if the sample itself is perfectly still. Everything you can think of—the book on your desk, the shoe on your foot, even the foot inside the shoe—is made up of moving particles.

You know that moving things have kinetic energy. Because they are in constant motion, the particles that make up matter have kinetic energy. The faster the particles move, the more kinetic energy they have. **Temperature** is a measure of the average kinetic energy of the particles in a sample of matter. The higher the temperature of a material, the faster its particles are

MINI-Lab

Can you "create" energy?
Pour sand into a plastic foam cup until the cup is about half full. Measure the temperature of the sand to the nearest tenth of a degree. Remove the thermometer and place a lid on the cup. While holding the lid firmly in place, shake the cup vigorously for several minutes. Stop shaking, remove the lid, and measure the temperature of the sand immediately. What effect did shaking have on the temperature of the sand? Was energy "created"? Explain.

OPTIONS

Meeting Different Ability Levels

For Section 5-2, use the following **Teacher Resource Masters** depending upon individual students' needs.

◆ **Study Guide Master** for all students.

● **Reinforcement Master** for students of average and above average ability levels.

▲ **Enrichment Master** for above average students.

Additional Teacher Resource Package masters are listed in the OPTIONS box throughout the section. The additional masters are appropriate for all students.

◆ STUDY GUIDE 23

STUDY GUIDE   Chapter 5
Temperature and Heat   Text Pages 118–121

In each of the following statements, the italicized term has been scrambled. Unscramble the term and write it on the line provided.

temperature	1. A measure of the average kinetic energy of the particles in a sample of matter is an object's *pentamrurte*.
thermal energy	2. The total energy of the particles that make up a material is *mathrel genry*.
heat energy	3. Energy that flows from something with a higher temperature to something with a lower temperature is *eath genery*.
potential energy	4. Thermal energy includes both kinetic energy and *laptoinn nergey*.
kinetic energy	5. The higher the temperature of a material, the faster its particles are moving and the greater their average *citniek rengy*.

For each group of three terms, write a sentence that explains how the terms are related. Underline the terms in your sentences. Answers will vary. Be sure students include all of the necessary characteristics and use complete sentences.

1. thermal energy, particles, energy
   Thermal energy is the total energy (kinetic and potential) of the particles that make up a material.

2. temperature, particles, kinetic energy
   Temperature is a measure of the average kinetic energy of the particles that make up a sample of matter.

3. heat energy, temperature, flow
   Heat energy is the flow of energy from something with a higher temperature to something with a lower temperature.

4. joules, heat, work
   Heat and work are measured in units called joules.

5. thermal energy, kinetic energy, potential energy
   Thermal energy is a measure of the kinetic energy and the potential energy of the particles that make up a material.

Copyright Glencoe Division of Macmillan/McGraw-Hill
Users of Merrill Physical Science have the publisher's permission to reproduce this page.   23

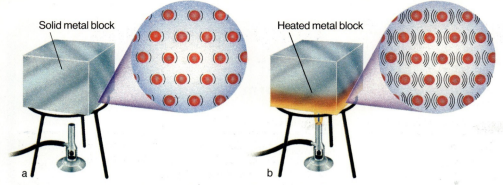

Figure 5-9. The drawing illustrates the motion of the particles of a material when it is cool (a) and when it is hot (b).

moving and the greater their average kinetic energy. Similarly, the lower the temperature of a material, the more slowly its particles are moving. Which particles are moving faster, those in a cup of hot tea or those in the same amount of iced tea?

Thermal Energy

If you place an ice-cold teaspoon on top of a scoop of ice cream, nothing will happen. But suppose you place a hot teaspoon on the ice cream. Now the ice cream under the spoon starts to melt. The hot spoon causes the ice cream to change because it transfers energy to the ice cream. Where does this energy come from? The spoon isn't moving, and its position is the same as that which the cold spoon had. So the energy is not due to motion or position of the spoon. It must be related to the temperature of the spoon.

The change in the ice cream is caused by thermal energy. Like temperature, thermal energy is related to the energy of the particles that make up matter. **Thermal energy** is the total energy of the particles that make up a material. This total includes both kinetic and potential energy.

Now suppose you stack two hot teaspoons and place them on a scoop of ice cream. What will happen? The two spoons will melt more ice cream than the single spoon did in the same amount of time. The stacked spoons have twice as much mass and, therefore, twice as many moving particles. The more mass a material has, the greater its thermal energy.

Figure 5-10. An ice-cold spoon (a) has no effect on ice cream. Two hot spoons (c) have more thermal energy than one hot spoon (b), so they melt more ice cream.

119

MINI-Lab

Materials: sand, plastic foam cup with lid, thermometer

Teaching Tips
► Enough granular material should be used to just submerge the bulb of the thermometer.
► Preliminary help and practice should be given in reading the thermometer and making estimates of tenths of degrees.

Answers to Questions
► The kinetic energy of each particle converts with each collision to higher *molecular* kinetic energy, resulting in higher temperature. No energy was "created."

2 TEACH

Key Concepts are highlighted.

CONCEPT DEVELOPMENT

► Make sure students understand the mathematical concept of average. Point out that the average of any group of numbers, for example, 1, 2, 4, and 5, is their sum (12) divided by the size of the group (4). The average, in this example, 3, is a way of describing the group and is not necessarily a number in the group. Likewise, the average kinetic energy of the particles is an indication of the kinetic energy of a representative particle of the sample. Real particles in a sample will have kinetic energies that range from above the average kinetic energy to below it.

PROGRAM RESOURCES

From the **Teacher Resource Package** use:

Activity Worksheets, page 45, Mini-Lab: Can you "create" energy?

Transparency Masters, pages 19-20, Cool and Hot Matter.

Use **Color Transparency** number 10, Cool and Hot Matter.

CONCEPT DEVELOPMENT

▶ Have students use the operational definition of energy to discuss the difference between temperature and heat. Have them consider the difference in the effects of being splashed by icy-cold water from a cup and from a bucket.

TEACHER F.Y.I.

▶ Temperature is an *intrinsic* quality. It is independent of the amount of substance. Thermal energy is an *extrinsic* quantity; it depends upon the amount of substance.

CROSS CURRICULUM

▶ **Life Science:** Have students research *thermogenesis*.

PROBLEM SOLVING

▶ Because both drinks are essentially water, and assuming the same size, the thermal energy of the tea was greater than the thermal energy of the soft drink.

Think Critically: Because the temperature of the tea was greater than the temperature of its surroundings, the heat flowed from the tea to the environment. The soft drink had a lower temperature than its surroundings, so heat flowed from the environment to the soft drink.

PROBLEM SOLVING

A Cold Cup of Tea and a Warm Soft Drink

Carol and Alicia were tired after playing a hard game of soccer. Shortly after arriving at Alicia's house and sitting down on the back porch, Alicia's grandmother peeked her head out the door.

"I am preparing myself a cup of herbal tea," she said. "Would you girls like some?"

"That sounds good," replied Carol. "I'm thirsty."

Alicia was thirsty too but didn't want hot tea. She told her grandmother, "No, I'll just have a cold soft drink."

They had just taken a sip of their drinks when Alicia suggested that they listen to a new cassette tape of her favorite group. The girls left their drinks and went to listen to the tape. When they finally returned to finish their drinks, Carol's tea was cold, and Alicia's soft drink was warm. How did the thermal energy of the two drinks compare when the girls first got the drinks?

Think Critically: Explain how heat was transferred in both drinks while the girls were listening to the tape.

EcoTip

Thermal energy must be used to heat water. Take a shower instead of a bath. A shower uses one-third the amount of hot water a bath does.

Different kinds of matter have different thermal energies, even when mass and temperature are the same. For example, a 5-g sample of sand has a different thermal energy than a 5-g sample of pudding at the same temperature. This difference is due mainly to the ways in which the particles of the materials are arranged.

It is important to remember that the thermal energy of a material depends on the total energy of its particles. The energy of the material itself has no effect on its thermal energy. For example, at 20°C a golf ball has the same thermal energy whether it's sitting on the ground or speeding through the air.

Heat

On a warm day, what would happen if you pressed your left hand against a cool tile wall? Your hand would feel cooler. Its temperature would have decreased. If you

---

OPTIONS

INQUIRY QUESTIONS

▶ **How can thermal energy be used to explain both hotness and coldness?** *Hotness can be explained as the presence of thermal energy. Coldness can be explained as the absence of thermal energy.*

▶ **Are heat and work properties of matter?** *No, heat is thermal energy transferred between matter at two different temperatures. Work represents the energy transferred to matter by motion.*

PROGRAM RESOURCES

From the **Teacher Resource Package** use:
Activity Worksheets, page 5, Flex Your Brain.

touched the same spot on the wall with your right hand, the spot wouldn't feel as cool as it did. The temperature of the spot would have increased when you touched it with your left hand. Energy flowed from your warm hand to the cool tile. **Heat is the energy that flows from something with a higher temperature to something with a lower temperature.** It is important to remember that heat always flows from warmer to cooler materials—never from cooler to warmer.

Like work, heat is measured in joules. That's not the only similarity between heat and work. Both involve transfers of energy. Heat is energy transferred between objects at different temperatures. Work is energy transferred when a force acts over a distance.

The next time you listen to a weather report, think about the difference between temperature and heat. And when you drop an ice cube into your drink, think about how the cooling occurs. Does the melting ice cause the liquid to cool? Or does heat flowing from the liquid to the ice, cool the drink and cause the ice to melt?

Figure 5-11. Heat flows from hot cocoa to your hand, making your hand feel hot. Heat flows from your hand to an ice cube, making your hand feel cold.

SECTION REVIEW

1. If temperature is not a direct measure of how much thermal energy something contains, why does a bottle of soda left in the sun have a higher temperature than one left in an ice chest?
2. Which has more thermal energy, a 5-kg bowling ball that has been resting on a hot driveway for 4 hours on a 35°C day, or the same bowling ball rolling down a lane in an air-conditioned bowling alley?
3. **Apply:** Using your understanding of temperature and heat, explain what happens when you heat a pan of soup on the stove, then put some leftover warm soup in the refrigerator.

☑ Concept Mapping

Create a network tree that shows how the following words and phrases are related: *energy, potential energy of particles, energy transfer (higher or lower temperature), heat, kinetic energy of particles,* and *thermal energy.* If you need help, refer to Concept Mapping in the **Skill Handbook** on pages 684 and 685.

Skill Builder

Skill Builder

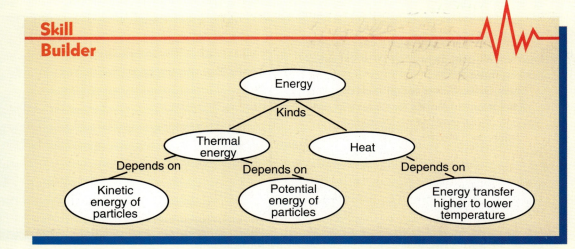

► Make sure students realize that heat is the thermal energy that flows *spontaneously* from warmer to cooler materials. Devices, such as refrigerators and air conditioners, can be used to reverse the flow, but require additional sources of energy.

MINI QUIZ

Use the Mini Quiz to check students' recall of chapter content.

❶ **What is thermal energy?** *the total energy of the particles that make up a material*
❷ **What is heat?** *energy that flows from something with a higher temperature to something with a lower temperature*

CHECK FOR UNDERSTANDING

Ask questions 1-2 and the **Apply** Question in the Section Review.

RETEACH

Have students repeat the first motivation activity. Discuss and explain their observations using the terms *work, temperature, thermal energy,* and *heat.*

EXTENSION

For students who have mastered this section, use the **Reinforcement** and **Enrichment** masters or other OPTIONS provided.

3 CLOSE

⁇ FLEX Your Brain

Use the Flex Your Brain activity to have students explore HEAT.

SECTION REVIEW ANSWERS

1. The soda absorbs energy from the sun and the average kinetic energy of the particles goes up. There is no outside source of energy to increase the energy of soda kept in an ice chest.
2. The ball that rested in the sun for several hours has more thermal energy.
3. Apply: Energy from the stove burner is transferred to the particles of soup. When the warm soup is placed in a cold refrigerator, heat will flow from the soup to the air in the refrigerator.

 **SCIENCE & SOCIETY** **5-3**

Energy from the Oceans and Earth

PREPARATION

SECTION BACKGROUND
▶ Geothermal energy refers to thermal energy found in molten magma beneath Earth's surface. Thermal energy can be used to produce steam for heating and for generating electricity.

PREPLANNING
▶ Obtain a small piece of granite rock, tongs, a medicine dropper, and a gas burner for the Motivation demonstration.

1 MOTIVATE

▶ **Demonstration:** Using tongs, heat a small piece of granite rock over a gas flame. When very hot, carefully place it on a heat proof pad and let a drop of water fall on it. Have students observe the water vaporizing. Ask them to discuss how rising steam could be used to do work on a turbine and produce electricity.

TYING TO PREVIOUS KNOWLEDGE:
Have students recall seeing geysers. Point out that geysers are fountains of steam formed when water comes into contact with hot rocks under ground.

OBJECTIVES AND SCIENCE WORDS:
Have students review the objectives and science words to become familiar with this section.

PROGRAM RESOURCES

From the **Teacher Resource Package** use:

Critical Thinking/Problem Solving, page 11, Is the Oil Age Ending?

Activity Worksheets, page 5, Flex Your Brain.

New Science Words

magma

Objectives

▶ Explain why ocean waters and subsurface rock may represent possible new sources of thermal energy.
▶ Discuss the benefits and drawbacks of proceeding with research and development of these new energy sources.

Exploring New Energy Resources

Scientists are always searching for new sources of energy and improved methods of using our present energy sources. Two new possibilities being explored involve the harnessing of thermal energy present in oceans waters and in rocks beneath Earth's surface.

You have learned that heat flows from regions of higher temperature to regions of lower temperature. In some ocean areas the temperature difference between surface water and deeper water is as much as 15°C. Scientists believe that they can use some of the thermal energy that flows between such regions of different temperature to produce electricity.

Another possible source of energy is **magma** (MAG muh), the molten rock that lies several kilometers beneath Earth's surface. Scientists are working on the idea of drilling deep wells in order to use the thermal energy stored in the magma.

Both of these proposed projects are ambitious and, if successful, could be of tremendous benefit to all peoples of the world. However, possible drawbacks must be considered. Each of these projects will be very expensive and will take

122 ENERGY

OPTIONS

Meeting Different Ability Levels
For Section 5-3, use the following **Teacher Resource Masters** depending upon individual students' needs.
◆ **Study Guide Master** for all students.
● **Reinforcement Master** for students of average and above average ability levels.
▲ **Enrichment Master** for above average students.

◆ **STUDY GUIDE** **24**

STUDY GUIDE   Chapter 5
Energy from the Oceans and Earth   Text Pages 122-123

Use the words listed below to fill in the blanks in the paragraphs.

deep	kinetic energy	more
electricity	law of conservation of energy	potential energy
energy	lower	surface
higher	magma	thermal energy

The ___law of conservation of energy___ states that energy can change from one form to another, but it cannot be created or destroyed under ordinary conditions. By applying this law, scientists hope to harness some of the ___thermal energy___ that lies in rocks beneath Earth's surface and in ocean water.

Molten rock that lies several kilometers beneath Earth's surface is called ___magma___. Scientists hope to drill deep wells into Earth to tap the stored, or ___potential energy___ in magma. This energy may then be changed into forms of energy that are useful to society.

Heat is one form of ___energy___. Temperature is a measure of the average ___kinetic energy___ of the particles in a sample of matter. Heat energy flows from regions of ___higher___ temperature to regions of ___lower___ temperature.

The surface water of the ocean has a higher temperature and ___more___ kinetic energy than deeper water. Heat energy flows form the warm ___surface___ water to the cooler ___deep___ water.

Scientists believe that they can harness some of this heat energy and convert it into ___electricity___.

24   Copyright Glencoe Division of Macmillan/McGraw-Hill
                     Users of Merrill Physical Science have the publisher's permission to reproduce this page

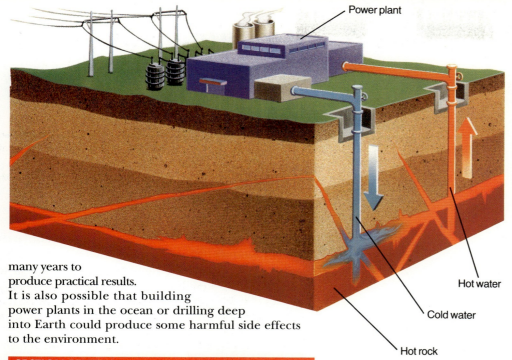

Power plant

Hot water

Cold water

Hot rock

many years to
produce practical results.
It is also possible that building
power plants in the ocean or drilling deep
into Earth could produce some harmful side effects
to the environment.

SECTION REVIEW

1. Explain how temperature differences at different depths of the ocean provide a possible energy source.
2. Why do you think projects like the ones mentioned in this section are so expensive and take so long to complete?

You Decide!

The growing demand for electricity combined with diminishing natural sources of fuel has made the need for new sources of energy used to produce electricity essential. All possible methods of developing new energy sources should be examined and evaluated carefully. It is equally important, however, to consider the negative aspects of proceeding with such projects as those described here. The most obvious negative aspects include possible harmful effects on the environment and the huge cost in time and money. Should tax dollars be used to support research and development of projects designed to provide new energy sources? If not, who should foot the bill?

SCIENCE & SOCIETY

123

2 TEACH

Key Concepts are highlighted.

CONCEPT DEVELOPMENT
▶ **Demonstration:** Heat water in a Pyrex beaker over a gas burner, but do not boil it. Add a few drops of food coloring to the water. Observe the currents.
▶ Introduce the word *geothermal*. Have students brainstorm its meaning.

CHECK FOR UNDERSTANDING
Ask questions 1 and 2 in the Section Review.

RETEACH
Cooperative Learning: Assign Numbered Heads Together groups to sketch methods of producing electricity by thermal energy sources in the oceans or Earth.

EXTENSION
For students who have mastered this section, use the **Reinforcement** and **Enrichment** masters or other OPTIONS provided.

3 CLOSE

? **FLEX Your Brain**

Use the Flex Your Brain activity to have students explore GEOTHERMAL ENERGY.
▶ Ask the You Decide question in the Section Review.

SECTION REVIEW ANSWERS
1. Energy in the form of heat flows from regions of higher to lower temperature. Scientists believe that they can devise methods of using some of this energy to produce electricity.
2. The projects require extensive time and preparation. Scientists must ensure that the projects are safe for the environment.

SCIENCE & SOCIETY

YOU DECIDE!

Answers should reflect ways of funding energy projects.

PREPARATION

SECTION BACKGROUND

▶ The specific heat of a material can be used to quantitatively describe a change in its thermal energy. By definition, the specific heat is the amount of energy needed to change the temperature of one kilogram of a material by one Celsius degree. Its unit is J/kg • °C.

PREPLANNING

▶ Obtain four Pyrex beakers, 50 g of sand, two thermometers, and a gas burner and stand for the Motivation demonstration.

1 MOTIVATE

▶ **Demonstration:** Fill two beakers each with 50 mL of water at room temperature. Measure their temperatures using two thermometers. Heat 50 mL of water in a beaker and 50 g of sand in a similar beaker to a temperature of 100°C. Carefully pour each, separately into the first two beakers. Have students read the resulting temperatures and calculate the temperature changes. Ask students to conjecture about the reasons for the difference in the temperature changes.

TYING TO PREVIOUS KNOWLEDGE: Have students recall the metric units and, where appropriate, the instruments used to measure energy, mass, and temperature. Tell students that they will use this knowledge to learn more about changes in thermal energy as something is heated or cooled.

New Science Words

specific heat

Objectives

▶ Define *specific heat*.
▶ Calculate changes in thermal energy.

Specific Heat

Have you ever jumped into a swimming pool or lake on a hot summer day and found the water surprisingly cold? Even though lots of radiant energy has been transferred to the water from the sun, the temperature of the water is still cooler than that of the surroundings. Different materials need different amounts of heat to produce similar changes in their temperatures. The materials have different specific heats. The **specific heat** (*C*) of a material is the amount of energy it takes to raise the temperature of 1 kg of the material 1 degree Celsius. Specific heat is measured in joules per kilogram per degree Celsius (J/kg • °C). Table 5-1 shows the specific heats of some familiar materials. How does the specific heat of water compare with the specific heats of the other materials?

Now that you see how high the specific heat of water is compared to other materials, do you understand why jumping into the water took your breath away on that hot day? The materials around the water heat up much faster than the water itself. So the water seems cold in comparison with its surroundings. Even if the water is 20°C, it seems much colder than air at 20°C. The water can take heat away from your body more quickly, because its specific heat is much higher than that of air.

Figure 5-12. Because of its high specific heat, water warms up more slowly than its surroundings.

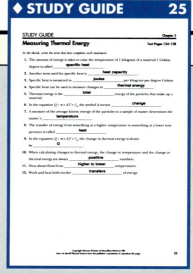

OPTIONS

Meeting Different Ability Levels

For Section 5-4, use the following **Teacher Resource Masters** depending upon individual students' needs.

◆ **Study Guide Master** for all students.

● **Reinforcement Master** for students of average and above average ability levels.

▲ **Enrichment Master** for above average students.

Additional Teacher Resource Package masters are listed in the OPTIONS box throughout the section. The additional masters are appropriate for all students.

◆ **STUDY GUIDE** 25

STUDY GUIDE   Chapter 5
Measuring Thermal Energy   Text Pages 124–128

In the blank, write the term that best completes each statement.

1. The amount of energy it takes to raise the temperature of 1 kilogram of a material 1 Celsius degree is called _____**specific heat**_____

2. Another term used for specific heat is _____**heat capacity**_____

3. Specific heat is measured in _____**joules**_____ per kilogram per degree Celsius.

4. Specific heat can be used to measure changes in _____**thermal energy**_____

5. Thermal energy is the _____**total**_____ energy of the particles that make up a material.

6. In the equation $Q = m \times \Delta T \times C_p$ the symbol Δ means _____**change**_____

7. A measure of the average kinetic energy of the particles in a sample of matter determines the matter's _____**temperature**_____

8. The transfer of energy from something at a higher temperature to something at a lower temperature is called _____**heat**_____

9. In the equation $Q = m \times \Delta T \times C_p$ the change in thermal energy is shown by _____**Q**_____

10. When calculating changes in thermal energy, the change in temperature and the change in thermal energy are always _____**positive**_____ numbers.

11. Heat always flows from _____**higher to lower**_____ temperatures.

12. Work and heat both involve _____**transfers**_____ of energy.

Table 5-1

SPECIFIC HEAT OF SOME COMMON MATERIALS*	
Water 4190	Iron 450
Alcohol 2450	Copper 380
Aluminum......................920	Silver 235
Carbon (Graphite)............710	Clay 130
Sand...............................664	*(J/kg • °C)

T E C H N O L O G Y

Infrared Weather Eyes

The satellite picture that you see on your TV weather show is usually an infrared image captured by a GOES satellite. GOES (**G**eostationary **O**perational **E**nvironmental **S**atellite) satellites remain directly above the same point on Earth's surface. Each satellite monitors a circular region of the surface 10 000 kilometers across. Within this circle, clouds appear white and the Earth's surface appears gray. A meteorologist can point out a line of clouds that indicates a weather front and run a sequence of images to demonstrate how that front is moving.

The satellite's sensors measure many bands of infrared radiation. One band detects moisture in the air. Dry air appears black and moist air appears in varying shades of gray. Because bad weather often breaks out when dry air intrudes into moist air, these water vapor images can be used to predict storms. Other bands of radiation reveal information about wind speed and direction, rainfall, fog, snow, and ice. Newer satellites, with a "sharper eye," may one day provide data for making accurate global weather forecasts 30 to 90 days in advance.

Think Critically: In addition to weather forecasting, what are some other uses for satellite data from infrared sources?

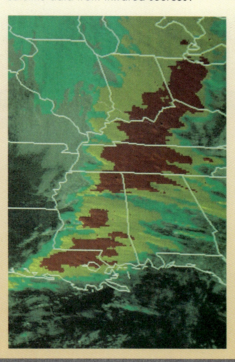

OBJECTIVES AND SCIENCE WORDS: Have students review the objectives and science words to become familiar with this section.

2 TEACH

Key Concepts are highlighted.

CONCEPT DEVELOPMENT

▶ Specific heat can be thought of as the amount of energy absorbed or released by a kilogram of material for each degree of change in temperature. The energy gained or lost per kilogram is expressed in J/kg and the temperature change of one degree is expressed as °C. Thus the unit of specific heat is
(J/kg)/°C = J/kg × 1/°C = J/kg • °C

▶ By comparing the values of the specific heat of different materials, one can compare the amount of energy materials will absorb or lose under similar circumstances. For example, the specific heat of aluminum is almost four times that of silver. Undergoing similar temperature changes, an aluminum spoon will absorb four times as much thermal energy as a silver spoon of the same weight.

T E C H N O L O G Y

For additional information on weather satellites, see "Ready, Set, GOES: Weather Eyes for the 21st Century," by Joanne Heckman, *Space World,* July 1987, pp. 23-26.

Think Critically: Satellite monitoring of infrared sources could provide information on ocean currents, patterns of thermal pollution, forest fires, volcanic activity, etc.

CONCEPT DEVELOPMENT

▶ You may wish to discuss changes in temperature and changes in thermal energy using the definition of ΔT as $T_{final} - T_{initial}$. Ask students to describe what a positive ΔT indicates. (The temperature of the material rose.) Point out that a positive ΔT means that the value of Q is also positive. Ask them what a positive value of Q means. (The material gained heat.) Now have students consider what is meant by a negative ΔT. (The temperature of the material fell.) Because ΔT is negative, so is the value of Q. Explain that the negative value of Q means that thermal energy left the material.

TEACHER F.Y.I.

▶ Historically, the specific heat of water is measured as a calorie (c), which is the amount of energy needed to raise the temperature of one gram of water by one Celsius degree. This unit is not recognized as an SI unit. However, dieticians measure the energy equivalent of foods in kilocalories (C). These values are often found in dieting books and listed among the nutritional information found on labels of food products. A kilocalorie equals 4180 joules.

CROSS CURRICULUM

▶ **History:** Have students research the experiments conducted by James Prescott Joule quantitatively relating thermal energy and work.

PRACTICE PROBLEMS ANSWERS

1. $Q = \Delta T \times m \times C_p$
   $= (90°C - 12°C) \times 230\ kg \times 4190\ J/kg \cdot °C$
   $= 78°C \times 230\ kg \times 4190\ J/kg \cdot °C$
   $= 75\ 000\ J$

2. $Q = \Delta T \times m \times C_p$
   $C_p = \dfrac{Q}{\Delta T \times m} = \dfrac{180\ 480\ J}{12°C \times 45\ kg}$
   $= \dfrac{180\ 480\ J}{540\ kg \cdot °C}$
   $= 334\ J/kg \cdot °C$

Thermometer
Stirrer
Cover
Inner chamber
Insulated flask (outer chamber)

Figure 5-13. Devices like this simple calorimeter are used to measure thermal energy transfer.

Using Specific Heat

Changes in thermal energy cannot be measured directly. No instrument can make such measurements. However, specific heat can be used to measure changes in thermal energy. For example, suppose you take a 3.1-g ball of aluminum foil from a pot of water at a temperature of 30°C and allow it to cool to room temperature, which is 15°C. You now have enough information to find out the change in the thermal energy of the ball of foil using the following equation:

$$\text{Change in thermal energy} = \text{mass} \times \text{Change in temperature} \times \text{specific heat}$$

$$Q = m \times \Delta T \times C_p$$

The symbol Δ (delta) means change, so ΔT is the change in temperature. "Change" is included in Q, which is the variable for energy change.

$$\Delta T = T_{final} - T_{initial}$$

When ΔT is positive the object has increased in temperature and gained heat. When ΔT is negative the object has decreased in temperature and given off heat.

EXAMPLE PROBLEM: Calculating Changes in Thermal Energy

Problem Statement: A 3.1-g ball of aluminum foil cools from 30°C to 15°C. What is the change in its thermal energy?

Known Information:
Strategy Hint: Make sure you're using the appropriate units.

Mass = m = 3.1 g = 0.0031 kg
T_{final} = 15.0°C
$T_{initial}$ = 30.0°C
Specific heat (C_p) = 920 J/kg • °C

Unknown Information: Energy change (Q)

Equation to Use:
$Q = \Delta T \times m \times C_p$
$\Delta T = T_{final} - T_{initial}$

Solution:
$Q = (T_{final} - T_{initial}) \times m \times C_p$
$= (15.0°C - 30.0°C) \times 0.0031\ kg \times 920\ J/kg \cdot °C$
$= -43\ J$

The foil ball loses 43 J of thermal energy as it cools.

OPTIONS

INQUIRY QUESTIONS

▶ **If water takes longer to heat up than its surroundings, why does it take away heat from your body so quickly?** *Although water has a large specific heat, the conductivity of the water is high and thermal energy is quickly spread throughout the water resulting in a longer time for the water to become heated. The conductivity of water is more than that of air, and the heat from your body is transferred to the surrounding water more quickly resulting in a rapid drop in skin temperature.*

▶ **Why do you think the unit of specific heat is J/kg • °C rather than J/L • °C?** *The volume of a material depends upon its temperature and therefore, the specific heat would be different at each temperature. However, the mass of a material does not depend upon its temperature.*

PRACTICE PROBLEMS

<u>Strategy Hint:</u> Will your answer be a positive or negative number?

<u>Strategy Hint:</u> What is the unknown information?

1. Calculate the change in thermal energy when 230 g of water warms from 12°C to 90°C.

2. A 45-kg brass sculpture gains 180 480 J of thermal energy as its temperature increases from 28°C to 40°C. What is the approximate specific heat of brass?

With your new knowledge of specific heat, think about temperature changes you've observed in objects around your home or in your neighborhood. Now you have an idea about why a kettle of water takes so long to boil. And why a sandy beach heats up quickly on a sunny day.

Figure 5-14. Computers will not work at high temperatures, so heat must be removed by an internal fan.

SECTION REVIEW

1. A bucket of sand and a bucket of water are side by side in direct sunlight. Which warms faster? Why?

2. Use Table 5-1 on page 125 to calculate the change in thermal energy when a 55-g iron nail cools from 90°C to 25°C.

3. **Apply:** If you wanted to quickly cool a piece of hot metal, would it be smarter to plunge it into a container of water or a container of sand at the same temperature?

☑ Interpreting Data

Equal amounts of clay, iron, water, and sand, all at the same temperature, were placed in an oven and heated. Use the data in Table 5-1 on page 125 to match each final temperature with the appropriate material: 30°C, 5°C, 160°C, and 23°C. If you need help, refer to Interpreting Data in the **Skill Handbook** on page 683.

Skill Builder

ENRICHMENT

▶ Have students research the calorimeter, an instrument used to measure thermal energy released in physical changes and chemical reactions.

PROGRAM RESOURCES

From the **Teacher Resource Package** use:
Concept Mapping, pages 15-16.
Use **Laboratory Manual**, Heat Transfer.

CHECK FOR UNDERSTANDING

Ask questions 1-2 and the **Apply** Question in the Section Review.

RETEACH

Ask students to look at Table 5-1. The values of the specific heats are ranked from high to low. Have the students recall the results of the Motivation demonstration or perform the demonstration now. Relate the results of the demonstration to the specific heats listed on the table. Ask students to predict the results of repeating the demonstration using 50 g of clay instead of sand.

EXTENSION

For students who have mastered this section, use the **Reinforcement** and **Enrichment** masters or other OPTIONS provided.

3 CLOSE

▶ Have students recall the conservation of mechanical energy statement from Section 5-1. Ask them if they have any evidence that thermal energy is also conserved.

SECTION REVIEW ANSWERS

1. The sand heats more quickly than the water because it has a lower specific heat than water.

2. $Q = \Delta T \times m \times C_p$
$Q = -65°C \times 0.055$ kg $\times$ 450 J/kg°C
$= -1609$ J

3. Apply: Plunge the metal into water. With its higher specific heat, water takes more heat from the metal as its temperature rises.

Skill Builder

160°C = clay, 5°C = water, 30°C = iron, 23°C = sand

ACTIVITY 5-2
40 minutes

OBJECTIVE: Measure the heat delivered by a hair curler over a 5-minute period.

PROCESS SKILLS applied in this activity:
▶ **Measuring** in Procedure Steps 4 and 5.
▶ **Using Numbers** in Analyze Statement 3.
▶ **Interpreting** in Conclude and Apply Question 5.

COOPERATIVE LEARNING Divide class into Science Investigation teams of three. Teams will develop conclusions after comparing lab results.

TEACHING THE ACTIVITY

Troubleshooting: Do not allow the water in the cup to overflow into the curler. The water inside the curler provides an even flow of heat to the thermometer.
▶ One set of hair curlers will serve the entire class. The type with a hard plastic outer covering is recommended.
▶ Heat the set of curlers to maximum temperature prior to class. Warn students not to touch metal interiors of the cylinders.
▶ Assign different sized curlers to different teams.
▶ Heat loss to air is ignored in this activity, but could become part of the follow up discussion. Placing a lid over the cup would control most of the heat loss during the 5-minute procedure.
▶ A class discussion period after completing **Analyze** is recommended.

PROGRAM RESOURCES
From the **Teacher Resource Package** use:
Activity Worksheets, pages 41-42, Activity 5-2: Specific Heat.

ACTIVITY 5-2
Specific Heat

Problem: *How much heat will curl your hair?*

Materials
- set of electric hair curlers
- thermometers, Celsius (2)
- plastic foam cup
- graph paper
- balance
- graduated cylinder

Procedure
1. Prepare a data table like the one shown.
2. Measure the mass of the plastic foam cup. Fill the cup about halfway with cool water and measure its mass again. Determine the mass of the water in kilograms.
3. Carefully remove a heated curler from its heating unit. **CAUTION:** *Don't touch any hot metal parts.* Stand the curler, open end up, on the table and pour in 2 mL of cool water.
4. Using two thermometers, measure and record the temperature of the water in the cup and the temperature of the water in the curler.
5. Carefully lower the curler into the cup of water. Measure and record the water temperatures every minute for five minutes.
6. Prepare a time-temperature graph, with time along the x-axis and temperature along the y-axis. Plot both heating and cooling curves.

Analyze
1. What happened to the water in the cup? Explain in terms of heat.
2. What was the change in temperature of the water in the cup over the 5-minute interval?
3. Using the formula below, find the change in thermal energy (Q), in joules, of the water in the cup.

$$Q = m \times \Delta T \times C_p$$

128 ENERGY

Data and Observations   Sample Data

Time in Minutes	Water Temperature (°C)	
	in curler	in cup
0	78	21
1	73	24
2	67	26
3	64	28
4	61	30
5	60	31

Conclude and Apply
4. Does the curler still have thermal energy available to continue heating the water after five minutes? How do you know?
5. Compare your results with those of your classmates. Do some curlers provide more heat than others? Which curlers provide the most heat?
6. How do the starting temperatures of all the curlers compare?
7. Which statement is more accurate: "Some curlers are hotter than others," or "Some curlers contain more thermal energy than others?" Explain your answer.

ANSWERS TO QUESTIONS

1. The water became hotter; its temperature rose. Heat produced by electricity was transferred to and stored in the curler. The stored heat was transferred to the water in the cup.
2. Probably about 10°C.
3. Most results will be in the 1000 to 2000 range.
4. Yes. The temperature inside the curler is still higher than the surrounding water.
5. Yes. The smaller curlers have less heat to deliver.
6. The starting temperatures are all nearly the same.

7. "Hotter" refers to temperature, or average kinetic energy of the particles. Thermal energy refers to total energy, both kinetic and potential.

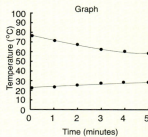

CHAPTER REVIEW

SUMMARY

5-1: Energy and Work

1. Energy is the ability to cause change. Energy may be in the form of motion (kinetic energy) or it may be stored (potential energy).
2. Energy exists in many different forms, and it can change from one form to another with no loss of energy.
3. Work is the transfer of energy through motion. Work is done only when force produces motion in the direction of the force.

5-2: Temperature and Heat

1. All matter is made up of tiny particles that are in constant motion. This motion is not related to or dependent on the motion of the matter.
2. Heat and temperature are related, but they are not the same. The temperature of a material is a measure of the average kinetic energy of the particles that make up the material. Heat is the energy that flows from a warmer to a cooler material.

3. The thermal energy of a material is the total energy—both kinetic and potential—of the particles that make up the material.

5-3: Science and Society: Energy from the Oceans and Earth

1. Temperature differences between layers of ocean waters and the energy of magma beneath Earth's surface represent two possible new sources of thermal energy.
2. The benefits and drawbacks of projects to develop new energy sources should be thoroughly investigated and evaluated before the projects are allowed to proceed.

5-4: Measuring Thermal Energy

1. Different materials have different heat capacities, or specific heats. Thus, their thermal energies change at different rates.
2. The specific heat of a material can be used to calculate changes in the thermal energy of the material.

KEY SCIENCE WORDS

a. energy
b. heat
c. kinetic energy
d. law of conservation of energy
e. magma
f. mechanical energy
g. potential energy
h. specific heat
i. temperature
j. thermal energy
k. work

UNDERSTANDING VOCABULARY

Match each phrase with the correct term from the list of Key Science Words.

1. the ability to cause change
2. energy of motion
3. under normal conditions, energy cannot be created or destroyed
4. energy required to raise the temperature of 1 kg of a material 1 degree Celsius
5. total energy of the particles in a material
6. the transfer of energy through motion
7. flows from warmer to cooler materials
8. stored energy
9. measure of the average kinetic energy of the particles in a material
10. the total amount of kinetic and potential energy in a system

ENERGY **129**

CHAPTER REVIEW

SUMMARY

Have students read the summary statements to review the major concepts of the chapter.

UNDERSTANDING VOCABULARY

1. a	6. k
2. c	7. b
3. d	8. g
4. h	9. i
5. j	10. f

OPTIONS

ASSESSMENT

To assess student understanding of material in this chapter, use the resources listed.

COOPERATIVE LEARNING

Consider using cooperative learning in the THINK AND WRITE CRITICALLY, APPLY, and MORE SKILL BUILDERS sections of the Chapter Review.

PROGRAM RESOURCES

From the **Teacher Resource Package** use:
Chapter Review, pages 13-14.
Chapter and Unit Tests, pages 28-31, Chapter Test.

CHAPTER
REVIEW

CHECKING CONCEPTS

1. b	6. b
2. a	7. a
3. a	8. c
4. c	9. c
5. c	10. b

UNDERSTANDING CONCEPTS

11. 1 Celsius degree
12. magma
13. velocity
14. change
15. energy

THINK AND WRITE CRITICALLY

16. Gravitational potential energy is the energy an object has due to its position above Earth's surface. Another type of potential energy is energy of a wound spring. Both of these types of energy are stored; kinetic energy is energy of motion.

17. At the top of a swing, a pendulum's potential energy is maximum; as it falls from this position, potential energy changes to kinetic energy. At the bottom of a swing, kinetic energy of the pendulum is at its greatest. As the pendulum moves up the other side of its swing, kinetic energy changes to potential energy. The total mechanical energy of the pendulum decreases with each swing as it is converted to thermal energy.

18. Thermal energy is the total kinetic and potential energy of all the particles that make up a material. Temperature is a measure of the average kinetic energy of the particles of a material. Heat is the transfer of energy due to a difference in temperature.

CHAPTER
REVIEW

CHECKING CONCEPTS

Choose the word or phrase that completes the sentence or answers the question.

1. The basic SI unit of energy is the _____.
   a. Calorie   c. newton
   b. joule   d. Kelvin
2. If the velocity of an object increases, the _____ of the object will also increase.
   a. kinetic energy   c. specific heat
   b. mass   d. potential energy
3. Which of these is not used to calculate change in thermal energy?
   a. volume   c. specific heat
   b. temperature change d. mass
4. The _____ of a material is a measure of the average kinetic energy of its particles.
   a. potential energy c. temperature
   b. thermal energy   d. specific heat
5. Which of these does not represent work done on a rock in the scientific sense?
   a. lifting a rock   c. holding a rock
   b. throwing a rock   d. moving a rock
6. The total amount of kinetic and potential energy in a closed system is called _____.
   a. specific heat   c. stored energy
   b. mechanical energy d. temperature
7. As the temperature of a material increases, the average _____ of its particles increases.
   a. kinetic energy   c. specific heat
   b. potential energy d. mass
8. Kinetic energy is directly related to _____.
   a. volume   c. mass
   b. force   d. position
9. The _____ of an object depends upon its position.
   a. kinetic energy   c. potential energy
   b. thermal energy   d. mechanical energy

10. The particles in a material all have _____.
    a. the same mass
    b. kinetic energy
    c. the same temperature
    d. the same velocity

UNDERSTANDING CONCEPTS

Complete each sentence.

11. Specific heat is the amount of energy needed to raise the temperature of a material _____.
12. _____ is molten rock below Earth's surface.
13. The kinetic energy of an object depends on the mass and _____ of the object.
14. Energy is the ability to cause _____.
15. Work is the transfer of _____ through motion.

THINK AND WRITE CRITICALLY

16. Describe two types of potential energy. How does this energy differ from kinetic energy?
17. Describe the energy changes that occur in a swinging pendulum. Explain how energy is conserved, even as a pendulum slows down and eventually stops swinging.
18. Compare and contrast heat, temperature, and thermal energy.
19. A copper bowl and a clay bowl of equal mass were heated from 27°C to 100°C. Which required more heat? Explain.
20. Describe some possible benefits and drawbacks of developing ways to convert thermal energy of the oceans and magma to useful purposes.

130 ENERGY

19. Because the specific heat of copper is greater than that of clay, more heat was needed to raise the temperature of the copper pot than was needed to produce the same temperature change in the clay pot.

20. The benefits are that both energy sources are inexhaustible and relatively clean, and their use would conserve Earth's dwindling supply of fossil fuels. The drawbacks include the expense involved in research and the possible harmful effects on the environment.

21. While performing a chin-up, Carlos raises himself 0.8 m. How much work does Carlos, who weighs 600 N, accomplish doing a chin-up?
22. A football player picks up a football, runs with it, and then throws it to a teammate. Describe the work done on the ball.
23. Wind has more kinetic energy than does still air. Why does air feel cold on a windy winter day and hot on a calm summer day?
24. How much thermal energy does 420 g of liquid water gain when it is heated from its freezing point to its boiling point?
25. 50 g of water and 50 g of sand each absorb 200 J of solar energy. What will be the temperature change?

MORE SKILL BUILDERS

If you need help, refer to the Skill Handbook.

1. **Comparing and Contrasting:** Compare and contrast heat and work.
2. **Sequencing:** Equal amounts of the following materials listed in Table 5-1 (page 125) are sitting in the sun: carbon, silver, alcohol, copper, and aluminum. List the materials in order of the average kinetic energies of their particles, from highest to lowest, after they have been in the sun for several hours.
3. **Measuring in SI:** A non-SI unit often used to measure thermal energy is the calorie, which is equal to 4.18 J. The number of calories needed to raise the temperature of 1-kg samples of three different materials 1 degree Celsius are given below. Use the factor-label method to convert each value to joules.

Material	Calories
wood	420
glass	120
mercury	33

4. **Hypothesizing:** Propose a hypothesis to explain why a person with a fever often feels chills, even in a warm room.
5. **Concept Mapping:** Below is a blank concept map of the energy changes of a gymnast bouncing on a trampoline. Complete the map by indicating the type of energy—kinetic, potential, or both—the gymnast has at each of the following stages in his or her path: a. halfway up; b. the highest point; c. halfway down; d. the lowest point, just before hitting the trampoline.

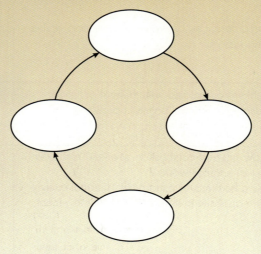

PROJECTS

1. Research and write a paper about the life of Albert Einstein. Describe how he explained the law of conservation of mass and energy.
2. Make a poster showing possible energy sources other than burning fossil fuels. Note the advantages and disadvantages of each and indicate which you think is the best resource to develop further and why.

ENERGY **131**

21. $W = F \times d$
   $= 600 \text{ N} \times 0.8 \text{ m}$
   $= 480 \text{ J}$
22. Work is done on the ball when the player picks it up and when the ball is thrown to a teammate. No work is done on the ball when the player carries it.
23. Cold air feels cold because the particles of air have lower average kinetic energy, regardless of whether the air is moving or not. Warm air feels warm because the particles of air have higher average kinetic energy.
24. $Q = \Delta T \times m \times C_p$
   $= 100°C \times 0.420 \text{ kg} \times 4190 \text{ J/kg} \cdot °C$
   $= 175\ 980 \text{ J}$
25. $Q = mC_p \Delta T$; solving for ΔT,
   $\Delta T = Q/mC_p$
   $\Delta T_{water} = (200 \text{ J})/(0.05 \text{ kg})(4190 \text{ J/kg} \cdot °C)$
   $\Delta T_{water} = 0.95°C$
   $\Delta T_{sand} = (200 \text{ J})/(0.05 \text{ kg})(664 \text{ J/kg} \cdot °C)$
   $\Delta T_{sand} = 6.0°C$

MORE SKILL BUILDERS

1. **Comparing and Contrasting:** Both heat and work involve the transfer of energy, and both are measured in joules. Energy is transferred as heat when two materials are at different temperatures. Energy is transferred as work when a force acts through a distance.
2. **Sequencing:** The order will be from the substance with the lowest specific heat to that with the highest specific heat: silver, copper, carbon, aluminum, and alcohol.
3. **Measuring in SI:** Wood: 420 cal × 4.18 J/cal = 1756 J
   Glass: 120 cal × 4.18 J/cal = 502 J
   Mercury: 33 cal × 4.18 J/cal = 138 J
4. **Hypothesizing:** When a person has a fever, the person perspires because of an elevated body temperature. Heat is carried away from the body as the perspiration evaporates, causing the person to feel cool, a condition known as chills.
5. **Concept Mapping:** See map at left.

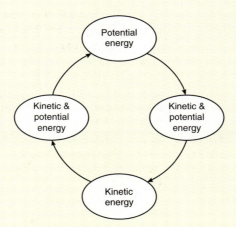

6 Using Thermal Energy

CHAPTER SECTION	OBJECTIVES	ACTIVITIES
6-1 Moving Thermal Energy (2 days)	1. **Compare** and **contrast** the transfer of thermal energy by conduction, convection, and radiation. 2. **Differentiate** between conductors and insulators. 3. **Explain** how insulation affects the transfer of energy.	**Activity 6-1:** *Convection,* p. 141
6-2 Heating Systems (2 days)	1. **Describe** three types of conventional heating systems. 2. **Explain** how solar energy can be used to heat buildings. 3. **Explain** the differences between passive and active solar heating systems.	**MINI-Lab:** *Can the sun be used to cook food?* p. 144
6-3 Thermal Pollution Science & Society (1 day)	1. **Identify** problems associated with thermal pollution. 2. **Discuss** solutions for thermal pollution problems.	
6-4 Using Heat to Do Work (2 days)	1. **Describe** how internal combustion engines and external combustion engines work. 2. **Explain** how a heat mover can transfer thermal energy in a direction opposite to that of its natural movement.	**Activity 6-2:** *The Four-stroke Engine,* p. 152
Chapter Review		

ACTIVITY MATERIALS

FIND OUT	ACTIVITIES		MINI-LABS
Page 133 lamp with bare bulb extension cord masking tape	**6-1 Convection, p. 141** colored ice cubes tongs thermometer 250-mL beaker salt stirring rod	**6-2 The Four-stroke Engine, p. 152** matches 250-mL flask glass or plastic "T" 2 pinch clamps large syringe, plastic 3 pcs. rubber tubing small piece of cloth or yarn rubber stopper, 2-hole, with glass tubing	**Can the sun be used to cook food? p. 144** glue aluminum foil poster board string wire coat hangers hot dog

CHAPTER FEATURES	TEACHER RESOURCE PACKAGE	OTHER RESOURCES
Problem Solving: *The Warm House,* p. 138 **Skill Builder:** *Using Variables, Constants, and Controls,* p. 140	**Ability Level Worksheets** ◆ **Study Guide,** p. 26 ● **Reinforcement,** p. 26 ▲ **Enrichment,** p. 26 **Activity Worksheet,** pp. 47, 48 **Cross-Curricular Connections,** p. 10	**Lab Manual 11,** Conduction of Heat **Lab Manual 12,** Specific Heats of Metals
Skill Builder: *Making and Using Tables,* p. 145	**Ability Level Worksheets** ◆ **Study Guide,** p. 27 ● **Reinforcement,** p. 27 ▲ **Enrichment,** p. 27 **MINI-Lab Worksheet,** p. 53 **Concept Mapping,** pp. 17, 18 **Science and Society,** p. 10 **Transparency Masters,** pp. 21, 22	**Color Transparency 11,** Heating Systems
You Decide! p. 147	**Ability Level Worksheets** ◆ **Study Guide,** p. 28 ● **Reinforcement,** p. 28 ▲ **Enrichment,** p. 28	
Technology: *Cooling Crystals,* p. 150 **Skill Builder:** *Concept Mapping,* p. 151	**Ability Level Worksheets** ◆ **Study Guide,** p. 29 ● **Reinforcement,** p. 29 ▲ **Enrichment,** p. 29 **Activity Worksheet,** pp. 49, 50 **Critical Thinking/Problem Solving,** p. 12 **Technology,** pp. 9, 10 **Transparency Masters,** pp. 23, 24	**Color Transparency 12,** Four-stroke Engine **Lab Manual 13,** Thermal Energy from Foods
Summary Think & Write Critically Key Science Words Apply Understanding Vocabulary More Skill Builders Checking Concepts Projects Understanding Concepts	**Chapter Review,** pp. 15, 16 **Chapter Test,** pp. 32-35	**Chapter Review Software** **Test Bank**

◆ **Basic**   ● **Average**   ▲ **Advanced**

ADDITIONAL MATERIALS

SOFTWARE	AUDIOVISUAL	BOOKS/MAGAZINES
Home Energy Conservation, EME. *The Solar Option,* EME. *Heat Energy and Temperature,* Focus. *Investigating Thermal Energy,* IBM.	*How to Make a Solar Heater,* film, Handel. *Mr. Wizard's World: Heat Transfers,* Macmillan/McGraw-Hill School Division. *Heat and How We Use It,* film, EBEC. *The Flow of Heat Energy,* video, Focus. *Heat: Molecules in Motion,* laserdisc, AIMS Media.	Chapman, Alan J. *Fundamentals of Heat Transfer,* 3rd ed. New York: Macmillan, 1987. McGuigan, Dermot and Amanda McGuigan. *Heat Pumps, An Efficient Heating and Cooling Alternative.* Pownal, VT: Storey Comm., 1981.

THEME DEVELOPMENT: The chapter discusses the transfer, production, and uses of thermal energy. Energy conversions and conservation should be stressed in each section.

CHAPTER OVERVIEW

▶ **Section 6-1:** The three types of thermal energy transfer—conduction, convection, and radiation—are discussed in this section. Thermal conductors and insulators are compared and contrasted.

▶ **Section 6-2:** This section discusses the three primary types of home-heating systems in terms of energy conversions and thermal energy transfers. Passive and active solar heating methods are introduced.

▶ **Section 6-3: Science and Society:** The environmental problem of thermal pollution of water systems is discussed and students are asked to evaluate the advantages and disadvantages associated with building an industrial plant that may produce thermal pollution in a local river.

▶ **Section 6-4:** Heat engines are introduced as devices that change thermal energy into mechanical energy by doing work. Internal and external combustion engines, refrigerators, and heat pumps are discussed.

CHAPTER VOCABULARY

conduction	cooling
fluid	towers
convection	heat engines
radiation	combustion
insulators	internal
radiator	combustion
solar energy	engine
solar	external
collectors	combustion
thermal	engine
pollution	heat mover
combustion	heat pump

CHAPTER

6 Using Thermal Energy

132

OPTIONS

For Your Gifted Students

Students can test various metals for their ability to conduct heat. Have them take nails made from different metals (steel, aluminum, brass, and so on) and place a drop of wax on the end of the nail. They should hold the nail with a pair of tongs and heat the opposite end with a candle. They will record the time it takes for the wax to melt. Have them hypothesize whether the size of the nail will affect the speed of heat transfer, then test the hypothesis.

The clothes you wear can make you feel warmer or cooler. They affect the amount of thermal energy that reaches and leaves your body. How else can the movement of thermal energy be affected?

FIND OUT!

Do this simple activity to find out how you can affect the movement of thermal energy.

Turn on a lamp with a bare light bulb. *Being careful not to touch the bulb,* put your hand near it. Do you feel warmth from the bulb? How is thermal energy getting to your hand? What happens if you move your hand nearer to the bulb or farther away? What happens if you put a book between your hand and the lamp? Suppose you use only a piece of paper instead of a whole book. Find some other things that you can put between your hand and the light bulb. Do some seem to block heat better than others? Feel the objects after they've been near the light bulb. Do some feel warmer than others? How can you explain the differences?

Gearing Up
Previewing this Chapter
Use this outline to help you focus on important ideas in this chapter.

Section 6-1   Moving Thermal Energy
► Conduction
► Convection
► Radiation
► Reducing Movement of Thermal Energy

Section 6-2   Heating Systems
► Conventional Heating Systems
► Solar Heating

Section 6-3   Science and Society
Thermal Pollution
► Not So Hot!

Section 6-4   Using Heat to Do Work
► Heat Engines
► Heat Movers

Previewing Science Skills
► In the Skill Builders, you will use variables, constants, and controls, make and use tables, and map concepts.
► In the Activities, you will observe, collect and organize data, sequence, analyze, and infer.
► In the MINI-Lab, you will observe and hypothesize.

What's next?

You have discovered that you can exert some control over the movement of thermal energy. Now you will learn about how thermal energy moves and how that movement can be put to useful purposes.

INTRODUCING THE CHAPTER
Use the Find Out activity to introduce students to the concept of heat transfer by convection and radiation.

FIND OUT!
Preparation: If you plan to conduct the activity in the classroom, have students bring in small desk lamps that use incandescent light bulbs. Obtain several electrical extension cords and wide masking tape.

Materials: lamp and bare light bulb for each group of three students, extension cords, and masking tape

Cooperative Learning: Assign Problem Solving Teams to quantitatively investigate how the temperature of the air above a lit light bulb changes with distance or how the wattage of a lit light bulb affects the temperature of the air at a certain distance from the bulb.

Teaching Tips
► **CAUTION:** *Hot light bulbs are not to be handled. Secure extension cords with masking tape to avoid tripping.*
► A string of well-insulated outdoor decoration lights may be used to supply a classroom with light bulbs for individual or small-group investigations. Replace any colored bulbs with clear or frosted bulbs for better results.
► Cardboard frames used for overhead transparencies can be used to mount different materials, such as paper, clear plastic wrap, foil wrap, and construction paper. Have students observe the effects of these materials on the transfer of thermal energy.

Gearing Up
Have students study the Gearing Up feature to familiarize themselves with the chapter. Discuss the relationships of the topics in the outline.

What's Next?
Before beginning the first section, make sure students understand the connection between the Find Out activity and the topics to follow.

For Your Mainstreamed Students
Students can test various brands of polystyrene foam cups from fast-food restaurants for their effectiveness. They should place the same amount of the same temperature hot and cold water in the various cups. A thermometer should be placed in the water and the top covered with plastic wrap. Students should record the temperature after 5 and then 10 minutes. The change in heat energy of the various cups can be charted. Results may be shared with the restaurants.

PREPARATION

SECTION BACKGROUND

▶ Thermal energy is spontaneously transferred from a material at a higher temperature to a material at a lower temperature in three ways: conduction, convection, and radiation. Heat is transferred by conduction mostly in solids. Convection is the predominant method of heat transfer in fluids. Thermal energy can also be transferred by radiation.

▶ Materials can be classified as thermal conductors or thermal insulators. Materials, such as metals, in which the atoms are close enough to easily transmit vibrational kinetic energy are good thermal conductors. Materials that lack this property are good insulators.

PREPLANNING

▶ To prepare for Activity 6-1, make several trays of ice cubes dyed with food coloring.

1 MOTIVATE

▶ Have students compare and contrast frying, grilling, roasting, and even solar cooking of a hot dog.

▶ **Demonstration:** Cut a spiral from a piece of construction paper and suspend it by a thread above an unlit light bulb. Have students note that the spiral begins to rotate only after the light is turned on. Allow students to conjecture on the possible causes of the spiral's motion.

6-1 Moving Thermal Energy

New Science Words

conduction
fluid
convection
radiation
insulators

Objectives

▶ Compare and contrast the transfer of thermal energy by conduction, convection, and radiation.
▶ Differentiate between conductors and insulators.
▶ Explain how insulation affects the transfer of energy.

Conduction

You have learned that thermal energy travels as heat from a material at higher temperature to a material at lower temperature. You see examples of this energy transfer all the time. If you pick up an ice cube, heat from your hand is transferred to the ice, causing it to melt. If you pick up a hot spoon, the heat from the spoon moves to your hand, causing you to drop the spoon. The question is, how does the thermal energy move from place to place?

One way thermal energy travels is by conduction. **Conduction** is the transfer of energy through matter by direct contact of particles. Recall that all matter is made up of tiny particles that are in constant motion. The temperature of a material is a measure of the average kinetic energy of its particles.

Energy is transferred when particles moving at different speeds bump into each other, or collide. When faster-moving particles collide with slower-moving particles, some of the energy of the faster-moving particles is passed along, or transferred, to the slower-moving particles. The faster particles slow down and the slower particles speed up. Thus, energy is transferred by means of conduction.

Heat may be transferred by conduction through a given material or from one material to another. Think about what happens when one end of a metal spoon is placed in boiling water. Heat from the water is transferred to the spoon. The end of the spoon in the water becomes

What is conduction?

EcoTip
When cooking or baking, leave the tops on the pots and keep the oven door closed. This will prevent energy from escaping and being wasted.

134 USING THERMAL ENERGY

OPTIONS

Meeting Different Ability Levels

For Section 6-1, use the following **Teacher Resource Masters** depending upon individual students' needs.

◆ **Study Guide Master** for all students.
● **Reinforcement Master** for students of average and above average ability levels.
▲ **Enrichment Master** for above average students.

Additional Teacher Resource Package masters are listed in the OPTIONS box throughout the section. The additional masters are appropriate for all students.

◆ STUDY GUIDE 26

STUDY GUIDE   Chapter 6
Moving Thermal Energy   Text Pages 134–141

In each of the following statements, a term has been scrambled. Unscramble the term and write it on the line provided.

conduction	1. The transfer of thermal energy through matter by direct contact of particles is called *doctnuicon.*
gases	2. Conduction can take place in solids, liquids, and *sages.*
convection	3. The transfer of energy by the movement of matter is called *invcetonoc.*
fluid	4. Any material that can flow is *luifd.*
conductor	5. Any material that allows heat to pass through it easily is a *roctoncud.*
radiation	6. The type of heat transfer that does not require matter is *iadrtonia.*
waves	7. Radiation is the transfer of energy in the form of invisible *svaes.*
insulator	8. Any material that does not allow heat to pass through it easily is an *rntouisla.*
metals	9. Many conductors, such as silver and copper, are *lmtaes.*
radiant energy	10. Energy that travels by radiation is often called *dariota greeny.*
heat	11. Insulators, such as wood and air, are poor conductors of *thea.*
matter	12. The transfer of thermal energy by convection and conduction both require *atoms.*

On the lines provided, explain the differences between conduction, convection, and radiation. Use the information in the exercise above to help you. Write your answers in complete sentences.

Answers will vary. Check to make sure that students' answers are written in complete sentences.

26

Figure 6-1. Part of the spoon is heated by contact with the hot water (left). Heat is transferred through the metal spoon, particle by particle (center), until the entire spoon is hot (right).

hotter than the other end of the spoon. But eventually the entire spoon becomes hot. Figure 6-1 shows the energy transfer involved in this situation.

Conduction can take place in solids, liquids, and gases. Because their particles are packed closer together, solids usually conduct heat better than liquids or gases. However, some solids conduct heat better than others. Metals such as silver, copper, and aluminum are good heat conductors, while wood, plastic, glass, and fiberglass are poor conductors of heat. Why do you think cooking pots are made of metal? What are the handles usually made of?

Convection

You know that liquids and gases are different from solids. Liquids and gases can move about more readily—they can flow. Any material that can flow is a **fluid.** The most important way thermal energy is transferred in fluids is by convection. **Convection** is the transfer of energy by the movement of matter. How does this differ from conduction? In conduction, energy moves from particle to particle, but the particles themselves remain in place. In convection, the particles move from one location to another, "carrying" energy with them.

When heat is added to a fluid, the particles of the fluid begin to move faster, just as the particles of a solid do. However, the particles of a fluid have more freedom of movement. So they spread out—they move farther apart.

Figure 6-2. The motion of the sawdust shows that a convection current is present in the liquid.

Convection current

Sawdust

TYING TO PREVIOUS KNOWLEDGE: Point out that students already know that heat naturally moves from warmer materials to cooler materials. In this section they will learn three methods of how this occurs.

OBJECTIVES AND SCIENCE WORDS: Have students review the objectives and science words to become familiar with this section.

2 TEACH

Key Concepts are highlighted.

CONCEPT DEVELOPMENT

▶ **Demonstration:** Dip the heads of several small thumbtacks into melted wax and attach them at 5-cm intervals along the shaft of a long, metal spatula or fork used for outdoor grilling. Hold the far end of the spatula or fork in the flame of a laboratory burner. Have the students observe the order in which the thumbtacks fall as heat is conducted along the shaft and melts the wax. Repeat the demonstration using a heat resistant glass stirring rod of similar dimensions. Have students note the difference in the time intervals between the thumbtacks falling in each demonstration.

▶ **Demonstration:** Fill a clear plastic shoe box two-thirds full of water. At one end of the box place an immersion heater and at the other end place a sealed plastic bag of ice cubes against the outside wall. Using a slide projector, cast the shadow of the box on the chalkboard. Have students note the vertical convection currents as the water is heated. Repeat the demonstration on an overhead projector and have students note that convection currents are set up horizontally.

STUDENT TEXT QUESTION

▶ Page 135, paragraph 1: **Why do you think cooking pots are made of metal?** *Metals are good conductors of thermal energy.* **What are the handles usually made of?** *plastic or wood (poor thermal energy conductors)*

Cooperative Learning: Assign Numbered Heads Together groups to explain the motion of the spiral demonstrated in the Motivation.

CROSS CURRICULUM

▶ **Language Arts:** Have students look up the words *conduction*, *convection*, and *radiation* in a dictionary. Students should find that the words come from the Latin roots *conducere* (to carry), *convehere* (to bring together), and *radius* (ray), respectively. Ask volunteers to explain how the meaning of each word reflects its root.

CHECK FOR UNDERSTANDING

Use the Mini Quiz to check for understanding.

MINI QUIZ

Use the Mini Quiz to check students' recall of chapter content.

1 _____ is the transfer of energy through matter by direct contact of particles. *Conduction*

2 _____ is the transfer of energy in the form of invisible waves. *Radiation*

RETEACH

Demonstration: Have six students seat themselves side-by-side in a row across the front of the classroom to represent a solid. Have them pass a ball from one end of the row to the other to represent heat being conducted through a solid. Now have the six students represent a fluid by moving their chairs apart so that their fingertips can barely touch those of their neighbors. Have them again pass the ball to represent conduction of heat through a fluid. Have three of the students stand on one side of the class and the other three on the opposite side. Have them toss the ball back and forth across the classroom to represent thermal energy being transferred by radiation.

EXTENSION

For students who have mastered this section, use the **Reinforcement** and **Enrichment** masters or other OPTIONS provided.

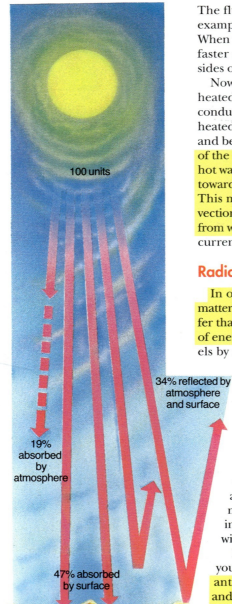

100 units

19% absorbed by atmosphere

34% reflected by atmosphere and surface

47% absorbed by surface

The fluid is said to expand. A hot-air balloon is a good example of the expansion of a fluid upon being heated. When the air in the balloon is heated, the particles move faster and farther apart. The air particles striking the sides of the balloon exert force, causing it to inflate.

Now think about what happens when a pot of water is heated. The stove burner heats the bottom of the pot by conduction. Water touching the bottom of the pot is also heated by conduction. As this water is heated, it expands and becomes less dense. Cooler, denser water at the top of the pot sinks and pushes the hot water upward. As the hot water rises, it cools, becomes more dense, and moves toward the bottom again, forcing warmer water to rise. This movement of particles within a fluid creates convection currents. These currents transfer thermal energy from warmer to cooler parts of the fluid. Wind and ocean currents are examples of convection currents.

Radiation

In order for conduction or convection to take place, matter must be present. There is a third type of heat transfer that does not require matter. **Radiation** is the transfer of energy in the form of invisible waves. Energy that travels by radiation is often called radiant energy. Radiant energy from the sun travels 150 million kilometers through mostly empty space to reach Earth. When this energy reaches Earth, some of it is reflected, or "bounced back," toward space, and some is absorbed. Only radiant energy that is absorbed is changed to thermal energy.

Different materials absorb radiant energy differently. Shiny materials reflect radiant energy; dull materials absorb it. Dark-colored materials absorb more radiant energy than light-colored materials do. This fact explains why summer clothing is usually made of lighter-colored materials than winter clothing.

If you hold your hand near a lighted electric bulb, your hand feels hot. This heat is produced when radiant energy from the bulb is absorbed by your hand and changed to thermal energy.

Figure 6-3. Only the radiant energy that is absorbed by Earth's surface is converted to thermal energy.

OPTIONS

INQUIRY QUESTIONS

▶ Air (oxygen) is necessary for a candle or the wick of a lantern to burn. Why does the flame of a candle or lantern glow more brightly if a glass chimney is placed around it? *Convection currents are formed in the chimney above the flame. These currents cause fresh air to enter at the base of the chimney and aid burning.*

▶ Why won't you get burned if you grab the hot handle of a pan with a dry dishcloth, but you might if you grab the handle with a wet dishcloth? *The tiny spaces among the fibers*

of a dry dishcloth are filled with air, which is a poor conductor of heat. However, the spaces among the fibers of a wet dishcloth are filled with water, which conducts heat more readily.

▶ Why does a nail inserted in a potato decrease the time it takes for the potato to bake in a conventional oven? *The nail conducts heat better to the center of the potato than does the potato itself.*

Reducing Movement of Thermal Energy

When the weather is really cold, doesn't it feel good to wrap yourself up in a thick sweater or curl up under a fluffy quilt? And in hot weather, wouldn't you rather have juice from a bottle that has been inside a picnic cooler than one that has been sitting out on a table?

What do these two situations have in common? In each case, some material is used to reduce the flow of heat by conduction, convection, or radiation. In the first case, the material of the sweater or quilt traps your body heat and keeps it from escaping to the open air. In the second case, the material of the picnic cooler keeps heat from flowing to the juice.

Earlier you learned that good conductors are materials that allow heat to move easily through them. Now you're finding out about good insulators—materials that do not allow heat to move easily through them. Some insulators, such as wood, plastic, glass, and fiberglass, have already been identified as being poor conductors.

Gases such as air are excellent insulators. Many types of insulation consist of materials that contain many tiny "pockets" of trapped air. These pockets are too small to allow convection currents to form, so the trapped air acts as an insulator. Plastic foam is a type of insulation commonly used in beverage cups and picnic coolers. This "foam" is mostly tiny pockets of trapped air. Down jackets and quilts are stuffed with tiny feathers or fibers that trap air.

Buildings are insulated to keep them warm in winter and cool in summer. In cold weather, a heated building is warmer than its surroundings. Heat tends to flow from the building to the outside. Insulation can help to reduce the amount of heat lost this way. In the United States, about 10 percent of all energy produced is used to heat buildings, so you can see why it is important to prevent as much heat loss as possible. In warm weather, air conditioners use a lot of energy to remove heat from building interiors. Insulation reduces the amount of heat that flows into a cool building from the outside, thus keeping the inside of the building cooler.

Building insulation is usually made of some fluffy material, such as fiberglass, cellulose, or treated paper. The insulation, which is packed into outer walls and under

Science and READING

Form a team to design and develop an energy-efficient home. Each member of the team should draw up a house plan, and the team should select the best one. Then each member researches one aspect of the new house for the best energy conservation ideas.

Figure 6-4. Air trapped in its shaggy coat keeps this polar bear warm.

TEACHER F.Y.I.

▶ Thermal energy is radiated from matter as electromagnetic radiation in the form of infrared energy. Excited electrons in a material lose energy by emitting photons of electromagnetic energy at values slightly less than that of visible light, hence the name *infrared,* which means "below red." Like other forms of electromagnetic energy, such as visible light, infrared energy can propagate through a vacuum, reflect from, refract through, and be absorbed by matter.

CONCEPT DEVELOPMENT

▶ Discuss how trapped air in snow, crumpled newspapers, and layered clothing provides good insulation.

Science and READING

Areas of responsibility include: roof, windows/doors, exterior siding, heating/cooling system, appliances, and so on. A local building contractor can provide valuable information.

REVEALING MISCONCEPTIONS

▶ Some students may think that materials are intrinsically cold or hot. For example, ask them why bathroom tiles feel cold to bare feet but a shaggy rug on top of the tiles feels warm. The discussion may reveal that students believe tiles are always cold and rugs are always warm. The feelings that the students experience are correct; however, both materials are at the same temperature. Make sure students are aware that the tile feels cool because it absorbs heat from a bare foot and cools the foot. The trapped air among the fibers of the rug provides insulation which dramatically reduces heat conduction and, therefore, reduces heat loss.

CROSS CURRICULUM

▶Life Science: Have students research how arctic animals have adapted to survive in extremely low temperatures.

PROBLEM SOLVING

Think Critically: The aluminum backing reduces heat loss due to radiation. The insulation and thermal windows all contain pockets of trapped air that reduce the transfer of thermal energy because air is a poor conductor of heat.

PROBLEM SOLVING

The Warm House

Mary and her family lived in a small house near the Canadian border. Because their house had become too small for their needs, the family was having a larger house built nearby.

One day Mary went to the new house with her father to check on a few things. They wanted to make sure that the house was being properly constructed to withstand the cold winters in the area. Mary's father had her check all the exterior walls to see that they were insulated. Mary found that the workers had used foam insulation backed with aluminum foil. Next Mary's father went up to the attic to make sure that rolls of fiberglass insulation had been installed between the rafters. Meanwhile, Mary checked to see that all the windows had stickers indicating that they were double-paned thermal windows. Satisfied that their new house would be nice and warm, Mary and her father returned home.

Think Critically: What was the purpose of the aluminum backing on the exterior wall insulation? What do the foam insulation, the fiberglass insulation, and the thermal windows have in common that helps them to prevent the loss of heat?

What does the *R* indicate in R-values?

roofs, is sometimes covered with shiny aluminum foil. By reflecting radiant energy back toward its source, the foil cuts down on energy transfer due to radiation.

Many materials are used in building construction. To help consumers understand the energy-transfer qualities of these different materials, a rating system has been established in which each material is given an R-value. The *R* indicates resistance to heat flow. Table 6-1 shows the R-values for some common building materials.

In order to have a well-insulated house, materials with an R-value of at least 19 should be used in the outer walls

138 USING THERMAL ENERGY

OPTIONS

INQUIRY QUESTIONS

▶**Both adobe bricks used to build pueblos and ice blocks used to build igloos have very good insulation properties. How do their functions differ?** *The adobe brick does not conduct heat from the warmer air outside the pueblo to the cooler air inside during the daytime and vice versa at night. The ice blocks do not conduct heat from the warmer air inside the igloo to the colder air outside.*

▶**Why do birds fluff their feathers and mammals fluff their fur to keep warm?** *The fluffing increases the amount of air trapped in the* feathers or fur, which increases their insulating properties.

▶**Does blubber have a high or low R-value? Explain.** *Blubber has a high R-value because it acts as an insulator in arctic mammals.*

▶**Why do the instructions for foods that are heated in a microwave oven sometimes indicate that the container should remain unopened for a few minutes after heating?** *The time is needed for heat to be conducted throughout the food.*

and those with R-values of 30-44 in the roof or ceilings. Higher R-values are needed for roofs and ceilings because the warmest air inside the house is carried upward by convection currents.

Even though glass isn't a good conductor, energy transfer does occur through windows. A single pane of glass has an R-rating of only 1, but the use of double-pane windows can reduce heat loss considerably. Such windows have a thin "sandwich" made of air trapped between two panes of glass. The air is an excellent insulator, and the space is too narrow to allow convection currents to form in the air.

In some double-pane windows, air is replaced with a harmless, colorless gas. This gas is a better insulator than air, thus giving the windows a higher R-value. Keep in mind that high R-values help keep buildings cool during hot weather, too.

Glass

Glass

Dead-air space

Figure 6-5. The air trapped in this double-pane window serves as a layer of insulation.

Table 6-1

R-VALUES OF VARIOUS MATERIALS

Material	R-Value
Brick	0.08/cm
Plasterboard (drywall)	0.35/cm
Stucco	0.08/cm
Wood siding	0.60/cm
Air space	1.82-3.56/cm
Fiberglass (bolts)	1.22/cm
Loose cellulose	1.46/cm
Aluminum siding	0.01/cm
Loose foam	1.89/cm
Loose vermiculite	1.09/cm

▶ Students should think of the R-value of a material as a rate of resistance to heat flow for each centimeter-thickness of insulating material. For example, a building brick is about 20 cm × 9 cm × 6 cm. Normally, a brick is placed in a wall with a depth of 9 cm. In this way, its R-value is 0.72 (9 cm × 0.08/cm). However, if the brick is placed in a wall lengthwise, its R-value would be 1.6 (20 cm × 0.08/cm). Why isn't the latter building method normally used? Explain to students that bricks are used to support rather than to insulate. The cost would be prohibitive because more than twice as many bricks would have to be used in the latter method. Other insulation materials are far less expensive.

▶ Students should also be made aware that the R-value of a wall or ceiling made of several layered materials is the sum of the individual R-values for each material. For example, a wall made of 1-cm layers of plasterboard, brick, and wood siding would have an R-value of 1.03 (0.35 + 0.08 + 0.60).

INQUIRY QUESTIONS
▶**What is the R-value of a wall made of bricks that are 9 cm thick?** *R-value = 0.72; 9 cm × 0.08/cm = 0.72*
▶**How thick would a solid brick wall have to be to have an R-value of 19?** *19 ÷ 0.08/cm = 240 cm*
▶**Houses are built with a dead air space between the interior and exterior brick walls. How thick would the walls be to have an R-value of 19?** *The two brick layers would have an R-value of 0.72 each, or 1.4. The R-value of the air must be 19 – 1.4, or 17.6. 17.6 ÷*
2.5/cm, roughly the average R-value of air, yields 7 cm. The thickness of the wall would be 25 cm, 18 cm for the bricks and 7 cm for the air space.

PROGRAM RESOURCES
From the **Teacher Resource Package** use:
  Cross-Curricular Connections, page 10, Asbestos.
Use **Laboratory Manual,** Conduction of Heat; Specific Heats of Metals.

CHECK FOR UNDERSTANDING

Ask questions 1-3 and the **Apply** Question from the Section Review.

RETEACH

Explain how a vacuum bottle keeps cold materials cold. Have students explain how the same bottle can keep hot materials hot.

EXTENSION

For students who have mastered this section, use the **Reinforcement** and **Enrichment** masters or other OPTIONS provided.

3 CLOSE

▶ Invite a representative from a local professional builders' association or utility company to discuss insulating materials with the class.

SECTION REVIEW ANSWERS

1. Conduction is the transfer of thermal energy by direct contact of particles. Convection is the transfer of energy by the movement of matter from one location to another. Radiation is the transfer of energy in the form of waves.
2. Heat is not transferred easily through a poor conductor. For this reason, poor conductors can be used to prevent heat from moving from one place to another.
3. Wood and plastic are poor conductors (good insulators) of heat. Heat cannot move easily through these materials from hot pots and pans.
4. Apply: The plastic foam contains hundreds of tiny air bubbles which act as insulation, keeping the heat from leaving the food, thus keeping the food warm.

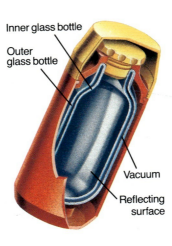

Inner glass bottle
Outer glass bottle
Vacuum
Reflecting surface

Figure 6-6 . This cutaway drawing of a vacuum bottle shows that its construction is similar to that of a double-pane window.

You may have used a vacuum bottle to carry cold or hot liquids for lunch. This bottle works much like a double-pane window; but instead, it has a double glass wall with a vacuum between the two glass layers. One side of each layer is coated with aluminum to reduce heat transfer by radiation.

Adding insulation and special windows are not the only ways to reduce heat loss from buildings. Many buildings, especially older ones, have cracks and gaps around windows and doors through which heat can escape. These "heat leaks" should be filled with caulking, putty, or weather stripping to reduce energy loss and fuel bills.

Now that you know more about how thermal energy is transferred, think about things you can do to influence the amount of energy that affects you. You can sit under a shady umbrella or put on a sweater. You can close a window or wear light-colored clothing. These are just a few examples of ways to cool off or warm up. What other ways can you think of?

SECTION REVIEW

1. Name and describe three methods by which thermal energy is transferred.
2. Explain why poor conductors of heat are good insulators of heat.
3. Why do many pots and pans used for cooking have wood or plastic handles?
4. **Apply:** Many fast-food restaurants serve their hot sandwiches in plastic foam containers. Why don't they just wrap the sandwiches in paper, which is much less expensive than plastic foam?

Skill Builder

☑ **Using Variables, Constants, and Controls**

Design an experiment to find out which material makes the best insulation: plastic foam pellets, shredded newspaper, or crumpled plastic bags. Remember to state your hypothesis and indicate what factors must be held constant. If you need help, refer to Using Variables, Constants, and Controls in the **Skill Handbook** on page 682.

Skill Builder

Example Experiment

Hypothesize: Different materials do not insulate equally.
Objective: to compare the insulating abilities of plastic foam pellets, shredded newspaper, and crumpled plastic bags in keeping an ice cube from melting
Procedure: Place three similarly sized ice cubes, one each into three plastic sandwich bags. Twist tie the bags. Center each of these bags into identical empty soup cans and pack each with a different insulating material. Place all three cans in direct sunlight. After 30 minutes remove the bags and note the amount of melted ice water in each bag. The best insulator will have the least amount of water.
Controls: size of ice cubes, size of cans, amount of insulating material, time exposed to the sun

ACTIVITY 6-1
Convection

Problem: *Where does ice go when it melts?*

Materials

- colored ice cubes
- tongs
- thermometer
- beaker, 250-mL
- salt
- stirring rod

Procedure

1. Prepare a data table like the one shown.
2. Fill the beaker with warm water.
3. Obtain an ice cube that has been strongly dyed with food coloring. Using tongs, *gently* place the ice cube in the warm water. Do not stir or mix. Keep the beaker and water as still as possible.
4. Observe the ice-water mixture for several minutes. Then measure the temperature at the surface and at the bottom of the mixture, and at three levels in between. Record the temperatures in your data table.
5. Empty the beaker and refill it with warm water. Add as much salt as will dissolve in the water, stirring vigorously as you pour.
6. Repeat Steps 3 and 4 with the salt water solution.

Data and Observations Sample Data

Fresh Water		Salt Water	
Depth	**Temp (°C)**	**Depth**	**Temp (°C)**
surface	19	surface	8
2 cm	19	2 cm	18
4 cm	19	4 cm	19
6 cm	18	6 cm	19
bottom	8	bottom	19

Analyze

1. As the ice melts, what happens to the meltwater in the fresh water? In the salt water?
2. Does the meltwater blend readily with the warm water or does it tend to remain separate from it?
3. Describe the changes in temperature within the meltwater-warm water mixtures.

Conclude and Apply

4. If the three fluids involved in this activity—fresh water, salt water, and meltwater—which is the most dense? How do you know?
5. Why does convection occur between fresh water and meltwater but not between salt water and meltwater?
6. What would happen if you were to add warm water to the bottom of a beaker of cold water?

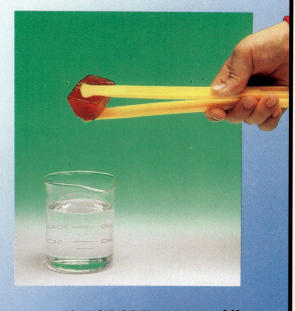

OBJECTIVE: **Explore** relationships between convection currents and fluid density.

PROCESS SKILLS applied in this activity:
▶ **Observing** in Procedure Steps 3 and 5.
▶ **Collecting and Organizing Data** in Procedure Step 4.
▶ **Inferring** in Conclude and Apply Questions 4 and 5.

COOPERATIVE LEARNING
Use the Science Investigation Team strategy in pairs. Do not divide the class into freshwater and saltwater groups.

TEACHING THE ACTIVITY
Troubleshooting: Prepare ice cubes the day before; allow two ice cubes per team.
▶ Provide about 70 grams of salt to each team. Most or all should dissolve with considerable stirring.
▶ It is assumed that students understand density or at least have the idea that "heavy" things sink and "light" things float.

PROGRAM RESOURCES
From the **Teacher Resource Package** use:

Activity Worksheets, pages 47-48, Activity 6-1: Convection.

ANSWERS TO QUESTIONS

1. In fresh water, the cold meltwater can be seen streaming to the bottom and forming a layer. In salt water, the melted ice layers on top.

2. Cold and hot water do not seem to mix.

3. Temperature changes sharply at the boundary of the colored layer.

4. Salt water is the most dense. Cold meltwater sinks in fresh water but floats in salt water.

5. Convection occurs when the more dense fluid is released at the top.

6. If less dense fluid were released at the bottom, it should rise to the top. (Demonstrate this by pouring warm, colored water into a long stem funnel that has its tip at the bottom of a beaker of ice water.)

PREPARATION

SECTION BACKGROUND

▶ The most common types of heating systems are hot water, steam, and forced hot air. Hot water and forced hot air are predominantly used in smaller dwellings, whereas steam heating is used in many large residential and commercial buildings.

▶ In homes containing passive or active solar heating, it is used primarily in conjunction with conventional heating systems or to supplement heating water for washing and bathing.

1 MOTIVATE

▶ Ask students to describe the heating systems in their homes. Based on the descriptions, have the class create categories and classify the systems.

▶ Have students identify the energy sources and the type of energy used in their home-heating systems. From a class poll, rank the energy sources from most used to least used.

New Science Words

radiator
solar energy
solar collectors

Objectives

▶ Describe three types of conventional heating systems.
▶ Explain how solar energy can be used to heat buildings.
▶ Explain the differences between passive and active solar heating systems.

Conventional Heating Systems

What is the weather like where you live? Is it cold part of the year or is it warm all year round? Even in warm climates, sometimes the weather is cold enough so that buildings need to be heated. For this reason, most buildings have some sort of heating system.

All heating systems must have a source of heat, such as fuel or electricity. The simplest type of heating system is one in which fuel is burned right in the area to be heated, such as in a stove or fireplace. The ==energy released by the burning fuel is transferred to the surrounding air by conduction, convection, and radiation.==

Many heating systems use radiators to transfer energy. A **radiator** is a device with a large surface area designed to heat the air near it by conduction. Convection currents then circulate the heat to all parts of the room.

In some heating systems, radiators are heated by electricity. However, most systems are set up so that fuel is

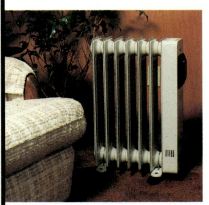

Figure 6-7. The design of this radiator permits large quantities of air to be heated by contact with its surface.

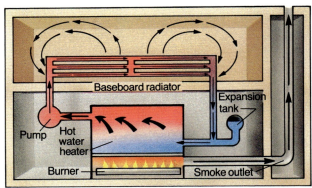

Figure 6-8. In this heating system, water is heated by the furnace and the hot water is pumped to the radiators to heat the rooms of the house.

Baseboard radiator
Expansion tank
Pump
Hot water heater
Burner
Smoke outlet

142 USING THERMAL ENERGY

OPTIONS

Meeting Different Ability Levels

For Section 6-2, use the following **Teacher Resource Masters** depending upon individual students' needs.

◆ **Study Guide Master** for all students.
● **Reinforcement Master** for students of average and above average ability levels.
▲ **Enrichment Master** for above average students.

Additional Teacher Resource Package masters are listed in the OPTIONS box throughout the section. The additional masters are appropriate for all students.

◆ **STUDY GUIDE** 27

burned in a furnace, and the heat is transported to radiators throughout the building. In one such system, the energy released in the furnace is used to heat water, which is then pumped through the pipes to the radiators in the system. After the water has given up some of its thermal energy, it is returned to the furnace to be heated again.

In a similar type of heating system, the furnace heats water to its boiling point, producing steam. The steam travels through insulated pipes to the radiators of the system. As it gives up its thermal energy, the steam condenses to water, which is returned to the furnace. Steam-heating systems need only about one-fiftieth as much water as hot-water systems, but the pipes and furnace in a steam-heating system need special insulation to keep the steam from condensing before it reaches the radiators.

Another type of heating system is the forced-air system, in which energy released in the furnace is used to heat air. A blower forces the heated air through a system of large pipes, called ducts, to openings, called vents, in each room. In the rooms the warm air circulates by convection. When the air has cooled, it passes through other vents and ducts and returns to the furnace to be heated again.

Some buildings are heated entirely by electricity. Heating coils are enclosed within floors or ceilings, and these are heated by electrical energy. Nearby air is heated by conduction, and people and materials in the room are also heated by radiation. Such systems, sometimes called radiant electric heating systems, provide even heating but are usually expensive to operate due to the high cost of electricity.

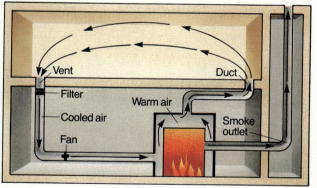

Figure 6-9. In a forced-air heating system, air heated by the furnace is used to heat the rooms of the house.

Vent
Duct
Filter
Warm air
Cooled air
Smoke outlet
Fan

TYING TO PREVIOUS KNOWLEDGE: Point out that in the last section students learned the three ways in which thermal energy is transferred. In this section they will learn how these methods help warm their homes.

OBJECTIVES AND SCIENCE WORDS: Have students review the objectives and science words to become familiar with this section.

2 TEACH

Key Concepts are highlighted.

Cooperative Learning: Assign Numbered Heads Together groups and have them identify and explain energy conversions and thermal energy transfers that take place in the heating systems shown in Figures 6-8 and 6-9.

PROGRAM RESOURCES

From the **Teacher Resource Package** use:

Transparency Masters, pages 21-22, Heating Systems.

Use **Color Transparency** number 11, Heating Systems.

● REINFORCEMENT 27

REINFORCEMENT   Chapter 6
Heating Systems   Text Pages 142–145

Answer Questions 1–10 about the heating system represented in the flowchart.

A. Furnace heats water to boil.

B. Steam provided by boiling water travels through pipes to a radiator.

C. Steam gives up thermal energy inside radiator and condenses to water.

D. Thermal energy of heated radiator heats air in room.

1. Is the system in the flowchart a hot-water system or a steam-heating system? **steam-heating**
2. How does the furnace get the energy needed to heat the water? **by burning a fuel**
3. How is the thermal energy produced by the furnace transferred to the water? **by conduction and convection**
4. Why do the pipes carrying the steam to the radiator need to be insulated? **to keep the steam from losing thermal energy**
5. How is the thermal energy from the steam transferred to the radiator? **by conduction**
6. How is the thermal energy of the radiator transferred to the surrounding air? **by conduction**
7. What happens to the steam as it gives up thermal energy inside the radiator? **It condenses into water.**
8. How is heat from the air surrounding the radiator transferred to the air in the rest of the room? **It is carried by pipes back convection**
9. What happens to the water that is formed inside the radiator? **It is carried by pipes back to the furnace to be reheated.**
10. What is a radiator? **a device with a large surface area designed to heat the air near it by conduction**

Copyright Glencoe Division of Macmillan/McGraw-Hill
Users of *Merrill Physical Science* have the publisher's permission to reproduce this page.   27

▲ ENRICHMENT 27

ENRICHMENT   Chapter 6
Heating Systems   Text Pages 142–145

HOME HEATING

Analyze the heating system in your home. Find someone who knows the heating system well. Maybe a parent or a brother or sister could help you. Other sources of help are a heating and cooling service person, a representative of a utility company, and literature on energy conservation measures. Once you have found someone, have him/her help you answer the following questions.

1. What type of heating system does your home have? **Either radiator, forced air, electric radiant heating, solar, or combinations of these are possible types.**
2. What type of fuel is used to heat your home? **natural gas, fuel oil, propane, electricity (from coal, nuclear, hydro, etc.)**
3. How much does it cost to heat your home per year? **Example: small ranch home, gas forced air, $50 per month for a year-long budget plan = $600 per year.**
4. What kind of low-cost actions could you take to help conserve heat in your home? **clean furnace filter monthly, insulate hot water and steam pipes, caulk around doors and windows, put insulating plastic on exterior of windows, keep fireplace flue closed when not in use, pull curtains at night to help insulate windows, open drapes during day to allow sunlight to heat the inside**
5. Suppose you had to replace your old heating system. What options are available to you? **New gas furnaces and hot-water boilers are much more efficient than older ones. Heat pumps can help heat in the winter and cool in the summer. Solar collectors can be used to supplement heating systems.**
6. Suppose you already had a highly efficient heating system. What kind of major improvements could you do to make your home even more heating efficient? **add insulation to the attic or walls, install new thermal replacement windows, add solar collectors**
7. Your heating system should have maintenance done on an annual basis. Why is this important? **Cleaning and proper adjustment allow the heating system to function at its maximum efficiency. It also makes sure that the fuel is burning properly. Improperly burned fuel could allow deadly carbon monoxide gas to be released into the home.**

Copyright Glencoe Division of Macmillan/McGraw-Hill
Users of *Merrill Physical Science* have the publisher's permission to reproduce this page.   27

▶ Make sure students understand that the major difference between passive and active solar heating systems is in the peripheral equipment. Passive solar heating systems use no mechanical means of transferring energy, whereas an active solar heating system does. Both systems heat matter by absorbing radiant energy from the sun.

CROSS CURRICULUM

▶ **Earth Science:** Have students explain why the windows of a house built in the northern hemisphere should face south for maximum sunlight. Then have them state in which direction the windows of a house built in the southern hemisphere should face.

MINI-Lab
Materials: Strips of poster board about 30 cm × 100 cm
▶ The board should be stiff enough to hold a smooth curve.
Teaching Tips
▶ The activity involves a good deal of inventing and experimenting by students. Encourage students to learn from each other's successes and failures.
▶ The arc will be closer to a parabola than to a circle.
▶ Many factors are involved: curvature, time of day, weather, and so on.
Answers to Questions: The hottest region would be where the reflected rays of the sun converge. The concentration of the radiant energy would make this region hot.

MINI-Lab

Can the sun be used to cook food?
Make a solar cooker by gluing aluminum foil to a large piece of poster board. Bend the board into an arc so that the ends of the board are nearly parallel to one another. Hold the board in this shape with string stretched between its corners. Use wire coat hangers to make a mount that will hold the board with its arc pointed directly at the sun. Using another coat hanger, fashion a device to hold a hot dog. Position the hot dog at the hottest region within the arc. Where is this region and why is it hot? The solar cooker is a passive system that converts radiant energy into thermal energy to heat the hot dog.

Figure 6-10. The passive (left) and active (right) solar heating systems change the sun's energy to thermal energy.

Solar Heating

If you have ever gotten into a car that has been sitting in direct sunlight for any length of time, you know that energy from the sun can be changed to thermal energy. Energy from the sun is known as **solar energy.** Because solar energy is free, the idea of using it to heat buildings is especially appealing.

Two basic types of systems have been designed to capture solar energy and convert it to thermal energy for use in heating buildings. The first type is passive solar heating. Passive systems use no fans or mechanical devices to transfer heat from one area to another. Some materials in the system absorb radiant energy during the day, convert it to thermal energy, and radiate the thermal energy after dark.

A house with a passive solar heating system usually has a wall of large windows on the south side to receive maximum sunlight. The other exterior walls are heavily insulated and have few windows. During the day, sunlight passes through the windows and is absorbed by some material, such as water or concrete. The radiant energy is converted to thermal energy, which is stored in the absorbing material. Later, when the house begins to cool, the stored energy radiates from the material, warming the rooms.

As you may have guessed, the second type of heating system using solar energy is called an active solar heating system. Most active solar heating systems include **solar collectors,** devices that absorb radiant energy from the sun. The collectors are usually installed on the roof or south side of a building. ❷

Use the Mini Quiz to check students' recall of chapter content.

❶ A(n) _____ is a device used to heat air by conduction. *radiator*
❷ A solar collector is a device that absorbs _____ from the sun. *radiant energy*

OPTIONS

INQUIRY QUESTIONS

▶ **Why is it more efficient to have heating elements near the floor than in the ceiling?** *With heating coils at floor level, convection currents can form and distribute the heat; however, with coils in the ceiling, no convection currents can form.*

▶ **Why is it better to have slightly moist air than dry air in a heated room?** *Water vapor causes moist air to have a higher specific heat than dry air; thus, the moist air can absorb and transfer more thermal energy than drier air.*

▶ **Why is water used rather than other fluids in home heating systems?** *The specific heat of water is very high compared to other fluids.*

PROGRAM RESOURCES
From the **Teacher Resource Package** use:
Activity Worksheets, page 53, Mini-Lab: Can the sun be used to cook food?
Science and Society, page 10, Solar Rights.

Figure 6-11 shows one type of solar collector. The metal plate absorbs radiant energy from the sun. Why do you think it's painted black? The glass or plastic sheets reduce energy loss due to convection. Water-filled pipes are located just beneath the metal plate. When radiant energy is absorbed, it is converted to thermal energy, which heats the water in the pipes. A pump circulates the heated water to radiators in the system. When the water is cooled, it is returned to the collector to be reheated. Some systems also have large, insulated tanks for storing heated water to be used as needed.

What type of a heating system is in the building where you live? If you were asked to redesign your building, what type of heating system would you install? What would you use for insulation in your building, and where would you install it? What other steps would you take to keep the building comfortable in all kinds of weather?

Figure 6-11. In an active solar system, the liquid heated in the solar collector is circulated throughout the house.

SECTION REVIEW

1. What are the main differences between electrical heating systems and more conventional radiator and forced-air systems?
2. Compare and contrast active and passive solar heating systems.
3. **Apply:** Suppose you are an architect who has always designed buildings for cold climates. You're asked to design a building for Phoenix, Arizona, where the average temperature is 22°C, and temperatures can reach 50°C in summer. How would you use what you know about keeping buildings warm to design a building that will stay cool in hot weather?

☑ Making and Using Tables

Skill Builder

In a table, organize information about the kinds of heating systems discussed in this chapter. Include any type of information you think is important. If you need help, refer to Making and Using Tables in the **Skill Handbook** on page 686.

Skill Builder

Type of Heating System	Specific Name	Heating Method
Conventional	Radiator	Conduction/convection
	Forced-air	Convection
	Radiant electric	Conduction/radiation
Solar	Passive	Radiation
	Active	Radiation/conduction

STUDENT TEXT QUESTION

▶ Page 145, paragraph 1: **Why do you think the plate of a solar collector is painted black?** *A plate painted black absorbs more radiant energy than a similar plate painted a lighter color.*

CHECK FOR UNDERSTANDING

Ask questions 1-2 and the **Apply** Question from the Section Review.

RETEACH

Have students list the three types of thermal energy transfer that take place in a radiator and rank them from most predominant method to least predominant method. Ask them to explain why the term *radiator* does not appropriately describe a radiator's primary method of heat transfer.

EXTENSION

For students who have mastered this section, use the **Reinforcement** and **Enrichment** masters or other OPTIONS provided.

3 CLOSE

▶ Have the students compare the tables they construct in the Skill Builder with the categories of home-heating systems the class compiled in the Motivation section.

SECTION REVIEW ANSWERS

1. Electrical heating systems have no furnaces, and no fuel is burned in the building being heated by them.
2. In passive systems, solar energy is used directly to heat an area. No devices are used to circulate the energy, and little energy storage takes place. In active systems, energy is collected, stored, transferred, and circulated by mechanical devices, such as pumps and fans.
3. Apply: Student responses will vary, but should incorporate ideas about using insulation and solar heating systems. Accept reasonable answers.

PROGRAM RESOURCES

From the **Teacher Resource Package** use:

   Concept Mapping, pages 17-18.

SCIENCE & SOCIETY 6-3

6-3 Thermal Pollution

PREPARATION

SECTION BACKGROUND

▶ Thermal pollution is a change in the natural fluctuations of temperature in an environment by artificial means. The change is usually detrimental to the ecological balance of the environment.

1 MOTIVATE

▶ Have students identify where they have seen water cooling towers.

▶ **Demonstration:** Moisten a cotton ball with ethanol and wrap it around the bulb of a thermometer. Have students note that the temperature reading of the thermometer decreases as the alcohol evaporates. Have students hypothesize how evaporation is used to cool materials.

TYING TO PREVIOUS KNOWLEDGE: Point out that students have learned how heat is transferred. In this section they will learn that heat transferred to the environment can harm it.

OBJECTIVES AND SCIENCE WORDS: Have students review the objectives and science words to become familiar with this section.

2 TEACH

Key Concepts are highlighted.

CONCEPT DEVELOPMENT

▶ Cooling towers cool water in one of two ways. In one method, the hot water is cooled by conduction. Heated water is exposed directly to the atmosphere. In the second method, hot water in a primary system of pipes is cooled when it heats and evaporates water in a secondary set of pipes which surround the primary system.

New Science Words

thermal pollution
cooling towers

Objectives

▶ Identify problems associated with thermal pollution.
▶ Discuss solutions for thermal pollution problems.

Not So Hot!

Have you ever been in a city on a warm day, surrounded by cars, large buildings, and concrete? If so, you may have noticed that it seems to be hotter there than in the suburbs, where there's less traffic and less activity. Well you're right. It is hotter in the city. Much of the energy used in everyday life—electrical, chemical, mechanical, radiant, or nuclear energy—ends up as waste thermal energy that is given off into the surroundings. And the heat removed from buildings and vehicles by air conditioners is released to the outside air, just as heat is released into a kitchen by a refrigerator.

The release of waste thermal energy into the environment can reach unhealthy levels. **Thermal pollution is a problem caused when waste thermal energy raises the temperature of the environment.** Thermal pollution is a particular problem in areas where power plants and factories use water to cool their buildings and equipment, raising the temperature of the water in the process. When the warmed water is dumped into a nearby river, lake, or ocean, the added heat may cause problems for the plants and animals living there.

146 USING THERMAL ENERGY

OPTIONS

Meeting Different Ability Levels

For Section 6-3, use the following **Teacher Resource Masters** depending upon individual students' needs.

◆ **Study Guide Master** for all students.
● **Reinforcement Master** for students of average and above average ability levels.
▲ **Enrichment Master** for above average students.

◆ **STUDY GUIDE** 28

STUDY GUIDE   Chapter 6
Thermal Pollution   Text Pages 146-147

Write the vocabulary term from this section that best completes each statement in the space provided.

1. The problem caused when waste thermal energy raises the temperature of the environment is _____ **thermal pollution** _____

2. Devices in which water is cooled by fans or evaporation before being released into the environment are _____ **cooling towers** _____

Use the words in the box to fill in the blanks.

temperature	25°C	buildings	pollution	heat	plants
factories	hours	raising	ocean	equipment	fish
animals	lake	increases	species	thermal	

Thermal _____ **pollution** _____ is a problem caused when waste _____ **thermal** _____ energy raises the _____ **temperature** _____ of the environment. Power plants and _____ **factories** _____ use water to cool their _____ **buildings** _____ and _____ **equipment** _____. Dumping this water after _____ **raising** _____ the temperature into a nearby river, _____ **lake** _____ or _____ **ocean** _____ adds _____ **heat** _____ and may cause problems for _____ **plants** _____ and _____ **animals** _____. Animals especially sensitive to _____ **increases** _____ in water temperature are _____ **fish** _____. Some _____ **species** _____ of fish will die within _____ **hours** _____ in water warmer than _____ **25°C** _____.

28   Copyright Glencoe Division of Macmillan/McGraw-Hill
            Users of Merrill Physical Science have the publisher's permission to reproduce this page.

Fish are especially sensitive to increases in water temperature. Some species will die within hours in water warmer than 25°C.

Thermal pollution can be reduced by releasing small amounts of warm water at a time, mixed with plenty of cooler water. Some factories and power plants use **cooling towers,** devices in which water is cooled by fans or evaporation. After cooling, the water can be released into the environment without causing harm. Another solution is to put the extra thermal energy to use by heating greenhouses or other buildings.

SECTION REVIEW

1. Thermal pollution may encourage the growth of certain water plants. Why might this be a problem?
2. A company plans to build several greenhouses to get rid of waste heat from cooling water. Suggest reasons why this plan might not be sufficient. What might the company do to improve the plan?

You Decide!

A company wants to build a factory by a river that runs through your city. Many new jobs will be created, but the factory will generate waste thermal energy. What steps would you take to find out whether the environment will be damaged? Should the company be allowed to build its factory?

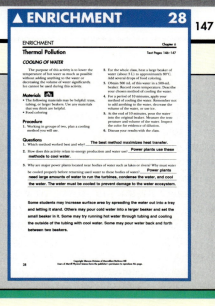

147

CHECK FOR UNDERSTANDING
Ask questions 1-2 from the Section Review.

RETEACH

 FLEX Your Brain

Use the Flex Your Brain activity to have students explore THERMAL POLLUTION.

EXTENSION
For students who have mastered this section, use the **Reinforcement** and **Enrichment** masters or other OPTIONS provided.

3 CLOSE

► Have students discuss their responses to the You Decide question.
► Have students identify and discuss sources of atmospheric thermal pollution, such as air conditioning and automobile exhaust.

SECTION REVIEW ANSWERS
1. Extremely heavy plant growth might prevent light from penetrating a body of water. As the plants die, their decay could use much of the oxygen from the water, making it unfit for other plants and animals to live.
2. Student answers will vary, but may include that building greenhouses would only use some of the heat. It would be necessary to use other methods of safely removing excess heat, such as building cooling towers.

YOU DECIDE!

The answer depends on local climate. Greenhouses need to be cooled instead of warmed in spring and summer. Build auxiliary cooling towers. Allow water to drain slowly into stream.

PROGRAM RESOURCES
From the **Teacher Resource Package** use:

Activity Worksheets, page 5, Flex Your Brain.

PREPARATION

SECTION BACKGROUND

▶ Heat engines convert thermal energy to mechanical energy; this implies that heat can do work. An internal combustion engine converts the chemical potential energy in fuel to thermal energy as the fuel burns. Thermal energy causes gases produced by the burned fuel to expand and do work against a piston. The mechanical energy of the piston produces motion.

▶ By reversing the processes of a heat engine, heat can be transferred from a material at a lower temperature to a material at a higher temperature. Work must be done on a system to reverse the natural flow of heat.

PREPLANNING

▶ Ask to borrow working models of internal combustion engines from the instructor at a local technical high school for demonstrations.

1 MOTIVATE

▶ Have students list various devices that contain internal combustion engines. Have students list the function of the engine in each case. For example, the function of the engine on a riding mower is to move the mower and rotate the cutting blade.

▶ Ask students to discuss how their lives would be different without the internal combustion engine.

6-4 Using Heat to Do Work

New Science Words

heat engines
combustion
internal combustion engine
external combustion engine
heat mover
heat pump

Objectives

▶ Describe how internal combustion engines and external combustion engines work.
▶ Explain how a heat mover can transfer thermal energy in a direction opposite to that of its natural movement.

Heat Engines

1 **Heat engines** are devices that convert thermal energy into mechanical energy. These engines burn fuel in a process called combustion. **Combustion** means rapid burning. The two main types of heat engines are classified according to where combustion happens—inside the engine or outside the engine.

2 In an **internal combustion engine,** fuel burns inside the engine, in chambers called cylinders. Gasoline engines and diesel engines, such as the ones used in cars and trucks, are examples of internal combustion engines.

Figure 6-12 shows what the cylinders look like inside the gasoline engine of a car. Each cylinder has two openings that open or close with valves. A piston inside each cylinder moves up and down, turning a rod called a crankshaft. The motion of the crankshaft is transferred to the wheels of the car through a series of moving parts. The wheels exert a force on the road, through the tires. The equal and opposite force of the road on the tires accelerates the car forward.

Each movement of the piston up or down is called a stroke. A gasoline engine is called a four-stroke engine because the piston makes four strokes in each cycle. Follow the steps of the four-stroke cycle in Figure 6-12.

1. *Intake stroke.* In another part of the engine called the carburetor (CAR buh ray tur), gasoline is broken up into fine droplets and mixed with air. In the cylinder, the intake valve opens and the piston moves downward, drawing the fuel-air mixture into the cylinder

OPTIONS

Meeting Different Ability Levels

For Section 6-4, use the following **Teacher Resource Masters** depending upon individual students' needs.

◆ **Study Guide Master** for all students.
● **Reinforcement Master** for students of average and above average ability levels.
▲ **Enrichment Master** for above average students.

Additional Teacher Resource Package masters are listed in the OPTIONS box throughout the section. The additional masters are appropriate for all students.

◆ **STUDY GUIDE**   **29**

STUDY GUIDE   Chapter 6
Using Heat to Do Work   Text Pages 148–152

Match each term in Column II with its description in Column I. Write the letter of the correct term in the space provided.

	Column I	Column II
c	1. rapid burning	a. internal combustion engine
f	2. device that moves thermal energy from one location and transfers it to another location at a different temperature	b. external combustion engine
b	3. burns fuel on the outside	c. combustion
d	4. device that converts thermal energy into mechanical energy	d. heat engine
a	5. burns fuels inside chambers called cylinders	e. heat pump
e	6. two-way heat mover	f. heat mover
g	7. movement of a piston up or down	g. stroke

The steps of the four-stroke cycle of a gasoline engine are described below. Use the terms compression stroke, power stroke, exhaust stroke, or intake stroke to correctly label each step. Write your labels in the blanks.

intake stroke	1. The piston moves downward and draws a fuel-air mixture into the cylinder through the intake valve.
compression stroke	2. The intake valve closes. The piston moves up squeezing the fuel-air mixture into a smaller space.
power stroke	3. A spark produced by a spark plug ignites the fuel-air mixture. Hot gases expand, forcing the piston down.
exhaust stroke	4. The piston moves up again, compressing the waste products from the burning of the fuel-air mixture. The waste products leave the cylinder through a valve.

29

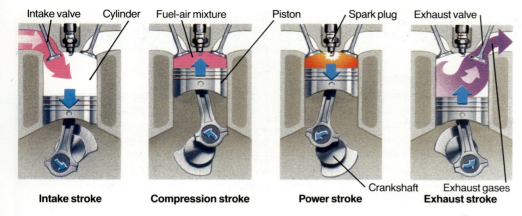

Intake valve Cylinder Fuel-air mixture Piston Spark plug Exhaust valve

| Intake stroke | Compression stroke | Power stroke | Exhaust stroke |

Crankshaft

Exhaust gases

2. *Compression stroke.* The intake valve closes, and the piston moves up. The fuel-air mixture is squeezed, or compressed, into a smaller space.

3. *Power stroke.* When the piston is almost at the top of the cylinder, a spark plug produces a hot spark that ignites the fuel-air mixture. As the mixture burns, hot gases expand, forcing the piston down. Energy is transferred from the piston to the wheels of the car, through the crankshaft and other moving parts.

4. *Exhaust stroke.* The piston moves up again, compressing the waste products left over from burning the fuel-air mixture. The exhaust valve opens to let the waste products out.

Some engines have fuel injectors instead of carburetors. In fuel injector engines, only air enters the cylinder during the intake stroke. During the compression stroke, fine droplets of fuel are injected directly into the compressed air in the cylinder. The other steps are the same as in an engine with a carburetor.

In a diesel engine, fuel also is injected into compressed air in the cylinder. But the engine has no spark plugs. The fuel-air mixture is compressed so much that it becomes hot enough to ignite without a spark.

In an internal combustion engine, only part of the thermal energy produced by burning fuel is converted to mechanical energy. The rest is left over as waste thermal energy. Gasoline engines convert only about 12 percent of the chemical potential energy in the fuel to mechanical energy. Diesel engines convert about 25 percent of the potential energy to mechanical energy.

Figure 6-12. This drawing shows what takes place during each stroke of a four-stroke engine.

How do fuel injectors operate?

149

2 TEACH

Key Concepts are highlighted.

CONCEPT DEVELOPMENT

▶ Engines may have several cylinders. The piston in each cylinder goes through a four-stroke cycle. However, in an engine with more than one cylinder, the strokes in the various cylinders will differ. For example, in a four-cylinder engine, each piston is at a different stroke in a four-stroke cycle. This produces a more continuous supply of motion to the crankshaft. One power stroke is supplied to the crankshaft during each step of the cycle. Point out that in a one-cylinder engine only one power stroke is supplied during the four steps of the cycle.

▶ Students may recall that as more air is pumped into a bicycle tire, the tire becomes warm. This warming is due to the rise in temperature of the air as work is done on it to compress it inside the tire. Much the same happens to the compressed air mixture inside the cylinder of a diesel engine. Point out that as a gas expands, the opposite effect takes place—the gas cools. Students may recall that a pressurized can of paint cools as the paint is released.

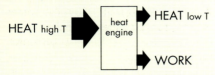
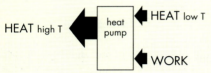
▲ T E C H N O L O G Y

Cooling Crystals

A conventional refrigerator works on the principle that when a liquid is allowed to evaporate and expand, it absorbs heat from its surroundings. Scientists are now working on an entirely different approach to refrigeration. This new approach is based on the fact that certain crystals give off heat when they are magnetized and absorb heat when demagnetized.

One substance that shows this behavior is a clear crystal called gadolinium gallium garnet. To create a continuous cycle of heat exchange, scientists have mounted crystal wafers of this substance on the outside of the wheel. The wheel is then positioned so that the wafers rotate in and out of a magnetic field. As they rotate, they alternately absorb and give off heat. This magnetic refrigerator can attain temperatures colder than a conventional refrigerator, reaching temperatures close to absolute zero.

Possible applications for this refrigerator include the cooling of infrared sensors on satellites and spacecraft, cooling medical research equipment, and cooling the components of future super computers.
Think Critically: What factor would determine how cold a gas-cycle refrigerator could get?

In an **external combustion engine,** fuel is burned outside the engine. In old-fashioned steam engines, such as those used to power early locomotives, fuel was burned to boil water in a chamber outside the engine. The steam produced passed through a valve in the engine, where it pushed a piston. The motion of the piston was transferred to the wheels of the locomotive.

Modern steam engines, such as those used in electrical power stations, don't have pistons. Instead, steam is directed onto huge, fanlike devices called turbines. The steam pushes against the turbine blades, and the turbine rotates rapidly.

Heat Movers

When you put warm food into the refrigerator, the food gets cooler. Where does the thermal energy in the food go? Feel the back of the refrigerator, and you'll notice that it's warm. But you know that heat always flows

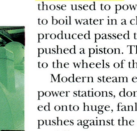

Figure 6-13. Turbines are used to convert thermal energy to mechanical energy.

OPTIONS

from warmer to cooler areas. So how can heat flow from the cool refrigerator to the warm room? It can't unless work is done. The energy to do the work comes from the electricity that powers the refrigerator.

A refrigerator is an example of a heat mover. **A heat mover is a device that removes thermal energy from one location and transfers it to another location at a different temperature.** Refrigerators use the process of evaporation to remove heat from the food inside. A liquid is pumped through coils inside the refrigerator. In most cooling systems, liquid Freon is used because it evaporates at low temperatures. As the liquid evaporates and becomes a gas, it absorbs heat, cooling the inside of the refrigerator. The Freon gas is then pumped to a compressor on the outside of the refrigerator. Compressing the Freon causes its temperature to rise above room temperature. So the Freon loses heat to the air around it and becomes liquid again. The excess heat is transferred into the room, sometimes with the help of fans.

An air conditioner is another kind of heat mover, removing thermal energy from a warm house and transferring it to the even warmer outdoor surroundings.

A **heat pump** is a two-way heat mover. In warm weather, it operates like an air conditioner. But in cold weather, it removes thermal energy from the cool outside air and transfers it to the inside of the house.

Figure 6-14. In a heat mover, such as a refrigerator, thermal energy is removed from one location and is released in another location.

SECTION REVIEW

1. What are the main differences between a diesel engine and a gasoline engine? How are they alike?
2. In a heat engine, chemical energy in the fuel is converted to thermal energy. What happens to the thermal energy?
3. **Apply:** On a hot day, a friend suggests you leave the refrigerator door open to make your house cooler. Is this a good idea? Explain your answer.

☑ Concept Mapping

Make a cycle concept map to show the steps in one cycle of a four-stroke internal combustion engine. If you need help, refer to Concept Mapping in the **Skill Handbook** on pages 684 and 685.

Skill Builder

Skill Builder

Four-stroke Internal Combustion Engine
(One cycle)

RETEACH

Cooperative Learning: Using the Paired Partners strategy, have students make flash cards with the names of the strokes of the four-stroke cycle. On the reverse side of each card, describe the stroke. Partners can then test each other by shuffling the cards and sequencing them both by name and description. Students can alter the cards to represent the four-stroke cycle of a diesel engine.

EXTENSION

For students who have mastered this section, use the **Reinforcement** and **Enrichment** masters or other OPTIONS provided.

3 CLOSE

▶ Invite a representative from a utilities company to discuss the advantages and disadvantages of heat pump and heating/air-conditioning systems.

SECTION REVIEW ANSWERS

1. Diesel fuel is different from gasoline; diesel engines do not use spark plugs or carburetors. Both types are four-stroke engines; each is an internal combustion engine.

2. Some of the thermal energy is converted to mechanical energy in the power stroke, forcing the piston to move; the rest is wasted thermal energy transferred to the environment.

3. Apply: No; the more heat allowed to enter the refrigerator, the more heat the refrigerator will move back into the kitchen. Much electrical energy will be wasted.

PROGRAM RESOURCES

From the **Teacher Resource Package** use:

Critical Thinking/Problem Solving, page 12, New Refrigerators.

Use **Laboratory Manual,** Thermal Energy from Foods.

ACTIVITY 6-2
30 minutes

OBJECTIVE: **Construct** and **analyze** a model of a four-stroke engine.

PROCESS SKILLS applied in this activity:
▶ **Observing** in Procedure Steps 4-7.
▶ **Analyzing** in Analyze Question 1.

👥 COOPERATIVE LEARNING

Use the Science Investigation Team strategy. Each member can operate a different part of the engine: carburetor, intake and exhaust valves, and piston.

TEACHING THE ACTIVITY

Troubleshooting: Insert glass tubing prior to the activity. This will both save time and increase safety.
▶ Students should prepare by reading pages 148-149 about internal combustion engines.
▶ Touch paper can be used to generate smoke. Otherwise, you should use paper towels.
▶ Soft rubber tubing and strong pinch clamps are needed to avoid gas leaks.
▶ Use the activity to discuss the use of models to study specific parts of a complex problem.

PROGRAM RESOURCES

From the **Teacher Resource Package** use:

Activity Worksheets, pages 49-50, Activity 6-2: The Four-stroke Engine.

ACTIVITY 6-2
The Four-stroke Engine

Problem: *When does potential energy change to kinetic energy?*

Materials

- matches
- flask, 250-mL
- glass or plastic "T"
- pinch clamps (2)
- large syringe, plastic
- rubber tubing (3 pieces)
- small piece of cloth or yarn
- rubber stopper, 2-hole, with glass tubing

Procedure

1. Set up a model four-stroke engine as shown.
2. Prepare a data table like the one shown. As you complete each step, identify the stroke and record your observations.
3. Ignite a small piece of cloth or yarn and drop it in the flask. **CAUTION:** *Exercise caution when using open flames.* Allow the flask, representing the carburetor, to fill with smoke.
4. With the piston inside the cylinder, open the intake valve and pull the piston down.
5. Close the intake valve and push the piston up into the cylinder.
6. Release the piston and observe what happens.
7. Open the exhaust valve and push the piston up into the cylinder.
8. Close the exhaust valve and repeat Steps 4-7.

Analyze

1. During which stroke are the smoke particles most widely separated?
2. What happens to the smoke particles when the intake valve is closed and the piston moves into the cyinder?
3. What happens when the piston is released?
4. What happens to the smoke particles when the exhaust valve is opened and the piston moves into the cylinder?
5. During what strokes are both valves closed?

Conclude and Apply

6. In this model, what does the smoke represent in Steps 4 and 5? In Step 7?
7. When would be the best instant to explode a fuel-air mixture?
8. In which stroke is kinetic energy changed to potential energy? potential to kinetic?

Data and Observations

Sample Data

Step	Stroke	Observations
4	intake	intake valve open; piston moves out of cylinder; smoke from carburetor fills cylinder
5	compression	both valves closed; piston moves into cylinder; particles of smoke squeezed together
6	power	both valves closed; pressure of gases squeezed at top of cylinder forces piston to move out
7	exhaust	exhaust valve open; piston moves into cylinder; smoke is pushed out through exhaust valve

ANSWERS TO QUESTIONS

1. intake stroke
2. The smoke particles are compressed—squeezed together.
3. It moves downward in the cylinder.
4. Smoke particles are pushed out through the valve by the piston.
5. during the compression and power strokes
6. In Steps 4 and 5, the smoke represents the fuel-air mixture; in Step 7, it represents exhaust gases.
7. when the piston is at the top of its stroke and the fuel-air mixture is compressed

8. Kinetic energy is changed to potential energy during the compression stroke. Potential energy is changed to kinetic energy during the power stroke.

SUMMARY

6-1: Moving Thermal Energy

1. Thermal energy can be transferred by conduction, convection, and radiation. Conduction and convection can only occur when matter is present. Radiation does not require matter.

2. Materials that do not allow heat to move through them easily are insulators. Conductors allow heat to move through them easily.

3. Insulation slows down or prevents the movement of thermal energy.

6-2: Heating Systems

1. Heating systems are generally identified by the medium that transfers the thermal energy. The three most common types of heating systems are hot water, steam, and hot air.

2. A solar heating system converts radiant energy from the sun to thermal energy.

3. Passive solar systems have no devices to transfer heat from one part of the system to another.

Active systems use fans or pumps to serve this purpose.

6-3: Science and Society: Thermal Pollution

1. Thermal pollution can adversely affect living things.

2. Specific practices have been identified that can greatly reduce thermal pollution at the source.

6-4: Using Heat to Do Work

1. Heat engines are devices that convert thermal energy produced by burning fuel into mechanical energy. In an internal combustion engine, fuel is burned inside the engine. In an external combustion engine, fuel is burned outside the engine.

2. Heat movers remove thermal energy from one place and release it in another place. In many cases, this transfer is from cooler to warmer regions.

KEY SCIENCE WORDS

a. combustion
b. conduction
c. convection
d. cooling towers
e. external combustion engine
f. fluid
g. heat engines
h. heat mover
i. heat pump
j. insulators
k. internal combustion engine
l. radiation
m. radiator
n. solar collectors
o. solar energy
p. thermal pollution

UNDERSTANDING VOCABULARY

Match each phrase with the correct term from the list of Key Science Words.

1. energy transfer by direct contact of particles
2. energy transfer by movement of particles from place to place
3. energy transfer by invisible waves
4. materials that resist the flow of heat
5. devices that absorb the sun's radiant energy
6. devices that convert thermal energy into mechanical energy
7. rapid burning
8. a device that transfers thermal energy from one place to another
9. devices in which warm water is cooled by fans or by evaporation
10. a device designed to heat the air that comes in contact with it

USING THERMAL ENERGY **153**

SUMMARY

Have students read the summary statements to review the major concepts of the chapter.

UNDERSTANDING VOCABULARY

1. b	6. g
2. c	7. a
3. l	8. h
4. j	9. d
5. n	10. m

OPTIONS

ASSESSMENT

To assess student understanding of material in this chapter, use the resources listed.

COOPERATIVE LEARNING

Consider using cooperative learning in the THINK AND WRITE CRITICALLY, APPLY, and MORE SKILL BUILDERS sections of the Chapter Review.

PROGRAM RESOURCES

From the **Teacher Resource Package** use:
Chapter Review, pages 15-16.
Chapter and Unit Tests, pages 32-35, Chapter Test.

CHAPTER
REVIEW

CHECKING CONCEPTS

1. b	6. b
2. a	7. c
3. d	8. a
4. a	9. d
5. a	10. d

UNDERSTANDING CONCEPTS

11. air
12. Thermal pollution
13. valves
14. power
15. convection

THINK AND WRITE CRITICALLY

16. Initially, the bottom of the pot and the soup near the pot bottom are heated by conduction. Some of the energy of the burner top is transferred to the particles of the pot bottom, which transfers energy to the soup. As the bottom portion of the soup becomes warm, the cooler, denser liquid sinks, forcing the warmer liquid to rise. This movement transfers heat throughout the liquid by convection.

17. Convection currents are created when one part of a fluid is heated. The cooler, denser fluid moves down and forces the warmer, less dense fluid to rise, creating a convection current. Winds and ocean currents are examples of convection currents in nature.

18. Darker materials absorb radiation more effectively. When layers of clothing are worn, a thin layer of insulating air will be present between each layer of clothing.

19. In passive solar heating, radiant energy is directed onto a material that will absorb the energy, convert it to thermal energy, and transfer it to the surroundings as heat. In active solar heating, the thermal energy is transferred by the use of mechanical devices. Both systems are based on the idea that radiant energy is changed to thermal energy when it is absorbed.

20. Most thermal pollution is produced by industries that use water as a coolant, and then release heated water back into the body of water from which

CHECKING CONCEPTS

Choose the word or phrase that completes the sentence or answers the question.

1. Which is not a method of heat transfer?
   a. conduction   c. radiation
   b. insulation   d. convection

2. In _____, fuel is burned inside chambers called cylinders.
   a. internal combustion engines
   b. external combustion engines
   c. heat pumps
   d. steam engines

3. Waste gases are removed during the _____ of a four-stroke engine.
   a. power stroke   c. compression engine
   b. intake stroke   d. exhaust stroke

4. Which material is a poor insulator of heat?
   a. aluminum   c. air
   b. feathers   d. plastic

5. A _____ is an example of a heat mover.
   a. refrigerator   c. radiator
   b. steam engine   d. four-stroke engine

6. In which of these forms is water not a fluid?
   a. liquid water   c. water vapor
   b. ice   d. steam

7. Heat can move easily through a good _____.
   a. insulator   c. conductor
   b. convector   d. collector

8. Which of these does not require the presence of particles of matter?
   a. radiation   c. convection
   b. conduction   d. combustion

9. In order for radiant energy to change to thermal energy, it must be _____.
   a. reflected   c. convected
   b. conducted   d. absorbed

10. A(n) _____ is a two-way heat mover.
    a. refrigerator   c. air conditioner
    b. steam engine   d. heat pump

UNDERSTANDING CONCEPTS

Complete each sentence.

11. Double-pane windows have a thin layer of _____ trapped between two panes of glass.

12. _____ results when waste energy raises the temperature of the environment.

13. In an internal combustion engine, the flow of gases is controlled by _____ that open and close.

14. The _____ stroke of a four-stroke engine begins when the fuel-air mixture is ignited.

15. A radiator heats the air in a room by conduction and _____.

THINK AND WRITE CRITICALLY

16. Describe all of the ways in which energy is transferred while a bowl of soup is heated on an electric stove. Indicate how each type of energy transfer takes place.

17. Explain how convection currents are created. Describe two examples of convection currents that occur in nature.

18. Why is winter clothing generally darker in color than summer clothing? Explain why wearing two or three layers of clothing helps to keep you warmer than one thick layer in cold weather.

19. Compare and contrast passive and active solar heating. What basic principle are both systems based on?

20. Describe some causes and effects of thermal pollution. Suggest some solutions to this environmental problem.

it came. The effect of this action is to raise the temperature of the body of water, which can make it unfit for plant and animal life to exist. The best way to prevent such pollution is to cool the water before returning it to the environment.

APPLY

21. Student responses will vary, but may include such analogies as energy being passed on to a pack of billiard balls when one ball is struck.

22. Radiant energy from the sun strikes materials inside a car and is absorbed, changing to thermal energy. Thermal energy is transferred as heat. The increase in heat causes the temperature inside the car to rise.

23. Student answers will vary, but should include dark-colored materials that will absorb radiant energy and layers of fibers that will trap air and reduce the loss of body heat.

24. Increasing the number of valves increases the amount of fresh air taken into the cylinder during the intake stroke and decreases the amount of exhaust remaining. More air can burn more fuel. The fuel injectors provide

APPLY

21. The energy transfer shown in Figure 6-1 takes place at the particle level of matter. Thus, the transfer of energy cannot be observed directly. Think of an analogy or model using visible objects that you could use to demonstrate the process of conduction.

22. Explain why the inside of an automobile left sitting in direct sunlight for several hours becomes very warm.

23. Design a line of clothing to be used on an Arctic expedition. Describe the articles of clothing and explain why each will keep the wearer warm in extremely cold conditions.

24. The engines of many high-performance cars have four valves per cylinder rather than the usual two-valve arrangement. These engines also have fuel injectors at each cylinder rather than a single carburetor. How do these differences improve the performance of the engine?

25. Describe how an automobile air conditioner using Freon gas works. Explain why the engine must be running in order for the air conditioner to work.

MORE SKILL BUILDERS

If you need help, refer to the Skill Handbook.

1. Interpreting Data: Using the R-values given in Table 6-1, design an energy-efficient house. Indicate the type and thickness of the different materials to be used in constructing the walls and ceilings.

2. Sequencing: Order the events that occur in the removal of heat from an object by a refrigerator. Start with the placing of a warm object in the refrigerator and finish with the change in Freon from a gas to a liquid.

3. Concept Mapping: Complete the following events chain to show how an active solar heating system works.

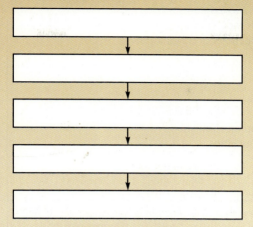

4. Recognizing Cause and Effect: Describe the probable effect of each of the following problems that might occur in a fuel-injected gasoline engine. Indicate the engine stroke that will be affected. (a) stuck exhaust valve; (b) clogged fuel injector; (c) bad spark plug; (d) intake valve will not close.

5. Using Variables, Constants, and Controls: Design an experiment to test the effects of surface area and length of a material on heat conduction. Indicate your hypothesis, controls, and constants. How will you organize and interpret your data?

PROJECTS

1. Design and construct an insulated container using household materials.

2. Research the development of the automobile engine. Construct a time line showing the most significant events.

USING THERMAL ENERGY **155**

---

a more even distribution of fuel. Both help to increase efficiency of combustion and thus increase power.

25. As liquid Freon moves through the air conditioner it evaporates, removing thermal energy from the interior of the car. This thermal energy is then released to the warmer air outside the car. This process requires work to be done by the car's engine.

MORE SKILL BUILDERS

1. Interpreting Data: Student responses will vary, but the combinations of suggested materials and/or their thicknesses should give total R-values of at least 19 for the walls and 30 for the roof.

2. Sequencing: Liquid Freon evaporates, removing thermal energy from the interior of the refrigerator; compressing the gas raises its temperature; heat flows from the gas to the exterior air, causing the Freon gas to condense to a liquid.

3. Concept Mapping:

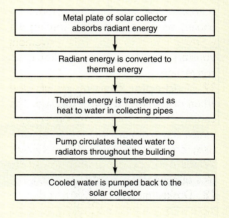

---

4. Recognizing Cause and Effect: (a) Exhaust gases will not be removed during the exhaust stroke, which will limit the amount of fuel-air mixture entering during the intake stroke. (b) The amount of fuel being mixed with air during the intake stroke will be reduced, thus reducing the effectiveness of the power stroke. (c) The fuel-air mixture will not be properly ignited, thus reducing the power stroke. (d) The fuel-air mixture that enters during the intake stroke will be pushed out of the stuck valve during the compression stroke, thus reducing the power stroke.

5. Using Variables, Constants, and Controls: Student responses will vary, but a sample hypothesis is that increasing surface area increases thermal conduction. Controls would include varying the surface area. Constants would include the type of material tested. Data analysis should include a line graph.

7 Machines

CHAPTER SECTION	OBJECTIVES	ACTIVITIES
7-1 Why We Use Machines (2 days)	1. **Explain** how machines make work easier. 2. **Calculate** mechanical advantage.	**Activity 7-1:** *Using Machines,* p. 162
7-2 The Simple Machines (2 days)	1. **Describe** the six types of simple machines. 2. **Calculate** the mechanical advantage for different types of simple machines.	**Activity 7-2:** *Levers,* p. 171
7-3 Human-Powered Flying Machines Science & Society (1 day)	1. **Analyze** the simple machines in a human-powered aircraft. 2. **Consider** the value of experiments with no obvious practical value.	
7-4 Using Machines (2 days)	1. **Recognize** the simple machines that make up a complex machine. 2. **Calculate** efficiency of a machine. 3. **Describe** the relationship between work, power, and time.	**MINI-Lab:** *Can you measure the power of a toy car?* p. 177
Chapter Review		

ACTIVITY MATERIALS

FIND OUT	ACTIVITIES		MINI-LABS

Page 157
 round pencils (several)
 ruler
 2 books
	7-1 Using Machines, p. 162
	 brick
	 book
	 string
	 2 pencil-sized dowels
	 hard board
	 pulley
	 ring stand with ring
		7-2 Levers, p. 171
		 sheet of paper,
		   20 cm x 28 cm
		   (8-1/2 " × 11")
		 3 coins (quarter,
		   dime, nickel)
		 balance
		 metric ruler
			Can you measure the power of a toy car? p. 177
			 wind up toy car
			 inclined plane board
			 stopwatch or timer
			   with second hand
			 meterstick
			 balance

CHAPTER FEATURES		TEACHER RESOURCE PACKAGE	OTHER RESOURCES
Skill Builder: *Recognizing Cause and Effect,* p. 161		**Ability Level Worksheets** ◆ **Study Guide,** p. 30 ● **Reinforcement,** p. 30 ▲ **Enrichment,** p. 30 **Activity Worksheet,** pp. 55, 56 **Transparency Masters,** pp. 9, 10	
Problem Solving: *How Do You Use Your Arm as a Lever?* p. 165 **Skill Builder:** *Making and Using Tables,* p. 170		**Ability Level Worksheets** ◆ **Study Guide,** p. 31 ● **Reinforcement,** p. 31 ▲ **Enrichment,** p. 31 **Activity Worksheet,** pp. 57, 58 **Critical Thinking/Problem Solving,** p. 13 **Transparency Masters,** pp. 25, 26	**Color Transparency 13,** Classes of Levers **Lab Manual 14,** Balanced Levers **Lab Manual 15,** Pulleys
You Decide! p. 173		**Ability Level Worksheets** ◆ **Study Guide,** p. 32 ● **Reinforcement,** p. 32 ▲ **Enrichment,** p. 32 **Cross-Curricular Connections,** p. 11	
Technology: *Micromachines,* p. 177 **Skill Builder:** *Concept Mapping,* p. 178		**Ability Level Worksheets** ◆ **Study Guide,** p. 33 ● **Reinforcement,** p. 33 ▲ **Enrichment,** p. 33 **MINI-Lab Worksheet,** p. 61 **Concept Mapping,** pp. 19, 20 **Science and Society,** p. 11 **Transparency Masters,** pp. 27, 28	**Color Transparency 14,** A Compound Machine **Lab Manual 16,** The Bicycle: A Well-Engineered Machine
Summary Key Science Words Understanding Vocabulary Checking Concepts Understanding Concepts	Think & Write Critically Apply More Skill Builders Projects	**Chapter Review,** pp. 17, 18 **Chapter Test,** pp. 36–39 **Unit Test,** pp. 40, 41	**Chapter Review Software** **Test Bank**

◆ **Basic**   ● **Average**   ▲ **Advanced**

ADDITIONAL MATERIALS		
SOFTWARE	**AUDIOVISUAL**	**BOOKS/MAGAZINES**
Simple Machines, Carolina Biological. *Simple Machines,* Micro-Ed. *Work and Machines,* Queue.	*The Lever,* film, BFA. *Work and Power,* filmstrip, EBEC. *Simple Machines,* EBEC. *Mr. Wizard's World: Simple Machines.* Macmillan/McGraw-Hill School Division. *Work and Play Made Easier: Using Simple Machines,* video, Focus. *Simple and Compound Machines: How they Work,* laserdisc, AIMS Media.	Bulliet, Richard W. *The Camel and the Wheel.* New York: Columbia University Press, 1990. Grannis, Gary E. *Modern Power Mechanics.* New York: Macmillan Publishing Inc., 1979. Stover, Dawn. "Reinventing the Wheel," *Science Digest,* June, 1985, p. 14.

THEME DEVELOPMENT: A simple machine is a system that has work done on it; it, in turn, does work on an object or another system. Emphasize the input-output nature of simple and compound machines throughout the chapter.

CHAPTER OVERVIEW

▶ **Section 7-1:** Simple machines are introduced and characterized in this section. The concept of mechanical advantage is developed.

▶ **Section 7-2:** This section classifies simple machines into six types and discusses how they can be conceptualized into two broad categories: levers and inclined planes.

▶ **Section 7-3: Science and Society:** A report on human-powered flight asks students to query the advantages and disadvantages of research that doesn't have apparent or immediate application.

▶ **Section 7-4:** Compound machines are discussed using a bicycle as an example. The concepts of efficiency and power of a machine are introduced and developed.

CHAPTER VOCABULARY

machine	pulley
simple machine	wheel and
effort force	axle
resistance force	inclined plane
ideal machine	screw
mechanical	wedge
advantage	compound
lever	machine
fulcrum	efficiency
effort arm	power
resistance arm	watt

CHAPTER

7 Machines

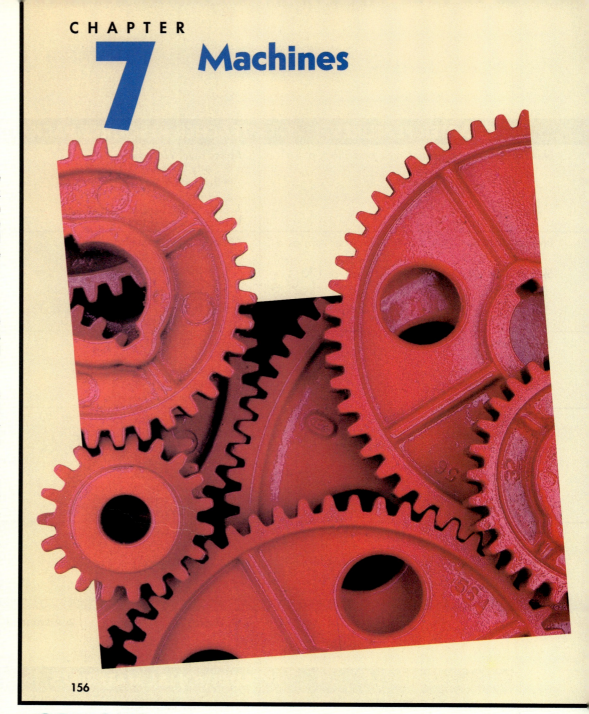

156

OPTIONS

⚡ For Your Gifted Students

▶ Have students design and build a compound machine that performs a task. They should name the machine and create an advertisement for their invention. The students can present their advertisements to the class as they might appear on radio, television, or in a magazine. Students should be able to identify the simple machines involved. They may wish to research how one receives a patent and contact the U.S. Patent Office.

▶ Have students create rubber-band vehicles. They can test them to see which one can climb the steepest inclined plane or carry the heaviest load.

When you think of machines, you might think of gears. Not all machines have gears, though. Some have no moving parts at all. One way that people make jobs easier is by using machines. You might use a claw hammer to pull out a nail or a cart to help you carry a heavy load. How do devices such as these make work easier?

FIND OUT!

Do this activity to show how you can reduce effort needed to move an object.

Stack two books on a flat desk or table. Use one hand to push them along the surface. Observe the amount of effort you exert. Now put several round pencils under the bottom book and try again to push the books. Are they easier to push?

Remove the pencils and position the books so that they just hang over the edge of the desk. Place your fingertips under the bottom book and try to lift the books with your fingers. Set the books flat on the surface again and slide a ruler under the edge of the bottom book. Push up on the ruler to lift the books. (Make sure the books are not so heavy that the ruler will break.) Is it easier to lift the books using the ruler?

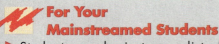

Gearing Up

Previewing the Chapter

Use this outline to help you focus on important ideas in this chapter.

Section 7-1   Why We Use Machines
▶ What Are Simple Machines?
▶ Advantages of Simple Machines

Section 7-2   The Simple Machines
▶ Levers
▶ Pulleys
▶ Wheel and Axle
▶ Inclined Plane
▶ Screw and Wedge

Section 7-3   Science and Society
Human-Powered Flying Machines
▶ Pedaling through the Sky

Section 7-4   Using Machines
▶ Compound Machines
▶ Efficiency
▶ Power

Previewing Science Skills

▶ In the **Skill Builders,** you will recognize cause and effect, make and use tables, and map concepts.
▶ In the **Activities,** you will observe, classify, measure in SI, and analyze.
▶ In the **MINI-Lab,** you will observe and measure in SI.

What's next?

You've shown that work can be made easier by reducing friction and using simple devices to reduce the amount of force you have to exert to move something. Now find out about some different devices used to make work easier, how they operate, and how much easier they make your work.

157

Use the Find Out activity to introduce students to the concept of machines as devices that make doing a job or task easier.

FIND OUT!

Materials: Obtain stiff rulers and several boxes of round pencils for the activity and a large coffee can, its plastic lid, and enough marbles to fill the lid for the demonstration.

Cooperative Learning: Have Problem Solving Teams determine if the length of the ruler inserted under the books has any effect on making the books easier to lift.

Teaching Tips
▶ To increase the sturdiness of the rulers, secure two together with tape or rubber bands.
▶ **Demonstration:** Fill the plastic lid of a coffee can with marbles and place the can on top of them. Allow students to turn the can. Point out that the marbles demonstrate how ball bearings are devices that reduce effort.

Gearing Up

Have students study the Gearing Up feature to familiarize themselves with the chapter. Discuss the relationships of the topics in the outline.

What's Next?

Before beginning the first section, make sure students understand the connection between the Find Out activity and the topics to follow.

For Your Mainstreamed Students

▶ Students can brainstorm a list of 20 machines that can easily be identified as containing simple machines. Assign each student to reseach one invention. Collectively create a time line that depicts the machines and the date each was invented.

▶ Have students contribute objects and pictures of simple machines to form a display. Students can label the objects and pictures and categorize them by the type of simple machine or compound machine each represents.

PREPARATION

SECTION BACKGROUND

▶ A machine can be thought of as a system that transfers mechanical energy through work. Work is done on the machine, and the machine, in turn, does work on another object or system. The most elementary system is a simple machine that transfers energy in one movement.

▶ A machine can multiply forces or multiply speeds at which the forces are delivered; because of the conservation of energy, it cannot do both simultaneously.

▶ The mechanical advantage of a machine indicates the factor by which it multiplies an effort force.

PREPLANNING

▶ Prepare for Activity 7-1 by obtaining one brick for each lab group.

1 MOTIVATE

▶ Have students list various simple tasks done at home or at school and discuss how different tools or devices help make doing the tasks easier. Have the discussions focus on identifying the task, the tool or device, and how it functions. For example, to tighten a screw into a piece of wood (the task), the student would probably choose a screwdriver (the tool). The blade of a screwdriver turns the head of the screw and drives it into the wood as the handle of the screwdriver is turned (how it functions).

Cooperative Learning: Using the Numbered Heads Together strategy, divide the class into groups and have each group decide upon an example of a complex machine and an example of a simple machine. Have the groups share their examples. Discuss how each group defined the terms *machine, complex,* and *simple.* Stress the commonality among the definitions.

7-1 Why We Use Machines

New Science Words

machine
simple machine
effort force
resistance force
ideal machine
mechanical advantage

Objectives

▶ Explain how machines make work easier.
▶ Calculate mechanical advantage.

What Are Simple Machines?

Have you used any machines today? You probably know that a bicycle is a machine. Pencil sharpeners and can openers are also machines. Even if you haven't used any of these things, you have probably used at least one machine today. If you turned a doorknob or twisted off a bottle cap, you have used a machine. **A machine is a device that makes work easier.**

Some machines are powered by engines or electric motors; others are "people-powered." Some machines are very complex; others are quite simple. **A simple machine is a device that does work with only one movement.** There are six types of simple machines, examples of which are pictured below. You'll learn more about each type in a later section of this chapter.

OPTIONS

Meeting Different Ability Levels

For Section 7-1, use the following **Teacher Resource Masters** depending upon individual students' needs.

◆ **Study Guide Master** for all students.
● **Reinforcement Master** for students of average and above average ability levels.
▲ **Enrichment Master** for above average students.
Additional Teacher Resource Package masters are listed in the OPTIONS box throughout the section. The additional masters are appropriate for all students.

◆ **STUDY GUIDE** 30

STUDY GUIDE   Chapter 7
Why We Use Machines   Text Pages 158–162

In each of the following statements, a term has been scrambled. Unscramble the term and write it on the line provided.

resistance	1.	The force applied by a machine to overcome gravity or friction is the *strenoca* force.
effort	2.	The force that is applied to the machine is the *offert* force.
work	3.	When a force is applied through a distance, *krow* is done.
machine	4.	A device that makes work easier is a *himcare.*
input	5.	The work done on a machine is work *putin.*
ideal	6.	A machine in which work input is equal to work output is an *ideal* machine.
simple	7.	A device that does work with only one movement is a *plesmo* machine.
advantage	8.	The number of times a machine multiplies the effort force is the mechanical *gaavandte.*
output	9.	The work done by a machine is work *poutut.*
force	10.	A machine makes work easier by changing the size or direction of the *ceorf* exerted on it.

In the blank write the term that correctly completes each statement about the equations given.
11. In the equation MA = F_r / F_e
   a. MA stands for   mechanical advantage
   b. F_r stands for   resistance force
   c. F_e stands for   effort force
12. In the equation W = F × d,
   a. W stands for   work
   b. F stands for   force
   c. d stands for   distance
13. In the equation W_{in} = F_e × d_e
   a. W_{in} stands for   work input
   b. d_e stands for   the distance the effort force is exerted
14. In the equation W_{out} = F_r × d_r
   a. W_{out} stands for   work output
   b. d_r stands for   the distance the resistance force moves

30   Copyright Glencoe Division of Macmillan/McGraw-Hill
                    Users of Merrill Physical Science have the publisher's permission to reproduce this page.

Advantages of Simple Machines

Suppose you wanted to pry the lid off a paint can with a screwdriver. You'd slip the end of the screwdriver blade under the edge of the can lid and push down on the handle. You would do work on the screwdriver and the screwdriver would do work on the lid.

Recall from Chapter 5 that work is done when a force is exerted through a distance. A machine makes work easier by changing the size or direction of the force you exerted on it, or both. For example, when you use a screwdriver to lift a can lid, as shown in the photo on the right, both the size and direction of the force you exert on the screwdriver are changed. The force you exert on the screwdriver is less than the force exerted by the screwdriver on the lid. And when you push down, the lid moves up.

When you use a simple machine, you are trying to move something that resists being moved. You are trying to overcome some force of resistance, usually gravity (weight) or friction, or both. For example, when you use a crowbar to move a large rock, you are working against gravity—the weight of the rock. When you use a screwdriver to move a paint can lid, you are working against friction—the friction between the lid and the can.

❷ Two forces are always involved when a machine is used to do work. The force applied *to* the machine is called the ❸ **effort force (F_e)**. The force applied *by* the machine to overcome resistance to gravity or friction is called **resistance force (F_r)**. In the screwdriver example, the effort force is the force you apply to the screwdriver handle. The resistance force is the force the screwdriver applies to the lid.

There are also two kinds of work to be considered when a machine is used—the work done *on* the machine and the work done *by* the machine. The work done on the machine is called work input (W_{in}); the work done by the machine is called work output (W_{out}). Recall that work is the product of force and distance: $W = F \times d$. Work input is the product of the effort force and the distance that force is exerted: $W_{in} = F_e \times d_e$. Work output is the product of the resistance force and the distance that force moves: $W_{out} = F_r \times d_r$.

It is important to remember that energy is always conserved. So, you can never get more work out of a machine than you put in. In other words, W_{out} can never be greater than W_{in}. In reality, whenever a machine is used, some

What forces are always involved when a machine is used to do work?

Figure 7-1. To lift the lid with the screwdriver, the effort distance (d_e) must be greater than the resistance distance (d_r).

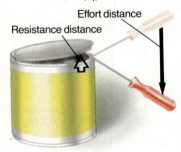

Effort distance

Resistance distance

159

TYING TO PREVIOUS KNOWLEDGE: Have students recall from Section 5-1 the scientific meaning of work. Point out that in this section they will use this definition to learn how machines make accomplishing work easier.

OBJECTIVES AND SCIENCE WORDS: Have students review the objectives and science words to become familiar with this section.

2 TEACH

Key Concepts are highlighted.

CONCEPT DEVELOPMENT

▶ Students should realize that the equation $W_{in} = W_{out}$ is a consequence of the conservation of energy. To transfer mechanical energy to a machine, work is done on the machine. The machine, in turn, does work on the object. Because the amount of energy transferred to a machine must equal the energy transferred by the machine,

$$W_{in} = W_{out}$$

▶ In an ideal machine, all the work done to the machine will appear as useful work done by the machine. However, in the real world, some mechanical energy is converted to heat through work done to overcome friction. Therefore, the amount of *observed* output work is always less than the amount of input work.

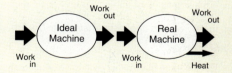

REVEALING MISCONCEPTIONS

▶ Some students may think that machines make work easier by reducing the amount of work that has to be done. Point out that machines actually require more work than does the task itself. Machines allow us to multiply our effort or speed, but not our energy.

▶ Point out that because $MA = F_r/F_e$, $F_e \times MA = F_r$. The value of MA indicates how much the effort force has been multiplied by the machine.

CHECK FOR UNDERSTANDING

Use the Mini Quiz to check for understanding.

MINI QUIZ

Use the Mini Quiz to check students' recall of chapter content.

① A simple machine is a device that does work with only one _____ . *movement*

② The force applied to a machine is called the _____ . *effort force*

③ The force applied by a machine is called the _____ . *resistance force*

④ The number of times a machine multiplies the effort force is the _____ of the machine. *mechanical advantage*

RETEACH

Demonstration: Set up the demonstration as shown below.

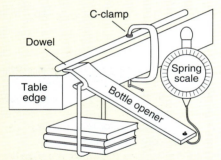

Have a volunteer measure the force delivered to the opener by carefully raising it as shown with the spring scale. Remove the books and weigh them. Sketch the demonstration on the chalkboard.

EXTENSION

For students who have mastered this section, use the **Reinforcement** and **Enrichment** masters or other OPTIONS provided.

PRACTICE PROBLEM ANSWER

1.
$$MA = \frac{F_r}{F_e}$$
$$F_e = \frac{F_r}{MA} = \frac{2000\text{ N}}{10} = 200\text{ N}$$

EcoTip

Use a simple machine and save energy resources. Use hand-operated tools to trim your lawn or remove snow from your sidewalk. You'll help to save natural resources and you'll get a little exercise, too.

kinetic energy is changed to heat due to friction. So, W_{out} is always smaller than W_{in}.

To understand how machines work, it helps to imagine a frictionless machine, in which no energy is converted to heat. Such an **ideal machine** is one in which work input equals work output. For an ideal machine,

$$W_{in} = W_{out}$$
$$F_e \times d_e = F_r \times d_r$$

In most cases, a machine multiplies the force applied to it—F_r is greater than F_e. So, in order for work input to equal work output, the effort force must travel farther than the resistance force—d_e must be greater than d_r.

Think once again about the screwdriver and the can lid. The distance you move the screwdriver handle (d_e) is greater than the distance the screwdriver blade moves the lid (d_r). So, the blade must exert more force on the lid (F_r) than you exert on the handle (F_e). The machine multiplies your effort.

④ The number of times a machine multiplies the effort force is the **mechanical advantage (MA)** of the machine. To calculate mechanical advantage, you divide the resistance force by the effort force.

$$MA = \frac{\text{resistance force}}{\text{effort force}} = \frac{F_r}{F_e}$$

EXAMPLE PROBLEM: Calculating Mechanical Advantage

Problem Statement: A worker applies an effort force of 10 N to pry open a window that has a resistance of 500 N. What is the mechanical advantage of the crowbar?

Known Information:
Strategy Hint: Mechanical advantage has no units.

resistance force, F_r = 500 N
effort force, F_e = 10 N

Unknown Information: mechanical advantage (MA)

Equation to Use: $MA = \dfrac{F_r}{F_e}$

Solution: $MA = \dfrac{500\text{ N}}{10\text{ N}} = 50$

PRACTICE PROBLEM

Strategy Hint: Rearrange the equation.

1. Find the effort force needed to lift a 2000-N rock, using a jack with a mechanical advantage of 10.

OPTIONS

INQUIRY QUESTIONS

▶ **How does the bending of a crowbar as it is being used affect its MA?** *The MA decreases because some force applied to the bar does work in bending it. Thus, the amount of work delivered by the machine is less.*

▶ **In the Example Problem on this page, the window moved 1 cm and the end of the crowbar moved 60 cm. How much mechanical energy was converted to heat?**
W_{in} = 10 N × 0.60 m = 6 J W_{out} = 500 × 0.01 m = 5 J
$W_{in} - W_{out}$ = 6 J – 5 J = 1 J

Some machines don't multiply force. Instead, they change the direction of the effort force. For example, when you pull down on the cord of window blinds, the blinds go up. Only the direction of the force changes; the effort force and resistance force are equal, so the mechanical advantage is 1.

Other machines have mechanical advantages less than 1. Such machines are used to increase the distance an object moves or the speed at which it moves.

Think again about all the machines you've seen in use today. What kind of work went into each machine, and what came out? Was the mechanical advantage greater than, less than, or equal to 1?

SECTION REVIEW

1. Explain how simple machines can make work easier without violating the law of conservation of energy.
2. A carpenter uses a claw hammer to pull a nail from a board. The nail has a resistance of 2500 N. The carpenter applies an effort force of 125 N. What is the mechanical advantage of the hammer?
3. **Apply:** Give an example of a simple machine you've used recently. How did you apply effort force? How did the machine apply resistance force?

☑ Recognizing Cause and Effect

Skill Builder

When you operate a machine, it's often easy to observe cause and effect. For example, when you turn a doorknob, the latch in the door moves. Give five examples of machines and describe one cause-and-effect pair in the action of each machine. If you need help, refer to Recognizing Cause and Effect in the **Skill Handbook** on page 679.

Skill Builder

Answers will vary. Examples are:
1. Screwdriver—turn the handle and screw is driven into wood
2. C-clamp—turn the lever and objects are forced together
3. Hatchet—strike wood and it splits
4. Nutcracker—apply force on the handles and nut cracks
5. Bottle lid—turn lid and bottle opens or closes

CROSS CURRICULUM
▶ **Social Studies:** Have students research the inventions of Leonardo da Vinci.

CONCEPT DEVELOPMENT
▶ Have students consider a tennis racket with an MA of 1/2. Make sure students realize that the MA indicates that if a player swings the racket with a force of 60 N, the racket will deliver a force of only 30 N to the ball. However, point out that if the player is delivering the effort force to the handle of the racket at a speed of 5 m/s, the racket strings will strike the ball at a speed of 10 m/s.

TEACHER F.Y.I.
▶ From the equation, $W_{in} = W_{out}$, it follows that $F_e \times d_e = F_r \times d_r$. The equation can be rearranged as
$$d_e/d_r = F_r/F_e$$
Take notice that the right side of the equation is the definition of MA. The left side is defined as the *ideal mechanical advantage, IMA*. The MA of the machine is always less than its IMA because some mechanical energy is converted to heat.

3 CLOSE
▶ Invite a patent attorney to discuss his or her career with the class.
▶ Ask questions 1-2 and the **Apply** Question in the Section Review.

SECTION REVIEW ANSWERS
1. Machines can multiply force so that work is made easier. However, machines cannot multiply work. When a machine multiplies an effort force, the distance that force must travel is greater than the distance traveled by the resistance force. Energy is always conserved.

2. $MA = \dfrac{F_r}{F_e} = \dfrac{2500 \text{ N}}{125 \text{ N}} = 20 \text{ N}$

3. Apply: Student responses will vary. Be sure they identify a simple machine and indicate an understanding of the effort force and how the machine changed that force. Accept all reasonable answers.

ACTIVITY 7-1
30 minutes

OBJECTIVE: Invent ways to use common implements as simple machines to accomplish a given task.

PROCESS SKILLS applied in this activity:
▶ **Experimenting** in Procedure Steps 2 and 4.
▶ **Communicating** in Analyze Questions 1 and 5.
▶ **Classifying** in Analyze Question 2.

👥 COOPERATIVE LEARNING
Divide the class into Science Investigation teams. Teams should interact to test the validity of their written instructions.

TEACHING THE ACTIVITY
Alternate Materials: Add other items such as chopsticks, masking tape, a wooden block, or cardboard.

Troubleshooting: Remind students to focus on accomplishing the task of moving the brick rather than on identifying simple machines.

▶ Add any additional restrictions you think necessary, but leave room for creativity.

ACTIVITY 7-1
Using Machines

Problem: *Can you invent a machine?*

Materials
- brick
- book
- string
- dowel, pencil-sized (2)
- hard board
- pulley
- ring stand and ring

NOTE: While conducting this activity, follow these simple rules:
   Do not touch the brick with your hands.
   Only one person at a time may apply force on the brick.

Procedure
1. Place the brick and the book about 30 cm apart on the table top.
2. Use any of the materials or combinations of materials to move the brick until it rests on top of the book.
3. Make a written record of your attempts. Describe what you did and what happened. Explain any failures as best you can.
4. Try as many different ways as you can think of to accomplish the task.

Analyze
1. Prepare a set of instructions for one of the methods you devised for moving the brick.
2. Identify the kind(s) of machine(s) you used in each of the steps in your method.

Conclude and Apply
3. Of the different methods you tried, describe the one you like best and explain why you prefer it.
4. Of the machines you used, which provided the greatest mechanical advantage?
5. Give your set of instructions for moving the brick to another team. See if they can use your method successfully.

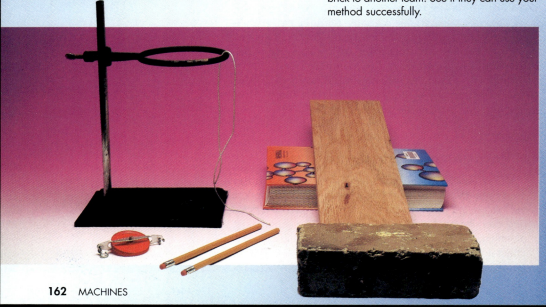

ANSWERS TO QUESTIONS
1. Let the team work together to develop one set of written instructions.
2. Encourage students to write down whatever terms come to mind, which may include nonmachine terms such as rope and platform. Sort these out in later discussion.
3. All reasons are acceptable as long as they are clearly stated.

4. It is most likely that the pointed dowel will have the greatest *MA* if it is used as a lever.
5. The real test of communication is whether or not someone understands the message. Each team should watch (but not talk to) another team as they try to follow the written instructions.

The Simple Machines 7-2

Objectives

▶ Describe the six types of simple machines.
▶ Calculate the mechanical advantage for different types of simple machines.

New Science Words

lever
fulcrum
effort arm
resistance arm
pulley
wheel and axle
inclined plane
screw
wedge

Levers

If you've ever ridden a seesaw, pried the cap from a bottle of soda pop, or swung a tennis racket, you have used a lever. A **lever** is a bar that is free to pivot, or turn, about a fixed point. The fixed point of a lever is called the **fulcrum** (FUL krum). The part of the lever on which the effort force is applied is called the **effort arm.** The part of the lever that exerts the resistance force is called the **resistance arm.**

Suppose you are using a crowbar to pry the lid from a crate. You can see in Figure 7-2 that the edge of the crate acts as the fulcrum. You push down on the effort arm of the crowbar. The bar pivots about the fulcrum, and the resistance arm exerts a force on the lid, lifting it upward.

Figure 7-2. The crowbar is being used as a lever. The edge of the crate acts as the fulcrum.

PREPARATION

SECTION BACKGROUND

▶ The six types of simple machines—lever, pulley, wheel and axle, inclined plane, wedge, and screw—fall into two broad categories: levers and inclined planes. Because pulleys and wheels and axles can be conceptualized as leverlike machines, they are grouped with levers. Wedges and screws are grouped with inclined planes.
▶ The mechanical advantage of every simple machine depends upon its design and is calculated by comparing its F_r to its F_e.

1 MOTIVATE

Cooperative Learning: Assign Problem Solving teams to demonstrate that a single pulley can have two different *MAs* depending on how it is used.
▶ Have students discuss how various kitchen utensils, such as knives, spoons, spatulas, whisks, and trussing nails, fit the definition of a simple machine. Ask students to find similarities among the functions and shapes of the utensils.

TYING TO PREVIOUS KNOWLEDGE: Have students recall from the last section the definition of *mechanical advantage*. Point out that in this section they will learn how the design of a simple machine affects its mechanical advantage.

OPTIONS

INQUIRY QUESTIONS

▶ **What is the approximate *MA* of the screwdriver shown in Figure 7-1 on page 159?** *determined from photo by approximating* L_e/L_r **What class of lever is it?** *first* **How could it be used as a second-class lever to open the lid?** *Pivot the screwdriver at its tip and push up.* **Would the screwdriver used as a second-class lever have a greater or lesser *MA* than used as shown? Explain.** *The MA would be less. In both levers, the L_e is the same. However, when the screwdriver is used as a second-class lever, L_r is greater, which* reduces the ratio of L_e to L_r.
▶ **Why can't a second-class lever be designed to have an *MA* less than 1?** *In a second-class lever, L_e is always longer than L_r, because the resistance force must be located between the fulcrum and the location of the effort force. Thus, L_e is always greater than L_r, and their ratio, MA, is always greater than 1.* **Can a third-class lever have an *MA* greater than 1?** *no*

OBJECTIVES AND SCIENCE WORDS: Have students review the objectives and science words to become familiar with this section.

Key Concepts are highlighted.

CONCEPT DEVELOPMENT

▶ Provide students with many opportunities to manipulate levers. Allow ample time for them to locate the fulcrum and identify the effort arm and resistance arm in each lever.

TEACHER F.Y.I.

▶ The mechanical advantages discussed in this section are ideal mechanical advantages of simple machines. The two terms are synonymous if we assume that no mechanical energy is converted to heat.

Science and WRITING

By changing the position of your hands on a bat, you are changing the ratio of L_e to L_r. "Choking up on the bat" decreases the ratio of L_e to L_r; that is, the MA of the bat decreases. The smaller MA will increase the speed at which the bat can deliver the resistance force to the ball.

CROSS CURRICULUM

▶ **Language Arts:** Have students look up the word *lever* in a dictionary. Students should find that it comes from the Latin root *levare* (to lift). Ask a volunteer to explain how the meaning of the word reflects its root.

PRACTICE PROBLEM ANSWER

$$MA = \frac{L_e}{L_r} = \frac{140 \text{ cm}}{20 \text{ cm}} = 7$$

PROGRAM RESOURCES

From the **Teacher Resource Package** use:

Transparency Masters, pages 25-26, Classes of Levers.

Use **Color Transparency** number 13, Classes of Levers.

Science and WRITING

When you are playing baseball or softball, your coach may tell you to "choke up on the bat." The bat is a lever. Explain how changing the position of your hands on the bat affects the operation of this simple machine.

The type of lever shown in Figure 7-2 makes work easier by multiplying your effort force. Like all simple machines, this lever has a mechanical advantage. You've learned that the mechanical advantage of any machine can be calculated by dividing the resistance force by the effort force. You can also use the lengths of the arms of a lever to find the mechanical advantage of the lever. The length of the effort arm is the distance from the fulcrum to the point where effort force is applied. The length of the resistance arm is the distance from the fulcrum to the point where the resistance force is applied. The following equation can be used to find the mechanical advantage of any lever:

$$MA = \frac{\text{length of effort arm}}{\text{length of resistance arm}} = \frac{L_e}{L_r}$$

EXAMPLE PROBLEM: Mechanical Advantage of a Lever

Problem Statement:

A worker uses an iron bar to raise a manhole cover weighing 65 N. The effort arm of the lever is 60 cm long. The resistance arm is 25 cm long. What is the mechanical advantage of the bar?

Known Information:
Strategy Hint: Which equation for mechanical advantage will you use?

length of effort arm, L_e = 60 cm
length of resistance arm, L_r = 25 cm

Unknown Information:

mechanical advantage (MA)

Equation to Use:

$$MA = \frac{L_e}{L_r}$$

Solution:

$$MA = \frac{60 \text{ cm}}{25 \text{ cm}} = 2.4$$

PRACTICE PROBLEM

Strategy Hint: Find the lengths of the effort arm and the resistance arm.

1. You use a crowbar 160 cm long as a lever to lift a large rock. The rock is 20 cm from the fulcrum. You push down on the other end of the crowbar. What is the MA of the lever?

There are three different types, or classes, of levers. These classes are based on the positions of the effort force, resistance force, and fulcrum. Figure 7-3 shows the three classes of levers.

164 MACHINES

OPTIONS

Meeting Different Ability Levels

For Section 7-2, use the following **Teacher Resource Masters** depending upon individual students' needs.

◆ **Study Guide Master** for all students.
● **Reinforcement Master** for students of average and above average ability levels.
▲ **Enrichment Master** for above average students.
Additional Teacher Resource Package masters are listed in the OPTIONS box throughout the section. The additional masters are appropriate for all students.

◆ STUDY GUIDE   31

STUDY GUIDE   Chapter 7

The Simple Machines   Text Pages 163-171

Short crypts are lists of related words written in a simple code in which a different set of letters has been substituted for the correct letters. The title of each list will give you a hint as to the subject of the list. Remember, the same code is used for the entire list. For example, if c stands for k in one word, c will stand for k in every word on the list. Each list has its own code. One word in each list has been done for you.

Code
A C D E F G I J K L N O R T U W X
e r h l c t o s m v d u t g a f n

Prying into Things
1. GALAC   lever
2. WOGFCOK   fulcrum
3. AWWICR UCK   effort arm
4. CAJEJRUXFA UCK   resistance arm
5. KAFDUXEFUG UNLUXRUTA   mechanical advantage
6. NECAFREIX   direction
7. FGUJJ   class

Code
A B C D E F I J L N O Q R S T U V W X Z
i e l o s h u s a b k t w y d g c n p r

Keeping It Simple
8. XICCBS   pulley
9. RFBBC LWT LJCB   wheel and axle
10. AWVCAWBT XCLWB inclined plane
11. EVNBR   screw
12. NCDVO LWT QLVOCB   block and tackle
13. UBLZ   gear

In the space at the left, write the term that best completes each statement. Use the terms listed below.

block and tackle   screw   inclined planes   pulley   wheel and axle

screw   14. An inclined plane wrapped around a cylindrical post is a _____.
wheel and axle   15. A doorknob is an example of a _____.
pulley   16. A grooved wheel with a rope or chain running along the groove is a _____.
inclined planes 17. Screws and wedges are types of _____.
block and tackle 18. A system of pulleys is called a _____.

Copyright Glencoe Division of Macmillan/McGraw-Hill
Users of Merrill Physical Science have the publisher's permission to reproduce this page.   31

First class

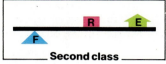
Second class

Third class

If you look at the examples of third-class levers, you will see that the effort arm is always shorter than the resistance arm. So, the *MA* of a third-class lever is always less than 1. This means that a third-class lever does not multiply force. A third-class lever multiplies the distance the effort force travels.

Figure 7-3. The classes of levers differ in the positions of the effort force, the resistance force, and the fulcrum.

PROBLEM SOLVING

How Do You Use Your Arm as a Lever?

The muscles and bones of your body work together as levers. Try contracting your biceps muscle to see how a simple body lever works.

The two bones in your forearm act as the bar of the lever. Because the elbow is the point where the arm lever pivots, it is the fulcrum. The bones in your forearm are attached to the upper arm bone by ligaments at the elbow. When you contract your biceps, this muscle exerts an effort force on the forearm bones to pull them upward. The entire forearm is the resistance force. What class of lever is being demonstrated when you raise your forearm?

Think Critically: Identify the fulcrum, effort force, and resistance force when you lower your arm, using the triceps muscle on the back of your upper arm.

165

TEACHER F.Y.I.

▶ It isn't necessary to know the exact location of F_e, F_r, and the fulcrum to classify a lever. All one needs to know is what is "in-between." In a first-class lever, the fulcrum is located somewhere between the effort force and the resistance force. In a second-class lever, F_r is in-between, and in a third-class lever, F_e is in-between.

CHECK FOR UNDERSTANDING

Use the Mini Quiz to check for understanding.

MINI QUIZ

Use the Mini Quiz to check students' recall of chapter content.

1. A _____ is a bar that is free to turn about a fixed point. *lever*
2. The fixed point of a lever is called the _____ . *fulcrum*
3. The _____ is the part of a lever on which the effort force is applied. *effort arm*
4. The _____ is the part of a lever that exerts the resistance force. *resistance arm*

RETEACH

Cooperative Learning: Assign Problem Solving teams to identify as levers bones shown in cardboard skeletons displayed at Halloween. From the functioning of each bone, have the team determine if it is a first-, second-, or third-class lever.

EXTENSION

For students who have mastered this section, use the **Reinforcement** and **Enrichment** masters or other OPTIONS provided.

PROBLEM SOLVING

When you raise your forearm, the muscles and bones are a third-class lever.

Think Critically: The elbow is the fulcrum. The effort force is exerted by the triceps. The bones of the forearm are the resistance force.

CONCEPT DEVELOPMENT

▶ **Demonstration:** Show that each strand of a single, movable pulley system supports half the resistance force. Weigh the pulley and a small attached weight. Attach a spring scale to each end of the cord that passes through the pulley and suspend the pulley and weight from the scales. Have a volunteer read each scale. Remove one spring scale and attach that end of the string to a ring stand. Have a volunteer read the spring scale supporting the pulley. Stand a meterstick behind the pulley system and have a volunteer measure the distance the weight moves as you pull the spring scale upward 20 cm. From the values of d_e and d_r show that the MA of a single, movable pulley is 2.

▶ **Demonstration:** Show how a single, fixed pulley is related to a first-class lever by placing a piece of brightly colored tape across the diameter of a large pulley. Use it as a single, fixed pulley to lift a small weight. Have students observe that the tape rotates around the center of the wheel much like a lever. Have the students identify the fulcrum, L_e, and L_r. Point out that a single, fixed pulley can be conceptualized as a first-class lever with an MA of 1. (L_e and L_r are equal.) Repeat the demonstration using the pulley as a single, movable pulley. Have students observe that the tape rotates around the end opposite the effort force. From their observations have them realize that a single, movable pulley can be conceptualized as a second-class lever with an MA of 2. (L_e is twice as long as L_r.)

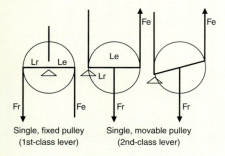

Single, fixed pulley (1st-class lever)   Single, movable pulley (2nd-class lever)

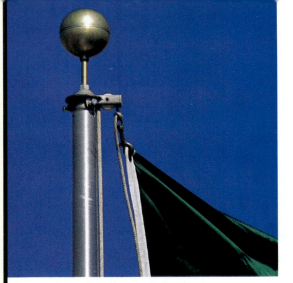

Figure 7-4. This single fixed pulley changes the direction of the effort force.

Pulleys

Have you ever seen someone raise a flag on a flagpole? A pulley is used to help get the flag to the top of the pole. A **pulley** is a grooved wheel with a rope or a chain running along the groove. Figure 7-4 shows a typical pulley.

A pulley works something like a first-class lever. Instead of a bar, a pulley has a rope. The two ends of the rope are the effort arm and the resistance arm. The wheel of the pulley acts like the fulcrum.

Pulleys can be fixed or movable. A fixed pulley is attached to something that doesn't move, such as a ceiling, wall, or tree. A fixed pulley can change the direction of an effort force. When you pull down on the effort arm of the rope, the pulley raises the object attached to the resistance arm. Because the resistance arm and effort arm are of equal length, the MA of a fixed pulley is 1. Thus, a fixed pulley does not multiply the effort force.

A movable pulley is attached to the object being moved, as shown in Figure 7-5. The difference between a fixed pulley and a movable pulley is shown in Figure 7-6. Unlike the fixed pulley, a movable pulley does multiply the effort force. Because a movable pulley multiplies force, its MA is greater than 1. In fact, the MA of a single movable pulley is 2. This means that an effort force of 1 N will lift a weight (resistance) of 2 N. In order to conserve energy, the effort distance must be twice as large as the resistance distance.

Fixed and movable pulleys can be combined to make a system of pulleys called a block and tackle. Depending on the number of pulleys used, a block and tackle can have a large mechanical advantage. The mechanical advantage of any ideal pulley or pulley system is equal to the number of ropes that support

Figure 7-5. A movable pulley is attached to the resistance. A block and tackle, like the one shown, multiplies the effort force and changes its direction.

OPTIONS

INQUIRY QUESTIONS

▶ **The MA of a single fixed pulley is 1. What, then, is gained by using a fixed pulley? Give two examples.** *Answers will vary but should reflect the idea that it allows a change of direction. A fixed pulley allows a person to use his or her weight to exert a downward force to raise an object. In addition, exerting a downward force is more convenient. Fixed pulleys may be used to raise objects to high places while the person stays at ground level.*

▶ **A worker uses a board that is 4.0 m long to pry up a large rock. A smaller rock is used for a fulcrum and is placed 0.5 m from the resistance end of the lever. What is the MA of the lever? If an effort force of 250 N is needed, what is the weight of the large rock?** *The effort arm of the lever is 4.0 m − 0.5 m = 3.5 m. Therefore, the MA = effort arm/resistance arm = 3.5 m/0.5 m = 7. For any machine, MA = resistance force/effort force. So, 7 = resistance force/250 N. Resistance force = 250 N × 7 = 1750 N.*

MA = 1
Single Fixed Pulley

MA = 2
Single Movable Pulley

MA = 4
Block and Tackle

Figure 7-6. The mechanical advantage of each type of pulley can be found by counting every rope except the effort rope.

the resistance weight. As Figure 7-6 shows, the only rope that does not support the resistance weight is the rope leading from the pulley system to the effort force.

Wheel and Axle

Look closely at a doorknob or a water faucet. Do they look like simple machines to you? Do they help you make work easier? If you don't think so, remove the knob or handle from its narrow shaft. Now try opening the door or turning on the water by rotating that shaft with your fingers. After a few minutes, you'll appreciate the fact that the knob and handle, together with their shafts, do make work easier. They are machines.

Doorknobs and faucets are examples of a wheel and axle. A **wheel and axle** is a simple machine consisting of two wheels of different sizes that rotate together. An effort force is usually applied to the larger wheel. The smaller wheel, called the axle, exerts the resistance force. In many cases the larger wheel doesn't look like a typical circular wheel. It may be a crank handle, like that of an ice cream freezer or a meat grinder. But it always travels in a circle.

Figure 7-7. A water faucet is an example of a wheel and axle. Without the faucet handle (wheel), the shaft of the faucet (axle) is difficult to turn.

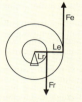
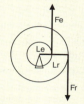

CONCEPT DEVELOPMENT

▶ Have students refer to the two sets of gears shown in Figure 7-9. Ask them to identify the set in which the gears will move in the same direction (drive chain) and the set in which they will move in opposite directions (mesh teeth).

TEACHER F.Y.I.

▶ In mesh teeth gears, the MA is equal to the number of teeth on the effort gear, N_e, divided by the number of teeth on the resistance gear, N_r. In mesh gears, the size and number of teeth must be precise for the gears to operate smoothly.

CROSS CURRICULUM

▶ **Mathematics:** Supply the students with silhouettes of several common wheels and axles, such as screwdrivers, house keys, and beaters from an electric mixer; or ask them to trace similar items at home and bring the tracings to class. Have them cut out the silhouettes or tracings, fold each along the center of the wheel and axle, unfold the paper, and measure the approximate radius of the wheel and the radius of the axle for each item. Allow the students to use calculators to determine the MA of each item and relate this value to the task that the item is used for.

PRACTICE PROBLEM ANSWER

$$MA = \frac{r_w}{r_a} = \frac{24 \text{ cm}}{4 \text{ cm}} = 6$$

Figure 7-8. The length of the crank handle represents the radius of the wheel in this simple machine.

It might help to think of a wheel and axle as being a lever attached to a shaft. The radius of the wheel is the effort arm, and the radius of the axle is the resistance arm. The center of the axle is the fulcrum. As with the lever, the mechanical advantage of a wheel and axle can be calculated by dividing the radius of the wheel ("effort arm") by the radius of the axle ("resistance arm").

$$MA = \frac{\text{radius of wheel}}{\text{radius of axle}} = \frac{r_w}{r_a}$$

EXAMPLE PROBLEM: Calculating MA of a Wheel and Axle

Problem Statement: In the ice-cream freezer shown in Figure 7-8, the wheel has a radius of 20 cm. The axle has a radius of 2 cm. What is the mechanical advantage of the wheel and axle?

Known Information: radius of wheel, r_w = 20 cm
Strategy Hint: What happens to the units when you divide? radius of axle, r_a = 2 cm

Unknown Information: mechanical advantage (MA)

Equation to Use: $MA = \dfrac{r_w}{r_a}$

Solution: $MA = \dfrac{20 \text{ cm}}{2 \text{ cm}} = 10$

PRACTICE PROBLEM

Strategy Hint: Use the diameter to find the radius of circle.

1. An automobile steering wheel having a diameter of 48 cm is used to turn the steering column, which has a radius of 4 cm. What is the MA of this wheel and axle?

OPTIONS

ENRICHMENT

▶ Have students research various types of gears, such as *helical, bevel, planetary,* and *worm;* display them to the class as working models and discuss their uses.

▶ Have interested students research how simple machines were used in early civilizations such as Babylon, Egypt, China, and Inca.

▶ Have interested students research and build an Archimedes' screw.

Gears are modified wheel and axle machines. A gear is a wheel with teeth along its circumference. Figure 7-9 shows two ways gears work. Effort is exerted on one of the gears, causing the other gear to turn. In most gears, the larger gear is the effort gear. The mechanical advantage of a pair of gears is found by dividing the radius of the effort gear by the radius of the resistance gear. This is known as the gear ratio of the pair.

Figure 7-9. In both cases, turning one gear causes the other gear to turn.

Inclined Plane

⑤ Suppose you had to move a heavy box from the ground up onto a porch. Would you rather lift the box straight up or slide it up a ramp? The ramp would make your job easier. A ramp is a type of **inclined plane,** a sloping surface used to raise objects.

The amount of work done on the box is the same whether you lift it straight up or slide it up the ramp. But remember that work has two parts, force and distance. When you lift the box straight onto the porch, the distance is small, but you must exert a large force. Using the ramp, you have to cover more distance, but you exert less force.

You can calculate mechanical advantage of an ideal inclined plane using distances, just as you did for a lever.

$$MA = \frac{\text{effort distance}}{\text{resistance distance}} = \frac{\text{length}}{\text{height}} = \frac{l}{h}$$

Figure 7-10. The ramp is an example of an inclined plane.

Screw and Wedge

⑥ The screw and the wedge are both examples of inclined planes that move. A **screw** is an inclined plane wrapped in a spiral around a cylindrical post. If you look closely

7-2 THE SIMPLE MACHINES **169**

Ask questions 1-2 and the **Apply** Question in the Section Review.

RETEACH

Demonstration: From colored construction paper, cut a set of three arrows, about 10 cm wide and 10, 20, and 30 cm long. Make a similar set in another color. Using a wide marker, label each arrow in the first set F_e. Label the second set F_r. Collect three or four examples of each type of simple machine. Begin the demonstration by explaining that the arrows represent different amounts of effort and resistance force. Ask a volunteer to choose a machine and use an arrow from each pile that represents the relative size of F_e and F_r. Showing the locations and directions of F_e and F_r, have the class agree upon the labels and classify the machine. Repeat the demonstration until students have exhausted all the examples.

EXTENSION

For students who have mastered this section, use the **Reinforcement** and **Enrichment** masters or other OPTIONS provided.

3 CLOSE

Cooperative Learning: Using the Numbered Heads Together strategy, have groups determine that the slider of a zipper is a simple machine, classify it as a wedge, and agree that its MA is greater than 1.

SECTION REVIEW ANSWERS

1. Student responses will vary. Accept all reasonable responses.
2. Students should describe how pulleys and wheel and axle machines are modifications of the lever. Wedges and screws are modifications of the inclined plane.
3. Apply: Responses may vary but could include the fact that friction makes it possible for people to walk up a ramp and keeps people from sliding down the ramp. Accept all reasonable responses.

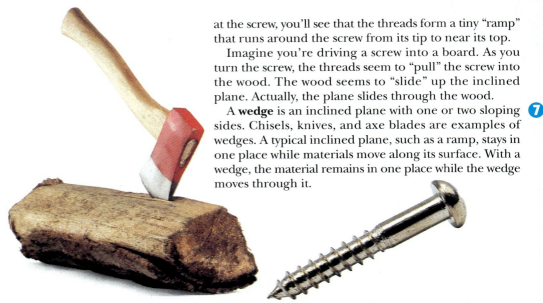

Figure 7-11. The blade of the axe and the threads of the screw are special types of inclined planes.

at the screw, you'll see that the threads form a tiny "ramp" that runs around the screw from its tip to near its top.

Imagine you're driving a screw into a board. As you turn the screw, the threads seem to "pull" the screw into the wood. The wood seems to "slide" up the inclined plane. Actually, the plane slides through the wood.

A **wedge** is an inclined plane with one or two sloping sides. Chisels, knives, and axe blades are examples of wedges. A typical inclined plane, such as a ramp, stays in one place while materials move along its surface. With a wedge, the material remains in one place while the wedge moves through it.

While reading about the six types of simple machines, perhaps you've noticed that they are all variations of two basic machines—the lever and the inclined plane. As you go about your daily activities, look for examples of each type of simple machine. See if you can tell how each makes work easier.

SECTION REVIEW

1. Give one example of each kind of simple machine. Use examples different from the ones in the text.
2. Explain why the six kinds of simple machines are really variations on just two basic machines.
3. **Apply:** When would the friction of an inclined plane be useful?

Skill Builder ☑ Making and Using Tables

Organize information about the six kinds of simple machines into a table. Include the type of machine, an example of each type, and a brief description of how it works. You may include other information if you wish. If you need help, refer to Making and Using Tables in the **Skill Handbook** on page 686.

Skill Builder

Student tables should reflect information included in the chapter about each type of machine.

ACTIVITY 7-2
Levers

Problem: *Can you measure mass with a lever?*

Materials

- sheet of paper, 20 cm × 28 cm (8½″ × 11″)
- coins, 3 (quarter, dime, nickel)
- balance
- metric ruler

Procedure

1. Make a lever by folding the paper into a strip 3 cm wide by 28 cm long.
2. Mark a line 2 cm from one end of the paper strip. Label this line "Resistance."
3. Slide the other end of the paper strip over the edge of a table until the strip begins to teeter on the edge. Mark a line across the paper at the table edge and label this line "Effort."
4. Measure the mass of the paper to the nearest 0.1 g. Write this mass on the "Effort" line.
5. Center a dime on the "Resistance" line.
6. Locate the fulcrum by sliding the paper strip until it begins to teeter on the edge. Mark the balance line. Label it "Fulcrum #1."
7. Measure the lengths of the resistance arm and the effort arm to the nearest 0.1 cm.
8. Calculate the MA of the lever.
9. Multiply the MA times the mass of the lever to find the mass of the coin.
10. Repeat Steps 5 through 9 with the nickel and then with the quarter. Mark the fulcrum line #2 for the nickel and #3 for the quarter.

Analyze

1. In this activity, is the effective total length of the lever a constant or a variable?
2. Are the lengths of the resistance and effort arms constants or variables?
3. What provides the effort force?
4. What does it mean if the MA is less than 1.0?

Conclude and Apply

5. Is it necessary to have the resistance line 2.0 cm from the end of the paper?
6. The calculations are done as if the entire weight of the paper is located at what point?
7. Why can mass units be used in place of force units in this kind of problem?

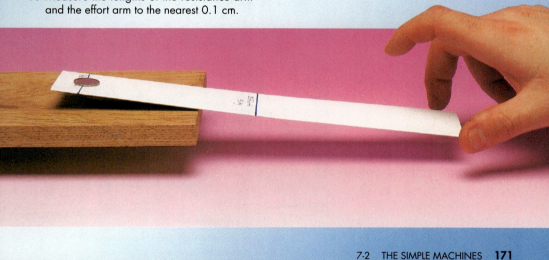

OBJECTIVE: **Calculate** the mechanical advantage of levers to balance unequal forces.

PROCESS SKILLS applied in this activity:
▶ **Measuring** in Procedure Steps 1-7.
▶ **Using Numbers** in Procedure Steps 8 and 9.
▶ **Interpreting** in Analyze Questions 1-3.

TEACHING THE ACTIVITY

Alternate Materials: Various sized washers can be substituted for the coins.

Troubleshooting: Because of the multiple steps in the procedure, it is advisable to demonstrate the activity before students work in the lab.

▶ This activity applies the idea that a rigid object can act as though its entire mass is located at its center of gravity. One end of the lever is located at the center of gravity of the paper, and the other end is located at a convenient position near one end of the paper. The coin is placed with its center of gravity right on the lever's end mark.

▶ Have students draw the effective lever and fulcrum on the paper between the effort and resistance lines. Point out that the rest of the paper is not considered part of the lever but serves to provide effort force and support.

▶ Allow students to check mass calculations by using a balance.

PROGRAM RESOURCES

From the **Teacher Resource Package** use:

Activity Worksheets, pages 57-58, Activity 7-2: Levers.

ANSWERS TO QUESTIONS

1. The lever's total length is a constant.
2. The lengths of effort and resistance arms are variables.
3. Gravity provides the effort force.
4. The force to move the lever is more than the weight that is moved.
5. No, the resistance line can be placed at any convenient location.
6. at the center of gravity of the paper
7. The forces on both ends of the lever are caused by gravity acting with the same ratio of force to mass.

PREPARATION

SECTION BACKGROUND

▶ Human-powered flight has fascinated scientists and inventors for centuries. The first demonstrably successful human-powered flight took place on August 23, 1977, when Bryan Allen flew the *Gossamer Condor* along a 1.6 km, figure-8 course to capture the £50,000 Kremer prize. The prize was established in 1959 by Henry Kremer, a British industrialist, to stimulate research into human-powered flight.

1 MOTIVATE

▶ **Demonstration:** Blow across a strip of paper held close to your mouth to demonstrate that moving air can provide lift. Make sure students understand that an airplane is lifted by the air moving under the wing, not by the propeller. The propeller moves the plane forward through the air.

TYING TO PREVIOUS KNOWLEDGE: Have students recall the function of gears. Point out that in this section they will learn how gears help to produce human-powered flight.

OBJECTIVES AND SCIENCE WORDS: Have students review the objectives and science words to become familiar with this section.

2 TEACH

Key Concepts are highlighted.

CONCEPT DEVELOPMENT

▶ Have students compare the Daedalus and a small-engine plane. Ask students to identify and explain how the energy source of each craft operates.

 **7-3:** # Human-Powered Flying Machines

Objectives

▶ Analyze the simple machines in a human-powered aircraft.
▶ Consider the value of experiments with no obvious practical value.

Pedaling through the Sky

Can you imagine how it would feel to pedal a bicycle through the air? That's probably how Greek cycling champion Kanellos Kanellopoulos felt in 1988, when he flew the Daedalus, a human-powered aircraft, 115 kilometers across the Aegean Sea.

Designed at the Massachusetts Institute of Technology, the Daedalus has pedals like a bicycle. The pilot applies an effort force to the pedals, and the force is transferred, through gears, to a propeller. The plane is human-powered because the pilot's legs are the only source of power.

OPTIONS

Meeting Different Ability Levels

For Section 7-3, use the following **Teacher Resource Masters** depending upon individual students' needs.

◆ **Study Guide Master** for all students.

● **Reinforcement Master** for students of average and above average ability levels.

▲ **Enrichment Master** for above average students.

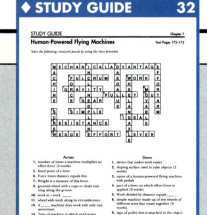

◆ STUDY GUIDE 32

In designing the plane, engineers did experiments to find out exactly how much power would be needed to fly it. One earlier model required about 1.5 watts of power for every pound the pilot weighed. That wasn't good enough—even a well-conditioned pilot would be able to provide enough power to fly the plane only 80 kilometers. By redesigning the aircraft, the engineers came up with a version that needed less power.

Kanellopoulos bicycled 800 kilometers a week to train for the flying feat. During the flight, he pedalled for nearly four hours, swigging a special high-energy drink until he complained that his stomach was full and "sloshing around."

As Kanellopoulos soared 12 meters above the sea, the director of the Daedalus project mused, "This is insane, but wonderful." Just 9 meters away from shore, a gust of wind snapped the tail off the Daedalus, and the plane fell, landing on an inflatable raft. Daedalus was a mess, but Kanellopoulos was safe, and the flight was declared a success.

SECTION REVIEW

1. Look at the simple diagram of the Daedalus. How many simple machines can you identify?
2. Would you feel differently about the value of the Daedalus project if Kanellopoulos had been hurt when the plane fell into the sea?

You Decide!

The researchers who worked on Daedalus often are asked if the project had any practical value. Can you think of any useful applications of their research? Do you think it is ever worthwhile to spend time and money on research that has no immediate practical applications? What would help you decide whether a research project is worth doing?

SCIENCE & SOCIETY

● **REINFORCEMENT** 32

▲ **ENRICHMENT** 32

173

CONCEPT DEVELOPMENT

▶ Students may not realize that an energy production of 1.5 watts/pound is quite large. A student (70 lb) climbing a flight of stairs produces about 2 watts/pound. Ask them if they think they could maintain that rate for four hours. Students may be surprised to know that maintaining that power output for four hours would be the equivalent of climbing 20 000 steps!

CHECK FOR UNDERSTANDING

Ask questions 1 and 2 in the Section Review.

RETEACH

Demonstration: Fly a rubber-band powered model airplane. Have students compare the time of flight and the complexities of the Daedalus to those of the model airplane.

EXTENSION

For students who have mastered this section, use the **Reinforcement** and **Enrichment** masters or other OPTIONS provided.

3 CLOSE

FLEX Your Brain

Use the Flex Your Brain activity to have students explore IMPROVING THE DAEDALUS.

SECTION REVIEW ANSWERS

1. Responses will vary. Accept all reasonable responses.
2. Student responses will vary.

YOU DECIDE!

SCIENCE & SOCIETY

Student responses will vary but should indicate some reasonable consideration of the ideas presented in this section.

PROGRAM RESOURCES

From the **Teacher Resource Package** use:

Cross-Curricular Connections, page 11, The Myth of Daedalus.

Activity Worksheets, page 5, Flex Your Brain.

PREPARATION

SECTION BACKGROUND
► Compound machines are systems containing two or more simple machines. The output work of one of the simple machines becomes the input work of the other.
► How effectively a machine transfers energy is measured by its efficiency. The rate at which it transfers energy is measured by its power.

PREPLANNING
► You will need a wind-up toy car for each group conducting the Mini-Lab.

1 MOTIVATE

Cooperative Learning: Using the Numbered Heads Together strategy, have groups attempt to classify a fingernail clipper.
► Have students identify the simple machines that make up some common devices, such as pencil sharpeners, rotary beaters, food mills, and bicycles.

TYING TO PREVIOUS KNOWLEDGE: Have students recall what a simple machine does. In this section they will see how combining simple machines also makes work easier.

OBJECTIVES AND SCIENCE WORDS: Have students review the objectives and science words to become familiar with this section.

PROGRAM RESOURCES
From the **Teacher Resource Package** use:

Transparency Masters, pages 27-28, A Compound Machine.

Concept Mapping, pages 19-20.

Use **Color Transparency** number 14, A Compound Machine.

7-4 Using Machines

New Science Words

compound machine
efficiency
power
watt

Objectives

► Recognize the simple machines that make up a complex machine.
► Calculate efficiency of a machine.
► Describe the relationship between work, power, and time.

Compound Machines

Many machines that you use, such as a lawn mower or a pencil sharpener, are made up of several simple machines. 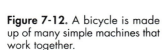 A combination of two or more simple machines is a **compound machine.** Even a tool as simple as an axe is a compound machine made up of a wedge and a lever.

Often the simple machines that make up a compound machine are concealed. However, in one familiar compound machine—the bicycle—many of the simple machines are visible and easily recognized.

Look at the bicycle in Figure 7-12. The pedal mechanism is a wheel-and-axle system made up of two wheels

Figure 7-12. A bicycle is made up of many simple machines that work together.

Screw

Lever

Wheel and axle

OPTIONS

Meeting Different Ability Levels
For Section 7-4, use the following **Teacher Resource Masters** depending upon individual students' needs.

◆ **Study Guide Master** for all students.
● **Reinforcement Master** for students of average and above average ability levels.
▲ **Enrichment Master** for above average students.
Additional Teacher Resource Package masters are listed in the OPTIONS box throughout the section. The additional masters are appropriate for all students.

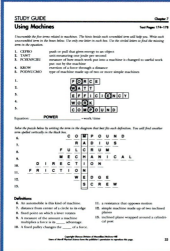

◆ STUDY GUIDE 33

STUDY GUIDE   Chapter 7
Using Machines   Text Pages 174-178

Unscramble the five terms related to machines. The hints beside each scrambled term will help you. Write each unscrambled term in the boxes below. Use only one letter in each box. Use the circled letters to find the missing term in the equation.

1. CEFRO — push or pull that gives energy to an object
2. TAWT — unit measuring one joule per second
3. FCYENFICIEI — measure of how much work put into a machine is changed to useful work put out by the machine
4. KROW — exertion of a force through a distance
5. PODNUCMO — type of machine made up of two or more simple machines

1. F O R C E
2. W A T T
3. E F F I C I E N C Y
4. W O R K
5. C O M P O U N D

Equation: **POWER** = work/time

Solve the puzzle below by writing the term in the diagram that best fits each definition. You will find another term spelled vertically in the black box.

6. C O M P O U N D
7. R A D I U S
8. F U L C R U M
9. M E C H A N I C A L
10. D I R E C T I O N
11. F R I C T I O N
12. W E D G E
13. S C R E W

Definitions
6. An automobile is this kind of machine.
7. distance from center of a circle to its edge
8. fixed point on which a lever rotates
9. A measure of the amount a machine multiplies a force is its _____ advantage.
10. A fixed pulley changes the _____ of a force.
11. a resistance that opposes motion
12. simple machine made up of two inclined planes
13. inclined plane wrapped around a cylindrical post

attached to the same axle. Each pedal moves in a circle, like a wheel. The axle is a gear. The effort force exerted on the pedals by the rider turns this pedal gear. The bicycle chain transfers the force to a smaller gear attached to the rear wheel. This wheel gear is actually the effort wheel of the rear wheel-and-axle system. As the wheel gear turns, it causes the rear wheel to turn, and the wheel exerts the resistance force, through the tires, on the road. Because the wheel gear is smaller than the pedal gear that drives it, the rear wheel turns faster than the pedals do.

The overall mechanical advantage of a bicycle is the ratio of the resistance force exerted by the tires on the road to the effort force exerted by the rider on the pedals. The bicycle shown in Figure 7-12 has only two gears. Its gear ratio is fixed, so its mechanical advantage cannot be changed. This makes it a one-speed bike. A ten-speed bike has two pedal gears and five wheel gears. By shifting gears, the rider can change gear ratios, thus changing the mechanical advantage of the bicycle.

A bicycle has many other simple machines. Some of these machines are shown in Figure 7-12. See if you can tell what each does. Can you think of any others?

Efficiency

You learned earlier that some of the energy put into a machine is "lost" as thermal energy produced as a result of friction. So the work put out by a machine is always less than the work put into the machine.

② **Efficiency is a measure of how much of the work put into a machine is changed to useful work put out by a machine. The higher the efficiency of a machine, the greater the amount of work input is changed to useful work output.** Efficiency is calculated by dividing work output by work input and is usually expressed as a percentage.

$$\text{efficiency} = \frac{W_{out}}{W_{in}} \times 100\% = \frac{F_r \times d_r}{F_e \times d_e} \times 100\%$$

Why must the efficiency of a machine always be less than 100 percent? Can you think of ways to increase the efficiency of a machine?

Figure 7-13. The rear wheel of a ten-speed bicycle has five different gears.

Did You Know?

Talk about a complex machine! The longest tandem bicycle is about 20 meters long and weighs about 1100 kilograms. With this vehicle you could take 34 of your friends along for a ride.

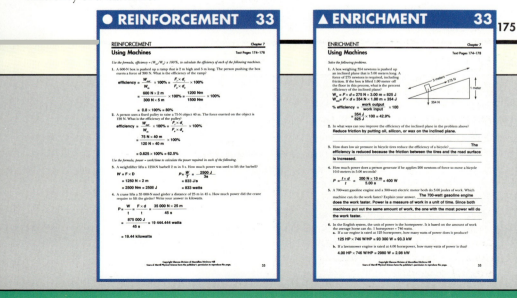

● **REINFORCEMENT** 33

▲ **ENRICHMENT** 33

175

Key Concepts are highlighted.

CONCEPT DEVELOPMENT

▶ **Demonstration:** Set up a meterstick as a lever with a fulcrum located at the 0-cm mark. Hang a heavy weight at the 30-cm mark and connect a single, moveable pulley to the meterstick with a wire tie at the 99-cm mark. Raise and lower the lever using the pulley string. Have students determine that the machine is a compound machine by identifying the lever and pulley. The resistance force of the pulley is actually driving the lever. Have students identify the meterstick as a second-class lever and have them calculate its *MA*.

$MA = L_e/L_r = 99\text{ cm}/33\text{ cm} = 3$

Have them recall that the *MA* of a single, moveable pulley is 2. Attach a spring scale to the string and record the force needed to raise and lower the lever. Measure the weight. From these values, calculate the *MA* of the compound machine.

▶ The following diagram illustrates energy transfers in a compound machine.

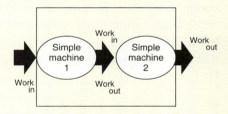

Compound machine

STUDENT TEXT QUESTION

▶ Page 175, paragraph 5: **Why must the efficiency of a machine always be less than 100 percent?** *In any machine, the work put out by a machine (W_{out}) is always less than the work put into it (W_{in}) because some mechanical energy is converted to thermal energy in the machine.*

CONCEPT DEVELOPMENT

▶ The mechanical advantage of a compound machine is the product of the individual mechanical advantages of the simple machines that make it up. In a simple machine, the output force is equal to the input force multiplied by the *MA* of the machine: $F_r = F_e \times MA$. In a compound machine, the output force of one of its simple machines becomes the input force of another. For a compound machine made of two simple machines,

$$F_r = MA_2 \times MA_1 \times F_e$$

PRACTICE PROBLEM ANSWER

Given: $F_r = 65$ N; $F_e = 72$ N
$d_r = d_e$

$$\text{efficiency} = \frac{F_r \times d_r}{F_e \times d_e} \times 100\%$$

$$= \frac{65\text{ N}}{72\text{ N}} \times 100\%$$

efficiency = 90%

REVEALING MISCONCEPTIONS

▶ Have students discuss their understanding of efficiency. Have them focus their discussion on doing a task, such as mowing a lawn. Some will interpret efficiency as doing a task quickly. Others may interpret efficiency as doing a task with less energy. As you develop the concept of efficiency, contrast its meaning with these misconceptions.

MINI QUIZ

Use the Mini Quiz to check students' recall of chapter content.

1 A(n) _____ is a combination of two or more simple machines. *compound machine*

2 _____ is a measure of how much of the work put into a machine is changed to useful work put out by a machine. *Efficiency*

EXAMPLE PROBLEM: Calculating Efficiency

Problem Statement:	A piece of furniture weighing 1500 N is pushed up an inclined plane that is 4.0 m long and 1.0 m high. A worker pushing the furniture uses a force of 500 N. What is the efficiency of the inclined plane?
Known Information: Strategy Hint: Can your answer be greater than 100 percent?	resistance force, $F_r = 1500$ N resistance distance, $d_r = 1.0$ m effort force, $F_e = 500$ N effort distance, $d_e = 4.0$ m
Unknown Information:	efficiency
Equation to Use:	$\text{efficiency} = \dfrac{F_r \times d_r}{F_e \times d_e} \times 100\%$
Solution:	$\text{efficiency} = \dfrac{1500\text{ N} \times 1.0\text{ m}}{500\text{ N} \times 4.0\text{ m}} \times 100\% = 75\%$

PRACTICE PROBLEM

Strategy Hint: How is this problem different from the sample problem?

1. Using a fixed pulley, you exert a 72-N force to raise a 65-N object. What is the efficiency of the pulley?

Many machines can be made more efficient by reducing friction. This is usually done by adding a lubricant, such as oil or grease, to surfaces that rub together. After a time, dirt will build up on the grease or oil, and the lubricant will lose its effectiveness. The dirty lubricant should be wiped off and replaced with clean grease or oil. Can you think of any other ways to increase the efficiency of a machine?

Power

Suppose you and a friend are pushing boxes of books up a ramp to load them into a truck. The boxes weigh the same, but your friend is able to push a box a little faster than you can. Your friend moves a box up the ramp in 30 seconds. It takes you 45 seconds. Do you both do the same amount of work? Yes. This is true because the boxes weighed the same and were moved the same distance. The only difference is in the time it takes you and your friend to do the work.

OPTIONS

INQUIRY QUESTIONS

▶ **What part of the axe is a lever?** *the handle* **What class of lever is it?** *third* **What are the benefits of attaching a wedge to a lever to make an axe?** *The axe increases the speed of the effort force through the lever and changes the direction of the effort force through the wedge.*

▶ **Use the information presented in the text to explain if the MA of a one-speed bike is greater or less than 1.** *Because the rear wheel goes faster that the pedal wheel, the* resistance distance is greater than the effort distance. The MA *must be less than 1 because* d_e *is less than* d_r. **What do you gain by using a one-speed bike?** *speed* **What do you lose?** *force*

Micromachines

Imagine a robot the size of a flyspeck. Thousands of these robots could be injected into your bloodstream to clean out deposits or to identify and destroy bacteria, viruses, and cancer cells. This is the future predicted by a new group of engineers called micromechanical engineers.

These engineers use a sculpting process similar to that used in microelectronics to create mechanical devices a few microns thick. (A human hair is about 75 microns

across.) The sculpting is done in silicon, which at this size demonstrates a strength similar to that of steel.

Micromechanical sensors are already widely used to detect pressure, acceleration, and temperature. However, these sensors are passive. Tiny robots will reduce micromachines that can make things move. Recently, scientists at the University of California at Berkeley constructed a rotary motor that is only about two-thirds the diameter of a human hair. The central motor is 0.002 inches across, and the rotor arm is about the size of a red blood cell. Although working on this very small scale still involves many unknowns, the possibilities are unlimited.

Think Critically: What are some of the problems encountered by mechanical engineers that may be quite different in machines constructed at the micron level?

Your friend has more power than you have. **Power** is the rate at which work is done. In other words, ==power is a measure of the amount of work done in a certain amount of time. To calculate power, divide the work done by the time required to do the work.==

$$\text{power} = \frac{\text{work}}{\text{time}}$$

$$P = \frac{W}{t}$$

Power is measured in watts, named for James Watt, the inventor of the steam engine. A **watt (W)** is one joule per second. A watt is pretty small—about equal to the power used to raise a glass of water from your knees to your

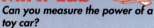

MINI-Lab

Can you measure the power of a toy car?

Wind up a toy car and place it at the bottom of an inclined plane. Adjust the angle of the inclined plane so the car will reach the top at the *slowest* speed possible. Measure the time in seconds for the car to travel to the top. Measure the *weight* of the car in newtons. Measure the height of the inclined plane in meters. Use weight and height to calculate the work in joules. Divide work by time to get power in watts.

7-4 USING MACHINES **177**

▶ For more information on micromachines, see "Micromachine Magic" by Robert Gannon, *Popular Science*, March 1989, pp. 89-92.
▶ Have students observe a silicon chip and a human hair together under a microscope. Use this comparison to develop the concept of scale and to introduce the micron.
Think Critically: At the micron level, qualities such as smoothness, friction, and lubrication may be very different from the same qualities in objects of normal size.

CONCEPT DEVELOPMENT

▶ To introduce the concept of power, pose the following questions. Suppose two students are asked to unpack identical cartons of books and place them on identical sets of shelves. One student completes the job in 10 minutes, whereas the other takes 20 minutes. Which student worked the "hardest"? Which student did the most work? Students are likely to say the first student worked "harder," although they may admit that both students did the same amount of work. Develop the idea of power, the rate of work, by asking students what they mean when they say someone worked harder at a task.

MINI-Lab

Materials: inclined plane board, stopwatch, meterstick, balance, and wind-up car
Teaching Tips
▶ Multiply the mass of the car in kilograms by 9.80 m/s^2 to determine its weight.
▶ Any toy that will travel up an incline can be used. Encourage students to bring their own.
Answers to Questions
▶ Answers will vary. Expect answers in the 0.01 watt range.

ENRICHMENT

▶ Have interested students demonstrate the gears of a ten-speed bike. Ask them to discuss the ten possible combinations of gears between the two pedal gears and the five rear-wheel gears. Have them relate the function of each combination in terms of starting, gaining speed, and climbing.
▶ Have interested students compile a listing of power ratings and efficiency ratings for various appliances. Encourage them to investigate if the two are related.

PROGRAM RESOURCES

From the **Teacher Resource Package** use:
Activity Worksheets, page 61, Mini-Lab: Can you measure the power of a toy car?
Science and Society, page 11, Will Robots Take Away Jobs?
Use **Laboratory Manual,** The Bicycle: A Well-Engineered Machine.

CONCEPT DEVELOPMENT

▶ Power is the rate at which energy is converted. For example, a 100-W light bulb converts 100 joules of electrical energy into 100 joules of radiant energy and heat during one second.

▶ Machines and appliances can be compared by their power ratings.

CROSS CURRICULUM

▶ **Health:** Nutritionists recommend a daily diet of about 5 000 000 J (1200 C) to maintain health. Show students that this diet would generate an average power of 58 W.

$$\frac{5\ 000\ 000\ J}{24\ h \times 60\ min/h \times 60\ s/min}$$

PRACTICE PROBLEM ANSWER

$$P = \frac{F \times d}{t} = \frac{25\ 000\ N \times 30\ m}{60\ s}$$
$$= 12\ 500\ W\ or\ 12.5\ kW$$

CHECK FOR UNDERSTANDING

Ask questions 1-2 and the **Apply** Question from the Section Review.

RETEACH

👥 **Cooperative Learning:** Have Problem Solving teams determine a method for calculating the amount of power a student generates while climbing a flight of stairs.

EXTENSION

For students who have mastered this section, use the **Reinforcement** and **Enrichment** masters or other OPTIONS provided.

3 CLOSE

▶ Have students explain why a car is more powerful than a bicycle but less efficient.

SECTION REVIEW ANSWERS

1. Student responses will vary. Accept all reasonable responses.

2. By definition, power is a measure of the amount of work done in a given amount of time.

3. Apply: For a given amount of work put into the mower, the work put out by the mower will increase.

EXAMPLE PROBLEM: Calculating Power

Problem Statement:	A figure skater lifts his partner, who weighs 450 N, 1 m in 3 s. How much power is required?
Known Information: Strategy Hint: Remember that work = force × distance.	force, F = 450 N distance, d = 1 m time, t = 3 s
Unknown Information:	power (P)
Equation to Use:	$P = \dfrac{W}{t} = \dfrac{F \times d}{t}$
Solution:	$P = \dfrac{450\ N \times 1\ m}{3\ s} = 150\ W$

PRACTICE PROBLEM

Strategy Hint: Should your answer be in watts or kilowatts?

1. A 500-N passenger is inside a 24 500-N elevator that rises 30.0 m in exactly 1 minute. How much power is needed for the elevator's trip?

mouth in one second. Because the watt is such a small unit, large amounts of power often are expressed in kilowatts. One kilowatt (kW) equals 1000 watts.

SECTION REVIEW

1. Give an example of a compound machine. What are the simple machines that make it up?
2. How are power, work, and time related?
3. **Apply:** You buy a secondhand lawn mower with an efficiency of 30 percent. By repairing and lubricating it, you increase its efficiency to 40 percent. How does this affect the work put out by the lawn mower for a given amount of work put in?

Skill Builder

☑ **Concept Mapping**

Make an events chain concept map to show how some of the simple machines in a bicycle work together to move the bicycle. Start with the feet applying force to the pedals. If you need help, refer to Concept Mapping in the **Skill Handbook** on pages 684 and 685.

Skill Builder

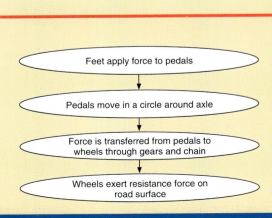

Feet apply force to pedals

↓

Pedals move in a circle around axle

↓

Force is transferred from pedals to wheels through gears and chain

↓

Wheels exert resistance force on road surface

7-1: Why We Use Machines

1. A machine makes work easier by changing the size of the force applied to it, the direction of that force, or both.

2. The number of times a machine multiplies the force applied to it is the mechanical advantage of the machine.

7-2: The Simple Machines

1. A lever is a bar that is free to pivot about a fixed point called a fulcrum. A pulley is a grooved wheel with a rope running along the groove. A wheel and axle consists of two different-sized wheels that rotate together. An inclined plane is a sloping surface used to raise objects. The screw and the wedge are special types of inclined planes.

2. Each type of simple machine has a specific equation for calculating its mechanical advantage. Each equation is related to the distance the effort force moves divided by the distance the resistance force moves.

7-3: Science and Society: Human-Powered Flying Machines

1. Simple machines can be combined to increase force and transfer that force from one place to another. Using a combination of simple machines, a human was able to propel a specially built airplane for a distance of more than 100 kilometers. The effort force for this flight was exerted by the pilot's legs.

2. Any experiment may have practical value that is not obvious at first.

7-4: Using Machines

1. A combination of two or more simple machines is called a compound machine.

2. The efficiency of any machine is a ratio of the work put into a machine to the useful work put out by the machine.

3. Power is a measure of the amount of work done in a certain amount of time. The SI unit of power is the watt, which is equivalent to one joule per second.

KEY SCIENCE WORDS

a. **compound machine**
b. **efficiency**
c. **effort arm**
d. **effort force**
e. **fulcrum**
f. **ideal machine**
g. **inclined plane**
h. **lever**
i. **machine**
j. **mechanical advantage**
k. **power**
l. **pulley**
m. **resistance arm**
n. **resistance force**
o. **screw**
p. **simple machine**
q. **watt**
r. **wedge**
s. **wheel and axle**

UNDERSTANDING VOCABULARY

Match each phrase with the correct term from the list of Key Science Words.

1. any device that accomplishes work with only one movement
2. force applied by a machine
3. a device in which work output equals work input
4. a bar that pivots about a fixed point
5. two different-sized wheels that rotate together
6. a combination of simple machines
7. the work output of a machine divided by the work input
8. the rate at which work is done
9. the fixed point of a lever
10. an inclined plane wrapped around a cylinder

MACHINES **179**

CHAPTER
REVIEW

SUMMARY

Have students read the summary statements to review the major concepts of the chapter.

UNDERSTANDING VOCABULARY

1. p   **6.** a
2. n   **7.** b
3. f   **8.** k
4. h   **9.** e
5. s   **10.** o

OPTIONS

ASSESSMENT

To assess student understanding of material in this chapter, use the resources listed.

COOPERATIVE LEARNING

Consider using cooperative learning in the THINK AND WRITE CRITICALLY, APPLY, and MORE SKILL BUILDERS sections of the Chapter Review.

PROGRAM RESOURCES

From the **Teacher Resource Package** use:

Chapter Review, pages 17-18.

Chapter and Unit Tests, pages 36-39, Chapter Test.

Chapter and Unit Tests, pages 40-41, Unit Test.

CHAPTER
REVIEW

1. b   6. b
2. b   7. a
3. a   8. b
4. c   9. b
5. d   10. a

UNDERSTANDING CONCEPTS

11. less than
12. resistance
13. effort
14. Power
15. 2

THINK AND WRITE CRITICALLY

16. Simple machines can make work easier by: (a) multiplying the effort force, as with a first-class lever; (b) changing the direction of the applied force, as with a single, fixed pulley; (c) increasing the distance through which the resistance force moves, as with a third-class lever.
17. Most machines increase the amount of work done by increasing the amount of friction involved in doing the work.
18. A fixed pulley changes the direction of the effort force; it does not multiply that force. A fixed pulley is similar to a first-class lever. A single, movable pulley moves with the resistance. It multiplies the force by 2. Such a pulley is similar to a second-class lever.
19. The *MA* of an inclined plane can be increased by increasing its length (or decreasing its height). Sharpening a knife has the effect of increasing the length of the "inclined plane."
20. Oil lubricates engine parts, thereby reducing friction and making the engine more efficient.

CHAPTER
REVIEW

CHECKING CONCEPTS

Choose the word or phrase that completes the sentence or answers the question.

1. There are _____ types of simple machines.
   a. 3   c. 8
   b. 6   d. 10
2. Which of these cannot be done by a machine?
   a. multiply force
   b. multiply energy
   c. change direction of a force
   d. all of these
3. In an ideal machine, the work input _____ work output.
   a. is equal to   c. is less than
   b. is greater than   d. none of these
4. The _____ of a machine is the number of times it multiplies the effort force.
   a. efficiency   c. mechanical advantage
   b. power   d. resistance
5. To raise a resistance 4 meters, the effort rope of a fixed pulley must move _____.
   a. 2 meters   c. 1 meter
   b. 8 meters   d. 4 meters
6. The mechanical advantage of a pulley system in which 5 ropes support an object is _____.
   a. 2.5   c. 10
   b. 5   d. 25
7. In a wheel and axle, the resistance force is usually exerted by the _____.
   a. axle   c. gear ratio
   b. larger wheel   d. pedals
8. The *MA* of an inclined plane 8 meters long and 2 meters high is _____.
   a. 2   c. 16
   b. 4   d. 8
9. As the efficiency of a machine increases, the _____ of the machine increases.
   a. work input   c. friction
   b. work output   d. *MA*

10. The *MA* of an inclined plane can be increased by _____.
    a. increasing the length
    b. increasing the height
    c. decreasing the length
    d. all of these

UNDERSTANDING CONCEPTS

Complete each sentence.

11. In an actual machine, the work output is almost always _____ than the work input.
12. In order to increase the *MA* of a first-class lever, move the fulcrum toward the _____.
13. In a wheel and axle, the _____ force is usually applied to the larger wheel.
14. _____ is measured in watts.
15. If the effort rope of a single movable pulley is pulled 4 meters, the resistance will be moved _____ meters.

THINK AND WRITE CRITICALLY

16. Describe three ways that a simple machine can make work easier. Give examples of each.
17. If machines make work easier, explain why most machines actually increase the amount of work you do in accomplishing a task.
18. Distinguish between a fixed pulley and a single movable pulley and describe the advantages of using each. Compare each type of pulley to its corresponding class of lever.
19. How can the mechanical advantage of an inclined plane be increased? Explain how sharpening a knife changes its *MA*.
20. The efficiency of an automobile is usually expressed in terms of gas mileage. How can changing the engine oil increase the gas mileage of the automobile?

APPLY

21. $MA = \dfrac{F_r}{F_e} = \dfrac{52 \text{ N}}{8 \text{ N}} = 6.5$
22. The fulcrum should be moved toward the adult, which increases the length of the effort arm of the child's lever. Thus, *MA* of the child's lever is increased, and the effort force exerted by the child is multiplied.
23. The screwdriver is being used as a wheel and axle, with the handle acting as the wheel. Thus, the short screwdriver with the fat handle will have a greater *MA*.

24. $\text{efficiency} = \dfrac{W_{out}}{W_{in}}$

    $= \dfrac{2000 \text{ N} \times 2 \text{ m}}{1250 \text{ N} \times 4 \text{ m}} \times 100 = 80\%$

25. $P = \dfrac{W}{t} = \dfrac{F \times d}{t}$

    $= \dfrac{500 \text{ N} \times 3 \text{ m}}{5 \text{ s}}$

    $= 300 \text{ watts or } 0.3 \text{ kW}$

APPLY

21. A cyclist applies a force of 8 N to the pedals of a bicycle. If the rear wheel applies a force of 52 N to the road surface, what is the *MA* of the bicycle?

22. An adult and a small child get on a seesaw that has a movable fulcrum. When the fulcrum is in the middle, the child can't lift the adult. How should the fulcrum be moved so that the two can seesaw? Explain your answer.

23. You have two screwdrivers. One is long with a thin handle, and the other is short with a fat handle. Which would you use to drive a screw into a board? Explain your choice.

24. Using a ramp 4 meters long, workers apply an effort force of 1250 N to move a 2000-N crate onto a platform 2 meters high. What is the efficiency of the ramp?

25. How much power does a person weighing 500 N need to climb a 3-meter ladder in 5 seconds?

MORE SKILL BUILDERS

If you need help, refer to the Skill Handbook.

1. **Outlining:** Make an outline describing the six types of simple machines. Be sure the outline indicates the two major types of simple machines and includes the following for each type of machine: (1) a description; (2) how it works; (3) a method for finding its *MA*; (4) an example.

2. **Making and Using Graphs:** A lever has a fixed effort arm length of 40 cm. Calculate effort force needed to raise a 10-N object with these resistance arm lengths: 80 cm, 40 cm, 20 cm, and 10 cm. Construct a line graph relating these resistance arm lengths to effort force. Describe the relationship between these two variables.

3. **Interpreting Scientific Illustrations:** Study the diagram of a garden hoe and answer the questions.
   a. What type of machine does the diagram represent? (Be specific.)
   b. What does the lower arrow represent?
   c. What does point A represent?
   d. What is represented by segment AC? segment AB?
   e. What is the *MA* of this machine?
   f. How does this machine make work easier?

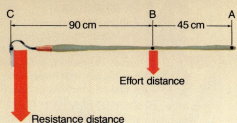

Effort distance

Resistance distance

4. **Measuring in SI:** The SI unit of power, the watt, is a derived unit. Using the definition of power, develop the formula for calculating power and determine the fundamental SI units for expressing power.

PROJECTS

1. Divide the class into teams of 3 or 4 students each. Have the members of each team spend one week daily identifying, describing, and classifying as many simple machines as they can find at school and at home. At the end of the week, each team should report their findings. Members should be prepared to support their own classifications and to challenge classifications they feel are incorrect.

2. Design a human-powered machine of some kind. Describe the simple machines used in your design and tell what each of these machines does.

4. **Measuring in SI:** Power is the rate at which work is done, or $P = W/t$. Power is expressed in watts. Using $F \times d$ to represent work, the formula for power becomes $P = (F \times d)/t$. So, a watt is the name for the derived unit newton • meter per second.

1. **Outlining:** Outlines may vary somewhat, but should resemble the following general scheme. Each lettered subhead should have the three subdivisions shown for A.
   I. Levers
      A. lever
         1. description
         2. method for finding *MA*
         3. examples
      B. pulley
      C. wheel and axle
   II. Inclined Planes
      A. ramp
      B. screw
      C. wedge

2. **Making and Using Graphs:**

$MA = \dfrac{L_e}{L_r}$	$F_e = \dfrac{F_r}{MA}$
$\dfrac{40}{80} = 0.5$	$\dfrac{10}{0.5} = 20$ N
$\dfrac{40}{40} = 1$	$\dfrac{10}{1} = 10$ N
$\dfrac{40}{20} = 2$	$\dfrac{10}{2} = 5$ N
$\dfrac{40}{10} = 4$	$\dfrac{10}{4} = 2.5$ N

Effort force and length of resistance arm are directly related.

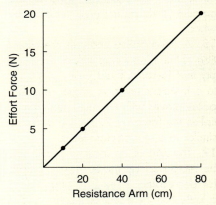

3. **Interpreting Scientific Illustrations:**
   a. third-class lever
   b. the distance the resistance moves
   c. fulcrum
   d. AC = resistance arm; AB = effort arm
   e. $MA = \dfrac{L_e}{L_r} = \dfrac{0.5 \text{ m}}{1.5 \text{ m}} = 0.33$
   f. The machine increases the distance the resistance moves for a given movement of the effort.

Objective
In this unit-ending feature, the unit topic, "Energy and Motion," is extended into other disciplines. Students will see how energy and motion are related to events occurring around the planet.

Motivate
Cooperative Learning: Assign one Connection to each group of students. Using the Expert Teams strategy have each group research to find out more about the geographic location of the Connection—its climate, culture, flora and fauna, and ecological issues.

Teaching Tips
▶ Ask students to look for the relationship between energy and motion in each of the items in this feature.
▶ Ask students to explain the motion involved in each Connection. Then ask them to describe the kind of energy involved in each one.

Wrap-Up
Conclude this lesson by asking students to describe how energy changes form in each of the Connections.

OCEANOGRAPHY
Background: Earth rotates once on its axis every 24 hours, while the moon orbits Earth. Before the moon returns to the same position overhead, Earth has rotated for 24 hours, 50 minutes. High tides occur when the moon is overhead or exactly on the opposite side of Earth. Because of this, high tides usually occur every 12 hours, 15 minutes.
Discussion: Ask students how tides might differ if Earth had two moons.
Answer to Question: Although the sun has much more mass than the moon, it is much farther away. The effect of the sun's gravity on Earth is more even than the moon's.
Extension: Have students find out how the Amazon River in South America is affected by tides.

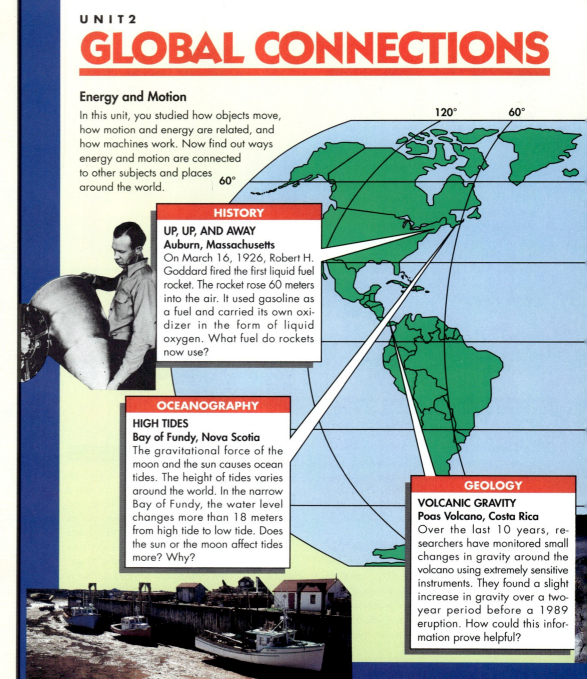

UNIT 2
GLOBAL CONNECTIONS

Energy and Motion
In this unit, you studied how objects move, how motion and energy are related, and how machines work. Now find out ways energy and motion are connected to other subjects and places around the world.

120°   60°

60°

HISTORY
UP, UP, AND AWAY
Auburn, Massachusetts
On March 16, 1926, Robert H. Goddard fired the first liquid fuel rocket. The rocket rose 60 meters into the air. It used gasoline as a fuel and carried its own oxidizer in the form of liquid oxygen. What fuel do rockets now use?

OCEANOGRAPHY
HIGH TIDES
Bay of Fundy, Nova Scotia
The gravitational force of the moon and the sun causes ocean tides. The height of tides varies around the world. In the narrow Bay of Fundy, the water level changes more than 18 meters from high tide to low tide. Does the sun or the moon affect tides more? Why?

GEOLOGY
VOLCANIC GRAVITY
Poas Volcano, Costa Rica
Over the last 10 years, researchers have monitored small changes in gravity around the volcano using extremely sensitive instruments. They found a slight increase in gravity over a two-year period before a 1989 eruption. How could this information prove helpful?

HISTORY
Background: The Chinese had used rockets during the Middle Ages. But until the 20th century rockets used gunpowder which is a fuel mixed with an oxidizer.
Discussion: Discuss with students the importance of an oxidizer to a rocket in traveling in space. Ask why a rocket traveling to the moon needs to carry a supply of liquid oxygen.
Answer to Question: Rockets now use liquid hydrogen as fuel and still carry liquid oxygen as the oxidizer.
Extension: Have students prepare a poster showing the structure of different kinds of rockets.

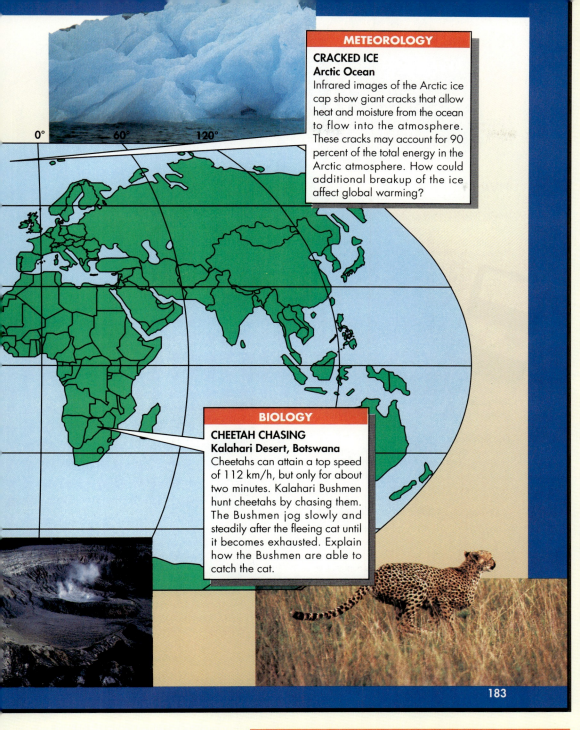

METEOROLOGY

CRACKED ICE
Arctic Ocean
Infrared images of the Arctic ice cap show giant cracks that allow heat and moisture from the ocean to flow into the atmosphere. These cracks may account for 90 percent of the total energy in the Arctic atmosphere. How could additional breakup of the ice affect global warming?

BIOLOGY

CHEETAH CHASING
Kalahari Desert, Botswana
Cheetahs can attain a top speed of 112 km/h, but only for about two minutes. Kalahari Bushmen hunt cheetahs by chasing them. The Bushmen jog slowly and steadily after the fleeing cat until it becomes exhausted. Explain how the Bushmen are able to catch the cat.

183

GEOLOGY

Background: Researchers inferred that the increase in gravity was likely due to the intrusion of dense molten magma into the volcano's cone before the eruption.

Discussion: Tell students that gravity decreased before the eruption of another volcano, probably because gas pockets formed in the magma, lowering its density. Discuss the possibility and practicality of determining a characteristic profile of each volcano in order to predict eruptions.

Answer to Question: The information might be used to help predict volcanic eruptions before they occur.

Extension: Have students research other methods that scientists use to predict volcanic eruptions.

METEOROLOGY

Background: The temperature of the ocean beneath the Arctic ice cap is about 40 degrees warmer than the Arctic air. Human activities which added more energy to the atmosphere could increase the breakup of the ice caps.

Discussion: Discuss the effects of global warming on the polar ice caps. Tell students that melting of the ice caps could raise sea level as much as 60 meters. Ask what effect this would have on the United States.

Answer to Question: If more energy escapes into the atmosphere, it could increase global warming.

Extension: Have students draw on a map the areas of the United States that would be below sea level if the polar ice caps melted.

BIOLOGY

Background: When comparing the speeds of various animals and humans, the maximum speeds attained are measured over varying distances. For a cheetah (112 km/h) to catch a gazelle (80 km/h), the cheetah must first get close enough so it can quickly catch the gazelle.

Discussion: In track, the cheetah could be compared to a sprinter, while the Bushmen are like marathon runners. Ask students to describe the motion of both in terms of speed and acceleration.

Answer to Question: The Bushmen can outlast the cheetah and catch up to the cat, which must slow down.

Extension: Have students research the maximum speeds of various other animals.

HVAC TECHNICIAN

Background: HVAC technicians may be self-employed or they may work for companies that install and service equipment. The technicians travel from location to location to install and service equipment. Some companies have HVAC technicians on staff to service the equipment in their buildings.

Related Career	Education
Machinist	high school
Boiler operator	high school
Power plant operator	technical school
Mechanical engineer	college degree

Career Issue: Refrigerators and air conditioners use coolants that contain ozone-eroding CFCs. In the process of servicing and repairing these units, technicians sometimes release these gases into the air. Technology exists to capture these gases, rather than release them into the atmosphere.

What do you think? Ask students if they think technicians should be required to capture and recycle CFCs from refrigeration units.

AERONAUTICAL ENGINEER

Background: Aeronautical engineers work for private companies or for the federal government. Some aeronautical engineers specialize in the design of spacecraft.

Related Career	Education
Air traffic controller	college degree
Commercial pilot	college degree
Aircraft mechanic	technical school
Tool and die maker	high school

Career Issue: Many people think more research and testing should be done to assure the safety of airplanes.

What do you think? Do students believe airplanes are safe enough now? Should the government require stricter safety standards?

HVAC TECHNICIAN

Heating, ventilation, and air-conditioning (HVAC) technicians work on equipment that heats and cools homes, schools, offices, and other buildings. Some technicians specialize in one of these areas, while others are skilled in all of them. They install, maintain, and repair units from the size of a room air conditioner to a central heating and cooling system for a large building.

If you're interested in becoming an HVAC technician you should take high school classes in math and physics and have mechanical aptitude. Some technicians learn the trade by working for several years as helpers with experienced technicians. Others take a two- or three-year program at a vocational or technical school.

For Additional Information
Contact the American Association of Heating, Refrigeration, and Air-Conditioning Engineers, 345 E. 47th Street, New York, New York 10017.

AERONAUTICAL ENGINEER

Aeronautical engineers design airplanes. They usually begin with a drawing that uses mathematics and engineering principles. Often they use computers to help them in the study and design of airplanes. Aeronautical engineers also use computers to simulate how the airplane they are designing will perform in flight. When the engineer has completed a design, a small model is built based on the design.

If you're interested in becoming an aeronautical engineer you should take classes in mathematics and physics in high school. Aeronautical engineers must have a college degree in engineering and may have advanced degrees.

For Additional Information
Contact the American Institute of Aeronautics and Astronautics, 1290 Avenue of the Americas, New York, New York 10019.

UNIT READINGS

▶ Laithwaite, Eric. *Force: The Power Behind Movement.* Danbury, CT: Watts, 1986.
▶ Santray, Laurence. *Heat.* Mahwah, NJ: Troll, 1985.
▶ Zubrowski, Bernard. *Raceways: Having Fun With Balls and Tracks.* New York: Morrow, 1985.

184

UNIT READINGS

Background
▶ *Force: The Power Behind Movement* looks at the basic principles that bridge the gap between pure science and the everyday world.
▶ *Heat* is an introduction to thermodynamics.
▶ *Machines and How They Work* describes the six simple machines.
▶ *Raceways: Having Fun With Balls and Tracks* includes activities that demonstrate velocity and acceleration.

More Readings
1. Watson, Philip. *Super Motion.* New York, NY: Lothrop, 1982. This book contains experiments to explore aspects of force and motion.
2. Kilgore, Jim. "The Art and Science of Punting." *Scholastic Science World.* November 20, 1987, pp. 28–29. Explains how a football punter can take advantage of the laws of projectile motion.

Dolphins

by Jacques-Yves Cousteau and Philippe Diole

This passage that follows is a brief account of Jacques Cousteau's first encounter with dolphins.

The cruiser *Primauguet* cut through the water at full speed, its prow rising and falling among the waves and raising a great wave of its own as it pushed irresistibly through the liquid wall of the sea. It was an impressive sight. The cruiser, a ship of the French Navy, had just been released from dry dock and we were testing her in the waters of the Far East. At that moment, the *Primauguet's* engines were wide open, and we were moving at a speed of 33.5 knots.

I was standing on the bridge, enthralled by the performance of the mighty cruiser as it cut through the sea with incredible violence. Then, I glanced to starboard. A school of dolphins was alongside, their fins regularly appearing then disappearing beneath the surface, their dark backs moving with graceful power through the rough water. I watched. And suddenly I realized that the dolphins were moving faster than the *Primauguet*. Swimming some thirty or forty feet away from the cruiser and parallel to her, they were passing her! I could hardly believe my eyes.

Then, suddenly, the lead dolphin altered his course and cut toward our prow.

When he reached the crest of the wave raised by the thrust of the *Primauguet's* engines, he hovered there until he was displaced by another dolphin, and then another. The dolphins had devised a game which they played in the midst of the waves: one by one, in turn, they rode the crest of the cruiser's wave, directly before our prow, for two or three minutes, then let themselves be carried to starboard or port so that the next dolphin could have his turn. It was an astonishing spectacle, but its importance to me at that time was practical rather than aesthetic. I realized that the school of dolphins, in catching up to and then passing the *Primauguet* as it moved at full power, must have been swimming at a speed of no less than fifty miles per hour!

That was forty years ago. Since then, I have had many encounters with dolphins, but I have never forgotten my first impression of those great mammals as they materialized in front of the *Primauguet's* stern—faster, and infinitely more maneuverable, than the best machines that human ingenuity had yet been able to devise.

In Your Own Words

▶Write a brief, descriptive essay about energy and motion involved in an encounter you have had with an animal.

185

Classics

Walker, Jeral. *Roundabout: The Physics of Rotation in the Everyday World.* New York, NY: Freeman and Company, 1985. Explains circular motion and how Newton's laws apply.

Source: Jacques-Yves Cousteau and Philippe Diole. *Dolphins.* New York, NY: A & W Visual Library, 1975.
Biography: Jacques-Yves Cousteau has dedicated his life to exploration of the sea. In 1950, he converted a minesweeper into a research vessel. Since then, he and the crew of the *Calypso* have traveled the world on scientific expeditions. He has filmed many of his adventures for television and has authored numerous books. Philippe Diole is a journalist, archaeologist, and diver. He has dived on many of *Calypso's* expeditions and been coauthor of many of Cousteau's books.

TEACHING STRATEGY

Have students read through the passage by Cousteau. Then have them respond to the discussion questions below.

Discussion Questions

1. **From the passage given here, why does Cousteau feel his observations about dolphins are important?** *Although he is impressed by the aesthetics of the dolphins' movements, he is more interested in the practical information he has learned—that is, the incredible speed of the dolphins and their ability to change directions.*

2. **From the passage given here, how does Cousteau compare dolphins with machines?** *He describes dolphins as being faster and much more maneuverable than the best machines yet devised by humans.*

Other Works

▶ Other books by Cousteau and Diole include: *Diving for Sunken Treasure; The Whale: Mighty Monarch of the Sea;* and *Octopus and Squid: The Soft Intelligence.*

In Unit 3, students are introduced to the physical and chemical classification of matter. The unit begins by describing the characteristics of the states of matter by the kinetic theory, continues by differentiating between physical and chemical properties, introduces the periodic table as a means of organizing elements, and relates chemical properties to atomic structure.

CONTENTS

ADVANCE PREPARATION

Activities
▶ **Activity 11-1, page 273,** calls for egg cartons. Have students begin saving them now.

Field Trips and Speakers
▶ Arrange to visit the auto shop at a local vocational school.
▶ Arrange to visit a darkroom at a local high school or photographer's studio.

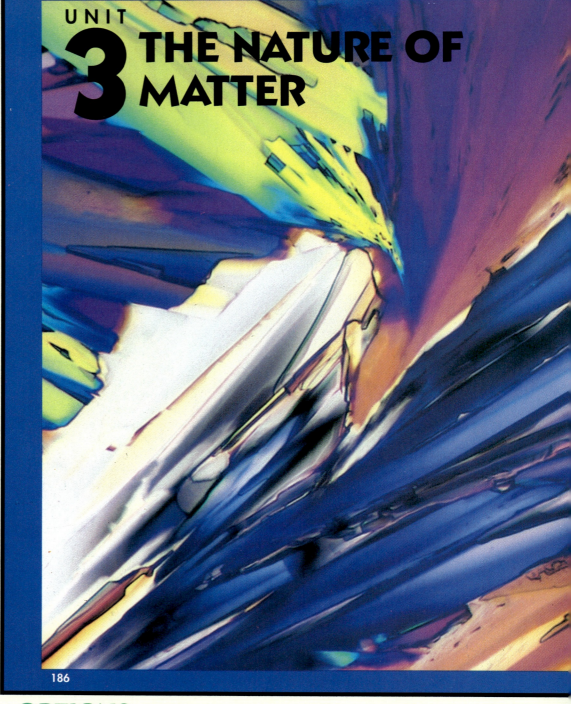

UNIT

3 THE NATURE OF MATTER

186

OPTIONS

Cross Curriculum
Have students list symbols that are introduced in other classes and their meanings.

Science at Home
Have students monitor television and newspapers to find the uses of models. Have them list the circumstances and how the model was used to convey information.

What's Happening Here?

The micrograph at the left shows a crystal of sodium thiosulfate ($Na_2S_2O_3$). Photographed in polarized light sodium thiosulfate, called *hypo*, is one of the chemicals used to develop photos. The atomic structure of sodium thiosulfate caused its crystals to form in this way. Atomic structure is one of the topics you'll study in Unit 3. Is matter made of other structures besides crystals? How is matter classified? What bonds hold it together? In Unit 3 you'll find the answers to these questions.

UNIT CONTENTS

187

INTRODUCING THE CHAPTER

What's Happening Here?
▶ Have students look at the photos and read the text. Ask them to tell you what's happening here. Point out to students that in this unit they will be studying the structure of matter and how its structure determines its characteristics and behavior.

▶ **Background:** In an electron microscope, beams of electrons are reflected by matter and then are refracted, that is focused—not by lenses as light is in an optical microscope, but by electric fields—onto a phosphorescent screen which is then photographed. The properties of electrons and their role in the structure of matter are discussed in Chapter 13.

▶ Sodium thiosulfate is used as a "fixer" in developing photographic film. It stops further light-sensitive chemical reactions on the surface of the negative.

Previewing the Chapters
▶ Have students use the figures and charts displayed in the unit to investigate the ways in which matter can be classified, such as state (pages 190-193); mixture or substance, element or compound (page 222); ionic compound or covalent compound (pages 276-277). Have them discuss into what categories they can place sodium thiosulfate now and what new information they would have to obtain to further classify it.

Tying to Previous Knowledge
▶ Have students discuss characteristics they use to classify materials as solids, liquids, and gases.

▶ Have students identify changes that occur when one bakes a cake. Lead them through mixing the dry ingredients, adding eggs, milk, and flavoring to the dry mixture, and baking it. Ask them to discuss what clues (visual, tactile, olfactory) they use to determine if a change has happened. Ask them to list other processes that indicate chemical changes.

▶ Use the **inquiry questions** in the OPTIONS box below to discuss classifying materials as solids, liquids, and gases.

Multicultural Awareness
Have interested students research historical cultural differences in explaining the basic types of matter and how they are related.

Inquiry Questions
▶ **How would you classify ice? Why?** *Solid. Accept all reasonable answers. It is "hard."*
▶ **How would you classify water? Why?** *Liquid. Accept all reasonable answers. It "pours."*
▶ **Discuss the characteristics you would use to classify butter and fog.** *Butter keeps its shape and melts at a certain temperature; therefore, it is a solid. Fog has the characteristics of air, so it must be a gas. However, it feels wet, so it must contain liquid, too.*

Solids, Liquids, and Gases

CHAPTER SECTION	OBJECTIVES	ACTIVITIES
8-1 Matter and Temperature (2 days)	1. **Describe** the four states of matter. 2. **Use** the kinetic theory of matter to explain the characteristics of solids, liquids, and gases. 3. **Explain** the thermal expansion of matter.	**Activity 8-1:** *Properties of Liquids,* p. 197
8-2 Water—Earth's Vital Liquid **Science & Society** (1 day)	1. **Describe** how people use and pollute water. 2. **Discuss** how people can save water and stop pollution.	
8-3 Changes in State (1 day)	1. **Interpret** state changes in terms of the kinetic theory of matter. 2. **Account** for the energy of the heats of fusion and vaporization in state changes.	**MINI-Lab:** *What energy changes take place during evaporation?* p. 201
8-4 Behavior of Gases (2 days)	1. **Explain** how a gas exerts pressure on its container. 2. **State** and **explain** how the pressure of a container of gas is affected when the volume is changed. 3. **Explain** the relationship between the temperature and volume of a gas.	**Activity 8-2:** *Temperature and Volume Relations,* p. 208
8-5 Uses of Fluids (2 days)	1. **State** Archimedes' principle and **predict** whether an object will sink or float in water. 2. **State** Pascal's principle and **describe** the operation of a machine that uses Pascal's principle. 3. **State** Bernoulli's principle and **describe** a way that Bernoulli's principle is applied.	**MINI-Lab:** *How does applied pressure affect different areas of a fluid?* p. 210
Chapter Review		

ACTIVITY MATERIALS

FIND OUT	ACTIVITIES		MINI-LABS	
Page 189 soccer ball 1 pump 1 inflation needle 1 gauge	**8-1 Properties of Liquids, p. 197** dropper food coloring wooden stick paper cup graduated cylinder 4% solution of powdered borax, in water 4% solution of polyvinyl alcohol (PVA) goggles, apron	**8-2 Temperature and Volume Relations, p. 208** string, marking pen meterstick container of ice water heat-proof glove/tongs beaker of boiling water thermometer goggles 2 medium, round balloons	**What energy changes take place during evaporation? p. 201** dropper rubbing alcohol	**How does applied pressure affect different areas of a fluid? p. 210** dropper 2-liter plastic soda bottle

CHAPTER FEATURES	TEACHER RESOURCE PACKAGE	OTHER RESOURCES
Problem Solving: *Breakfast with Grandmother,* p. 196 **Skill Builder:** *Making and Using Tables,* p. 196	**Ability Level Worksheets** ◆ *Study Guide,* p. 34 ● *Reinforcement,* p. 34 ▲ *Enrichment,* p. 34 **Activity Worksheet,** pp. 63, 64 **Transparency Master,** pp. 29, 30	**Color Transparency 15,** States of Matter **Lab Manual 17,** Density of a Liquid; **18,** Densities of Solutions
You Decide! p. 199	**Ability Level Worksheets** ◆ *Study Guide,* p. 35 ● *Reinforcement,* p. 35 ▲ *Enrichment,* p. 35 **Cross-Curricular Connections,** p. 12 **Science and Society,** p. 12	
Skill Builder: *Concept Mapping,* p. 203	**Ability Level Worksheets** ◆ *Study Guide,* p. 36 ● *Reinforcement,* p. 36 ▲ *Enrichment,* p. 36 **Concept Mapping,** pp. 21, 22 **MINI-Lab Worksheet,** p. 69	
Technology: *Gaseous Research Grants,* p. 206 **Skill Builder:** *Hypothesizing,* p. 207	**Ability Level Worksheets** ◆ *Study Guide,* p. 37 ● *Reinforcement,* p. 37 ▲ *Enrichment,* p. 37 **Activity Worksheet,** pp. 65, 66	**Lab Manual 19,** Behavior of Gases
Skill Builder: *Measuring in SI,* p. 214	**Ability Level Worksheets** ◆ *Study Guide,* p. 38 ● *Reinforcement,* p. 38 ▲ *Enrichment,* p. 38 **Critical Thinking/Problem Solving,** p. 14 **MINI-Lab Worksheet,** p. 70 **Transparency Master,** pp. 31, 32	**Color Transparency 16,** Archimedes' Principle
Summary Think & Write Critically Key Science Words Apply Understanding Vocabulary More Skill Builders Checking Concepts Projects Understanding Concepts	**Chapter Review,** pp. 19, 20 **Chapter Test,** pp. 53-56	**Chapter Review Software** **Test Bank**

◆ **Basic**　　● **Average**　　▲ **Advanced**

ADDITIONAL MATERIALS

SOFTWARE	AUDIOVISUAL	BOOKS/MAGAZINES
Gas Laws, ComPress. *General Gas Laws,* Microphys. *The Earth's Water,* Queue.	*Matter and Energy: Properties of Matter,* filmstrip, SVE. *Particles in Motion: States of Matter,* film, National Geographic. *Solids, Liquids, and Gases,* film, McGraw-Hill. *Water: A Clear and Present Danger,* video, ABC News Close-Up, Coronet/MTI. *It's Chemical: Density in Gases/Density in Liquids,* laserdisc, Aims Media. *It's Chemical: Density in Solids/Phase Changes,* laserdisc, Aims Media.	Walton, Alan J., *Three Phases of Matter.* 2nd ed. New York: Oxford University Press, 1983. Turner, M.W. and B. Hulme. *Plasma Proteins: An Introduction.* Woodstock, NY: Beekman Publishing Inc., 1971.

THEME DEVELOPMENT: The energy content, or temperature, of particles plays a major role in determining their state of matter. The kinetic theory of matter enables the student to visualize atoms and molecules in motion and form a mental model of the states of matter.

CHAPTER OVERVIEW

▶ **Section 8-1:** The kinetic theory of matter explains why solids, liquids, gases, and plasmas behave differently.

▶ **Section 8-2: Science and Society:** Students learn how they use, pollute, and can conserve water.

▶ **Section 8-3:** The kinetic theory is applied to explain how thermal energy affects changes of state.

▶ **Section 8-4:** After *pressure* is defined, the relationships between volume, pressure, and temperature in gases are explored.

▶ **Section 8-5:** Characteristics of fluids are discussed by exploring the discoveries of Archimedes, Pascal, and Bernoulli.

CHAPTER VOCABULARY

states of matter	pressure
kinetic theory	pascal
of matter	Boyle's Law
crystals	Charles's Law
plasma	buoyant force
thermal	Archimedes'
expansion	principle
polluted water	Pascal's
evaporation	principle
condensation	Bernoulli's
heat of fusion	principle
heat of	
vaporization	

CHAPTER

8 Solids, Liquids, and Gases

188

OPTIONS

For Your Gifted Students

Have students form a hypothesis about the effect of fluid density on the buoyant force exerted on an object. Use water and saturated salt solution for comparison. Determine the density of each by measuring the mass of a known volume. For objects that will sink, buoyant force can be measured directly by hanging the object by a thread from a spring scale and observing the apparent weight loss when it is immersed. For floating objects, determine, in addition to the weight, how much weight must be added to the object to sink it.

Perhaps you have seen bicycle tires or a soccer ball lose pressure and soften with a change of the seasons. Do objects lose pressure only if they leak air? Or does this mean a change in temperature affects pressure?

FIND OUT!

Do this activity to find out if the temperature and pressure of air are related.

Using a hand pump, pressure gauge, and an inflation needle, inflate a soccer ball until the gauge reads 20 lb/sq in. Drop the ball and have a partner measure the height of the first bounce. Next, submerge the ball in a bucket of ice water for 10 minutes and then use the needle and gauge to measure the pressure of the ball. Drop the cold ball from the same height as before and have your partner measure its first bounce. Then submerge the ball in warm water for 10 minutes (or longer) and repeat both measurements. Do the pressure and bounce heights vary with temperature?

Previewing Science Skills
- ▶ In the *Skill Builders,* you will make and use a table, make a concept map, hypothesize, and measure in SI.
- ▶ In the *Activities,* you will observe, organize and collect data, infer, communicate, measure, and classify.
- ▶ In the *MINI-Labs,* you will observe and hypothesize.

What's next?

You have shown that temperature affects the pressure of air. You will learn more about the behavior of gases as you read the pages that follow.

189

INTRODUCING THE CHAPTER
Use the Find Out activity to introduce students to the relationship that exists between temperature and pressure of gases. Inform students that they will be learning more about temperature and its effects on matter as they read the chapter.

FIND OUT!
Preparation: Obtain soccer balls and inflation equipment from students or from your school's athletic department.
Materials: one soccer ball, one pump, one inflation needle, and one gauge per group
Teaching Tips
- ▶ If you have gauges that read in kilopascals, inform students that 20 lb/sq in is about 140 kPa.
- ▶ Do not allow students to hold the ball underwater with their hands. Use a plumber's helper or a similar item to hold the ball.
- ▶ Remind students to drop ball from the same height each time. Therefore, they will have to measure the height of the first drop.
- ▶ Three or four setups should be enough to get good comparisons. Do as a demonstration if you have materials for only one setup.

Gearing Up
Have students study the Gearing Up feature to familiarize themselves with the chapter. Discuss the relationships of the topics in the outline.

What's Next?
Before beginning the first section, make sure the students understand the connection between the Find Out activity and the topics to follow.

For Your Mainstreamed Students

This chapter deals with the changes matter undergoes as a result of temperature. There is little substitute for tactile and/or visual experiences with matter. The aim should be to make sure students can correctly identify a state of matter and relate its overall characteristics. Changes in state can easily be related to the events students observe in the kitchen.

Special effort should be made to have mainstreamed students perform Activity 8-2. All students, especially those with impaired vision, will benefit greatly from the observations of this lab.

PROGRAM RESOURCES
From the **Teacher Resource Package** use:

Transparency Masters, pages 29-30, States of Matter.

Use the **Color Transparency** number 15, States of Matter.

PREPARATION

SECTION BACKGROUND

▶ All true solids are crystalline. Their crystal shape reflects the original arrangement of atoms and molecules.

▶ The kinetic theory of matter assumes that particles of matter are in constant motion and undergo perfectly elastic collisions. That is, they lose no energy in collisions.

▶ Particles of liquids have little, if any, more spacing than those of solids. For water, liquid particles are actually closer together than those of the solid. Thus, ice is less dense and floats in liquid water.

▶ As more molecules of air are added to a tire, the number of collisions per second increases as the distance between molecules decreases. A single gas molecule undergoes several billion collisions per second.

▶ Because it is made of charged particles, plasma is greatly affected by electric and magnetic fields.

PREPLANNING

▶ For Activity 8-1, make enough 4% sodium borate and polyvinyl alcohol solutions for your lab groups.

1 MOTIVATE

▶ Ask your students if they have ever heard of fuel line freeze-up or engine vapor lock. With vapor lock, fuel vaporizes at a hot spot causing a fuel line to partially fill with gas. A car's fuel pump is designed to pump a liquid, not a gas. In summer, the gasoline can vaporize in the fuel line. In winter, water from condensation in the gas tank can freeze and block the fuel line. Discuss with students how temperature affects the state of matter.

8-1 Matter and Temperature

New Science Words

states of matter
kinetic theory of matter
crystals
plasma
thermal expansion

Objectives

▶ Describe the four states of matter.
▶ Use the kinetic theory of matter to explain the characteristics of solids, liquids, and gases.
▶ Explain the thermal expansion of matter.

Figure 8-1. Water can exist in nature as a solid, a liquid, or a gas.

States of Matter

When was the last time you poured solid water into a glass? It was probably just after you grabbed a handful of ice cubes from the freezer. If you let the solid cubes sit at room temperature, they melted into liquid water. If you heated the liquid water in a pan on the stove, the liquid water changed to a gas called water vapor, or steam. Ice, liquid water, and steam are examples of the three most familiar states of matter—solid, liquid, and gas.

All matter takes up space and has mass, yet matter can exist in different states. There are four **states of matter**— solid, liquid, gas, and plasma. The state of a sample of matter depends on its temperature. For example, water ordinarily exists as ice at low temperatures and as liquid water at moderate temperatures. At higher temperatures, water changes to the gas state as water vapor. At still higher temperatures, the matter in water would become plasma. Each state has characteristics that are used to identify it, as you'll see. **①**

Solids

A metal spoon, a cube of sugar, and a piece of cement are classified as solids. Every solid has a definite shape and a definite volume. For example, a metal spoon stays spoon-shaped whether it's in your hand or in a glass of water. And because no ordinary amount of force can squeeze the spoon into a smaller space, it has a definite volume. **②**

190 SOLIDS, LIQUIDS, AND GASES

OPTIONS

Meeting Different Ability Levels

For Section 8-1, use the following **Teacher Resource Masters** depending upon individual students' needs.

◆ **Study Guide Master** for all students.

● **Reinforcement Master** for students of average and above average ability levels.

▲ **Enrichment Master** for above average students.

Additional Teacher Resource Package masters are listed in the OPTIONS box throughout the section. The additional masters are appropriate for all students.

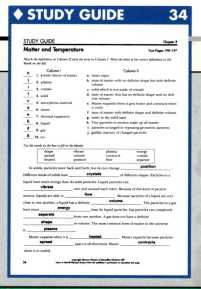

◆ STUDY GUIDE 34

STUDY GUIDE   Chapter 8
Matter and Temperature   Text Pages 190–197

Match the definition in Column II with the term in Column I. Write the letter of the correct definition on the blank on the left.

Column I
h   1. kinetic theory of matter
j   2. plasma
i   3. crystals
f   4. solid
c   5. amorphous material
a   6. steam
e   7. thermal expansion
b   8. liquid
d   9. gas
g   10. ice

Column II
a. water vapor
b. state of matter with no definite shape but with definite volume
c. solid which is not made of crystals
d. state of matter that has no definite shape and no definite volume
e. matter expands when it gets hotter and contracts when it cools.
f. state of matter with definite shape and definite volume
g. water in the solid state
h. Tiny particles in motion make up all matter.
i. particles arranged in repeating geometric patterns
j. gaslike mixture of charged particles

Use the words in the box to fill in the blanks.

shape   vibrate   plasma   energy
spread   volume   contracts   crystals
heated   position   flow   separate

In solids, particles move back and forth, but do not change _____position_____.

Different kinds of solids have _____crystals_____ of different shapes. Particles in a liquid have more energy than do solid particles. Liquid particles can _____vibrate_____ over and around each other. Because of this kind of particle motion, liquids are able to _____flow_____. Because particles of a liquid are very close to one another, a liquid has a definite _____volume_____. The particles in a gas have more _____energy_____ than do liquid particles. Gas particles can completely _____separate_____ from one another. A gas does not have a definite _____shape_____ or volume. The most common form of matter in the universe is _____plasma_____.

Matter expands when it is _____heated_____. Matter expands because particles _____spread_____ apart in all directions. Matter _____contracts_____ when it is cooled.

34   Copyright Glencoe Division of Macmillan/McGraw-Hill
            Users of Merrill Physical Science have the publisher's permission to reproduce this page.

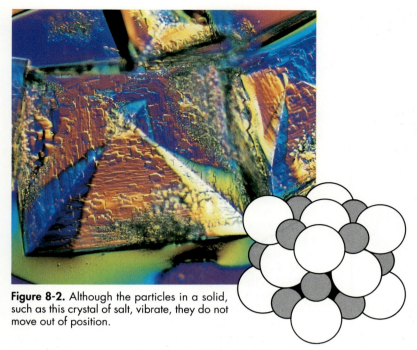

Figure 8-2. Although the particles in a solid, such as this crystal of salt, vibrate, they do not move out of position.

What accounts for the characteristics of solids? Tiny particles in constant motion make up all matter. This idea is called the **kinetic theory of matter.** The particles in solid matter are held very close together by forces between them. This is why a solid can't be squeezed into a smaller space. The particles can vibrate against their neighbors, but can't move out of position. Thus, they can't move over or around each other. This explains why a solid holds its shape.

In solids, the particles are arranged in repeating geometric patterns. These arrangements form **crystals.** Different kinds of solids have crystals of different shapes. With a magnifier you can see that salt crystals are little cubes. A snowflake is a crystal of water that has the shape of a hexagon.

Some materials such as glass, many plastics, and some kinds of wax, appear to be solids but are not made of crystals. They are often called amorphous solids. The word *amorphous* means having no form. Many scientists think some of these noncrystalline materials should be classified as very thick liquids.

Why does a solid hold its shape?

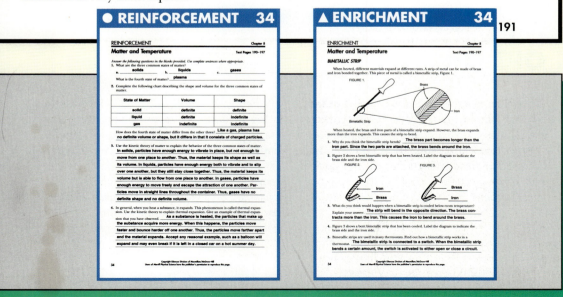
191

TYING TO PREVIOUS KNOWLEDGE: Remind students that their bodies contain three of the four states of matter. Ask them to give examples such as bones, blood, and exhaled air.

▶ Students should realize that temperature changes cause changes in matter. Ask if they have ever noticed cracking or clanking noises when a furnace or radiator is turned on. The noises come from the expansion of the pipes as they heat up.

OBJECTIVES AND SCIENCE WORDS: Have students review the objectives and science words to become familiar with this section.

2 TEACH

Key Concepts are highlighted.

CONCEPT DEVELOPMENT

▶ If possible, obtain some moth crystals to use in teaching this section. As you discuss solids, have a student place some moth crystals in a test tube. Stopper the tube and pass it around the class so students can observe the crystalline form.

▶ Have students observe the regular shape of salt crystals under a microscope or with a hand lens.

Cooperative Learning: Assign Problem Solving Teams. Have each team prepare a written statement explaining how refineries solve the problems of fuel line freeze-up and vapor lock. They will find that refineries change gasoline blends for different seasons and different geographical locations.

CONCEPT DEVELOPMENT

▶ As you discuss liquids, melt the moth crystals using boiling water. Relate the role of energy to the melting process. Use the kinetic theory to explain to your students what is happening on a molecular level.

▶ The smell of the vaporized moth crystals will provide evidence that the molecules (dichlorobenzene) are also present as a gas.

▶ Using a series of containers of varying sizes and shapes, pour a liquid from one container to another. Relate students' observations to the particle model of a liquid.

Cooperative Learning: Use the Science Investigation strategy with groups of three. Have one student place 5 drops of vanilla flavoring into a balloon, blow up the balloon, and tie it closed. Have a second student smell near the surface of the balloon. The student should be able to detect the smell of vanilla as it evaporates inside the balloon. The balloon may feel cool where the liquid is evaporating on the inside. Have the third student monitor, confirm, and record the group's observations. Ask the group to explain their observations using the kinetic theory. They should conclude that the moving molecules of vanilla aroma passed between the molecules of the stretched balloon. Introduce the term *diffusion* if it is appropriate for your class.

TEACHER F.Y.I.

▶ Some liquids can be instantaneously changed into solids by high voltage. These liquids are called ER (electro-rheological) fluids. In the future these ER fluids may be used in robots.

Liquids

When heated, most solids will change into liquids. A liquid does not have a definite shape, but it does have a definite volume. So a liquid flows and takes the shape of its container. However, like solids, liquids can't normally be squeezed to a smaller volume. If you push down on a liter of water with a moderate amount of force, its volume will remain a liter.

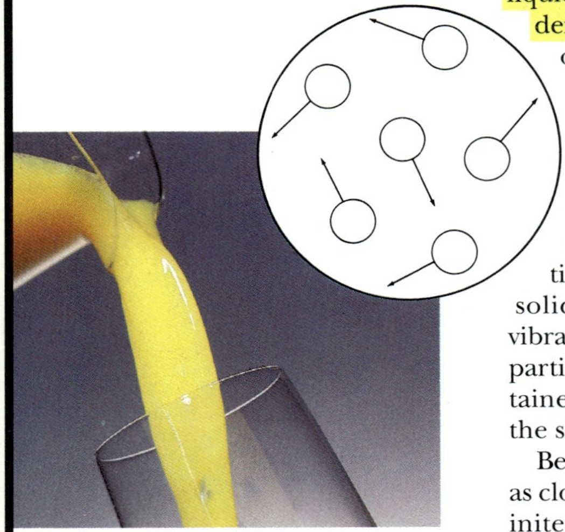

Just as the kinetic theory explains the properties of solids, it also explains the properties of liquids. Because a liquid can't be squeezed, its particles must also be very close together, like those of a solid. However, they have enough kinetic energy to vibrate over and around each other. This movement of particles lets a liquid flow and take the shape of its container. Thus, orange juice poured into a glass will take the shape of the glass.

Because its particles are held very close together, almost as close as those of a solid, liquid matter does have a definite volume. If you pour 1 liter of orange juice into a 2-liter bottle, it will not spread out to fill the bottle. Likewise, you couldn't force the liter of juice into a half-liter container. The two containers in Figure 8-4 contain the same volume of juice.

Figure 8-3. The particles in a liquid are close together, but have enough energy to vibrate over and around one another.

Figure 8-4. Although its volume does not change, the shape of a liquid depends on the shape of its container.

192 SOLIDS, LIQUIDS, AND GASES

OPTIONS

INQUIRY QUESTIONS

▶ Sometimes expensive glassware is called "crystal." Explain why this term is incorrectly used. *Glass is not crystalline; it is amorphous.*

▶ Is there anything wrong with saying, "This bottle is half filled with carbon dioxide gas?" *Yes, a gas occupies all the space available in its container.*

▶ When water changes from the liquid state to the solid state, it expands and becomes less dense. What happens during freezing, in terms of particle spacing and arrangement? List a physical property of ice that results from this change. *The particles change from a jumbled arrangement to a regular arrangement. The spacing is greater in the solid than in the liquid. Ice floats in liquid water.*

Gases

A gas has neither a definite shape nor a definite volume. You may have pumped air into a basketball, tire, or balloon and noticed that the air takes the shape of the object. ==Gases are springy—they expand or contract to fill the space available to them and can be squeezed into a smaller space.==

According to the kinetic theory of matter, the particles of a gas have enough energy to separate completely from one another. Therefore, the particles are free to move in all directions until they have spread evenly throughout their container. Because the particles are not close together, they can also be squeezed into a smaller space. When you pump up a bicycle tire, you are forcing more and more air particles into the same space.

Compare the models of a solid, a liquid, and a gas shown in Figure 8-6. How are they different?

Plasma

So far you've learned about the three familiar states of matter. But none of these is the most common state of matter in the universe. For example, 99 percent of the

Figure 8-5. The particles in a gas have enough energy to spread widely apart from one another.

Figure 8-6. The diagrams below show the spacing and arrangements of the particles in the three familiar states of matter.

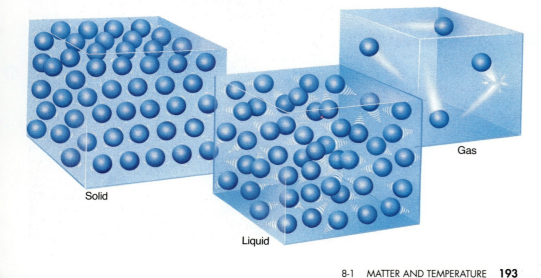

Solid

Liquid

Gas

▶ Many students have the impression that the particle spacing of liquids is somehow intermediate between the spacing in solids and gases. If this were true, liquids would be "springy" like a gas, and hydraulic machines would not work. In addition, the expansion of water upon freezing directly contradicts this assumption.

CONCEPT DEVELOPMENT

▶ **Demonstration:** On the overhead projector, in a clear plastic lid from a box of greeting cards, place five marbles. Agitate the box to simulate gas molecules in motion. Increase the amount of agitation of the box lid to simulate the effect of increasing the temperature of a gas. Point out the more frequent and forceful collisions. Relate student observations to the properties and particle model of a gas.

CROSS CURRICULUM

▶ **Art and Design:** As students visit shopping malls, have them observe how the states of matter are used to decorate and make shopping more pleasant. Have them write about what they saw, such as waterfalls, helium balloons, marble floors, fluorescent and neon lighting.

STUDENT TEXT QUESTION

▶ Page 193, paragraph 3: **How are the models of solids, liquids, and gases different?** *The particles of solids are close together in a regular arrangement. The particles of liquids are close together but jumbled. The particles of gases are far apart and are not in an arrangement.*

ENRICHMENT

▶ Have a student research how synthetic diamonds are made and report to the class.
▶ Have a student research superconducting crystals.
▶ Cryogenics is the study of matter at very low temperatures. Ask a student to research how a solid's properties change near absolute zero.

PROGRAM RESOURCES

Use **Laboratory Manual,** Density of a Liquid.

Figure 8-7. Most of the matter in the universe is in the plasma state. The stars at the center of this nebula and the sun contain plasma.

Did You Know?

The sun is getting smaller, losing over 400 km of radius in the past 50 years.

mass of our solar system is contained in the sun. The most common form of matter in the universe is the type found in stars like the sun. Such matter is called plasma. **Plasma** is a gaslike mixture of positively and negatively charged particles. Besides light from the sun, you can observe the effects of plasma in your home or school. When a fluorescent light is switched on, electricity causes particles of mercury gas inside the tube to form plasma.

You know that particles of matter move faster as the matter is heated to higher temperatures. The faster they move, the greater the force with which they bump into other particles, or collide. As matter is heated to *very* high temperatures, the particles begin to collide violently. As a result, the particles break up into the smaller particles they are made of. These particles are electrically charged.

Thermal Expansion

You have learned how the kinetic theory accounts for characteristics of different states of matter you see and touch every day. The kinetic theory also explains other things you may have observed.

For example, have you ever noticed the strips of metal that run across the floors and up the walls in long hallways of concrete and steel buildings? Maybe you've seen these strips in your school. These strips usually cover gaps in the building structure called expansion joints. Expansion joints allow the building to expand in hot weather and shrink in cold weather without cracking the concrete. As you drive onto or off a bridge, you will usually pass over a large steel expansion joint as shown in Figure 8-8.

Almost all matter expands as it gets hotter and contracts when it cools. This characteristic of matter is called **thermal expansion.** How does the kinetic theory of matter explain thermal expansion? In a solid, forces between the particles hold them together. As the solid is heated, these particles move faster and faster and vibrate against each other with more force. As a result, the particles spread apart slightly in all directions and the solid expands. The same effect also occurs in liquids and gases.

You can compare thermal expansion to a crowd of people. When the people are quiet and still, they are able to stand close together. As the people become restless, they jostle one another and the crowd spreads out.

Figure 8-8. Expansion joints in a bridge allow the structure to expand in warm weather without cracking.

What is the purpose of expansion joints in buildings?

⑤

EcoTip

Make your own air freshener. Put vinegar, a few spices, and a little cinnamon in a small glass jar. Heat the jar in the microwave oven for one minute and then place it where you need it most.

CHECK FOR UNDERSTANDING

Use the Mini Quiz to check for understanding.

MINI QUIZ

Use the Mini Quiz to check students' recall of chapter content.

① **Name the four states of matter.** *solid, liquid, gas, plasma*

② **Which state of matter has definite shape and definite volume?** *solid*

③ **According to kinetic theory, what is all matter composed of?** *tiny particles in constant motion*

④ **What happens to the speed of the particles of matter as it is heated?** *It increases.*

⑤ **What happens to most matter when it is heated?** *It expands.*

RETEACH

Provide the students who have not demonstrated mastery with the crossword puzzle and have them write the clues for each word. Then give the entire class a blank crossword and the clues to solve it.

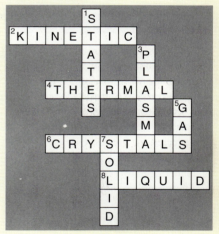

EXTENSION

For students who have mastered this section, use the **Reinforcement** and **Enrichment** masters or other OPTIONS provided.

ENRICHMENT

▶ Have students investigate and report on plasmas. They should include fusion reactions as well as everyday objects. They could also report on methods used to contain a plasma in a magnetic bottle.

▶ Ask students to think about what would happen if the collisions between particles of matter were not perfectly elastic. The particles would lose kinetic energy in collisions. Inform them that the top of a person's head undergoes nine billion collisions per second with molecules making up air.

▶ A group of students could prepare a chart and present it to the class. It could list the four states of matter, information about their shape, volume, relative densities, particle models, and so on.

PROGRAM RESOURCES

Use **Laboratory Manual,** Density by Percent.

PROBLEM SOLVING

This method of opening jars can easily be demonstrated to the class. Remind students that most metals have a much lower specific heat than glass or plastic. Therefore, the lid increases in temperature much faster than the jar does.

Think Critically: As the lid's temperature rises, it undergoes thermal expansion making it a little looser on the jar.

PROGRAM RESOURCES

From the **Teacher Recource Package** use:

Activity Worksheets, page 5, Flex Your Brain.

3 CLOSE

▶ Ask questions 1-3 and the **Apply** Question in the Section Review.

 FLEX Your Brain

Use the Flex Your Brain activity to have students explore STATES OF MATTER. Guide students to associate the states with their physical characteristics and their particle models. You could direct students to explore state changes in preparation for Section 8-3.

▶ Have a group of students prepare a bulletin board on the states of matter and their particle models.

SECTION REVIEW ANSWERS

1. Both solids and liquids have a definite volume because their particles are closely packed. Solids have a definite shape, but liquids take the shape of the container. The particles of solids are held in place by attractive forces. The particles of liquids have enough energy to tumble over and around one another.

2. The material is a gas because it expanded to occupy all the space available in the container.

3. The particles of copper move more slowly as it cools. Attractive forces then pull them closer together.

4. Apply: Glass is not a solid but is, rather, a very thick liquid. Over time it flows downward.

PROBLEM SOLVING

Breakfast with Grandmother

Juan was visiting his grandmother for the weekend. On Saturday morning, he woke to the smell of muffins baking. The smell made him hungry, so he dressed quickly and ran down the stairs and into the kitchen.

Grandmother was taking the muffins out of the oven. After placing them on the table, she asked Juan to get a jar of jam from the cabinet and open it. Juan tried to remove the metal lid from the glass jar, but no matter how hard he tried, the lid would not budge. At his grandmother's suggestion, Juan ran hot water over the lid before trying again to remove the lid, and then it came off easily.

Think Critically: How did hot water affect the metal lid of the jar? Why was the lid easier to remove after running hot water over it?

SECTION REVIEW

1. Compare the characteristics of solids and liquids.
2. You pour 500 mL of a green material into a 1-liter flask and stopper it. The material completely fills the flask. What state of matter is the material? Explain how you know.
3. In terms of particle motion, explain why copper shrinks when it cools.
4. **Apply:** In very old houses, the window glass is thicker at the bottom of the panes than at the top. How can you account for this thickening?

Skill Builder

☑ **Making and Using Tables**

Make a table to classify several materials as a solid, liquid, gas, or plasma. Include columns for properties and a description of particles for each state. If you need help, refer to Making and Using Tables in the **Skill Handbook** on page 686.

Skill Builder

Possible Solution

State	Properties	Particle description	Examples
Solid	Definite shape and volume	Closely packed; do not change position	ice, sugar
Liquid	Definite volume; takes shape of container	Closely packed; able to move past one another	milk, mercury in thermometer
Gas	Occupies shape and volume of container	Spread apart; free to move in all directions	oxygen, steam
Plasma	Occupies shape and volume of container	Gaslike mix of negatively and positively charged particles	mercury vapor in fluorescent tube, sun and stars

ACTIVITY 8-1
Properties of Liquids

Problem: *How can properties of a material be used to classify it?*

Materials

- dropper
- food coloring
- wooden stick
- paper cup
- graduated cylinder
- 4% solution of powdered borax, in water
- 4% solution of polyvinyl alcohol (PVA)
- goggles
- apron

Procedure

1. Copy the data table and use it to record your observations of the new material.
2. Using a graduated cylinder, measure 30 mL (cm^3) of PVA solution into a paper cup. Add two drops of food coloring.
3. Using a dropper, add about 3 mL (cm^3) of borax solution to the PVA in the cup and begin to stir vigorously with a wooden stick.
4. After stirring for 2 minutes, what is the consistency of the material?
5. Transfer the material to your hand. **CAUTION:** *Do not taste or eat the material and be sure to wash your hands after the activity.* Rate the ease with which the material flows.
6. Form the material into a ball and then place it in the cup to test its ability to take the shape of its container.
7. Compare the volume of the new material with the volume of the original material before stirring.

Analyze

1. Is the new material more like a gas, a liquid, or a solid?
2. What other materials have you seen that have similar properties to this one?
3. Considering the slow flow of the new material, how would you rate the strength of the attraction among its particles?

Conclude and Apply

4. Using the kinetic theory of matter, how would you describe the closeness of the particles of matter in the new material?
5. How can properties of this material be used to classify it?

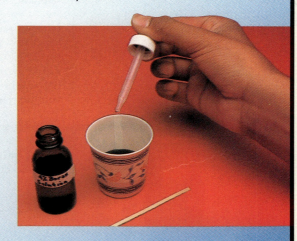

Data and Observations

Sample Data

Property	Observation	Interpretation
Ability to flow	Yes, but slowly (high viscosity)	Molecules hold to each other, but not as much as solids
Shape changes	Does change shape	Molecules do allow movement
Volume changes	No change	Molecules are not totally free to fill up any volume

---

ANSWERS TO QUESTIONS

1. a liquid
2. Slime, gelatin dessert, jellies, mucus
3. The particles are fairly strongly attracted. They hold into a certain volume and do not fill the container as a gas would. However, unlike a solid they are not attracted strongly enough to hold the material into a specific shape.
4. The particles are close together because the material cannot be pressed into a smaller space.
5. It exhibits the properties of flow, indefinite shape, and constant volume. Therefore, it is classified as a liquid.

PROGRAM RESOURCES

From the **Teacher Resource Package** use:
Activity Worksheets, pages 63-64, Activity 8-1: Properties of Liquids.

OBJECTIVE: Observe the properties of a material and classify its state of matter.

PROCESS SKILLS applied in this activity:
▶ **Measuring** in Procedure Steps 2 and 3.
▶ **Classifying** in Analyze Questions 1 and 2.
▶ **Formulating models** in Conclude and Apply Question 4.

COOPERATIVE LEARNING

Organize Science Investigation groups. If possible, have no more than three students per group. Have three or four groups compare results and form generalized conclusions.

TEACHING THE ACTIVITY

▶ **Troubleshooting:** In order to properly mix the borax and PVA, students must stir the solutions quickly and continuously. Do not allow students to taste the resulting gel or take it out of the classroom. Spills may be cleaned up with water.

▶ The new material is a polymer that is very much like products sold in toy stores under names like Slime. Encourage students to make comparisons to commercial products.

▶ The PVA can be obtained from several chemical companies. It is a dry powder. You can prepare the solution by adding about 40 g of PVA to about one liter of tap water. Stir vigorously.

▶ To prepare 4% borax solution, dissolve 12 g sodium borate in 288 mL of hot water with constant stirring. Cool before using.

▶ To prepare 4% PVA solution, add 40 g of 98% hydrolyzed PVA to 960 mL H_2O. Heat to 80°C with stirring. Cool before using.

PREPARATION

SECTION BACKGROUND

▶ Find out what the water sources for your community are and how water for human consumption is treated. Is water in short supply in your area? Why? Is polluted water a problem where you live? Why? You may want to assign these tasks to students.

1 MOTIVATE

▶ **Demonstration:** Fill a graduated cylinder to the 100-mL mark with water. Ask a student to remove one milliliter using a medicine dropper and place it on a watch glass. This is a rough scale model of the amount of fresh water on Earth.

TYING TO PREVIOUS KNOWLEDGE: Ask students to list the ways they have used water since they awoke this morning. Ask them how much of the water was reusable when they finished with it.

OBJECTIVES AND SCIENCE WORDS: Have students review the objectives and science words to become familiar with this section.

2 TEACH

Key Concepts are highlighted.

CONCEPT DEVELOPMENT

▶ **Demonstration:** Before class, mix dirt and water to make a liter of muddy water. Filter a small amount using filter paper in a funnel. Add a drop or two of food coloring to the remaining muddy water. Filter as before. Point out that dissolved contaminants cannot be filtered out.

SCIENCE & SOCIETY **8-2** # Water—Earth's Vital Liquid

New Science Words	Objectives
polluted water	▶ Describe how people use and pollute water.
	▶ Discuss how people can save water and stop pollution.

Will There Be Enough Water?

What percentage of the water on Earth is available fresh water?

For living things, like yourself, the most important liquid on Earth is fresh water. It is not as abundant as you might think. Fresh water, which is water that is not salty, makes up only 0.75 percent of the water available on Earth in the liquid state.

How much water do you think you use in a day? Take a guess. Did you say 1700 gallons? For the average person in the United States, that's the correct answer! Each person uses about 200 gallons a day for cooking, bathing, toilet use, and heating and cooling homes. Add to this the 750 gallons per person a day used to produce materials and energy, and another 750 gallons per person a day used to water crops. Table 8-1 lists only a few ways you use water indirectly as well as directly.

Table 8-1

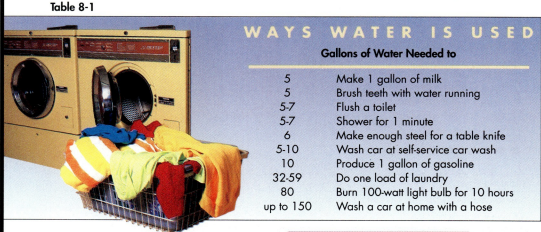

WAYS WATER IS USED

Gallons of Water Needed to

5	Make 1 gallon of milk
5	Brush teeth with water running
5-7	Flush a toilet
5-7	Shower for 1 minute
6	Make enough steel for a table knife
5-10	Wash car at self-service car wash
10	Produce 1 gallon of gasoline
32-59	Do one load of laundry
80	Burn 100-watt light bulb for 10 hours
up to 150	Wash a car at home with a hose

198 SOLIDS, LIQUIDS, AND GASES

OPTIONS

Meeting Different Ability Levels

For Section 8-2, use the following **Teacher Resource Masters** depending upon individual students' needs.

◆ **Study Guide Master** for all students.

● **Reinforcement Master** for students of average and above average ability levels.

▲ **Enrichment Master** for above average students.

STUDY GUIDE 35

STUDY GUIDE   Chapter 8
Water, Earth's Vital Liquid   Text Pages 198–199

Complete the following sentences using words from pages 198–199 in your textbook. Then look for these words in the word search.

1. For living things, the most important liquid on Earth is __fresh water__. (2 words)
2. Water __pollution__ is the result of making water dirty.
3. People sometimes dump __toxic__ materials down drains.
4. Chemical __fertilizer__, herbicides, and pesticides pollute water.
5. __Thermal__ pollution is the heating of rivers and lakes.
6. Heating the __environment__ of water organisms often kills them.
7. Water in a lake or a __river__ is fresh water.
8. __Motor oil__, paint thinner, bleach, and drain cleaners are examples of toxic materials. (2 words)
9. Organisms can quickly break down __biodegradable__ materials.
10. __Industry__ pollutes water by dumping raw sewage, chemicals, and radioactive materials into it.

F O R O A N P S M S C A S
W D E T A W H S E R P L E
B R G N X M O T O R D I I
A Z I N O C A P R Z I P A
R O R W V S I J A N O M
C L N U O I V E R W E L R
Q I N D O E G R D A B L E
T R X U O S O N H E S U
G H A O D S L B N S J T T
S E D E V L T H M M T I N
O U K R H O L R R A E O L
D A O N D R Y A J N G N A
L P M E I B F E G S R E T

Copyright Glencoe Division of Macmillan/McGraw-Hill
Users of Merrill Physical Science have the publisher's permission to reproduce this page.   35

Not only do people use huge amounts of fresh water, they also pollute their natural supplies of this liquid. **Polluted water** is water that is dirty and unfit for living things. Motor oil, paint thinner, bleach, and drain cleaners are a few examples of toxic materials that people dump down drains or on the ground. From there, the materials may move into water supplies.

Industry pollutes water by dumping raw sewage, toxic industrial chemicals, and radioactive materials into it. The farming industry pollutes water with chemical fertilizers, herbicides, and pesticides. Another form of pollution is the heating of rivers and lakes called thermal pollution. Hot water produced by electric power plants flows into and heats bodies of water where organisms live. This heating often kills the organisms.

Many toxic materials that pollute water stay in their original form for many years. Scientists are trying to develop products that are safe for the environment. For example, they are trying to make materials that are biodegradable. Organisms can break down biodegradable materials, changing them into harmless forms.

Many people seem to think fresh, clean water will always be plentiful. But, for reasons you have read about, some environmental scientists disagree.

SECTION REVIEW

1. What are two main reasons that there could be a shortage of clean water?
2. List five sources of water pollution.

You Decide!

The amount of water used by each person can be reduced 15 to 25 percent without any noticeable change in lifestyle. What are five things you could do to use less water or reduce water pollution?

SCIENCE & SOCIETY

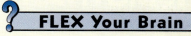

● **REINFORCEMENT** 35   ▲ **ENRICHMENT** 35 199

PROGRAM RESOURCES

From the **Teacher Resource Package** use:

Cross-Curricular Connections, page 12, Watersheds and Water Quality.

Science and Society, page 12, Is Your Water Safe?

Activity Worksheets, page 5, Flex Your Brain.

CHECK FOR UNDERSTANDING
▶ Ask questions 1-2 in the Section Review.

RETEACH
▶ **Demonstration:** Filter vinegar through filter paper. Test the filtrate with litmus paper to show that dissolved chemicals cannot be filtered out.

EXTENSION
For students who have mastered this section, use the **Reinforcement** and **Enrichment** masters or other OPTIONS provided.

3 CLOSE

FLEX Your Brain

Use the Flex Your Brain activity to have students explore WATER POLLUTION.

SECTION REVIEW ANSWERS
1. the wasteful use of water and pollution of water
2. Answers will vary, but may include toxic industrial chemicals, toxic household chemicals, chemical fertilizers, pesticides, herbicides, radioactive materials, raw sewage, heat from electric power plants.

YOU DECIDE!

SCIENCE & SOCIETY

Answers will vary, but should include (a) ways to use less water, such as taking short showers, turning off water while brushing teeth, and reporting leaky faucets and open hydrants; and (b) using nontoxic or biodegradable materials at home; and (c) participating in the political process.

PREPARATION

SECTION BACKGROUND

▶ Substances with high melting temperatures have strong attractive forces between particles.

▶ Substances that have weak intermolecular forces evaporate easily and melt or boil at relatively low temperatures.

▶ Before a substance reaches its melting or boiling point, added energy increases the motion (kinetic energy) of the particles and the temperature increases.

▶ At the melting point and boiling point, added energy allows the position (potential energy) of the particles to change.

PREPLANNING

▶ The Mini-Lab requires rubbing alcohol and droppers.

1 MOTIVATE

▶ **Demonstration:** Solid iodine sublimes easily. Place a few crystals of solid iodine in a stoppered test tube or glass flask. A pale violet color will be visible to students. **CAUTION:** *Iodine vapors are toxic.* Ask students to suggest a mechanism for this phenomenon based on the particle models of the states of matter.

TYING TO PREVIOUS KNOWLEDGE: Ask students to recall how cold they felt when they got out of the water after swimming when a strong breeze was blowing.

▶ Ask your class if anyone has seen dry ice subliming. Ask them to describe what they saw. If possible, obtain a piece for your students to observe.

New Science Words

evaporation
condensation
heat of fusion
heat of vaporization

Objectives

▶ Interpret state changes in terms of the kinetic theory of matter.
▶ Account for the energy of the heats of fusion and vaporization in state changes.

Kinds of State Changes

If you've ever seen ice cream melt before you could eat it, you have seen matter change state. Solid ice crystals in the ice cream melt when they change from the solid state to the liquid state. In melting, a solid changes into a liquid. You put water in the freezer to make ice cubes. In freezing, matter changes from the liquid state to the solid state.

When you boil water, you observe another change of state, called vaporization. In boiling, you add heat to a liquid until it reaches a temperature at which it changes to bubbles of gas below its surface. Many liquids don't need to boil to change to a gas. In **evaporation,** a liquid changes to a gas gradually at temperatures below the boiling point. When you come out of a pool into warm air,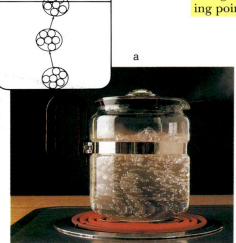

Figure 8-9. When water boils, bubbles of gas particles form below the surface, rise to the top, and escape (a). When a liquid evaporates, individual gas particles escape from the surface (b).

a

b

OPTIONS

Meeting Different Ability Levels

For Section 8-3, use the following **Teacher Resource Masters** depending upon individual students' needs.

◆ **Study Guide Master** for all students.
● **Reinforcement Master** for students of average and above average ability levels.
▲ **Enrichment Master** for above average students.

Additional Teacher Resource Package masters are listed in the OPTIONS box throughout the section. The additional masters are appropriate for all students.

◆ **STUDY GUIDE** 36

STUDY GUIDE   Chapter 8
Changes in State   Text Pages 200–203

Solve the following crossword puzzle by using the clues provided.

Across
3. The state of a material depends on this.
5. change of a solid directly to a gas
9. When ice melts, the particles of solid water ____ energy.
10. gaseous water
13. energy needed to change a material from solid to liquid (3 words)
15. change of a liquid to gas below the boiling point
16. has definite volume but no definite shape
17. The kinetic energy of a substance is the ____ kinetic energy of its particles.
18. to change from a liquid to a gas at temperatures above those normal to the liquid state
19. process that occurs during boiling

Down
1. to change from solid to liquid
2. energy needed to change a material from liquid to gas (5 words)
4. occurs when a gas cools and changes to a liquid
6. Liquids have a definite volume and ____.
7. a unit of heat
8. no definite shape, no definite volume
11. theory used to explain changes of state
12. has a definite volume and shape
14. determined by motion and spacing of particles

36

Copyright Glencoe Division of Macmillan/McGraw-Hill
Users of Merrill Physical Science have the publisher's permission to reproduce this page.

water on your skin soon evaporates. You'll see later how this drying helps cool you.

Have you noticed that ice cubes seem to shrink when they've been in the freezer a long time? This shrinkage happens because of another change of state called sublimation. In sublimation, a solid changes directly to a gas without going through the liquid state. ③

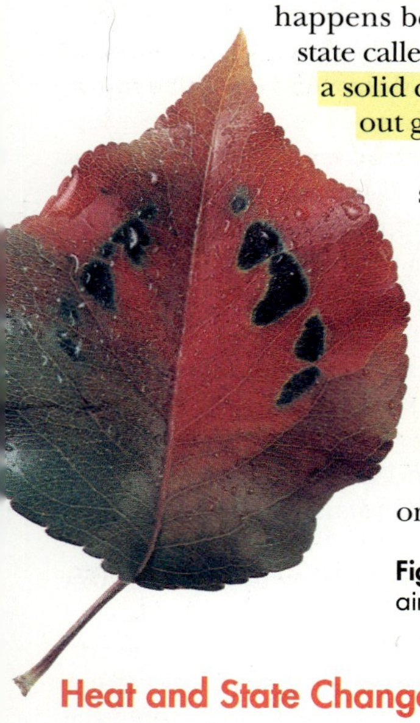

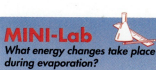

You see another change of state when your glass of ice-cold soft drink "sweats." The drops of water on your glass appear when gaseous water condenses on the cold surface. Condensation takes place when a gas changes to a liquid. ④ Generally, a gas will condense when cooled to or below its boiling point.

Figure 8-10. Gaseous water in the air often condenses on cool surfaces.

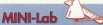

MINI-Lab

What energy changes take place during evaporation?
Use a dropper to place five drops of rubbing alcohol on the back of your hand. Wait for two minutes. What sensations did you feel? What change of state did you observe? Is energy entering or leaving your hand? Where does the energy for this process come from?

Heat and State Changes

The kinetic theory of matter explains changes of state. Suppose you take some ice cubes from your freezer, put them in a beaker, and heat them. Then, you measure the temperature of the cubes every 30 seconds. You will find that the temperature rises steadily as the cubes absorb thermal energy. Figure 8-11 on the next page plots these temperature changes.

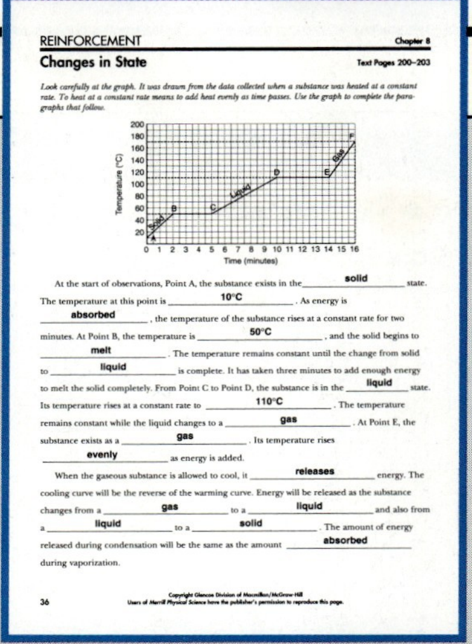

After 5 minutes, the cubes warm up to 0°C and begin to melt. But the temperature stops rising and stays at 0°C while the cubes melt. What is happening to the energy? The particles of the solid water are absorbing energy. This energy enables them to overcome forces that hold them in place. Then the particles are free to tumble over one another. In other words, they have become particles of water in the liquid state.

The amount of energy needed to change a material from the solid state to the liquid state is the **heat of fusion** of that material. For water, the heat of fusion is 334 kJ/kg. This means that it takes 334 kJ of energy to melt 1 kg of ice without changing its temperature from 0°C.

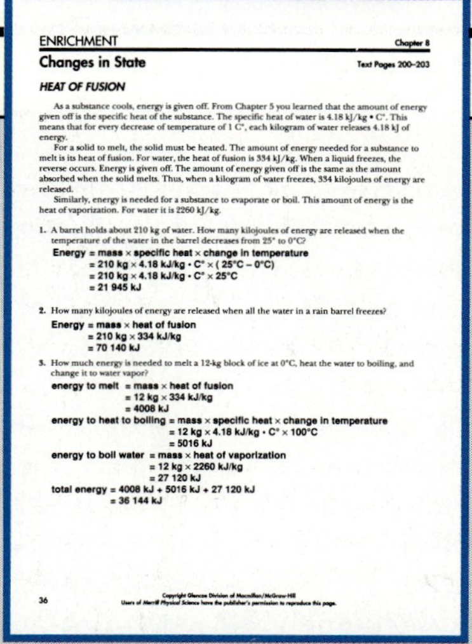

What is the heat of fusion of a material? ⑤

201

OBJECTIVES AND SCIENCE WORDS: Have students review the objectives and science words to become familiar with this section.

2 TEACH

Key Concepts are highlighted.

CONCEPT DEVELOPMENT

▶ Remind students that melting and freezing as well as boiling and condensing are reversible changes. The substance is unchanged in these physical changes.

▶ It is important that students realize that a substance melts and freezes at the same temperature; it is the energy content, or heat of fusion, that determines the state of the substance.

MINI-Lab

Materials: dropper, rubbing alcohol

Teaching Tips

▶ Emphasize that an input of energy is required for continued evaporation.

▶ Discuss the function of perspiration during hot weather and physical exertion.

Results: In a short time, the alcohol will evaporate completely. Students will feel a cooling sensation.

▶ Have students compare what they feel in still air and when blowing gently across the hand.

Answers to Questions
Hands felt cooler. Evaporation was observed. Energy for evaporation came mostly from the skin.

PROGRAM RESOURCES

From the **Teacher Resource Package** use:

Activity Worksheets, page 69, Mini-Lab: What energy changes take place during evaporation?

---

1 Define melting. *A solid changes to a liquid.*

2 Define evaporation. *A liquid gradually changes to a gas below the boiling point.*

3 Define sublimation. *A solid changes directly to a gas.*

4 Define condensation. *A gas changes to a liquid.*

5 How much energy is needed to melt 1000 grams of ice at 0°C? *334 kJ*

CROSS CURRICULUM

▶ **Geology:** Have students read about the mechanism and energy source for geysers. Yellowstone Park's Old Faithful geyser is a well known example of a change in state involving the boiling of water. Geothermal energy provides the heat of vaporization.

REVEALING MISCONCEPTIONS

▶ Students tend to believe that ice is always at its freezing temperature. In reality, it can become colder like any other solid after freezing.

CONCEPT DEVELOPMENT

▶ When a liquid evaporates, the molecules are becoming a vapor at the surface only. When a liquid boils, the molecules are becoming a vapor throughout the liquid.

▶ The amount of energy required to change liquid particles to gas particles depends on the pressure applied to them. The greater the pressure, the more energy is required to separate particles in a liquid to form a gas. Thus, water inside a pressure cooker boils at a temperature much higher than water's normal boiling point. Conversely, water at high altitudes boils at a lower temperature. The normal boiling point given in tables of information is at one atmosphere of pressure.

▶ Remind students that the sloped portions of the graphs in Figure 8-11 represent a change in temperature. The horizontal portions indicate that a state change is occurring.

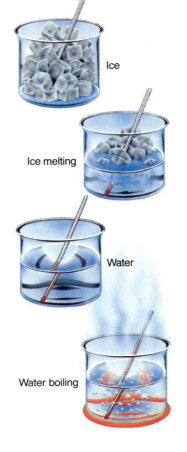

Ice

Ice melting

Water

Water boiling

Suppose it takes 5 minutes for all the cubes to melt, and you continue to heat the liquid water. You observe that the temperature rises once again. After another 10 minutes the water begins to boil. The temperature has reached 100°C and rises no further. Again, the water particles are absorbing energy, which enables them to overcome attractive forces holding them together in the liquid state. After absorbing energy, the particles can separate to great distances from one another. They are becoming particles of gaseous water, steam. The amount of energy needed to change a material from a liquid to a gas is the **heat of vaporization** of that material. For water, the heat of vaporization is 2260 kJ/kg.

After some time, the water has boiled away, and the temperature of the remaining steam rises rapidly. Suppose you could condense the steam back into liquid water and then freeze the liquid into ice. You would remove all the energy you added before. And the temperature would stay at 100°C while the steam condensed and at 0°C while the ice froze.

You can also use the kinetic theory to explain how water evaporates from your skin and how it cools you. When a liquid evaporates, the particles do not all have the same kinetic energy. Some move faster than others. Many of these are moving fast enough to break away from the liquid and become a gas. As these fast-moving water particles leave, the average kinetic energy of the remain-

Figure 8-11. The warming and melting of ice (a). The warming and boiling of water (b).

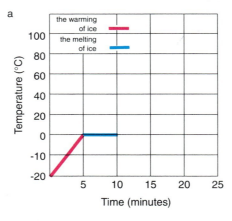

a

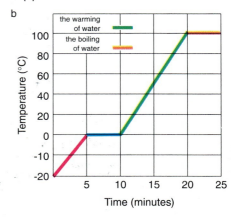

b

OPTIONS

INQUIRY QUESTIONS

▶ Some liquids have much stronger attractive forces between particles than others. Suggest how the amount of attractive force affects the boiling point of a liquid. *The higher the attractive force, the higher the boiling point— provided other factors are equal.*

▶ Under the oceans, hot lava erupts from cracks in Earth's crust. The water boils when heated by the molten rock. Explain why steam bubbles are never observed at the ocean's surface. *The steam loses heat and condenses as it rises.*

PROGRAM RESOURCES

From the **Teacher Resource Package** use:
Concept Mapping, page 21.

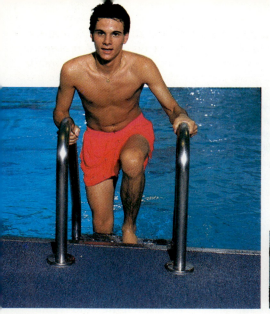
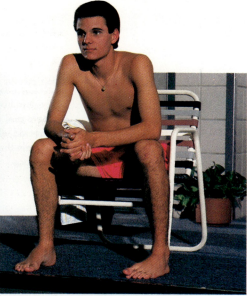

Figure 8-12. In warm air, water soon evaporates from wet skin and hair.

ing particles becomes less. As a result the temperature of the remaining water goes down. Because the water is now cooler than your skin, it takes heat from your skin and cools you.

SECTION REVIEW

1. Name and describe the state changes in which another state changes to a gas.
2. Use the kinetic theory to explain melting.
3. What happens to the energy put into a liquid during boiling?
4. **Apply:** Steam must lose its heat of vaporization in order to condense. How does this fact help explain why steam causes more severe skin burns than water at its boiling point?

☑ Concept Mapping

Use a cycle map to show the changes in particles as cool water boils, changes to steam, and then changes back to cool water. If you need help, refer to Concept Mapping in the **Skill Handbook** on pages 684 and 685.

Skill Builder

Skill Builder

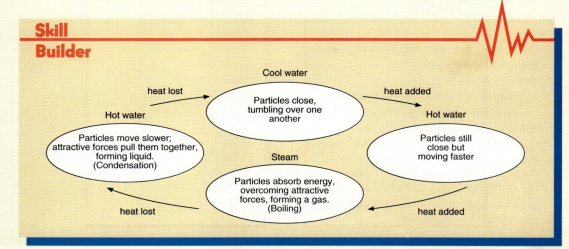

Ask questions 1-3 and the **Apply** Question in the Section Review.

RETEACH

Cooperative Learning: Use the Paired Partner strategy. Have each partner draw and label a particle model of one of the three common states of matter and write a state change that could occur starting from the state drawn. Students should then exchange papers and make a particle sketch representing the indicated state change. Repeat until all states and possible changes are exhausted.

EXTENSION

For students who have mastered this section, use the **Reinforcement** and **Enrichment** masters or other OPTIONS provided.

3 CLOSE

▶ **Demonstration:** In novelty stores, one can purchase a "drinking bird." If a student has one, have him or her bring it to class and explain how it works. The water evaporates from the head to cool and condense the vapors of the volatile liquid inside.

SECTION REVIEW ANSWERS

1. Boiling: Gas bubbles form within the liquid at the boiling point. Sublimation: A solid changes directly to a gas. Evaporation: Particles of a liquid gain enough energy to escape from the surface of the liquid.
2. Particles absorb energy and become free enough to tumble over one another.
3. The energy is used in overcoming the attractive forces that hold the liquid particles close to one another.
4. Apply: If steam touches the skin, steam will condense and give up its heat of vaporization there. Liquid water at its boiling temperature does not have heat of vaporization to lose.

PREPARATION

SECTION BACKGROUND

▶ Gas molecules are much smaller than the distance between the molecules.

▶ The gas laws treat gases as though they are ideal gases. In ideal gases, each molecule has no volume, and there is no attraction between molecules.

▶ Most gases behave almost like ideal gases at normal pressures and temperatures.

PREPLANNING

▶ A supply of ice will be needed for Activity 8-2. Two balloons will be needed per lab team.

1 MOTIVATE

▶ **Demonstration:** Fill a small fruit juice glass to overflowing with water. Hold a 3 x 5-inch card on top of the glass and invert it. Ask your students what they think will happen if you take your hand away. Remove your hand from beneath the card. Air pressure will hold the card on the inverted glass. Use this demonstration to introduce the lesson on pressure and to point out that air pressure acts in all directions.

▶ To emphasize that a pascal is a very small unit, remind students that a newton is about the weight of a stick of butter. If they imagine the butter spread over a square meter surface, they have an idea of a pascal of pressure.

TEACHER F.Y.I.

▶ Safety, handling, and gas mileage suffer when drivers fail to inflate automobile tires properly. Some expensive cars have in-wheel pressure sensors that cause a light on the instrument panel to go on if any tires are underinflated.

8-4 Behavior of Gases

New Science Words

pressure
pascal
Boyle's law
Charles's law

Objectives

▶ Explain how a gas exerts pressure on its container.
▶ State and explain how the pressure of a container of gas is affected when the volume is changed.
▶ Explain the relationship between the temperature and volume of a gas.

Figure 8-13. The force of colliding particles of air in constant motion keeps a tire inflated.

Pressure

Every time you feel the wind on your face, you observe the behavior of a gas—rather, the mixture of gases that is Earth's air, or atmosphere. Even when the wind is calm, the air exerts a force called pressure.

What causes the pressure of a gas? Particles of matter are very small—many billions of particles of air fill an inflated toy balloon. When riding on a bike or in a car, you're riding on pockets of colliding air particles inside your tires. You have learned that the particles of air, like those in all gases, are constantly moving. They're free to fly about and collide with anything in their way. The collisions keep the balloons or tires inflated and cause the force that you feel when you squeeze them.

The total amount of force exerted by a gas depends on the size of its container. **Pressure is the amount of force exerted per unit of area.** ❶

$$P = F/A$$

The **pascal** (Pa) is the SI unit of pressure. One pascal ❷ of pressure is a force of one newton per square meter. This is a very small pressure unit, so most pressures are given in kilopascals (kPa).

Earth's atmosphere exerts a pressure on everything within it. At sea level, atmospheric pressure is 101.3 kPa. This means that at Earth's surface, the atmosphere exerts a force of about 100 000 newtons on every square meter. This amount of force is equal to a weight of 100 000 newtons—about the weight of a large truck.

OPTIONS

Meeting Different Ability Levels

For Section 8-4, use the following **Teacher Resource Masters** depending upon individual students' needs.

◆ **Study Guide Master** for all students.
● **Reinforcement Master** for students of average and above average ability levels.
▲ **Enrichment Master** for above average students.

Additional Teacher Resource Package masters are listed in the OPTIONS box throughout the section. The additional masters are appropriate for all students.

◆ **STUDY GUIDE** 37

STUDY GUIDE — Chapter 8
Behavior of Gases — Text Pages 204-208

Use the words in the box to fill in the blanks.

force	constantly	size	absolute	liquids
increase	volume	boiling	decrease	pressure
kinetic	particles	kilopascals	larger	decrease
pressure	Charles's	Boyle's	temperature	increased

Gases in Earth's atmosphere exert **pressure** on everything. According to the **kinetic** theory, the particles of a gas are **constantly** moving. Every time gas particles hit something and bounce off, they exert a tiny force. Pressure is this amount of **force** exerted per unit of area. Air pressure at sea level is 101.3 **kilopascals**.

The amount of force exerted by a gas depends on the **size** of its container. **Boyle's** law states that if a sample of gas is kept at constant **temperature**, decreasing the volume will **increase** the pressure the gas exerts. If you increase the volume, the pressure will **decrease**. According to the kinetic theory, if you do not change the amount of gas or its temperature but **decrease** the size of the container, the particles will strike the walls more often and the pressure will rise. When the size of the container is **larger**, the pressure is smaller because the **particles** hit the walls less often.

According to **Charles's** law, if a sample of gas is kept at constant **pressure**, the volume increases if the temperature is **increased**. Charles's measurements suggested that the **volume** of a gas would become zero at a temperature of –273°C. The temperature –273°C is called **absolute** zero. All gases become **liquids** when cooled to their **boiling** points.

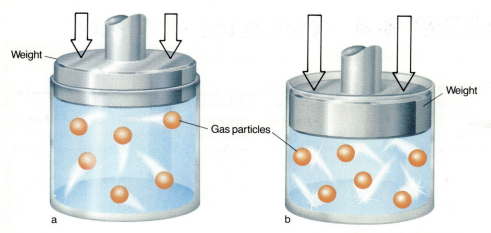

Weight

Gas particles

Weight

a

b

Boyle's Law

Suppose you have some gas in a sealed flexible container, such as a balloon. You can squeeze or stretch the container without changing the amount of gas trapped inside.

The pressure of a gas depends on how often its particles strike the walls of the container. If you squeeze some gas into a smaller space, its particles will strike the walls more often, giving an increased pressure. This behavior explains why when you squeeze a balloon into a smaller space, it causes the balloon to push back with more force. The reverse happens too. If you give the gas particles more space, they will hit the walls less often and the gas pressure will be reduced. Robert Boyle (1627-1691), a British scientist, described this property of gases. According to **Boyle's law,** if you decrease the volume of a container of gas, the pressure of the gas will increase, provided the temperature does not change. Increasing the volume causes pressure to drop. As you'll see, it is important that the temperature remain constant.

Charles's Law

If you've seen a hot-air balloon being inflated, you know gases expand when heated. Jacques Charles (1742-1823) was a French scientist who studied gases. According to **Charles's law,** the volume of a gas increases with increasing temperature, provided the pressure does not change. As with Boyle's law, the reverse is true, also. A

Figure 8-14. If you increase the pressure on air in an enclosed space (a), the volume of the air in the enclosed space decreases, (b).

❸

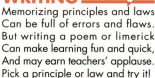

Science and WRITING

Memorizing principles and laws
Can be full of errors and flaws.
But writing a poem or limerick
Can make learning fun and quick,
And may earn teachers' applause.
Pick a principle or law and try it!

❹

205

TYING TO PREVIOUS KNOWLEDGE: Ask a student who swims frequently to describe the feeling he or she has when diving below the surface. The skin is sensitive to pressure only when it is not normal atmospheric pressure.

OBJECTIVES AND SCIENCE WORDS: Have students review the objectives and science words to become familiar with this section.

2 TEACH

Key Concepts are highlighted.

CONCEPT DEVELOPMENT

▶ **Demonstration:** Place an empty aluminum cola can containing 20 mL of water on a hot plate to boil. After the can has filled with steam, grasp it with tongs or a hot pad and quickly plunge the can *inverted* into a large beaker of ice water. Atmospheric pressure will quickly crush the can.

MINI QUIZ

Use the Mini Quiz to check students' recall of chapter content.

❶ **Force per unit area is a measure of _____.** *pressure*

❷ **Average sea level air pressure is _____ kPa.** *101.3*

❸ **With temperature held constant, when the volume of a gas increases, the pressure will _____ .** *decrease*

❹ **With pressure held constant, as a gas is heated, the volume will _____ .** *increase*

Science and WRITING

Cooperative Learning: Use the Problem Solving Team strategy here to cooperatively create a poem or limerick, such as:

Constant, rapid, random motion.
Not a liquid, not a lotion.
It's a gas.

For more information on research balloons, see "NASA's Giant Research Balloons Are Out of Sight," by James R. Chiles, *Smithsonian*, Jan. 1987, pp. 82-91.

Think Critically: Balloons are less expensive than rockets and satellites. Balloons can float within the atmosphere at a controlled altitude carrying instruments that can make measurements in the immediate surroundings, rather than observing the surroundings from above.

CONCEPT DEVELOPMENT

▶ Discuss with the class that a complete description of a gas will include the volume, mass, pressure, and temperature.

▶ Explain that the relationship between volume and pressure (Boyle's law) is inverse while the relationship between volume and absolute temperature (Charles's law) is direct.

CROSS CURRICULUM

▶ **Meteorology:** Bring an aneroid barometer to class. Have the students record the pressure each day and the outside weather conditions for several days. Ask them to search the data for correlations. They may observe that on days of low pressure it tends to be cloudy with precipitation while on days of high pressure it may be clear.

CHECK FOR UNDERSTANDING

Ask questions 1-2 and the **Apply** Question in the Section Review.

RETEACH

Have students place a small air sample in a re-sealable plastic bag in the freezer overnight. Remove the bag from the freezer, and with the bag sealed, warm it with a hair dryer. Have them explain their observations. Remind them of Charles's law if necessary.

EXTENSION

For students who have mastered this section, use the **Reinforcement** and **Enrichment** masters or other OPTIONS provided.

TECHNOLOGY

Gaseous Research Giants

Imagine a balloon so immense that, when fully inflated, it will hold a volume of gas equivalent to 168 Goodyear blimps! Scientists are sending such balloons into the stratosphere, the layer of the atmosphere that is above 99 percent of Earth's air. These giant balloons are filled with helium gas, which gives them their lift. One of these balloons may hoist a load higher than a cruising jumbo jet, but lower than an orbiting satellite in space. The initial volume of helium required to lift the load might be the size of a small house. In the stratosphere, the volume may reach the size of 283 of the houses!

Scientists use the balloons for research. For example, a load of equipment may gather data on how ozone gas is formed in the upper atmosphere. Ozone helps protect life by absorbing a dangerous form of energy given off by the sun. Because the sky is clear in the stratosphere, another load may be a telescope for studying the energy given off by the sun and other stars. Such studies help scientists understand the make-up and behavior of matter.

Think Critically: For some kinds of research, why do scientists launch giant balloons into the stratosphere instead of launching satellites into outer space where there is no air?

gas shrinks with decreasing temperature. Figure 8-15 shows a demonstration of Charles's law.

Using his law, Charles was able to calculate the temperature at which a gas would have a volume of zero. The kinetic theory would say that this is the temperature at which all particle motion of matter should stop. Charles found this temperature to be −273°C, or 0 K, also called absolute zero. In reality, gases cannot be cooled to zero volume. Instead, they condense to liquids when cooled to their boiling points.

OPTIONS

INQUIRY QUESTIONS

▶ **Scuba divers breathe compressed air. Will a full tank of air last longer if the diver is ten meters below the surface or is at twenty meters?** *ten meters*

▶ **When a helium-filled rubber balloon is released outdoors, will it break or come down to Earth intact? Explain your answer.** *The pressure on the balloon decreases with altitude. It will expand and burst.*

▶ **Yeast put into bread dough reacts with sugar to produce carbon dioxide gas, which becomes trapped in the dough. During baking, the yeast organisms are killed, but the bread continues to rise. Explain why.** *The trapped gas expands with increasing temperature.*

▶ **In theory, a gas at a temperature of absolute zero would have zero volume. Why would it never actually achieve this volume?** *It condenses into a liquid and freezes into a solid.*

You can explain Charles's law by using the kinetic theory of matter. As a gas is heated, its particles move faster and faster, and its temperature increases. Because the gas particles move faster, they begin to strike the walls of their container more often and with more force. If the walls are free to move, the gas pushes the walls out and expands.

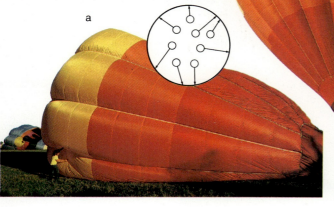

Figure 8-15. If you increase the temperature of the air in a balloon (a), the volume of the air in the balloon also increases (b).

SECTION REVIEW

1. When you bounce a basketball on the floor, the air pressure inside the ball increases for a moment. Explain why this increase occurs.
2. Why does a closed, empty 2-liter plastic soft-drink bottle "cave in" when placed in a freezer?
3. **Apply:** Labels on cylinders of compressed gases state the highest temperature to which the cylinder may be exposed. Give a reason for this warning.

☑ Hypothesizing

A bottle of ammonia begins to leak in an empty room. An hour later you walk into the room and can smell ammonia almost everywhere. The smell is stronger near the leaking bottle. State a hypothesis to explain your observations. If you need help, refer to Hypothesizing in the **Skill Handbook** on page 682.

Skill Builder

ENRICHMENT

▶ An air thermometer is a long tube filled with dry air. One end of the tube is sealed and the other end is connected to a pressure gauge that is calibrated to read degrees. Have students find out how this type of thermometer works. As temperature increases, the pressure inside the tube increases proportionally because of constant volume. (The tube itself expands very little.) Thus, it is possible to calibrate a pressure gauge to read in degrees.

PROGRAM RESOURCES

From the **Teacher Resource Package** use:
Activity Worksheets, page 5, Flex Your Brain.
Use **Laboratory Manual,** Behavior of Gases.

---

3 CLOSE

? FLEX Your Brain

Use the Flex Your Brain activity to have students explore BEHAVIOR OF GASES. This could be made more concrete by asking students to visualize the behavior of gases trapped in balloons or inflated balls during changes of temperature, pressure, or volume.

▶ Invite a local TV meteorologist to visit your classroom to discuss the relationship between atmospheric pressure and weather along with the causes for high and low pressure.

SECTION REVIEW ANSWERS

1. The ball is momentarily compressed to a smaller volume resulting in a momentary increase in pressure according to Boyle's law.
2. The air particles in the "empty" bottle decrease in average velocity as the temperature drops. Thus they collide less frequently with the walls of the bottle. The pressure inside the bottle decreases, but the atmospheric pressure on the outside remains the same. Because the walls are relatively flexible, the bottle decreases in volume according to Charles's law.
3. **Apply:** With increasing temperatures, gas particles move faster and faster, striking the walls of their container more frequently. If the walls are not free to move, the gas cannot expand. Thus, the pressure builds up instead, and the cylinder may explode. Every gas container will have a maximum safe pressure, thus a maximum safe temperature.

Skill Builder

The bottle of ammonia gives off ammonia gas. Gases are made of particles that spread farther and farther apart as they move from a bottle into a room. Thus, the ammonia is more concentrated near the bottle and less concentrated farther away.

ACTIVITY 8-2
40 minutes

OBJECTIVE: **Measure** and **infer** the relationship between the temperature and volume of a gas.

PROCESS SKILLS applied in this activity:
▶ **Measuring** in Procedure Steps 3, 6, 7, and 8.
▶ **Inferring** in Analyze Questions 1 and 2.
▶ **Predicting** in Conclude and Apply Question 4.

COOPERATIVE LEARNING
Use the Science Investigation group strategy with groups of four. One pair can handle the heating while another does the chilling.

TEACHING THE ACTIVITY
▶ **Troubleshooting:** Two balloons are used at room temperature so that one may be exposed to cold while the other is exposed to hot. If only one balloon is used for both extremes, there is a greater risk of breaking the balloon.
▶ Make sure students use tongs when holding the balloons over steam.
▶ When producing the graph, students may have to estimate the best straight line.
▶ A picnic ice chest works for the cold environment. A large beaker of boiling water on an electric hot plate works well for the hot environment.
▶ Students should use the average volume of the two room temperature balloons for the medium temperature data.
▶ Review with students how to cube a number. The volume formula is derived from
$V = 4/3 \ \pi r^3$ and $r = C/2\pi$

ACTIVITY 8-2
Temperature and Volume Relations

Problem: *How is volume of air affected by changing temperature?*

Materials
- string
- marking pen
- meterstick
- container of ice water
- tongs
- heat-proof glove or tongs
- beaker of boiling water
- thermometer
- goggles
- 2 medium, round balloons

Procedure
1. Copy the data table. Measure and record the room temperature.
2. Inflate two balloons to about the same size and tie them closed.
3. Use string to measure the circumference of each balloon at room temperature. For later use, place an ink dot where the string went around each balloon. Then use a meterstick to measure the length of the string.
4. Cube the circumference and then divide by 59 to find volume: $V = c^3/59$.
5. Place one balloon in ice water for 5 minutes. Measure and record the temperature of the ice water.
6. Remove the balloon and quickly use the string to measure the new circumference, using the ink dot as a guide, as shown in the drawings.
7. Using a heat-proof glove, place the second balloon in the steam above boiling water for 5 minutes. **CAUTION:** *Steam causes burns.* Measure and record the temperature of the steam.
8. Repeat Step 6 for this balloon.

Data and Observations Sample Data

State	Circumference	Volume	Temperature
Room	36 cm	780 cm^3	24°C
Cold	33 cm	609 cm^3	1°C
Hot	42 cm	1256 cm^3	98°C

Analyze
1. Using the temperatures and volumes in your data table, make a line graph. What is the relationship between the temperature and volume of a gas?
2. Your graph should suggest a straight line. If you extended the line to zero volume, to what temperature would it correspond?

Conclude and Apply
3. Using the kinetic theory, explain how the movements of air particles inside each balloon are causing the volume to change.
4. Aerosol cans often bear the warning "Do not incinerate, contents under pressure." How can you apply what you have seen in this activity to explain this caution?

208 SOLIDS, LIQUIDS, AND GASES

ANSWERS TO QUESTIONS

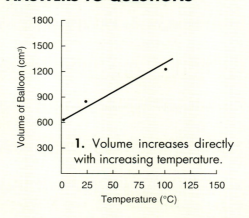

1. Volume increases directly with increasing temperature.

2. absolute zero, −273°C
3. Particles move faster with increasing temperature. Thus, they strike the wall of the balloon more frequently and with more force. Because the wall is flexible, the balloon expands. Cooling the gas gives the opposite effect.
4. The aerosol can is not free to expand like the balloon. Therefore, the gas pressure inside would increase instead. Soon the strength of the metal is exceeded and the can explodes.

Uses of Fluids

Objectives

▶ State Archimedes' principle and predict whether an object will sink or float in water.

▶ State Pascal's principle and describe the operation of a machine that uses Pascal's principle.

▶ State Bernoulli's principle and describe a way that Bernoulli's principle is applied.

New Science Words

buoyant force
Archimedes' principle
Pascal's principle
Bernoulli's principle

Archimedes' Principle

Have you ever relaxed by floating quietly on your back in a swimming pool? You seem weightless as the water supports you. If you climb slowly out of the pool you feel as if you gain weight. The farther out you climb, the more you have to use your muscles to support yourself. When you were in the pool, you experienced buoyancy. Buoyancy is the ability of a fluid—a liquid or a gas—to exert an upward force on an object immersed in it. This force is called **buoyant force.**

The amount of buoyant force determines whether an object will sink or float in a fluid. If the buoyant force is

Figure 8-16. Forces acting on person lying on the floor beside a pool (a) and in water (b).

Weight

Support force from floor

Weight

Buoyant force from water

8-5   USES OF FLUIDS   **209**

PREPARATION

SECTION BACKGROUND

▶ An object's density, not its weight, determines whether it will sink or float.

▶ As with any other machines, those that employ Pascal's principle are limited in that the work done by the machine cannot be greater than the work done on the machine.

▶ Bernoulli's principle applies to both liquids and gases.

PREPLANNING

▶ Check the margin for materials needed in the demonstrations to determine in advance which ones you will choose to do.

1 MOTIVATE

▶ **Demonstration:** Place an egg in a beaker of tap water. It sinks. Place another egg in a beaker of saturated salt solution. It floats. Discuss swimming in a freshwater pool and in the ocean as it relates to buoyancy.

▶ **Demonstration:** Use a toy airplane glider, and show the difference between dropping it and throwing it. When the wing moves forward, lift is created by the air flow.

TYING TO PREVIOUS KNOWLEDGE: Ask students to recall when they have seen hydraulic or pneumatic devices being used. Common examples are bulldozers, jackhammers, door closers, and pneumatic impact tools. All of these devices make use of Pascal's principle.

OBJECTIVES AND SCIENCE WORDS: Have students review the objectives and science words to become familiar with this section.

OPTIONS

INQUIRY QUESTIONS

▶ **Air-filled soap bubbles sink at a slower rate than a small balloon of equal size. Explain why.** *Buoyant force acts on both. However, the rubber compresses the air and adds more weight. Therefore, the net downward force is greater on the balloon.*

▶ **When a weather balloon is released, it is partially filled with helium gas. Describe what happens to the balloon's volume as it goes up.** *Atmospheric pressure decreases; volume increases.*

PROGRAM RESOURCES

From the **Teacher Recource Package** use:

Critical Thinking/Problem Solving, page 14, Hydraulics.

Transparency Masters, pages 31-32, Archimedes' Principle.

Use **Color Transparency** number 16, Archimedes' Principle.

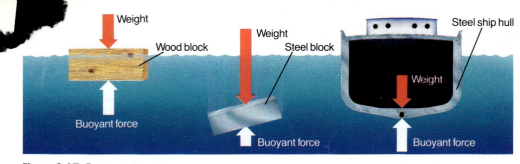

Figure 8-17. Forces acting on a wood block, a steel block, and a steel ship hull in water.

2 TEACH

Key Concepts are highlighted.

CONCEPT DEVELOPMENT

▶ Discuss with your class how each of the following demonstrations makes Archimedes' principle visible. Use the principle to explain why the various objects sink or float.

▶ **Demonstration:** Place an unopened can of diet cola and a can of non-diet cola in a water-filled aquarium. The can of sugar-free cola is less dense and will float. Make sure cans are aluminum, not steel.

▶ **Demonstration:** Connect rubber tubing to the stem of a small funnel. Connect the tubing to a natural gas jet and dip the funnel in a bubble-blowing liquid. Turn on the gas to produce methane-filled soap bubbles. Gently shake the bubbles from the funnel and watch them rise. Methane, CH_4, is much less dense than air.

▶ **Demonstration:** Place an ice cube in a beaker of water. It floats. Place an ice cube in a beaker of alcohol. It sinks.

MINI-Lab

Materials: dropper, 2-liter plastic soda bottle

Teaching Tips

▶ Adjust the dropper in a beaker or wide-mouth jar before placing it in the bottle.

▶ This activity illustrates both Archimedes' and Pascal's principles. Have students account for their observations using both principles.

Answers to Questions

▶ As more water enters the dropper, the density increases.

▶ The pressure on the bottle is transmitted evenly throughout. The pressure forces more water into the dropper, and it sinks.

PROGRAM RESOURCES

From the **Teacher Recource Package** use:

Activity Worksheets, page 70, Mini-Lab: How does applied pressure affect different areas of a fluid?

MINI-Lab

How does applied pressure affect different areas of a fluid?
Draw water into a dropper and place it into a water-filled 2-L soft drink bottle. Suck in or squeeze out water from the dropper until it just barely floats. How does increasing the amount of water inside the dropper affect its density? Put the cap back on the bottle. Squeeze the bottle. What is the effect of applied pressure on the dropper?

210 SOLIDS, LIQUIDS, AND GASES

less than the object's weight, the object will sink. If the buoyant force equals the object's weight, the object floats. Sometimes the buoyant force on an object is greater than its weight. This force is what seems to pull a helium-filled balloon upward in the air. When the balloon is released, the unbalanced buoyant force causes the balloon to accelerate upward.

① Archimedes, a Greek mathematician who lived in the third century B.C. made a discovery about buoyancy. According to **Archimedes' principle**, the buoyant force on an object in a fluid is equal to the weight of the fluid displaced by the object. If you place a block of pine wood in water, it will push water out of the way as it begins to sink—but only until the weight of the water it displaces equals the block's weight. The block floats at this level, as shown in Figure 8-17.

Suppose you drop a solid steel block the same size as the wood block into water. When the steel block is placed into the water, the steel block begins to push aside water as it sinks. Buoyant force begins to push up on the block. However, the density of steel is much greater than that of wood. So the buoyant force never becomes great enough to equal the weight of the steel block, and it sinks to the bottom.

How, then, does a steel ship float? Suppose you formed the steel block into a large hollowed-out bowl shape. As this shape sinks into water, it displaces much more water than the solid block. Soon, it displaces enough water to equal the weight of the steel, and it floats.

Pascal's Principle

If you dive underwater, you can feel the pressure of the water all around you. You live at the bottom of Earth's atmosphere, which also is a fluid that exerts a pressure.

OPTIONS

Meeting Different Ability Levels

For Section 8-5, use the following **Teacher Resource Masters** depending upon individual students' needs.

◆ **Study Guide Master** for all students.

● **Reinforcement Master** for students of average and above average ability levels.

▲ **Enrichment Master** for above average students.

Additional Teacher Resource Package masters are listed in the OPTIONS box throughout the section. The additional masters are appropriate for all students.

◆ **STUDY GUIDE** 38

STUDY GUIDE   Chapter 8
Uses of Fluids   Text Pages 209–214

Match the definitions in Column II with the terms in Columns I. Write the letter of the correct definition on the blank on the left.

	Column I		Column II
b	1. fluid	a.	the ability of a fluid to exert an upward force on an object immersed in it
e	2. Archimedes' principle	b.	a gas or a liquid
d	3. pressure	c.	Pressure applied to a fluid is transmitted unchanged throughout the fluid.
f	4. hydraulic lift	d.	force per unit area
g	5. Bernoulli's principle	e.	The buoyant force on an object in a fluid is equal to the weight of the fluid displaced by the object.
a	6. buoyancy	f.	operates on Pascal's principle
c	7. Pascal's principle	g.	As the velocity of a fluid increases, the pressure exerted by the fluid decreases.

Use the words in the list to fill in the blanks.

Bernoulli's   Archimedes'   less   faster   farther   floats
hydraulic   piston   buoyant force   pressure   areas
sinks   liquid   connected   Pascal's   upward

The amount of ____buoyant force____ determines whether an object will sink or float in a fluid. If the buoyant force is less than an object's weight, the object ____sinks____.

If the buoyant force equals an object's weight, the object ____floats____.

____Archimedes'____ principle can be used to explain the buoyant force on an object submerged in a fluid.

Machines such as a ____hydraulic____ lifts that multiply forces use ____Pascal's____ principle. In a hydraulic lift, a ____liquid____ is placed in two ____connected____ cylinders. Each cylinder has a ____piston____ that can move up and down. Also, the cylinders have different cross sectional ____areas____. In this device, the ____pressure____ on each piston will be the same. However, the force will be greater on the piston with larger area.

____Bernoulli's____ principle explains why a pitched baseball curves and how airplanes fly. Air travels ____farther____ over the top of the wing than over the bottom. Thus, the air travels ____faster____ over the top of the wing than over the bottom. Pressure above the wing is ____less____ than pressure below it. There is net ____upward____ force on the wing.

38   Copyright Glencoe Division of Macmillan/McGraw-Hill
                       Users of Merrill Physical Science have the publisher's permission to reproduce this page.

210 CHAPTER 8

This pressure is also all around you, even though you don't feel it. Blaise Pascal (1623-1662), a French scientist, discovered a useful property of fluids. **Pascal's** **principle** states that pressure applied to a fluid is transmitted unchanged throughout the fluid. For example, when you squeeze one end of a balloon, the balloon pops out on the other end. When you squeeze one end of a toothpaste tube, toothpaste emerges from the other end.

State Pascal's principle.

Figure 8-18. When you apply pressure on one end of an inflated balloon, the pressure is transmitted throughout the fluid—that is, the air—in the balloon.

Hydraulic machines that move very heavy loads use Pascal's principle. Maybe you've a seen car raised using a hydraulic lift. Look at Figure 8-19 to see how a machine of this type works. A small cylinder and a large cylinder are connected by a pipe. The cross section of the small cylinder has an area of 5 cm². The cross section of the large cylinder is 50 cm². Each cylinder is filled with a hydraulic fluid, usually oil, and has a piston that rests on the oil's surface.

Suppose you apply 500 N of force to the small piston. Therefore the pressure on the small piston is:

$$P = F/A = 500 \text{ N}/5 \text{ cm}^2 = 100 \text{ N/cm}^2.$$

Pascal's principle says that this pressure is transferred unchanged throughout the liquid. Therefore, the large piston will also have a pressure of 100 N/cm² applied to it. But the area of the large piston is 50 cm². So, the total force on the large piston is 100 N/cm² × 50 cm² = 5000 N. With this hydraulic machine, you could use your weight to lift something ten times as heavy as yourself. What action must be increased when using this machine?

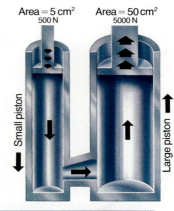

Figure 8-19. A hydraulic lift is a machine that makes use of Pascal's principle.

Area = 5 cm²
500 N

Area = 50 cm²
5000 N

Small piston

Large piston

211

CHECK FOR UNDERSTANDING
Use the Mini Quiz to check for understanding.

MINI QUIZ

Use the Mini Quiz to check students' recall of chapter content.

❶ **The cause of buoyant force was first explained by _____ .** *Archimedes*

❷ **The discovery that pressure is exerted in all directions throughout a fluid was made by _____ .** *Pascal*

❸ **Hydraulic jacks that move heavy loads make use of _____ principle.** *Pascal's*

RETEACH
Have students test several objects that sink or float in water. Encourage students to explain why each object sinks or floats. Have students use density, volume, and mass in their explanations.

EXTENSION
For students who have mastered this section, use the Reinforcement and Enrichment masters or other OPTIONS provided.

STUDENT TEXT QUESTION
▶ Page 211, paragraph 4: **What action must be increased when using a hydraulic lift?** *the distance the effort force moves*

CONCEPT DEVELOPMENT

▶ Use the following demonstrations to illustrate Bernoulli's principle.

▶ **Demonstration:** Connect the hose to the exhaust side of a wet vac. Use a vertical stream of air to support a ping pong ball.

▶ **Demonstration:** Connect a water aspirator to a lab sink's faucet. Connect about a meter of tubing to the aspirator arm. Turn on the water and allow students to experience the low pressure created by the rapid flow of water through the wasp-waisted shape of the aspirator's venturi.

CROSS CURRICULUM

▶ **History:** Ask three students to research the scientists studied in this section. Have them report on the weapons of war, means of transportation, and general living conditions in each scientist's country during his lifetime. Archimedes (287-212 B.C., Greece); Blaise Pascal (1623-1662, France); Daniel Bernoulli (1700-1782, Switzerland)

PROGRAM RESOURCES

From the **Teacher Resource Package** use:

Technology, pages 11-12, How Are Oil Spills Cleaned Up?

Bernoulli's Principle

It took humans thousands of years to learn to do what birds do naturally—fly, glide, and soar. Obviously it was no simple task to build a machine that could lift itself off the ground and fly with people aboard. The ability of an airplane to rise into the air is an example of another property of fluids called Bernoulli's principle. Daniel Bernoulli (1700-1782) was a Swiss scientist who studied the properties of moving fluids such as water and air. He published his discovery in 1738. According to **Bernoulli's principle**, as the velocity of a fluid increases, the pressure exerted by the fluid decreases.

Figure 8-20. If you hang a piece of paper and then blow across its surface, the paper rises.

To demonstrate Bernoulli's principle, blow across the surface of a sheet of paper, as in Figure 8-20. The paper will rise. The velocity of the air you blew over the top surface of the paper is greater than that of the quiet air below it. As a result, the downward air pressure above the paper decreases. The higher air pressure below the paper exerts a net force that pushes the paper upward.

OPTIONS

ENRICHMENT

▶ Use tape and rubber bands to seal a plastic garbage bag around a wet-vac hose attached to the exhaust side. Place a cafeteria tray on top of the flattened plastic bag. Place a large mass on the tray and raise it by inflating the bag. Fire rescue trucks use air bags to upright flipped cars and trucks at an accident scene.

▶ If the auto shop at your local vocational school has a hydraulic lift, arrange for your students to see it in operation. Point out that, unlike the idealized diagram shown in the text, the lift has no single narrow column. Rather, there may be a reciprocating piston and a valve system that allow more oil to enter on each stroke. Also, there may be other types of oil pressure pumps.

Figure 8-21. The design of airplane wings is an application of Bernoulli's principle.

Now look at the curvature of the airplane wing in Figure 8-21. As the wing moves forward, the air passing over the wing must travel farther than air passing below it. Yet all the air takes the same time to get to the rear of the wing. Therefore, air must travel faster over the top of the wing than below it. Consequently, the pressure above the wing is less than the pressure below it. The result is a net upward force on the wing. This upward force makes up most of the force that lifts an airplane in flight.

Baseball pitchers also take advantage of Bernoulli's principle. If the pitcher puts a spin on the ball, air moves faster along the side of the ball that is spinning away from the direction of the throw. Look at Figure 8-22 on the next page. The ball's spin results in a net force that pushes the ball toward the low-pressure direction. The force gives the ball an unexpected curve that the pitcher hopes the batter won't be able to predict.

Fluids flow faster when forced to flow through narrow spaces. As a result of this speed increase, the pressure of the fluid drops. This reduction in pressure in these spaces is a special case of Bernoulli's principle called the Venturi effect. A dramatic demonstration of the Venturi effect

How does a difference in air pressure help an airplane to fly?

CONCEPT DEVELOPMENT
▶ If someone in your school is an expert baseball pitcher, ask him or her to demonstrate the various pitches that take advantage of Bernoulli's principle. This is probably best done outdoors.
🖼 **Cooperative Learning:** Organize Science Investigation teams to design a paper airplane that can be folded from a single sheet of paper. Have teams compare their planes for longest distance, duration of flight, and height of flight. Several books on constructing paper airplanes have been published. One is *Paper Airplane Book,* published in 1985 by the AAAS.

CROSS CURRICULUM
▶ **Geology:** Have a student form a sloping stream bed out of wet sand. Have the width of the stream bed vary. Notice that water speeds up as it passes through the narrow area (Venturi effect). Have students notice the rate of erosion of the banks.

ENRICHMENT
▶ Have students determine the masses of several small objects. Include objects that will sink and float in water. Place each object in a graduated cylinder half filled with water. Be sure students record the volume readings before and after immersion of the object. Record the volume of the water displaced. Using the density of water 1 gram/milliliter, determine the mass of the water displaced. Compare this value with the mass of each object. Students should discover that objects that float displace their mass in water, while objects that sink displace less.

▶ The density of a submarine can be varied by filling areas with water or air. Have a student research and report on how submarines surface and dive.

▶ Submarines, like airplanes, also have control surfaces that use Bernoulli's principle. A student could research how these surfaces aid in steering, diving, and stabilization.

CHECK FOR UNDERSTANDING

Ask questions 1-3 and the **Apply** Question in the Section Review.

RETEACH

Flight simulators that run on PCs are popular and available. Have students work with a simulator to make the plane climb, dive, bank, and so on. Challenge them to explain how Bernoulli's principle plays a part in the maneuvers.

EXTENSION

For students who have mastered this section, use the **Reinforcement** and **Enrichment** masters or other OPTIONS provided.

3 CLOSE

 FLEX Your Brain

Use Flex Your Brain activity to have students explore PROPERTIES OF FLUIDS.

SECTION REVIEW ANSWERS

1. Shape the concrete into a hollowed-out boat shape so that it displaces its weight in water before sinking.

2. The machine in the example multiplies forces by ten. Therefore, a force of 2000 N would have to be applied to the small piston.

3. As the velocity of a fluid increases, the pressure exerted by the fluid decreases. Air is a fluid. An airplane's wing is shaped such that air flows at a greater velocity over its upper surface. The difference in pressure above and below the wing creates a net upward force that helps lift the plane.

4. Apply: The air in the balloon is compressed compared to normal air and thus has a greater density. The weight of the denser air along with the weight of the rubber itself is greater than the buoyant force of the surrounding air. Therefore, the balloon sinks.

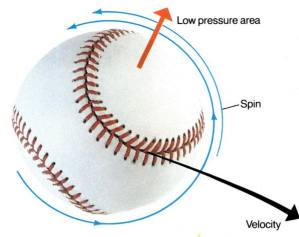

Figure 8-22. Air moves faster along the side of a spinning ball that is moving away from the direction of the throw.

has occurred in cities where the wind is forced to blow between rows of skyscrapers. The reduced air pressure outside of buildings during strong winds has caused windows to be forced out by the higher air pressure inside the buildings.

SECTION REVIEW

1. How is it possible that a boat made of concrete can float?
2. If you wanted to lift an object weighing 20 000 N, how much force would you have to apply to the small piston in Figure 8-19?
3. State Bernoulli's principle and tell how it helps produce lift on an airplane.
4. **Apply:** If you blow up a balloon with air and release it, it will fall to the floor. Why does it fall instead of floating?

 **Skill Builder** ☑ **Measuring in SI**

The density of water is 1.0 g/cm³. How many kilograms of water does a submerged 120-cm³ block displace? One kilogram weighs 9.8 N. What is the buoyant force on the block? If you need help, refer to Chapter 2 and to Measuring in SI in the **Skill Handbook** on page 680.

Skill Builder

A submerged block of 120 cm³ displaces 120 cm³ of water. The mass of water displaced is therefore 120 cm³ × 1.0 g/cm³ = 120 g. Converting to kilograms, 120 g ÷ 1000 g/kg = 0.12 kg. The buoyant force on the block is then 0.12 kg × 9.8 N/kg = 1.2 N.

You can extend the Skill Builder by posing the following question. **Suppose the mass of the block is 90 grams. If a diver carries it underwater, will it float or sink?** *It will float because the downward force of gravity is about 0.9 N, which is less than the upward buoyant force.*

SUMMARY

8-1: Matter and Temperature
1. There are four states of matter: solid, liquid, gas, and plasma.
2. According to the kinetic theory, all matter is made of constantly moving particles.
3. Most matter expands when heated and contracts when cooled.

8-2: Science and Society: Water—Earth's Vital Liquid
1. Fresh water on Earth is scarce, and this water is often wasted or polluted.
2. There are many ways in which people can save water and stop its pollution.

8-3: Changes in State
1. Changes of state can be interpreted in terms of the kinetic theory of matter.
2. The energy of the heat of fusion and vaporization overcomes attractive forces between particles of matter.

8-4: Behavior of Gases
1. The pressure of a gas is caused by collisions of its moving particles.
2. Boyle's law states that the volume of a gas decreases when the pressure increases, at constant temperature.
3. Charles's law states that the volume of a gas increases when the temperature increases, at constant pressure.

8-5: Uses of Fluids
1. Archimedes' principle states that the buoyant force on an object in a fluid is equal to the weight of the fluid displaced.
2. Pascal's principle states that pressure applied to a fluid is transmitted unchanged throughout the fluid.
3. Bernoulli's principle states that the pressure exerted by a fluid decreases as its velocity increases.

KEY SCIENCE WORDS

a. **Archimedes' principle**
b. **Bernoulli's principle**
c. **Boyle's law**
d. **buoyant force**
e. **Charles's law**
f. **condensation**
g. **crystals**
h. **evaporation**
i. **heat of fusion**
j. **heat of vaporization**
k. **kinetic theory of matter**
l. **pascal**
m. **Pascal's principle**
n. **plasma**
o. **polluted water**
p. **pressure**
q. **states of matter**
r. **thermal expansion**

UNDERSTANDING VOCABULARY

Match each phrase with the correct term from the list of Key Science Words.

1. the volume of a gas is reduced when the temperature is decreased
2. water that is dirty and unfit for living things
3. liquid changes to gas below the boiling point
4. amount of force exerted per unit of area
5. the buoyant force on an object in a fluid equals the weight of the displaced fluid
6. the SI unit of pressure
7. particles are arranged in regular patterns
8. a gaslike mixture of charged particles
9. matter is made of tiny, moving particles
10. energy needed for a liquid to boil

SUMMARY

Have students read the summary statements to review the major concepts of the chapter.

UNDERSTANDING VOCABULARY

1. e
2. o
3. h
4. p
5. a
6. l
7. g
8. n
9. k
10. j

OPTIONS

ASSESSMENT
To assess student understanding of material in this chapter, use the resources listed.

👥 COOPERATIVE LEARNING
Consider using cooperative learning in the THINK AND WRITE CRITICALLY, APPLY, and MORE SKILL BUILDERS sections of the Chapter Review.

PROGRAM RESOURCES
From the **Teacher Resource Package** use:
Chapter Review, pages 19 to 20.
Chapter and Unit Tests, pages 53-56, Chapter Test.

CHAPTER REVIEW

CHECKING CONCEPTS

1.	a	**6.**	a
2.	d	**7.**	a
3.	c	**8.**	b
4.	b	**9.**	d
5.	c	**10.**	c

UNDERSTANDING CONCEPTS

11. amorphous
12. condensation
13. Pascal's
14. temperature
15. Charles's

THINK AND WRITE CRITICALLY

16. Some water is suitable for watering plants, gardens, and lawns. Some used wash water is suitable for presoaking clothes yet to be washed. Other answers are possible.

17. Since gases can be squeezed into smaller spaces, more gas can be added to a room, no matter how much is already present.

18. The hot tea transfers energy to particles in the glass and the ice. The tea cools, because its particles now have a lower average kinetic energy. The glass warms as its particles absorb energy from the tea. The ice absorbs energy from the tea. Ice will melt after its temperature is raised to 0°C and energy equal to its heat of fusion is absorbed.

19. Water vapor in the air is cooled by the glass. The particles lose energy and condense.

20. The deeper water exerts a much greater buoyant force on your body, reducing the downward force of your feet on the rocks.

CHAPTER REVIEW

CHECKING CONCEPTS

Choose the word or phrase that completes the sentence.

1. The temperature at which all particle motion of matter would stop is _____.
   a. absolute zero **c.** 0°C
   b. its melting point **d.** 273°C

2. The state of matter that has a definite volume and a definite shape is _____.
   a. gas **c.** plasma
   b. liquid **d.** solid

3. The most common state of matter is _____.
   a. gas **c.** plasma
   b. liquid **d.** solid

4. Most pressure is measured in _____.
   a. grams **c.** newtons
   b. kilopascals **d.** pascals

5. Pascal's principle is the basis for _____.
   a. aerodynamics **c.** hydraulics
   b. buoyancy **d.** changes of state

6. Bernoulli's principle explains why _____.
   a. airplanes fly **c.** pistons work
   b. boats float **d.** ice melts

7. Particles separate completely from each other in a(n) _____.
   a. gas **c.** solid
   b. liquid **d.** amorphous material

8. The state of the matter in the sun and other stars is primarily _____.
   a. amorphous **c.** liquid
   b. plasma **d.** gas

9. In general, as a solid is heated, it _____.
   a. becomes a gas **c.** contracts
   b. condenses **d.** expands

10. A material's heat of fusion gives the amount of energy needed to _____.
    a. condense a gas **c.** melt a solid
    b. boil a liquid **d.** evaporate a liquid

216 SOLIDS, LIQUIDS, AND GASES

UNDERSTANDING CONCEPTS

Complete each sentence.

11. Materials that appear to be solid but are not made of crystals are _____.

12. _____ is the process by which a gas changes to a liquid.

13. The fact that pressure applied to a fluid is transmitted unchanged throughout the fluid is _____ principle.

14. The state of a sample of matter depends on its _____.

15. When a balloon is placed in warmer air, its volume increases. This is an example of _____ law.

THINK AND WRITE CRITICALLY

16. How might waste water in the home be recycled instead of being poured into the sewer system?

17. Why would it be incorrect to say, "This room is full of air"?

18. What energy changes occur when hot tea is poured over ice?

19. Use the kinetic theory to explain why liquid water forms on the outside of a glass of cold lemonade.

20. Why might rocks in a creek hurt your feet more than the same rocks would in deeper water?

21. Use Charles's and Boyle's laws to explain why you should check your tire pressure when the temperature changes.
22. Explain how food might get "freezer burn." How might you prevent it?
23. Alcohol evaporates more quickly than does water. What can you tell about the forces between the alcohol particles?
24. Why do aerosol cans have a "do not incinerate" warning?
25. Applying pressure lowers the melting point of ice. Why might an icy road at −1°C be more dangerous than an icy road at −10°C?

MORE SKILL BUILDERS

If you need help, refer to the Skill Handbook.

1. **Observing and Inferring:** Infer the effect related to air pressure that a large truck passing a small car would have on the car.
2. **Making and Using Graphs:** A group of students heated ice until it melted and then turned to steam. They measured the temperature each minute and graphed the results. Their graph is provided below. In terms of the energy involved, explain what is happening at each letter (a, b, c, d) in the graph.

3. **Sequencing:** Sequence the processes that occur when ice is heated until it becomes steam and then the steam is cooled until it is ice again.
4. **Interpreting Data:** As elevation increases, boiling point decreases. List each of the following locations as at sea level, above sea level, or below sea level. (Boiling point of water in °C is given.)
   Death Valley (100.3), Denver (94), Madison (99), Mt. Everest (76.5), Mt. McKinley (79), New York City (100), Salt Lake City (95.6), San Francisco (100)
5. **Recognizing Cause and Effect:** List possible effects for each of the following causes.
   a. Perspiration evaporates.
   b. Pressure on a balloon decreases.
   c. Your buoyant force equals your weight.

PROJECTS

1. What would happen to an unprotected person at the bottom of the ocean or in outer space? Research the effects of pressure changes on the human body and write a report.
2. Research crystal growing and what conditions are needed to grow a perfect crystal. Grow crystals of several different materials and display them.

SOLIDS, LIQUIDS, AND GASES **217**

21. According to Charles's law, as the temperature of a gas changes, so does the volume. As the volume changes, so does the pressure, according to Boyle's law. Point out that "bleeding" hot tires to lower the pressure is not advisable.
22. Ice in the food sublimes, drying out the food. This can be prevented by wrapping the food in airtight packaging such as foil or by using heavy plastic containers.
23. The forces between the water particles are probably stronger than those between the alcohol particles.
24. According to Charles's law, as temperature increases, gases tend to expand. However, since the can is not free to expand, pressure builds up and the can may explode.
25. If the ice is just below its normal melting point, pressure, such as that applied by tires, will melt it and form a slippery layer of liquid water on the ice. At lower temperatures, the pressure of the tires may not be enough to melt the ice.

MORE SKILL BUILDERS

1. **Observing and Inferring:** When the car and truck are side by side, the space between them is narrow. The air passing through this space must travel faster. This lowers the air pressure and the higher pressure, on the other side of the car pushes the car toward the truck.
2. **Making and Using Graphs:**
   a. Ice is warming to its melting point.
   b. Ice is absorbing energy equal to its heat of fusion. Ice melts.
   c. Liquid water warms.
   d. Liquid absorbs energy equal to its heat of vaporization. Liquid boils.
3. **Sequencing:** melting, boiling, condensation, freezing
4. **Interpreting Data:** Above: Denver, Madison, Mt. Everest, Mt. McKinley, Salt Lake City
   At: New York City, San Francisco
   Below: Death Valley
5. **Cause and Effect:** Student answers may vary. Sample answers are given.
   a. Skin feels cooler.
   b. Volume increases.
   c. You float.

9 Classification of Matter

CHAPTER SECTION	OBJECTIVES	ACTIVITIES
9-1 Composition of Matter (2 days)	1. **Distinguish** between substances and mixtures. 2. **Compare** and **contrast** solutions, colloids, and suspensions.	**Activity 9-1:** *Elements, Compounds, and Mixtures,* p. 225
9-2 Smog, A Mixture in the Environment Science & Society (1 day)	1. **Identify** smog as a harmful colloid by its properties. 2. **Describe** how smog is formed and suggest several ways to eliminate it.	
9-3 Describing Matter (2 days)	1. **Give examples** of physical properties. 2. **Distinguish** between physical and chemical changes. 3. **Distinguish** between chemical and physical properties. 4. **State** and **explain** the law of conservation of mass.	**Activity 9-2:** *A Chemical Change,* p. 236
Chapter Review		

ACTIVITY MATERIALS

FIND OUT	ACTIVITIES		MINI-LABS	
Page 219 crushed calcium carbonate tablets (10 g) 20 g sand 30 g small gravel 5 g water paper cup	**9-1 Elements, Compounds, and Mixtures, p. 225** plastic freezer bag containing tagged items: copper foil small package of salt piece of solder aluminum foil baking soda in a vial piece of granite sugar water in a vial	**9-2 A Chemical Change, p. 236** goggles 0.5 g baking soda small evaporating dish hand lens 1 cm³ of 1M hydro- chloric acid 10 cm³ graduated cylinder electric hot plate		

CHAPTER FEATURES	TEACHER RESOURCE PACKAGE	OTHER RESOURCES
Problem Solving: *Jason Makes a Colloid,* p. 223 **Skill Builder:** *Concept Mapping,* p. 224	**Ability Level Worksheets** ◆ **Study Guide,** p. 39 ● **Reinforcement,** p. 39 ▲ **Enrichment,** p. 39 **Activity Worksheet,** pp. 72, 73 **Concept Mapping,** pp. 23, 24 **Transparency Masters,** pp. 33, 34	**Color Transparency 17,** Classification of Matter **Lab Manual 20,** Chromatography
You Decide! p. 227	**Ability Level Worksheets** ◆ **Study Guide,** p. 40 ● **Reinforcement,** p. 40 ▲ **Enrichment,** p. 40	
Technology: *Aerogels—Next to Nothing at All,* p. 231 **Skill Builder:** *Observing and Inferring,* p. 235	**Ability Level Worksheets** ◆ **Study Guide,** p. 41 ● **Reinforcement,** p. 41 ▲ **Enrichment,** p. 41 **Activity Worksheet,** pp. 74, 75 **Critical Thinking/Problem Solving,** p. 15 **Cross-Curricular Connections,** p. 13 **Science and Society,** p. 13 **Transparency Masters,** pp. 35, 36	**Color Transparency 18,** Conservation of Matter **Lab Manual 21,** Properties of Matter
Summary Think & Write Critically Key Science Words Apply Understanding Vocabulary More Skill Builders Checking Concepts Projects Understanding Concepts	**Chapter Review,** pp. 21, 22 **Chapter Test,** pp. 57-60	**Chapter Review Software** **Test Bank**

◆ **Basic**   ● **Average**   ▲ **Advanced**

ADDITIONAL MATERIALS		
SOFTWARE	**AUDIOVISUAL**	**BOOKS/MAGAZINES**
Structure of Matter, Classroom Consortia Media. *Solutions,* J&S Software. *Physical or Chemical,* EME.	*Mixtures, Solutions, and Compounds,* filmloop, Science Software. *Solution Process and Theory,* filmstrip, Science Software. *Pollution of the Upper and Lower Atmosphere,* video, LCA.	Cornell, John. *Experiments with Mixtures.* 2nd ed. New York: Wiley, John & Sons, Inc., 1990. Matsubara, T. *The Structure and Properties of Matter.* New York: Springer-Verlag New York Inc., 1982. Zubrowski, Bernie. *Messing Around with Baking Chemistry: A Children's Museum Activity Book.* Boston, MA: Little, Brown & Co., 1981.

THEME DEVELOPMENT: Patterns of change is one of the major themes emphasized in this text. In Chapter 9 the student learns to classify matter by observing the patterns that occur when it undergoes physical and chemical change.

CHAPTER OVERVIEW

▶ **Section 9-1:** This section introduces the student to the vocabulary used by scientists when classifying matter. Also, it distinguishes between true substances and various kinds of mixtures.

▶ **Section 9-2: Science and Society:** Students learn how smog is made. The class will be asked to think about long-term solutions to air pollution.

▶ **Section 9-3:** Physical and chemical properties and physical and chemical changes are described and related to the students' daily living in this section.

CHAPTER VOCABULARY

element
compounds
substance
heterogeneous mixture
homogeneous mixture
solution
colloid
suspension
Tyndall effect
smog
physical property
physical change
chemical change
chemical property
law of conservation of mass

CHAPTER

9 Classification of Matter

218

OPTIONS

For Your Gifted Students

Have students add equal amounts of soil, clay, sand, gravel, and pebbles into a gallon jar. Enough water should be added so the jar is almost full. Students should stir or shake the mixture thoroughly and then observe. Have them predict the order in which the materials will settle and explain why. They should prepare a list of variables that would control the rate of settling. Have them test salt water, hot water, and cold water to see if the order and rate of deposition changes. Can they reseparate the sediment using filter paper and screens?

Did you ever watch a construction crew pour concrete for a building? What is this material? Actually, you can't classify fresh concrete as one of the states of matter. Rather, it is a mixture of solids—portland cement, sand, rocks—and a liquid, water.

FIND OUT!

Do this activity to make some classroom concrete and observe its properties.

Mix together 10 g of crushed calcium carbonate tablets; 20 g of sand; 30 g of small, clean rocks; and 5 g of water. Mix thoroughly in a paper cup. Describe the appearance and state of the mixture. Allow to dry overnight and observe again.

Gearing Up
Previewing the Chapter

Use this outline to help you focus on important ideas in this chapter.

Section 9-1   Composition of Matter
- ▶ Substances
- ▶ Mixtures
- ▶ Solutions
- ▶ Colloids and Suspensions

Section 9-2   Science and Society
Smog, a Mixture in the Environment
- ▶ Visible Air Pollution

Section 9-3   Describing Matter
- ▶ Physical Properties
- ▶ Physical Changes
- ▶ Chemical Changes
- ▶ Chemical Properties
- ▶ The Conservation of Mass

Previewing Science Skills
- ▶ In the **Skill Builders,** you will make a concept map and observe and infer.
- ▶ In the **Activities,** you will classify, model, observe, and hypothesize.

What's next?

You have made a model of concrete, a useful mixture. Study Chapter 9 for a better understanding of mixtures and the physical and chemical properties of matter.

219

SECTION BACKGROUND

▶ In science, the word *substance* is limited to elements and compounds. More than nine million substances are known to chemists. A system of classification is necessary.

▶ A heterogeneous mixture is one that is composed of more than one phase. A phase is any region with a uniform set of properties.

▶ Solutions are not necessarily liquid. Air is a gaseous solution. Most alloys of metals are solid solutions.

▶ Colloids are composed of two phases, the dispersed phase and the continuous phase.

PREPLANNING

▶ To prepare for Activity 9-1, label seven items and place them in a plastic bag for each activity group.

▶ Several demonstrations are offered. Scan them to see which ones you want to do and gather the materials needed.

▶ Begin using the wall periodic table to point out element names and symbols. Becoming familiar with the table now will serve students well in upcoming chapters.

1 MOTIVATE

▶ **Demonstration:** Obtain five small clear glass bottles. In the first, place some Cu metal and label it. In the second, place some sulfur and label it. Leave the third empty and label it oxygen. In the fourth bottle, place a little copper and sulfur. Leave plenty of space. The fifth bottle should contain copper(II) sulfate, $CuSO_4$. Use these bottles to demonstrate elements, compounds, and mixtures. Aid students in forming mental models of chemically combined compounds versus mixtures.

New Science Words

element
compounds
substance
heterogeneous mixture
homogeneous mixture
solution
colloid
suspension

Objectives

▶ Distinguish between substances and mixtures.
▶ Compare and contrast solutions, colloids, and suspensions.

Substances

You can easily tell whether a line is drawn in ink or pencil. The lines look different because they are made of different materials. Look at the parts of a pencil. Notice that it's made of several kinds of materials. You could classify the materials of the pencil according to the four states of matter. Another way to classify materials is by the particles they are made of.

The particles that make up all matter are called atoms. **If all the atoms in a sample of matter are alike, that kind of matter is an element.** ➊ The carbon in a pencil point, the oxygen in the air, and the copper in a penny are all examples of elements. Altogether, there are 109 elements. The names of all the elements are in the periodic table on pages 258-259. You will learn more about the other information in the table in later chapters.

Materials called compounds are made from atoms of two or more elements that are combined. ➋ The ratio of the different atoms in a compound is always the same. For example, the elements hydrogen and oxygen can combine to form the compound water. The atoms of elements in water are present in the ratio of two hydrogen atoms to one oxygen atom.

Figure 9-1. A pencil is made up of several different materials.

OPTIONS

Meeting Different Ability Levels

For Section 9-1, use the following **Teacher Resource Masters** depending upon individual students' needs.

◆ **Study Guide Master** for all students.
● **Reinforcement Master** for students of average and above average ability levels.
▲ **Enrichment Master** for above average students.
Additional Teacher Resource Package masters are listed in the OPTIONS box throughout the section. The additional masters are appropriate for all students.

◆ **STUDY GUIDE** 39

STUDY GUIDE — Chapter 9
Composition of Matter — Text Pages 220-225

One key term has been scrambled in each of the following statements. Unscramble the term. On the lines provided, rewrite the entire statement with the unscrambled term. Then find each unscrambled key term in the hidden word puzzle.

1. A(n) *tthgneosuroe* mixture has different materials that are spread out unevenly.
   A **heterogeneous** mixture has different materials that are spread out unevenly.

2. A(n) *oidolo* is a heterogeneous mixture whose particles never settle and are large enough to scatter light. A **colloid** is a heterogeneous mixture whose particles never settle and are large enough to scatter light.

3. A homogeneous mixture in which particles are so small that they cannot be seen without a microscope is a(n) *lusoion*. A **homogeneous** mixture in which particles are so small that they cannot be seen without a microscope is a **solution**.

4. A(n) *ssiinospue* is a liquid heterogeneous mixture in which visible particles settle.
   A **suspension** is a liquid heterogeneous mixture in which visible particles settle.

5. A(n) *oouodmpc* is a material made from atoms of two or more combined elements.
   A **compound** is a material made from atoms of two or more combined elements.

6. If all the atoms in a sample of matter are alike, that kind of matter is a(n) *tnemeel*.
   If all the atoms in a sample of matter are alike, that kind of matter is a(n) **element**.

7. A(n) *oogenusmoh* mixture has substances which are uniformly spread out.
   A **homogeneous** mixture has substances which are uniformly spread out.

Figure 9-2. Sugar is a compound of carbon, oxygen, and hydrogen.

When was the last time you ate a compound whose elements are a black solid and two invisible gases? One compound that fits this description is sugar. You can recognize sugar by its white crystals and sweet taste. But the elements in sugar—carbon, hydrogen, and oxygen—are neither white nor sweet, Figure 9-2. Like sugar, compounds are usually very different from the elements that make them up.

Oxygen, carbon, water, sugar, and salt are examples of materials classified as substances. A **substance** is either an element or a compound.

Mixtures

When you have a sore throat, do you gargle with salt water? Salt water is classified as a mixture. A mixture is a material made up of two or more substances, and salt and water are different substances.

Unlike compounds, mixtures do not always contain the same amounts of different substances. You may be wearing clothing made of permanent-press fabric. This fabric is woven from fibers of two compounds—polyester and cotton. The fabric may contain 45 percent polyester and 55 percent cotton, or 65 percent polyester and 35 percent cotton, as shown Figure 9-3. Fabric with more polyester is more resistant to wrinkling than fabric with less polyester.

Figure 9-3. Permanent-press fabrics are mixtures that have variable composition.

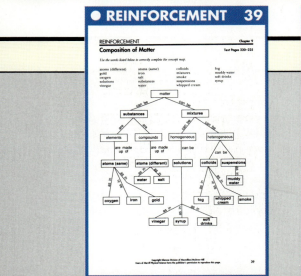

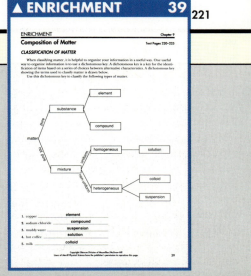

221

CONCEPT DEVELOPMENT

► **Demonstration:** Partially fill a petri dish with water and place it on the overhead projector. Place a crystal of potassium permanganate, $KMnO_4$, in the water, and have the students observe the purple streamers as you stir the water *very* gently. Emphasize that a solution is completely homogeneous on a molecular level because particles of matter are in constant motion (kinetic theory).

► **Demonstration:** Place sugar in a glass of cold tea so that some remains undissolved on the bottom of the glass (heterogeneous). Transfer the mixture to a beaker and warm gently, stirring until the sugar dissolves in the hot tea (homogeneous). Introduce the idea that temperature (energy) sometimes determines the form of a mixture.

TEACHER F.Y.I.

► Dr. Linus Pauling, a two-time Nobel prize winner, reported an observation regarding sickle-cell anemia. In this disease, an abnormal form of hemoglobin is present and it is not water soluble. The abnormal form cannot carry oxygen in the blood, and the sickle-shaped cells clog capillaries.

CROSS CURRICULUM

► **Language Arts:** Have a group of volunteers prepare a crossword puzzle using the vocabulary words of this lesson. Shown here is one possibility.

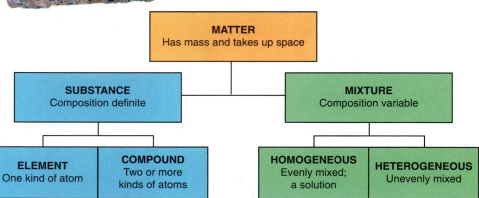

A mixture in which different materials are spread out unevenly is called a **heterogeneous mixture.** Permanent-press fabrics are heterogeneous mixtures because you can detect the different materials by sight or with a microscope. Gravel, concrete, and dry soup mixes are examples of other heterogeneous mixtures.

MATTER
Has mass and takes up space

SUBSTANCE
Composition definite

MIXTURE
Composition variable

ELEMENT
One kind of atom

COMPOUND
Two or more kinds of atoms

HOMOGENEOUS
Evenly mixed; a solution

HETEROGENEOUS
Unevenly mixed

Figure 9-4. Every sample of matter is an element, a compound, or a mixture.

Figure 9-5. Vinegar is a liquid solution containing acetic acid and water.

Solutions

The salt water you gargle with looks like water and tastes salty. Like a polyester-cotton fabric, salt water is in some ways similar to both of the substances it contains. But you can't see the particles in salt water even with a microscope. A material in which the substances are uniformly spread out is classified as a **homogeneous mixture.**

Have you ever looked closely at a bottle of white vinegar? Vinegar is a liquid solution made mostly of acetic acid and water. It appears clear, even though it is made up of particles of acetic acid in water. A **solution** is another name for a homogeneous mixture. Particles in solutions are so small that they cannot be seen even with a microscope. The particles have diameters of about 0.000 000 001 m (1 nm). The particles will also never settle to the bottom of their container. Solutions remain constantly and uniformly mixed.

OPTIONS

INQUIRY QUESTIONS

► **When a soft drink is opened, the solution becomes a heterogeneous mixture. Describe what happens and explain why the result is heterogeneous.** *The pressure of carbon dioxide in the bottle is reduced by opening the bottle, and the excess dissolved gas bubbles out of solution.*

► **Explain why a solution is always a mixture, but not every mixture is a solution.** *All solutions are homogeneous mixtures because they are mixed at the molecular level. Some mixtures are heterogeneous and therefore* cannot be a solution.

► **How would you explain to a person that paint is not a substance?** *True substances, elements and compounds, cannot be separated physically. Paint, left standing, will separate and must be stirred before using. In addition, the person can see that the paint contains materials that evaporate, leaving dry paint behind.*

PROBLEM SOLVING

Jason Makes a Colloid

Jason makes a colloid to use on sandwiches. His friends think that his colloid tastes better than store-bought mayonnaise, although it is similar.

To make the colloid, Jason pours 60 cm³ vinegar into a blender. He then adds 30 cm³ sugar and blends until dissolved. Next, he adds 5 cm³ dry mustard, one clove of fresh garlic, a pinch of salt, and one egg. He blends these ingredients until they are well mixed. While the blender is still on, he slowly adds 180 cm³ vegetable oil in a steady stream. He continues blending until the colloid is thick.

At what stages in the preparation of his recipe does Jason have homogeneous and heterogeneous mixtures?

Think Critically: How can mayonnaise be distinguished from a solution?

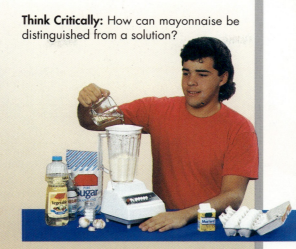

Colloids and Suspensions

When you drink a glass of whole or low-fat milk, you are drinking a mixture of water, fats, proteins, and other substances. Milk is a colloid. A **colloid** is a heterogeneous mixture that, like a solution, never settles. Unlike the particles in a solution, the particles in a colloid are large enough to scatter light. Milk appears white because its particles scatter light. Gelatin is a colloid that may seem to be clear until you shine a light on it. Then you see that its particles also scatter light.

In what way is a colloid like a solution?

Figure 9-6. A beam of light goes straight through a solution (left) but is scattered by a colloid (right).

ENRICHMENT

▶ Have a student prepare and present a brief report on Brownian motion and its cause. Brownian motion can be seen in a suspension of very fine dust, pollen, or bacteria in water. The student could set up a microscope and slide to demonstrate the effect. High magnification is needed.

▶ Some gas masks use the principle of adsorption to filter poisonous gases from the air. Because they are so finely divided, colloidal particles have a very large surface area compared to a solid chunk of the same

material. Have interested students research how gas masks work. Be sure they discover the concept of surface adsorption by colloidal particles.

| PROGRAM RESOURCES |
From the **Teacher Resource Package** use: **Concept Mapping,** page 23.

PROBLEM SOLVING

Answers to Questions: The vinegar is homogeneous. Adding sugar gives a heterogeneous mixture until the sugar dissolves. At this point, the mixture is again homogeneous. After the mustard is added, the mixture remains heterogeneous.

Think Critically: Mayonnaise, like milk, appears white and opaque because it scatters light. Therefore, it is a colloid.

CONCEPT DEVELOPMENT

▶ The motion of colloidal particles is called Brownian motion. This motion is direct evidence for the kinetic theory of matter.

▶ Some medications are suspensions that must be shaken before using. Ask students why it is important to follow directions to shake well, rather than shaking only one or two times, before taking a medication.

CROSS CURRICULUM

▶ **Biology and Medicine:** Have interested students research the use of electrophoresis in DNA fingerprinting and the separation of materials in kidney dialysis.

CHECK FOR UNDERSTANDING

Use the Mini Quiz to check for understanding.

MINI QUIZ

Use the Mini Quiz to check students' recall of chapter content.

❶ If all the atoms of a sample of matter are alike, the matter is a(n) _____ . *element*

❷ Substances made from a combination of two or more elements are called _____ . *compounds*

❸ A mixture that is not the same throughout is called a(n) _____ mixture. *heterogeneous*

❹ A mixture that is the same throughout is called a(n) _____ mixture or _____ . *homogeneous, solution*

❺ A heterogeneous mixture that never settles is called a(n) _____ . *colloid*

224 CHAPTER 9

RETEACH

Fill a large jar with water and exhibit. Using a large stainless steel spoon, dissolve some sugar in the water. Follow this with some food coloring. Pour in some sand and stir. Finally, add a dropperful of milk. Stop stirring and allow everything to stand. Have a student describe the contents of the jar at each step using terms from this section. Note: Don't forget the metal spoon at the end. Stainless steel is a solid solution (alloy) containing iron, chromium, and other metals.

EXTENSION

For students who have mastered this section, use the **Reinforcement** and **Enrichment** masters or other OPTIONS provided.

3 CLOSE

▶ Ask questions 1-2 and the **Apply** Question in the Section Review.

▶ Have a scientist from a nearby water treatment plant come and describe how mud, algae, bacteria, and harmful chemicals are detected and removed from your drinking water. As an alternative, have a team videotape an interview at the water treatment plant.

SECTION REVIEW ANSWERS

1. The hydrogen and oxygen are separate, uncombined elements. The water vapor is a compound made from these elements.

2. A substance is either an element or a compound. It has a specific composition. A mixture contains two or more substances. The composition of a mixture can vary.

3. Apply: The label indicates that the juice must contain materials that have settled out and must be resuspended.

Table 9-1

COMPARING SOLUTIONS, COLLOIDS, AND SUSPENSIONS

Description	Solutions	Colloids	Suspensions
Settle upon standing	No	No	Yes
Can be separated using filter paper	No	No	Yes
Sizes of particles	0.1-1 nm	1-100 nm	Greater than 100 nm
Scatter light	No	Yes	Yes

Have you ever been playing on a wet field and kicked a ball into a puddle of muddy water? Some mixtures, such as muddy water, are neither solutions nor colloids. If you fill a glass with tap water after a heavy rainstorm, the water may be slightly muddy. If you let it stand long enough, the silt will fall to the bottom of the glass and the water will clear. Muddy water is an example of a suspension. A **suspension** is a heterogeneous mixture containing a liquid in which visible particles settle.

You can use the information in Table 9-1 to classify different kinds of mixtures.

SECTION REVIEW

1. How is a container of hydrogen and oxygen different from a container of water vapor?
2. Distinguish between a substance and a mixture.
3. **Apply:** Why do the words "Shake well before using" on a bottle of fruit juice indicate that the juice is a suspension?

Skill Builder

☑ **Concept Mapping**

Make a network tree to show types of liquid mixtures. Include these terms: *homogeneous mixtures, heterogeneous mixtures, solutions, colloids,* and *suspensions.* If you need help, refer to Concept Mapping in the **Skill Handbook** on pages 684 and 685.

Skill Builder

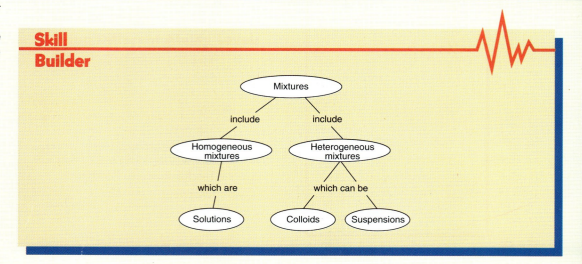

ACTIVITY 9-1
Elements, Compounds, and Mixtures

Problem: *What are the differences among elements, compounds, and mixtures?*

Materials
- plastic freezer bag containing tagged items
- copper foil
- small package of salt
- piece of solder
- aluminum foil
- baking soda or chalk (calcium carbonate)
- piece of granite
- sugar water in a vial

Procedure
1. Copy the data table and use it to record your observations.
2. Obtain a prepared bag of numbered objects.
3. Use the list above to identify each object.
4. The names of all the elements appear in the periodic table on pages 258-259. Use the table to classify any of the objects as elements.
5. Any of the objects that are compounds have been named as examples in Section 9-1.

Analyze
1. If you know the name of a substance, how can you find out if it is an element?
2. How is a compound different from a mixture?
3. Were the mixtures you identified homogeneous or heterogeneous?

Conclude and Apply
4. Examine the contents of your refrigerator at home. Classify what you find as elements, compounds, or mixtures.
5. All materials can be classified with some descriptions. What are the differences among elements, compounds, and mixtures?

Data and Observations   Sample Data

Object	Identity	Classification
1	copper	element
2	salt	compound
3	solder	homogeneous mixture
4	aluminum	element
5	chalk	compound
6	granite	heterogeneous mixture
7	sugar/water	homogeneous mixture

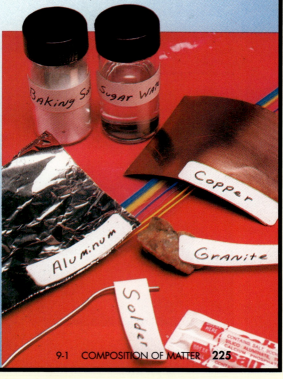

9-1   COMPOSITION OF MATTER   **225**

ACTIVITY 9-1
25 minutes

OBJECTIVE: **Classify** materials based on their appearance and chemical makeup.

PROCESS SKILLS applied in this activity:
▶ **Observing** in Procedure Steps 3, 4, and 5.
▶ **Modeling** in Conclude and Apply Question 5.

COOPERATIVE LEARNING
Use the Science Investigation strategy in groups of three. One student can examine the periodic table to search for elements. Have another student identify compounds and mixtures. The third can collect and evaluate decisions and fill out the data table.

TEACHING THE ACTIVITY
Alternate Materials: Any equivalent assortment that students can identify may be substituted. Pictures of materials may be substituted for actual objects.
Troubleshooting: Make sure vials are tightly sealed.
▶ Introduce formulas for the compounds or have students look them up.
▶ If you have not done so already, this would be a good time to hang a large periodic table on the wall.

PROGRAM RESOURCES
From the **Teacher Resource Package** use:

Activity Worksheets, pages 72-73, Activity 9-1: Elements, Compounds, and Mixtures.

ANSWERS TO QUESTIONS
1. See if it appears on the periodic table.
2. A compound is a substance that consists of chemically combined elements. A mixture consists of various substances not chemically combined.
3. Solder and sugar water were homogeneous. Granite was heterogeneous.
4. Answers will vary but may include: milk, heterogeneous mixture; water, compound; and tea, homogeneous mixture. Students will find few, if any, elements.

5. Elements are homogeneous materials having a specific composition consisting of only one kind of atom. Compounds are also homogeneous and have a specific composition, but they consist of two or more kinds of atoms chemically combined. Mixtures do not have a specific composition and may consist of varying amounts of two or more substances.

PREPARATION

SECTION BACKGROUND

▶ The internal combustion engine operates at temperatures greater than 1000°C. At this high temperature, oxygen and nitrogen in the air can combine to form nitrogen oxides. These nitrogen oxides, NO and NO_2, are part of an automobile's exhaust.

▶ The word *smog* was first used in 1905 as a combination of *smoke* and *fog*. Today smog contains pernitric acid, carbon monoxide, ozone, organic peroxy compounds, and aldehydes.

1 MOTIVATE

▶ **Demonstration:** In an empty aquarium, place a large empty pan. On a stand inside the aquarium, react a small piece of copper wire with nitric acid in a crucible. Cover the aquarium to keep the poisonous gas out of the room. Use a sprinkling can to simulate rain through polluted air. Place a sample of water from the sprinkling can in a test tube and another sample of collected "rainwater" from the pan at the bottom of the aquarium in a second test tube. Use a universal indicator or pH paper in both test tubes to show the change in pH. Use this demonstration to connect polluted air and acid rain in the students' minds.

TYING TO PREVIOUS
KNOWLEDGE: Have students recall and discuss where they have observed litter or pollution caused by improperly discarded items. Point out that air pollution is equivalent to littering the air with waste gases and particles.

OBJECTIVES AND
SCIENCE WORDS: Have students review the objectives and science words to become familiar with this section.

9-2 Smog, a Mixture in the Environment

New Science Words

Tyndall effect
smog

Objectives

▶ Identify smog as a harmful colloid by its properties.
▶ Describe how smog is formed and suggest several ways to eliminate it.

Did You Know?

One out of three Americans lives in an area where the air standards of the Clean Air Act are violated.

Visible Air Pollution

Have you ever watched the beam of a searchlight zoom across the night sky? The beam forms when light from the searchlight is scattered by invisible bits of dust and droplets of water in the air. The scattering of light by particles in a mixture is called the **Tyndall effect.** You can see the Tyndall effect in all colloids. As you recall, a colloid is a mixture in which the particles are invisible and never settle. However, the particles in the mixture are large enough to scatter light. Fog is a mixture of water droplets in air. The water droplets scatter light, causing the fog to appear cloudy or hazy. The air above large cities sometimes appears hazy. The haze is often smog. **Smog is a form of air pollution.** It is a colloid of small, invisible pieces of solid materials mixed with the gases that make up air. Some of the solid material in smog is dust. The dust can occur naturally. It may come from

226 CLASSIFICATION OF MATTER

---

loose soil blown upward by the wind or from ash from volcanic eruptions and forest fires. However, smog also contains solid materials that are not produced naturally. In the early 1900s, ash and soot from burning coal produced most of the dust in smog. Today, unburned compounds in automobile exhaust account for most of the particles of solids in smog. Other sources of solid materials in the air are gasoline stations, industrial plants, hair sprays, and spray paints.

Normally, warm air will rise in the atmosphere. However, sometimes a layer of warm air will be trapped beneath a layer of colder air. Smog forms in this layer of warm, trapped air. The constant motion of the warm air mixes the dust and other solid particles in the air, producing the colloid. Within the smog, new compounds that are harmful to humans begin to form. These compounds cause eye irritation and can cause lung damage. Sometimes smog becomes so severe that city governments must declare smog alerts. These alerts advise elderly people and people with respiratory problems to remain indoors. Industries are asked to cut back their use of fuels, and nonessential traffic is restricted. Winds eventually blow smog away from the cities over which it forms.

SECTION REVIEW

1. Why does smog appear hazy?
2. How does smog form?

You Decide!

One way to reduce air pollution is to reduce the consumption of gasoline. Suppose there was a bill in Congress to raise gasoline taxes and use the proceeds to help clean up the environment. Would you want your representatives to vote for the higher taxes? Why or why not?

SCIENCE & SOCIETY

● REINFORCEMENT 40

REINFORCEMENT   Chapter 9
Smog, A Mixture in the Environment   Text Pages 226–227

WHEN DO 50 + 50 = 95?

Read the following paragraphs. Answer the questions and make drawings in the spaces provided.

Karen did an activity in science class. She measured 50 mL of alcohol into one graduated cylinder and 50 mL of water into another graduated cylinder. She then emptied the 50 mL of alcohol into a 100-mL graduated cylinder. Then she emptied the 50 mL of water into the same 100-mL graduated cylinder that contained the alcohol. She then observed and recorded the total volume as 95 mL. Karen thought that she made a mistake in measuring, so she repeated the entire procedure and again observed that the total volume was 95 mL.

How could this be? She asked her teacher what she had done wrong. Her teacher said that Karen would be able to explain the results if she thought about it for a while.

Karen went home from school and made some popcorn. To 500 mL of popped popcorn she added 25 mL of salt and noted that the total volume did not go above 500 mL. Karen then watched her four-year-old neighbor playing in his sandbox. He emptied a container of sand into a pail filled with pebbles, but his pail did not overflow. These are organic materials that escape from gasoline tanks or are emitted during incomplete combustion of day. She could now explain how 50 + 50 = 95.

1. What explanation was Karen going to give in science class? _There could be small spaces between the particles of alcohol and water. The water particles go in between the alcohol particles and take up some of this empty space._

2. Make drawings to help you explain.

a. water particles   b. alcohol particles   c. alcohol and water particles

3. How can Karen's science class explanation help you explain how smog conditions worsen in a city in a period of one day? _There is a lot of empty space between air particles. This empty space can hold more pollution particles if the air is trapped over the city._

40

▲ ENRICHMENT 40

ENRICHMENT   Chapter 9
Smog, A Mixture in the Environment   Text Pages 226–227

PHOTOCHEMICAL SMOG

Photochemical smog is a type of smog caused by the action of sunlight on exhaust gases from factories and automobiles. The chemicals involved in photochemical smog include the following.

A. Nitrogen monoxide (NO). It is formed in the atmosphere from oxygen and nitrogen and from combustion in automobiles.

B. Nitrogen dioxide (NO_2). It is made from the reaction of nitrogen monoxide and oxygen in the atmosphere. It has a pungent, irritating odor and has an orange-brown color.

C. Ozone (O_3). It is produced from the photochemical reaction of nitrogen monoxide, nitrogen dioxide, and sunlight. It is a powerful oxidant and can crack rubber, corrode metals, and damage plant and animal tissues.

D. Hydrocarbons. These are organic materials that escape from gasoline tanks or are emitted during incomplete combustion of gasoline. These can cause burning eyes, are

harmful to people with respiratory or heart disease, can injure plants, and can damage rubber and paint.

Data Table. Chemicals in Photochemical Smog

Time	Hydrocarbons	NO	NO_2	O_3
Midnight	0.18	0.07	0.06	0.01
2 AM	0.18	0.09	0.06	0.02
4 AM	0.19	0.10	0.06	0.02
6 AM	0.26	0.12	0.09	0.03
8 AM	0.40	0.11	0.15	0.04
10 AM	0.35	0.03	0.14	0.07
Noon	0.28	0.01	0.08	0.12
2 PM	0.21	0.02	0.07	0.15
4 PM	0.18	0.02	0.07	0.12
6 PM	0.17	0.04	0.06	0.07
8 PM	0.17	0.05	0.06	0.02
10 PM	0.07	0.07	0.06	0.01

Analyze and Conclude

1. At what time do the concentrations of both nitrogen oxides and hydrocarbons peak? _about 8 AM_
What could cause these high concentrations? _morning rush hour traffic—more auto-mobile exhaust gases_

2. As the concentration of NO_2 is increasing, the concentration of NO is decreasing. How can you explain this? _NO + oxygen make NO_2_

3. Ozone in the upper atmosphere is important in protecting us from ultraviolet light. Near the ground ozone is a pollutant. Using the data table, determine which chemicals are near minimum levels when ozone is at its maximum level. _NO, NO_2, students may include hydrocarbons_
What does this tell you about the production of ozone in polluted air? _These chemicals, along with sunlight, make ozone._

4. What steps can be taken to reduce photochemical smog? _Sample answers include: Reduce the level of polluting chemicals. Put less reliance on polluting fuels—convert to cleaner fuels._

40

PREPARATION

SECTION BACKGROUND

▶ Physical properties may be divided into groups. Extensive properties depend on the amount of matter present (mass, length, volume). Intensive properties do not depend on the amount of matter (malleability, luster, conductivity, brittleness).

▶ Physical changes don't alter the identity of a substance. Pounding, pulling, cutting, dissolving, melting, or boiling don't produce a new substance with new properties, the mark of a chemical change.

▶ Evidence that a chemical change has occurred includes formation of a precipitate, evolution or absorption of heat or light, evolution of a gas, or a color change.

▶ Chemical properties cannot be tested without altering the identity of the substance being tested.

▶ Since Einstein wrote $E = mc^2$, mass and energy have been thought of as being equivalent. Mass can be changed into energy and energy can be changed into mass. However, the law of conservation of mass, as stated here, holds true for everyday physical and chemical changes.

▶ The French scientist Lavoisier first stated the law of conservation of mass. He was executed in 1794 during the French Revolution.

PREPLANNING

▶ For Activity 9-2, you will need to prepare dilute hydrochloric acid.

▶ Several demonstrations are offered. Scan them to see which ones you want to do and gather the materials needed.

STUDENT TEXT QUESTIONS

▶ Page 228, paragraph 1: **Does all matter have properties?** *Yes. All matter can be described by its properties.*

▶ Page 228, paragraph 2: **What physical property of a nail is measured with a balance?** *its mass*

New Science Words

physical property
physical change
chemical change
chemical property
law of conservation of mass

Objectives

▶ Give examples of physical properties.
▶ Distinguish between physical and chemical changes.
▶ Distinguish between chemical and physical properties.
▶ State and explain the law of conservation of mass.

Physical Properties

You can bend an empty aluminum can. But you can't bend a piece of chalk. Chalk doesn't bend—it breaks. Brittleness is a characteristic that describes a piece of chalk. Its color and shape also describe the chalk. A **physical property** is any characteristic of a material that you can observe easily without changing the substances that make up the material. You can describe matter using physical properties. Does all matter have properties?

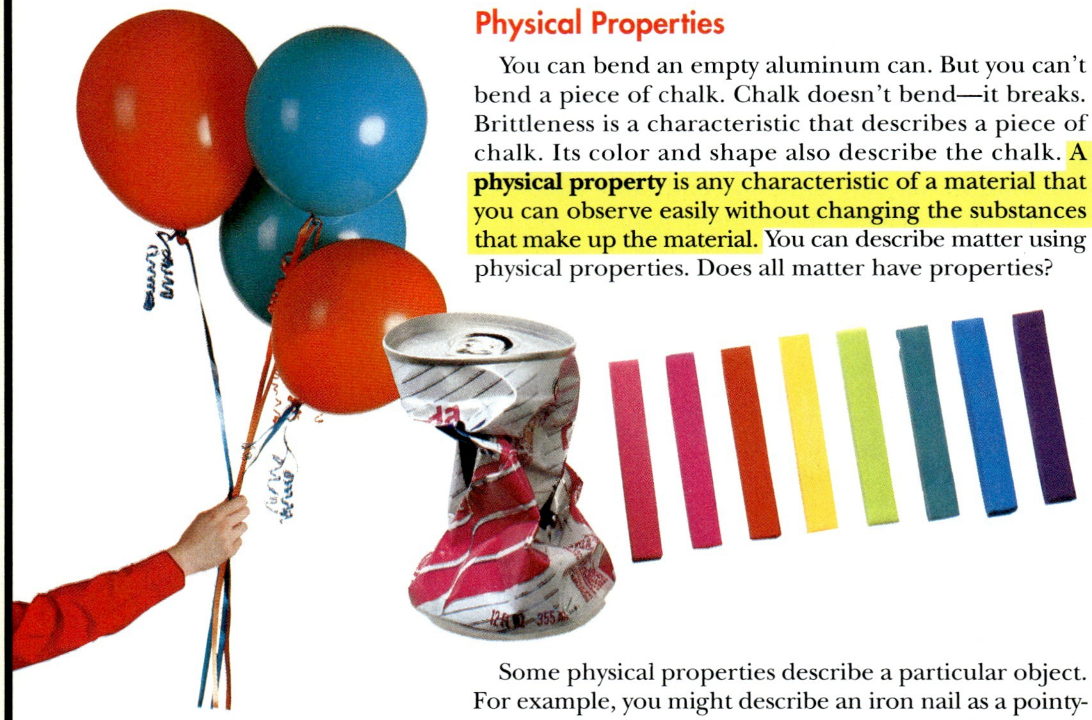

Figure 9-7. What are the physical properties of the balloons and the gas inside them?

Some physical properties describe a particular object. For example, you might describe an iron nail as a pointy-ended cylinder made of dull, gray-colored solid. By describing the shape, color, and state of the nail, you have listed several of its physical properties. Some physical properties can be measured. For instance, you could use a metric ruler to measure another property of the nail—its length. What physical property of the nail is measured with a balance?

OPTIONS

Meeting Different Ability Levels

For Section 9-3, use the following **Teacher Resource Masters** depending upon individual students' needs.

◆ **Study Guide Master** for all students.
● **Reinforcement Master** for students of average and above average ability levels.
▲ **Enrichment Master** for above average students.

Additional Teacher Resource Package masters are listed in the OPTIONS box throughout the section. The additional masters are appropriate for all students.

◆ STUDY GUIDE   41

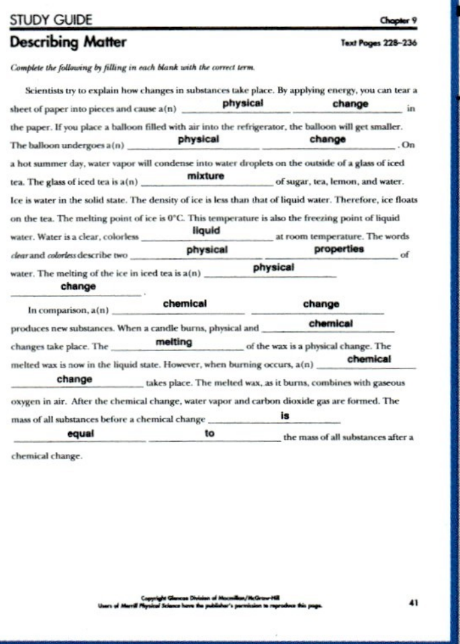

STUDY GUIDE   Chapter 9
Describing Matter   Text Pages 228-236

Complete the following by filling in each blank with the correct term.

Scientists try to explain how changes in substances take place. By applying energy, you can tear a sheet of paper into pieces and cause a(n) _____**physical**_____ _____**change**_____ in the paper. If you place a balloon filled with air into the refrigerator, the balloon will get smaller. The balloon undergoes a(n) _____**physical**_____ _____**change**_____. On a hot summer day, water vapor will condense into water droplets on the outside of a glass of iced tea. The glass of iced tea is a(n) _____**mixture**_____ of sugar, tea, lemon, and water. Ice is water in the solid state. The density of ice is less than that of liquid water. Therefore, ice floats on the tea. The melting point of ice is 0°C. This temperature is also the freezing point of liquid water. Water is a clear, colorless _____**liquid**_____ at room temperature. The words clear and colorless describe two _____**physical**_____ _____**properties**_____ of water. The melting of the ice in iced tea is a(n) _____**physical**_____ _____**change**_____.

In comparison, a(n) _____**chemical**_____ _____**change**_____ produces new substances. When a candle burns, physical and _____**chemical**_____ changes take place. The _____**melting**_____ of the wax is a physical change. The melted wax is now in the liquid state. However, when burning occurs, a(n) _____**chemical**_____ _____**change**_____ takes place. The melted wax, as it burns, combines with gaseous oxygen in air. After the chemical change, water vapor and carbon dioxide gas are formed. The mass of all substances before a chemical change _____**is**_____ _____**equal**_____ _____**to**_____ the mass of all substances after a chemical change.

If you had some water in a test tube, you might measure its volume and temperature and describe its odor. Each characteristic is a physical property. Some physical properties describe a material or a substance. As you may know, all objects made of iron are attracted by a magnet. Attraction by a magnet is a property of the substance iron. Every substance has physical properties that distinguish it from other substances. ==Examples of physical properties you have learned about are color, shape, size, density, melting point, and boiling point.==

Do you pick out the grapes in a fruit salad and eat them first, last, or maybe not at all? If you do, you are using physical properties to identify the grapes and separate them from the other fruits in the mixture. Figure 9-8 shows a mixture of pebbles and sand. You can identify the pebbles and grains of sand by differences in color, shape, and size. By sifting the mixture, you can quickly separate the pebbles from the grains of sand because they have different sizes.

Look at the mixture of iron filings and sand shown in Figure 9-9. It would be impossible to separate this mixture with a sieve because the filings and grains of sand are the same size. A more efficient way is to pass a magnet through the mixture. When you pass a magnet through the mixture, the magnet attracts the iron filings and pulls them from the sand. In this way, the difference in a physical property, such as attraction to a magnet, can be used to separate substances in a mixture.

Figure 9-8. This mixture of pebbles and sand could be separated with a sifter.

Figure 9-9. A mixture of sand and iron filings can be separated with a magnet. The iron filings are magnetic. The sand is not.

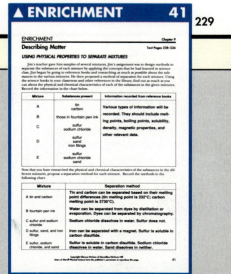

229

▶ **Demonstration:** Place 1 g $Cu(NO_3)_2$ in the bottom of a 500-mL Erlenmeyer flask. Dissolve 4 g of NaOH in 10 mL of water and pour the solution into a test tube. **CAUTION:** *NaOH is caustic. $Cu(NO_3)_2$ is toxic and a strong oxidizer.* Place the test tube upright in the flask containing the $Cu(NO_3)_2$. Stopper the flask and measure the mass of the system on a balance. Carefully tip the stoppered flask so that the NaOH solution mixes with the $Cu(NO_3)_2$. Take the mass again. Students will observe physical properties, chemical changes, and the law of conservation of mass.

TYING TO PREVIOUS KNOWLEDGE: A common remedy for a sore throat is to gargle with salt water. Dissolving salt, NaCl, in water is a physical change. The action of the salt on the bacteria is also physical in that it kills the cells by dehydrating them. Salt has been used as a preservative for meat for centuries.

OBJECTIVES AND SCIENCE WORDS: Have students review the objectives and science words to become familiar with this section.

2 TEACH

Key Concepts are highlighted.

CONCEPT DEVELOPMENT
▶ Be sure students understand that "without changing the substances" in the definition of physical property means that the *composition* of the substances is not changed.

List five examples of physical changes in water.

Physical Changes

If you break a piece of chalk, it loses its original size and shape. You have caused a change in some of its physical properties. But you have not changed the substances that make up the chalk.

The changes of state that you studied in Chapter 8 are all examples of physical changes. When water—or any substance—freezes, boils, evaporates, sublimates, or condenses, it undergoes physical changes. There are energy changes during these changes in state, but the kind of substance—the identity of the element or compound—does not change.

As shown in the picture above, iron, like water, will change states if it absorbs enough energy. In each state it will have physical properties that can be used to identify it as the substance iron. A change in size, shape, color, or state of matter is called a **physical change.** Physical changes do not change the substances in a material.

Just as physical properties can be used to separate mixtures, so can physical changes. For example, if you let salt water stand, you'll find at a later time that

TECHNOLOGY

Aerogels—Next to Nothing at All

Imagine a block of gelatin dessert in which all of the liquid has been replaced with air. It might look like a frozen cloud and would be called an aerogel.

Light passing through the tiny pores and microscopic framework of an aerogel is bent, giving the aerogel a bluish color against a dark background and a yellowish color in the light. Unlike a solid, the framework is so weakly connected that the aerogel is a poor conductor of heat. Therefore, an aerogel is an excellent insulator. The insulating property of aerogels has caught the interest of industry. Thus, you may soon see aerogels used as insulation in everything from refrigerators to double pane windows.

Think Critically: What property of aerogels might limit their use as an insulator in double pane windows?

the water has evaporated, leaving salt crystals inside the glass. The process of evaporating water from salty seawater is used to produce drinking water.

Chemical Changes

In any physical change of a material, the substances in the material do not change their identities. But you know that substances do change their identities. Fireworks explode, matches burn, eggs rot, and bikes and car bodies rust. What do changes in these materials have in common?

Burned toast, burned soup, and burned steak all smell burned. The smell is different from the smell of bread, soup, or steak. The odor is a clue that a new substance

For more information on aerogels, see "Super Fluff" by Robert Pool, *Discover*, Aug. 1990, p. 26, and "The Art of Making Insubstantial Things" by Ivan Amato, *Science News*, Nov. 17, 1990, p. 316.

Think Critically: The bluish or yellowish color may limit its use in standard windows.

CONCEPT DEVELOPMENT

▶ Students enjoy learning about chemical changes by seeing them occur. You can demonstrate each evidence of a chemical change.

▶ **Demonstration:** A precipitate can be formed by mixing copper(II) nitrate solution (2 g in 10 mL water) and sodium hydroxide solution (4 g in 10 mL water). **CAUTION:** *These chemicals are toxic and caustic, respectively.* Copper(II) hydroxide forms. The heat of the reaction can change the blue copper(II) hydroxide into black copper(II) oxide. If this does not occur, warm the beaker to produce the color change, another evidence that a chemical change has occurred.

▶ **Demonstration:** The evolution of heat and light can be demonstrated by striking a match and letting it burn.

▶ **Demonstration:** The evolution of a gas can be demonstrated by mixing baking soda with vinegar in the bottom of a large flask or jar. Carbon dioxide gas, water, and sodium acetate are the products. Pour the denser-than-air carbon dioxide gas onto a burning candle to show students how it can be used in fire extinguishers.

TEACHER F.Y.I.

▶ Physical and chemical changes are always accompanied by energy changes. The energy changes occur between a system and its surroundings. A system is that piece of the universe under consideration, for example, a flask and its contents. Everything else is the surroundings.

ENRICHMENT

▶ Some of the chemical changes that occur in the body take in energy, and others release energy. Have students gather information about the Calorie content of some common foods. Then have them research activities to find out how many Calories are used. Students should compute the energy value of a typical meal and then determine how long they would have to perform various activities in order to use up that energy. Be sure students include basal metabolic rates.

PROGRAM RESOURCES

From the **Teacher Resource Package** use: **Cross-Curricular Connections,** page 13, Physical and Chemical Properties and Changes.

MINI QUIZ

Use the Mini Quiz to check students' recall of chapter content.

1 Which kind of property can be determined without changing the identity of a material? *physical property*

2 A change in size, color, shape, or state of matter is called a(n) _____ change. *physical*

3 A change of one substance into a different substance is a(n) _____ change. *chemical*

4 Rusting is a chemical change because iron and oxygen combine to form a new _____ . *substance*

CROSS CURRICULUM

▶ **History:** Nitrates are a primary ingredient in explosives and gun powder. Before World War I, Germany had to import nitrates from South America. Because the British navy could have cut off this supply, Germans looked for alternate sources of nitrates. Fritz Haber discovered a way to make ammonia from nitrogen and hydrogen. Friedrich Ostwald later discovered a method to oxidize the ammonia to form nitrate. The motivation for these scientists' research was not to enable Germany to make explosives, but to make inexpensive fertilizer available to Europe's worn out farm land. Interested students could read about Haber's and Ostwald's lives and work.

STUDENT TEXT QUESTION

▶ Page 233, paragraph 2: **What physical property do these bottles have in common?** *They are opaque or they transmit little light.*

has been produced. A change of one substance in a material to a different substance is a **chemical change.** There are many signs that can tell you when a chemical change has taken place. For example, the foaming of an antacid tablet in a glass of water and the smell in the air after a thunderstorm indicate that new substances have been produced. In some chemical changes a rapid production of energy, such as the light and sound of an exploding firecracker, is a clue. **③**

When iron is exposed to the oxygen and water in the air, the iron and oxygen slowly form a new substance, rust. When hydrogen gas is burned in a rocket engine, the elements hydrogen and oxygen combine to form water. Burning and rusting are chemical changes because different substances are produced. **④**

OPTIONS

INQUIRY QUESTIONS

▶ Classify each of the following as chemical or physical changes: (a) fading of dye in cloth; (b) growth of a plant; (c) formation of clouds in the air. *(a) chemical; (b) chemical; (c) physical*

▶ Classify each of the following as heterogeneous mixture, element, compound, or solution: (a) air; (b) table salt; (c) apple; (d) silver; (e) hot tea; (f) box of cake mix; (g) copper. *(a) mixture; (b) compound; (c) mixture; (d) element; (e) solution; (f) mixture; (g) element*

PROGRAM RESOURCES

From the **Teacher Resource Package** use:

Critical Thinking/Problem Solving, page 15, Ethanol versus Gasoline.

Science and Society, page 13, Motor Vehicle Pollution.

Chemical Properties

Look at Figure 9-10. You have probably seen this warning on cans of paint thinners and lighter fluids for charcoal grills. The warning indicates that they burn quickly. The tendency of a substance to burn is an example of a chemical property. **A chemical property** is a characteristic of a substance that indicates if it can undergo a certain chemical change. Many substances are flammable. Knowing which materials contain substances that have this chemical property allows you to use them safely.

Figure 9-10. Flammability is a chemical property of some materials used in the home.

If you look around a drugstore, you might notice that many medicines are stored in dark bottles. These medicines contain compounds with a similar chemical property. Chemical changes will take place in the compounds if they are exposed to light. What physical property do these bottles have in common?

Even though there are thousands of substances and billions of mixtures, they do share a few common physical and chemical properties. You can use these properties to study matter further.

Science and READING

When iron has turned to rust, why do you have so much more rust than you originally had iron?

EcoTip

Cleaners with the words *warning*, *caution*, or *poison* on them can be dangerous to you and to the environment. Call the local EPA to find out how to dispose of them when they are no longer needed.

9-3   DESCRIBING MATTER   **233**

Science and READING

Nearly all chemistry books discuss rusting in some detail as a basic example of chemical change. When iron rusts, it combines with oxygen from the air. After rusting, all the iron that was originally there is still there. The added oxygen results in an increased mass. Rust has the formula Fe_2O_3.

CONCEPT DEVELOPMENT

▶ The chemical properties of a substance depend on the action of the substance in the presence of other substances.

▶ Some examples of chemical properties are (1) changes in the presence of light, (2) flammability, (3) reacts with oxygen in air, (4) reacts with water, (5) reacts with acid, (6) is decomposed by electricity, (7) produces a gas when heated, and (8) forms a precipitate in the presence of base.

▶ Examples of reactions that occur from the above list of chemical properties are (1) photographs and dyes fade, (2) paper and wood burn, (3) white phosphorus ignites in air, (4) Li, Na, and K react in water, (5) zinc metal reacts in acid, (6) electrolysis of water, (7) metal carbonates produce CO_2 in acid, and (8) some metals form insoluble hydroxides.

▶ You can use the two lists above to prepare a matching quiz for students who like to be challenged.

REVEALING MISCONCEPTIONS

▶ Use the Ecotip on page 233 to clear up this common misconception: The proper disposal of all household chemicals is to put them down the drain.

▶ Have students make posters for display in their homes that give specific disposal instructions for common household chemical wastes such as paint, used oil, outdated medications, and so on.

ENRICHMENT

▶ Ask a student to research how crude oil can be obtained from shale or oil sands through chemical and physical means. In one method, the shale is crushed and then placed into a retort, where it is heated with superheated steam, which vaporizes the oil. The vapors are condensed, and the oil is refined.

▶ A shortage of drinking water is a problem in some parts of the world. Ask a student to investigate various methods used to produce pure water from seawater. Have the student pay attention to state changes and other physical processes involved. Students can find information on solar distillation, conventional evaporation, electrodialysis, vapor compression, flash evaporation, reverse osmosis, and freezing.

▶ Refer to the demonstration on page 229 in the Motivate section. This demonstration provides experimental evidence regarding the law of conservation of mass.

▶ You may want to contrast an ordinary chemical reaction with a nuclear reaction when you discuss the law of conservation of mass. The formula $E = mc^2$ shows that mass is converted to energy in a nuclear reaction. When nuclear reactions are considered, the law becomes the law of conservation of mass-energy. This law simply states that the sum of mass and energy remains constant.

CHECK FOR UNDERSTANDING

Use the Mini Quiz to check for understanding.

MINI QUIZ

Use the Mini Quiz to check students' recall of chapter content.

5 Which kind of property indicates whether a substance can undergo a certain chemical change? *chemical*

6 Which law states that matter can be neither created nor destroyed during a chemical change? *law of conservation of mass*

7 The mass of substances remaining after a chemical change _____ the mass of substances present before the change. *equals*

RETEACH

Cooperative Learning: Use the Paired Partner strategy to have students prepare two sets of flash cards. Have students write the definitions of words in this section on the reverse side of one set. On the other set, write examples for each term. Use the cards to provide drill and practice for students who need remediation.

EXTENSION

For students who have mastered this section, use the **Reinforcement** and **Enrichment** masters or other OPTIONS provided.

What are some signs of a chemical change when a log burns?

The Conservation of Mass

Suppose you burn a large log on a campfire until nothing is left but a small pile of ashes. During the burning, smoke, heat, and light are given off. It's easy to see that a chemical change occurs. At first, you might also think that matter was lost during this change, because the pile of ashes looks much smaller than the log. In fact, if you could measure both the mass of the log and the mass of the ashes, the mass of the ashes would be less than that of the log. But suppose that during the burning, you could collect all the oxygen in the air that was combined with the log during the burning. And suppose you could also collect all the smoke and gases that escape from the burning log and measure their masses, too. Then you would find that there is no loss of mass during the burning.

Not only is there no loss of mass during burning; there is no loss or gain of mass during any chemical change. In other words, matter is neither created nor destroyed during a chemical change. This statement is known as the **law of conservation of mass.** According to this law, the mass of all substances present before a chemical change equals the mass of all the substances remaining **6**

Figure 9-11. Although you can't see the gases used or formed when a log burns, there is no loss or gain of mass.

234 CLASSIFICATION OF MATTER

OPTIONS

ENRICHMENT

▶ Chemical changes occur when some photosensitive chemicals are exposed to light. If your school has a darkroom, have interested students develop film and print pictures and enlargements. For more depth, students could find books and articles on photographic chemistry. There may be a student photographer who is willing to demonstrate the use of the darkroom and chemicals used in photography to interested students after school.

PROGRAM RESOURCES

From the **Teacher Resource Package** use:

Transparency Masters, pages 35-36, Conservation of Matter.

Use **Color Transparency** number 18, Conservation of Matter.

Use **Laboratory Manual,** Properties of Matter.

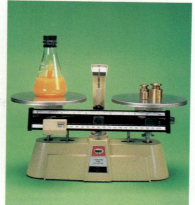

Figure 9-12. A chemical change between two compounds illustrates the law of conservation of mass.

7 after the change. Figure 9-12 shows a chemical change inside a flask. What evidence is there that a chemical change has occurred? How do the pictures demonstrate the law of conservation of mass?

SECTION REVIEW

1. What physical properties could you use to distinguish between iron and aluminum?
2. In terms of substances, explain why evaporation of water is a physical change and not a chemical change.
3. Give an example of a chemical change that occurs when you prepare a meal.
4. Why is being flammable a chemical property rather than a physical property?
5. **Apply:** The law of conservation of mass applies to physical changes as well as to chemical changes. How might you demonstrate this law for melting ice?

☑ Observing and Inferring

Observe a burning candle. What evidence do you have that there are chemical and physical changes in the candle as it burns? If you need help, refer to Observing and Inferring in the **Skill Handbook** on page 678.

Skill Builder

Skill Builder

Evidence of chemical changes includes the production of heat and light, the smell of something burning, the darkening of the wick, and the production of smoke (soot) and water vapor. Evidence of physical changes includes the melting and hardening (solidification) of the wax; the change in the shape, mass, and length of the candle; and the shortening of its wick.

In the 19th century, Michael Faraday wrote a book for young people on the changes occurring during the burning of a candle. Its title is *The Chemical History of a Candle.* The book has been reprinted in modern form and should be available at many libraries.

STUDENT TEXT QUESTIONS

▶ Page 235, paragraph 1: **What evidence is there that a chemical change has occurred?** *A new substance apparently has formed.* **How do these pictures demonstrate the law of conservation of mass?** *Even though a change takes place, no mass is lost or gained.*

3 CLOSE

❓ FLEX Your Brain

Use the Flex Your Brain activity to have students explore CHEMICAL CHANGES.

▶ Students may want you to repeat their favorite demonstration from the ones that you did for them. Have them explain the significance of the demonstration as you do it. If the demonstration is relatively safe to do, students could perform it themselves.

▶ Ask questions 1-4 and the **Apply** Question in the Section Review.

SECTION REVIEW ANSWERS

1. Answers may vary but could include color, hardness, density, and magnetic attraction.

2. In evaporation, the water merely changes from a liquid to a gas. There is no change in the composition of the substance.

3. Answers may vary but could include toasting bread, rising and browning of pancakes on a grill, searing of meat in a pan. Processes involving only melting or mixing should not be included.

4. Flammability is a material's tendency to catch fire in air. Burning is a chemical change because substances change to new substances.

5. Apply: Measure the mass of a closed container of ice. Allow the ice to melt and measure the mass again. There should be no change in mass.

PROGRAM RESOURCES

From the **Teacher Resource Package** use:

Activity Worksheets, page 5, Flex Your Brain.

ACTIVITY 9-2
40 minutes

OBJECTIVE: Observe and **describe** evidence for a chemical change.

PROCESS SKILLS applied in this activity:
▶ **Observing** in all Procedure steps.
▶ **Hypothesizing** in Conclude and Apply Question 4.

![icon] COOPERATIVE LEARNING
Use the Science Investigation group strategy. It is important that one student be free to monitor the drying process continuously.

TEACHING THE ACTIVITY
▶ **CAUTION:** *It is recommended that only actual laboratory evaporating dishes be used in this activity. Substituting other containers could result in heat shattering.*
Alternate Materials: A vinegar solution may be used instead of HCl. You will need about 10 cm³ to react with 0.5 g of baking soda.
Troubleshooting: Be sure students do not turn hot plates too high. The solution should not spatter.
▶ Proper technique is to remove the dish with tongs or turn off the hot plate while the mixture is approaching dryness. The residual heat will complete the drying.
▶ Some HCl fumes will be given off near the end of the drying process. Caution students to avoid looking downward into the dish.
▶ The reaction proceeds according to the following equation:
$$NaHCO_3 + HCl \rightarrow$$
$$NaCl + CO_2 + H_2O.$$
▶ Prepare dilute HCl (4M) by adding 330 cm³ of stock concentrated HCl (12M) slowly to 670 cm³ of water with stirring.

PROGRAM RESOURCES
From the **Teacher Resource Package** use:
  Activity Worksheets, pages 74-75, Activity 9-2: A Chemical Change.

ACTIVITY 9-2
A Chemical Change

Problem: *What is considered evidence for a chemical change?*

Materials
- safety goggles
- 0.5 g baking soda
- small evaporating dish
- hand lens
- 3 cm³ of dilute hydrochloric acid
- 10 cm³ graduated cylinder
- electric hot plate

Procedure
1. Make a chart like the one shown to record your data. Place 0.5 g of baking soda in an evaporating dish. Examine the substance with a hand lens and record your observations.
2. Slowly add 1 cm³ of dilute hydrochloric acid to the 0.5 g of baking soda in the dish. **CAUTION:** *Hydrochloric acid is corrosive and can burn the skin.* Record your observations of any changes.
3. Slowly add 1 cm³ more hydrochloric acid to the dish. Heat the dish until the contents become dry, and let it cool. Examine the contents of the dish with the hand lens and record your observations.
4. Add another 1 cm³ of acid to the material in the dish. Record your observations.

236   CLASSIFICATION OF MATTER

Data and Observations   Sample Data

Appearance of baking soda	white powder
Effect of adding acid	bubbles produced
Appearance after adding acid	small granules or crystals appear
Effect of adding final acid	no change

Analyze
1. What differences do you notice in the appearances of the materials under the magnifying lens?
2. How did adding the final 1 cm³ of acid help you know a chemical change took place with the earlier additions of acid?

Conclude and Apply
3. What is the evidence that a chemical change took place between the substances you mixed? In general, what evidence must be present to conclude that a chemical change has taken place?
4. Baking soda can neutralize acids. In what type of consumer products might you find baking soda?

ANSWERS TO QUESTIONS
1. Baking soda is a powder of irregularly shaped small pieces. The new product (salt) is more granular and composed of small cubic crystals.
2. Adding the final acid to the white product results in no visible reaction. This shows that the product has properties different from those of the starting material.

3. A gas which was probably a new substance bubbled off. The solid residue appeared to be a different substance. Chemical changes can be detected when there is evidence the new substances were formed.
4. antacids, cleaning products

CHAPTER
REVIEW

CHAPTER
REVIEW

9-1: Composition of Matter

1. Elements and compounds are substances; a mixture is composed of two or more substances.
2. A liquid solution is a homogeneous mixture. Colloids and suspensions are two kinds of heterogeneous mixtures.

9-2: Science and Society: Smog, a Mixture in the Environment

1. Smog is a form of air pollution that can be identified as a colloid by the Tyndall effect.
2. Ways to eliminate smog include reducing the use of materials responsible for air pollution.

9-3: Describing Matter

1. Physical properties are characteristics of materials that you can observe without changing substances.
2. In physical changes, substances in materials do not change. In chemical changes, substances in materials change to different substances.

3. Physical properties can be observed without changing substances; chemical properties indicate chemical changes substances can undergo.
4. The law of conservation of mass states that during any chemical change, matter is neither created nor destroyed.

KEY SCIENCE WORDS

a. **chemical change**
b. **chemical property**
c. **colloid**
d. **compounds**
e. **element**
f. **heterogeneous mixture**
g. **homogeneous mixture**
h. **law of conservation of mass**
i. **physical change**
j. **physical property**
k. **smog**
l. **solution**
m. **substance**
n. **suspension**
o. **Tyndall effect**

UNDERSTANDING VOCABULARY

Match each phrase with the correct term from the list of Key Science Words.

1. a colloidal form of air pollution
2. mixture in which different materials are spread out unevenly
3. all atoms in a sample are alike
4. change in color, size, shape, or state
5. change of substance to a different substance
6. combined atoms of two or more elements
7. either an element or a compound
8. mixture that scatters light and never settles
9. an indication of whether a chemical change can occur in a substance
10. In a chemical change, matter is neither created nor destroyed.

SUMMARY

Have students read the summary statements to review the major concepts of the chapter.

UNDERSTANDING VOCABULARY

1. k		**6.** d
2. f		**7.** m
3. e		**8.** c
4. i		**9.** b
5. a		**10.** h

OPTIONS

ASSESSMENT

To assess student understanding of material in this chapter, use the resources listed.

👥 COOPERATIVE LEARNING

Consider using cooperative learning in the THINK AND WRITE CRITICALLY, APPLY, and MORE SKILL BUILDERS sections of the Chapter Review.

PROGRAM RESOURCES

From the **Teacher Resource Package** use:
Chapter Review, pages 21-22.
Chapter and Unit Tests, pages 57-60, Chapter Test.

CHAPTER
REVIEW

CHECKING CONCEPTS

1. b	**6.** a
2. a	**7.** d
3. b	**8.** c
4. a	**9.** b
5. d	**10.** b

UNDERSTANDING CONCEPTS

11. Tyndall
12. homogeneous
13. suspension
14. heterogeneous
15. solution

THINK AND WRITE CRITICALLY

16. Answers might include color, mass, smell, taste, temperature, state of milk, state of carton, volume, texture, density, and shape.

17. Table salt has properties different from those of sodium or chlorine alone.

18. Gels and many thick liquids such as paints and glues are actually colloids.

19. The iron in the nail is not lost. It merely combines with oxygen. The mass of the rusty nail equals the mass of the original nail plus the mass of the oxygen that reacted with it.

20. Many substances are dissolved in ocean water, forming a solution. There are also many small particles suspended in the water. These particles will settle out upon standing.

CHAPTER
REVIEW

CHECKING CONCEPTS

Choose the word or phrase that completes the sentence or answers the question.

1. A copper wire will bend. This is an example of _____.
  a. a chemical property   **c.** conservation
  b. a physical property   **d.** an element

2. Which of the following is *not* an element?
  a. water   **c.** oxygen
  b. carbon   **d.** hydrogen

3. An example of a chemical change is _____.
  a. boiling   **c.** evaporation
  b. burning   **d.** melting

4. Whipped cream is an example of a _____.
  a. colloid   **c.** substance
  b. solution   **d.** suspension

5. A sunbeam is an example of _____.
  a. an element **c.** a suspension
  b. a solution **d.** the Tyndall effect

6. Most smog is now caused by _____.
  a. automobile exhaust   **c.** dust
  b. burning coal   **d.** factories

7. The red color of a rose is a _____.
  a. chemical change   **c.** physical change
  b. chemical property **d.** physical property

8. The process of evaporating water from seawater for drinking is a _____.
  a. chemical change   **c.** physical change
  b. chemical property **d.** physical property

9. Which warning label indicates a chemical property of the material being labeled?
  a. "Fragile"   **c.** "Handle with Care"
  b. "Flammable"   **d.** "Shake Well"

10. Which of the following is a substance?
  a. colloid   **c.** mixture
  b. element   **d.** solution

UNDERSTANDING CONCEPTS

Complete each sentence.

11. The scattering of light by particles in a mixture is called the _____ effect.

12. When substances that make up a material are uniformly spread out, the material is said to be _____.

13. A heterogeneous mixture in which visible particles will settle is a(n) _____.

14. When different materials are spread out unevenly, the mixture is _____.

15. Another name for a homogeneous mixture is a(n) _____.

THINK AND WRITE CRITICALLY

16. Describe a carton of milk using its physical properties.

17. The soft metal sodium and the greenish gas chlorine change to form table salt, sodium chloride. How do you know table salt is a compound?

18. The word *colloid* means "gluelike." Why was colloid chosen for these mixtures?

19. Use a nail rusting in air to explain the law of conservation of mass.

20. Mai says that ocean water is a solution. Ed says that ocean water is a suspension. Are they both correct?

21. Rust is formed from oxygen and iron. How might you keep an iron pipe from rusting?
22. By mistake, sugar was put into some dry rice. How might you separate the mixture?
23. Not all solutions are liquid. Why is a metal alloy, such as brass, considered a solution?
24. Use what you know about suspensions to explain why deltas form at the mouths of large rivers.
25. Why do many medications have instructions to "shake well before using"?

MORE SKILL BUILDERS

If you need help, refer to the Skill Handbook.

1. **Recognizing Cause and Effect:** List at least two causes of smog and two effects of smog.
2. **Making and Using Tables:** Different colloids may involve different states. For example, gelatin is formed from solid particles in a liquid. Complete the following table, using these common colloids: smoke, marshmallow, fog, paint.

Colloid	Example
Gas in solid	
Solid in liquid	
Solid in gas	
Liquid in gas	

3. **Comparing and Contrasting:** In terms of suspensions and colloids, compare and contrast a glass of milk and a glass of grapefruit juice.
4. **Interpreting Data:** From a 25-cm^3 sample of pond water, Joe poured 5 cm^3 through filter paper. He repeated this four more times. He dried each piece of filter paper and measured the mass of the sediment. Why did the last sample have a higher mass than did the first sample?
5. **Using Variables, Constants, and Controls:** Marcos took a 100-cm^3 sample of a suspension, shook it well, and divided it equally into four different test tubes. He placed one test tube in a rack, one in very hot water, one in warm water, and the fourth in ice water. He then observed the time it took for each suspension to settle. What was the variable in the experiment? What were the constants?

PROJECTS

1. Research the smog problem in Los Angeles. Report on what causes the problem, what health and other problems are caused by the smog, and possible solutions to the problem.
2. Make a display of an example of a solution, a heterogeneous mixture, a colloid, and a suspension. Label each and explain their differences.

CLASSIFICATION OF MATTER **239**

21. Coat the iron with paint, grease, or other material that will prevent oxygen from coming into contact with the iron. Water is also necessary for common rusting, but students may not know that.
22. A possible solution would be to dissolve the sugar in water and filter the mixture.
23. Brass is a homogeneous mixture of atoms of different metals, primarily copper and zinc.
24. As the river water flows rapidly, particles are kept suspended by the water's motion. As the river widens at the delta, the water slows down, allowing particles to settle out.
25. Because some liquid medications are suspensions, some of their substances will settle out. These substances need to be resuspended evenly before the medication is used.

MORE SKILL BUILDERS

1. **Determining Cause and Effect:** Causes include dust, ash, unburned materials, and spray products. Effects include health problems, restrictions on industry and traffic, and a drop in tourism.
2. **Making and Using Tables:** The table should be completed as follows: gas in solid, marshmallow; solid in liquid, paint; solid in gas, smoke; liquid in gas, fog.
3. **Comparing and Contrasting:** They are alike in that both have small particles suspended in a liquid. The particles of the juice will settle out. Thus, the juice is a suspension. The milk does not settle and is therefore a colloid.
4. **Interpreting Data:** The pond water was a suspension that was settling as the experiment progressed. Thus, each succeeding filter paper received more sediment.
5. **Using Variables, Constants, and Controls:** The variable was temperature. Constants include the volume and constituents of each sample.

10 Atomic Structure and the Periodic Table

CHAPTER SECTION	OBJECTIVES	ACTIVITIES
10-1 Structure of the Atom (2 days)	1. **List** the names and symbols of common elements. 2. **Describe** the present model of the atom. 3. **Describe** how electrons are arranged in an atom.	**Activity 10-1:** *Models of Atomic Structure, p. 247*
10-2 Smaller Particles of Matter **Science & Society** (1 day)	1. **Identify** quarks as particles of matter that make up protons and neutrons. 2. **Explain** how protons can be broken apart.	
10-3 Masses of Atoms (2 days)	1. **Compute** the atomic mass and mass number of an atom. 2. **Identify** and **describe** isotopes of common elements. 3. **Interpret** the average atomic mass of an element.	**Activity 10-2:** *Isotopes and Atomic Mass, p. 254*
10-4 The Periodic Table (2 days)	1. **Describe** the periodic table of elements and use it to find information about an element. 2. **Distinguish** between a group and a period. 3. **Use** the periodic table to classify an element as a metal, nonmetal, or metalloid.	**MINI-Lab:** *What are the advantages of a periodic table? p. 257*
Chapter Review		

ACTIVITY MATERIALS

FIND OUT	ACTIVITIES		MINI-LABS
Page 241 assorted small nuts, bolts, and washers toothpicks	**10-1 Models of Atomic Structure, p. 247** magnetic board about 20 cm × 27 cm 1 0.5-cm piece and 24 2-cm pieces of rubber magnetic strips circles of white paper 4-cm wide marker	**10-2 Isotopes and Atomic Mass, p. 254** 4 red and 3 green candy-coated peanuts 2 red and 3 green candy-coated chocolates	**What are the advantages of a periodic table? p. 257** assorted pencils and pens large table surface

CHAPTER FEATURES	TEACHER RESOURCE PACKAGE	OTHER RESOURCES
Skill Builder: *Concept Mapping,* p. 246	**Ability Level Worksheets** ◆ **Study Guide,** p. 42 ● **Reinforcement,** p. 42 ▲ **Enrichment,** p. 42 **Cross-Curricular Connections,** pp. 15, 16 **Activity Worksheet,** pp. 78, 79	
You Decide! p. 249	**Ability Level Worksheets** ◆ **Study Guide,** p. 43 ● **Reinforcement,** p. 43 ▲ **Enrichment,** p. 43	
Problem Solving: *Ivan's Isotopes,* p. 252 **Skill Builder:** *Making and Using Tables,* p. 253	**Ability Level Worksheets** ◆ **Study Guide,** p. 44 ● **Reinforcement,** p. 44 ▲ **Enrichment,** p. 44 **Critical Thinking/Problem Solving,** p. 16 **Activity Worksheet,** pp. 80, 81	
Technology: *Seeing Atoms,* p. 261 **Skill Builder:** *Making and Using Graphs,* p. 262	**Ability Level Worksheets** ◆ **Study Guide,** p. 45 ● **Reinforcement,** p. 45 ▲ **Enrichment,** p. 45 **Concept Mapping,** pp. 25, 26 **Cross-Curricular Connections,** p. 14 **Science and Society,** p. 14 **MINI-Lab Worksheet,** p. 84 **Transparency Masters,** pp. 37-40	**Color Transparency 19,** The Periodic Table **Color Transparency 20,** The Periodic Table—Blank **Lab Manual 22,** Chemical Activity
Summary Think & Write Critically Key Science Words Apply Understanding Vocabulary More Skill Builders Checking Concepts Projects Understanding Concepts	**Chapter Review,** pp. 23, 24 **Chapter Test,** pp. 61-64	**Chapter Review Software** **Test Bank**

◆ **Basic**   ● **Average**   ▲ **Advanced**

ADDITIONAL MATERIALS

SOFTWARE	AUDIOVISUAL	BOOKS/MAGAZINES
The Structure of Matter, Queue. *Classifying Elements,* Queue. *Element Hunt,* ComPress. *The Periodic Table,* Focus. *Investigating Atomic Models,* IBM.	*Periodic Table,* film, EME. *Matter and Molecules: Into the Atom,* filmstrip and cassette, SVE. *Periodic Table Videodisc: Reactions of the Elements,* laserdisc, JCE: Software.	Bohr, Niels. *Atomic Theory and the Description of Nature.* Woodbridge, CT: OxBow Press, 1987. Dean, John A., *Lange's Handbook of Chemistry.* New York: McGraw-Hill Publishing Co., 1985.

CHAPTER

10

ATOMIC STRUCTURE AND THE PERIODIC TABLE

THEME DEVELOPMENT: Scale and structure as a theme are developed through a presentation of atomic structure and the periodic table. The structure of an atom is related to its position on the periodic table.

CHAPTER OVERVIEW

- **Section 10-1:** This section introduces the atom's general structure. The make-up of the nucleus and electron cloud are detailed.
- **Section 10-2: Science and Society:** The student learns how a supercollider can reveal subatomic particles.
- **Section 10-3:** In this section, the student learns that atoms of different elements have different masses. The term *isotope* is introduced, and the concept of average atomic mass is developed.
- **Section 10-4:** The student learns how the periodic table organizes elements into groups and periods related to atomic structure. Students are introduced to dot diagrams of atoms.

CHAPTER VOCABULARY

chemical symbol
nucleus
electrons
protons
neutrons
atomic number
electron cloud
quarks
mass number
isotopes
average atomic mass
periodic table
groups
dot diagram
periods
metals
nonmetals
metalloids

CHAPTER

10 Atomic Structure and the Periodic Table

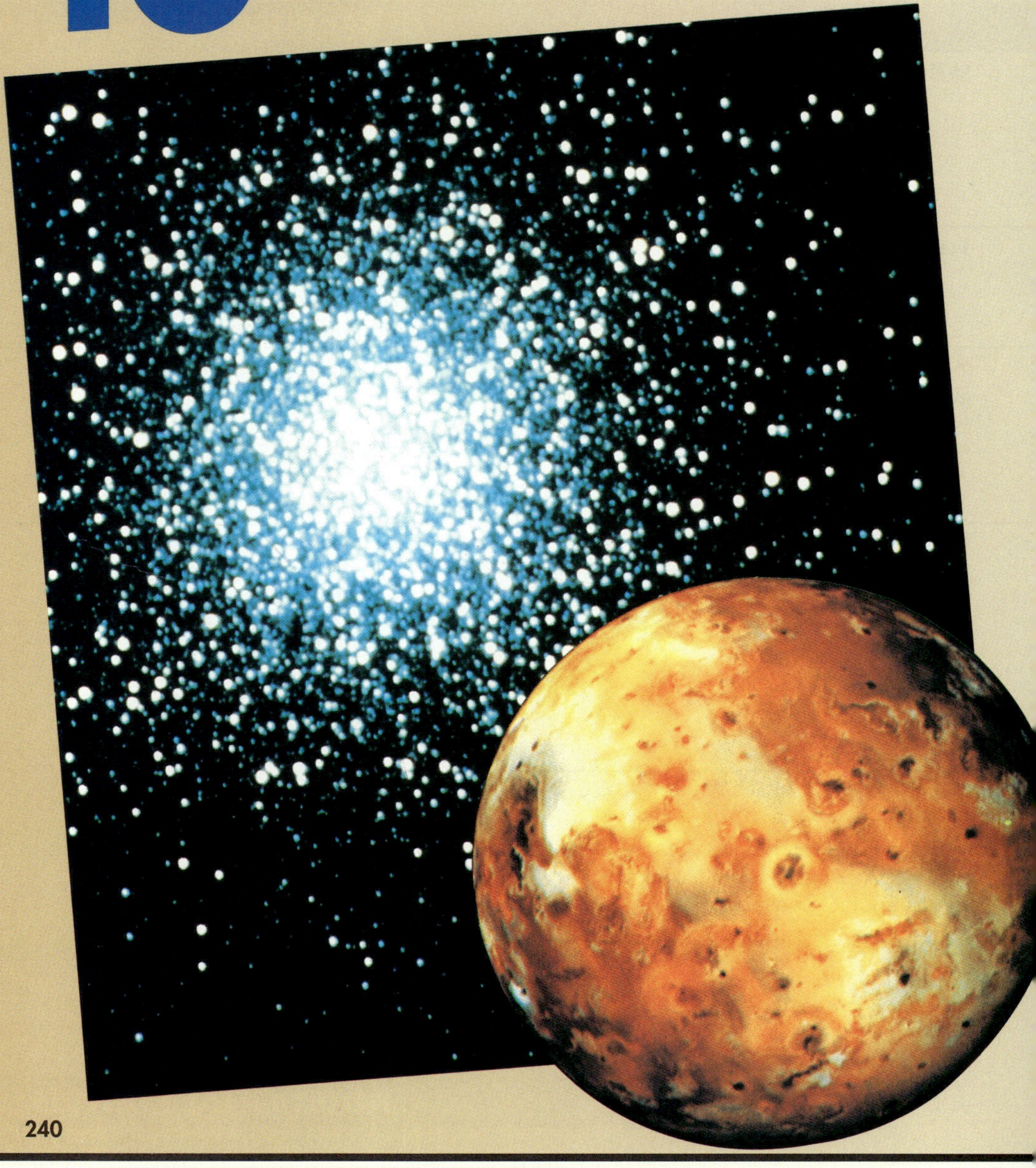

240

OPTIONS

For Your Gifted Students

Have students create their own element. They should name it and predict its physical characteristics. Have them diagram the electron arrangement in the appropriate energy levels, the number of protons, and the number of neutrons. Students should find the correct position of their element in the periodic table according to group and period. Unless students have designed a very large atom, they will find an existing element in the same position. They should check the properties, the number of protons and neutrons, and the electron arrangement of the element against their predictions.

Did you ever go stargazing at a planetarium? If so, you may have seen a globular cluster like the one in the picture. The appearance of this collection of stars resembles one model of the structure of the atom. What are some other models of the atom?

FIND OUT!

In this activity, you will make another kind of model of an atom.

Your teacher will give you a certain number of bolts, nuts, and/or washers. Each group in the class will get different numbers of the pieces of hardware. Bury your hardware in a piece of modeling clay. Form the clay into a ball so that you can't see the hardware. Trade clay balls with another group that started with different kinds and/or numbers of hardware pieces. You have made a kind of model of an atom. Using toothpicks that you stick into the ball, try to find out how many of each hardware piece are hidden in the clay without pulling it apart. Now you have used indirect evidence, as scientists do, to identify and count the hidden parts of your model atom.

Gearing Up

Previewing the Chapter

Use this outline to help you focus on important ideas in this chapter.

Section 10-1   Structure of the Atom
▶ Chemical Symbols
▶ Matter and Atoms
▶ Models of the Atom
▶ Energy Levels of Electrons

Section 10-2   Science and Society
Smaller Particles of Matter
▶ Looking for Quarks

Section 10-3   Masses of Atoms
▶ Atomic Mass
▶ Mass Number
▶ Isotopes

Section 10-4   The Periodic Table
▶ Structure of the Periodic Table
▶ Groups of Elements
▶ Periods of Elements

Previewing Science Skills
▶ In the Skill Builders, you will make a concept map, make and use a table, and make and use a graph.
▶ In the Activities, you will build models, infer, predict, and control variables.
▶ In the MINI-Lab, you will observe and infer.

What's next?

You have investigated one simple model of an atom. In the pages that follow, you will learn about scientists' models of atoms.

241

For Your Mainstreamed Students

Obtain samples of several elements, such as tin, sulfur, copper, carbon, iron, aluminum, lead, zinc, gold, silver. Let students examine and record the characteristics of each element. They should look for such properties as color, hardness, texture, brittleness, and the like. Students can compare their lists. They can play a game in which one student lists characteristics and others try to identify the element.

INTRODUCING THE CHAPTER
Use the Find Out activity to introduce students to atomic structure and the problems that faced scientists who tried to determine atomic structure. Inform students that they will be learning more about the structure of atoms as they read the chapter.

FIND OUT!
Preparation: Collect small nuts, bolts, and washers. Determine how much clay will be needed to bury a cluster of hardware.
Materials: assorted small nuts, bolts, and washers; toothpicks
Cooperative Learning: Use Science Investigation groups of three. Have one student form the model out of sight of the other two.
Teaching Tips
▶ Have students prepare the clay balls the day before the activity. Have lumps of clay contain one, two, or three pieces of hardware.
▶ Have students prepare a detailed, full-scale map of the interior of the clay ball. Have students stick a broken-off toothpick in a permanent location on the ball as a point of reference. Record the position of each toothpick probe and the result. An *0* on the map means the probe hit nothing; an *X* on the map indicates that the probe touched a piece of hardware.

Gearing Up
Have students study the Gearing Up feature to familiarize themselves with the chapter. Discuss the relationships of the topics in the outline.

What's Next?
Before beginning the first section, make sure students understand the connection between the Find Out activity and the topics to follow.

SECTION BACKGROUND

▶ The use of letters as chemical symbols is a relatively modern addition to chemistry begun by Berzelius (1779-1848).

▶ The International Union of Pure and Applied Chemistry (IUPAC) has adopted a three-letter symbol for elements beyond 103. The symbols represent the names, which themselves are made up of Latin and Greek prefixes for the corresponding atomic numbers.

▶ In 400 B.C., Democritus proposed that all matter was composed of small particles he called *atomos*. It wasn't until 1808 that Dalton restated this as a part of the atomic theory of matter.

▶ Atomic numbers were first assigned to elements as a result of the work of Henry Moseley. In 1913, Moseley used X rays to differentiate among the atomic nuclei of different elements.

▶ In 1913, Bohr described the planetary model of the atom. Schrödinger later used quantum mechanics to describe the electron clouds around the nucleus.

PREPLANNING

▶ Try to have a wall-size copy of the periodic table available to refer to during this and following chapters. This display will help reinforce the use of the table as a source of information about elements.

▶ To prepare for Activity 10-1, cut and glue the magnetic tape to the backs of the paper circles. Allow the glue to dry overnight. As an alternative, obtain magnetic tape that has one peel-and-stick side.

STUDENT TEXT QUESTION

▶ Page 242, paragraph 2: **Which symbols in Table 10-1 might come from Latin?** *Cu, Au, Fe, Hg, K, Ag, Na*

10-1 Structure of the Atom

New Science Words

chemical symbol
nucleus
electrons
protons
neutrons
atomic number
electron cloud

Objectives

▶ List the names and symbols of common elements.
▶ Describe the present model of the atom.
▶ Describe how electrons are arranged in an atom.

Table 10-1

Chemical Symbols

Do the letters C, Al, He, and Ag mean anything to you? Each letter or pair of letters is a **chemical symbol,** which **①** **is a shorthand way to write the name of an element.** The black material on a burned match is carbon—C. You may wrap food in foil made of aluminum—Al. Did you ever lose a balloon filled with helium—He? You often use coins that contain copper—Cu.

Most chemical symbols consist of one capital letter or a capital letter plus a small letter. For some elements, the symbol is the first letter of the element's name. For other elements, the symbol is the first letter of the name plus another letter from its name. Some symbols, such as Ag, are derived from Latin. *Argentum* is Latin for silver. Which symbols in Table 10-1 might come from Latin?

SYMBOLS OF SOME ELEMENTS

Aluminum	Al	Gold	Au	Mercury	Hg
Calcium	Ca	Hydrogen	H	Nitrogen	N
Carbon	C	Helium	He	Oxygen	O
Chlorine	Cl	Iodine	I	Potassium	K
Copper	Cu	Iron	Fe	Silver	Ag
Fluorine	F	Magnesium	Mg	Sodium	Na

Matter and Atoms

The idea of atoms began more than 2400 years ago with Greek thinkers, who defined atoms as the smallest parts of matter. Today scientists consider atoms to be the basic building blocks of matter. The atom consists

OPTIONS

Meeting Different Ability Levels

For Section 10-1, use the following **Teacher Resource Masters** depending upon individual students' needs.

◆ **Study Guide Master** for all students.

● **Reinforcement Master** for students of average and above average ability levels.

▲ **Enrichment Master** for above average students.

Additional Teacher Resource Package masters are listed in the OPTIONS box throughout the section. The additional masters are appropriate for all students.

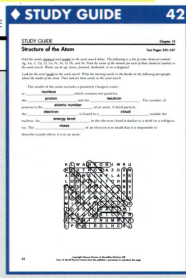

of a positively charged center, or **nucleus.** Moving around the nucleus are negatively charged particles called **electrons.** The two major kinds of particles in the nucleus are **protons** and **neutrons.** The mass of a proton is about the same as that of a neutron. The mass of an electron is about 1/2000 the mass of a proton. The electron's mass is so small that it is considered negligible. Therefore, the nucleus contains most of the mass of the atom.

A neutron is neutral, which means it has no charge. A proton has a positive charge. As a result, the net charge on the nucleus is positive. A proton's positive charge is equal to the negative charge of an electron. Table 10-2 summarizes this information about the three particles in an atom.

② Science and READING

The element platinum has an interesting history. Find out why it was called fool's silver.

Table 10-2

COMPARISON OF PARTICLES IN AN ATOM

	Relative Mass	Charge	Location in the Atom
Proton	1	1+	Part of nucleus
Neutron	1	none	Part of nucleus
Electron	0	1−	Moves around nucleus

The **atomic number** of an atom is the number of protons in its nucleus. Every atom of the same element has the same number of protons. Atoms of different elements have different numbers of protons. For example, every carbon atom has 6 protons. Therefore, it has the atomic number 6.

③

The number of electrons in an atom is equal to the number of protons. A carbon atom, then, has 6 electrons because it has 6 protons. Because the numbers of positively charged protons and negatively charged electrons in an atom are equal, the atom as a whole is electrically neutral.

How is the number of electrons in an atom related to the number of protons?

Table 10-3

ATOMIC NUMBER OF SOME ELEMENTS

Atom	Number of Protons	Number of Electrons	Atomic Number
Carbon	12	12	12
Aluminum	13	13	13
Helium	2	2	2
Silver	47	47	47

● REINFORCEMENT 42

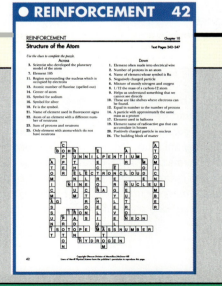

▲ ENRICHMENT 42 **243**

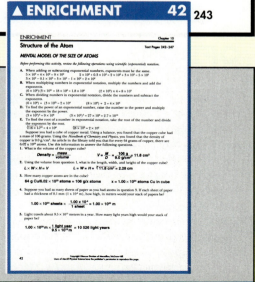

① MOTIVATE

▶ Obtain a periodic table that is in Spanish or French from your school's foreign language teacher. Explain that the chemical symbols are the same for all languages.

TYING TO PREVIOUS KNOWLEDGE:
Have students recall the standardized shapes and symbols used on street signs to convey safety information. Students will probably know a few names and chemical formulas for some common substances, such as table salt, NaCl; cane sugar, $C_{12}H_{22}O_{11}$; and water, H_2O. Encourage your students by informing them that they will learn many more symbols and formulas during this and the next chapter.

OBJECTIVES AND SCIENCE WORDS:
Have students review the objectives and science words to become familiar with this section.

② TEACH

Key Concepts are highlighted.

CONCEPT DEVELOPMENT

▶ For students who enjoy history, you can share the following information. By 1700, thirteen elements had been identified in their pure form. When Mendeleev proposed his periodic table in 1869, chemists knew of 26 elements. In 1908, Moseley used X rays to determine the atomic numbers of 81 elements. Today, 109 elements have been discovered or synthesized.

CONCEPT DEVELOPMENT

▶ You may want to review Rutherford's gold foil experiment with the class. Alpha particles hit gold foil. Most passed through, indicating that the atom is mostly empty space. However, some particles were deflected by a small, dense, positively charged nucleus. Details may be found in all high school chemistry texts.

▶ Emphasize that Bohr's planetary model of the atom is not the best model for science students to visualize. Encourage them to think about electrons occupying probability clouds.

▶ **Demonstration:** Place a small scoop of sesame seeds inside a balloon. Inflate it and tie it closed. Shake the seeds around the balloon to simulate electrons moving about the nucleus. Their pattern of motion mimics that of electrons in an electron cloud.

STUDENT TEXT QUESTION

▶ Page 244, paragraph 2: **Why is the Bohr model called the planetary model?** *It has electrons orbiting in paths like planets around a sun.*

REVEALING MISCONCEPTIONS

▶ Students often do not realize the importance of capital and lowercase letters in chemical symbols. For example, *CO* and *Co* do not have the same meaning. Point out that carbon monoxide is not the same as an atom of cobalt.

CROSS CURRICULUM

▶ **Design and Engineering:** Both engineers and scientists often use models to predict the behavior of actual objects. An airplane model is constructed and tested in a wind tunnel before the prototype is built. Design flaws can be corrected because a model behaves just like the real thing. Sometimes computer models are used instead of physical models. Our model of the atom should also allow us to explain how the real atom behaves.

Figure 10-1. A globe is a physical model, unlike a scientific model, which is a mental picture.

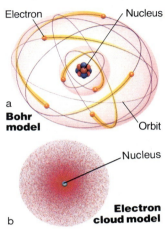

a **Bohr model**

b **Electron cloud model**

Figure 10-2. The top illustration is an early model of an atom with defined paths for electrons. The lower illustration is a later model showing a region where electrons are likely to be.

Figure 10-3. In an atom as wide as a football field, the nucleus would be as wide as a paper clip wire.

Models of the Atom

As scientists continued to study matter and atoms, they tried to form a mental picture or model of what an atom might look like. ==A model helps us understand something we cannot see directly. A good model of the atom must explain all the information about matter and atoms.== As more information was collected, scientists changed their models. Therefore, the model of the atom we use today is the result of the work of many scientists.

One of the earliest models of an atom looked like the one in Figure 10-2a. It was developed by Niels Bohr in 1913. Bohr pictured the atom as having a central nucleus with electrons moving around it in well-defined paths, or orbits. Can you explain why Bohr's model is also called the planetary model of the atom?

In 1926, scientists developed a better model of the atom. In this model, ==the electrons moved about in a region called an **electron cloud**== (Figure 10-2b). This cloud surrounds the nucleus of the atom. It describes the region where an electron is likely to be, at any time. The diameter of the nucleus is about 1/100 000 the diameter of the electron cloud. Suppose you built a model of an atom with an electron cloud as wide as a football field. The atom's nucleus would be about the thickness of the wire in a paper clip!

Because the electron's mass is so small, it is impossible for you—or anyone—to describe exactly where it is as it moves in the atom. All anyone can give

OPTIONS

INQUIRY QUESTIONS

▶ **Democritus stated his belief that matter was composed of atoms in 400 B.C. John Dalton proposed his atomic theory in 1808 A.D. Science has advanced rapidly since the acceptance of the atomic theory. Why didn't the ancient Greeks make similar advances? Hint: Research the influence of Aristotle's ideas about matter.** *Aristotle's idea that matter was continuous prevailed. Many of Aristotle's ideas were accepted without question until the 17th and 18th centuries.*

▶ **Hydrazine, N_2H_4, is a fuming, corrosive liquid used in rocket fuels. Ammonia, NH_3, is a gas that dissolves in water to form a cleaning solution. What is the difference in their chemical formulas?** *Hydrazine has two atoms of hydrogen for every one atom of nitrogen. Ammonia has three atoms of hydrogen for every one atom of nitrogen.*

Figure 10-4. You can compare the spray of water from a lawn sprinkler to an electron cloud.

is its probable location. Describing the electron's location around a nucleus is like trying to describe your location in your science class at any given moment. Your most probable location during the class is at your desk. Other possible, though less probable, locations are at the pencil sharpener, in the supply closet, and at the teacher's desk.

The electron cloud represents the probable locations of electrons within an atom. You can compare the electron cloud to the spray of water drops from a lawn sprinkler. Each drop represents a probable location of an electron in the cloud. As you can see in Figure 10-4, most of the drops are concentrated near the center of the spray. In an atom, the most probable location of electrons is in the electron cloud, distributed about the nucleus.

What does the electron cloud represent?

Energy Levels of Electrons

All the electrons in an atom are contained in the electron cloud. Within the electron cloud, electrons are at various distances from the nucleus. Electrons near the nucleus have low energy. Electrons farther away have higher energy. You can represent the energy differences of the electrons by picturing the atom as having energy levels.

These energy levels are like the shelves of a refrigerator door. A carton on the lowest shelf represents an electron in the lowest energy level. The difference in spacing of the shelves indicates differences in the amount of energy the electrons in that level can have. Shelves of a refrigerator door can usually hold the same number of cartons. Unlike these shelves, each energy level of an atom has a maximum number of electrons it can hold.

Did You Know?

One ounce of gold can be made into a wire 50 miles long.

CONCEPT DEVELOPMENT

▶ A dart board and one dart can be used as a model of the hydrogen atom with its one electron. The pattern of holes in the dart board represents the electron cloud around the nucleus.

▶ A multi-electron atom can have concentric spheres of electron clouds, called energy levels, around the nucleus. Students have seen layers of clouds in the sky when lower clouds are covered by a higher overcast.

REVEALING MISCONCEPTIONS

▶ Be certain that your students understand that the electron does not go around the nucleus like a train on a track.

CROSS CURRICULUM

▶ **Meteorology:** Fog can vary in density as is measured by visibility. Some aircraft need 1200 feet of visibility to take off. The density of the electron probability cloud varies also. It is less dense near and far from the nucleus. It has maximum density in the center of the cloud.

CHECK FOR UNDERSTANDING

Use the Mini Quiz to check for understanding.

MINI QUIZ

Use the Mini Quiz to check students' recall of chapter content.

1 A shorthand way to write an element's name is to use a(n) _____ . *chemical symbol*

2 An atom's nucleus contains _____ . *protons and neutrons*

3 An atom's atomic number is the number of _____ in its nucleus. *protons*

4 Electrons move around the nucleus in a region called an electron _____ . *cloud*

5 Electrons near the nucleus have low _____ . *energy*

6 The electron capacities of the first three energy levels are 2, 8, and _____ . *18*

ENRICHMENT

▶ By assigning each student a scientist to research, you can have the class prepare a time line mural on the bulletin board to show how each contributed to our knowledge of the atom. You can assign the following names: Democritus, Aristotle, Newton, Boyle, Lavosier, Proust, Dalton, Avogadro, Gay-Lussac, Millikan, J. J. Thomson, Geiger, Rutherford, Bohr, De Broglie, Planck, Chadwick, Pauli, Schrödinger, Einstein, Heisenberg, Becquerel, and Curie.

PROGRAM RESOURCES

From the **Teacher Resource Package** use:
Cross-Curricular Connections, page 15, Alchemy.
Cross-Curricular Connections, page 16, The Name Game.

RETEACH

RETEACH

Have each student complete a duplicate of Table 10-2 that has one item missing from each of the three lines of information.

EXTENSION

For students who have mastered this section, use the **Reinforcement** and **Enrichment** masters or other OPTIONS provided.

3 CLOSE

▶ Ask questions 1-3 and the Apply Question in the Section Review.

? FLEX Your Brain

Use the Flex Your Brain activity to have students explore ATOMIC STRUCTURE.
▶ **Demonstration:** To make this section more concrete, allow students to see a cloud chamber in operation. Dry ice, methanol, a plastic box, a bright light source, and a radioactive source are needed. Your school district's physics teacher may have a cloud chamber. The alpha particles, helium nuclei, will cause the cold alcohol vapors to condense.

SECTION REVIEW ANSWERS

1. C, Al, H, O, Na
2. proton: positive, nucleus; neutron: no charge, nucleus; electron: negative, cloud surrounding nucleus
3. the region where electrons are likely to be in an atom
4. Apply: The visual blur formed by the moving blades can be a model for an electron cloud surrounding the nucleus of an atom. The blades form a blurry cloud and appear to be everywhere at once. Unlike electrons, the blades move in a flat plane in definite paths, whereas electrons have a spherical distribution.

PROGRAM RESOURCES

From the **Teacher Resource Package** use:

Activity Worksheets, page 5, Flex Your Brain.

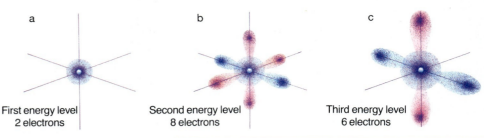

Figure 10-5. A sulfur atom has 16 electrons in three energy levels. Each of the colored regions at each level can hold two electrons. To get a complete picture, place (b) and (c) on top of (a).

The lowest energy level can hold just two electrons. The second energy level can hold eight electrons, and the third energy level can hold 18 electrons.

Sulfur's atomic number is 16. It has 16 protons and 16 electrons. Two of these electrons are in the first energy level, eight are in the second energy level, and six are in the third energy level. The electron arrangement of sulfur is shown in Figure 10-5.

Table 10-4

ELECTRONS IN ENERGY LEVELS	
Energy Level in Atom	**Maximum Number of Electrons**
1	2
2	8
3	18
4	32

SECTION REVIEW

1. Write the chemical symbols for the elements carbon, aluminum, hydrogen, oxygen, and sodium.
2. List the names, charges, and locations of three kinds of particles in an atom.
3. What does an electron cloud represent?
4. **Apply:** How might an electric fan that is turned on be a model of an atom? How is the fan unlike an atom?

☑ Concept Mapping

Make a concept map for the parts of an atom. Include the following terms: *electron cloud, nucleus, electrons, protons,* and *neutrons.* Also provide the charge of each part. If you need help, refer to Concept Mapping in the **Skill Handbook** on pages 684 and 685.

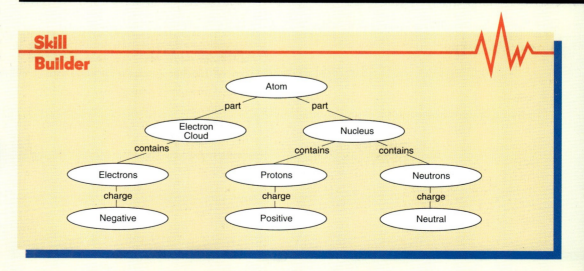

ACTIVITY 10-1
Models of Atomic Structure

Problem: *How can using a model allow you to predict similarities in atomic structure?*

Materials
- magnetic board about 20 cm × 27 cm
- one 0.5-cm piece and 24 2-cm rubber magnetic strips
- circles of white paper 4 cm wide
- marker

Procedure
1. Choose an element with an atomic number of 1 through 24. Determine the number of each kind of particle needed to make up an atom of that element.
2. Use a marker to write the number of protons and neutrons on a paper circle. This represents the nucleus of the atom.
3. Use a 0.5-cm magnetic strip to attach the model nucleus to one side of a magnetic board.
4. Use 2-cm magnetic strips to represent electrons. Arrange the model electrons in energy levels around the nucleus.

5. Remove either the model nucleus or the model electrons from the magnetic board and ask classmates to identify the element.
6. Repeat Steps 1 through 5 for another element.

Analyze
1. In a neutral atom, which particles will always be present in equal numbers?
2. What do you think would happen to the charge of an atom if one of the electrons was removed from the atom?
3. Except for hydrogen, how many first level electrons did each selected atom contain?

Conclude and Apply
4. How is this model of an atom similar to an actual atom?
5. Name two differences, other than size, between your model and an actual atom.
6. What happens to the atom if one proton is removed from the nucleus and one electron is also removed?

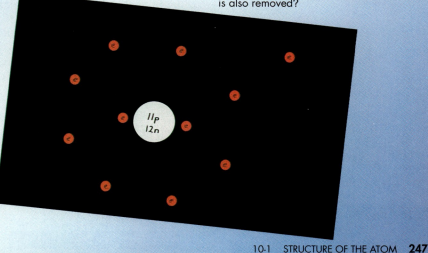

OBJECTIVE: Formulate models of atomic structure and **identify** atoms by their structures.

PROCESS SKILLS applied in this activity:
▶ **Formulating models** in Procedure Steps 2, 3, and 4.
▶ **Inferring** in Conclude and Apply Questions 5 and 6.

👥 COOPERATIVE LEARNING
Organize the class into Science Investigation groups of three or four. Have one student or pair construct the atom's nucleus and present it to the other two students, who must then decide on the electron arrangement.

TEACHING THE ACTIVITY
Alternate Materials: Painted steel rectangular snack trays may work well as magnetic boards. Use the bottom if there is a distracting design. Another possibility is to use carpet squares and the stiff half of Velcro strips.

Troubleshooting: Make sure the atom models are correctly constructed before having the class identify them. Going beyond element 20 requires a more detailed understanding of the distribution of electrons in energy levels.
▶ Review with students how to find the number of neutrons in an atom's nucleus when the atomic number is known.
▶ Peel-and-stick magnetic plastic tape is sold in most craft and hobby shops.

PROGRAM RESOURCES
From the **Teacher Resource Package** use:

Activity Worksheets, pages 78-79, Activity 10-1: Models of Atomic Structure.

ANSWERS TO QUESTIONS
1. protons and electrons
2. The atom would have an unbalanced proton and therefore would have a positive charge.
3. two
4. Answers will vary but should reflect the ideas that the numbers of protons and electrons are equal, the protons and neutrons are localized in the nucleus, and that electrons are distributed in energy levels outside the nucleus.

5. Answers will vary. Possible answers include the facts that electrons are not moving, the model is two-dimensional, and the electrons would be distributed much farther from the nucleus if the model were to scale.
6. The atom becomes a different element with an atomic number one less than that of the original atom.

PREPARATION

SECTION BACKGROUND

▶ Quarks are described as having properties called flavors, such as charm, truth, and beauty. Quarks also have properties called colors: red, green, and blue. These terms are simply arbitrary labels for properties.

▶ Protons and neutrons are thought to be made of quarks.

1 MOTIVATE

▶ **Demonstration:** Place a glass bottle in a heavy cloth bag. Drop it to break the bottle. Place the pieces on a newspaper. Ask students if they think they could reconstruct the bottle by studying the pieces. Relate this to the work of scientists who smash atoms in a supercollider. They study the pieces to learn more about the whole particle.

TYING TO PREVIOUS KNOWLEDGE:
Have students recall that National Transportation Safety Board investigators collect the pieces after an airplane crash to determine the cause of the accident.

OBJECTIVES AND SCIENCE WORDS:
Have students review the objectives and science words to become familiar with this section.

New Science Words

quarks

Objectives

▶ Identify quarks as particles of matter that make up protons and neutrons.
▶ Explain how protons can be broken apart.

Looking for Quarks

You know that protons and neutrons form the nucleus of atoms. What forms protons and neutrons? Many scientists agree that protons and neutrons are made of even smaller particles of matter called **quarks.** So far five different types of quarks have been postulated and there is evidence of a sixth type. Scientists hope someday to observe this type of quark by breaking apart protons with enough energy to release quarks.

The strong nuclear force holding quarks together gets stronger and stronger as quarks are pulled apart, just like a spring. So far, no collision has had enough energy to actually isolate individual quarks. Scientists will break protons apart by crashing them into other protons. How can scientists make protons crash into each other?

One way will be with a gigantic supercollider. The supercollider is expected to be completed at a cost of more than eight billion dollars early in the next cen-

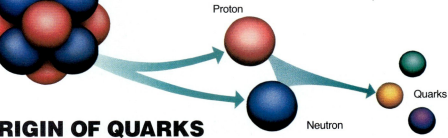

ORIGIN OF QUARKS

Proton

Neutron

Quarks

OPTIONS

Meeting Different Ability Levels

For Section 10-2, use the following **Teacher Resource Masters** depending upon individual students' needs.

◆ **Study Guide Master** for all students.
● **Reinforcement Master** for students of average and above average ability levels.
▲ **Enrichment Master** for above average students.

◆ **STUDY GUIDE** **43**

STUDY GUIDE — Chapter 10
Smaller Particles of Matter — Text Pages 248–249

Circle the correctly spelled vocabulary word in each row.

1. quark — qarck — qwark — (quark)
2. (proton) — protahn — protan — prohton
3. nutron — neutran — (neutron) — nuetron
4. (research) — resurch — reserch — research
5. (nucleus) — neucleus — nuclius — nuclea
6. elament — (element) — elliment — ellament
7. elektron — electran — (electron) — elecktron
8. What is a supercollider? Briefly, describe how a supercollider can be used to study the nature of matter. **A supercollider is a gigantic accelerator that is used to accelerate two beams of protons going in opposite directions. When they are going at almost 300 000 m/s the two beams are aimed in such a way that there is a head-on collision. The impact of the collision will break the protons into quarks.**

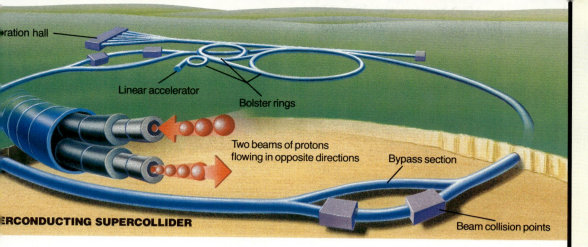

ration hall

Linear accelerator

Bolster rings

Two beams of protons
flowing in opposite directions

Bypass section

ERCONDUCTING SUPERCOLLIDER

Beam collision points

tury near the town of Waxahachie, Texas. The supercollider will include a 80-km track surrounded by more than 8500 magnets. These powerful magnets will force protons into two beams whirling in opposite directions inside the supercollider track. Accelerated by magnetic forces, the protons in each beam will move faster and faster. When the protons are moving at almost 300 000 000 m/s, the two beams will meet in a head-on collision. Large detectors and computers will record the particles produced by the destruction of the protons.

SECTION REVIEW

1. What are quarks?
2. Describe the supercollider and its research use.

You Decide!

Supporters of the supercollider say that it will help scientists to better understand what matter is made of and how matter behaves. They point out that the money spent will create thousands of new jobs. It will also create new technology just as the space program did. However, critics argue that important, smaller research projects may be cancelled because of lack of funds due to the supercollider's high costs. What factors do you think are important in evaluating scientific research like the supercollider? Why?

SCIENCE & SOCIETY

249

---

2 TEACH

Key Concepts are highlighted.

CONCEPT DEVELOPMENT

▶ **Demonstration:** The magnets referred to are electromagnets, which can change polarity quickly to alternately pull and push the protons. Use a 6-volt battery connected to many turns of insulated wire wrapped around a large nail to demonstrate an electromagnet.

CHECK FOR UNDERSTANDING

Ask questions 1-2 in the Section Review.

RETEACH

Discuss the Science and Society feature and You Decide with the class. Use the discussion to refocus attention on how and why a supercollider is used.

EXTENSION

For students who have mastered this section, use the **Reinforcement** and **Enrichment** masters or other OPTIONS provided.

3 CLOSE

▶ Have students do library research to determine the current status of the supercollider project.

SECTION REVIEW ANSWERS

1. Quarks are small particles of matter that make up protons and neutrons.
2. The supercollider consists of an 80-km track surrounded by thousands of powerful magnets.

SCIENCE & SOCIETY

YOU DECIDE!

Answers will vary. Students should give sound support for their positions. If your class has students accustomed to debate, you could organize two teams to research and debate the topic.

PREPARATION

SECTION BACKGROUND

▶ The choice of the first atomic mass standard was arbitrary. For a long time chemists used an atomic mass scale based on oxygen-16. In 1961, it was agreed to use carbon-12 as the standard for atomic mass.

▶ The term *atomic weight* is incorrect even though it has been used for many years. Your students will quickly learn from your correct examples and frequent use of *atomic mass*.

▶ Be certain students understand that isotopes of the same element are exactly alike chemically, but different in mass.

▶ The atomic number is designated by the letter *Z* and the mass number by the letter *A*. The number of neutrons in an atom can be calculated using the formula *A* − *Z*.

PREPLANNING

▶ To prepare for Activity 10-2, you will need to obtain the candy-coated peanuts and candy-coated chocolates. Sort out the needed number of different colors and place them in plastic bags.

1 MOTIVATE

▶ Use the Problem Solving feature on page 252 to show your students the relevance of the topic.

TYING TO PREVIOUS KNOWLEDGE: Students have previously studied mass in different contexts. Refresh their memories by asking them to relate their concepts of mass. Make sure they are not confusing mass with size.

New Science Words

mass number
isotopes
average atomic mass

Objectives

▶ Compute the atomic mass and mass number of an atom.
▶ Identify and describe isotopes of common elements.
▶ Interpret the average atomic mass of an element.

Atomic Mass

What is the atom mass unit?

You may have guessed that the mass of an atom is *very* small. Yet, scientists are able to measure that mass with great accuracy. They can even measure the masses of protons and neutrons. The unit of measurement of those particles is the atomic mass unit (u). In fact, the mass of a proton or a neutron is almost equal to 1 u. This is not a coincidence—the unit was defined that way. ❶ The atomic mass unit is defined as one-twelfth the mass of a carbon atom containing six protons and six neutrons. Remember that the mass of a carbon atom is in its nucleus because the atom's six electrons have a negligible mass. Therefore, each of the 12 particles in the nucleus must have a mass nearly equal to one-twelfth the mass of the carbon atom. Thus, a proton or a neutron has a mass of about 1 u.

To help you understand this, suppose you have a egg carton containing six brown eggs and six white eggs, as shown in Figure 10-6. You could define a mass unit as one-twelfth the mass of the entire dozen. Because the carton itself has very little mass, the mass of each egg, brown or white, would be equal to your defined unit.

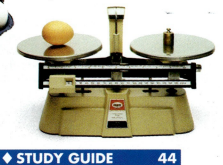

Figure 10-6. You can compare a carton of eggs to a carbon atom.

OPTIONS

Meeting Different Ability Levels

For Section 10-3, use the following **Teacher Resource Masters** depending upon individual students' needs.

◆ **Study Guide Master** for all students.
● **Reinforcement Master** for students of average and above average ability levels.
▲ **Enrichment Master** for above average students.

Additional Teacher Resource Package masters are listed in the OPTIONS box throughout the section. The additional masters are appropriate for all students.

◆ **STUDY GUIDE** 44

STUDY GUIDE — Chapter 10
Masses of Atoms — Text Pages 250–254

Use the terms in the box to complete the following paragraph about atomic mass. Terms may be used more than once.

| number | standard | neutron(s) | proton(s) | mass |

The electron has very little mass compared to the _____**proton**_____ or _____**neutron**_____. The mass of the atom depends on the nucleus and how many _____**protons**_____ and _____**neutrons**_____ it has. The sum of the protons and neutrons is the _____**number**_____ of an atom. The number of neutrons in an atom can be found by subtracting the atomic number from the _____**mass**_____ number. The mass of the atom is so small that there is a measure called the atomic _____**mass**_____ unit with a symbol of "μ."

Use the terms in the box to complete the following paragraph about isotopes. Terms may be used more than once.

| many | mixtures | protons | neutrons | between | number |
| element | one | isotopes | six protons | electrons | |

The nuclei of all atoms of a given element always have the same number of _____**protons**_____. They will also have the same number of _____**electrons**_____ around the nucleus. Some atoms may have more or fewer _____**neutrons**_____ than will other atoms of the same element. Atoms of the same element with different numbers of neutrons are called _____**isotopes**_____. Hydrogen has three isotopes. A hydrogen atom may contain zero, one, or two _____**neutrons**_____. Every atom of carbon must contain _____**six protons**_____, but some contain six neutrons and others have eight neutrons. Some elements have only _____**one**_____ natural isotope; however, other elements may have _____**many**_____ isotopes.

One way of showing the difference between isotopes of an element is to put the mass _____**number**_____ after the name of the element. The second way of showing an isotope is to write the mass number and the atomic number with the symbol of the _____**element**_____. In nature, most elements are _____**mixtures**_____ of isotopes. In chlorine gas, there are two isotopes and the average mass of this element is _____**between**_____ the two.

44

Mass Number

The **mass number** of an atom is the sum of the number of protons and the number of neutrons in an atom. Put another way, the mass number is the number of particles in the nucleus of an atom. As you can see in Table 10-5, the mass number of an atom is almost equal to its mass expressed in atomic mass units. ②

If you know the mass number and the atomic number of an atom, you can then calculate the number of neutrons. The number of neutrons is equal to the atomic number subtracted from the mass number:

number of neutrons = mass number − atomic number

Table 10-5

MASS NUMBERS OF SOME ATOMS					
Element	Symbol	Protons	Neutrons	Mass Number	Atomic Mass*
Boron	B	5	6	11	10.81
Carbon	C	6	6	12	12.01
Oxygen	O	8	8	16	16.00
Sodium	Na	11	12	23	22.99
Copper	Cu	29	34	63	63.55

* to two decimal places

Isotopes

③ Not all the atoms of an element have the same number of neutrons. Atoms of the same element that have different numbers of neutrons are called **isotopes**.

Suppose you have a sample of the element boron, which is a dark gray powder. Naturally occurring atoms of boron have mass numbers of 10 or 11. How many neutrons are there in a boron atom? It depends upon which boron atom you are referring to. Look at Table 10-5 and use the formula above to calculate that a boron atom may contain five or six neutrons. Use the example on the left to help you.

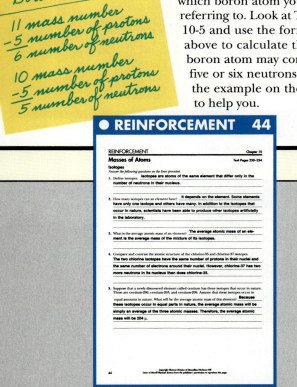

B
Boron

11 mass number
−5 number of protons
6 number of neutrons

10 mass number
−5 number of protons
5 number of neutrons

Figure 10-7. Boron has two naturally occurring isotopes.

● **REINFORCEMENT 44**

▲ **ENRICHMENT 44**

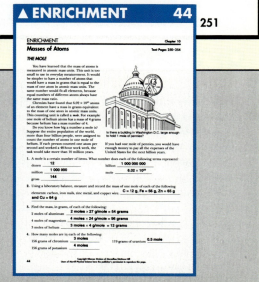

2 TEACH

Key Concepts are highlighted.

CONCEPT DEVELOPMENT

▶ The proton, 1.0073 u, and the neutron, 1.0087 u, are essentially equal in mass. The mass of the electron is extremely small, 0.000 549 u, or about 1/2000 the mass of a proton.

▶ Emphasize the fact that nearly all the mass of the atom is located in the nucleus.

▶ For most calculations in science, the average atomic mass is used rather than the mass of just one isotope.

REVEALING MISCONCEPTIONS

▶ The word *isotope* sometimes conjures up thoughts of dangerous radioactive materials. Before discussing isotopes, have members of the class tell what the word brings to mind. They should understand that nearly all elements exist as mixtures of isotopes and that many are not radioactive.

CROSS CURRICULUM

▶ **Medicine:** Nuclear radiation therapy is very successful for some cancers. Have interested students research the production and medical uses of radioactive isotopes.

TEACHER F.Y.I.

▶ Eighty percent of all nuclear waste comes from hospitals where nuclear medicine is practiced.

STUDENT TEXT QUESTION

▶ Page 251, paragraph 4: **Calculate that a boron atom may contain 5 or 6 neutrons.** *Mass number − protons = neutrons. 10 − 5 = 5; 11 − 5 = 6*

CHECK FOR UNDERSTANDING

Use the Mini Quiz to check for understanding.

MINI QUIZ

Use the Mini Quiz to check students' recall of chapter content.

① One-twelfth of the mass of carbon-12 is defined as one atomic _____ . *mass unit*

② The sum of the protons and neutrons in an atom is the atom's _____ . *mass number*

③ Atoms of the same element that have a different mass are called _____ . *isotopes*

④ Most elements have more than one isotope, so the mass number on the periodic table is a(n) _____ . *average*

RETEACH

To model the concept of average atomic mass, determine the average weight of the students in your class after each records his or her weight, to the nearest ten pounds, on a folded piece of paper.

EXTENSION

For students who have mastered this section, use the **Reinforcement** and **Enrichment** masters or other OPTIONS provided.

PROBLEM SOLVING

Think Critically: Refer students to the first two sections of Chapter 24 for additional information on this topic. The iodine-131 atom has too many neutrons for the number of protons to be stable. With too few or too many neutrons, the isotope is likely to be radioactive.

 Proton

 Neutron

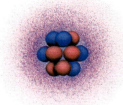
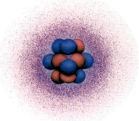

Figure 10-8. The two isotopes of boron have different numbers of neutrons and different mass numbers.

Figure 10-8 shows the two isotopes of boron. Because the numbers of neutrons in the isotopes are different, the mass numbers are also different. You use the name of the element followed by the mass number of the isotope to identify each isotope: boron-10 and boron-11. Because most elements have more than one isotope, each element is given an average atomic mass. The **average atomic mass** of an element is the average mass of the mixture of its isotopes.

PROBLEM SOLVING

Ivan's Isotopes

After carrying out many medical tests, the doctor found a tumor in Ivan's thyroid gland. The doctor decided to treat the tumor with iodine-131, an isotope of iodine. Ivan asked her how the treatment would work. She explained that atoms of some isotopes, like iodine-131, are unstable. One of these atoms has too many neutrons for the number of protons. The nucleus in an unstable isotope rearranges itself spontaneously, resulting in the release of energy called radiation.

The thyroid gland absorbs iodine because the gland needs iodine to function properly. The doctor told Ivan the tumor cells in his thyroid are more sensitive to radiation than the healthy thyroid cells. A controlled dose of radiation from the iodine-131 would kill the tumor cells but would not affect the healthy cells.

Think Critically: Why is iodine-131 unstable? Why is the number of neutrons in an atom important in the field of medicine?

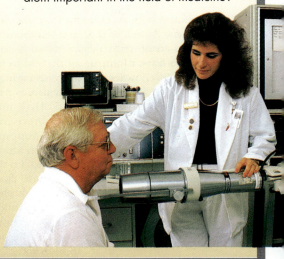

OPTIONS

INQUIRY QUESTIONS

▶ Both X-ray radiation and nuclear radiation can be used in the treatment of cancer. How do they differ? How do they work against a tumor? *The X ray is a form of radiant energy. Nuclear radiation can be of two types—particle radiation such as alpha and beta, or an energy wave called gamma radiation. All can disrupt the DNA molecules of actively dividing tumor cells.*

PROGRAM RESOURCES

From the **Teacher Resource Package** use:
Critical Thinking/Problem Solving, page 16, Carbon-14 Dating.

For example, four out of five atoms of boron are boron-11, and one out of five is boron-10, as shown in Figure 10-8. Thus, in an average sample of five atoms of boron, four atoms are likely to have a mass of 11 u. One atom will have a mass of 10 u. If you measured the mass of the five atoms, you would find it to be 54 u. The average atomic mass of the boron mixture is 54 u divided by five, or 10.8 u. That is, the average atomic mass of the element boron is 10.8 u. Note that the average atomic mass of boron is close to the mass of its most abundant isotope, boron-11.

For another example, hydrogen has three isotopes—H-1, H-2, and H-3. Each has one proton. How many neutrons does each have? The most abundant isotope is H-1, and the element's average atomic mass is 1.008.

The average atomic mass of each element can be found in the periodic table of elements. As you will see later, the periodic table also holds much more information about the elements.

EcoTip

Many batteries contain the elements mercury and cadmium. These are hazardous materials that contaminate landfills when the batteries break apart. Reduce waste. Use rechargeable batteries.

SECTION REVIEW

1. A chlorine atom has 17 protons and 18 neutrons. What is its mass number? What is its atomic number?
2. How are the isotopes of an element alike and how are they different?
3. The atomic number of magnesium is 12. The three naturally occurring isotopes of magnesium are Mg-24, Mg-25, and Mg-26. The average atomic mass of magnesium is 24.3 u. Why does this indicate that most magnesium atoms contain 12 neutrons?
4. **Apply:** An isotope of phosphorus used to treat bone cancer is P-30. Another isotope of phosphorus is P-31. What are two reasons why most of the phosphorus in your food must be P-31 and not P-30?

☑ Making and Using Tables

Construct a table organizing information about the atomic numbers, atomic mass numbers, and the number of protons, neutrons, and electrons in atoms of oxygen-16 and oxygen-17. If you need help, refer to Making and Using Tables in the **Skill Handbook** on page 686.

Skill Builder

3 CLOSE

▶ Ask questions 1-3 and the **Apply** Question in the Section Review.

▶ Have a doctor or nurse from your local hospital's radiation therapy or nuclear medicine department talk to the class about how treatments are done and what the results are. Perhaps a team of students with a video camera could go to the hospital and record a tour and interview to share with the class if the doctor cannot come to the school.

SECTION REVIEW ANSWERS

1. 35, 17

2. They have the same number of protons (atomic number) but different numbers of neutrons (mass number).

3. An atom of magnesium has 12 protons. Because the average atomic mass is close to 24, most atoms of magnesium would have 12 neutrons, giving a mass number of 24.

4. Apply: Living things that make up our food source could not themselves survive with large quantities of a radioactive isotope. The average atomic mass of phosphorus is very near 31, indicating that most naturally occurring atoms of phosphorus are P-31, which is not radioactive.

Skill Builder

Comparing Isotopes of Oxygen

Isotope	O-16	O-17
Atomic number	8	8
Protons	8	8
Electrons	8	8
Neutrons	8	9
Mass number	16	17

ENRICHMENT

Have students work these problems.

▶ What is the weighted average for a class of 24 students on a quiz if 5 students earn a grade of 100, and 19 students earn a grade of 80? *84%*

▶ What is the average atomic mass of silicon if 92.21% of its atoms have mass 27.977 u, 4.70% have mass 28.976 u, and 3.09% have mass 29.974 u? *28.1 u*

▶ What is the average atomic mass of hafnium if, out of every 100 atoms, 5 have mass 176 u, 19 have mass 177 u, 27 have mass 178 u, 14 have mass 179 u, and 35 have mass 180 u? *179 u*

▶ Compute the average atomic mass of silver if 51.83% of the atoms in nature have a mass of 106.905 u and 48.17% have a mass of 108.905 u. *107.9 u*

OBJECTIVE: Model the concept of average atomic mass by using an analogy.

PROCESS SKILLS applied in this activity:
▶ **Separating and controlling variables** in Procedure Steps 4 and 5.
▶ **Calculating** in Analyze Question 2.
▶ **Predicting** in Conclude and Apply Questions 3 and 4.

COOPERATIVE LEARNING
Use the Paired Partners strategy to conduct this activity. Have students reverse roles in Procedure Step 5.

TEACHING THE ACTIVITY
Alternate Materials: Several popular brands of candy will meet the needs of this activity.
Troubleshooting: Work out one example using different candy ratios.
▶ Use small paper cups or plastic bags to organize the candy before the activity. It may prevent some time delays and confusion.

PROGRAM RESOURCES
From the **Teacher Resource Package** use:

Activity Worksheets, pages 80-81, Activity 10-2: Isotopes and Atomic Mass.

ACTIVITY 10-2
Isotopes and Atomic Mass

Problem: *How do isotopes affect average atomic mass?*

Materials
- 4 red and 3 green candy-coated peanuts
- 2 red and 3 green candy-coated chocolates

Procedure
1. Copy the data table and use it to record your observations.
2. Make a pile of four red candy-coated peanuts and two red candy-coated chocolates. The two different kinds of candy represent isotopes of the same element.
3. Assume that a red peanut has a mass of two candy units and a red chocolate has a mass of one candy unit.
4. To calculate the average mass of the element, multiply the number of red peanuts by its mass expressed in candy units. Do the same for the red chocolates. Combine the two values and divide this total mass by the total number of candies. Record your calculations.
5. Repeat Steps 2 through 4, but use three green peanuts and three green chocolates. Assume a green peanut has a mass of four units and a green chocolate has a mass of three units.

Analyze
1. There were six red and six green candies. Why were their average masses not the same?
2. If a sample of element X contains 100 atoms of X-12 and ten atoms of X-14, what is the average mass of X?

Conclude and Apply
3. An element needed for most nuclear reactors is uranium. Its two major isotopes are U-235 and U-238. Look at the mass of uranium on the periodic table. Which isotope is the most common? Explain.
4. How do the masses of isotopes affect the average atomic mass of an element so that it is often not a whole number?

Data and Observations

Sample Data

| | Peanut | Chocolate | Average |
	candy × mass	candy × mass	$\dfrac{\text{total mass}}{\text{total candies}}$
Red	4 × 2 = ⑧	2 × 1 = ②	$\dfrac{8+2}{4+2} = 1.7$
Green	3 × 4 = ⑫	3 × 3 = ⑨	$\dfrac{12+9}{3+3} = 3.5$

ANSWERS TO QUESTIONS
1. A greater proportion of the red candies were peanuts, which had a larger mass.
2. $100 \times 12 = 1200$
   $10 \times 14 = 140$

   Average mass $= \dfrac{1200 + 140}{100 + 10}$

   $= \dfrac{1340}{110} = 12.2$

3. Students should infer that U-238 is most common because the average atomic mass of uranium is very near 238.

4. Average atomic mass is a weighted average of all isotopes of an element. Significant proportions of isotopes other than the most abundant one will cause the average to vary from a whole number. Chlorine (average atomic mass = 35.45) is a good example. It consists of approximately 75% Cl-35 and 25% Cl-37.

The Periodic Table 10-4

Objectives

▶ Describe the periodic table of elements and use it to find information about an element.
▶ Distinguish between a group and a period.
▶ Use the periodic table to classify an element as a metal, nonmetal, or metalloid.

New Science Words

periodic table
groups
dot diagram
periods
metals
nonmetals
metalloids

Structure of the Periodic Table

Remember the last time you sat on a swing and moved back and forth, over and over? Your movement was periodic. *Periodic* means "repeated in a pattern." Look at a calendar. The days of the week are periodic because they repeat themselves every seven days. The calendar is a periodic table of days. You use calendars to organize your time.

In the late 1800s, Dimitri Mendeleev, a Russian chemist, searched for a way to organize the elements. He arranged all the elements known at that time in order of increasing atomic masses. He discovered that there was a pattern to the properties of the elements. This pattern was periodic. The arrangement of elements according to repeated changes in properties is called a **periodic table** of elements. Look at the early periodic table at the right.

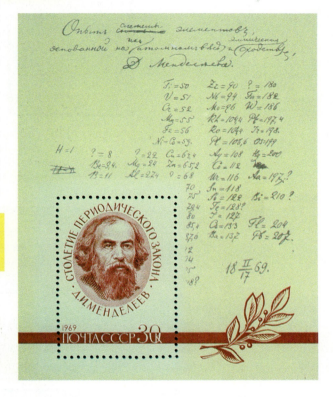

Figure 10-9. In his first periodic table, Mendeleev wrote question marks in spaces for elements not yet discovered.

SECTION 10-4

PREPARATION

SECTION BACKGROUND

▶ Dimitri Ivanovich Mendeleev was born in Siberia, the last of 14 or 17 children, depending on which record you accept. His father died when Mendeleev was very young. His mother took him to St. Petersburg (Leningrad) for education. She died shortly after their arrival. He graduated from college at the top of his class and then studied in France and Germany. In 1866, he became professor of chemistry at the University of St. Petersburg.
▶ Mendeleev predicted the existence of six undiscovered elements—scandium, gallium, germanium, technetium, rhenium, and polonium.
▶ Mendeleev's first three predictions, made in 1871, were confirmed by 1885.

PREPLANNING

▶ Collect assorted pens and pencils for the Mini-Lab on page 257.
▶ If you have not already obtained one, you should have a display-size periodic table available.

1 MOTIVATE

▶ **Demonstration:** Using a battery-powered conductivity tester, touch the instrument's probes to samples of elements. Your high school physics teacher may have a conductivity tester that you can borrow. Students can begin to classify elements as conductors and nonconductors. Use this activity to lead into a discussion about the need to classify elements.

OPTIONS

INQUIRY QUESTIONS

Ask these questions as students study pages 255-257.
▶ **The nitrogen family of elements begins with a nonmetal and ends with a metal, bismuth. Can you explain such a wide variety of properties within group 15? Hint: The less attracted the outer-level electrons are, the more metallic the element.** *The size of the atom increases as you go down the family. Thus, the attraction for the outer electrons is less. Nitrogen is much smaller and has five closely held outer electrons.*

▶ **The noble gases (group 18) are chemically inert under most reaction conditions. What does chemically "inert" mean? What feature of outer electron structure do all noble gases share?** *The elements usually do not react with other elements. With the exception of helium, all have eight outer-level electrons.*

Mendeleev's periodic table had blank spaces. He looked at the properties and atomic masses of the elements surrounding these blank spaces. From this information he predicted the properties and the mass numbers of new elements that had not yet been discovered. Sometimes you make predictions like this. Suppose someone crossed out a date on a calendar, as shown. You could predict the missing date by looking at the surrounding dates. **Mendeleev's predictions proved to be quite accurate.** Scientists later discovered elements, such as germanium, having the properties that he had predicted (Table 10-6).

The periodic table of the elements is shown on pages 258 and 259. It's not as complex as it may seem to be. Each box in the table contains information about the elements that you studied earlier in this chapter. Look

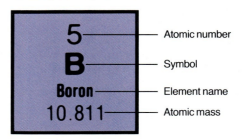

Figure 10-10. The periodic table shows the symbol, name, atomic number, and atomic mass of each element.

at Figure 10-10. This box represents the element boron. The atomic number, chemical symbol, name, and average atomic mass are included in this box. **The boxes for all of the elements are arranged in order of their atomic numbers.**

Table 10-6

"EKASILICON" (GERMANIUM)		
Properties	**Predicted**	**Actual**
Atomic mass	72	72.6
Density	5.5 g/cm³	5.35 g/cm³
Color	dark gray	gray-white
Effect of water	none	none
Effect of acid	slight	HCl: no effect
Effect of base	slight	KOH: no effect

256 ATOMIC STRUCTURE AND THE PERIODIC TABLE

Groups of Elements

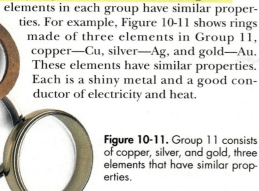

The vertical columns in the periodic table are called **groups.** The groups are numbered 1 through 18. The elements in each group have similar properties. For example, Figure 10-11 shows rings made of three elements in Group 11, copper—Cu, silver—Ag, and gold—Au. These elements have similar properties. Each is a shiny metal and a good conductor of electricity and heat.

Figure 10-11. Group 11 consists of copper, silver, and gold, three elements that have similar properties.

Why do elements in a group have similar properties? It is because they have similar electron arrangements. Think about how the properties of different kinds of balls are related to their shape. You expect a soccer ball and a basketball to bounce in similar ways because they have similar shapes. But a football will bounce differently, because it has a different shape.

Atoms of different elements have different numbers of electrons. However, atoms of different elements may have the same number of electrons in their outer energy levels. It is the number of electrons in the outer energy level that determines the properties of the element. Different elements with the same number of electrons in their outer energy level have similar properties. These outer electrons are so important that a special way to represent them has been developed. A **dot diagram** uses the symbol of the element and dots to represent the electrons in the outer energy level.

MINI-Lab
What are the advantages of a periodic table?
Observe the mass and other properties of your pen or pencil, such as color and composition. With your class, develop a "periodic table" of pens and pencils. Arrange similar pens and pencils in columns and in order of mass. What can you say about (a) the properties of the elements and (b) the masses of the elements in a column, or group, of the periodic table?

257

MINI-Lab
Materials: assorted pencils and pens, large table surface
Teaching Tips:
► Discuss with students the reasons for their arrangements. Make sure they have examined the properties of objects as they are arranged within columns.

Expected Results
Students should be able to place all wooden pencils in one column, mechanical pencils in another column, stick pens in another column, retractable pens in another column, and so on.

Answers to Questions
Within a column on the periodic table, the elements have similar properties and the same number of electrons in their outer energy level.

CONCEPT DEVELOPMENT
► Take every opportunity to point out elements on the periodic table and stress the relationship between electron structure and an element's position on the table.
► Point out that Groups one and two have one and two outer electrons, respectively. The number of outer electrons in groups 13 through 18 can be determined by subtracting ten from the group number.
► The number of outer electrons determines the element's properties. How tightly they are attracted to the nucleus determines their metallic nature. The "looser" the outer electrons are, the more metallic the element is.

PROGRAM RESOURCES
From the **Teacher Resource Package** use:

Activity Worksheets, page 84, Mini-Lab: What are the advantages of a periodic table?

Use **Laboratory Manual,** Chemical Activity.

CONCEPT DEVELOPMENT

▶ The spectrum of color across the periodic table shown here is designed to illustrate and reinforce the increasing nonmetallic character of elements as you read from left to right across the table. The redder the coloration of the element box, the greater the metallic character of the element. The bluer the box, the more nonmetallic the element. Notice that the elements along the stairstep line have both metallic and nonmetallic characteristics. These elements are the metalloids.

▶ Note also that the elements with the greatest metallic character are in the lower left corner of the table. Atoms of these elements are large, having several levels of electrons. As a result, their outer electrons are relatively distant from the nucleus and thus are loosely held. This fact causes the elements to be highly reactive because they lose outer electrons easily.

▶ Elements that are most nonmetallic are in the upper right of the table (disregarding the noble gases, Group 18). Atoms of these elements are small and have nearly full outer electron levels. Consequently, these elements attract electrons strongly and are highly reactive.

▶ The noble gases are technically nonmetals in physical character, but are extremely unreactive and therefore form a separate group with their own distinct properties.

▶ Hydrogen, by its electron arrangement, is part of group 1. However, because it has only one electron energy level which can hold only two electrons, it has its own unique set of properties. Therefore, it is colored differently from the other elements.

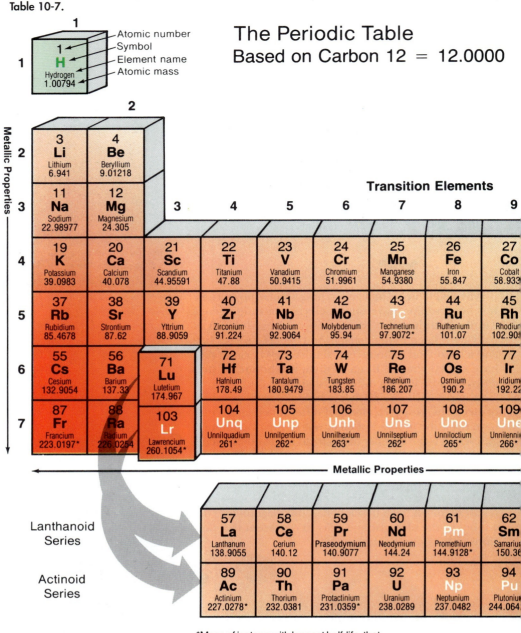

Table 10-7.

The Periodic Table
Based on Carbon 12 = 12.0000

*Mass of isotope with longest half-life, that is, the most stable isotope of the element

OPTIONS

INQUIRY QUESTIONS

▶ Iodine is used in many commercial chemicals and dyes. What is the name of the group to which iodine belongs? What is the meaning of the group name? *halogens, Greek for "salt formers"*

▶ Calcium compounds in the soil are absorbed by grass which is eaten by cows and made into milk. In your body, calcium is found in teeth and bones. Assume that some radioactive strontium-90 has accidentally been released into the atmosphere. Is there cause for concern? Explain. *Yes. Sr-90 will*

take the place of Ca because it is in the same group. After the Chernobyl accident in 1986, milk had to be discarded because it was radioactive.

▶ There are seven numbered rows on the periodic table. What does this tell you about atoms of elements in the seventh row? *These atoms have electrons in seven energy levels.*

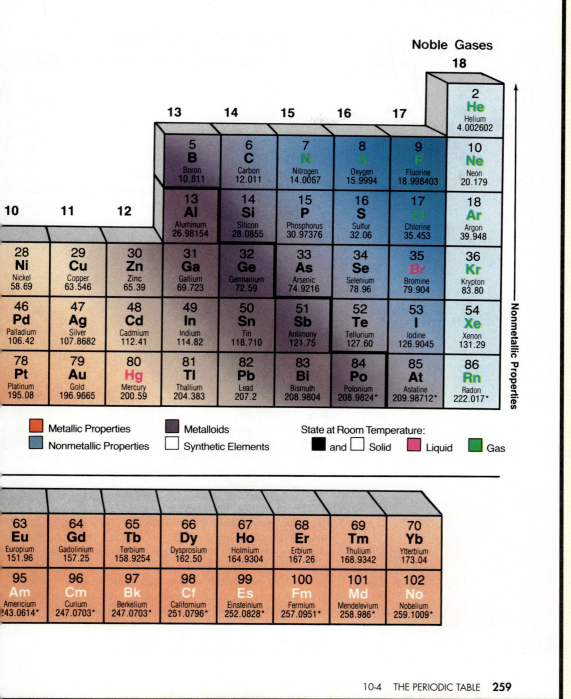

Noble Gases

					18
13	**14**	**15**	**16**	**17**	2 **He** Helium 4.002602
5 **B** Boron 10.811	6 **C** Carbon 12.011	7 **N** Nitrogen 14.0067	8 **O** Oxygen 15.9994	9 **F** Fluorine 18.998403	10 **Ne** Neon 20.179

Metallic Properties
Nonmetallic Properties
Metalloids
Synthetic Elements

State at Room Temperature:
■ and □ Solid ■ Liquid ■ Gas

Nonmetallic Properties

CONCEPT DEVELOPMENT

▶ You may have older tables in which groups are numbered with Roman numerals and letters. The American Chemical Society in recent years has recommended the use of periodic tables numbered 1 through 18.

▶ Remind students that all atoms of the same element contain the same number of protons.

▶ Inform students that scientists use the periodic table to make predictions every day. Atomic and ionic radii, ionization energy, electron affinity, electronegativity, melting point, and oxidation number can all be predicted from the periodic table.

▶ Learning to draw dot diagrams will help students in the future as they relate reactivity to the outer arrangement of electrons. The octet of outer electrons is particularly stable, as are filled and half-filled sublevels.

MINI QUIZ

Use the Mini Quiz to check students' recall of chapter content.

1 The arrangement of elements according to repeated changes in properties is called the _____ . *periodic table*

2 _____ used his table to make predictions about undiscovered elements. *Mendeleev*

3 The elements on the periodic table are arranged in order of increasing atomic _____ . *number*

4 Vertical columns on the periodic table are called _____ . *groups*

5 The number of outermost electrons determines the _____ of an element. *properties*

ENRICHMENT

▶ Have students use reference books to determine the origin of the symbols for the following elements: copper, gold, iron, lead, tin, mercury, silver, sodium, potassium, antimony, and tungsten. Copper: Cu, cuprum; Gold: Au, aurum; Iron: Fe, ferrum; Lead: Pb, plumbum; Tin: Sn, stannum; Mercury: Hg, hydroargyrum; Silver: Ag, argentum; Sodium: Na, natrium; Potassium: K, kalium; Antimony: Sb, stibnum; Tungsten: W, wolfram

PROGRAM RESOURCES

From the **Teacher Resource Package** use:

Cross-Curricular Connections, page 14, La Tabla Periodica.

Transparency Masters, pages 37-38, The Periodic Table.

Transparency Masters, pages 39-40, The Periodic Table—Blank.

Use **Color Transparency** number 19, The Periodic Table.

Use **Color Transparency** number 20, The Periodic Table—Blank.

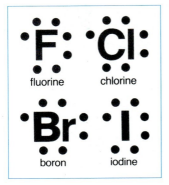

Figure 10-12. In each of these dot diagrams, the seven dots represent seven outer electrons.

fluorine   chlorine
boron   iodine

For example, the dot diagrams of the atoms of the elements in Group 17, called the halogens, are shown in Figure 10-12. They all have seven electrons in their outer energy levels. One similar property of the halogens is the ability to form compounds with elements in Group 1. The elements in Group 18 are known as noble gases. Noble gases do not usually form compounds. We say they are stable. The atoms of all the noble gases except helium have outer energy levels that contain eight electrons, as shown in Figure 10-13. You will learn more about the significance of electron arrangement of halogens, noble gases, and other elements in later chapters.

6

7

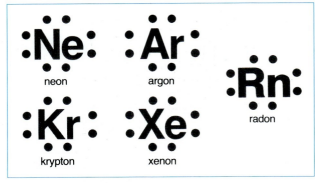

neon   argon
krypton   xenon   radon

Figure 10-13. In each of these dot diagrams, the eight dots represent eight outer electrons.

Periods of Elements

The horizontal rows of elements in the periodic table are called **periods.** Notice the stair-step line on the right side of the periodic table. All the elements to the left of this line, except hydrogen, are metals. **Metals** are elements that have several properties in common. Iron, zinc, and copper are examples of metals. Most metals are solids at room temperature. They are shiny and good conductors of heat and electricity.

8

Figure 10-14. Gallium is a metal that has a low melting point.

260 ATOMIC STRUCTURE AND THE PERIODIC TABLE

TECHNOLOGY

Seeing Atoms

For more than 50 years, scientists have been able to see extremely tiny things with electron microscopes. But it was less than ten years ago that scientists first saw atoms with scanning probe microscopes. These microscopes are the result of a new approach to how we see objects. Instead of shining light or a beam of electrons on an object, these new microscopes drag a probe across the surface of an object. The position of the probe is then changed and it is dragged across the surface again. This process, called scanning, is repeated many times to build an image of the peaks and valleys on the surface of the object. Scanning is like going into a dark room and using your hand as a probe to feel a chair to determine its shape, instead of shining a light on it.

The key development in the invention of the scanning probe microscope was a system that moves the probe in precise steps smaller than the width of an atom. In addition to seeing atoms, these probes enable scientists to move single atoms. Scientists at IBM used xenon atoms to spell out "IBM" in letters only five atoms tall! This ability to handle materials on an atom-by-atom basis could lead to ways of developing new materials that, up until now, were just not possible.

Think Critically: Scientists are using scanning probe microscopes to view atoms. Atoms range in radius from 0.053 nm for hydrogen to 0.27 nm for francium. What everyday objects, like two kinds of balls, would represent this range in size?

Those elements to the right of the stair-step line on the periodic table are classified as **nonmetals.** Oxygen, nitrogen, and carbon are examples of nonmetals. At

---

TECHNOLOGY

For more information on imaging atoms, read "Seeing Atoms" by James Trefil, *Discover*, June 1990, pp. 55-60.

Think Critically: The radii given are in a ratio of approximately 1:5. Size comparisons could include a golf ball and a volleyball.

CHECK FOR UNDERSTANDING

Use the Mini Quiz to check for understanding.

MINI QUIZ

Use the Mini Quiz to check students' recall of chapter content.

6 The halogens are found in which group? *17*

7 The noble gases are found in which group? *18*

8 Horizontal rows on the periodic table are called _____ . *periods*

9 Elements next to the stair-step line are called _____ . *metalloids*

10 Groups 4 through 12 are called the _____ metals. *transition*

RETEACH

Cooperative Learning: Using an appropriate strategy such as Expert Teams, organize eight class groups. Have them devise dot diagrams for the first 18 elements in the periodic table. Each group should be assigned one of the major groups—1, 2, and 13 through 18. Once the correct diagrams are established, have the groups enter their diagrams in a large table on the chalkboard or on roll paper. Point out the electron similarity in each group and the repeating pattern in the periods.

EXTENSION

For students who have mastered this section, use the **Reinforcement** and **Enrichment** masters or other OPTIONS provided.

ENRICHMENT

▶ Have a student use a calendar to illustrate the concept of periodicity.

▶ The radius of an atom increases down through a group. Ask students to explain why this occurs. There are additional energy levels around the nucleus.

▶ Research the activity series of the metals. Point out that an element's activity is related to its position on the periodic table.

PROGRAM RESOURCES

From the **Teacher Resource Package** use:
Concept Mapping, pages 25-26.
Science and Society, page 14, Steel and Aluminum Beverage Cans.

▶ Ask questions 1-3 and the **Apply** Question in the Section Review.

? FLEX Your Brain

Use the Flex Your Brain activity to have students explore the PERIODIC TABLE.

SECTION REVIEW ANSWERS

1. N, nitrogen, 7, 14.01
   Ca, calcium, 20, 40.08
   Kr, krypton, 36, 83.80
   W, tungsten, 74, 183.85
   Note: Atomic masses are rounded to two decimal places.
2. nitrogen, period 2, group 15
   sodium, period 3, group 1
   iodine, period 5, group 17
   mercury, period 6, group 12
3. K, potassium, metal
   Si, silicon, metalloid
   Ba, barium, metal
   S, sulfur, nonmetal
4. **Apply:** It is a liquid at room temperature, but like other metals, it conducts electricity.

Skill Builder

The graph should indicate 77% of the elements are metals, 8% are metalloids, and 15% are nonmetals.

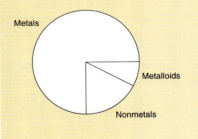

Metals
Metalloids
Nonmetals

Figure 10-15. Freshly mined sulfur is a nonmetal that is a brittle solid.

Where are the metalloids located in the periodic table?

room temperature, most nonmetals are gases and some are brittle solids. Most nonmetals do not conduct heat and electricity well.

⑨ The elements next to the stair-step line are classified as **metalloids,** because they have properties of both metals and nonmetals. Boron and silicon are examples of metalloids.

⑩ Elements in Groups 3 through 12 are called the transition elements. They are metals but have properties not found in elements of other groups. Copper and iron are examples of common transition elements. Others, such as platinum, are much more rare.

SECTION REVIEW

1. Use the periodic table to find the name, atomic number, and average atomic mass of the following elements: N, Ca, Kr, and W.
2. Give the period and group in which each of these elements is found: nitrogen, sodium, iodine, and mercury.
3. Write the name of each of these elements and classify it as a metal, a nonmetal, or a metalloid: K, Si, Ba, and S.
4. **Apply:** What property of mercury makes it different from other metals and also makes it useful in thermometers and "silent" light switches?

Skill Builder   ☑ **Making and Using Graphs**

Construct a pie graph showing the elements classified as metals, metalloids, and nonmetals. If you need help, refer to Making and Using Graphs in the **Skill Handbook** on page 687.

OPTIONS

ENRICHMENT

▶ Have an artistic student research alchemists' symbols and use them to prepare a bulletin board.

▶ Barium compounds are very toxic. Small doses are fatal. Determine why barium compounds are used when making gastrointestinal X rays. Barium sulfate is opaque to X rays. It is also very insoluble in water. Therefore, there is little danger in having barium sulfate in the intestines. Very little barium would pass into the bloodstream.

PROGRAM RESOURCES

From the **Teacher Resource Package** use: **Activity Worksheets,** page 5, Flex Your Brain.

CHAPTER
REVIEW

CHAPTER
REVIEW

SUMMARY

10-1: Structure of the Atom
1. A chemical symbol is a shorthand way of writing the name of an element.
2. An atom consists of a nucleus made of protons and neutrons surrounded by an electron cloud.
3. The electrons in an atom are arranged in several energy levels, each of which is able to hold a certain number of electrons.

10-2: Science and Society: Smaller Particles of Matter
1. Quarks are particles of matter that make up protons and neutrons.
2. Protons can be broken into quarks by having them collide while traveling at the speed of light.

10-3: Masses of Atoms
1. The number of neutrons in an atom can be computed by subtracting the atomic number from the mass number.
2. The isotopes of an element are atoms of that same element that have different numbers of neutrons.
3. The average atomic mass of an element is the average mass of the mixture of its isotopes.

10-4: The Periodic Table
1. The periodic table of elements is an arrangement of elements according to repeated changes in properties.
2. In the periodic table, the 109 elements are arranged in 18 vertical columns, or groups, and seven horizontal rows, or periods.
3. Metals are found at the left of the periodic table, nonmetals at the right, and metalloids along the line that separates the metals from the nonmetals.

KEY SCIENCE WORDS

a. atomic number
b. average atomic mass
c. chemical symbol
d. dot diagram
e. electron cloud
f. electrons
g. groups
h. isotopes
i. mass number
j. metalloids
k. metals
l. neutrons
m. nonmetals
n. nucleus
o. periodic table
p. periods
q. protons
r. quarks

UNDERSTANDING VOCABULARY

Match each phrase with the correct term from the list of Key Science Words.

1. a shorthand way to write the name of an element
2. atomic particles with no charge
3. atoms of the same element with different numbers of neutrons
4. average mass of the mixture of isotopes
5. positively charged center of an atom
6. particles that make up protons and neutrons
7. the region occupied by electrons
8. the number of protons in the nucleus
9. total number of particles in the nucleus
10. horizontal rows in the periodic table

ATOMIC STRUCTURE AND THE PERIODIC TABLE **263**

SUMMARY

Have students read the summary statements to review the major concepts of the chapter.

UNDERSTANDING VOCABULARY

1. c
2. l
3. h
4. b
5. n
6. r
7. e
8. a
9. i
10. p

OPTIONS

ASSESSMENT
To assess students' understanding of material in this chapter, use the resources listed.

COOPERATIVE LEARNING
Consider cooperative learning in the THINK AND WRITE CRITICALLY, APPLY, and MORE SKILL BUILDERS sections of the Chapter Review.

PROGRAM RESOURCES
From the **Teacher Resource Package** use:
Chapter Review, pages 23-24.
Chapter and Unit Tests, pages 61-64, Chapter Test.

C H A P T E R
REVIEW

CHECKING CONCEPTS

1. d		**6.** c	
2. c		**7.** d	
3. b		**8.** a	
4. b		**9.** d	
5. a		**10.** b	

UNDERSTANDING CONCEPTS

11. electrons
12. properties
13. groups
14. isotopes
15. 48

THINK AND WRITE CRITICALLY

16. The tendency of the moving electron to escape is balanced by the electrical attraction of the positive nucleus for the negative electron.

17. Because the names of several elements may start with the same letter, a second letter is needed to distinguish them.

18. Silver atoms have an atomic number of 47 and therefore contain 47 protons.

Mass of atoms in sample
$$= 52 (60 + 47) + 48 (62 + 47)$$
$$= 52 \times 107 + 48 \times 109$$
$$= 5564 + 5232$$
$$= 10\,796$$

Average atomic mass
$$= \frac{10\,796}{52 + 48} = 107.96$$

19. Answers will vary. Students may say that some quarks have mass whereas others have charge. Scientists believe that both protons and neutrons are made up of three quarks. You may want to give students this information for further speculation.

20. They are called nucleons because they are the particles that make up the nucleus.

CHECKING CONCEPTS

Choose the word or phrase that completes the sentence or answers the question.

1. The state of matter of most of the elements to the left of the stair-step line in the periodic table is _____.
- **a.** gas
- **b.** liquid
- **c.** plasma
- **d.** solid

2. If a pattern repeats itself, it is _____.
- **a.** isotopic
- **b.** metallic
- **c.** periodic
- **d.** transition

3. _____ is an element that would have similar properties to those of neon.
- **a.** Aluminum
- **b.** Argon
- **c.** Arsenic
- **d.** Silver

4. Boron is a _____.
- **a.** metal
- **b.** metalloid
- **c.** noble gas
- **d.** nonmetal

5. The element potassium is a _____.
- **a.** metal
- **b.** metalloid
- **c.** nonmetal
- **d.** transition element

6. The element bromine is a _____.
- **a.** metal
- **b.** metalloid
- **c.** nonmetal
- **d.** transition element

7. The halogens are those elements in Group _____.
- **a.** 1
- **b.** 11
- **c.** 15
- **d.** 17

8. In its group, nitrogen is the only element that is a _____.
- **a.** gas
- **b.** metalloid
- **c.** metal
- **d.** liquid

9. _____ is a shiny element that conducts electricity and heat well.
- **a.** Chlorine
- **b.** Sulfur
- **c.** Hydrogen
- **d.** Magnesium

10. The atomic number of Re is 75. The atomic mass of one of its isotopes is 186. How many neutrons are in an atom of this isotope?
- **a.** 75
- **b.** 111
- **c.** 186
- **d.** 261

UNDERSTANDING CONCEPTS

Complete each sentence.

11. Negatively charged particles called _____ move around the nucleus.

12. Elements are arranged in the periodic table according to repeated changes in their _____.

13. Vertical columns of elements in the periodic table are called _____.

14. Hafnium-178 and hafnium-179 are examples of _____.

15. Cadmium's atomic number is 48. The number of protons in a cadmium atom is _____.

THINK AND WRITE CRITICALLY

16. Why do electrons keep moving around the nucleus and not away from the atom?

17. Why do some chemical symbols have one letter and some have two letters?

18. A silver sample contains 52 atoms, each having 60 neutrons, and 48 atoms, each having 62 neutrons. What is the sample's average atomic mass?

19. Using Table 10-2 on page 243, what might be the masses and charges of quarks that make up protons?

20. Why are protons and neutrons also known as "nucleons"?

21. We know that properties of elements are periodic. List at least two other things in nature that are periodic.

22. Lead and mercury are two pollutants in the environment. From information about them in the periodic table, why are they called "heavy metals"?

23. Ge and Si are used in making semiconductors. Are these two elements in the same group or the same period?

24. U and Pu are named for objects in nature. What are these objects, and what other element is named after a similar object?

25. Ca is used by the body to make bones and teeth. Radioactive Sr is in nuclear waste. Why is this Sr hazardous to people?

MORE SKILL BUILDERS

If you need help, refer to the Skill Handbook.

1. Making and Using Tables: Use the periodic table to list a metal, a metalloid, and a nonmetal with 5 outer-level electrons.

2. Comparing and Contrasting: From the information found in the periodic table and reference books, compare and contrast the properties of chlorine and bromine.

3. Interpreting Data: If scientists have determined that a neutral atom of rubidium has an atomic number of 37 and a mass number of 85, how many protons, neutrons, and electrons does the atom have?

4. Sequencing: What changes in the periodic table would occur in Periods 1 through 4 if the elements are arranged according to increasing average atomic mass instead of atomic number? How do we know that arrangement by atomic number is correct?

5. Concept Mapping: As a star dies, it becomes more dense. Its temperature rises to a point where He nuclei are combined with other nuclei. The atomic numbers of the other nuclei are increased by 2 because each gains the two protons contained in the He nucleus. For example, Cr fused with He becomes Fe. Complete the concept map below showing the first four steps in He fusion.

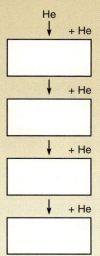

PROJECTS

1. Do research on the attempts made by Johann Dobereiner and John Newlands to classify the elements. Write a report on your findings.

2. Make a display of samples or pictures of several elements. List the name, symbol, atomic number, average atomic mass, and several uses for each element.

3. Research and report on models of the atom from the time of the ancient Greeks until the present.

21. Possible answers are tides, time of day, seasons, and moon phases.
22. They have relatively high atomic masses.
23. the same group
24. They are planets. Neptunium is also named for a planet.
25. Calcium and strontium are in the same group and therefore have similar properties. Strontium, like calcium, is easily absorbed into the body.

MORE SKILL BUILDERS

1. Making and Using Tables: metal, bismuth; metalloid, antimony or arsenic; nonmetal, nitrogen or phosphorus

2. Comparing and Contrasting: The chemical properties of chlorine and bromine would be similar because they are in the same group. At room temperature, bromine occurs as a liquid, whereas chlorine is a gas. Bromine atoms have a greater mass than chlorine atoms. It is also reasonable to assume that a bromine atom is larger than a chlorine atom because the bromine atom has one more level of electrons.

3. Interpreting Data: 37 protons, 37 electrons, 48 neutrons

4. Sequencing: Argon and potassium would be reversed as would nickel and cobalt. The resulting arrangement would cause the elements to appear in groups with other elements that do not share their properties.

5. Concept Mapping: See below.

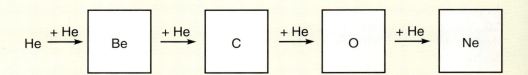

CHAPTER
11 Chemical Bonds

CHAPTER SECTION	OBJECTIVES	ACTIVITIES
11-1 Why Atoms Combine (2 days)	**1. Describe** how a compound differs from the elements it is composed of. **2. Explain** what a chemical formula represents. **3. State** a reason why chemical bonding occurs.	**Activity 11-1:** *Models of Combining Atoms*, p. 273
11-2 Hazardous Compounds at Home Science & Society (1 day)	**1. Describe** the dangers posed by hazardous compounds in the home. **2. Demonstrate** an understanding of ways to avoid hazardous compounds or ways to use them safely.	
11-3 Kinds of Chemical Bonds (2 days)	**1. Describe** ionic bonds and covalent bonds. **2. Identify** the particles produced by ionic bonding and by covalent bonding. **3. Distinguish** between a nonpolar covalent bond and a polar covalent bond.	**Activity 11-2:** *Covalent and Ionic Bonds*, p. 281
11-4 Formulas and Names of Compounds (2 days)	**1. Explain** how to determine oxidation numbers. **2. Write formulas** for compounds from their names. **3. Name** compounds from their formulas. **4. Describe** hydrates and their formulas.	**MINI-Lab:** *How does heat affect a hydrate?* p. 287
Chapter Review		

ACTIVITY MATERIALS

FIND OUT	ACTIVITIES		MINI-LABS
Page 267 steel wool 2 test tubes of the same size 1 beaker or jar	**11-1 Models of Combining Atoms, p. 273** modified egg carton marbles	**11-2 Covalent and Ionic Bonds, p. 281** 1 tablespoon each of crushed ice, sugar, and salt 3 test tubes wire test tube holder laboratory burner goggles	**How does heat affect a hydrate? p. 287** white paper glass stirring rod solution containing 1 g $CoC_{12} \cdot 6H_2O$ in 35 mL of water

CHAPTER FEATURES	TEACHER RESOURCE PACKAGE	OTHER RESOURCES
Skill Builder: *Making and Using Tables,* p. 272	**Ability Level Worksheets** ◆ **Study Guide,** p. 46 ● **Reinforcement,** p. 46 ▲ **Enrichment,** p. 46 **Science and Society,** p. 15 **Activity Worksheet,** pp. 86, 87 **Transparency Masters,** pp. 41, 42	**Color Transparency 21,** Chemical Bonding **Lab Manual 23,** The Six Solutions Problem
You Decide! p. 275	**Ability Level Worksheets** ◆ **Study Guide,** p. 47 ● **Reinforcement,** p. 47 ▲ **Enrichment,** p. 47 **Concept Mapping,** pp. 27, 28 **Critical Thinking/Problem Solving,** p. 17	
Technology: *Bond Busters,* p. 279 **Skill Builder:** *Concept Mapping,* p. 280	**Ability Level Worksheets** ◆ **Study Guide,** p. 48 ● **Reinforcement,** p. 48 ▲ **Enrichment,** p. 48 **Activity Worksheet,** pp. 88, 89	**Lab Manual 24,** Chemical Bonds
Problem Solving: *The Packet of Mystery Crystals,* p. 288 **Skill Builder:** *Using Variables, Constants, and Controls,* p. 288	**Ability Level Worksheets** ◆ **Study Guide,** p. 49 ● **Reinforcement,** p. 49 ▲ **Enrichment,** p. 49 **Cross-Curricular Connections,** p. 17 **MINI-Lab Worksheet,** p. 92 **Transparency Masters,** pp. 43, 44	**Color Transparency 22,** Oxidation Numbers of Elements
Summary — Think & Write Critically Key Science Words — Apply Understanding Vocabulary — More Skill Builders Checking Concepts — Projects Understanding Concepts	**Chapter Review,** pp. 25, 26 **Chapter Test,** pp. 65-68 **Unit Test,** pp. 69, 70	**Chapter Review Software Test Bank**

◆ **Basic**   ● **Average**   ▲ **Advanced**

ADDITIONAL MATERIALS

SOFTWARE	AUDIOVISUAL	BOOKS/MAGAZINES
Elements, Compounds, and Mixtures, Focus. *Atomic Structure and Bonding,* Focus. *Compounds,* Queue. *Chemical Formulas and Equations,* ComPress.	*Chemical Reactions,* video, Focus. *All About Matter,* video, Focus.	Gray, Harry B. *Chemical Bonds: An Introduction to Atomic and Molecular Structure.* Redwood City, CA: Benjamin-Cummings Publishing Co., 1973. Murrell, John N. *The Chemical Bond.* 2nd ed. New York: Wiley, John & Sons Inc., 1987.

THEME DEVELOPMENT: Stability as a theme of the textbook is described in terms of chemical stability. The relationship between an atom's electron structure and its stability is discussed. A study of chemical bonding further develops the theme. Chemical properties such as corrosiveness, flammability, and toxicity are related to stability.

CHAPTER OVERVIEW

▶ **Section 11-1:** Atoms react to form chemically stable substances, which are held together by chemical bonds and are represented by chemical formulas.

▶ **Section 11-2: Science and Society:** Students learn that care must be exercised when using many chemicals found in the home.

▶ **Section 11-3:** Ionic, polar covalent, and covalent bonds are conceptualized in this section as are the resulting polar and nonpolar molecules.

▶ **Section 11-4:** Oxidation numbers are used to introduce formula writing and naming for both binary and polyatomic compounds. This section also introduces students to hydrates.

CHAPTER VOCABULARY

chemical formula	covalent bond
chemically stable	polar molecule
chemical bond	nonpolar molecule
toxic	oxidation number
corrosive	binary compound
ion	polyatomic ion
ionic bond	hydrate

CHAPTER

11 Chemical Bonds

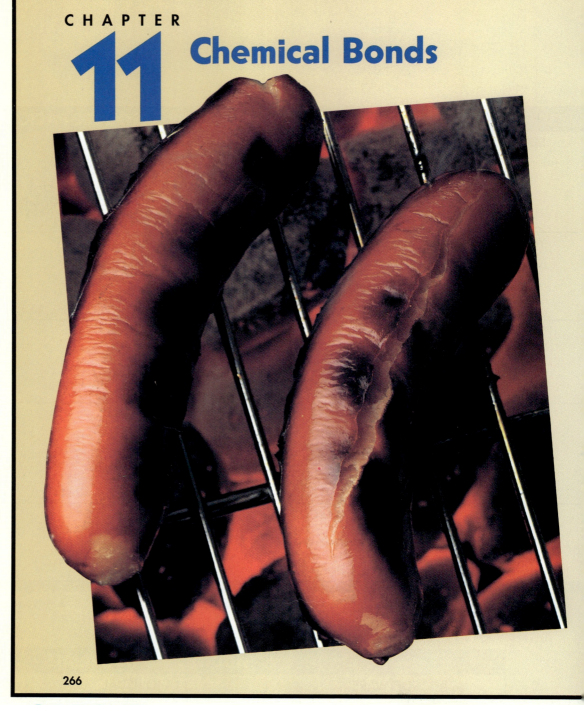

266

OPTIONS

For Your Gifted Students

Gifted students who have shown an interest in the topic of chemistry throughout Chapters 8, 9, and 10 should now be encouraged to study the subject in more depth in a current high school chemistry text. A concept that is particularly important for them to grasp is the relationship between an element's electron structure and the way it combines with other elements. If equipment and facilities are available, students should conduct laboratory experiments from a lab manual associated with their chemistry text. These should be done only with your prior approval and supervision.

Whenever you watch charcoal burning, you observe a change in which chemical bonds form. These bonds form between the carbon in the charcoal and oxygen in the air. What is another chemical change in which oxygen bonds with another element?

FIND OUT!

Do this simple activity to find out how oxygen can bond with another element.

Stuff some wet steel wool into the bottom of a test tube. Invert the test tube in a beaker of water. Invert a tube containing only air beside the first one. Adjust the water levels in both tubes so that they are equal, with the water rising about 1 cm above the openings of the test tubes. Let the tubes stand a few days. What evidence of chemical change do you observe?

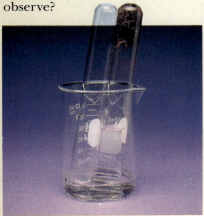

Previewing Science Skills
► In the Skill Builders, you will make and use a table, make a concept map, and use variables, constants, and controls.
► In the Activities, you will observe, compare, classify, and hypothesize.
► In the MINI-Lab, you will observe and infer.

What's next?

You have shown that moist iron rusts as it combines with the oxygen in a test tube of air. You will learn more about how elements combine as you read the pages that follow.

INTRODUCING THE CHAPTER
Use the Find Out activity to introduce students to chemical bonding. Inform students that they will be learning more about chemical formulas and bonds as they read the chapter.

FIND OUT!
Preparation: Some steel wool has an oily coating to prevent rust. If you suspect this, wash the steel wool in soapy water and rinse thoroughly before using.

Materials: steel wool, two test tubes of the same size, and one beaker or jar for each group

Cooperative Learning: Use the Paired Partners strategy if you have enough materials. Have students speculate on the reason for the empty test tube. Ask them to form a common hypothesis about the results.

Teaching Tips
► Students can adjust water levels in tubes by tilting them slightly near the surface of the water.
► Tubes should rest securely on bottom of beaker. If they tend to float, pour some water out of the beaker.
► If you have some very large test tubes, set up a large-scale version of the activity as a demonstration.
► Water should rise one-fifth of the way up the tube with steel wool. Remind students that the air is 20 percent oxygen, as the activity demonstrates. The remainder is mainly nitrogen and argon.

Gearing Up
Have students study the Gearing Up feature to familiarize themselves with the chapter. Discuss the relationships of the topics in the outline.

What's Next?
Before beginning the first section, make sure students understand the connection between the Find Out activity and the topics to follow.

For Your Mainstreamed Students
Students can make a survey of all the hazardous materials found in their homes and school. They could prepare a poster display using magazine pictures of these materials and write a paragraph for each that lists the hazards and the proper disposal of the material.

The use of physical models to show atomic structure and bonding is particularly important for students who have impaired vision.

PREPARATION

SECTION BACKGROUND

▶ Formulas of chemical compounds are simple whole-number ratios of the atoms of the elements that make up the compound.

▶ An atom with eight outer electrons is chemically stable, or unreactive. This is a basic principle of chemistry called the octet rule.

▶ Electrons can be simultaneously attracted between two nuclei. The attractive force is called a chemical bond.

▶ Most metals have three or fewer outer electrons and tend to lose electrons to form positive ions.

▶ Most nonmetals have five or more outer electrons and tend to gain electrons to form negative ions.

PREPLANNING

▶ To prepare for Activity 11-1, prepare modified egg carton and package marbles for each laboratory team.

1 MOTIVATE

▶ **Demonstration:** Two elements combining in a dramatic way can be shown by reacting 3 g of zinc dust with 2 g of iodine crystals. Combine them in a test tube. Shake to mix, and then clamp the tube securely upright. Add 1 mL water from a dropper to start the reaction. **CAUTION:** *The reaction gives off heat. Do not hold the tube. Perform only outdoors or in a fume hood.* Point out to the class that the elements became more stable by combining. Tell them that they will learn to name and write the formula for the product of this reaction, zinc iodide.

STUDENT TEXT QUESTION

▶ Page 268, paragraph 3: **How are the properties of salt different from those of sodium and chlorine?** *Salt is a white, crystalline, nonpoisonous solid.*

New Science Words

chemical formula
chemically stable
chemical bond

Objectives

▶ Describe how a compound differs from the elements it is composed of.
▶ Explain what a chemical formula represents.
▶ State a reason why chemical bonding occurs.

Did You Know?

In the last two centuries, humans have increased the amount of CO_2 in the air by 25 percent. This is one of the main factors responsible for the greenhouse effect.

Figure 11-1. When iron rusts, iron and oxygen combine to form a new substance.

Compounds

Most of the matter around you is in the form of compounds or mixtures of compounds. The water you drink, the carbon dioxide you exhale, and the salt you put on food are examples of compounds.

Some of the matter around you is in the form of elements, such as iron and oxygen. But, like many other pairs of elements, iron and oxygen tend to unite chemically to form a compound when the conditions are right. You know how iron in moist steel wool exposed to oxygen forms rust, a compound. Rusting is a chemical change because a new substance, rust, is produced.

Compounds have properties unlike those of their elements. Salt, for example, is composed of the elements sodium and chlorine. Sodium is a shiny, soft, gray metal that reacts violently with water. Chlorine is a greenish-yellow gas that can kill an animal that inhales a few deep breaths of the gas. These elements combine to form table salt, or sodium chloride. Look at Figure 11-2. How are the properties of salt different from those of sodium and chlorine?

OPTIONS

Meeting Different Ability Levels

For Section 11-1, use the following **Teacher Resource Masters** depending upon individual students' needs.

◆ **Study Guide Master** for all students.
● **Reinforcement Master** for students of average and above average ability levels.
▲ **Enrichment Master** for above average students.

Additional Teacher Resource Package masters are listed in the OPTIONS box throughout the section. The additional masters are appropriate for all students.

◆ STUDY GUIDE 46

STUDY GUIDE — Chapter 11
Why Atoms Combine — Text Pages 268-273

The definitions of several key terms about how atoms combine are given below. In the blanks, write the term from the word list that makes each definition complete.

| atoms | chemical symbol | compound | electrons | force |
| number | ratios | elements | energy level | |

1. Chemical formula: tells what **elements** make up a **compound** and the **ratios** of the atoms of those elements.
2. Subscript: a **number** in a chemical formula written after a **chemical symbol** that tells how many atoms of an element are in a unit of the compound.
3. Chemically stable: condition of an atom when outer **energy level** is completely filled with **electrons**.
4. Chemical bond: in a compound, the **force** that holds the **atoms** together.

Use the diagram below to select eight letters to form a word found in this chapter. Use the statements as hints to help you select the correct letters. Circle each letter as you find it in the diagram. Write the word in the space provided. Then define the term.

1. The first letter must be in the triangle and in the circle, but not in the rectangle.
2. The second letter must be in the triangle only.
3. The third letter must be in the circle, triangle, and rectangle.
4. The fourth letter must be in the rectangle only.
5. The fifth letter must be in the circle only.
6. The sixth letter must be in both the rectangle and the triangle, but not in the circle.
7. The seventh letter must be in both the rectangle and circle, but not in the triangle.
8. The eighth letter must be in the part of the rectangle that is below the triangle.

The word is **c o m p o u n d**. Definition: A **compound** is a substance composed of two or more elements chemically combined.

Figure 11-2. Sodium, a soft, gray metal, combines with chlorine, a greenish-yellow gas, to form sodium chloride, a white crystalline solid.

Formulas

Do you recall that the chemical symbols Na and Cl represent sodium and chlorine? When written as NaCl, the symbols make up a formula, or chemical shorthand for the compound sodium chloride. Another formula you may recognize is H_2O, for water. The formula is a combination of the symbols H and O and the subscript number 2. *Subscript* means "written below." A subscript number written after a symbol tells how many atoms there are of that element in a unit of the compound. If a symbol has no subscript, there's one atom of that element. The formula H_2O, then, shows there are two atoms of hydrogen for one atom of oxygen in one unit of the compound water. Put another way, the ratio of hydrogen atoms to oxygen atoms in water is 2 to 1.

Look at the formula for rust: Fe_2O_3. The symbol for iron, Fe, is followed by the subscript 2, and the symbol for oxygen, O, is followed by the subscript 3. For two atoms of iron there are three atoms of oxygen in the compound. That is, the ratio of iron atoms to oxygen atoms in rust is 2 to 3.

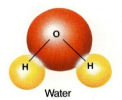

Water

Carbon dioxide

Figure 11-3. These models show the ratios and the arrangements of atoms in water and carbon dioxide.

269

CROSS CURRICULUM

▶ **Geology:** The names that geologists use for gemstones and other crystals are not the same names used by chemists. A quartz crystal is silicon dioxide. Fool's gold, iron pyrite, is named iron sulfide, and fluorite is calcium fluoride. Have students research common names, chemical names, and chemical formulas for other gems and minerals.

CONCEPT DEVELOPMENT

▶ To help your students better understand chemical stability, you can use the concept of potential energy. A book held above a desk has potential energy depending on its height above the desk. The book can become more stable by falling to the desk, losing energy in the process. When atoms bond together and become more stable, energy is also given off.

STUDENT TEXT QUESTIONS

▶ Page 270, paragraph 1: **What elements are in each compound listed in Table 11-1? What is the ratio of atoms in each compound?** *Refer to Table 11-1. Aid students in picking individual element symbols out of formulas and in interpreting the formulas.*

Science and READING

Students may think that the names of chemical compounds listed on product labels are the correct chemical names for those ingredients. For example, some anticavity toothpastes contain stannous fluoride. The correct name is tin(II) fluoride. Manufacturers also can give a trade name to a chemical that will be sold by their companies.

Table 11-1

SOME FAMILIAR COMPOUNDS

Familiar Name	Chemical Name	Formula
Lye	Sodium hydroxide	$NaOH$
Vinegar	Acetic acid	$HC_2H_3O_2$
Ammonia	Ammonia	NH_3
Grain alcohol	Ethanol	C_2H_5OH
Sand	Silicon dioxide	SiO_2
Battery acid	Sulfuric acid	H_2SO_4
Stomach acid	Hydrochloric acid	HCl
Milk of magnesia	Magnesium hydroxide	$Mg(OH)_2$
Cane sugar	Sucrose	$C_{12}H_{22}O_{11}$

The **chemical formula** for any compound tells what elements it contains and the ratio of the atoms of those elements. What elements are in each compound listed in Table 11-1? What is the ratio of atoms in each compound?

Chemically Stable Atoms

What causes elements to form compounds? Look again at the periodic table on pages 258 and 259. It lists 109 elements, most of which can, and often do, combine with other elements. But the six noble gases in Group 18 seldom combine with other elements. Why do the noble gases almost never form compounds? The reason is that the arrangement of electrons in their atoms makes them chemically stable, or resistant to change.

What electron arrangements make atoms stable? An atom is **chemically stable** if its outer energy level is completely filled with electrons. 2 For the atoms of most elements, the outer energy level is filled when it contains eight electrons. Atoms of the noble gases neon, argon, krypton, xenon, and radon all contain eight electrons in the outermost energy level. For atoms of helium, the outermost energy level is filled when it has two electrons.

Figure 11-4 shows dot diagrams of some of the noble gases. Remember that a dot diagram of an atom shows

Science and READING

Check the labels on the products you find in such places in your home as the medicine cabinet, the refrigerator, and the cupboard under the sink. Match the name of the active ingredient with a formula, and vice versa, for as many products as you can.

OPTIONS

INQUIRY QUESTIONS

▶ **Hot packs are used by athletic trainers. When the chemicals inside the plastic bag are mixed, a chemical reaction occurs. Describe what you think is happening in terms of an atom's electrons.** *Some atoms lose and some atoms gain electrons. As they become more stable, energy is released in the form of heat.*

▶ **Atoms of some elements will bond with another atom of the same element. The molecules they form are called diatomic molecules. The oxygen gas you breathe is diatomic, O_2. Why would like atoms bond together?** *They share electrons, giving each atom eight electrons in the outer energy level.*

▶ **Potassium permanganate is used to control odors around paper mills and animal feedlots. How many oxygen atoms are in its formula, $KMnO_4$?** *4*

▶ **When would a chemist want to produce a chemical that was unstable?** *rocket fuel, explosive*

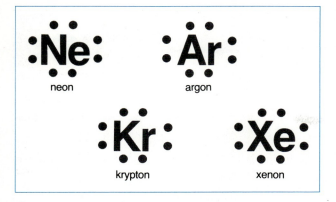

Figure 11-4. Dot diagrams of neon—Ne, krypton—Kr, argon—Ar, and xenon—Xe

the number of electrons in its outer energy level. Notice that each of these elements has eight outer electrons. Because each noble gas has an outer level that is filled to capacity with electrons, each of these elements is chemically stable. Thus, the noble gases don't form compounds naturally. A few compounds of xenon and radon do exist, but these have been prepared in the laboratory under special conditions. Each atom of all the elements *except* the noble gases has from one to seven electrons in its outer energy level. These atoms tend to lose, gain, or share electrons with other atoms. It is the gaining, losing, or sharing of electrons that causes chemical changes to happen. In one of these ways, an atom may have its outer energy level filled, like a noble gas.

Losing, gaining, and sharing electrons are the means by which atoms form chemical bonds. A chemical bond is a force that holds together the atoms in a compound. When a chemical bond forms between sodium and chlorine, each sodium atom loses one electron and each chlorine atom gains one. As a result, each atom in sodium chloride, NaCl, has eight electrons in its newly formed outer energy level, as shown in Figure 11-5. Why is the compound sodium chloride stable?

What is a chemical bond?

Figure 11-5. When sodium combines with chlorine, each sodium atom loses an electron and each chlorine atom gains an electron.

sodium atom   chlorine atom   sodium chloride

11-1   WHY ATOMS COMBINE   **271**

▶ Page 272, paragraph 1: **How is the bond in Cl₂ different from the bond in NaCl?** *It is formed by sharing electrons rather than by electron transfer.*

CHECK FOR UNDERSTANDING

Ask questions 1-3 and the **Apply** Question in the Section Review.

RETEACH

▶ Have students look up water (H_2O) and hydrogen peroxide (H_2O_2) in a dictionary. Ask the students to explain why they are different substances even though they are made of the same elements. Emphasize that the different chemical properties are due to compounds' different formulas.

▶ Have students interpret the formulas in Table 11-1 on page 270. Ask them what elements and how many atoms of each are present. Ask why they think each is a stable compound. The answer in all cases is that all atoms present are stable because they have an outer level with eight electrons.

EXTENSION

For students who have mastered this section, use the **Reinforcement** and **Enrichment** masters or other OPTIONS provided.

3 CLOSE

? FLEX Your Brain

Use the Flex Your Brain activity to have students explore COMPOUNDS.

▶ Bring in a box of baking soda. The label on the box says that it is $NaHCO_3$, sodium hydrogen carbonate. Have students name the elements present and tell in what ratio they are present.

SECTION REVIEW ANSWERS

1. The properties of the elements are replaced by the properties of the compound they form.

2. (a) CaF_2, (b) Al_2S_3

3. The compounds that are formed are chemically more stable than the elements.

4. Apply: sodium, carbon, and oxygen, in the ratio of 2 to 1 to 3

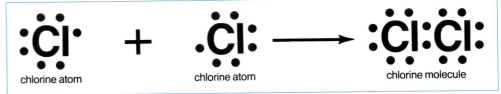

Figure 11-6. Dot diagram for the formation of chlorine gas, Cl_2, from two atoms of chlorine

Chlorine is a gas made up of particles in which two chlorine atoms share electrons. In its formula, Cl_2, the subscript 2 shows that there are two atoms bonded together. Look at Figure 11-6. How is the bond in Cl_2 different from the bond in NaCl?

As you read at the start of this section, compounds, rather than elements, make up most of the matter around you. Why is this so? The answer is that the arrangements of electrons in most atoms make them chemically unstable. Thus, ==atoms combine with other atoms by sharing or transferring electrons. By doing so, the atoms achieve more stable arrangements of electrons.==

What makes most atoms chemically unstable?

SECTION REVIEW

1. What happens to the properties of elements when they form compounds?
2. Write formulas for (a) a compound with one atom of calcium and two atoms of fluorine and (b) a compound with two atoms of aluminum and three atoms of sulfur.
3. Why do most elements tend to form compounds?
4. **Apply:** The label on a box of washing soda states that it contains Na_2CO_3. Name the elements in this compound. In what ratio are they present?

Skill Builder ☑ Making and Using Tables

The compounds in Table 11-1 on page 270 that contain carbon are classified as organic, and the others are classified as inorganic. Reorganize the contents of the table using these groups. If you need help, refer to Making and Using Tables in the **Skill Handbook** on page 686.

Skill Builder

Type of Compound	Familiar Name	Chemical Name	Formula
Organic	vinegar	acetic acid	$HC_2H_3O_2$
	grain alcohol	ethanol	C_2H_5OH
	cane sugar	sucrose	$C_{12}H_{22}O_{11}$
Inorganic	lye	sodium hydroxide	NaOH
	ammonia	ammonia	NH_3
	sand	silicon dioxide	SiO_2
	battery acid	sulfuric acid	H_2SO_4
	stomach acid	hydrochloric acid	HCl
	milk of magnesia	magnesium hydroxide	$Mg(OH)_2$

ACTIVITY 11-1
Models of Combining Atoms

Problem: *How can a model show the way atoms lose, gain, or share electrons?*

Materials
- modified egg carton
- marbles

Procedure
1. Obtain a modified egg carton and marbles from your teacher. The carton will represent the first and second energy levels of an atom, and the marbles will represent electrons.
2. Place one marble in each receptacle of the carton. Start with the pair of receptacles representing the first energy level of the atom.
3. Place the remaining marbles in receptacles representing the second energy level. In which column would your element appear on the periodic chart?
4. Compare your model with those of your classmates. Find one or more other cartons that, when combined with yours, will make it possible for each of the two cartons to have eight marbles in its second energy level.
5. Make a list of the combinations you were able to make with your classmates' models.

Analyze
1. Generally, do groups of metals on the periodic table have more or fewer electrons in their outer energy levels than nonmetals?
2. The combinations you found could represent chemical formulas. Why did some formulas require more than one atom of an element?

Conclude and Apply
3. Would your model be more likely to represent a metal or a nonmetal atom? Explain.
4. What group of elements would your model be in if you received eight marbles? Explain.

OBJECTIVE: Infer chemical formulas by **making models** of outer electron levels.

PROCESS SKILLS applied in this activity:
▶ **Classifying** in Procedure Step 3.
▶ **Hypothesizing** in Analyze Question 2.

COOPERATIVE LEARNING
Use the Science Investigation team strategy in pairs. Further group five teams together to find all compound possibilities.

TEACHING THE ACTIVITY
Alternate Materials: Substitutes for marbles could include buttons, candy, or beans.

Troubleshooting: Remind students that these examples do not include the transition metals. These egg carton "atoms" can represent the elements in the first two rows of the periodic table.
▶ Using the egg carton, tape off two of the egg receptacles and review with students the capacity of first and second energy levels.
▶ Give different numbers of marbles to different students so that all elements from lithium to neon are represented. Depending on the size of your class, have students add or remove marbles to change their element models and increase the number of matchup possibilities.
▶ Monitor students so that they discover simple matchups such as LiF and progress to compounds such as BeF_2, Li_2O, BeO, and Be_3N_2. Remind them that atoms can achieve stability by both losing and gaining electrons.

ANSWERS TO QUESTIONS
1. Metals have fewer outer level electrons than nonmetals.

2. Some formulas require more than one atom of each element because two atoms combined do not provide enough electrons for both to have eight.

3. Answers will vary. Usually fewer than four outer electrons indicates a metal. More than four usually indicates a nonmetal.

4. Eight marbles indicates a Group 16 element. These atoms have six outer electrons.

PROGRAM RESOURCES
From the **Teacher Resource Package** use:
Activity Worksheets, pages 86-87, Activity 11-1: Models of Combining Atoms.

SCIENCE & SOCIETY

11-2 Hazardous Compounds at Home

PREPARATION

SECTION BACKGROUND

▶ Common sense is the first defense against harm from household items. Take into account the people present. Are any allergic to a common material or food? All potentially hazardous items should be out of reach of small children.

▶ One quart of oil can contaminate one million liters of drinking water because it forms a very thin film on the surface of the water.

1 MOTIVATE

▶ Have students brainstorm a list of household chemicals they think are corrosive, toxic, or flammable.

TYING TO PREVIOUS KNOWLEDGE:
Have students recall and discuss where they have personally observed litter or pollution caused by improperly discarded items.

OBJECTIVES AND SCIENCE WORDS:
Have students review the objectives and science words to become familiar with this section.

2 TEACH

Key Concepts are highlighted.

CONCEPT DEVELOPMENT

▶ Nearly every chemical has potential benefits and associated risks. The use of DDT is an old example. Debate over DDT still goes on in regions where malaria is prevalent.

New Science Words

toxic
corrosive

Objectives

▶ Describe the dangers posed by hazardous compounds in the home.
▶ Demonstrate an understanding of ways to avoid hazardous compounds or ways to use them safely.

Corrosive, Flammable, and Toxic Compounds

In 1989, the oil tanker *Exxon Valdez* spilled 11 million gallons of oil. This was one of the worst oil spills in history. People were shocked and outraged. But think about this. Every year do-it-yourself oil changers improperly dispose of 176 million gallons of oil. This is equal to 16 *Exxon Valdez* spills! One quart of oil can contaminate 250 000 gallons of drinking water. Many common household products are hazardous. This means that they contain compounds that can affect the health and safety of people.

Hazardous household chemicals can be toxic, corrosive, or flammable. **Compounds that are toxic are poisonous.** Toxic compounds are in products such as disinfectants, insect sprays, medicine, antifreeze, and nail polish remover. **Compounds that are corrosive attack and destroy metals, human tissues, and other materials.** Corrosive compounds are found in battery acid, drain cleaners, oven cleaners, bleach, and toilet cleaners. **Compounds that are flammable burn readily.** Flammable compounds include ingredients of gasoline, paint thinner, oil-based paint, and some aerosols.

Toxic, corrosive, and flammable compounds threaten the health and safety of people in their homes. These materials can poison children and pets and pose fire hazards. They may cause cancer and other diseases. When people handle or dispose of hazardous chemicals improperly, they can pollute air, soil, and water. Many times people dump these materials into sewer systems. Hazardous compounds can pass unchanged through septic systems and water treatment plants and into clean

274 CHEMICAL BONDS

OPTIONS

Meeting Different Ability Levels

For Section 11-2, use the following **Teacher Resource Masters** depending upon individual students' needs.

◆ **Study Guide Master** for all students.
● **Reinforcement Master** for students of average and above average ability levels.
▲ **Enrichment Master** for above average students.

◆ STUDY GUIDE 47

STUDY GUIDE   Chapter 11
Hazardous Compounds at Home   Text Pages 274–275

Use the definitions of the types of hazardous compounds given below to decide if each of the materials described is toxic, corrosive, or flammable. In the space provided, write T for toxic, C for corrosive, and F for flammable.

T = **toxic:** poisonous
C = **corrosive:** substance that can attack, weaken, and destroy metals, human tissues, and other materials
F = **flammable:** burns readily

C   1. After working with a car battery, you should wash your hands carefully and avoid contact between the battery acid and your clothing. Battery acid can weaken and cause holes to form in a fabric.
T   2. An insecticide is a chemical preparation used to kill unwanted insect pests.
T   3. Flea sprays and roach sprays are commonly used insecticides.
F   4. Gasoline ignites easily in the presence of a spark or a flame.
T   5. Each year many pets die from drinking water from puddles that have been contaminated with antifreeze.
C   6. Maria poured some liquid drain cleaner into her sink. Later, she discovered that the drain was no longer clogged, but a hole had formed in the pipe.
F   7. Petroleum products, such as oil and kerosene, can be highly explosive.
C   8. Too much bleach in a washer can weaken fabric and cause holes to form.
T   9. Herbicides are chemical preparations used to kill weeds.

Answer the following questions on the lines provided.
1. What is a hazardous compound? **a compound that contains materials that can affect the health and safety of people**

2. Some aerosols contain petroleum products. Are these aerosols corrosive, toxic, or flammable? **flammable**

Copyright Glencoe Division of Macmillan/McGraw-Hill
Users of Merrill Physical Science have the publisher's permission to reproduce this page.   47

Table 11-2

ALTERNATIVES TO HAZARDOUS HOME CHEMICALS

Product	Safe Alternatives
Aerosols	Use gels, lotions, and nonaerosol sprays.
Chlorine bleach	Use dry bleach or borax.
Moth balls	Use cedar chips.
Toilet bowl cleaners	Use nonphosphate detergents and baking soda.
Drain cleaners	Use a plumbing snake or a plunger to unplug drains.
Window cleaner	Use 2 teaspoons of vinegar in a quart of water and wipe dry with newspaper.
Insecticides	Provide houses and the proper environment in your yard to attract birds, bats, toads, and snakes to eat insects.

water supplies. Hazardous chemicals dumped on soil and in landfills seep into and pollute groundwater supplies. Freon from refrigerators and air conditioners and evaporated gasoline and paint products are examples of chemicals that pollute the air and destory the ozone layer.

How can you and your family remain healthy and safe and prevent pollution? Some suggestions are: (1) Use safe alternatives to hazardous materials, as suggested in Table 11-2. (2) Do not pour automotive fluids into the sewer or on the ground. (3) Recycle oil, antifreeze, and used batteries. (4) If you must purchase a hazardous product, buy only the amount you need and give the excess to someone who will use it. (5) Store hazardous materials in their original containers, away from children. (6) Keep hazardous materials that easily evaporate in tightly closed containers, to prevent the escape of vapors. (7) Share your knowledge of the problem of hazardous household compounds with others.

EcoTip

Instead of using poisonous chemical sprays, chase away insect pests by planting chrysanthemums near your doorways or in your garden.

SECTION REVIEW

1. What are three dangerous properties of hazardous compounds in many household products?
2. What are five ways you can protect yourself and the environment from hazardous materials?

You Decide!

Your neighbor changes his own automobile oil. Several times you have seen him dump the used liquids at the edge of his property and yours. What should you do?

SCIENCE & SOCIETY

275

PROGRAM RESOURCES

From the **Teacher Resource Package** use:

Concept Mapping, page 27.
Critical Thinking/Problem Solving, page 17, Groundwater Pollution.
Activity Worksheets, page 5, Flex Your Brain.

CHECK FOR UNDERSTANDING

Ask questions 1 and 2 in the Section Review.

RETEACH

Cooperative Learning: Have Expert Teams survey their apartments or houses for toxic, corrosive, or flammable chemicals.

EXTENSION

For students who have mastered this section, use the **Reinforcement** and **Enrichment** masters or other OPTIONS provided.

3 CLOSE

FLEX Your Brain

Use the Flex Your Brain activity to have students explore HAZARDOUS COMPOUNDS.

SECTION REVIEW ANSWERS

1. corrosive, toxic, or flammable
2. Sample answers are given. (1) Substitute safe materials. (2) Do not pour hazardous materials on the ground or allow them to evaporate. (3) Store hazardous materials in a safe place in their original containers. (4) Recycle materials. (5) Educate others.

YOU DECIDE!

SCIENCE & SOCIETY

Find out from your local environmental agency how to dispose properly of such materials. Explain to your neighbor why it is dangerous to dump the materials and offer the advice you learned about disposal.

PREPARATION

SECTION BACKGROUND

▶ An atom's electronegativity is the tendency of the atom to attract a pair of electrons in a bond.

▶ Excluding noble gases, elements in the upper right of the periodic table have high electronegativities. Those in the lower left have low electronegativities.

▶ An ionic bond results from electron transfer between two atoms that differ greatly in electronegativity.

▶ A covalent bond results from the sharing of a pair of electrons between two atoms that are close in electronegativity.

▶ In a polar covalent bond between two atoms, there is unequal sharing of the electron pair due to a moderate difference in electronegativity.

PREPLANNING

▶ For Activity 11-2 you will need sugar, salt, and finely crushed ice.

▶ If you have not done so, consider making magnetic "electrons" to manipulate on the chalkboard in order to model bonding between atoms.

1 MOTIVATE

▶ **Demonstration:** The formation of an ionic bond occurs when a piece of magnesium ribbon is burned. **CAUTION:** *Hold the burning ribbon inside a can so that the bright light cannot be directly observed.* The reaction is

$$2Mg + O_2 \rightarrow 2MgO.$$

New Science Words

ion
ionic bond
covalent bond
polar molecule
nonpolar molecule

Objectives

▶ Describe ionic bonds and covalent bonds.
▶ Identify the particles produced by ionic bonding and by covalent bonding.
▶ Distinguish between a nonpolar covalent bond and a polar covalent bond.

Ions and Ionic Bonds

The brilliant flash in the photograph shows what happens when sodium is put in a flask of chlorine gas. (**CAUTION:** *It is very dangerous to handle or mix sodium and chlorine—do not try it.*) Recall how the atoms of these elements—sodium and chlorine—bond chemically when mixed. An atom of sodium has one electron in its outer energy level, as shown in Figure 11-7. When the atom loses that electron, its second energy level is then outermost and complete, because it contains eight electrons. But the atom now has 11 protons, with a total charge of 11+, and 10 electrons, with a total charge of 10−. Because (11+) + (10−) = 1+, the atom has a net positive charge of 1+. <mark>Atoms that have charges are called ions.</mark> Thus, the sodium atom, Na, that has lost an electron is now a sodium ion, Na⁺. You write the symbol for the ion with a superscript plus sign to indicate its charge. *Superscript* means "written above." ❶

Figure 11-7. Dot diagrams for sodium atom becoming a sodium ion (top), and chlorine atom becoming a chloride ion (bottom)

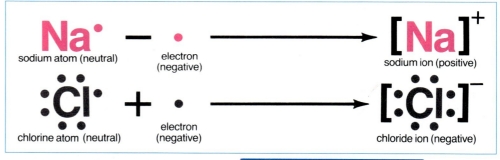

Na•	− • →	[Na]⁺
sodium atom (neutral)	electron (negative)	sodium ion (positive)
:Cl̈:	+ • →	[:Cl̈:]⁻
chlorine atom (neutral)	electron (negative)	chloride ion (negative)

OPTIONS

Meeting Different Ability Levels

For Section 11-3, use the following **Teacher Resource Masters** depending upon individual students' needs.

◆ **Study Guide Master** for all students.
● **Reinforcement Master** for students of average and above average ability levels.
▲ **Enrichment Master** for above average students.

Additional Teacher Resource Package masters are listed in the OPTIONS box throughout the section. The additional masters are appropriate for all students.

A chlorine atom has seven electrons in its outer energy level, as shown in Figure 11-7. When the atom gains an electron, its outermost energy level contains eight electrons. But the atom now has 17 protons, with a total charge of 17+, and 18 electrons, with a total charge of 18–. Because (17+) + (18–) = 1–, the atom has a net negative charge of 1–. In other words, it is now a chloride ion, which you write with a superscript minus sign, Cl^-, to indicate its charge. The compound NaCl as a whole, however, is neutral, because the total net positive charge equals the total net negative charge.

An **ion** is an atom that is either positively or negatively charged. Compounds made up of ions are ionic compounds, and the bonds that hold them together are ionic bonds. An **ionic bond** is the force of attraction between the opposite charges of the ions in an ionic compound. 2

Figure 11-9 shows another example of ionic bonding—the formation of magnesium fluoride, MgF_2. When magnesium reacts with fluorine, a magnesium atom loses two electrons and becomes a positively charged ion, Mg^{2+}. Notice that you write 2+ on the symbol for magnesium to indicate the ion's net charge. At the same time, each of the two fluorine atoms gains one electron each and becomes a negatively charged fluoride ion, F^-. The compound as a whole is neutral. Why? Because the sum of the net charges on all three ions is zero.

Figure 11-8. Dot diagram for sodium chloride, NaCl

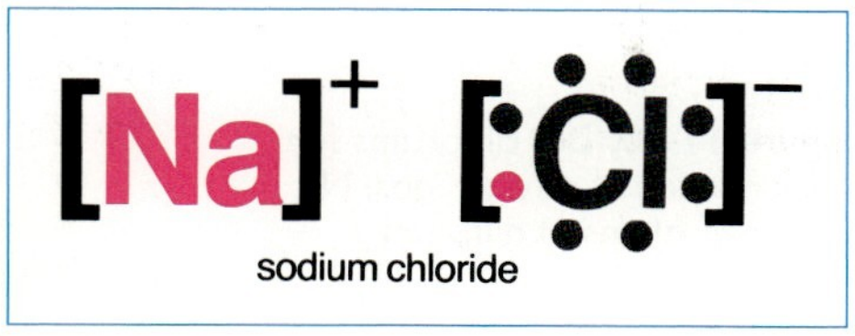

Why is the charge on a magnesium ion positive?

Molecules and Covalent Bonds

3 Most atoms become more chemically stable by sharing electrons, rather than by losing or gaining electrons. In Figure 11-6 on page 272, you saw how two chlorine atoms share electrons. Notice that the chlorine parti-

Figure 11-9. Dot diagram for magnesium fluoride, MgF_2

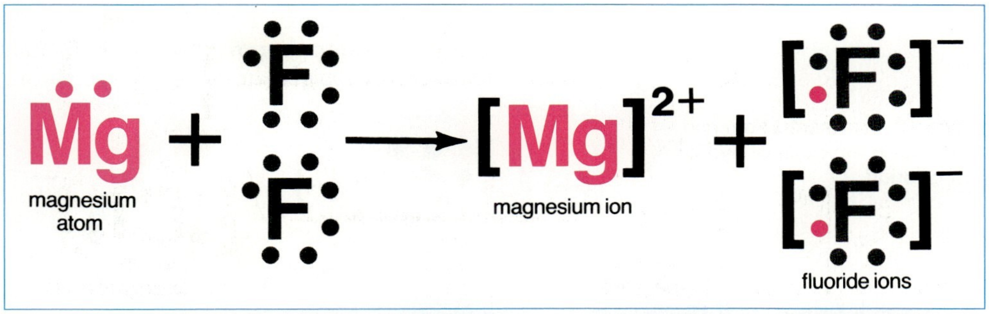

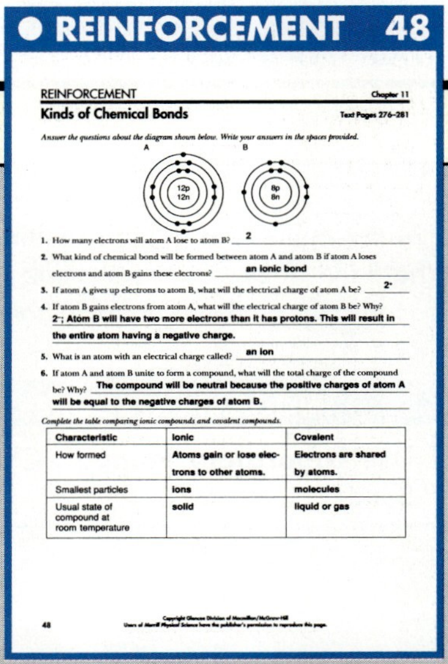

● REINFORCEMENT 48

REINFORCEMENT Chapter 11

Kinds of Chemical Bonds Text Pages 276–281

Answer the questions about the diagram shown below. Write your answers in the spaces provided.

A B

12p 12n 8p 8n

1. How many electrons will atom A lose to atom B? **2**
2. What kind of chemical bond will be formed between atom A and atom B if atom A loses electrons and atom B gains these electrons? **an ionic bond**
3. If atom A gives up electrons to atom B, what will the electrical charge of atom A be? **2+**
4. If atom B gains electrons from atom A, what will the electrical charge of atom B be? Why? **2–; Atom B will have two more electrons than it has protons. This will result in the entire atom having a negative charge.**
5. What is an atom with an electrical charge called? **an ion**
6. If atom A and atom B unite to form a compound, what will the total charge of the compound be? Why? **The compound will be neutral because the positive charges of atom A will be equal to the negative charges of atom B.**

Complete the table comparing ionic compounds and covalent compounds.

Characteristic	Ionic	Covalent
How formed	**Atoms gain or lose electrons to other atoms.**	**Electrons are shared by atoms.**
Smallest particles	**ions**	**molecules**
Usual state of compound at room temperature	**solid**	**liquid or gas**

48

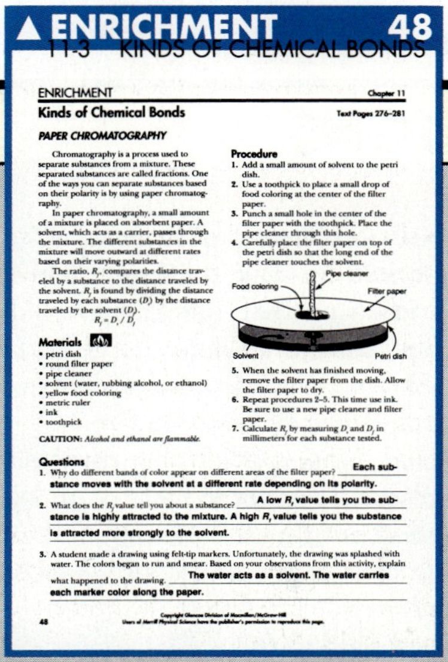

▲ ENRICHMENT 48

ENRICHMENT Chapter 11

Kinds of Chemical Bonds Text Pages 276–281

PAPER CHROMATOGRAPHY

Chromatography is a process used to separate substances from a mixture. These separated substances are called fractions. One of the ways you can separate substances based on their polarity is by using paper chromatography.

In paper chromatography, a small amount of a mixture is placed on absorbent paper. A solvent, which acts as a carrier, passes through the mixture. The different substances in the mixture will move outward at different rates based on their varying polarities.

The ratio, R_f, compares the distance traveled by a substance to the distance traveled by the solvent. R_f is found by dividing the distance traveled by each substance (D_s) by the distance traveled by the solvent (D_f).

$$R_f = D_s / D_f$$

Materials
- petri dish
- round filter paper
- pipe cleaner
- solvent (water, rubbing alcohol, or ethanol)
- yellow food coloring
- metric ruler
- ink
- toothpick

CAUTION: *Alcohol and ethanol are flammable.*

Procedure
1. Add a small amount of solvent to the petri dish.
2. Use a toothpick to place a small drop of food coloring at the center of the filter paper.
3. Punch a small hole in the center of the filter paper with the toothpick. Place the pipe cleaner through this hole.
4. Carefully place the filter paper on top of the petri dish so that the long end of the pipe cleaner touches the solvent.

Pipe cleaner
Food coloring
Filter paper
Solvent
Petri dish

5. When the solvent has finished moving, remove the filter paper from the dish. Allow the filter paper to dry.
6. Repeat procedures 2–5. This time use ink. Be sure to use a new pipe cleaner and filter paper.
7. Calculate R_f by measuring D_s and D_f in millimeters for each substance tested.

Questions
1. Why do different bands of color appear on different areas of the filter paper? **Each substance moves with the solvent at a different rate depending on its polarity.**
2. What does the R_f value tell you about a substance? **A low R_f value tells you the substance is highly attracted to the mixture. A high R_f value tells you the substance is attracted more strongly to the solvent.**
3. A student made a drawing using felt-tip markers. Unfortunately, the drawing was splashed with water. The colors began to run and smear. Based on your observations from this activity, explain what happened to the drawing. **The water acts as a solvent. The water carries each marker color along the paper.**

48

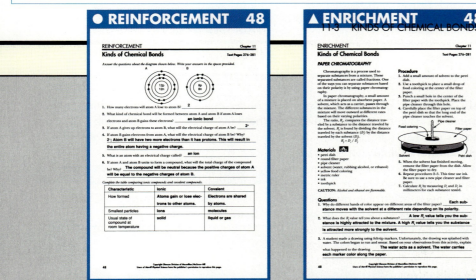

TYING TO PREVIOUS KNOWLEDGE: Recall that elements with three or fewer electrons are metals. Metals tend to lose electrons to form positive ions. Nonmetals generally have five or more outer electrons. Nonmetals tend to gain electrons to form negative ions.

OBJECTIVES AND SCIENCE WORDS: Have students review the objectives and science words to become familiar with this section.

2 TEACH

Key Concepts are highlighted.

CONCEPT DEVELOPMENT

▶ The ionic bond is very strong as is indicated by the high melting points for ionic compounds. Ask students to hypothesize about the differences in melting points between ionic and covalent compounds. Ask them to give reasons for their hypotheses.

▶ A covalent bond can be thought of as a spring that allows the bonded atoms to stretch and bend back and forth.

REVEALING MISCONCEPTIONS

▶ Students often think that a chemical bond physically links atoms just as a nail holds two pieces of wood together. Emphasize that the bond is an attractive force.

CROSS CURRICULUM

▶ **Medicine:** Cyanoacrylate, known as Super Glue, can be used in place of sutures in some types of surgery. Super Glue forms chemical bonds with the surface molecules that are being joined together.

▶ **Art:** After students study types of bonds, have them convey their impressions of two atoms in each type of bond using color, form, and modeling to emphasize differences in bond type.

Why is a chlorine molecule neutral?

cle, Cl_2, is not charged—it is neutral. The chlorine is not in the form of ions, but molecules. Neutral particles formed as a result of electron sharing are called molecules.

A bond that forms between atoms when they share electrons is known as a **covalent bond.** In the case of chlorine, a covalent bond is formed between two atoms of the same element. Covalent bonds also form between atoms of nitrogen, the gas that makes up most of the air. As you can see in Figure 11-10, two atoms of nitrogen in N_2 share three electrons, forming three covalent bonds between the atoms.

Figure 11-10. Dot diagrams for the formation of nitrogen gas, N_2, from two atoms of nitrogen

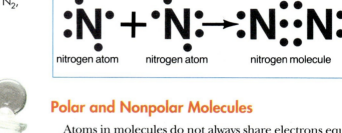

nitrogen atom   nitrogen atom   nitrogen molecule

Polar and Nonpolar Molecules

Atoms in molecules do not always share electrons equally. An example is a molecule of hydrogen chloride, HCl. A water solution of HCl is hydrochloric acid, which is used in laboratories, to clean metal, and in your stomach to digest food. The chlorine atom has a stronger attraction for electrons than does the hydrogen atom. As a result, the electrons they share in hydrogen chloride will spend more time near the chlorine atom than near the hydrogen atom. This type of molecule is called polar. *Polar* means "having two opposite ends." A **polar molecule** is one that has a positive end and a negative end.

Water is another example of a compound with polar molecules, as shown in Figure 11-12. A water molecule contains two polar covalent bonds, one between each hydrogen atom and the oxygen atom. The oxygen atom

Figure 11-11. Dot diagram and model for a molecule of hydrogen chloride

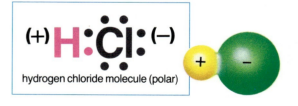

hydrogen chloride molecule (polar)

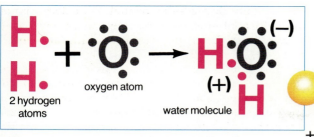

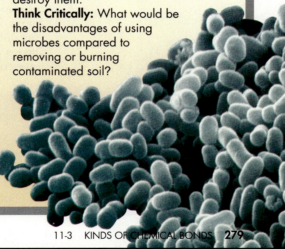

Figure 11-12. Dot diagram and model for a molecule of water

oxygen atom

2 hydrogen atoms

water molecule

has a stronger attraction for electrons than the hydrogen atoms do. As a result, the oxygen end of the water molecule is negative and the hydrogen end of the molecule is positive.

TECHNOLOGY

Bond Busters

Toxic compounds with names such as vinyl chloride, benzene, and pentachlorophenol are among the pollutants that human activities generate in huge amounts and that damage the environment. One way to get rid of toxic compounds is to change them chemically into other, harmless compounds. That is, the chemical bonds holding together the atoms in molecules of toxic compounds must be broken. Then the atoms are bonded into different molecules of harmless substances.

Scientists are now enlisting new strains of microbes as bond busters to change toxic compounds into nontoxic ones. The microbes eat the compounds, which change chemically as they are digested. To create a strain of pollutant-eating microbes, scientists first add a pollutant to a population of microbes. Most of the microbes die, leaving only the hardiest ones to reproduce. Scientists then seed polluted soil with these microbes and add fertilizer and oxygen to

promote their growth. The microbes break down the toxic compounds and then, with the food source gone, the microbes die.

At least 1000 different strains of bacteria and fungi are now helping to get rid of pollutants. The biggest advantage of the microbial approach is that instead of relocating the pollutants—by moving toxic substances to other places—the microbes destroy them.

Think Critically: What would be the disadvantages of using microbes compared to removing or burning contaminated soil?

3 CLOSE

Figure 11-13. Sugar is an example of a covalent compound that has polar molecules.

As a group, do ionic compounds have higher or lower melting points than covalent compounds?

Some molecules, such as those of nitrogen, are nonpolar. Because the two nitrogen atoms share their electrons equally, the molecule's ends are neither positive or negative. A **nonpolar molecule** is one that does not have oppositely charged ends. Look again at the diagram of a nitrogen molecule in Figure 11-10 on page 278.

You have read about two main ways chemical bonding takes place, producing two kinds of compounds—ionic and covalent. These groups of compounds have contrasting properties. For example, like sodium chloride, most ionic compounds are crystalline solids with high melting points. Like water, most covalent compounds are liquids or gases at room temperature. But some covalent compounds, such as sugar, are solids. In later chapters, you will learn more about compounds of each type.

SECTION REVIEW

1. Compare ionic and covalent bonds.
2. What type of particle is formed by the following bonds: (a) ionic (b) polar covalent (c) nonpolar covalent?
3. **Apply:** The label on a tube of toothpaste states that it contains the decay preventative sodium fluoride, NaF. Draw a dot diagram of sodium fluoride, which is an ionic compound.

Skill Builder   ☑ Concept Mapping

Using the following terms, make a network tree concept map of chemical bonding: *ionic, covalent, ions, positive ions, negative ions, molecules, polar, nonpolar.* If you need help, refer to Concept Mapping in the **Skill Handbook** on pages 684 and 685

Skill Builder

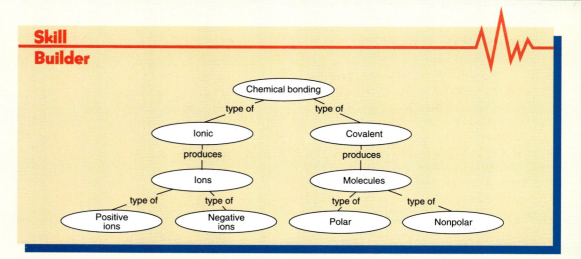

ACTIVITY 11-2
Covalent and Ionic Bonds

Problem: *How can melting point be used to compare covalent and ionic substances?*

Materials
- 1 tablespoon each of crushed ice, sugar, and salt
- wire test-tube holder
- 3 test tubes
- goggles
- laboratory burner

Procedure
1. Copy the data table below and use it to record your observations.
2. Place a tablespoon each of crushed ice, sugar, and salt in separate test tubes.
3. Wearing goggles and using a wire test-tube holder, heat each test tube with a laboratory burner for no longer than five minutes.
4. Observe and record the appearance of each substance at one-minute intervals.
5. Rank the three materials from the easiest to the most difficult to melt.

Analyze
1. Which one of the three compounds do you believe to be ionic?
2. What is the role of energy during a change of state, such as melting?

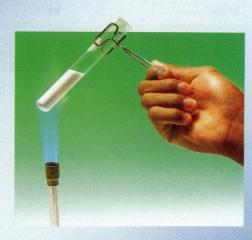

Conclude and Apply
3. Butter is a common material that is easy to melt. Would you conclude that butter is composed of mainly covalent compounds or of ionic compounds?
4. In general, how do the melting points of covalent compounds and ionic compounds compare?

Data and Observations

Sample Data

Substance	Appearance after Heating				
	1 min	2 min	3 min	4 min	5 min
Salt	No change	Some moisture present, but no change	No change	No change	No change
Sugar	Begins to melt	Melting and browning; sweet smell	Black paste and smoke	Bubbling from paste and burnt smell	Paste hardens; still black
Ice	Some melting	Liquid forms	May begin to boil	Boiling away	May continue to boil or may have boiled away

OBJECTIVE: Compare melting properties of several substances and **infer** the type of bonding present.

PROCESS SKILLS applied in this activity:
▶ **Observing** in Procedure Step 4.
▶ **Inferring** in Analyze Question 1 and Conclude and Apply Question 3.
▶ **Comparing** in Conclude and Apply Question 4.

TEACHING THE ACTIVITY
Alternate Materials: Solid shortening may be used as another example of a covalently bonded material.

Troubleshooting: Under typical lab conditions the table salt will not melt. This indicates a very high melting point. The students should not continue heating beyond five minutes.
▶ If necessary, remind students how to adjust a burner and where the hottest part of the flame is located. Their placement of tubes should be consistent.

ANSWERS TO QUESTIONS
1. NaCl, or table salt, is ionic.
2. During a change of state, energy is used to overcome the forces of attraction between the particles. Refer students to Chapter 8 if they have trouble with this question.
3. Because it melts so easily, it is likely made up of covalently bonded substances.
4. Generally, ionically bonded materials are difficult to melt because of the high temperatures required. In general, covalent compounds melt at lower temperatures than do ionic compounds.

PROGRAM RESOURCES
From the **Teacher Resource Package** use:
Activity Worksheets, pages 88-89, Activity 11-2: Covalent and Ionic Bonds.

PREPARATION

SECTION BACKGROUND

▶ As a general rule, the oxidation number of metals can be predicted based on their outer electron configuration. Metals with one outer-level electron (Group 1) have oxidation numbers of 1+. Those with two electrons have oxidation numbers of 2+ and so on. Most transition metals have variable oxidation numbers.

▶ The oxidation number of nonmetals can be predicted based on their outer electron configuration. Those with seven outer-level electrons (one less than eight) have oxidation number of 1– and so on.

▶ The noble gases have oxidation numbers of zero because they have eight outer electrons.

▶ Many compounds have water molecules as a part of the crystal. The compounds are referred to as hydrates.

PREPLANNING

▶ Cobalt(II) chloride hexahydrate is needed for the Mini-Lab in this section. You may want to have some plaster of paris, calcium sulfate dihydrate, available too.

1 MOTIVATE

▶ **Demonstration:** Exhibit 4 g of powdered sulfur and 7 g of iron filings. Point out the yellow color of sulfur and the magnetic properties of iron. Mix them on a piece of paper and pour into a test tube. Behind a shield, heat the tube using a burner until the contents glow red. Then, plunge it into a beaker of water to break the test tube. The students will notice that the product is not yellow or magnetic.

$$Fe + S \longrightarrow FeS.$$

Use the demonstration to introduce oxidation numbers, formula writing, and naming.

11-4 Formulas and Names of Compounds

New Science Words

oxidation number
binary compound
polyatomic ion
hydrate

Objectives

▶ Explain how to determine oxidation numbers.
▶ Write formulas for compounds from their names.
▶ Name compounds from their formulas.
▶ Describe hydrates and their formulas.

Oxidation Numbers

The two people in these pictures seem to have little in common. Yet, in a sense, ==the medieval alchemist is the ancestor of the modern chemist.== Both are shown at work investigating matter. Notice how each would write symbols for the elements silver and sulfur. Tarnish is silver sulfide, a compound of silver and sulfur. If the alchemist knew the composition of tarnish, how might he write its formula? The modern chemist does know its composition; she would write it Ag_2S. When you get to the end of this section, you, too, will know how to write such formulas.

What two elements are present in tarnish?

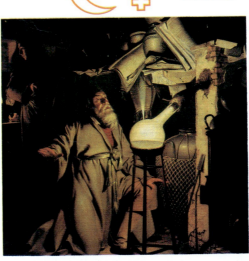

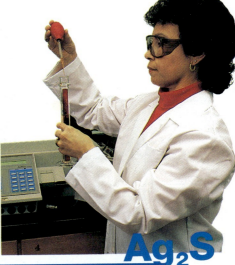

Ag_2S

OPTIONS

Meeting Different Ability Levels

For Section 11-4, use the following **Teacher Resource Masters** depending upon individual students' needs.

◆ **Study Guide Master** for all students.
● **Reinforcement Master** for students of average and above average ability levels.
▲ **Enrichment Master** for above average students.

Additional Teacher Resource Package masters are listed in the OPTIONS box throughout the section. The additional masters are appropriate for all students.

◆ **STUDY GUIDE** 49

STUDY GUIDE   Chapter 11
Formulas and Names of Compounds   Text Pages 282–288

Match each term in Column II with its description in Column I. Write the letter of the correct term in the space provided.

	Column I	Column II
j	1. prefix meaning six	a. bi-
g	2. prefix meaning many	b. ion
a	3. prefix meaning two	c. binary
c	4. compound composed of two elements	d. anhydrous
b	5. positively or negatively charged atom	e. polyatomic ion
e	6. positively or negatively charged group of atoms	f. subscript
i	7. compound that has water chemically attached to its ions	g. poly-
h	8. number assigned to an element to show its combining ability in a compound	h. oxidation number
d	9. without water	i. hydrate
f	10. number that tells how many atoms of an element are in a unit of the compound	j. hexa-

The words in each group below are related. Write a sentence, using all the words in the group, that shows how the words are related.

Student responses may vary. Check to be sure students have written complete sentences using all terms.

Example:
compound, properties, elements
The properties of a compound differ from the properties of the elements making up the compound.

1. hydrate, water, ions   A hydrate is a compound that has water chemically attached to its ions.

2. oxidation number, element, compound   The oxidation number of an element can be used to determine its combining ability in a compound.

3. zero, oxidation numbers, noble gases   The oxidation numbers of the noble gases are zero.

4. oxidation number, Roman numeral, element   The name of a compound containing an element with more than one oxidation number must include a Roman numeral after the name of the element.

Copyright Glencoe Division of Macmillan/McGraw-Hill
Users of Merrill Physical Science have the publisher's permission to reproduce this page.   49

You can figure out formulas with the help of oxidation numbers. What are these numbers? An **oxidation number** is a positive or negative number assigned to an element to show its combining ability in a compound. In other words, an oxidation number indicates how many electrons an atom has gained, lost, or shared when bonding with other atoms. For example, when sodium forms an ion, it loses an electron and has a charge of 1+. So the oxidation number of sodium is 1+. And when chlorine forms an ion, it gains an electron and has a charge of 1−. So the oxidation number of chlorine is 1−.

Oxidation numbers are often a periodic property of elements. The red numbers printed on the periodic table shown in Figure 11-14 are the oxidation numbers for many elements in binary compounds. *Bi-* means "two," and a **binary compound** is one that is composed of two elements. Sodium chloride is an example of a binary compound.

Like sodium, each metal in Group 1 loses its one outer electron in bonding, so each of these elements has an oxidation number of 1+. Remember, losing electrons produces a positive oxidation number in an element. Each metal in Group 2 loses both its outer electrons in bonding, so each has an oxidation number of 2+.

Like chlorine, each of the nonmetals in Group 17 gains one electron in bonding, so each of these elements has an oxidation number of 1−. Remember, gaining electrons

❶

What does an oxidation number indicate?

❷

❸

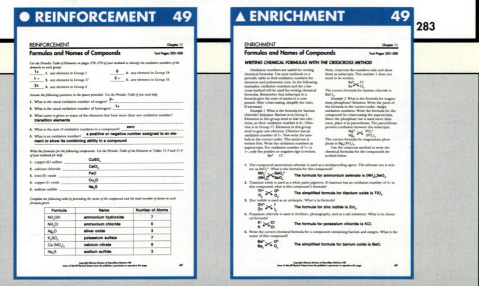

Figure 11-14. Part of the periodic table, with oxidation numbers for elements in Groups 1, 2, 13, 14, 15, 16, 17, and 18.

* In Group 14, Sn and Pb also exhibit 2+ oxidation states.

The lanthanoid and actinoid elements are not shown in this table.

TYING TO PREVIOUS KNOWLEDGE: Ask students to write on the chalkboard the chemical formulas for as many compounds as they remember. Use the formulas to introduce oxidation numbers, formula writing, and naming.

OBJECTIVES AND SCIENCE WORDS: Have students review the objectives and science words to become familiar with this section.

2 TEACH

Key Concepts are highlighted.

CONCEPT DEVELOPMENT

▶ Give each student a blank copy of the periodic table. Have students write the oxidation number of Groups 1, 2, 13, 14, 15, 16, 17, and 18 at the top of each column.

▶ These general rules for oxidation numbers will help students write correct formulas.

Rule 1. The oxidation number of any free element is zero.

Rule 2. The oxidation number of a monatomic ion is equal to the charge on the ion.

Rule 3. The oxidation number of hydrogen in most compounds is 1+.

Rule 4. The oxidation number of oxygen in most compounds is 2−.

Rule 5. The sum of the oxidation numbers of all the atoms in a particle must equal the charge of that particle.

Rule 6. In compounds, the elements of Groups 1 and 2 and aluminum have positive oxidation numbers of 1+, 2+, and 3+ respectively.

▶ It is best that students not be required to memorize oxidation numbers but rather relate them to atomic structure and to an atom's position on the periodic table, when possible.

▶ Explain that oxidation numbers are used as an aid in understanding atomic structure and writing formulas correctly. Formula writing is not just a reasoning exercise but represents a way of predicting the composition of actual chemical substances formed in real chemical processes.

CROSS CURRICULUM

▶ **Geology:** Geologists use oxidation numbers to infer what conditions were present in past geologic periods. The presence of iron(III) indicates shoreline deposition where plenty of oxygen was available. Iron(II) indicates the sediment was deposited in deeper water where oxygen was lacking.

CONCEPT DEVELOPMENT

▶ The authors do not recommend using the technique that has students cross oxidation numbers to get subscripts in a formula. This shortcut can result in many errors. The summing-to-zero method in this text is a reasonably accurate model of the electron changes that atoms actually undergo when combining chemically.

▶ At this level, it is not recommended that students memorize the ion charges. They should be provided that information in tables when taking tests.

Cooperative Learning: Use Problem Solving Teams to do the Practice Problems together. Switch to Expert Teams and have one group make up plausible compound names while the other makes up plausible formulas. Have one group write names for the other group's formulas and vice versa.

PRACTICE PROBLEM ANSWERS

1. 2+   2–
   Ca   0
   (2+) + (2–) = 0
   Therefore, the formula is CaO.
2. CuS

---

copper(I)	Cu^+
copper(II)	Cu^{2+}
iron(II)	Fe^{2+}
iron(III)	Fe^{3+}
chromium(II)	Cr^{2+}
chromium(III)	Cr^{3+}
lead(II)	Pb^{2+}
lead(IV)	Pb^{4+}

Figure 11-15. Here are some elements that have variable oxidation numbers.

produces a negative oxidation number in an element. Each nonmetal in Group 16 gains two electrons in bonding, so each has an oxidation number of 2–.

Some elements have more than one oxidation number. Copper, as you can see in Figure 11-15, can be both Cu^+ and Cu^{2+}. In the name of a compound of copper, the Roman numeral equals the oxidation number of copper in that compound. Thus, the oxidation number of copper in copper(II) oxide is 2+. Iron may be Fe^{2+} or Fe^{3+}. Thus, the oxidation number of iron in iron(III) oxide is 3+.

④

Formulas for Binary Compounds

Once you know how to find the oxidation numbers of elements in binary compounds, you can write formulas by using these rules: (1) Write first the symbol of the element with the positive oxidation number. Hydrogen and all metals have positive oxidation numbers. (2) Then write the symbol of the element with the negative oxidation number. (3) Add subscripts so that the sum of the oxidation numbers of all the atoms in the formula is zero.

⑤

EXAMPLE PROBLEM: Writing Formulas for Binary Compounds

Problem Statement :

What is the formula of a compound composed of sulfur and aluminum?

Problem-Solving Steps:

1. Write the symbol of the positive element followed by the symbol of the negative element.

   Al   S

2. Look up oxidation numbers for each element. Write oxidation numbers above the symbols.

   3+   2–
   Al   S

3. Write in subscripts so that the sum of the oxidation numbers is zero.

   3+   2–
   Al_2 S_3

4. Check to see if the sum of the oxidation numbers is zero.

   $2(3+) + 3(2–) = (6+) + (6–) = 0$

Solution:

Final Formula: Al_2S_3

PRACTICE PROBLEMS

<u>Strategy Hint:</u> Be sure to use the smallest possible subscript numbers to make the sum zero.

<u>Strategy Hint:</u> The Roman numeral II tells you the oxidation number of copper.

1. Write the formula for a compound of calcium and oxygen.
2. Write the formula of a compound of copper(II) and sulfur.

OPTIONS

INQUIRY QUESTIONS

▶ Determine the oxidation number of chlorine in the following compounds: HClO, $HClO_2$, $HClO_3$, $HClO_4$, HCl, and Cl_2. *1+, 3+, 5+, 7+, 1–, 0*

▶ Write the name for each of the following binary compounds:
a. **KBr** *potassium bromide*
b. **CaO** *calcium oxide*
c. **CuI** *copper(I) iodide*
d. **Al_2S_3** *aluminum sulfide*

▶ Determine the oxidation number of S in sulfuric acid, H_2SO_4. *6+*

▶ What is wrong with the way the following formulas are written? Rewrite them correctly:

Al3Cl: *Formulas should use subscripts, not coefficients; $AlCl_3$ is correct.*

NaO: *Oxidation numbers do not sum to zero in this ratio; Na_2O is correct.*

$(Ca)_1(Br)_2$: *The numeral 1 is not used in formulas. Parentheses are used only with polyatomic ions; $CaBr_2$ is correct.*

Naming Binary Compounds

You can name a binary compound from its formula by using these rules: (1) Write the name of the first element. (2) Write the root of the name of the second element. (3) Add the ending *-ide* to the root. Table 11-3 lists several elements and their *-ide* counterparts. For example, $CaCl_2$ is named calcium chloride.

To name compounds of elements having two oxidation numbers you must first figure out the oxidation numbers of the elements. Study the next example problem and do the practice problems.

Figure 11-16. Many binary compounds of transition elements are brightly colored.

EXAMPLE PROBLEM: Naming Some Binary Compounds

Problem Statement:

What is the name of CrO?

Problem-Solving Steps:

1. Look up the oxidation number of the negative element.

2. Figure out the oxidation number of the positive element.

$$\begin{array}{cc} & 2- \\ Cr & O \end{array}$$

$? + (2-) = 0; ? = 2+$

$$\begin{array}{cc} Cr & O \end{array}$$

3. Write the name of the compound, using a Roman numeral for the positive oxidation number if necessary.

$(2+) + (2-) = 0$

$$\begin{array}{cc} Cr & O \end{array}$$

Solution:

chromium(II) oxide

PRACTICE PROBLEM

Strategy Hint: For names of elements with more than one oxidation number, remember to include the Roman numeral. For names of nonmetals in binary compounds use Table 11-3.

1. Name the following compounds:
   Li_2S, MgF_2, FeO, CuCl

Table 11-3

ELEMENTS IN BINARY COMPOUNDS

Element	*-ide* Naming
Chlorine	Chloride
Fluorine	Fluoride
Nitrogen	Nitride
Oxygen	Oxide
Phosphorus	Phosphide
Sulfur	Sulfide

► There are computer programs that provide practice naming binary compounds. Ask your school's media specialist if your district has one.

► Students can better visualize the compounds they are naming if they make models of them. If modeling kits are not available, use gumdrops of different colors and toothpicks, or use chalkboard models with magnetic "electrons."

► Emphasize that a Roman numeral indicates the oxidation number of an ion whose oxidation number varies. It is as important as the name of the element.

MINI QUIZ

Use the Mini Quiz to check students' recall of chapter content.

1. An element's combining ability in a compound is designated by its _____ . *oxidation number*

2. A compound formed from two elements is called a(n) _____ . *binary compound*

3. Elements that lose one electron take on an ion charge of _____ . *1+*

4. How do you show the oxidation number of a metal having more than one oxidation number when naming a compound? *Use a Roman numeral.*

5. In a correct formula, the oxidation numbers of all atoms add up to _____ . *zero*

PRACTICE PROBLEM ANSWERS

Note: Have students check Figure 11-15 on page 284 for elements with variable oxidation numbers. Many more elements than the ones in the list are variable. However, those listed are the only variable elements used in this text unless specifically stated in a problem.

1. lithium sulfide
2. magnesium fluoride
3. iron(II) oxide
4. copper(I) chloride

INQUIRY QUESTIONS

► Write the formula for each of the following:

a. magnesium nitride Mg_3N_2
b. aluminum oxide Al_2O_3
c. lithium fluoride LiF
d. lead(IV) oxide PbO_2
e. chromium(II) bromide $CrBr_2$

► Element A has oxidation numbers of 2+ and 3+. Element Z has oxidation numbers of 2– and 3–. What are possible formulas if A and Z bond together? AZ, A_3Z_2, A_2Z_3

PROGRAM RESOURCES

From the **Teacher Resource Package** use:

Cross-Curricular Connections, page 17, Restoration of the Sistine Chapel.

Transparency Masters, pages 43-44, Oxidation Numbers.

Use **Color Transparency** number 22, Oxidation Numbers.

CONCEPT DEVELOPMENT

▶ Remind students that polyatomic ions act as a single group. Thus, they should be treated very much like a single element when writing formulas.

▶ Students will probably want to use parentheses in formulas when they are not needed. Remind them that parentheses are to be used only around polyatomic ions when more than one is needed to make the formula electrically neutral.

▶ **Demonstration:** To show that like charges repel and opposites attract to form chemical compounds, place two 25-cm-long pieces of cellophane tape on a plastic surface side by side. Pull both up at the same time. They will then have like charges. Bring the two pieces toward each other and watch them repel. Then put one piece down on the plastic surface. Place a second piece on top of it. Pull them off the plastic surface, and then separate them. They will have opposite charges, and, as you bring them close together, they will attract.

STUDENT TEXT QUESTIONS

▶ Page 286, paragraph 1: **What four elements does NaHCO₃ contain?** *sodium, hydrogen, carbon, and oxygen*
▶ Page 286, paragraph 2: **What is the name of Sr(OH)₂?** *strontium hydroxide*

PRACTICE PROBLEM ANSWERS

1. 1+   2–
  Na   SO₄
Therefore, Na_2SO_4 gives a sum of zero for charges.
2. 2+   1–
  Mg   ClO₃
Therefore, the formula is $Mg(ClO_3)_2$.

Table 11-4

POLYATOMIC IONS		
Charge	Name	Formula
1+	Ammonium	NH_4^+
1–	Acetate	$C_2H_3O_2^-$
	Chlorate	ClO_3^-
	Hydroxide	OH^-
	Nitrate	NO_3^-
2–	Carbonate	CO_3^{2-}
	Sulfate	SO_4^{2-}
3–	Phosphate	PO_4^{3-}

Compounds with Polyatomic Ions

Not all compounds are binary. Have you ever used baking soda in cooking, as a medicine, or to brush your teeth? Baking soda, which has the formula $NaHCO_3$, is an example of a compound that is not binary. What four elements does it contain? Some compounds, including baking soda, are composed of more than two elements because they contain polyatomic ions. The prefix *poly-* means "many," so *polyatomic* means "having many atoms." A **polyatomic ion** is a positively or negatively charged group of atoms. So the compound as a whole contains three or more elements.

Table 11-4 lists several polyatomic ions. To name a compound that contains one of these ions, write first the name of the positive element. For a compound of the ammonium ion, NH_4^+, write ammonium first. Then use Table 11-4 to find the name of the polyatomic ion. For example, K_2SO_4 is potassium sulfate. What is the name of $Sr(OH)_2$?

To write formulas for compounds containing polyatomic ions, follow the rules for writing formulas for binary compounds, with one addition. Write parentheses around the group representing the polyatomic ion when more than one of that ion is needed.

EXAMPLE PROBLEM: Writing Formulas with Polyatomic Ions

Problem Statement: What is the formula for calcium nitrate?
Problem-Solving Steps:

1. Write symbols and oxidation numbers for calcium and the nitrate ion.

  2+   1–
  Ca   NO₃

2. Write in subscripts so that the sum of the oxidation numbers is zero. Enclose the NO_3 in parentheses.

  2+   1–
  Ca (NO₃)₂

Solution: Final formula: $Ca(NO_3)_2$

PRACTICE PROBLEMS

<u>Strategy Hint:</u> When only one polyatomic ion is needed in a formula, do not enclose the ion in parentheses.
<u>Strategy Hint:</u> Because the subscript 3 in ClO_3 is part of the ion, it should not be changed when written as part of a formula.

1. What is the formula for sodium sulfate?

2. What is the formula for magnesium chlorate?

OPTIONS

INQUIRY QUESTIONS

▶ Use Table 11-4 to write the formulas for the following:
a. iron(III) nitrate $Fe(NO_3)_3$
b. calcium carbonate $CaCO_3$
c. aluminum acetate $Al(C_2H_3O_2)_3$
d. ammonium phosphate $(NH_4)_3PO_4$

▶ Use Table 11-4 to write the names of the following compounds:
a. NaOH   *sodium hydroxide*
b. KClO₃   *potassium chlorate*
c. CuSO₄   *copper(II) sulfate*
d. NH₄Cl   *ammonium chloride*

Hydrates

Some ionic compounds may have water molecules as part of their structure and written into their formulas. These compounds are called hydrates. ==A **hydrate** is a compound that has water chemically attached to its ions.== *Hydrate* comes from a word that means water. For example, when a water solution of cobalt chloride evaporates, pink crystals that contain six water molecules for each unit of cobalt chloride are formed. The formula for this compound is $CoCl_2 \cdot 6H_2O$ and its name is cobalt chloride hexahydrate. *Hexa-* means "six." ==You can remove water from these crystals by heating them. The resulting blue compound is called anhydrous,== which means without water. The blue paper in Figure 11-17 has been soaked in cobalt chloride solution and heated.

Like many anhydrous compounds, cobalt chloride gains water molecules easily. You may have seen "weather predictors" made from blue paper that turns pink in humid air. The paper contains cobalt chloride. How does it detect water vapor?

Have you ever made a mold or cast with plaster of paris? If so, you have made a hydrate. Plaster of paris is the anhydrous form of calcium sulfate dihydrate, $CaSO_4 \cdot 2H_2O$. When you mix plaster of paris with water, it absorbs water and changes chemically into the hydrate.

Water in a hydrate has lost its properties because it is chemically attached. Not all crystals are hydrates. The only way to detect the presence of water in crystals is to heat the solid material and see if it gives off steam and changes to powder. For example, if you heat hardened plaster of paris, it will give off steam, crumble, and become powdery. How would you write the formula for this powder?

You have learned how to write formulas of binary ionic compounds and of compounds containing polyatomic ions. Using oxidation numbers to write formulas, you can predict the ratio in which atoms of elements may combine to form compounds. You have also seen how hydrates have water molecules as part of their structure and formulas. As you study the chapters that follow, you will see many uses of formulas.

Figure 11-17. The paper strips have been soaked in a solution of $CoCl_2$. The blue strips have been heated to drive water molecules out of the crystals.

MINI-Lab

How does heat affect a hydrate?
Using a light pink solution of $CoCl_2 \cdot 6H_2O$ as ink and a glass rod as a pen, write your name on white paper. After you have allowed the writing to air dry, it should be nearly invisible. Next, *carefully* wave the paper above a flame until the writing starts to appear blue. What part of the $CoCl_2 \cdot 6H_2O$ was changed? How does heat affect a hydrate? What term is applied to the remainder of the hydrate?

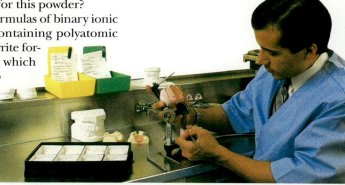

11-4   FORMULAS AND NAMES OF COMPOUNDS   **287**

CROSS CURRICULUM

▶ **Geology:** Calcium sulfate dihydrate is plaster of paris. It is also called gypsum. When seawater evaporated from shallow pools, beds of gypsum were formed. One of these gypsum beds is the Paris Basin in France.

STUDENT TEXT QUESTIONS

▶ Page 287, paragraph 2: **How does cobalt chloride detect water vapor?** *by changing color as it forms a hydrate*
▶ Page 287, paragraph 4: **How would you write the formula for this powder (anhydrous plaster of paris)?** $CaSO_4$

CONCEPT DEVELOPMENT

▶ **Demonstration:** Some substances are said to be *deliquescent*. Have students look up this term. If you have some calcium chloride, you can demonstrate deliquescence by pouring some into an open dish and allowing it to stand. A deliquescent substance is so hygroscopic that it will take up enough water from the air to dissolve itself.

MINI-Lab

Materials: white paper, glass stirring rod, solution containing 1 g $CoCl_2 \cdot 6H_2O$ in 35 mL of water
Teaching Tips
▶ Try the activity before class to determine drying time and the best technique around the flame.
▶ **CAUTION:** *Be sure students are patient when drying the sheets and do not allow the paper to ignite. Demonstrate proper technique to students.*
Answers to Questions
▶ The water of hydration was driven off.
▶ Heat can remove water from a hydrate.
▶ anhydrous

ENRICHMENT

▶ Have students look up the word *hygroscopic* and share its meaning with the class. Explain how it relates to hydrates. Ask if there are any examples of hygroscopic materials in students' kitchens. The ions of some anhydrous substances have such a strong attraction for water that the dehydrated crystal will recapture and hold water molecules from the air. Crackers and cookies that become stale and soggy are examples.

PROGRAM RESOURCES

From the **Teacher Resource Package** use:
Activity Worksheets, page 92, Mini-Lab: How does heat affect a hydrate?
Activity Worksheets, page 5, Flex Your Brain.

PROBLEM SOLVING

Think Critically: The silica gel would absorb the water and form a hydrate. It was packed with the VCR to absorb water molecules, thus helping to prevent corrosion of the metal parts of the VCR.

CHECK FOR UNDERSTANDING

Ask questions 1-3 and the **Apply** Question in the Section Review.

RETEACH

Cooperative Learning: Organize Expert Teams. Have one group from each team prepare flash cards showing positive ions and their names. The other group should prepare a similar set of flash cards showing negative ions. Teams should get back together and draw one card from each "pack." Have them determine the formula and name of the resulting compounds.

EXTENSION

For students who have mastered this section, use the **Reinforcement** and **Enrichment** masters or other OPTIONS provided.

3 CLOSE

❓ FLEX Your Brain

Use the Flex Your Brain activity to have students explore CHEMICAL FORMULAS.

▶ Have students write their own definitions of the word *chemical*. Their definitions should approximate the definition of substance in Chapter 9. The definition should be rational and without the negative connotations so often given it in popular media.

SECTION REVIEW ANSWERS

1. sodium iodide, iron(III) iodide, potassium sulfate, ammonium bromide
2. (a) Li_2S, (b) $Ca(C_2H_3O_2)_2$, (c) BaO
3. (a) $CoCl_2$, (b) $CaSO_4 \cdot 2H_2O$
4. **Apply:** KNO_3

PROBLEM SOLVING

The Packet of Mystery Crystals

When a new video cassette recorder (VCR) was delivered to Peter's home, he was eager to start using it to tape programs. So he asked for and got the job of unpacking the VCR. When he lifted the instrument from the carton, a small flat packet fell out. A label on the packet read "Contains silica gel. Do not eat."

Peter was curious about the contents of the packet, so he looked up "silica gel" in a reference book. There he read that silica gel is the anhydrous form of silica, a mineral that consists mainly of silicon(IV) oxide, SiO_2.

Think Critically: What would silica gel do if water molecules were in the air? Why was the packet of silica gel placed in the carton with the VCR?

SECTION REVIEW

1. Name the following: NaI, FeI_3, K_2SO_4, NH_4Br.
2. Write formulas for compounds composed of (a) lithium and sulfur, (b) calcium and the acetate ion, and (c) barium and oxygen.
3. Write formulas for the following: (a) the anhydrous form of $CoCl_2 \cdot 6H_2O$ and (b) calcium sulfate dihydrate.
4. **Apply:** The label on a package of plant food lists potassium nitrate as one ingredient. What is the formula for this compound?

Skill Builder

☑ Using Variables, Constants, and Controls

Design an experiment to distinguish between crystals that are hydrates and those that are not. Include crystals of iron(II) chloride, copper(I) nitrate, and crystals of sucrose. If you need help, refer to Using Variables, Constants, and Controls in the **Skill Handbook** on page 682.

Skill Builder

Heat crystals of each substance and observe whether or not they give off steam and turn powdery. Add water to the powder. If the original types of crystals form, then the substance was a hydrate. Crystals of iron(III) chloride and copper(II) nitrate are both hydrates, whereas sucrose is not. When sucrose is heated, it decomposes and gives off water vapor, leaving black carbon as a residue that will not dissolve in water nor form sugar crystals.

SUMMARY

11-1: Why Atoms Combine

1. The properties of compounds are generally different from those of the elements they are composed of.

2. The symbols and subscripts in a chemical formula for a compound indicate the composition of a unit of the compound.

3. Chemical bonding occurs when atoms of most elements become more stable by gaining, losing, or sharing electrons.

11-2: Science and Society: Hazardous Compounds at Home

1. Compounds that are toxic, corrosive, or flammable are hazardous.

2. There are many ways in which people can protect their health and the environment from hazardous compounds in the home.

11-3: Kinds of Chemical Bonds

1. Ionic bonds between atoms are formed by the transfer of electrons, and covalent bonds are formed by the sharing of electrons.

2. Ionic bonding produces charged particles called ions. Covalent bonding produces particles called molecules.

3. The unequal sharing of electrons produces polar compounds, and the equal sharing of electrons produces nonpolar compounds.

11-4: Formulas and Names of Compounds

1. An oxidation number indicates how many electrons an atom has gained, lost, or shared when bonding with other atoms.

2. In the formula of an ionic compound, the element or ion with the positive oxidation number is written first, followed by the one with the negative oxidation number.

3. The name of a binary compound is derived from the names of the two elements it is composed of.

4. A hydrate is a compound that has water chemically attached to its ions and written into its formula.

KEY SCIENCE WORDS

a. **binary compound**
b. **chemical bond**
c. **chemical formula**
d. **chemically stable**
e. **corrosive**
f. **covalent bond**
g. **hydrate**
h. **ion**
i. **ionic bond**
j. **nonpolar molecule**
k. **oxidation number**
l. **polyatomic ion**
m. **polar molecule**
n. **toxic**

UNDERSTANDING VOCABULARY

Match each phrase with the correct term from the list of Key Science Words.

1. a charged group of atoms

2. a compound composed of two elements

3. a molecule with a charge on each end

4. a positively or negatively charged atom

5. bond formed by transfer of electrons

6. bond formed from shared electrons

7. crystalline substance that contains water molecules

8. outer energy level is filled with electrons

9. shows an element's combining ability

10. tells what elements are in a compound and their ratios

SUMMARY

Have students read the summary statements to review the major concepts of the chapter.

UNDERSTANDING VOCABULARY

1. l   **6.** f
2. a   **7.** g
3. m   **8.** d
4. h   **9.** k
5. i   **10.** c

ASSESSMENT

To assess student understanding of material in this chapter, use the resources listed.

👥 COOPERATIVE LEARNING

Consider using cooperative learning in the THINK AND WRITE CRITICALLY, APPLY, and MORE SKILL BUILDERS sections of the Chapter Review.

PROGRAM RESOURCES

From the **Teacher Resource Package** use:

Chapter Review, pages 25-26.

Chapter and Unit Tests, pages 65-68, Chapter Test.

Chapter and Unit Tests, pages 69-70, Unit Test.

C H A P T E R
REVIEW

CHECKING CONCEPTS

1. b
2. c
3. c
4. c
5. a

6. d
7. b
8. b
9. a
10. d

UNDERSTANDING CONCEPTS

11. molecule
12. one
13. nonpolar
14. subscript
15. hazardous

THINK AND WRITE CRITICALLY

16. The molecule is composed of one atom of carbon and two atoms of oxygen.

17. Atoms can lose, gain, or share electrons to become more stable.

18. Chromium is a transition element and has two different oxidation numbers.

19. The hydroxide ion, OH^-, in $Mg(OH)_2$ is a polyatomic ion that acts as a unit when it combines with the magnesium ion.

20. XZ, X_2Z_3, X_2Z_5, X_3Z_5

CHECKING CONCEPTS

Choose the word or phrase that completes the sentence or answers the question.

1. The elements that are least likely to react with other elements are the _____.
   a. metals
   b. noble gases
   c. nonmetals
   d. transition elements

2. The oxidation number of Fe in Fe_2S_3 is _____.
   a. 1+
   b. 2+
   c. 3+
   d. 4+

3. The name of CuO is _____.
   a. copper oxide
   b. copper(I) oxide
   c. copper(II) oxide
   d. copper(III) oxide

4. The formula for iron(III) chlorate is _____.
   a. $FeClO_3$
   b. $FeCl$
   c. $Fe(ClO_3)_3$
   d. $FeCl_3$

5. Which of the following is a nonpolar molecule? _____
   a. N_2
   b. H_2O
   c. NaCl
   d. HCl

6. The number of electrons in the outer energy level of Group 17 elements is _____.
   a. 1
   b. 2
   c. 17
   d. 7

7. An example of a binary compound is _____.
   a. O_2
   b. NaF
   c. H_2SO_4
   d. $Cu(NO_3)_2$

8. An example of an anhydrous compound is _____.
   a. H_2O
   b. $CaSO_4$
   c. $CuSO_4 \cdot 5H_2O$
   d. $CaSO_4 \cdot 2H_2O$

9. An atom that has gained an electron is a _____.
   a. negative ion
   b. positive ion
   c. polar molecule
   d. nonpolar molecule

10. An example of a covalent compound is _____.
    a. sodium chloride
    b. calcium fluoride
    c. calcium chloride
    d. water

UNDERSTANDING CONCEPTS

Complete each sentence.

11. An uncharged group of covalently bonded atoms is a(n) _____.

12. An iodine atom can form an ionic compound by accepting _____ electron(s) from a metal.

13. A molecule that has no charge on either end is said to be _____.

14. In a formula, a(n) _____ written after a symbol tells how many atoms of that element are in that compound.

15. Household products that are _____ may be toxic, flammable, or corrosive.

THINK AND WRITE CRITICALLY

16. What does the formula CO_2 tell you about a molecule of carbon dioxide?

17. By what three ways can atoms become chemically stable?

18. How can chromium form two different compounds with oxygen?

19. Why is the formula for milk of magnesia written $Mg(OH)_2$ instead of MgO_2H_2?

20. What compounds can be formed from element X, with oxidation numbers 3+ and 5+, and element Z, with oxidation numbers 2− and 3−? Write their formulas.

APPLY

21. Anhydrous calcium chloride attracts water and is used on dusty roads. Draw a dot diagram of calcium chloride.

22. Write the formula for a compound that is safe to use for cleaning. For help in answering, see Table 11-2 on page 275 and Table 11-4, page 286.

23. Artificial diamonds are made using thallium carbonate. If thallium has an oxidation number of 1+, what is the formula for the compound?

24. Ammonium sulfate is used as a fertilizer. What is its chemical formula?

25. The formula for a compound that can cause kidney stones is $Ca_3(PO_4)_2$. What is the chemical name of this compound?

MORE SKILL BUILDERS

If you need help, refer to the Skill Handbook.

1. **Comparing and Contrasting:** Compare and contrast polar and nonpolar molecules.

2. **Interpreting Scientific Illustrations:** Write the name and formula for the compound illustrated below.

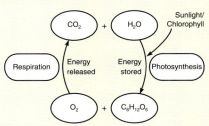

3. **Hypothesizing:** Several uses of HCl were given to you in Section 11-3. HF is another acid and is used to etch glass. If HCl is hydrochloric acid, what would be the name of HF?

4. **Observing and Inferring:** Ammonia gas and water react to form household ammonia, NH_4OH. If the formula for water is H_2O, what is the formula for ammonia gas?

5. **Concept Mapping:** In photosynthesis, green plants, in sunlight, convert carbon dioxide and water to glucose, $C_6H_{12}O_6$, and oxygen, O_2. In respiration, glucose and oxygen react to produce carbon dioxide and water and release energy. In the following map, write in the formulas of the molecules and the names of the processes.

PROJECTS

1. One common form of phosphorus, white phosphorus, has the formula P_4 and is formed by four covalently bonded phosphorus atoms. Make a model of this molecule, showing that all four atoms are now chemically stable.

2. More sulfuric acid, H_2SO_4, is made in the United States than is any other chemical. Research the production and uses of sulfuric acid and write a report on your findings.

APPLY

21.

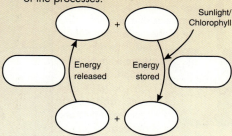

22. $NaHCO_3$ (baking soda)
23. Tl_2CO_3
24. $(NH_4)_2SO_4$
25. calcium phosphate

MORE SKILL BUILDERS

1. **Comparing and Contrasting:** Both molecules have covalent bonds. Polar molecules always have polar bonds and a slight charge on each end. Nonpolar molecules have no charged ends.

2. **Interpreting Scientific Illustrations:** hydrogen sulfide, H_2S

3. **Hypothesizing:** hydrofluoric acid

4. **Observing and Inferring:** NH_3

5. **Concept Mapping:**

Objective

In this unit-ending feature, the unit topic, "The Nature of Matter," is extended into other disciplines. Students will see how knowledge of matter influences events around the planet.

Motivate

Cooperative Learning: Assign one Connection to each group of students. Using the Expert Teams strategy, have each group research to find out more about the geographic location of the Connection—its climate, culture, flora and fauna, and ecological issues.

Teaching Tips

▶ Tell students to keep in mind while they are reading this feature the connection between knowledge about the nature of matter and how that knowledge is applied.

▶ Ask students to hypothesize about how new knowledge about the nature of matter might affect their lives in the future.

Wrap-Up

Conclude this lesson by having students discuss how the events discussed in these Connections affected other parts of the world.

METEOROLOGY

Background: Hail is a form of precipitation that occurs mostly during the warm, summer months. It consists of lumps of ice that form within cumulonimbus clouds—the clouds that produce thunderstorms.

Discussion: Discuss the effects of a hailstorm on crops, buildings, cars, etc.

Answer to Question: Hailstones start as ice crystals (solids) within a storm cloud. Strong updrafts within the cloud toss the crystals up and down, and droplets of water (liquid) freeze in layers (solid) around the ice crystals. When the hailstones become too heavy, they fall to the ground.

Extension: Have students describe experiences they have had with hailstorms.

UNIT 3
GLOBAL CONNECTIONS

The Nature of Matter

In this unit, you studied what matter is, how it is classified, and how it is put together. Now find out how matter is connected to other subjects and places around the world.

120°   60°

60°

METEOROLOGY

THE SKY IS FALLING
Central Kansas
The largest hailstone ever measured fell in Kansas during a September, 1970, thunderstorm. It was almost 14 cm in diameter—the size of a grapefruit. The noise of the hailstones hitting buildings during the storm sounded like exploding bombs. How do hailstones form and what changes in state are involved?

SOCIAL STUDIES

STEAM POWER
New Orleans, Louisiana
By the early 1900s, boats with steam-driven paddle wheels traveled the length of the Mississippi River, carrying passengers and farm goods and opening up the frontier to settlers. Find out how the development of steam engines also affected farming in the Midwest.

BIOLOGY

DEEP-SEA LIFE
Galapagos Islands
Ocean vents that release mineral-rich hot water form the basis of food chains that do not depend on light or photosynthesis. Bacteria around the vents obtain energy from the oxidation of sulfur compounds from the vent. In what lake have scientists found similar vents?

BIOLOGY

Background: In 1977, in the Pacific Ocean near the Galapagos Islands, the first vents were found. Vents have been discovered in 20 areas on the ocean floor.

Discussion: Discuss how, up to the time of this discovery, scientists believed that all food chains depended on organisms that used sunlight to produce food in the process of photosynthesis. Ask students to predict what might happen to the life around the vents if the chemicals given off at the vents changed.

Answer to Question: Scientists have recently discovered the first freshwater vents in Lake Baikal in Siberia.

Extension: Have students research the variety of life found around the ocean vents.

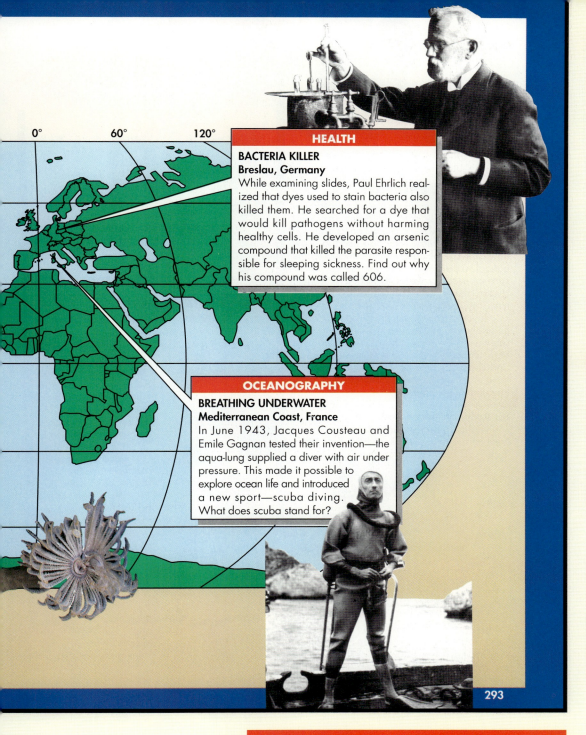

HEALTH

BACTERIA KILLER
Breslau, Germany
While examining slides, Paul Ehrlich realized that dyes used to stain bacteria also killed them. He searched for a dye that would kill pathogens without harming healthy cells. He developed an arsenic compound that killed the parasite responsible for sleeping sickness. Find out why his compound was called 606.

OCEANOGRAPHY

BREATHING UNDERWATER
Mediterranean Coast, France
In June 1943, Jacques Cousteau and Emile Gagnan tested their invention—the aqua-lung supplied a diver with air under pressure. This made it possible to explore ocean life and introduced a new sport—scuba diving. What does scuba stand for?

293

OCEANOGRAPHY

Background: Before the invention of the aqualung, divers had to use a heavy diving suit that required a lifeline with air pumped down from the surface.

Discussion: Discuss how the behavior of gases allowed the aqualung to be invented. Ask students what happens to air remaining in the tank, as the diver uses up some of the air.

Answer to Question: *Scuba* stands for <u>s</u>elf-<u>c</u>ontained <u>u</u>nderwater <u>b</u>reathing <u>a</u>pparatus.

Extension: Have students find out why scuba divers sometimes suffer from "the bends" and how this condition is related to the gas laws.

SOCIAL STUDIES

Background: The steamboat was important in the United States because so much of the country was linked by large rivers. Competition among builders of steamboats led to rapid improvement in their designs and speed.

Discussion: Ask students to describe the change of state that occurs in steam engines and how Boyle's and Charles's laws are involved in a steam engine.

Answer to Question: With steam-powered threshers, farmers could thresh 30 times more wheat per day than they could have by hand.

Extension: Ask students to prepare biographical sketches of some of the early pioneers in the development of steam engines.

HEALTH

Background: The painstaking methods Ehrlich used for finding chemicals to kill bacteria and other pathogens opened the way for the discovery of many other medicines.

Discussion: Tell students that 606 was later discovered to be a cure for syphilis. Discuss the significance of finding chemical compounds that could cure diseases.

Answer to Question: Ehrlich tested every arsenic-based compound he could find on laboratory mice, but most would not kill bacteria. Finally the 606th one he tested worked.

Extension: Ask students to find out how research on new drugs is carried out.

CAREERS

HYDRAULIC ENGINEER

Background: Some hydraulic engineers work for county, state, or federal government agencies. Others work for large construction companies that build bridges and dams.

Related Career	Education
Construction worker	high school
Hydrologist	college degree
Equipment operator	technical school
Architect	college degree

Career Issue: Many groups are against the construction of new dams for flood control, to create recreational areas, or power generation because of the damage it does to the environment. **What do you think?** Ask students to discuss how they would decide whether or not a new dam should be built on a river in your area.

CHEMISTRY TEACHER

Background: Chemistry teachers must not only have a good understanding of chemistry, but also must be able to explain the subject to students. Chemistry teachers teach in public and private schools, as well as in colleges.

Related Career	Education
Research chemist	graduate degree
Teacher's aide	high school
Science supervisor	college degree
School nurse	college degree

Career Issue: Some people think that students should be required to take more science classes, particularly chemistry and physics, to better prepare them for the technological world in which they live. **What do you think?** Lead students in a discussion of their own attitudes toward more stringent science requirements in high school.

HYDRAULIC ENGINEER

Hydraulic engineers use a knowledge of fluids to design bridges and dams. They must study bodies of water to find out about drainage and water supplies. They also need to know how a bridge or dam will be affected by the normal water pressure, as well as extra pressure exerted by water from heavy storms. Hydraulic engineers must be sure that the structures they design will not collapse after a storm.

If you're interested in becoming a hydraulic engineer you should like working with measurements, formulas, statistics, and graphs. In high school, you should take math, physics, and chemistry classes. Hydraulic engineers have at least a bachelor's degree, and many have advanced degrees.

For Additional Information
Contact the American Society of Civil Engineers, 345 E. 47th Street, New York, New York 10017.

UNIT READINGS

▶ Hamilton, J.H. and Maruhn, J.A. "Exotic Atomic Nuclei." *Scientific American,* July, 1986, pp. 80-89.
▶ Maxwell, James C. *Maxwell on Molecules and Gases.* Cambridge, MA: MIT Press, 1986.
▶ Sprackling, Michael. *Liquids and Solids.* New York: Methuen, 1985.

294

CHEMISTRY TEACHER

A *chemistry teacher* works with students to help them learn about chemistry and how it is a part of their everyday lives. Chemistry teachers must make daily lesson plans, set up laboratory activities, demonstrate experiments, and work with students having different backgrounds and interests.

If you're interested in becoming a chemistry teacher, you should enjoy math and science classes, and should like working with young people. Many colleges and universities offer programs for bachelor's and master's degrees in chemical education.

For Additional Information
Contact the National Science Teachers Association, 1742 Connecticut Avenue, NW, Washington, DC 10009-1171.

UNIT READINGS

Background
▶ *Maxwell on Molecules and Gases* is a collection of classic writings.
▶ *Liquids and Solids* describes properties of these familiar states of matter.

More Readings
1. Mebane, Robert C. and Rybolt, Thomas R. *Adventures with Atoms and Molecules: Chemistry Experiments for Young People.* Hillside, NJ: Enslow, 1985. Thirty experiments that answer fundamental questions about the nature of matter.

Classics
▶ Chester, Michael. *Particles.* New York, NY: Macmillan, 1978. An introduction to the world of atomic and subatomic particles.

Connections

by James Burke

The passage that follows describes the invention of the barometer.

In June 1644, Torricelli wrote to a colleague and friend in Rome, Michelangelo Ricci, to explain an experiment carried out by his own assistant Vincenzo Viviani, to which he added drawings in the margin. Viviani had filled a 6-foot long tube with mercury and upended it in a dish full of the same metal, with the open end of the tube beneath the surface of the mercury in the dish. When he took his finger away from the open end of the tube, the mercury in it ran out into the dish, but stopped when the mercury column left in the tube was still about 30 inches above the dish. Torricelli reasoned that the weight of the air pressing on the mercury in the dish had to be exactly equal to the weight of the mercury left in the tube. If there were no weight of air, all the mercury in the tube would have run out into the dish. If this were so, he wrote, "we live submerged at the bottom of an ocean of air." What was more, in the space at the top of the tube left by the mercury was the thing thought to be impossible: a vacuum. Torricelli wrote that if he was right, the pressure of the air in our atmospheric ocean must vary according to how far up or down in the ocean we are.

Ricci, realizing that current church opinion in Rome would not take kindly to these arguments (since if they were true several things followed, such as the existence of interplanetary vacuum, with sun-orbiting planets), made a copy of Torricelli's letter and sent it to a priest in Paris, Father Marin Mersenne. . . . the first thing he did was send another copy of it to a friend who was interested in the same problem, the son of a Paris tax inspector, Blaise Pascal. Two years after receiving the letter (he had been busy meanwhile in the Paris gambling halls working on laws-of-chance mathematics) Pascal found himself in Rouen. It was here that he repeated Torricelli's experiment, to check it; only he did it full-scale, with water. Unfortunately he was in no position to check the second part of the argument—there were no mountains around Rouen. However, Pascal had a brother-in-law called Francois Perier who lived in central France, in Clermont Ferrand, which is surrounded by mountains. So Pascal wrote to Perier, asking him to take things to the next stage.

In Your Own Words

1. Pascal asked his brother-in-law, Perier, to take things to the next stage. If you had been Perier, what would you have done next?
2. How might Pascal's knowledge of Torricelli's barometer influenced him in his discovery of Pascal's principle?

295

Source: Burke, James. *Connections.* Little, Brown and Company, Boston MA: 1978.

Biography: James Burke was born in 1936 in England and is a graduate of Oxford University. He was the BBC's chief reporter on the Apollo moon missions. The book is the companion volume to the television series produced by the BBC and broadcast over PBS stations in 1979. Burke served as the host of the television series. Research and filming for the television series and the book took Burke to 23 countries and took over two years to complete.

TEACHING STRATEGY

Have students read through the passage by James Burke. Then have them respond to the discussion questions below.

Discussion Questions

1. **How does Burke say the Church in Rome would react to Torricelli's discoveries? Why do you think this is the case?** *The text says the church would not take kindly to the discoveries. The Roman Catholic church was very powerful during the 1600s and if any scientist disagreed with the position of the church, he could be tried for heresy.*
2. **What significance does Burke give to Father Mersenne?** *Father Mersenne served as the link between the scientists of the day. If he had not had so many contacts, and had not copied and sent letters, many scientists would have been unaware of what others were working on and what discoveries had been made.*

Other Works

▶ Other books on this subject include: Middleton, W.E. Knowles. *The History of the Barometer.* Baltimore, MD: John Hopkins University Press, 1964. Mesnard, Jean. *Pascal, His Life and Works.* London: Harvill Press, 1952.

UNIT
4
KINDS OF SUBSTANCES

In Unit 4, students are introduced to a broad classification of substances—elements and compounds. The common properties and uses of elements categorized as metals, nonmetals, mixed groups, and synthetic elements are discussed and related to their position in the periodic table. The common structure and characteristics of organic and biological compounds are then explored. Students are then introduced to materials science with a discussion of alloys, ceramics, plastics, and composites.

CONTENTS

ADVANCE PREPARATION

Audiovisuals
▶ Show the slides/cassette *Metals*, Science Software.
▶ Show the slides/cassette *The Halogens*, Science Software.
▶ Show the film *The Noble Gases*, Science Software.
▶ Show the filmstrip *Organic Chemistry*, Science Software.

Field Trips and Speakers
▶ Arrange for a certified gemologist to visit your class.
▶ Arrange for a representative from your school's food service department to visit your class.

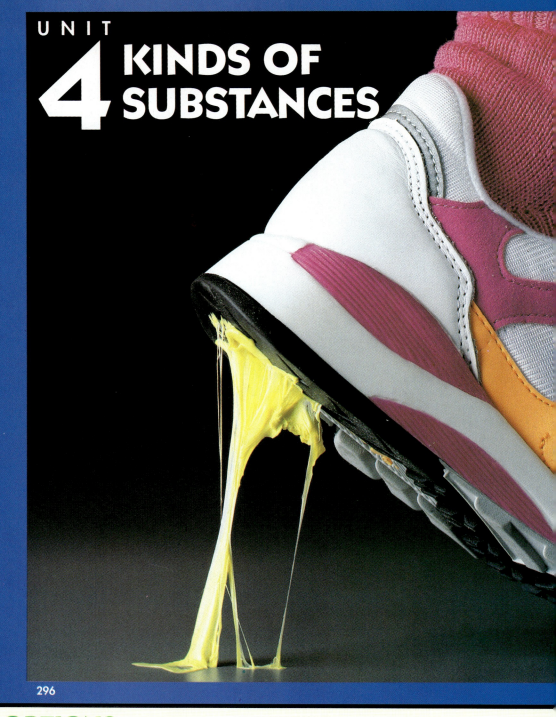

UNIT
4
KINDS OF SUBSTANCES

296

OPTIONS

Cross Curriculum
▶ Have students begin research on the composition of coins used in the United States and other countries.

Cooperative Learning: Have students track the price of gold or crude oil by monitoring television and newspapers. Ask them to present the data as graphs and discuss the results. Have them relate any fluctuations in the prices to world events discussed in social studies.

Science at Home
Cooperative Learning: Assign groups of students to track the disposal of various materials such as metals, paper, and plastics, suggested by manufacturers on the products' labels or by community refuse collectors. Have them conjecture why proper disposal of these materials is important.

▶ Have students list various products found around the home that include imitation or artificial flavorings or scents. Have students research what these artificial scents and flavorings are and how they are made.

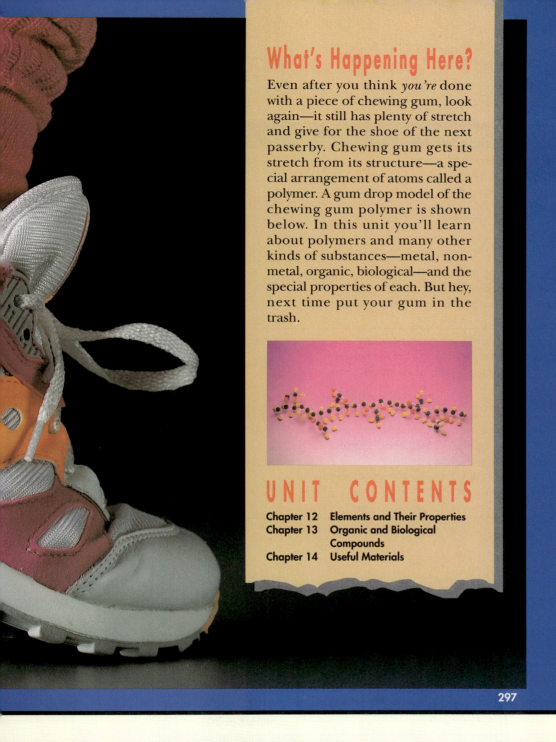

What's Happening Here?

Even after you think *you're* done with a piece of chewing gum, look again—it still has plenty of stretch and give for the shoe of the next passerby. Chewing gum gets its stretch from its structure—a special arrangement of atoms called a polymer. A gum drop model of the chewing gum polymer is shown below. In this unit you'll learn about polymers and many other kinds of substances—metal, non-metal, organic, biological—and the special properties of each. But hey, next time put your gum in the trash.

UNIT CONTENTS

297

Multicultural Awareness

Have interested students research the contributions of Oriental, African, and Native American cultures to the development of ceramics and metallurgy.

Inquiry Questions

Use the following discussion questions to focus a discussion on the properties of organic and synthetic compounds.

▶ **What characteristic does this chewing gum display?** *Accept all reasonable answers.* "stretchiness," elasticity, "rubbery"

▶ **What other materials displayed in the photograph have similar characteristics?** *Sole of shoe (tennis shoe, sneaker)*

▶ **How is this characteristic useful in materials and products that you are familiar with?** *Elastic material in cuffs, waistbands, and neck openings keep clothing in place; clothing made from latex material are form fitting for more comfort, less hazardous for exercising and biking; rubber soles give bounce and cushion the feet; "rubber" surgery gloves afford dexterity and protection.*

INTRODUCING THE CHAPTER

What's Happening Here?

▶ Point out to students that in this unit they will be studying how the atomic or molecular structure of a substance accounts for its properties and its uses. They will also study how substances can be altered to produce new materials.

▶ **Background:** Chewing gum contains a gum base which gives it its elastic properties. At one time, most gum bases consisted of *chicle*, a coagulation of the latex obtained from the sapodilla tree. This material was first used as a chewing gum by natives of the Yucatán peninsula centuries ago and is similar to the latex used to make natural rubber. Today most gum base consists of synthetic polymers of polyvinyl acetate.

$$- CH_2 - \underset{\underset{\underset{CH_3}{|}}{\underset{\underset{C=O}{|}}{\overset{\overset{H}{|}}{\underset{O}{C}}}}{} - CH_2 - \underset{\underset{\underset{CH_3}{|}}{\underset{\underset{C=O}{|}}{\overset{\overset{H}{|}}{\underset{O}{C}}}}{} - CH_2 - \underset{\underset{\underset{CH_3}{|}}{\underset{\underset{C=O}{|}}{\overset{\overset{H}{|}}{\underset{O}{C}}}}{}$$

or [unvulcanized] styrene-butadiene rubber (most common synthetic rubber),

both of which are manufactured from petroleum products.

Previewing the Chapters

▶ **Cooperative Learning:** Have groups of students classify the materials in classroom objects using charts and photographs in this unit.

Tying to Previous Knowledge

▶ Have students collect high-tech mail order catalogues and read advertisements for new and improved products and the materials from which they are made. Have students list the materials and their properties.

▶ Use the **inquiry questions** in the OPTIONS box below to discuss organic and synthetic compounds.

12 Elements and Their Properties

CHAPTER SECTION	OBJECTIVES	ACTIVITIES
12-1 Metals (2 days)	1. **Describe** the properties of a typical metal. 2. **Identify** the alkali and alkaline earth metals. 3. **Differentiate** among three groups of transition elements.	**MINI-Lab:** *How is metallic bonding related to the flexibility of a metal?* p. 301
12-2 Synthetic Elements **Science & Society** (1 day)	1. **Distinguish** among elements classified as lanthanoids, actinoids, and transuranium elements. 2. **Compare** the pros and cons of making synthetic elements.	
12-3 Nonmetals (2 days)	1. **Recognize** hydrogen as a typical nonmetal. 2. **Compare** and **contrast** properties of the halogens. 3. **Describe** properties and uses of the noble gases.	**Activity 12-1:** *Nonmetal Reaction,* p. 315
12-4 Mixed Groups (2 days)	1. **Distinguish** among metals, nonmetals, and metalloids in Groups 13 through 16 of the periodic table. 2. **Describe** the nature of allotropes. 3. **Recognize** the significance of differences in crystal structure in carbon.	**Activity 12-2:** *Carbon and Graphite,* p. 322
Chapter Review		

ACTIVITY MATERIALS

FIND OUT	ACTIVITIES		MINI-LABS
Page 299 paper clips tongs sodium chloride strontium chloride copper(II) sulfate burner (gas) distilled water small beakers	**12-1 Nonmetal Reaction, p. 315** large test tube large wooden match 20 mL liquid laundry bleach (5% sodium hypochlorite) 0.5 g cobalt chloride goggles	**12-2 Carbon and Graphite, p. 322** nut and bolt powdered graphite 6 pieces of thin spaghetti polystyrene sheet marking pen	**How is metallic bonding related to the flexibility of a metal? p. 301** pieces of thin iron wire (such as hairpins) tongs burner beaker of cold water

CHAPTER FEATURES	TEACHER RESOURCE PACKAGE	OTHER RESOURCES
Technology: *Metallic Moments,* p. 305 **Skill Builder:** *Interpreting Scientific Illustrations,* p. 307	**Ability Level Worksheets** ◆ **Study Guide,** p. 50 ● **Reinforcement,** p. 50 ▲ **Enrichment,** p. 50 **MINI-Lab Worksheet,** p. 100 **Critical Thinking/Problem Solving,** p. 18 **Cross-Curricular Connections,** p. 18 **Transparency Masters,** pp. 45, 46	**Color Transparency 23,** Metallic Bonding
You Decide! p. 309	**Ability Level Worksheets** ◆ **Study Guide,** p. 51 ● **Reinforcement,** p. 51 ▲ **Enrichment,** p. 51	
Skill Builder: *Making and Using Graphs,* p. 314	**Ability Level Worksheets** ◆ **Study Guide,** p. 52 ● **Reinforcement,** p. 52 ▲ **Enrichment,** p. 52 **Activity Worksheet,** pp. 94, 95 **Science and Society,** p. 16	**Lab Manual 25,** Preparation of Carbon Dioxide **Lab Manual 26,** Preparation of Hydrogen **Lab Manual 27,** Preparation of Oxygen
Problem Solving: *The "Lead" in a Pencil,* p. 318 **Skill Builder:** *Concept Mapping,* p. 321	**Ability Level Worksheets** ◆ **Study Guide,** p. 53 ● **Reinforcement,** p. 53 ▲ **Enrichment,** p. 53 **Activity Worksheet,** pp. 96, 97 **Concept Mapping,** pp. 29, 30 **Transparency Masters,** pp. 47, 48	**Color Transparency 24,** Allotropes of Carbon
Summary Think & Write Critically Key Science Words Apply Understanding Vocabulary More Skill Builders Checking Concepts Projects Understanding Concepts	**Chapter Review,** pp. 27, 28 **Chapter Test,** pp. 80-83	**Chapter Review Software** **Test Bank**

◆ **Basic**　　● **Average**　　▲ **Advanced**

ADDITIONAL MATERIALS		
SOFTWARE	**AUDIOVISUAL**	**BOOKS/MAGAZINES**
Chemaid: Introduction to the Periodic Table, Ventura Educational Systems. *Hydrogen Spectrum,* Scott Foresman & Co.	*Matter and Molecules: The Matter of Elements,* filmstrip, Singer Media Corporation. *Metals of Groups I-A and II-A,* filmstrip, Science Software. *Metals,* slides/cassette, Science Software. *The Noble Gases,* filmstrip, Science Software. *The Halogens,* slides/cassette, Science Software.	Colin, Norman. "Uranium Enrichment," *Science,* May 22, 1987, pp. 906-908. Donohue, Jerry. *The Structures of the Elements.* Melbourne, FL: Krieger, 1982. Matthews, G. J. *Origin and Distribution of the Elements.* Teaneck, NJ: World Scientific Pub., 1988. Ruben, Samuel. *Handbook of the Elements.* Peru, IL: Open Court Publishing Co., 1985.

THEME DEVELOPMENT: Scale and structure as a theme of the textbook is developed through a presentation of metallic and nonmetallic properties of elements and their positions on the periodic table as a consequence of their atomic structures.

CHAPTER OVERVIEW

▶ **Section 12-1:** The properties of metals are presented and explained by a study of metallic bonding. The alkali and alkaline earth families, as well as transition elements, are studied in detail.

▶ **Section 12-2: Science and Society:** The student is introduced to the synthetic elements and learns that they are important in some useful devices.

▶ **Section 12-3:** The properties of hydrogen, the halogens, and noble gases are developed in detail. The properties of nonmetals are contrasted with those of metals.

▶ **Section 12-4:** Within some groups on the periodic table there are nonmetals, metalloids, and metals. These groups are studied in Section 12-4.

CHAPTER VOCABULARY

malleable	transuranium
ductile	element
metallic	diatomic
bonding	molecule
radioactive	sublimation
element	semiconductors
transition	allotropes
elements	

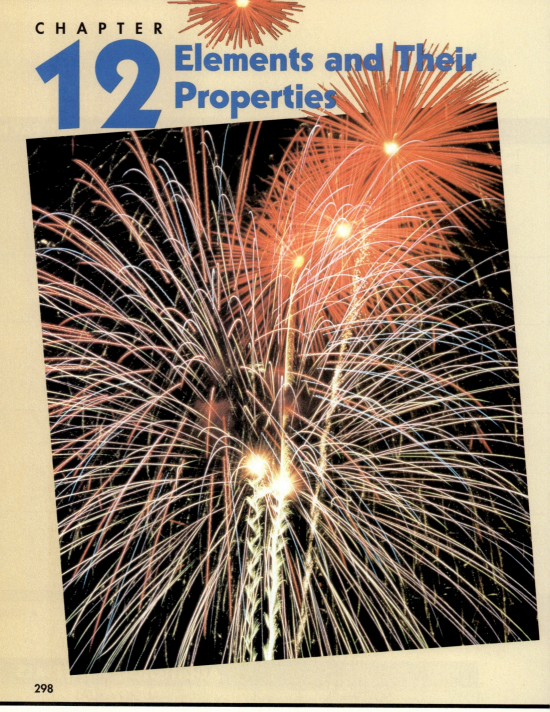

CHAPTER

12 Elements and Their Properties

298

OPTIONS

For Your Gifted Students

Gifted students should continue to supplement their study with high school chemistry texts and lab manuals. Students could observe flame tests for various metallic elements. Single-displacement reactions in which the more active halogen, chlorine, replaces less active halogens, bromine and iodine, from their halide salts are also interesting. In addition, these reactions illustrate and reinforce the pattern of varying chemical activity within a family. Similar reactions in which a more active metal displaces a less active metal from its salt may be performed. Observe proper precautions when allowing students to perform any laboratory experiments.

Did you know that the Chinese invented fireworks hundreds of years ago? They used certain substances mixed with gunpowder —which they also invented—to produce colorful explosions.

FIND OUT!

In this activity, observe the colors some compounds give to a flame.

Using tongs, hold a clean paper clip in a flame until no color is added to the flame. Dip the paper clip in a solution of sodium chloride and hold it in the flame again. Observe and record the color produced. Repeat the procedure using strontium chloride, and again using copper(II) sulfate. How might you find out which element in each compound causes the color? Test your hypothesis. Besides fireworks, what do you think is another use for brightly colored flames?

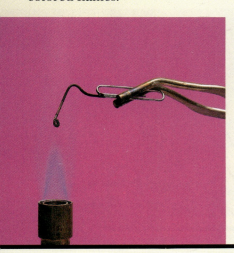

Gearing Up
Previewing the Chapter
Use this outline to help you focus on important ideas in this chapter.

Previewing Science Skills
▶ In the Skill Builders, you will interpret scientific illustrations, make and use a graph, and make a concept map.
▶ In the Activities, you will observe, classify, predict, infer, and build a model.
▶ In the MINI-Lab, you will observe and draw a conclusion.

What's next?

Read Chapter 12 to learn more about elements that give colors to flames. You will also study other properties of elements.

299

INTRODUCING THE CHAPTER
Use the Find Out activity to introduce students to metals and nonmetals. Inform students that they will be learning about the properties of elements as they read the chapter.

FIND OUT!
Preparation: Make three concentrated salt solutions before class using distilled water.
Materials: paper clips, tongs, sodium chloride, strontium chloride, copper(II) sulfate, gas burner, distilled water, small beakers
Cooperative Learning: Use the Science Investigation team strategy to answer the questions. Each member of the group should test one element in the flame.
Teaching Tips
▶ **CAUTION:** *Have students wear goggles and aprons and be cautious working with open flames. The paper clip will become very hot.*
▶ It is important that the burners be adjusted to a blue flame. In a darkened room, sodium compounds give a fluffy yellow flame, strontium compounds give a red flame, and copper compounds give a pale green flame.
▶ For a dramatic demonstration darken the room and place one of the three salts in a paper or plastic bag. Shake the bag and then open it near the air intake of the burner. The flame will turn color and will be visible all over the room as the dust enters the burner flame.
▶ **Answers to Questions:** Test other combinations of the same ions. For instance, test a different sodium compound and a different chlorine compound. Uses include signal and warning flares.

Gearing Up
Have students study the Gearing Up feature to familiarize themselves with the chapter. Discuss the relationships of the topics in the outline.

What's Next?
Before beginning the first section, make sure students understand the connection between the Find Out activity and the topics to follow.

For Your Mainstreamed Students

The principal goal of this chapter is to show students that certain properties characterize classes of elements (metals and nonmetals) and that elements of the same group have similar properties. Elements have certain practical applications as a consequence of those properties. Try to have mainstreamed students distinguish between metals and nonmetals on the basis of their properties. Since metals are used much more often in their elemental form than are nonmetals, students should make surveys of how metals are used in the home and relate those uses to metallic properties. Examples include heat conductivity (cooking utensils and radiators), electrical conductivity (wiring and plugs), and malleability and strength (the structure of washers, ranges, and refrigerators). A class presentation would benefit all.

PREPARATION

SECTION BACKGROUND

▶ As the atomic numbers of the alkali metals increase: the atoms become larger, the outer electrons are farther from the nucleus, lower level electrons shield the effect of the larger nucleus, and outer electrons are held less tightly. This results in more active atoms.

▶ The transition elements are those elements whose highest-energy electrons are in the *d* sublevels. These partially filled *d* sublevels cause the chemical properties to be different from the other metals.

1 MOTIVATE

▶ **Demonstration:** Have a student wearing leather gloves attempt to tear an aluminum can into two pieces by gripping the ends and twisting in one direction. It will twist but not tear. Use a stiff, L-shaped piece of metal to scratch the protective plastic film off the inside of the can in a line around the middle. Put 125 mL of water into the can. Then add 100 mL concentrated hydrochloric acid. **CAUTION:** *Hydrochloric acid is corrosive and gives off harmful fumes. Place can inside a large beaker.* After a few minutes the acid will partially dissolve the can. Rinse completely. You can now easily tear the treated can as you introduce the properties of metals.

TYING TO PREVIOUS KNOWLEDGE:
Ask your students why they wear metallic jewelry. They wear it because they know and like to display properties of metals such as luster and malleability. Ask them why they don't wear a piece of sulfur (nonmetal) as a necklace.

12-1 Metals

New Science Words

malleable
ductile
metallic bonding
radioactive element
transition elements

Objectives

▶ Describe the properties of a typical metal.
▶ Identify the alkali and alkaline earth metals.
▶ Differentiate among three groups of transition elements.

Properties of Metals

Have you ever seen very old jewelry or statues made of gold and copper? These were the two first metals that people discovered, thousands of years ago. The use of silver and tin soon followed. Then came iron. But aluminum—the metal used in your soft drink cans—wasn't discovered until a little more than 100 years ago.

Gold, copper, silver, tin, iron, and aluminum are typical metals. What do these and other metals have in common? ==Most metals are hard, shiny solids. Metals are also good conductors of both heat and electricity.== These properties make metals suitable for uses ranging from kitchen pots and pans to wires for electric appliances. Because metals reflect light well, they are used in mirrors. ==Metals are **malleable,**== which means they can be hammered or rolled into sheets. ==Metals are also **ductile**,== which means they can be drawn into a wire. ❶

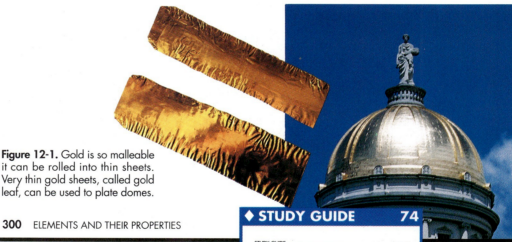

Figure 12-1. Gold is so malleable it can be rolled into thin sheets. Very thin gold sheets, called gold leaf, can be used to plate domes.

300 ELEMENTS AND THEIR PROPERTIES

OPTIONS

Meeting Different Ability Levels

For Section 12-1, use the following **Teacher Resource Masters** depending upon individual students' needs.

◆ **Study Guide Master** for all students.
● **Reinforcement Master** for students of average and above average ability levels.
▲ **Enrichment Master** for above average students.

Additional Teacher Resource Package masters are listed in the OPTIONS box throughout the section. The additional masters are appropriate for all students.

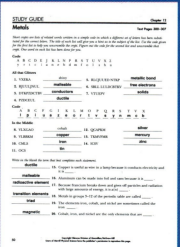

Figure 12-2. Metals are ductile, which means they can be drawn into a wire.

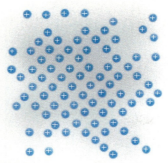
Figure 12-3. In metallic bonding, an electron cloud surrounds positively charged ions.

The atoms of metals generally have from one to three electrons in their outer energy levels. Metals tend to give up electrons easily. Remember from Chapter 11 what happens when metals combine with nonmetals. The atoms of the metals tend to lose electrons to the atoms of nonmetals, forming ionic bonds. The other type of bond you have studied is the covalent bond, which generally forms between atoms of nonmetals. ②

A third type of bonding, neither ionic nor covalent, occurs among the atoms in a metal. In metallic bonding, positively charged metallic ions are surrounded by a "sea of electrons." Outer level electrons are not held tightly to their particular nucleus. Rather, the electrons move freely among many positively charged ions. The electrons form a cloud around the ions of the metal as shown in Figure 12-3.

Metallic bonding explains many of the properties of metals. For example, when a metal is hammered or drawn into a wire, it does not break because the ions are in layers that slide past one another. And because the outer level electrons are free to move, metals are good conductors of electricity.

Look at the periodic table on pages 258-259. How many of the elements in the table are classified as metals? Except for hydrogen, all the elements in Groups 1 through 12 are metals. You will read about metals in some of these groups in this section. Some other metals are discussed in later sections.

MINI-Lab

How is metallic bonding related to the flexibility of a metal?
Carefully, using tongs, hold two pieces of thin wire in a flame until they are red hot. Drop one wire into a beaker of cold water. Let the other wire slowly cool. Be sure both wires cool to room temperature. Try to quickly bend both pieces of wire. What do you observe about the flexibility of the wires? How can metallic bonding be used to explain what you observe?

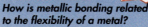 REINFORCEMENT 50

 ENRICHMENT 50

301

2 TEACH

Key Concepts are highlighted.

CONCEPT DEVELOPMENT

▶ Have your students learn the properties of metals so they can list them from memory. They will not have to memorize the properties of nonmetals because they are opposite to those of metals. For example, metals are malleable while nonmetals are hard and brittle.

MINI-Lab

Materials: pieces of thin iron wire, such as hairpins; tongs; burner; beaker of cold water
Teaching Tips
▶ **CAUTION:** *Students should wear goggles. Warn students to be careful not to drop red-hot wires.*
▶ Place the cold water near the flame so that the wire is thoroughly hot when it is immersed.
▶ **Expected Results:** The slow-cooled wire retains its normal flexibility while the quick cooled wire becomes brittle.
▶ **Answers to Questions:** Layers of atoms can move past one another. When heated, the structure becomes jumbled and unstable. Quick cooling "freezes" the atoms in these positions. Slow cooling allows the atoms to resume normal positions.

PROGRAM RESOURCES

From the **Teacher Resource Package** use:

Activity Worksheets, page 100, Mini-Lab: How is metallic bonding related to the flexibility of a metal?

1
3 **Li** Lithium 6.941
11 **Na** Sodium 22.98977
19 **K** Potassium 39.0983
37 **Rb** Rubidium 85.4678
55 **Cs** Cesium 132.9054
87 **Fr** Francium 223.0197*

The Alkali Metals

The elements in Group 1 of the periodic table are the alkali metals. Like metals generally, these metals are shiny, malleable, and ductile. They are good conductors of both heat and electricity. ==The alkali metals are the most highly reactive of all metals.== For this reason, they are found in nature only in the combined state.

Each atom of an alkali metal has one electron in its outer energy level. This electron is given up when an alkali metal combines. The result is a positively charged ion in a compound such as sodium chloride, NaCl, or potassium bromide, KBr. As shown in Figure 12-4, you can use flame tests to identify compounds of alkali metals.

Alkali metals and their compounds have many and varied uses. You and other living things need potassium and sodium compounds—such as table salt, NaCl—to stay healthy. Doctors use lithium compounds to treat manic-depressive disease. The operation of some photocells depends upon rubidium or cesium compounds.

Francium, the last element in Group 1, is radioactive. ==The nucleus of a **radioactive element** breaks down and gives off particles, radiation, and large amounts of energy.== You will study radioactive elements later.

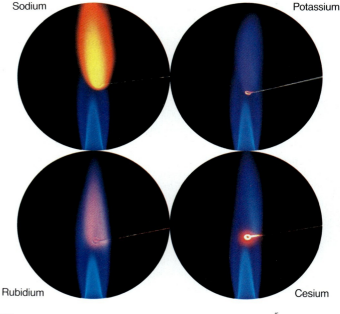

Figure 12-4. Alkali metals and their compounds give distinctive colors to flames.

The Alkaline Earth Metals

5 The alkaline earth metals make up Group 2 of the periodic table. Like the alkali metals, these metals are shiny, malleable, ductile, and so reactive that they are not found free in nature. Each atom of an alkaline earth metal has two electrons in its outer energy level. These electrons are given up when an alkaline earth metal combines. The result is a positively charged ion in a compound such as calcium fluoride, CaF_2, or barium chloride, $BaCl_2$.

Emeralds and aquamarines are gemstone forms of beryl, a mineral that contains beryllium. Do you watch fireworks on the Fourth of July? The brilliant red in fireworks is produced by compounds of strontium.

Magnesium can be made into a ribbon that burns so brightly that it is used in some photographic flashbulbs. Magnesium metal is also used in fireworks to produce brilliant white. Magnesium's lightness and strength account for its use in cars, planes, and spacecraft. Magnesium is also used to make such things as household ladders and baseball and softball bats.

Calcium is almost never used as a free metal, but its compounds are needed for life. Calcium carbonate in your bones helps make them strong. Marble and lime-

2
4 **Be** Beryllium 9.01218
12 **Mg** Magnesium 24.305
20 **Ca** Calcium 40.078
38 **Sr** Strontium 87.62
56 **Ba** Barium 137.33
88 **Ra** Radium 226.0254

Figure 12-5. Bones contain calcium carbonate (a); magnesium burns easily (b); and magnesium is used in bats (c).

a   b   c

TEACHER F.Y.I.

▶ Barium compounds are very toxic. They can be used to assist radiologists by making the intestinal tract easier to see on X rays. Since barium sulfate is insoluble, very little enters the tissues of the body.

CONCEPT DEVELOPMENT

▶ You may wish to inform your students that radioactive tracers are used to help diagnose disease. Radioactive iodine-131 is used for thyroid diagnosis and radioactive technetium-99 for kidney disorders. Nuclear medicine is a career field some students might want to research.

▶ Students may ask why the transition elements have multiple oxidation numbers. The *d* electrons can be lost one at a time after the outer *s* electrons have been lost.

▶ The brightly colored compounds of the transition elements should be shown to students. Nickel (green), chromium (yellow and orange), copper (blue and green), and cobalt (red) compounds will attract their attention. **CAUTION:** *The dust of some of these chemicals is both toxic and carcinogenic. It is best to display them in closed, clear bottles.*

▶ An interested student may want to research why the transition elements have colored compounds. Have them look under coordination compounds in a chemistry textbook.

▶ You may have a student who has a rock collection that includes some gems. If you have a locked display area, the student may be willing to lend the collection to the school for a science display.

CROSS CURRICULUM

▶ **Astronomy:** The flame tests the students observed demonstrate that each element has its own identifying emission spectrum. Astronomers use this fact when they analyze the light spectrum from stars to accurately determine their composition.

What metal is part of the compound chlorophyll?

stone are calcium carbonate. Most life on Earth depends upon chlorophyll, a magnesium compound that enables plants to make food. 6

Some barium compounds are used to diagnose digestive disorders. The patient swallows a barium compound, which absorbs X rays. As the barium compound goes through the digestive tract, a doctor can study the X rays. Radium, the last element in Group 2, is radioactive. It was once used to treat cancers. Today, other radioactive substances are replacing radium in cancer therapy.

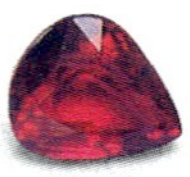

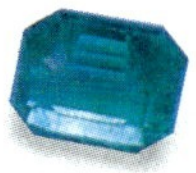

Figure 12-6. The colors of these gems are due to compounds of transition elements.

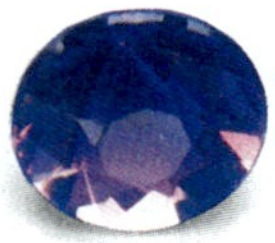

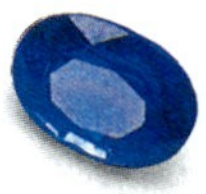

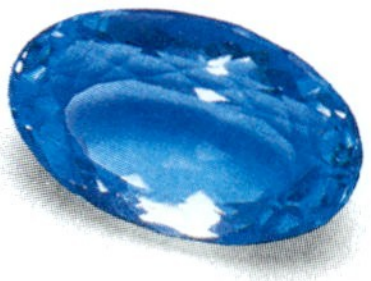

Transition Elements

An iron nail, a copper wire, and a silver dime are examples of objects made from transition elements. The **transition elements** are those elements in Groups 3 through 12 of the periodic table. Typical transition elements are metals and have one or two electrons in the outer energy level. These metals are less active than those in Groups 1 and 2. 7

Many gems contain brightly colored compounds of transition elements. Brilliant cadmium yellow and cobalt blue paints are made from compounds of transition elements. But cadmium and cobalt paints are so toxic that their use is now limited.

Iron, Cobalt, and Nickel

Which elements are able to create a magnetic field?

Iron, cobalt, and nickel form an unusual cluster of transition elements. The first elements in Groups 8, 9, and 10, respectively, these three metals are known as the iron triad. The iron triad elements are the only substances known to create a magnetic field. 8

25 **Mn** Manganese 54.9380	26 **Fe** Iron 55.847	27 **Co** Cobalt 58.9332	28 **Ni** Nickel 58.69	29 **Cu** Copper 63.546
43 **Tc** Technetium 97.9072*	44 **Ru** Ruthenium 101.07	45 **Rh** Rhodium 102.9055	46 **Pd** Pallidium 106.42	47 **Ag** Silver 107.8682

OPTIONS

INQUIRY QUESTIONS

▶ **How does a radioactive element affect cancer cells in a tumor?** *Alpha and beta particles can cause damage to the DNA molecule of the cell. The energy of gamma rays can also disrupt DNA, causing the cell to die or fail to reproduce.*

▶ **Iron forms part of the protein hemoglobin in our blood. What is the function of iron in hemoglobin?** *The iron attracts and binds to oxygen. The blood then provides a source of oxygen for cell respiration.*

PROGRAM RESOURCES

From the **Teacher Resource Package** use:

Critical Thinking/Problem Solving, page 18, How Much Is Your Penny Worth?

Cross-Curricular Connections, page 18, Metal Cations in Nutrition.

Iron is second only to aluminum among the metals in abundance in Earth's crust. As the main component of steel, iron is the most widely used of all metals. Some steels also contain cobalt. Nickel is added to other metals to give them strength. Nickel is also often used to give a shiny, protective coating to other metals, as shown in the picture above.

 ## T E C H N O L O G Y

Metallic Moments

A large radio antenna was folded into a compact shape and launched into space. Once in orbit it absorbed heat from the sun and unfolded as a working antenna! This antenna was made of Nitinol, a mixture of nickel and titanium.

Nitinol is one of a class of metal mixtures, or alloys, that is able to remember an earlier shape. About 20 of the transition elements can form shape memory alloys (SMAs). If you bend and then heat an object made from an SMA, it returns to its original shape. Products made from SMAs include eyeglass frames, orthodontic wires, and electrical connectors.

Because SMAs absorb heat and convert it to mechanical energy, they are used in heat engines. A device that delivers small doses of medication into veins uses SMA power.

Think Critically: Elements that can form SMAs are found in Groups 3 through 12 of the periodic table. What are some other common properties of these elements?

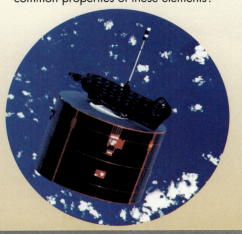

▶ **Metallurgy:** Iron is a very versatile element especially when alloyed with combinations of carbon, nickel, chromium, and cobalt to form various steels. Interested students may want to read and report on how various kinds of steel are made and used.

TEACHER F.Y.I.

▶ At ordinary temperatures, the crystalline structure of iron is body-centered cubic. Above 910°C iron crystals take on a face-centered structure. The amount of carbon in the iron affects its structure and properties.

CHECK FOR UNDERSTANDING

Use the Mini Quiz to check for understanding.

MINI QUIZ

Use the Mini Quiz to check students' recall of chapter content.

6 What metal is found in chlorophyll? *magnesium*

7 Groups 3 through 12 are known as the _____ elements. *transition*

8 What unique property does the iron triad of iron, cobalt, and nickel have? *magnetism*

9 Copper, silver, and gold are known as the _____ metals. *coinage*

10 The only metal that is a silvery liquid at room temperature is _____ . *mercury*

RETEACH

Have each student make one flash card listing an element, its group (or "transition element" if it is one) and its properties. Use the cards to provide review and reinforcement of the entire section.

EXTENSION

For students who have mastered this section, use the **Reinforcement** and **Enrichment** masters or other OPTIONS provided.

Copper, Silver, and Gold

11
29 **Cu** Copper 63.546
47 **Ag** Silver 107.8682
79 **Au** Gold 196.9665

Can you name the main metals in the coins in the photograph below? They are copper, silver, and gold, the three elements in Group 11. They are so unreactive that they are found as elements in nature. For centuries, these metals have been widely used as coins. For this reason, they are known as the coinage metals. **9**

Copper is often used in electric wiring, because of its superior ability to conduct electricity and its low cost. Can you imagine a world without photographs and movies? Because silver iodide and silver bromide break down when exposed to light, these compounds are used to make photographic film and paper. Much silver is also used in jewelry. The yellow color, relative softness, and rarity of gold account for its use in jewelry.

Zinc, Cadmium, and Mercury

12
30 **Zn** Zinc 65.39
48 **Cd** Cadmium 112.41
80 **Hg** Mercury 200.59

Zinc, cadmium, and mercury make up Group 12 of the periodic table. Zinc combines with oxygen in the air to form a thin protective coating of zinc oxide on the surface of the metal. Zinc is often used to coat, or plate, other metals, such as iron. Cadmium is also used in plating and in rechargeable batteries. **10**

Mercury is a silvery, liquid metal used in thermometers, thermostats, switches, and batteries. Mercury is poisonous, and mercury compounds may accumulate in the body. People have died of mercury poisoning that resulted from eating fish from mercury-contaminated water.

306   ELEMENTS AND THEIR PROPERTIES

OPTIONS

INQUIRY QUESTIONS

▶ There are many types of batteries available for many different uses today. Find out the application to which each of the following batteries is best suited: carbon-zinc, lithium, nickel-cadmium, silver, lead-acid, and alkaline. *C-Zn in flashlights, Li—ten year battery, has good shelf life, Ni-Cd can be recharged, Ag in calculators and watches, lead-acid in automobiles where rechargeability and large capacity are important, alkaline in electronic equipment needing a longer life than a C-Zn battery can provide.*

PROGRAM RESOURCES

From the **Teacher Resource Package** use: **Activity Worksheets,** page 5, Flex Your Brain.

Figure 12-7. Mercury is liquid at room temperature (left). Metallic copper is found in nature (right).

Look again at the periodic table on pages 258-259. Which elements do you think of when you think of typical metals? Probably transition elements, such as iron or copper. The reason is that Group 1 and Group 2 metals are not found in nature except in compounds. But many transition elements occur in nature as elements, and thus are the most familiar metals.

Why are transition metals more familiar than Group 1 and Group 2 metals?

SECTION REVIEW

1. You are given a piece of the element palladium. How would you test it to see if it is a metal?
2. On the periodic table, how does the arrangement of the iron triad differ from the arrangements of the coinage metals and of the zinc group?
3. **Apply:** If X stands for a metal, how can you tell from the formulas XCl and XCl$_2$ which compound contains an alkali metal and which contains an alkaline earth metal?

☑ **Interpreting Scientific Illustrations**

Draw dot diagrams to show the similarity among chlorides of three alkali metals: lithium chloride, sodium chloride, and potassium chloride. If you need help, refer to Interpreting Scientific Illustrations in the **Skill Handbook** on page 689.

❓ FLEX Your Brain

Use the Flex Your Brain activity to have students explore PROPERTIES OF ELEMENTS.

👥 **Cooperative Learning:** Glue a small periodic table to a piece of cardboard. Have students using the Expert Team strategy choose a metal and report on its proper-ties and uses to the class. Have that team glue a sample of the metal to a square of cardboard lettered to match that metal's square on the periodic table. Arrange the squares to form a partial periodic table. For those metals that are unobtainable or are unsafe to handle, use only the square. Aid students by exhibiting samples of these metals if you have them.

▶ Ask questions 1-2 and the **Apply** Question in the Section Review.

SECTION REVIEW ANSWERS

1. Find out if it is hard and shiny, is a good conductor of heat and electricity, and is malleable and ductile.

2. Iron, cobalt, and nickel are successive metals in the same period. Copper, silver, and gold are all in Group 11. Zinc, cadmium, and mercury are all in Group 12.

3. Apply: Chlorine bonds by gaining or sharing one electron. Alkali metals can lose one electron, so they would form the compound XCl. Alkaline earth metals have two outer electrons, so they would form compounds XCl$_2$.

Skill Builder

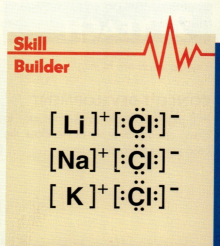

INQUIRY QUESTIONS

▶ **Silver conducts electricity better than gold and is less expensive. However, gold is used to plate electrical contacts in high-quality switches and in computers. Why is gold preferable to silver for this use?** *Silver is more reactive than gold and tarnishes by combining with pollutants in air.*

▶ **Catalytic converters on cars contain platinum, palladium, and rhodium. Research the purpose of the converter and how these elements work in the converter.** *The converter cleans the exhaust gases of unburned hydro-* carbons. *The elements are surface catalysts. The combustion products are held on the hot surface of the metal and further reacted with oxygen.*

▶ **Platinum spark plugs are now being used in car engines. Older plugs had to be replaced every 10 000 miles. The platinum plugs work for 60 000 miles but cost more. Find out the advantages of platinum spark plugs.** *burn more cleanly, more reliable, better fuel economy, less downtime in the shop resulting in lower labor charges*

PREPARATION

SECTION BACKGROUND

▶ Elements with atomic numbers greater than 100 have been produced using other elements to bombard target elements.

1 MOTIVATE

▶ Ask the class if they have ever heard of Merlin in King Arthur's court. He was an alchemist. He tried to change common metals into gold. Today this can be accomplished in a nuclear reactor. Ask your class why they think today's scientists do not convert iron into gold. Mined gold is cheaper.

TYING TO PREVIOUS KNOWLEDGE:
Ask your students what they know about synthetic elements. They may respond that they don't last very long (short half-lives). Inform them that they will be surprised how synthetic elements are used to improve our standard of living.

OBJECTIVES AND SCIENCE WORDS:
Have students review the objectives and science word to become familiar with this section.

2 TEACH

Key Concepts are highlighted.

CONCEPT DEVELOPMENT

▶ Bring a portable smoke detector to class, open it and show the class the case where the americium is.

SCIENCE & SOCIETY ■ 12-2

Synthetic Elements

New Science Words

transuranium element

Objectives

▶ Distinguish among elements classified as lanthanoids, actinoids, and transuranium elements.
▶ Compare the pros and cons of making synthetic elements.

What synthetic element is used in smoke alarms?

Why Make Synthetic Elements?

Did you know that the smoke alarm in your home may contain americium? This element does not form naturally. Because it can be made only in a laboratory, americium is called a synthetic element. There are 19 synthetic elements. One of these, technetium, is a period-5 transition metal. The other synthetic elements are found in periods 6 and 7.

Lanthanoids and Actinoids

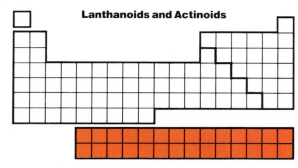

If you look at the periodic table on pages 258-259, you will see breaks in periods 6 and 7. The first break includes a series of 14 elements with atomic numbers of 57 through 70. The second break include those elements with atomic numbers ranging from 89 to 102. The two series include elements that have similar electron structures and similar properties. They also include many synthetic elements.

The picture tube in your color TV contains pigments that glow bright red when struck by electrons. These pigments are oxides of europium and ytterbium, two lanthanoids. A lanthanoid is an element with an atomic

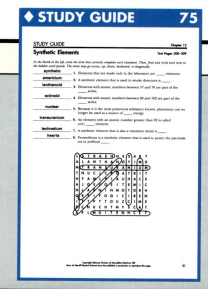

308 ELEMENTS AND THEIR PROPERTIES

OPTIONS

Meeting Different Ability Levels

For Section 12-2, use the following **Teacher Resource Masters** depending upon individual students' needs.

◆ **Study Guide Master** for all students.
● **Reinforcement Master** for students of average and above average ability levels.
▲ **Enrichment Master** for above average students.

◆ **STUDY GUIDE** 75

STUDY GUIDE   Chapter 12
Synthetic Elements   Text Pages 308–309

In the blank at the left, write the term that correctly completes each statement. Then, and circle each term in the hidden word puzzle. The terms may go across, up, down, backward, or diagonally.

synthetic
americium
lanthanoid
actinoid
nuclear
transuranium
technetium
hearts

1. Elements that are made only in the laboratory are _____ elements.
2. A synthetic element that is used in smoke detectors is _____
3. Elements with atomic numbers between 57 and 70 are part of the _____ series.
4. Elements with atomic numbers between 89 and 102 are part of the _____ series.
5. Because it is the most poisonous substance known, plutonium can no longer be used as a source of _____ energy.
6. An element with an atomic number greater than 92 is called a(n) _____ element.
7. A synthetic element that is also a transition metal is _____
8. Promethium is a synthetic element that is used to power the pacemakers in artificial _____

number of 57-70. The lanthanoid series contains one synthetic element, promethium, used to power pacemakers and artificial hearts.

3 Americium is one of the ten synthetic elements in the actinoid series. An actinoid is an element with an atomic number of 89-102. One important actinoid you may have heard of is uranium.

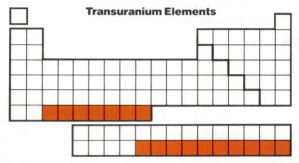

Transuranium Elements

All elements with atomic numbers higher than that of uranium are synthetic elements called transuranium ele-
4 ments. A **transuranium element** has an atomic number greater than 92. One of these is plutonium.

Plutonium has been used in nuclear reactors and in nuclear warheads. Because it is the most poisonous substance known, its production has been banned. Other transuranium elements in the actinoid series are used as nuclear energy sources for generating electric power and in nuclear weapons. However, like all synthetic elements, they are radioactive and some can be very harmful.

The other transuranium elements are presently being used to research the structure of matter. Perhaps these elements will provide future sources of energy.

SECTION REVIEW

1. Compare the lanthanoid and actinoid series.
2. What are the transuranium elements?

You Decide!

Plutonium was banned after much debate. Suppose you had to vote on a petition to ban the production of another synthetic element. What information would you want to help you decide how to vote?

EcoTip

The amount of hazardous waste produced each year in the United States is equal to the weight of a car for each U.S. citizen.

SCIENCE & SOCIETY

309

● **REINFORCEMENT** 51

REINFORCEMENT   Chapter 12
Synthetic Elements   Text Pages 308–309

Use the periodic table on pages 258–259 of your textbook to answer questions 1–8.

1. What is the name of the group of elements with atomic numbers of 57–70?   lanthanoid series
2. What is the name of the group of elements with atomic numbers 89–102?   actinoid series
3. In what period do the elements in the actinoid series belong?   period 7
4. In what period do the elements in the lanthanoid series belong?   period 6
5. How many elements make up the lanthanoid series?   14
6. a. Which element in the lanthanoid series has the highest atomic number?   ytterbium
   b. What is the atomic mass of this element?   173.04
7. a. Which element in the actinoid series has the greatest atomic number?   nobelium
   b. How many protons are in the nucleus of one atom of this element?   102
8. List the names of the elements that make up the lanthanoid series in order from greatest atomic mass to least atomic mass.   ytterbium, thulium, erbium, holmium, dysprosium, terbium, gadolinium, europium, samarium, promethium, praseodymium, cerium, lanthanum
9. How does the lanthanoid series compare to the actinoid series?   They both include elements that have similar electron structures and similar properties.

Conclude and Apply

10. What is one practical use of the elements europium and ytterbium?   Oxides of these elements are used in the picture tubes of television sets.
11. Which elements in the actinoid series are transuranium elements?   neptunium, plutonium, americium, curium, berkelium, californium, einsteinium, fermium, mendelevium, and nobelium

▲ **ENRICHMENT** 51

ENRICHMENT   Chapter 12
Synthetic Elements   Text Pages 308–309

NAMING OF NEW ELEMENTS

You have just discovered a new element that has an atomic number of 110. In the past, you could have named the element as you wished. But what happens if another person discovered and named the element about the same time? What would be the official name of the element?

Scientists in both the United States and the Soviet Union claim discovery of elements 104 and 105. Because of the confusion about what to name these new elements, the International Union for Pure and Applied Chemistry (IUPAC) decided that a system was needed to officially name new elements. The systematic names are alternatives to the already trivial names approved by the IUPAC for elements 101, 102, and 105 (mendelevium, nobelium, and lawrencium). Any new element must be named using the approved names.

The IUPAC guidelines for new chemical names are as follows.
1. The name is derived directly from the atomic number of the element using the

following numerical roots:
0 - nil
1 - un
2 - bi
3 - tri
4 - quad
5 - pent
6 - hex
7 - sept
8 - oct
9 - enn

2. The roots are put together in order of the digits which make up the atomic number. The name is ended by two to spell out the name. The final n of enn is removed when it occurs before nil. The final i of bi and tri is removed when it occurs before ium.
3. The symbol of the element is composed of the initial letters of the numerical roots which make up the name.
4. The numerical root un is pronounced with a long u, to rhyme with moon.

Conclude and Apply

1. Write the IUPAC approved names and the symbols for the elements that would have the following atomic numbers. The first one is given as an example.

104	Unnilquadium	Unq	108	Unniloctium	Uno
105	Unnilpentium	Unp	109	Unnilennium	Une
106	Unnilhexium	Unh	110	Ununnilium	Uun
107	Unnilseptium	Uns	120	Unbinilium	Ubn

2. What are the advantages and disadvantages of using the IUPAC system to name new compounds?   advantage, no confusion over naming elements; disadvantage, takes some of the uniqueness out of finding and naming elements

MINI QUIZ

Use the Mini Quiz to check students' recall of chapter content.

1 **Of the 109 known elements, how many are synthetic?** *19*
2 **Elements having atomic numbers between 57 and 70 are classified as _____ .** *lanthanoids*
3 **Elements having atomic numbers between 89 and 102 are classified as _____ .** *actinoids*
4 **A transuranium element has an atomic number greater than _____ .** *92*

RETEACH

Have your students use a blank copy of the periodic table to record the symbol, name, and atomic number of the 19 synthetic elements.

EXTENSION

For students who have mastered this section, use the **Reinforcement** and **Enrichment** masters or other OPTIONS provided.

3 CLOSE

SECTION REVIEW ANSWERS

1. Both series contain 14 elements. The lanthanoids are in Period 6 and contain one synthetic element. Actinoids are in Period 7 and contain 10 synthetic elements.
2. Period 7 elements with atomic numbers greater than 92

YOU DECIDE!

Answers will vary. Students should discuss its technological and economic benefits (medicine, national security) and its liabilities (toxicity, disposal problems).

SECTION BACKGROUND

▶ Atoms of most nonmetals have five or more outer electrons, and tend to gain electrons to complete their outer energy levels.

▶ Hydrogen has unique properties and is usually considered as a group by itself. Hydrogen can react by gaining, losing, or sharing electrons.

▶ As the atomic numbers of the halogens increase, the atoms become larger, the outer electrons are farther from the nucleus, the nucleus has less attraction for electrons of other atoms, and the atoms become less active.

▶ The noble gases were considered to be inert until 1962 when xenon and oxygen difluoride were combined in a nickel tube at 300°C under pressure to produce xenon difluoride.

PREPLANNING

▶ To prepare for Activity 12-1 you will need laundry bleach and wooden matches.

▶ You may want to prepare a collection of nonmetals to have on display for the class to see. A piece of roll sulfur, some coal, and a few crystals of iodine in a sealed bottle can be used.

1 MOTIVATE

▶ **Demonstration:** Use a piece of roll sulfur to visually reinforce the properties of nonmetals. Show the class the dull surface before you cover it with a cloth and using a hammer, break off a piece. Students will see that it is brittle and powdery, not malleable. Use an electrical conductivity checker to demonstrate that sulfur is a nonconductor.

▶ Remind students that the properties of metals are the opposite of nonmetals.

12-3 Nonmetals

New Science Words

diatomic molecule
sublimation

Objectives

▶ Recognize hydrogen as a typical nonmetal.
▶ Compare and contrast properties of the halogens.
▶ Describe properties and uses of the noble gases.

Properties of Nonmetals

Figure 12-8 shows that you're mostly made of oxygen, carbon, hydrogen, and nitrogen. Calcium, a metal, and other elements make up the remaining four percent of your body's weight. Phosphorus, sulfur, and chlorine are among other elements found in your body. These elements are among those classified as nonmetals.

Look at the periodic table on pages 258 and 259. How many elements are nonmetals? **Notice that most nonmetals are gases at room temperature.** Several nonmetals are solids, and one nonmetal is a liquid.

In contrast to metals, **solid nonmetals are dull. Because they are brittle and powdery, they are neither malleable nor ductile.** The electrons in nonmetals are tightly held and are not free to move as in metals. So **nonmetals are poor conductors of heat and electricity.**

Most nonmetals form both ionic and covalent compounds. When nonmetals gain electrons from metals, the nonmetals become negative ions in ionic compounds. An example is potassium

carbon 18%
calcium 2.0%
nitrogen 3.0%
hydrogen 10%
other elements 2.0%
oxygen 65%

TOTAL: 100%

Figure 12-8. Most of your body weight consists of compounds of nonmetals.

OPTIONS

Meeting Different Ability Levels

For Section 12-3, use the following **Teacher Resource Masters** depending upon individual students' needs.

◆ **Study Guide Master** for all students.

● **Reinforcement Master** for students of average and above average ability levels.

▲ **Enrichment Master** for above average students.

Additional Teacher Resource Package masters are listed in the OPTIONS box throughout the section. The additional masters are appropriate for all students.

◆ STUDY GUIDE 52

STUDY GUIDE   Chapter 12
Nonmetals   Text Pages 310-315

Use the clues given below and the letters you have been given to identify each of the missing terms in the puzzle. Write one letter in each space.

Clues
1. only nonmetal on left side of the periodic table
2. only liquid nonmetal
3. kind of bond that forms a salt
4. Two atoms of the same element, when bonded, form a(n) _____ molecule.
5. most chemically active element
6. type of bond formed when nonmetals combine with other nonmetals
7. process by which a solid, such as iodine, changes directly to a gas
8. Its name means "salt-former."
9. common name for the elements that make up group 18 of the periodic table

1. H Y D R O G E N
2. B R O M I N E
3. I O N I C
4. D I A T O M I C
5. F L U O R I N E
6. C O V A L E N T
7. S U B L I M A T I O N
8. H A L O G E N
9. N O B L E G A S E S

52

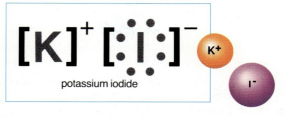

potassium iodide

Figure 12-9. Nonmetals form both ionic and covalent compounds.

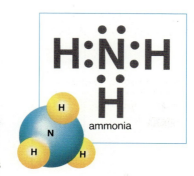

ammonia

iodide, KI, which is found in iodized table salt. KI is formed from the nonmetal iodine and the metal potassium. On the other hand, when bonded with other nonmetals, atoms of nonmetals usually share electrons and form covalent compounds. An example is ammonia, NH_3, the gas you may smell when you open a bottle of household ammonia.

The noble gases, Group 18, make up the only group of elements that are all nonmetals. Group 17 elements, except for astatine, are also nonmetals. Several other nonmetals, found in Groups 13 through 16, will be discussed later. Except for hydrogen, all of the nonmetals are located on the right side of the periodic table.

Hydrogen

Do you know that 90 percent of all the atoms in the universe are hydrogen? Most hydrogen on Earth is found in the compound water. When water is broken down into its elements, hydrogen forms as a gas made up of diatomic molecules. A **diatomic molecule** consists of two atoms of the same element. Thus, the formula for hydrogen gas is H_2.

Hydrogen is highly reactive. A hydrogen atom has a single electron, which the atom shares when it combines with other nonmetals. Hydrogen burns in oxygen to form water, H_2O. In forming water, hydrogen shares electrons with oxygen. Hydrogen also shares electrons with chlorine to produce hydrogen chloride, HCl.

Hydrogen may gain an electron when it combines with alkali and alkaline earth metals. The compounds formed are hydrides, such as sodium hydride, NaH.

Figure 12-10. Hydrogen gas, which consists of diatomic molecules, combines with oxygen in an oxyhydrogen torch.

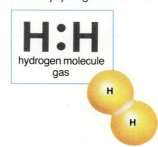

hydrogen molecule gas

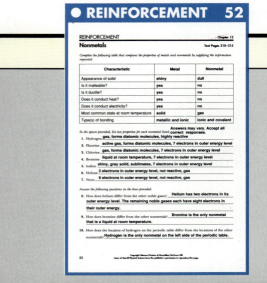

● **REINFORCEMENT 52**

▲ **ENRICHMENT 52**

311

TYING TO PREVIOUS KNOWLEDGE: Many students have seen a picture of the airship *Hindenburg* when it crashed in New Jersey in 1937. The hydrogen gas explosion and fire brought an end to commercial lighter-than-air craft service. Ask students what they can infer about the properties of hydrogen.

OBJECTIVES AND SCIENCE WORDS: Have students review the objectives and science words to become familiar with this section.

2 TEACH

Key Concepts are highlighted.

CONCEPT DEVELOPMENT

▶ **Demonstration:** A small amount of hydrogen gas can be generated by placing a piece of mossy zinc in a large test tube. Add 4 mL of 6M sulfuric acid and stopper the test tube with a 1-hole stopper fitted with a 90° glass bend. **CAUTION:** *The acid is corrosive.* Use an empty, inverted test tube to collect the hydrogen gas by the downward displacement of air. A burning wood splint can be used to show that the gas is flammable. **CAUTION:** *Use an explosion shield. Never produce more than a small test tube of explosive hydrogen gas.*

▶ Tell students that hydrogen gas is being investigated as a nonpolluting fuel for autos, buses, and planes. The flammable gas can be used to heat homes in winter with no danger of carbon monoxide poisoning.

REVEALING MISCONCEPTIONS

▶ Ask students what gas is used to fill balloons that are lighter than air. Some think that hydrogen rather than helium is used. Help students eliminate this confusion between the two gases by asking why helium is used instead of hydrogen gas. Show a picture of the burning *Hindenburg* to help students remember the flammability of hydrogen gas.

TEACHER F.Y.I.

▶ In the USA and Canada, 50 percent of the people drink fluoridated water. The fluoride ion is incorporated into the tooth enamel which is hardened and becomes more resistant to tooth decay.

CONCEPT DEVELOPMENT

▶ **Demonstration:** Place some chlorine bleach on a cloth. Ask the class if they smell anything familiar. A characteristic odor can be used to identify compounds. The other halogens have similar odors.

▶ Students can be reminded that the halogens are the smallest atoms in their period. Thus, they have a strong attraction for electrons. This helps to account for the fact that they are very reactive.

▶ Remind the class that atomic size and mass increase as you go down a group. These increases result in differences in state. Point out that fluorine and chlorine are gases, but bromine is a liquid, and iodine is a solid.

▶ **Demonstration:** To exhibit purple iodine vapors, place a crystal in a test tube and seal the top. The iodine will sublime faster if the tube is placed in warm water. Place a drop of liquid bromine in a test tube and seal. It will vaporize to fill the tube with reddish brown vapors. Chlorine gas can be produced *only* in a fume hood by mixing together 10 mL of chlorine bleach with 5 mL of water and 5 mL of concentrated hydrochloric acid in a 125-mL Erlenmeyer flask. The gas will collect above the liquid. Seal the flask only after the reaction stops. **CAUTION:** *All three elements are very toxic.*

CROSS CURRICULUM

▶ **Writing:** Have several student volunteers each write a different toothpaste company asking for scientific test results that show the effectiveness of their fluoride treatment for teeth. Have the letter writers share the companies' responses with the class.

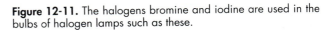

17
9 **F** Fluorine 18.998403
17 **Cl** Chlorine 35.453
35 **Br** Bromine 79.904
53 **I** Iodine 126.9045
85 **At** Astatine 209.98712*

The Halogens

Look how bright these high-tech lamps are in Figure 12-11. Their light and that of the headlights of some cars is supplied by halogen light bulbs. You may have seen these bulbs. They contain small amounts of bromine or iodine. These elements, as well as fluorine and chlorine, are called halogens and are found in Group 17. 3

Figure 12-11. The halogens bromine and iodine are used in the bulbs of halogen lamps such as these.

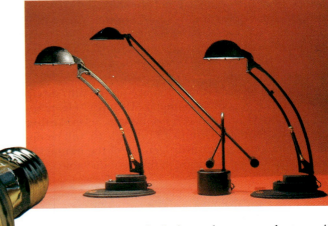

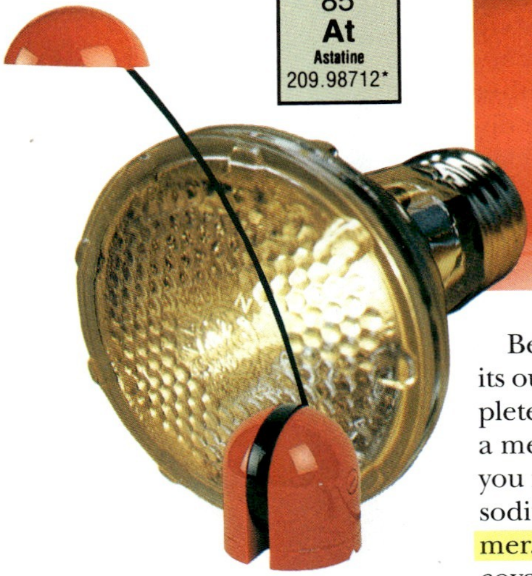

Because an atom of a halogen has seven electrons in its outer energy level, only one electron is needed to complete this energy level. If a halogen gains an electron from a metal, an ionic compound, called a salt, is formed. As you recall, sodium chloride, or table salt, is formed from sodium and chlorine. The word *halogen* means "salt former." In the gaseous state, the halogens form diatomic covalent molecules and can be identified by their distinctive colors.

Fluorine is the most chemically active of all the elements. Hydrofluoric acid, a mixture of hydrogen fluoride and water, is used to etch glass and to "frost" the inner surfaces of light bulbs. Other fluorides are added to toothpastes and to city water systems to prevent tooth decay. Does your community add fluorides to its water? 4

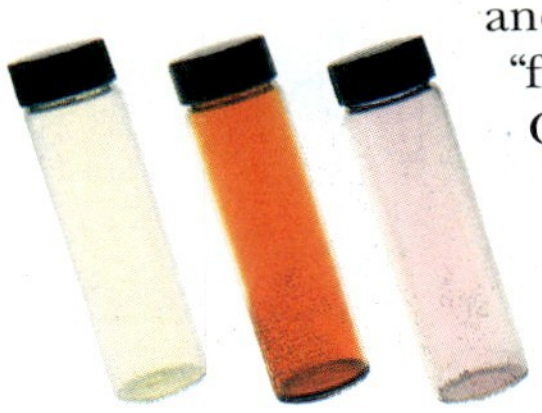

Figure 12-12. In the gaseous state, the halogens chlorine, bromine, and iodine have distinctive colors.

OPTIONS

INQUIRY QUESTIONS

▶ **What can you say about the outer electron structure in a group of elements?** *It is the same.*

▶ **How many outer electrons are there in an atom of each of the halogens? How is this related to the activity?** *Each has seven. Each halogen tends to gain one electron so as to fill its outer energy level and become stable. Thus, halogens are very active chemically.*

▶ **How many outer electrons are in each of the noble gases and how is this related to their chemical properties?** *Each has eight. The element has a filled outer level and is therefore stable.*

▶ **What is the difference between a hydrogen ion and a hydride ion?** *The hydride ion has gained an electron and has a negative one charge. The hydrogen ion has lost an electron and has a positive one charge.*

Are you familiar with the harsh odor near swimming pools? It's the odor of chlorine. Chlorine compounds are used to disinfect the water in these pools. Chlorine, the most abundant halogen, is obtained from seawater. Household bleach and industrial bleaches used to whiten flour and paper contain chlorine compounds.

Bromine, the only nonmetal that is liquid at room temperature, is extracted from compounds in seawater. Other bromine compounds are used as dyes in cosmetics.

Iodine, a shiny gray solid, is obtained from brine. When heated, iodine changes directly to a purple vapor. The process of a solid changing directly to a vapor without forming a liquid is called **sublimation.** Recall that sublimation accounts for ice cubes shrinking in freezers. Iodine is essential in your diet to prevent goiter, an enlarging of the thyroid gland in the neck.

As you have read, both silver iodide and silver bromide are also used to produce photographic paper and film.

Astatine, the last member of Group 17, is radioactive and very rare. But it has many properties similar to those of the other halogens.

The Noble Gases

Why are the noble gases called "noble"? It was known that these gases did not naturally form compounds. Thus, they were thought of as the nobility of elements, because nobles did not mix with common folk. Scientists were later able to prepare some compounds of noble gases.

Figure 12-14. "Neon" signs contain several noble gases.

Figure 12-13. Dyes in some cosmetics contain bromine compounds.

18
2 **He** Helium 4.002602
10 **Ne** Neon 20.179
18 **Ar** Argon 39.948
36 **Kr** Krypton 83.80
54 **Xe** Xenon 131.29
86 **Rn** Radon 222.017*

TEACHER F.Y.I.

▶ In 1962, xenon gas reacted with other elements for the first time. Neils Bartless conducted the experiment. See *Science*, Vol. 138, October 12, 1962, for an example of the initial reports.

CONCEPT DEVELOPMENT

▶ Reinforce the chemical properties of both aluminum and the noble gases by pointing out that aluminum cannot be welded in air but must be welded in an inactive atmosphere. Helium and argon are used to provide this atmosphere.

▶ Ask students to bring in pictures of "neon" signs from magazines. The different colors observed are red-orange from neon, yellow from helium, blue from xenon, purple from argon, and white from krypton.

▶ **Demonstration:** Hydrofluoric acid will etch glass, but is too dangerous to work with in a school lab. A safer way to show this effect is to dip a glass plate into hot paraffin, thoroughly coating both sides. Use a piece of metal wire to scratch through the cooled wax, making an exposed design. Wearing rubber gloves and goggles, in a fume hood, place 12 g of calcium fluoride in a plastic dish. Add enough concentrated sulfuric acid to the dish to cover the glass plate. **CAUTION:** *Acid is corrosive.* Place the glass plate in the dish and cover it with a plastic lid for 20 minutes. Use tongs to remove the glass plate and rinse the acid off in water. Use a large beaker of boiling water to remove the wax from the glass plate. The HF fumes will have etched the design onto the glass plate.

ENRICHMENT

▶ Polychlorinated biphenyls, PCBs, have had effects on human health. Have a student research PCBs. Why they were invented; what their use was; and how scientists are removing them from the environment are some of the questions the student's research should answer. They are a group of chlorinated hydrocarbons that are nonflammable, inexpensive, and stable, but carcinogenic. They were used to cool transformers on power lines. They are difficult to remove from the environment.

PROGRAM RESOURCES

From the **Teacher Resource Package** use:
Science and Society, page 16, Americium and Smoke Detectors.
Use **Laboratory Manual,** Preparation of Hydrogen and Preparation of Oxygen.
Use **Laboratory Manual,** Preparation of Carbon Dioxide.

CHECK FOR UNDERSTANDING

Use the Mini Quiz to check for understanding.

MINI QUIZ

Use the Mini Quiz to check students' recall of chapter content.

1 In what state are most nonmetals at room temperature? *gases*

2 When hydrogen burns in air what product forms? *water*

3 Group 17 elements are also called _____ . *halogens*

4 Which element is the most chemically active nonmetal? *fluorine*

5 Which nonmetal is a liquid at room temperature? *bromine*

RETEACH

Have the students bring in pictures of items made with the elements that have been studied to make a bulletin board display.

EXTENSION

For students who have mastered this section, use **Reinforcement** and **Enrichment** masters or other OPTIONS provided.

3 CLOSE

▶ Ask questions 1-3 and the **Apply** Question in the Section Review.

SECTION REVIEW ANSWERS

1. by sharing an electron or by gaining an electron to form a hydride

2. Like other halogens, bromine has 7 outer-level electrons and gains one electron to form a negative ion. It also bonds covalently with other atoms and exists as diatomic molecules. Bromine is the only halogen in the liquid state at room temperature.

3. They are chemically stable. Therefore they can be used to maintain a chemically inert environment around reactive materials.

4. Apply: Hydrofluoric acid is very reactive and will react with glass. It must be stored in bottles made of more inert material.

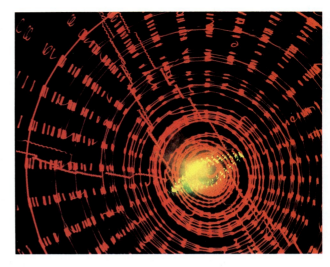

Figure 12-15. Noble gases are used in laser light shows.

What are some uses of the noble gases?

As you recall, each element in Group 18 is stable because its outer energy level has eight electrons, except helium, which has two electrons. The stability of the noble gases plays an important role in their uses, such as those shown in Figures 12-14 and 12-15.

Both the halogens and the noble gases illustrate the family relationships in vertical columns of the periodic table. Each element in a group, or family, has some similar properties. But each element also has unique properties and uses.

SECTION REVIEW

1. What are two ways in which hydrogen combines with other elements?
2. Compare bromine to the other halogens.
3. What property of noble gases makes them useful?
4. **Apply:** Why must hydrofluoric acid always be stored in plastic bottles?

Skill Builder ☑ Making and Using Graphs

Prepare a bar graph comparing nonmetals and metals as solids, liquids, and gases at room temperature. If you need help, refer to Making and Using Graphs in the **Skill Handbook** on page 687.

314 ELEMENTS AND THEIR PROPERTIES

Skill Builder

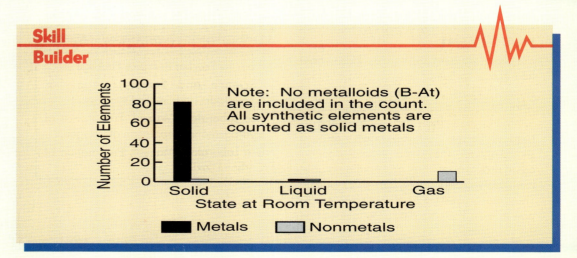

Note: No metalloids (B-At) are included in the count. All synthetic elements are counted as solid metals

■ Metals   ☐ Nonmetals

ACTIVITY 12-1
Nonmetal Reaction

Problem: *How can oxygen be produced from a common substance?*

Materials
- large test tube
- large wooden match
- 20 mL liquid laundry bleach (5% sodium hypochlorite)
- 0.5 g cobalt chloride
- goggles

Procedure
1. Put on safety goggles.
2. Carefully pour about 20 mL of liquid laundry bleach into a large test tube.
3. Add about 0.5 g of cobalt chloride to the bleach.
4. A gas will start to form in the liquid. Place your thumb loosely over the opening of the tube until you feel some slight pressure, but do not attempt to prevent the escape of the gas from the tube.
5. Have a classmate carefully bring a lighted match near the opening of the tube.
6. Blow out the flame of the match and insert the glowing end of the match into the upper half of the tube.

Analyze
1. An increase in the amount of oxygen in a container can cause a glowing match to burst into flame. Were the bubbles given off in your tube oxygen? Explain your answer.
2. Look at the formula for sodium hypochlorite present in bleach, NaClO. What two nonmetals does this compound contain?

Conclude and Apply
3. Liquid bleach is sometimes used as a disinfectant in kitchens. As the sodium hypochlorite in bleach decomposes, or breaks down, what product do you predict might appear?
4. Sunlight can also decompose hypochlorite. Examine the materials used to make containers of different sizes and brands of bleach. In what way are the containers all alike? Suggest a reason for this similarity.

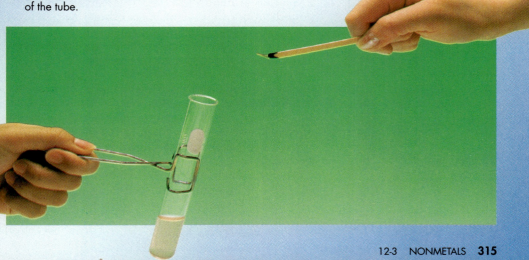

ACTIVITY 12-1
25 minutes

OBJECTIVE: **Observe** some of the properties of oxygen, a typical non-metal.

PROCESS SKILLS applied in this activity:
▶ **Observing** in Procedure Step 6.
▶ **Predicting** in Conclude and Apply Question 3.
▶ **Classifying** in Conclude and Apply Question 4.

COOPERATIVE LEARNING
Use the Paired Partners strategy, dividing the tasks of the activity and having students work together to answer questions.

TEACHING THE ACTIVITY
Alternate Materials: Crystals of $CuSO_4$ or $FeSO_4$ should also work well with chlorine bleach. Try before using.

Troubleshooting: Try out the reaction using materials students will use. The reaction mixture may foam upward. Make sure the tubes are large enough to contain the reaction. Adjust quantities if needed.

▶ The 0.5 g of $CoCl_2$ does not need to be exact. You could measure out the quantity and exhibit to students so they can approximate the amount. This will save time in measuring.

▶ The reaction mixture will turn black when the $CoCl_2$ is added.

▶ Demonstrate the proper technique for gently placing the thumb over the tube.

ANSWERS TO QUESTIONS
1. Yes. The glowing match burst into flame.
2. chlorine and oxygen
3. Oxygen could be a product of bleach decomposition. So might chlorine.
4. Containers are made of opaque materials. This keeps out light which could decompose the bleach.

PROGRAM RESOURCES

From the **Teacher Resource Package** use:
Activity Worksheets, pages 94-95, Activity 12-1: Nonmetal Reaction.

PREPARATION

SECTION BACKGROUND

▶ Of the elements in Group 13, aluminum has the greatest number of practical uses. With three outer electrons, it is less metallic than the Group 1 and 2 metals.

▶ The elements of Group 14 generally react by sharing electrons. However, the tendency of these elements to lose electrons—their metallic nature—increases as the atomic number increases.

▶ Pure oxygen is extracted from liquefied air, compressed, and sold in cylinders. It is most often used in the production of steel and in medicine, rocket fuel, and welding torches.

▶ Recent research suggests that the ozone layer has been thinning at a rate of 2.5 percent over the last decade. The CFCs, chlorofluorocarbons, currently in the atmosphere will persist for many years. A treaty that calls for the gradual reduction in the use of CFCs went into effect in 1989.

PREPLANNING

▶ Assemble the materials needed for Activity 12-2. The polystyrene foam sheets can be obtained from a hardware store or a vinyl siding company. Students can bring spaghetti, nuts, and bolts from home.

1 MOTIVATE

▶ Have the class recall that life on this planet is based primarily on the chemistry of carbon, oxygen, and nitrogen. Ask them if they think it is possible for other life-forms to exist in the universe. Ask students which elements could be a basis of those life-forms. Very different life-forms have been found deep in oceans near volcanic vents. They thrive on normally poisonous gases such as hydrogen sulfide.

12-4   Mixed Groups

New Science Words

semiconductors
allotropes

Objectives

▶ Distinguish among metals, nonmetals, and metalloids in Groups 13 through 16 of the periodic table.
▶ Describe the nature of allotropes.
▶ Recognize the significance of differences in crystal structure in carbon.

What kind of properties do metalloids have?

Locating the Mixed Groups

Can an element be both a metal and a nonmetal? In a sense, some elements are. They are the metalloids, which have both metallic and nonmetallic properties. A metalloid may conduct electricity better than a nonmetal but not as well as a metal. In the periodic table on pages 258-259 the metalloids are the elements located along the stair-step line. The mixed groups—13, 14, 15, and 16—contain some metals, some nonmetals, and some metalloids.

The Boron Group

Boron, a metalloid, is the first element in Group 13. If you look around your home, you may find two compounds of boron. One of these is boric acid, a mild antiseptic. The other is borax, used in laundry products to soften water. Less familiar are the boranes, compounds of boron used in fuels for rockets and jet planes.

Aluminum, a metal, is also in Group 13. Aluminum is the most abundant metal in Earth's crust. You use aluminum in soft drink cans, foil wrap, and cooking pans. You may also see aluminum on the sides of buildings, where it's used because it doesn't rust. And because aluminum is both strong and light, it is used to build airplanes.

When you operate electronic equipment, such as calculators and computers, you may be using one of the other metals in Group 13. These metals are gallium, indium, and thallium, used in the electronics industry to

13

5 **B** Boron 10.811
13 **Al** Aluminum 26.98154
31 **Ga** Gallium 69.723
49 **In** Indium 114.82
81 **Tl** Thallium 204.383

316   ELEMENTS AND THEIR PROPERTIES

OPTIONS

Meeting Different Ability Levels

For Section 12-4, use the following **Teacher Resource Masters** depending upon individual students' needs.

◆ **Study Guide Master** for all students.
● **Reinforcement Master** for students of average and above average ability levels.
▲ **Enrichment Master** for above average students.

Additional Teacher Resource Package masters are listed in the OPTIONS box throughout the section. The additional masters are appropriate for all students.

◆ STUDY GUIDE   53

STUDY GUIDE   Chapter 12
Mixed Groups   Text Pages 316–322

In each of the following statements, one key term has been scrambled. Unscramble each term and write it on the line provided.

metalloids   1. Elements with properties of both metals and nonmetals are called *tallemoids*.
semiconductors   2. Metals from group 13 are used to produce *smonicconud* substances that conduct electricity under certain conditions.
allotropes   3. Diamond and graphite are *spllatore* of carbon.
oxygen   4. About 20% of the air is made up of the element *geonxy*.
metals   5. All of the elements in the Boron group except boron are *metals*.
diatomic   6. Oxygen exists in the air as *diatomic* molecules.
ozone   7. The form of oxygen that protects living things from damage caused by the sun is called *ezon*.
molecular   8. Allotropes are different forms of an element with different *ecolumlar* structures.

Use the terms from the list below to fill in the following table. You will use some terms more than once. Some terms may not be used.

metal   14   nonmetal   toxic in large amounts
13   metalloid   15   semiconductor
allotrope   building material fertilizer   16

Element	Group Number	Metal, Nonmetal, or Metalloid	Other Properties
Gallium	13	metal	semiconductor
Sulfur	16	nonmetal	allotrope
Phosphorus	15	nonmetal	fertilizer
Selenium	16	nonmetal	toxic in large amounts
Carbon	14	nonmetal	allotrope
Aluminum	13	metal	building material

produce semiconductors. **Semiconductors** are substances that conduct an electric current under certain conditions. You will learn more about semiconductors in Chapter 23.

The Carbon Group

Each element in Group 14, the carbon family, has four electrons in its outer energy level. But here much of the similarity ends. Carbon is a nonmetal; silicon and germanium are metalloids; tin and lead are metals.

What do the diamond in a diamond ring and the graphite in your pencil lead have in common? It may surprise you to learn that they are both pure carbon. How can this be? Diamond and graphite are examples of allotropes. **Allotropes** are different forms of the same element having different molecular structures. Look at the diagrams below. Graphite is a black powder that consists of hexagonal layers of carbon atoms. In the hexagons,

14

6
C
Carbon
12.011

14
Si
Silicon
28.0855

32
Ge
Germanium
72.59

50
Sn
Tin
118.710

82
Pb
Lead
207.2

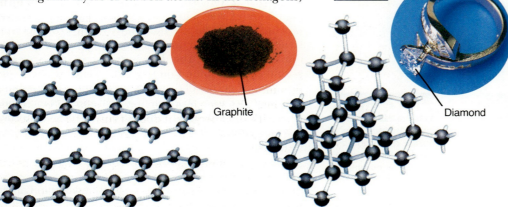

Graphite

Diamond

● **REINFORCEMENT** 53

REINFORCEMENT   Chapter 12
Mixed Groups   Text Pages 316–322

The elements that make up groups 13–16 of the periodic table are listed below. Classify each element as a metal, nonmetal, or metalloid by writing its name under the correct heading in the table. Use the periodic table of the elements on pages 258–259 of your textbook if you need help.

Boron Group	Nitrogen Group	Carbon Group	Oxygen Group
boron	nitrogen	carbon	oxygen
aluminum	phosphorus	silicon	sulfur
gallium	arsenic	germanium	selenium
indium	antimony	tin	tellurium
thallium	bismuth	lead	polonium

Metals	Nonmetals	Metalloids
aluminum	carbon	boron
gallium	nitrogen	silicon
indium	phosphorus	germanium
thallium	oxygen	antimony
tin	sulfur	tellurium
lead	selenium	polonium
bismuth		arsenic

Allotropes are different forms of the same element having different molecular structures. Diamond and graphite are allotropes of carbon. Look at the diagrams. Label each drawing as the structure for graphite or the structure for diamond.

Diamond

Graphite

Copyright Glencoe Division of Macmillan/McGraw-Hill
Users of Merrill Physical Science have the publisher's permission to reproduce this page.   53

▲ **ENRICHMENT** 53

ENRICHMENT   Chapter 12
Mixed Groups   Text Pages 316–322

DIAMOND AND GRAPHITE

Alchemists of the Middle Ages sweated over their stoves while trying to turn metals like lead, copper, and zinc into gold. They may have been better off trying to turn their glowing coals into diamonds. Charcoal and diamonds are made of the same element, carbon.

Carbon is found in nature in at least six crystalline forms. Each form is called an allotrope. Allotropes are different forms of the same element having different molecular structures. The best known allotropes are diamond and graphite.

In diamond, each carbon atom is bonded to four other carbon atoms. There are four carbon atoms at the corners of a tetrahedron around the central carbon atom. In graphite, each carbon atom is bonded to only three other carbon atoms. The result is that graphite is composed of hexagonal rings arranged in a flat sheet. The rings of graphite are aromatic, which means the rings contain alternating single and double bonds. In diamond, neighboring carbon atoms are joined by single covalent bonds.

Diamond   Graphite

These atomic arrangements explain the differences in physical properties of diamond and graphite. Since all the valence electrons of diamond are tied up in single bonds, there are no mobile electrons, thus diamond doesn't conduct electricity. Graphite's aromatic system has many mobile electrons. These account for its electrical and thermal conductivity. In fact,

graphite is the only nonmetal found in nature that conducts electricity.

Since graphite is inert, it is used to make electrodes for electrochemical applications. The many double bonds of graphite cause it to absorb light of all wavelengths. This explains its opaque, black color. This contrasts with the colorless transparency of pure diamond.

Conclude and Apply

1. Using the description and diagram above, tell why graphite is one of the most slippery solids known, while diamond is one of the hardest. **Graphite is bonded only in two dimensions. There are no bonds between the flat sheets. The resulting flat sheets readily slide over each other. The tight packing and three-dimensional bonding of atoms makes diamond a hard substance.**

2. What are some uses for graphite? **pencil lead, high-temperature lubricant, electrode**

3. What are some uses for diamond? **jewelry, rugged lenses, diamond-tipped saws, cutting instruments**

Copyright Glencoe Division of Macmillan/McGraw-Hill
Users of Merrill Physical Science have the publisher's permission to reproduce this page.   53

TYING TO PREVIOUS KNOWLEDGE: Help students to recall information about Groups 13-16 presented in Chapter 10 when they learned about the periodic table. Remind students about the number of outer electrons in each group and how these electrons relate to the element's chemical behavior.

OBJECTIVES AND SCIENCE WORDS: Have students review the objectives and science words to become familiar with this section.

2 TEACH

Key Concepts are highlighted.

CONCEPT DEVELOPMENT

▶ Build a model of a boron or aluminum compound to show students. There are three bonds directed at a 120° bond angle. The structure is trigonal planar.

▶ **Demonstration:** Have a student remove the label from an empty tin (actually iron) can and leave the can outside for two days and nights. Beside it, place a similar aluminum can. Bring both cans to class on the third day. The oxidation resistance of aluminum will be obvious. Ask students why they think the iron reacted while the aluminum did not. Iron atoms are larger and electrons are farther away from the nucleus and less tightly held.

▶ If you have an old calculator that doesn't work, remove the circuit board with the computer chip on it. Show this to the class as you discuss semiconductors. Save the board for Chapter 23.

▶ As you discuss carbon, display a large lump of coal, graphite flakes, and a fake diamond. This visual emphasis will help students remember allotropes.

PROBLEM SOLVING

If possible, have assorted grades of pencils available for students to try. A book that uses the pencil as a central theme in a discussion of design and engineering technology is *The Pencil: A History of Design and Circumstance* by Henry Petroski, New York: Knopf, 1990.

Think Critically: Because graphite acts as a lubricant, it is safe to assume that the softest pencil (No. 1) contains more graphite than the hardest pencil (No. 3).

CROSS CURRICULUM

▶ **Business:** Ask each student to bring to class a pencil that has an advertisement or message on it. Tape the student's name to it and then display pencils for all of the classes to see. Pencils are big business. Specially engineered machines print messages on pencils. Ask students if they think this is an effective use of advertising budgets.

CONCEPT DEVELOPMENT

▶ **Demonstration:** Each student can build one unit cell of a diamond. The cells can then be connected to make a model that accurately demonstrates why a diamond is so hard. Duplicate four equilateral triangles for each student. Have the student cut out each triangle, leaving a tab on each edge. Tape or glue the triangles together to form a tetrahedron. Stack the tetrahedrons together in a clear plastic sweater storage box. The interlocking network of tetrahedrons represents the rigid crystal structure of a diamond.

👥 **Cooperative Learning:** Send an Expert Team to a jewelry store to interview a jeweler about diamonds. Have students make an appointment in advance so they can talk to a certified gemologist about a stone's carat weight, cut, and clarity. Perhaps the jeweler could visit the school and talk to the class.

PROBLEM SOLVING

The "Lead" in a Pencil

In a pencil factory, ground graphite crystals are mixed with clay to make the pencil "lead." The graphite-clay mixture is then shaped into long thin rods.

The rods are cut, dried, and heated. Grooves shaped to fit the rods are cut into half blocks of wood. The grooves are coated with glue, and then the rods are placed into the grooves. The other half of the block of wood is placed on the first half. After the glue has dried, the block is cut into individual pencils. After the pencils are painted, metal bands and erasers are added to make finished pencils.

Think Critically: What makes up the lead of a pencil? How do the amounts of graphite in hard (No. 3), medium (No. 2), and soft (No. 1) pencils compare? Explain your answer.

Did You Know?

Synthetic diamonds, used extensively in industry, are made by subjecting graphite to extremely high pressure and temperature.

each carbon atom is bonded to three other carbon atoms. The fourth electron of each atom is bonded weakly to the layer below. This structure allows the layers to slide easily past one another, making graphite an excellent lubricant.

A diamond is clear and extremely hard. In a diamond, each carbon atom is bonded to four other carbon atoms at the vertices, or corner points, of a tetrahedron. In turn, many tetrahedrons join together to form a giant molecule in which the atoms are held tightly in a strong crystal structure. This structure accounts for the hardness of diamond. Look at the drawings of the structures of graphite and diamond on page 317. How are the structure and properties of diamond unlike those of graphite?

Carbon occurs as an element in coal and as compounds in oil, natural gas, and foods. Carbon in these materials may combine with oxygen to produce carbon dioxide, CO_2. Plants combine CO_2 with water to make food. In Chapter 13, you will study other carbon compounds—many essential to life.

Silicon is second only to oxygen in abundance in Earth's crust. Most silicon is found in sand, silicon dioxide, SiO_2,

318 ELEMENTS AND THEIR PROPERTIES

OPTIONS

INQUIRY QUESTIONS

▶ **The carbon family of Group 14 has both metallic and nonmetallic members. How can you distinguish between them?** *The metals have typical metallic properties (luster, conductivity, malleability, and so on) and have positive oxidation numbers. The nonmetals have typical semimetallic properties (brittleness, nonconductivity, and so on) and have negative oxidation numbers.*

PROGRAM RESOURCES

From the **Teacher Resource Package** use:
Transparency Masters, pages 47-48, Allotropes of Carbon.
Use **Color Transparency** number 24, Allotropes of Carbon.

and in almost all rocks and soil. The crystal structure of silicon dioxide is similar to the tetrahedrons found in diamond. Silicon, too, occurs as two allotropes. One of these is a hard, gray substance, and the other is a brown powder.

What compound has a structure similar to that of diamond?

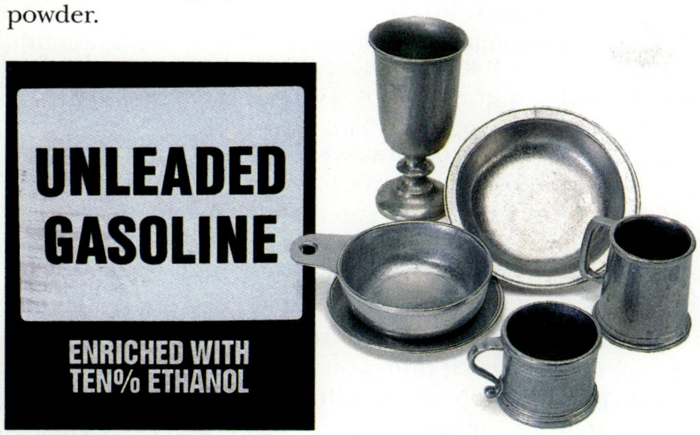

Figure 12-16. Most gasolines are no longer leaded (left). Pewter contains tin and other metals (right).

5 Both silicon and germanium, the other metalloid in the carbon group, are used in making semiconductors, which you'll learn about in Chapter 23. Tin and lead are typical metals. Tin is used to coat other metals to prevent corrosion. Tin is also combined with other metals to produce bronze and pewter. Lead was once used widely in paints and antiknock gasoline. But lead is poisonous, so it has been largely replaced in these materials.

The Nitrogen Group

6 The nitrogen family makes up Group 15. Each element has five electrons in its outer energy level. These elements tend to share electrons and to form covalent compounds with other elements.

7 Each breath you take is about 80 percent gaseous nitrogen, as diatomic molecules, N_2. If you look again at Figure 12-8 on page 310, you'll see that nitrogen is the element fourth in abundance in your body. Yet you and other animals and plants can't use nitrogen as N_2. The nitrogen must be combined into compounds, such as nitrates—compounds that contain the nitrate ion, (NO_3^-). Much nitrogen is used to make nitrates and ammonia, NH_3, both of which are used in fertilizers.

15
7 **N** Nitrogen 14.0067
15 **P** Phosphorus 30.97376
33 **As** Arsenic 74.9216
51 **Sb** Antimony 121.75
83 **Bi** Bismuth 208.9804

REVEALING MISCONCEPTIONS

▶ The words *silicon* and *silicone* are often interchanged in everyday usage. Silicon is an element. Silicones are long chains of Si and O bonded to carbon atoms. Help students avoid confusing these words by making sure they pronounce them correctly.

▶ Students often hear the term *tin can*. In reality, the metal cans in which food is preserved are iron cans. At one time, all were coated with tin. Today, many have a plastic film lining.

TEACHER F.Y.I.

▶ Some computer bulletin boards have had recipes for making explosives. Advise your students *never* to try making these high-powered nitrogen explosives.

CROSS CURRICULUM

▶ **Political Science:** Nitrogen compounds can include ammonia and nitrate fertilizers that help feed the world's population as well as drugs to help treat disease. They also include trinitrotoluene, TNT, that is used in bombs and rockets and other compounds used in poisonous gases. Chemicals are neither good nor bad. People decide how chemicals are to be used. Have a panel discussion on whether scientists should work on development of explosives and poisons.

MINI QUIZ

Use the Mini Quiz to check students' recall of chapter content.

1. **How do we classify an element that has both metallic and nonmetallic properties?** *as a metalloid*
2. **What is the most abundant metal in the Earth's crust?** *aluminum*
3. **What do we call substances that conduct an electric current under certain conditions?** *semiconductors*
4. **Different forms of the same element are called _____ .** *allotropes*
5. **Most semiconductors are made from silicon or _____ .** *germanium*

ENRICHMENT

▶ Have a student research the meaning of the Greek word *graphein* from which we get our word, *graphite*. It means "to write."

▶ Black lung disease occurs among coal miners. Have a student research the disease and its causes. Have a second student report on how mining practices and equipment have changed to help prevent the disease.

▶ Have students find out why both germanium and silicon are used to make computer chips.

PROGRAM RESOURCES

From the **Teacher Resource Package** use:
Concept Mapping, page 29.

► Point out that phosphorus occurs as P_4 molecules. These molecules stack in different ways to form white, red, and black phosphorus allotropes.

► **Demonstration:** Oxygen can be easily produced in a beaker, and the gas can be repeatedly tested using a glowing splint. Students will observe that oxygen supports combustion but does not burn. Place 1 g of MnO_2 in a 600-mL beaker. Slowly add 3% hydrogen peroxide to the beaker. Oxygen gas will be produced and will fill the beaker. Lower a glowing splint into the beaker. The splint will burst into flame.

CHECK FOR UNDERSTANDING

Use the Mini Quiz to check for understanding.

MINI QUIZ

Use the Mini Quiz to check students' recall of chapter content.

6 How many outer electrons are present in each member of the nitrogen family? *five*

7 The air contains _____ percent nitrogen gas. *about eighty*

8 The air contains _____ percent oxygen gas. *about twenty*

9 What is the chemical formula for ozone? O_3

10 Which Group 16 element is very toxic but is needed in your diet in trace amounts? *selenium*

RETEACH

Have each student in the class prepare a flash card listing one element from Groups 13-16. On one side show the name and symbol, and on the other side write the properties and uses. Use these cards for drill and practice. To review the chapter, have students assemble sets of cards for all elements discussed.

EXTENSION

For students who have mastered this section, use the **Reinforcement** and **Enrichment** masters or other OPTIONS provided.

Phosphorus is a nonmetal. Uses of phosphorus compounds range from water softeners to fertilizers to match heads. Antimony is a metalloid, and bismuth is a metal. Both elements are used with other metals to lower their melting points. It is because of this property that the metal in automatic fire sprinkler heads contains bismuth.

16

8
O
Oxygen
15.9994

16
S
Sulfur
32.06

34
Se
Selenium
78.96

52
Te
Tellurium
127.60

84
Po
Polonium
208.9824*

The Oxygen Group

The oxygen group makes up Group 16 on the periodic table. You can't live for more than a short time without the nonmetal oxygen, which makes up about 20 percent of the air. Oxygen exists in the air as diatomic molecules, O_2. During electric storms some oxygen molecules, O_2, change into ozone molecules, O_3. Do you see that O_2 and O_3 are allotropes?

Nearly all living things on Earth need free oxygen, as O_2, for respiration. Living things also depend on a layer of ozone, O_3, around Earth for protection from some of the sun's radiation, as you will learn in later chapters.

Sulfur is a nonmetal that can exist in several allotropes—as different-shaped crystals, as a noncrystalline solid, and in a liquid form. Sulfur combines with metals to form sulfides of such distinctive colors that they are used as pigments in paints.

Figure 12-17 Eight-sided and needlelike crystals are two of the allotropes of sulfur.

OPTIONS

ENRICHMENT

► Silicon dioxide (quartz) crystals can be clear and colorless. When they have impurities they become colored gem stones. Research which impurities are in amethyst, emerald, aquamarine, jade, garnet, opal, onyx, and moonstone. For example, Mn and Fe cause quartz to become purple amethyst. An oxide of chromium causes the emerald to be green.

► Have students research glass, china and its glazes, and ceramics. Ceramics are clay products such as brick, tile, and terra cotta.

► Asbestos contains the element silicon. Ask a student to report on asbestos, its uses, and why it is being removed from buildings.

► Photovoltaic solar cells convert sunlight into electricity. Ask a student to read and report on solar cell research.

► Fiber optics are used for communication. Have a student report on how these fibers are made and how they work. Fibers are pulled from a melt of pure quartz crystals. The light reflects off the interior walls of the fiber.

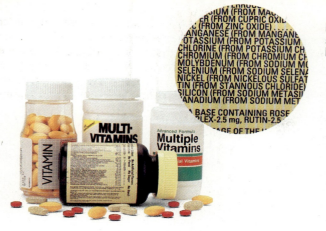

The nonmetal selenium and two metalloids, tellurium and polonium, are the other Group 16 elements. Selenium is the most common of these. This element is one of several that you need in trace amounts in your diet. Larger amounts of selenium are toxic, however.

One thing is certain—your life would be impossible without the elements in the mixed groups. From oxygen, present in a large amount in your body, to selenium, present in a very minute amount, you are these elements.

SECTION REVIEW

1. Why are Groups 14 and 15 better representatives of mixed groups than Group 13 or Group 16?
2. How do the allotropes of sulfur differ?
3. Why is graphite a lubricant while a diamond is the hardest gem known?
4. **Apply:** Today aluminum is one of the most plentiful and least expensive of metals. Yet Napoleon III set the table for his most important guests with knives, forks, and spoons made of aluminum instead of silver or gold. Why?

Science and WRITING

Fluorescent lamps have been described as a major advantage in the energy conservation movement. Explain how they work and why they are so much better than the incandescent bulb.

☑ Concept Mapping

Make a concept map for allotropes of carbon, using the terms *graphite*, *diamond*, *hexagon*, and *tetrahedron*. If you need help, see Concept Mapping in the **Skill Handbook** on pages 684 and 685.

Skill Builder

12-4 MIXED GROUPS **321**

Science and WRITING

The filament emits electrons that collide with mercury vapor in the tube. Mercury atoms emit ultraviolet light that causes the phosphor coating on the inside of the tube to glow (fluoresce). Fluorescent lights use about 1/4 the energy of incandescent lights of equivalent brightness. Despite the savings, many people cannot afford the initial cost of conversion

3 CLOSE

▶ Ask each student in class to write five ways his or her life would be different if elements in Groups 13-16 became scarce on Earth.

▶ Ask questions 1-3 and the **Apply** Question in the Section Review.

SECTION REVIEW ANSWERS

1. Group 13 contains no elements that are clearly nonmetals. Group 16 contains no elements that are clearly metals.

2. It can exist as different shaped crystals, a noncrystalline (amorphous) solid or a liquid.

3. In graphite, carbon is arranged in flat sheets of atoms bonded in a hexagonal pattern. Because the sheets can slide over one another, graphite is a good lubricant. A diamond consists of a network of tetrahedrally bonded carbon atoms. Thus the crystal is essentially a giant molecule which results in an extremely hard gem.

4. Apply: At the time of Napoleon III, who ruled from 1850 to 1870, no reliable method of extracting aluminum from its compounds had been found. As a result, aluminum metal was costly and rare. Aluminum tableware was a sign of great wealth and prestige.

Skill Builder

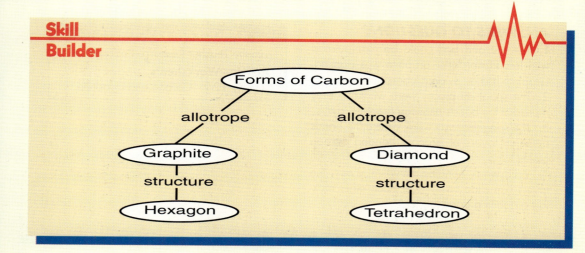

ACTIVITY 12-2
25 minutes

OBJECTIVE: **Model** the structure of graphite and **determine the cause and effect** relationship between its structure and properties.

PROCESS SKILLS applied in this activity:
▶ **Making and Using Models** in Procedure Steps 3, 4, and 5.
▶ **Inferring** in Conclude and Apply Question 3.

COOPERATIVE LEARNING
Use the Science Investigation group strategy to take advantage of different skills that group members have.

TEACHING THE ACTIVITY
Alternate Materials: Hexagons could be cut from corrugated cardboard also.

Troubleshooting: Powdered graphite can be messy. Have students use it over sheets of newspaper and wipe it off thoroughly with towels or a cloth.
▶ Cut out hexagonal patterns to distribute to students to help them save time.
▶ Use thin styrene foam sheets available at hardware stores. These are sometimes found as shims in appliance packaging.
▶ Have students compare lines made by pencils of various hardness grades and relate these to the activity.
▶ Be sure students realize that the spaghetti, which will break when the model is pushed, represents the weak, easily broken bonds between layers of hexagonally bonded carbon atoms.

ACTIVITY 12-2
Carbon and Graphite

Problem: *Why can graphite be used as a lubricant?*

Materials
- nut and bolt
- powdered graphite
- 6 pieces of thin spaghetti
- polystyrene sheet
- marking pen

Procedure
1. Put together and then take apart a nut and bolt.
2. Coat the threads of the nut with powdered graphite, and then repeat Step 1.
3. Construct a model of graphite as follows. Cut out two polystyrene hexagons with sides about 10 cm long. Use a marking pen to label the intersections of sides with the letter *C*.
4. Insert six 10-cm pieces of thin spaghetti between the hexagons so that they pierce the letter *C* on each hexagon.
5. Set your finished two-layer model on your desk. Gently press down on the top layer and push the model forward.

Analyze
1. Compare your observations in Step 1 and Step 2. How do you account for any difference you noticed?
2. When you applied pressure to your model of graphite, what were the weakest parts of the structure?

Conclude and Apply
3. Your model represents the bonding of carbon in graphite. How is the way the spaghetti breaks related to the bond structure in graphite?
4. Why do the bonding and structure of graphite make it a good lubricant?

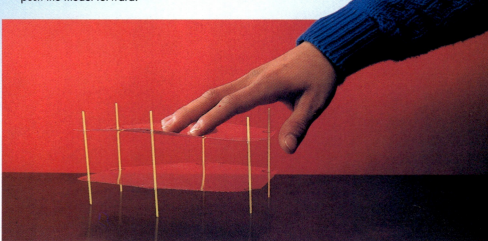

ANSWERS TO QUESTIONS
1. The nut and bolt could be manipulated with less friction after graphite was applied. Graphite has an evident lubricating property.
2. The spaghetti pieces were weakest. They represent the bonds between graphite layers.
3. The spaghetti was weak as are the bonds between layers of strongly bonded carbon atoms.
4. With weak bonding between layers, the layers can slide easily over each other making graphite a good lubricant.

PROGRAM RESOURCES
From the **Teacher Resource Package** use:
Activity Worksheets, pages 96-97, Activity 12-2: Carbon and Graphite.

SUMMARY

12-1: Metals

1. A typical metal is a hard, shiny, solid that—due to metallic bonding—is malleable, ductile, and a good conductor of heat and electricity.
2. Groups 1 and 2 on the periodic table are the alkali and alkaline earth metals, which have some similar and some contrasting properties.
3. The iron triad, the coinage metals, and the zinc, cadmium, mercury group are among the transition elements, which make up Groups 3 through 12 on the periodic table.

12-2: Science and Society: Synthetic Elements

1. The lanthanoids and actinoids have atomic numbers 57-70 and 89-102, respectively, whereas transuranium elements have atomic numbers greater than 92.
2. The making of synthetic elements is a controversial issue.

12-3: Nonmetals

1. As a typical nonmetal, hydrogen is a gas that forms compounds by sharing electrons with other nonmetals and also with metals.
2. All the halogens, Group 17, have seven outer electrons and form both covalent and ionic compounds, but each halogen has some properties unlike the others.
3. The noble gases, Group 18, are elements whose properties and uses are related to their chemical stability.

12-4: Mixed Groups

1. Groups 13 through 16 of the periodic table include metals, nonmetals, and metalloids.
2. Allotropes are different forms of the same element having different molecular structures.
3. The properties of two forms of carbon, graphite and diamond, depend upon the differences in their crystal structure.

KEY SCIENCE WORDS

a. allotropes
b. diatomic molecule
c. ductile
d. malleable
e. metallic bonding
f. radioactive element
g. semiconductors
h. sublimation
i. transuranium element
j. transition elements

UNDERSTANDING VOCABULARY

Match each phrase with the correct term from the list of Key Science Words.

1. can be drawn out into a wire
2. appears after uranium on the periodic table
3. can be hammered into a thin sheet
4. change directly from a solid to a gas
5. will conduct an electric current under certain conditions
6. different structural forms of the same element
7. composed of two atoms of the same element
8. breaks down and gives off particles, radiation, and energy
9. Groups 3 through 12 on the periodic table
10. Positively charged ions are surrounded by freely moving electrons.

ELEMENTS AND THEIR PROPERTIES **323**

CHAPTER
REVIEW

SUMMARY

Have students read the summary statements to review the major concepts of the chapter.

UNDERSTANDING VOCABULARY

1. c
2. i
3. d
4. h
5. g
6. a
7. b
8. f
9. j
10. e

OPTIONS

ASSESSMENT

To assess student understanding of material in this chapter, use the resources listed.

👥 COOPERATIVE LEARNING

Consider using cooperative learning in the THINK AND WRITE CRITICALLY, APPLY, and MORE SKILL BUILDERS sections of the Chapter Review.

PROGRAM RESOURCES

From the **Teacher Resource Package** use:
Chapter Review, pages 27-28.
Chapter and Unit Tests, pages 80-83, Chapter Test.

CHAPTER REVIEW

CHAPTER REVIEW

CHECKING CONCEPTS

1. b	6. c
2. a	7. d
3. d	8. d
4. c	9. a
5. a	10. d

UNDERSTANDING CONCEPTS

11. graphite
12. halogens
13. alkaline earth
14. transition elements
15. stability

THINK AND WRITE CRITICALLY

16. francium, because it is at the bottom of Group 1 and at the left of the table

17. oxygen, silicon, aluminum, and iron, respectively

18. Atoms of gaseous elements other than the noble gases have unstable electron structures. These atoms acquire stable structures by sharing electrons in diatomic molecules. The atoms of a noble gas, on the other hand, are stable and thus do not share electrons to form diatomic molecules. Instead, they occur in monatomic form.

19. Elements are grouped on the periodic table according to their atomic numbers and electron arrangements. Hydrogen is placed first because its atomic number is 1. It is placed above the alkali metals because, like those elements, it has one electron in its outer energy level. Note, however, that hydrogen's properties differ from those of Group 1 metals in several significant ways.

20. Zinc, cadmium, and nickel are three metals used to coat other metals to form a protective layer that resists corrosion.

CHECKING CONCEPTS

Choose the word or phrase that completes the sentence or answers the question.

1. When magnesium and fluorine react, what type of bond is formed?
   - a. metallic
   - b. ionic
   - c. covalent
   - d. diatomic

2. What type of bond is found in a piece of pure gold?
   - a. metallic
   - b. ionic
   - c. covalent
   - d. diatomic

3. Because electrons move freely in metals, metals are _____.
   - a. brittle
   - b. hard
   - c. dull
   - d. conductors

4. The _____ make up the most reactive group of all metals.
   - a. iron triad
   - b. coinage metals
   - c. alkalis
   - d. alkaline earths

5. The most reactive of all elements is _____.
   - a. fluorine
   - b. uranium
   - c. hydrogen
   - d. oxygen

6. The element _____ is always found in nature combined with other elements.
   - a. copper
   - b. gold
   - c. magnesium
   - d. silver

7. The least magnetic of these metals is _____.
   - a. cobalt
   - b. iron
   - c. nickel
   - d. titanium

8. The synthetic element _____ was banned after much controversy.
   - a. ytterbium
   - b. promethium
   - c. americium
   - d. plutonium

9. An example of a radioactive element is ____.
   - a. astatine
   - b. bromine
   - c. chlorine
   - d. fluorine

10. The only group that is completely nonmetallic is Group _____.
    - a. 1
    - b. 2
    - c. 17
    - d. 18

UNDERSTANDING CONCEPTS

Complete each sentence.

11. The crystal structure of the form of carbon called _____ makes it useful as a lubricant.

12. A group of elements named for their reactions in which salts are formed are the _____.

13. Red and white fireworks may be produced by two metals in the _____ group.

14. The class of elements that generally have from one to three outer electrons is the _____.

15. Many uses of the noble gases are related to their property of _____.

THINK AND WRITE CRITICALLY

16. Reading from top to bottom on the periodic table, metallic properties of elements *increase*, reading from left to right, metallic properties *decrease*. Which element is the most metallic of all? Explain your answer.

17. The most abundant elements in Earth's crust are a nonmetal, a metalloid, and two metals. List the four elements.

18. Why do oxygen and nitrogen occur in the air as diatomic molecules, but argon, neon, krypton, and xenon occur as monatomic molecules?

19. Explain why hydrogen, a nonmetal, is on the metal side of the periodic table.

20. Name three metals used to coat other metals. Why is one metal used to coat another?

21. Why was mercury used in clinical thermometers, and why is it no longer used for that purpose?
22. The density of hydrogen is so low that it can be used to fill balloons to make them lighter than air. Why is helium used more frequently?
23. Why is aluminum used instead of steel in building airplanes?
24. Why are silver compounds used in photography? Name two nonmetals extracted from brine that are also part of these compounds.
25. Like selenium, chromium is poisonous but is needed in trace amounts in your diet. How does this information apply to the safe use of vitamin-mineral pills?

MORE SKILL BUILDERS

If you need help, refer to the Skill Handbook.

1. **Making and Using Tables:** Use the periodic table to classify each of the following as a lanthanoid or actinoid: californium, europium, cerium, nobelium.
2. **Comparing and Contrasting:** Aluminum is close to carbon on the periodic table. Explain why aluminum is a metal and carbon is not.
3. **Observing and Inferring:** You are shown two samples of phosphorus. One is white and burns if exposed to air. The other is red and burns if lit. Infer why the properties of two samples of the same element differ.
4. **Recognizing Cause and Effect:** Plants need nitrogen compounds. Nitrogen-fixing changes free nitrogen into nitrates. Lightning and legumes are both nitrogen-fixing. What are the cause and effect of nitrogen fixing?
5. **Concept Mapping:** Complete the concept map located to the right for some common metals. You may use symbols for the elements.

PROJECTS

1. Research the pros and cons of using nuclear energy to produce electricity. Prepare a report which includes data as well as your informed opinion on the subject. If several class members do research, conduct a debate on the issue.
2. Research the source, composition, and properties of asbestos. What properties made it suitable for use in construction in the past? How did these same properties cause asbestos to become a health hazard, and what is being done now to eliminate the hazard?

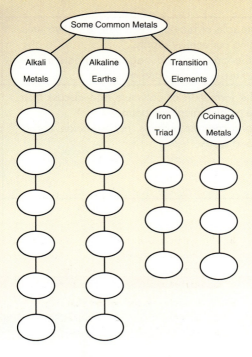

ELEMENTS AND THEIR PROPERTIES   **325**

21. Mercury remains a liquid throughout the ordinary temperature range and expands as temperature increases. Mercury is poisonous.
22. Hydrogen burns readily in air. Helium is a noble gas and therefore is stable.
23. Aluminum is strong but light in density. Therefore, it is more fuel efficient than steel.
24. Some silver compounds change chemically when exposed to light. Bromine and iodine, used to make silver bromide and silver iodide, are obtained from brine.
25. Do not take more than the recommended dosage. Exceeding the trace amounts needed may produce toxic reactions.

MORE SKILL BUILDERS

1. Making and Using Tables: lanthanoids: europium, cerium; actinoids: californium, nobelium
2. Comparing and Contrasting: Aluminum has metallic properties such as being malleable and ductile, and it transfers electrons when it combines with nonmetals. Carbon has none of these properties.
3. Observing and Inferring: They are allotropes of phosphorus, that is, forms of the element with different properties because they have different structures.
4. Recognizing Cause and Effect: Cause: lightning and legumes; Effect: changing atmospheric nitrogen into nitrogen compounds
5. Concept Mapping:

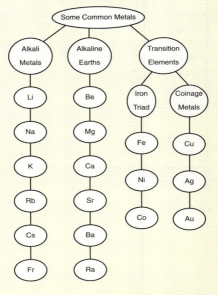

13 Organic and Biological Compounds

CHAPTER SECTION	OBJECTIVES	ACTIVITIES
13-1 Simple Organic Compounds (2 days)	1. **Describe** structures of organic compounds and explain why carbon forms so many compounds. 2. **Distinguish** between saturated and unsaturated hydrocarbons. 3. **Identify** isomers of organic compounds.	**MINI-Lab:** *What structures can octane have?* p. 330
13-2 Other Organic Compounds (2 days)	1. **Describe** characteristics of aromatic compounds. 2. **Classify** groups of organic compounds as substituted hydrocarbons.	**Activity 13-1:** *Alcohols and Organic Acids,* p. 337
13-3 Alternative Sources of Energy Science & Society (1 day)	1. **Describe** the role of biomass as a source of two fuels for increasing our energy supply. 2. **Analyze** the positive and negative effects of the widespread use of ethanol and gasohol.	
13-4 Biological Compounds (2 days)	1. **Describe** the formation of polymers and **discuss** their importance as biological compounds. 2. **Compare** and **contrast** proteins, nucleic acids, carbohydrates, and lipids.	**Activity 13-2:** *Biological Polymers,* p. 346
Chapter Review		

ACTIVITY MATERIALS

FIND OUT	ACTIVITIES		MINI-LABS
Page 327 white bread white paper laboratory burner or hot plate test tubes	**13-1 Alcohols and Organic Acids, p. 337** test tube and stopper dropper pipet graduated cylinder ethyl alcohol 6 M sodium hydroxide 0.01 M potassium permanganate	**13-2 Biological Polymers, p. 346** paper clips notecards	**What structures can octane have? p. 330** gum drops of one color raisins toothpicks

CHAPTER FEATURES		TEACHER RESOURCE PACKAGE	OTHER RESOURCES
Problem Solving: *The Case of the Overripe Tomatoes,* p. 332 **Skill Builder:** *Making and Using Graphs,* p. 333		**Ability Level Worksheets** ◆ **Study Guide,** p. 54 ● **Reinforcement,** p. 54 ▲ **Enrichment,** p. 54 **MINI-Lab Worksheet,** p. 108 **Cross-Curricular Connections,** p. 19 **Transparency Masters,** pp. 49, 50	**Color Transparency 25,** Hydrocarbon Structure
Skill Builder: *Interpreting Scientific Illustrations,* p. 336		**Ability Level Worksheets** ◆ **Study Guide,** p. 55 ● **Reinforcement,** p. 55 ▲ **Enrichment,** p. 55 **Activity Worksheet,** pp. 102, 103 **Critical Thinking/Problem Solving,** p. 19 **Technology,** pp. 13, 14	
You Decide! p. 339		**Ability Level Worksheets** ◆ **Study Guide,** p. 56 ● **Reinforcement,** p. 56 ▲ **Enrichment,** p. 56	
Technology: *Fake Fats,* p. 344 **Skill Builder:** *Concept Mapping,* p. 345		**Ability Level Worksheets** ◆ **Study Guide,** p. 57 ● **Reinforcement,** p. 57 ▲ **Enrichment,** p. 57 **Activity Worksheet,** pp. 104, 105 **Concept Mapping,** pp. 31, 32 **Science and Society,** p. 17 **Transparency Masters,** pp. 51, 52	**Color Transparency 26,** Biological Polymers **Lab Manual 28,** The Breakdown of Starch **Lab Manual 29,** Testing for a Vitamin
Summary Key Science Words Understanding Vocabulary Checking Concepts Understanding Concepts	Think & Write Critically Apply More Skill Builders Projects	**Chapter Review,** pp. 29, 30 **Chapter Test,** pp. 84-87	**Chapter Review Software** **Test Bank**

◆ **Basic** ● **Average** ▲ **Advanced**

ADDITIONAL MATERIALS

SOFTWARE	AUDIOVISUAL	BOOKS/MAGAZINES
Organic Chemistry, J&S Software. *Polymer Chemistry,* American Chemical Society. *Chemistry of Life,* Queue.	*Carbon and Its Compounds,* 2nd ed., film, Coronet/MTI. *The Carbon Compounds,* film, SVE. *Organic Chemistry,* filmstrip, Science Software. *Special Topics in Chemistry,* video, Focus.	Buscall, R. *Science and Technology of Polymer Colloids.* NY: Elsevier Science Publishing Co., Inc., 1985. Gallant, K.W. and J.M. Railey. *Physical Properties of Hydrocarbons,* Vol. 2, 2nd ed. Houston, TX: Gulf Publishing Co., 1984. Kahn, M.A. and R.H. Stanton. *Toxicology of Halogenated Hydrocarbons: Health and Ecological Effects.* Elmsford, NY: Pergamon Press Inc., 1981.

THEME DEVELOPMENT: Scale and structure as a theme of the textbook is developed through a presentation of organic compounds and related biopolymers. The relationships that exist between the structure of organic molecules and the properties of those molecules are described and developed.

CHAPTER OVERVIEW

▶ **Section 13-1:** The unique chemistry of carbon as it forms many different molecular shapes is presented in this section. The student is introduced to saturated and unsaturated hydrocarbons as well as isomers.

▶ **Section 13-2:** Aromatic compounds and substituted hydrocarbons are described in this section.

▶ **Section 13-3: Science and Society:** Biomass conversion as an alternate energy source is described in detail.

▶ **Section 13-4:** This section introduces biochemistry and describes the structure of the main classes of biochemicals, proteins, fats, and carbohydrates. The concept of polymerization is presented to unify the section.

CHAPTER VOCABULARY

organic compounds	biomass
hydrocarbon	biogas
saturated	energy
hydrocarbons	farming
unsaturated	gasohol
hydrocarbons	polymers
isomers	proteins
aromatic compound	nucleic acids
substituted	carbohydrates
hydrocarbons	lipids
alcohol	

CHAPTER

13 Organic and Biological Compounds

326

OPTIONS

⚡ For Your Gifted Students

Have students research the structure of DNA and its mode of operation in controlling cell functions and in cell reproduction. They can research the bases adenine, guanine, cytosine, and thymine. Have students show the chemical structure of the bases. They can make a three-dimensional model of the double helix and show how the four bases pair. Some students could research the way base sequences code for amino acids in proteins. The students will need to find out how protein is synthesized as a consequence of the DNA code.

Have you heard the saying "You are what you eat"? Actually, many of the same compounds in foods are found in your body. And one special element is basic to these compounds and to other substances made by living things.

FIND OUT!

Do this activity to observe the element that forms from the breakdown of some kinds of materials when they are heated.

Place a small piece of bread in a test tube. Hold the test tube over the flame of a laboratory burner. What do you observe? Using a clean test tube and a small amount of paper instead of bread, repeat the procedure. What do you observe this time?

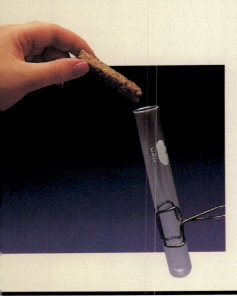

Gearing Up
Previewing the Chapter

Use this outline to help you focus on important ideas in this chapter.

Section 13-1   Simple Organic Compounds
► Organic Compounds
► Hydrocarbons
► Isomers

Section 13-2   Other Organic Compounds
► Aromatic Compounds
► Substituted Hydrocarbons

Section 13-3   Science and Society
Alternative Sources of Energy
► Why Not New Fuels?

Section 13-4   Biological Compounds
► Proteins
► Nucleic Acids
► Carbohydrates
► Lipids

Previewing Science Skills

► In the Skill Builders, you will make and use a graph, interpret scientific illustrations, and make a concept map.
► In the Activities, you will observe, predict, and build models.
► In the MINI-Lab, you will build a model, compare, and contrast.

What's next?

You have observed evidence of the presence of carbon in bread and paper, which contain organic compounds. As you study this chapter, you will find out more about organic compounds.

For Your Mainstreamed Students

Ask students to make models of organic compounds. They can paint polystyrene foam balls various colors for the specific elements (carbon—black, hydrogen—yellow, and so forth). Have them combine the atoms to make models of the molecules shown in this chapter. This will afford opportunities for visual, tactile, and kinesthetic learning.

INTRODUCING THE CHAPTER

Use the Find Out activity to introduce students to organic and biological compounds. Inform students that they will be learning more about their special chemistry, formulas, and reactions as they read the chapter.

FIND OUT!

Preparation: Cut fresh bread and paper into thin strips 2 cm long, that will fit into a test tube.

Materials: white bread, white paper, laboratory burner or hot plate, test tubes

Teaching Tips
► Suggest to students that they record the time they begin heating both samples and the time that the first observable change is noticed.
► Use this activity to reinforce the evidences of a chemical reaction—color change, odor, and evolution of a gas (water vapor).
► Students will notice that both paper and bread turn black. Both will give off water vapor which will condense inside the test tube.
► Because cellulose and starch are chemically similar, students observe similar reactions when paper and bread are heated. Ask the class if this means they can digest paper. The negative answer implies a difference in structure between the two. Digestive enzymes are structurally specific.

Gearing Up

Have students study the Gearing Up feature to familiarize themselves with the chapter. Discuss the relationships of the topics in the outline.

What's Next?

Before beginning the first section, make sure students understand the connection between the Find Out activity and the topics to follow.

PREPARATION

SECTION BACKGROUND

▶ Organic compounds can be classified as aromatic and aliphatic. Aromatic compounds contain one or more benzene rings. All other hydrocarbons are classified as aliphatic.

▶ A chain compound in which all carbon-carbon bonds are single bonds is called an alkane. This is also called a saturated compound. The general formula for alkanes is C_nH_{2n+2}.

▶ A group of atoms that is attached to a main chain is called a branch or substituent.

▶ Alkenes are unsaturated hydrocarbons that contain double bonds. The general formula for an alkene is C_nH_{2n}.

▶ Alkynes are unsaturated hydrocarbons that contain triple bonds. The general formula for an alkyne is C_nH_{2n-2}.

PREPLANNING

▶ To prepare for the Mini-Lab on page 330, obtain soft gum drops, raisins, and toothpicks.

1 MOTIVATE

▶ **Demonstration:** Organic compounds, called esters, that smell like pineapple, banana, and wintergreen can easily be prepared by reacting an organic acid with an alcohol. Place 6 mL each of an acid and an alcohol in a test tube. Add 5 drops of concentrated sulfuric acid, mix and heat in a warm water bath. **CAUTION:** *Acid is corrosive. Alcohols are flammable. Butyric acid has a foul odor.*

butyric acid + ethanol = pineapple
acetic acid + ethanol = apple
acetic acid + isopentanol = banana
acetic acid + 1-octanol = orange
salicylic acid + methanol = wintergreen

13-1 Simple Organic Compounds

New Science Words

organic compounds
hydrocarbon
saturated hydrocarbons
unsaturated hydrocarbons
isomers

Objectives

▶ Describe structures of organic compounds and explain why carbon forms so many compounds.
▶ Distinguish between saturated and unsaturated hydrocarbons.
▶ Identify isomers of organic compounds.

Organic Compounds

How many covalent bonds can a carbon atom form?

What do cassette tapes and CDs, the paper and ink in this book, and you and your athletic shoes have in common? Each is made up mostly of substances called organic compounds. **Organic compounds** are compounds that contain the element carbon. More than 90 percent of all compounds are organic compounds.

You probably recognize that the word *organic* is related to *organism*. At one time, scientists assumed that only living organisms having a "vital force" could produce organic compounds. However, by 1830 scientists were making organic compounds artificially in laboratories. But scientists didn't change the name of these carbon-containing compounds. Today, most of the millions of different organic compounds that exist are synthetic. In fact, the manufacturing of organic compounds is one of world's largest industries. A chemical plant is shown in Figure 13-1 on the next page.

You may be wondering why there are so many organic compounds. There are several reasons, each related to the element carbon. First, a carbon atom has four electrons in its outer energy level. Recall that this electron arrangement means that each atom can form four covalent bonds with atoms of carbon or other elements. Four is a large number of bonds compared to the number of bonds that atoms of other elements can form. When carbon atoms bond to form the molecules of some organic compounds, they form long chains. These chains may

OPTIONS

Meeting Different Ability Levels

For Section 13-1, use the following **Teacher Resource Masters** depending upon individual students' needs.

◆ **Study Guide Master** for all students.
● **Reinforcement Master** for students of average and above average ability levels.
▲ **Enrichment Master** for above average students.

Additional Teacher Resource Package masters are listed in the OPTIONS box throughout the section. The additional masters are appropriate for all students.

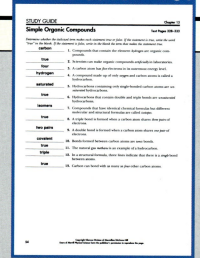

◆ **STUDY GUIDE** 54

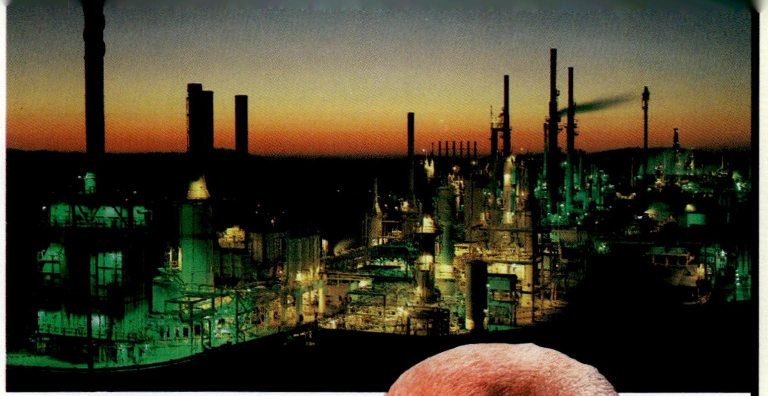

Figure 13-1. Many useful organic compounds are made in petrochemical plants like this one.

be continuous or branched. In other compounds the carbon atoms form closed rings. Molecules of organic compounds may contain from one to several thousand carbon atoms.

Second, a carbon atom can form a single, double, or triple bond with another carbon atom. There also can be many different arrangements of single, double, and triple bonds between carbon atoms. Each arrangement forms a molecule of a different organic compound. Finally, a carbon atom can bond with atoms of many other elements, such as hydrogen, oxygen, nitrogen, and chlorine. Carbon forms an enormous number of compounds with hydrogen alone. A compound made up of only carbon and hydrogen atoms is called a **hydrocarbon.** You can learn a lot about other organic compounds by studying hydrocarbons.

Hydrocarbons

Does the furnace, stove, or water heater in your home burn natural gas? Almost all the natural gas people use for these purposes is the hydrocarbon methane. The chemical formula of methane is CH_4. There are two other ways to represent methane. The structural formula in Figure 13-3 shows how the atoms are arranged in a molecule.

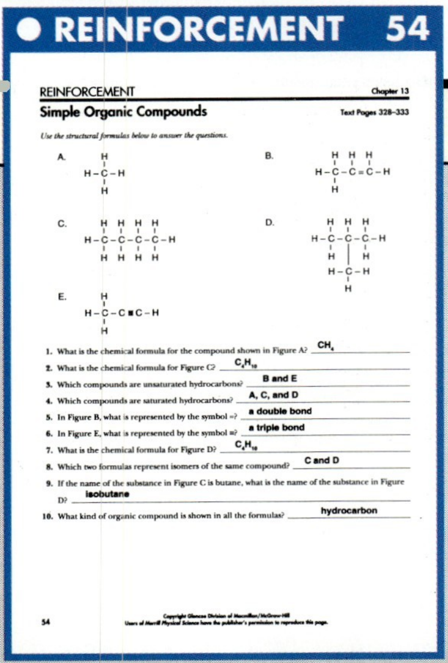

Figure 13-2. Natural pigments like the color of this flamingo are organic compounds.

Figure 13-3. Natural gas is mostly methane, CH_4.

methane
CH_4

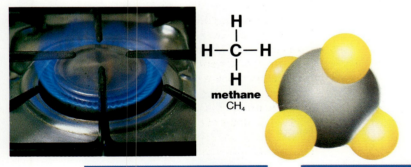

● **REINFORCEMENT** 54

▲ **ENRICHMENT** 54

REINFORCEMENT   Chapter 13
Simple Organic Compounds   Text Pages 328–333

ENRICHMENT   Chapter 13
Simple Organic Compounds   Text Pages 328–333
ISOMERS

TYING TO PREVIOUS KNOWLEDGE: There are both expensive and inexpensive perfumes. Ask your class what they think the difference is. Some fine perfumes are still made from natural ingredients, such as oil extracted from rose petals. Inexpensive perfumes usually use synthetic esters to imitate the natural esters (oils).

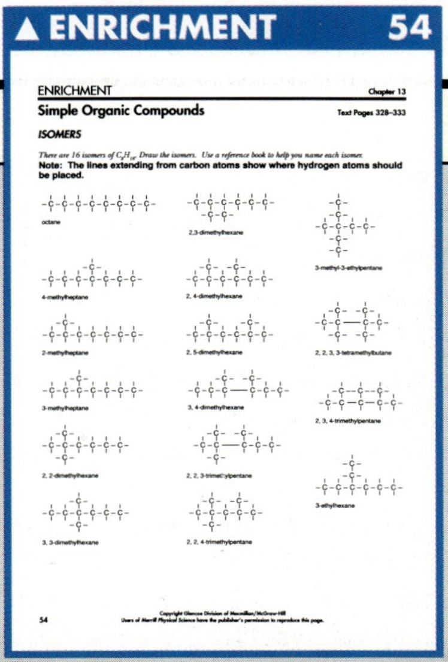

OBJECTIVES AND SCIENCE WORDS: Have students review the objectives and science words to become familiar with this section.

2 TEACH

Key Concepts are highlighted.

CONCEPT DEVELOPMENT

▶ Ask students to think about organic chemicals that they have used since they awoke this morning.

▶ Discuss with the class some of the common medicines that they use or see people use each day. Point out that knowledge of your own body chemistry can help you lead a healthier life.

▶ Ask students what is used as a source of raw materials to make organic chemicals. Petroleum is a complex mixture of organic compounds that are used as building blocks for other organic chemicals.

▶ Show a ball-and-stick model of methane, ethane, propane, and butane. Point out the structural similarities in a homologous series such as the alkanes.

▶ Bring to class a small propane torch commonly used by plumbers, a butane lighter, and a methane-fired Bunsen burner. Point out that the small molecular masses of these fuels result in their being gases at room temperature. Butane is a liquid in the lighter only because it is under pressure. Intermolecular forces are much weaker in small hydrocarbons than in water, which has a similar molecular mass but also has polar attractions.

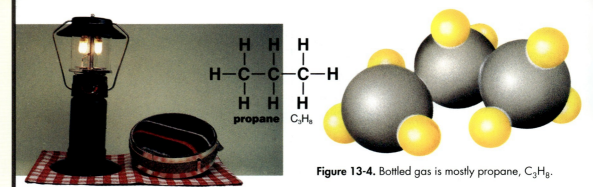

Figure 13-4. Bottled gas is mostly propane, C_3H_8.

MINI-Lab

What structures can octane have?

Octane, C_8H_{18}, is a hydrocarbon in gasoline. Using gum drops for carbon atoms, raisins for hydrogen atoms, and toothpicks for bonds that join the "atoms," make a model of one possible structure of octane. Each carbon atom can have four bonds and each hydrogen atom one bond. Compare the structure of your model to those of your classmates.

Each line between atoms represents a single covalent bond. As you recall, a covalent bond is formed when two atoms share a pair of electrons. The space-filling model in Figure 13-3 shows the relative volumes of the electron clouds in the molecule.

Methane and other hydrocarbons account for more than 90 percent of the energy sources used in homes, schools, industry, and transportation. Hydrocarbons are also important in manufacturing almost all the organic compounds used in products ranging from fertilizers to skateboards.

Some stoves, most outdoor grills, and hot-air balloons burn the bottled gas propane, another hydrocarbon. Its chemical formula is C_3H_8. Look at Figure 13-4. How many

Table 13-1

SOME HYDROCARBONS		
Name	**Chemical Formula**	**Structural Formula**
Methane	CH_4	H–C–H with H above and below
Ethane	C_2H_6	H–C–C–H
Propane	C_3H_8	H–C–C–C–H
Butane	C_4H_{10}	H–C–C–C–C–H
Pentane	C_5H_{12}	H–C–C–C–C–C–H

Octane has 18 isomers. Shown here are the carbon chains for the isomers.

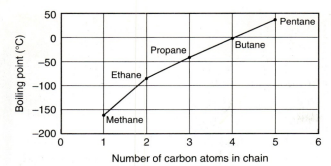

Figure 13-5. Boiling Points of Hydrocarbons in Natural Gas

atoms of each element are in a molecule of propane? How many covalent bonds are in each molecule?

In some hydrocarbons, the carbon atoms are joined by single covalent bonds. Hydrocarbons containing single-bonded carbon atoms are called **saturated hydrocarbons.** The carbon atoms in a molecule of propane are bonded by single covalent bonds. Propane is a saturated hydrocarbon. As you can see, the carbon atoms in propane seem to form a short chain. Propane is a member of a group of saturated hydrocarbons in which the carbon atoms form chains. Table 13-1 lists methane, propane, and three other similar hydrocarbons. Notice how each carbon atom appears to be a link in the chain within the molecule. Figure 13-5 shows a graph of the boiling points of these hydrocarbons. What happens to the boiling point as the number of carbon atoms in the chain increases?

Do you like bananas? They are among the many fruits and vegetables that are often ripened with the help of ethylene. Ethylene is the common name of the hydrocarbon ethene, C_2H_4. Did you ever watch a welder using an acetylene torch? Acetylene is the common name of the hydrocarbon ethyne, C_2H_2. Look at the structural formulas for ethene and ethyne. The double lines between the carbon atoms in ethene represent a double covalent bond. A double covalent bond is the sharing of two pairs of electrons—in other words, four electrons. The three lines in ethyne represent a triple covalent bond. How many pairs of electrons are shared in a triple covalent bond?

Hydrocarbons such as ethene and ethyne that contain double or triple bonds between carbon atoms are called **unsaturated hydrocarbons.** Remember that *saturated*

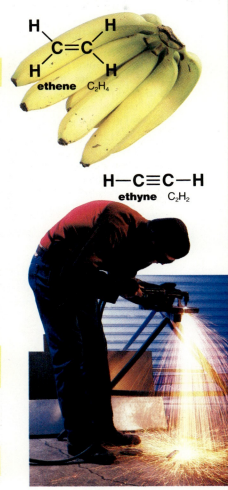

ethene C_2H_4

ethyne C_2H_2

13-1   SIMPLE ORGANIC COMPOUNDS   **331**

OPTIONS

INQUIRY QUESTIONS

▶ The general formula for saturated hydrocarbons is C_nH_{2n+2}. Determine the formulas for pentane, which has five carbon atoms, and hexane, which has six. C_5H_{12}, C_6H_{14}.

▶ Write a formula for a nine-carbon saturated hydrocarbon. C_9H_{20}

▶ Which compound—pentane, hexane, or octane—would have the highest boiling point? Give a reason. *octane, because it has the greatest molecular mass*

▶ Write the formulas for ethane, ethene, and ethyne. C_2H_6, C_2H_4, C_2H_2

PROGRAM RESOURCES

From the **Teacher Resource Package** use:
Activity Worksheets, page 108, Mini-Lab: What structures can octane have?
Transparency Masters, pages 49-50, Hydrocarbon Structure.
Use **Color Transparency** number 25, Hydrocarbon Structure.

REVEALING MISCONCEPTIONS

▶ Emphasize to students that not all compounds that contain carbon are classified as organic. The oxides of carbon, CO and CO_2, cyanides, and carbonates are considered inorganic.

CONCEPT DEVELOPMENT

▶ The use of models is very helpful for the student. Ask student volunteers to construct models of each compound mentioned in the text.

▶ Bring to class examples of saturated and unsaturated fats. Have students read the labels on butter, margarine, solid vegetable shortening, and liquid cooking oils. Discuss the dietary recommendations of health organizations such as the cancer, diabetes, and heart societies. If there is little knowledge among students about this important topic, make research assignments.

▶ **Demonstration:** Bromine bonds to hydrocarbons having double bonds. You can show the presence and reactivity of double bonds by adding a few mL of bromine water to cyclohexene in a test tube. Stopper and shake. Use cyclohexane as a comparison. **CAUTION:** *Hydrocarbons are both flammable and toxic.* Repeat this test for unsaturation by using various fats and oils.

STUDENT TEXT QUESTIONS

▶ Page 331, paragraph 1: **How many atoms of each element are there in a molecule of propane?** *8 hydrogen, 3 carbon.* **How many covalent bonds are in each molecule?** *10*

▶ Page 331, paragraph 2: **What happens to the boiling points of hydrocarbons as the number of carbon atoms in the chain increases?** *The boiling points become higher.*

▶ Page 331, paragraph 3: **How many pairs of electrons are shared in a triple covalent bond?** *three (six electrons total)*

PROBLEM SOLVING

Think Critically: The avocado was already overripe, so the ripening process continued until it rotted. Ethylene gas given off by the overripe avocado was trapped in the bag, causing the tomatoes to ripen more rapidly than expected.

CONCEPT DEVELOPMENT

▶ Students may want to know that most organic compounds have isomers. The unbranched isomers have higher melting and boiling points than highly branched isomers.

TEACHER F.Y.I.

▶ Nonane has 35 possible isomers, and decane has 75 isomers.

CHECK FOR UNDERSTANDING

Use the Mini Quiz to check for understanding.

MINI QUIZ

Use the Mini Quiz to check students' recall of chapter content.

1 Organic compounds contain the element _____ . *carbon*

2 How many bonds do carbon atoms form? *four*

3 What do you call a compound that is made of only carbon and hydrogen atoms? *hydrocarbon*

4 Hydrocarbons that contain only single-bonded carbon atoms are _____ . *saturated*

5 Unsaturated hydrocarbons contain what kinds of bonds between carbon atoms? *double or triple*

6 Compounds that have identical chemical formulas but different molecular structures are called _____ . *isomers*

RETEACH

On a handout, draw structural formulas for several hydrocarbons. Have students write the molecular formula for each and decide if it is a saturated or unsaturated hydrocarbon.

EXTENSION

For students who have mastered this section, use the **Reinforcement** and **Enrichment** masters or other OPTIONS provided.

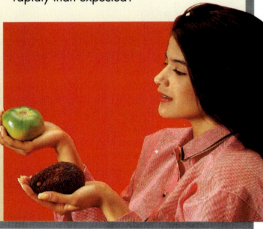

PROBLEM SOLVING

The Case of the Overripe Tomatoes

Maria helped out at home by preparing dinner on Mondays and Thursdays. She was also responsible for buying any groceries needed to prepare the meals. One Monday Maria bought an overripe avocado to use for guacamole sauce that evening and some green tomatoes to use for a salad on Thursday. She thought the tomatoes would be juicy but still firm by Thursday evening. The grocery clerk put the avocado and tomatoes in a brown paper bag.

When Maria arrived at home, her father decided to take the family out to dinner. So she didn't have to prepare dinner that evening.

On Thursday, Maria opened the paper bag. The avocado was rotten, and the tomatoes were overripe—not firm as she had expected. Maria knew that fruits give off ethylene gas as they ripen. But the tomatoes ripened more quickly than they should have.

Think Critically: Why did the avocado rot? What caused the tomatoes to ripen more rapidly than expected?

hydrocarbons contain only single bonds. As you will read in a later section, fats and oils can also be classified as unsaturated or saturated because parts of their molecules are similar to hydrocarbon molecules.

Isomers

Perhaps you have seen or know about butane, a gas sometimes burned in camping stoves and lighters. The chemical formula of butane is C_4H_{10}. Another hydrocarbon also has the same chemical formula as butane. How can this be? The answer lies in the arrangement of the four carbon atoms. Look at Figure 13-6. In a molecule of butane, the carbon atoms form a continuous chain. The carbon chain of isobutane is branched. The arrangement of carbon atoms in each compound changes the shape of the molecule. Isobutane and butane are isomers.

OPTIONS

INQUIRY QUESTIONS

▶ Extend your knowledge of hydrocarbons by predicting the shape of a cyclobutane molecule. *It is square.*

▶ Explain why a double bond is expected to be stronger than a single bond. *The electron cloud created by four electrons has a greater attraction for the two nuclei.*

▶ What can you infer about the length of a double bond when compared to a single bond? *The double bond is shorter because the extra electrons attract the nuclei closer together.*

PROGRAM RESOURCES

From the **Teacher Resource Package** use:

Cross-Curricular Connections, page 19, How Fattening Is Your Food?

Activity Worksheets, page 5, Flex Your Brain.

Table 13-2

PROPERTIES OF BUTANE ISOMERS

	Butane	Isobutane
Description	Colorless gas	Colorless gas
Density	0.6 kg/L	0.6 kg/L
Melting point	−138°C	−160°C
Boiling point	−0.5°C	−12°C

Isomers are compounds that have identical chemical formulas but different molecular structures and shapes. There are thousands of isomers among the hydrocarbons. Table 13-2 summarizes several properties of the two isomers of butane. As you can see, the structure of an isomer does affect some of the compound's properties.

(6)

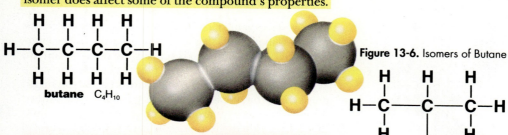

butane C_4H_{10}

Figure 13-6. Isomers of Butane

isobutane
C_4H_{10}

SECTION REVIEW

1. Why can carbon form so many organic compounds?
2. Compare and contrast ethane, ethene, and ethyne.
3. How is an unsaturated hydrocarbon different from a saturated hydrocarbon?
4. **Apply:** Cyclopropane is a saturated hydrocarbon containing three carbon atoms. In this compound, each carbon atom is bonded to two other carbon atoms. Draw its structural formula. Are cyclopropane and propane isomers? Explain.

☑ Making and Using Graphs

Make a graph of Table 13-1. For each compound, plot the number of carbon atoms on one axis and the number of hydrogen atoms on the other axis. Use the graph to predict the formula of hexane, which has six carbon atoms. If you need help, refer to Making and Using Graphs in the **Skill Handbook** on page 686.

Skill Builder

Skill Builder

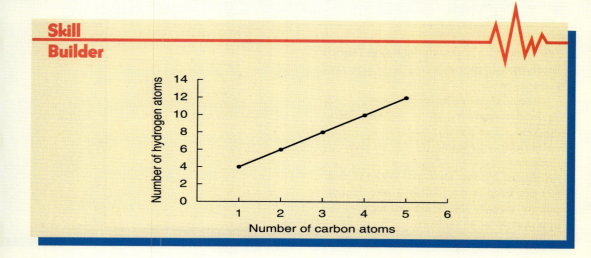

CONCEPT DEVELOPMENT

▶ **Demonstration:** The reactivity of the triple bond can be shown by producing acetylene, ethyne. Place a piece of calcium carbide in water and collect gas by water displacement in an inverted test tube. Hold the tube with tongs, keeping the mouth of the test tube down, and ignite. **CAUTION:** *The gas will flame and may pop.*

CROSS CURRICULUM

▶ **Art:** Have students use the molecular models that they have made to build a large mobile.

3 CLOSE

▶ Ask questions 1-3 and the **Apply** Question in the Section Review.

❓ FLEX Your Brain

Use the Flex Your Brain activity to have students explore ORGANIC COMPOUNDS.

SECTION REVIEW ANSWERS

1. Carbon can form four covalent bonds with other atoms, including other carbon atoms. Thus carbon atoms can form long, branched chains. Also, the bonds can be single, double, or triple.

2. The three compounds are hydrocarbons, each containing two carbon atoms. Ethane is a saturated hydrocarbon; ethene and ethyne are unsaturated hydrocarbons. Ethene contains a double covalent bond and ethyne contains a triple covalent bond.

3. A saturated hydrocarbon contains only single bonds between carbon atoms. An unsaturated hydrocarbon contains one or more double or triple bonds between carbon atoms.

4. Apply:

Cyclopropane, C_3H_6, is not an isomer of propane, C_3H_8, because it has a different chemical formula.

PREPARATION

SECTION BACKGROUND

▶ The benzene ring possesses great stability because it has a system of delocalized electrons.

▶ Aromatic compounds are economically important to many chemical industries including rubber, plastics, fibers, explosives, paint, and petroleum.

▶ Substituted hydrocarbons are generally more reactive than unsubstituted compounds. A halogen derivative has a halogen substituted for a hydrogen atom.

▶ Many organic compounds contain oxygen. Alcohols, ethers, aldehydes, ketones, carboxylic acids, and esters are classifications of oxygen-containing organic chemicals.

▶ The symbol R– represents any hydrocarbon radical. Thus R–OH is the general formula for alcohols, and R–COOH is the general formula for organic acids.

PREPLANNING

▶ For Activity 13-1, prepare a 0.01M solution of potassium permanganate, and a 6.0M solution of sodium hydroxide. Allow the base solution to cool overnight before using.

1 MOTIVATE

▶ Have students turn ahead to the Unit 5 opener on pages 376-377. Stinging insects, such as wasps and ants, are well known. Ask students if they know what causes the pain when they get stung. In some cases, it is formic acid, HCOOH, the simplest organic acid. Now that the class knows that it is an acid, ask for suggestions on how to counteract the venom. Have them explain why a baking soda paste and household ammonia are effective treatments.

New Science Words

aromatic compound
substituted hydrocarbon
alcohol

Objectives

▶ Describe characteristics of aromatic compounds.
▶ Classify groups of organic compounds as substituted hydrocarbons.

Aromatic Compounds

Do you like vanilla ice cream or vanilla yogurt? Perhaps you know that vanilla flavor, like many flavors, is due largely to smell. What you taste is actually the smell of vanillin, the compound in vanilla extract that produces the vanilla flavor. Another word for smell is aroma. So you might guess that aromatic compounds are smelly—and indeed most of them are. An **aromatic compound** is a compound that contains the benzene ring structure. Look at a model of benzene, C_6H_6, and its structural formula, Figure 13-8. As you can see, the benzene molecule has six carbon atoms bonded into a ring. The electrons in the three double bonds and three single bonds that form the ring are actually shared by all six carbon atoms in the ring. The sharing of these electrons causes the benzene molecule to be very stable. Because many compounds contain this stable ring structure, it is given a special symbol, as shown in (c).

Knowing the structure of benzene can help you to picture hundreds of different aromatic organic compounds.

Figure 13-7. Vanilla extract comes from the dried pod of the vanilla orchid, shown above.

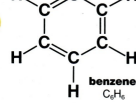 

Figure 13-8. Benzene, C_6H_6, can be represented by (a) a space-filling model, (b) a structural formula, or (c) the benzene ring symbol.

benzene
C_6H_6

OPTIONS

Meeting Different Ability Levels

For Section 13-2, use the following **Teacher Resource Masters** depending upon individual students' needs.

◆ **Study Guide Master** for all students.
● **Reinforcement Master** for students of average and above average ability levels.
▲ **Enrichment Master** for above average students.

Additional Teacher Resource Package masters are listed in the OPTIONS box throughout the section. The additional masters are appropriate for all students.

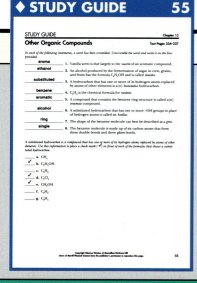

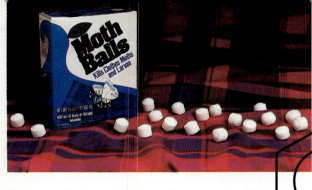

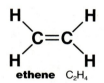

Figure 13-9. Moth crystals are naphthalene.

naphthalene
$C_{10}H_8$

One example is naphthalene. Can you recognize the odor of moth crystals? Moth crystals are naphthalene, as shown in Figure 13-9. Notice that naphthalene is made up of two ring structures.

Substituted Hydrocarbons

Usually, a cheeseburger is a hamburger covered with melted American cheese and served on a bun. However, you can make a cheeseburger with Swiss cheese and serve it on slices of bread. If you ate this cheeseburger, you would notice how the substitutions affect the taste.

Chemists make similar changes to hydrocarbons. These changes produce compounds called substituted hydrocarbons. ==A **substituted hydrocarbon** has one or more of its hydrogen atoms replaced by atoms of other elements.==

❸ For example, a compound used in dry cleaning, tetrachloroethene, C_2Cl_4, is a substituted hydrocarbon. The prefix *tetra-* means "four," and *chloro-* refers to chlorine. Figure 13-10 shows how C_2Cl_4 is formed when four chlorine atoms replace the hydrogen atoms in ethene, C_2H_4.

Have you ever used rubbing alcohol to soothe aching muscles after too much exercise? Did you know you were using a substituted hydrocarbon? Alcohols are an important group of organic compounds. ==An **alcohol**❹ is formed when –OH groups replace one or more hydrogen atoms in a hydrocarbon,== as shown in Figure 13-11. Ethanol, C_2H_5OH, is an alcohol produced by the fermentation of sugar in corn and other grains, and in many fruits. Alcoholic beverages contain ethanol. As you will learn in the next section, this alcohol is sometimes added

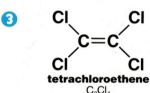

ethene C_2H_4

tetrachloroethene C_2Cl_4

Figure 13-10. Tetrachloroethene is a substituted hydrocarbon.

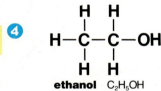

ethanol C_2H_5OH

Figure 13-11. Ethanol is one of many alcohols.

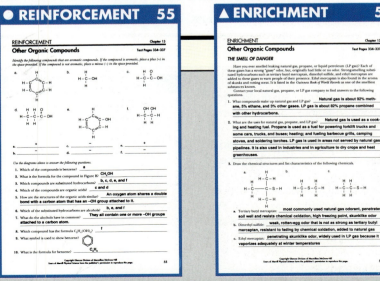
335

TYING TO PREVIOUS KNOWLEDGE: Have students recall and discuss when they have seen explosives such as TNT detonated on TV or in movies. Make a model of benzene. Then, in front of the class, remove a hydrogen atom and replace it with a methyl, $-CH_3$, group. Now you have toluene. Replace the two hydrogens on either side of the methyl group with two nitro, $-NO_2$, groups. Remove the hydrogen opposite the methyl and replace it with a third nitro group. You now have a model of trinitrotoluene, TNT.

OBJECTIVES AND SCIENCE WORDS: Have students review the objectives and science words to become familiar with this section.

2 TEACH

Key Concepts are highlighted.

CONCEPT DEVELOPMENT

▶ Students may want to know that alcohols are defined as poisons because they adversely affect enzyme systems that regulate the speed of chemical reactions. Alcohol slows down the brain's chemistry.

CHECK FOR UNDERSTANDING

Use the Mini Quiz to check for understanding.

MINI QUIZ

Use the Mini Quiz to check students' recall of chapter content.

❶ A compound that contains a benzene ring is classified as a(n) _____ compound. *aromatic*

❷ Why is the benzene molecule very stable? *Electrons are shared by all six carbon atoms.*

❸ Which element has been replaced in a substituted hydrocarbon? *hydrogen*

❹ When a hydrogen atom is replaced with an –OH group, the compound is called a(n) _____ . *alcohol*

3 CLOSE

▶ Ask questions 1-2 and the **Apply** Question in the Section Review.

SECTION REVIEW ANSWERS

1. All aromatic compounds contain the benzene ring.

2. (a) Chlorine atoms have replaced the hydrogen atoms in a hydrocarbon; (b) an −OH group has replaced a hydrogen atom in a hydrocarbon; (c) a −COOH group has replaced a hydrogen atom in a hydrocarbon.

3. Apply: A poisonous substance is added to ethanol to cause someone trying to drink it to become ill.

Skill Builder

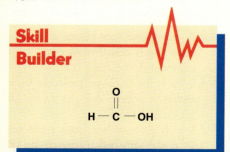

Table 13-3

COMMON ALCOHOLS					
		Methanol	Ethanol	Isopropyl alcohol (rubbing alcohol)	Phenol
		$H-C-OH$ (with H above and below C)	$H-C-C-OH$	$H-C-C-C-H$ (with OH on middle C)	(benzene ring)−OH
Uses	Fuel	✓	✓		
	Cleaner	✓	✓	✓	
	Disinfectant		✓	✓	✓
	Manufacturing chemicals	✓		✓	✓

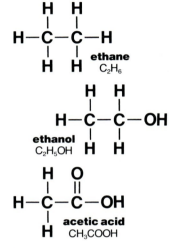

Figure 13-12. The structures of these compounds are similar.

to gasoline. Ethanol is also a good cleaning fluid because it can dissolve substances that don't dissolve in water. Denatured alcohol is a mixture of ethanol and a poisonous substance such as methanol. It is used as a solvent. Several alcohols are listed in Table 13-3.

You may recall that vinegar contains acetic acid. Acetic acid is an example of a compound called an organic acid. Many fruit juices contain similar organic acids. Look at Figure 13-12. The structures of ethane, ethanol, and acetic acid are very similar. Do you see how this similarity indicates that acetic acid is a substituted hydrocarbon? Substituted hydrocarbons account for millions of organic compounds.

SECTION REVIEW

1. What do all aromatic compounds have in common?
2. How is each of the following a substituted hydrocarbon: (a) tetrachloroethene, (b) ethanol, (c) acetic acid?
3. **Apply:** Why is ethanol intended for use as a solvent denatured by the addition of a poisonous substance?

Skill Builder

☑ **Interpreting Scientific Illustrations**

Formic acid, HCOOH, is the simplest organic acid. Draw its structural formula by referring to Figure 13-12. If you need help, refer to Interpreting Scientific Illustrations in the **Skill Handbook** on page 683.

OPTIONS

INQUIRY QUESTIONS

▶ Write the chemical formula for trichloromethane, commonly called chloroform. $CHCl_3$

▶ Write a formula for methanol. Methyl alcohol or wood alcohol are common names. CH_3OH

▶ When −COOH is substituted for a hydrogen atom, an organic acid forms. Write the formula for ethanoic acid, also known as acetic acid and vinegar. CH_3COOH

PROGRAM RESOURCES

From the **Teacher Resource Package** use:

Technology, pages 13-14, Making Paper Less Perishable.

Critical Thinking /Problem Solving, page 19, Reformulated Gasoline.

ACTIVITY 13-1
Alcohols and Organic Acids

Problem: *What new compound can be formed from an alcohol?*

Materials

- test tube and stopper
- 1 mL 0.01 *M* potassium permanganate solution
- 1 mL 6 *M* sodium hydroxide solution
- 3 drops of ethanol
- goggles
- apron

Procedure

1. Pour 1 mL of 0.01 *M* potassium permanganate solution and 1 mL of 6 *M* sodium hydroxide solution into a test tube. **CAUTION:** *Handle both of these chemicals with care; immediately flush any spill with water.*
2. Add three drops of ethanol to the test tube.
3. Stopper the test tube and gently shake it for one minute. Observe and record any changes you notice in the tube for the next five minutes.

Data and Observations   Sample Data

Changes in Mixture
Within a few seconds the mixture should change from purple to green. Over the next few minutes the solution should turn brown.

Analyze

1. What is the structural formula for ethanol?
2. What part of a molecule identifies a compound as an alcohol?
3. What part of a molecule identifies a compound as an organic acid?

Conclude and Apply

4. What evidence did you observe of a chemical change taking place in the test tube?
5. In the presence of potassium permanganate, an alcohol may undergo a chemical change into an acid. If the alcohol used is ethanol, what would you predict to be the formula of the acid produced?
6. The acid from ethanol is found in a common household product. What is the acid's name? In what common household product is the acid found?

13-2   OTHER ORGANIC COMPOUNDS   **337**

ANSWERS TO QUESTIONS

1.

2. the hydroxyl group, –OH
3. the carboxylic acid group, –COOH
4. The color changes from purple to green to brown.

5.

6. acetic acid; in vinegar

PREPARATION

SECTION BACKGROUND

▶ Synfuels or synthetic fuels are derived from organic sources that are more difficult to convert or environmentally less acceptable than traditional fuels. Grains, sugars, and wood can produce ethanol and methanol. Tar sands in Canada, oil shales in the western U.S., and coal can be used to produce synthetic fuels.

1 MOTIVATE

▶ **Demonstration:** Place a small amount of ethanol in an evaporating dish. Slowly add enough saturated calcium acetate solution to cause the alcohol to solidify. Show the class the jellied alcohol, then darken the room and ignite it. **CAUTION:** *Keep flammable materials clear.* Point out that the flame is burning clean and blue in color. This demonstration shows the class one way that fuels can be modified; burning solids is safer than burning liquids.

TYING TO PREVIOUS KNOWLEDGE: Ask students what a windmill is and where they have seen windmills used. Experimental windmill farms to generate electricity have been built in California. Windmills are still used today to pump water for animals in remote areas of farms and ranches. These are alternative sources of energy.

OBJECTIVES AND SCIENCE WORDS: Have students review the objectives and science words to become familiar with this section.

 **13-3 Alternative Sources of Energy**

New Science Words

biomass
biogas
energy farming
gasohol

Objectives

▶ Describe the role of biomass as a source of two fuels for increasing our energy supply.
▶ Analyze the positive and negative effects of the widespread use of ethanol and gasohol.

Why Not New Fuels?

What fuels have you used today? Probably the main sources of energy you use are natural gas, coal, or petroleum. But did you know that most people in the world rely on biomass for their energy supply? **Biomass refers to all animal and plant material, both dead and alive.** Wood, leaves, animal and human wastes, and food waste are all biomass.

What is the composition of biomass?

If plant and animal wastes are allowed to rot in the absence of air, bacteria break down the wastes to produce biogas. **Biogas is mainly methane, just like natural gas.** People in rural areas in Third World countries cook, heat their homes, and generate electricity with biogas. China has some four million factories that produce biogas. This fuel is such a promising source of additional energy supplies that proposals have been made for energy farming. **Energy farming involves growing plants for use as fuel.** One proposal is to use the troublesome water hyacinth that clogs waterways.

338 ORGANIC AND BIOLOGICAL COMPOUNDS

OPTIONS

Meeting Different Ability Levels

For Section 13-3, use the following **Teacher Resource Masters** depending upon individual students' needs.

◆ **Study Guide Master** for all students.
● **Reinforcement Master** for students of average and above average ability levels.
▲ **Enrichment Master** for above average students.

◆ **STUDY GUIDE** 56

STUDY GUIDE — Chapter 13
Alternative Sources of Energy — Text Pages 338–339

Solve the following crossword puzzle by using the clues provided.

Across
1. compound with benzene ring structure
2. type of bonds in organic compounds
6. shape formed by a benzene molecule
8. compound of only carbon and hydrogen
11. gas produced when bacteria break down plant and animal wastes in the absence of oxygen
12. prefix used for isomers
13. type of bond in saturated hydrocarbons
15. hydrocarbon with one or more hydrogen atoms replaced by atoms of other elements
17. hydrocarbons with double or triple bonds
19. Aromatic compounds contain this ring
20. hydrocarbons with only single bonds

Down
1. organic substance with an OH group
2. element in all organic compounds
3. growing of plants for use as fuels (2 words)
4. kind of bond formed when three pairs of electrons are shared
5. compounds with identical chemical formulas but different molecular structures
7. fuel made from ethanol and petroleum
9. all plant and animal material
10. name for a carbon-containing compound
14. natural gas with the formula CH_4
16. kind of bond formed when two pairs of electrons are shared
18. prefix meaning four

Did you ever see a sign like the one to the right? **Gasohol** is a combination of ethanol and gasoline. If you have ridden in a car fueled with gasohol, you have used a product of biomass. Recall that fermentation produces the ethanol found in alcoholic beverages. The same process of fermentation is also used with a variety of grains and fruits to produce ethanol for use as a fuel. Pure ethanol can be used in cars if the engines are modified slightly. Car engines do not have to be modified to burn gasohol. When gasoline is in short supply because of a lack of petroleum, gasohol finds wider use. Is gasohol the answer to our periodic shortages of petroleum?

At first, biogas and gasohol seem like ideal energy sources. Yet producing them commercially results in numerous environmental problems. Among these are disturbing the ecosystem, fertilizer runoff, erosion, and air pollution. The decision for or against large-scale production of biogas and gasohol may not be an easy one.

Clearly the conversion of biomass to easily handled fuels such as methane and ethanol is an interesting possibility for supplying part of our energy needs. But, large-scale tests of energy production from biomass have not yet been carried out in the United States, and energy farming may have as yet unknown effects on our environment.

EcoTip

If you have a garden, grow beans or peas between other plants. The peas and beans supply the soil with nitrogen which is needed by other plants.

SECTION REVIEW

1. In what two major ways is biomass used as a source of fuels?
2. What are the main pros, cons, and concerns related to the use of ethanol in gasohol?

You Decide!

Increasing the production and use of both biogas and gasohol may help the United States to cope with petroleum shortages. Should government agencies encourage the production of these fuels? Why or why not?

SCIENCE & SOCIETY

339

PREPARATION

SECTION BACKGROUND

▶ Approximately one-half of our non-water mass consists of proteins. These form muscle, cartilage, and tendons. One-half of the protein in the human body is used as biological catalysts called enzymes.

▶ Nucleic acids are polymers of nucleotides. The nucleotide is composed of three parts—a nitrogen base, a sugar, and a phosphate group.

▶ The carbohydrates glycogen, starch, and cellulose differ simply in the way glucose monomers are linked together. The process of breaking down carbohydrates into CO_2 and H_2O is the chief energy source of an organism.

▶ Lipids can be divided into different groups. One group is fats which are esters formed from glycerol and fatty acids. Fatty acids are carboxylic acids with 12 to 20 carbon atoms in the chain. Steroids are another group of lipids that contain a tetracyclic ring system. Some vitamins are lipids and form another group. Vitamins aid enzyme reactions.

PREPLANNING

▶ To prepare for Activity 13-2, you will need index cards and paper clips. Crayons or colored markers can be used if available.

1 MOTIVATE

▶ **Demonstration:** Before class, prepare a 70-cm-long chain of paper clips and place it in a small box with one end of the chain clipped at the edge of the box. In class, add loose paper clips, monomers, to the same box. Cover the box with your hand and gently shake to simulate a polymerization reaction. Uncover the box and pull out the previously connected paper clips to the amazement of your students.

New Science Words

polymers
proteins
nucleic acids
carbohydrates
lipids

Objectives

▶ Describe the formation of polymers and discuss their importance as biological compounds.
▶ Compare and contrast proteins, nucleic acids, carbohydrates, and lipids.

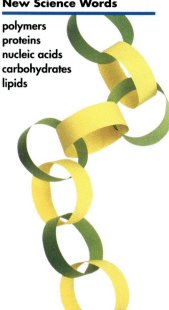

Proteins

Did you ever loop together strips of paper to make paper chains for decorations? Have you ever strung paper clips together as a prank? Both a paper chain and a string of paper clips are very much like polymers. **Polymers are huge molecules made of many smaller organic molecules that have formed new bonds and linked together. The smaller molecules are called monomers.** Monomers are usually very similar in size and structure. You can picture a monomer as an individual loop of paper or an individual paper clip. The photograph on the left shows this model of a polymer. As you will see in Chapter 14, plastics are polymers. Many of the important biological compounds in your body also are polymers. Among them are the proteins.

Proteins make up many of the tissues in your body, such as muscles and tendons, as well as your hair and fingernails. A protein in your blood called hemoglobin carries oxygen, Figure 13-13. The enzymes that control chemical reactions in your body are proteins. In fact, proteins account for 15 percent of your weight. That's about half the weight of all materials other than water in your body.

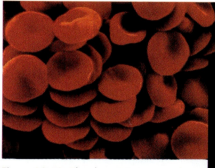

Figure 13-13. Blood contains a complex protein called hemoglobin.

OPTIONS

Meeting Different Ability Levels

For Section 13-4, use the following **Teacher Resource Masters** depending upon individual students' needs.

◆ **Study Guide Master** for all students.
● **Reinforcement Master** for students of average and above average ability levels.
▲ **Enrichment Master** for above average students.

Additional Teacher Resource Package masters are listed in the OPTIONS box throughout the section. The additional masters are appropriate for all students.

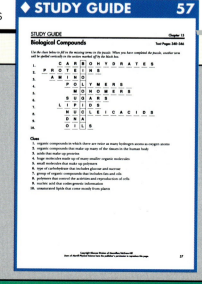

◆ **STUDY GUIDE** 57

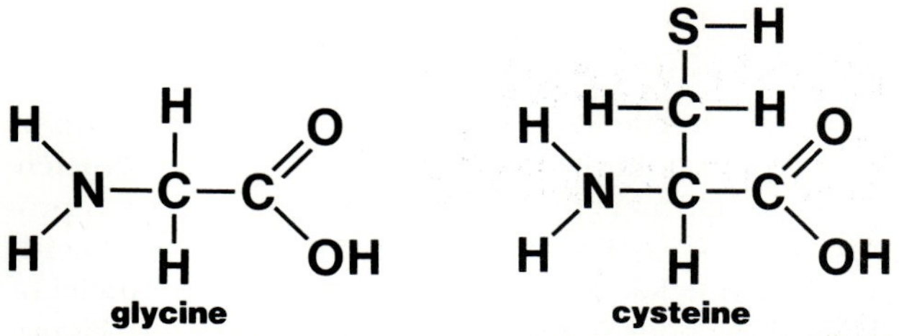

glycine   cysteine

Figure 13-14. Two Amino Acids

③ <mark>Proteins are polymers formed from organic compounds called amino acids.</mark> Even though there are millions of different proteins, there are only 20 common amino acids. Two amino acids are shown in Figure 13-14.

Notice that each molecule of an amino acid contains a –COOH group and a –NH_2 group. The –COOH group is called the carboxylic acid group. If you look again at Figure 13-12 on page 336, you'll see that the structure of this group appears also in acetic acid. The –NH_2 group is called the amine group. Both groups appear in every amino acid.

In a protein polymer, peptide bonds link together molecules of amino acids. Peptide bonds form when the amine group of one amino acid combines with the organic acid group of another amino acid. Look at Figure 13-16. You might think of the 20 amino acids as letters of an alphabet. Each protein is a word spelled with these letters. However, unlike English words, words in this alphabet may contain hundreds of letters. Actually, some proteins may contain thousands of amino acids.

Your body makes proteins from amino acids. The amino acids come from eating and digesting foods that contain proteins. Digestion breaks the protein polymers into monomers of amino acids, which your body uses to make new proteins.

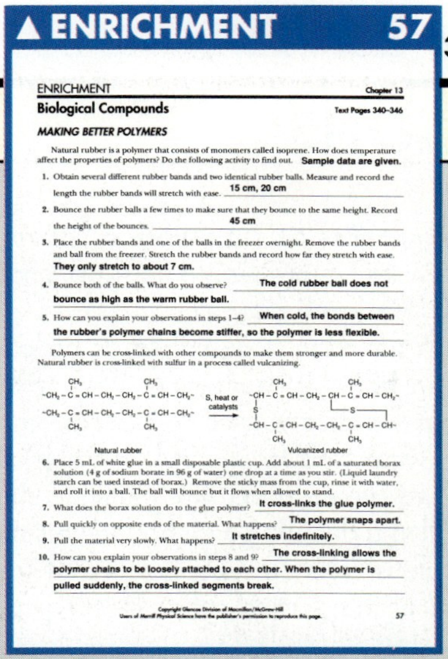

Figure 13-15. Some High-Protein Foods

Figure 13-16. The protein molecule contains many peptide bonds.

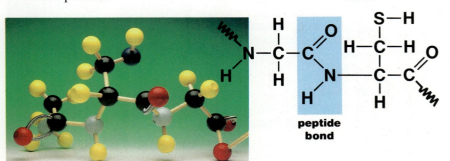

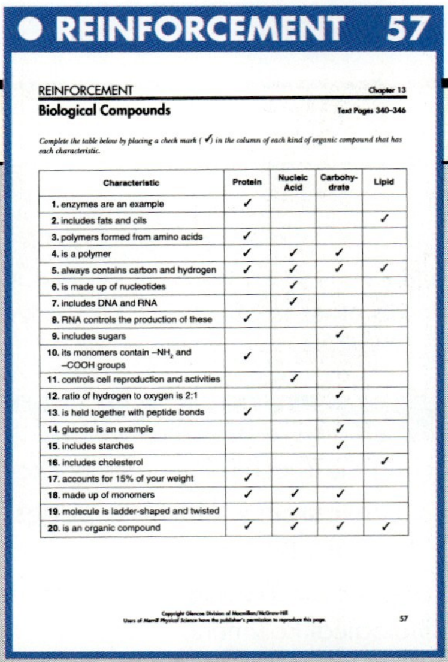

peptide bond

341

TYING TO PREVIOUS KNOWLEDGE: In the party supplies section of toy stores you can find a spray can of string confetti. This polymer can be shown to students by spraying a string from the can. A 100-g can will produce about 100 meters of polymer for about $2.00.

OBJECTIVES AND SCIENCE WORDS: Have students review the objectives and science words to become familiar with this section.

2 TEACH

Key Concepts are highlighted.

CONCEPT DEVELOPMENT

▶ **Demonstration:** Show students a polymer being formed by making nylon. Commercially available solutions of sebacoyl chloride and 1,6-diaminohexane are available from your science supplier. The two solutions are layered in a small beaker. Using forceps, pick up the center of the "film" that forms at the interface of the two liquids. Slowly pull the nylon string from the beaker and roll it up on a graduated cylinder that has been wrapped with a paper towel.

▶ **Demonstration:** Plastics are polymers and some are foamed by having gas blown into them. Place a small amount of acetone or alcohol in the bottom of a 600-mL beaker. Add to the solvent a large volume of the polystyrene foam "peanuts" used in shipping containers. Allow the acetone to evaporate overnight. A disc of solid polystyrene will remain.

TEACHER F.Y.I.

▶ Americans use 2.5 million plastic bottles every hour.

REVEALING MISCONCEPTIONS

▶ To many people, *polymer* is another name for plastic. Be certain students understand that plastic is only one of many kinds of polymers.

CROSS CURRICULUM

▶ **Language Arts:** Percy Lavon Julian (1899-1975) synthesized progesterone, testosterone, and cortisone. These are steroids. Have some students research medical uses of steroids, such as treatment of inflammation and estrogen replacement therapy during menopause. Other students could research effects of using steroids in sports and body building. All students should write reports documenting their findings. The school librarian should be advised in advance of this assignment.

CONCEPT DEVELOPMENT

▶ **Demonstration:** Nucleic acids are polymer chains that are cross linked. These cross links are somewhat like the rungs on a ladder. You can demonstrate cross linking by placing 5 mL of Elmer's white glue in a small disposable plastic cup. Add saturated borax solution, 4 g sodium borate in 96 mL water, dropwise as you stir the white glue. About 1 mL of borax solution will be required. A sticky ball will form. Remove it from the cup and rinse it with tap water. Roll it into a ball and bounce it. The borax cross links the polymer chains in the white glue to form a synthetic rubber.

▶ Point out to students the cross linking in DNA using the models pictured in Figure 13-17. In humans, cytosine pairs with thymine while adenine pairs with guanine to form the cross links. The genetic code is the order in which these bases occur.

Nucleic Acids

The nucleic acids are another important group of organic compounds that are necessary for life. **Nucleic acids are polymers that control the activities and reproduction of cells.** One kind of nucleic acid, deoxyribonucleic acid (DNA), is found in the nuclei of cells. DNA codes and stores genetic information. Figure 13-17 shows a model and the formula for a portion of the DNA polymer. It resembles a twisted ladder. Like other polymers, DNA is made up of monomers. With the genetic code, DNA controls the production of ribonucleic acid (RNA), another kind of nucleic acid. RNA, in turn, controls the production of proteins that will make new cells.

The monomers that make up DNA are called nucleotides. Each nucleotide looks like one-half of a ladder rung with an attached side piece. As you can see, each pair of nucleotides forms a rung on the ladder, while the side pieces give the ladder a little twist. Because the nucleotides may be made up of four different organic compounds, all the ladder rungs are not the same. Unless you're an identical twin, your DNA differs from that of every other person because the nucleotides and their locations are not the same in any two polymers.

Did You Know?

Rubber is an organic substance that was named because it could be used to rub out pencil marks.

What are nucleotides?

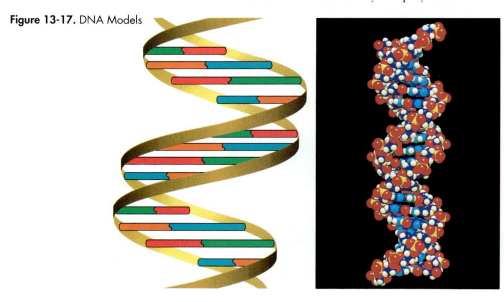

Figure 13-17. DNA Models

342   ORGANIC AND BIOLOGICAL COMPOUNDS

OPTIONS

INQUIRY QUESTIONS

▶ **What similarities exist between a colored paper chain and a protein?** *Both have small units (monomers) linked together.*

▶ **The DNA molecule is described as a double helix in biology courses. In your textbook, what words are used to describe this structure?** *twisted ladder*

▶ **When two amino acids link together, the bond is called a peptide bond, and the resulting molecule is called a dipeptide. What science word in this section refers to polypeptides?** *proteins*

▶ **Use the percentage value given in the text to calculate the amount of protein in a person whose mass is 50 kg (110 lb of weight).** *7.5 kg (16.5 lb)*

PROGRAM RESOURCES

From the **Teacher Resource Package** use:

Transparency Masters, pages 51-52, Biological Polymers.

Use **Color Transparency** number 26, Biological Polymers.

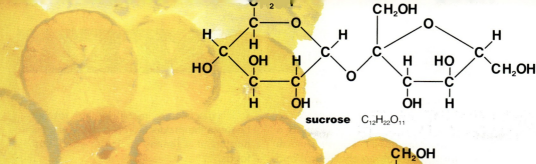

sucrose $C_{12}H_{22}O_{11}$

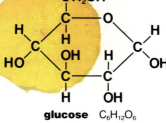

glucose $C_6H_{12}O_6$

Figure 13-18. Sucrose and glucose are sugars found in foods. Fruits contain glucose.

Carbohydrates

If you hear the word *carbohydrate*, you may think of a sweet fruit or sugary treat. Do you also think of carbohydrate loading by athletes? Runners, for example, often prepare for a long-distance race by eating, or "loading," carbohydrates in starchy foods such as vegetables and pasta. Starches provide high-energy, clean-burning fuel for the body.

5 **Carbohydrates** are organic compounds in which there are twice as many hydrogen atoms as oxygen atoms. One group of carbohydrates is the sugars, as shown in Figure 13-18. The sugar, glucose, is found in your blood and also in many sweet foods such as grapes and honey. The sugar, sucrose, is common table sugar. By counting the hydrogen and oxygen atoms in each formula, you will see that these sugars are carbohydrates.

Figure 13-19 shows a part of a starch molecule. **Starch**
6 **is a carbohydrate that is also a polymer.** During digestion, sucrose and starch are broken down into monomers of glucose and similar sugars.

What is the formula for the sugar found in your blood?

Figure 13-19. Starch is the major component of pasta.

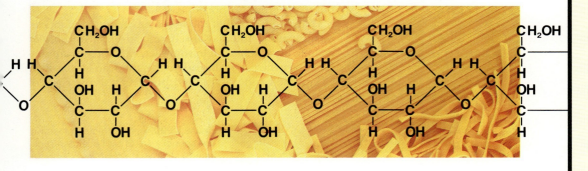

TECHNOLOGY

For more information on fake fats, see "Ersatz Fat: Do New Synthetic Foodstuffs Mean Worry-Free Indulgence?" by Virginia DeMoss, *Bicycling*, June 1990, pp. 112-113.

Think Critically: Although these compounds occur in nature, they are not chemically combined. Once combined, they form a new substance with an entirely new set of properties.

CONCEPT DEVELOPMENT

▶ Ask students to check their home kitchens to see what type of oil is used in cooking. Materials rich in unsaturated fatty acids from plants are generally oils at room temperature. Saturated fats, such as those from animals and plant oils that have been hydrogenated, tend to be solids at room temperature.

▶ Bring in an empty box of margarine. Have a student read the label to the class. Hydrogenation (adding hydrogen to double bonds) changes vegetable oils into fats.

▶ Interested students might want to research the relationship of the lipid, cholesterol, to heart and artery disease. Autopsies performed on young males show that there is some evidence of artery occlusion at age 12.

CHECK FOR UNDERSTANDING

Use the Mini Quiz to check for understanding.

MINI QUIZ

Use the Mini Quiz to check students' recall of chapter content.

5 Organic compounds that contain twice as many hydrogen atoms as oxygen atoms are classified as _____ . *carbohydrates*

6 Starch is a carbohydrate that is also a(n) _____ . *polymer*

7 Fats, oils, and related compounds make up a group of organic compounds known as _____ . *lipids*

8 Does cholesterol have any good use in the body? *Yes, it is used to build cell membranes.*

Fake Fats

Scientists at a company that produces processed foods have synthesized a molecule that promises the look and "mouth feel" of fats, but with no cholesterol and fewer calories. In a process involving heat and pressure, soybean or some other oil is combined with sugar. The result is a very large, complex molecule called a sucrose polyester. The enzyme responsible for breaking down fats during digestion has no effect on the sucrose polyester. So this "fake fat" passes through the body mostly unchanged.

A second fat substitute has been announced by another company. Because this product is made by combining water with egg or milk protein, its makers maintain that it is all natural. Special techniques shape the proteins into spheres to give the substance the smooth feel of fats. This compound substitutes protein and water for fat, so it is much lower in calories than fat. But because the product forms a gel when it is heated, it is limited to use in uncooked foods.

Think Critically: Both the sugar and oils used in one "fake fat" occur naturally. Why is this fat substitute considered synthetic?

Lipids

Fats, oils, and related compounds make up a group of organic compounds known as **lipids.** Lipids include animal fats, such as butter, and vegetable oils, such as corn oil. Lipids contain the same elements as carbohydrates, but in different proportions.

Have you heard that eating too much saturated fat can be unhealthy? You may also have heard that you should include unsaturated fat in your diet. Fats and oils are similar in structure to hydrocarbons, so they can be classified as saturated and unsaturated, according to the types of

Figure 13-20. At room temperature, fats are normally solids and oils are usually liquids.

OPTIONS

INQUIRY QUESTIONS

▶ Which of the biological compound classifications would you apply to milk? *Milk contains minerals, water, lactose (a carbohydrate), casein (protein), vitamins, and fat. All three classifications apply.*

▶ Why do you think unsaturated vegetable oil is less likely to contribute to artery and heart disease than saturated animal fat? *The double bonds in the unsaturated oil are more chemically reactive than single bonds. Thus, the unsaturated oil can be broken down more easily by enzymes in the cell.*

PROGRAM RESOURCES

From the **Teacher Resource Package** use:

Science and Society, page 17, The Cholesterol Controversy.

Concept Mapping, page 31.

Activity Worksheets, page 5, Flex Your Brain.

Use **Laboratory Manual,** The Breakdown of Starch and Testing for a Vitamin.

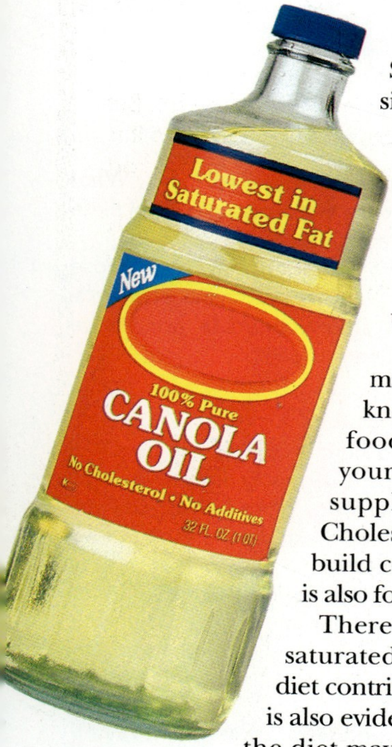

Figure 13-21. Fats can be classified by the types of bonds in their carbon chains.

bonds in their carbon chains. Saturated fats contain only single bonds between carbon atoms and unsaturated fats contain at least one double bond. Most animal fats contain a great deal of saturated fats, whereas oils from most plants are mainly unsaturated.

Another lipid found in animal foods is cholesterol. Do you know that even if you never eat foods containing cholesterol, your body would make its own supply? The reason is simple. Cholesterol is used by the body to build cell membranes. Cholesterol is also found in bile, a digestive fluid. There is evidence that too much saturated fat and cholesterol in the diet contributes to heart disease. There is also evidence that unsaturated fats in the diet may help to prevent heart disease. A properly balanced diet includes some fats, just as it includes some proteins and carbohydrates.

Which fats, animal or plant, are mainly unsaturated?

Science and MATH

Molecular mass is the sum of the masses of the atoms in a molecule. Which substance has the greatest molecular mass: ethanol, propane, or formic acid?

SECTION REVIEW

1. What is a polymer? Why are polymers important organic compounds?
2. Compare and contrast proteins and nucleic acids.
3. **Apply:** Is ethanol a carbohydrate? Explain.

☑ Concept Mapping

Use a network tree to describe types of fats using the terms *saturated fats, unsaturated fats, single bonds,* and *double bonds.* If you need help, refer to Concept Mapping in the **Skill Handbook** on pages 684 and 685.

Skill Builder

13-4 BIOLOGICAL COMPOUNDS **345**

Skill Builder

Fats
- include → Saturated fats
  - which have → Only single bonds
- include → Unsaturated fats
  - which have → Both single and double bonds

Science and MATH

Compound	Molecular Mass
Ethanol (C_2H_5OH)	46.0
Propane (C_3H_8)	44.0
Formic acid (HCOOH)	46.0

To one decimal place, ethanol and formic acid have the same molecular mass.

3 CLOSE

▶ Ask a representative from your school's food service department to come and explain to the class how the menu items are selected for the school lunch program and how they meet the nutritional needs of a teenager.
▶ Ask questions 1-2 and the **Apply** Question in the Section Review.

❓ FLEX Your Brain

Use the Flex Your Brain activity to have students explore BIOLOGICAL COMPOUNDS.

SECTION REVIEW ANSWERS

1. A polymer is a large molecule made up of smaller molecules, called monomers, chemically bonded together. Many important biological compounds are polymers.

2. Proteins are formed when amino acids form polymers. They are important in making body tissues and enzymes. Nucleic acids are polymers of nucleotides. They contain a code that controls cell activities.

3. Apply: No. A molecule of ethanol does not have twice as many hydrogen atoms as oxygen atoms.

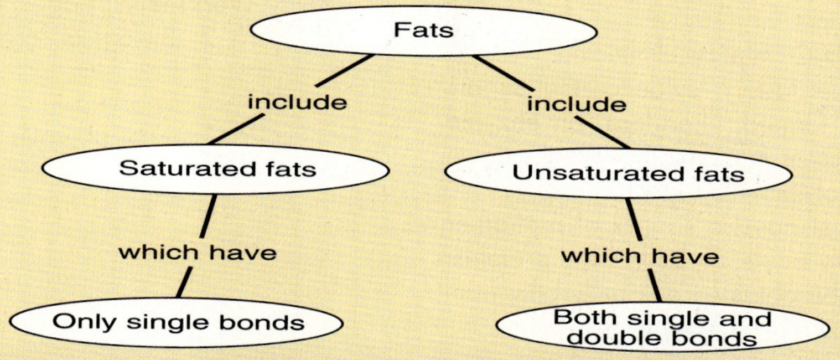

ACTIVITY 13-2
30 minutes

OBJECTIVE: Model the polymeric structure of starch and protein.

PROCESS SKILLS applied in this activity:
▶ **Building Models** in Procedure Steps.
▶ **Predicting** in Analyze Question 2.
▶ **Inferring** in Conclude and Apply Questions 3 and 4.

🤝 COOPERATIVE LEARNING
Use the Paired Partner strategy to draw structures on cards.

TEACHING THE ACTIVITY
Alternate Materials: More permanent monomers could be made from stiff plastic sheets. Use a paper punch to make holes for paper clips.

Troubleshooting: It is necessary that the structures be drawn on the cards in the positions described.

▶ Point out that monomers do not just link. Rather, a chemical bond must form. Lead students to discover that an H– and an –OH must be eliminated between the two molecules to make room for a bond. The H– and –OH form a water molecule.

▶ The glucose linkages recommended here form a model of one type of starch called *amylose*. Other linkages are possible.

▶ For amino acids, use the structures shown on page 341. You may want to show other amino acid structures to reinforce the idea that all amino acids have common structured features.

ACTIVITY 13-2
Biological Polymers

Problem: *What is the structure of some biological polymers?*

Materials
- index cards
- 4 paper clips

Procedure
1. Draw the structure of glucose, as shown on page 343, on an index card. Make the drawing large enough to fill the card.
2. Insert a paper clip where the OH appears at the left edge of the card and another paper clip where the H appears at the right edge of the card.
3. With your classmates, use the paper clips to join the glucose molecules on all your cards.
4. Your teacher will give you the structural formula of an amino acid. Draw its structure on another index card so that it fills the card. Place the acid group next to the right edge of the card and the amine group next to the bottom edge of the card.
5. Insert a paper clip through the card between the OH of the acid group and an H of the NH_2 (amine group).
6. With your classmates, use the paper clips on your cards to join together all the cards in the class.

Analyze
1. Starches and proteins are polymers. What are the monomers that make up each of these kinds of polymers?
2. For a bond to form between two glucose molecules or between two amino acid molecules, what small molecule has to be eliminated in each case?

Conclude and Apply
3. If you chew a starchy cracker and hold it in your mouth as it begins to digest, you may detect a sweet taste. What process can you suggest that would explain the change from starch into sugar?
4. The body builds its own proteins by forming peptide bonds between amino acids. Why, then, is it necesary for you to eat foods that contain protein?

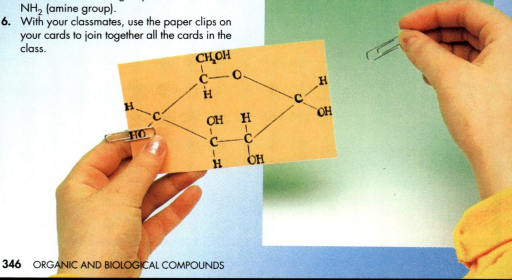

346 ORGANIC AND BIOLOGICAL COMPOUNDS

ANSWERS TO QUESTIONS
1. Starches are composed of glucose monomers. Proteins are composed of amino acid monomers.

2. Water, H_2O, must be eliminated.

3. The sweet taste is evidence that sugars have been formed. Therefore, an enzyme must be present in saliva that breaks down the starch polymer into sugars.

4. You must have a supply of monomer units, amino acids, to build new proteins. These can be obtained efficiently only from the breakdown of other proteins.

PROGRAM RESOURCES
From the **Teacher Resource Package** use:
Activity Worksheets, pages 104-105, Activity 13-2: Biological Polymers.

SUMMARY

13-1: Simple Organic Compounds

1. Carbon is an element with a structure that enables it to form a very large number of compounds, known as organic compounds.

2. Saturated hydrocarbons contain only single bonds between carbon atoms, and unsaturated hydrocarbons contain double or triple bonds.

3. Isomers of organic compounds have identical formulas but different molecular shapes.

13-2: Other Organic Compounds

1. Aromatic compounds, many of which have odors, contain the benzene ring structure.

2. A substituted hydrocarbon contains one or more atoms of other elements that have replaced hydrogen atoms.

13-3: Science and Society: Alternative Sources of Energy

1. Biomass is the source of biogas and gasohol, two fuels that can be used to increase our energy supply.

2. Ethanol and gasohol are useful as substitutes for gasoline, but their production may damage the environment.

13-4: Biological Compounds

1. Many important biological compounds are polymers—huge organic molecules made of many smaller units, or monomers.

2. Proteins, nucleic acids, carbohydrates, and lipids are major groups of biological compounds found in organisms.

KEY SCIENCE WORDS

a. **alcohol**
b. **aromatic compound**
c. **biogas**
d. **biomass**
e. **carbohydrates**
f. **energy farming**
g. **gasohol**
h. **hydrocarbon**
i. **isomers**
j. **lipids**
k. **nucleic acids**
l. **organic compounds**
m. **polymers**
n. **proteins**
o. **saturated hydrocarbons**
p. **substituted hydrocarbon**
q. **unsaturated hydrocarbons**

UNDERSTANDING VOCABULARY

Match each phrase with the correct term from the list of Key Science Terms.

1. a combination of ethanol and gasoline
2. hydrocarbons containing only single bonds
3. all animal and plant material
4. an –OH group replaces one or more hydrogen atoms in a hydrocarbon
5. compounds with identical chemical formulas but different molecular structures
6. hydrocarbons containing double or triple bonds between carbons
7. contains the benzene ring structure
8. fats, oils, and related compounds
9. formed from plant and animal waste
10. growing plants for use as fuel

ORGANIC AND BIOLOGICAL COMPOUNDS **347**

CHAPTER
REVIEW

SUMMARY

Have students read the summary statements to review the major concepts of the chapter.

UNDERSTANDING VOCABULARY

1. g	**6.** q
2. o	**7.** b
3. d	**8.** j
4. a	**9.** c
5. i	**10.** f

OPTIONS

ASSESSMENT

To assess student understanding of material in this chapter, use the resources listed.

COOPERATIVE LEARNING

Consider using cooperative learning in the THINK AND WRITE CRITICALLY, APPLY, and MORE SKILL BUILDERS sections of the Chapter Review.

PROGRAM RESOURCES

From the **Teacher Resource Package** use:

Chapter Review, pages 29-30.

Chapter and Unit Tests, pages 84-87, Chapter Test.

CHECKING CONCEPTS

1. b	6. a
2. c	7. b
3. b	8. c
4. a	9. d
5. d	10. d

UNDERSTANDING CONCEPTS

11. substituted
12. polymers
13. proteins
14. carbohydrates
15. nucleic acids

THINK AND WRITE CRITICALLY

16. Organic compounds make up all living things, or things that have lived. In addition to these, many are made artificially. Also, organic compounds have a large amount of structural variation.

17. In a single bond, two atoms share a pair of electrons. In a double bond, the atoms share two pairs of electrons. In a triple bond, three pairs of electrons are shared. (Student diagrams should show four bonds for each carbon atom.)

H—C—C—C≡C—C—C≡C—H

Single bond   Double bond   Triple bond

18. Marshes have abundant plant and animal life and the water provides a medium for the air-free decomposition of dead organisms.

19. All amino acids contain an –NH_2 (amine) group and a –COOH (carboxylic acid) group.

20. One possible answer is shown.

C=C—C=C—C=C

CHECKING CONCEPTS

Choose the word or phrase that completes the sentence or answers the question.

1. A benzene ring is very _____.
   a. rare
   b. stable
   c. unstable
   d. saturated

2. Alcohols and organic acids are both _____ hydrocarbons.
   a. aromatic
   b. saturated
   c. substituted
   d. unsaturated

3. Two examples of _____ are a dog and a tree.
   a. biogas
   b. biomass
   c. energy farming
   d. hydrocarbons

4. Polymers are made from _____.
   a. monomers
   b. isomers
   c. plastics
   d. carbohydrates

5. Some examples of _____ are enzymes and hemoglobin.
   a. carbohydrates
   b. lipids
   c. nucleic acids
   d. proteins

6. DNA codes and stores _____.
   a. genetic information
   b. nucleic acids
   c. proteins
   d. lipids

7. DNA is made up of _____.
   a. amino acids
   b. nucleotides
   c. polymers
   d. carbohydrates

8. Glucose and fructose, both $C_6H_{12}O_6$, are _____.
   a. amino acids
   b. alcohols
   c. isomers
   d. polymers

9. If a carbohydrate has 16 oxygen atoms, how many hydrogen atoms does it have?
   a. 4
   b. 8
   c. 16
   d. 32

10. Cholesterol is a type of _____.
    a. sugar
    b. starch
    c. protein
    d. lipid

UNDERSTANDING CONCEPTS

Complete each sentence.

11. A _____ hydrocarbon has at least one of its hydrogen atoms replaced by atoms of another element.

12. Huge organic molecules made from many smaller ones are _____.

13. The organic compounds that make up muscle tissues in the body are _____.

14. Organic compounds called _____ have twice as many hydrogen atoms as oxygen atoms.

15. Polymers that control cell reproduction are _____.

THINK AND WRITE CRITICALLY

16. Why are more than 90 percent of all compounds organic compounds?

17. Use a diagram to explain single, double, and triple bonds in hydrocarbons. Draw a chain of carbon atoms that shows each type of bond.

18. Explain why a marsh provides an environment that produces biogas.

19. Show how the structure of an amino acid explains the term *amino acid*.

20. Some fats are polyunsaturated. Draw a chain of carbon atoms that would be polyunsaturated.

21. Too much saturated fat in the diet is unhealthful. What is the difference in the composition of saturated fat and unsaturated fat?
22. Rubbing alcohol is isopropyl alcohol. How does this differ from propyl alcohol?
23. Carbon tetrachloride, a former dry cleaning fluid, is formed when all the hydrogen in methane is replaced by chlorine. Write the formula for carbon tetrachloride.
24. Explain how biomass has been used as an energy source throughout history.
25. Some vitamins are lipids and won't dissolve in water but will dissolve in other lipids. What is one reason we need fat in our diet?

MORE SKILL BUILDERS

If you need help, refer to the Skill Handbook.

1. **Making and Using Graphs:** Using the following table, plot the number of carbon atoms on one axis and the boiling point on the other axis. Use the graph to predict the boiling points of butane, octane, and dodecane ($C_{12}H_{26}$).

GRAPH DATA		
Name	**Formula**	**Boiling Point (°C)**
Methane	CH_4	−162
Ethane	C_2H_6	−89
Propane	C_3H_8	−42

2. **Interpreting Scientific Illustrations:** Which of the following terms apply to the illustration below? Terms: alcohol, aromatic, carbohydrate, hydrocarbon, lipid, organic compound, polymer, saturated, substituted hydrocarbon, unsaturated

3. **Comparing and Contrasting:** In terms of DNA, compare and contrast identical twins and two people who are not identical twins.
4. **Recognizing Cause and Effect:** Our society has a definite need for more energy farming. List several causes and several effects of this need.
5. **Hypothesizing:** Sarah decided to go on a weight reduction diet. She is eating only lettuce and fruit. What do you predict will happen to Sarah as a result?

PROJECTS

1. Research hydrocarbons containing five carbon atoms. Draw diagrams of their structures, name them, and tell their uses.
2. Survey local gasoline stations and find out if they sell gasohol or sell gasoline. Find out how much of each fuel is sold per month. Display results in a table or graph.
3. Research ways crops are used as energy resources. Report your findings. Suggest how these ways could be implemented locally.

ORGANIC AND BIOLOGICAL COMPOUNDS **349**

21. Saturated fats contain only single bonds between carbon atoms. Unsaturated fats contain one or more double bonds between carbon atoms.
22. Both compounds contain the same number of each kind of atom, but the arrangements of atoms are different.
23. CCl_4
24. Answers will vary. Answers may include use of wood and peat for fuel.
25. One reason is that fats must be present to dissolve certain vitamins. This group of vitamins is called fat-soluble vitamins.

MORE SKILL BUILDERS

1. **Making and Using Graphs:** Answers should be close to -1°C, 126°C, and 216°C respectively.
2. **Interpreting Scientific Illustrations:** hydrocarbon, organic compound, unsaturated
3. **Comparing and Contrasting:** Characteristics of identical twins are the same because the order of nucleotides in the DNA ladder is the same. Other people are different because the order of nucleotides in the DNA ladder is different.
4. **Recognizing Cause and Effect:** Answers will vary. Causes may include need for a renewable resource and dwindling supply of fuel. Possible effects include usage of food-producing land, environmental damage, and increased fuel supply.
5. **Hypothesizing:** Answers will vary. Answers may include negative effects of protein and lipid deficiencies.

CHAPTER SECTION	OBJECTIVES	ACTIVITIES
14-1 Materials with a Past (2 days)	1. **Identify** common alloys and ceramics. 2. **Compare** and **contrast** alloys and ceramics.	**Activity 14-1:** *Preparing an Alloy,* p. 359
14-2 Recycling **Science & Society** (1 day)	1. **Explain** the importance of recycling solid wastes. 2. **Discuss** ways in which state and local governments encourage recycling of solid waste materials.	
14-3 New Materials (2 days)	1. **Compare** and **contrast** plastics and synthetic fibers. 2. **Describe** a composite.	**Activity 14-2:** *Composite Model,* p. 368
Chapter Review	.	

ACTIVITY MATERIALS

FIND OUT	ACTIVITIES		MINI-LABS	
Page 351 ruler biology textbook	**14-1 Preparing an Alloy, p. 359** copper penny zinc, 30 mesh laboratory burner ring stand nitric acid, HNO_3, dilute sodium hydroxide solution, NaOH dilute 2 evaporating dishes tongs	**14-2 Composite Model, p. 368** plaster of paris paper clips water aluminum foil, heavy duty measuring cup beaker hammer paper towels		

CHAPTER FEATURES	TEACHER RESOURCE PACKAGE	OTHER RESOURCES
Problem Solving: *Plastics Around You,* p. 355 **Skill Builder:** *Concept Mapping,* p. 358	**Ability Level Worksheets** ◆ *Study Guide,* p. 58 ● *Reinforcement,* p. 58 ▲ *Enrichment,* p. 58 **Activity Worksheet,** pp. 110, 111 **Critical Thinking/Problem Solving,** p. 20 **Cross-Curricular Connections,** p. 20 **Transparency Masters,** pp. 53, 54	**Color Transparency 27,** Steel Alloys
You Decide! p. 361	**Ability Level Worksheets** ◆ *Study Guide,* p. 59 ● *Reinforcement,* p. 59 ▲ *Enrichment,* p. 59	
Technology: *Plastic Parts Instantly,* p. 365 **Skill Builder:** *Observing and Inferring,* p. 367	**Ability Level Worksheets** ◆ *Study Guide,* p. 60 ● *Reinforcement,* p. 60 ▲ *Enrichment,* p. 60 **Activity Worksheet,** pp. 112, 113 **Concept Mapping,** pp. 33, 34 **Science and Society,** p. 18 **Transparency Masters,** pp. 55, 56	**Color Transparency 28,** Production of Nylon
Summary Key Science Words Understanding Vocabulary Checking Concepts Understanding Concepts Think & Write Critically Apply More Skill Builders Projects	**Chapter Review,** pp. 31, 32 **Chapter Test,** pp. 88-91 **Unit Test,** pp. 92, 93	**Chapter Review Software Test Bank**

◆ **Basic**   ● **Average**   ▲ **Advanced**

ADDITIONAL MATERIALS

SOFTWARE	AUDIOVISUAL	BOOKS/MAGAZINES
	The Rock That Glowed: The Importance of Recycling, video, Focus. *Plastics, The World of Imagination,* video, Modern Talking Picture Service.	Arzt, E. and L. Schultz. *New Materials by Mechanical Alloying Techniques.* NY: IR Publications, Limited, 1989. Jenkins, Gwyn M. and K. Kawamura. *Polymeric Carbons-Carbon Fibre, Glass, and Charcoal.* Ann Arbor, MI: Books on Demand. Salmang, Hermann. *Ceramics: Physical and Chemical Fundamentals.* Ann Arbor, MI: Books on Demand. Salmen, L. et al. *Composite Systems From Natural & Synthetic Polymers.* Elsevier, NY: Science Publishing Co., Inc., 1986.

THEME DEVELOPMENT: Scale and structure as a theme of the textbook is developed by introducing the student to the structure of alloys, ceramics, plastics, synthetic fibers, and composite materials. A discussion of recycling causes the student to think about the scale on which these materials are used and discarded.

CHAPTER OVERVIEW

▶ **Section 14-1:** The section differentiates between an alloy and an amalgam. The uses and properties of ceramic and glass materials are also presented.

▶ **Section 14-2: Science and Society:** Recycling is the focus of this section. Reasons are given for recycling and why recycling is sometimes economically impractical.

▶ **Section 14-3:** This section describes the properties and uses of plastics, synthetic fibers, and composite materials.

CHAPTER VOCABULARY

alloy	cermets
amalgam	recycling
ores	plastic
ceramic	synthetic fiber
glass	composite

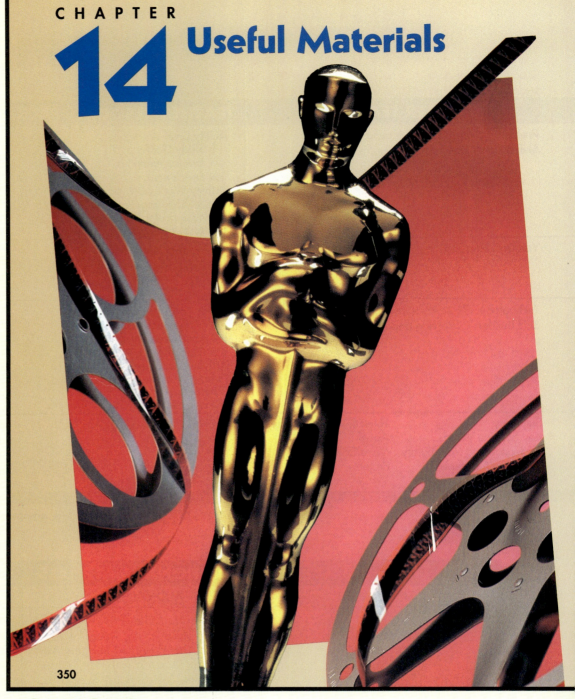

CHAPTER

14 Useful Materials

350

OPTIONS

For Your Gifted Students

Ask students to research the history of the development of plastics. They should find out how plastics have influenced the way we live and how they have affected the environment. Students can make a mural showing the development of plastics, highlighting the historic changes that have taken place in their development.

21. Too much saturated fat in the diet is unhealthful. What is the difference in the composition of saturated fat and unsaturated fat?
22. Rubbing alcohol is isopropyl alcohol. How does this differ from propyl alcohol?
23. Carbon tetrachloride, a former dry cleaning fluid, is formed when all the hydrogen in methane is replaced by chlorine. Write the formula for carbon tetrachloride.
24. Explain how biomass has been used as an energy source throughout history.
25. Some vitamins are lipids and won't dissolve in water but will dissolve in other lipids. What is one reason we need fat in our diet?

MORE SKILL BUILDERS

If you need help, refer to the Skill Handbook.

1. **Making and Using Graphs:** Using the following table, plot the number of carbon atoms on one axis and the boiling point on the other axis. Use the graph to predict the boiling points of butane, octane, and dodecane ($C_{12}H_{26}$).

GRAPH DATA		
Name	**Formula**	**Boiling Point (°C)**
Methane	CH_4	−162
Ethane	C_2H_6	−89
Propane	C_3H_8	−42

2. **Interpreting Scientific Illustrations:** Which of the following terms apply to the illustration below? Terms: alcohol, aromatic, carbohydrate, hydrocarbon, lipid, organic compound, polymer, saturated, substituted hydrocarbon, unsaturated

3. **Comparing and Contrasting:** In terms of DNA, compare and contrast identical twins and two people who are not identical twins.
4. **Recognizing Cause and Effect:** Our society has a definite need for more energy farming. List several causes and several effects of this need.
5. **Hypothesizing:** Sarah decided to go on a weight reduction diet. She is eating only lettuce and fruit. What do you predict will happen to Sarah as a result?

PROJECTS

1. Research hydrocarbons containing five carbon atoms. Draw diagrams of their structures, name them, and tell their uses.
2. Survey local gasoline stations and find out if they sell gasohol or sell gasoline. Find out how much of each fuel is sold per month. Display results in a table or graph.
3. Research ways crops are used as energy resources. Report your findings. Suggest how these ways could be implemented locally.

21. Saturated fats contain only single bonds between carbon atoms. Unsaturated fats contain one or more double bonds between carbon atoms.
22. Both compounds contain the same number of each kind of atom, but the arrangements of atoms are different.
23. CCl_4
24. Answers will vary. Answers may include use of wood and peat for fuel.
25. One reason is that fats must be present to dissolve certain vitamins. This group of vitamins is called fat-soluble vitamins.

MORE SKILL BUILDERS

1. **Making and Using Graphs:** Answers should be close to -1°C, 126°C, and 216°C respectively.
2. **Interpreting Scientific Illustrations:** hydrocarbon, organic compound, unsaturated
3. **Comparing and Contrasting:** Characteristics of identical twins are the same because the order of nucleotides in the DNA ladder is the same. Other people are different because the order of nucleotides in the DNA ladder is different.
4. **Recognizing Cause and Effect:** Answers will vary. Causes may include need for a renewable resource and dwindling supply of fuel. Possible effects include usage of food-producing land, environmental damage, and increased fuel supply.
5. **Hypothesizing:** Answers will vary. Answers may include negative effects of protein and lipid deficiencies.

14 Useful Materials

CHAPTER SECTION	OBJECTIVES	ACTIVITIES
14-1 Materials with a Past (2 days)	1. **Identify** common alloys and ceramics. 2. **Compare** and **contrast** alloys and ceramics.	**Activity 14-1:** *Preparing an Alloy,* p. 359
14-2 Recycling Science & Society (1 day)	1. **Explain** the importance of recycling solid wastes. 2. **Discuss** ways in which state and local governments encourage recycling of solid waste materials.	
14-3 New Materials (2 days)	1. **Compare** and **contrast** plastics and synthetic fibers. 2. **Describe** a composite.	**Activity 14-2:** *Composite Model,* p. 368
Chapter Review	.	

ACTIVITY MATERIALS

FIND OUT	ACTIVITIES		MINI-LABS	
Page 351 ruler biology textbook	**14-1 Preparing an Alloy, p. 359** copper penny zinc, 30 mesh laboratory burner ring stand nitric acid, HNO_3, dilute sodium hydroxide solution, NaOH dilute 2 evaporating dishes tongs	**14-2 Composite Model, p. 368** plaster of paris paper clips water aluminum foil, heavy duty measuring cup beaker hammer paper towels		

The Oscar is an award given for motion-picture excellence. It is a statue 25 centimeters high having a mass of 3.18 kilograms. The Oscar is made of a mixture of copper and tin that is covered with a very thin coating of pure gold. The total value of these materials is less than a few hundred dollars. If the Oscar were made of solid gold, it would be worth more than $40 000. Like Oscar, your body is made up of a combination of elements. How much do you think those elements are worth?

FIND OUT!

Do this activity to examine the elements that make up the human body.

Scientists have found that six elements—oxygen, carbon, hydrogen, nitrogen, calcium, and phosphorus—make up about 99 percent of a human body by weight. The remaining 1 percent of the body's weight is made up of other elements, including very tiny trace amounts of gold.

Just how much are all these elements worth? If you weigh 34 kilograms, the total value of all the elements in your body is about $3.88 at today's prices. Sorry about that!

Now try to guess what elements make up most of the following parts of the human body: muscles, bones, teeth, blood, fats, and water.

Gearing Up

Previewing the Chapter

Use this outline to help you focus on important ideas in the chapter.

Section 14-1   Materials with a Past
▶ Alloys
▶ Ceramics

Section 14-2   Science and Society
Recycling
▶ Why Recycle?

Section 14-3   New Materials
▶ Plastics
▶ Composites

Previewing Science Skills

▶ In the **Skill Builders,** you will map concepts and observe and infer.
▶ In the **Activities,** you will observe and infer and hypothesize.

What's next?

You have learned that the value or importance of an object often cannot be judged by the value of the materials of which it is composed. Now find out about the composition and properties of some very useful materials.

351

INTRODUCING THE CHAPTER

Use the Find Out activity to introduce students to useful materials. Inform students that they will be learning more about new and old products of science as they read the chapter.

FIND OUT!

Preparation: Have a high school biology book available for each team.
Materials: ruler, biology textbook

Cooperative Learning: Use the Problem Solving team strategy. After the team has assigned roles, have the reader read the problem. The clarifier and solver can use the biology book's index. The recorder should prepare a grid and check off the elements as the team decides.

Teaching Tips

▶ You may want to prepare a grid for each team. Write the elements across the top of the paper and the body tissues down the edge of the paper.
▶ Set a time limit for this activity. Fifteen minutes is usually sufficient.
▶ Duplicate the grid on an overhead transparency. Have each recorder check off the team's findings using a different color marking pen for each team.
▶ Elements and percent by mass are: oxygen, 65%; carbon, 18%; hydrogen, 10%; nitrogen, 3%; calcium 2%; phosphorus, 1%; potassium, 0.4%; sulfur, 0.25%; sodium, 0.15%; chlorine, 0.15%; magnesium, 0.05%; and iron, 0.005%. Percentage values will vary from source to source.

Gearing Up

Have students study the Gearing Up feature to familiarize themselves with the chapter. Discuss the relationships of the topics in the outline.

What's Next?

Before beginning the first section, make sure students understand the connection between the Find Out activity and the topics to follow.

PREPARATION

SECTION BACKGROUND

▶ Many common metals are not pure elements, but alloys. Some pairs of metals are soluble in each other in all proportions. Homogeneous examples are Cu/Ni, Cu/Au, W/Mo, Pt/Au. Some pairs that do not dissolve completely and therefore form heterogeneous alloys are Al/Si, Pd/Sn, Cu/Sn, and Ag/Cu.

▶ The solubility of one metal in another is determined mainly by the size of the atoms. Metals with atoms of similar size tend to be soluble in each other. Also, elements whose atoms are very much smaller than the other element are usually soluble. For example, hydrogen dissolves in palladium.

▶ Steel is an alloy of iron and carbon containing up to two percent carbon. Stainless steel is made by adding carbon, chromium, and nickel to iron. Adding tungsten produces a steel that is hard even at high temperatures. It is used to make cutting tools for metalworking. Manganese steels are very hard and used for parts of bank vaults and rock crushers. Vanadium steel is tough and is used in automobile engine crankshafts. Silicon steel has electrical properties that make it useful in the cores of many transformers.

▶ Some dental alloys are also made from silver and tin. Polymers that are cured with ultraviolet light are used where the filling must match the color of the tooth. The metal amalgam filling is more resistant to wear than the polymer fillings.

PREPLANNING

▶ To prepare for Activity 14-1, ask students to bring to class bright, shiny pennies. If bright pennies are not available, dilute the nitric acid and prepare the sodium hydroxide solution in advance.

14-1 Materials with a Past

New Science Words

alloy
amalgam
ores
ceramic
glass
cermets

Objectives

▶ Identify common alloys and ceramics.
▶ Compare and contrast alloys and ceramics.

EcoTip

In the United States, 70 percent of all metals used are discarded after a single use.

What is an alloy?

Alloys

Imagine interstate highways without steel bridges, cities without brick buildings, and rooms without glass windows. It's almost impossible because such materials as steel, brick, and glass are part of your everyday life. As you will see, these and many more familiar materials are rooted in discoveries made thousands of years ago.

When a marching band goes by, you can easily recognize the brass section. The instruments are brilliant in both sound and color. Trumpets, trombones, and tubas are made of an alloy called brass. An **alloy** is a mixture of a metal and one or more other elements. Brass is a mixture of copper and zinc. The brass used in musical instruments and in some hardware is composed of about 80 percent copper and 20 percent zinc. These percentages indicate that a 10-gram brass key contains 8 grams of copper and 2 grams of zinc. Brass of this quality is a solid solution of the two metals. As you recall from Chapter 9, a solution is a homogeneous mixture. Any brass that contains more than 40 percent zinc is a heterogeneous mixture. This means that the mixture of molecules of the two metals is not completely uniform.

Have you ever been awarded a plaque or trophy? Chances are it is made of bronze, an alloy similar to brass. About 5000 years ago, people discovered that a new material could be made by mixing melted copper and tin. The new material—bronze—was stronger and

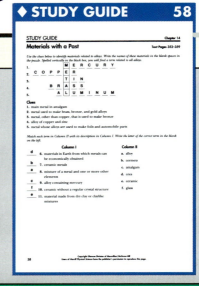

Figure 14-1. This bronze helmet is centuries old.

OPTIONS

Meeting Different Ability Levels

For Section 14-1, use the following **Teacher Resource Masters** depending upon individual students' needs.

◆ **Study Guide Master** for all students.
● **Reinforcement Master** for students of average and above average ability levels.
▲ **Enrichment Master** for above average students.

Additional Teacher Resource Package masters are listed in the OPTIONS box throughout the section. The additional masters are appropriate for all students.

◆ **STUDY GUIDE** 58

STUDY GUIDE   Chapter 14
Materials with a Past   Text Pages 352–359

Use the clues below to identify materials related to alloys. Write the names of these materials on the blank spaces in the puzzle. Spelled vertically in the black box, you will find a term related to all alloys.

1.   M E R C U R Y
2.   C O P P E R
3.   T I N
4.   B R A S S
5.   A L U M I N U M

Clues
1. main metal in amalgam
2. metal used to make brass, bronze, and gold alloys
3. metal, other than copper, that is used to make bronze
4. alloy of copper and zinc
5. metal whose alloys are used to make foils and automobile parts

Match each term in Column II with its description in Column I. Write the letter of the correct term in the blank on the left.

	Column I	Column II
d	6. materials in Earth from which metals can be economically obtained	a. alloy
b	7. ceramic metals	b. cermets
a	8. mixture of a metal and one or more other elements	c. amalgam
c	9. alloy containing mercury	d. ores
f	10. ceramic without a regular crystal structure	e. ceramic
e	11. material made from dry clay or claylike mixtures	f. glass

58

more durable than either copper or tin. This first known alloy became so popular and so widely used that a 2000-year span of history is known as the Bronze Age. The Bronze Age ended with the discovery of iron.

Bronze is more expensive than brass, because tin is more expensive than zinc. However, bronze is especially useful in plumbing fixtures and hardware that will be exposed to salt water. Brass is not suitable for such items as boat propellers, because the zinc reacts with minerals in salt water, leaving porous copper behind. The tin in bronze does not react with saltwater minerals.

==Metals can be combined with other elements in different amounts to produce many different mixtures.== Table 14-1 lists some common alloys. Thousands of alloys have been created since the time bronze was first made.

Table 14-1

COMMON ALLOYS		
Name	**Composition**	**Use**
Bronze	copper, tin	jewelry, marine hardware
Brass	copper, zinc	hardware
Sterling silver	silver, copper	tableware
Pewter	tin, copper	tableware
Solder	lead, tin	plumbing
Wrought iron	lead, copper, magnesium	porch railings, fences

==An alloy has properties that are different from and more useful than the properties of the elements in it.== Look at the bracelet shown in Figure 14-2. It appears to be made of gold. It is actually made of an alloy. As you know, gold is a very bright, very expensive element. It is

Figure 14-2. Like this bracelet, most gold jewelry is made of a gold-copper alloy.

▶**Demonstration:** Obtain clay from the school's art teacher. Have a student divide the clay into two parts. Shape each part into a useful object. Ask the art teacher to fire one piece in a kiln. Allow the second piece to air dry. Have the students examine both ceramic pieces and describe the properties of each. Ask them why they think the properties of the fired and unfired pieces are so different.

TYING TO PREVIOUS KNOWLEDGE: Ask students if they have ever had "gold" chains turn their necks or wrists green. The alloy was mostly copper with very little gold. Emphasize that alloys can vary in composition.

OBJECTIVES AND SCIENCE WORDS: Have students review the objectives and science words to become familiar with this section.

Key Concepts are highlighted.

CONCEPT DEVELOPMENT
▶Remind students that the strong metallic bond of structural metals, such as iron, chromium, and nickel, makes them hard and strong. In general, transition metals are the hardest and strongest because of delocalized *d* electrons. It is possible to strengthen some of the elements that have fewer delocalized electrons by combining them with other metals to form alloys.

CONCEPT DEVELOPMENT

▶ It is important that students realize that alloys have properties different from those of pure elements.

▶ Bring samples of alloys to class. Hardware stores have brass nuts and bolts that students can examine. Bronze, stainless steel, pewter, and gold jewelry are possible alloys you can show the class.

▶ Perform, repeat, or review the demonstration on page 305 in Chapter 12. Iron and carbon form the alloy called steel. Steel is a very useful material because it can be heat treated. Softened or annealed steel can be easily shaped into car body parts due to its large crystal size. Hardened steel is used when wear resistance is necessary. Hardened steel is brittle because of its small crystal size. Tempered steel is both hard and strong. It has a springiness because of its intermediate crystal size.

REVEALING MISCONCEPTIONS

▶ Some people believe that galvanized steel is an alloy. Be certain students realize galvanized steel has been dipped into molten zinc. A thin layer of zinc metal coats the surface. If possible, bring a piece of galvanized metal to class. Students can see the zinc metal crystals on the surface using a hand lens.

CROSS CURRICULUM

▶ **Language Arts:** Have students write a science fiction story that makes use of a new alloy with unique properties. In the story, have them tell how the alloy is made and what the properties are. An example is the legend surrounding Jim Bowie's knife. It was said to be made from the metal of a meteorite he found. The metal blade was said to be indestructible, and never needed sharpening.

also a soft metal that bends very easily. Copper, on the other hand, is a somewhat dull, inexpensive, hard metal. When melted gold and copper are mixed and then allowed to cool, an alloy is formed. It has most of the brilliance of gold and most of the sturdiness of copper. By varying the amounts of gold and copper, alloys with properties designed for different purposes can be produced. Figure 14-3 shows several gold alloys.

The alloys shown in Figure 14-3 contain only two metals. All alloys are not that simple. Do you or someone you know wear dental braces? The wire used in the braces is an alloy of gold, silver, platinum, palladium, zinc, and copper.

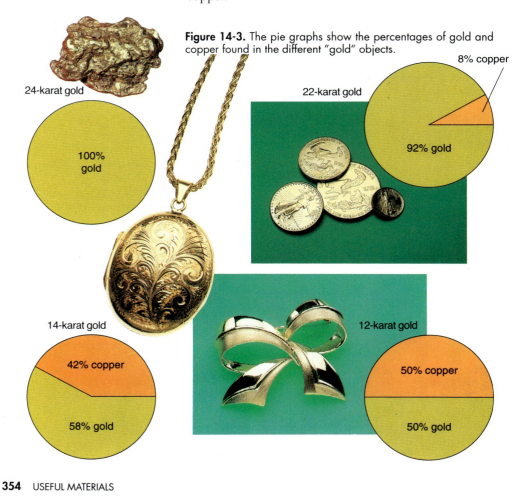

Figure 14-3. The pie graphs show the percentages of gold and copper found in the different "gold" objects.

24-karat gold — 100% gold

22-karat gold — 8% copper, 92% gold

14-karat gold — 42% copper, 58% gold

12-karat gold — 50% copper, 50% gold

OPTIONS

INQUIRY QUESTIONS

▶ **Look at the periodic table and find the locations of copper and zinc. What can be said about the relative sizes of these two elements' atoms? What alloy is formed by mixing Cu and Zn? What role do you think the relative size of the atoms plays in the formation of this alloy?** *The alloy is brass. The atoms are nearly the same size. Elements that have atoms of about the same size tend to form alloys easily.*

▶ **What properties would you expect an alloy of iron and chromium to have?** *Iron has*

great physical strength and chromium is corrosion resistant. You would expect the alloy to have both these properties.

▶ **What advantages and disadvantages would brass have over gold even though they both are the same color?** *Advantages: Brass is cheaper and harder than gold. Disadvantages: Brass will tarnish or oxidize but gold will not.*

PROBLEM SOLVING

Plastics Around You

Your writing pen, the cover of your notebook, a sandwich bag, and the covering on school desks are all plastics.

Plastics are stronger and more flexible than many natural products. They resist chemical change and wear. They are easy to clean and can be made in a variety of colors.

Many plastics are thermoplastics, which are plastics that soften or fuse when heated and harden again when cooled. The molecules in thermoplastics are linked together to form unbranched chains. Polyethylene, polystyrene, polyvinyl chloride, and nylon are some common thermoplastics.

Thermosets make up another group of plastics. Thermosets become permanently rigid when heated and will not melt again and reharden. The molecules in thermosets are linked in set chains. Common thermosets are Formica and Bakelite. What is one advantage of thermoplastics over thermosets?

Think Critically: Classify the materials in the first paragraph as thermoplastics or thermosets.

Some other alloys used by dentists are called amalgams. **An amalgam is an alloy that contains mercury.** Dental amalgams consist of mercury, silver, and zinc. You may have one in your mouth right now. They are used as fillings for cavities.

As you may have guessed by now, most metallic objects are manufactured from alloys. Various types of steel make up an important group of alloys. **Steel production is greater than that of any other alloy. All types of steel are alloys of iron and carbon.** You may have seen advertisements for carving knives with blades made of high-carbon steel. The carbon content of this alloy ranges from 1.0 percent to 1.7 percent. Because this steel

Figure 14-4. Surgical steel is used to join bones together

14-1   MATERIALS WITH A PAST   **355**

ENRICHMENT

▶ Have a student who wears dental braces talk to his or her orthodontist and ask which properties are important in the alloy the doctor uses.

▶ Ask a student to ask a dentist about dental amalgams. Why are they preferred over plastic fillings? How are amalgams made? Have the student ask about and research the issue of possible health effects of mercury amalgams.

▶ Ask a student to contact a jeweler and ask about the compositions of gold alloys. Have the student report to the class the meaning of 10-, 14-, and 24-carat gold found in jewelry.

PROBLEM SOLVING

Answers to Questions: Unlike thermosets, thermoplastics can be remelted and used again.
Think Critically: The pen, notebook cover, and plastic bag are thermoplastics. The desk coverings are thermosets.

CONCEPT DEVELOPMENT

▶ Ask students what happens when they bite down on a piece of aluminum foil. Those who have metal fillings are likely to experience pain. Unlike metals in an electrolyte (saliva) produce an electric current.

▶ **Demonstration:** Use a wire with alligator clips at both ends to connect a 15-cm piece of clean copper wire to one electrode of a flashcube. Connect the other electrode of the flashcube to a 20-cm piece of magnesium ribbon that has been coiled by wrapping it around a pencil. Clamp the flashcube and electrodes to a ring stand. Raise a 150-mL beaker that contains 50 mL of water and 50 mL of concentrated hydrochloric acid until the Mg and Cu electrodes are simultaneously immersed. The current produced will fire the flash bulb in the flashcube.

MINI QUIZ

Use the Mini Quiz to check students' recall of chapter content.

1 **What kinds of substances make up an alloy?** *a metal and one or more other elements*
2 **Bronze is a mixture of what two elements?** *copper and tin*
3 **How does an alloy compare with the elements it is composed of?** *The properties of the alloy are different from those of the elements.*
4 **An alloy that contains mercury is called a(n) _____ .** *amalgam*
5 **All types of steel are alloys of iron and _____ .** *carbon*

CHAPTER 14   **355**

Table 14-2

		SOME STEEL ALLOYS	
Name	Composition	Properties	Uses
Manganese	10–18% Mn	very hard	railroads, armor plate, conveyors
Duriron	12–15% Si	acid resistant	pipes, condensers, containers
Nickel	2–5% Ni	elastic, corrosion resistant	gears, drive shafts, cables
Invar	36% Ni	does not expand or contract	measuring tapes, pendulums
Permalloy	78% Ni	magnetic	cables
Stainless	14–19% Cr 7–9% Ni	strong, corrosion resistant	surgical instruments, knives, flatware
High speed	14–20% W, 4% Cr or 6–12% Mo, 4% Cr	keeps hardness at high temperatures	cutting tools, drill bits, saw blades

REVEALING MISCONCEPTIONS

▶Many students believe that the only reason aluminum cans should be recycled is to eliminate the litter a discarded can creates or to delay the filling up of landfills. A better economic reason is that large amounts of electricity are required to convert bauxite ore into Al metal. For every one can produced from ore, twelve cans can be produced from recycled cans using the same amount of electricity. Therefore, it is much cheaper to produce cans from recycled aluminum than from ore.

CROSS CURRICULUM

▶**Economic Geography:** Have students locate the following countries on a world map. Make signs that show the major elements that are extracted from ores mined in these countries. Canada: Ni, Cu, Nb, Ga, Ta, Zn, Cd, Cs; Mexico: Zn, Sb, Cd, Sr; Brazil: Nb, Mn, Ta; Bolivia: Ag, Sn; Jamaica: Al; Zaire: Co, Cu, Sn, Nb, Ta, Au, W, diamonds; South Africa: Cr, Mn, V, Pt; Botswana: Cr, diamonds; Zambia: Co, Au, Mn; Gabon: Mn; U.K.: Pt; Germany: Ga, Cs; Belgium: Co, Sb; Norway: Ni; France: Mn; Commonwealth of Independent States: Cr, Pt; Turkey: Cr; China: Sb; Philippines: Cr; Indonesia: Sn; Malaysia: Ta, Sn; Australia: Al, Mn, Cd; New Caledonia: Ni
Use this map-making exercise to demonstrate how technology depends on Earth's resources.

CONCEPT DEVELOPMENT

▶The photograph at the bottom of this page shows silver ore. The silver appears black because it is chemically combined as silver sulfide.
▶**Demonstration:** An empty aluminum soft-drink can may be used to demonstrate the strength of this lightweight metal. The aluminum skin of an airplane must flex many times without tearing. Have a student wearing rubber gloves attempt to tear a soft-drink can into two pieces by gripping the ends and twisting in one direction. The can will usually twist but will not tear.

EcoTip

During a three-month period, Americans throw away enough aluminum to totally rebuild our entire commercial airline fleet.

is very hard, the knife blades will stay very sharp. As you can see from Table 14-2, steels of different compositions are made for different uses.

Aluminum alloys are the second largest group of alloys produced. Aluminum alloys are used to manufacture products ranging from foils used in food wraps to automobile bodies.

In the last decade, aluminum-lithium alloys have become very important. Because lithium is the lightest metal, these alloys are lightweight, yet exceedingly strong. Unlike other alloys, aluminum-lithium alloys maintain their strength at very high temperatures. In the future these alloys may be used to make the bodies of aircraft that will travel near the outer limits of Earth's atmosphere.

Most of the elements needed to make alloys are obtained from ores. **Ores are materials in Earth from which metals can be economically obtained.** If you look ❻ closely at the photo to the left, you can see the silver in the ore. Earth also contains clay. As you will see, clay is used in the manufacturing of another important group of useful materials.

OPTIONS

INQUIRY QUESTIONS

▶**What is the percent of aluminum metal in a sample of the ore, bauxite, if 25 g of pure aluminum is processed from 1000 grams of ore?** *2.5 percent*
▶**If an iron ore contains two percent iron, how much must be processed to produce one kilogram of iron?** *50 kg*
▶**A sample of uranium ore, called pitchblende, is found to contain five percent uranium. How many metric tons of pure uranium can be extracted from 1000 metric tons of ore?** *50 metric tons*

PROGRAM RESOURCES

From the **Teacher Resource Package** use:
Critical Thinking/Problem Solving, page 20, Mercury in Dental Amalgam.
Cross-Curricular Connections, page 20, Recycling.
Transparency Masters, pages 53-54, Steel Alloys.
Use **Color Transparency** number 27, Steel Alloys.

Ceramics

Have you ever watched a potter making a bowl? If you have, you know that the potter spins wet clay on a wheel while shaping it into a bowl by hand. The bowl is then heated in a very hot oven to dry it. The bowl is removed from the oven and hardens as it cools. The bowl is made of a material called ceramic. **A ceramic is a material made from dried clay or claylike mixtures.** People began making ceramic containers thousands of years ago to store food and carry water.

As with alloys, there are thousands of different ceramics. Is your school building made of bricks? Does it have tiled hallways? Bricks and tiles are examples of a group of ceramics called structural ceramics. Structural ceramics are used by the construction industry because of their rigidity and strength. These ceramics contain silicon or aluminum. Recall that these elements can form many covalent bonds. These bonds make the ceramics strong and chemically stable. The porcelain ceramics used on sinks and bathtubs are called whitewares. Figure 14-6 shows examples of several important types of ceramics.

Look at some bricks or bathroom tiles, or at the porcelain enamel around the burner plates of a stove. You'll probably see small breaks in their surfaces. These breaks are evidence of one disadvantage of some ceramics: they are so rigid that they crack. If you've ever picked up the

Figure 14-5. This ancient ceramic pottery is made of a mixture of clay and water.

Figure 14-6. The photographs show structural ceramics (left), whitewares (center), and porcelain enamel (right).

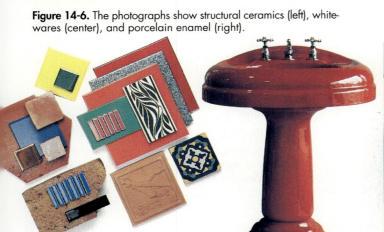

▶ Ceramics are inorganic, nonmetallic solids that are stable at high temperatures. Ceramics can be either crystalline or noncrystalline.

▶ **Demonstration:** Glass is amorphous, which means it has no crystal structure. As in a liquid, the molecules can move past one another. To demonstrate this very slow movement, you can use water glass to make a solid, white "rubber ball." Mix 25 mL of water glass, sodium silicate, with 25 mL of water. In another beaker mix 18 mL of 95% ethanol with 7 mL of water. Pour the alcohol solution into the beaker containing the water glass solution. Swirl the beaker to mix the two solutions. A white solid forms. Drain off the excess solution. Stack 7–10 paper towels. Dump the solid onto the towels. Gently squeeze the white mass and shape it into a ball. The ball will bounce if you drop it. Place the ball on the lab table. After about 15 minutes have students observe the bottom of the ball. Even though the material seems solid, it has flattened.

TEACHER F.Y.I.

▶ Living organisms produce ceramic materials, but the processing methods are not well understood. Understanding the growth of biocrystals is the first step to biomimetic processing of ceramics. Bacteria can produce magnetite particles, and yeast can produce small crystals of cadmium sulfide.

CHECK FOR UNDERSTANDING
Use the Mini Quiz to check for understanding

MINI QUIZ
Use the Mini Quiz to check students' recall of chapter content.

6 Metals are obtained from materials in Earth called _____ . *ores*

7 From what are ceramic materials made? *clay or claylike mixtures*

8 A ceramic that does not have a regular crystal structure is called a(n) _____ . *glass*

9 Glass is made from sand. What elements make up sand? *silicon and oxygen*

10 Materials that have properties of both ceramics and alloys are called _____ . *cermets*

ENRICHMENT

▶ Kidney stones and gallstones are ceramic-like materials that form in the human body. Ask two students to research one of these and report their findings to the class. How do they form and how can they be prevented? Students may be able to conduct a telephone interview with a doctor.

▶ Have students conduct a survey of ceramic and glass objects they find at home and at school. Students can share their written findings in class the next day. Figure 14-6 will give them some ideas.

▶ Interested students could research high-temperature ceramics, ceramic-metal composites, polymer-ceramic composites, biomimetic ceramics, and oxide-ceramic superconductors.

▶ Pyroceramic materials like Corning Ware, were originally developed as missile nose cones. Pyroceramics can withstand large temperature changes without shattering. Have students research the properties that make them good for the home as well as for nose cones.

3 CLOSE

? FLEX Your Brain

Use the Flex Your Brain activity to have your students explore ALLOYS AND CERAMICS.

▶ Activity 14-1, Preparing an Alloy, is an activity that students enjoy. The questions are especially useful in bringing this section to closure.

▶ Ask questions 1-4 and the **Apply** Question in the Section Review.

SECTION REVIEW ANSWERS

1. An alloy is a mixture of a metal and another element. Responses will vary, but should include examples of alloys discussed in the section.

2. Alloys combine the useful properties of different metals into one material.

3. A ceramic is a material made of dried clay or claylike mixtures. Responses will vary but should include examples of ceramics discussed in the section.

4. A ceramic contains silicon or aluminum, which are elements whose atoms can form many covalent bonds.

5. Apply: Ceramic magnets have the magnetic properties of iron.

Figure 14-7. The different colors of the glass in this window are produced by pigments added to the glass. Such pigments include cadmium sulfide (red), cerium oxide (yellow), and cobalt oxide (blue).

pieces of a dinner plate you accidentally dropped, you are well aware of this.

Almost half of the ceramics produced today are classified as glasses. A **glass** is a ceramic without a regular crystal structure. Like all mixtures, glasses come in thousands of varieties. You are probably most familiar with the type of glass that you see in windows and drinking tumblers. This glass contains mostly oxygen and silicon, with smaller amounts of sodium and calcium, and a trace of aluminum. The major ingredient that is used to make glass is silicon dioxide—sand. **8**

9

As with other ceramics, glasses can be made to have desired properties by changing the kinds and proportions of elements that make them up. Crystal pendants, vases, and chandeliers are made from glass that contains lead as well as silicon and oxygen. Food storage dishes that you can pull from a freezer and place in an oven to heat are also made of glass. These modern glasses contain boron and magnesium or lithium. As you can see in Figure 14-7, the addition of pigments to a glass alters its appearance.

Do you have magnets stuck to your refrigerator door? If so, chances are they are ceramic magnets. These magnets are examples of cermets. **Cermets,** or ceramic-metals, are materials designed and made to have properties of both ceramics and alloys. They are new materials with ancient pasts. **10**

SECTION REVIEW

1. What is an alloy? List names and uses of several alloys.
2. Why are alloys produced?
3. What is a ceramic? List names and uses of several ceramics.
4. Why are ceramics very strong materials?
5. **Apply:** Ceramic magnets demonstrate properties of alloys of what element?

Skill Builder

☑ Concept Mapping

Make a network tree to describe the composition of common alloys using the alloys and elements mentioned in this section. If you need help, refer to Concept Mapping in the **Skill Handbook** on pages 684 and 685.

Skill Builder

You may want to supply students with a list of the alloys to work with.

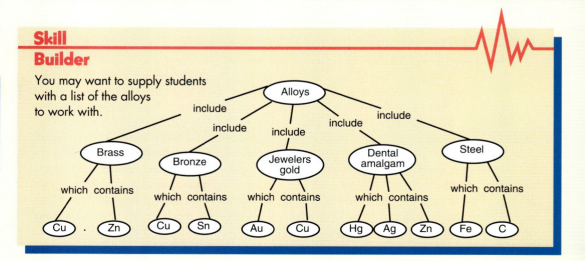

ACTIVITY 14-1
Preparing an Alloy

Problem: *How can two metals be combined to form an alloy?*

Materials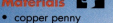

- copper penny
- zinc, 30-mesh
- hot plate
- nitric acid, HNO_3, dilute
- sodium hydroxide solution, NaOH, dilute
- evaporating dishes (2)
- tongs

CAUTION: *Acids and bases can cause burns. Rinse spills immediately.*

Procedure

1. CAREFULLY pour enough dilute HNO_3 into one evaporating dish to half fill the dish. Using tongs, grasp the penny and hold it in the acid for about 20 seconds.
2. Still using tongs, remove the penny from the acid and rinse it with cold tap water.
3. Place one teaspoon of 30-mesh zinc in the second evaporating dish. CAREFULLY add dilute NaOH to the dish to a depth of about 2 cm above the zinc.
4. Using tongs, carefully place the penny on top of the zinc. GENTLY heat the contents of the dish until the penny turns a silver color.
5. Set the control of the hot plate on medium high. Using tongs, carefully remove the penny from the dish and rinse it in cold tap water. Dry the penny and place it directly on the preheated hot plate until the penny has a golden color.

Analyze

1. Describe the appearance of the penny after it was immersed in the nitric acid. Why did its appearance change?
2. In Step 3, the penny turned a silver color. Was it actually becoming silver? Was it, at this point, an alloy?

Conclude and Apply

3. Do alloys require specific amounts of ingredients to form?
4. What alloy has this procedure produced?
5. Why is heat usually necessary for two metals to combine to form an alloy?

OBJECTIVE: **Observe** that the properties of an alloy differ from those of the component metals.

PROCESS SKILLS applied in this activity:
▶ **Observing** in Procedure Steps 4 and 5 and Analyze Question 1.
▶ **Inferring** in Conclude and Apply Questions 3 and 4.

COOPERATIVE LEARNING
If possible, have students work as Paired Partners. This activity does not lend itself to large groups. Have partners plan and share the laboratory tasks and cooperate on the questions.

TEACHING THE ACTIVITY

Alternate Materials: If you start with clean, shiny pennies, you can have students bypass Procedure Steps 1 and 2. Try to do this if possible. Small pieces of copper can be substituted for pennies. If you do not have 30-mesh zinc, try out any granulated zinc and adjust the time according to your results.

Troubleshooting: The penny should stay in contact with the zinc long enough to become uniformly coated. Turn the penny or push it into the zinc if needed. Warming speeds the reaction.

▶ **CAUTION:** *Do not permit students to carry the coin to the sink to rinse it because acid or alkali will drip on clothes or floor.*

▶ Newer pennies that are made of copper-plated zinc can be used if they are shiny and do not require an acid cleaning.

▶ Pennies can also be held with tongs and heated gently at the tip of a burner flame. *Use open flame precautions with this method.* The hot-plate method gives more reliable results.

▶ To prepare dilute nitric acid, carefully add 15 mL of concentrated acid to 85 mL of distilled water with constant stirring.

▶ To prepare dilute sodium hydroxide, dissolve 80 g NaOH in 1000 mL of distilled water. Because the solution will become hot, it should be made well in advance of the activity.

ANSWERS TO QUESTIONS

1. The dark penny became bright. The nitric acid reacted with surface corrosion and removed it.

2. No, the penny was being coated with fresh zinc. It was not an alloy at this point because the metal atoms had not mixed with each other.

3. No. Most alloys are formed from elements that can dissolve in each other in all proportions.

4. brass

5. Heating increases the motion of the metal atoms, causing the zinc to mix with the copper.

PROGRAM RESOURCES
From the **Teacher Resource Package** use:
Activity Worksheets, pages 110-111, Activity 14-1: Preparing an Alloy.

SCIENCE & SOCIETY **14-2 Recycling**

New Science Words

recycling

Objectives

▶ Explain the importance of recycling solid wastes.
▶ Discuss ways in which state and local governments encourage recycling of solid waste materials.

Science and MATH

Choose an item that you could recycle, such as aluminum cans or newspapers. Save that item for one week, weigh the collected items, and find out how much money they are worth. Calculate how much you could make by recycling for a year.

Figure 14-8. Most solid wastes are still buried in sanitary landfills like the one shown here.

Why Recycle?

Think about all the different things that get discarded every day. Paper products, bottles and cans, bicycles and automobiles—the list is endless. In the past few years, major efforts have been made in this country toward recycling some of our solid wastes. **Recycling is the recovering and processing of waste materials to regain them for human use.** ❶

The reasons for recycling materials can be summed up in two words—*preservation* and *conservation*. We need to preserve and conserve natural resources.

Preserving the environment doesn't just mean picking up litter in our parks and along highways. Solid waste must be reduced. Most solid waste is deposited in landfills. Although today's landfills are a great improvement over the old municipal dumps, they are still smelly, unpleasant environmental eyesores. But perhaps more important, many of America's more populous areas are running out of space. For example, some states, such as New Jersey, ❷ are forced to transport much of their solid waste to landfills in other states, at considerable costs in money and energy. There's just no room for any more landfills. So, we have to find new ways to deal with solid waste. Recycling is one important way to reduce the amount of solid waste material.

When you think of conservation, you should think of these two things: conserving the raw materials and conserving

OPTIONS

energy. Consider the three most commonly recycled materials—aluminum, glass, and paper. When an aluminum can or a newspaper is recycled, some aluminum ore is conserved or a tree is saved. But of equal importance, much less energy is needed to process the recycled can or paper. For example, to produce one aluminum can from ore takes 12 times as much electricity as is needed to produce the same can from recycled aluminum.

③ Thus, recycling helps to conserve our fossil fuels and reduces air and water pollution. In the case of glass, the raw materials—mostly sand—are not in short supply. However, the amount of energy saved by recycling glass is significant.

If recycling is so beneficial, why don't we recycle more materials? There are several reasons. For one thing, most factory machines are designed to use raw materials. And in many cases, it is actually less expensive to make something from scratch than it is to use recycled materials. The entire process of recovering and reusing materials is a very complex one.

In some states the recycling of certain materials is required by law. People must separate recyclable materials and place them by the curb for pickup. Many states
④ have deposit laws that require people to pay a deposit on all canned and bottled beverages. The deposit is refunded when the bottle or can is returned to the store. As space and raw materials become scarcer, more and more states will turn to recycling. Recycling is definitely the wave of the future.

SECTION REVIEW

1. What are the main reasons for recycling solid wastes?
2. In what two major ways is recycling encouraged in some states?

You Decide!

Assume you are a member of the city council of a town of 200 000 people. Your town is running out of space for storing solid wastes, but the city department responsible for collecting the 400 metric tons of solid waste produced daily is currently spending its total budget. Would you vote for or against a tax increase to develop a program of collecting recyclable materials? Why?

SCIENCE & SOCIETY

● REINFORCEMENT 59

▲ ENRICHMENT 59

361

REINFORCEMENT Chapter 14
Recycling Text Pages 360–361

Use the words increases, decreases, more, or less, to complete each statement below. In the space provided, write the word that makes each statement correct.

1. As the amount of solid waste produced by people increases, the need for a way to dispose of these wastes ____increases____.

2. The amount of solid waste that will have to be buried in landfills ____decreases____ as recycling becomes more widely used.

3. When paper products are recycled, the number of trees that need to be cut down for use as paper ____decreases____.

4. It takes about twelve times ____more____ energy to produce one aluminum can from raw materials as it takes to recycle one aluminum can.

5. If more people recycle their aluminum cans, ____less____ aluminum ore will need to be mined.

6. Recycling often uses ____less____ electricity than does making products from raw materials.

7. If less energy (electricity) is needed to recycle materials than to produce the same products from raw materials, recycling can ____decrease____ the amount of fossil fuels used to produce electricity.

8. If fewer fossil fuels are used to produce electricity, the amount of air pollution created by burning fossil fuels ____decreases____.

9. One drawback to recycling is that in many cases it is ____more____ expensive to recycle materials than it is to create new products from raw materials.

10. Even without recycling, the need for other ways to dispose of solid wastes ____increases____.

Answer the following questions on the lines provided.

11. Besides newspapers, what paper products do you use that could be recycled? Answers will vary but may include grocery bags, typing paper, and notebook paper.

12. Why is recycling a good idea? Recycling cuts back on wastes stored in landfills, uses less electricity than making new products, reduces air and water pollution, and conserves natural resources.

Copyright Glencoe Division of Macmillan/McGraw-Hill
Users of Merrill Physical Science have the publisher's permission to reproduce this page. 59

ENRICHMENT Chapter 14
Recycling Text Pages 360–361

RECYCLING OLD TIRES

No one is really sure how many old, worn out tires are littering the American landscape. Americans are generating scrap tires at the rate of about one tire per person per year. That adds up to about 250 million tires annually. It is estimated that 60% or more of these tires are disposed of improperly or illegally.

Not only are these tires unsightly, but they also pose a threat to our health and the environment. Tire piles are fire hazards. They give off dense, black smoke when burned. Tires are extremely difficult to put out and may burn for weeks or months. Tires are also ideal breeding grounds for disease-carrying mosquitos. The recently discovered Asian tiger mosquito is believed to have been introduced into the U.S. in tires imported from the Far East.

Discarded tires are bulky and almost indestructible. When the tire casings are compressed by dirt, they slowly spring back into shape and work their way back to the surface. This makes tires unwanted items in many landfills and disposal sites.

Collecting and recycling or disposing of scrap tires is expensive. A profitable way to convert old tires into another product has not yet been found.

1. Who should take responsibility for disposing of scrap tires—tire companies, tire dealers, or state or local government? Explain your answer. Answers will vary, but may include the following. Tire companies should take responsibility since they make the tires. They should find a way to recycle or dispose of them. Tire dealers should take responsibility since they sell the tires. These dealerships would be a good place to return used tires. Government should take responsibility by making laws and providing money to citizens for recycling or properly disposing of scrap tires.

2. What uses can you think of for discarded tires? Shredded tires could be burned to produce energy or reprocessed to make new tires. Whole tires could be used as erosion control devices or in playground equipment.

3. Why is it not a good idea to leave scrap tires lying around? They can burn easily and they provide a breeding area for mosquitos.

Copyright Glencoe Division of Macmillan/McGraw-Hill
Users of Merrill Physical Science have the publisher's permission to reproduce this page. 59

CHECK FOR UNDERSTANDING

Use the Mini Quiz to check for understanding.

MINI QUIZ

Use the Mini Quiz to check students' recall of chapter content.

❶ What is recycling? *recovering and processing of waste materials to regain them for use*

❷ What is the problem with currently used landfills? *They are running out of space to put trash.*

❸ How does recycling help save energy? *Glass and aluminum can be made from scratch but that requires more energy than using recycled glass and aluminum.*

❹ What is a deposit law? *A cash deposit is refunded when the item is returned to the store.*

RETEACH

Remind students of the law of conservation of mass. It is impossible to throw matter away. There is no "away" because matter is not destroyed in ordinary reactions.

EXTENSION

For students who have mastered this section, use the **Reinforcement** and **Enrichment** masters or other OPTIONS provided.

3 CLOSE

▶ Ask questions 1 and 2 in the Section Review.

SECTION REVIEW ANSWERS

1. We are running out of space for landfills. We can save money by recycling rather than manufacturing from scratch.

2. Recycling is encouraged in some states by laws requiring recycling and deposits on beverage containers.

YOU DECIDE!

SCIENCE & SOCIETY

Student responses may vary but should reflect the importance of preservation of the environment and the conservation of raw materials and energy.

PREPARATION

SECTION BACKGROUND

▶ Plastics made by addition polymerization are polyethylene, polypropylene, polyvinyl chloride, polyvinyl acetate, polystyrene, Teflon, and acrylics. In the process of addition polymerization, compounds with double bonds add on to each other end-to-end to form the polymer.

▶ Plastics can also be made by condensation polymerization. Polyesters and polyurethane are made this way. To form a polymer, one molecule loses a hydrogen and the next loses a hydroxyl group. The lost groups combine to form water.

▶ Graphite imbedded in a plastic is a composite that has found uses in sports equipment such as golf clubs, tennis rackets, and fishing rods. It is also being used to replace aluminum panels in aircraft skins. It is lighter, stronger, and for military aircraft it can be made to absorb radar.

PREPLANNING

▶ For Activity 14-2, you will need paper clips and plaster of paris. Pipe cleaners can be used by some students.

1 MOTIVATE

▶ **Demonstration:** Prepare nylon using premixed solutions of sebacoyl chloride and 1,6 diaminohexane. Kits for this demonstration are available from science supply houses. Layer the two solutions in a beaker. Using forceps, pick up the center of the film that forms at the interface of the two liquids. Slowly pull the nylon fiber from the beaker and roll it up on a graduated cylinder that has been covered with a paper towel.

New Science Words

plastic
synthetic fiber
composite

Objectives

▶ Compare and contrast plastics and synthetic fibers.
▶ Describe a composite.

Plastics

Think how often you and your family use the telephone. How often have you accidentally dropped the receiver or knocked a telephone over? Did the phone still work? A telephone never seems to wear out. It lasts because it is made mostly of plastics. The first plastic was made only about a century ago. You may be thinking that one hundred years is a long time. However, if you remember that alloys and ceramics have been around for thousands of years, you'll realize that plastics are really modern materials.

Recall from the last chapter that a polymer is a gigantic molecule formed from thousands of smaller organic molecules, such as hydrocarbons. Molecules that form polymers are called monomers. You are made of natural polymers, such as proteins and nucleic acids. Polymers that do not form naturally can be manufactured from organic compounds. These polymers are called synthetic polymers. A **plastic** is a material made from synthetic polymers.

You are probably familiar with the rolls of plastic bags that you find in the produce section of supermarkets. These bags are made of polyethylene (pahl ee ETH uh leen), one of the world's most widely produced and used plastics. Polyethylene is used to make, among other things, food storage containers, bottles, and the bands used around beverage six-packs. This synthetic polymer

Figure 14-9. The versatility and ruggedness of plastics make them ideal for use in objects that receive a lot of rough handling.

OPTIONS

Meeting Different Ability Levels

For Section 14-3, use the following **Teacher Resource Masters** depending upon individual students' needs.

◆ **Study Guide Master** for all students.
● **Reinforcement Master** for students of average and above average ability levels.
▲ **Enrichment Master** for above average students.

Additional Teacher Resource Package masters are listed in the OPTIONS box throughout the section. The additional masters are appropriate for all students.

◆ **STUDY GUIDE** **60**

STUDY GUIDE   Chapter 14
New Materials   Text Pages 362–368

In each of the following statements, a term has been scrambled. Unscramble the term and write it in the blank on the left.

polymer	1. A gigantic molecule formed from thousands of smaller organic molecules is called a *yplmoer.*
monomers	2. The molecules that form polymers are called *momenors.*
synthetic	3. Polymers that are made artificially in a laboratory are called *thesticyn* polymers.
plastic	4. A common material made from synthetic polymers is *clapsit.*
ethene	5. Polyethylene is a polymer formed from monomers of *theone.*
fiber	6. A strand of a synthetic polymer is called a synthetic *breif.*
petroleum	7. Most of the raw materials to make synthetic materials come from *trumloepe* products.
fiberglass	8. A glass-fiber composite used to make the hulls of boats is *lsafgibser.*
composite	9. A mixture of two materials made by embedding one material in the other is called a *stoipmoce.*
organic	10. Plastics are made from *groinca* compounds.

In the spaces below, list five products that you use every day that are made from plastics.
11. food wrap or food storage bags
12. telephones
13. food storage containers
14. pens, markers, push pins
15. computers, phonograph records, cassette storage containers

Answers will vary. Suggested answers are given. Accept all logical responses.

Copyright Glencoe Division of Macmillan/McGraw-Hill
Users of *Merrill Physical Science* have the publisher's permission to reproduce this page.

60

is made of monomers of ethene, an unsaturated hydro-carbon. The structural formula of ethene is shown to the right.

FOPS, Chapter 14, **363**

Basically, polyethylene is formed by breaking the double bonds of many ethene molecules and allowing the molecules to reform as a polymer. Part of the polymer of polyethylene is shown below.

Because so many different organic compounds can be used as monomers, there are many different plastics, as shown in Table 14-3.

Table 14-3

COMMON PLASTICS

Name	Polymer Structure	Uses
Polypropylene		Rope, protective clothing, textiles, carpet
Polystyrene		Containers, boats, coolers, insulation, furniture, models
Polyvinyl chloride (PVC)		Rubber substitute, cable covering, tubing, rainwear, gaskets
Teflon (polytetrafluorethane)		Nonstick cookware surfaces
Saran (polyvinylidene chloride)		Clinging food wraps

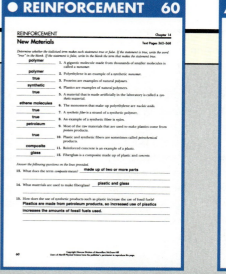

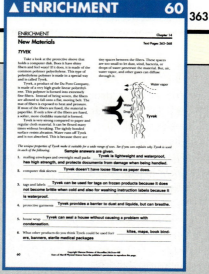

363

2 TEACH

Key Concepts are highlighted.

CONCEPT DEVELOPMENT

► Have a student give a brief report on the Bronze Age. Then ask the class if they believe they are living in the Plastic Age.

► Skin is composed mostly of proteins. A protein is a polymer. Ask the students if they think they are plastic wrapped. In a sense, they are. Skin is tough yet flexible. It is water proof and provides a barrier against infection. It is also a mixture of polymers. Skin has many of the characteristics of a good plastic.

REVEALING MISCONCEPTIONS

► Many people believe that all plastics get soft and melt when heated. Many plastics do soften when heated. They are called thermoplastic materials. The chains of thermosetting polymers are cross-linked. Heating causes more cross-links to form and the plastic gets harder. See the Problem Solving feature on page 355.

CROSS CURRICULUM

► **Art:** Have students bring in different small items that are made from plastic. Arrange them using stiff wire and string to form a mobile. Hang the mobile from the ceiling under a sign that reads "New Materials."

CONCEPT DEVELOPMENT

▶ **Demonstration:** Each student will want to prepare a sample of this cross-linked polymer. When dry it will be a hard, plastic sheet. Each student will need 20 mL of 4% polyvinyl alcohol solution and 6 mL of 4% sodium borate solution. To prepare the polyvinyl alcohol solution, a combination magnetic stirrer-hot plate is helpful. While stirring, slowly add 40g of 98% hydrolyzed polyvinyl alcohol powder to 960 mL of water. Heat this suspension to 80°C while stirring. Add a few drops of food coloring. This will prepare enough for 50 students. The cross linker (borax) is prepared by dissolving 12 g of sodium borate in 288 mL of hot water while stirring. Into a small disposable paper or plastic cup, pour 20 mL of the 4% alcohol solution and add 6 mL of the 4% borax solution while stirring. The short polymer chains will cross link like the rungs on a ladder. Stir until a solid forms. Remove the solid from the cup and roll it into a ball. It will flow very slowly when draped over your hand, but will break if pulled quickly. Allow the plastic to flow in one direction, then turn it 90° and allow it flow in another direction so as to form a square. Drape the plastic over a 2-liter plastic soda bottle that has its label removed. The square will flow over the bottle and dry to form a plastic sheet. Plastic sheets can be formed when polymer chains are cross linked.

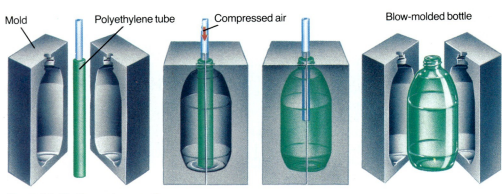

Figure 14-10. The major use of high-density polyethylene (HDPE) is to make blow-molded products, such as bottles for milk and other consumer products.

Do you know that making plastic soft drink bottles is similar to blowing up a balloon? Refer to Figure 14-10 as you read how polyethylene bottles are manufactured. First, a tube of warm polyethylene is placed inside a bottle-shaped mold. Then the mold is closed, sealing the bottom of the tube. Next, compressed air is blown into the polyethylene tube; the tube expands and takes the shape of the mold. The mold is then opened and the bottle is removed.

Table 14-4

COMMON POLYMERS		
Name	**Structural**	**Uses**
Dacron (a polyester)	$\cdots C - \bigcirc - C - OCH_2CH_2O - C - \bigcirc - C - OCH_2CH_2O \cdots$	Textiles, arterial grafts
Nylon 66	$\cdots C(CH_2)_4 - CN(CH_2)_6N - C(CH_2)_4C - N(CH_2)_6N \cdots$	Tire cord, textiles, brush bristles, netting, carpet, athletic turf, sutures
Polyethylene	$\cdots CH_2 - CH_2 - CH_2 - CH_2 - CH_2 - CH_2 \cdots$	Tubing, prosthetic devices, packaging materials, kitchen utensils, paper coating
Orlon (polyacrylonitrile)	$\cdots C - C - C - C - C - C \cdots$ (with H, CN substituents)	Textiles

364 USEFUL MATERIALS

OPTIONS

INQUIRY QUESTIONS

▶ **Some plastics have properties similar to those of rubber. What does this indicate about the chemical structure of rubber?** *Rubber is also a polymer.*

▶ **Why are synthetic fibers necessary in order to clothe the world's population?** *Natural fibers rely on agricultural processes. Land that will grow cotton and graze sheep is also needed to produce food. Oil wells don't require much land and can yield the raw materials needed to produce synthetic fibers.*

▶ **Silk is made by a caterpillar that eats the leaves of mulberry trees. Compare the cost of a man's silk tie to a polyester one. Why is there a price difference? Why are silk ties still preferred?** *The production of silk requires more labor, which is expensive. Silk is also in shorter supply than are synthetic fibers. However, silk usually gives a better appearance.*

TECHNOLOGY

Plastic Parts Instantly

All over the world, powerful computer systems are being used to create electronic, three-dimensional models of the products of tomorrow. These systems, called CAD systems, have greatly reduced the amount of time needed to determine the size and shape of new products. Once a new product is designed, the next step is the construction of a model that can be held in your hand. This model is called a prototype, and it is tested to be sure that it works as the designer intended.

Now a process invented by Charles W. Hull permits engineers to grow a prototype from liquid plastic, using the information from the CAD electronic model. Software slices the electronic model into a series of horizontal layers. A laser under computer control is directed at the surface of a vat of photosensitive plastic. Each pass of the laser

causes the plastic to harden. The hardened part sinks to the bottom of the vat, and the next laser pass adds another layer of hardened plastic. In this way the prototype actually grows from the bottom up. This technique, called stereolithography, should drastically reduce the time and expense required to bring many new products to market.

Think Critically: What properties make a material useful for building prototypes or models?

The clothing you are wearing may be made of fabrics that have been woven from synthetic fibers. **A synthetic fiber** is a strand of a synthetic polymer. Some synthetic fibers have amazing properties. For example, a strand of a synthetic fiber called Kevlar is five times stronger than a similar strand of steel. It is so strong it is used to make bulletproof vests. Synthetic fibers are used to weave both indoor and indoor-outdoor carpeting, upholstery coverings, and other textiles. Today, the use of synthetic fibers is greater than that of natural fibers. Table 14-4 lists the names and polymer structures of several familiar synthetic fibers. Fabrics with new properties are made by weaving natural fibers, such as cotton and silk, with synthetic fibers. If you look at the label of a permanent-press shirt, you will see that the fabric is a mixture of natural and synthetic fibers.

②

Figure 14-11. Wrinkle-resistant materials can be produced by combining synthetic fibers and natural fibers.

Think Critically: The properties will depend on the type of testing the prototype will undergo. The material used to make a prototype which is to be used only to evaluate shape needs only be moldable. If the prototype is to be used to evaluate function, the material may need to be strong, durable, waterproof, or have other characteristics.

CONCEPT DEVELOPMENT

Cooperative Learning: Send an Expert Team to interview a fire prevention officer to determine if there is a danger in having curtains, drapes, carpeting, and upholstery made of synthetic fibers. Have students ask what gaseous products form when various fibers burn.

▶ Ask your students if they have observed the construction of a new house that was wrapped in a white paper-like material. This Kevlar wrap is used to help make the house draft-free. This will result in energy conservation.

▶ Students may be interested that today's army helmets are also made from light weight Kevlar fibers.

Cooperative Learning: Send an Expert Team to a local carpet store to interview a salesperson about the different fibers used in carpet manufacture. Have them determine the advantages and disadvantages of the various carpet fibers.

CROSS CURRICULUM

▶ **Art:** Have each student bring in a swatch of cloth made from synthetic fibers. Have the class decide on a picture they would like and draw a rough sketch on heavy card stock. "Paint" the picture by cutting and gluing the cloth over the rough sketch.

ENRICHMENT

▶ Have students investigate the monomers that go into the production of synthetic fibers such as Saran, Kodel, Acrilan, Dynel, and Mylar. Saran is a copolymer of vinyl chloride. Kodel is a copolymer of ethylene glycol and terephthalic acid. Acrilan is a polymer of acrylonitrile. Dynel is a copolymer of acrylonitrile and vinyl chloride. Mylar is a copolymer of ethylene glycol and terephthalic acid.

PROGRAM RESOURCES

From the **Teacher Resource Package** use:

Concept Mapping, page 33.

Science and Society, page 18, Bottle Bill.

Transparency Masters, pages 55-56, Production of Nylon.

Use **Color Transparency** number 28, Production of Nylon.

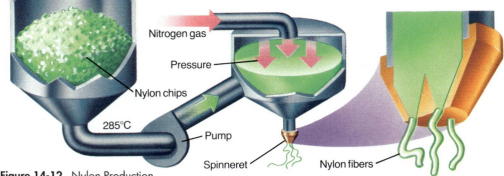
Figure 14-12. Nylon Production

CONCEPT DEVELOPMENT

▶ A car body shop can be a source of a composite that has been removed from a collision-damaged fiberglass car body. Students are interested to see how the epoxy and fiberglass mat has been used to form a car body panel. **CAUTION:** *Students should handle the broken material only while wearing gloves.* Body shops may have other high-strength plastics used in cars.

▶ Graphite composites are being used to form panels on modern airplanes. An Air Force recruiter may have a picture of the stealth fighter F117A that is constructed using graphite composite panels.

▶ Ask a student who has a graphite composite golf club, tennis racket, or fishing rod to bring it to class and show the other students. The strength and flexibility of fiberglass and graphite composites have caught the attention of track and field athletes. Ask a track coach if you can show the class a fiberglass composite pole used in the pole vault event.

CHECK FOR UNDERSTANDING

Use the Mini Quiz to check for understanding.

MINI QUIZ

Use the Mini Quiz to check students' recall of chapter content.

1 A material made from a synthetic polymer is called a(n) _____ . *plastic*

2 A strand of synthetic polymer is called a(n) _____ . *synthetic fiber*

3 Most plastics and synthetic fibers are made from the raw materials _____ . *petroleum and natural gas*

4 When one material is embedded in another material, the mixture is called a(n) _____ . *composite*

RETEACH

Have students make flash cards with names of modern materials on one side and examples listed in the text-book on the reverse side.

Figure 14-12 shows how nylon fibers are manufactured. (a) Nylon chips are heated until they melt. (b) The melted nylon is pumped into a high-pressure chamber. (c) It is then forced through tiny openings of a nozzle called a spinneret. As it cools, the nylon forms long strands. **3** You may wonder where the raw materials—the hydrocarbons and organic compounds—used to produce plastics and synthetic fibers come from. Most of them are found in petroleum—crude oil—and in natural gas. Can you explain why plastics and synthetic fibers are sometimes called petrochemical products? As the production of plastics and synthetic fibers continues to increase, so will the demand for crude oil.

Composites

Have you ever seen a picture of a face made from cut-up photographs of famous people? These pictures are called composite pictures. The word *composite* means "made of two or more parts." Some materials are also composites.

Figure 14-13 shows a bridge being built of reinforced concrete. As you can see, the concrete has long steel rods

Figure 14-13. The steel "skeleton" adds strength and flexibility to the concrete used to build this bridge.

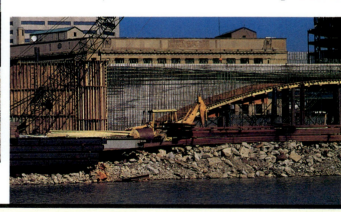

OPTIONS

INQUIRY QUESTIONS

▶ **Since fiberglass composites don't rust, why aren't they used instead of steel to make car bodies?** *Steel is cheaper and can be stamped into body panels. Composites must be molded.*

▶ **Plastics will last a long time and don't biodegrade in a landfill. Why have plastic bottles recently become more popular than the glass bottles that have been used for centuries?** *Plastics are lighter in weight, which reduces shipping costs, and they seldom break in shipment.*

▶ **Synthetic fibers resist wrinkling, are color-fast, windproof, and wear resistant. Why is cotton so popular? Why is it blended with synthetic fibers such as polyester?** *Cotton allows fabric to breathe. Some synthetics do not allow perspiration or air to pass through. Some synthetics feel hot in summer and cold in winter. The addition of cotton to the synthetic can help overcome these problems.*

Figure 14-14. The composite material used in this artificial limb makes it strong, yet light in weight.

running through it. These rods reinforce the concrete, giving it additional strength and support. Reinforced concrete is an example of a composite.  **A composite is a mixture of two materials, one embedded in the other.**

Have you ever heard of cars with fiberglass bodies or boats with fiberglass hulls? These bodies and hulls are made of a glass-fiber composite. This composite is a mixture of small threads, or fibers, of glass, imbedded in a plastic. The structures of the fiberglass reinforce the plastic, making a strong, lightweight composite. A glass-fiber composite is an example of a ceramic imbedded in a plastic. How would you describe reinforced concrete? Many different composites can be made using various metals, plastics, and ceramics. Figure 14-14 shows an example. New composites are being produced every year. In the future you may be driving a car, working in a building, and living in a house that are made almost entirely of composites.

SECTION REVIEW

1. Name several plastics and synthetic fibers.
2. Compare and contrast plastics and synthetic fibers.
3. Describe a composite.
4. **Apply:** What advantages would an automobile engine made of a metal-ceramic composite have compared to one made of an alloy?

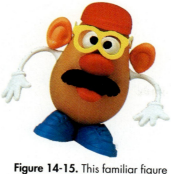

Figure 14-15. This familiar figure is a composite of the "potato" and whatever facial features are added to it.

Did You Know?

The organs a spider uses to spin the fibers for its web are called spinnerets. The manufacture of nylon fibers mimics this natural process.

☑ **Observing and Inferring**

Look at the figures in this section. Describe a way to manufacture a roll of polyethylene bags. If you need help, refer to Observing and Inferring in the **Skill Handbook** on page 678.

Skill Builder

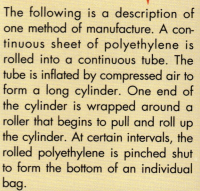

ACTIVITY 14-2
40 minutes

OBJECTIVE: Compare the properties of a composite and a non-composite material of similar composition.

PROCESS SKILLS applied in this activity:
▶ **Interpreting Data** in Conclude and Apply Question 4.
▶ **Predicting** in Analyze Question 3.

🔴 COOPERATIVE LEARNING
Have Science Investigation teams divide the activity tasks into measuring, mixing, and constructing. Have a reader give instructions and monitor each task. See the suggestions under Alternate Materials below.

TEACHING THE ACTIVITY
Alternate Materials: Have each group test a different reinforcing material. In addition to paper clips, students could use a piece of window screen, a piece of gauze, pipe cleaners, string, fishing line, and other practical materials suggested by students. Most soft or fine materials should be thoroughly wet with thin plaster of Paris before embedding. The recorder from each team should post the team's results.

Troubleshooting: Students should construct the tray first so that it is ready when the plaster is ready. Be sure the reinforcing materials will stick to the plaster or wet them with plaster first.
▶ If possible, try the plaster mix ahead of time so that you can tell students how long to wait before pouring it. The plaster should become thick enough to support the reinforcing materials but not so firm that it will not adhere.
▶ For best results, observe the 24-hour drying time.
▶ Be sure each block is completely wrapped in a towel before students strike it with a hammer.

ACTIVITY 14-2
Composite Model

Problem: What new properties can result from combining materials?

Materials
- plaster of Paris
- paper clips
- water
- aluminum foil, heavy-duty
- measuring cup
- beaker
- hammer
- paper towels

Procedure
1. Shape the aluminum foil into a rectangle with a dividing ridge down the center. The approximate dimensions should be 20 cm long by 20 cm long, with sides about 3 cm high.
2. Measure 2/3 cup of water and 1 cup of plaster of Paris. Add the plaster of Paris slowly to the water.
3. Gently mix the two ingredients and let stand for five minutes.
4. Stir the mixture and pour approximately 1/4 of it into each side of the dividing ridge. Next, carefully place several paper clips on the surface of the plaster of Paris on one side of the divider.
5. After waiting five minutes, pour the rest of the mixture equally into the two compartments, covering the paper clips that are in one of the compartments. Let this set for 24 hours or more.

6. After 24 hours, remove the aluminum foil from the blocks and examine the outward appearance of both blocks.
7. Wrap each block in a towel. Using the hammer, firmly strike each block. (**CAUTION:** *Wear goggles. Do not strike too sharply.*) If nothing happens, strike the blocks again.

Analyze
1. Before striking the blocks with the hammer, was there any noticeable difference between the two blocks? If so, describe the difference.
2. How did the hammer blow affect each block?
3. If you had made the composite with pipe cleaners instead of paper clips, what differences might you have noticed?

Conclude and Apply
4. What can you conclude about the properties of the composite material made of plaster of Paris and paper clips?
5. In what way is the structure that you made similar to some concrete structures?

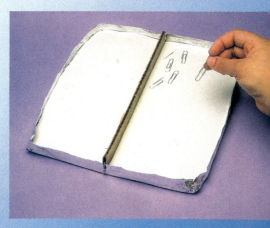

ANSWERS TO QUESTIONS
1. The blocks should appear to be the same when viewed or handled.

2. The unreinforced plaster block should shatter into several pieces. The reinforced block should crack but cling together.

3. Pipe cleaners provide a more continuous support and tighter adhesion and should give the block more resistance to crumbling.

4. The addition of paper clips to plaster of Paris gives it the ability to crack without breaking apart.

5. It is similar to steel-reinforced concrete which has increased strength resulting from embedded metal rods.

PROGRAM RESOURCES
From the **Teacher Resource Package** use:
Activity Worksheets, pages 112-113, Activity 14-2: Composite Model.

CHAPTER REVIEW

CHAPTER REVIEW

SUMMARY

14-1: Materials with a Past

1. People have been making and using alloys and ceramics for thousands of years. Some common alloys include bronze, brass, amalgams, and various alloys of iron. Some common ceramics include structural ceramics, such as brick and tile, and various kinds of glass.

2. An alloy is a mixture of a metal with one or more other elements. Alloys exhibit metallic properties. Ceramics are composed of clay or claylike mixtures. Except for cermets—ceramic metals—ceramics generally have nonmetallic properties.

14-2: Science and Society: Recycling

1. There are two important reasons for recycling materials: preservation of the environment and conservation of natural resources.

2. State and local governments encourage recycling through educational programs and by passing laws requiring that certain materials be recycled.

14-3: New Materials

1. Plastics and synthetic fibers are materials made from synthetic polymers. Plastics can be produced in many forms, ranging from very thin films to thick slabs or blocks. Synthetic fibers are produced in thin strands that can be woven into fabrics.

2. A composite is a mixture of two materials, one embedded in the other. Reinforced concrete is an example of a composite.

KEY SCIENCE WORDS

a. **alloy**
b. **amalgam**
c. **ceramic**
d. **cermets**
e. **composite**
f. **glass**
g. **ores**
h. **plastic**
i. **recycling**
j. **synthetic fiber**

UNDERSTANDING VOCABULARY

Match each phrase with the correct term from the list of Key Science Words.

1. a strand of a synthetic polymer
2. ceramic with no regular crystal structure
3. mixture consisting of a metal and one or more other elements
4. made from dried clay or claylike mixtures
5. material made from synthetic polymers
6. mined sources of metals
7. mixture of one material embedded in another
8. recovering waste materials and reprocessing them for reuse
9. have properties of ceramics and alloys
10. alloy containing mercury

USEFUL MATERIALS **369**

SUMMARY

Have students read the summary statements to review the major concepts of the chapter.

UNDERSTANDING VOCABULARY

1. j	**6.** g
2. f	**7.** e
3. a	**8.** i
4. c	**9.** d
5. h	**10.** b

OPTIONS

ASSESSMENT

To assess student understanding of material in this chapter, use the resources listed.

COOPERATIVE LEARNING

Consider using cooperative learning in the THINK AND WRITE CRITICALLY, APPLY, and MORE SKILL BUILDERS sections of the Chapter Review.

PROGRAM RESOURCES

From the **Teacher Resource Package** use:
Chapter Review, pages 31-32.
Chapter and Unit Tests, pages 88-91, Chapter Test.
Chapter and Unit Tests, pages 92-93, Unit Test.

CHAPTER
REVIEW

CHECKING CONCEPTS

1.	d	6.	b
2.	a	7.	a
3.	a	8.	c
4.	c	9.	b
5.	a	10.	c

UNDERSTANDING CONCEPTS

11. cermets
12. Polyethylene
13. iron
14. conserve
15. composite

THINK AND WRITE CRITICALLY

16. The primary raw material is silicon dioxide, sand. It is abundant and inexpensive and the production process is relatively simple.

17. Preservation is keeping things as they are. Conservation is saving a resource by using less of it or by finding a substitute.

18. It takes less energy to produce glass from recycled materials than to produce it from raw materials.

19. Copper can be found in its elemental form in nature. Iron is found only in a combined state and must be separated chemically to be usable.

20. Steel is an alloy of a metal with a nonmetal, carbon. The other alloys are made from two or more metals.

CHAPTER
REVIEW

CHECKING CONCEPTS

Choose the word or phrase that completes the sentence.

1. The production of _____ is greater than that of any other alloy.
   - **a.** amalgam
   - **b.** brass
   - **c.** bronze
   - **d.** steel

2. Steel is an alloy of iron and _____.
   - **a.** carbon
   - **b.** mercury
   - **c.** tin
   - **d.** zinc

3. Structural ceramics contain silicon or _____.
   - **a.** aluminum
   - **b.** carbon
   - **c.** copper
   - **d.** lithium

4. The source of the materials used to make plastics is _____.
   - **a.** clay
   - **b.** ore
   - **c.** petroleum
   - **d.** synthetic fiber

5. The most commonly recycled metal is _____.
   - **a.** aluminum
   - **b.** glass
   - **c.** iron
   - **d.** paper

6. Brass and bronze both contain _____.
   - **a.** mercury
   - **b.** copper
   - **c.** tin
   - **d.** zinc

7. _____ alloys are very lightweight and strong.
   - **a.** Aluminum-lithium
   - **b.** Copper-zinc
   - **c.** Copper-tin
   - **d.** Iron-carbon

8. Most elements needed to make alloys are obtained from _____.
   - **a.** amalgams
   - **b.** ceramics
   - **c.** ores
   - **d.** recycling

9. Clay is used to make _____.
   - **a.** alloys
   - **b.** ceramics
   - **c.** ores
   - **d.** plastics

10. Most solid waste is _____.
    - **a.** recycled
    - **b.** in usable form
    - **c.** deposited in landfills
    - **d.** burned

UNDERSTANDING CONCEPTS

Complete each sentence.

11. Many magnets are made of ceramic-metals, known as _____.
12. _____ is formed by breaking the double bonds of many ethene molecules and allowing the molecules to reform as a polymer.
13. The Bronze Age ended when _____ was discovered.
14. Recycling helps to _____ fossil fuels.
15. Reinforced concrete is an example of a(n) _____.

THINK AND WRITE CRITICALLY

16. Explain why most glass products are relatively inexpensive.
17. Explain the difference between preservation and conservation.
18. Explain why it is important to recycle glass when the raw materials for making it are so plentiful.
19. Iron bonds more readily with other elements than does copper. Why do you think copper was discovered so much earlier than iron was?
20. In what way is steel different from such alloys as brass, bronze, and most aluminum alloys?

21. Describe three ways you can conserve energy in your home.
22. List two reasons why you would choose to use recycled materials, even though other materials may cost less.
23. A lower carat gold has less gold in it than a higher carat gold. Why might you prefer a ring that is 10 carat gold over a ring that is 20 carat gold?
24. Explain how we contribute to air and water pollution when we don't recycle.
25. A synthetic fiber might be preferred over a natural fiber for use outdoors because it will not rot. Why might this property become a negative feature in the environment?

MORE SKILL BUILDERS

If you need help, refer to the Skill Handbook.

1. **Comparing and Contrasting:** Compare and contrast alloys and ceramics.
2. **Measuring in SI:** A bronze trophy has a mass of 952 grams. If the bronze is 85 percent copper, how many grams of tin are contained in the trophy?
3. **Interpreting Data:** Aluminum recycling saves 95 percent of the energy it takes to produce an aluminum product from ore. On the average, each American uses 320 aluminum beverage cans per year. If all 320 cans are recycled into other cans, how many new cans could be produced from ore for the same amount of energy used?
4. **Recognizing Cause and Effect:** Americans use 215 million aluminum cans per day. Compare the effects of recycling these cans to the effects of throwing them away.

5. **Concept Mapping:** Draw a network tree classifying matter, moving from the most general term to the most specific. Use the terms *compounds, elements, heterogeneous, heterogeneous mixtures, homogeneous, homogeneous mixtures, materials, solutions, substances.* Check (✔) the most specific term that describes an alloy and underline the most specific term that describes a composite.

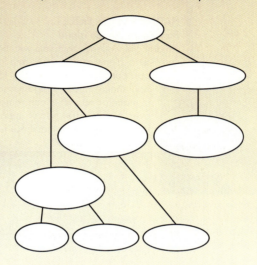

PROJECTS

1. Research gold, its alloys, and "carats." Find out several uses for gold and its alloys and what carat gold is used for each.
2. Make a poster of the floor plan of your school or an area of the school. On the floor plan, list locations where ceramics are used and the types of ceramics used there.
3. Research the production of silk fabric and compare it to production of synthetic fabrics such as nylon. Display samples of each.

USEFUL MATERIALS **371**

21. Answers will vary, but may include turning off lights, lowering the thermostat, and not leaving hot water running.
22. Answers will vary, but may include the fact that using recycled materials conserves energy and resources. Also, the recycling process may produce less pollution, thereby preserving the environment.
23. The 10-carat ring will be less expensive, and less easily bent, worn away, or scratched.
24. Answers will vary, but may include the facts that more energy is used, industrial wastes are produced, and unrecycled materials are discarded, thus contributing to land and water pollution.
25. Some synthetic fibers will not decompose and may be found in the environment thousands of years later.

MORE SKILL BUILDERS

1. **Comparing and Contrasting:** Both alloys and ceramics are mixtures designed to use the most favorable properties of their components. Alloys are mixtures of two or more metals. Ceramics are mixtures of nonmetals, or a nonmetal and a metal.
2. **Measuring in SI:** 143 grams
3. **Interpreting Data:** 16 cans
4. **Recognizing Cause and Effect:** Recycling the cans will conserve aluminum and the energy required to produce it. Recycling will also decrease the amount of solid waste discarded in landfills or as litter.

5. **Concept Mapping:**

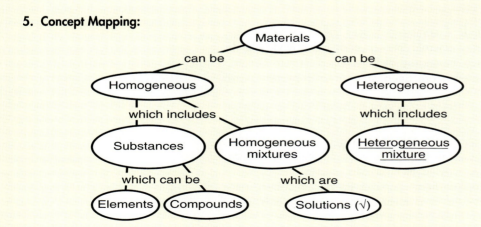

Objective

In this unit-ending feature, the unit topic, "Kinds of Substances," is extended to other disciplines. Students will see how different chemical substances affect other places around the world.

Motivate

Cooperative Learning: Assign one Connection to each group of students. Using the Expert Teams strategy, have each group research to find out more about the geographic location of the Connection—its climate, culture, flora and fauna, and ecological issues.

Teaching Tips

▶ Tell students to keep in mind the connection between chemical substances and their uses or effects as they are reading this feature.

▶ Ask students to brainstorm about new products and/or technologies that might exist in the future.

Wrap-Up

Conclude this lesson by having students discuss how the Connections presented here also affect other parts of Earth.

BIOLOGY

Background: The Providence system is set up in a greenhouse, with a series of vats containing swamp-like ecosystems. In marshes and swamps, sunlight bleaches some pollutants from water. Others are broken down by bacteria or are removed by plants such as cattails.

Discussion: Ask students to compare the organisms in the artificial wetland with those that would occur in a natural ecosystem.

Answer to Question: Organic matter and heavy metals would pollute any areas, either land or water, where they were released.

Extension: Have students research how Biosphere II plans to treat its sewage.

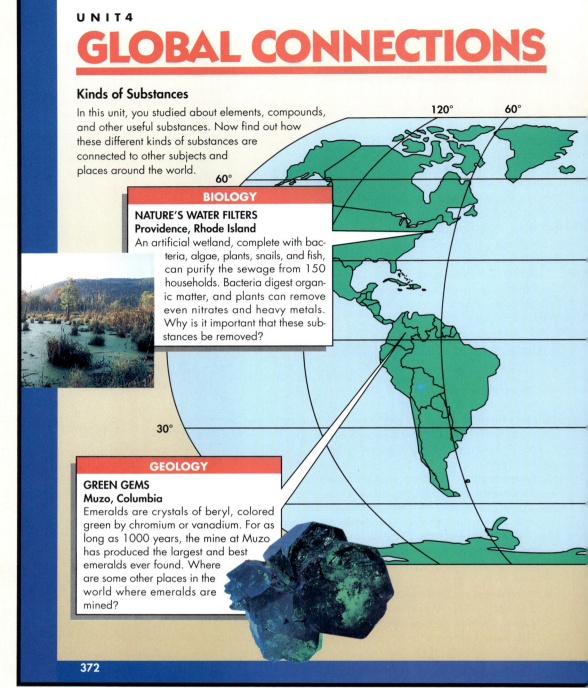

UNIT4
GLOBAL CONNECTIONS

Kinds of Substances

In this unit, you studied about elements, compounds, and other useful substances. Now find out how these different kinds of substances are connected to other subjects and places around the world.

BIOLOGY

NATURE'S WATER FILTERS
Providence, Rhode Island
An artificial wetland, complete with bacteria, algae, plants, snails, and fish, can purify the sewage from 150 households. Bacteria digest organic matter, and plants can remove even nitrates and heavy metals. Why is it important that these substances be removed?

GEOLOGY

GREEN GEMS
Muzo, Columbia
Emeralds are crystals of beryl, colored green by chromium or vanadium. For as long as 1000 years, the mine at Muzo has produced the largest and best emeralds ever found. Where are some other places in the world where emeralds are mined?

372

GEOLOGY

Background: Colombia produces half of the billion dollars' worth of emeralds mined yearly in the world. Beryls are minerals composed of beryllium aluminum silicate. Only those that are deep green and transparent are emeralds.

Discussion: Discuss with students how modern chemical analysis has changed what is called an emerald. Before then, almost any green stone was called an emerald. Gemologists can often determine the mine site of an emerald by studying the emerald.

Answer to Question: Zambia, Brazil, Zimbabwe, and Pakistan are the other major producers of emeralds.

Extension: Have students find out how synthetic emeralds are manufactured.

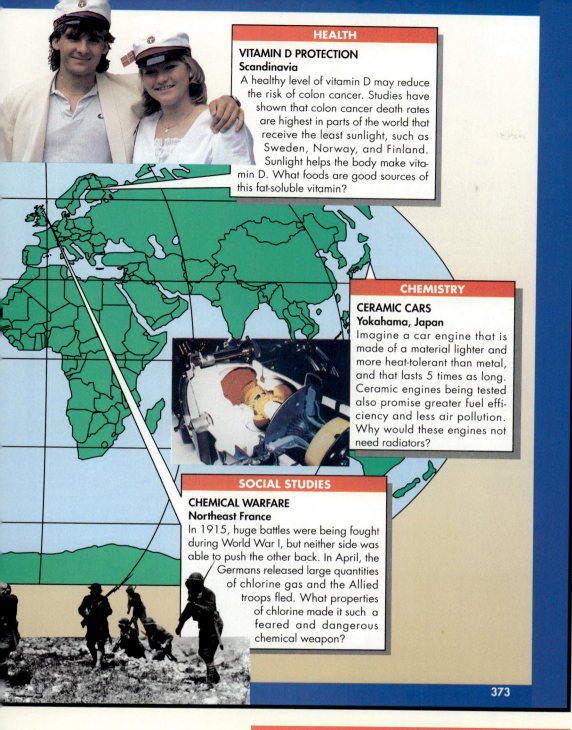

VITAMIN D PROTECTION
Scandinavia

A healthy level of vitamin D may reduce the risk of colon cancer. Studies have shown that colon cancer death rates are highest in parts of the world that receive the least sunlight, such as Sweden, Norway, and Finland. Sunlight helps the body make vitamin D. What foods are good sources of this fat-soluble vitamin?

CHEMISTRY

CERAMIC CARS
Yokahama, Japan

Imagine a car engine that is made of a material lighter and more heat-tolerant than metal, and that lasts 5 times as long. Ceramic engines being tested also promise greater fuel efficiency and less air pollution. Why would these engines not need radiators?

SOCIAL STUDIES

CHEMICAL WARFARE
Northeast France

In 1915, huge battles were being fought during World War I, but neither side was able to push the other back. In April, the Germans released large quantities of chlorine gas and the Allied troops fled. What properties of chlorine made it such a feared and dangerous chemical weapon?

373

SOCIAL STUDIES

Background: The use of chlorine gas was the first recorded use of poison gas in chemical warfare. Mustard gas ($C_4H_8Cl_2S$), an oily liquid which evaporates to a poison gas that causes blindness, burns, and death, was also used during World War I.

Discussion: By international agreement, the use of chemical weapons has been banned. However, not all countries have adhered to the ban.

Answer to Question: Chlorine is a poisonous gas that is heavier than air and settled in the trenches. It is very irritating to the nose, throat, and lungs.

Extension: Have students research the use of the chlorine compound 2,4,5-T, which was used as a chemical defoliant during the Vietnam war.

HEALTH

Background: Vitamin D is dissolved in and transported through the body in fat. It can be stored in fatty tissues, and toxic levels can build up if a person takes more than the recommended amount.

Discussion: Discuss with students why extra exposure to sunlight might not be the answer to the colon cancer risk. Point out that exposure to UV radiation from sunlight increases the risk for skin cancer.

Answer to Question: Fortified milk, liver, and fatty fishes are good sources of vitamin D.

Extension: Ask students to find out other environmental and lifestyle risk factors for cancer.

CHEMISTRY

Background: One Japanese car company has test driven a ceramic-engine prototype car over 5000 kilometers at speeds up to 150 km/hour.

Discussion: Point out to students that one disadvantage of many ceramics is that they are brittle. Ask what problems this could cause in car engines.

Answer to Question: Ceramics can withstand temperatures that would melt metal engines, so a radiator, whose purpose is to cool an engine, is not needed.

Extension: Have students prepare reports on some of the elements used in ceramics: titanium, zirconium, aluminum, silicon, carbon, nitrogen, and oxygen.

FARMER

Background: Farmers may work on family farms, as tenant farmers who live and work on property owned by others, or as hired hands who live elsewhere.

Related Career	Education
Farm-equipment mechanic	technical school
Animal nutritionist	college degree
Aerial crop sprayer	technical school
Feed salesperson	high school

Career Issue: Many farmers are concerned about contamination of groundwater from agricultural runoff. Some people want to see the use of certain agricultural chemicals restricted or banned.

What do you think? Lead students in a discussion of their own attitudes about the use of farm chemicals. Reducing the use of fertilizers and pesticides might result in smaller crops and higher prices. Would they be willing to pay more for food to reduce chemical use on farms?

PHARMACIST

Background: Dispensing pharmacists work in drugstores, clinics, and hospitals. Other pharmacists work for pharmaceutical laboratories testing drugs for purity and strength.

Related Career	Education
Crime lab technician	technical school
Quality control technician	technical school
Biomedical engineer	college degree
Pharmaceutical technician	technical school

Career Issue: Unless a physician specifies on a prescription that a generic drug may be substituted for a brand name, a pharmacist must dispense the brand name drug, usually at a higher cost to the patient.

What do you think? Do students think pharmacists should be allowed to make generic substitutions without the approval of the doctor? without the approval of the patient?

PHARMACIST

A *pharmacist* dispenses drugs and medicines prescribed by physicians and dentists. He or she also advises consumers on the uses and possible side effects of medicines—both prescription and nonprescription. A pharmacist must know about the chemical properties of drugs and their effects on the body.

If you're interested in becoming a pharmacist, you should take high school classes in biology, chemistry, and mathematics. Pharmacists attend college for four to six years. All states require a pharmacist to pass a licensing examination.

For Additional Information
Contact the American Pharmaceutical Association, 2215 Constitution Avenue NW, Washington, DC 20037.

UNIT READINGS

► Corrick, James A. *Recent Revolutions in Chemistry.* Danbury, CT: Watts, 1986.
► "Elements Show They're Metal." *New Scientist,* April 9, 1987, pp. 32-35.
► Ponte, Lowell. "Dawn of the New Stone Age." *Reader's Digest,* July, 1987, pp. 128-133.

FARMER

Because modern farming is so complex, a *farmer* needs business skills, as well as an understanding of and experience in methods and problems of farming. Different kinds of farming include dairy production, livestock production, crop production, orchards, and vineyards.

To be a farmer, you should be in good physical condition, enjoy working outdoors, and be interested in working with plants and animals. You also need a good background in biology, chemistry, mathematics, and good mechanical ability.

Many farmers receive on-the-job training while working with relatives or as hired hands. Some farmers take vocational classes to expand and update their knowledge. Others take 2- or 4-year college courses in agriculture.

For Additional Information
Contact the American Farm Bureau Federation, 225 Touhy Avenue, Park Ridge, Illinois 60668.

UNIT READINGS

Background
► *Recent Revolutions in Chemistry* presents discoveries such as silicon chips and polymers in a clear, understandable way.
► "Elements Show They're Metal" describes some unusual properties of metals subjected to high temperatures and pressures.
► "Dawn of the New Stone Age" discusses the uses of new ceramic compounds.

More Readings
1. Ward, Fred. "Emeralds." *National Geographic.* July 1990, pp. 38-69. Describes the often dangerous world of emerald mining and buying.
2. Canby, Thomas Y. "Advanced Materials—Reshaping Our Lives." *National Geographic.* December 1989, pp. 746-781.

The Art of Pottery

The passage that follows discusses an ancient technique for making pottery and a woman, Margaret Tafoya, who uses the technique to create highly prized pieces.

How and where pottery originated remains unknown, but early pottery can be traced back for about 9000 years. At some point, it was discovered that when dried clay bowls were placed in a fire and heated, they became hard and retained their shape—they became pottery, the first ceramics. Pottery could hold liquids, such as oil or water, which baskets could not.

In the areas of North America where pottery making flourished, three basic techniques were used—coiling, molding, and coiling and molding. Most pots were made by coiling or by a combination of coiling and molding. Coiling is done by forming a clay ball into a flat disk to serve as a base. Additional clay balls are rolled out to form coils and placed on top of one another to form the walls of the pot. Coiled pots are usually covered with slips to make the surface smooth for polishing, carving, or painting. Slip is made by mixing fine clay with water until it has the consistency of heavy cream. The pots are then polished with smooth, round polishing stones. The completed pots are fired in shallow pits or directly on the ground in fires of cedar wood. Potters can tell by the color of the fire when the pots are done.

Margaret Tafoya, a Pueblo potter from Santa Clara, New Mexico, uses the same methods to create her pottery that were used 1500 years ago by her Anasazi ancestors. She and other members of her family have dug clay from the same area for generations. She then shapes the clay, coil by coil, into a pot. The decorations she carves into her pots are symbols of the Santa Clara people. Her deeply carved redware and blackware are highly prized. She says the secret to the brilliant shine on her pottery is the polishing. She spends hours carefully rubbing her pots before firing them. The polishing stones she uses have been passed down from mother to daughter for generations.

In 1984, Margaret Tafoya was named a National Heritage Fellow by the National Endowment for the Arts. Since 1982 the Endowment has recognized, through its Folk Art Program, exceptional artists who have preserved their cultural and artistic traditions.

In Your Own Words

► Does a person have to be a painter or sculptor to be considered an artist? Write an essay supporting your position.

375

Biography: Margaret Tafoya is a member of the Tafoya-Naranjo family, known since the 1930s for their polished, carved, black and red pottery. Four generations of the family currently carry on the pottery-making tradition.

TEACHING STRATEGY

Have students read through the article on pottery. Then have them respond to the discussion questions below.

Discussion Questions

1. The designs for Margaret Tafoya's pottery are inspired by old myths of her people and include water serpents, buffalo horns, and bear paws. If you were going to make pottery, what kinds of designs would you use to represent your ethnic or cultural heritage? *Allow students to describe symbols they would use and encourage them to explain the personal significance of the symbols.*

2. Margaret Tafoya regards her polishing stones as her most valuable family heirlooms. Would you consider items such as these heirlooms? What items would be considered family heirlooms in your family? *Family heirlooms are items that have special meaning and emotional attachment for family members. Margaret Tafoya's polishing stones have been used for generations to carry on the art of pottery. Family heirlooms that students could mention might include such things as items of furniture, books, old photo albums, or any other item that helps hold a family tradition or culture together.*

Classics

► Street, A. and Alexander, W. *Metals in the Service of Man.* New York, NY: Penguin, 1962.

Other Works

► Books and articles on Native American pottery include: Wormington, H.M. *The Story of Pueblo Pottery.* Denver, Colo: Denver Museum of Natural History. Museum Pictorial, No. 2, 1974. Fenstermarker, Gerald, B. "Iroquois Pottery." *Pennsylvania Archaeologist.* January 1937. Dockstader, Frederick. *Naked Clay: Unadorned Pottery of the American Indian.* New York, NY: Museum of the American Indian, 1972.

In Unit 5, students are introduced to broad categories of physical and chemical changes in matter. Common properties of solutions and their behaviors are discussed. Chemical changes in matter are categorized as chemical reactions which can be represented by chemical equations. Four broad classes of chemical reactions are discussed as well as the role of energy in determining chemical reactions. The unit concludes with a discussion of acids and bases.

CONTENTS

ADVANCE PREPARATION

Audiovisuals
▶ Show the filmstrip/cassette *Chemical Reactions,* Science Software.
▶ Show the filmstrip *All About Acids and Bases,* Science Software.

Field Trips and Speakers
▶ Arrange for a county extension agent to visit your class to discuss testing soil acidity and alkalinity.

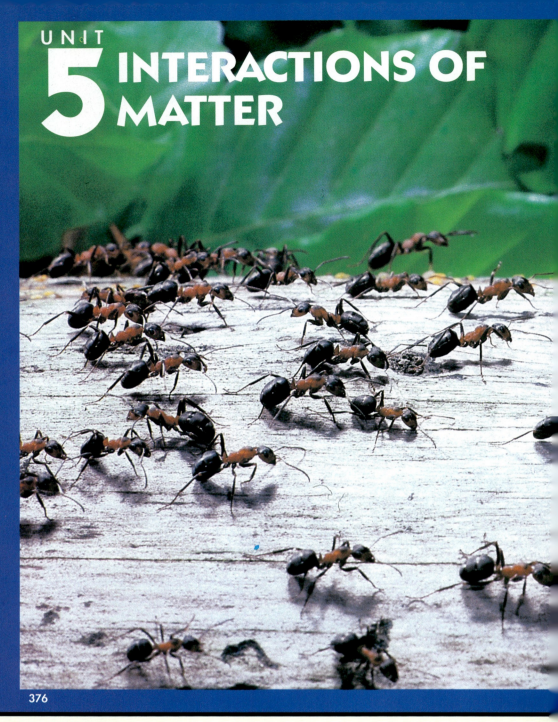

UNIT
5 INTERACTIONS OF MATTER

376

OPTIONS

Cross Curriculum
Have students research how the shelf-life of a food product is increased with preservatives. Have students research the two main types of preservatives: antimicrobials and antioxidants. Have them consider the economic and social benefits and also potential harm that food preservatives afford.

Science at Home
Cooperative Learning: Have groups of students begin collecting labels from empty containers of household materials that contain acids and bases that have safety statements and instructions for emergency antidotal procedures. Have students prepare a household alert bulletin board to describe dangers, proper uses, and first-aid procedures.

What's Happening Here?

What puts the fire in a fire ant's sting—and what in an aspirin takes the fire out? Acids are responsible in both cases. The itching and burning from the ant's bite are caused by formic acid. The easing of pain, fever, and swelling that an aspirin provides is caused by acetylsalicylic acid. How do acid solutions react with other substances to cause such different effects? You'll learn more about solutions and chemical reactions in this unit.

UNIT CONTENTS

377

Multicultural Awareness

Pickling, a process of food preservation that depends upon the chemical process of fermentation and the prohibition of bacterial growth in a highly acidic solution, is found in the cuisine of many cultures. Have students research different pickling processes and prepare lists of how and what products are pickled in different cultures. You may want to enlist the aid of the cafeteria director to assemble pickled foods from various cultures for a tasting.

Inquiry Questions

Use the following questions to focus a discussion of acids and acid solutions.

▶ **Suppose you have to take a pill (prescribed by a doctor) which you can't swallow. You might want to dissolve it in water. What things can you do to make it dissolve more quickly or completely?** *Stir it into the water; warm the water; crush the tablet into smaller pieces.*

▶ **Vinegar, lemon juice, and tomato juice contain organic acids. What common characteristic do they share?** *They taste sour.*

INTRODUCING THE CHAPTER

What's Happening Here?
▶ Have students look at the photos and read the text. Ask them to tell you what's happening here. Point out to students that in this unit they will learn that acids and other groups of substances can be classified by their chemical properties. They will also learn what happens to substances during chemical reactions and how the products of chemical reactions can be predicted.

▶ **Background:** Formic acid and acetylsalicylic acid are organic acids. Their respective structural formulas are

$$H - \underset{\underset{H}{|}}{C} = O \qquad CH_3 - \underset{\underset{O}{||}}{C} - O - \hexagon - \underset{\underset{O}{||}}{C} - OH$$

Formic acid destroys proteins and has deleterious effects similar to the methanol from which it is metabolized. Acetylsalicylic acid reduces pain by interfering with the production of hormones that affect the signals transmitted across the synapses of sensory nerves.

Previewing the Chapters
▶ Have students identify photographs in the chapters that indicate chemical changes have taken place.
▶ Have students identify photographs that show chemical reactions with which they are familiar.

Tying to Previous Knowledge
▶ Have students recall the structural formula of formic acid that they were asked to write in the Skill Builder from Section 13-2, on page 336. Draw the structure of acetylsalicylic acid on the chalkboard. Have them determine how many saturated and unsaturated bonds are in each.

▶ Have students conjecture on how instant hot-packs and cold-packs used to treat sport injuries work. Students should infer that chemical reactions are taking place.

▶ Use the **inquiry questions** in the OPTIONS box below to discuss acid solutions.

CHAPTER SECTION	OBJECTIVES	ACTIVITIES
15-1 How Solutions Form (2 days)	1. **Classify** solutions into three types and **identify** their solutes and solvents. 2. **Explain** the dissolving process. 3. **Describe** the factors that affect the rates at which solids and gases dissolve in liquids.	**MINI-Lab:** *How does solute surface area affect dissolving?* p. 383
15-2 Oceans—The World's Largest Solution Science & Society (1 day)	1. **Explain** why an ocean is considered a solution. 2. **Compare** and **contrast** methods of desalination.	
15-3 Solubility and Concentration (2 days)	1. **Discuss** how solubility varies among different solutes and for the same solute at different temperatures. 2. **Demonstrate** an understanding of solution concentrations. 3. **Compare** and **contrast** a saturated, unsaturated, and supersaturated solution.	**Activity 15-1:** *A Saturated Solution,* p. 394
15-4 Particles in Solution (2 days)	1. **Compare** and **contrast** the behavior of polar and non-polar substances in forming solutions. 2. **Relate** the processes of dissociation and ionization of solutions that conduct electricity. 3. **Explain** how the addition of solutes to solvents affects the freezing and boiling points of solutions.	**Activity 15-2:** *Boiling Points of Solutions,* p. 398
Chapter Review		

ACTIVITY MATERIALS

FIND OUT	ACTIVITIES		MINI-LABS
Page 379 1 paper or foam cup 1/3 c. clean sand 1/2 c. fine gravel 1 or 2 pieces of barbecue charcoal crushed into powder	**15-1 A Saturated Solution, p. 394** potassium bromide (KBr) distilled water lab burner large test tube graduated cylinder test tube holder 2 hole stopper thermometer balance apron goggles	**15-2 Boiling Points of Solutions, p. 398** 400 mL distilled water Celsius thermometer ringstand 72 g table salt, NaCl laboratory burner 250-mL beaker	**How does solute surface area affect dissolving? p. 383** 4 sugar cubes 2 100-mL beakers 2 stirring rods

CHAPTER FEATURES		TEACHER RESOURCE PACKAGE	OTHER RESOURCES
Problem Solving: *Derrick's Dilemma,* p. 394 **Skill Builder:** *Comparing and Contrasting,* p. 385		**Ability Level Worksheets** ◆ **Study Guide,** p. 61 ● **Reinforcement,** p. 61 ▲ **Enrichment,** p. 61 **MINI-Lab Worksheet,** p. 122 **Concept Mapping,** pp. 35, 36 **Science and Society,** p. 19 **Transparency Masters,** pp. 57, 58	**Color Transparency 29,** The Solution Process **Lab Manual 30,** Solutions
You Decide! p. 387		**Ability Level Worksheets** ◆ **Study Guide,** p. 62 ● **Reinforcement,** p. 62 ▲ **Enrichment,** p. 62	
Technology: *Replacing a Super Solvent,* p. 392 **Skill Builder:** *Making and Using Graphs,* p. 393		**Ability Level Worksheets** ◆ **Study Guide,** p. 63 ● **Reinforcement,** p. 63 ▲ **Enrichment,** p. 63 **Activity Worksheet,** pp. 116, 117 **Cross-Curricular Connections,** p. 21	**Lab Manual 31,** Solubility
Skill Builder: *Concept Mapping,* p. 397		**Ability Level Worksheets** ◆ **Study Guide,** p. 64 ● **Reinforcement,** p. 64 ▲ **Enrichment,** p. 64 **Activity Worksheet,** pp. 118, 119 **Critical Thinking/Problem Solving,** p. 21 **Transparency Masters,** pp. 59, 60	**Color Transparency 30,** Disassociation and Ionization
Summary Key Science Words Understanding Vocabulary Checking Concepts Understanding Concepts	Think & Write Critically Apply More Skill Builders Projects	**Chapter Review,** pp. 33, 34 **Chapter Test,** pp. 101-104	**Chapter Review Software** **Test Bank**

◆ **Basic**   ● **Average**   ▲ **Advanced**

ADDITIONAL MATERIALS		
SOFTWARE	**AUDIOVISUAL**	**BOOKS/MAGAZINES**
Solubility, EME. *Soluble, Programs for Learning Solutions,* Focus.	*Mr. Wizard's World: Chemistry in the Kitchen,* video, Macmillan/McGraw-Hill School Division.	Cohen, I. Bernard. *Theory of Solutions & Stereo-Chemistry.* Salem, NH: Ayer Co. Pub. 1981. DeRenzo, D.J. *Solvents Safety Handbook.* Park Ridge, NJ: Noyes Press, 1986. Markham, Ursula. *Crystal Workbook: A Complete Guide to Working With Crystals.* New York: Sterling Pub., 1988.

THEME DEVELOPMENT: Systems and Interactions is a theme of this textbook that is clearly developed in Chapter 15. The interaction of solute and solvent is developed by discussing the dissolving process. The solute interacts with the solvent and changes the physical characteristics of the solvent.

CHAPTER OVERVIEW

▶ **Section 15-1:** The different types of solutions are described. The dissolving process is presented in detail as are the factors that affect the rate of dissolving.

▶ **Section 15-2: Science and Society:** Students discover that the ocean could become the world's source of fresh water.

▶ **Section 15-3:** Solubility is defined and developed in this section. Ways used to describe solution concentration are presented. Unsaturated through supersaturated solutions are discussed.

▶ **Section 15-4:** The effect of solute and solvent polarity on solubility is presented in this section. Electrolytes are introduced and students learn that solutes have an effect on a solvent's boiling and freezing points.

CHAPTER VOCABULARY

solute	unsaturated
solvent	solution
desalination	supersaturated
distillation	solution
solubility	dissociation
saturated	ionization
solution	electrolyte
nonelectrolyte	

CHAPTER

15 Solutions

378

OPTIONS

For Your Gifted Students

Gifted students should continue to supplement their study by using a high school chemistry text and lab activities. They should find out how nonpolar solutes dissolve, be able to describe the equilibrium that exists between solute and solid in a saturated solution, and show how chemical theory explains Raoult's law. In addition, students could extend Activity 15-1 by obtaining more data and drawing a graph of solubility versus temperature. Activity 15-2 could be extended by using different salts and including freezing point.

Did you know that people in the United States consume about 1.5 trillion liters of water daily from sources such as the Colorado River? Almost all of this water is put through filtration.

FIND OUT!

Do this activity to find out what things are removed from water in the filtering process.

Use a sharp pencil to poke ten holes in the bottom of a foam cup. Place 1 cm of fine gravel in the cup. Then add 3 cm of clean sand. Place 1 cm of powdered charcoal on top of the sand. Finally, place another layer of fine gravel on top of the charcoal. Now your model filtration system is ready.

Slowly pour about 100 mL of dirty water through the cup. Catch the water that passes through the filtration system in a clear plastic cup. How does the filtered water compare to the original water? **CAUTION:** *This water is not suitable to drink.*

Gearing Up
Previewing the Chapter
Use this outline to help you focus on important ideas in this chapter.

Previewing Science Skills
▶ In the Skill Builders, you will compare and contrast, make and use a graph, and use a concept map.
▶ In the Activities, you will observe, organize, and collect data, and hypothesize.
▶ In the MINI-Lab, you will observe and infer.

What's next?

You have shown that filtering dirty water removes some contaminants. You will learn why all of them can't be removed by filtration alone when you read the pages that follow.

379

INTRODUCING THE CHAPTER
Use the Find Out activity to introduce students to solutions. Inform students that they will be learning more about how substances dissolve to form solutions as they read the chapter.

FIND OUT!
Preparation: Before lab, outside the building, place the charcoal in a cloth sack and pound with a hammer until it is a powder. You may choose to purchase activated charcoal used in aquarium filters.

Materials: one paper or foam cup, one-third cup clean sand, one-half cup fine gravel, one or two pieces of barbecue charcoal crushed into a powder for each group.

Teaching Tips
▶ Holes should be carefully punched so they are small. A straightened wire paper clip can also be used to punch holes.
▶ Students should observe that the filtered water is much clearer than the original water.
▶ After the students have used their filters to clear the muddy water, you can ask them if they think the filters could be used indefinitely. No. The sand and gravel can become clogged. The charcoal filter will become saturated with chemical contaminants.

Gearing Up
Have students study the Gearing Up feature to familiarize themselves with the chapter. Discuss the relationships of the topics in the outline.

What's Next?
Before beginning the first section, make sure students understand the connection between the Find Out activity and the topics to follow.

For Your Mainstreamed Students

Students can observe what happens when soluble and insoluble substances in a liquid are passed through a filter. They should stir table salt into 50 mL of water until no more salt will dissolve. Then they should add 5 mL of powdered chalk to the solution, and stir. Have them line a funnel with filter paper and pour the liquid through quickly. They should observe the substance on the filter paper after it has dried. Have them determine the identity of the remaining liquid by allowing it to evaporate to dryness and observing the crystals that remain.

PREPARATION

SECTION BACKGROUND

▶ Because there are three common states of matter, there are nine possible combinations of solvent-solute pairs. Not all possible combinations are presented in this introduction.

▶ Without stirring, the dissolving process slows as the solution reaches saturation around each piece of solute. Eventually the process reaches equilibrium as the number of particles leaving the surface of the solute equals the number of particles returning to the surface. Stirring brings a fresh supply of solvent near the solute.

▶ Most solids have positive enthalpies of solution, and are more soluble in hot water than in cold. Gases and some solids have negative enthalpies of solution and are more soluble in cold than in hot water.

▶ The mass of a gas that will dissolve in a liquid at a given temperature varies directly with the partial pressure of that gas. This is why solutions of gases in water such as soda pop must be maintained under pressure.

PREPLANNING

▶ To prepare for the Mini-Lab, obtain four sugar cubes per laboratory team.

1 MOTIVATE

▶ **Demonstration:** Place 20 g each of calcium acetate and potassium nitrate in separate, labeled beakers that contain 50 mL of water each. Stir, and observe that the calcium acetate dissolves but the potassium nitrate is only partially soluble. Then heat both beakers on a hot plate and stir occasionally. More potassium nitrate will dissolve while the calcium acetate will come out of solution.

New Science Words

solute
solvent

Objectives

▶ Classify solutions into three types and identify their solutes and solvents.
▶ Explain the dissolving process.
▶ Describe the factors that affect the rates at which solids and gases dissolve in liquids.

Figure 15-1. Examples of Gaseous and Liquid Solutions

Types of Solutions

To you the word *solution* may mean a kind of liquid mixture, like salt water or soda. Both these liquids are examples of solutions. But did you know that you also breathe a solution? Yes, air is a solution—and so is the sterling silver used to make fine jewelry. Solutions, then, can be gaseous or solid as well as liquid, as the examples show in Figure 15-1 and Figure 15-2. What makes all these mixtures solutions? Recall that a solution is a homogeneous mixture, in which the particles of the mixing substances are evenly distributed throughout.

There are three types of solutions, as shown in Table 15-1: gaseous solutions, liquid solutions, and solid solutions. A gaseous solution is a mixture of two or more gases. A liquid solution results when a gas, liquid, or solid is dissolved in a liquid solvent. A solid solution forms when a liquid and a solid or two or more solid substances

Table 15-1

COMPOSITION OF SOLUTIONS		
	Types of Solutions	**Examples**
Gaseous Solutions	gas + gas	air
Liquid Solutions	liquid + gas liquid + liquid liquid + solid	club soda vinegar sugar water
Solid Solutions	solid + liquid solid + solid	dental amalgam steel, brass

OPTIONS

Meeting Different Ability Levels

For Section 15-1, use the following **Teacher Resource Masters** depending upon individual students' needs.

◆ **Study Guide Master** for all students.
● **Reinforcement Master** for students of average and above average ability levels.
▲ **Enrichment Master** for above average students.

Additional Teacher Resource Package masters are listed in the OPTIONS box throughout the section. The additional masters are appropriate for all students.

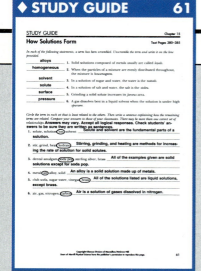

◆ **STUDY GUIDE**   61

STUDY GUIDE   Chapter 15
How Solutions Form   Text Pages 380–385

Figure 15-2. These objects are made of solid solutions called alloys.

are melted, mixed, and cooled. Solid solutions containing metals are usually called alloys.

To describe a solution, you may say that one substance is dissolved in another. ==The substance being dissolved is the **solute**. The substance that dissolves the solute is the **solvent**.== When a solid dissolves in a liquid, the solid is the solute and the liquid is the solvent. Thus, in salt water, sodium chloride is the solute, and water is the solvent. In a liquid-gas solution, the gas is the solute. In soda, carbon dioxide is the solute and water is the solvent.

In some solutions, either substance could be the solute or solvent. Generally, ==the substance present in the largest amount is considered to be the solvent.== Air is 78 percent nitrogen, 21 percent oxygen, and 1 percent argon. Thus, nitrogen is the solvent. In the alloy sterling silver, made of 92.5 percent silver and 7.5 percent copper, silver is the solvent and copper is the solute.

2

In air—a gaseous solution—which substance is the solvent?

The Dissolving Process

A good way to make lemonade is to prepare a solution of sugar in water before you add the lemon juice and ice. By what process do a solid and a liquid, such as sugar and water, form a solution? The dissolving of a solid in a liquid occurs at the surface of the solid. For water solutions, keep in mind two things you have learned about water. Like the particles of any liquid, water molecules are constantly moving. You also know that a water molecule is polar, which means it has a positive end and negative end. Molecules of sugar are also polar.

Figure 15-3. To prepare a glass of lemonade, it helps to first dissolve the sugar in water.

OBJECTIVES AND SCIENCE WORDS: Have students review the objectives and science words to become familiar with this section.

2 TEACH

Key Concepts are highlighted.

CONCEPT DEVELOPMENT

▶ **Demonstration:** Students can observe the dissolving process when you partially fill a petri dish with water and place it on the overhead projector. Place a crystal of potassium permanganate in the dish. Have students note the purple streamers as the water is stirred *gently*.

▶ The Motivate demonstration on page 380 makes use of the following solubility data per 100 mL water.

	0°C	100°C
Calcium acetate	37.4 g	29.7 g
Potassium nitrate	13.3 g	247.0 g

Potassium nitrate has a positive enthalpy of solution while calcium acetate has a negative enthalpy of solution.

▶ **Demonstration:** If students did not perform Activity 14-1 in which an alloy was formed, you may want to present it now as a demonstration. Point out that the brass that forms on the penny's surface is an alloy, a solution of a solid in a solid.

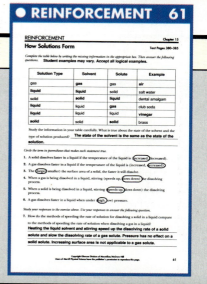

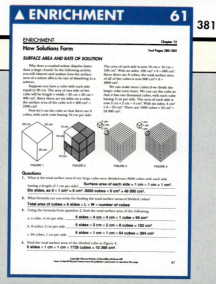

381

► There is a big difference between a liquid and a solution, but many people fail to see the difference and use the words interchangeably. Discuss the difference with your students. In addition, people often believe that the word *solution* always refers to a water solution. Whenever possible, reinforce the idea that it is possible to have solutions in other solvents.

CROSS CURRICULUM

► **Dietetics:** People who are trained in food preparation and nutrition know the economy of buying concentrates and diluting them to make the desired solutions. Show the class how tomato paste can become tomato sauce which can become tomato juice by adding water to a small sample. Shipping costs and fuel consumption are reduced when you add the water at the destination.

CONCEPT DEVELOPMENT

► **Demonstration:** To show the polarity of water, blow up a balloon and rub its surface with a wool cloth or fur. Turn on the water faucet so it delivers a thin stream. Bring the statically charged balloon near the stream and observe as the stream bends dramatically. Polar solvents attract and dissolve polar solutes.

TEACHER F.Y.I.

► The U.S. Navy recommends that divers using compressed air not dive below 38 meters. This recommendation is based on the fact that too much nitrogen and oxygen from the air will dissolve in the blood. This high concentration causes a type of intoxication called "rapture of the deep."

STUDENT TEXT QUESTION

► Page 382, paragraph 3: **What causes the particles in an alloy to be evenly spread out?** *The components are originally mixed as a liquid solution.*

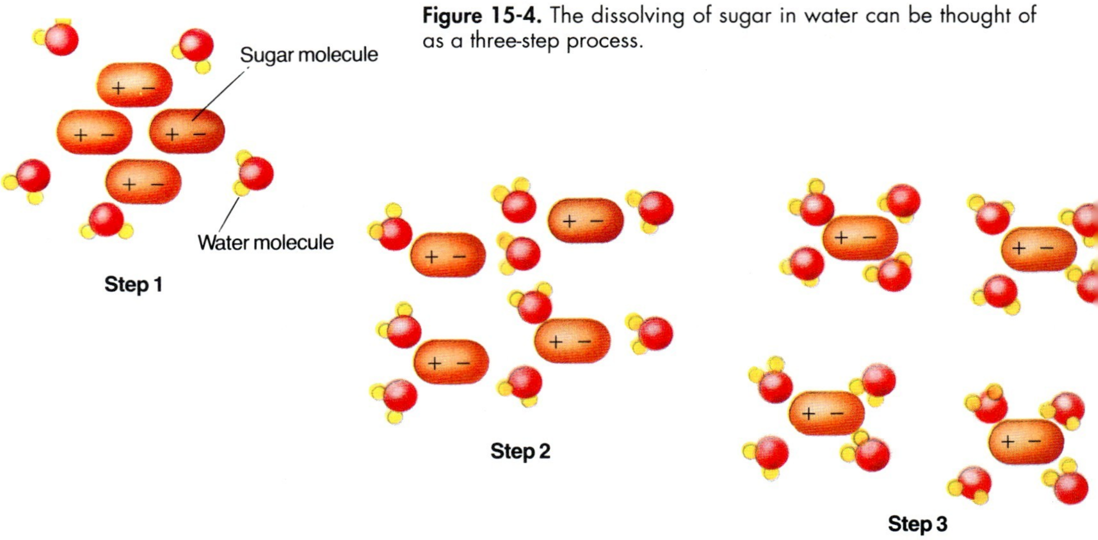

Figure 15-4. The dissolving of sugar in water can be thought of as a three-step process.

Sugar molecule

Water molecule

Step 1

Step 2

Step 3

When sugar dissolves in water, why are the water molecules attracted to the sugar molecules?

Study Figure 15-4 and the following steps to see how a sugar crystal dissolves in water.

Step 1: The moving water molecules cluster around the sugar molecules. The negative ends of the water molecules are attracted to the positive ends of the sugar molecules.

Step 2: The water molecules pull the sugar molecules into solution.

Step 3: The moving water molecules spread the sugar molecules out equally throughout the solution.

The process repeats itself as layer after layer of sugar molecules move away from the crystal until all the molecules are evenly spread out. The same three steps occur when any polar or ionic compound dissolves in a polar liquid. A similar process also occurs when a gas dissolves in a liquid.

You know from your study of fluids in Chapter 8 that particles of liquids and gases move much more freely than the particles of solids. When gases dissolve in gases, or when liquids dissolve in liquids, this movement results in uniform distribution. Alloys are made by first melting and then mixing the components. What causes the particles in an alloy to be evenly spread out?

382 SOLUTIONS

OPTIONS

INQUIRY QUESTIONS

► **When a glass of iced tea has some undissolved sugar on the bottom, why doesn't it dissolve and the tea become sweeter?** *The solution becomes concentrated around the sugar. Thus there are fewer free water molecules near the crystals. Also, the cold temperature reduces molecular movement.*

► **An opened bottle of carbonated soft drink goes "flat" upon standing. How do you think this occurs?** *The dissolved gas molecules are in motion and migrate out of the solution and into the air.*

Rate of Dissolving

Think again about making a sugar solution for lemonade. When you add the sugar to the water, you stir it. Stirring a solution speeds up dissolving because it brings more fresh solvent in contact with more solute. The rapid movement of liquid solvent particles causes the solid solute to move into solution faster.

A second way to speed the dissolving of a solid in a liquid is to grind large crystals into smaller ones. Suppose you had to use a 5-g crystal of rock candy, which is made of sugar, to sweeten your lemonade. If you put the crystal into a glassful of water, it might take two minutes to dissolve even with stirring. However, 5 g of powdered rock candy would dissolve in the same amount of water in a few seconds with stirring.

Why does powdering a crystal cause it to dissolve faster? Breaking the crystal into smaller pieces greatly increases its surface area, as you can see in Figure 15-5. Because dissolving takes place at the surface of the solid, increasing the surface area allows more solvent to come in contact with more solid solute. Thus, the speed of the solution process increases.

A third way to increase the rate at which most solids dissolve is to increase the temperature of a solvent. Think of making a sugar solution for lemonade. You can make the sugar dissolve faster by putting it in hot water instead of cold water. Increasing the temperature of a solvent speeds up the movement of its particles. This causes more solvent particles to bump into the solute. As a result, solute particles break loose from the surface faster.

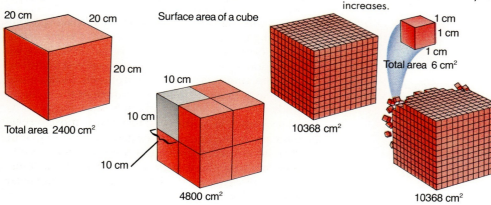

Figure 15-5. As a crystal is broken down into smaller pieces, the total surface area of the crystal increases.

Surface area of a cube

20 cm 20 cm
20 cm
Total area 2400 cm²

10 cm
10 cm
10 cm
4800 cm²

1 cm
1 cm
1 cm
Total area 6 cm²

10368 cm²

10368 cm²

CONCEPT DEVELOPMENT

▶ Students have read that solution rate is a function of the kinetic energy (temperature) of the solvent particles. The faster the solvent particles are moving, the more often they will collide with the crystal particles.

▶ **Demonstration:** To demonstrate the effect of temperature on rate of solution, place two petri dishes on an overhead projector. Into one dish place hot water and into the second place ice water. Then drop a sugar cube or uncoated aspirin tablet into each dish at the same time. Ask students to explain their observations based on their reading.

CROSS CURRICULUM

▶ **Health and Recreation:** Have a student trainer talk about the use of hot and cold packs. Striking the pack brings a dry chemical in contact with water. As the chemical dissolves the temperature will rise if the dissolving process is exothermic as with calcium chloride; it will go down if the process is endothermic as with ammonium chloride.

ENRICHMENT

▶ Ask students to think of ways to demonstrate the dissolving process or rates of dissolving. One may suggest Alka Seltzer tablets in hot and cold water with an uninflated balloon over the top of the flask. Although this process involves a chemical change, the substances must dissolve before reacting.

▶ Ask students to tell specifically how some home appliances, such as a mixer, food processor, stove, and microwave oven speed the dissolving process.

PROBLEM SOLVING

Have students examine packages of powdered sugar at home before answering the questions.

Think Critically: The constants were the amount of sugar, amount of water, size of cup, and temperature of water. Packaged powdered sugar often contains cornstarch, which will not dissolve in cold water.

CONCEPT DEVELOPMENT

▶ Pressure has little effect on solutions unless the solute is a gas. Ask students to use the particle model of a gas to explain increased solubility at higher pressures. At higher pressures, gas molecules are closer together (more concentrated) over the solvent and therefore enter solution more readily.

CHECK FOR UNDERSTANDING

Use the Mini Quiz to check for understanding.

MINI QUIZ

Use the Mini Quiz to check students' recall of chapter content.

❶ List five different types of solutions with an example of each. *See Table 15-1 for possible answers.*

❷ What are two parts that make up a solution? *solute and solvent*

❸ Polar solvents are able to dissolve which types of solute? *polar and ionic*

❹ How can the speed of solvent particles be increased? *increase the temperature*

RETEACH

▶ Have students give oral interpretations of what is happening in Figure 15-4 on page 382. Ask them to explain why each step occurs.

▶ Make a list of factors that affect the rate of solution for different types of solutions.

EXTENSION

For students who have mastered this section, use the **Reinforcement** and **Enrichment** masters or other OPTIONS provided.

Derrick's Dilemma

Derrick's teacher asked the students to think about the dissolving process. She asked them to think of ways to speed up the rate of dissolving a solid in a liquid.

Derrick knew that granulated sugar dissolves faster than sugar cubes. He hypothesized that powdered sugar would dissolve even faster than granulated sugar.

Derrick tested his hypothesis at home. He placed one level spoonful of powdered sugar in one cup and the same amount of granulated sugar in an identical cup. He added 250 mL of water at the same temperature to each cup. To his surprise, all the powdered sugar didn't dissolve. His mother suggested he read the ingredients on the powdered sugar package.

Think Critically: What four factors did Derrick keep constant in his experiment? How can you explain why all the powdered sugar did not dissolve?

Why does soda in an opened bottle bubble up when shaken?

How do you think these same factors will affect a gas-liquid solution? When you shake or stir an opened bottle of soda, it bubbles up and usually spills over—or squirts out. Did you ever wonder why? Stirring or shaking a solution of a gas in a liquid causes the gas to come out of solution faster. This happens because as you shake or stir the solution, more gas molecules are exposed to the surface. These molecules escape more freely. Shaking and stirring also increase the temperature of the solution slightly.

How might you do the opposite—cause the gas to dissolve faster in the liquid? The answer is simple: cool the liquid solvent and increase the pressure of the gas. In a soda bottling plant, both of these things are done. The machinery cools the solution and keeps it under pressure.

384 SOLUTIONS

OPTIONS

ENRICHMENT

▶ Have students look up the term *miscible* and explain what it means to say that two liquids are completely miscible. The liquids dissolve in each other in all proportions.

▶ Have students make clay cubes 10 cm on a side. Have them calculate the surface area of the six faces (600 cm²). Cut each cube into quarters, 5 cm on a side, and calculate the total surface area again. Each cube's area is 6 faces × 25 cm²/face = 150 cm². Therefore the total surface area is 8 cubes × 150 cm²/cube = 1200 cm². The surface area doubles.

▶ Have students look up the term *effervescence* and describe the difference in effervescence when opening bottles of cold soda and warm soda. The effervescence is greater in the warm soda.

Figure 15-6. When bottles of soda are opened, more gas comes out of solution in the warm bottle than in the cold one.

Maybe you have noticed the difference between opening a bottle of cold soda and a bottle of warm soda, Figure 15-6. Carbon dioxide gas is more soluble in cold water than in warm water. All gases are more soluble in cooler solvents. As shown in Figure 15-7, an unopened bottle of soda has no bubbles of carbon dioxide on its sides. In the sealed bottle, increased pressure keeps all of the gas dissolved. When the bottle is opened, the pressure of the carbon dioxide is greatly reduced. Then the carbon dioxide comes out of solution quickly.

Figure 15-7. Reduced pressure inside an opened bottle of soda causes the gas to come out of solution.

SECTION REVIEW

1. What are the three types of solutions? Give an example of each type.
2. What are three ways to increase the rate of dissolving a solid in a liquid?
3. **Apply:** Amalgams, sometimes used in tooth fillings, are alloys of mercury with other metals. Is an amalgam a solution? Explain.

☒ Comparing and Contrasting

Compare and contrast the effects on the rate of dissolving (1) a solid in a liquid and (2) a gas in a liquid, when (a) the solution is cooled, (b) it is stirred, and (c) the pressure on it is lowered. If you need help, refer to Comparing and Contrasting in the **Skill Handbook** on page 679.

Skill Builder

PREPARATION

SECTION BACKGROUND
▶ Because people are concerned about water quality, reverse osmosis water purification systems are sold for home use.

1 MOTIVATE

▶ **Demonstration:** Distill some water that has food coloring added to it. If you do not have a cold water condenser, just pass the steam through glass tubing. The separation of clear and colored water is visible.

Science and WRITING
Have students research the extraction of metals from their salts once the salts have been isolated from seawater.

TYING TO PREVIOUS
KNOWLEDGE: Have students discuss lifeboat rescue movies. They may recall that a stored fresh water supply was crucial to survival.

OBJECTIVES AND
SCIENCE WORDS: Have students review the objectives and science words to become familiar with this section.

2 TEACH

Key Concepts are highlighted.

CONCEPT DEVELOPMENT
▶ Ask students how long they think they can survive without water. Most students know that you can survive only a few days in the best of conditions.
▶ Point out to the class that many people around the world do not have pure water or enough water to drink. Many of these people cannot afford the energy costs to desalinate water.

SCIENCE & SOCIETY 15-2

Oceans—The World's Largest Solution

New Science Words
desalination
distillation

Science and WRITING
Prepare a report for the class explaining how minerals are mined from the ocean.

Objectives
▶ Explain why an ocean is considered a solution.
▶ Compare and contrast methods of desalination.

Can Oceans Be Used as Fresh Water Sources?

About 97 percent of the water on Earth is in our salty oceans. Although the most abundant salt in the oceans is sodium chloride, the oceans also contain many other dissolved salts. Thus, the oceans make up the world's largest solution. Do we need this solution as a source of fresh water?

The need for fresh water in the world is greater today then ever before. Several reasons contributing to an increased need for fresh water are:

1. Increase in the world's population,
2. High concentration of people living in selected areas,
3. Increase in the uses of fresh water,
4. Increase in the pollution of existing sources of fresh water, and
5. Development of areas where water has always been scarce.

To meet this need, scientists are turning to desalination. Any method that removes dissolved salts from ocean water to produce fresh water is called **desalination.**
In 1989, two billion gallons of fresh water were produced per day by more than 1500 desalination plants

386 SOLUTIONS

OPTIONS

Meeting Different Ability Levels
For Section 15-2, use the following **Teacher Resource Masters** depending upon individual students' needs.
◆ **Study Guide Master** for all students.
● **Reinforcement Master** for students of average and above average ability levels.
▲ **Enrichment Master** for above average students.

◆ STUDY GUIDE   62

STUDY GUIDE   Chapter 15
Oceans—The World's Largest Solutions   Text Pages 386–387

Twelve terms related to desalination are included in the puzzle below. Use the clues and the letters you have been given to identify each of the missing terms. Write one letter in each space.

1. S O D I U M C H L O R I D E
2. F R E E Z E M E T H O D
3. F R E S H W A T E R
4. E V A P O R A T E
5. S O L V E N T
6. D I S T I L L A T I O N
7. C O N D E N S A T I O N
8. V A C U U M
9. S O L A R S T I L L
10. L I Q U I D
11. S O L U T E
12. O C E A N W A T E R

Clues
1. most common salt in ocean water (2 words)
2. process by which fresh water is obtained from frozen ocean water (2 words)
3. wanted end product of desalination (2 words)
4. The first step in distillation is to ____ the water from the solution.
5. In a solution of ocean water, water is the ____.
6. process by which a liquid is separated from solution through evaporation and condensation
7. process by which a liquid is obtained by cooling a gas
8. type of chamber used in freeze method or in flash distillation
9. Simplest method of desalination uses this device. (2 words)
10. type of solution ocean water forms
11. In a solution of ocean water, NaCl is the ____.
12. Ninety-seven percent of Earth's water is ____. (2 words)

Answer the following question.
13. What is desalination? **any process by which dissolved salts are removed from ocean water**

62

throughout the world. The most common desalination methods used by these plants are distillation and freezing.

In **distillation,** water is evaporated from a solution. The water vapor is cooled, condensed, and collected as fresh water. The simplest and cheapest type of distillation uses a solar still. Heat from the sun evaporates the water. The water vapor condenses on the reservoir's transparent cover and runs into collecting trays.

Another type of distillation is flash distillation. Flash distillation makes use of the fact that water boils at a much lower temperature in a vacuum or reduced-pressure chamber. In flash distillation, ocean water is pumped into a vacuum chamber where it starts to boil. The salt-free water vapor is collected and condensed to form fresh water.

The freeze method also is being used to desalinate water. When salt water is cooled sufficiently, the ice that forms is salt-free. In the freeze method, ocean water enters a vacuum freezing chamber. The vapor produced is condensed directly to fresh water. The water that freezes is rinsed and then melted to form fresh water.

Many people are looking to our oceans as a vast resource of fresh water. But removing the solute from this solution is not a simple process.

Figure 15-8. In the freeze process ocean water is frozen. This ice is rinsed and then melted to produce salt-free water.

SECTION REVIEW

1. Why are the oceans a solution?
2. Describe how distillation and freezing ocean water can be used to produce fresh water.

You Decide!

Suppose that you were in charge of building a desalination plant in a desert area. Large amounts of ocean water could be brought to the area. Which desalination method would you use and why?

SCIENCE & SOCIETY

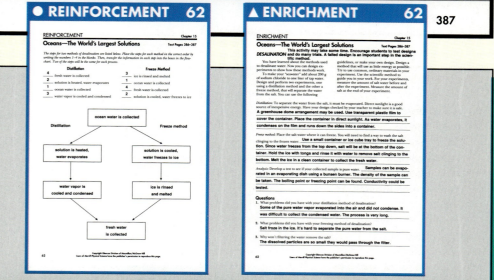

387

CROSS CURRICULUM

▶ **Literature:** Samuel T. Coleridge wrote in *The Rime of the Ancient Mariner* these words:

Water, water, everywhere,
And all the boards did shrink;
Water, water, everywhere
Nor any drop to drink.

Cooperative Learning: Ask Paired Partners to interpret the Coleridge poem using the knowledge gained in this section.

CHECK FOR UNDERSTANDING

Have students answer questions 1-2 in the Section Review.

RETEACH

Point out that the salts dissolved in ocean water, do not evaporate easily. With that in mind, have students interpret the process of distillation stepwise and explain why it yields pure water.

EXTENSION

For students who have mastered this section, use the **Reinforcement** and **Enrichment** masters or other OPTIONS provided.

3 CLOSE

▶ Have students prepare a list of ways that society uses fresh water. Combine the individual lists into one large list. After examining the list of uses for fresh water, ask the students which ones would produce the greatest conservation if eliminated or reduced.

SECTION REVIEW ANSWERS

1. There are many salts dissolved in the oceans.

2. In distillation, ocean water is evaporated, leaving salts behind. The vapor is condensed to yield fresh water. When salt water is frozen, the ice that forms is salt-free and can be melted to yield fresh water.

YOU DECIDE!

SCIENCE & SOCIETY

Answers will vary. Make sure students can support their answers. They should consider the types of energy available in the area. Is there sunlight only or is there abundant electricity and/or fuel?

SECTION BACKGROUND

▶ Solubility differences can be used to separate a mixture of different substances. If a water solution of two salts is allowed to evaporate, the least soluble one at the temperature of evaporation will crystallize first.

▶ In science, more solutions are expressed in mass percentages than volume percentages.

▶ A saturated solution is in a state of equilibrium. The number of particles leaving the crystal surface (dissolving) is equal to the number returning to the surface (crystallizing).

▶ Supersaturation is possible because solids will not crystallize unless there is a suitable surface such as a crystal, upon which to start crystallization.

PREPLANNING

▶ To prepare for Activity 15-1, you will need to prepare a copper wire stirrer for each team.

▶ To save lab time and improve results, you may want to prepare the 9-gram samples of potassium bromide in test tubes.

1 MOTIVATE

▶ Show the students a bottle of contact lens solution. Read the ingredients and their concentrations. Ask them if concentration is important to their eye health. Too much salt or too little can cause damage to living tissue.

▶ Point out that in this chapter students will learn how to duplicate a solution's concentration so it is the same every time it is prepared. Just as the contact lens solution is the same month after month in the pharmacy.

15-3 Solubility and Concentration

New Science Words

solubility
saturated solution
unsaturated solution
supersaturated solution

Objectives

▶ Discuss how solubility varies among different solutes and for the same solute at different temperatures.

▶ Demonstrate an understanding of solution concentrations.

▶ Compare and contrast a saturated, unsaturated, and supersaturated solution.

Solubility

Sugar, you know, dissolves easily in water. Suppose you want to make super sweet lemonade. You stir two, three, four—or more—teaspoons of sugar into a cup of water, and it all dissolves. But eventually you add another teaspoon of sugar and it no longer dissolves, Figure 15-9.

Change the scene from your kitchen to a laboratory. Suppose now you measure out 1.3 g of lithium carbonate and add it to 100 g of water at 20°C. You observe that all of the lithium carbonate dissolves. But if you add more lithium carbonate to the same solution, none of it dissolves. However, you could add 34 g of potassium chloride to 100 g of water before no more will dissolve. You would have shown that the amount of these two substances that dissolves in 100 g of water at 20°C varies greatly.

Generally, the **solubility** of a substance is the maximum number of grams of the substance that will dissolve in 100 g of solvent at a certain temperature. Table 15-2 shows how the solubility of several substances varies at 20°C. For solutes that are gases, the pressure must also be given, for a reason you will learn soon. ❶

Figure 15-9. The amount of sugar that can dissolve in a glass of water is limited.

OPTIONS

Meeting Different Ability Levels

For Section 15-3, use the following **Teacher Resource Masters** depending upon individual students' needs.

◆ **Study Guide Master** for all students.

● **Reinforcement Master** for students of average and above average ability levels.

▲ **Enrichment Master** for above average students.

Additional Teacher Resource Package masters are listed in the OPTIONS box throughout the section. The additional masters are appropriate for all students.

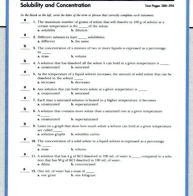

◆ **STUDY GUIDE** 63

STUDY GUIDE — Chapter 15
Solubility and Concentration — Text Pages 388–394

In the blank at the left, write the letter of the term or phrase that correctly completes each statement.

__a__ 1. The maximum number of grams of solute that will dissolve in 100 g of solvent at a certain temperature is the ____ of the solute.
   a. solubility   b. dilution

__a__ 2. Different substances have ____ solubilities.
   a. different   b. the same

__b__ 3. The concentration of a mixture of two or more liquids is expressed as a percentage by ____.
   a. mass   b. volume

__a__ 4. A solution that has dissolved all the solute it can hold at a given temperature is ____.
   a. unsaturated   b. saturated

__a__ 5. As the temperature of a liquid solvent increases, the amount of solid solute that can be dissolved in the solvent ____.
   a. increases   b. decreases

__b__ 6. Any solution that can hold more solute at a given temperature is ____.
   a. unsaturated   b. saturated

__a__ 7. Each time a saturated solution is heated to a higher temperature, it becomes ____.
   a. saturated   b. supersaturated

__b__ 8. A solution that contains more solute than a saturated one at a given temperature is ____.
   a. unsaturated   b. supersaturated

__b__ 9. Lines on a graph that show how much solute a solvent can hold at a given temperature are called ____.
   a. solution graphs   b. solubility curves

__a__ 10. The concentration of a solid solute in a liquid solvent is expressed as a percentage by ____.
   a. mass   b. volume

__a__ 11. A solution that has 4 g of KCl dissolved in 100 mL of water is ____ compared to a solution that has 80 g of KCl dissolved in 100 mL of water.
   a. dilute   b. concentrated

__a__ 12. One mL of water has a mass of ____.
   a. one gram   b. one kilogram

Copyright Glencoe Division of Macmillan/McGraw-Hill
Users of Merrill Physical Science have the publisher's permission to reproduce this page.   63

Table 15-2

SOLUBILITY OF SUBSTANCES IN WATER AT 20°C	
Solid Substances	**Solubility in g/100 g of Water**
Barium sulfate	0.00025
Lithium carbonate	1.3
Potassium chloride	34.0
Sodium nitrate	88.0
Lithium bromide	166.0
Sucrose (sugar)	204.0
Gaseous Substances*	
Hydrogen	0.00017
Oxygen	0.005
Carbon dioxide	0.16

*when pressure = 1 atmosphere

Concentration

Suppose you added one spoonful of lemon juice to a glass of water to make lemonade. Your friend decided to add four spoonfuls of lemon juice to a glass. You could say that your glass of lemonade is dilute. Your friend's glass of lemonade is concentrated. It would have more lemon flavor than yours. A concentrated solution is one in which there is a large amount of solute in the solvent. A dilute solution is one in which there is a small amount of solute in the solvent.

Concentrated and *dilute* are not precise terms. But there are ways to describe solution concentrations precisely. One of these ways is to state the percentage by volume of the solute. Do you ever have a fruit juice drink in a box with your lunch or for a snack? Next time you do, read the label to see how much actual juice you are getting. The percentage by volume of the cherry juice in the drink shown in Figure 15-11 is 10 percent cherry juice and about 90 percent water. Ten mL of cherry juice plus 90 mL of water makes 100 mL of cherry drink. Generally, if two or more liquids are being mixed, the concentration is often given in percentage

Dilute Solution

Concentrated Solution

Figure 15-10. The concentrated solution of lemonade contains more solute (lemon juice) than the dilute solution.

Figure 15-11. The concentrations of fruit juices are often given in percent by volume.

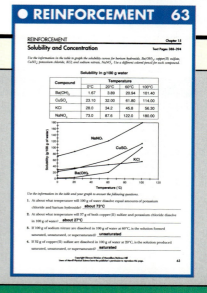

● REINFORCEMENT 63

▲ ENRICHMENT 63

389

TYING TO PREVIOUS KNOWLEDGE: Ask students to check at home to see if there is a very old jar of honey on a shelf. As the water slowly evaporates from the honey, sugar crystals begin to form and cause the honey to have a coarse texture. The solution has become saturated.

OBJECTIVES AND SCIENCE WORDS: Have students review the objectives and science words to become familiar with this section.

2 TEACH

Key Concepts are highlighted.

CONCEPT DEVELOPMENT

Cooperative Learning: An opportunity to use the Science Investigation group strategy occurs when you provide teams with the chemicals to determine the solubility of an unknown substance by repeatedly adding 1 g samples to 100 mL of water at 20°C. When the solution is saturated, ask students to analyze their solubility data and determine the identity of their unknown. Use information from Tables 15-2, 15-3, and from reference books for other substances. Use only substances that are safe.

► Ask students where they have seen percentage concentration figures printed on labels. Have samples with labels available from your kitchen, garage, and bathroom that students can read to the class. Mouthwash may be 15% alcohol; bleach is usually 5% sodium hypochlorite; and so on.

REVEALING MISCONCEPTIONS

► Many students believe that all concentrated acids are 100% acid. Have small labeled bottles of concentrated hydrochloric, nitric, and sulfuric acids on display. Have students read from the label the percentage of acid in each.

► **Music:** Have students fill stemmed glasses with water colored with food coloring. Adjust the water level in each glass so that a different note is produced when a wet finger tip is rubbed around the rim. Glasses can be tuned to duplicate one octave of music. Have a talented student or team of students play a melody on the solution-filled glasses.

CONCEPT DEVELOPMENT

► Prepare an overhead transparency or a chalkboard presentation of the example problem on page 390. Use it to go through this example in detail. Emphasize the problem-solving steps.
► Encourage students to bring calculators to class to solve the solution concentration problems.

PRACTICE PROBLEM ANSWERS

$1.0 L = 1000 mL$
$40 g/1000 mL = 0.040 g/mL$
$0.040 g/mL \times 20 mL = 0.80 g$ NaOH

MINI QUIZ

Use the Mini Quiz to check students' recall of chapter content.

1 The maximum number of grams of a substance that will dissolve in 100 g of solvent at a specific temperature is known as the _____ of the substance. *solubility*

2 When there is a large amount of solute in the solvent, the solution is said to be _____ . *concentrated*

3 Use Table 15-2 to determine how much sucrose would dissolve in 100 g and in 50 g of water at 20°C. *204 g and 102 g*

4 The concentration of a solution of a solid in a liquid is usually expressed as a percentage by _____ . *mass*

5 A solution that contains all the solute it can hold at a given temperature is said to be _____ . *saturated*

---

by volume, stated in number of milliliters of solute plus enough solvent to make 100 mL of solution.

You can express concentration of a solid dissolved in a liquid as percentage by mass. This is the mass in grams of solute plus enough solvent to make 100 g of solution. Because 1 mL of water has a mass of 1 g, you would mix 10 g of sodium chloride with 90 mL of water to make a 10 percent solution of sodium chloride. **4**

You can also express concentration as mass of solute in a liter of solution. When a certain volume of solution is measured out, the number of grams of solute it contains can easily be calculated.

EXAMPLE PROBLEM: Calculating the Mass of Solute/Liter of Solution

Problem Statement:	A potassium chloride solution contains 88 g of KCl in 1.0 L of solution. How many grams of solute are in 50 mL of solution?
Problem-Solving Steps:	
1. Change 1.0 L to mL	$1.0 L = 1000 mL$
2. Figure out the number of g of solute in 1 mL of solution.	$88 g/1000 mL = 0.088 g/mL$
3. Use equation:	Mass of solute = concentration of 1 mL solution × volume of solution
Solution:	Mass = $0.088 g/mL \times 50 mL = 4.4 g$

PRACTICE PROBLEM

Strategy Hint: Move decimal in 40.0 g three places to the left to find the mass of solute in 1 mL of solution.

1. Forty grams of lye (NaOH) was dissolved in enough water to make 1.0 L of solution. How many grams of lye would be in 20 mL of the solution?

Limits of Solubility

If you add 30.0 g of potassium chloride, KCl, to 100 g of water at 0°C, only 28 g will dissolve. You have a saturated solution because no more KCl can dissolve. **A saturated solution is a solution that has dissolved all the solute it can hold at a given temperature.** But if you heat the mixture to a higher temperature, more KCl can dissolve. As the temperature of the liquid solvent increases, the amount of solid that can dissolve also increases. Table 15-3 gives the amounts of a few solutes that can dissolve in water at different temperatures, forming saturated solutions. **5**

What is a saturated solution?

OPTIONS

INQUIRY QUESTIONS

► A sodium nitrate solution contains 40 g of NaNO₃ dissolved in 1.0 L of solution. How many grams of sodium nitrate can be recovered when 100 mL of solution is evaporated to dryness? *4 grams*
► Use Table 15-2 to determine how much sodium nitrate will dissolve in 1000 g of water at 20°C. *880 g*
► A 50.0-mL sample of salt solution is found to contain 0.040 g of sodium chloride. How much salt would be in 1.0 L of solution? *0.80 g*

Table 15-3

Compound	Formula	Solubility in g/100 g Water at the Temperature Indicated			
		0°C	20°C	60°C	100°C
Ammonium chloride	NH_4Cl	29.4	37.2	55.3	77.3
Barium hydroxide	$Ba(OH)_2$	1.67	3.89	20.94	101.40
Copper(II) sulfate	$CuSO_4$	23.1	32.0	61.8	114
Lead(II) chloride	$PbCl_2$	0.67	1.00	1.94	3.20
Potassium bromide	KBr	53.6	65.3	85.5	104
Potassium chloride	KCl	28.0	34.0	45.8	56.3
Potassium nitrate	KNO_3	13.9	31.6	109	245
Sodium acetate	$NaC_2H_3O_2$	36.2	46.4	139	170.15
Sodium chlorate	$NaClO_3$	79.6	95.9	137	204
Sodium chloride	NaCl	35.7	35.9	37.1	39.2
Sodium nitrate	$NaNO_3$	73.0	87.6	122	180
Sucrose (sugar)	$C_{12}H_{22}O_{11}$	179.2	203.9	287.3	487.2

Another way to picture the effect of higher temperatures on solubility is with line graphs, like those in Figure 15-12. The lines are called solubility curves. You can use the curves to figure out the amount of solute that will dissolve at any temperature given on the graph. For example, at 47°C, about 82 g of both KBr and KNO_3 form saturated solutions with 100 g of water. About how much NaCl will form a saturated solution with 100 g of water at the same temperature?

6 An **unsaturated solution** is any solution that can dissolve more solute at a given temperature. Each time a saturated solution is heated to a higher temperature, it may becomes unsaturated. The term *unsaturated* isn't precise. At 20°C, 37.2 g of NH_4Cl dissolved in 100 g water is a saturated solution. However, an unsaturated solution of NH_4Cl could be any amount less than 37.2 g in 100 g of water at 20°C.

Figure 15-12. The solubilities of substances in water change with temperature.

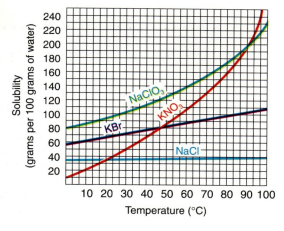

15-3   SOLUBILITY AND CONCENTRATION   **391**

CONCEPT DEVELOPMENT
▶ Being able to read information correctly from a table is an important skill that is included on most standardized tests. Quiz your students randomly about information on Table 15-3. For example, ask how many grams of potassium chloride will dissolve in 100 g of water at 60°C (45.8 g).
▶ **Demonstration:** Prepare 50 mL of a saturated solution of any substance from Table 15-3 except lead(II) chloride and barium hydroxide. Place a small amount of this solution in a petri dish on the overhead projector. Place a small amount of the same solution in a second petri dish and add water to make it unsaturated. Have a student drop a crystal of the salt into each petri dish and slowly stir both solutions. The class will observe the crystal dissolve in the unsaturated solution, but it will remain visible in the saturated solution.
▶ Emphasize to your students that the term unsaturated is not a precise indicator of how concentrated a solution is. Concentrated and dilute also do not convey any quantitative information about a solution.
▶ In class, place a seed crystal of sodium acetate on a watch glass. Slowly pour supersaturated solution on the crystal. The class will observe a stalagmite-like solid form on the glass as you pour. The crystals can be reused.

REVEALING MISCONCEPTIONS
▶ Most people believe that all solid solutes become more soluble in water as the temperature increases. Calcium acetate's solubility data shows that this is a misconception. At 0°C, 37.4 g will dissolve in 100 mL of water while at 100°C only 29.7 g is soluble. The slope of the solubility graph for such a substance is negative.

STUDENT TEXT QUESTION
▶ Page 391, paragraph 1: **How much NaCl will form a saturated solution with 100 g of water at 47°C?** *about 36.7 g*

ENRICHMENT
▶ "Oil and water do not mix" is a simplistic statement, but it generally means that organic solutes are dissolved by organic solvents and not by water. Ask a student to demonstrate for the class how best to clean a paint brush that has been used with a water-based latex paint and one that has an oil based paint in it. **CAUTION:** *Paint thinner is flammable. Never use gasoline as a substitute.*

▶ Sealed plastic bags containing a supersaturated solution of sodium acetate and a metal disk are sold in stores as reusable hot packs. When the metal disk is pressed, the solution crystallizes. Have a student bring one from home and demonstrate its use for the class. The pack is made reusable by placing it in boiling water to redissolve the solute.

For more information on replacing CFCs see "Atmosphere of Uncertainty" by Deborah Erickson, *Scientific American*, April 1990, pp. 77-78.

Think Critically: Answers will vary. Examples include shoe polish, car waxes, water-repellent products, and stain-resistant products.

CONCEPT DEVELOPMENT

▶ **Demonstration:** In advance, prepare a supersaturated solution for each class by adding 50 to 75 g of sodium acetate trihydrate to a very clean 250-mL Erlenmeyer flask. Warm the flask on a hot plate until the crystals melt. Use a wash bottle filled with distilled water to rinse down the sides of the flask with about 8 mL of water. Gently swirl the flask to mix, then cover it and allow to cool.

 FLEX Your Brain

Use the Flex Your Brain activity to have students explore SOLUBILITY.

CHECK FOR UNDERSTANDING

Use the Mini Quiz to check for understanding.

MINI QUIZ

Use the Mini Quiz to check students' recall of chapter content.

6 A solution that can dissolve more solute at a given temperature is said to be _____ . *unsaturated*

7 A solution that contains more solute than a saturated one has at a specific temperature is said to be _____ . *supersaturated*

8 If you add a solute crystal to an unsaturated solution, the crystal will _____ . *dissolve*

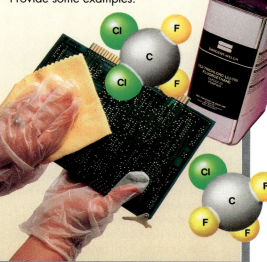
Replacing a Super Solvent

Scientists the world over are involved in a struggle to replace chlorofluorocarbons, often called CFCs. One of these compounds, named CFC-113, has been described as a super solvent. This compound doesn't bead up like water, so it is a better wetting agent. This means, for example, that CFC-113 can flow into all the tiny spaces on a printed circuit board to clean it up. This CFC has been used to clean sensitive equipment on the space shuttle and the electronic chips responsible for emission control in cars.

If this solvent is so fantastic, why are scientists trying to replace it? This super solvent has a serious drawback. Like other CFCs, it is damaging Earth's protective ozone layer, high in the atmosphere. As you will read in the next chapter, radiation from the sun splits off chlorine atoms from CFCs, and these chlorine atoms destroy ozone.

Thus, scientists need to develop solvents that can do the same jobs as CFCs but contain no chlorine. Recently, two new compounds called hydrochlorofluorocarbons, or HCFCs, have been tested. HCFCs work almost as well as the CFCs as solvents and cleaning agents, but they contain less chlorine and so cause less damage to the ozone layer. The HCFCs may be the new super solvents. They can be used until solvents containing no chlorine at all are available for use.

Think Critically: The inability of one substance to wet another is important in the development of many products. Provide some examples.

If you make a saturated solution of potassium nitrate 100°C and then let it cool to 20°C, part of the solute comes out of solution. You can see why—at the lower temperature, a saturated solution is formed with less solute. Most other saturated solutions behave in a similar way when cooled. But if you cool a saturated solution of sodium acetate from 100°C to 20°C, no solute comes out. This solution is supersaturated. A supersaturated **solution** contains more solute than a saturated one has at that temperature. This kind of solution is unstable.

OPTIONS

Figure 15-13. A supersaturated solution of sodium acetate (left) crystallizes out when a crystal of sodium acetate is added (right).

When a small crystal of the solute is added to a supersaturated solution, the excess solute quickly crystallizes out. Figure 15-13 shows this behavior in a supersaturated solution of sodium acetate.

Suppose you add a solute crystal to a solution. If the crystal dissolves, the solution is unsaturated. If the crystal does not dissolve, the solution is saturated. And if excess solute comes out, the solution is supersaturated. How would you explain each of these possible results? **8**

SECTION REVIEW

1. Do all solutes dissolve to the same extent in the same solvent? How do you know?
2. Using Table 15-3 on page 391, state the following: the mass of $NaNO_3$ that would have to be dissolved in 100 g of water to form a saturated, an unsaturated, and a supersaturated solution of $NaNO_3$ at 20°C.
3. **Apply:** By volume, orange drink is 10 percent orange juice and 10 percent corn syrup. A 1500-mL can of the drink costs $0.95. A 1500-mL can of orange juice is $1.49, and 1500 mL of corn syrup is $1.69. How could you make orange drink? Is it cheaper to make or to buy?

☑ Making and Using Graphs
Skill Builder

Using Table 15-3 on page 391, make a graph showing the solubility curves for $CuSO_4$ and $NaNO_3$. How would you make a saturated water solution of each substance at 80°C? If you need help, refer to Making and Using Graphs in the **Skill Handbook** on page 687.

Skill Builder

Mass of solute / 100 g water (g) vs Temperature (°C)

NaNO₃

CuSO₄

Masses of substances to add to 100 g of water at 80°C to make saturated solutions:
$NaNO_3$ - about 148 g
$CuSO_4$ - about 86 g

---

3 CLOSE

ACTIVITY 15-1
40 minutes

OBJECTIVE: **Compare** the solubility of a salt at various temperatures.

PROCESS SKILLS applied in this activity:
▶ **Measuring** in Procedure Steps 2 and 5.
▶ **Calculating** in Analyze Question 1.
▶ **Inferring** in Conclude and Apply Questions 4 and 5.

👫 COOPERATIVE LEARNING
If you have enough materials, you can save time by using the Science Investigation strategy with groups of six. The groups are subdivided into three pairs. Each pair conducts the activity with one of the three water amounts.

TEACHING THE ACTIVITY
Alternate Materials: Other salts, such as KNO_3, that have a linear solubility change over this temperature range may be used.
Troubleshooting: Do not use NaCl. Its solubility varies only slightly over this temperature range.
▶ Bend the wire so that it has a small loop on the bottom that will slip around the thermometer.
▶ Lubricate thermometers well before inserting through stopper.
▶ Once students have calculated solubilities at the different temperatures, have them construct a graph of solubility versus temperature. The graph should be a nearly straight line with a positive slope.

PROGRAM RESOURCES
From the **Teacher Resource Package** use:

Activity Worksheets, pages 116-117, Activity 15-1: A Saturated Solution.

ACTIVITY 15-1
A Saturated Solution

Problem: *How does temperature affect the solubility of a salt?*

Materials
- 9.0 g potassium bromide, KBr
- distilled water
- copper wire stirrer
- laboratory burner
- large test tube
- test tube holder
- thermometer inserted in one hole of a 2-hole stopper

Procedure
1. Copy the data table and use it to record your observations.
2. Place 10 mL distilled water and 9.0 g potassium bromide in a large test tube.
3. Obtain a 2-hole stopper with a thermometer inserted in one hole. Place a copper wire stirrer through the second hole. Place the stopper in the test tube, as shown.
4. Using the wire stirrer, stir the contents of the tube while slowly heating it over a burner to 80°C. Remove the heat when all the KBr has dissolved.
5. Observe the solution as it cools. As soon as you see crystals begin to form, record the temperature. This is the saturation temperature.
6. Add 2 more mL of water to the tube and then repeat Steps 4 and 5.
7. Repeat Step 6.

Data and Observations   Sample Data

g KBr	mL H₂O	Saturation Temperature	g KBr per 100 g H₂O
9.0	10	68°C	90
9.0	12	41°C	75
9.0	14	24°C	64

394 SOLUTIONS

Analyze
1. Use your data to calculate the mass of KBr that would dissolve in 100 mL of water at the three different saturation temperatures you measured. Do this by setting up mathematical proportions. Write these masses in the right column of your data table.
2. How did the saturation temperature change as more water was added?
3. How does the mass of KBr that would dissolve in 100 mL of water change as temperature changes?

Conclude and Apply
4. Using your data and calculations, write a statement about how temperature affects the solubility of KBr in water.
5. In making hard candy, a solution of sugar in water is heated until a thick syrup forms. When the syrup is cooled and flavored, hard candy forms. Using what you have learned in this activity, explain what happens in this process.

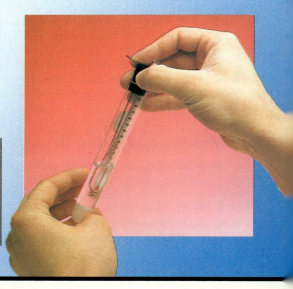

ANSWERS TO QUESTIONS
1. Aid students in calculating values. For example, if 9 g of KBr in 12 g of water gives a saturation temperature of 41°C, the solubility per 100 g water must be $9/12 \times 100 = 75$ g. If students can do proportions, they can calculate

$$\frac{9 \text{ g KBr}}{12 \text{ g H}_2\text{O}} = \frac{x \text{ g KBr}}{100 \text{ g H}_2\text{O}}$$

2. The temperature became lower.
3. It became less as the temperature went down.

4. The solubility of KBr in water decreases with decreasing temperature. Students can also say it increases with increasing temperature.

5. As the solution cools, the solubility of sugar decreases. The sugar crystallizes from solution forming hard candy.

Particles in Solution 15-4

Objectives

▶ Compare and contrast the behavior of polar and nonpolar substances in forming solutions.
▶ Relate the processes of dissociation and ionization to solutions that conduct electricity.
▶ Explain how the addition of solutes to solvents affects the freezing and boiling points of solutions.

New Science Words

dissociation
ionization
electrolyte
nonelectrolyte

Solvents and Solutes

Why do you have to shake an oil and vinegar salad dressing, Figure 15-14, immediately before you use it? Oil and vinegar do not form a solution. Oil does not dissolve in vinegar.

Why does a substance dissolve in one solvent but not in another? Solvents with nonpolar molecules dissolve solutes with nonpolar molecules. Benzene dissolves grease because both substances have nonpolar molecules. Similarly, polar solvents dissolve polar solutes. Water is a polar solvent, and it dissolves sucrose, a polar solute. Polar solvents also dissolve ionic solutes, such as sodium chloride. A polar solvent won't normally dissolve a nonpolar solute. That's why oil, which is nonpolar, won't dissolve in vinegar, which is polar. In general, when predicting which solutes will dissolve in which solvents, remember the phrase, "like dissolves like."

Some substances form solutions with both polar and nonpolar solutes, because their molecules have a polar and a nonpolar end. Ethanol is such a molecule, Figure 15-15. The polar end dissolves polar substances, and the nonpolar end dissolves nonpolar substances. Thus, ethanol dissolves iodine, which is nonpolar, and water, which is polar.

Figure 15-14. Vinegar and oil don't form a solution. You can see oil drops in vinegar even when the mixture is shaken.

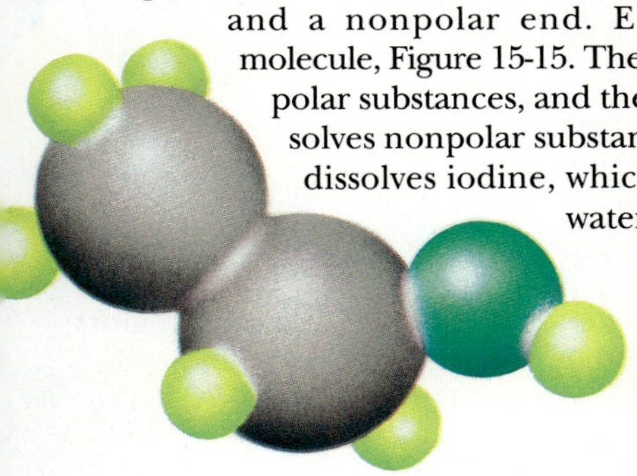

Figure 15-15. Ethanol has a polar –OH group at one end and a nonpolar –CH$_3$ group at the other end.

15-4 PARTICLES IN SOLUTION **395**

Skill Builder

Compounds that dissolve in water

conduct electricity — do not conduct electricity

Electrolytes — Nonelectrolytes

type — type — type

Ionic compounds — Certain polar compounds — Other polar compounds

process — process

Dissociation — Ionization

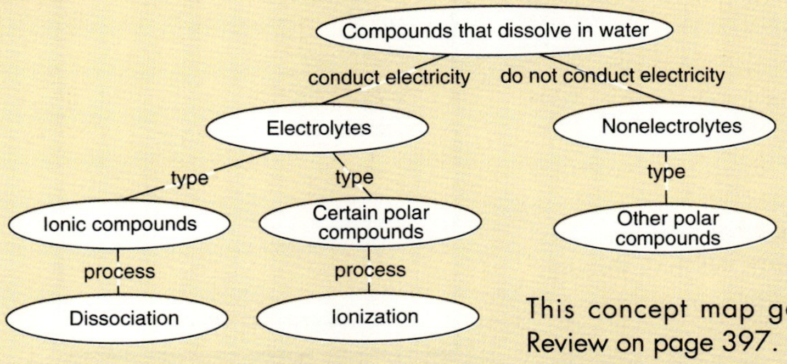

This concept map goes with the Section Review on page 397.

SECTION 15-4

PREPARATION

SECTION BACKGROUND

▶ Polar molecules are a result of polar covalent chemical bonds in unsymmetrical molecules. The pair of electrons is not shared equally which results in one end of the bond having a partial positive charge and the other end a partial negative charge.
▶ In 1887, Arrhenius offered an explanation of why acids and bases conduct an electric current. These substances ionize in water to produce ions. He called the charged particles ions (wanderers).

1 MOTIVATE

▶ **Demonstration:** Clamp a large dill pickle on a ring stand. Place a nail in each end of the pickle so that the points are about 1 to 2 cm apart. Using an electrical cord that has two alligator clips at one end, connect the clips to the nails. Plug the electric cord into any regular 110 volt outlet. **CAUTION:** *Do not touch any part of the setup while the cord is plugged in. Make sure the stand is not on a conductive surface and that students do not approach.* Turn off the lights and observe the pickle glow. Ask students to interpret the phenomenon. The pickling solution contains an electrolyte and conducts electricity.

PROGRAM RESOURCES

From the **Teacher Resource Package** use:

Critical Thinking/Problem Solving, page 21, Denatured Alcohol.

Transparency Worksheets, pages 59-60, Dissociation and Ionization.

Use **Color Transparency** number 30, Dissociation and Ionization.

KNOWLEDGE: Ask students why it is unwise to take a bath while an electric appliance is plugged into an outlet nearby. Ask them if they know why a person can be electrocuted.

▶ In colder climates, chemicals are put on streets and sidewalks to melt ice and snow. Ask the class if they know how this works.

OBJECTIVES AND SCIENCE WORDS: Have students review the objectives and science words to become familiar with this section.

2 TEACH

Key Concepts are highlighted.

CONCEPT DEVELOPMENT

▶ **Demonstration:** Using a conductivity checker, show the class that *distilled* water is a nonelectrolyte. Place the electrodes in a beaker of dry salt, NaCl, crystals to show no conduction. Then with the electrodes submerged in *distilled* water, slowly add salt to the water while stirring. The meter or light bulb will show increasing conductivity as the number of ions in solution increases. Use great caution if the apparatus uses line voltage.

REVEALING MISCONCEPTIONS

▶ Many people believe that water conducts electricity when, in fact, pure water is a poor conductor. Ask students why they must take precautions when using electricity near water. Most tap water contains enough dissolved salts to make it conductive.

CROSS CURRICULUM

▶ **Environmental Science:** Water a potted plant with a dilute NaCl solution to simulate what happens to plants along highways in areas where salt is spread to melt snow. If possible, use fresh water on a second plant as a control.

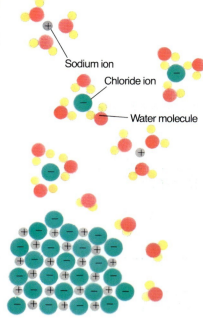

Sodium ion

Chloride ion

Water molecule

Figure 15-16. When sodium chloride dissolves in water, H_2O molecules surround, pull apart, and separate the Na^+ and Cl^- ions.

Solutions as Conductors

Why should you never use a hair dryer when standing on a wet bathroom floor? You take such precautions because, as you may have discovered in a safer situation, you are an excellent conductor of electricity. Your body is about 70 percent water with many ionic compounds dissolved in it. Like the metals used to wire lamps and appliances, water solutions of ionic compounds and of some polar compounds conduct electricity.

When an ionic solid dissolves in water, the positive and negative ions separate from one another. This separation process is called **dissociation.** For example, sodium chloride dissociates when it dissolves in water, as shown in Figure 15-16. When certain polar substances dissolve in water, the water pulls their molecules apart. This process is called **ionization.** Hydrogen chloride ionizes in water, as shown in Figure 15-17 below. A substance that separates into ions or forms ions in a water solution is called an **electrolyte.** Thus, both NaCl, which dissociates, and HCl, which ionizes, are examples of electrolytes.

Pure water does not conduct electricity. If a water solution is a conductor, the solute must be an electrolyte. But many polar substances, such as sugar and alcohol, do not ionize when they dissolve in water. These solutions do not conduct electricity. A substance whose water solutions are nonconducting is a **nonelectrolyte.**

Figure 15-17. When hydrogen chloride dissolves in water, H_2O molecules surround and pull apart HCl molecules, forming the ions H_3O^+ and Cl^-.

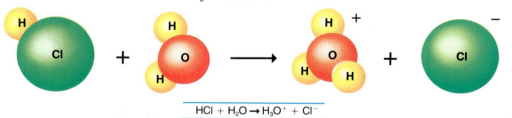

$$HCl + H_2O \rightarrow H_3O^+ + Cl^-$$

Effects of Solute Particles

Antifreeze that you may add to water in a car radiator prevents freezing. Adding a solute to a solvent lowers the freezing point of the solvent. How much the freezing

OPTIONS

Meeting Different Ability Levels

For Section 15-4, use the following **Teacher Resource Masters** depending upon individual students' needs.

◆ **Study Guide Master** for all students.

● **Reinforcement Master** for students of average and above average ability levels.

▲ **Enrichment Master** for above average students.

Additional Teacher Resource Package masters are listed in the OPTIONS box throughout the section. The additional masters are appropriate for all students.

◆ **STUDY GUIDE**   **64**

STUDY GUIDE   Chapter 15
Particles in Solution   Text Pages 395–398

Match the terms in Column II with the definitions in Column I. Write the number of the correct term in the correct box in the grid. If you correctly complete the grid, the sum of the numbers in each horizontal and vertical row will be the same. The first one is done for you.

Column I	Column II
A. homogeneous mixture	1. mixture
B. solution of metals	2. concentrated
C. charged atom	3. solution
D. any method used to remove salts from ocean water	4. solvent
E. substance being dissolved	5. supersaturated solution
F. substance that dissolves a solute	6. unsaturated solution
G. process by which a liquid is evaporated and then condensed to separate it from solution	7. dissociation
H. number of grams of solute that will dissolve in 100 g of solvent	8. nonelectrolyte
I. substance whose solutions do not conduct electricity	9. ion
J. substance that separates into ions in a water solution	10. conductor
K. contains more solute than a saturated solution does at a given temperature	11. ionization
L. substance that allows electricity to pass through it	12. alloy
M. solution that has all the solute it can hold at a given temperature	13. saturated solution
N. process by which ions split apart when dissolved	14. solute
O. process by which polar substances are pulled apart in water	15. dilute
P. any solution that can dissolve more solute at a given temperature	16. distillation
	17. desalination
	18. saturated solution
	19. electrolyte
	20. filtration

Answer Box				Totals
A 3	B 13	C 10	D 17	43
E 14	F 4	G 16	H 9	43
I 8	J 19	K 5	L 11	43
M 18	N 7	O 12	P 6	43
Totals 43	43	43	43	

64

Copyright Glencoe Division of Macmillan/McGraw-Hill
Users of *Merrill Physical Science* have the publisher's permission to reproduce this page.

point goes down depends upon how many solute particles you add.

How does antifreeze work? As a substance freezes, its particles organize themselves into an orderly pattern. The solute particles interfere with the formation of this orderly pattern. This prevents the solvent from freezing at its normal freezing point. To overcome this interference, a lower temperature is required to freeze the solvent.

You may also know that antifreeze raises the boiling point of the water in a car radiator. As a result, the radiator does a better job of removing the heat from the engine in hot weather. The amount that the boiling point is raised depends upon the number of solute particles present. Generally, the more solute present, the higher the boiling point becomes. What causes this effect? Solute particles interfere with the evaporation of solvent particles. Thus, more energy is needed to allow the solvent particles to evaporate. And the solution boils at a higher temperature.

Whatever the weather, solutions of antifreeze in water are part of your life every time you ride in a car or bus. And, as you read earlier, solutions such as lemonade and ocean water are also part of your everyday life.

Why do particles of solute lower the freezing point of water?

EcoTip

Antifreeze has a sweet odor and taste, but is deadly to pets. If antifreeze leaks onto the driveway, wash it away immediately. Never pour antifreeze into street gutters.

Why do particles of solute raise the boiling point of water?

SECTION REVIEW

1. Explain why (a) water dissolves sugar, (b) water does not dissolve oil, and (c) benzene does dissolve oil.
2. What kinds of solute particles are present in water solutions of (a) electrolytes and (b) nonelectrolytes?
3. **Apply:** In very cold weather, people often put salt on ice that forms on sidewalks and driveways. The salt helps melt the ice forming a saltwater solution. Explain why this solution may not refreeze.

☑ Concept Mapping

Draw a concept map to show the relationship among the following terms: *electrolytes, nonelectrolytes, dissociation, ionization, ionic compounds, certain polar compounds, other polar compounds.* If you need help, refer to Concept Mapping in the **Skill Handbook** on pages 684 and 685.

Skill Builder

CONCEPT DEVELOPMENT

▶ **Demonstration:** Fill two 400-mL beakers with crushed ice, then add water and a thermometer to each beaker. Stir and have a student read the temperature of each beaker. Add 75 g of NaCl to one beaker and stir. Read the thermometers again and notice the 4- to 6-degree change.

CONCEPT DEVELOPMENT

▶ **Demonstration:** Fill two 400-mL beakers with crushed ice, then add water and a thermometer to each beaker. Stir and have a student read the temperature of each beaker. Add 75 g of NaCl to one beaker and stir. Read the thermometers again and notice the 4- to 6-degree change.

CHECK FOR UNDERSTANDING

Use the Mini Quiz to check for understanding.

MINI QUIZ

Use the Mini Quiz to check students' recall of chapter content.

1. When an ionic solid dissolves in water, the separation process is called _____ . *dissociation*
2. When a polar solute is pulled apart by water, the process is called _____ . *ionization*
3. What happens to the freezing point of a solvent when a solute is added? *It is lowered.*

RETEACH

▶ Have students look at and describe the processes taking place in the diagrams in Figures 15-15, 15-16, and 15-17. Perform or repeat the conductivity demonstration on page 396.

EXTENSION

For students who have mastered this section, use the **Reinforcement** and **Enrichment** masters or other OPTIONS provided.

3 CLOSE

▶ Ask questions 1-2 and the **Apply** Question in the Section Review.

SECTION REVIEW ANSWERS

1. a. Both are polar. b. Water is polar but oil is not. c. Both are nonpolar.
2. a. ions; b. molecules
3. Apply: The freezing point of the water from the melted ice is lowered by the presence of sodium and chloride ions from the salt. As long as the temperature does not drop lower than the new freezing point of the solution, the water will remain a liquid.

Skill Builder is on page 395.

ACTIVITY 15-2
35 minutes

OBJECTIVE: **Interpret data** and **draw conclusions** regarding the effect of a solute on the boiling point of water.

PROCESS SKILLS applied in this activity:
▶ **Measuring** in Procedure Steps 2-5.
▶ **Graphing** in Procedure Step 6.

👥 COOPERATIVE LEARNING
Use Science Investigation groups. Have one student in a group measure out the additional NaCl needed while others handle heating. Students should work on graphs in groups.

TEACHING THE ACTIVITY
Alternate Materials: Other soluble ionic compounds, such as calcium chloride, will also raise the boiling point.
Troubleshooting: Be sure students have thermometer bulbs immersed when reading temperatures and that thermometers read clearly in a range above 100°C. Determine the boiling point of water for your altitude from a handbook.
▶ The following is a graph using sample data. Students should obtain similar graphs.

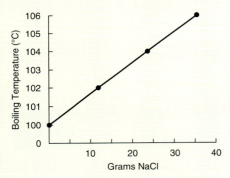

▶ It is possible to do the activity by adding successive 12-gram amounts of NaCl to the same beaker, but it will not give accurate results because of water loss.
▶ To save time, you could have students use level teaspoons (approximately 12 grams) of NaCl. It would be better, though, to reinforce science concepts by having them use a balance.

ACTIVITY 15-2
Boiling Points of Solutions

Problem: *How is boiling point affected by the addition of a solute?*

Materials
- 400 mL distilled water
- thermometer
- ring stand
- 12 g table salt, NaCl
- laboratory burner
- 250-mL beaker

Procedure
1. Copy the data table and use it to record your observations.
2. Bring 100 mL of distilled water in a 250-mL beaker to a gentle boil. Record the temperature.
3. Dissolve 12 g of NaCl in 100 mL of distilled water. Bring this solution to a gentle boil and record its boiling point. **CAUTION:** *Always keep the thermometer away from the flame.*
4. Repeat Step 2, using 24 g of NaCl.
5. Repeat Step 2 again, using 36 g of NaCl.
6. Plot your results on a graph that shows boiling point on the vertical axis and g of NaCl on the horizontal axis.

398 SOLUTIONS

Data and Observations Sample Data

Grams of NaCl Solute	Boiling Point (°C)
0	~100
12	~102
24	~104
36	~106

Analyze
1. What difference is there between the boiling point of a pure solvent and a solution?
2. Instead of doubling the amount of NaCl in Step 4, what would have been the effect of doubling the amount of water?
3. What would be the result of using tap water instead of distilled water?

Conclude and Apply
4. In cooking, why would adding salt to water cause some foods to cook faster?
5. If you continued to add more salt, would you predict that your graph would continue in the same pattern or level off? Explain your prediction.

ANSWERS TO QUESTIONS
1. The boiling point of the solution is higher.
2. The boiling point would have gone down but would still be higher than the boiling point of pure water.
3. Most tap water contains dissolved salts, so its boiling point would be above 100°C.
4. The salt water solution would boil at a little higher temperature.
5. The graph would continue until saturation was reached. Then it would level off because no more salt would dissolve.

SUMMARY

15-1: How Solutions Form

1. Solutions are classified into three types according to their final state: gaseous, liquid, and solid.
2. Dissolving occurs when constantly moving solvent molecules attract particles of solute and surround them with solvent.
3. Stirring, surface area, temperature, and pressure are factors that affect the rate of dissolving.

15-2: Science and Society: Oceans— The World's Largest Solution

1. The oceans form the world's largest solution because they contain, in addition to dissolved sodium chloride, many other dissolved salts.
2. Methods being used to salinate ocean water include distillation, flash distillation, and freezing followed by melting.

15-3: Solubility and Concentration

1. Solubility of substances varies among different solutes and for the same solute at different temperatures.
2. Two precise ways to express solution concentrations are (1) percentage by volume and (2) percentage by mass.
3. A solution may be saturated, unsaturated, or supersaturated.

15-4: Particles in Solution

1. Usually, among polar and nonpolar solvents and solutes, "like dissolves like."
2. Ionic compounds dissociate when dissolved in water, and some covalent compounds ionize when dissolved in water.
3. Adding a solute to a solvent lowers its freezing point and raises its boiling point.

KEY SCIENCE WORDS

a. desalination
b. dissociation
c. distillation
d. electrolyte
e. ionization
f. nonelectrolyte
g. saturated solution
h. solubility
i. solute
j. solvent
k. supersaturated solution
l. unsaturated solution

UNDERSTANDING VOCABULARY

Match each phrase with the correct term from the list of Key Science Words.

1. a solution that can dissolve more solute at a given temperature
2. the substance being dissolved
3. has more solute than a saturated solution has at that temperature
4. is ionized in a water solution
5. molecules are pulled apart in solution
6. separation of negative and positive ions
7. the most solute in grams, that will dissolve in 100 g of solvent at a certain temperature
8. a solution that has dissolved all the solute it can hold at a given temperature
9. the substance that dissolves a solute
10. the general term for any method that removes salt from ocean water

---

CHAPTER
REVIEW

SUMMARY

Have students read the summary statements to review the major concepts of the chapter.

UNDERSTANDING VOCABULARY

1. l
2. i
3. k
4. d
5. e
6. b
7. h
8. g
9. j
10. a

OPTIONS

ASSESSMENT

To assess student understanding of material in this chapter, use the resources listed.

COOPERATIVE LEARNING

Consider using cooperative learning in the THINK AND WRITE CRITICALLY, APPLY, and MORE SKILL BUILDERS sections of the Chapter Review.

PROGRAM RESOURCES

From the **Teacher Resource Package** use:
Chapter Review, pages 33-34.
Chapter and Unit Tests, pages 101-104, Chapter Test.

CHAPTER
REVIEW

CHECKING CONCEPTS

1. d
2. a
3. b
4. d
5. a
6. b
7. b
8. a
9. b
10. c

UNDERSTANDING CONCEPTS

11. concentrated
12. nonelectrolyte
13. unsaturated
14. solute
15. solvent

THINK AND WRITE CRITICALLY

16. The boiling point of salt is much higher than that of water. Salt is a strongly bonded ionic compound.

17. The negative ends of polar water molecules attract the positive copper ions at the surface of the solid and pull them into solution. The positive ends of water molecules attract the negative sulfate ions at the surface of the solid and pull them into solution.

18. There is no set amount of solute that makes a solution concentrated or dilute.

19. Answers may vary. One possibility is to add 25 mL of apple juice to 75 mL of water.

20. Solutions may be prepared using solvents other than water. For example, iodine dissolves in alcohol to produce a solution (tincture of iodine). Water also could be the solute in a solution. An example would be rubbing alcohol, which is 70 percent isopropanol.

CHECKING CONCEPTS

Choose the word or phrase that completes the sentence or answers the question.

1. Which of the following is not a solution?
   a. a glass of soda
   b. air in a SCUBA tank
   c. bronze (an alloy)
   d. muddy water

2. Solutions may not be _____.
   a. colloidal
   b. gaseous
   c. liquid
   d. solid

3. When iodine is dissolved in alcohol, the alcohol is the _____.
   a. alloy
   b. solvent
   c. solution
   d. solute

4. If a bronze alloy is 85 percent copper and 15 percent tin, tin is the _____.
   a. alloy
   b. solvent
   c. solution
   d. solute

5. Forty-nine mL of water has a mass of _____.
   a. 49 g
   b. 51 g
   c. 100 g
   d. 4900 g

6. A polar solvent will dissolve _____.
   a. any solute
   b. a polar solute
   c. a nonpolar solute
   d. no solute

7. If a water solution conducts electricity, the solute must be a(n) _____.
   a. gas
   b. electrolyte
   c. liquid
   d. nonelectrolyte

8. In a water solution, an ionic compound undergoes _____.
   a. dissociation
   b. electrolysis
   c. ionization
   d. no change

9. A gas becomes more soluble in a liquid when you increase _____.
   a. particle size
   b. pressure
   c. stirring
   d. temperature

10. Solute may come out of a solution that is ____.
   a. unsaturated
   b. saturated
   c. supersaturated
   d. all of these

UNDERSTANDING CONCEPTS

Complete each sentence.

11. A solution that contains a large amount of solute is said to be _____.

12. If a water solution of a compound does not conduct electricity, the compound is a(n) ____.

13. A(n) _____ solution contains less than the maximum amount of solute at a given temperature.

14. In the ocean, salt is a(n) _____.

15. In a solution, the substance present in the greatest amount is the _____.

THINK AND WRITE CRITICALLY

16. As the first step of distillation, salt water is boiled and the water vaporizes. Why doesn't the salt also vaporize?

17. Explain what happens when copper(II) sulfate, $CuSO_4$, an ionic compound, dissolves in water.

18. Why are *concentrated* and *dilute* not exact terms?

19. Explain how you would make a 25 percent solution of apple juice.

20. Why is the statement "Water is the solvent in a solution" not always true?

APPLY

21. Explain why tetrachloroethene, a dry cleaning fluid, will dissolve grease and water will not.

22. Why might a tropical lake have more minerals dissolved in it than a lake in Minnesota?

23. Explain why salt will melt ice on a sidewalk.

24. Why might potatoes cook quicker in salt water than in unsalted water?

25. Explain why an unrefrigerated glass of soda will go "flat" quicker in hot weather.

MORE SKILL BUILDERS

If you need help, refer to the Skill Handbook.

1. **Comparing and Contrasting**: Compare and contrast the processes of ionization and dissociation.
2. **Hypothesizing:** You are stocking a pond in a tropical climate and a pond in a temperate climate with fish. Both ponds contain about the same amount of water. Based on the amount of oxygen dissolved in the water, to which pond would you be able to add more fish? Explain why.
3. **Interpreting Data:** The label on a bottle of rubbing alcohol might read "70% isopropanol by volume." Assuming the rest of the solution is water, what does this label tell you about the contents and preparation of the solution in the bottle?
4. **Measuring in SI:** 153 g of potassium nitrate have been dissolved in enough water to make 1.00 L of solution. You use a graduated cylinder to measure 80.0 mL of solution. What mass of potassium nitrate do you have in the 80.0-mL sample?
5. **Making and Using Tables:** Using the data in Table 15-3 on page 391, fill in the following table. Use the words *saturated, unsaturated,* and *supersaturated.*

Compound	g Dissolved in 100 g Water at 20°C	Type of Solution
$Ba(OH)_2$	2.96	
$CuSO_4$	32.0	
KCl	45.8	
KNO_3	31.6	
$NaClO_3$	79.6	

PROJECTS

1. Research crystal growing using saturated and supersaturated solutions. Grow several crystals and display them. Accompany the display with a report explaining what you did.
2. Do research on a titanium alloy. Report on its production, composition, and uses.
3. Visit a SCUBA shop. Find out about the composition of the gas used in the tanks. In terms of solution, report your findings.

21. Tetrachloroethene and grease are both composed of nonpolar molecules. Water is polar and is not attracted to nonpolar grease molecules.
22. A tropical lake is likely to be warmer. Most solutes are more soluble in water at higher temperatures.
23. The salt dissociates into ions when it dissolves. The presence of these ions lowers the freezing point of water. Unless it is very cold, the dissolved salt will keep the water liquid.
24. The salted water boils at a slightly higher temperature than unsalted water because of the presence of dissolved ions. At the higher temperature, the potatoes cook more quickly.
25. The higher room temperature in summer causes decreased solubility of carbon dioxide gas in water. Thus, more of the gas comes out of solution more rapidly.

MORE SKILL BUILDERS

1. **Comparing and Contrasting:** Both processes result in ions in solution. Dissociation involves the separation of ions in an ionic compound. Ionization involves the pulling apart of polar molecules into ions.
2. **Hypothesizing:** In theory, more fish could live in the temperate climate. At the colder temperature, more oxygen would dissolve in the water.
3. **Interpreting and Using Data:** For every 100 mL of the rubbing alcohol, 70 mL are alcohol, and 30 mL are water. The alcohol was most likely prepared by combining the ingredients in this ratio.
4. **Measuring in SI:**

$$\frac{153 \text{ g } KNO_3}{1000 \text{ mL solution}} \times 80.0 \text{ mL solution}$$
$$= 12.2 \text{ g } KNO_3$$

5. **Making and Using Tables:**
$Ba(OH)_2$ — unsaturated
$CuSO_4$ — saturated
KCl — supersaturated
KNO_3 — saturated
$NaClO_3$ — unsaturated

CHAPTER
16 Chemical Reactions

CHAPTER SECTION	OBJECTIVES	ACTIVITIES
16-1 Chemical Changes in Matter (2 days)	1. **Identify** reactants and products in a chemical reaction. 2. **Explain** how a chemical reaction satisfies the law of conservation of mass. 3. **Interpret** chemical equations.	**MINI-Lab:** *Does mass change in a reaction?* p. 405
16-2 The Hole in the Ozone Layer Science & Society (1 day)	1. **Describe** the role of the ozone layer in protecting life on Earth. 2. **Explain** the role of CFCs in the threat to the ozone layer.	
16-3 Chemical Equations (2 days)	1. **Explain** what is meant by a balanced chemical equation. 2. **Demonstrate** how to write balanced chemical equations.	**MINI-Lab:** *Must the sums of reactant and product coefficients be equal?* p. 412
16-4 Types of Chemical Reactions (2 days)	1. **Describe** four types of chemical reactions using their generalized formulas. 2. **Classify** various chemical reactions by type.	**Activity 16-1:** *Displacement Reactions,* p. 416
16-5 Energy and Chemical Reactions (2 days)	1. **Differentiate** between an exothermic reaction and an endothermic reaction. 2. **Describe** the effects of catalysts and inhibitors on the speed of chemical reactions.	**Activity 16-2:** *Catalyzed Reaction,* p. 420
Chapter Review		

ACTIVITY MATERIALS

FIND OUT	ACTIVITIES		MINI-LABS	
Page 403 2 darkened pennies table salt vinegar medicine dropper paper towel plastic wrap one dish per group	**16-1 Displacement Reactions, p. 416** 3 test tubes test tube stand small pieces of copper, Cu; zinc, Zn; and magnesium, Mg 15 mL dilute hydrochloric acid, HCl graduated cylinder wooden splint	**16-2 Catalyzed Reactions, p. 420** 3 medium-sized test tubes and stand 15 mL H_2O_2 graduated cylinder laboratory spatula manganese dioxide, MnO_2 wooden splint hot plate sand beaker of hot water	**Does mass change in a reaction? p. 405** medicine dropper bottle dilute NaOH solution dilute $FeCl_3$ solution soap balance	**Must the sums of reactant and product coefficients be equal? p. 412** cards markers

CHAPTER FEATURES	TEACHER RESOURCE PACKAGE	OTHER RESOURCES
Problem Solving: *Metals and the Atmosphere,* p. 406 **Skill Builder:** *Recognizing Cause and Effect,* p. 407	**Ability Level Worksheets** ◆ **Study Guide,** p. 65 ● **Reinforcement,** p. 65 ▲ **Enrichment,** p. 65 **MINI-Lab Worksheet,** p. 130	**Lab Manual 32,** Conservation of Mass
You Decide! p. 409	**Ability Level Worksheets** ◆ **Study Guide,** p. 66 ● **Reinforcement,** p. 66 ▲ **Enrichment,** p. 66 **Concept Mapping,** pp. 37, 38 **Transparency Masters,** pp. 61, 62	**Color Transparency 31,** CFCs and Ozone
Skill Builder: *Observing and Inferring,* p. 412	**Ability Level Worksheets** ◆ **Study Guide,** p. 67 ● **Reinforcement,** p. 67 ▲ **Enrichment,** p. 67 **MINI-Lab Worksheet,** p. 131 **Cross-Curricular Connections,** p. 22 **Transparency Masters,** pp. 63, 64	**Color Transparency 32,** Chemical Equations **Lab Manual 33,** Reaction Rates and Temperature
Skill Builder: *Hypothesizing,* p. 415	**Ability Level Worksheets** ◆ **Study Guide,** p. 68 ● **Reinforcement,** p. 68 ▲ **Enrichment,** p. 68 **Activity Worksheet,** pp. 124, 125 **Critical Thinking/Problem Solving,** p. 22 **Science and Society,** p. 20 **Transparency Masters,** pp. 65, 66	**Color Transparency 33,** Types of Chemical Reactions **Lab Manual 34,** Chemical Reactions
Technology: *Catalytic Converters,* p. 419 **Skill Builder:** *Concept Mapping,* p. 419	**Ability Level Worksheets** ◆ **Study Guide,** p. 69 ● **Reinforcement,** p. 69 ▲ **Enrichment,** p. 69 **Activity Worksheet,** pp. 126, 127	
Summary Think & Write Critically Key Science Words Apply Understanding Vocabulary More Skill Builders Checking Concepts Projects Understanding Concepts	**Chapter Review,** pp. 35, 36 **Chapter Test,** pp. 105-108	**Chapter Review Software** **Test Bank**

◆ **Basic**   ● **Average**   ▲ **Advanced**

ADDITIONAL MATERIALS

SOFTWARE	AUDIOVISUAL	BOOKS/MAGAZINES
Reactions, J&S Software. *Chemical Reactions,* ComPress.	*Chemical Change All About Us,* film, Coronet/MTI. *Investigating Matter,* Chemical Reaction, filmstrip/cassette, EBE. *Chemical Reactions,* filmstrip/cassette, Science Software. *Oxidation and Reduction Reactions,* filmstrip/cassette, Science Software. *Special Topics in Chemistry,* video, Focus.	Baer, Michael. *Theory of Chemical Reaction Dynamics.* Boca Raton, FL: CRC Press, 1985. Compton, R.G. *Comprehensive Chemical Kinetics.* New York: Elsevier, 1988. Sykes, Peter. *A Guidebook to Mechanism in Organic Chemistry.* New York: Wiley, 1986.

THEME DEVELOPMENT: Patterns of change as a theme of the textbook is developed through a presentation of how chemical changes are classified and represented by balanced chemical equations.

CHAPTER OVERVIEW

▶ **Section 16-1:** The chemical equation is introduced as a way of representing chemical reactions in a way that complies with the law of conservation of mass.

▶ **Section 16-2: Science and Society:** This section describes how the ozone layer is affected by CFCs.

▶ **Section 16-3:** How to balance a chemical equation is presented in this section.

▶ **Section 16-4:** Four common types of chemical reactions are presented. This section demonstrates how chemists are able to predict products for a chemical reaction.

▶ **Section 16-5:** Energy as a product or reactant in a chemical change is discussed. Catalysts and inhibitors are introduced.

CHAPTER VOCABULARY

chemical reaction
reactants
products
coefficients
chlorofluorocarbons (CFCs)
balanced chemical equation
synthesis reaction
decomposition reaction
single displacement reaction
precipitate
double displacement reaction
endothermic reactions
exothermic reactions
catalyst
inhibitor

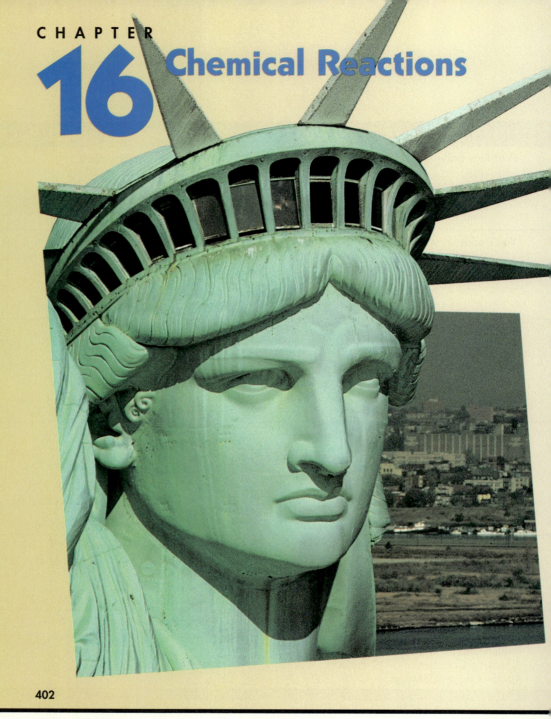

CHAPTER

16 Chemical Reactions

402

OPTIONS

For Your Gifted Students

Challenge students to balance the following equations. The equations are given here in balanced form. Rewrite them, leaving out the coefficients.

1. $2KNO_3 \rightarrow 2KNO_2 + O_2$
2. $2C_2H_6 + 7O_2 \rightarrow 4CO_2 + 6H_2O$
3. $2Na + 2H_2O \rightarrow 2NaOH + H_2$
4. $3O_2 + CS_2 \rightarrow CO_2 + 2SO_2$
5. $2KClO_3 \rightarrow 2KCl + 3O_2$
6. $C_4H_8 + 6O_2 \rightarrow 4CO_2 + 4H_2O$
7. $2C_5H_{10} + 15O_2 \rightarrow 10\ CO_2 + 10\ H_2O$
8. $Cu + 2H_2SO_4 \rightarrow CuSO_4 + SO_2 + 2H_2O$
9. $3SiF + 3H_2O \rightarrow 2H_2SiF_6 + H_2SiO_3$
10. $4Na + O_2 \rightarrow 2Na_2O$
11. $2IrCl_3 + 3NaOH \rightarrow Ir_2O_3 + 3HCl + 3NaCl$
12. $Cu_2S + 12HNO_3 \rightarrow Cu(NO_3)_2 + CuSO_4 + 10NO_2 + 6H_2O$
13. $2KBr + 3H_2SO_4 + MnO_2 \rightarrow 2KHSO_4 + MnSO_4 + 2H_2O + Br_2$

You may not realize it, but the Statue of Liberty is made of copper. Why is it green? Brand new pennies are bright and shiny. Older pennies are black and quite dull. Some very old pennies often have a green layer on them. What causes pennies and copper statues to lose their shiny surfaces and turn green?

FIND OUT!

Do this activity to find out why copper surfaces often turn green.

Obtain two dark copper pennies. Sprinkle some table salt on them. Drop about five or six drops of vinegar on the salt-covered pennies. Observe the pennies for about 20 minutes and then rinse them with water. How do the pennies look now?

Place one of the pennies in a piece of plastic wrap. Wrap the penny so that no air can get to it. Set this penny aside. Place the other penny on a saucer. Add just enough water to the saucer so that the penny is not completely covered. Let this coin remain in the water overnight. Observe the pennies the next day. How do they compare? What caused the changes that you observed?

Previewing Science Skills
► In the **Skill Builders,** you will recognize cause and effect, observe and infer, hypothesize, and make a concept map.
► In the **Activities,** you will observe, infer, and classify.
► In the **MINI-Labs,** you will observe and infer.

What's next?

You have seen what happens to a penny when it is exposed to air. You will learn more about this chemical change and others as you read the pages that follow.

403

INTRODUCING THE CHAPTER
Use the Find Out activity to introduce students to chemical reactions. Inform students that they will be learning more about kinds of chemical reactions and how to describe them as they read the chapter.

FIND OUT!
Preparation: Have students refer to the chapter opening photo of the Statue of Liberty as you discuss this activity. Have students bring in pennies from home.
Materials: two darkened pennies, table salt, vinegar, medicine dropper, paper towel, plastic wrap, one dish per group
Teaching Tips
► This activity works well at home. It is safe, and the student can do other things during the twenty minutes required for the reaction to occur.
► The patina coating on the Statue of Liberty is basic copper(II) sulfate, $CuSO_4 \bullet 3Cu(OH)_2$, which is called brochantite. This protective patina has preserved the original copper skin. Only about four percent has been eroded so far, but acid rain can increase the rate of erosion.
► For copper to turn green, it must oxidize and then be exposed to water and sulfur compounds in air that has a relative humidity of at least 75 percent. This process is very slow.

Gearing Up
Have students study the Gearing Up feature to familiarize themselves with the chapter. Discuss the relationships of the topics in the outline.

What's Next?
Before beginning the first section, make sure students understand the connection between the Find Out activity and the topics to follow.

For Your Mainstreamed Students
Have students make a crossword puzzle of the key science words found at the end of the chapter. Definitions for the terms can be found within the chapter and used as clues. Computer programs that construct crossword puzzles are available. Your school may have one.

PREPARATION

SECTION BACKGROUND

▶ A correct chemical equation shows what changes take place. It also shows the relative amounts of substances that take part in these changes.

▶ The symbols used in a chemical equation are the same in all languages around the world.

▶ The symbols used to indicate the state of matter have changed recently in scientific literature. The (s) for solid has been replaced with (cr) for crystalline solid. If the material is not crystalline, it is not a true solid, and the symbol (amor) for amorphous is used.

1 MOTIVATE

▶ **Demonstration:** Prepare a soap solution by adding 160 mL of water to a 400-mL beaker, with 25 mL of liquid detergent and 5 mL of glycerine. In a separate beaker, dissolve 5 g of sucrose in 60 mL of water. Gently mix the two solutions. Connect one end of a length of rubber tubing to the gas outlet and the other end to a small funnel. Invert the funnel into the beaker of soap mixture. Make a bubble using the gas. Darken the room. Dislodge bubbles by turning the funnel sideways and gently shaking. As the bubble rises, ignite it with a burning candle taped to a meterstick. **CAUTION:** *Be sure there are no flammable materials nearby.*

TYING TO PREVIOUS KNOWLEDGE:
Remind students of the indications that a chemical change has occurred: color change, evolution of gas, heat, light, formation of a precipitate, production of electric current.

STUDENT TEXT QUESTION

▶ Page 404, paragraph 3: **What are the reactants and products in photosynthesis?** *reactants—carbon dioxide and water; products—sugar and oxygen*

New Science Words

chemical reaction
reactants
products
coefficients

Objectives

▶ Identify reactants and products in a chemical reaction.
▶ Explain how a chemical reaction satisfies the law of conservation of mass.
▶ Interpret chemical equations.

Reactants and Products

In Chapter 9 you learned about chemical changes. These changes are taking place all around you and even inside your body. One of the most important chemical changes on Earth is photosynthesis. During photosynthesis plants use sunlight, carbon dioxide, and water to make sugar and oxygen. Another important chemical change takes place in the cells in your body. This change combines sugar and oxygen to produce energy, carbon dioxide, and water.

A **chemical reaction** is a well-defined example of a chemical change. In a chemical reaction, one or more substances are changed to new substances. The substances you start with are called **reactants.** The new substances formed are called **products.** This relationship can be written as follows:

$$\text{reactants} \xrightarrow{\text{produce}} \text{products}$$

What are the reactants and products in the photosynthesis reaction described above?

Conservation of Mass

In the early 1700s, scientists wondered what happened to the masses of the reactants and products in a chemical reaction. The French chemist Antoine Lavoisier performed many experiments to find out. In one experiment, Lavoisier placed a carefully measured amount of solid

Figure 16-1. Antoine Lavoisier used precise balances to perform experiments that led to the law of conversation of mass.

OPTIONS

Meeting Different Ability Levels

For Section 16-1, use the following **Teacher Resource Masters** depending upon individual students' needs.

◆ **Study Guide Master** for all students.

● **Reinforcement Master** for students of average and above average ability levels.

▲ **Enrichment Master** for above average students.

Additional Teacher Resource Package masters are listed in the OPTIONS box throughout the section. The additional masters are appropriate for all students.

◆ STUDY GUIDE 65

STUDY GUIDE
Chemical Changes in Matter   Text Pages 404–407

Solve the puzzle below by writing the term in the diagram that fits each definition. You will find another term spelled vertically in the black box.

1.   Y I E L D S
2.   A Q U E O U S
3.   F O R M U L A
4. C H E M I C A L R E A C T I O N
5.   P R O D U C T S
6.   C O E F F I C I E N T S
7.   S Y M B O L S
8. R E A C T A N T S

Hints
1. The arrow in a chemical equation means produces or _____.
2. means dissolved in water
3. combination of chemical symbols used to represent a compound
4. well-defined example of a chemical change (2 words)
5. substances produced in a chemical reaction
6. numbers before a symbol that represent the relative number of atoms taking part in a reaction
7. letters used to represent elements
8. substances that react to produce a chemical change

Some symbols that are used in chemical equations are listed in the first column of the table below. Complete the table by writing in the second column the term represented by each symbol.

Symbol	Meaning
→	yields or produces
(cr)	solid
(l)	liquid
(g)	gas
(aq)	aqueous or dissolved in water

Copyright Glencoe Division of Macmillan/McGraw-Hill
Users of Merrill Physical Science have the publisher's permission to reproduce this page.   65

mercury(II) oxide into a sealed flask. When he heated this flask, oxygen gas and liquid mercury were produced:

solid mercury(II) oxide plus heat produces oxygen gas plus liquid mercury

Lavoisier found that the mass of the oxygen gas and the mercury produced was equal to the mass of the mercury(II) oxide that he started with:

mercury(II) oxide produces oxygen plus mercury
10.0 g   =   0.7 g + 9.3 g

3 This and many other experiments allowed Lavoisier to state the law of conservation of mass: in a chemical reaction matter cannot be created or destroyed; therefore, mass is conserved. In Chapter 9, you read how this law applies generally to chemical changes. For a chemical reaction, this law means that the mass of the reactants must equal the mass of the products. As you will see, the law of conservation of mass must be satisfied when describing a chemical reaction.

Describing Chemical Reactions

If you wanted to describe the chemical reaction shown in Figure 16-2, it might look something like this:

solid lead(II) nitrate, dissolved in water plus
solid potassium iodide, dissolved in water produce
solid lead(II) iodide plus potassium nitrate,
dissolved in water

This series of words is rather long and cumbersome. But, all information in this expression is important. The

Figure 16-2. The beakers contain solutions of lead(II) nitrate and potassium iodide (a). When these solutions are mixed, a bright yellow solid forms (b). The yellow solid, lead(II) iodide, settles to the bottom of the beaker. The solution in the beaker is potassium nitrate (c).

a   b   c

● REINFORCEMENT 65   ▲ ENRICHMENT 65   405

OBJECTIVES AND SCIENCE WORDS: Have students review the objectives and science words to become familiar with this section.

2 TEACH

Key Concepts are highlighted.

CONCEPT DEVELOPMENT

► **Demonstration:** Place a very small amount of iodine crystals and zinc powder in an evaporating dish. Add a few drops of water to the dish in the fume hood. **CAUTION:** *This is an exothermic reaction that produces toxic fumes.* The zinc reacts with the diatomic iodine to form zinc iodide, ZnI_2 in a synthesis reaction.

► As students are introduced to equation balancing and the use of coefficients, they often use the coefficient when they should use a subscript to make the sum of the oxidation numbers equal zero. Beginning students may try to put the coefficient in the middle of the chemical formula, writing Pb2I instead of the correct PbI_2.

CONCEPT DEVELOPMENT

► **Demonstration:** To easily illustrate the law of conservation of mass, burn a piece of magnesium ribbon in a darkened room. Use tongs to hold the piece of burning ribbon inside a can so the students cannot see the flame directly. This is the same reaction that occurs in some flashbulbs. Determine the mass of a flashbulb on the balance. Fire the flashbulb. Show that the magnesium has oxidized inside the bulb, but there has been no change in mass.

► Continue to emphasize the difference between a subscript and a coefficient.

► It will be helpful if you provide each student a copy of the periodic table for reference throughout the chapter.

► Remind students that an arrow usually indicates the direction to go. In a chemical reaction, the arrow indicates the direction the reaction proceeds.

CHECK FOR UNDERSTANDING

Use the Mini Quiz to check for understanding.

MINI QUIZ

Use the Mini Quiz to check students' recall of chapter content.

1 A chemical reaction begins with substances called _____ . *reactants*

2 The new substances formed in a chemical reaction are called _____ . *products*

3 In a chemical reaction, if you begin with 12.5 g of reactants, what mass of products can you expect to form? *12.5 g*

4 Numbers used in a chemical equation to represent the relative amounts of atoms taking part in a reaction are called _____ . *coefficients*

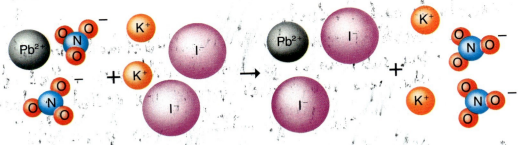

Figure 16-3. One unit of $Pb(NO_3)_2$ reacts with two units of KI to produce one unit of PbI_2 plus two units of KNO_3.

What is a chemical equation?

Table 16-1

SYMBOLS USED IN CHEMICAL EQUATIONS	
Symbol	**Meaning**
→	produces or forms
+	plus
(cr)	solid
(l)	liquid
(g)	gas
(aq)	aqueous, a solid is dissolved in water
heat →	the reactants are heated
light →	the reactants are exposed to light
elect. →	an electric current is applied to the reactants

same is true of descriptions of most chemical reactions—many words are needed to state all the important information. So scientists have developed a shorthand method to describe chemical reactions. A chemical equation is an expression that decribes a chemical reaction using chemical formulas and other symbols. In Chapter 11, you learned how to use chemical symbols and formulas. Some of the other symbols used in chemical equations are listed in Table 16-1.

What would the chemical equation for the reaction in Figure 16-2 look like?

$$Pb(NO_3)_2(aq) + 2KI(aq) \rightarrow PbI_2(cr) + 2KNO_3(aq)$$

The symbols to the right of the formulas are (cr) for solid and (aq) for aqueous, which means dissolved in water.

What do the numbers to the left of the formulas for reactants and products mean? Remember that the law of conservation of mass states that matter cannot be created or destroyed. Atoms can be rearranged during chemical reactions, but never lost or destroyed. These numbers, called **coefficients, represent the relative amounts of atoms taking part in a reaction.** They show you what is really happening inside the reaction flask. For example, in the above reaction one unit of $Pb(NO_3)_2$ reacts with two units of KI to produce one unit of PbI_2 and two units of KNO_3. Figure 16-3 will help you visualize this reaction.

You don't always have to analyze the reaction mixture to find out what the coefficients in a chemical reaction are. In the next section you will find out how to choose coefficients for a chemical equation.

OPTIONS

INQUIRY QUESTIONS

► **Magnesium metal will react with hydrochloric acid solution, HCl, to produce a salt solution, magnesium chloride, and diatomic hydrogen gas. Which substances are reactants?** *Mg and HCl*

► **In the above reaction, what symbols and formulas would be used to represent each reactant and each product?** *Mg(cr), HCl(aq), $MgCl_2$(aq), H_2(g)*

► **What would you expect to happen to the amount of products present as a chemical reaction proceeds?** *The amount increases*

because products are being produced during a chemical reaction.

► **From the following formulas and coefficients, determine the number of atoms of each element present:**

$2C_6H_{14}$	*12 carbon, 28 hydrogen*
$5NaCH_3COO$	*5 sodium, 10 carbon, 15 hydrogen, 10 oxygen*

PROBLEM SOLVING

Metals and the Atmosphere

When metals are exposed to air, they often corrode. Rusting is one type of corrosion. Rust is iron(III) oxide.

Aluminum also reacts with oxygen in the air to form the white solid aluminum oxide. Unlike rust, which crumbles and exposes more iron to the air, aluminum oxide adheres to the aluminum surface on which it forms. This coating protects the aluminum underneath from further corrosion.

Copper is another metal that corrodes when exposed to air. When copper corrodes, a green coating called basic copper sulfate is formed. You may have seen this type of corrosion on the Statue of Liberty.

Think Critically: Identify the reactants and products in the corrosion of iron and aluminum. When the Statue of Liberty was restored, the green coating was not removed. Why?

SECTION REVIEW

1. Identify the reactants and the products in the following chemical equation
$$2B(cr) + 3I_2(g) \rightarrow 2BI_3(cr)$$
2. What is the name and state of matter of each substance in the following reaction?
$$4Al(cr) + 3O_2(g) \rightarrow 2Al_2O_3(cr)$$
3. **Apply:** Soap (sodium stearate) is made as follows:

fat plus sodium hydroxide produce soap plus glycerin

When 890 g of fat reacts totally with 120 g of sodium hydroxide, 92 g of glycerin is formed. How many grams of soap must be formed to satisfy the law of conservation of mass?

☑ Recognizing Cause and Effect

Lavoisier heated mercury(II) oxide in a sealed flask. Explain the effect on the mass of the products of the reaction if he had used an open flask. If you need help, refer to Recognizing Cause and Effect in the **Skill Handbook** on page 679.

Skill Builder

16-1   CHEMICAL CHANGES IN MATTER   **407**

PREPARATION

SECTION BACKGROUND

▶ When ultraviolet light strikes an oxygen molecule, the O_2 molecule is broken apart to form two oxygen atoms. These oxygen atoms will react with other O_2 molecules to form ozone. This process takes place between 15 and 30 km above the surface of Earth.

▶ Ultraviolet energy has a devastating effect on the DNA molecules that control the function of living cells of many microorganisms. These organisms include many of those in the sea that produce the oxygen we breathe.

1 MOTIVATE

▶ **Demonstration:** In a darkened room, use an ultraviolet lamp to show how some chemicals glow when exposed to ultraviolet light. Boxes of detergent are often printed with fluorescent inks. Discuss how ultraviolet light differs from visible light.

TYING TO PREVIOUS
KNOWLEDGE:
Have students recall and discuss when they have been sunburned. Discuss ways to prevent and treat sunburns.

OBJECTIVES AND
SCIENCE WORDS:
Have students review the objectives and science words to become familiar with this section.

2 TEACH

Key Concepts are highlighted.

CONCEPT DEVELOPMENT

▶ Bring a can of auto air-conditioner refrigerant to class to show the students. Read the list of ingredients.

16-2 The Hole in the Ozone Layer

New Science Words

chlorofluorocarbons (CFCs)

Objectives

▶ Describe the role of the ozone layer in protecting life on Earth.
▶ Explain the role of CFCs in the threat to the ozone layer.

How Do CFCs Affect Ozone?

Have you heard that a decrease of ozone in Earth's atmosphere has led to an increase in skin cancer? That is probably so, but it is only the beginning. Far more serious might be widespread damage to crops or total destruction of life in the ocean. Normally, the ozone layer absorbs much of the ultraviolet (UV) radiation from the sun. UV radiation is invisible, high-energy waves that can harm living things. ❶

Ozone, remember, consists of O_3 molecules. Ozone can form from ordinary oxygen, O_2, under certain conditions. Near the ground, ozone is a major pollutant in smog produced from automobile exhausts. Even in minute amounts, the ozone in smog irritates the eyes and makes breathing difficult. ❷

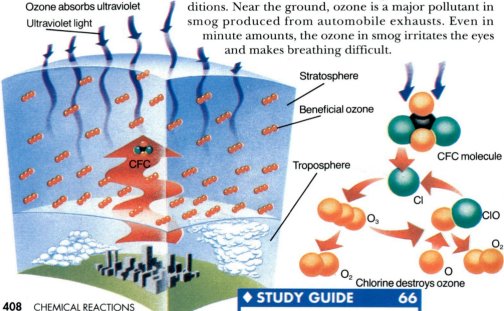

Ozone absorbs ultraviolet
Ultraviolet light

Stratosphere
Beneficial ozone
Troposphere

CFC molecule
Cl
ClO
O_3
O_2
O
Chlorine destroys ozone

408 CHEMICAL REACTIONS

OPTIONS

Meeting Different Ability Levels

For Section 16-2, use the following **Teacher Resource Masters** depending upon individual students' needs.

◆ **Study Guide Master** for all students.
● **Reinforcement Master** for students of average and above average ability levels.
▲ **Enrichment Master** for above average students.

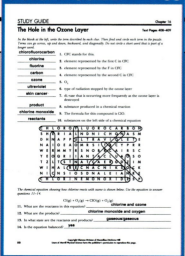

◆ STUDY GUIDE   66

STUDY GUIDE   Chapter 16
The Hole in the Ozone Layer   Text Pages 408–409

However, scientists have become concerned about a far more important ozone problem—the loss of more than three percent of the ozone high in Earth's atmosphere. Satellite photos of Antarctica, like the one to the right, show that every year the hole in the ozone layer, which is the size of the United States, gets bigger. And as the hole gets bigger, more and more life-damaging UV radiation can reach Earth.

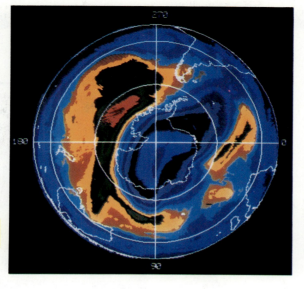

Scientists believe that the ozone destruction is largely due to compounds called chlorofluorocarbons. **Chlorofluorocarbons (CFCs) are a group of compounds of chlorine, fluorine, and carbon.** Some CFCs are used in refrigerators and air conditioners. When CFCs are released into the air, they move into the upper atmosphere. There, UV radiation causes the CFCs to break down and release atoms of chlorine. A chlorine atom destroys an ozone molecule, forming chlorine monoxide and oxygen:

$$Cl(g) + O_3(g) \rightarrow ClO(g) + O_2(g)$$

The chlorine monoxide, ClO, then breaks apart, setting free the chlorine atom, which repeats the process. In this way, a single chlorine atom can destroy 100 000 ozone molecules. The governments of 25 countries hope to totally stop the use of CFCs by the year 2000. But CFCs already in the atmosphere may continue to destroy the ozone for hundreds of years.

SECTION REVIEW

1. Why is the ozone layer in the atmosphere important?
2. Write an equation to show how a chlorine atom from a CFC destroys ozone.

You Decide!

Many businesses are calling for CFC recycling programs to prevent the CFCs from getting into the atmosphere. Will recycling solve the problem?

Ask questions 1 and 2 in the Section Review.

RETEACH
Have students draw molecules to represent the reaction in which ozone is destroyed. All bonds are covalent.

EXTENSION
For students who have mastered this section, use the **Reinforcement** and **Enrichment** masters or other OPTIONS provided.

3 CLOSE

❓ FLEX Your Brain

Use the Flex Your Brain activity to have students explore THE OZONE HOLE.

Cooperative Learning: Have an Expert Team conduct a telephone survey of the auto repair shops to determine how much CFC is used in your area to recharge auto air conditioners each year. This CFC is replacing what has been lost from the autos to the atmosphere.

SECTION REVIEW ANSWERS

1. It shields living things on Earth from harmful UV radiation from the sun.
2. $Cl(g) + O_3(g) \rightarrow ClO(g) + O_2(g)$

YOU DECIDE!

Opinions will vary. Students may say that recycling would help only if it goes on indefinitely. They could consider whether it is possible for recycling to compensate for leaks.

PROGRAM RESOURCES

From the **Teacher Resource Package** use:

Activity Worksheets, page 5, Flex Your Brain.

Concept Mapping, page 37.

Transparency Masters, pages 61–62, CFCs and Ozone.

Use **Color Transparency** number 31, CFCs and Ozone.

SCIENCE & SOCIETY

SECTION BACKGROUND

▶ Balanced equations have the same kind and number of atoms on each side.

▶ Coefficients are used to balance an equation; subscripts are never changed. To change a subscript is to change the identity of a substance.

▶ A balanced chemical equation accurately represents what actually happens in a chemical reaction. The relative amounts of each substance are shown in the equation. The law of conservation of mass is observed in a balanced chemical equation not just as a formality, but because reacting substances obey this law.

1 MOTIVATE

▶ Representing balanced chemical equations can best be done using models. If you do not have commercial kits, substitute candy gum drops and toothpicks.

▶ To model the reaction on page 410, give each student four red, four white, and two black gum drops. The white ones represent silver atoms; the red ones represent hydrogen atoms; the black ones represent sulfur atoms.

▶ Have students draw an arrow on a sheet of paper. Ask them to place their models on the paper to show the balanced equation that appears on page 411.

TYING TO PREVIOUS KNOWLEDGE: Give students a simple addition problem followed by a simple multiplication problem. Inform the class that if they got both problems correct, they can balance equations.

OBJECTIVES AND SCIENCE WORDS: Have students review the objectives and science words to become familiar with this section.

New Science Words

balanced chemical equation

Objectives

▶ Explain what is meant by a balanced chemical equation.
▶ Demonstrate how to write balanced chemical equations.

Checking for Balance

Where does the tarnish on silver come from? As you read in Chapter 11, tarnish is silver sulfide, Ag_2S. It forms when sulfur-containing compounds in the air or food react with the silver. Suppose you write this chemical equation for tarnishing:

$$Ag(cr) + H_2S(g) \rightarrow Ag_2S(cr) + H_2(g)$$

Now, examine the equation. Remember that matter is never created or destroyed in a chemical reaction. Notice that one silver atom appears in the reactants, $Ag + H_2S$. However, two silver atoms appear in the products, $Ag_2S + H_2$. As you know, one silver atom can't just become two. The equation must be balanced so it shows a true picture of what takes place in the reaction. ==A **balanced chemical equation** has the same number of atoms of each element on both sides of the equation.== To find out if this equation is balanced, make a chart like that shown in Table 16-2. ❶

The number of hydrogen and the number of sulfur atoms are balanced. However, there are two silver atoms on the right side of the equation and only one on the left side. This equation isn't balanced. ==Never change subscripts of a correct formula to balance an equation. Instead, place whole number coefficients to the left of the formulas of the reactants and products so that there are equal numbers of silver atoms on both sides of the equation.== If no number is present, the coefficient is one. ❷

Choosing Coefficients

How do you find out which coefficients to use to balance an equation? This decision is a trial-and-error process. With practice, the process becomes simple to perform.

Table 16-2

ATOMS IN UNBALANCED EQUATION		
Kind of Atom	Number of Atoms $Ag + H_2S \rightarrow Ag_2S + H_2$	
Ag	1	2
H	2	2
S	1	1

OPTIONS

Meeting Different Ability Levels

For Section 16-3, use the following **Teacher Resource Masters** depending upon individual students' needs.

◆ **Study Guide Master** for all students.

● **Reinforcement Master** for students of average and above average ability levels.

▲ **Enrichment Master** for above average students.

Additional Teacher Resource Package masters are listed in the OPTIONS box throughout the section. The additional masters are appropriate for all students.

◆ STUDY GUIDE 67

STUDY GUIDE   Chapter 16
Chemical Equations   Text Pages 410–412

In the chemical equation for tarnishing, you found that both the sulfur atoms and the hydrogen atoms were already balanced. Putting a coefficient before those formulas that contain these atoms might make matters worse. So, look at the formulas containing silver atoms: Ag and Ag_2S. There are two atoms of silver on the right side and only one on the left side. If you put a coefficient of two before Ag, the equation is balanced, as shown in Table 16-3.

$$2Ag(cr) + H_2S(g) \rightarrow Ag_2S(cr) + H_2(g)$$

Writing Balanced Chemical Equations

When a piece of magnesium ribbon burns in a flask of oxygen, a white powder called magnesium oxide is formed. To write a balanced chemical equation for this and most other reactions, follow these four steps:

Step 1 Describe the reaction in words, putting the reactants on the left side and the products on the right side.

magnesium plus oxygen produces magnesium oxide

Step 2 Write a chemical equation for the reaction using formulas and symbols. Review how to write formulas for compounds in Section 11-3. The formulas for elements are generally just their symbols. However, as you read in Chapter 12, some elements ordinarily exist as diatomic molecules as shown in Table 16-4. Oxygen is a diatomic molecule.

$$Mg(cr) + O_2(g) \rightarrow MgO(cr)$$

Step 3 Check the equation for balance. Set up a chart like Table 16-5 to help you.

The magnesium atoms are balanced, but the oxygen atoms are not. Therefore, this equation isn't balanced.

Step 4 Choose coefficients that balance the equation. Remember, never change subscripts of a correct formula to balance an equation. Try putting a coefficient of two before MgO to balance the oxygen.

$$Mg(cr) + O_2(g) \rightarrow 2MgO(cr)$$

Now there are two Mg atoms on the right side and only one on the left side. So a coefficient of two is needed next to Mg also.

$$2Mg(cr) + O_2(g) \rightarrow 2MgO(cr)$$

Table 16-6 indicates that the equation is now balanced.

Table 16-3

ATOMS IN BALANCED EQUATION		
Kind of Atom	Number of Atoms $2Ag + H_2S \rightarrow Ag_2S + H_2$	
Ag	2	2
H	2	2
S	1	1

Table 16-4

DIATOMIC MOLECULES	
Name	Formula
Hydrogen	H_2
Oxygen	O_2
Nitrogen	N_2
Fluorine	F_2
Chlorine	Cl_2
Bromine	Br_2
Iodine	I_2

Table 16-5

ATOMS IN UNBALANCED EQUATION		
Kind of Atom	Number of Atoms $Mg + O_2 \rightarrow MgO$	
Mg	1	1
O	2	1

Table 16-6

ATOMS IN BALANCED EQUATION		
Kind of Atom	Number of Atoms $2Mg + O_2 \rightarrow 2MgO$	
Mg	2	2
O	2	2

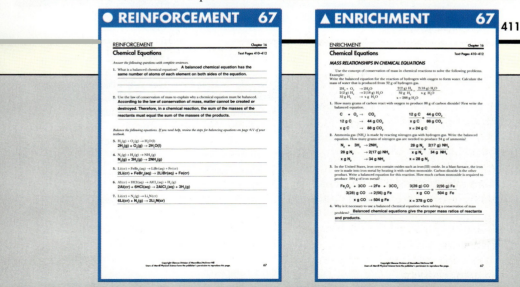

3 CLOSE

▶ Ask questions 1 and 2 and the **Apply** Question in the Section Review.
▶ If you performed the Motivate demonstration on page 404, you can present the following equations for the burning of fuel gases, in unbalanced form, and challenge students to balance them. Natural gas (mostly methane):
$CH_4(g) + 2O_2(g) \rightarrow CO_2(g) + 2H_2O(g)$
Propane:
$C_3H_8(g) + 5O_2(g) \rightarrow 3CO_2(g) + 4H_2O(g)$

SECTION REVIEW ANSWERS

1. to accurately show what takes place in a reaction and to show that matter is conserved
2. (a) $2Cu(cr) + S(cr) \rightarrow Cu_2S(cr)$
  (b) $2Na(cr) + 2H_2O(l) \rightarrow 2NaOH(aq) + H_2(g)$
3. Apply: $4Fe(cr) + 3O_2(g) \rightarrow 2Fe_2O_3(cr)$

Skill Builder

$Ca(NO_3)_2(aq) + Na_2CO_3(aq) \rightarrow 2NaNO_3(aq) + CaCO_3(cr)$
The $CaCO_3$ precipitates as a white solid.

Table 16-7

Kind of Atom	Number of Atoms $AgNO_3 + NaCl \rightarrow AgCl + NaNO_3$	
ATOMS IN AgCl FORMATION		
Ag	1	1
N	1	1
O	3	3
Na	1	1
Cl	1	1

④ Work through the following example
The photo to the right shows that when a silver nitrate solution is mixed with a sodium chloride solution, a white, insoluble solid is formed. This solid is silver chloride. The sodium nitrate formed remains in solution. Write a balanced equation for this reaction.
Step 1 Describe the reaction in words:
  aqueous silver nitrate plus aqueous sodium chloride produces solid silver chloride plus aqueous sodium nitrate
Step 2 Write the chemical equation:
  $AgNO_3(aq) + NaCl(aq) \rightarrow AgCl(cr) + NaNO_3(aq)$
Step 3 Check the equation for balance:
There are already equal numbers of each element on both sides of the equation. This equation is balanced.
Step 4 Choose coefficients:
  This equation is balanced, so no coefficients other than one are needed.

SECTION REVIEW

1. What are two reasons for balancing equations for chemical reactions?
2. Write balanced chemical equations for the following reactions: (a) copper metal plus sulfur produces copper(I) sulfide, (b) sodium metal plus water produces aqueous sodium hydroxide plus hydrogen gas.
3. **Apply:** Rust, iron(III) oxide, is formed when iron is exposed to oxygen in the air. Write a balanced equation for this reaction.

Skill Builder ☑ Observing and Inferring

Hard water contains ions of calcium, magnesium, and/or iron. When Na_2CO_3 is added to hard water, it is softened because these ions are removed as a white solid. For Mg, this reaction may occur:
  $MgCl_2(aq) + Na_2CO_3(aq) \rightarrow MgCO_3(cr) + 2NaCl(aq)$
Write an equation showing how water containing $Ca(NO_3)_2$ could be softened. If you need help, refer to Observing and Inferring in the **Skill Handbook** on page 678.

412 CHEMICAL REACTIONS

OPTIONS

Types of Chemical Reactions

Objectives

▶ Describe four types of chemical reactions using their generalized formulas.

▶ Classify various chemical reactions by type.

New Science Words

synthesis reaction
decomposition reaction
single displacement reaction
precipitate
double displacement reaction

Classifying Chemical Reactions

There are hundreds of kinds of chemical reactions. Rather than try to memorize them, it is easier to group reactions by their similarities. When you have classified a reaction in this way, you can then learn a great deal about it by comparing it to others in the group.

Scientists have developed a system of classification based upon the way the atoms rearrange themselves in a chemical reaction. Most reactions can be placed in one of four groups: synthesis, decomposition, single displacement, or double displacement reactions.

Synthesis Reactions

❶ The easiest reaction to recognize is a synthesis reaction. In a **synthesis reaction,** two or more substances combine to form another substance. The generalized formula for this reaction type is:

$$A + B \rightarrow AB$$

The reaction in which hydrogen burns in oxygen to form water is an example of a synthesis reaction:

$$2H_2(g) + O_2 \rightarrow (g)\ 2H_2O(g)$$

This reaction between hydrogen and oxygen occurs between two elements. It takes place very rapidly and it is explosive. One type of rocket fuel is hydrogen, which burns in oxygen when the rocket is fired.

Sulfuric acid is one of the most important manufactured chemicals. The final step in making sulfuric acid

Did You Know?

The novocaine that dentists use to deaden pain is a stable, easy-to-synthesize isomer of cocaine with few side effects.

What type of reaction is the burning of hydrogen in oxygen?

INQUIRY QUESTIONS

▶ Two components of smog are NO and NO_2. When NO_2 is exposed to sunlight it forms NO and O atoms. What type of reaction is this? *decomposition*

▶ A lab technician was estimating the amount of material needed for the production of sulfuric acid. The technician used the equation $SO_2 + O_2 \rightarrow SO_3$. What type of equation is it and why was the technician unable to correctly estimate the amounts of chemicals needed? *The reaction is synthesis. The equation is not balanced.*

PROGRAM RESOURCES

From the **Teacher Resource Package** use:
Critical Thinking/Problem Solving, page 22, Metal Corrosion.
Science and Society, page 20, Fuel Cells.
Transparency Masters, pages 65-66, Types of Chemical Reactions.
Use **Color Transparency** number 33, Types of Chemical Reactions.
Use **Laboratory Manual,** Chemical Reactions.

SECTION 16-4

PREPARATION

SECTION BACKGROUND

▶ From the name, one might expect synthesis reactions to be the most common method of preparing new compounds. However, these reactions are rarely as practical as the other three types.

▶ The energy necessary to decompose a compound can be in the form of heat, light, mechanical shock, or electricity.

▶ Chemists are able to predict the products of decomposition reactions because they often follow known patterns. For example, some metal carbonates produce metal oxides and carbon dioxide gas. Some metal chlorates yield metal chlorides and oxygen gas. Some metal hydroxides decompose into metal oxides and water.

▶ There are many reactions in which positive and negative ions of two compounds are interchanged. The formation of a precipitate or gas causes separation of the products and drives the reaction to completion.

PREPLANNING

▶ To prepare for Activity 16-1, safely dilute hydrochloric acid by adding concentrated acid to water and prepare the small pieces of metal.

1 MOTIVATE

▶ **Demonstration:** A decomposition reaction that can be easily performed is the decomposition of sugar. Place some sucrose in a test tube and heat it until it burns. Carbon remains. Water vapor and carbon dioxide gas are released. Compare this reaction to what happens when sugar is digested and then metabolized in a living cell.

TYING TO PREVIOUS KNOWLEDGE:
Discuss what students have previously learned in health class about chemical reactions associated with digestion. Ask the class how they would describe the chemical reactions that occur when a car's engine burns gasoline.

OBJECTIVES AND SCIENCE WORDS:
Have students review the objectives and science words to become familiar with this section.

2 TEACH

Key Concepts are highlighted.

CONCEPT DEVELOPMENT

▶ **Demonstration:** A single displacement reaction can be shown by placing a piece of mossy zinc metal in dilute sulfuric acid. Hydrogen gas is produced along with zinc sulfate, which remains dissolved in the water.
CAUTION: *Acid is corrosive. Hydrogen gas is flammable.*

REVEALING MISCONCEPTIONS

▶ Students often confuse elements in their pure form with elements in compounds. For example, students believe that copper in copper sulfate is the same as copper metal. Both use the symbol Cu. Point out that one form is an ion, whereas the other form is an unchanged atom.

CROSS CURRICULUM

▶ **Language Arts:** Have students look up the word *decompose* in a dictionary. Write a paragraph relating decomposition reactions to a possible solution to the problem of solid waste disposal caused by the closing of landfills.

Figure 16-4. Because sulfuric acid is used to manufacture so many different products, more of it is produced than any other chemical.

Figure 16-5. Copper in a wire replaces silver in silver nitrate, forming a blue solution. The silver precipitates onto the wire.

is a synthesis reaction between two compounds, sulfur trioxide and water:

$$SO_3(g) + H_2O(l) \rightarrow H_2SO_4(aq)$$

In the next chapter you will learn more about the importance of this acid and others.

Decomposition Reactions

The opposite of a synthesis reaction is a decomposition reaction. The drawing below illustrates this

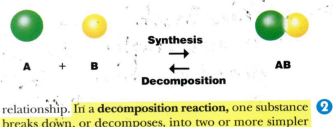

relationship. In a **decomposition reaction,** one substance breaks down, or decomposes, into two or more simpler substances. The generalized formula for this type of reaction is:

$$AB \rightarrow A + B$$

Most decomposition reactions require the use of heat, light, or electricity.

The decomposition of water by an electric current produces hydrogen and oxygen.

$$2H_2O(l) \xrightarrow[\text{current}]{\text{electric}} 2H_2(g) + O_2(g)$$

Displacement Reactions

A **single displacement reaction** occurs when one element replaces another in a compound. There are two generalized formulas for this type of reaction.

In the first case, A replaces B as follows:

$$A + BC \rightarrow AC + B$$

In the second case D replaces C as follows:

$$D + BC \rightarrow BD + C$$

In Figure 16-5, a copper wire is put into a solution of silver nitrate. Because copper is a more active metal than silver, it replaces the silver, forming a blue copper(II) nitrate solution. The silver forms an insoluble solid, or **precipitate.**

OPTIONS

Meeting Different Ability Levels

For Section 16-4, use the following **Teacher Resource Masters** depending upon individual students' needs.
◆ **Study Guide Master** for all students.
● **Reinforcement Master** for students of average and above average ability levels.
▲ **Enrichment Master** for above average students.
Additional Teacher Resource Package masters are listed in the OPTIONS box throughout the section. The additional masters are appropriate for all students.

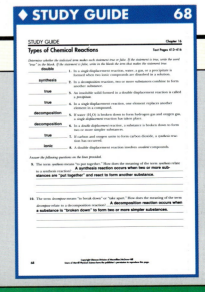

If a zinc strip is put into a copper(II) nitrate solution, the copper precipitates out.

$$Zn(cr) + Cu(NO_3)_2(aq) \rightarrow Zn(NO_3)_2(aq) + Cu(cr)$$

Zinc replaced the copper, so zinc must be a more active metal than copper. Table 16-8 summarizes the activity of some metals.

A **double displacement reaction** takes place if a precipitate, water, or a gas forms when two ionic compounds in solution are combined. In a double displacement reaction, the positive ion of one compound replaces the positive ion of the other compound to form two new compounds. The generalized formula for this type of reaction is:

$$AB + CD \rightarrow AD + CB$$

The reaction of silver nitrate with sodium chloride is an example of this type of reaction. As shown in the picture on page 412, a precipitate—silver chloride—is formed. The chemical equation is:

$$AgNO_3(aq) + NaCl(aq) \rightarrow AgCl(cr) + NaNO_3(aq)$$

You have seen just a few examples of chemical reactions classified into types. Many more reactions of each type occur around you.

SECTION REVIEW

1. Classify the following reactions by type:
   (a) $2KClO_3(cr) \rightarrow 2KCl(cr) + 3O_2(g)$
   (b) $CaBr_2(aq) + Na_2CO_3(aq) \rightarrow CaCO_3(cr) + 2NaBr(aq)$
   (c) $Zn(cr) + S(cr) \rightarrow ZnS(cr)$
   (d) $2Li(cr) + FeBr_2(aq) \rightarrow 2LiBr(aq) + Fe(cr)$
2. **Apply:** The copper bottoms of some cooking pans turn black after being used. The copper reacts with oxygen forming black copper(II) oxide. Write a balanced chemical equation for this reaction.

☑ Hypothesizing

Skill Builder

Group 1 metals replace hydrogen in water in reactions that are often very violent. A sample equation for one reaction is: $2K(cr) + 2HOH(l) \rightarrow 2KOH(aq) + H_2(g)$.

Use Table 16-8 to help you hypothesize about why these metals are often stored in kerosene. If you need help, refer to Hypothesizing in the **Skill Handbook** on page 682.

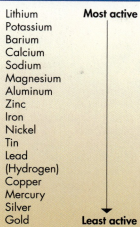

Table 16-8

ACTIVITY SERIES OF METALS

Lithium	**Most active**
Potassium	
Barium	
Calcium	
Sodium	
Magnesium	
Aluminum	
Zinc	
Iron	
Nickel	
Tin	
Lead	
(Hydrogen)	
Copper	
Mercury	
Silver	
Gold	**Least active**

CHECK FOR UNDERSTANDING
Use the Mini Quiz to check for understanding.

MINI QUIZ

Use the Mini Quiz to check students' recall of chapter content.

❶ **What type of reaction occurs when two substances combine to form one?** *synthesis*
❷ **What type of reaction occurs when one substance breaks down into two?** *decomposition*
❸ **An insoluble solid that forms from a solution is a(n) _____ .** *precipitate*

RETEACH
Students usually learn to balance equations and classify reactions only through drill and practice. Provide additional equations to balance and classify. Most introductory chemistry texts and problem-solving books are good sources.

EXTENSION
For students who have mastered this section, use the **Reinforcement** and **Enrichment** masters or other OPTIONS provided.

3 CLOSE

▶ Ask question 1 and the **Apply** Question in the Section Review.

SECTION REVIEW ANSWERS
1. (a) decomposition; (b) double displacement; (c) synthesis; (d) single displacement
2. Apply: $2Cu(cr) + O_2(g) \rightarrow 2CuO(cr)$

Skill Builder
Evidence that these metals are very active is their position near the top of the activity series. Because they are very active, Group 1 metals will react with water vapor and oxygen in the air. Therefore they must not come in contact with air.

ACTIVITY 16-1
30 minutes

OBJECTIVE: Compare the activity of different metals in the presence of acid.

PROCESS SKILLS applied in this activity:
► **Observing** in Analyze Questions 1 and 2.
► **Predicting** in Conclude and Apply Question 5.
► **Inferring** in Conclude and Apply Question 6.

🔴 COOPERATIVE LEARNING
Use the Science Investigation group strategy in teams of three. Have each student demonstrate one of the tests to the others and then pool resources to draw conclusions and answer questions.

TEACHING THE ACTIVITY
Troubleshooting: If the zinc is old, there may be no immediate reaction visible. Warming the tube between hands or in warm water may help.
► Use approximately 0.1M HCl prepared by adding 9 mL of concentrated HCl to a liter of water. If this does not work well with your materials, increase the HCl concentration. Too strong a solution will give a reaction with magnesium that is too fast.
► Collect hydrogen gas in an empty test tube inverted over the tube with magnesium. The tube must be inverted and ready when the metal is added.
► Do not use zinc or magnesium *powder*. The reactions will be too rapid and possibly violent.
► Cut pieces from magnesium ribbon and copper wire.

ACTIVITY 16-1
Displacement Reactions

Problem: *Which metals can displace hydrogen from an acid?*

Materials
- 3 test tubes
- test-tube stand
- small pieces of copper, Cu; zinc, Zn; and magnesium, Mg
- 15 mL dilute hydrochloric acid, HCl
- graduated cylinder
- wooden splint

CAUTION: *Handle acid with care. If spillage occurs, rinse area with plenty of water.*

Procedure
1. Copy the data table and use it to record your observations.
2. Set three test tubes in a test tube stand. Carefully pour 5 mL of dilute hydrochloric acid into each tube.
3. Place a small piece of metal in each test tube: copper in the first tube, zinc in the second tube, and magnesium in the third tube.

Data and Observations   Sample Data

Tube	Substances Mixed	Observations
1	HCl + Cu	no change
2	HCl + Zn	bubbles form
3	HCl + Mg	bubbles form more rapidly than in tube 2 and tube feels slightly warm

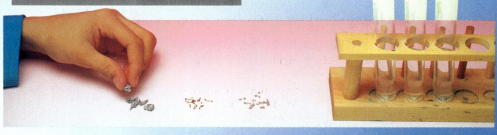

Analyze
1. What evidence of chemical reaction did you observe? In which tubes did a reaction occur?
2. When ignited, hydrogen burns rapidly. With your teacher's permission, trap some of the gas from tube 3. Bring a lighted splint near the gas. What happens? What do you infer about the identity of the gas?
3. Write a balanced equation for the reaction in tube 3. Magnesium reacts with an oxidation state of 2+.

Conclude and Apply
4. Examine your balanced equation in 3. What happens to an element that is displaced by another element?
5. From the activity series of metals, Table 16-8, on page 415, select another element that would have the same behavior as copper. Select another element that would have the same behavior as zinc and magnesium.
6. An outstanding physical property of hydrogen gas is its low density—about 1/15th of the density of air. Although hydrogen is used to fill weather balloons, it is not used to fill blimps. What chemical property of hydrogen that you observed in this activity prevents its use in blimps?

ANSWERS TO QUESTIONS
1. A gas was produced in the tubes with zinc and magnesium. There was no reaction in the tube with copper.
2. The gas ignites with a pop. The gas is likely to be hydrogen.
3. $Mg(cr) + 2HCl(aq) \rightarrow MgCl_2(aq) + H_2(g)$
4. It becomes a free element.
5. Point out to students that both zinc and magnesium lie above hydrogen in the activity series, whereas copper lies below. All metals above hydrogen will displace hydrogen from acids as magnesium does. Mercury, gold, and silver will act in a way similar to copper.

6. It burns in air readily.

PROGRAM RESOURCES

From the **Teacher Resource Package** use:
Activity Worksheets, pages 124-125, Activity 16-1: Displacement Reactions.

Energy and Chemical Reactions

Objectives

▶ Differentiate between an exothermic reaction and an endothermic reaction.

▶ Describe the effects of catalysts and inhibitors on the speed of chemical reactions.

New Science Words

endothermic reactions
exothermic reactions
catalyst
inhibitor

Energy Changes in Chemical Reactions

Did you ever watch the explosion of dynamite at a construction site? An explosion results from a very violent chemical reaction. In all chemical reactions energy is either released or absorbed. This energy can take many forms. It might be in the form of heat, light, sound, or even electricity. The explosion of dynamite produces heat, light, and sound.

Where does the energy to be released or absorbed come from? Whenever a chemical reaction takes place, some chemical bonds in the reactants must be broken. To break chemical bonds, energy must be provided. In order for products to be produced, new bonds must be formed. Bond formation releases energy.

Endothermic Reactions

Sometimes, more energy is required to break bonds than to form new ones in a chemical reaction. In these reactions, called **endothermic reactions,** energy must be provided for the reaction to take place.

When some endothermic reactions proceed, so much heat is absorbed that their containers feel cold to the touch. In other endothermic reactions, so little heat is absorbed that you would need a thermometer to determine that a temperature change has occurred.

Have you ever been at an athletic event where a player was injured and then applied a cold pack to the injury? Cold packs take advantage of an endothermic reaction.

Figure 16-6. The explosion of dynamite produces heat, light, and sound.

What is one kind of evidence that heat is absorbed in a reaction?

16-5 ENERGY AND CHEMICAL REACTIONS **417**

Skill Builder

This is the answer to the Skill Builder on page 419.

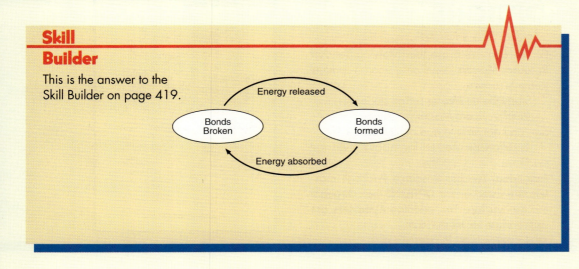

Bonds Broken → (Energy released) → Bonds formed

Bonds formed → (Energy absorbed) → Bonds Broken

SECTION 16-5

PREPARATION

SECTION BACKGROUND

▶ Exothermic reactions generally take place spontaneously. Endothermic reactions are generally not spontaneous.

▶ A system in nature tends to go from a state of higher energy to a state of lower energy.

▶ Most heterogeneous catalysts work by absorbing one of the reactants on the catalyst's surface.

PREPLANNING

▶ For Activity 16-2, obtain sand and manganese dioxide.

1 MOTIVATE

▶ **Demonstration:** You can simulate the action of both a hot pack and a cold pack used by athletic trainers. In advance, place some calcium chloride, such as that used to melt ice, in a zip-closed bag for the hot pack. Place a smaller zip-closed plastic bag containing water inside the bag containing the $CaCl_2$. Have the same setup available for each class, but use ammonium chloride for the cold pack. In class, open the inner bag containing the water and close the outer bag. Mix the contents. Have students feel the outside of the bag. Repeat this for the cold pack.

TYING TO PREVIOUS KNOWLEDGE: Ask your students to describe how they feel when they have a fever. Ask them why the body gets hot. Guide the students' thinking toward the making and breaking of chemical bonds with the associated release of energy. Some of this energy is released in the form of heat which raises the body temperature.

OBJECTIVES AND SCIENCE WORDS: Have students review the objectives and science words to become familiar with this section.

Key Concepts are highlighted.

CONCEPT DEVELOPMENT

▶ **Demonstration:** To show the effect of a catalyst, dissolve 25 g of potassium sodium tartrate in 300 mL of very hot water in a 600-mL beaker. Then add 100 mL of six percent hydrogen peroxide to the beaker and heat to 85°C. Nothing happens until 3 grams of cobalt chloride, the catalyst, are added and stirred. The beaker may overflow, so place it on a tray.

REVEALING MISCONCEPTIONS

▶ **Demonstration:** The reaction of a sparkler burning is very exothermic, but some students are confused because you have to light it. They think the activation energy means that the reaction is endothermic.

CHECK FOR UNDERSTANDING

Use the Mini Quiz to check for understanding.

MINI QUIZ

Use the Mini Quiz to check students' recall of chapter content.

1 When more energy is required to break bonds than to form new ones, the reaction will be _____ . *endothermic*

2 If energy is given off, a reaction is said to be _____ . *exothermic*

3 How does a catalyst affect the rate of a chemical reaction? *increases it*

4 A catalyst in a living organism is called a(n) _____ . *enzyme*

5 How does an inhibitor affect the rate of a chemical reaction? *decreases it*

Figure 16-7. When the inner capsule in a cold pack is broken, the chemicals mix, and a lower temperature results.

The cold pack contains ammonium chloride sealed in a container inside a larger plastic bag filled with water. When you break the inner container, the ammonium chloride mixes with the water. The reaction absorbs so much heat from the water that the pack feels very cold.

Exothermic Reactions

Most chemical reactions aren't endothermic. In most chemical reactions, less energy is required to break old bonds than to form new ones. In these reactions, called **exothermic reactions,** energy is given off by the reaction. **2** The heat given off causes the reaction mixture to feel hot.

The burning of wood and the explosion of dynamite are exothermic reactions. They are exothermic because they give off energy as the reaction proceeds. Rusting is also exothermic, but the reaction proceeds so slowly that it is difficult to detect the temperature change caused by the release of energy.

Catalysts and Inhibitors

Some reactions are so slow that you would have to wait for a long time for the desired product to be formed.

To speed up these reactions you can add a catalyst. A **catalyst** is a substance that speeds up a chemical reaction without itself being permanently changed. When you **3** add a catalyst to a reaction, you end up with the same amount of the catalyst that you started with.

Certain proteins known as enzymes act as catalysts in living organisms. Enzymes allow reactions to occur at faster rates and lower temperatures than would otherwise be possible. Without these enzymes, life as we know **4** it would not be possible.

Some reactions need to be slowed down. The food preservations BHT and BHA slow down the spoilage of certain foods. BHT and BHA are inhibitors. Any substance that slows down a reaction is called an **inhibitor.** **5**

Figure 16-8. The burning of wood is an example of an exothermic reaction. Energy is released in the form of heat and light.

How do enzymes affect reactions in living oranisms?

418   CHEMICAL REACTIONS

OPTIONS

Meeting Different Ability Levels

For Section 16-5, use the following **Teacher Resource Masters** depending upon individual students' needs.

◆ **Study Guide Master** for all students.

● **Reinforcement Master** for students of average and above average ability levels.

▲ **Enrichment Master** for above average students.

Additional Teacher Resource Package masters are listed in the OPTIONS box throughout the section. The additional masters are appropriate for all students.

◆ **STUDY GUIDE** 69

STUDY GUIDE   Chapter 16
Energy and Chemical Reactions   Text Pages 417–420

TECHNOLOGY

Catalytic Converters

The exhaust systems of cars today are equipped with catalytic converters that use rhodium and platinum as the catalysts. These catalysts speed up reactions of three types of toxic compounds given off by cars. These compounds are unburned hydrocarbons, carbon monoxide, and nitrogen oxides. Catalytic converters change these compounds into harmless compounds.

Two types of reactions are catalyzed. In one type of reaction, oxygen is added. Adding oxygen converts carbon monoxide to carbon dioxide, and unburned hydrocarbons to carbon dioxide and water. In the other type of reaction, oxygen is removed. Removing oxygen converts nitrogen oxides to nitrogen, water, and carbon dioxide.

Think Critically: Why is it not necessary to add more rhodium and platinum to a catalytic converter as these substances are used?

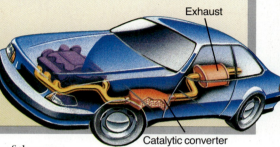

Exhaust

Catalytic converter

Using catalysts and inhibitors are just a few of the ways scientists control chemical reactions. With further research, scientists will learn more about these very useful chemicals.

SECTION REVIEW

1. What is the difference between exothermic and endothermic reactions?
2. Rusting takes place much faster in the presence of water. What role does water play in this reaction?
3. **Apply:** Suppose you wanted to develop a product for warming people's hands at outdoor winter events. Would you choose an exothermic reaction or an endothermic reaction to use in your device? Why?

Science and WRITING

The development of the chemical accelerator was a major factor in the making of new materials through chemical reactions. Explain how it works.

☑ Concept Mapping

Construct a concept map to show the relationship between energy and bond formation and bond breakage. If you need help, refer to Concept Mapping in the **Skill Handbook** on pages 684 and 685.

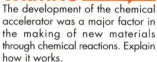

Skill Builder

TECHNOLOGY

For more information on catalytic converters, read "They Forgot More Chemistry Than I Ever Knew" by Dennis Simanaitis, *Road and Track*, May 1985, page 154.

Think Critically: Rhodium and platinum are catalysts and are therefore not consumed.

RETEACH

Discuss how homes are heated, cars are fueled, and cooking is done. Have students identify where exothermic chemical reactions play a role.

EXTENSION

For students who have mastered this section, use the **Reinforcement** and **Enrichment** masters or other OPTIONS provided.

Science and WRITING

It accelerates ions and molecules to high energy states that would normally require temperatures of 10 000°C to 100 000°C.

CROSS CURRICULUM

▶ **Language Arts:** Have students determine the meanings of the roots *endo-*, *exo-*, and *therm-*. Ask a volunteer to explain how the roots of the word reflect its meaning.

3 CLOSE

▶ Ask questions 1 and 2 and the **Apply** Question in the Section Review.

SECTION REVIEW ANSWERS

1. An exothermic reaction releases energy. An endothermic reaction absorbs energy.

2. Water acts as a catalyst in the reaction.

3. **Apply:** You would choose an exothermic reaction so that the heat given off could be used to warm cold hands.

Note: Skill Builder answer is on page 417.

● **REINFORCEMENT** 69   ▲ **ENRICHMENT** 69   419

REINFORCEMENT   Chapter 16
Energy and Chemical Reactions   Text Pages 417–420

Answer the following questions with complete sentences.

1. What is a catalyst? **A catalyst is a chemical substance that speeds up a chemical reaction without undergoing a permanent change itself.**

2. What is an exothermic reaction? **An exothermic reaction is a reaction that gives off more energy than it requires.**

3. What is an inhibitor? **An inhibitor is any substance that slows down a reaction.**

4. What is an endothermic reaction? **An endothermic reaction requires energy for the reaction to take place.**

Identify whether each reaction described involves a catalyst, an inhibitor, or neither. Write C for catalyst, I for inhibitor, or N for neither in the space at the left.

N 5. Placing oil on a metal part helps to keep the part from rusting. Is the oil a catalyst, an inhibitor, or neither?

C 6. In the human body, proteins called enzymes help to speed up chemical processes. The proteins are not changed during these chemical processes. Are the enzymes catalysts, inhibitors, or neither?

N 7. Painting a metal surface keeps water from touching the metal and causing the metal to rust. Is the paint a catalyst, an inhibitor, or neither?

I 8. Food preservatives called BHT and BHA slow down the spoilage of certain foods. Are BHT and BHA catalysts, inhibitors, or neither?

C 9. Nickel is used to increase the rate of methane formation from the addition of hydrogen and carbon monoxide. Nickel does not permanently change. Is nickel a catalyst, inhibitor, or neither?

Identify whether each reaction described below is endothermic or exothermic. In the blank, write EN for endothermic or EX for exothermic.

EX 10. When a lit match is placed in alcohol, the alcohol ignites producing heat and light.

EN 11. Energy in the form of electricity can be added to water to break apart the water molecules into hydrogen gas and oxygen gas.

EX 12. A piece of coal placed in a furnace gives off heat and light before turning to ash.

EN 13. When ammonium chloride mixes with water, the solution formed feels cold.

ENRICHMENT   Chapter 16
Energy and Chemical Reactions   Text Pages 417–420

HOT CHEMICAL PACKS

Have your muscles ever felt sore after work or exercise? If so, a chemical hot pack may be just the thing to make your sore muscles feel better.

A hot pack uses a process called an exothermic reaction. One type of hot pack uses an outer plastic bag with an inner paper bag perforated by very small holes. The paper bag contains a mixture of powdered iron, sodium chloride, activated charcoal, and sawdust, all dampened with water. When the paper bag is removed from the outer plastic bag and shaken vigorously, it gets hot. The reaction of iron with the oxygen in the air produces rust and heat. The sodium chloride, charcoal, and sawdust make the crystals grow faster. The exothermic reaction is the result of the rapid rusting of the iron.

You can make your own instant hot pack. Get about 500 g of sodium thiosulfate hydrate (sold in many photo stores), two self-locking plastic bags of different sizes, a 500 mL glass mixing cup, a measuring spoon, a metal stirring spoon, and a large pan for heating.

Put about 440 g of the crystal sodium thiosulfate hydrate into the measuring cup. Add about 2 tablespoons of water. Place the cup in a pan of water at room temperature. (The water can't be too deep, or the cup will tip over.) Heat the water to a gentle boil. Stir until the crystals completely dissolve, then heat and stir a few more minutes.

Turn off the heat. Let the liquid stand in the water bath until it cools to room temperature. Pour the liquid into a self-locking plastic bag and seal the bag. Place this bag inside a second self-locking bag. Place a few crystals of sodium thiosulfate hydrate in the second bag between the two bags. Your pack may be stored like this.

To use the heat pack, open the outer bag and get two or three crystals. Open the inner bag and drop the seed crystals into different areas of the liquid. Reseal both bags. Your pack should produce heat at a steady temperature of 48 degrees Celsius for about an hour.

To recharge your heat pack, remove the solid sodium thiosulfate hydrate from the bag and melt it as before. Pour the liquid into a fresh inner bag. You can recycle the sodium thiosulfate hydrate indefinitely.

Questions

1. What are several uses for a hot pack? **sore muscles, hand warmer**

2. Suppose you have a hot pack that uses iron and oxygen. You start the exothermic reaction by shaking the bag. Is there any way for you to stop the reaction? Explain. **Since the reaction needs oxygen, you can put the paper bag into an airtight plastic bag. If no oxygen is available to combine with the iron, the exothermic reactions stops.**

Teacher note: If students have trouble obtaining solid sodium thiosulfate hydrate, check with chemical stores. This activity could then be done as a small group activity. If this chemical is not found anywhere, suggest making the hot pack with iron, sodium chloride, sawdust, and activated charcoal as per paragraph two above.

CHAPTER 16 **419**

ACTIVITY 16-2
30 minutes

OBJECTIVE: Operationally define a catalyst and **observe** its action.

PROCESS SKILLS applied in this activity:
▶ **Observing** in Procedure Step 3.
▶ **Classifying** in Analyze Questions 3, 4, and 5.
▶ **Operationally defining** in Conclude and Apply Question 6.

TEACHING THE ACTIVITY

Troubleshooting: Students should have the glowing splint ready when the MnO_2 is placed in the peroxide solution. Demonstrate the technique for students. Hydrogen peroxide must be freshly opened.

▶ Blood or small pieces of raw liver contain an enzyme that catalyzes the breakdown of H_2O_2. Save some blood from a beef roast and demonstrate its catalytic activity to students by substituting it for MnO_2.

▶ Repeat the activity as a demonstration by using larger test tubes and larger quantities.

▶ Ordinary 3 percent H_2O_2 available from drugstores should work well if it is fresh.

PROGRAM RESOURCES

From the **Teacher Resource Package** use:

Activity Worksheets, pages 126-127, Activity 16-2: Catalyzed Reaction.

ACTIVITY 16-2
Catalyzed Reaction

Problem: How does a catalyst affect hydrogen peroxide?

Materials

- 3 medium-sized test tubes
- test-tube stand
- 15 mL hydrogen peroxide, H_2O_2
- graduated cylinder
- small plastic spoon
- sand
- manganese dioxide, MnO_2
- wooden splint
- hot plate
- beaker of hot water

CAUTION: *Hydrogen peroxide can irritate skin and eyes. Wear goggles and apron.*

Procedure

1. Set three test tubes in a test-tube stand. Pour 5 mL of hydrogen peroxide into each tube.
2. Place about 1/4 spoonful of sand in tube 2 and the same amount of manganese dioxide in tube 3.
3. In the presence of some substances that act as catalysts, H_2O_2 decomposes rapidly, producing oxygen gas, O_2. A glowing splint placed in O_2 will relight. Test the gas produced in any of the tubes as follows. Light a wooden splint, blow out the flame, and insert the glowing splint into the tube.
4. Place all three tubes in a beaker of hot water. Heat on a hot plate until all the remaining H_2O_2 is driven away and there is no liquid left in the tubes.

Analyze

1. What changes did you observe when the solids were added to the tubes?
2. In which tube was oxygen produced rapidly, and how do you know?

3. Which substance, sand or manganese dioxide, caused the rapid production of gas from the hydrogen perioxide?
4. How did you identify the gas produced?
5. What remained in each tube after the hydrogen peroxide was driven away?

Conclude and Apply

6. What are the two characteristics of a catalyst? Which substance in this activity has both characteristics?
7. The word *catalyst* has uses beyond chemistry. If a person who is added to a basketball team acts as a catalyst, what effect is that person likely to have on the team?

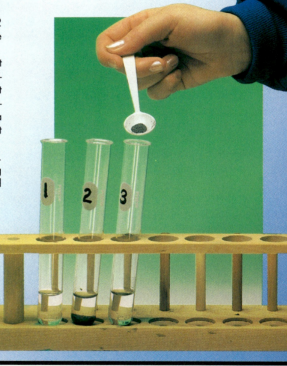

ANSWERS TO QUESTIONS

1. tube with H_2O_2 alone—no change; tube with H_2O_2 and sand—no change; tube with H_2O_2 and MnO_2—rapid bubbling

2. Oxygen was produced in the tube containing H_2O_2 and MnO_2. Bubbles appear and the glowing splint test for oxygen was positive.

3. MnO_2

4. The glowing splint burst into flame.

5. tube with H_2O_2 alone—nothing; tube with H_2O_2 and sand—sand; tube with H_2O_2 and MnO_2—MnO_2

6. A catalyst speeds up a chemical reaction.

A catalyst is not permanently changed by a reaction.

7. The person energizes the team and causes the team to be more active than it would normally be.

SUMMARY

16-1: Chemical Changes in Matter

1. In a chemical reaction, the reactants are changed into the products, which are different substances.

2. According to the law of conservation of mass, the mass of the reactants in a chemical reaction equals the mass of the products.

3. A chemical equation is a shorthand way of describing a chemical reaction using symbols, coefficients, and formulas.

16-2: Science and Society: The Hole in the Ozone Layer

1. The ozone layer helps protect life on Earth by absorbing much of the ultraviolet radiation from the sun.

2. In the upper atmosphere, CFCs release atoms of chlorine that destroy ozone molecules.

16-3: Chemical Equations

1. A balanced chemical equation has the same number of atoms of each element on both sides of the equation.

2. The final step in the process of balancing a chemical equation is the choice of the correct coefficients.

16-4: Types of Chemical Reactions

1. Generalized formulas are used to describe four reaction types—synthesis, decomposition, single displacement, and double displacement.

2. Many specific chemical reactions can be classified as one of four types.

16-5: Energy and Chemical Reactions

1. In an exothermic reaction, energy is released; in an endothermic reaction, energy is absorbed.

2. A catalyst increases the speed of a chemical reaction; an inhibitor decreases the speed of a chemical reaction.

KEY SCIENCE WORDS

a. balanced chemical equation
b. catalyst
c. chemical reaction
d. chlorofluorocarbons (CFCs)
e. coefficients
f. decomposition reaction
g. double displacement reaction
h. endothermic reactions
i. exothermic reactions
j. inhibitor
k. precipitate
l. products
m. reactants
n. single displacement reaction
o. synthesis reaction

UNDERSTANDING VOCABULARY

Match each phrase with the correct term from the list of Key Science Words.

1. energy is given off
2. has same number of atoms on both sides
3. energy is absorbed
4. an element replaces another in a compound
5. slows down a reaction rate
6. substance breaks down into simpler substances
7. two ionic compounds are in solution and precipitate forms
8. two or more substances combine
9. group of compounds that contains chlorine, fluorine, and carbon
10. well-defined example of chemical change

SUMMARY

Have students read the summary statements to review the major concepts of the chapter.

UNDERSTANDING VOCABULARY

1. i	**6.** f
2. a	**7.** g
3. h	**8.** o
4. n	**9.** d
5. j	**10.** c

OPTIONS

ASSESSMENT

To assess student understanding of material in this chapter, use the resources listed.

COOPERATIVE LEARNING

Consider using cooperative learning in the THINK AND WRITE CRITICALLY, APPLY, and MORE SKILL BUILDERS sections of the Chapter Review.

PROGRAM RESOURCES

From the **Teacher Resource Package** use:

Chapter Review, pages 35-36.

Chapter and Unit Tests, pages 105-108, Chapter Test.

CHAPTER REVIEW

CHECKING CONCEPTS

1. d	**6.** a
2. b	**7.** c
3. a	**8.** d
4. a	**9.** b
5. c	**10.** c

UNDERSTANDING CONCEPTS

11. catalyst
12. Coefficients
13. precipitate
14. reactants
15. products

THINK AND WRITE CRITICALLY

16. Equations will vary, but for all equations, the number of atoms of each element in the reactants must equal the number of atoms of each element in the products.

17. Zinc will replace copper in $Cu(NO_3)_2$ because zinc is the more active metal. Copper metal will form a precipitate. No reaction will occur in the other case.

18. $PbSO_4(cr)$

19. Changing subscripts changes the identity of a substance.

20. $2CuO(cr) \rightarrow 2Cu(cr) + O_2(g)$

CHAPTER REVIEW

CHECKING CONCEPTS

Choose the word or phrase that completes the sentence.

1. An example of a chemical reaction is _____.
  a. bending   **c.** melting
  b. evaporation   **d.** photosynthesis

2. Lavoisier's experiments gave examples of the law of _____.
  a. chemical reaction
  b. conservation of mass
  c. coefficients
  d. gravity

3. An element that is more _____ will replace another element in a compound.
  a. active   **c.** inhibiting
  b. catalytic   **d.** soluble

4. In the expression $4Ca(NO_3)_2$, the 4 is a _____.
  a. coefficient   **c.** subscript
  b. formula   **d.** symbol

5. BHA is an example of a(n) _____.
  a. catalyst   **c.** inhibitor
  b. formula   **d.** product

6. If a substance is dissolved in water, _____ follows its formula in an equation.
  a. *(aq)*   **c.** *(g)*
  b. *(cr)*   **d.** *(l)*

7. In tarnishing, Ag_2S is a(n) _____.
  a. catalyst   **c.** product
  b. inhibitor   **d.** reactant

8. In the burning of hydrogen, O_2 is a(n) _____.
  a. catalyst   **c.** product
  b. inhibitor   **d.** reactant

9. _____ is a substance that absorbs UV radiation.
  a. O_2 **b.** O_3 **c.** Cl   **d.** Cl_2

10. If a substance is a solid, _____, follows its formula in an equation.
  a. *(l)*   **b.** *(g)*   **c.** *(cr)*   **d.** *(aq)*

UNDERSTANDING CONCEPTS

Complete each sentence.

11. A(n) _____ speeds up a reaction without being permanently changed.

12. _____ represent the relative number of units taking part in a reaction.

13. An insoluble product of a reaction that comes out of solutions is a(n) _____.

14. When nitrogen and oxygen react to form nitrogen dioxide, nitrogen and oxygen are _____.

15. The new substances formed in a chemical reaction are the _____.

THINK AND WRITE CRITICALLY

16. Write a balanced chemical equation and use it to explain the law of conservation of mass.

17. If a strip of Zn is placed in a solution of $Cu(NO_3)_2$, and a strip of Cu is placed in a $Zn(NO_3)_2$ solution, what reaction takes place? Explain.

18. $PbCl_2$ and Li_2SO_4 react to form LiCl and what other substance?

19. Why should subscripts not be changed to balance an equation?

20. Write a balanced equation for the decomposition of copper(II) oxide.

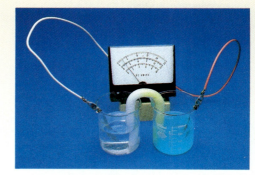

21. Chromium is produced by reacting its oxide with aluminum. If 76 g of Cr_2O_3 and 27 g of Al react to form 51 g of Al_2O_3 how many grams of Cr are formed?

22. Propane, $C_3H_8(g)$, burns in oxygen to form carbon dioxide and water vapor. Write a balanced equation for burning propane.

23. $Cl(g) + O_3(g) \rightarrow ClO(g) + O_2(g)$ plays a role in ozone destruction. What is the source of the monatomic chlorine, Cl?

24. In one reaction of a catalytic converter, nitrogen(II) oxide reacts with hydrogen to form ammonia and water vapor. Write a balanced equation for this reaction.

25. If lye, NaOH, is put in water, the solution gets hot. What kind of reaction is this?

MORE SKILL BUILDERS

If you need help, refer to the Skill Handbook.

1. **Observing and Inferring:** What belongs in the parentheses in the following double displacement reaction?

   $BaCl_2(aq) + K_2CO_3(aq) \rightarrow BaCO_3(\ ) + 2KCl(aq)$

2. **Recognizing Cause and Effect:** Sucrose, table sugar, is a disaccharide. This means that sucrose is composed of two simple sugars chemically bonded together. Sucrose can be separated by digestion or by heating it in a sulfuric acid solution. Find out what products are formed by breaking sucrose. What role does the acid play?

3. **Interpreting Data:** When 46 g of sodium were exposed to dry air, 62 g of sodium oxide formed over a period of time. How many grams of oxygen from the air were used?

4. **Outlining:** Make an outline with the general heading "Chemical Reactions." Include the

four types of reactions, with a description and example of each.

5. **Concept Mapping:** The arrow in a chemical equation tells the reaction direction. Some reactions are reversible, because they don't go in only one direction. Sometimes the bond formed is weak, and a product breaks apart as it's formed. A double arrow used in the equation indicates this reaction. Fill in the cycle, using the words *product(s)* and *reactant(s)*. In the blanks in the center, fill in the formulas for the substances appearing in the reversible reaction:

$H_2(g) + I_2(g) \rightleftarrows 2HI(g)$

PROJECTS

1. Research common chemical reactions that occur safely in your home. Demonstrate one of these reactions. Tell what type of reaction it is and how it is used. Write a balanced equation for the reaction.

2. Investigate the label on a package of cold cuts. Research as many of the chemicals added as possible. Is anything added as an inhibitor? Report on your findings.

21. 76 g Cr_2O_3 + 27 g Al = 51 g Al_2O_3 + X g Cr
mass of Cr = 52 g

22. $C_3H_8(g) + 5O_2(g) \rightarrow 3CO_2(g) + 4H_2O(g)$

23. decomposition of ClO

24. $2NO(g) + 5H_2(g) \rightarrow 2NH_3(g) + 2H_2O(g)$

25. exothermic

MORE SKILL BUILDERS

1. **Observing and Inferring:** The symbol *cr* would be used. A precipitate must be formed.

2. **Recognizing Cause and Effect:** The simple sugars glucose and fructose are formed. The acid is a catalyst.

3. **Interpreting Data:** 46 g Na + X g O_2 = 62 g Na_2O
mass of O_2 = 16 g

4. **Outlining:** Sample outline:

I. Chemical reactions

   A. Synthesis
      1. Two or more substances react to form another substance.
      2. Example: $2H_2(g) + O_2(g) \rightarrow 2H_2O(g)$

   B. Decomposition
      1. A substance breaks down into other substances.
      2. Example: $2HI(g) \rightarrow H_2(g) + I_2(g)$

   C. Single displacement
      1. One element replaces another from a compound.
      2. Example: $Zn(cr) + 2AgNO_3(aq) \rightarrow 2Ag(cr) + Zn(NO_3)_2(aq)$

   D. Double displacement
      1. Takes place when two ionic compounds combine and a gas or precipitate is formed.
      2. Example: $NaCl(aq) + AgNO_3(aq) \rightarrow AgCl(cr) + NaNO_3(aq)$

5. **Concept Mapping:**

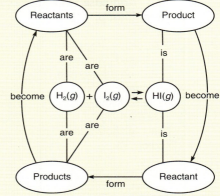

CHAPTER SECTION	OBJECTIVES	ACTIVITIES
17-1 Acids and Bases (2 days)	1. **Define** acid and base. 2. **Describe** the characteristic properties of acids and bases. 3. **List** the names, formulas, and uses of some common acids and bases. 4. **Relate** the processes of ionization and dissociation to the formation of acids and bases.	**MINI-Lab:** Do acids and bases conduct an electric current? p. 428
17-2 Strength of Acids and Bases (2 days)	1. **Explain** what determines the strength of an acid or a base. 2. **Differentiate** between strength and concentration. 3. **Define** pH. 4. **Describe** the relationship between pH and the strength of an acid or a base.	**Activity 17-1:** Strong and Weak Acids, p. 437
17-3 Acid Rain Science & Society (1 day)	1. **Describe** the factors contributing to the formation of acid rain. 2. **Discuss** the problems acid rain is causing and how these problems might be solved.	
17-4 Acids, Bases, and Salts (2 days)	1. **Describe** a neutralization reaction. 2. **Explain** what a salt is and how salts form. 3. **Differentiate** between soaps and detergents. 4. **Explain** how esters are made and what they are used for.	**Activity 17-2:** Acid-Base Reactions, p. 446
Chapter Review		

ACTIVITY MATERIALS

FIND OUT	ACTIVITIES		MINI-LABS
Page 425 soda water marble chips salt water balance filter paper funnel heat lamp or portable hair dryer	**17-1 Strong and Weak Acids, p. 437** typing paper (22 cm $\times$ 28 cm), marked with rectangles thick cardboard (22 cm $\times$ 28 cm), marked with rectangles scissors 2 test tubes 2 medicine droppers graduated cylinder dilute hydrochloric acid (HCl) dilute acetic acid (CH$_3$COOH)	pH paper timer, with second hand **17-2 Acid-Base Reactions, p. 446** test tube 2 medicine droppers graduated cylinder carbonated beverage, colorless dilute sodium hydroxide (NaOH) phenolphthalein indicator, 1%	**Do acids and bases conduct an electric current? p. 428** conductivity tester orange juice cleaner containing ammonia small jars or beakers

CHAPTER FEATURES	TEACHER RESOURCE PACKAGE	OTHER RESOURCES
Technology: *Book Decay,* p. 429 **Skill Builder:** *Comparing and Contrasting,* p. 433	**Ability Level Worksheets** ◆ *Study Guide,* p. 70 ● *Reinforcement,* p. 70 ▲ *Enrichment,* p. 70 MINI-Lab Worksheet, p. 139 Concept Mapping, pp. 39, 40 Transparency Masters, pp. 67, 68	**Color Transparency 34,** Acids in Solutions
Skill Builder: *Concept Mapping,* p. 436	**Ability Level Worksheets** ◆ *Study Guide,* p. 71 ● *Reinforcement,* p. 71 ▲ *Enrichment,* p. 71 Activity Worksheet, pp. 133, 134 Critical Thinking/Problem Solving, p. 23 Transparency Masters, pp. 69, 70	**Color Transparency 35,** The pH Scale **Lab Manual 35,** Acids, Bases, and Indicators
You Decide! p. 439	**Ability Level Worksheets** ◆ *Study Guide,* p. 72 ● *Reinforcement,* p. 72 ▲ *Enrichment,* p. 72	**Lab Manual 36,** Acid Rain
Problem Solving: *Julio's Experiment,* p. 441 **Skill Builder:** *Interpreting Data,* p. 445	**Ability Level Worksheets** ◆ *Study Guide,* p. 73 ● *Reinforcement,* p. 73 ▲ *Enrichment,* p. 73 Activity Worksheet, pp. 135, 136 Cross-Curricular Connections, p. 23 Science and Society, p. 21 Technology, pp. 15, 16	
Summary　　Think & Write Critically Key Science Words　　Apply Understanding Vocabulary　　More Skill Builders Checking Concepts　　Projects Understanding Concepts	**Chapter Review,** pp. 37, 38 **Chapter Test,** pp. 109-112 **Unit Test,** pp. 113, 114	**Chapter Review Software Test Bank**

◆ **Basic**　　● **Average**　　▲ **Advanced**

ADDITIONAL MATERIALS

SOFTWARE	AUDIOVISUAL	BOOKS/MAGAZINES
Acid Base Problems, J & S Software. *Titration Lab,* EME. *Acids and Bases,* COMPress. *Acid Rain,* AIT.	*Acids, Bases, and Salts,* film, Coronet/MTI Films. *All About Acids and Bases,* filmstrip, Science Software. *Introduction to Titration,* video, EME. *Mr. Wizard's World: Chemical Tests,* Macmillan/McGraw-Hill School Division. *Acid Rain,* video, Focus.	Pearson, R.G., ed. *Hard and Soft Acids and Bases.* NY: Van Nostrand Reinhold, 1973. Stewart. *How to Understand Acid-Base: A Quantitative Acid Base Primer for Biology and Medicine.* NY: Elsevier Science Publishing Co., Inc., 1981.

THEME DEVELOPMENT: Systems and interactions as a theme of the textbook are developed through a presentation of the Arrhenius system of acids and bases. The interactions that occur between an acid and base to produce a salt and the corrosive interactions between an acid and other substances are developed in the chapter.

CHAPTER OVERVIEW

▶ **Section 17-1:** Acids and bases are defined in this section. Their properties are described and explained according to the theory of ionization. Common acids and bases are named.

▶ **Section 17-2:** This section explains what determines acid or base strength. The concept of pH and how it relates to the strength of an acid or base is developed in detail.

▶ **Section 17-3: Science and Society:** Acid rain's probable causes are presented along with possible solutions to this environmental problem.

▶ **Section 17-4:** This section describes how a salt is formed in a neutralization reaction. The section also introduces the student to a saponification reaction and explains the difference between a soap and a detergent.

CHAPTER VOCABULARY

acid	pH
indicator	acid rain
dehydrating agent	plankton
pickling	neutralization
base	salt
hydronium ion	titration
strong acid	soaps
weak acid	saponification
strong base	detergents
weak base	ester

CHAPTER

17 Acids, Bases, and Salts

424

OPTIONS

📌 For Your Gifted Students

▶ Students can do research to determine where in the U.S. and Canada there are indications of forest or wildlife damage as a result of acid rain. They can also research the level of damage at different altitudes. Have students draw a map of North America. The map can be color coded to indicate areas of dense population, industrialization, forest damage, and wildlife damage, including damage to bodies of water.

▶ Students who are interested in chemistry could do quantitative titrations using volumetric apparatus and standard solutions of known molarity. Others could learn about different indicators and the pH range in which each changes color. A chemistry teacher could probably furnish apparatus and materials for these investigations.

Do you know what is causing this marble statue to deteriorate at an alarming rate?

FIND OUT!

Do this simple activity to find out how a solution can change a rock.

Marble is mostly calcite, $CaCO_3$, a mineral found in many rocks. Normal rainwater does not have much effect on calcite. However, in places where there is a lot of air pollution, certain chemical pollutants dissolve in rainwater and change its chemical makeup. This rainwater-pollutant solution reacts with calcite, causing it to weaken and eventually crumble.

Let's simulate this reaction. Weigh out exactly 5.0 g of marble chips and place them in a beaker. Next add about 50 mL of soda

water, which is similar in some ways to the rainwater-pollutant solution. Observe the mixture for several minutes. Then stir the mixture vigorously and let it sit until it stops moving. Pour the mixture through a filter paper. Dry the marble chips and mass them again. Has their mass changed? How do your conclusions relate to acid rain?

Previewing Science Skills
- ▶ In the **Skill Builders,** you will compare and contrast, make a concept map, and interpret data.
- ▶ In the **Activities,** you will use models, hypothesize, measure, observe, and predict.
- ▶ In the **MINI-Lab,** you will observe and infer.

What's next?

You have seen that contact with some solutions can produce a change in a mineral. Now find out what kinds of solutions produce such changes.

425

INTRODUCING THE CHAPTER
Use the Find Out activity to introduce students to acids and bases. Inform students that they will be learning more about neutralization reactions and salts as they read the chapter.

FIND OUT!
Preparation: Mass samples of marble chips ahead of time. A heat lamp or portable hair dryer will be needed.
Materials: soda water, marble chips, salt water, balances, filter paper, funnels, heat lamp or portable hair dryer

Cooperative Learning: Use the Science Investigation group strategy to carry out this research problem. Have half the group do the test using salt water.
Teaching Tips
▶ Measure the 5-gram samples of marble chips into small beakers with the mass recorded on a taped label to eliminate wasted time as students wait for a balance. Each group of four students will need two samples. If you have one electronic balance, this can be completed very quickly.
▶ Several portable hair dryers will quickly dry the calcium carbonate chips so they can be re-massed during the same laboratory period.

Gearing Up
Have students study the Gearing Up section to familiarize themselves with the chapter. Discuss the relationships of the topics in the outline.

What's Next?
Before beginning the first section, make sure students understand the connection between the Find Out activity and the topics to follow.

For Your Mainstreamed Students
▶ Have students make a crossword puzzle or word search from the key science words found at the end of the chapter. Clues for the puzzle can be definitions or descriptions of those words found in the chapter. Students could also make flash cards. On one side they can place the word and on the other side the definition. They can quiz each other using the cards.

▶ Special effort should be made to have mainstreamed students perform or assist in Activity 17-2. Some students could carry out their own titrations of vinegar, lemon juice, and orange juice to compare the acidity with that of carbonated beverages. Mainstreamed students might like to perform the suggested extension of this activity in which they compare the acidity of different brands and types of beverages.

PREPARATION

SECTION BACKGROUND

▶ This text limits the discussion of acids and bases to the Arrhenius theory. The theories proposed by Bronsted, Lowry, and Lewis build on the Arrhenius theory and extend the definitions of acids and bases.

▶ Binary acids contain only two elements. The salts of these acids end in the suffix -ide.

▶ Ternary acids contain three elements. Oxy-acids end in suffix -ic or -ous, and their salts end in -ate and -ite.

PREPLANNING

▶ To prepare for the Mini-Lab on page 428, obtain a conductivity tester, orange juice, and ammonia cleaner.

1 MOTIVATE

▶ **Demonstration:** To establish a need to know more about acids, bases, and salts, prepare two solutions. The acid solution is made by adding 0.6 mL of concentrated (18M) sulfuric acid to 99.4 mL of water. Add 10 mL of this solution to 90 mL of water to prepare a 0.01M acid solution. Separately prepare a base solution by adding 0.32 g of Ba(OH)$_2$•8H$_2$O to 100 mL of water. This gives a 0.01M solution.

▶ Add the 0.01M sulfuric acid solution to the beaker of a conductivity apparatus so that the beaker is half-filled with acid. Place the electrodes in the beaker. While stirring the solution, add the 0.01M Ba(OH)$_2$ solution dropwise. Have students observe both the salt formation and the decreasing conductivity as fewer ions are present in the solution. Barium sulfate is insoluble.

New Science Words

acid
indicator
dehydrating agent
pickling
base
hydronium ion

Objectives

▶ Define *acid* and *base*.
▶ Describe the characteristic properties of acids and bases.
▶ List the names, formulas, and uses of some common acids and bases.
▶ Relate the processes of ionization and dissociation to the formation of acids and bases.

Figure 17-1. This indicator turns red in the presence of an acid.

Properties of Acids

What comes to mind when you hear the word *acid*? Do you think about something that has a sour taste? Do you think of a substance that can burn your skin, or even burn a hole through a piece of metal? Although many acids are not strong enough to burn through metal, or even burn your skin, these characteristics are, indeed, properties of acids.

Acids make up a very important group of compounds. All of these compounds contain hydrogen. When an acid is dissolved in water, some of the hydrogen is released as hydrogen ions (H$^+$). Thus, an **acid** is a substance that produces hydrogen ions (H$^+$) in solution. It is the presence of the H$^+$ ions that gives acids their characteristic properties. A brief description of these acid properties follows. ❶

Acids taste sour. The familiar sour taste of such foods as citrus fruits and tomatoes is due to the presence of acids. *However, taste should* **NEVER** *be used to test for the presence of acids.* Some acids can produce painful burns and damage to tissues. ❷

Acids are electrolytes. Because they always contain some ions, acid solutions conduct electricity.

Acids are corrosive. Some acids react strongly with certain metals, seeming to "eat away" the metals as metallic compounds and hydrogen gas are produced.

Acids react with certain compounds, called indicators, to produce a predictable change in color. An **indicator** is an organic compound that changes color in an acid or a base.

OPTIONS

Meeting Different Ability Levels

For Section 17-1, use the following **Teacher Resource Masters** depending upon individual students' needs.

◆ **Study Guide Master** for all students.
● **Reinforcement Master** for students of average and above average ability levels.
▲ **Enrichment Master** for above average students.

Additional Teacher Resource Package masters are listed in the OPTIONS box throughout the section. The additional masters are appropriate for all students.

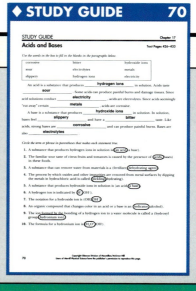

Common Acids

Many familiar items that you use every day contain acids. Acids are components of many foods. The gastric juices in your stomach contain acid that helps to break down food during digestion. Car batteries, some flashlight batteries, and some household cleaners also contain acids. Table 17-1 gives the names and formulas of a few common acids and tells where they are found.

In addition to these acids that you come in contact with every day, certain acids are vital to industry. The four most important industrial acids are sulfuric acid, phosphoric acid, nitric acid, and hydrochloric acid.

Sulfuric acid, H_2SO_4, is the most widely used chemical in the world. Almost 30 billion kilograms of this acid are produced in the United States annually. More than half of this acid is used by industries in this country. The rest is exported.

Sulfuric acid is a thick, oily liquid. Because of its use in automobile storage batteries, sulfuric acid is sometimes called battery acid. Most sulfuric acid produced is

Did You Know?

In the 8th century, a mixture of nitric acid and hydrochloric acid was known as *aqua regia*, meaning "kingly water," because it was able to dissolve gold.

Table 17-1

SOME COMMON ACIDS		
Name	Formula	Where Found
Acetic acid	CH_3COOH	Vinegar
Acetylsalicylic acid	$HOOC-C_6H_4-OOCCH_3$	Aspirin
Ascorbic acid (vitamin C)	$C_5H_9O_5-COOH$	Citrus fruits, tomatoes, vetetables
Boric acid	H_3BO_3	Eyewash solutions
Carbonic acid	H_2CO_3	Carbonated drinks
Hydrochloric acid	HCl	Gastric juices in stomach
Nitric acid	HNO_3	Fertilizers, explosives (TNT)
Phosphoric acid	H_3PO_4	Detergents, fertilizers
Sulfuric acid	H_2SO_4	Car batteries, fertilizers

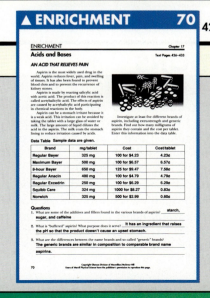

427

TYING TO PREVIOUS KNOWLEDGE: Ask students to name foods that taste sour. They might name lemon (citric acid), apple (malic acid), grapefruit (ascorbic acid), grape (tartaric acid), or vinegar (acetic acid). Point out to them that the Latin word *acidus* means "sour." Remind students how slippery their hands feel when they use soap. Bases feel slippery.

OBJECTIVES AND SCIENCE WORDS: Have students review the objectives and science words to become familiar with this section.

2 TEACH

Key Concepts are highlighted.

CONCEPT DEVELOPMENT

▶ Students will retain information that they have experienced. Each of the properties of acids can be easily demonstrated.

▶ **Demonstration:** Acids taste sour. Cut a lemon into thin slices and then cut the slices into smaller pieces. Distribute these to each student to taste.

▶ **Demonstration:** Acids are electrolytes. Materials to make a lemon or potato clock are available from commercial science suppliers. Copper and zinc electrodes connected to a digital clock are placed 1 cm apart in a lemon and the clock operates. A voltmeter can be used to show that the Cu/Zn electrodes in a lemon do produce a voltage.

▶ **Demonstration:** Acids are corrosive. Place a piece of magnesium ribbon in a petri dish on the overhead projector. Add dilute HCl dropwise to the metal. The class will be able to see the hydrogen gas being evolved. Try the demonstration with warm lemon juice.

▶ **Demonstration:** Acids cause indicators to change color. Place a few milliliters of water containing universal indicator in a petri dish on the overhead projector. Add vinegar to the petri dish dropwise. The color changes will be visible to the entire class. Blue litmus paper can also be used.

► Students have the misconception that all acids are very strong. Bring in some common items found at home that contain acids. You can include vitamin C (ascorbic acid), eye wash (boric acid), drink mixes (citric acid), and soft drinks (phosphoric acid). Students should know that most acids are weak acids.

CROSS CURRICULUM

► **Geology:** Earth scientists use dilute hydrochloric acid to test different rocks for the presence of carbonate. A piece of limestone will react and give off carbon dioxide gas when a few drops of dilute HCl are added.

TEACHER F.Y.I.

► Acids and bases cause indicator dyes to change color. Litmus is such a dye. It is extracted from lichens that grow on rocks and trees. Blue litmus turns red when touched with a drop of acid.

MINI-Lab

Materials: conductivity tester, orange juice, cleaner containing ammonia, small jars or beakers

Cooperative Learning: Extra hands may be needed here. Use the Paired Partner strategy having one student hold the conductivity apparatus in the solution while the other steadies the beaker and reads the meter.

Teaching Tips

► Have students test other juices and other bases, such as milk of magnesia, $Mg(OH)_2$.

► **CAUTION:** *Tell students not to taste any of the substances being tested.*

► Do not allow students to use 110-volt conductivity meters. Use only battery-powered apparatus.

Answers to Questions

The juice does conduct electricity. It contains ascorbic acid (vitamin C) and citric acid. The ammonia cleaner conducts electricity. It contains NH_4^+ and OH^- ions. Typically, acids produce H^+ ions and bases produce OH^- ions in solution.

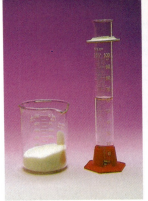

Figure 17-2. Sulfuric acid reacts with the hydrogen and oxygen in sugar, removing them as water and leaving only carbon.

used in the manufacture of fertilizer. It is also used in petroleum refining, steel manufacture, and in the production of plastics, drugs, dyes, and other acids.

What is a dehydrating agent?

 Another important use for sulfuric acid is as a dehydrating agent. A **dehydrating agent** is a substance that can remove water from materials. As Figure 17-2 illustrates, organic compounds are dehydrated by removing hydrogen and oxygen in the form of water from the compounds, leaving only carbon. When sulfuric acid comes in contact with human tissue, this dehydrating action produces painful burns.

Phosphoric acid, H_3PO_4, is another acid important to industry in the United States. Eighty percent of the phosphoric acid produced is used to make fertilizers.

Dilute phosphoric acid has a slightly sour but pleasant taste and is used in soft drinks. It is also used to make phosphates, which are added to detergents to enhance their cleaning power. Unfortunately, these phosphates cause pollution problems in lakes and streams.

Nitric acid, HNO_3, is best known for its use in making explosives. However, like sulfuric and phosphoric acids, most of the nitric acid produced is used in the manufacture of fertilizers. Concentrated nitric acid is a colorless liquid. When exposed to light, the acid slowly changes to a yellow liquid. This change in color occurs because some of the nitric acid decomposes into nitrogen dioxide, NO_2, which is a brownish gas. Nitric acid can cause serious burns on human skin. Contact with light-colored skin causes yellow stains. This yellow color is a test for protein.

MINI-Lab

Do acids and bases conduct an electric current?
What term is used to describe a substance that, when dissolved in water, conducts an electric current? Carefully place the electrodes of a conductivity tester into a glass of orange juice. Did the juice conduct electricity? What acids are present in orange juice? (**CAUTION:** *Do not taste the juice.*) Try the same conductivity procedure with an ammonia cleaner. Did this solution conduct electricity? What base is present in the cleaner? What are the most important ions formed in aqueous solutions of acids? of bases?

428 ACIDS, BASES, AND SALTS

OPTIONS

INQUIRY QUESTIONS

► Active metals such as zinc can remove hydrogen from acids. Write a balanced chemical equation that shows this reaction occurring with sulfuric acid. $Zn(cr) + H_2SO_4(aq) \rightarrow H_2(g) + ZnSO_4(aq)$

► A water solution of HF is called hydrofluoric acid, and HCl is named hydrochloric acid. Using this pattern, name the acids HBr and HI. *hydrobromic acid, hydroiodic acid (actually hydriodic acid)*

► Almost 30 billion kilograms of sulfuric acid is produced in the U.S. each year. If a kilogram of sulfuric acid has a retail value of $3.50, what is the economic value of the acid produced each year? *105 billion dollars*

PROGRAM RESOURCES

From the **Teacher Resource Package** use:
Activity Worksheets, page 139, Mini-Lab: Do acids and bases conduct an electric current?

Hydrogen chloride is a colorless gas. When this gas is dissolved in water, hydrochloric acid, HCl, is formed. The HCl fumes given off by the hydrochloric acid can harm the lungs, eyes, and skin.

Hydrochloric acid, which is commonly called muriatic acid, is used in industry to clean surfaces of materials. Large quantities of the acid are used by the steel industry for pickling. **Pickling** is a process in which oxides and other impurities are removed from metal surfaces by dipping the metals in hydrochloric acid.

Figure 17-3. Pickling removes impurities from metal surfaces.

TECHNOLOGY

Book Decay

New technologies often bring new problems. When paper made from flax or cotton was replaced by paper made from wood fiber, the life expectancy of the paper was severely reduced. Paper made from wood fiber must be treated with sizing. When this paper is exposed to heat and humidity, the sizing reacts to form an acid. The acid then decomposes the wood fiber in the paper. If the acid is not neutralized or removed, the paper will last only about 50 years.

The Library of Congress currently contains 16 million books and manuscripts that are in danger of acid decay. Several technologies are being developed to remove acid from paper. One involves vacuum drying the books and adding a magnesium compound to neutralize the acid. A second method dips books in a mixture of Freon and magnesium oxide. The most exotic technique exposes the books to diethylzinc (DEZ) gas for neutralization. DEZ, however, is explosive, making the process hard to engineer. Recently, manufacturers have started to produce paper that is alkaline and, therefore, more durable.

Think Critically: What could be done to reduce the rate of paper deterioration while scientists search for an efficient and inexpensive neutralization technique?

17-1   ACIDS AND BASES   **429**

CONCEPT DEVELOPMENT
▶ **Demonstration:** Place a piece of aluminum foil in tomato sauce or juice overnight. Have students examine the foil the next day. Ask the class if tomato-based foods should be stored in aluminum cookware or covered with aluminum foil. Ask students how the presence of aluminum ions in the food affects taste. They should suggest that it tastes metallic.

▶ **Demonstration:** The brown ring test for a protein is mentioned in the textbook. Fry or boil an egg and bring the white of the egg to class. Place a drop of nitric acid on the egg white. Students will observe the yellow-brown discoloration that indicates the presence of a protein.

TECHNOLOGY

To learn more about the preservation of books, see "Paper Progress" by John Mattill, *Technology Review*, April 1989, p. 11. Ask students to search for examples of old, brittle books at home. Have them bring in the books to exhibit to the class. If you have a brittle book of little value, test some of the paper with pH paper or indicators to see if you can detect the acidity.

Think Critically: Because heat and moisture promote the release of acid, books could be stored in cool, dry areas.

MINI QUIZ

Use the Mini Quiz to check students' recall of chapter content.

❶ **What kind of ions are produced by an acid in water solution?** *hydrogen ions*

❷ **List four properties that are common to acids.** *Acids taste sour, conduct electricity, cause indicators to change color, and are corrosive.*

❸ **List four common industrial acids.** *sulfuric, phosphoric, nitric, and hydrochloric acids*

❹ **A substance that can remove water from another substance is called a(n) _____ agent.** *dehydrating*

❺ **What happens when a metal is pickled?** *It is dipped in hydrochloric acid to remove oxides and other impurities.*

ENRICHMENT
▶ Ask a student to use an encyclopedia to research the life and work of Svante Arrhenius. The student should prepare a report for the class.

▶ Have a student contact the local soil and water conservation office or county extension agent to find out how soil is tested to determine its acidity or alkalinity, what the test costs, and what soils are like in your area. Even if you live in a large city, these offices and services may be available.

▶ Have each student bring in a small sample of cleaning agent that is used in his or her home. Use red and blue litmus paper to test the acidity or alkalinity of each. Record the results on a bulletin board. Students are surprised that many cleaners are acidic.

EcoTip

Many detergents and household cleaners contain phosphates which pollute lakes, streams, and groundwater when released in wastewater. Read labels carefully and select cleansing agents that do not contain phosphates.

What properties do acids and bases have in common?

Figure 17-4. Many household materials contain bases.

There are several methods for making phosphoric, nitric, and hydrochloric acids. But one general method can be used to make all three acids. This method involves reacting concentrated sulfuric acid with a compound containing the negative ion of the desired acid.

$$Ca_3(PO_4)_2(cr) + 3H_2SO_4(aq) \rightarrow 2H_3PO_4(aq) + 3CaSO_4(cr)$$
$$NaNO_3(cr) + H_2SO_4(aq) \rightarrow HNO_3(g) + NaHSO_4(aq)$$
$$NaCl(cr) + H_2SO_4(aq) \rightarrow HCl(g) + NaHSO_4(aq)$$

Properties of Bases

Like acids, bases are an important group of chemical compounds. Although acids and bases seem to have some features in common, the two groups are actually quite different.

6 A **base** is a substance that produces hydroxide ions (OH^-) in solution. Does this OH combination look familiar? You may recall from Chapter 13 that an alcohol has a hydroxyl group, $-OH$, as part of its molecule. This hydroxyl group is not an ion and should not be confused with the OH^- ions that are present in all bases. Alcohols are not bases.

The hydroxide ions present in all basic solutions are negative ions, whereas the hydrogen ions present in acid solutions are positive ions. This difference in charge accounts for some of the differences between acids and bases.

In the pure, undissolved state, most bases are crystalline solids. In solution, bases feel slippery and have a bitter taste. Like acids, strong bases are corrosive, and contact with the skin may result in severe burns and tissue damage. *Therefore, taste and touch should **NEVER** be used to test for the presence of a base.* Basic solutions are electrolytes. This property is due to the presence of ions in the solutions. Finally, bases react with indicators to produce predictable changes in color.

OPTIONS

INQUIRY QUESTIONS

▶ **Why do your eyes burn when you get shampoo in them?** *One reason is that the shampoo contains a base, which irritates the eyes.*

▶ **Antacid tablets are advertised for an upset stomach. How would you classify magnesium hydroxide, which is present in some antacids? Why would antacids help calm the stomach?** *It is a base. The stomach normally contains acid. Sometimes too much acid is produced. Bases react with acids to form neutral solutions.*

▶ **Write an equation to show how calcium hydroxide breaks apart in solution to form ions.** $Ca(OH)_2(cr) \rightarrow Ca^{2+}(aq) + 2OH^-(aq)$

Common Bases

Many household products contain bases. Most soaps, for example, contain bases, which explains their bitter taste and slippery feel. Table 17-2 contains the names and formulas of some common bases and tells how the bases are used.

Table 17-2

COMMON BASES AND THEIR USES		
Name	Formula	Uses
Aluminum hydroxide	$Al(OH)_3$	Deodorant, antacid
Ammonium hydroxide	NH_4OH	Household cleaner
Calcium hydroxide	$Ca(OH)_2$	Leather production, manufacture of mortar and plaster
Magnesium hydroxide	$Mg(OH)_2$	Laxative, antacid
Sodium hydroxide	NaOH	Drain cleaner, soap making

Although you won't find it listed in the table, the most widely used base is ammonia, NH_3. Pure ammonia is a colorless gas with a very distinctive, irritating odor. When ammonia gas is dissolved in water, some of its molecules react with water molecules, forming ammonium ions (NH_4^+) and hydroxide ions.

$$NH_3(g) + H_2O(l) \rightarrow NH_4^+(aq) + OH^-(aq)$$

The solution containing ammonium ions and hydroxide ions is called ammonium hydroxide, or ammonia water. However, ammonium hydroxide exists as a solid compound only at temperatures below $-79°C$. Ammonia water is an excellent household cleaning agent. Ammonia is also used as a fertilizer and in the production of rayon, nylon, and nitric acid.

Another widely used base is calcium hydroxide, $Ca(OH)_2$. Commonly called caustic lime, this base is a white crystalline powder that is only slightly soluble in water. Calcium hydroxide is used in the production of mortar and plaster and to "sweeten" acidic soils.

Sodium hydroxide, NaOH, is a strong, very corrosive base. This compound, commonly called lye, dissolves readily in water. Its corrosive nature makes sodium hydroxide an effective oven cleaner and drain cleaner. It reacts with such organic materials as oils and fats to produce soap and glycerine.

Figure 17-5. Ammonia is an important ingredient of these products.

17-1 ACIDS AND BASES **431**

CONCEPT DEVELOPMENT

▶**Demonstration:** Metal oxides react with water to form a basic solution. Burn a few centimeters of magnesium ribbon. **CAUTION:** *Do not look directly at the bright light.* Place the white powder, MgO, in a test tube and add a milliliter of water. Heat to near boiling. Test the resulting $Mg(OH)_2$ with an indicator such as litmus.

▶ After the above demonstration, remind students that lime, CaO, is used in cement mixes. The dust can settle on skin and react with perspiration to form $Ca(OH)_2$, which can result in chemical burns.

CROSS CURRICULUM

▶**Language Arts:** The old name for sulfuric acid was oil of vitriol. Have students use a dictionary to look up *vitriol* and *vitriolic*. Ask them to use *vitriolic* in a sentence.

REVEALING MISCONCEPTIONS

▶ Scientists use specific words carefully. Be certain students understand the difference between the words *dissociation* (separation of ions in solution) and *ionization*. In the ionization of a weak electrolyte, the solvent plays an active role in bond breaking.

CHECK FOR UNDERSTANDING

Use the Mini Quiz to check for understanding.

MINI QUIZ

Use the Mini Quiz to check students' recall of chapter content.

6 **What do scientists call a substance that produces hydroxide ions in solution?** *a base*

7 **Give the name and formula for the ions that form when ammonia gas reacts with water.** *ammonium, NH_4^+, and hydroxide, OH^-, ions*

8 **Solutions that contain hydrogen ions are _____ .** *acids*

9 **What is the symbol and charge of a hydronium ion?** H_3O^+

10 **When an ionic compound is pulled apart by the solvent, the process is called _____ .** *dissociation*

Solutions of Acids and Bases

It is important to understand that the compounds that produce acids or bases when dissolved in water are not, themselves, acids or bases. **The terms *acid* and *base* refer to aqueous (water) solutions. Solutions that contain H^+ ions are acids; those that contain OH^- ions are bases.** **8**

All compounds that produce acids when dissolved in water are made up of polar molecules. When such a compound is dissolved in water, the molecules are pulled apart, forming positive and negative ions. Recall from Chapter 15 that this process is called ionization. The positive hydrogen ion is attracted to and held by the negative end of a water molecule, forming a new ion, as shown in Figure 17-6. **The ion formed by the bonding of a hydrogen ion, H^+, to a water molecule is called a hydronium ion, H_3O^+.** **9**

What is a hydronium ion?

Figure 17-6. When an acid dissolves in water, hydrogen ions from the acid combine with water molecules to produce hydronium ions.

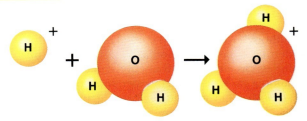

Figure 17-7 shows what happens when hydrogen chloride gas dissolves in water. Because the solution contains H^+ ions, it is an acid—hydrochloric acid, HCl. As described earlier, the H^+ ions bond with water molecules to form H_3O^+ ions.

Figure 17-7. When hydrogen chloride gas dissolves in water, it ionizes to produce H^+ ions and Cl^- ions.

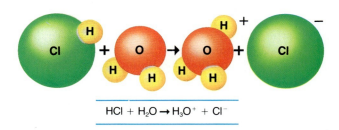

$$HCl + H_2O \rightarrow H_3O^+ + Cl^-$$

The equation below shows the ionization of acetic acid, CH_3COOH, which is an organic acid.

$$CH_3COOH(l) + H_2O(l) \rightarrow H_3O^+(aq) + CH_3COO^-(aq)$$

432   ACIDS, BASES, AND SALTS

OPTIONS

INQUIRY QUESTIONS

▶**What ion is responsible for acidic properties?** *hydrogen ion or hydronium ion*

▶**What ion is responsible for basic properties?** *hydroxide ion*

▶**An organic acid is classified as a carboxylic acid and contains the –COOH group. Acetic acid has the formula CH_3COOH. Which of the four hydrogens present in the formula is responsible for the acidic properties?** *The hydrogen in the –COOH group.*

▶**How can ammonia gas, NH_3, exhibit basic properties when dissolved in water even though it has no hydroxide ion in its formula?** *The action of ammonia in splitting the water into H^+ and OH^- ions results in hydroxide ions being present in the solution.*

As the equation shows, when an organic acid ionizes, the H at the end of the –COOH group combines with water to form the hydronium ion.

Except for ammonia, nearly all compounds that produce bases in aqueous solution are ionic compounds. That is, they are already made up of ions. As the equation below shows, when such a compound dissolves, the ions dissociate, or pull apart, and exist as individual ions in solution.

$$NaOH(cr) \xrightarrow{H_2O} Na^+(aq) + OH^-(aq)$$

Ammonia is a polar compound. In solution, ionization takes place when the ammonia molecule attracts a hydrogen atom from a water molecule, as shown in Figure 17-8.

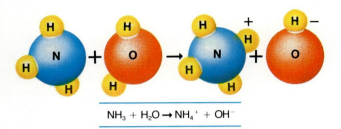

$$NH_3 + H_2O \rightarrow NH_4^+ + OH^-$$

Figure 17-8. Even though ammonia is not a hydroxide, it reacts with water to produce some OH^- ions.

The next time you sip a soft drink, wash your hands with soap, or use any of the products described in this section, stop and think for a minute. Think about what properties the product has and why it has them.

SECTION REVIEW

1. Why are acids and bases electrolytes?
2. Name three important acids and three important bases and describe some uses of each.
3. **Apply:** When you are stung by a bee or a wasp, it injects formic acid, HCOOH, into your body. What kind of acid is formic acid? How do you know? Write an equation showing how formic acid ionizes.

☑ Comparing and Contrasting

List as many ways as you can think of that acids and bases are similar. Make a second list of the ways in which they are different. If you need help, refer to Comparing and Contrasting in the **Skill Handbook** on page 679.

Skill Builder

SECTION 17-2

PREPARATION

SECTION BACKGROUND

▶ The binary acids HCl, HBr, and HI are strong; all other binary acids and HCN are weak.

▶ Ternary acids contain oxygen. Strong ternary acids include HNO_3, H_2SO_4, and $HClO_3$. Examples of weak ternary acids are HClO, H_2CO_3, and H_3AsO_4.

▶ Polyprotic acids are those that have more than one ionizable hydrogen. Examples are H_2SO_4 and H_3PO_4.

▶ Hydroxides of Group 1 and 2 metals (except beryllium) are strong bases. All others are weak.

PREPLANNING

▶ For Activity 17-1, prepare 0.1*M* hydrochloric acid and 0.1*M* acetic acid. If dropping bottles are available, you will need only a few drops of each acid per group.

1 MOTIVATE

▶ **Demonstration:** Place two petri dishes, each containing a small piece of magnesium ribbon, on an overhead projector. Place several drops of 6*M* HCl on one piece of Mg and a similar amount of vinegar on the other Mg piece. Students will see that the action of a strong acid contrasts greatly to that of a weak acid. Use the demonstration to introduce this section and its concepts.

PROGRAM RESOURCES

From the **Teacher Resource Package** use:

Critical Thinking/Problem Solving, page 23, Is Acid Rain a Threat?

Transparency Masters, pages 69-70, The pH Scale.

Use **Color Transparency** number 35, The pH Scale.

Use **Laboratory Manual,** Acids, Bases, and Indicators.

17-2 Strength of Acids and Bases

New Science Words

strong acid
weak acid
strong base
weak base
pH

Objectives

- ▶ Explain what determines the strength of an acid or a base.
- ▶ Differentiate between strength and concentration.
- ▶ Define *pH.*
- ▶ Describe the relationship between pH and the strength of an acid or a base.

Strong and Weak Acids and Bases

You have learned that all acids have certain properties in common. Yet, some acids are safe enough to swallow or put in your eyes, whereas other acids destroy human tissue and corrode metal. Obviously, all acids are not alike. Some acids are stronger than others. The same is true of bases. Table 17-3 lists some strong and weak acids and bases.

The strength of an acid or base depends on how completely a compound is pulled apart to form ions when dissolved in water. An acid that ionizes almost completely in solution is a **strong acid.** Conversely, an acid that only partly ionizes in solution is a **weak acid.** 1

How do strong acids differ from weak acids?

Strong acids contain large numbers of hydronium ions. Look at the equations for the ionization of hydrochloric acid, a strong acid, and acetic acid, a weak acid.

$$HCl(g) + H_2O(l) \rightarrow H_3O^+(aq) + Cl^-(aq)$$

$$CH_3COOH(l) + H_2O(l) \rightleftarrows H_3O^+(aq) + CH_3COO^-(aq)$$

In the equation for the formation of hydrochloric acid, note that no HCl molecules are present in solution. All of the HCl ionizes, and the H^+ ions produced combine with water to form H_3O^+ ions. In the equation for acetic acid, not all of the CH_3COOH molecules ionize. Some of the molecules remain intact in solution. Thus, only a few H^+ ions are produced to form H_3O^+ ions.

The strength of a base is determined by its solubility in water. Remember, most bases are ionic compounds

Figure 17-9. H_2SO_4 is a strong acid; CH_3COOH is a weak acid.

OPTIONS

Meeting Different Ability Levels

For Section 17-2, use the following **Teacher Resource Masters** depending upon individual students' needs.

◆ **Study Guide Master** for all students.

● **Reinforcement Master** for students of average and above average ability levels.

▲ **Enrichment Master** for above average students.

Additional Teacher Resource Package masters are listed in the OPTIONS box throughout the section. The additional masters are appropriate for all students.

◆ STUDY GUIDE 71

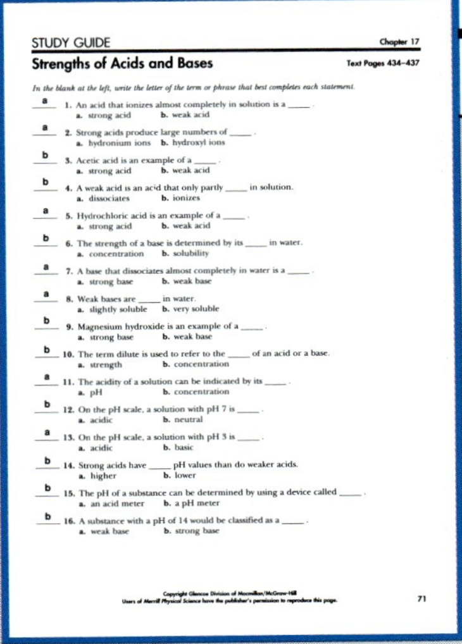

STUDY GUIDE — Chapter 17

Strengths of Acids and Bases — Text Pages 434–437

In the blank at the left, write the letter of the term or phrase that best completes each statement.

a 1. An acid that ionizes almost completely in solution is a ____.
a. strong acid b. weak acid

a 2. Strong acids produce large numbers of ____.
a. hydronium ions b. hydroxyl ions

b 3. Acetic acid is an example of a ____.
a. strong acid b. weak acid

b 4. A weak acid is an acid that only partly ____ in solution.
a. dissociates b. ionizes

a 5. Hydrochloric acid is an example of a ____.
a. strong acid b. weak acid

b 6. The strength of a base is determined by its ____ in water.
a. concentration b. solubility

a 7. A base that dissociates almost completely in water is a ____.
a. strong base b. weak base

a 8. Weak bases are ____ in water.
a. slightly soluble b. very soluble

b 9. Magnesium hydroxide is an example of a ____.
a. strong base b. weak base

b 10. The term dilute is used to refer to the ____ of an acid or a base.
a. strength b. concentration

a 11. The acidity of a solution can be indicated by its ____.
a. pH b. concentration

b 12. On the pH scale, a solution with pH 7 is ____.
a. acidic b. neutral

a 13. On the pH scale, a solution with pH 3 is ____.
a. acidic b. basic

b 14. Strong acids have ____ pH values than do weaker acids.
a. higher b. lower

b 15. The pH of a substance can be determined by using a device called ____.
a. an acid meter b. a pH meter

b 16. A substance with a pH of 14 would be classified as a ____.
a. weak base b. strong base

 71

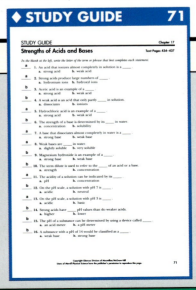

that dissociate to produce individual ions when they dissolve. Thus, the more soluble an ionic compound is, the greater will be its degree of dissociation.

A **strong base** is one that dissociates almost completely in solution. Strong bases are very soluble, and their water solutions contain large numbers of hydroxide ions. A **weak base** is one that only partly dissociates in solution. Weak bases are only slightly soluble in water. The equations show the dissociation of sodium hydroxide, a strong base, and magnesium hydroxide, a weak base.

$$\text{NaOH}(cr) \xrightarrow{\text{H}_2\text{O}} \text{Na}^+(aq) + \text{OH}^-(aq)$$

$$\text{Mg(OH)}_2(cr) \underset{\longleftarrow}{\longrightarrow} \text{Mg}^{2+}(aq) + 2\text{OH}^-(aq)$$

Often, the *strength* of an acid or base is confused with its *concentration*. As you learned in Chapter 15, *dilute* and *concentrated* are terms used to indicate the concentration of a solution.

The concentration of an acid or base has nothing to do with its strength. Strong acids and bases are always strong; weak acids and bases are always weak. It is possible to have dilute concentrations of strong acids or bases and concentrated solutions of weak acids or bases.

pH of a Solution

If you have a pool or keep tropical fish, you know that the pH of the water must be controlled. **pH** is a measure of the concentration of hydronium ions in a solution. It indicates acidity. To determine pH, a scale ranging from 0 to 14 has been devised, as shown in the diagram below.

Table 17-3

STRENGTHS OF SOME ACIDS AND BASES		
Acid	**Strength**	**Base**
Hydrochloric, HCl Sulfuric, H_2SO_4 Nitric, HNO_3	STRONG	Sodium hydroxide, NaOH Potassium hydroxide, KOH Magnesium hydroxide, $Mg(OH)_2$
Phosphoric, H_3PO_4	MODERATE	Calcium hydroxide, $Ca(OH)_2$
Acetic, CH_3COOH Carbonic, H_2CO_3 Boric, H_3BO_3	WEAK	Ammonium hydroxide, NH_4OH Aluminum hydroxide, $Al(OH)_3$ Iron(III) hydroxide, $Fe(OH)_3$

Did You Know?

The pH of human blood is 7.4. The lungs, kidneys, and circulatory system itself help to maintain that basic level.

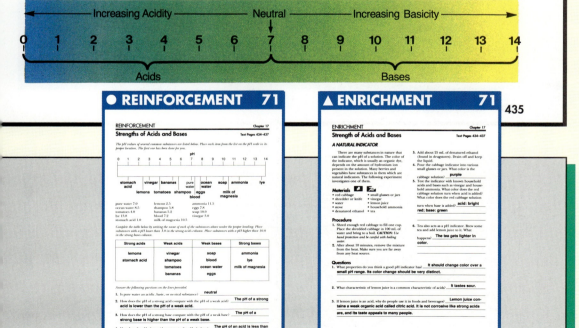

435

TYING TO PREVIOUS KNOWLEDGE: Ask students if they have ever experienced pain when foods such as lemon or tomato catsup came into contact with a sore spot in their mouths. These foods contained acids that were strong enough to burn exposed tissue.

OBJECTIVES AND SCIENCE WORDS: Have students review the objectives and science words to become familiar with this section.

2 TEACH

Key Concepts are highlighted.

CONCEPT DEVELOPMENT

▶ **Demonstration:** Conductivity apparatus can be used to show the relative ion concentrations that determine acid or base strength. Prepare four solutions of acetic acid to be tested. The 6.0M solution is prepared by adding 34.5 mL of concentrated (glacial) acetic acid to 65.5 mL of water. Prepare a 1.0M solution by adding 5.8 mL of the 6.0M acid solution to 94.2 mL of water. Dilute the 1.0M to form a 0.1M solution by adding 10 mL of 1.0M acid to 90 mL of water. Finally, in a similar way, dilute the 0.1M solution to make a 0.01M acetic acid solution. Conductivity is directly related to the concentration of ions in solution. This demonstration will help students see that the percent of ionization varies with concentration.

Acetic Acid Concentration	Percent of Ionization
6.0M	0.2%
1.0M	0.4%
0.1M	1.3%
0.01M	4.2%

What will amaze them is that the more concentrated acid is actually the weaker acid solution. A greater number of water molecules causes more acid molecules to ionize. This increased percentage of ionization will result in a greater conductivity as evidenced by a brighter light bulb or a higher meter reading.

3 CLOSE

Figure 17-10. When matched with a color chart, the color of the pH paper will show that the solution being tested is a base.

As the diagram shows, solutions with a pH lower than 7 are acidic. The lower the value, the more acidic the solution. Solutions with pH greater than 7 are basic, and the higher the pH, the more basic the solution. A solution with a pH of exactly 7 is neutral—neither acidic nor basic. Pure water has a pH of 7. **3**

Strong acids will have lower pH values—be more acidic—than weak acids of the same concentration. This is because strong acids ionize more completely, thus forming larger numbers of H_3O^+ ions. Similarly, strong bases, which contain large numbers of OH^- ions, will have higher pH values than weak bases of the same concentration.

Determining pH

A pH meter like the one shown can be used to determine the pH of a solution. This meter is operated by simply immersing the electrodes in the solution to be tested and reading the dial. Small, battery-operated pH meters with digital readouts make measuring the pH of materials even more convenient.

If a pH meter is not available, a universal indicator or pH paper can be used. Both of these undergo a color change in the presence of H_3O^+ ions and OH^- ions in solution. The final color of the solution or the pH paper is matched with colors in a chart to find the pH, as shown in Figure 17-10.

SECTION REVIEW

1. What determines the strength of an acid? a base?
2. How can you make a dilute solution of a strong acid? Include an example as part of your explanation.
3. **Apply:** What does the pH of each of the solutions indicate about the solution? Rainwater, 5.8; soda water, 3.0; drain cleaner, 14.0; seawater, 8.9; pure water, 7.0.

Skill Builder

☑ **Concept Mapping**

Make a concept map of pH values. Start with three boxes labeled acidic, neutral, and basic and indicate the pH range of each box. Below each box, give some examples of solutions that belong in each pH range and give the pH of each. If you need help, refer to Concept Mapping in the **Skill Handbook** on pages 684 and 685.

Skill Builder

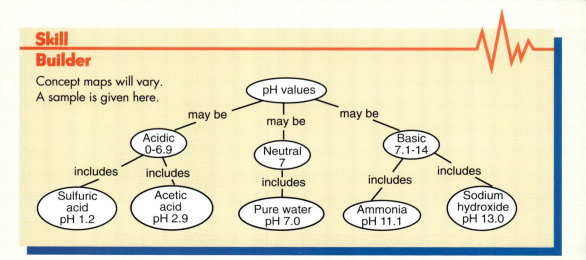

ACTIVITY 17-1
Strong and Weak Acids

Problem: *How do strong acids differ from weak acids?*

Materials:

- typing paper (22 cm x 28 cm), marked with rectangles
- thick cardboard (22 cm x 28 cm), marked with rectangles
- scissors
- test tubes (2)
- medicine droppers (2)
- graduated cylinder
- dilute hydrochloric acid (HCl)
- dilute acetic acid (CH₃COOH)
- pH paper
- timer, with second hand

Procedure

1. Prepare a data table like the one shown.
2. Make sure your paper and cardboard are marked with equal numbers of rectangles. Mark every other rectangle with a plus sign (+) to represent hydronium ions. Then mark the blank rectangles with a minus sign (−) to represent negative ions.
3. Using scissors, cut the typing paper into as many of its individual rectangles as possible in ten seconds.

4. Repeat Step 3 with the piece of cardboard.
5. Obtain 2 mL each of dilute HCl and dilute CH₃COOH in test tubes. **CAUTION:** *Handle these acids with care. Avoid contact with the skin or clothing. Report any spills to your teacher immediately.*
6. Using a different dropper for each acid, add two drops of each to separate strips of pH paper. Determine their respective pH values and record them in the data table.

Data and Observations   Sample Data

8-12	ions removed from typing paper	1	pH of HCl solution
4-6	ions removed from cardboard	2	pH of acetic acid solution

Analyze

1. Which was easier to "separate" into ions, the typing paper or the cardboard?
2. Which acid separated into ions most easily? How do you know?

Conclude and Apply

3. Which acid is stronger, HCl or CH₃COOH? How do you know?
4. Which represents the stronger acid, the typing paper or the cardboard? Explain your answer.
5. Which has the stronger bonds between fibers, the typing paper or the cardboard? Explain your answer.
6. Which acids have stronger bonds within their molecules, strong acids or weak acids? Explain your answer.

17-2   STRENGTH OF ACIDS AND BASES   **437**

ACTIVITY 17-1
20 minutes

OBJECTIVE: **Distinguish** between weak and strong acids by **comparing** ease of ionization.

PROCESS SKILLS applied in this activity:
▶ **Using models** in Conclude and Apply Questions 4 and 5.
▶ **Hypothesizing** in Conclude and Apply Question 6.

COOPERATIVE LEARNING

The Paired Partner strategy should work well in this activity. Pairs should divide up the manipulative tasks and work together to interpret data and answer questions.

TEACHING THE ACTIVITY

Troubleshooting: Caution students to cut at a steady pace and not to rush. If the cardboard is very hard to cut, extend the time by an appropriate amount.

▶ To emphasize the difference in the separation of paper ions versus the cardboard ions, make a chalkboard data table for the entire class and have each team record its results.

▶ To save time, have the rectangles marked on the paper and cardboard before class.

▶ Use 0.1M concentrations of HCl and CH₃COOH. You may wish to have 2-mL samples of each solution available for students.

▶ To prepare 0.1M acetic acid, dilute 5.9 mL of concentrated (17M, glacial) acetic acid to 1.0 L with distilled water. It is important to use distilled water when making very dilute solutions of acids or bases.

▶ To prepare 0.1M hydrochloric acid, dilute 8.4 mL of concentrated (12M) hydrochloric acid to 1.0 L with distilled water.

▶ This activity is meant to model the ease with which strong and weak acids ionize. Although a time factor is used in the cutting of paper and cardboard ions, the actual ionization of acids in water is not time-dependent. A more precise model might have equal amounts of force attempting to pull apart paper ions and the cardboard ions.

ANSWERS TO QUESTIONS

1. The ions on the typing paper were easier to separate.

2. The HCl separated more easily. It had a lower pH, indicating a greater concentration of H₃O⁺ ions.

3. The HCl is the stronger acid. The acids were of the same concentration, but HCl was more ionized.

4. The typing paper represented the stronger acid. It separated more readily.

5. The cardboard was more strongly bonded because it was more difficult to separate.

6. Weak acids are more strongly bonded. The attractions of water molecules do not cause them to break into ions as readily as do strong acids.

PROGRAM RESOURCES

From the **Teacher Resource Package** use:
Activity Worksheets, pages 133-134, Activity 17-1: Strong and Weak Acids.

PREPARATION

SECTION BACKGROUND

▶ Acid rain harms living organisms. As the acidity of lake water increases, metal ions such as aluminum dissolve from the rocky lake bed. The presence of these metals interferes with the reproductive cycle of some fish.

1 MOTIVATE

▶ **Demonstration:** In a fume hood, ignite a pea-sized piece of sulfur in a deflagrating spoon. Lower it into a wide-mouth gas collecting bottle that contains 25 mL of water. Cover the bottle with a glass plate until the sulfur flame is smothered. Remove the spoon, stopper, and shake. Test the solution with universal indicator or litmus. The solution will be acidic.

TYING TO PREVIOUS KNOWLEDGE:
Have students recall and discuss where they have observed marble or limestone objects that show the effects of weathering.

OBJECTIVES AND SCIENCE WORDS:
Have students review the objectives and science words to become familiar with this section.

2 TEACH

Key Concepts are highlighted.

CONCEPT DEVELOPMENT

Cooperative Learning: Have Expert Teams research photochemical smog. The library will have information on California air quality. This state has taken a lead role in improving the quality of air that citizens breathe.

New Science Words

acid rain
plankton

Objectives

▶ Describe the factors contributing to the formation of acid rain.
▶ Discuss the problems acid rain is causing and how these problems might be solved.

What Is Acid Rain?

Fish are disappearing from lakes. The surfaces of sculptures and buildings are wearing away. Crops are growing more slowly, and forests are dying. What is the cause of all these problems? The answer could be acid rain. You might be surprised to learn that the term *acid rain* was first used in 1872 by Angus Smith. Smith wrote a book about the polluted air and rain near large cities in England. In the 1970s, people first started to regard acid rain as a serious problem in the northeastern United States and Canada. Now acid rain seems to be a problem in all industrialized countries.

Normal rain has a pH of 5.6. This acidity is due to the reaction of carbon dioxide gas with rainwater to form carbonic acid.

$$CO_2(g) + H_2O(l) \rightarrow H_2CO_3(aq)$$

Carbonic acid is weak. Thus, the carbon dioxide in the air does not contribute very much to the problem of acid rain.

Any form of precipitation having a pH lower than 5.6 is called **acid rain.** Scientists think that acid rain forms when oxides of sulfur and nitrogen in the atmosphere react with rainwater. These oxides are released when fossil fuels are burned. Oxides of sulfur and nitrogen can combine with rainwater to produce strong acids such as sulfuric acid and nitric acid. Although these acids are quite dilute, they can harm the environment. The problem becomes particularly bad in densely populated industrial regions where large quantities of gasoline and high-sulfur fuels are burned.

Figure 17-11. This tree shows the effects of acid rain.

438 ACIDS, BASES, AND SALTS

OPTIONS

Meeting Different Ability Levels

For Section 17-3, use the following **Teacher Resource Masters** depending upon individual students' needs.

◆ **Study Guide Master** for all students.
● **Reinforcement Master** for students of average and above average ability levels.
▲ **Enrichment Master** for above average students.

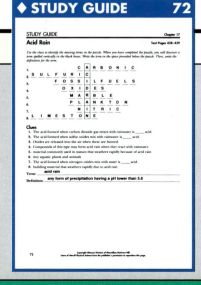

◆ **STUDY GUIDE** 72

STUDY GUIDE Chapter 17
Acid Rain Text Pages 438–439

Use the clues to identify the missing terms in the puzzle. When you have completed the puzzle, you will discover a term spelled vertically in the black boxes. Write the term in the space provided below the puzzle. Then, write the definition for the term.

1. C A R B O N I C
2. S U L F U R I C
3. F O S S I L F U E L S
4. O X I D E S
5. M A R B L E
6. P L A N K T O N
7. N I T R I C
8. L I M E S T O N E

Clues
1. The acid formed when carbon dioxide gas mixes with rainwater is ____ acid.
2. The acid formed when sulfur oxides mix with rainwater is ____ acid.
3. Oxides are released into the air when these are burned.
4. Compounds of this type may form acid rain when they react with rainwater.
5. material commonly used in statues that weathers rapidly because of acid rain
6. tiny aquatic plants and animals
7. The acid formed when nitrogen oxides mix with water is ____ acid.
8. Building material that weathers rapidly due to acid rain

Term: acid rain
Definition: any form of precipitation having a pH lower than 5.6

72

When acid rain falls to Earth, the soil and water become increasingly acidic. Among the first organisms to suffer are plankton. **Plankton** are tiny aquatic plants and animals. These organisms form the base of the food chain for small fish. When the plankton die, the fish that depend on them as a food source soon die also.

Acid rain also has a harmful effect on soil and land plants. As acid rain moves through the soil, it dissolves important mineral nutrients and carries them away. Plants deprived of these nutrients will not grow at a normal rate. Crops and forests are damaged.

Acid rain also causes rapid weathering of buildings and statues made of limestone and marble. For example, the Parthenon in Greece has survived for more than 2000 years. Today, it is rapidly being destroyed by acid rain.

Figure 17-12. The deterioration of this building is due to the chemical reaction of acid rain with calcite, the principal mineral in marble and limestone.

SECTION REVIEW

1. What are the main causes of acid rain?
2. What are the effects of acid rain?

You Decide!

Assume you live in an area whose main industry is mining high-sulfur coal. The coal is burned by the local power company. A law is passed requiring the local company to reduce its sulfur dioxide emissions. Plant owners are faced with two choices: (1) They can buy low-sulfur coal from a neighboring state, which would not result in increased electric rates. (2) They can use local coal and increase electric rates ten percent to cover the costs of removing sulfur and sulfur compounds. Which choice would you support?

SCIENCE & SOCIETY

REINFORCEMENT 72

ENRICHMENT 72

439

CHECK FOR UNDERSTANDING

Ask questions 1-2 in the Section Review.

RETEACH

Is a damaged environment easily repaired? Ask students to discuss how technology's impact can be minimized.

EXTENSION

For students who have mastered this section, use the **Reinforcement** and **Enrichment** masters or other OPTIONS provided.

3 CLOSE

▶ Ask students to discuss which is better—to treat statues with preservatives like polyurethane coatings and lakes with basic compounds such as lime, CaO, or to remove the offending oxides from exhausts by using catalytic converters and smokestack scrubbers and use alternative energy sources. Should we be doing both at the same time?

▶ Ask students to discuss the role of economics in finding a solution. The Clean Air Act will be expensive.

SECTION REVIEW ANSWERS

1. The main cause of acid rain is the reaction of rainwater with oxides released into the air by the burning of fossil fuels.

2. Acid rain is harmful to plants and animals and causes rapid deterioration of many stone structures.

SCIENCE & SOCIETY

YOU DECIDE!

Student responses may vary, but the most reasonable response is probably (2), raising rates to cover the costs of removing sulfur from local coal supplies. This choice would result in cleaner air and the continuing operation of the local coal mines, the major economic base of the community.

PREPARATION

SECTION BACKGROUND

▶ Analytical chemists often need to find the concentration of a solution. Titration is a quantitative analytical method used in volumetric analysis. Burets are accurately calibrated to deliver measured volume.

▶ When an alcohol reacts with either an organic acid or an organic acid anhydride, an ester is formed. This type of reaction is called esterification.

▶ An ester can be split into an alcohol and carboxylic acid by the addition of water, called hydrolysis.

▶ If a metallic base is used instead of water, the metal salt of the carboxylic acid is obtained, not the acid. This process is called saponification. Soap is a metal salt of a fatty acid. The natural fat or oil is an ester.

PREPLANNING

▶ To prepare for Activity 17-2, purchase clear carbonated beverages. Prepare a 0.20M NaOH solution.

1 MOTIVATE

▶ Use the chemical equations shown below to introduce students to neutralization reactions that are important to keeping them healthy. Human blood is buffered primarily by HCO_3^-, the hydrogen carbonate ion. This ion can react with excess acid or base in the blood to maintain the pH at 7.4. The reaction with excess hydronium ions from acid is $HCO_3^- + H_3O^+ \rightarrow H_2CO_3 + H_2O$. When the H_2CO_3 reaches the lungs it decomposes into CO_2 and water vapor. The reaction with excess hydroxide ions from base is $HCO_3^- + OH^- \rightarrow H_2O + CO_3^{2-}$.

New Science Words

neutralization
salt
titration
soaps
saponification
detergents
ester

What is neutralization?

Did You Know?

In 1990, a ten-year-long study of acid rain costing 500 million dollars was completed. The study concluded with a 15 000 page report indicating that scientists on both sides of the controversy had overstated their cases.

Objectives

▶ Describe a neutralization reaction.
▶ Explain what a salt is and how salts form.
▶ Differentiate between soaps and detergents.
▶ Explain how esters are made and what they are used for.

Neutralization

You have probably seen television commercials for antacids that describe how effectively these products neutralize excess stomach acid. Would the pH of such a product be higher or lower than 7? If you answered higher, you are correct. Only a base can neutralize the effects of an acid.

Neutralization is a chemical reaction between an acid and a base. During a neutralization reaction, hydronium ions from the acid combine with hydroxide ions from the base to produce water. ❶

$$H_3O^+(aq) + OH^-(aq) \rightarrow 2H_2O(l)$$

As the reactive ions are removed from the solution, the acidic and basic properties of the reactants are cancelled, or neutralized.

The equation above accounts for only half of the ions present in the solution. What happens to the remaining ions? They react to form a salt. A **salt** is a compound formed when the negative ions from an acid combine with the positive ions from a base. ❷

Neutralization reactions are ionic. The following equations show what happens to all of the ions during a neutralization reaction:

$$HCl(aq) + NaOH(aq) \rightarrow$$
$$H_3O^+(aq) + Cl^-(aq) + Na^+(aq) + OH^-(aq)$$

Water Formation: $H_3O^+(aq) + OH^-(aq) \rightarrow 2H_2O(l)$

Salt Formation: $Na^+(aq) + Cl^-(aq) \rightarrow NaCl(cr)*$

*Note: The formation of crystalline NaCl occurs only if the water is removed by boiling or evaporation.

OPTIONS

Meeting Different Ability Levels

For Section 17-4, use the following **Teacher Resource Masters** depending upon individual students' needs.

◆ **Study Guide Master** for all students.

● **Reinforcement Master** for students of average and above average ability levels.

▲ **Enrichment Master** for above average students.

Additional Teacher Resource Package masters are listed in the OPTIONS box throughout the section. The additional masters are appropriate for all students.

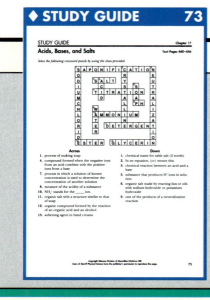

◆ **STUDY GUIDE** 73

STUDY GUIDE   Chapter 17
Acids, Bases, and Salts   Text Pages 440–646

Solve the following crossword puzzle by using the clues provided.

Across
1. process of making soap
4. compound formed when the negative ions from an acid combine with the positive ions from a base
7. process in which a solution of known concentration is used to determine the concentration of another solution
8. measure of the acidity of a substance
10. NH_4^+ stands for the ____ ion.
11. organic salt with a structure similar to that of soap
12. organic compound formed by the reaction of an organic acid and an alcohol
13. softening agent in hand creams

Down
1. chemical name for table salt (2 words)
2. In an equation, (cr) means this.
3. chemical reaction between an acid and a base
5. substance that produces H^+ ions in solution
6. organic salt made by reacting fats or oils with sodium hydroxide or potassium hydroxide
9. one of the products of a neutralization reaction

Copyright Glencoe Division of Macmillan/McGraw-Hill
Users of Merrill Physical Science have the publisher's permission to reproduce this page.   73

PROBLEM SOLVING

Julio's Experiment

Julio went to the doctor with stomach pains. The doctor told Julio that he had excess stomach acid and advised him to purchase an over-the-counter antacid and take it according to the directions on the package.

Julio wants to determine the best antacid to use. He thinks the best antacid will neutralize the greatest amount of hydrochloric acid.

He went to the drugstore and purchased several antacids that he had seen advertised on television. His science instructor said he would allow Julio to conduct his experiment during study hall and advised Julio to use bromothymol blue as his indicator because it turned pale green at pH 7. What was Julio's hypothesis?

Think Critically: How could Julio design an experiment to determine which antacid is most effective in neutralizing stomach acid?

Salts

Many substances that you come in contact with every day are salts. Of course, the most familiar salt is sodium chloride—common table salt. Table 17-4 on page 442 contains information about some common salts. As the table shows, most salts are composed of a metal and a nonmetal other than oxygen, or a metal and a polyatomic ion. Ammonium salts contain the polyatomic ammonium ion, NH_4^+, rather than a metal. Salts also form when acids react with metals. Hydrogen gas is released during such reactions.

How do salts form?

$$\text{Acid} + \text{Metal} \rightarrow \text{Salt} + \text{Hydrogen}$$
$$H_2SO_4(aq) + Zn(cr) \rightarrow ZnSO_4(aq) + H_2(g)$$
$$6HCl(aq) + 2Fe(cr) \rightarrow 2FeCl_3(aq) + 3H_2(g)$$

Reactions between metals and acids are replacement reactions in which the metal displaces hydrogen from the acid and replaces it. ❸

● **REINFORCEMENT** 73

▲ **ENRICHMENT** 73

441

PROBLEM SOLVING

Answers to Questions: Julio's hypothesis was that the best antacid would be the one that neutralized the most hydrochloric acid.

Think Critically: Julio could add each antacid to equal quantities of dilute hydrochloric acid containing bromothymol blue. The most effective antacid would be the one that changed the color of the acid solution pale green using the smallest amount of antacid. **CAUTION:** The one that neutralizes the most acid may cause irritation.

TYING TO PREVIOUS KNOWLEDGE: Ask students if they have ever taken something to relieve stomach discomfort. Stomach remedies contain a base to neutralize the hydrochloric acid. Magnesium and calcium hydroxides are common bases used.

OBJECTIVES AND SCIENCE WORDS: Have students review the objectives and science words to become familiar with this section.

2 TEACH

Key Concepts are highlighted.

CONCEPT DEVELOPMENT

▶ **Demonstration:** Grind up two tablets of a common stomach remedy. Dissolve them in warm water. Add a few drops of universal indicator. Slowly add a few drops of dilute 0.1M HCl to the beaker with stirring. Students will observe that the base can react with a small amount of acid. But as you continue to add acid, the base is used and the indicator changes color. Use this demonstration to introduce the ideas of neutralization and endpoints.

▶ Slowly evaporate the solution from the above demonstration in a warm oven overnight. The students will be able to observe the salt formed by the reaction of the acid and base.

Table 17-4

SOME COMMON SALTS			
Name	Formula	Common Name	Uses
Sodium chloride	NaCl	Salt	Food preparation; manufacture of chemicals
Sodium hydrogen carbonate	$NaHCO_3$	Sodium bicarbonate (baking soda)	Food preparation; in fire extinguishers
Calcium carbonate	$CaCO_3$	Calcite (chalk)	Manufacture of paint and rubber tires
Potassium nitrate	KNO_3	Saltpeter	In fertilizers; manufacture of explosives
Potassium carbonate	K_2CO_3	Potash	Manufacture of soap and glass
Trisodium phosphate	Na_3PO_4	TSP	In detergents
Ammonium chloride	NH_4Cl	Sal ammoniac	In dry cells

REVEALING MISCONCEPTIONS

▶When an acid reacts with a base, a salt and water are the products. Because the term *neutralization* is applied to the reaction of an acid with a base, many people think that the resulting salt solution always has a neutral pH of 7. This is true when the acid and base are both strong or when weak bases neutralize weak acids. When a strong acid neutralizes a weak base, the salt solution has an acid pH. When a strong base neutralizes a weak acid, the salt solution has a basic pH.

CONCEPT DEVELOPMENT

▶**Demonstration:** Use medicine droppers to show students that equal volumes of strong acid and strong base of the same concentration produce a neutral solution. Use an overhead projector and a small beaker. Place 50 drops of 0.1M HCl in the beaker with a drop of universal indicator. Then slowly add, with swirling, 50 drops of 0.1M NaOH. Have students match the final color with the chart that comes with universal indicator.

TEACHER F.Y.I.

▶Alkaloids are naturally occurring bases that contain nitrogen. Like ammonia, the nitrogen base in these substances attracts hydrogen from water, leaving hydroxide ions. This results in a basic solution. Some alkaloids are listed below.

Quinine—found in cinchona bark; used to treat malaria

Morphine—narcotic found in opium poppy flower; used to relieve pain

Caffeine—a stimulant found in coffee beans and tea leaves

Nicotine—a stimulant found in tobacco leaves

Mescaline—a hallucinogen found in peyote cactus

Figure 17-13. The apparatus is set up to perform a titration of a base.

Titration

It is sometimes necessary to find the concentration of an acidic or basic solution. This can be accomplished by titration. **Titration** is the process in which a solution of known concentration is used to determine the concentration of another solution. Most titrations involve acid-base neutralizations.

In a titration, a solution of known concentration, called the standard solution, is added drop by drop to a solution of unknown concentration to which an indicator has been added. If the solution of unknown concentration is a base, a standard acid solution is used, and vice versa.

As an example, assume that you need to find the concentration of an acid solution. First, you would add a few drops of phenolphthalein (feen ul THAYL een) indicator to a carefully measured amount of this solution. Phenolphthalein is colorless in an acid, but is pink in a base.

A standard base solution is added to this acid one drop at a time. At some point, one drop of the base just begins to turn the acid solution pink. This is known as the endpoint of the titration. Just enough standard solution has been added to neutralize the acid. The volume of the base used to neutralize the known volume of acid is determined, and the concentration of the acid can be calculated.

OPTIONS

INQUIRY QUESTIONS

▶**There are four areas of taste found on the tongue—sweet, sour, salty, and bitter. Which three relate to the words in the title of Section 17-4?** *acids—sour, bases—bitter, salts—salty*

▶**In one or two sentences, describe the process in which a base neutralizes an acid.** *The hydronium ion from the acid and the hydroxide ion from the base unite to form water, while the other ions unite to form a salt when the water is evaporated.*

▶**What is the purpose of performing a titration?** *to determine the concentration of an unknown solution*

▶**What is an endpoint in a titration experiment?** *when just enough acid has been added to react with the base to produce color change in an indicator*

Soaps and Detergents

5 **Soaps** are organic salts. Soaps are made by reacting fats or oils with sodium hydroxide or potassium hydroxide. One formula for soap made using sodium hydroxide is $C_{17}H_{35}COONa$. The structural formula for this soap is provided below.

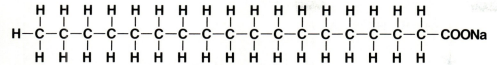

A soap made using potassium hydroxide might have the formula $C_{15}H_{31}COOK$. Below is the structural formula for this soap.

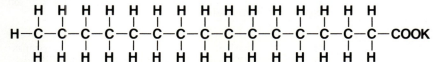

Sodium hydroxide produces solid soaps. Potassium hydroxide makes liquid soaps. Another product of this reaction is glycerin, which is a softening agent in hand creams.

6 The process of making soap is called **saponification**. Soaps increase the cleaning action of water. When soap is put into water, it ionizes as follows:

$$C_{17}H_{35}COONa\,(cr) \rightarrow C_{17}H_{35}COO^-\,(aq) + Na^+\,(aq)$$

The negative ion consists of two parts: an ionic head and a long, nonpolar hydrocarbon tail. Remember that grease is composed of hydrocarbon molecules. These molecules are similar in structure to the long hydrocarbon tail of the soap molecule.

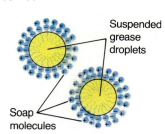

Figure 17-14. Soap removes grease by breaking it up into tiny droplets.

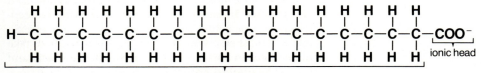

When you use soap to wash your hands, the nonpolar hydrocarbon tail dissolves any fat or grease that may be on them. The ionic head dissolves in the water and carries the dirt away.

17-4   ACIDS, BASES, AND SALTS   **443**

▶ **Demonstration:** Detergents can form more suds in hard water than soap and retard the formation of soap scum. Dissolve a small piece of soap overnight in water. Place a few drops of this soap solution in a test tube half-filled with hard water. Hard water can be made by adding small amounts of Ca and Mg salts to water. Place the same number of drops of liquid detergent in another test tube half-filled with hard water. Stopper and shake both tubes the same amount. Examine the amount of foam and the amount of insoluble solids formed.

▶ **Demonstration:** Esters can be produced by reacting an organic carboxylic acid with an alcohol in the presence of an acid catalyst. Esters can be prepared by placing 6 mL of each reactant into a test tube with 5 drops of concentrated sulfuric acid. **CAUTION:** *Sulfuric acid is corrosive, and alcohols are flammable.* Heat the test tube in a warm water bath. Pineapple smell can be created by reacting butyric acid with ethanol. The odor of apples can be synthesized by reacting acetic acid with ethanol. Wintergreen aroma can be duplicated by reacting salicylic acid and methanol.

MINI QUIZ

Use the Mini Quiz to check students' recall of chapter content.

7 **What do scientists call an organic salt that has a structure similar to soap?** *detergent*

8 **Which ions in hard water react with soap to form a precipitate known as soap scum?** *Ca, Mg, and Fe ions*

9 **What forms when an organic acid reacts with an alcohol?** *an ester*

10 **What do esters contribute to flowers, fruits, and many foods?** *flavors and odors*

7 **Detergents** are organic salts having structures similar to those of soaps. The most common detergent in use today has the following structural formula:

Like soap, the negative ions of detergents have a nonpolar hydrocarbon tail and an ionic head. Detergents enhance the cleaning action of water in a manner similar to that of soap.

When soap is used in hard water, it forms soap scum, or "bathtub ring." This scum forms because hard water contains compounds of calcium, magnesium, and iron. **8** The calcium, magnesium, and iron ions react with the soap to form a precipitate, which is the undesirable scum. Detergents do not form this scum. Therefore, most laundry products are detergents, not soaps.

Organic Acids and Esters

9 An **ester** is an organic compound formed by the reaction of an organic acid with an alcohol. The reaction is different from neutralization in that it needs a compound that will split a molecule of water out of the organic acid and alcohol. In Section 17-1 you learned that concentrated sulfuric acid is a powerful dehydrating agent. So this acid must be present for the organic reaction to take place. Figure 17-15 shows the reaction of acetic acid and methyl alcohol to produce an ester—methyl acetate—and water.

10 Esters are responsible for the many wonderful odors and flavors of flowers, fruits, and other foods. Sometimes esters are added to gelatin desserts or candy to give the characteristic flavors of strawberry, banana, or apple.

What is an ester?

OPTIONS

INQUIRY QUESTIONS

▶ Complete and balance the following acid-base reaction:

$LiOH + HBr \rightarrow$
$LiOH + HBr \rightarrow LiBr + H_2O$

▶ Complete and balance the following equation to show the products that form when barium hydroxide neutralizes perchloric acid.

$Ba(OH)_2 + 2HClO_4 \rightarrow$
$Ba(OH)_2 + 2HClO_4 \rightarrow Ba(ClO_4)_2 + 2H_2O$
barium perchlorate and water

▶ If 20 drops of a solution of HCl exactly neutralize 10 drops of a solution of NaOH, what can be said about the concentrations of the two solutions? *The HCl solution is half as concentrated as the NaOH solution.*

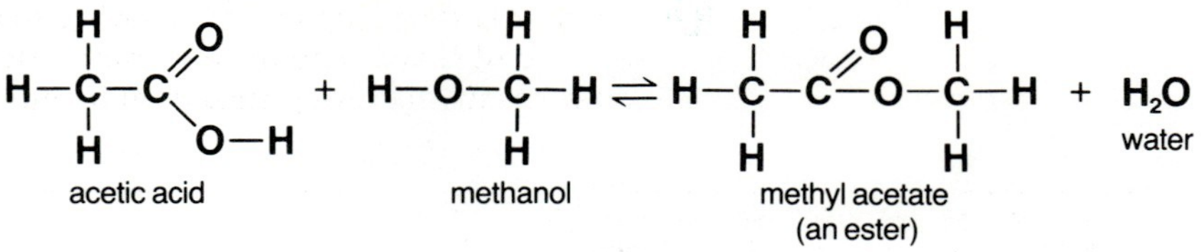

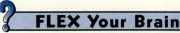

acetic acid + methanol ⇌ methyl acetate (an ester) + H₂O water

Synthetic fibers known as polyesters are made from an organic acid that has two –COOH groups and an alcohol that has two –OH groups. Because the two compounds form long chains with the ester linkage, a polymer results.

Figure 17-15. This structural equation shows the formation of an ester, methyl acetate, by the reaction of an organic acid and an alcohol.

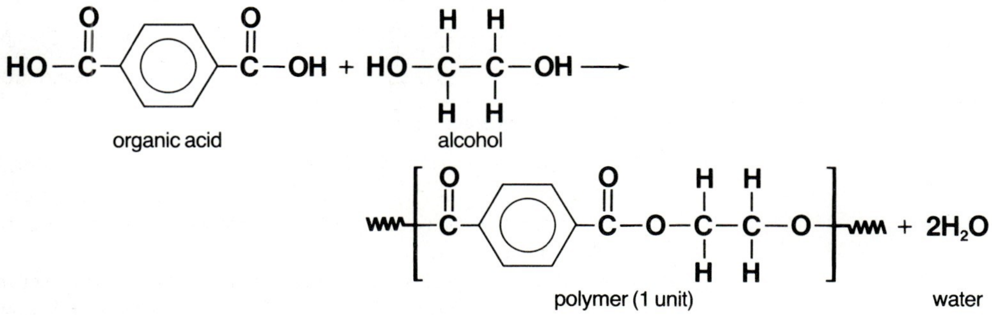

organic acid + alcohol ⟶

polymer (1 unit) + 2H₂O water

SECTION REVIEW

1. What is a neutralization reaction? What are the products of such reactions?
2. When doing laundry, what advantage does using a detergent have over using a soap?
3. **Apply:** Give the names and formulas of the salt that will form in these neutralizations:
   a. hydrochloric acid and ammonium hydroxide
   b. nitric acid and potassium hydroxide
   c. carbonic acid and aluminum hydroxide

☑ Interpreting Data

Skill Builder

Three salts — calcium sulfate, sodium chloride, and potassium nitrate — were obtained in reactions of the acid-base pairs shown here. Match each salt with the acid-base pair that produced it. If you need help, refer to Interpreting Data in the **Skill Handbook** on page 683.

$HCl + NaOH$ $HNO_3 + KOH$ $H_2SO_4 + Ca(OH)_2$

17-4   ACIDS, BASES, AND SALTS   **445**

ACTIVITY 17-2
30 minutes

OBJECTIVE: Observe the process of a neutralization reaction.

PROCESS SKILLS applied in this activity:
▶ **Measuring** in Procedure Step 2.
▶ **Observing** in Procedure Step 5.
▶ **Predicting** in Conclude and Apply Question 4.

COOPERATIVE LEARNING
The Science Investigation group strategy applies especially well to this activity because there are several manipulative, observing, and recording tasks to be done.

TEACHING THE ACTIVITY
Alternate Materials: Any strong base will work in this activity, but NaOH is probably the most widely available. If you have small Erlenmeyer flasks, they will work better than test tubes.

Troubleshooting: Students often believe that dropping or pouring one solution into another automatically mixes them. Make sure students swirl the solution after every drop. Try the beverage you plan to use the day before the activity. If too little NaOH is required, you should reduce the NaOH concentration or try to find a more acidic beverage.

▶ Use 0.20*M* NaOH solution. To prepare this solution, dissolve 8.0 g of NaOH pellets in enough water to make 1.0 L of solution. **CAUTION:** *Sodium hydroxide is caustic. Do not touch the pellets or the solution.*

▶ Most carbonated beverages will be relatively saturated with CO_2. Therefore, all should give the same result. In reality, many beverages will contain additional acids such as phosphoric acid and/or citric acid. These acids, if present, contribute to overall acidity and must be neutralized before the phenolphthalein will change color. Students may find it interesting to titrate equal volumes of different beverages to see which one has the highest acidity.

ACTIVITY 17-2
Acid-Base Reactions

Problem: *What happens when a base is added to an acid?*

Materials
- test tube
- medicine dropper (2)
- graduated cylinder
- carbonated beverage, colorless
- dilute sodium hydroxide (NaOH)
- phenolphthalein indicator, 1%

Procedure
1. Prepare a data table like the one shown.
2. Open a container of a colorless carbonated beverage. Measure 5 mL of the beverage and pour it into a test tube.
3. Add 2 drops of 1% phenolphthalein to the test tube.
4. Using a clean dropper, add dilute NaOH solution to the test tube, one drop at a time. **CAUTION:** *Handle the NaOH solution carefully. Avoid contact with your skin or clothing and report any spills to your teacher immediately.*
5. Count the drops as you add them, gently swirling the solution in the test tube after each drop is added. Stop adding NaOH to the test tube as soon as the solution turns pink and the color remains.
6. Discard the solution as directed by your teacher. Rinse the test tube and droppers thoroughly, dry them, and repeat Steps 1- 4. Find the average number of drops of NaOH used in the two trials.

Data and Observations Sample Data

	Trial 1	Trial 2	Average
Number of drops of NaOH solution needed	15	21	18

446 ACIDS, BASES, AND SALTS

Analyze
1. What name is used to identify the type of reaction that takes place between the NaOH and the carbonated beverage?
2. Phenolphthalein turns pink in a solution of pH 8 or higher. Why didn't the carbonated beverage turn pink as soon as the phenolphthalein was added? Why did the solution turn pink after NaOH was added?
3. One of the acids present in the carbonated beverage is carbonic acid, H_2CO_3. Write a chemical reaction to show how this acid reacts with NaOH.

Conclude and Apply
4. How many drops of NaOH were needed to neutralize the 5-mL sample of the carbonated beverage? Suppose a solution of NaOH half as concentrated as the one used were added to the carbonated beverage. About how many drops would be needed to cause the same effect?
5. Describe how you might use this experimental design to compare acid levels of several different carbonated beverages.

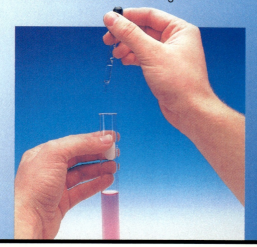

ANSWERS TO QUESTIONS
1. neutralization
2. The beverage was acidic. The acid was neutralized, and the pH increased to 8 or more.
3. $H_2CO_3 + 2NaOH \rightarrow Na_2CO_3 + 2H_2O$
4. Answers will depend on the acidity of the beverage and the size of the drops. If the NaOH were half as concentrated, twice as many drops would be needed.
5. Students should suggest titrating equal volumes of each beverage while holding the temperature, freshness, and strength of NaOH solution constant. The greater the number of drops needed to produce a color change in a particular beverage, the greater the acidity of that beverage.

PROGRAM RESOURCES
From the **Teacher Resource Package** use:
Activity Worksheets, pages 135-136, Activity 17-2: Acid-Base Reactions.

SUMMARY

17-1: Acids and Bases

1. An acid is a substance that produces hydrogen ions (H^+) in solution. A base produces hydroxide ions (OH^-) in solution.

2. Acids and bases have characteristic properties that are due, in part, to the presence of the H^+ and OH^- ions.

3. Common acids include hydrochloric acid, sulfuric acid, nitric acid, and phosphoric acid. Common bases include sodium hydroxide, calcium hydroxide, and ammonia.

4. Acids form when certain polar compounds ionize as they dissolve in water. Except for ammonia, bases form when certain ionic compounds dissociate upon dissolving in water.

17-2: Strength of Acids and Bases

1. The strength of an acid or base is determined by the number of ions present in solution.

2. Strength and concentration are not related. Concentration involves the relative amounts of solvent and solute in a solution.

3. pH is a measure of the hydrogen ion concentration of a solution.

4. For acid solutions of equal concentration, the stronger the acid, the lower its pH; for basic solutions of equal concentration, the stronger the base, the higher the pH.

17-3: Science and Society: Acid Rain

1. Acid rain is produced when substances in the air react with rainwater to make it acidic. Acid rain production is increased by the release of certain oxides into the air when fossil fuels are burned.

2. Acid rain is harmful to plants and animals and increases the rate of weathering of some building materials.

17-4: Acids, Bases, and Salts

1. In a neutralization reaction, the H_3O^+ ions from an acid react with the OH^- ions from a base to produce water molecules. The products of neutralization are a salt plus water.

2. Salts form when the negative ions from an acid combine with the positive ions from a base.

3. Soaps and detergents are organic salts. Unlike soaps, detergents do not react with compounds in hard water to form scum deposits.

4. Esters are organic compounds formed by the reaction of an organic acid and an alcohol.

KEY SCIENCE WORDS

a. acid
b. acid rain
c. base
d. dehydrating agent
e. detergents
f. ester
g. hydronium ion
h. indicator
i. neutralization
j. pH
k. pickling
l. plankton
m. salt
n. saponification
o. soaps
p. strong acid
q. strong base
r. titration
s. weak acid
t. weak base

UNDERSTANDING VOCABULARY

Match each phrase with the correct term from the list of Key Science Words.

1. a hydrogen ion bonded to a water molecule
2. a reaction between an acid and a base
3. acid that ionizes completely in solution
4. base that partly dissociates in solution
5. can remove water from materials
6. formed when negative ions from an acid combine with positive ions from a base
7. removes impurities from metal surfaces
8. measures the concentration of H_3O^+ ions
9. produces hydrogen ions in solution
10. the process of making soap

ACIDS, BASES, AND SALTS **447**

CHAPTER
REVIEW

SUMMARY

Have students read the summary statements to review the major concepts of the chapter.

UNDERSTANDING VOCABULARY

1. g
2. i
3. p
4. t
5. d
6. m
7. k
8. j
9. a
10. n

OPTIONS

ASSESSMENT

To assess student understanding of material in this chapter, use the resources listed.

COOPERATIVE LEARNING

Consider using cooperative learning in the THINK AND WRITE CRITICALLY, APPLY, and MORE SKILL BUILDERS sections of the Chapter Review.

PROGRAM RESOURCES

From the **Teacher Resource Package** use:

Chapter Review, pages 37-38.

Chapter and Unit Tests, pages 109-112, Chapter Test.

Chapter and Unit Tests, pages 113-114, Unit Test.

CHAPTER
REVIEW

CHECKING CONCEPTS

1. a
2. a
3. b
4. d
5. a
6. a
7. c
8. b
9. d
10. c

UNDERSTANDING CONCEPTS

11. titration
12. Soap
13. ester
14. base
15. plankton

THINK AND WRITE CRITICALLY

16. HCl ionizes, forming H^+ and Cl^- ions.

17. In alcohol, OH forms the hydroxyl group, which is not ionized. In a base, OH forms the hydroxide ion, OH^-.

18. In water, ammonia molecules react with water molecules, producing ammonium ions and hydroxide ions.

19. A concentrated acid contains more solute and less water than does a dilute acid. The terms have nothing to do with how much an acid dissociates in water, which is the measure of its strength.

20. Ashes were used as the source of hydroxide ions. These ashes were mixed with animal fat to make soap.

CHAPTER
REVIEW

CHECKING CONCEPTS

Choose the word or phrase that completes the sentence.

1. HF reacts strongly with metals; CH_3COOH does not. HF is more _____.
   a. acidic
   b. basic
   c. corrosive
   d. sour

2. Sulfuric acid is also known as _____.
   a. battery acid
   b. citric acid
   c. stomach acid
   d. vinegar

3. Most sulfuric acid is used to produce _____.
   a. batteries
   b. fertilizer
   c. petroleum products
   d. plastics

4. _____ is used to make phosphoric, nitric, and hydrochloric acids.
   a. Dehydration
   b. A base
   c. Pickling
   d. Sulfuric acid

5. The most widely used base is _____.
   a. ammonia
   b. caustic lime
   c. lye
   d. milk of magnesia

6. Carrots have a pH of 5.0, so carrots are _____.
   a. acidic
   b. basic
   c. neutral
   d. an indicator

7. Pure water has a pH of _____.
   a. 0
   b. 5.2
   c. 7
   d. 14

8. Certain materials can act as indicators because they change _____.
   a. acidity
   b. color
   c. pH
   d. taste

9. KBr is an example of a(n) _____.
   a. acid
   b. base
   c. indicator
   d. salt

10. You might use a solution of _____ to titrate an oxalic acid solution.
    a. HBr
    b. $Ca(NO_3)_2$
    c. NaOH
    d. NH_4Cl

UNDERSTANDING CONCEPTS

Complete each sentence.

11. The process in which a solution of known concentration is used to determine the concentration of another solution is _____.

12. _____ forms when a fat or oil reacts with sodium or potassium hydroxide.

13. When an organic acid and an alcohol react in the presence of sulfuric acid, a(n) _____ and water are formed.

14. A substance that produces hydroxide ions in solution is a(n) _____.

15. Tiny plant and animals that live in water and may be killed by acid rain are _____.

THINK AND WRITE CRITICALLY

16. When hydrogen chloride, HCl, is dissolved in water to form hydrochloric acid, what happens to the HCl?

17. Explain how the hydroxide ion differs from the –OH group in an alcohol.

18. Why is ammonia considered a base, even though it contains no hydroxide ions?

19. Explain why a concentrated acid is not necessarily a strong acid.

20. Ashes from a wood fire are basic. Explain how early settlers used this fact when making soap.

APPLY

21. Explain why you should never use taste to test for an acid, even though acetic, citric, and dilute phosphoric acids are in things you eat and drink.
22. How would the pH of a dilute solution of HCl compare with the pH of a concentrated solution of the same acid? Explain.
23. Acid rain containing sulfuric acid, H_2SO_4, will react with iron objects. What products will result from this reaction?
24. Chalk, $CaCO_3$, is a salt. What acid and what base react to form this salt?
25. Suppose you have hard water in your home. Would you use a soap or a detergent for washing your clothes and dishes? Explain your answer.

MORE SKILL BUILDERS

If you need help, refer to the Skill Handbook.

1. **Making and Using Tables:** Make a table that lists the chemical and physical properties of acids and bases.
2. **Recognizing Cause and Effect:** Complete the following table by describing the cause and effect of each change listed in the left-hand column.

Process	Cause	Effect
Saponification		
Esterification		
Acid rain		
Neutralization		
Corrosion		

3. **Comparing and Contrasting:** Compare and contrast the reactions that would be produced by pouring sulfuric acid on a piece of paper and burning a marshmallow.
4. **Observing and Inferring:** You have equal amounts of three colorless liquids, A, B, and C. You add several drops of phenolphthalein to each liquid. A and B remain colorless, but C turns pink. Next you add some of liquid C to liquid A and the pink color disappears. You add the rest of C to liquid B and the mixture remains pink. What can you infer about each of these liquids? Which liquid probably has a pH of 7?
5. **Interpreting Data:** A soil test indicates that the pH of the soil in a field is 4.8. To neutralize the soil, would you add a substance containing H_3PO_4 or one containing $Ca(OH)_2$? Explain your answer.

PROJECTS

1. Make a display and write a report on common household acids and bases, how they are used, and cautions to be taken.
2. Do research to find out how acids are used in making fertilizer. Name several acids and tell why each is needed and how their proportions may vary from fertilizer to fertilizer. Conduct an investigation by growing seedlings using different fertilizers. Describe your results in a report.

ACIDS, BASES, AND SALTS **449**

APPLY

21. Acids that you eat are weak. Strong acids can cause severe burns.
22. The pH of the concentrated solution would be lower (more acidic) than that of the dilute solution. In the dilute solution, the hydronium ions are less concentrated than in the concentrated solution.
23. hydrogen gas and iron(II) sulfate
24. calcium hydroxide, $Ca(OH)_2$, and carbonic acid, H_2CO_3
25. You would use a detergent because a detergent will not react with minerals in the water to form a scum (precipitate).

MORE SKILL BUILDERS

1. **Making and Using Tables:** Tables may vary, but should resemble the following.

	Physical Properties	Chemical Properties
Acid	sour taste, electrolyte	corrosive, reacts with indicators, forms H_3O^+ in solution
Base	bitter taste, feels slippery, electrolyte	corrosive, reacts with indicators, forms OH^- in solution

2. **Recognizing Cause and Effect:** See table at bottom of page.
3. **Comparing and Contrasting:** Both processes involve dehydration of an organic material, removing the water and leaving only carbon. Thus, both final products are dark in appearance. They differ in that acid is used as a dehydrating agent on the paper, and heat drives off the water in the marshmallow.
4. **Comparing and Contrasting:** Liquid C is a base because it turns phenolphthalein pink. Liquids A and B are not bases. Liquid A is an acid because it turns the pink base solution colorless. Liquid B is probably not acid and is most likely to have a pH of 7.
5. **Interpreting Data:** You would use $Ca(OH)_2$. The soil has a pH of 4.8, indicating that it is acidic. To neutralize this acidic soil, a base should be added.

Answer to More Skill Builders, number 2.

Process	Cause	Effect
Saponification	NaOH or KOH and fat react	soap and glycerine formed
Esterification	organic acid and alcohol react	ester and water formed
Acid rain formation	pollutants from burning fossil fuels react with water in air	destruction of life, soil, metal, minerals
Neutralization	acid and base react	salt and water formed
Corrosion	metal reacts with a corrosive agent	metal forms a compound and loses strength

UNIT 5
GLOBAL CONNECTIONS

Objective

In this unit-ending feature, the unit topic, "Interactions of Matter," is extended into other disciplines. Students will see how interactions of matter are occurring around the planet.

Motivate

Cooperative Learning: Assign one Connection to each group of students. Using the Expert Teams strategy, have each group find out more about the geographical location of the Connection—its climate, culture, flora and fauna, and ecological issues.

Teaching Tips

▶ Ask students to describe the kind of interaction of matter that is occurring in each Connection.

Wrap-Up

Conclude this lesson by having students predict other places besides the ones shown here where similar interactions of matter might occur.

METEOROLOGY

Background: Great Salt Lake is the remnant of Lake Bonneville, formed 16 000 years ago during the last glacial period. The lake now covers an area about the size of Delaware.

Discussion: Discuss how varying weather conditions affect this lake. Ask students to hypothesize what weather conditions might have lead to the lake's lowest level, reached in 1963. Ask how the lake's salinity would have been affected.

Answer to Question: More water would enter the lake, but less water would evaporate so the salinity would probably decrease.

Extension: Have students use salt and water to make salt solutions that represent the maximum and minimum concentrations of Great Salt Lake.

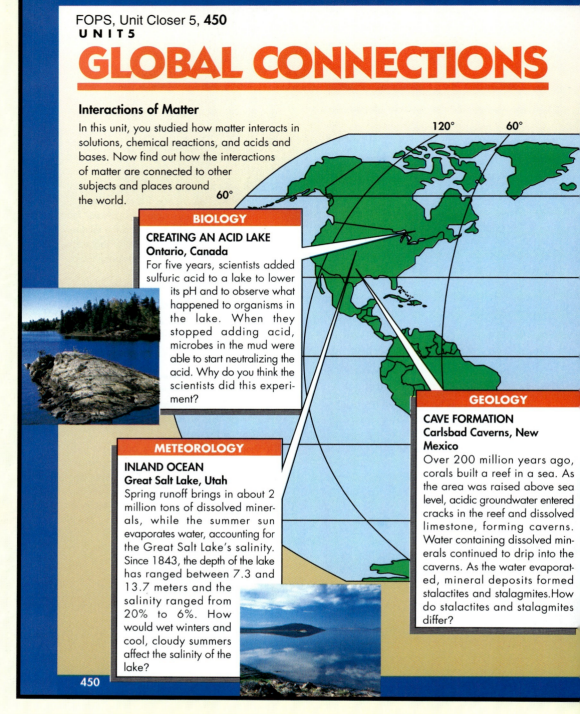

GLOBAL CONNECTIONS

Interactions of Matter

In this unit, you studied how matter interacts in solutions, chemical reactions, and acids and bases. Now find out how the interactions of matter are connected to other subjects and places around the world.

BIOLOGY
CREATING AN ACID LAKE
Ontario, Canada

For five years, scientists added sulfuric acid to a lake to lower its pH and to observe what happened to organisms in the lake. When they stopped adding acid, microbes in the mud were able to start neutralizing the acid. Why do you think the scientists did this experiment?

METEOROLOGY
INLAND OCEAN
Great Salt Lake, Utah

Spring runoff brings in about 2 million tons of dissolved minerals, while the summer sun evaporates water, accounting for the Great Salt Lake's salinity. Since 1843, the depth of the lake has ranged between 7.3 and 13.7 meters and the salinity ranged from 20% to 6%. How would wet winters and cool, cloudy summers affect the salinity of the lake?

GEOLOGY
CAVE FORMATION
Carlsbad Caverns, New Mexico

Over 200 million years ago, corals built a reef in a sea. As the area was raised above sea level, acidic groundwater entered cracks in the reef and dissolved limestone, forming caverns. Water containing dissolved minerals continued to drip into the caverns. As the water evaporated, mineral deposits formed stalactites and stalagmites. How do stalactites and stalagmites differ?

450

GEOLOGY

Background: About 95% of Carlsbad's formations are now dry, and very little cave building is occurring. The area above ground is now desert. Cave temperatures remain fairly constant year round.

Discussion: Discuss the chemistry of cave formation. Tell students that when carbon dioxide dissolves in water, weak carbonic acid forms. The acid reacts with limestone (calcium carbonate) to form calcium bicarbonate, which dissolves in the water.

Answer to Question: Stalactites form as water with dissolved minerals drips down from cavern ceilings. Stalagmites form from the ground up as water drips down stalactites to end up on the cavern floor.

Extension: Have students use dilute HCl to observe how acidic water can dissolve limestone.

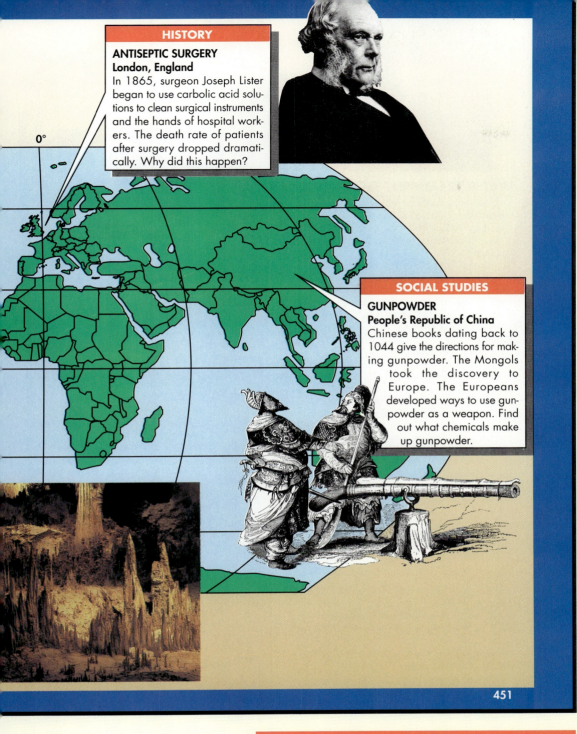

ANTISEPTIC SURGERY
London, England
In 1865, surgeon Joseph Lister began to use carbolic acid solutions to clean surgical instruments and the hands of hospital workers. The death rate of patients after surgery dropped dramatically. Why did this happen?

0°

SOCIAL STUDIES

GUNPOWDER
People's Republic of China
Chinese books dating back to 1044 give the directions for making gunpowder. The Mongols took the discovery to Europe. The Europeans developed ways to use gunpowder as a weapon. Find out what chemicals make up gunpowder.

451

HISTORY

Background: Lister had learned about Pasteur's germ theory of disease. He hypothesized that deaths occurring after surgery might be caused by germ infections. He also realized the germs could be coming from the doctors' hands or their instruments, so he used carbolic acid in an attempt to kill the germs.
Discussion: Discuss the importance of Lister's discovery. Point out that before this, patients often died even though their surgery was successful.
Answer to Question: Carbolic acid acts as an antiseptic and kills germs that cause infections.
Extension: Have students research other antiseptics and their chemical makeup.

BIOLOGY

Background: Researchers at Canada's Experimental Lakes Area sacrificed a lake in Ontario to see if ecosystems in seemingly lifeless lakes damaged by acid rain could be brought back. As they lowered the pH from 6.5 to 5.1, fish stopped reproducing and other organisms died off. As the pH rose to 5.4, fish started reproducing again, but all species did not return to the lake.
Discussion: Discuss what scientists hoped to learn from the experiment. Ask students to discuss the advantages of using a real lake for the experiment rather than a laboratory.
Answer to Question: Scientists hoped to find out if the lake would recover and if populations of organisms would return to the lake.
Extension: Have students find out about other research being done on lakes damaged by acid rain.

SOCIAL STUDIES

Background: Evidence indicates that the Chinese had invented gunpowder by the year 250, but used it primarily for fireworks. It was not extensively used in warfare until it reached Europe.
Discussion: Discuss how knowledge of gunpowder led to the development of cannons. Ask students to discuss how this invention changed warfare in Europe.
Answer to Question: The chemicals in gunpowder are saltpeter, charcoal, and sulfur.
Extension: Have students research the development of cordite, the explosive that replaced gunpowder on the battlefield.

PAINT ANALYST

Background: Paint analysts work for companies that manufacture paints. In addition to developing different colors, many paint analysts work on the development of specialty paints, such as marine paints and mildew-resistant paints.

Related Career	Education
Art restorer	graduate degree
Automotive painter	high school
Painter	high school
Lithographic artist	technical school

Career Issue: Some specialty paints, such as those designed to protect boat hulls from marine organisms and those designed to protect objects from mildew, contain chemical additives that some people worry about. They think these paints can harm the environment.

What do you think? Have students discuss of the pros and cons of using chemical additives in certain paints.

WATER-TREATMENT PLANT TECHNICIAN

Background: Water treatment technicians may work in industrial plants, municipal plants, or state and federal centers. Because water treatment is a 24-hour-a-day operation, technicians work different shifts.

Related Career	Education
Hydrologist	college degree
Water-treatment plant operator	high school
Agricultural technician	technical school
Instrumentation technician	technical school

Career Issue: In some areas, municipal wells have had to be closed down because of contamination from agricultural chemicals, industrial pollutants, or chemicals used on icy roads.

What do you think? Lead students in a discussion about their attitudes toward groundwater pollution. How do they think this problem should be dealt with? What role should water-treatment technicians play?

WATER TREATMENT TECHNICIAN

A *water treatment technician* works wherever there is a possibility of water contamination. The technician collects and prepares water samples for laboratory examination.

Some technicians test drinking-water supplies from municipal water plants or wells to make sure the water is safe to use and drink. They add chemicals, such as chlorine or fluorides to the water supply. Other technicians work in waste-water plants, making sure the waste is clean enough to be released back into the environment.

If you're interested in becoming a water treatment technician, you should take high school classes in chemistry, mathematics, and biology. Since some technicians in smaller communities also perform maintenance duties, such as repairing pumps, you should also have mechanical aptitude. Most technicians complete a two-year course at a technical school.

For Additional Information

Contact the National Environmental Training Association, 148 S. Napoleon Street, Valparaiso, IN 46383.

UNIT READINGS

▶ Cobb, Vicki. *Chemically Active!* Philadelphia: Lippincott, 1985.
▶ Mohnen, Volker A. "The Challenge of Acid Rain." *Scientific American*, August, 1988, pp. 30-38.
▶ Whyman, Dathryn. *Chemical Changes*, Danbury, CT: Gloucester, 1986.

PAINT ANALYST

Paint analysts develop new colors of paints. They mix together basic colors to create hundreds of different colors. You have probably seen these on paint chips in paint or hardware stores. Once you have selected the color you want, a worker at the store mixes the paint according to directions that were provided by the paint analyst.

If you're interested in becoming a paint analyst, you should have good color vision and artistic skills. High school classes in art and chemistry are also helpful. Although some paint analysts receive on-the-job training, most have college degrees in chemistry.

For Additional Information

Contact the American Chemical Society, 1155 16th Street NW, Washington, DC 20036.

UNIT READINGS

Background

▶ *Chemically Active!* describes how to make solutions and how to separate mixtures.
▶ "The Challenge of Acid Rain" discusses advancements that help provide solutions to the acid rain problem.
▶ *Chemical Changes* illustrates some basic principles of science.

More Readings

1. Zubrowski, Bernie. *Messing Around with Baking Chemistry.* Boston, MA: Little, 1980. Presents experiments to explore what happens when batter and dough turn into cake and bread.
2. Walters, Derek. *Chemistry.* New York, NY: Watts, 1982. Easy experiments that highlight the applications of chemistry to everyday life.

Snow

by Ruth Kirk

The passage that follows gives Ruth Kirk's perspective on the use of salt for snow control on roads.

Tests show salt damage as far as one hundred feet from the edge of pavement. It harms soil structure and by upsetting osmotic balance causes water to be drawn out of plants' roots instead of into them. (The flow is toward the greater salt concentration, which normally is in the root sap.) Gardeners at Arlington National Cemetery have reported the loss of privet hedges and bluegrass lawns because of salt, and at Walter Reed Hospital street maples and parking lot hemlocks have died because of salt-laden snow piled up outside curbing where its melt seeped into the ground. In New Hampshire, Massachusetts, Vermont, and Connecticut, tests of afflicted and dying trees indicate excess sodium in leaf tissue and a high total salt concentration in sap. Maples seem the most affected, sugar maples more so than red maples. The New Hampshire tests noted damage along state roads, which are salted, but not along roads of the same area where de-icing salts are not used.

Animals and human life suffers too. The death of pheasants, pigeons, quail and rabbits have been traced to salt poisoning in the Madison, Wisconsin, region. Deer drawn to roads to lick salt have been struck by cars. Dog owners protest damage to pets' feet. Doctors in several areas of high winter salt use recommend the purchase of distilled water by patients with congestive heart failure, certain kidney problems, or hypertension, and for many pregnant women. Widespread contamination of municipal wells has become commonplace and a few communities have been forced to close water supplies that had served for generations. Some of the trouble comes from snow scraped off streets and roads and dumped into rivers, lakes, and ponds; some is from seepage through the soil. Improper storage causes a high proportion of the problem. Salt piles should rest on an impermeable footing and be covered as protection from rain and snow, but often no effort at containment is made.

In Your Own Words

▶ Write an informative essay on the importance of finding alternatives to snow control, based on Ruth Kirk's writings.

453

Source: Ruth Kirk, *Snow*, New York: William Morrow and Company, 1978.
Biography: Ruth Kirk is well known for nature writings. Her previous magazine articles and books have dealt with subjects ranging from desert and rain forest ecology to archaeology. In researching this book, she studied hundreds of scientific reports, talked with experts, and traveled extensively.

TEACHING STRATEGY

▶ Have students read trhough the passage by Ruth Kirk. The have them respond to the discussion questions below.

Discussion Questions

1. **From the passage given here, how does Ruth Kirk describe the damage to plant and animal life caused by the use of road salts?** *Kirk refers to plant life, such as trees and grasses, as being killed by the salt "upsetting the osmotic balance," causing "water to be drawn out of plants' roots instead of into them." Birds and small mammals have been poisoned by salt; deer have been killed by vehicles when they lick salt from the roads; and salt injures dogs' feet.*

2. **Do research to learn more about what non-biological damage results from salting roads and highways. If you live in an area where it snows, but salt is not used, find out how snow on highways is treated and why salt is not used.** *Automobile magazines, general-interest magazines, and consumer publications are good sources. Encourage students to research this topic using Reader's Guide to Periodical Literature. Students may find out about damage to metal structures, deterioration of concrete, and damage to automobiles themselves. In areas that have snow but do not use salt, road crews may spread sand, stone, or cinders, or may simply rely on plowing. In some communities, salt may be outlawed. Students may be surprised to learn that salt may not be used because the climate is too cold for it to be effective.*

Classics

▶ Asimov, Isaac. *Asimov on Chemistry*. New York NY: Doubleday, 1974. A collection of essays on chemistry written between 1958 and 1965 for magazines.

Other Works

▶ Other books and articles that include information on snow removal techniques include: "Water Pollution and Associated Effects from Street Salting." Environmental Protection Technology Series. Environmental Protection Agency R2-73-257. Washington, D.C., May 1973. Stamps, David. "The Real Price of Road Salt." *National Wildlife*. December-January, 1989.

In Unit 6, students are introduced to wave phenomena. The properties and behavior of transverse mechanical waves are discussed and related to those of longitudinal waves. The various properties of sound are explained by its wave characteristics. Light is then introduced to demonstrate the wave characteristics of electromagnetic waves. The unit closes by having students explore optics and optical instruments.

CONTENTS

ADVANCE PREPARATION

Activities
▶ **Activity 18-2, page 471,** requires plastic pipe (2 1/2" to 4") that can be obtained in hardware or plumbing supply stores.

Audiovisuals
▶ Show the video *Mr. Wizard's World: Sound Instruments,* Macmillan/McGraw-Hill School Division.
▶ Show the video *Noise Pollution,* LCA.
▶ Show the film *Color From Light,* Churchill Films.
▶ Show the film *Light and Lenses,* Journal Films, Inc.

454

OPTIONS

Cross Curriculum
Cooperative Learning: Assign students to groups and have them keep journals indicating when terms related to the unit are used or discussed in classes other than science. Have them note the class, the circumstance, and if the term was used the same way. At the end of the unit, have students in each group compile their journals and discuss their findings with the class.

Science at Home
Have students list the titles of songs that they have heard on radio, TV, or cassettes, or have read on the covers of cassettes, albums, or sheet music that contain colors. Have them conjecture on how color is used to portray or affect a mood.

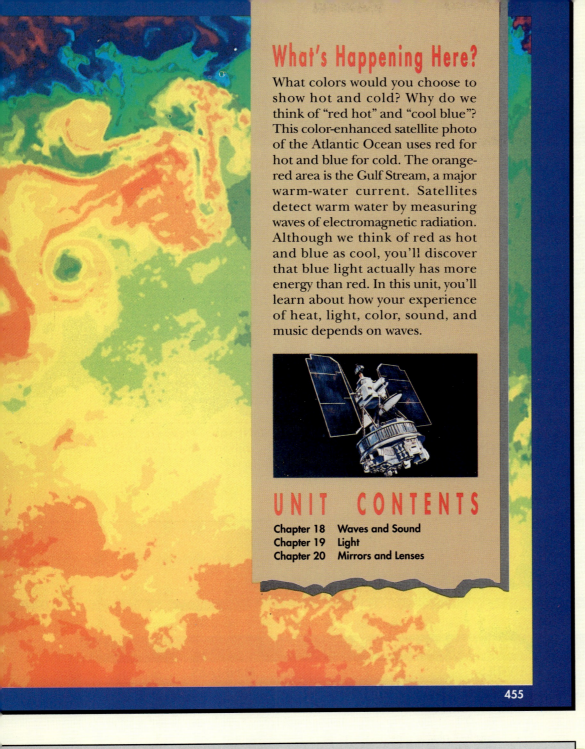

What's Happening Here?

What colors would you choose to show hot and cold? Why do we think of "red hot" and "cool blue"? This color-enhanced satellite photo of the Atlantic Ocean uses red for hot and blue for cold. The orange-red area is the Gulf Stream, a major warm-water current. Satellites detect warm water by measuring waves of electromagnetic radiation. Although we think of red as hot and blue as cool, you'll discover that blue light actually has more energy than red. In this unit, you'll learn about how your experience of heat, light, color, sound, and music depends on waves.

UNIT   CONTENTS

455

What's Happening Here?

▶ Have students look at the photos and read the text. Ask them to tell you what's happening here. Point out to students that in this unit they will learn how all electromagnetic energy, such as infrared radiation and visible light, and detectors of electromagnetic energy, such as the satellite's sensors and the human eye, have common characteristics.

▶ **Background:** The computer-enhanced image can be considered a thermograph or temperature picture of the area. All matter radiates thermal energy in the form of electromagnetic waves called infrared radiation. The frequency of the infrared radiation is precisely related to the temperature of the material from which it is radiated. The satellite detects the different frequencies of infrared radiation and relays the data to ground stations, where computers process the data to produce colored images. The colors used to enhance the image are chosen for psychological effect.

Previewing the Chapters

▶ Have students find and identify the photographs in the chapters that show (1) what noise and musical sounds look like; *Figure 18-9, page 474,* (2) an unappetizing picture of broccoli; *Figure 19-10b, page 494,* (3) something that they listen to that also makes colors; *Figure 19-20, page 505,* (4) an application of a laser *Figure 20-17, page 531.*

Tying to Previous Knowledge

▶ Have students recall other types of thermal energy transfer in matter. Have them explain how a satellite stays in orbit.

▶ Relate the following question to the Previewing the Chapter activity. (1) What does the photograph show? What is your interpretation of it? (2) Why is the broccoli unappetizing? How does the color of food affect its appeal? (3) Where else have you seen a similar effect? (4) What other laser applications are you familiar with?

▶ Use the **inquiry questions** in the OPTIONS box below to investigate light.

Multicultural Awareness

Have interested students research the cultural differences in the symbolic use of color. Students might be interested in surveying the use of color in flags of nations around the world.

Inquiry Questions

▶ **What part of the satellite detects the infrared radiation?** *Accept all reasonable answers. Small lenses or plates on surface of satellite.*

▶ **What human body organ detects infrared radiation?** *skin*

▶ **What organ detects light?** *eye*

▶ **What was the energy source [of the infrared radiation when this picture was taken?** *water*

▶ **What would be the energy source if the satellite took a picture using visible light?** *sun*

CHAPTER SECTION	OBJECTIVES	ACTIVITIES
18-1 Wave Characteristics (2 days)	1. **Sketch** a transverse wave and **identify** its characteristics. 2. **Discuss** the relationship between the frequency and wavelength in a transverse wave. 3. **Using** the relationship between wavelength, frequency, and velocity, **find** one variable when two are given.	**Activity 18-1:** *Transverse Waves,* p. 463
18-2 The Nature of Sound (2 days)	1. **Describe** the transmission of sound through a medium. 2. **Recognize** the relationships between amplitude and loudness and frequency and pitch. 3. **Illustrate** the Doppler effect with a practical example.	**MINI-Lab:** *How is sound different when it travels through solids?* p. 466 **Activity 18-2:** *Frequency of Sound Waves,* p. 471
18-3 Noise Pollution Science & Society (1 day)	1. **Analyze** the role of noise as one type of pollution. 2. **Suggest** three ways noise pollution can be reduced.	
18-4 Musical Sounds (2 days)	1. **Distinguish** between music and noise. 2. **Describe** why different instruments produce sounds of different quality. 3. **Explain** three types of wave interference.	**MINI-Lab:** *How can hearing loss change the sounds you hear?* p. 476
Chapter Review		

ACTIVITY MATERIALS

FIND OUT	ACTIVITIES		MINI-LABS	
Page 457 1 soda pop bottle water	**18-1 Transverse Waves, p. 463** small slinky stopwatch	**18-2 Frequency of Sound Waves, p. 471** length of plastic pipe rubber band metric ruler	**How is sound different when it travels through solids? p. 466** 1.5 m string metal objects	**How can hearing loss change the sounds you hear? p. 476** radio heavy pads

CHAPTER FEATURES		TEACHER RESOURCE PACKAGE	OTHER RESOURCES
Skill Builder: *Comparing and Contrasting,* p. 462		**Ability Level Worksheets** ◆ **Study Guide,** p. 74 ● **Reinforcement,** p. 74 ▲ **Enrichment,** p. 74 **Concept Mapping,** pp. 41, 42 **Science and Society,** p. 22 **Activity Worksheet,** pp. 141, 142 **Transparency Masters,** pp. 71, 72	**Color Transparency 36,** Wave Motion **Lab Manual 37,** Velocity of a Wave
Technology: *Window on the Deep?* p. 467 **Skill Builder:** *Concept Mapping,* p. 470		**Ability Level Worksheets** ◆ **Study Guide,** p. 75 ● **Reinforcement,** p. 75 ▲ **Enrichment,** p. 75 **Activity Worksheet,** pp. 143, 144 **MINI-Lab Worksheet,** p. 147 **Transparency Masters,** pp. 73, 74	**Color Transparency 37,** The Decibel Scale **Lab Manual 38,** Sound Waves and Pitch
You Decide! p. 473		**Ability Level Worksheets** ◆ **Study Guide,** p. 76 ● **Reinforcement,** p. 76 ▲ **Enrichment,** p. 76	
Problem Solving: *The Piano that Played Itself,* p. 475 **Skill Builder:** *Recognizing Cause and Effect,* p. 478		**Ability Level Worksheets** ◆ **Study Guide,** p. 77 ● **Reinforcement,** p. 77 ▲ **Enrichment,** p. 77 **Critical Thinking/Problem Solving,** p. 24 **Cross-Curricular Connections,** p. 24 **MINI-Lab Worksheet,** p. 148	
Summary Key Science Words Understanding Vocabulary Checking Concepts Understanding Concepts	Think & Write Critically Apply More Skill Builders Projects	**Chapter Review,** pp. 39, 40 **Chapter Test,** pp. 122-125	**Chapter Review Software** **Test Bank**

◆ **Basic**   ● **Average**   ▲ **Advanced**

ADDITIONAL MATERIALS

SOFTWARE	AUDIOVISUAL	BOOKS/MAGAZINES
Sound Waves, J&S Software. *Sound,* Cross Educational Software. *Waves and Sound Energy,* Focus. *Sound: A Microcomputer Based Lab,* Queue.	*A Look at Sound,* film, Time-Life. *Matter and Energy: Sound,* filmstrip and cassette, SVE. *Mr. Wizard's World: Sound Instruments,* video, Macmillan/McGraw-Hill School Division. *Noise Pollution,* video, LCA. *The World of Sound Energy,* video, Focus. *What is a Wave?,* video, Focus.	Knight, David C. *All About Sound.* Mahwah, NJ: Troll Assocs., 1983. Leitner, Bernhard. *Sound: Space.* New York: University Press, 1978. Wong, George S.K. "Slowing Down the Speed of Sound," *Science News.* June 21, 1986.

THEME DEVELOPMENT: Energy is one of the main themes of this chapter, as waves are rhythmic disturbances that carry energy. Emphasize how the amplification of waves increases the energy. Use examples to show both kinds of waves carrying energy.

CHAPTER OVERVIEW

▶ **Section 18-1:** This section introduces transverse waves. The parts of a wave are identified, and the relationship between frequency, wavelength, and velocity is discussed.

▶ **Section 18-2:** Compressional waves are explained. The differences between frequency and pitch and intensity and loudness are examined. A discussion of the Doppler effect concludes this section.

▶ **Section 18-3: Science and Society:** Noise pollution, its control, and its effects on the human ear are explored. The You Decide feature asks students to determine if skateboarders violate noise pollution codes.

▶ **Section 18-4:** This section contrasts music and noise. Musical quality and interference are illustrated.

CHAPTER VOCABULARY

waves	intensity
medium	loudness
transverse wave	noise
crests	pollution
troughs	music
wavelength	noise
amplitude	resonance
frequency	quality
compressional	interference
wave	reverberation
pitch	acoustics

456

OPTIONS

For Your Gifted Students

▶ Have students research the speeds of light and sound in different media, make a bar graph for each, and make a hypothesis about how the density of matter affects both light and sound.

▶ Have students determine the ratio of the speed of light and the speed of sound in air at a specific temperature.

Have you ever played a musical instrument? Perhaps you plucked the strings on a guitar, or made music by blowing air into a harmonica or a clarinet. Did you know you can even make music with a soda pop bottle?

FIND OUT!

Do this simple activity to find out how you can make music with a soda pop bottle.

You need a clean, empty soda pop bottle. First, place the empty bottle just below your lower lip so it touches your lip lightly. Take a big breath and blow a steady stream of air across the top of the bottle. Did you hear a musical tone? Fill the bottle halfway with water and make another musical tone. Did it sound lower or higher than the first tone you made? Pour some water out of the bottle. How do you expect the tone to sound now? It should be lower. Could you play a song with several other soda pop bottles with different water levels? Try it!

Previewing Science Skills
- ► In the Skill Builders, you will make a concept map and determine cause and effect.
- ► In the Activities, you will observe, measure, and hypothesize.
- ► In the MINI-Labs, you will observe, interpret, and hypothesize.

What's next?

Now that you know how to make music with a soda pop bottle, you can learn how sound waves are made. You can also find out how changing the length of the air column in the bottle affects the musical tone as you read this chapter.

457

For Your Mainstreamed Students

► Have a physician or nurse speak about hearing disorders and their detection and treatment.

► Play a radio in the classroom at a comfortable level of volume. Place different objects in front of the radio to determine how well they absorb sound. Objects you could try might include a balloon, a pillow, a book, and some paper. Rank the items you tested in order of how well they absorbed sound. Discuss the types of materials that could be used to soundproof buildings.

INTRODUCING THE CHAPTER

Use the Find Out activity to introduce students to musical pitches. Explain that as they read the chapter they will be learning what sound is and why each sound is unique.

FIND OUT!

Preparation: Several days before you begin this chapter, have students bring in clean, empty soda pop or juice bottles. Save these bottles to use in future activities.

Materials: one soda pop bottle for every three students; a container of water or access to a sink for each group

Cooperative Learning: Use the Science Investigation strategy in groups of three. Have one student describe and record the sounds heard, the second student adjust the water level, and the third student blow into the bottle.

Teaching Tips
- ► The cooperative learning suggestion above encourages student communication and raises the level of excitement.
- ► The bottles should be washed thoroughly after each use.
- ► The water level in the bottle during each test could be measured and recorded so students can infer the relationship between water level and sound.
- ► Have the class try to play a song.

Gearing Up

Have students study the Gearing Up section to familiarize themselves with the chapter. Discuss the relationships of the topics in the outline.

What's Next?

Before beginning the first section, make sure students understand the connection between the Find Out activity and the topics to follow.

18-1

18-1 Wave Characteristics

PREPARATION

SECTION BACKGROUND

▶ Although students sometimes name water waves as examples of transverse waves, these waves are actually a distinct kind of wave called a surface wave. In addition to moving up and down, the water molecules also move in circles.

▶ Earthquakes under the ocean floor can cause giant tidal waves called tsunamis. They move at speeds up to 800 km/h, and wave height can exceed that of a 20-story building.

▶ One hertz is one cycle per second.

PREPLANNING

▶ Obtain a class set of small Slinkys for Activity 18-1.

1 MOTIVATE

▶ Place a table tennis ball in a wide pan of water about halfway between the center and the edge of the pan. When the water is still, drop a rock into the pan. The wave moves, but the ball is still in the same place. Compare the motion of the wave to that of the energy.

▶ Have the class make a wave like those that spectators make at ball games. Join hands in a circle and emphasize that there must be a certain rhythm to each wave. Experiment with how many ways you can change the appearance of the wave (wavelength, frequency, amplitude, speed).

New Science Words

waves
medium
transverse wave
crests
troughs
wavelength
amplitude
frequency

Objectives

▶ Sketch a transverse wave and identify its characteristics.
▶ Discuss the relationship between the frequency and wavelength in a transverse wave.
▶ Using the relationship between wavelength, frequency, and velocity, find one variable when two are given.

Figure 18-1. The energy of a water wave does work on anything in its path.

What are waves?

Transverse Waves

Have you ever seen stadium waves created by enthusiastic fans at a baseball game? What do you think stadium waves have in common with water waves, microwaves, sound waves, and radio waves? These and all other types of waves transfer energy from one place to another. In this lesson, you will read about some of the characteristics of waves.

Water waves are probably the easiest type of wave to visualize. If you've been in a boat on a lake, you know that approaching waves bump against the boat but do not carry the boat along with them. The boat just moves up and down as the waves pass by. Like the boat, the water molecules on the surface of the lake move up and down, but not forward. Only energy carried by the waves moves forward.

Waves are rhythmic disturbances that carry energy through matter or space. Water waves transfer energy through the water. Earthquakes transfer energy in powerful shock waves that travel through Earth. Both types of waves travel through a **medium,** a material through which a wave can transfer energy. This medium may be a solid, a liquid, a gas, or a combination of these. Radio waves and light waves, however, are types of waves that can travel without a medium.

Two types of wave motion can carry energy. In one type, a **transverse wave,** the medium moves at right angles to the direction the wave travels. Figure 18-2 shows how you can make transverse waves by snapping the end of a rope up and down while your friend holds one end.

OPTIONS

Meeting Different Ability Levels

For Section 18-1, use the following **Teacher Resource Masters** depending upon individual students' needs.

◆ **Study Guide Master** for all students.
● **Reinforcement Master** for students of average and above average ability levels.
▲ **Enrichment Master** for above average students.

Additional Teacher Resource Package masters are listed in the OPTIONS box throughout the section. The additional masters are appropriate for all students.

◆ **STUDY GUIDE** 74

STUDY GUIDE · Chapter 18
Wave Characteristics · Test Pages 458-463

Use words from Section 18-1 to fill in the blanks in the reading passage below. Note that some of the blanks are numbered. Use the letters on these numbered blanks to complete the statement at the bottom of the sheet. This statement expresses an important concept from Section 18-1.

Waves are rhythmic disturbances. The easiest type of wave to visualize is a W A T E R wave. The highest points of such waves are called C R E S T S, and the lowest points are called T R O U G H S. The distance between the high point of one wave and the high point of the next wave is the W A V E L E N G T H.

The distance from the crest of a wave to the rest position of the medium is the A M P L I T U D E of the wave. The speed at which the wave crests move is the V E L O C I T Y. The number of wave crests that pass a point in one second is called the F R E Q U E N C Y of the wave, which is expressed in units called H E R T Z.

W A V E S   T R A N S F E R   E N E R G Y

74

The other type of wave motion will be described in the discussion of compressional waves in the next lesson.

The wave you made with the rope can be described by its characteristics. When you snapped the rope up and down, you may have noticed that high points and low points formed. **The highest points of a wave are called the crests,** and the lowest points are called the **troughs.** Waves are measured by their wavelength. **Wavelength is the distance between a point on one wave and the identical point on the next wave,** such as from crest to crest, or trough to trough. The wavelength between two crests is labeled on Figure 18-3. How could you measure the wavelength on other parts of the wave?

Ocean or lake waves can be described by how high they appear above the normal water level. Amplitude describes wave height. **Amplitude is the distance from the crest (or trough) of a wave to the rest position of the medium,** as shown in Figure 18-3. The amplitude corresponds to the amount of energy carried by the wave. Waves that carry great amounts of energy have large heights or amplitudes, and waves that carry less energy have smaller amplitudes.

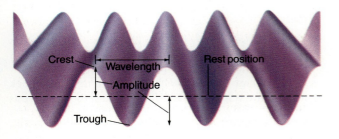

Wave Frequency

Do you know the frequency of your favorite radio station? When you tune your radio to a station, you are actually looking for waves of a certain frequency. The **frequency** of a wave is the number of wave crests that pass one place each second. Frequency is expressed in hertz (Hz). One hertz is the same as one wave per second.

Figure 18-2. You can model transverse waves with a rope.

What are the high points and low points of a wave called?

Figure 18-3. Parts of a Transverse Wave

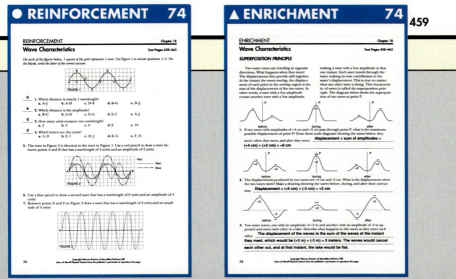

OBJECTIVES AND SCIENCE WORDS: Have students review the objectives and science words to become familiar with this section.

2 TEACH

Key Concepts are highlighted.

CONCEPT DEVELOPMENT

▶ To reinforce the comprehension of the major features of a transverse wave, let students demonstrate how amplitude, wavelength, and frequency can be varied by making waves on a rope or Slinky.

STUDENT TEXT QUESTION

▶ Page 459, paragraph 1: **How could you measure the wavelength on other parts of the wave?** *You can measure wavelength from any part on one wave to the same part of the next wave (crest to crest, trough to trough, and so on).*

▶ Demonstrate frequency by beating a pencil on your desk with a steady rhythm. Change the frequency and ask students to explain what has changed (the time intervals between taps and the number of taps per second).

▶ This is a good opportunity to emphasize that frequency and wavelength are inversely proportional if wave speed remains constant.

CROSS CURRICULUM

▶ **Math:** Students have learned that as wavelength increases, the frequency decreases if the speed of the wave is constant. Ask them what the relationship between wavelength and frequency is called (inversely proportional).

CHECK FOR UNDERSTANDING

Use the Mini Quiz to check for understanding.

MINI QUIZ

Use the Mini Quiz to check students' recall of chapter content.

❶ **What do waves transfer?** *energy*
❷ **In what unit is frequency usually expressed?** *Hertz*
❸ **What happens to the wavelength if the frequency increases?** *It decreases.*
❹ **The highest points of a wave are called _____ .** *crests*

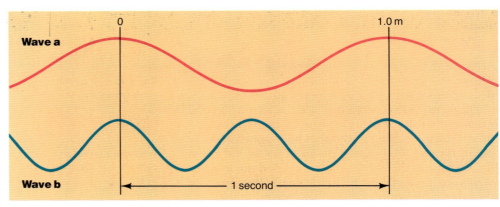

Figure 18-4. Wave a has a longer wavelength and a lower frequency than wave b. Both waves are traveling at the same speed.

How do you increase the frequency of a wave? To do this with a rope, you simply move the rope up and down faster, so you create more crests each second. Then, if the speed of the waves does not change, the frequency of the waves increases. As a result, the wavelengths must become shorter. In other words, as the frequency increases, the wavelength decreases. Using a rope, you can demonstrate this principle as shown in Figure 18-4. This relationship between wavelength and frequency will be discussed further in the next section and in Chapter 19.

What happens to the wavelength of a wave as the frequency increases?

Wave Velocity

Sometimes you may want to know how fast a wave is traveling. For example, earthquakes below the ocean can produce giant tidal waves. You would want to know how soon a tidal wave would reach you, if you needed to seek shelter. Wave velocity, *v*, describes how fast the wave crests move.

Wave velocity can be determined by multiplying the wavelength and frequency as shown below. Wavelength is represented by the Greek letter lambda, λ. If you know any two variables in the following equation, you can find the unknown variable.

$$velocity = wavelength \times frequency$$
$$v = \lambda \times f$$

The examples that follow show how you can use this equation to solve for the unknown variable.

Did You Know?

Lightning flashes move at speeds up to 140 000 km/s and last about 0.003 s, with temperatures of about 30 000°C (or 5 times greater than the temperature on the surface of the sun).

460   WAVES AND SOUND

OPTIONS

INQUIRY QUESTIONS

▶ **What other two variables would you need to know to find the wavelength of a water wave?** *velocity and frequency* **What formula would you use?** $\lambda = v/f$

▶ **Could you find the frequency of a wave if you knew how fast it was traveling and the distance from trough to trough?** *yes* **Explain your answer mathematically.** *frequency = velocity/wavelength*

PROGRAM RESOURCES

Use **Laboratory Manual,** Velocity of a Wave.

EXAMPLE PROBLEM: Calculating the Velocity of a Wave

Problem Statement:
A wave is generated in a wave pool at a water amusement park. The wavelength is 3.2 m. The frequency of the wave is 0.60 Hz. What is the velocity of the wave?

Known Information:
Strategy Hint: Another way to express Hertz is 1/second, therefore, m × 1/s = m/s.

wavelength, λ = 3.2 m
frequency, f = 0.60 Hz

Unknown Information:
velocity (v)

Equation to Use:
$v = \lambda \times f$

Solution:
$v = \lambda \times f = 3.2 \text{ m} \times 0.60 \text{ Hz} = 1.92 \text{ m/s}$

PRACTICE PROBLEM

Strategy Hint: Make sure all units correspond.

1. A wave moving along a rope has a wavelength of 1.2 m and a frequency of 4.5 Hz. How fast is the wave traveling along the rope?

EXAMPLE PROBLEM: Calculating the Frequency of a Wave

Problem Statement:
Earthquakes can produce three types of waves. One of these is a transverse wave called an S wave. A typical S wave travels at 5000 m/s. Its wavelength is about 417 m. What is its frequency?

Known Information:
Strategy Hint: Remember, Hz = 1/s, so m/s ÷ m = 1/s = 1 Hz

velocity, v = 5000 m/s
wavelength, λ = 417 m

Unknown Information:
frequency (f)

Equation to Use:
$v = \lambda \times f$

Solution:
$v = \lambda \times f$, so $f = v/\lambda$
$= (5000 \text{ m/s})/(417 \text{ m}) = 12 \text{ Hz}$

PRACTICE PROBLEM

Strategy Hint: What formula do you use to find frequency?

1. A tuning fork produces a sound wave with a wavelength of 0.20 m and a velocity of 25.6 m/s. What is the frequency of the tuning fork?

PRACTICE PROBLEM ANSWERS
Calculating the Velocity of a Wave
1. wavelength, λ = 1.2 m
   frequency, f = 4.5 Hz
   $v = \lambda \times f = 1.2 \text{ m} \times 4.5 \text{ Hz}$
   $= 5.4 \text{ m/s}$

PRACTICE PROBLEM ANSWERS
Calculating the Frequency of a Wave
1. velocity, v = 25.6 m/s
   wavelength, λ = 0.20 m
   $f = v/\lambda = (25.6 \text{ m/s})/(0.20 \text{ m})$
   $= 128 \text{ Hz}$

INQUIRY QUESTIONS

▶ **Three waves with frequencies of 1 Hz, 3 Hz, and 9 Hz travel at the same speed. Rank these waves in order of decreasing wavelength.** *1 Hz, 3 Hz, 9 Hz. As the frequency increases, the wavelength decreases.*

▶ **What happens to the wavelength and frequency of a wave if its velocity increases?** *The wavelength, the frequency, or both must increase.*

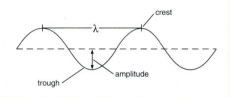

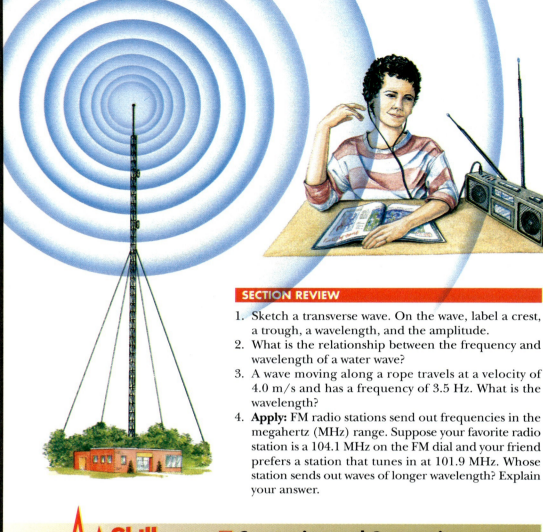

SECTION REVIEW

1. Sketch a transverse wave. On the wave, label a crest, a trough, a wavelength, and the amplitude.
2. What is the relationship between the frequency and wavelength of a water wave?
3. A wave moving along a rope travels at a velocity of 4.0 m/s and has a frequency of 3.5 Hz. What is the wavelength?
4. **Apply:** FM radio stations send out frequencies in the megahertz (MHz) range. Suppose your favorite radio station is a 104.1 MHz on the FM dial and your friend prefers a station that tunes in at 101.9 MHz. Whose station sends out waves of longer wavelength? Explain your answer.

Skill Builder

☑ **Comparing and Contrasting**

Use Figure 18-3 and information from this section to compare the frequency, amplitude, and wavelength of a wave. Which of these measurements depends on energy? Which is measured in meters? Which depends on the number of waves? If you need help, refer to Comparing and Contrasting in the **Skill Handbook** on page 679.

ACTIVITY 18-1
Transverse Waves

Problem: *How can wave energy be stored?*

Materials
- small Slinky
- stopwatch

Procedure
1. You and a partner should pull on each end of the Slinky until it is stretched about 1 meter.
2. Hold one end of the Slinky motionless and shake the other end to make the slinky vibrate in one segment.
3. Count the number of vibrations the spring makes in 10 seconds.
4. Make a second wave by moving the end of the spring from side to side twice as fast as before. Look for the spring to vibrate in two equal segments. Each segment will move in opposite directions.
5. Try to make the spring vibrate in three equal segments.

Analyze
1. Draw pictures of the spring for each of the three forms of waves you made. How many transverse waves does each picture represent?
2. The spring can store energy when the wave is the right size to exactly "fit" onto the spring. How many wavelengths fit onto the spring for each of the three forms of waves produced?

Conclude and Apply
3. If wave energy is to be stored in the spring, how must the length of the spring and the length of the wave compare?
4. Why could you store short wave energy in a long spring but are not able to store long wave energy in a short spring?

18-1 WAVE CHARACTERISTICS **463**

OBJECTIVE: Develop a hypothesis for energy storage waves.

PROCESS SKILLS applied in this activity:
- ▶ **Observing** in Procedure Step 3.
- ▶ **Inferring** in Conclude and Apply Question 3.
- ▶ **Interpreting** in Analyze Question 1.
- ▶ **Forming Hypotheses** in Conclude and Apply Question 4.

👥 COOPERATIVE LEARNING
Use the Science Investigation strategy in groups of three. One student can be given the task of timing the rate of vibration of the spring while the other two hold the spring. Have groups repeat observations after exchanging roles.

TEACHING THE ACTIVITY
Alternate Materials: The same work can be done with lengths of rope (2 meters or more in length), but the rope will not provide as strong a sensation of stored energy as that of the spring. Lengths of rubber laboratory tubing also may be used. Caution students to grip the spring, rope, or tube tightly.

Troubleshooting: Be sure students make waves with a smooth rhythm and do not try to fight the natural resonant frequencies of the spring.

▶ Use smaller Slinkys sold in toy stores. The larger Slinkys purchased from science supply houses require much more space and must be worked on a smooth floor.

▶ Warn students about overstretching the spring. This is a matter of judgment and depends on the kind of Slinky used.

▶ A review of transverse wave form will help students observe and interpret. They should be able to distinguish between the shape of a full wave and the shape of a half wave.

ANSWERS TO QUESTIONS
1. Drawings should show
   a. one half of a wave
   b. one full wave
   c. one and a half waves
2. The first—the spring holds one half of a wave. The second—the spring holds two halves of a wave. The third—the spring holds three halves of a wave.
3. Wave energy can be stored in the spring if the spring is some whole number or half number of waves in length.
4. In order to store wave energy, the spring must be at least a half wavelength long.

PREPARATION

SECTION BACKGROUND

▶ The speed of sound in air is called Mach 1. A common reference value for Mach 1 at a 12-km altitude is 1056 km/h. Altitude and air temperature affect this value.

▶ When an object exceeds the speed of sound, a sonic boom can be produced. A sonic boom is a sharp crack that is heard by listeners as the shock waves that follow a supersonic object reach their ears. Captain Chuck Yeager first broke the sound barrier in 1947.

▶ The speed of sound waves actually depends on the temperature and elasticity of the matter in the medium. Atoms are usually close together in elastic materials. As a result, solids transmit sound faster than air. Hunters of herd animals often put their ears to the ground to determine where the animals were.

▶ A person with a cold often loses his or her voice due to swollen vocal cords that can't vibrate enough to produce sound.

1 MOTIVATE

▶ Begin class by speaking without your voice. Mouth the words you want to say, but make no sound until students are curious. Then begin speaking normally. Ask them to explain what produces sound when you speak. Ask how your voice travels to their ears.

▶ Begin class by playing a current song on a tape player. Ask the students what produces the sound and what actually changes when the volume is turned up. Ask if they could listen to this song on the moon.

New Science Words

compressional wave
pitch
intensity
loudness

Objectives

▶ Describe the transmission of sound through a medium.
▶ Recognize the relationships between amplitude and loudness and frequency and pitch.
▶ Illustrate the Doppler effect with a practical example.

Compressional Waves

Think of all the sounds you've heard since you awoke this morning. Did you hear a blaring alarm, honking horns, human voices, and lockers slamming? Your ears allow you to recognize these different sounds, but do you know what they all have in common? These sounds are all produced by the vibrations of objects. For example, your voice is produced by the vibrations of your own vocal cords. The energy produced by these vibrations is carried to your friend's ears by sound waves.

The waves discussed in the last section were described as transverse waves because the matter moved at right angles to the direction the wave was traveling. You could produce this type of wave in a rope or spring by moving one end from side to side or up and down. Sound waves carry energy by a different type of wave motion. You can model sound waves with a coil spring. If you hold one end of a spring, squeeze the coils together, and then release the coils while holding the end of the spring, you will produce a compressional wave. ==Matter vibrates in the same direction as the wave travels in a **compressional wave.**== Figure 18-5 shows how the compressional wave you made should look.

Figure 18-5. You can demonstrate how compressional waves form with a spring.

OPTIONS

Meeting Different Ability Levels

For Section 18-2, use the following **Teacher Resource Masters** depending upon individual students' needs.

◆ **Study Guide Master** for all students.

● **Reinforcement Master** for students of average and above average ability levels.

▲ **Enrichment Master** for above average students.

Additional Teacher Resource Package masters are listed in the OPTIONS box throughout the section. The additional masters are appropriate for all students.

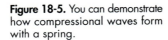

Notice that as the wave moves, some of the coils are squeezed together just as you squeezed the ones on the end of the spring. **This crowded area is called a compression. The compressed area then expands, spreading the coils apart, creating a less dense area. This less dense area of the wave is called a rarefaction.** Does the whole spring move forward? Tie a piece of string on one of the coils and observe its motion. The string moves back and forth with the coils. **Therefore, the matter in the medium does not move forward with the wave. Instead, the wave carries only the energy forward.**

Recall that transverse waves have wavelengths, frequencies, amplitudes, and velocities. Compressional waves also have these characteristics. **A wavelength in a compressional wave is made of one compression and one rarefaction** as shown in Figure 18-7. Notice that one wavelength is the distance between two compressions or two rarefactions of the same wave. **The frequency is the number of compressions that pass a place each second.** If you repeatedly squeeze and release the end of the spring three times each second, you will produce a wave with a frequency of 3 Hz. The amount of compression is like the amplitude of the transverse wave, and it depends on the energy content of the wave. Think about what you would do to increase the amount of compression in the coil spring. You would have to squeeze harder, and you would be putting more energy into the wave.

Media and the Speed of Sound

Perhaps while you were making compressional waves on a spring, you spoke to your friend. The vibrations generated by your vocal cords produced compressional waves that traveled through the air to your friend. This process is very similar to what you saw when you made compressional waves on a spring. Your voice causes compressions and rarefactions among the particles in the air.

Figure 18-6. The sound of this porpoise's voice travels slower in air than it does in water.

Figure 18-7. The spring vibrates back and forth, but the energy of this compressional wave moves forward.

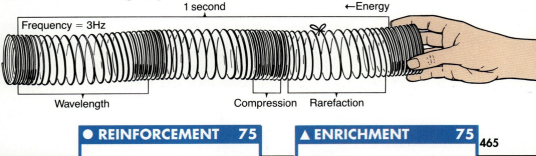

Frequency = 3Hz

1 second

←Energy

Wavelength   Compression   Rarefaction

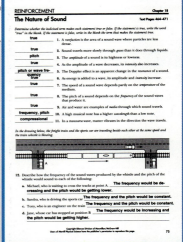

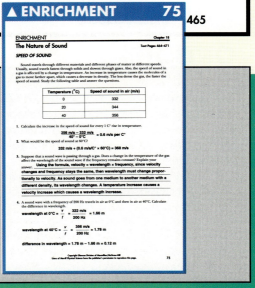

TYING TO PREVIOUS KNOWLEDGE: Ask students what they have to do to sing a tune. (They know they must make their voice go "higher" and "lower.") Explain that in this lesson they will find out what *higher* and *lower* really mean.

OBJECTIVES AND SCIENCE WORDS: Have students review the objectives and science words to become familiar with this section.

2 TEACH

Key Concepts are highlighted.

CONCEPT DEVELOPMENT

▶ It is very helpful to use a coil spring to actually do the exercises mentioned in the student text. The compressions and rarefactions can be easily identified. Have a student sketch a compressional wave on the board and identify how frequency and wavelength are measured.

▶ Students get excited when discussing space. When discussing the requirement for a medium for sound travel, ask them whether they could talk to each other on the moon. (Because there is no atmosphere, this wouldn't be possible without the aid of electronic equipment.)

The speed of light is 300 000 000 m/s, so the light gets there virtually instantaneously. The speed of sound is about 330 m/s, so the timed speed will be 0.6 s faster than the real speed.

CONCEPT DEVELOPMENT

▶ Have students place their hands gently over their throats and sing the musical scale, "do re mi fa so la ti do." Ask what they feel. (They should be able to tell that their vocal cords vibrate differently as they go up the scale.) Use this demonstration to introduce pitch.

MINI-Lab

▶Use about 1.5 meters of string per student.

▶Try a variety of metal objects—ring stand rods make excellent bell-like sounds. Curtain rods, metal tools, dinner knives, and forks could be tested. Oven racks give impressive results.

▶**Answer:** Low energy, low frequency sounds are not easily heard through air but travel well through the string, giving the objects sounds similar to large bells.

Science and MATH

The timer at a track meet starts the watch when he hears the sound of the gun rather than when he sees the smoke. If the gun is 200 m away from him, how much faster or slower would the recorded time be than the actual time?

MINI-Lab

How is sound different when it travels through solids?
Tie a metal object to the center of a piece of string. Wrap each of the two ends of the string around one finger on each hand. Place the fingers holding the string in your ears. Let the object swing until it bumps against the edge of a chair or table and listen to the sound. Compare this to the sound you hear from the object when your fingers are not in your ears. Which frequencies, high or low, seem to travel best through the string? What kinds of objects produce the most interesting sounds?

What is pitch?

The speed of sound waves depends on the medium through which the waves travel and its temperature. Air is the most common medium you hear sound waves through, but sound waves can be transmitted through any type of matter. Liquids and solids are even better conductors of sound than air because the individual particles in a liquid or solid are much closer together than the particles in air, making the transmission of energy easier. Sound waves transmit energy faster in substances with smaller spaces between the particles. Can sound be transmitted if there is no matter? Astronauts on the moon would find it impossible to talk to each other without the aid of modern electronic communication systems. Since the moon has no atmosphere, there is no air to compress and expand.

The temperature of the medium is also an important factor in determining the speed of sound waves. As the temperature of a substance increases, the molecules move faster and therefore collide more frequently. This increase in molecular collisions transfers more energy in a shorter amount of time. This allows the sound waves to be transmitted faster. Sound travels through air at 344 m/s if the temperature is 20°C, but at only 332 m/s when the temperature is 0°C.

The speed of sound is much slower than the speed of light. Have you ever tried to guess how far away a lightning bolt is by counting the time interval between when you see a lightning flash and when you hear the thunder? Have you seen fireworks explode in the sky before you heard the boom? You see the light before you hear the sound because light waves travel through air about one million times faster than sound waves.

Frequency and Pitch

If you have ever taken a music class, you are probably familiar with the scale "do re mi fa so la ti do." As you sing this scale, your voice starts low and becomes higher with each note. You hear a change in pitch. **Pitch** is the highness or lowness of a sound. The pitch you hear depends on the frequency of the sound waves. The higher the frequency, the higher the pitch, and the lower the frequency, the lower the pitch. A healthy human ear can hear sound frequencies from about 20 Hz to 20 000 Hz.

466 WAVES AND SOUND

OPTIONS

INQUIRY QUESTIONS

▶ If you are watching a space movie and two "starfighters" are firing weapons at each other in space, what sound effects should you hear? *Nothing — sound waves don't travel in a vacuum.*

▶ How can you increase the speed of sound waves in a substance? *Increase the temperature or density of the substance.*

PROGRAM RESOURCES

From the **Teacher Resource Package** use:

Activity Worksheets, page 147, Mini-Lab: How is sound different when it travels through solids?

As people age, they often have more trouble hearing high frequencies. Most people can't hear sound frequencies above 20 000 Hz, which are called ultrasonic waves. Bats, however, can detect frequencies as high as 100 000 Hz. Ultrasonic waves are used in sonar as well as in medical diagnosis and treatment. Sonar, or sound navigation ranging, is a method of using sound waves to estimate the size, shape, and depth of underwater objects. Infrasonic waves have frequencies below 20 Hz. These are produced by sources such as heavy machinery and thunder. Although you probably can't hear them, you may have sensed these sound waves as a disturbing rumble inside of your body.

Science and WRITING

You have just formed a new company, Ultrasonics Unlimited. Develop an advertisement for a product that uses this energy.

 # TECHNOLOGY

Window on the Deep?

Over 130 years ago, a side-wheel steamer, the *Central America*, disappeared in a hurricane off the coast of South Carolina. In its hold lay three tons of newly minted gold coins and bars worth over 50 million dollars in today's market. In 1987 the application of a sophisticated new sonar technology opened a window on the deep for a group of scientifically trained treasure hunters. The group found the wreck of the *Central America* and her rich cargo under more than 2800 m of water.

The treasure hunters used a low frequency sonar system to conduct their search. It could scan a 3-mile-wide section of ocean in a single pass. Signals from the sonar were processed by a computer which displayed images on its screen. When set to a narrower focus, the sonar can spot an object as small as 25 cm at a depth of 7000 m. This method of merging computer and sonar technologies can revolutionize the ways scientists investigate the oceans.

Think Critically: In what other ways do you think these technologies can help scientists study the ocean?

18-2   THE NATURE OF SOUND   **467**

Science and WRITING

An encyclopedia will describe many uses including scientific (oceanographic exploration and sonar), industrial (cleaning, flaw detection, and welding), medical (diagnosis, treatment, and sanitization), residential (burglar and pest control), and others.

 # TECHNOLOGY

For more information on the use of low frequency sonar to find underwater treasures see "Deep Quest" by Abe Dane, *Popular Mechanics*, Jan. 1990, pp. 56-59.

Think Critically: Scientists might be able to map the features of the ocean floor with great accuracy. They may also be able to locate biological organisms with this system.

TEACHER F.Y.I.

▶ The frequencies of the human voice range from about 250 to 2000 Hz in a normal conversation.

INQUIRY QUESTIONS

▶**How can you sense sounds you can't hear?** *Sound waves are caused by vibrations in matter, and they carry energy from these vibrations through a medium. You might feel the energy of the sound waves in your body tissues without it stimulating your eardrums.*

► Play a radio and adjust the volume knob to introduce the idea of loudness and intensity. Have students identify the wave property that changes with volume (a change in amplitude).

► Have the students brainstorm a list of common sounds. Write this list on the chalkboard. Next, have the students look at Table 18-1 and decide where each item in their list should be placed on the table.

Intensity and Loudness

Have you ever been told to turn down your stereo? If so, you probably adjusted the volume. The music still had the same notes, so the frequencies didn't change, but the amplitude of each sound wave was reduced. The **intensity** of a sound wave depends on the amount of energy in each wave. This, in turn, corresponds to the wave's amplitude. Intensity of a sound wave increases as its amplitude increases.

Loudness is the human perception of sound intensity. The higher the intensity and amplitude, the louder the sound. People vary in sensitivity to different frequencies. What seems loud to one person may not seem loud to you. The intensity of a sound is measured in units called decibels, abbreviated dB. On this scale, the faintest sound that can be heard by most humans is 0 dB. Sounds with intensities above 120 dB may cause pain and hearing loss. Sounds of this intensity occur during some rock concerts. Table 18-1 shows some familiar sounds and their intensities in dB.

2

Table 18-1

DECIBEL SCALE

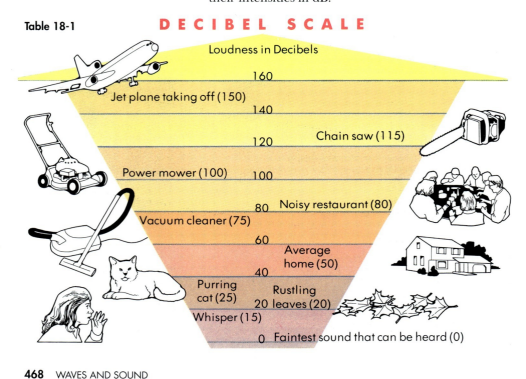

Loudness in Decibels

160
Jet plane taking off (150)
140
120 — Chain saw (115)
Power mower (100) — 100
80 — Noisy restaurant (80)
Vacuum cleaner (75)
60
Average home (50)
40
Purring cat (25) — Rustling leaves (20)
20
Whisper (15)
0 — Faintest sound that can be heard (0)

468 WAVES AND SOUND

OPTIONS

INQUIRY QUESTIONS

► What happens to the loudness, intensity, amplitude, and energy of sound waves when you turn up the volume on a radio? *All will increase.*

► How would you describe the relationship between loudness, intensity, amplitude, and energy in a sound wave? *They are all directly proportional—when one increases, so do the others.*

Figure 18-8. The pitch of the emergency vehicle's siren appears to be higher as it approaches because the sound waves are compressed in front of the moving vehicle.

Frequency and Pitch

Imagine the sound you hear when a firetruck with its siren on rapidly approaches and then passes you. As the truck is moving toward you, the pitch of the siren sounds higher. And as it travels away from you, the pitch sounds lower. The motion of the siren toward you compresses the sound waves closer together. This increases the frequency of the sound waves striking your ear. As a result, the pitch you hear is higher. As the siren moves away, the waves are pulled farther apart. This decreases the frequency and you hear a lower pitch. This apparent change in wave frequency is called the Doppler effect. Figure 18-8 illustrates this effect.

What would you expect would happen if you were moving past a stationary sound source? Suppose you were riding a school bus and passed by a building with a ringing alarm bell. The pitch would sound higher as you approached the building and lower as you rode away from it. The Doppler effect is observed when the source of sound is moving or when the observer is moving.

Think again of the alarm clock that woke you up this morning. Can you describe how the rhythmic vibrations of the clock produced compressional waves in the air?

When can the Doppler effect be observed?

CONCEPT DEVELOPMENT
▶ **Demonstration:** Cut a small door in the side of a Nerf ball. Place a piezo-electric buzzer connected to a battery inside the ball. Throw the ball from the front to the back of the room. The increased and decreased pitches caused by the Doppler effect should be audible.

CROSS CURRICULUM
▶ **History:** Have students research the first sonic boom. (See note in Section Background.)

CHECK FOR UNDERSTANDING
Ask your students if they would hear an alarm clock on the moon. There is no air on the moon for the compressional wave to travel through.

RETEACH
Model an alarm clock ringing on the moon. Place a ringing alarm clock under a bell jar on the pad of a vacuum pump. Ask what happens as you begin to pump the air out of the jar. (The ringing gets quieter.) Ask what happens as you slowly let air back into the jar. (The ringing returns to normal loudness.)

EXTENSION
For students who have mastered this section, use the **Reinforcement** and **Enrichment** masters or other OPTIONS provided.

INQUIRY QUESTIONS
▶ Suppose you were riding the same school bus described in paragraph 2 and you approached a fire truck that was parked beside an intersection. **Explain how the pitch of the fire truck's siren would change if the school bus approached the intersection, stopped for a red light, and then drove on.** *As the bus approaches the fire truck, the pitch of the siren would be higher than normal because the sound waves would have an increased frequency. As the bus stopped, the pitch would lower to normal. As the bus pulled away, the pitch of the siren would fall because the sound waves reaching your ears would have decreased in frequency.*

▶ **If you observed a speeding fire truck with a blaring siren, and you were not a passenger on that fire truck, is there any way you could NOT observe the Doppler effect?** *Only if you were moving at the same speed and in the same direction as the fire truck.*

3 CLOSE

▶ Make two different sounds for your class. Have students explain how the sound is created and is transferred, which sound has the greatest pitch, and which sound has the greatest intensity.

▶ Ask questions 1-4 and the **Apply** Question in the Section Review.

SECTION REVIEW ANSWERS

1. compressional waves; in the same direction the waves move, by colliding particles

2. Sound waves move faster at higher temperatures.

3. Intensity, amplitude, and loudness change.

4. No; there is no matter in space; compressional waves don't transfer energy in a vacuum.

5. Apply: The bat is flying toward the prey; the prey is flying toward the bat; or both are flying toward each other.

The sound waves carried energy to your ears through a series of compressions and rarefactions of air molecules. If your clock gives off high frequency vibrations, you hear a high pitch. The more intense the waves, or the more energy they carry, the louder your clock sounds.

SECTION REVIEW

1. What type of waves are sound waves and how do they transfer energy?
2. How does the temperature of the medium affect the speed of sound waves?
3. While on your way to school, you turned up the volume on the car radio. Which of the following quantities change as a result: velocity of sound, intensity, pitch, amplitude, frequency, wavelength, loudness?
4. While watching a "Star Trek" rerun, you hear the roaring approach of another ship in space. Is this possible? Explain your answer.
5. **Apply:** A bat in a dark cave sends out a high frequency sound wave and detects an increase in frequency after the sound reflects off the prey. Describe the possible motions of the bat and the prey.

Skill Builder   ☑ **Concept Mapping**

Prepare a concept map that shows the series of events that occur to produce sound. Include the terms *rarefaction*, *vibration*, and *compression*. If you need help, refer to Concept Mapping in the **Skill Handbook** on pages 684 and 685.

470 WAVES AND SOUND

Skill Builder

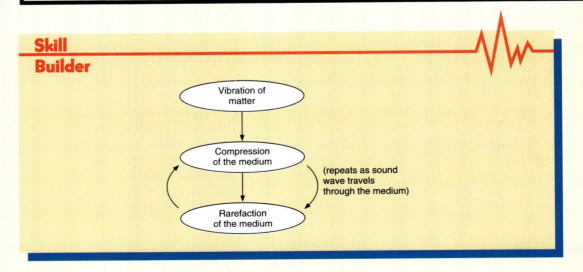

ACTIVITY 18-2
Frequency of Sound Waves

Problem: *What is the frequency of a musical note?*

Materials
- plastic pipe
- rubber band
- metric ruler

Procedure
1. Measure the length of the pipe and record it on the data table.
2. Stretch one end of a rubber band across the open end of the pipe and hold it firmly in place as shown. **CAUTION:** *Be careful not to release your grip on the ends of the rubber band.*
3. Hold the rubber band close to your ear and pluck it.
4. Listen for a *double* note.
5. Slowly relax the tightness of the rubber band. Listen for one part of the double note to change and the other part to remain the same.
6. Continue to adjust the tightness until you hear only one note.
7. Exchange pipes with another group and repeat the experiment.

Data and Observations   Sample Data

Sound Frequencies Produced by Open Pipes		
Length of pipe	Length of wave	Frequency of sound
0.2 m	0.4 m	855 Hz
0.5 m	1.0 m	342 Hz

Analyze
1. The wavelength you obtained in Step 6 is twice the length of the pipe. Calculate the wavelength.

2. Assume the velocity of sound to be 34 200 cm/s. Use the equation

    frequency = velocity/wavelength

    to calculate the frequency of the note.
3. What was the wavelength and frequency of the sound waves in the second pipe?

Conclude and Apply
4. How does the length of a pipe compare with the frequency and wavelength of the sound it can make?
5. A pipe organ uses pipes of different lengths to produce various notes. What other musical instruments use lengths of pipe to produce musical notes?
6. If you listen closely, you can hear longer pipes produce certain higher frequency sounds. How is this possible?

ACTIVITY 18-2
30 minutes

OBJECTIVE: Compare wavelength and frequency to the size of an object producing sound.

PROCESS SKILLS applied in this activity:
▶ **Observing** in Procedure Steps 3 and 4.
▶ **Measuring** in Procedure Step 1 and Analyze Question 3.
▶ **Using Numbers** in Analyze Questions 1 and 2.
▶ **Defining Operationally** in Conclude and Apply Question 1.

COOPERATIVE LEARNING
If you have enough materials, use the Paired Partner strategy. Students should trade equipment with other teams.

TEACHING THE ACTIVITY
Alternate Materials: Any kind of hard-walled pipe will work. Rolled paper will absorb sound without resonating.
Troubleshooting: Students can hear the resonant frequency of the pipe by tapping the open end with a pencil.
▶ Use PVC pipe sold in home supply or hardware stores. For best results, use thin-walled pipe of 1-inch diameter or more. Pipe can easily be cut with a hacksaw. Cut into various lengths from 20 cm to 1 meter. Mark each pipe with an identifying number.
▶ The pipe produces its fundamental frequency regardless of the frequency of the rubber band. But overtones of the fundamental can be heard as slightly louder sounds when the rubber band hits those frequencies.
▶ If a pitch-pipe, tuning fork, or musical instrument is available, have students match the sound of the pipe to a note of known pitch and frequency.

PROGRAM RESOURCES
From the **Teacher Resource Package** use:

   Activity Worksheets, pages 143-144, Activity 18-2: Frequency of Sound Waves.

ANSWERS TO QUESTIONS
1. longest wavelength = 2 × pipe length (Example) 2 × 20 cm = 40 cm
2. $\dfrac{32\ 200\ cm/se}{40\ cm} = 805$ Hz
3. Answers will vary. Wavelength will increase and frequency decrease as the pipes become longer.
4. The longer the pipe, the longer the wavelength and the lower its frequency.
5. All horns and woodwinds as well as the human voice use a vibrating air column. A xylophone uses open pipes to amplify the sound of the vibrating bars.
6. A series of shorter waves will "fit" the pipe if their wavelengths are 1×, 2/3×, 1/2×, 2/5× . . . the length of the pipe.

PREPARATION

SECTION BACKGROUND

▶ OSHA regulations require that workers exposed to sound intensities greater than 85 dB be provided with ear protection and have annual hearing exams.

1 MOTIVATE

▶ Have students make a list of sounds that really annoy them or make them uncomfortable. Ask where these sounds are encountered.

TYING TO PREVIOUS
KNOWLEDGE: Have the students recall that sound waves are capable of vibrating objects, including the eardrum. If the vibrations are too intense, damage to the ear can occur.

OBJECTIVES AND
SCIENCE WORDS: Have students review the objectives and science words to become familiar with this section.

2 TEACH

Key Concepts are highlighted.

CONCEPT DEVELOPMENT

▶ Borrow a model or large diagram of the human ear. Describe the function of the ear and show where damage can occur.

CROSS CURRICULUM

▶ **Language Arts:** Have students use the periodicals in the library to find an article describing a noise pollution situation. Have them critique the article and explain whether they agree with the author's position.

 **18-3** **Noise Pollution**

New Science Words

noise pollution

Objectives

▶ Analyze the role of noise as one type of pollution.
▶ Suggest three ways noise pollution can be reduced.

What Is Noise Pollution?

Are you aware that you can be fined for littering on a highway or in a public place? Littering is one of the most obvious types of pollution. There are other types of pollution which may not seem so obvious. One of these is noise pollution. **Noise pollution includes sounds that are loud, annoying, or harmful to the ear.** These sounds can come from sources such as a jackhammer, a jet engine, or highly amplified music. Noise pollution is becoming a problem that sometimes requires legal intervention.

Noise pollution can be harmful in several ways. Recall the way in which sound waves transfer energy through compressions and rarefactions. If the intensity of the sound waves is high enough, the energy carried can actually shatter windows and crack plaster. However, most laws that govern sound levels were created because loud sounds can damage the human ear.

When sound waves reach the human ear, the vibrations pass through its various parts. Extremely intense vibrations can rupture the eardrum, but loudness-related hearing loss usually develops gradually. Your brain perceives sound when the auditory nerve carries a nerve impulse to the brain. This nerve is composed of many tiny nerve fibers surrounded by a fluid inside your ear. Hearing loss occurs when intense compressional waves traveling through the fluid destroy these nerve fibers. Loud sounds in the frequency range of 4000 to 20 000 Hz cause most of the damage to these nerve fibers. Amplified music, motorcycles, and machinery are sources of sound in this frequency range that often cause hearing loss.

472 WAVES AND SOUND

OPTIONS

Meeting Different Ability Levels

For Section 18-3, use the following **Teacher Resource Masters** depending upon individual students' needs.

◆ **Study Guide Master** for all students.
● **Reinforcement Master** for students of average and above average ability levels.
▲ **Enrichment Master** for above average students.

◆ **STUDY GUIDE** 76

STUDY GUIDE   Chapter 18
Noise Pollution   Text Pages 472-473

Use the terms in the box to correctly complete each statement.

amplified	ear plugs	gradually	noise pollution
barriers	fibers	intensity	permanent
eardrums	frequency	legal	vibrations

1. Extremely intense sound can rupture the _____ **eardrums** _____.
2. _____ **Amplified** _____ music can be a source of noise pollution.
3. Noise pollution can cause _____ **permanent** _____ damage to the ears.
4. Sound _____ **vibrations** _____ pass through the various parts of the ear.
5. Loudness-related hearing loss usually develops _____ **gradually** _____.
6. Sometimes it requires _____ **legal** _____ intervention to control noise pollution.
7. Hearing loss occurs when nerve _____ **fibers** _____ are destroyed.
8. Most hearing loss is caused by sounds in the _____ **frequency** _____ range of 4000 to 20 000 Hz.
9. _____ **Ear plugs** _____ can be used to help protect your ears from noise pollution.
10. Sound waves of great _____ **intensity** _____ can shatter windows and crack plaster.
11. _____ **Noise pollution** _____ includes sounds that are loud or annoying.
12. Building high _____ **barriers** _____ along the sides of highways helps to reduce noise pollution in residential areas.

76

Can you suggest how the amount of noise pollution could be decreased? ==One way would be to reduce the intensities of the sound waves from sources that cause noise pollution.== Some scientists and engineers work on making quieter machinery and cars. ==Another way to reduce noise exposure is to insulate the loud areas with sound barriers.== Giant walls are built along the sides of highways to keep some of the sound from reaching residential areas. ==You can put the sound barriers over your own ears by wearing ear protection.==

Think about the other kinds of pollution you are familiar with. Littering, air pollution, and water pollution might come to mind. Now add noise pollution to the list. Rank your list from the most serious pollution problem to the least serious problem. Where does noise pollution rank? Can you explain your reasoning?

SECTION REVIEW

1. What is noise pollution?
2. How can loud sounds damage your hearing?
3. List at least two things that can be done to reduce the harmful effects of noise pollution.

You Decide!

Sometimes a noise can be irritating without being harmful. In one community, some teens built a large skateboarding ramp in the front yard of a house. Their neighbors have complained to the city officials about the ongoing noise the skating makes. The city officials have determined that the sound levels don't exceed the maximum intensities allowed in the city ordinance. Can this still be considered noise pollution? How might this problem be solved?

SCIENCE & SOCIETY

473

CHECK FOR UNDERSTANDING

Ask questions 1–3 in the Section Review.

RETEACH

One way to decrease noise pollution is to create a barrier for the sound. Have students put their hands over their ears as you speak. How does this affect the way you sound?

EXTENSION

For students who have mastered this section, use the **Reinforcement** and **Enrichment** masters or other OPTIONS provided.

3 CLOSE

Cooperative Learning: Use the Problem Solving Team strategy to have students analyze the You Decide situation. Encourage them to devise a solution that will satisfy both sides. Have them come to a consensus within their group and then as a class.

SECTION REVIEW ANSWERS

1. Noise pollution includes sounds that are loud, annoying, or harmful to the ear.
2. Loud sounds can damage the eardrum and cause a gradual hearing loss.
3. Reduce the intensities of sound waves at their source, or use sound barriers.

YOU DECIDE! **SCIENCE & SOCIETY**

Answers will vary. Lead students to discuss other sounds that might be annoying to one person but not to another. How would they reach a compromise?

PREPARATION

SECTION BACKGROUND

▶ When disturbed, an object made of elastic materials vibrates at a distinct set of frequencies, called its natural frequency. The natural frequency is determined by the elasticity and shape of the object. At this frequency, the minimum energy is required to begin the vibrations.

▶ Some objects can resonate much like waves. Consider the resonance and collapse of the Tacoma Narrows Bridge in Washington state.

PREPLANNING

▶ Find out which students in the class play musical instruments. Arrange for a "Musical Instrument Day" so they can bring their instruments to class to demonstrate.

1 MOTIVATE

▶ If you have musical talent, begin class by playing an instrument. Ask the students to explain how they think the instrument works.

▶ Play a musical tape while students are coming into class. Then bang a ruler on several objects with no apparent pattern. Ask the students if both sounds are music.

◼ 18-4 Musical Sounds

New Science Words

music
noise
resonance
quality
interference
reverberation
acoustics

Objectives

▶ Distinguish between music and noise.
▶ Describe why different instruments produce sounds of different quality.
▶ Explain three types of wave interference.

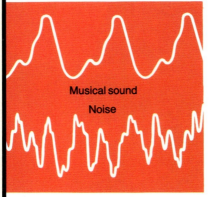

Figure 18-9. Music follows a pattern; noise does not.

How do music and noise differ?

What Is Music?

Has anyone ever commented that the music you were listening to sounded like a jumble of noise? Both music and noise are caused by vibrations, but there are some important differences. You can easily make a noise by just speaking a word or tapping a pencil on a desk, but it takes some deliberate actions to create music. Of course, you may be able to create music with your voice or your pencil if you try. **Music** is created using specific pitches and sound quality and by following a regular pattern. The most common kind of sound is **noise**, which has no set pattern and no definite pitch. Figure 18-9 shows a comparison of noise and music patterns. ❷

A stringed musical instrument, such as a guitar, generates a sound when you pluck a string. Plucking a string creates waves in the string. Because the ends of the string are fastened, the waves reflect back and forth between the ends causing the string to vibrate. The guitar string, like most objects, has a natural frequency of vibration. Plucking it causes the string to vibrate at its natural frequency.

What kind of sound would be produced if you held a guitar string tightly between your hands while a friend plucked it? You would hear a sound, but it would be much quieter than if the string was fixed on a guitar. Because the string is attached to the guitar, the guitar frame and the air inside the instrument absorb energy from the vibrating string. The vibration of the guitar and the air inside it is called a forced vibration. As a result of forced vibration, the sound of the string is made louder.

If the sound that reaches an object is at the same fre-

OPTIONS

Meeting Different Ability Levels

For Section 18-4, use the following **Teacher Resource Masters** depending upon individual students' needs.

◆ **Study Guide Master** for all students.

● **Reinforcement Master** for students of average and above average ability levels.

▲ **Enrichment Master** for above average students.

Additional Teacher Resource Package masters are listed in the OPTIONS box throughout the section. The additional masters are appropriate for all students.

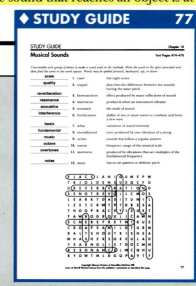

quency as the natural frequency of the object, the object will begin to vibrate at this frequency. This type of vibration is called **resonance.** As a result of resonance, the sound is amplified.

PROBLEM SOLVING

The Piano That Played Itself

Alan had started piano lessons in elementary school. After many years of practice, he became a member of a local rock band.

One afternoon as he was practicing for a gig, several friends stopped by. He decided to use the piano to play a trick on them. He said, "I bet this piano can play itself. I won't even touch a key." Ralph voiced everyone's reaction when he replied, "No way."

First, Alan pushed a pedal that released all the strings in the piano and left them free to vibrate. Then he asked his friends to join in as he sung a note. When everyone stopped singing, they heard the same note coming from the piano. How could the group cause a different note to come from the piano?

Think Critically: How did the piano play the note? Would this trick have worked if Alan hadn't released the piano strings? Explain why or why not.

Musical Sounds

If you were to play a note of the same pitch and loudness on a flute and on a piano, the sound wouldn't be the same. These instruments have a different quality of sound. This quality does not refer to how good or bad the instrument sounds. Sound **quality** describes the differences among sounds of the same pitch and loudness. All sounds are produced by vibrations of matter, but most objects vibrate at more than one frequency. Distinct sounds from musical instruments are produced by different combinations of these wave frequencies.

① Define sound quality.

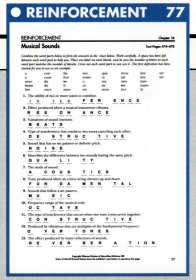

PROBLEM SOLVING

The group could sing a note at a different frequency.
Think Critically: The singing voices created compressional waves at the same frequency as the natural frequency of the piano string, causing the piano string to resonate. No; if Alan hadn't released the strings, they wouldn't have been free to vibrate.

TYING TO PREVIOUS KNOWLEDGE: Students have taken music at some point in their education. Ask what kinds of things the choir teacher looks for when directing a choir. (They should at least answer pitch and a specific rhythm.) This should introduce music as related to physics.

OBJECTIVES AND SCIENCE WORDS: Have students review the objectives and science words to become familiar with this section.

2 TEACH

Key Concepts are highlighted.

CONCEPT DEVELOPMENT

▶ If you have students who are in the school band, use actual demonstrations whenever possible in this section.
▶ Pluck a guitar string. Use a strobe light to show the standing wave vibrating on the string.
▶ **Demonstration:** Obtain two tuning forks of the same frequency mounted on a hollow box. Strike one with a rubber object. The other one should begin vibrating as the sound waves of the first tuning fork strike it. Use this demonstration to illustrate forced vibrations and resonance.

● REINFORCEMENT 77   ▲ ENRICHMENT 77   475

CONCEPT DEVELOPMENT

▶ Explain to the students that a standing wave is a transverse wave in which the crests and troughs do not travel along the medium. In the case of the guitar string mentioned in the text, the standing wave forms because both ends are in fixed positions.

MINI-Lab

Materials: one radio for not more than six students
▶ Work might be best done at home by individuals. Each listener needs two pads of several layers of cloth or small pillows to muffle sound.
Alternate Materials: A small radio or small speaker could be enclosed in a pad of cloth.
▶ **Answers:** Most hearing losses are in the higher frequencies of the speech range.
Most affected are women's voices and consonant sounds.
People with hearing losses should be spoken to face on, at a steady, unrushed pace with a slight emphasis on consanant sounds.

CHECK FOR UNDERSTANDING

Large symphonies produce a more intense sound than that of unamplified small bands. Have students use physics terms to explain why three cellos playing together sound louder than one. (If they are playing the same note at the same time, their compressions overlap to form a wave of greater amplitude and intensity. Thus, the music sounds louder.)

Did You Know?

The housefly hums at a pitch equivalent to the middle octave F on the piano.

Figure 18-10. This diagram illustrates some of the ways a string can vibrate to produce overtones. A string can vibrate in all these ways at once.

MINI-Lab

How can a hearing loss change the sounds you hear?
To simulate a hearing loss, tune a radio to a news or talk station. Turn the volume down to the lowest level you can hear and understand. Turn the bass to maximum and the treble to minimum. If the radio does not have these controls, mask out the higher frequency sounds with heavy pads over your ears. Which voices are hardest to understand, men's or women's? What letter sounds are the most difficult to hear, vowels or consonants? How could you help a person with a hearing loss understand what you say?

Imagine producing a tone by plucking a guitar string. The tone produced when the string vibrates in one piece is called the fundamental frequency. At the same time, each half of the string can vibrate in one piece. This produces the first overtone. Its frequency is twice the fundamental frequency. Overtones have frequencies that are multiples of the fundamental frequency. The intensity and number of overtones vary with each instrument to form a distinct quality of sound. Figure 18-10 illustrates the fundamental frequency and the first three overtones.

Music is written and played based on a musical scale of notes. The musical scale has eight notes, each of which has a characteristic frequency. The eight notes span a frequency range called an octave. The first and last notes in an octave are designated by the same letter. The highest note in an octave has exactly twice the frequency of the lowest note in that octave.

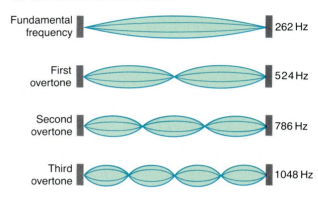

Fundamental frequency	262 Hz
First overtone	524 Hz
Second overtone	786 Hz
Third overtone	1048 Hz

Interference

In a band performance you may have heard several instruments playing the same notes at the same time. What is the purpose of having more than one instrument creating the same sound? The waves are combining to form a new wave. **Interference is the ability of two or more waves to combine and form a new wave.** Because the musicians are simultaneously playing the same note, their compressions overlap to form a greater compression. As a result, the music sounds much louder. Constructive interference occurs when the compressions of different waves arrive at the same place at the same time.

OPTIONS

INQUIRY QUESTIONS

▶ If the frequency of the first note of a scale—C—is 262 Hz, what is the frequency of the next C note up the scale? *524 Hz*
▶ What is the frequency of the C note one octave below the original C? *131 Hz*

PROGRAM RESOURCES

From the **Teacher Resource Package** use:
Activity Worksheets, page 148, Mini-Lab: How can a hearing loss change the sounds you hear?

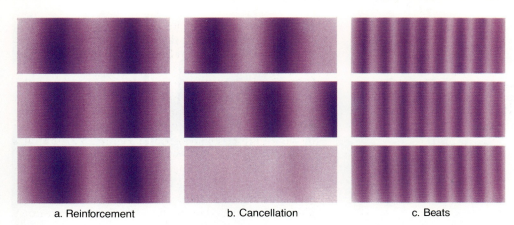

a. Reinforcement   b. Cancellation   c. Beats

Sometimes the compression of one wave will arrive with the rarefaction of another wave. They cancel each other, resulting in a decrease in loudness. This is an example of destructive interference.

If a tuning fork with a frequency corresponding to middle C is used to tune a piano, the piano frequency of middle C should blend perfectly with the tuning fork. If the piano produces a slightly different frequency than middle C, the compressions from the fork can't continue to arrive at the same time as the compressions from the piano. The musician will hear variations of sound intensity called beats. The sum of the amplitudes of the waves causes the loudness to regularly rise and fall. Have you ever heard two flutes play the same note when they weren't properly tuned? You could clearly hear the beats until the musicians correctly adjusted their instruments. The beats slowed and then stopped when the flutes were tuned. Figure 18-11 shows a comparison of the types of sound wave interference.

Acoustics

At a concert or a school assembly where a speaker sound system is used, someone usually speaks into the microphone to test the system. Sometimes you hear the sound linger for a couple of seconds. Perhaps you hear echoes of the sound. The sound reaches your ears at different times because it has been reflected off different walls and objects around you. This effect produced by many reflections of sound is called **reverberation.**

Figure 18-11. In (a) the sound compressions reinforce and produce a louder sound. In (b) compressions and rarefactions combine to cancel the sound waves. In (c) two different frequencies produce loud and soft beats.

What are beats?

EcoTip

When is sound noise? Not when it comes from birds and insects. Plant sunflowers and other plants that attract these musical friends to your yard.

18-4   MUSICAL SOUNDS   **477**

▶ Listen to a tape of a symphony or a popular hit. Identify examples of the ideas introduced in this section. For example, how many kinds of music qualities can you hear? Why is this music rather than noise? What part vibrates in each instrument to make a sound?

▶ Ask questions 1-3 and the **Apply** Question in the Section Review.

SECTION REVIEW ANSWERS

1. Music has definite pitches and a rhythmic pattern; noise has irregular patterns and random pitches.

2. their sound qualities

3. Compressions overlap, arrive together, and amplify sound in constructive interference; in destructive interference, cancellation occurs when compressions and rarefactions overlap.

4. Apply: If the glass is vibrated by the compressional waves and resonates at the same frequency, it might shatter.

Skill Builder

Constructive interference causes an increase in amplitude, intensity, and loudness of the sound heard. Destructive interference is caused when a compression arrives along with a rarefaction, nearly cancelling the sound wave. As a result, little sound is heard.

Concert halls and theaters are designed by scientists and engineers who specialize in **acoustics,** the study of sound. You will often see carpets and draperies lining the walls of concert halls. Soft, porous materials and special room shapes can reduce excess reverberation. Acoustic scientists also work on understanding human hearing and speaking processes.

SECTION REVIEW

1. Compare and contrast music and noise.
2. If you were to close your eyes and listen to middle C played both on a flute and on a cello, what musical property would enable you to distinguish one instrument from the other?
3. Explain the difference between constructive and destructive interference.
4. **Apply:** Intense high frequency sound can actually cause glass to shatter. What might be happening to the glass that causes it to break?

Skill Builder ☑ Recognizing Cause and Effect

What is the effect when waves interact by constructive interference? Describe the cause and effect sequence for destructive interference. If you need help, refer to Recognizing Cause and Effect in the **Skill Handbook** on page 679.

478 WAVES AND SOUND

OPTIONS

ENRICHMENT

▶ Have students investigate the architecture and design of some of the famous theaters, amphitheaters, and concert halls around the world. Have them identify ways that the engineers and architects designed and built these structures to improve sound quality.

CHAPTER
REVIEW

SUMMARY

18-1: Wave Characteristics

1. The medium moves at right angles to the direction a transverse wave travels. Wave characteristics include crests, troughs, wavelength, and amplitude.

2. If the speed of the waves doesn't change, and the frequency increases, the wavelength decreases.

3. The velocity of a wave can be found by multiplying its wavelength by its frequency.

18-2: The Nature of Sound

1. Sound begins as a vibration that is transferred through a medium in a series of compressions and rarefactions of the matter in the medium, called compressional waves.

2. The pitch of a sound becomes higher as the frequency increases, and lower as the frequency decreases. Both amplitude and intensity increase as energy is added to a wave. Loudness is the human perception of sound intensity.

3. The Doppler effect is an apparent change of frequency and pitch of a sound as a result of either the observer or the sound source or both moving with respect to each other.

18-3: Science and Society: Noise Pollution

1. Noise pollution includes sounds that are loud, annoying, or harmful to the ear.

2. Noise pollution can be reduced by producing less noise, building barriers, or by using protective wear over the ears.

18-4: Musical Sounds

1. Music is created using specific pitches, sound quality, and a regular set pattern. Noise has no definite pitch, or set pattern.

2. Musical instruments each have their own unique sound quality. Sound quality describes the differences among sounds of the same pitch and loudness.

3. Interference is the ability of two or more waves to combine and form a new wave.

KEY SCIENCE WORDS

a. **acoustics**
b. **amplitude**
c. **compressional wave**
d. **crests**
e. **frequency**
f. **intensity**
g. **interference**
h. **loudness**
i. **medium**
j. **music**
k. **noise**
l. **noise pollution**
m. **pitch**
n. **quality**
o. **resonance**
p. **reverberation**
q. **transverse wave**
r. **troughs**
s. **wavelength**
t. **waves**

UNDERSTANDING VOCABULARY

Match each phrase with the correct term from the list of Key Science Words.

1. distance between identical points on two waves
2. sounds that are loud, annoying, or harmful
3. the study of sound
4. matter vibrates in the same direction as the wave travels
5. the highness or lowness of a sound
6. material through which a wave travels
7. expressed in Hertz
8. the highest point of a transverse wave
9. distance from the rest position of a medium to the trough or crest of a wave
10. human perception of sound intensity

SUMMARY

Have students read the summary statements to review the major concepts of the chapter.

UNDERSTANDING VOCABULARY

1. s
2. l
3. a
4. c
5. m
6. i
7. e
8. d
9. b
10. h

ASSESSMENT

To assess student understanding of material in this chapter, use the resources listed.

COOPERATIVE LEARNING

Consider using cooperative learning in the THINK AND WRITE CRITICALLY, APPLY, and more SKILL BUILDERS sections of the Chapter Review.

PROGRAM RESOURCES

From the **Teacher Resource Package** use:
Chapter Review, pages 39-40.
Chapter and Unit Tests, pages 122-125, Chapter Test.

CHECKING CONCEPTS

1. b	6. d
2. a	7. a
3. b	8. b
4. d	9. a
5. c	10. c

UNDERSTANDING CONCEPTS

11. Destructive
12. at right angles
13. noise
14. overtones
15. increases

THINK AND WRITE CRITICALLY

16. In a transverse wave, amplitude is the distance between the rest position of the medium and the crest or trough; frequency is the number of crests that pass a point in one second; and wavelength is the distance between two consecutive crests or two troughs. In a compressional wave, amplitude is the amount of compression of the medium's particles; frequency is the number of compressions that pass a point in one second; and wavelength is the distance between two consecutive compressions or rarefactions.

17. All three occur when two waves meet. In constructive interference, waves of equal frequency meet crest-to-crest so that their amplitudes add up and loudness increases. In destructive interference, waves of equal frequency meet crest-to-trough so that their amplitudes cancel one another and loudness decreases. Beats are formed when waves of different frequencies meet, resulting in alternating periods of loudness (constructive interference) and softness (destructive interference).

18. A note played on a musical instrument is associated with a fundamental frequency. Whole number multiples of this frequency produce overtones. Each instrument has a different number of overtones for a given note. This produces distinct sound qualities that make the instruments sound different from one another.

CHAPTER
REVIEW

CHECKING CONCEPTS

Choose the word or phrase that completes the sentence.

1. Waves carry _____.
   a. matter
   b. energy
   c. matter and energy
   d. the medium
2. A wave that carries a large amount of energy will always have a _____.
   a. large amplitude
   b. small amplitude
   c. high frequency
   d. short wavelength
3. A sound with a low pitch always has a low _____.
   a. amplitude
   b. frequency
   c. wavelength
   d. wave velocity
4. As _____, sound intensity decreases.
   a. wave velocity decreases
   b. wavelength decreases
   c. quality decreases
   d. amplitude decreases
5. Sounds with the same pitch and loudness may differ in _____.
   a. frequency
   b. amplitude
   c. quality
   d. wavelength
6. Sound cannot travel through _____.
   a. solids
   b. liquids
   c. gases
   d. empty space
7. Variations in the loudness of sound that are caused by wave interference are called _____.
   a. beats
   b. standing waves
   c. reverberations
   d. forced vibrations
8. _____ is shown when a window pane vibrates at the same frequency as a thunderclap.
   a. The Doppler effect
   b. Resonance
   c. Reverberation
   d. Destructive interference

9. Wave frequency is measured in _____.
   a. hertz
   b. decibels
   c. meters
   d. meters/second
10. When a sound source passes by you, the sound's _____.
    a. velocity decreases
    b. loudness increases
    c. pitch decreases
    d. frequency increases

UNDERSTANDING CONCEPTS

Complete each sentence.

11. _____ interference causes a sound to become softer.
12. Particles of a medium move _____ to the direction of the wave in transverse waves.
13. A sound that does not have a definite pitch or a definite pattern is called _____.
14. Sound quality is determined by _____.
15. As the frequency of a wave _____, its wavelength decreases.

THINK AND WRITE CRITICALLY

16. Describe how amplitude, frequency, and wavelength are determined in transverse and compressional waves.
17. What do constructive interference, destructive interference, and the formation of beats have in common? How are they different?
18. Explain how different combinations of wave frequencies make a guitar and a trumpet sound different even when the same note is played.
19. In what ways can noise pollution be reduced?
20. Why does the ringing of an alarm clock enclosed in an airtight container become softer as the air is drawn out of the container?

19. Noise pollution can be reduced by reducing the intensity of the sound waves at the source, or by using sound proofing barriers.

20. Compressional waves need a medium to be transferred. As the density of the medium decreases, less energy is carried by the waves.

21. A wave has a wavelength of 6 m and a wave velocity of 420 m/s. What is its frequency?
22. A bus driver is rounding a curve approaching a railroad crossing. She hears a train's whistle and then hears the whistle's pitch become lower. What assumptions can she make about what she will see when she rounds the curve and looks at the crossing?
23. When a little boy blows a dog whistle, his dog comes even though the boy can't hear the whistle. Explain why the boy can't hear the whistle, but his dog can.
24. An earthquake beneath the middle of the Pacific Ocean produces a tidal wave that hits a remote island. Is the water that hits the island the same water that was above the earthquake? Explain.
25. Explain how a stethoscope helps a doctor listen to someone's heart.

MORE SKILL BUILDERS

If you need help, refer to the Skill Handbook.

1. **Hypothesizing:** Sound travels slower in air at high altitudes than at low altitudes. State a hypothesis to explain this observation.
2. **Observing and Inferring:** Infer the effect of increasing wave velocity on the wavelength of a compressional wave that has a constant frequency.
3. **Interpreting Scientific Illustrations:** Look at the two transverse waves in Figure 18-4 on page 460. Compare the frequencies, wavelengths, amplitudes, and energies of these waves. Draw another wave that has twice the frequency and energy of the bottom wave.
4. **Making and Using Graphs:** Construct a bar graph to analyze the following data. Order

the substances from most to least dense. Does this graph indicate any differences in the speed of each substance's particles?

Substance	Speed of Sound 25°C
air	343 m/s
brick	3650 m/s
cork	500 m/s
water	1498 m/s
steel	5200 m/s

5. **Making and Using Tables:** You have started a lawn mowing business during summer vacation. Your family's power lawn mower has a sound level of 100 decibels. Using the table below, determine how many hours a day you can safely work mowing lawns. If you want to work longer hours, what can you do to protect your hearing? If your family purchases a new lawn mower with a sound level of 95 dB, how will your business be affected?

OSHA RECOMMENDED NOISE EXPOSURE LIMITS	
Sound Level (decibels)	Time Permitted (hours per day)
90	8
95	4
100	2
105	1
110	0.5

PROJECTS

1. Research the uses of sonar and of ultrasonic waves in medicine. Prepare a written report.
2. Using materials you have at home, make a musical instrument. Play your instrument for your classmates and explain how you can change the pitch of your instrument.

WAVES AND SOUND **481**

21. Given: wavelength = 6 m
            velocity = 420 m/s

    Unknown: frequency
    Equation: $v = \lambda \times f$

    Solution: $420 \text{ m/s} = 6 \text{ m} \times f$

    $$f = \frac{420 \text{ m/s}}{6 \text{ m}} = 70 \text{ Hz}$$

22. She can assume that she will see that the engine of the train has passed the crossing because the drop in the pitch of the whistle indicates that the engine had been approaching the crossing and had then passed it.
23. The dog whistle must have had a frequency outside of the range of human hearing.
24. No. Waves transfer energy, not the matter in the media through which they move. The water that hits the shore was already near the shore.
25. Particles in a stethoscope are much closer together than particles in air and sound is transmitted more easily through media with closely packed particles.

MORE SKILL BUILDERS

1. **Hypothesizing:** Two possible hypotheses are:
   a. Air particles are farther apart at high altitudes.
   b. Air temperature is lower at high altitudes, and the slower moving particles do not transfer sound as quickly.
   The latter hypothesis is correct.
2. **Observing and Inferring:** The equation relating velocity, wavelength, and frequency is: $v = \lambda \times f$. If frequency does not change, then wavelength increases with velocity.
3. **Interpreting Scientific Illustrations:** Wave *a* has a longer wavelength and lower frequency. Both have the same amplitude and transfer the same amount of energy.

4. Making and Using Graphs:

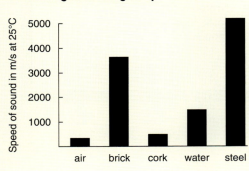

The temperature is constant, so the differences in sound velocity must be due to density. Sound travels faster in more dense substances, so in order from most to least dense are: steel, brick, water, cork, air. The graph does not indicate any differences in particle speed.

5. **Making and Using Tables:** You should wear earplugs or some other hearing protection device. You can work twice as long.

CHAPTER
19 Light

CHAPTER SECTION	OBJECTIVES	ACTIVITIES
19-1 Electromagnetic Radiation (2 days)	1. **Contrast** electromagnetic waves with other kinds of waves. 2. **Describe** the arrangement of electromagnetic waves on the electromagnetic spectrum. 3. **Explain** at least one application of each type of electromagnetic wave.	**MINI-Lab:** *Is fluorescent light hot?* p. 490
19-2 Light and Color (2 days)	1. **Describe** the differences among opaque, transparent, and translucent materials. 2. **Explain** how you see color. Describe the difference between light color and pigment color.	**Activity 19-1:** *Analysis of a Spectrum,* p. 497
19-3 Battle of the Bulbs Science & Society (1 day)	1. **Explain** how incandescent and fluorescent bulbs work. 2. **Analyze** the advantages and disadvantages of different light sources.	
19-4 Wave Properties of Light (2 days)	1. **State** and **give an example** of the law of reflection. 2. **Explain** how refraction is used to separate the colors of the spectrum in white light. 3. **Describe** how diffraction and interference patterns demonstrate the wave behavior of light.	**Activity 19-2:** *Refraction and Reflection,* p. 506
Chapter Review		

ACTIVITY MATERIALS

FIND OUT	ACTIVITIES		MINI-LABS
Page 483 objects in room	**19-1 Analysis of a Spectrum, p. 497** diffraction grating power supply with rheostat clear, tubular light bulb socket red, yellow, and blue colored pencils rope (5 m)	**19-2 Refraction and Reflection, p. 506** light bulb ceramic lamp base paper clip plastic box water	**Is fluorescent light hot? p. 490** incandescent light fluorescent light, same wattage as above styrofoam cup plastic food wrap thermometer

CHAPTER FEATURES	TEACHER RESOURCE PACKAGE	OTHER RESOURCES
Skill Builder: *Outlining,* p. 491	**Ability Level Worksheets** ◆ **Study Guide,** p. 78 ● **Reinforcement,** p. 78 ▲ **Enrichment,** p. 78 **Concept Mapping,** pp. 43, 44 **Science and Society,** p. 23 **MINI-Lab Worksheet,** p. 156 **Transparency Masters,** pp. 75, 76	**Color Transparency 38,** The Electromagnetic Spectrum **Lab Manual 40,** Light Intensity **Lab Manual 41,** Producing a Spectrum
Problem Solving: *Color in the Sunday Comics,* p. 496 **Skill Builder:** *Concept Mapping,* p. 496	**Ability Level Worksheets** ◆ **Study Guide,** p. 79 ● **Reinforcement,** p. 79 ▲ **Enrichment,** p. 79 **Cross-Curricular Connections,** p. 25 **Activity Worksheet,** pp. 150, 151	
You Decide! p. 499	**Ability Level Worksheets** ◆ **Study Guide,** p. 80 ● **Reinforcement,** p. 80 ▲ **Enrichment,** p. 80	
Technology: *Holograms—The Key to 3-D,* p. 504 **Skill Builder:** *Observing and Inferring,* p. 505	**Ability Level Worksheets** ◆ **Study Guide,** p. 81 ● **Reinforcement,** p. 81 ▲ **Enrichment,** p. 81 **Critical Thinking/Problem Solving,** p. 25 **Activity Worksheet,** pp. 152, 153 **Transparency Masters,** pp. 77, 78	**Color Transparency 39,** Wave Interference
Summary Key Science Words Understanding Vocabulary Checking Concepts Understanding Concepts Think & Write Critically Apply More Skill Builders Projects	**Chapter Review,** pp. 41, 42 **Chapter Test,** pp. 126-129	**Chapter Review Software** **Test Bank**

◆ **Basic**   ● **Average**   ▲ **Advanced**

ADDITIONAL MATERIALS

SOFTWARE	AUDIOVISUAL	BOOKS/MAGAZINES
Optics on Computer: Physical Science Simulations, Focus. *Waves and Light,* Queue. *Reflection and Refraction,* Queue.	*The World of Light Energy,* video, Focus. *Learning About Light,* film, EBEC. *Color From Light,* film, Churchill Films. *Mr. Wizard's World: Light Reflection; Light Refraction; Light Instruments,* video, Macmillan/McGraw-Hill School Division.	Ardley, Neil. *Sun and Light.* NY: Watts, Franklin, Inc., 1983. Morris, Richard. *Light: From Genesis to Modern Physics.* Macmillan Publishing Co., Inc., 1979. Simon, Hilda. *The Magic of Color.* Wooster, OH: Lathrop, Norman Enterprises, 1981.

THEME DEVELOPMENT: Electromagnetic radiation is energy, the major theme of this chapter. Help students make connections using applications of radiation they are already familiar with. Stress that visible light, as well as other types of radiation, is actually a form of energy.

CHAPTER OVERVIEW

▶ **Section 19-1:** This section introduces the electromagnetic spectrum and discusses each type of radiation with familiar examples.

▶ **Section 19-2:** The spectrum of visible light is used to explain colors and the difference between transparent and opaque objects is discussed. Pigments are explained.

▶ **Section 19-3: Science and Society:** The differences between incandescent and fluorescent bulbs are explored. Students are encouraged to make informed decisions as energy-conscious consumers.

▶ **Section 19-4:** Reflection and refraction are discussed. Diffraction and interference patterns are investigated.

CHAPTER VOCABULARY

radiation	gamma rays
electromagnetic	opaque materials
spectrum	transparent
photons	materials
radio waves	translucent
modulation	materials
microwaves	incandescent light
infrared radiation	flourescent light
visible radiation	reflection
ultraviolet	refraction
radiation	diffraction
X rays	diffraction
	grating

C H A P T E R

19 Light

482

OPTIONS

For Your Gifted Students

▶ Have students fold different colors of construction paper or fabric to form a sleeve. They should insert a thermometer into the sleeve and place it 10 inches from a light source. Have students record the temperature after 10 minutes. They should repeat the procedure with several colors, compare the results, and explain their findings to the class.

▶ Have students investigate the particle-wave theories of light.

Color is a very important part of our lives. How would you describe things around you without using color?

FIND OUT!

Do the following activity to find out how it feels not to use color.

Get together with a partner. Each of you should pick an object and form a clear picture of it in your own mind. Next, one of you should close your eyes. The other person must describe his or her object as completely as possible without using colors. Can you guess what it is? Switch roles and try it again. Why is it so difficult to describe or identify objects without the use of colors? You depend on light and color to see and describe everything in the world around you, from the food you eat to the clothes you wear.

Gearing Up
Previewing the Chapter

Use this outline to help you focus on important ideas in this chapter.

Previewing Science Skills
► In the **Skill Builders**, you will outline, make a concept map, and observe and infer.
► In the **Activities**, you will observe, communicate, predict, and formulate models.
► In the **MINI-Lab**, you will observe, interpret, and measure.

What's next?

Now that you have thought about how much you depend on light and color to see and describe objects around you, learn why objects have colors. Learn how light affects the color of objects, as well as the characteristics of light, as you read the following pages.

483

INTRODUCING THE CHAPTER

Use the Find Out activity to introduce the students to the idea of color. Explain that they'll be investigating the ways light affects color and how different colors occur.

FIND OUT!

Preparation: Place a few colorful objects or posters around the room so students have a variety of objects to describe.

Cooperative Learning: Use the Paired Partners strategy. After doing the activity once, they should switch roles.

Teaching Tips
► Have one person in each group turn toward the back of the room. Put a colorful object in front of the room. Have the partner describe it without color. Keep score of correct guesses and find out which group has the highest score.

Gearing Up

Have students study the Gearing Up section to familiarize themselves with the chapter. Discuss the relationships of the topics in the outline.

What's Next?

Before beginning the first section, make sure students understand the connection between the Find Out activity and the topics to follow.

For Your Mainstreamed Students

A student can observe refraction by placing a coin in the bottom of an empty cup and lowering his or her head so the coin is just hidden from sight by the edge of the cup. As the student maintains this line of sight, have another student slowly pour water into the cup. The coin should come into view.

PREPARATION

SECTION BACKGROUND

▶ Scientists now agree that light has both particle and wave nature, but there is a rich scientific history leading to this idea. In the fifth century B.C., Socrates and Plato thought light was made of streams of light emitted by the eye. Followers of Pythagoras thought luminous objects emitted light particles. Newton formed a particle theory of light at the same time Huygens concluded it was a wave. Einstein's theory of light as photons was published in an explanation of the photoelectric effect in 1905.

▶ The photoelectric effect is the ejection of electrons from certain photosensitive metals when photons of light are absorbed by an atom in the surface of the material. Each photon must contain a certain amount of energy to be absorbed by an atom. Otherwise, it will not knock an electron from the atom. This is evidence for the particle, or quantum, theory of light.

▶ Electromagnetic radiation is energy emitted from vibrating electric charges in atoms in the form of transverse waves. These waves are composed of an electric field and magnetic field oscillating at right angles to each other.

PREPLANNING

▶ To prepare for the Mini-Lab, obtain an incandescent bulb and a fluorescent bulb of the same voltage, a thermometer, a polystyrene cup, and some plastic wrap.

New Science Words

radiation
electromagnetic spectrum
photons
radio waves
modulation
microwaves
infrared radiation
visible radiation
ultraviolet radiation
X rays
gamma rays

Objectives

▶ Contrast electromagnetic waves with other kinds of waves.
▶ Describe the arrangement of electromagnetic waves on the electromagnetic spectrum.
▶ Explain at least one application of each type of electromagnetic wave.

The Electromagnetic Spectrum

Do you listen to the radio, watch television, play video games, or use a heat lamp or a microwave oven? These devices all make use of different kinds of electromagnetic waves. Light, radio waves, and microwaves are all examples of electromagnetic waves.

Electromagnetic waves are transverse waves produced by the motion of electrically charged particles. These waves radiate from the particles, so we often call them *electromagnetic radiation*. Therefore, the transfer of energy by electromagnetic waves is called **radiation.** One way these waves differ from those you learned about in Chapter 18 is that electromagnetic waves do not need a medium to transfer energy. They travel through a vacuum—empty space—at a speed of 300 000 km/sec. These waves travel slower when they pass through any type of matter, but they still travel very fast compared to the speed of sound waves or water waves.

Electromagnetic waves all travel at the same constant speed in each particular medium, but their frequencies and wavelengths may vary. The shorter the wavelength of a wave, the higher its frequency. Electromagnetic waves are classified according to their wavelengths on the **electromagnetic spectrum.** Figure 19-2 shows the range of the electromagnetic spectrum, which includes and lists all forms of energy—from low frequency, long wavelength radio waves to high frequency, short wavelength gamma rays.

Figure 19-1. Electromagnetic waves travel at the same speed but at different wavelengths and frequencies.

484 LIGHT

OPTIONS

Meeting Different Ability Levels

For Section 19-1, use the following **Teacher Resource Masters** depending upon individual students' needs.

◆ **Study Guide Master** for all students.
● **Reinforcement Master** for students of average and above average ability levels.
▲ **Enrichment Master** for above average students.

Additional Teacher Resource Package masters are listed in the OPTIONS box throughout the section. The additional masters are appropriate for all students.

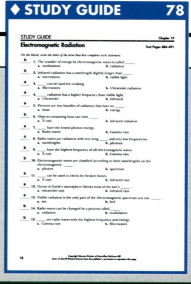

Scientists have observed that radiation not only carries energy, but also that it has momentum. This suggests that electromagnetic radiation has particle-like behavior. In 1905, Albert Einstein suggested that light is composed of tiny particles. These tiny bundles of radiation that have no mass are called **photons.** The photons with the highest energy correspond to light with the highest frequency. Very high energy photons can actually damage matter such as the cells in your body.

Radio Waves

When you tune your radio to a station, you are adjusting it to respond to radio waves of a certain wavelength. Even though radio waves are all around you right now, you can't feel them. **Radio waves** are the kind of electromagnetic radiation with very long wavelength and very low frequency. Thus, radio waves have the lowest photon energy. Locate radio waves on the electromagnetic spectrum in Figure 19-2.

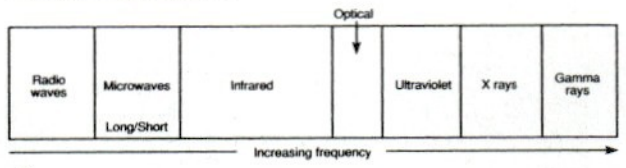

Figure 19-2. All electromagnetic waves are classified by their wavelengths on the electromagnetic spectrum.

Describe the wavelength and frequency of radio waves.

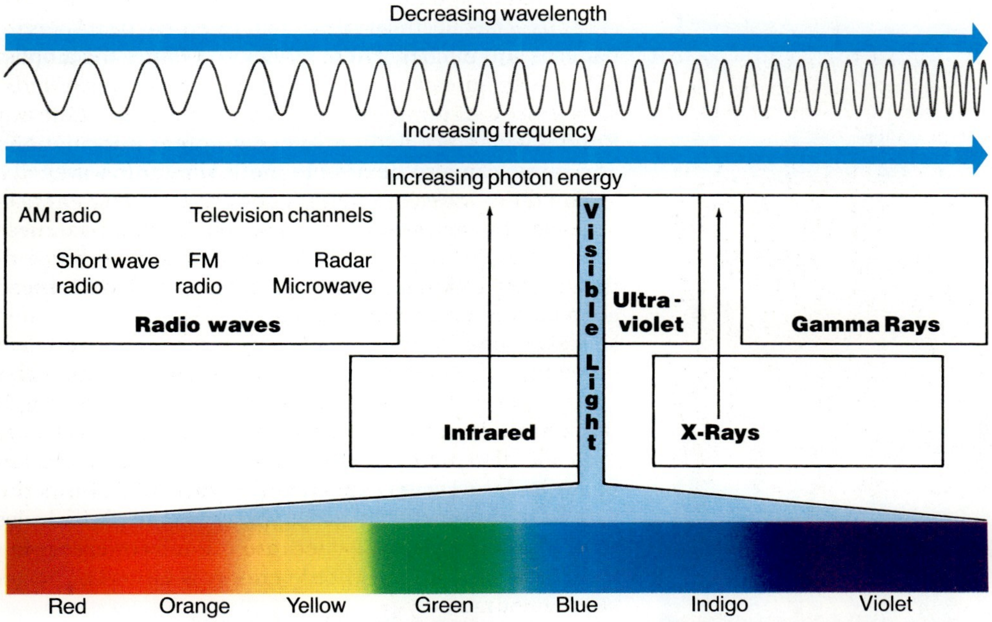

Decreasing wavelength

Increasing frequency

Increasing photon energy

| AM radio | Television channels |
| Short wave radio | FM radio | Radar Microwave |

Radio waves

Visible Light

Infrared

Ultra-violet

X-Rays

Gamma Rays

Red   Orange   Yellow   Green   Blue   Indigo   Violet

● REINFORCEMENT 78

▲ ENRICHMENT 78

▶ Ask the students how they can prove that electromagnetic radiation is all around them. You could demonstrate by turning on a radio.

▶ Make the classroom as dark as possible. Pose an interesting question. If you can't see colors in the dark, are the objects still colored? That should make students wonder how light helps us see color.

TYING TO PREVIOUS KNOWLEDGE: Emphasize that, like sound waves and water waves, electromagnetic waves carry energy. This energy can be used to do work. Ask them what happens if you remove the light source from a solar-powered calculator.

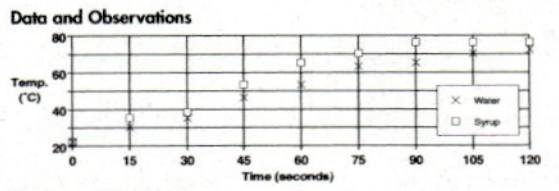

OBJECTIVES AND SCIENCE WORDS: Have students review the objectives and science words to become familiar with this section.

2 TEACH

Key Concepts are highlighted.

CONCEPT DEVELOPMENT

▶ Ask students where they would place sound waves in the electromagnetic spectrum. Sound waves are compressional waves and require a medium to transfer energy. Electromagnetic waves are vibrations of pure energy and can travel in a vacuum.

PROGRAM RESOURCES

From the **Teacher Resource Package** use:

Transparency Masters, pages 75-76, The Electromagnetic Spectrum.

Color Transparency, number 38, The Electromagnetic Spectrum

▶ Radio waves were originally used by clicking them on and off in Morse Code. This is how radio waves were first modulated.

CONCEPT DEVELOPMENT

▶ Bring a radio to class and have students tune it to AM and FM stations. Stress that radios are tuned in by the frequency of the carrier wave. List their favorite stations on the chalkboard in order of increasing frequency. Explain the difference between AM and FM.

▶ **Demonstration**: Illustrate the cooking pattern in a microwave oven. Saturate a paper towel in a concentrated solution of cobalt chloride. Place it on an empty cardboard box to elevate it several cm. Cook in 15-second intervals until you see areas of the towel dry and turn blue. Use this demonstration to show why it is important to rotate food while cooking it in a microwave.

STUDENT TEXT QUESTION

▶ Page 486, paragraph 2: **Why shouldn't you use metal containers in microwave ovens?** *Metal containers used in microwave ovens reflect the microwaves away from the food. The oven can be damaged.*

In addition to radio communications, radio waves are used in television, cellular telephones, and cordless telephones. How is your voice transmitted by radio waves on a cordless telephone? The sound waves produced by your voice are changed to varying electrical currents. These currents act as electrical signals that represent your speech patterns and pitches. These signals vary either the amplitudes or frequencies of radio waves that are transmitted. This process of varying radio waves is called **modulation**. Besides your voice, light images, computer information and music can also be used to modulate radio waves.

The radio waves of the highest frequency and energy are called **microwaves**. They are used in communications, but you are probably most familiar with microwaves for their speedy cooking abilities. Have you ever popped popcorn in a microwave oven? Do you wonder how the kernels pop so quickly? Microwaves carry energy into the molecules of the popcorn. When they receive this energy, the molecules vibrate faster and rotate. As a result, the kinetic energy and temperature of the molecules increases. The water inside the popcorn kernel turns to steam, and the kernel explodes due to the increased pressure. Materials such as glass, paper, and some plastics are used in microwave ovens because the microwaves pass through them easily and little energy is wasted in heating the container.

486 LIGHT

OPTIONS

INQUIRY QUESTIONS

▶ **Explain whether or not you can hear radio waves.** *No, you don't hear radio waves. What you do hear are sound waves that are generated by radio waves.*

▶ **If microwaves are really high frequency radio waves, how would the wavelengths of microwaves compare to those of radio waves?** *Microwaves are radiowaves with long wavelengths.*

PROGRAM RESOURCES

From the **Teacher Resource Package** use:
Concept Mapping, page 43.
Use **Laboratory Manual,** Light Intensity.

Infrared Radiation

Have you ever napped in a comfortable lawn chair on a hot summer day? Even with your eyes closed, could you feel when clouds moved in front of the sun? When the sunlight wasn't blocked by the clouds, you may have felt its warmth on your skin. This warm feeling is caused by the infrared radiation from the sun. **Infrared radiation has a wavelength slightly longer than visible light, as you can see by its location on the electromagnetic spectrum.** Your skin feels warm because it is actually absorbing some of the infrared radiation from the sun. This causes the molecules in your skin to vibrate more, increasing their kinetic energy and temperature.

Warmer objects, such as your body, give off more infrared radiation than do cooler objects. Some parts of your body are warmer than others and, as a result, give off more infrared radiation. Measurement of the body's emission of infrared radiation helps doctors make some medical diagnoses. A thermogram, such as the one shown in Figure 19-3b, can be produced by measuring the infrared radiation given off by different body parts. Tumors can sometimes be detected in a thermogram because they are warmer than the healthy tissue around them.

People using infrared-sensitive binoculars can see humans and animals in complete darkness. These binoculars can detect the infrared waves given off by warm bodies. Some home security systems are designed to

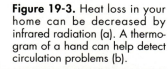
What objects give off infrared radiation?

Figure 19-3. Heat loss in your home can be decreased by infrared radiation (a). A thermogram of a hand can help detect circulation problems (b).

a

b

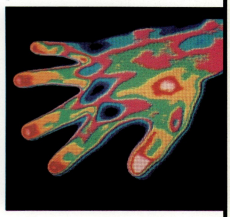

Figure 19-4. You may have seen infrared lamps, like these, in restaurants keeping food warm until it is served.

What are some uses of infrared radiation?

detect objects giving off infrared radiation, and to respond by activating light or an alarm.

Because infrared radiation raises the temperature of matter, it can be used to warm and dry objects. Infrared lamps are used in some restaurants to keep cooked food hot until it is served. Some auto paint shops use infrared radiation to dry car finishes. Can you think of any other uses of this form of radiant energy?

Visible Radiation

Visible radiation, or light, is the only part of the electromagnetic spectrum you can see. Can you find visible radiation on the electromagnetic spectrum diagram in Figure 19-2? Notice it covers a very small range of the spectrum compared to the other types of radiation.

Hot objects, such as the sun, radiate a great deal of electromagnetic energy. Much of this energy is in the visible range of the electromagnetic spectrum. Sunlight is a combination of light of all the different colors, and it appears white. Light and color will be discussed in Section 19-2.

Light can stimulate chemical reactions. It provides the energy for the process of photosynthesis in which green plants make their own food through a series of chemical reactions. Light also stimulates chemical reactions in your eyes that allow you to see.

488 LIGHT

Ultraviolet Radiation

Why do you wear sunglasses or use sunscreen when you're in the sunlight for several hours? These two products are designed to protect you from large doses of ultraviolet radiation. Where is ultraviolet radiation located with respect to visible light on the electromagnetic spectrum in Figure 19-2? **Ultraviolet radiation** has a higher frequency than visible light, and as a result its photons are more energetic and have greater penetrating power. Exposure to ultraviolet radiation enables the skin cells to produce vitamin D, which is needed for healthy bones and teeth. However, overexposure to ultraviolet radiation kills healthy cells. Prolonged and frequent overexposure can lead to sagging, dry skin, and even skin cancer. For this reason, it is important to use a sunscreen regularly if you spend a lot of time outdoors. Sunscreens absorb many of the ultraviolet rays before they penetrate your skin.

Earth's atmosphere has a natural filter, ozone, that blocks most of the sun's ultraviolet rays. Three oxygen atoms combine to make each ozone molecule. Therefore, ozone is a form of oxygen. Ozone molecules filter out much of the damaging ultraviolet radiation in the radiant energy from the sun. A reduction in the amount of ozone in Earth's atmosphere will result in an increase of the ultraviolet radiation reaching Earth's surface. Some chemicals can break down ozone molecules. Our use of spray-can propellants and refrigerants, which contain these chemicals, may be breaking down this layer, so we should limit our use of these compounds.

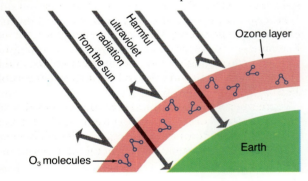

Figure 19-5. A layer of ozone molecules in Earth's atmosphere blocks most of the sun's ultraviolet rays.

CONCEPT DEVELOPMENT

▶ **Demonstration:** Show students how a "black light" can be used to cause certain minerals to fluoresce, or emit visible light, after absorbing the ultraviolet light. You can also turn out the lights and shine the black light on the students' clothes and teeth. Whiteners in clothing and natural tooth enamel fluoresce as well.

CROSS CURRICULUM

▶ **Medical Science:** Obtain some old X rays from a doctor's or dentist's office and view them. For reinforcement, ask students why only bony tissue is visible. Point out that when having X rays taken, patients usually wear protective lead aprons to cover body parts not being viewed.

CHECK FOR UNDERSTANDING

To find out if the students can distinguish between the various types of radiation, ask them to answer the following questions. **Which type of radiation**

(a) would you use to identify a fluorescent mineral? *ultraviolet*

(b) allows you to listen to the radio? *radio waves*

(c) is used in cancer therapy? *gamma*

(d) keeps food warm in restaurants? *infrared*

INQUIRY QUESTIONS

▶ **Lamps that generate ultraviolet radiation are called black lights. Would you expect to see the radiation given off by these lamps?** *No, because ultraviolet radiation is not a part of the visible spectrum.*

▶ **Light from black lamps, actually appears faintly purple. How can this be?** *Ultraviolet radiation is near the violet end of the visible spectrum, so the light given off by these lamps contains some violet light from the visible spectrum.*

MINI-Lab

Teaching Tips.

▶ **CAUTION:** *Bulbs will be hot. Students should not allow the cup or the window to touch them.*

▶ The heat collector will reach its heat capacity when it absorbs heat as fast as it radiates heat. Therefore, the temperature increase is a rough measure of the rate at which heat flows through the window.

▶ **Answer:** Even though the fluorescent light area is large, the heat flow is very small. The student will discover more heat flows from the incandescent light.

RETEACH

Cooperative Learning: Divide the class into seven groups. Present each group with a sign of one of the seven types of radiation. Give them about ten minutes to become "experts" on their topic, finding out the relative penetrating power and several applications. Have one speaker from each group carry their sign as they line up from the longest to shortest wavelength and make a short presentation.

EXTENSION

For students who have mastered this section, use the **Reinforcement** and **Enrichment** masters or other OPTIONS provided.

MINI-Lab
Is fluorescent light hot?
Use an incandescent light and a fluorescent light of identical wattage. Make a heat collector by covering the top of a plastic foam cup with a plastic food wrap "window." Push a thermometer through the side of the cup. Hold the window of the tester one centimeter from each light for two minutes. Determine the temperature change inside the "heat collector" for exposure to each bulb. What was the temperature change inside the cup for each bulb? Which bulb appears to give off more heat?

Because ultraviolet rays can penetrate cells, they can also be used to kill germs in food processing and in hospitals. Some minerals become fluorescent when exposed to ultraviolet light. Fluorescence occurs when a material absorbs ultraviolet radiation and changes some of the radiation into visible light.

X Rays and Gamma Rays

If you ever had a bad fall, you probably had to have an X ray taken to check for broken bones. **X rays** have a shorter wavelength and higher frequency than ultraviolet radiation. X-ray photons carry higher energy and have a greater penetrating power than any of the forms of electromagnetic radiation discussed so far. This higher energy allows X rays to travel through some types of matter, such as your skin and muscles. When X rays hit a more dense material, such as bone, they are absorbed. If you saw the X ray of your broken bone, it probably looked similar to the one in Figure 19-6. An X-ray photograph is a negative; thus, the bones appear much brighter than the surrounding tissues because they absorb most of the X rays.

Gamma rays have the highest frequency of all the electromagnetic waves. They are located at the opposite end of the electromagnetic spectrum from radio waves. Gamma rays are emitted from the nuclei of radioactive atoms. Earth receives some gamma radiation from space as well. Gamma rays are the most penetrating kind of electromagnetic radiation. Concentrated gamma rays are very destructive to human cells and are used to kill cancerous cells. People who undergo gamma radiation therapy for cancer frequently suffer side effects from the therapy because healthy cells are damaged.

Doctors and technicians who give gamma radiation therapy or take X-ray pictures protect themselves from this penetrating radiation by standing behind lead shields. These shields

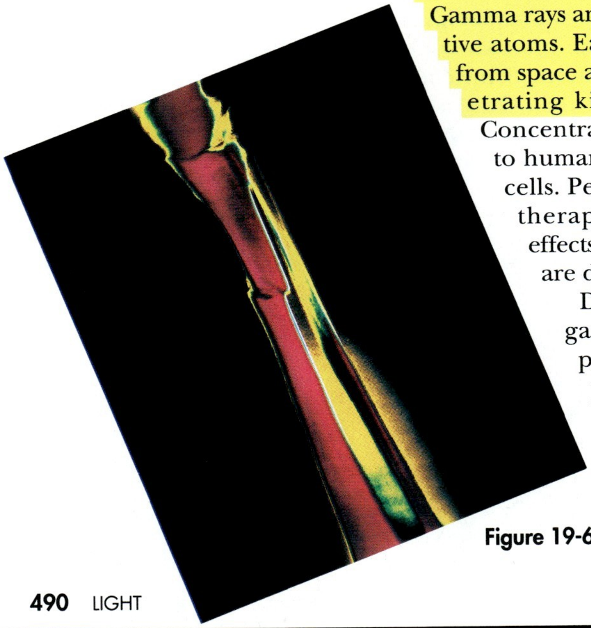

Figure 19-6. X rays can help locate the break in a bone.

OPTIONS

PROGRAM RESOURCES

From the **Teacher Resource Package** use:

Activity Worksheets, page 156, Mini-Lab: Is fluorescent light hot?

Science and Society, page 23, Food Irradiation.

Use **Laboratory Manual,** Producing a Spectrum.

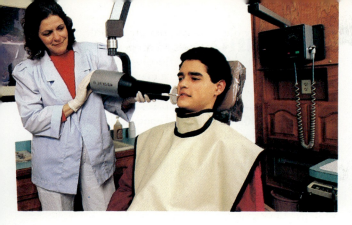

Figure 19-7. Exposure to X rays and gamma radiation can be harmful to workers if they don't use protective measures.

absorb the high-energy photons. Excess exposure to X rays and gamma radiation is even more harmful to your body than overexposure to ultraviolet radiation.

Think of all the uses of the waves of the electromagnetic spectrum that you read about in this section. Can you think of some uses that weren't mentioned? In the next section, you will learn more about the visible part of the spectrum, visible light.

SECTION REVIEW

1. Describe at least three ways electromagnetic waves differ from sound waves.
2. Arrange the following waves in order of decreasing wavelength: radio waves, gamma rays, ultraviolet rays, visible light, infrared radiation.
3. Explain how X rays can be used to photograph your bones.
4. How do microwaves cook food?
5. **Apply:** If someone told you that you were being exposed to radio waves and gamma radiation, which would you be the most concerned about? Explain your choice.

☑ **Outlining**

Skill Builder

Outline the major types of electromagnetic radiation discussed in this section. Include at least two uses for each type listed. If you need more help, refer to Outlining in the **Skill Handbook** on page 677.

▶ Ask students to locate where visible light is found on the electromagnetic spectrum. Emphasize that it is a very small wavelength range of the whole spectrum, but it is of special interest to us because we can see it. The next section will focus on visible light and color.

▶ Ask questions 1-4 and the **Apply** Question in the Section Review.

SECTION REVIEW ANSWERS

1. Electromagnetic waves don't need a medium to transfer energy. They are all transverse waves, and they travel much faster than sound waves through air.
2. radio, infrared, visible, ultraviolet, gamma
3. X rays can easily penetrate skin and muscle tissues, but are absorbed by bones. Those X rays that are not absorbed expose the photographic film. Those X rays that are absorbed by the bones create a shadow of the bones on the photographic film.
4. Energy from the microwaves is absorbed by food molecules, making these molecules vibrate faster and rotate. The temperature of the food increases with the kinetic energy of the molecules.
5. Apply: Gamma rays; they carry more energy and are more penetrating.

Skill Builder

I. Radio waves
  A. radio and television communications
  B. cellular and cordless telephones
II. Microwaves
  A. cooking
  B. communications
III. Infrared radiation
  A. medical diagnoses
  B. warming food
IV. Visible radiation
  A. stimulates chemical reactions
  B. helps you see color
V. Ultraviolet radiation
  A. helps skin make vitamin D
  B. kills germs in food processing
VI. X rays
  A. examine bones
  B. scan luggage in an airport
VII. Gamma rays
  A. cancer therapy
  B. can damage healthy cells too

PREPARATION

SECTION BACKGROUND

▶ Materials that are transparent to visible light are not necessarily transparent to other types of radiation. For example, glass is not transparent to ultraviolet radiation. This explains why you do not get a sunburn from light that has passed through a window.

▶ Determining the real color of something is difficult because color depends on the wavelengths of light produced by the source. People complain of looking "washed out" in fluorescent lights. This happens because fluorescent lamps produce visible light concentrated in wavelengths near the blue end of the spectrum. Hence, blue colors in skin stand out more than the reddish colors under fluorescent bulbs.

PREPLANNING

▶ Have students bring in a favorite picture or poster for the Close activity at the end of this section.

▶ Obtain the materials needed for Activity 19-1.

1 MOTIVATE

▶ **Demonstration:** Begin by convincing students that there is more than one color in visible white light. Aim an overhead projector toward a white screen. Narrow the light path by passing it through a slit and then aim the light beam through a prism. You should be able to project the spectrum on the wall. Remember that refraction isn't discussed until later in the chapter.

▶ Bring in three white or clear objects. Make sure one is opaque, one is transparent, and the other is translucent. Have students describe, as specifically as they can, the different ways light behaves when it shines on the objects.

19-2 Light and Color

New Science Words

opaque materials
transparent materials
translucent materials

Objectives

▶ Describe the differences among opaque, transparent, and translucent materials.
▶ Explain how you see color.
▶ Describe the difference between light color and pigment color.

Light and Matter

Have you ever been asleep in a dark room when someone suddenly opened the curtains and bright, white light came bursting into the room? You probably groaned as your eyes adjusted to the light. As you looked around, you could clearly see all the objects in the room and their colors. When no light was in the room, your eyes couldn't distinguish those objects or their colors. What you actually see depends on the amount and color of light the objects you are looking at are reflecting or absorbing. In order for you to see an object, it must reflect at least a little bit of light.

The type of matter in an object determines the amount of light it absorbs and reflects. For example, the curtains at the window kept the room dark when they were completely closed. The curtains are opaque. **Opaque materials** absorb or reflect all light and you cannot see objects through them. When the curtains were opened, bright sunlight came shining through the glass window panes. Most glass windows are transparent. **Transparent materials** allow light to pass through and you can clearly see objects through them. Other materials, such as frosted glass and wax paper, allow light to pass through but you cannot clearly see objects through them. These materials are **translucent materials.**

Figure 19-8. The lenses in the glasses are transparent, the vase is translucent, and the flowers are opaque.

492 LIGHT

OPTIONS

Meeting Different Ability Levels

For Section 19-2, use the following **Teacher Resource Masters** depending upon individual students' needs.

◆ **Study Guide Master** for all students.
● **Reinforcement Master** for students of average and above average ability levels.
▲ **Enrichment Master** for above average students.

Additional Teacher Resource Package masters are listed in the OPTIONS box throughout the section. The additional masters are appropriate for all students.

◆ STUDY GUIDE   79

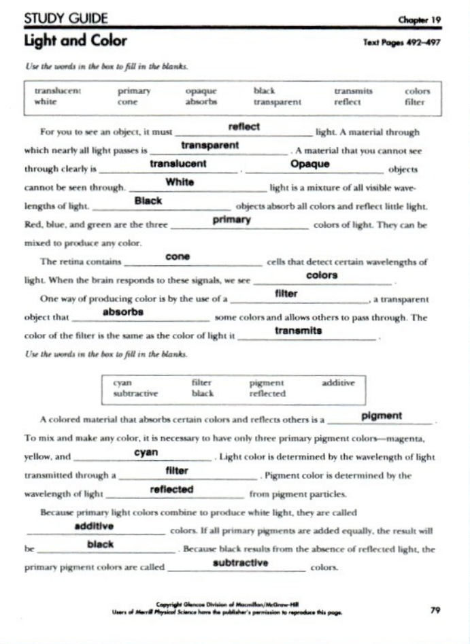

STUDY GUIDE   Chapter 19
Light and Color   Text Pages 492-497

Use the words in the box to fill in the blanks.

| translucent | primary | opaque | black | transmits | colors |
| white | cone | absorbs | transparent | reflect | filter |

For you to see an object, it must ___reflect___ light. A material through which nearly all light passes is ___transparent___. A material that you cannot see through clearly is ___translucent___. ___Opaque___ objects cannot be seen through ___White___ light is a mixture of all visible wavelengths of light. ___Black___ objects absorb all colors and reflect little light. Red, blue, and green are the three ___primary___ colors of light. They can be mixed to produce any color.

The retina contains ___cone___ cells that detect certain wavelengths of light. When the brain responds to these signals, we see ___colors___.

One way of producing color is by the use of a ___filter___, a transparent object that ___absorbs___ some colors and allows others to pass through. The color of the filter is the same as the color of light it ___transmits___.

Use the words in the box to fill in the blanks.

| cyan | filter | pigment | additive |
| subtractive | black | reflected | |

A colored material that absorbs certain colors and reflects others is a ___pigment___. To mix and make any color, it is necessary to have only three primary pigment colors—magenta, yellow, and ___cyan___. Light color is determined by the wavelength of light transmitted through a ___filter___. Pigment color is determined by the wavelength of light ___reflected___ from pigment particles.

Because primary light colors combine to produce white light, they are called ___additive___ colors. If all primary pigments are added equally, the result will be ___black___. Because black results from the absence of reflected light, the primary pigment colors are called ___subtractive___ colors.

79

Colors

Have you ever wondered why your blue jeans look blue or why grass looks green? What do you suppose your blue jeans and grass have in common? They are both opaque materials, either absorbing or reflecting nearly all of the light that strikes them. When struck by white light, your blue jeans reflect blue light back to your eyes and absorb all of the other colors. What color of light do you think a blade of grass reflects? White objects appear white because they reflect all colors of light in the visible spectrum. The colors of the spectrum, arranged in order of decreasing wavelengths, are red, orange, yellow, green, blue, indigo, and violet. Infrared radiation lies just outside of the red end of visible light on the electromagnetic spectrum. Infrared lamps often appear red because their filaments produce light with a range of wavelengths that include those of a red light and infrared radiation. Where do you think ultraviolet light is located on the spectrum with respect to visible light? When you see an object that is reflecting all colors of the spectrum, it appears white. Objects that appear black absorb all colors of light and reflect little or no light back to your eye. Why do you think colorful objects appear to be black in a dark room?

Figure 19-9. The colors of the flags depend on the wavelengths they absorb and reflect.

Why do some objects appear black?

STUDENT TEXT QUESTIONS

▶ Page 493, paragraph 1: **What color of light do you think a blade of grass reflects?** *A blade of grass reflects green light.*

▶ Page 493, paragraph 1: **Where do you think ultraviolet light is located on the spectrum with respect to visible light?** *Ultraviolet light is located next to violet light on the electromagnetic spectrum.*

▶ Page 493, paragraph 1: **Why do you think colorful objects appear to be black in a nearly dark room?** *Colorful objects appear to be black in a nearly dark room because there is so little light for them to reflect.*

TYING TO PREVIOUS KNOWLEDGE:
Ask students to describe sunlight. They will probably use the phrase *white light.* Point out that if you can see it, then it is part of the visible spectrum. This, in turn is a part of the electromagnetic spectrum, as they read in the last section.

OBJECTIVES AND SCIENCE WORDS:
Have students review the objectives and science words to become familiar with this section.

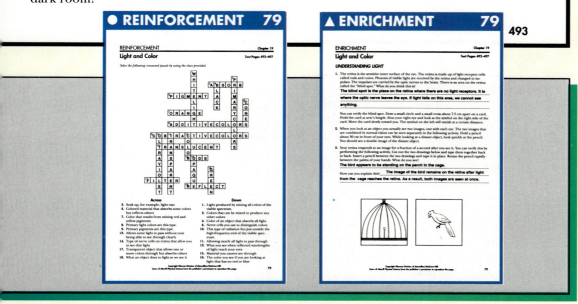

a
b

Figure 19-10. The broccoli appears green when viewed through a green filter (a) and black when viewed through a red filter (b).

Key Concepts are highlighted.

REVEALING MISCONCEPTIONS

▶ Ask students if they can name the three primary light colors. They may name the primary pigment colors instead. (Children learn red, yellow, and blue.) From their art education, they may have a working knowledge of color. Emphasize that the primary pigment colors are different from the primary light colors. We will investigate what makes things look green, blue, and red.

CONCEPT DEVELOPMENT

▶ **Demonstration:** Obtain sheets of red, blue, and green transparency film. Cut a 10-cm circle of each color. Place these on the overhead projector and shine combinations of these primary colors on a white screen to make other colors. Demonstrate how red and green overlap to make yellow, red and blue make magenta, and green and blue make cyan. Show how the combination of red, blue, and green light makes white light.

▶ Show how the demonstration above relates to Figure 19-11.

▶ Colored overhead transparencies can be used as light filters. They can be stacked easily in different combinations. Colored slides can also be used.

STUDENT TEXT QUESTION:

▶ Page 494, paragraph 1: **Why does [the broccoli] appear this way?** *Broccoli can appear to be very dark, almost black, when viewed through a red filter. The red filter absorbs green light, so there is none for the broccoli to reflect.*

Did you ever look at a white egg through a piece of colored plastic wrap? If you did, you know that the egg appeared the same color as the wrap. The plastic wrap is a filter. A filter is a transparent material that transmits one or more colors of light but absorbs all others. The color of a filter is the same as the color of light it transmits. What happens when you look at colored objects through colored filters? In white light, broccoli looks green because it reflects only the green light in the white light striking it. It absorbs light of all other colors. If you look at the broccoli through a green filter, the broccoli still looks green because the filter transmits the reflected green light. Figure 19-10b shows how the broccoli looks when you look at it through a red filter. Why does it appear this way? Red, green, and blue light, are called the primary colors of light. They can be mixed in different amounts to produce any color of light. Figure 19-11 shows how all three primary colors form white light.

How do you actually see colors? First, light enters your eye and is focused on the retina, which is made up of two main types of nerve cells. When these nerve cells, the rods and cones, absorb light, they send signals to your brain. The rods allow you to see dim light because they are more sensitive than the cones. The cones allow you to distinguish colors. There are three types of cones, each of which absorbs a different range of wavelengths. "Red" cones absorb mostly red and yellow, "green" cones absorb mostly yellow and green, and "blue" cones absorb mostly blue and violet.

What happens when you look at pure yellow

Figure 19-11. White light is produced when the three primary colors of light are mixed.

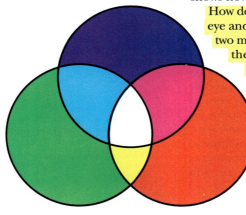

494 LIGHT

OPTIONS

INQUIRY QUESTIONS

▶ **How can a colored light bulb be like a filter?** *The color of the glass on the outside of the bulb is the same color as the light it transmits. The colored glass absorbs the other colors from the white light given off by the filament.*

▶ **Some people are color-blind, and as a result, can't distinguish between the colors red and green. Based on the discussion of cones above, what can you infer about this disorder?** *Color-blind people either don't have both red and green cones, or these cones are not properly stimulated by certain wavelengths of light, or if the cones exist, and are stimulated, the proper message doesn't reach the brain.*

light? Both your red and green cones respond, and your brain interprets the combined signal as yellow. Your brain would get the same signal if a mixture of red light and green light reached your eye. Again, your red and green cones would respond, and you would "see" yellow light because your brain can't perceive the difference.

You "see" white light when a mixture of all visible wavelengths of light enter your eye because all of your cones are stimulated. If a mixture of red, green, and blue light, the primary colors, reaches your eye, you would also see white light.

Pigments

A pigment is a colored material that absorbs some colors and reflects others. Pigments are used by artists to make various colors of paints. Paint pigments are usually made of powered insoluble chemicals such as titanium (IV) oxide, a bright white pigment, and lead (II) chromate, used in painting yellow lines on highways. Few people have exactly the same skin color because the amount of pigmentation in the skin varies.

You can make any pigment color by mixing different amounts of the three primary pigments—yellow, magenta, and cyan. A primary pigment's color depends on the color of light it reflects. For example, in white light the yellow pigment appears yellow because it reflects red and green light but absorbs blue light. The color of a mixture of two primary pigments is deteremined by the primary color of light that both pigments can reflect.

Look at Figure 19-12. Its center appears black because the three blended primary pigments absorb all the primary colors of light. Note that the primary colors of light combine to produce white light; they are called additive colors. But the primary pigment colors combine to produce black. Because black results from the absence of reflected light, the primary pigments are called subtractive colors.

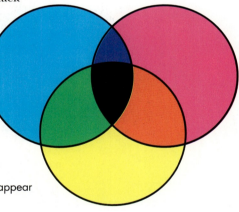

Figure 19-12. The three primary colors of pigment appear black when they are mixed.

What is a pigment?

Think Critically: A mixture of cyan and yellow dots makes the grass appear green. Cyan reflects blue and green and absorbs red; yellow reflects green and red and absorbs blue. Green is the only color reflected by both cyan and yellow ink.

3 CLOSE

FLEX Your Brain

Use the Flex Your Brain Activity to have students explore COLORS

▶ Write on the overhead projector with different colors of ink. Be sure to use transparent ink. Ask students what colors are absorbed, and what colors are transmitted (the ones you see).

▶ Ask questions 1-4 and the **Apply** Question in the Section Review.

SECTION REVIEW ANSWERS

1. Transparent materials transmit all light so objects can be seen clearly, such as a glass window. Opaque objects, like a wall, absorb or reflect all light. Translucent materials, such as waxed paper, allow light through, but objects can't be clearly seen.

2. red reflected, all others absorbed

3. Blue light is a part of the electromagnetic spectrum; blue pigment is a substance that reflects blue light and absorbs all the other colors.

4. Light enters your eye, focuses on nerve cells on the retina, which send signals to your brain. The red, green, and blue cones enable the brain to interpret colors.

5. Apply: White; yellow activates both red and green cones and blue activates the blue cones. The brain interprets this mixture as white. Yellow and blue are complimentary colors.

PROBLEM SOLVING

Color in the Sunday Comics

Becky looked forward to Sunday mornings because she liked to read the comics in the Sunday newspaper. One morning, as she was reading the comics, she wondered how color was produced in them. She decided to take a closer look, so she dug through her closet and located a hand lens.

She remembered from science class that the primary colors of pigments were magenta, cyan, and yellow. First, she examined the primary colors in the comics. The red areas were made of magenta dots, the blue areas of cyan dots, and the yellow areas of yellow dots. Next, she examined the other colors in the comics. She saw that an illustration of an orange school bus was made up of a mixture of cyan and yellow dots and one of a purple box was composed of a mixture of magenta and cyan dots. In the next cartoon frame, she examined a field of green grass.

Think Critically: What color dots do you think she found? How can you explain the reflection of green?

SECTION REVIEW

1. Contrast opaque, transparent, and translucent materials. Give at least one example of each.
2. If white light shines on a red shirt, what colors are reflected and what colors are absorbed?
3. What is the difference between blue light and blue pigment?
4. Explain how your eye sees color.
5. **Apply:** What color would your brain perceive if you were looking at a mixture of yellow and blue light? Explain your answer.

 **Skill Builder**

☑ **Concept Mapping**

   Design a concept map to show the chain of events that must happen for you to see a blue object. Work with a partner. If you need help, refer to Concept Mapping in the **Skill Handbook** on pages 684 and 685.

Skill Builder

| Visible light strikes blue object |
| Blue light reflected; other colors absorbed |
| Blue light strikes cones and rods on retina |
| Cones sensitive to blue absorb the light |
| Cones send the signal to brain |

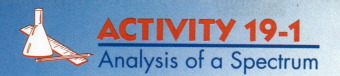

ACTIVITY 19-1
Analysis of a Spectrum

Problem: *What colors have the highest frequency and energy?*

Materials
- diffraction grating
- power supply with rheostat
- clear, tubular light bulb
- socket
- red, yellow, and blue colored pencils
- rope (5 m)

Procedure
1. Set the light bulb in an upright position and plug it into the power supply.
2. Adjust the light to its brightest setting.
3. Look toward the light through the diffraction grating. Look for a spectrum to the right and left of the light bulb.
4. Slowly turn down the power supply to the light. Notice which end of the spectrum (red or blue) disappears first.
5. Next, stretch the rope between you and another student. Hold one end of the rope still and make waves at the other end.
6. Make some waves as long as possible and others as short as possible. Notice which kind of waves need the most energy to produce.

Analyze
1. Make a drawing of the color spectrum you observed using red, yellow, and blue colored pencils.
2. Make a second drawing showing the spectrum with the power of the light turned down.
3. Draw the rope with a long wavelength. Make another drawing showing the rope with short wavelengths. Label one of these drawings "high frequency" and the other "low frequency."

Conclude and Apply
4. Which end of the light spectrum, red or blue, requires the highest energy to produce?
5. What wavelength on the rope requires the highest energy to produce, long or short?
6. What wavelength, long or short, has the highest frequency?
7. Use these observations to decide which end of the light spectrum represents the highest energy. Which end represents the longest wavelength?

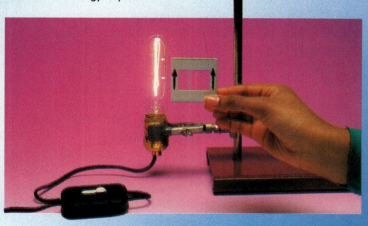

19-2 LIGHT AND COLOR **497**

OBJECTIVE: Relate the colors of the visible spectrum to the energy of the light source and **observe** the effect of color filters on a spectrum.

PROCESS SKILLS applied in this activity:
► **Observing** in Procedure Steps 2-5.
► **Interpreting Data** in Analyze Questions 2 and 3.
► **Inferring** in Conclude and Apply Questions 4, 5, 7, and 8.

TEACHING THE ACTIVITY
Alternate Materials: Use a clear, bright, showcase lamp like the one shown in the photo. If you can get photographic filter gels in the primary colors, use those instead of cellophane.

Troubleshooting: Be sure to try the activity ahead of time to be certain that the lamp is bright enough to give a full spectrum and to determine where the blue portion of the spectrum begins to disappear. Check the cellophane filters to see that they will absorb the expected parts of the spectrum. Use multiple layers to get the best effect.

► Verify that students have made the correct observations. After all groups have finished, leave the bulb turned on so that students can repeat any observations they feel are needed or experiment with different combinations of filters.

► The activity works best in a darkened room. The spectra can be seen to best effect under these conditions.

► When you find what thicknesses of cellophane give best results, you could mount these in ordinary slide mounts to reduce time spent on trial and error.

ANSWERS TO QUESTIONS
1. Answers will vary.
2. The drawing should show that the red end of the spectrum was brighter.
3.

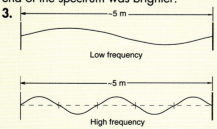

4. Blue light (with the highest frequency) requires the highest energy.

5. The short wavelength (high frequency) required the most energy.
6. The short wavelength had the higher frequency.
7. The violet end of the spectrum represents the highest energy and the shortest wavelength for visible light. Red has the longest wavelength for visible light.

PREPARATION

SECTION BACKGROUND

▶ Standard 60–75-watt incandescent bulbs can be replaced by 18-watt compact fluorescent bulbs. They use about 90 percent less electricity to produce the same amount of light.

1 MOTIVATE

▶ Classroom lights are usually fluorescent bulbs. Ask your students how these differ in appearance from those in lamps at home.

TYING TO PREVIOUS KNOWLEDGE: Ask students what a light bulb feels like after it has been on. It feels warm, because incandescent light is produced by heat.

OBJECTIVES AND SCIENCE WORDS: Have students review the objectives and science words to become familiar with this section.

2 TEACH

Key Concepts are highlighted.

CONCEPT DEVELOPMENT

▶ Emphasize that phosphors are fluorescent materials that give off visible light when struck with ultraviolet radiation. Make sure students do not confuse this with the element phosph*us*. They are not the same.

19-3 Battle of the Bulbs

New Science Words

incandescent light
fluorescent light

Objectives

▶ Explain how incandescent and fluorescent bulbs work.
▶ Analyze the advantages and disadvantages of different light sources.

Do Light Bulbs Make a Difference?

Are you using light from a light bulb to illuminate this page as you read it? Have you ever thought about what actually produces this light?

If you touch a light bulb after it has been on for a while, it may feel hot. If it feels hot, it is an incandescent light. **Incandescent light is produced by heat.** If you look into an incandescent light bulb, you will see a thin wire called a filament. It is usually made of the element tungsten. When you turn on the light, electricity flows through the filament. The filament heats up. When it gets hot, tungsten gives off visible light. **Over half of the energy given off by incandescent bulbs is heat.**

Fluorescent lighting is an alternative to incandescent lighting. A fluorescent bulb is filled with gas at a low pressure. The inner side of the bulb is coated with phosphors, fluorescent materials that give off visible light when they absorb ultraviolet light. When the electricity is turned on, electrons collide with the gas molecules to make them give off ultraviolet radiation. You can't see the ultraviolet light, but the phosphors absorb the ultraviolet radiation and glow to give off visible light that you can see.

A **fluorescent light** produces light without excessive loss of energy due to heat. These bulbs use as little as one-fifth the energy of ordinary incandescent bulbs. This

OPTIONS

Meeting Different Ability Levels

For Section 19-3, use the following **Teacher Resource Masters** depending upon individual students' needs.

◆ **Study Guide Master** for all students.
● **Reinforcement Master** for students of average and above average ability levels.
▲ **Enrichment Master** for above average students.

◆ STUDY GUIDE   80

energy difference can save you from $25 to $60 over the life of the fluorescent bulb.

The electricity used by a light bulb has been generated at a power plant. Whenever you turn on a light at home or at school, the electric company measures the amount of energy that the light bulb uses while it is on. The electric company then charges a fee for the energy that is used. By turning a light off when you leave a room, you are saving money as well as electricity.

About 20 percent of all electricity consumed in the United States is used for lighting. A great deal of this energy is wasted by lighting unoccupied rooms and using inefficient lighting sources. How efficient is the lighting in your home? You can find out.

SECTION REVIEW

1. Explain how light is produced in an ordinary incandescent bulb.
2. What are the advantages and disadvantages of using a fluorescent bulb instead of an incandescent bulb?

You Decide!

You are at the store to purchase a new study lamp. The fluorescent and incandescent lamps cost about the same, but the fluorescent bulb costs about ten times as much as the incandescent bulb. The fluorescent bulb is also guaranteed to last ten times longer than the incandescent bulb. Which would you buy? Explain your reasoning.

SCIENCE & SOCIETY

● **REINFORCEMENT 80**

REINFORCEMENT   Chapter 19
Battle of the Bulbs   Text Pages 498–499

1. Write a paragraph about lighting. Use the words listed below in your paragraph.
   light bulb   tungsten   phosphorus   visible light
   incandescent light   heat   coating   efficiency
   fluorescent light   filament   ultraviolet light
   Accept all reasonable paragraphs.

2. Observe incandescent and fluorescent lights in your home, in your school, and in a store or office.
   a. Where is each type of light more likely to be used? _Fluorescent lights are more likely to be used in stores and offices. Incandescent lights are used more extensively in homes._
   b. Compare and contrast the color and general appearance of fluorescent and incandescent lights. _In general, incandescent lights give a more pleasant and warmer color of light than do fluorescent lights. However, some fluorescent lights have special colors and are more like incandescent lights. Depending on the size of the bulb, both types of bulbs can give out plenty of light._
   c. Why do you think the types of lights were chosen for use in the places that you observed? _For home use, the color of the incandescent bulb is softer and has a warmer feel. Also, most home lamps are designed for incandescent bulbs. For business use, fluorescent lights are cooler and use far less energy. When a large number of fixtures in use, the cost of lighting a facility becomes a major consideration._

80   Copyright Glencoe Division of Macmillan/McGraw-Hill
                      Users of Merrill Physical Science have the publisher's permission to reproduce this page.

▲ **ENRICHMENT 80**

ENRICHMENT   Chapter 19
Battle of the Bulbs   Text Pages 498–499

SPECTRA OF LIGHT BULBS

Light bulbs vary in the method used to make light. They also vary in the kind of light they produce. The light emitted by a bulb can be separated into a spectrum by either a prism or a diffraction grating. You can observe light spectra by using a pocket spectroscope. Use a reference textbook or a classroom chart of common gas spectra to compare the observations described below.

1. Use the spectroscope to observe an incandescent bulb. Look through the slit to line up the light bulb directly. To view the spectrum, look at the scale of the spectroscope without moving the spectroscope. The numbers 4, 5, 6, and 7 should be visible at the bottom of the scale. Observe and draw the spectrum using colored pencils. Describe the spectrum.

   Red   Orange   Yellow   Green   Blue   Violet

   The spectrum of the incandescent bulb will be continuous, all of the colors are present.

2. Use the spectroscope to observe a fluorescent bulb. Observe and draw the spectrum, and describe the spectrum.

   Red   Yellow   Green   Blue   Violet

   The fluorescent bulb will give a bright line spectrum. Individual lines such as red, orange, yellow, green, and blue will be seen. Dark areas between the lines represent light waves that have been absorbed by the gas in the bulb.

3. Observe a sodium-vapor street lamp and a neon light if they are available. What do their spectra look like? _They are both bright line spectra._

4. Using a gas spectra chart, find out what gas is present in a fluorescent bulb. _mercury gas_

80   Copyright Glencoe Division of Macmillan/McGraw-Hill
                      Users of Merrill Physical Science have the publisher's permission to reproduce this page.

499

PREPARATION

SECTION BACKGROUND

▶ Light that falls on a rough surface strikes and is reflected in many directions. This phenomena is called diffuse reflection. You see most objects by diffuse reflection of light. Otherwise you would always see your own reflection in objects.

▶ The ratio of the speed of light in a vacuum to the speed of light in another material is the index of refraction. The higher this value is, the slower light travels through the other material.

▶ Did you know that you actually can see the sun a few minutes before the sun rises and after the sun falls below the horizon? Light entering Earth's atmosphere changes speeds due to the change in density, producing the index of refraction of 1.0003. The light rays from the sun are bent, causing the sun to appear higher in the sky than it is.

▶ Christian Huygens is usually considered the originator of the wave theory of light, which he published in 1690. Huygen's principle states that each wave front is actually composed of many smaller wave fronts or a new source of disturbance. Using this model, diffraction and interference are easier to understand.

PREPLANNING

▶ Gather the materials needed for Activity 19-2.

New Science Words

reflection
refraction
diffraction
diffraction grating

Objectives

▶ State and give an example of the law of reflection.
▶ Explain how refraction is used to separate the colors of the spectrum in white light.
▶ Describe how diffraction and interference patterns demonstrate the wave behavior of light.

Reflection

Just before you left for school this morning you might have glanced in a mirror one last time to make sure you looked okay. In order for you to see your reflection in the mirror, light had to reflect off you, hit the mirror, and be reflected off the mirror into your eye. **Reflection occurs when a wave strikes an object and bounces off.**

Reflection occurs with all types of waves: electromagnetic waves, sound waves, and water waves. Look at the water wave striking a barrier in Figure 19-14. The waves striking the barrier are called incident waves. The waves that bounce off the barrier are called reflected waves.

Notice that in Figure 19-14 a line is drawn perpendicular to the surface of the barrier. This line is called the *normal*. The angle formed by the incident wave and the normal is the angle of incidence, labeled *i*. The angle formed by the reflected wave and the normal is the angle of reflection, labeled *r*. Any reflected light, whether it is reflected from a mirror, a piece of foil, or the moon, follows the law of reflection. The law of reflection states that the angle of incidence is equal to the angle of reflection.

If you took a smooth piece of aluminum foil and looked into it, you would see a slightly distorted image of yourself. What if you crumpled up the foil and then unfolded it again? What would you see? The creases in the foil have created an uneven surface. Could you draw lines normal to every surface? These lines would go in many different

Figure 19-13. You can't see a clear image reflected from an uneven surface such as this one.

EcoTip

Turn out lights in your home when they are not needed. Exchange 100 watt bulbs with 60 watt bulbs to save energy.

②

OPTIONS

Meeting Different Ability Levels

For Section 19-4, use the following **Teacher Resource Masters** depending upon individual student' needs.

◆ **Study Guide Master** for all students.

● **Reinforcement Master** for students of average and above average ability levels.

▲ **Enrichment Master** for above average students.

Additional Teacher Resource Package masters are listed in the OPTIONS box throughout the section. The additional masters are appropriate for all students.

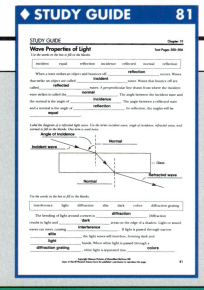

◆ **STUDY GUIDE** 81

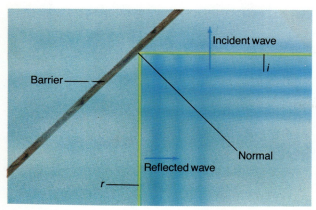

Barrier

Incident wave

i

Normal

Reflected wave

r

Figure 19-14. The water waves striking the barrier are incident waves and those bouncing off are reflected waves.

directions. You can't see an image of yourself because the reflected light, like the normal lines, is also scattered in different directions. Smooth surfaces reflect light in one direction, but rough surfaces scatter light in many directions.

Refraction

Stick your finger at an angle halfway into a glass of water and look at it through the side of the glass. Do you notice anything bizarre? Your finger appears to be bent or even split into two pieces once it enters the water. This happens because light waves bend when they move from air to water. They bend because the speed of light changes when light waves move from one medium to another.

❶ **Refraction is the bending of waves caused by a change in their speed. The amount of bending that occurs depends on the speed of light in both materials.** The greater the difference between the speeds of light in two mediums, the more the light is bent as it passes at an angle from one medium to another. When light is passing into a material that will slow it down, the light is refracted (bent) toward an imaginary line drawn perpendicular to the surface of the medium. This imaginary line is called the normal. When light passes into a material in which light travels faster, it will be refracted (bent) away from the normal.

The amount of refraction also depends on the wavelength of the light. In the visible spectrum, the wavelengths of light vary from the longer red waves to

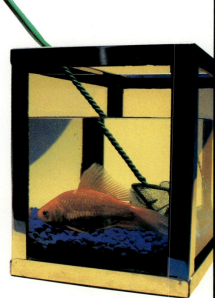

Figure 19-15. The ruler looks bent because of the refraction of the light waves as they change speed when they pass from the water to the air.

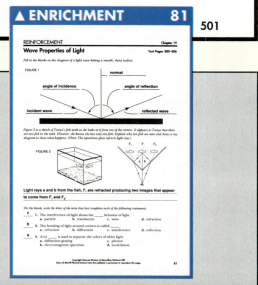

● **REINFORCEMENT 81**

▲ **ENRICHMENT 81**

501

ENRICHMENT   Chapter 19

Wave Properties of Light   Text Pages 500–506

LIGHT THEORY AND EVERYDAY PHENOMENA

Use the library to find information to explain the following phenomena.

1. What is a rainbow?   A rainbow forms when the sun is behind you and there are
water droplets in the air in front of you. When sunlight strikes the water droplets,
the light is bent, or refracted, to form the colors of the spectrum. The refracted
light is reflected by the water droplets. We see a rainbow when the angle of
reflected rays with the sun's rays is between 40°24' and 42°18'. Each color of the
rainbow is a certain angle in this range. Violet will be at the bottom of the band of
colors since it is refracted the most. Red will be at the top since it is refracted the
least.

2. Why are sunrises and sunsets sometimes red?   When the sun is low in the sky, light rays
pass through more atmosphere, dust particles, and water droplets than when the
sun is high in the sky. Short wavelengths of light such as blue are scattered
more than the longer wavelengths of light such as red and orange. As a result,
more of the orange and red reach us causing the sky to appear red.

3. What causes eyes to be blue and brown?   When a baby is born, its eyes are blue. Actually a baby's eyes do not have any color. The blue is due to the scattering of
light. When white light enters the iris, muscle tissue scatters it. The reds pass
through, but the scattered blue light is reflected. This makes the baby's eyes
appear blue. As the baby gets older, brown pigment forms on the back part of
the iris. If this pigment is dark and heavy, the person has brown eyes; the scattered blue light is not apparent. When the layer of pigment is lighter, the color
that results is a mixture of brown and the scattered blue. Since the amount of
pigment varies from person to person, eye color varies greatly.

4. Look at the side of a compact disc that is read by the laser during playing. What do you see?
colored bands of light

5. Explain your observation.   The compact disc is etched with many pits. The pits act
much like diffraction gratings and diffracted light waves are reflected.

Copyright Glencoe Division of Macmillan/McGraw-Hill
Users of Merrill Physical Science have the publisher's permission to reproduce this page.   81

REINFORCEMENT   Chapter 19

Wave Properties of Light   Text Pages 500–506

Fill in the blanks in this diagram of a light wave hitting a smooth, shiny surface.

FIGURE 1

normal

angle of incidence   angle of reflection

incident wave   reflected wave

Figure 2 is a sketch of Tanya's fish tank as she looks at it from one of the corners. It appears to Tanya that there are two fish in the tank. However, she knows she has only one fish. Explain why two fish are seen and draw a ray diagram to show what happens. (Hint: The aquarium glass refracts light rays.)

FIGURE 2

F_i F F_s

**Light rays a and b from the fish, F, are refracted producing two images that appear
to come from F_i and F_s**

On the blank, write the letter of the term that best completes each of the following statements.

__c__ 1. The interference of light shows the _____ behavior of light.
        a. particle   b. translucent   c. wave   d. refraction

__b__ 2. The bending of light around corners is called _____.
        a. refraction   b. diffraction   c. interference   d. reflection

__a__ 3. A(n) _____ is used to separate the colors of white light.
        a. diffraction grating   c. photon
        b. electromagnetic spectrum   d. modulation

Copyright Glencoe Division of Macmillan/McGraw-Hill
Users of Merrill Physical Science have the publisher's permission to reproduce this page.   81

1 MOTIVATE

▶ Ask students if they have ever seen a mirage, or wavering images above hot ground. What is it? Sometimes images of nearby objects appear inverted. A mirage occurs when a layer of hot air lies right above the ground. Light can move through hot air faster than through the colder air above. This causes a bending of light rays, and refracted images of objects can be seen.

▶ Shine a light on a compact disc and look at the colors reflected. Where does the color come from? The different wavelengths and colors of white light are separated by diffraction in the grooves in the disc.

REVEALING MISCONCEPTIONS

▶ Many people think that seeing a mirage on an extremely hot day is caused by mental confusion resulting from the heat. In most cases, there is a valid scientific explanation for it. See the explanation in the Motivate section.

TYING TO PREVIOUS KNOWLEDGE:

Ask students how the underwater portions of their bodies look when they are in a swimming pool. They probably will say that they look shorter and distorted. This is because the speed of light in water is different than the speed of light in air, causing light to refract and distort the image.

OBJECTIVES AND SCIENCE WORDS:

Have students review the objectives and science words to become familiar with this section.

2 TEACH

Key Concepts are highlighted.

CONCEPT DEVELOPMENT

▶ When discussing reflection, give the students some foil and mirrors and ask them to describe how their images differ in each one. Discuss the explanation given in the text.

Cooperative Learning: Use the Paired Partners strategy. Place a coin in the bottom of a cup. Have one person hold the cup at about the chest level of the other person. Move the cup until the coin is just hidden from view from the partner. Slowly pour water into the cup—the coin will become visible. Ask students for an explanation. The light reflected from the coin bends away from the normal as it emerges from the water. Because the ray of light reaching your eye is lowered, the image of the coin appears higher in the water than the coin is.

▶ **Demonstration:** Show that electromagnetic waves, sound waves, and water waves can be diffracted. Set up a "pond" in a large pan. Put a barrier in the pan. Drop a stone in the pan and watch how the waves bend around the barrier. If you have a wave generator, use it instead.

▶ To help students remember the colors of the spectrum from longest to shortest wavelength, use the fictitious character ROY G. BIV as a memory device. The name corresponds to the colors of the rainbow: red, orange, yellow, green, blue, indigo, violet.

STUDENT TEXT QUESTION

▶ Page 502, paragraph 2: **Have you ever noticed that the reddish colors are always on top and the bluish colors are always on the bottom of a rainbow?** *Red light is always at the top of a rainbow because it has a longer wavelength and refracts the least, violet refracts the most.*

a   b

Figure 19-16. A prism is an angular transparent object (a). White light is refracted into the colors of the visible spectrum as it passes through a prism (b).

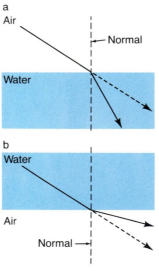

Figure 19-17. Light slows down and refracts toward the normal as it passes into a more dense medium (a), and light speeds up and bends away from the normal as it passes into a less dense medium (b).

the shorter violet waves. Figure 19-16 shows what happens when white light passes through a prism. The triangular prism refracts the light twice, once when it enters the prism and again when it leaves the prism and reenters the air. Because the shorter wavelengths of light are refracted more than the longer wavelengths, violet light is bent the most. Which color of light would you expect to bend the least? As a result of this varied refraction, the different colors are separated as they emerge from the prism.

Does the light leaving a prism remind you of a rainbow? If the sun shines during a rain shower, you might see a rainbow. Like prisms, rain droplets also refract light. The refraction of the different wavelengths can cause white light from the sun to separate into the individual colors of the visible light spectrum. Isaac Newton recognized that white light actually includes all of the seven colors of the rainbow. In order of decreasing wavelength, the colors you should see in the rainbow are red, orange, yellow, green, blue, indigo, and violet—the same order as the colors of the electromagnetic spectrum. Have you noticed that the reddish colors are always on top and the bluish colors are always on the bottom of a rainbow? Can you explain why this is so?

Diffraction and Interference

Have you heard bells or music played by vendors selling ice cream as they drive their trucks through your neighborhood? Or maybe you have heard cars drive by your home with blasting stereos. You can hear these sounds even when buildings or hills separate you from

OPTIONS

INQUIRY QUESTIONS

▶ **What makes stars twinkle?** *Light traveling through the atmosphere is refracted by varying amounts because the density and composition of the atmosphere along its path varies. Because some light from a star is refracted away from our line of sight because of the motion of various regions of the atmosphere that differ in density and composition, the star appears to turn on and off, that is, to twinkle.*

▶ **List the colors of visible light in order of most to least diffraction.** *violet, indigo, blue, green, yellow, orange, red*

▶ **If you walked by an open door, and music was playing inside the room, you would hear the music before you reached the doorway. How is this possible?** *Sound waves diffract, or bend around barriers. The sound waves of the music bend outward as they pass through the door.*

Figure 19-18. Water waves diffract around a barrier.

the sound. This happens because sound waves can bend around corners to reach you. **Diffraction is the bending of waves around a barrier.** ➌ In the 1600s, an Italian physicist, Francesco Grimaldi, observed light and dark areas on the edge of a shadow. If you observe the shadow formed when light passes through an open door, you'll notice no clearly defined boundary between light and dark. Instead, you will see a gradual transition. Grimaldi explained this phenomenon by suggesting that light could be bent around the edges of barriers.

Electromagnetic waves, sound waves, and water waves can all be diffracted. You can see water waves bend around you as you swim. The pattern of the waves changes as the waves are diffracted. Diffraction is important in the transfer of radio waves. Longer wavelengths, such as those used by AM radio stations, are easier to diffract than short FM waves. That is why AM reception is often better than FM reception around tall buildings and hills.

What waves can be diffracted?

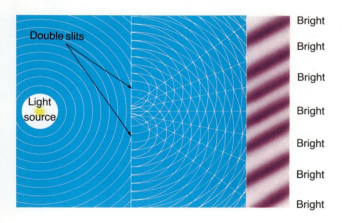

Double slits
Light source
Bright
Bright
Bright
Bright
Bright
Bright
Bright

Figure 19-19. Wave interference demonstrates how light behaves like waves.

▶Pass diffraction gratings around. Explain that there are many slits to let light pass through. Look through one while looking at a light source—what do you see? You see the colors of the spectrum because the different wavelengths of light are separated by diffraction.

CROSS CURRICULUM

▶**Language Arts:** Have students write a fictitious, creative short story explaining why the sky is blue. Then have them research and write the factual reason that the sky appears blue.

CHECK FOR UNDERSTANDING

Use the Mini Quiz to check for understanding.

MINI QUIZ

Use the Mini Quiz to check students' recall of chapter content.

➊ _____ occurs when waves bend due to a change in their speed. *Refraction*

➋ A line drawn perpendicular to the surface of the barrier is the _____ . *normal*

➌ _____ is the bending of waves around a barrier. *Diffraction*

➍ _____ is caused when light waves overlap each other. *Wave interference*

INQUIRY QUESTIONS

▶In the situation described above, which sounds would you expect to hear first, low frequency or high frequency? *Explain your reasoning. You would hear the low frequency sounds first because they have longer wavelengths, therefore, they are easier to diffract than the shorter wavelengths of high frequency sounds*

PROGRAM RESOURCES

From the **Teacher Resource Package** use:
Transparency Masters, pages 77-78, Wave Interference.
Use **Color Transparency,** number 39, Wave Interference.

► Trace the history of attempts to produce 3-D images in books, at the movies, and on TV.

► For more information on 3-D images, see Rennie, John. "Move Over, Mr. Spock." *Scientific American.* July 1990, pages 89-92.

Think Critically: A three-dimensional display would be advantageous in situations such as air traffic control, automobile design, architecture, etc.

RETEACH

Give each pair of students a cup of water and a round washer. Drop the washer in the cup. Try to put a pen or pencil through the hole in the washer. Have students explain why it is difficult to hit the hole directly. The light reflected from the washer bends away from the normal as it emerges from the water. Because the light ray that reaches your eye is lowered, the image of the washer appears higher in the water than the coin actually is.

EXTENSION

For students who have mastered this section, use the **Reinforcement** and **Enrichment** masters or other OPTIONS provided.

TECHNOLOGY

Holograms—The Key to 3-D

A hologram is a vivid three-dimensional image that appears to float in space. As you walk around a hologram you see the image from a slightly different angle.

Holograms are produced by illuminating the object you wish to make an image of with light from a laser. Laser light reflected from the object shines on photographic film simultaneously with light from a second laser of the same wavelength. The pattern created on the photographic film produces a hologram image when laser light shines through it.

A hologram conveys more information to your eye than a conventional two-dimensional photograph by controlling both the intensity and direction of the light that departs from the image. As a result, these vivid three-dimensional objects are very difficult to copy. For this reason, holographic images are used on credit cards and on the labels of some clothing to help prevent counterfeiting. Scientists are working on ways of displaying computer information on a three-dimensional screen. How would you like to play video games in 3-D?

Think Critically: What are some situations where a three-dimensional image or display would be a significant advantage over a two-dimensional image?

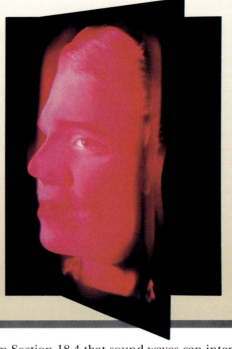

Recall from Section 18-4 that sound waves can interfere with each other to form constructive and destructive interference. In the early 1800s, Thomas Young, an English scientist, expanded the diffraction theory Grimaldi had developed. In a famous experiment, he passed light of a uniform wavelength through a narrow slit. The new diffraction pattern of the light waves then passed through a barrier with two slits. You can see the results, wave interference, in Figure 19-19. The wave crests are shown by the semicircles. The light from these slits was projected on a screen. Young observed light bands

504   LIGHT

OPTIONS

INQUIRY QUESTIONS

► Imagine you are walking down a narrow hallway in your school onto which classroom doors are opened. You can hear murmurs and voices in each room as you pass, but you can also hear the teacher in the room at the end of the hall lecturing in a loud voice. Describe the changes in sound you expect to hear as you approach the end of the hall. *The students should answer that they expect to hear alternating areas of clear sound and areas of silence or almost no sound due to interference of the sound waves.*

PROGRAM RESOURCES

From the **Teacher Resource Package** use: **Critical Thinking/Problem Solving,** page 25, Communications Innovations.

where two crests or two troughs combined, and dark areas where a crest and a trough crossed paths. This experiment shows how light behaves as a wave. Only waves have interference; particles do not.

You know that one way to separate colors of white light is by refraction in a prism. ==Colors can also be separated by interference using many slits. A **diffraction grating** is a piece of glass or plastic made up of many parallel slits.== Diffraction gratings commonly have as many as 12 000 slits per centimeter. When white light shines through a diffraction grating, the colors are separated by the interference pattern. Reflective materials can be ruled with closely spaced grooves to produce diffraction patterns. For example, shiny bumper stickers sometimes diffract light into a wide array of colors. You can also see the dazzling results of simple diffraction gratings by looking at the reflection of light provided from the grooves in a compact disc.

Recall that throughout this chapter, we have referred to light as both waves and particles. That is because, as you have read in this lesson, light demonstrates properties of both waves and particles. Do you recall the wave properties of light? What properties of light support the particle theory?

Figure 19-20. Compact discs can produce diffraction patterns.

☑ **Observing and Inferring**

Skill Builder

Imagine you are at the ocean shore and see waves moving toward you from behind a cliff. Waves are leaving the cliff at a slightly different angle than that of their approach. What would you infer is happening? If you need help, refer to Observing and Inferring in the **Skill Handbook** on page 678.

ENRICHMENT

▶ Have students investigate and describe the phenomena that causes the spectrum of colors to be seen in soap bubbles.

---

3 CLOSE

▶ Obtain a medium-sized cardboard box and cut off the top flaps and one side of the box. Attach a mirror to one end of the box and tape a maze (from a coloring book) to the bottom. Have several students try to draw through the maze while looking only at the reflection of the maze in the mirror. Discuss why this is difficult using incident and reflected light paths.

▶ Ask questions 1-3 and the **Apply** Question in the Section Review

STUDENT TEXT QUESTIONS

▶ Page 505, paragraph 2: **Do you recall the wave properties of light?** *reflection, refraction, diffraction, interference*

▶ Page 505, paragraph 2: **What properties of light support the particle theory?** *evidence of the existence of photons and measurements of their momentum; cell damage caused by high energy radiation*

SECTION REVIEW ANSWERS

1. The angle of incidence equals the angle of reflection.

2. Toward; light moves more slowly in glass.

3. A prism refracts light twice. The shortest wavelengths are refracted the most and the longest wavelengths are refracted the least.

4. Apply: Light spreads out as it passes through a diffraction grating; this behavior is characteristic of waves, not particles.

Skill Builder

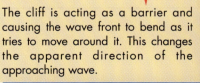

The cliff is acting as a barrier and causing the wave front to bend as it tries to move around it. This changes the apparent direction of the approaching wave.

ACTIVITY 19-2
40 minutes

OBJECTIVE: Predict how light reflects and refracts.

PROCESS SKILLS applied in this activity:
▶ **Observing** in Analyze Question 1.
▶ **Experimenting** in Analyze Question 2.
▶ **Formulating Models** in Conclude and Apply Question 3.
▶ **Predicting** in Conclude and Apply Question 4.

👥 COOPERATIVE LEARNING
Students can work in teams of not more than three. Up to four teams can share the same light source.

TEACHING THE ACTIVITY
Troubleshooting: The light should be taped down so it can't be removed during the experiment.
▶ Use a clear plastic box of rectangular shape. Size: 5 to 8 cm across and at least 3 cm deep. A clear glass baking dish can be used if you can't find a plastic box. Boxes with curved surfaces can be used for follow-up.
▶ The pencil **must** stand straight up. Use the edge of the box to check.
▶ Measurement of angles between rays and normals is not necessary for observation and description of the general effect.

PROGRAM RESOURCES
From the **Teacher Resource Package** use:
Activity Worksheets, pages 152-153, Activity 19-2: Refraction and Reflection.

ACTIVITY 19-2
Refraction and Reflection

Problem: *How do light rays refract and reflect?*

Materials
- light source
- pencil
- plastic box
- water
- notebook paper
- clay

Procedure
1. Fill the plastic box with water and place it on a sheet of notebook paper.
2. Outline the box on the paper.
3. Stand the pencil on end in the clay and place it on the paper in front of the box.
4. Place the lamp in an upright position near the paper and turn it on.
5. Adjust the position of the paper and the pencil so the pencil's shadow on the paper goes completely through the box.
6. Draw lines on the shadow where it enters and leaves the box. Draw a line on the shadow that reflects from the surface of the box.
7. Move the box. Connect the lines to show the shadow through the box.

Analyze
1. Draw a reference line (normal) at right angles to the box from the point where the shadow touches its surface. As the shadow enters the box, does it refract toward the reference line or away from it? What happens when the shadow leaves the other side of the box?
2. Alter the xperiment by changing the angle between the reference line and the shadow. What happens to the reflected and refracted shadows?

Conclude and Apply
3. Compare the angles of reflection and refraction for light striking the flat surface of water.
4. Would the angles of reflection or refraction change in Question 3 if the surface of the water was curved? Explain your answer.

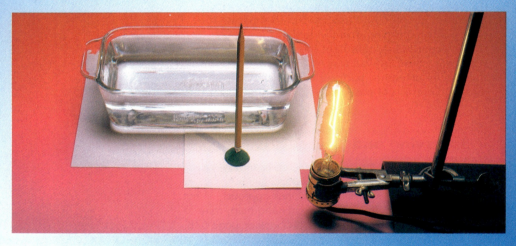

ANSWERS TO QUESTIONS
1. The shadow refracts toward the reference line when it enters the box and refracts away when it leaves.
2. The angles of the refracted and reflected rays increase when the angle of the incoming shadow is increased. (Students might also notice that the intensity of the reflected ray increases as the incident angle increases.)

3. It is always true that light rays *refract* to make smaller angles inside water than outside, but rays always *reflect* with the same angle as the incoming ray.
4. The statement is true for curved surfaces. For groups of rays the images are distorted with curved surfaces.

SUMMARY

19-1: Electromagnetic Radiation

1. Electromagnetic waves differ from other types of waves because they do not need a medium to transfer energy.

2. Electromagnetic waves are arranged on the electromagnetic spectrum in order of decreasing wavelengths.

3. Radio waves and microwaves are used in communications. Infrared radiation is used to detect tumors. Visible light is produced by light bulbs for illumination. Ultraviolet radiation causes fluorescent bulbs to glow. X rays are used for medical diagnosis. Gamma rays can be used to destroy cancer cells.

19-2: Light and Color

1. You can't see through opaque materials. You can see clearly through transparent materials. You can't see clearly through translucent materials.

2. You see color when light is reflected off objects and into your eye. Inside your eyes color cones respond to certain wavelengths.

3. Colored light can be made by mixing the three primary colors of light. Pigment colors can be made by mixing the three primary pigments.

19-3: Science and Society: Battle of the Bulbs

1. Incandescent bulbs produce light by heat. Fluorescent bulbs give off light when ultraviolet radiation produced inside the bulb causes a fluorescent coating inside the bulb to glow.

2. Although expensive to purchase, fluorescent bulbs waste less energy, last longer, and cost much less to use than incandescent bulbs.

19-4: Wave Properties of Light

1. The law of reflection states that the angle of incidence is equal to the angle of reflection.

2. White light can be separated into the colors of the visible spectrum because each wavelength refracts at a different angle as it passes into a medium.

3. Diffraction and interference patterns demonstrate wave patterns of light by showing that the waves bend around a barrier, and that they have crests and troughs.

KEY SCIENCE WORDS

a. **diffraction**
b. **diffraction grating**
c. **electromagnetic spectrum**
d. **fluorescent light**
e. **gamma rays**
f. **incandescent light**
g. **infrared radiation**
h. **microwaves**
i. **modulation**
j. **opaque materials**
k. **photons**
l. **radiation**
m. **radio waves**
n. **reflection**
o. **refraction**
p. **translucent materials**
q. **transparent materials**
s. **visible radiation**
t. **X rays**

UNDERSTANDING VOCABULARY

Match each phrase with the correct term from the list of Key Science Words.

1. energy transfer by electromagnetic waves
2. bundles of radiation with no mass
3. electromagnetic radiation that is felt as heat
4. objects that can't be seen through
5. light produced by heat
6. occurs when a wave strikes an object and then bounces off
7. the bending of waves around a barrier
8. contains many parallel slits that can separate white light into colors
9. highest frequency electromagnetic waves
10. radio waves with the greatest energy

SUMMARY

Have the students read the summary statements to review the major concepts of the chapter.

UNDERSTANDING VOCABULARY

1. l
2. k
3. g
4. j
5. f
6. n
7. a
8. b
9. e
10. h

OPTIONS

ASSESSMENT

To assess student understanding of material in this chapter, use the resources listed.

👥 COOPERATIVE LEARNING

Consider using cooperative learning in the THINK AND WRITE CRITICALLY, APPLY, and MORE SKILL BUILDERS sections of the Chapter Review.

PROGRAM RESOURCES

From the **Teacher Resource Package** use:
Chapter Review, pages 126 to 129.
Chapter and Unit Tests, pages 41 to 42, Chapter Test.

CHAPTER
REVIEW

CHECKING CONCEPTS

1. d		**6.** b
2. a		**7.** c
3. a		**8.** d
4. a		**9.** a
5. b		**10.** c

UNDERSTANDING CONCEPTS

11. black
12. blue
13. heat
14. equal to
15. increases

THINK AND WRITE CRITICALLY

16. Sound waves can be converted to electrical signals that correspond to the sound's characteristic patterns. These electrical signals can then be used to modulate or vary either the amplitude or frequency of a radio wave that correspond to the sound's characteristic patterns. This process is utilized in radio and television transmissions, cellular telephones, and cordless telephones.

17. Light color is determined by the wavelength of light transmitted while pigment color is determined by the color of light reflected.

18. Light reflects off a white wall or a mirror because of the law of reflection. Both the wall and mirror reflect all frequencies of light. Light reflected off a wall is scattered because the surface is rough and light reflected off a mirror is not scattered and comes off in parallel rays.

19. Rainbows are produced when white light from the sun passes through large droplets of water suspended in the atmosphere after a heavy rain. The water droplets act like prisms, refracting light of different wavelengths and separating colors into the visible spectrum.

20. Light behaves as a particle because it has momentum. Albert Einstein postulated that light is transmitted as tiny packets of energy called photons. Light can also be diffracted to

---

CHAPTER
REVIEW

CHECKING CONCEPTS

Choose the word or phrase that completes the sentence.

1. Electromagnetic waves are different from other types of waves in that they do not _____.
   a. have amplitude   c. transfer energy
   b. have frequency   d. need a medium

2. When radiation passes through matter, it ____.
   a. slows down
   b. speeds up
   c. travels at 300 000 km/sec
   d. stops

3. A contact lens is _____.
   a. transparent   c. opaque
   b. translucent   d. all of these

4. Electromagnetic waves with the longest wavelengths are _____.
   a. radio waves   c. X rays
   b. visible light   d. gamma rays

5. The process of changing the frequency or amplitude of radio waves in order to send a signal is _____.
   a. diffraction   c. reflection
   b. modulation   d. refraction

6. When food molecules absorb microwaves, they vibrate faster and their _____.
   a. kinetic energy decreases
   b. kinetic energy increases
   c. temperature decreases
   d. temperature remains constant

7. Your body gives off _____.
   a. radio waves   c. infrared radiation
   b. visible light   d. ultraviolet radiation

8. Fluorescence occurs when a material glows as it absorbs _____.
   a. microwaves   c. infrared radiation
   b. gamma rays   d. ultraviolet radiation

9. X rays are best absorbed by _____.
   a. bone   c. muscle
   b. hair   d. skin

10. Objects that partially scatter light that passes through them are called _____.
    a. reflective   c. translucent
    b. opaque   d. transparent

UNDERSTANDING CONCEPTS

Complete each sentence.

11. An object that absorbs all colors of light appears _____.
12. An _____ filter transmits blue light.
13. Fluorescent lights are more efficient than incandescent lights because they lose less energy as _____.
14. The angle of incidence of a wave is _____ its angle of reflection.
15. When light travels into a medium in which its speed _____, it will be bent from the normal.

THINK AND WRITE CRITICALLY

16. Explain how sound waves are converted to radio waves. Give some examples of uses of this process.
17. What is the difference between light color and pigment color?

---

show interference patterns. This suggests that light behaves as a wave. Light's wave-like behavior was studied by Francesco Grimaldi and Thomas Young.

APPLY

21. Blue light has a higher frequency than red light, and therefore its particles carry more energy. The hotter an object is, the more energy it gives off.

22. A blue filter will transmit the blue light reflected from the shirt, and the shirt will appear blue. Because the red and green filters each absorb blue light, blue light reflected from the shirt will be absorbed by either filter, and the shirt will appear black.

23. blue filter: blue cones; red filter: red cones; green filter: none

24. Violet slows down the most since it is bent the most by a prism and the greater the difference in the speed of light in two different media, the more it is refracted.

18. How is the reflection of light off a white wall similar to the reflection of light off a mirror? How is it different?
19. Explain how a rainbow is produced.
20. Describe the evidence that light behaves both as a wave and a particle and note the scientists who studied both behaviors.

APPLY

21. Heated objects often give off light of a particular color. Explain why an object that glows blue is hotter than one that glows red.
22. How would a blue shirt appear if a blue filter were placed in front of it? A red filter? A green filter?
23. What color cones in your eye would transmit signals to your brain as you looked at the purple shirt through each of the three filters described in Question 22?
24. Which color of visible light slows down the most when it passes through a prism? Explain.
25. Explain why you can hear a fire engine coming around a street corner but cannot see it.

MORE SKILL BUILDERS

If you need help, refer to the Skill Handbook.

1. **Sequencing:** List the types of radiation in the electromagnetic spectrum in order of decreasing penetrating power. Use Figure 19-2, the electromagnetic spectrum, as a reference.
2. **Making and Using Tables:** Construct a table to show the applications of each type of electromagnetic wave. Which type would an electronics engineer be most interested in? A doctor?
3. **Observing and Inferring:** Most mammals, such as dogs and cats, can't see colors. Infer how a cat's eye might be different from your eye.

4. **Concept Mapping:** Use the blank concept map below to show the five steps in the production of fluorescent light.

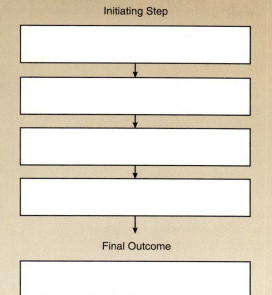

Initiating Step

Final Outcome

5. **Outlining:** Make an outline of Section 19-1. Be sure to include the types of energy on the electromagnetic spectrum and give one example of how each type of energy is used.

PROJECTS

1. Make a scrapbook of newspaper and magazine articles describing the dangers of ultraviolet radiation and the damage they cause to Earth's ozone layer. Write a short summary of each article.
2. Make a poster to show how the three primary pigments are combined to produce common colors such as blue, red, yellow, green, purple, brown, and black.

25. Waves with greater wavelengths are diffracted more easily than waves with shorter wavelengths. Sound has a much longer wavelength than light. Sound is therefore bent much more easily around a street corner than light.

MORE SKILL BUILDERS

1. **Sequencing:** Penetrating power is directly related to wave energy which is, in turn, directly related to wave frequency. Therefore, the order of decreasing penetrating power of electromagnetic waves is the same as the order of decreasing frequency: gamma rays, X rays, ultraviolet radiation, visible light, infrared radiation, microwaves, radio waves.
2. **Making and Using Tables:** A possible table is shown below, left. An electronics engineer would be most interested in radio waves, microwaves, and visible light, while a doctor would be more interested in infrared radiation, X rays, or gamma rays.
3. **Observing and Inferring:** The best inference would be that a cat's eye does not have the cone nerve cells that are in the human eye.
4. **Concept Mapping:** Possible answer is shown below.
5. **Outlining:** This outline will be similar to the one on TE page 491. Only one example of each type of energy should be listed.

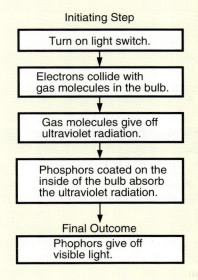

Initiating Step

Turn on light switch.

Electrons collide with gas molecules in the bulb.

Gas molecules give off ultraviolet radiation.

Phosphors coated on the inside of the bulb absorb the ultraviolet radiation.

Final Outcome

Phophors give off visible light.

Type of Radiation	Applications
Radio waves	Radio and TV transmissions, cordless telephones
Microwaves	Cooking, communication
Infrared radiation	Thermograms to detect tumors, warm food
Visible light	Solar-powered calculators, etc.
Ultraviolet radiation	Fluorescent lights, to kill germs, helps skin make Vitamin D
X rays	Medical diagnoses, airport security
Gamma rays	Cancer treatment

20 Mirrors and Lenses

CHAPTER SECTION	OBJECTIVES	ACTIVITIES
20-1 The Optics of Mirrors (2 days)	1. **Explain** how an image is formed in two types of mirrors. 2. **Identify** examples and uses of plane, concave, and convex mirrors.	**Activity 20-1:** *Reflections of Reflections,* p. 517
20-2 The Optics of Lenses (2 days)	1. **Describe** the types of images formed in convex and concave lenses. 2. **Cite examples** of how these lenses are used. 3. **Explain** how lenses are used to correct vision.	**MINI-Lab:** *Can lenses be made of liquids?* p. 520
20-3 Optical Instruments (2 days)	1. **Compare** refracting and reflecting telescopes. 2. **Explain** how a camera creates an image.	**MINI-Lab:** *What do telescopes see?* p. 523
20-4 The Hubble Space Telescope Science & Society (1 day)	1. **Describe** the development and goals of the Hubble Space Telescope. 2. **Evaluate** the need for a space telescope.	
20-5 Applications of Light (2 days)	1. **Describe** polarized light and the uses of polarizing lenses. 2. **Explain** how a laser produces coherent light and how it differs from incoherent light. 3. **Apply** the concept of total internal reflection to the uses of optical fibers.	**Activity 20-2:** *Polarized Light,* p. 534
Chapter Review		

ACTIVITY MATERIALS

FIND OUT	ACTIVITIES		MINI-LABS	
Page 511 metal spoons	**20-1 Reflections of Reflections, p. 517** 2 plane mirrors cellophane tape masking tape protractor paper clip light (with base)	**20-2 Polarized Light, p. 534** 2 polarizing filters light source objects with flat, hard surfaces	**Can lenses be made of liquids? p. 520** plastic bowl plastic wrap small objects	**What do telescopes see? p. 523** 2 pieces of aluminum foil needle light bulb

CHAPTER FEATURES	TEACHER RESOURCE PACKAGE	OTHER RESOURCES
Problem Solving: *Mirrors on the New Car,* p. 516 **Skill Builder:** *Recognizing Cause and Effect,* p. 516	**Ability Level Worksheets** ◆ **Study Guide,** p. 82 ● **Reinforcement,** p. 82 ▲ **Enrichment,** p. 82 **Activity Worksheet,** pp. 158, 159 **Concept Mapping,** pp. 45, 46 **Transparency Masters,** pp. 79, 80	**Color Transparency 40,** Optics of Concave Mirrors **Lab Manual 41,** Reflection of Light **Lab Manual 42,** Magnifying Power
Skill Builder: *Concept Mapping,* p. 521	**Ability Level Worksheets** ◆ **Study Guide,** p. 83 ● **Reinforcement,** p. 83 ▲ **Enrichment,** p. 83 **MINI-Lab Worksheet,** p. 164 **Science and Society,** p. 24 **Transparency Masters,** pp. 81, 82	**Color Transparency 41,** Vision Corrections
Skill Builder: *Hypothesizing,* p. 525	**Ability Level Worksheets** ◆ **Study Guide,** p. 84 ● **Reinforcement,** p. 84 ▲ **Enrichment,** p. 84 **MINI-Lab Worksheet,** p. 165 **Cross-Curricular Connections,** p. 26 **Critical Thinking/Problem Solving,** p. 26	
You Decide! p. 527	**Ability Level Worksheets** ◆ **Study Guide,** p. 85 ● **Reinforcement,** p. 85 ▲ **Enrichment,** p. 85	
Technology: *The Light Scalpel,* p. 533 **Skill Builder:** *Sequencing,* p. 533	**Ability Level Worksheets** ◆ **Study Guide,** p. 86 ● **Reinforcement,** p. 86 ▲ **Enrichment,** p. 86 **Activity Worksheet,** pp. 160, 161 **Technology,** pp. 17, 18	
Summary Think & Write Critically Key Science Words Apply Understanding Vocabulary More Skill Builders Checking Concepts Projects Understanding Concepts	**Chapter Review,** pp. 43, 44 **Chapter Test,** pp. 130-133 **Unit Test,** pp. 134, 135	**Chapter Review Software** **Test Bank**

◆ **Basic**   ● **Average**   ▲ **Advanced**

ADDITIONAL MATERIALS

SOFTWARE	AUDIOVISUAL	BOOKS/MAGAZINES
Lenses-Optics, Albion. *Mirrors and Lenses,* Microphys. *Special Senses—The Eye,* ComPress. *Optics on Computer: Physical Science Simulations,* Focus. *Optics and Light Democomp Series,* Focus.	*Light and Lenses,* film, Journal Films, Inc. *Mr. Wizard's World: Light Reflection, Light Refraction, Light Instruments,* Macmillan/McGraw-Hill School Division.	Middleton, Thomas H. *Light Refractions.* Old Lyme, CT: Verbatim Books, 1976. Safford, Edward L. *The Fiberglass and Laser Handbook.* Blue Ridge Summit, PA: Tab Books, 1982. Texereau, Jean. *How to Make a Telescope.* Richmond, VA: Willmann-Bell, 1984.

THEME DEVELOPMENT: This chapter discusses the principles and applications of geometric optics. Systems and interactions are a major theme of this chapter. Light interacts with mirrors and lenses to produce images. Mirrors and lenses allow us to take pictures, view distant stars and planets, and perform surgery using lasers and fiber optics.

CHAPTER OVERVIEW

▶ **Section 20-1:** This section introduces the optics of plane, concave, and convex mirrors. Methods of using the focal point to find virtual and real images from reflections are illustrated.

▶ **Section 20-2:** Concave and convex lenses are discussed, as well as how they affect vision.

▶ **Section 20-3:** This section explains the optics of telescopes, microscopes, and cameras.

▶ **Section 20-4: Science and Society:** NASA's Hubble Space Telescope project is presented, and students are asked to think about the relative importance of answering questions about the universe.

▶ **Section 20-5:** Technological applications of light are discussed. Polarized light, lasers, and fiber optics are highlighted.

CHAPTER VOCABULARY

plane mirror	reflecting telescope
virtual image	microscope
concave mirror	wide angle lenses
focal point	telephoto lenses
focal length	polarized light
real image	laser
convex mirror	coherent
convex lenses	incoherent
concave lenses	total internal
refracting	reflection
telescope	optical fibers

510

OPTIONS

For Your Gifted Students

▶ Have students cut a strip of graph paper and place it into a bottle of water. Have them observe the strip, comparing the spacing between the lines both vertically and horizontally to the paper outside the water. Have students relate any observable differences to the curvature of the bottle. Students may repeat these examinations using bottles of different curvatures.

Have you ever seen a magnified or distorted reflection of yourself? What kinds of objects cause this reflection?

FIND OUT!

Do the following activity to find out how light reflecting off surfaces of different shapes can produce different images.

Obtain a flat mirror and a shiny metal spoon. First look at your reflection in the flat mirror. What do you see? Is the reflection the same size as your face? Is it right side up? Now look at your image in the back of the spoon. Move the spoon close to your face and then far away. How does the image change? Turn the spoon over and look into the inside of the spoon. Move it back and forth. How do the images produced by these three shiny surfaces differ?

Gearing Up

Previewing the Chapter

Use this outline to help you focus on important ideas in this chapter.

Previewing Science Skills

▶ In the Skill Builders, you will recognize cause and effect, make a concept map, hypothesize, and sequence.
▶ In the Activities, you will observe, measure, predict, and infer.
▶ In the MINI-Labs, you will hypothesize, infer, and measure.

What's next?

You've seen how your reflection can change, depending on the shape and distance of the mirror you are looking into. As you read the next section, you'll find out how images are formed in three types of mirrors.

511

INTRODUCING THE CHAPTER

Use the Find Out activity to introduce students to images produced by reflection. Inform students that they will investigate how the shape of mirrors and lenses affects the kind of image produced.

FIND OUT!

Preparation: Gather enough shiny spoons for every two people in your class. You might be able to borrow some from the school cafeteria.
Materials: spoons

Cooperative Learning: Use the Paired Partners strategy for this activity. One student can look into the spoon while the other person records observations about the image for each position of the spoon. Have them change roles.
Teaching Tips
▶ Display a large concave and a large convex mirror and have students compare each part of the spoon to the mirrors. Have them view their images in the mirrors and find similarities between their images in the mirrors and those in the spoon.

Gearing Up

Have students study the Gearing Up section to familiarize themselves with the chapter. Discuss the relationships of the topics in the outline.

What's Next?

Before beginning the first section, make sure students understand the connection between the Find Out activity and the topics to follow.

For Your Mainstreamed Students

▶ Students can measure the magnifying power of a convex lens. Have students focus a convex lens over some narrowly lined paper. They will compare the number of spaces seen through the lens with the number of spaces seen outside the lens. For example, if there are eight spaces outside the lens to two through the lens, the lens magnifies four times (4×).

SECTION BACKGROUND

▶ Principles of reflection and refraction are consistent with the wave model of light. However, the analysis of images formed by mirrors and lenses is based on the ray model of light, which assumes that light travels in straight-line paths called rays. We assume light travels from objects to our eyes in straight paths.

▶ The defect present in spherical mirrors is called spherical aberration. This occurs when rays come to an imperfect focus at the focal point. The larger the mirror, the more blurred the image is likely to be. For this reason, mirrors in astronomical telescopes must be finely ground and calibrated. Spherical mirrors would form a sphere if the surface were extended. The focal length is equal to half the radius of the sphere.

PREPLANNING

▶ Gather a few full-sized mirrors, smaller makeup mirrors, and a collection of concave and convex lenses to use in demonstrations.

1 MOTIVATE

▶ Bring a door-sized plane mirror to class. Have one student hold the mirror. Stand with your nose against the side of the mirror, so that half your body is in front and half your body is in back. Now pick up your leg and flap your arms as if flying. Students looking into the mirror will see you "fly."

▶ Discuss other optical illusions and magic tricks that are produced with mirrors.

▶ Ask students if they have ever been in a store and thought it was much larger due to a reflection.

20-1 The Optics of Mirrors

New Science Words

plane mirror
virtual image
concave mirror
focal point
focal length
real image
convex mirror

Objectives

▶ Explain how an image is formed in two types of mirrors.
▶ Identify examples and uses of plane, concave, and convex mirrors.

Plane Mirrors

Recall the wave properties of light from Chapter 19—reflection, refraction, and diffraction. In this chapter, you will examine the properties of reflection and refraction more closely. First, you will read about how mirrors reflect light and lenses refract light to form images. Next you will study some of the practical applications of these concepts.

Now, close your eyes and picture your own face. You know what you look like because you have seen your reflection. In what objects have you seen your reflection? The most obvious answer is a mirror, but you probably have seen your reflection in objects such as windows and pieces of aluminum foil also. Any smooth object that reflects light to form an image is a mirror.

You are probably used to seeing your image in a plane mirror, one with a flat surface. What happens if you stand in front of the mirror and snap your fingers on your right hand? Your reflection seems to snap its left fingers because the left and right sides of the image appear to be reversed. Notice your reflection is also upright and the same size as you. Figure 20-1 shows how your image is formed by a plane mirror. The mirror is a piece of glass with a reflective coating on the front or the back. Light is reflected off of you toward the mirror. Then, the light rays are reflected by the mirror back to your eyes.

Your image appears to be behind the mirror because you perceive that the light forming the image is coming from somewhere beyond the mirror. Figure 20-1 shows how rays reflected from a plane mirror appear to form an image. Remember, reflected light rays do not exist *behind* the mir-

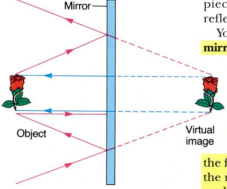

Figure 20-1. A plane mirror forms an upright, virtual image.

OPTIONS

Meeting Different Ability Levels

For Section 20-1, use the following **Teacher Resource Masters** depending upon individual students' needs.

◆ **Study Guide Master** for all students.

● **Reinforcement Master** for students of average and above average ability levels.

▲ **Enrichment Master** for above average students.

Additional Teacher Resource Package masters are listed in the OPTIONS box throughout the section. The additional masters are appropriate for all students.

---

ror because the mirror is opaque. The image you see in a plane mirror is called a virtual image. A **virtual image** is an image in which no light rays pass through the image. The virtual image formed by a plane mirror is erect and appears as far behind the mirror as the object is in front of it.

Concave Mirrors

Mirrors are not always flat. If the surface of a mirror is curved inward, like the inside of a spoon, it is a **concave mirror.** Look for your reflection in the bowl of a shiny spoon. Concave mirrors form images differently than plane mirrors do. The way an image is formed depends on the position of the object in front of the mirror. Figure 20-2 shows one way an image can be formed in a concave mirror. The straight line drawn through the center of the mirror is the optical axis. Light rays parallel to the optical axis approaching a concave mirror are all reflected to pass through one point on the optical axis, called the **focal point.** The distance from the center of the mirror to the focal point is called the **focal length.**

Suppose that the distance from the object to the mirror is a little greater than the focal length, as in Figure 20-2. Then, you can locate the image by following two rays. One ray is drawn through the focal point to the mirror. All rays that pass through the focal point on the way to the mirror are reflected parallel to the optical axis. From the same point on the object, a second ray is drawn parallel to the optical axis. This ray is reflected through the focal point. Find the point where these two reflected rays meet. This image is enlarged and upside down. Because

When can a virtual image be seen?

2

What is the focal length?

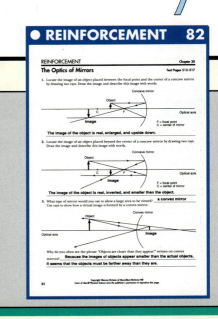

Figure 20-2. When the distance from the object to the concave mirror is a little greater than the focal length (a), you see an enlarged, inverted, real image (b).

Mirror surface

Object

a

Inverted real image

Focal point

Optical axis

b

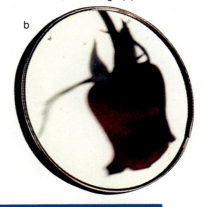

513

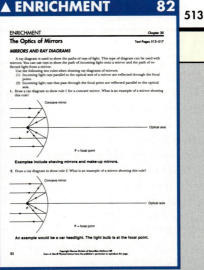

● **REINFORCEMENT** 82

▲ **ENRICHMENT** 82

TYING TO PREVIOUS KNOWLEDGE: Recall the law of reflection in the last chapter and the difference between looking in smooth and crumpled aluminum foil. In this section, the law of reflection will be applied to common types of mirrors.

OBJECTIVES AND SCIENCE WORDS: Have students review the objectives and science words to become familiar with this section.

2 TEACH

Key Concepts are highlighted.

CONCEPT DEVELOPMENT

▶ Have students stand in front of a plane mirror. Note that the right hand mirrors the left hand. Emphasize that the size of your image will be the same size as yourself if the image is located as far behind the mirror as you are in front.

Cooperative Learning: Ask students how large the mirror must be in order to see a full view of one's body. Place students in Paired Partners and have them make a prediction. Have students stand about one meter in front of a tall plane mirror; the partner should place a piece of tape where the other sees his or her head and another where he or she sees his or her feet. Compare your height to the distance between the pieces of tape. The distance between the tape should be half your height.

▶ Use the above setup to investigate the effect of distance from the mirror on image height. After marking the image with pieces of tape, take a few steps back and again mark the position of your head and feet in the mirror. Students will be surprised to find that although the image looks smaller from their point of view, the image height in the mirror is still the same. The size of the mirror needed does not depend on one's distance from the mirror.

CONCEPT DEVELOPMENT

▶ Place two plane mirrors in a v-shape with a narrow object in between. Look into one of the mirrors and observe the many images of the object produced.

▶ Take apart a flashlight and look at the concave mirror surrounding the light bulb. Ask students to explain the placement of the bulb in front of the mirror. The concave mirror reflects the light from the bulb in nearly parallel rays to form a more intense beam of light because the bulb is placed at the focal point.

MINI QUIZ

Use the Mini Quiz to check students' recall of chapter content.

① A _____ forms an upright, virtual image. *plane mirror*

② A _____ is curved like the inside of a spoon. *concave mirror*

③ What image do you see if you place the object at the focal point of a concave mirror? *no image*

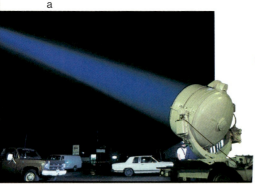
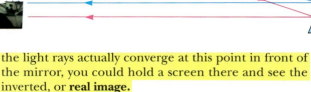

Figure 20-3. A beam of light forms (a) when a light is placed at the focal point of a concave mirror (b).

Figure 20-4. The image of the rosebud is magnified (a) when the rosebud is placed between the focal point and the surface of a concave mirror (b).

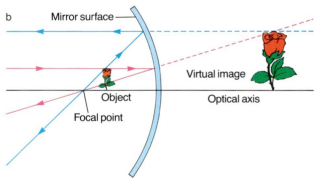

==the light rays actually converge at this point in front of the mirror, you could hold a screen there and see the inverted, or **real image.**==

What if you placed an object at the focal point of the concave mirror? Figure 20-3 shows that if the object is at the focal point, all light rays are reflected parallel to the optical axis. No image can be seen because the rays do not converge. However, a light placed at the focal point can be reflected in a beam. In devices such as car headlights, flashlights, and spotlights, the light bulb is placed at the focal point of a concave mirror to create a concentrated light beam of nearly parallel light rays. The light isn't exactly parallel because not all of the light bulb can be exactly at the focal point.

You may own a hand mirror that magnifies reflections. This, like the inside of the shiny spoon, is a concave mirror also. When you hold the mirror close to your face, your face is between the focal point and the mirror. Again,

OPTIONS

INQUIRY QUESTIONS

▶ **Suppose you wanted to buy a shaving or make up mirror. What kind would you buy and explain your choice?** *A concave mirror because its image is magnified.*

▶ **Assume you bought a concave mirror to use to apply makeup, but it reflected an image of your face that was enlarged and upside down. Is the mirror faulty and should you return it to the store?** *No, you need to stand closer to the mirror so your face is between the focal point and the mirror.*

PROGRAM RESOURCES

From the **Teacher Resource Package** use:
Transparency Masters, pages 79-80, Optics of Concave Mirrors.
Use **Color Transparency** number 40, Optics of Concave Mirrors.
Use **Laboratory Manual,** Reflection of Light.

two rays leave the object from the same point. One ray is drawn toward the mirror as if it had come through the focal point. It is reflected parallel to the optical axis. The second ray leaves the object parallel to the optical axis and reflects through the focal point. These rays never meet to form a real image. Instead, they appear to come from a single point behind the mirror. Rays from various points on the object form a virtual image that appears upright, enlarged, and behind the mirror.

Convex Mirrors

Have you ever seen a large mirror mounted above the aisles in a store? This type of mirror that curves outward is called a **convex mirror.** No matter where the object is, the convex mirror diverges, or spreads the rays. Figure 20-5 shows how convex mirrors produce an image. The reflected rays never meet, so the image is always virtual. The image is upright and smaller than the actual object.

Because convex mirrors spread out the reflected light, they allow large areas to be viewed. In addition to increasing the field of view in places like grocery stores and factories, convex mirrors can widen the view of traffic that can be seen in rear or side-view mirrors of automobiles. Your perception of distance can be distorted, however, because objects are always closer than they appear in a convex mirror.

So far, you have read about three ways that light can be reflected and form images. Can you recall the three types of mirrors and describe the image that each mirror produces? In Section 20-2, you will find out the ways in which light can be refracted to form images.

What kind of image does a convex mirror form?

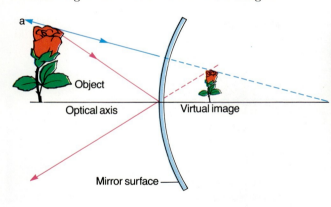

Figure 20-5. A convex mirror diverges reflected rays (a) to form a virtual image that is always upright and smaller than the object (b).

PROBLEM SOLVING

Joel's image in the plane mirror was virtual, upright, reversed from right to left, and the same size as his face. Joel's image in the convex mirror was virtual, upright, reversed from right to left, and smaller than his face.

Think Critically: Convex mirrors give drivers a wider view of the road. They are stamped with the warning so that drivers do not misjudge the distance of the car behind them.

3 CLOSE

▶ Ask questions 1-3 and the **Apply** Question in the Section Review.

▶ Have students make a list of as many situations as possible where mirrors are used. Divide the lists into the three types of mirrors studied here: plane, concave, and convex. Try to specify in each case the type of image produced: real or virtual, enlarged or smaller, and upright or inverted.

SECTION REVIEW ANSWERS

1. enlarged, upside down, and real

2. Convex mirrors are used to provide a wide view because they can form images that are smaller than the object.

3. plane mirrors—flat; concave mirrors—curved inward; convex mirrors—curved outward

4. Apply: Use a concave mirror to form a real image since the object is so far beyond the focal point. It converges the light so the image can be viewed.

Skill Builder
The role of the concave mirror is to reflect parallel light rays to make a concentrated beam of light. If the light is intense, it is likely that the mirror is broken and is scattering light in many directions.

PROBLEM SOLVING

Mirrors on the New Car

Joel and his father visited car dealerships for two weeks looking for a new car. They finally found one that had the features they both wanted.

When they went to pick up the new car, Joel's father disappeared with the salesman to complete the paperwork.

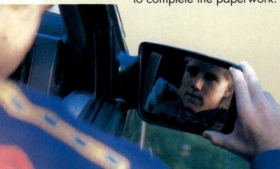

Joel decided to give the new car a quick once-over while he was waiting. He noticed that the mirror on the passenger side of the car was stamped with a warning stating "OBJECTS IN MIRROR ARE CLOSER THAN THEY APPEAR." He thought that was strange and looked at the driver's side mirror. It didn't have the warning. Joel compared his image in both mirrors and decided that the mirror on the driver's side was a plane mirror and the mirror on the passenger side was a convex mirror. Describe the images Joel saw in the two mirrors.

Think Critically: Explain why convex mirrors are sometimes used as outside rear view mirrors on cars. Why are they stamped with a warning?

SECTION REVIEW

1. Describe the image formed by a concave mirror when the object is beyond the focal point.
2. What are convex mirrors used for? Explain.
3. Contrast the differences between the surfaces of plane, concave, and convex mirrors.
4. **Apply:** If you were going to use a mirror to gather the light entering a telescope, what kind of mirror would you use to focus it? Explain.

Skill Builder ☒ Recognizing Cause and Effect

Suppose you drop a flashlight that has a concave mirror in it. When you turn the flashlight on, you notice the light is less intense than it was before you dropped it. What may have happened? If you need help, refer to Recognizing Cause and Effect in the **Skill Handbook** on page 679.

OPTIONS

PROGRAM RESOURCES
From the **Teacher Resource Package** use:
Concept Mapping, page 45.
Use **Laboratory Manual,** Magnifying Power.

ENRICHMENT
▶ Have students find out how large mirrors are made for telescopes so as to create a smooth finish on the mirror's surface.

ACTIVITY 20-1
Reflections of Reflections

Problem: *How do plane mirrors make images?*

Materials
- 2 plane mirrors
- cellophane tape
- masking tape
- protractor
- paper clip
- light source

Procedure
1. Lay the two mirrors side by side and tape them together so they will open and close. Label them *R* and *L* as shown.
2. Place the mirrors on a sheet of paper and using the protractor, close the mirrors to an angle of 72°. Mark the position of the *R* mirror on the paper.
3. Bend one leg of a paper clip up 90° and place it close to the front of the *R* mirror.
4. Count the number of paper-clip *R* and *L* images you see in the mirrors. Don't move the clip.
5. Count the images as you slowly open the mirrors to 90° and then to 120°.
6. Place the light behind the paper clip to form a shadow that extends from the surface of the *R* mirror to the *L* mirror. Look into each mirror along the paths of the reflected shadows.
7. Make a data table to record the number of images you can see when the mirrors are at 72°, 90°, and 120°.

Data and Observations   Sample Data

Angle of Mirrors	Number of Paper Clip Images	
	R	L
72°	2	2
90°	2	1
120°	1	1

Analyze
1. How does the direction of the shadow help you predict where the image of the paper clip will seem to be?
2. How is the number of paper-clip images affected by increasing the angle between the mirrors in Step 5?

Conclude and Apply
3. Considering that there are 360° in a circle, into how many "wedges" of space does each of the angles divide the circle?
4. What angle would divide space into six segments? How many images do you think would be produced by it?
5. Which is the best predictor of paper-clip images, numbers of mirror images, or numbers of space segments?

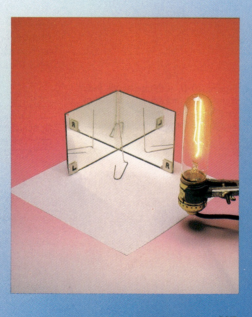

ACTIVITY 20-1
30 minutes

OBJECTIVE: Predict image formation by plane mirrors.

PROCESS SKILLS applied in this activity:
▶ **Measuring** in Procedure Steps 2, 3, and 5.
▶ **Predicting** in Conclude and Apply Questions 4 and 5.
▶ **Inferring** in Analyze Question 2 and Conclude and Apply Question 3.

👥 COOPERATIVE LEARNING
Arrange students in Problem Solving teams.

TEACHING THE ACTIVITY
▶ Use rectangular mirrors at least 5 cm across. Thin glass is better. Mirror tiles (hardware store) can be cut to size but sharp edges must be ground or taped.
▶ The intent of Procedure Step 6 and Analyze Step 2 is to show that images are located in the direction of reflected rays. Omit this step and question if time or equipment is a problem.
▶ Place a protractor on a copy machine and make lab worksheets upon which students can measure the appropriate angles.

PROGRAM RESOURCES
From the **Teacher Resource Package** use:
  Activity Worksheets, pages 158-159, Activity 20-1: Reflection of Reflections.

ANSWERS TO QUESTIONS
1. The shadow ray will seem to come from the direction of the image in the mirror.
2. The number of paper clip images in the mirrors is reduced as the angle between the mirrors increases.
3. Each number divides evenly into 360. As a result, the 360° space around the axis of the mirror pair is divided into five, four, and three equal segments.

4. The angle producing six segments is 360/6 = 60 degrees. Five images will be produced.
5. One paper clip can be seen in each "wedge" space segment. One of the wedges is real and the rest are virtual images.

PREPARATION

SECTION BACKGROUND

▶ Note that in both concave and convex lenses, the greatest bending of light rays occurs near the ends of the lens. Near the ends, the two glass surfaces are not parallel to one another and more refraction occurs. Light is refracted twice when passing through a lens, once entering and once leaving the lens. In the center of the lens, the glass sides are parallel to each other and the light ray passes straight through.

▶ Lenses are already somewhat familiar because so many people wear eyeglasses. Eyeglasses were used as early as the thirteenth century, and gems were used even earlier as natural magnifying glasses by the Greeks and Arabs.

1 MOTIVATE

▶ Laminate some small print from a text. Have students place a large drop of water on the text with an eyedropper. What happens to the text below the water? What does the shape of the droplet look like? The text looks slightly magnified. The droplet's surface curves up like a convex lens.

▶ Ask students how their eyes focus on both near and far away objects. The lens in your eye is flexible and can change shape.

New Science Words

convex lenses
concave lenses

Objectives

▶ Describe the types of images formed in convex and concave lenses.
▶ Cite examples of how these lenses are used.
▶ Explain how lenses are used to correct vision.

Did You Know?

The fastest camera, built for laser research, registers images at the rate of 33 million per second.

Convex Lenses

Do you wear glasses or contact lenses? If so, you use lenses to improve your ability to see. Like curved mirrors, lenses are described as convex or concave, depending on their shape.

Convex lenses are thicker in the middle than at the edges. Light rays approaching the lens parallel to the optical axis are refracted toward the center of the lens. ② They converge at the focal point, so they are capable of forming real images that can be projected on a screen.

The amount of refraction depends on the change in the speed of light as it passes through a material, and the amount of refraction also depends on the shape of the object. Thick lenses with very curved surfaces bend light a great deal more than thin ones with less curved surfaces. The focal length of the thick convex lens in Figure 20-6

Figure 20-6. A thick convex lens bends light more than a thin convex lens. Notice that the focal length is shorter for the thick lens.

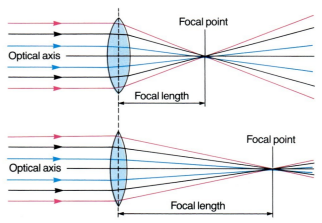

OPTIONS

Meeting Different Ability Levels

For Section 20-2, use the following **Teacher Resource Masters** depending upon individual students' needs.

◆ **Study Guide Master** for all students.
● **Reinforcement Master** for students of average and above average ability levels.
▲ **Enrichment Master** for above average students.

Additional Teacher Resource Package masters are listed in the OPTIONS box throughout the section. The additional masters are appropriate for all students.

◆ STUDY GUIDE 83

STUDY GUIDE   Chapter 20
The Optics of Lenses   Text Pages 518–521

Use the terms in the list below to fill in the blanks in the paragraphs about lenses.

concave   longer   larger   curved   convex   length   clearly
object   thick   shape   lens   retina   lens
refracting   inverted   muscles   virtual   cornea   astigmatism

Lenses are made of transparent material and have a _____**curved**_____ surface. A convex lens has thin edges and a _____**thick**_____ middle. Another type of lens is thicker at the edge than the middle and is called a _____**concave**_____ lens. All lenses work by _____**refracting**_____ light. Parallel rays of light are refracted toward each other and brought to a focal point in a _____**convex**_____ lens. Light is refracted both when it enters and leaves a _____**lens**_____. The amount of refraction depends on the change of the speed of light as it passes through a material and on the _____**shape**_____ of the lens. In a convex lens, the type of image formed depends on the position of the _____**object**_____ and the focal length of the lens. When the object is more than twice the focal length from the lens, the real image is smaller than the object and _____**inverted**_____. If the object is between one and two focal lengths, the image is _____**larger**_____ than the object and inverted. When the object is between the lens and the focal point, the image is larger and upright but is a _____**virtual**_____ image. Concave lenses are not able to produce real images and are used with convex lenses to create a _____**longer**_____ focal length.

The light we see enters our eyes through the transparent covering of the eye called the _____**cornea**_____. The light then passes through the pupil and converges on the back part of the eye called the _____**retina**_____. Images are properly focused on the retina by the convex lens in the eye, which is controlled by eye _____**muscles**_____. To focus images of distant objects, a longer focal _____**length**_____ is needed. To do this, the muscles relax, allowing the lens to be _____**less**_____ convex. People are farsighted when they can see things far away _____**clearly**_____ but have fuzzy vision at close range. To correct this problem, a _____**convex**_____ lens is used. A _____**concave**_____ lens is used to correct the vision of a nearsighted person. An eye problem caused by an unevenly curved cornea is _____**astigmatism**_____.

is shorter than that of the thin convex lens. ==Convex lenses are capable of producing many kinds of images, both real and virtual, upright, inverted, enlarged, or smaller. The type of image formed depends on the position of the object and the focal length of the lens.==

Have you ever photographed a faraway object? If so, it's likely the object was more than two focal lengths from the lens. If you follow the light paths in Figure 20-7a, you'll notice that the real image is smaller than the object, and inverted. The lens in your eye forms images in the same way.

If an object is between one and two focal lengths from the lens, as in Figure 20-7c, the real image is inverted and larger than the object. This is the method used to project a movie from a small film to the large screen of the theater. Can you think of other examples in which producing a larger, inverted image is desired?

Have you ever used a magnifying glass to closely examine an object? A magnifying glass is a convex lens, so you must hold it less than one focal length from the object. The light rays can't converge and an enlarged and upright virtual image is formed. Look at the position of the image in Figure 20-7c. Notice the object seems farther away than it really is.

Concave Lenses

==**Concave lenses** are thinner in the middle and thicker at the edges. Light passing through a concave lens bends toward the edges. The rays diverge and never form a real image. The virtual image is upright and smaller than the actual object.== The image formed by a concave lens is similar to the image produced by a convex mirror because they both diverge light to form virtual images.

Concave lenses are usually used in combination with other lenses. They can be used with convex lenses in telescopes and cameras to extend the focal length so you can see a clear image of a faraway object. Concave lenses are also used to correct nearsighted vision.

Lenses and Vision

What determines how well you can "see" the words on this page? Your ability to focus on these words depends

Figure 20-7. The image formed by a convex lens depends on the location of the object in relation to the focal length of the lens.

Figure 20-8. Light rays passing through a concave lens diverge and form a virtual image.

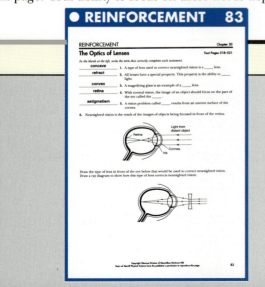
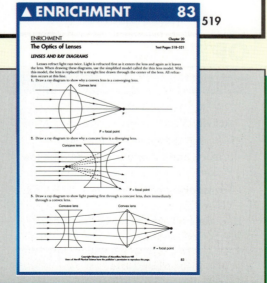

TYING TO PREVIOUS KNOWLEDGE: Many students wear corrective lenses, either as eyeglasses or contact lenses. What do the eyeglasses do? They change the light path from the object to your eyes by refracting the light before it enters your eyes.

OBJECTIVES AND SCIENCE WORDS: Have students review the objectives and science words to become familiar with this section.

2 TEACH

Key Concepts are highlighted.

CONCEPT DEVELOPMENT

▶ Distribute some convex lenses of varying focal lengths to your class. Show students how to find the focal length of a lens by focusing the shortest image of sunlight possible on a white piece of paper (held by a partner) and measuring the distance from the paper to the lens.

▶ Following the previous suggestion and a discussion of the kinds of images formed by convex lenses, pass out some concave lenses. Tell students to find the focal lengths of the concave lenses. They will not be able to focus the image because these lenses diverge light to form only virtual images.

CROSS CURRICULUM

▶ **Language Arts:** Have students write a paper about how convex and concave lenses are manufactured for use in eyeglasses and optical instruments.

STUDENT TEXT QUESTION

Page 519, paragraph 3: **Can you think of other examples in which producing a larger, inverted image is desired?** *the microscope*

▶ Ask local eye doctors if they will donate old eyeglass lenses or come to your class to demonstrate simple vision tests.

MINI-Lab
Teaching Tips
▶ Demonstrate safe procedures for using a sharp object.

▶ A margarine container makes a good holder. Cut the hole with a pocket knife or scalpel.

▶ The window must be stretched tight and have no wrinkles.

▶ The water drop forms a convex lens. Too large a drop will lose its curvature and too small a drop is hard to look through.

▶ Holding the drop close to the print will form a virtual image; magnified and upright. Holding the drop farther away will form a real image; small and upside down.

Answers to Questions
▶ The drop forms a convex lens.

▶ It can make two kinds of images if you adjust the focal length.

CHECK FOR UNDERSTANDING
Present the following situation to your class: **Keisha sits in the back of the room and can't read what is written on the chalkboard but has no trouble reading her text. What is the cause of her vision problem and what kind of lens could correct it?** *She is nearsighted, and the image focuses in front of the retina (the eyeball is too long or there is a bulging cornea). Correct this problem with a concave lens.*

RETEACH
Compare eyeglasses designed to correct nearsightedness and farsightedness. Have students examine near and far objects through each type of lens. Have students explain how each lens corrects vision problems.

EXTENSION
For students who have mastered this section, use the **Reinforcement** and **Enrichment** masters or other OPTIONS provided.

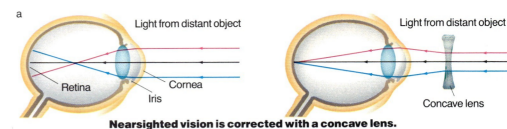

Nearsighted vision is corrected with a concave lens.

Farsighted vision is corrected with a convex lens.

Figure 20-9. Some vision problems can easily be corrected with concave and convex lenses.

MINI-Lab
Can lenses be made of liquids?
Make a water-drop lens holder by cutting a round hole in the bottom of a plastic bowl. Make the hole about 2 cm across. Stretch a piece of plastic wrap over the hole and tape it in place. Put a drop of water on the plastic window and look at this print through the drop. Look at other small objects. What kind of lens does the drop form? How can your lens make two kinds of images?

on the way your eye is designed. Light enters your eye through the transparent covering of your eye, the cornea. The light then passes through an opening called the pupil. The colored part of your eye, the iris, adjusts the pupil size to control how much light can pass through a convex lens behind the pupil. The light then converges to form an inverted image on your retina. The lens in your eye is soft; and flexible muscles in your eye can change its shape. When you look at a distant object, you need a longer focal length than that needed to look at nearby objects. Your eye muscles adjust your lens to a less convex shape. When you focus on a nearby object, the eye muscles will tighten to increase the curvature of the lens.

If you have healthy vision, you should be able to clearly see objects from a focal length of about 25 cm or more. Many people need their vision corrected with lenses to enjoy normal vision. To have normal vision, the image of an object should focus on the retina inside your eye. A nearsighted person has difficulty seeing distant objects clearly. The eyeball is too long or the cornea bulges out, causing the image to focus in front of the retina. Figure 20-9a illustrates how concave lenses correct this problem by diverging the light rays before they enter the eye.

Farsighted people can see faraway objects, but they can't focus clearly on nearby objects. Their eyeballs are

520 MIRRORS AND LENSES

OPTIONS

PROGRAM RESOURCES
From the **Teacher Resource Package** use:

Activity Worksheets, page164, Mini-Lab: Can lenses be made of liquids?

Science and Society, page 24, A New Vision.

Transparency Masters, pages 81-82, Vision Corrections.

Use **Color Transparency** number 41, Vision Corrections.

either too short or their corneas are too flat. Their lenses aren't convex enough to converge the rays on the retina. As a result, the image is focused behind the retina. Figure 20-9b shows how this condition can be corrected if an additional convex lens is used.

Another vision problem is astigmatism. Blurry vision from astigmatism is caused when the surface of the cornea is curved unevenly. Corrective lenses for this condition have an uneven curvature as well.

There are currently several ways to correct poor vision caused by lens problems in the eye. Artificial lenses in the form of eyeglasses or contacts can be worn. These prescription lenses are shaped to refract light before it enters the eye, so that the light will focus on the retina. As a result, the wearer will see clear images. Contact lenses can actually be worn over the cornea. Another way to correct the lens in the eye is by using surgery. Eye surgeons often use lasers to reshape the cornea.

Can you recall what all lenses have in common? They all refract light that passes through them. Convex lenses refract light toward the center of the lens, and concave lenses refract light away from the center of the lens. As you read the next section, you'll see how these two kinds of lenses are used in cameras, microscopes, and telescopes.

SECTION REVIEW

1. Distinguish between the characteristics of convex and concave lenses.
2. When using a slide projector, you put the slides in the projector upside down. Why must they be inserted this way?
3. What type of lens would you use to examine a tiny spider on your desk?
4. **Apply:** If you have difficulty reading the chalkboard from the back row, what is most likely your vision problem? How could it be corrected?

☑ Concept Mapping

Mirrors and lenses are the simplest optical devices. Design a network tree concept map to show some uses for each shape of mirror and lens. If you need help, refer to Concept Mapping in the **Skill Handbook** on pages 684 and 685.

Skill Builder

EcoTip

Collect and videotape all the trash your school throws away in one day. Classify the trash as recyclable or non-recyclable. Show the video to your classmates.

What do all lenses have in common?

Use the Mini Quiz to check students' recall of chapter content.

1 A(n) _____ lens causes light rays to diverge. *concave*
2 Light rays meet at the focal point after passing through a(n) _____ lens. *convex*
3 What kind of lens is found in your eye? *convex*

? FLEX Your Brain

Use the Flex Your Brain activity to have students explore LENSES AND VISION PROBLEMS.

3 CLOSE

▶ Ask questions 1-3 and the **Apply** Question in the Section Review.
▶ Ask students what would happen if you placed two lenses in a row or used a mirror to reflect focused light through a lens? Combinations of lenses and mirrors are used to create various optical instruments.

SECTION REVIEW ANSWERS

1. convex—thickest in center, converges light; concave—thickest at the edges, diverges light
2. The convex lens will form an enlarged inverted image because the slides are placed between one and two focal lengths from the lens.
3. A convex lens. Viewing the spider between the lens and the focal point will produce an enlarged virtual image.
4. Apply: You are nearsighted and should wear a concave lens to diverge the light rays entering your eye.

PROGRAM RESOURCES

From the **Teacher Resource Package** use:

Activity Worksheets, page 5, Flex Your Brain.

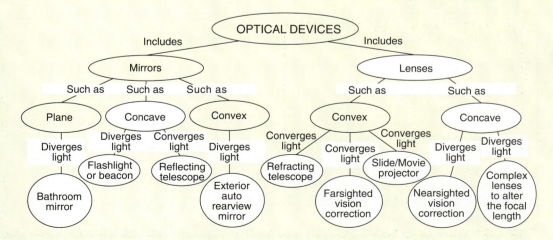

PREPARATION

SECTION BACKGROUND

▶ Galileo did not invent the telescope, but he was among the first to use it in monitoring the heavens. He discovered sunspots, some moons of Jupiter, and the design of the Milky Way galaxy, to name a few.

▶ The total magnification of a simple microscope is the product of the magnifications produced by each of the two lenses. Note that the eyepiece lens is also called the ocular.

▶ Maps of the moon actually show the moon as being upside down on the page. When you look through most astronomical telescopes, the image is upside down compared to how you would view it with the unaided eye (objects in space are only "right-side-up" because we see them that way). So the maps are drawn as you actually see the images.

PREPLANNING

▶ If your school does not have a telescope, try to borrow one for demonstrations. Bring in a microscope and several cameras.

20-3 Optical Instruments

New Science Words

refracting telescope
reflecting telescope
microscope
wide-angle lenses
telephoto lenses

Objectives

▶ Compare refracting and reflecting telescopes.
▶ Explain how a camera creates an image.

Figure 20-10. The moon can be seen in greater detail when viewed through a telescope as in the lower photo.

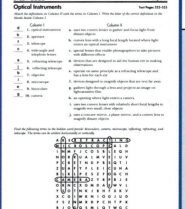

Telescopes

There are many uses for lenses and mirrors. They are important components in optical instruments—devices that are designed to aid the human eye in making observations. In this section you'll read about three common optical instruments that you are probably familiar with. The first of these is the telescope.

Have you ever looked at the moon through a telescope? It appears to be very different from the moon you see when you glance at the night sky, doesn't it? With a good telescope, you should be able to clearly see the craters and other features on the moon's surface. Telescopes are designed to magnify objects that are very far away. Much of the information we have today about the moon, the planets, and our galaxy and others has been gathered by viewing these celestial bodies through telescopes.

Early telescopes, like those used today, were built from lenses and mirrors. Around the year 1600, lensmakers in Holland constructed a telescope to view distant objects. In 1609, Galileo built and used his own telescope to discover the moons of Jupiter, the phases of Venus, and details of the Milky Way galaxy. Today, scientists use several kinds of telescopes with many design improvements.

522   MIRRORS AND LENSES

OPTIONS

Meeting Different Ability Levels

For Section 20-3, use the following **Teacher Resource Masters** depending upon individual students' needs.

◆ **Study Guide Master** for all students.
● **Reinforcement Master** for students of average and above average ability levels.
▲ **Enrichment Master** for above average students.

Additional Teacher Resource Package masters are listed in the OPTIONS box throughout the section. The additional masters are appropriate for all students.

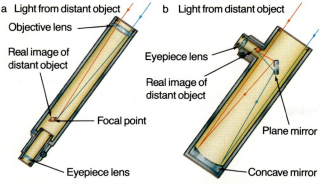

a Light from distant object
Objective lens
Real image of distant object
Focal point
Eyepiece lens

b Light from distant object
Eyepiece lens
Real image of distant object
Plane mirror
Concave mirror

Figure 20-11. A refracting telescope (a) and a reflecting telescope (b) magnify the images of distant objects.

One common telescope is the **refracting telescope.** A simple refracting telescope uses two convex lenses to gather and focus light from distant objects. Figure 20-11a is a diagram of a refracting telescope. Notice how light enters the telescope through a convex lens with a long focal length. This lens is called the objective lens. The real image formed by this lens is magnified by a second convex lens, called the eyepiece, with a shorter focal length. What you view through the eyepiece is an enlarged, virtual image of the real image. The image you see is also inverted.

There are several problems with refracting telescopes that may make another type of telescope more desirable to use. First of all, the objective lens must be quite large to allow enough light in to form a bright image. These heavy glass lenses are hard to make and quite costly. Their own weight can cause them to sag and distort the image. As a result, most large telescopes are reflecting telescopes.

A **reflecting telescope** uses a concave mirror, a plane mirror, and a convex lens to magnify distant objects. Figure 20-11b shows how light enters the telescope and is reflected by the concave mirror onto a plane mirror inside the telescope. The plane mirror reflects the rays to form an inverted real image in the telescope. The convex lens in the eyepiece then magnifies this image. The eyepiece can be replaced by a camera to photograph the real image.

Sometimes you might want to view distant objects so they appear upright. Imagine trying to watch a baseball game through binoculars if the image were upside down. Binoculars work on the same principle as a refracting telescope, except there are two lenses—one for each eye.

MINI-Lab

What do telescopes see?
Punch two closely spaced holes in a piece of aluminum foil with a needle. Have a friend hold it in front of a light bulb. Move away from the light bulb until you can barely see both holes. Make a tiny hole in a second piece of foil. Make two slightly larger holes in the second piece of foil. Hold the foil close to your eye and look through each hole at the two "stars." How does the image of the "stars" compare as seen through each of the three holes?

523

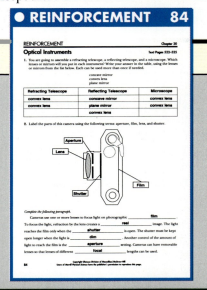
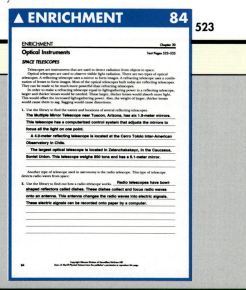
▶Have students examine the close-up photo of the moon's surface on the left page and compare it to the photo of the moon as it would look to the unaided eye. Discuss the ways in which optical devices, such as telescopes and cameras, have helped form our view of the world around us.

MINI-Lab
Teaching Tips
▶Several students can view the same light source, but each should make a set of viewing holes.
▶To make a very small hole, place the foil on a hard surface.
Answers to Questions
▶The larger holes, like large lenses and mirrors, provide better "resolution" of the two "stars." Diffraction of light through the small hole blurs the two "stars" to look like one.

TYING TO PREVIOUS KNOWLEDGE: Ask students if they have ever taken a blurry picture with a camera. Have them suggest why this might have happened. The function of a camera will be discussed in this section.

OBJECTIVES AND SCIENCE WORDS: Have students review the objectives and science words to become familiar with this section.

Key Concepts are highlighted.

CONCEPT DEVELOPMENT

▶ Obtain two convex lenses with short focal lengths. Mount them on a meterstick and focus them so that you see an enlarged image of a small, close-up object such as the print in this book. This is a simple microscope.

TEACHER F.Y.I.

▶ The magnification of a lens, such as that in a microscope or telescope, is given in terms of how much larger the image appears than the actual object. For example, a 140× magnification of a cell would produce an image that has a length 140 times that of the actual cell.

▶ If possible, obtain a telescope and microscope to dismantle in class to show students where the lenses are.

CROSS CURRICULUM

▶ **Art:** Find a book on photography and investigate what variables in a camera can be controlled to gain the desired effects in a photograph. Look up aperture, shutter speed, wide-angle and telephoto lenses, and flashes.

CHECK FOR UNDERSTANDING

Use the Mini Quiz to check for understanding.

MINI QUIZ

Use the Mini Quiz to check students' recall of chapter content.

1 A telescope which contains a concave mirror, a plane mirror, and a convex lens is called a(n) _____ telescope. *reflecting*

2 What optical instrument could you make to magnify close objects too small to see with the unaided eye? *microscope*

3 What kind of lens would you use if you wanted to photograph a person with his or her surroundings? *a wide-angle lens*

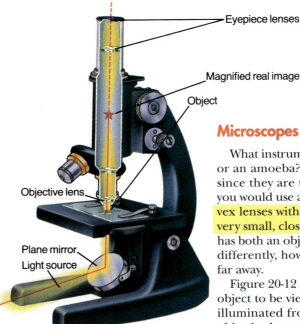

Figure 20-12. A microscope contains two convex lenses so it can magnify very small objects.

Did You Know?

The most powerful microscope is the IBM 1981 scanning tunneling microscope with the magnifying ability of 100 million X. This instrument resolves down to 1/100 the diameter of an atom and the tip of its probe is a single atom.

A third lens or a pair of reflecting prisms has been added to binoculars to invert the upside-down image so it appears upright. Terrestrial telescopes, such as those used for bird watching, are also designed to produce an upright image.

Microscopes

What instrument would you use to look at a cell, a hair, or an amoeba? You obviously wouldn't use a telescope since they are used to look at faraway objects. Instead, you would use a microscope. A **microscope** uses two convex lenses with relatively short focal lengths to magnify very small, close objects. A microscope, like a telescope, has both an objective lens and an eyepiece. It is designed differently, however, because the objects viewed are not far away.

Figure 20-12 shows the operation of a microscope. The object to be viewed is placed on a transparent slide and illuminated from below. The light travels through the objective lens and a real, enlarged image is formed. It is enlarged because it is farther from the lens than the object. The real image is magnified again by the eyepiece. The image you see is actually a virtual, enlarged image of the already magnified real image. This results in an image up to several hundred times larger than the actual object.

Cameras

Do you keep a photograph album with your favorite pictures? Have you ever wondered how these pictures were made? Of course, they were made with a camera, but have you ever wondered how a camera transfers an image onto film? A camera gathers light through a lens and projects an image on light-sensitive film.

When you take a picture with a camera, the light reflected off the subject of the photograph enters an opening in the camera called the aperture. A shutter on the aperture opens to allow light to enter the camera.

The light passes through the lens of the camera, which focuses the image on the photographic film. The image is real, inverted, and smaller than the actual object. The

OPTIONS

INQUIRY QUESTIONS

▶ **What happens inside a camera when you focus a picture?** *You are adjusting the focal length, or the distance between the film and the lens.*

▶ **What type of lens would you expect to find in a camera and why?** *A convex lens, because a concave lens can't focus light rays to form a real image.*

▶ **How is a camera like a human eye?** *The shutter is like an eyelid, the aperture is like an iris, and the image is focused on the film much like it is on the retina. The lenses in a camera and the lenses in your eye are adjustable convex lenses.*

size of the image depends on the focal length of the lens and how close the lens is to the film.

Imagine you and a friend are going to photograph the same object at the same distance, but with different types of cameras. Your picture would look different from that of your friend if the cameras had different lenses. Some lenses have short focal lengths that produce a relatively small image of the object but include much of its surroundings. These lenses are called **wide-angle lenses,** and they must be placed close to the film to focus the image with their short focal length. **Telephoto lenses** have longer focal lengths and are located farther from the film than wide-angle lenses. Telephoto lenses are easy to recognize because they protrude out from the camera to increase the distance between the lens and the film. The image seems enlarged and closer than the object actually is. These lenses are preferred when photographing people's faces from a distance.

Telescopes, microscopes, and cameras are just a few examples of instruments that contain mirrors and lenses and help you to make observations. What are some other types of optical instruments? See how many you can name.

Figure 20-13. The upper photo was taken with a wide-angle lens, and the lower photo was taken with a telephoto lens.

SECTION REVIEW

1. Compare and contrast reflecting and refracting telescopes.
2. If you wanted to photograph a single rose on a rosebush, what kind of lens would you use? Explain why you chose this lens.
3. Why are maps of the moon upside down?
4. **Apply:** Which optical instrument—a telescope, a microscope, or a camera—forms images in a way most like your eye? Explain.

☑ Hypothesizing

Skill Builder

You've noticed that all the objects in a photograph you've taken are blurry. Use your knowledge of lenses and focal lengths to form a hypothesis that could explain why the photo was blurred. If you need help, refer to Hypothesizing in the **Skill Handbook** on page 682.

3 CLOSE

PREPARATION

SECTION BACKGROUND

▶NASA has a teacher resource center that will provide free Hubble Space Telescope materials.

▶The mirrors and lenses in the telescope are large and were carefully ground and calibrated to produce clear images. But shortly after launching, a significant error was found in one of the main mirrors. Have students do some library research to find out what the mistake was.

1 MOTIVATE

▶Display photos of the Hubble Space Telescope in your classroom.

TYING TO PREVIOUS KNOWLEDGE:
Ask students if they have ever tried to retrieve a coin from a swimming pool. The light is refracted by the water, so they get a distorted image of the coin below the water. The atmosphere does the same thing to light reaching us from distant stars, so the Hubble telescope allows us to view this light before it is distorted by Earth's atmosphere.

OBJECTIVES AND
SCIENCE WORDS: Have students review the objectives and science words to become familiar with this section.

2 TEACH

Key Concepts are highlighted.

CONCEPT DEVELOPMENT

▶Draw a line 2.4 m long to show students how large the diameter of the primary mirror is. The large size allows the telescope to capture more light so that faint, distant stars can be observed. These stars could not be seen from Earth's surface.

The Hubble Space Telescope

Objectives

▶ Describe the development and goals of the Hubble Space Telescope.

▶ Evaluate the need for a space telescope.

Is It Worth It?

Imagine trying to read a sign from the bottom of a swimming pool. The water distorts your view of objects beyond the water. In a similar way, Earth's atmosphere blurs our view of many stars, planets, and other objects in space. Not even powerful telescopes positioned at high elevations can allow us to see distant objects clearly. On April 20, 1990, the National Aeronautics and Space Administration (NASA) launched the Hubble Space Telescope. ==The telescope has produced images sharper than powerful telescopes on Earth by allowing us to view the planets, stars, and distant galaxies from an orbit beyond Earth's atmosphere. It is designed to detect infrared and ultraviolet light in space that is usually blocked by Earth's atmosphere.==

The Hubble Space Telescope was placed into an orbit almost 600 kilometers above Earth by the space shuttle *Discovery*. The 13 m, 11 300 kg telescope is named after Edwin P. Hubble, an astronomer. Hubble is famous for his observations of many other galaxies beyond the Milky Way, and evidence that the universe appears to be expanding.

Look at the diagram of the Hubble Space Telescope on the opposite page. The solar panels provide electrical power to the system. A 2.4 m primary and a smaller secondary mirror collect and focus light to form an image. Various instruments on the telescope interpret the data and communicate it to scientists on Earth.

526 MIRRORS AND LENSES

OPTIONS

Meeting Different Ability Levels

For Section 20-4, use the following **Teacher Resource Masters** depending upon individual students' needs.

◆ **Study Guide Master** for all students.

● **Reinforcement Master** for students of average and above average ability levels.

▲ **Enrichment Master** for above average students.

Additional Teacher Resource Package masters are listed in the OPTIONS box throughout the section. The additional masters are appropriate for all students.

◆ **STUDY GUIDE** 85

STUDY GUIDE Chapter 20
The Hubble Space Telescope Text Pages 526–527

Determine whether the italicized term makes each statement true or false. If the statement is true, write the word "true" in the blank. If the statement is false, write in the blank the term that makes the statement true.

true	1. The Hubble Space Telescope is named after *Edwin P. Hubble,* an astronomer.
atmosphere	2. Our view of outer space from the surface of Earth is blurred by Earth's *ocean.*
ultraviolet	3. The Hubble Space Telescope is designed to detect infrared and *visible* light in space that usually cannot be detected by telescopes at Earth's surface.
solar panels	4. Electrical power is supplied to the telescope's system by the *electric company.*
Aeronautics	5. NASA is the abbreviation for the National *Airways* and Space Administration.
600	6. The Hubble Space Telescope is in an orbit about *100* kilometers above Earth.
billion	7. The final cost of the Hubble Space Telescope project is about 2 *million* dollars.
true	8. The Hubble Space Telescope was launched by *NASA* on April 20, 1990.
ten	9. The Hubble Space Telescope produces images that are *five* times sharper than powerful telescopes on Earth.
expanding	10. The universe appears to be *contracting.*

Answer the following question on the lines below. Use complete sentence.

11. What do scientists hope to learn by using the Hubble Space Telescope? What would you like to study in outer space? Why?
Scientists hope to learn how the universe began and whether there are inhabited planets circling distant stars. Accept all reasonable responses for students' preferences for study in outer space.

Copyright Glencoe Division of Macmillan/McGraw-Hill
Users of *Merrill Physical Science* have the publisher's permission to reproduce this page. 85

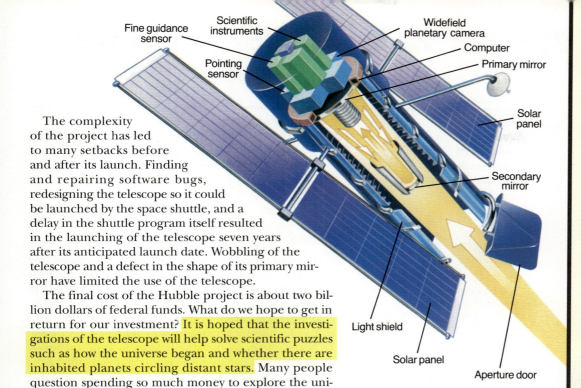

Fine guidance sensor
Scientific instruments
Pointing sensor
Widefield planetary camera
Computer
Primary mirror
Solar panel
Secondary mirror
Light shield
Solar panel
Aperture door

The complexity of the project has led to many setbacks before and after its launch. Finding and repairing software bugs, redesigning the telescope so it could be launched by the space shuttle, and a delay in the shuttle program itself resulted in the launching of the telescope seven years after its anticipated launch date. Wobbling of the telescope and a defect in the shape of its primary mirror have limited the use of the telescope.

The final cost of the Hubble project is about two billion dollars of federal funds. What do we hope to get in return for our investment? ==It is hoped that the investigations of the telescope will help solve scientific puzzles such as how the universe began and whether there are inhabited planets circling distant stars.== Many people question spending so much money to explore the universe when they believe there are so many unsolved problems on Earth. What do you think?

SECTION REVIEW

1. Why can a telescope in orbit above Earth form clearer images than a telescope on Earth?
2. What knowledge do we hope to gain from the Hubble Space Telescope?

You Decide!

Make a list of the major unsolved problems and questions our society faces today. Consider the future benefits from solving these problems. Where do you rank exploring the universe on your list? Do you think we should spend more billions of dollars to answer these questions about the universe? Some people are even in favor of launching more space telescopes. Do you think we need more?

SCIENCE & SOCIETY

● REINFORCEMENT 85

REINFORCEMENT   Chapter 20
The Hubble Space Telescope   Text Pages 536–527

Write a paragraph describing the Hubble Space Telescope. Use the following terms in your paragraph.

distortion   Hubble   primary mirror
images   galaxies   secondary mirror
orbit   universe   computer software
infrared   expanding   investigation
ultraviolet   solar panels

Accept all reasonable paragraphs.

Describe the problems and setbacks faced in launching the Hubble Space Telescope into orbit. Use the following terms in your description.

late   software   redesign   delay   testing

Accept all reasonable paragraphs.

▲ ENRICHMENT 85

ENRICHMENT   Chapter 20
The Hubble Space Telescope   Text Pages 536–527

ATMOSPHERIC REFRACTION

Light rays are bent, or refracted, when they move from one medium to another medium. Therefore, light entering Earth's atmosphere from space is refracted. This refraction of light causes images viewed from telescopes to be blurry. Orbiting satellites, such as the Hubble Space Telescope, are designed to work outside Earth's atmosphere. This allows a clearer view of distant objects.

1. Why are ground-based telescopes built on high mountains away from large cities?
The atmosphere at high altitudes is thinner and clearer. Light from cities can interfere with starlight.

2. Because of atmospheric refraction, you can see the sun in the evening for several minutes after it is really below the horizon. In the morning you can see it for several minutes before it is actually above the horizon. Draw a simple diagram to show this.

Light from the sun
Earth

3. How would the sun look from a planet with a very thick and dense, but still transparent, atmosphere? **The sun would seem to be flattened in the vertical direction. Light from the bottom edge would be more strongly refracted than light from the top edge.**

4. Locations of stars and planets are measured using altitude (degrees above the horizon) and azimuth (compass direction). What errors are possible when making measurements of star and planet locations? **Refraction causes light to be bent. The measurements will be off by the angle of refraction of the light.**

527

Ask questions 1-2 in the Section Review.

RETEACH
Reinforce the idea that the Hubble Space Telescope needs to be above Earth's atmosphere. Draw a sphere to represent Earth. Now surround the sphere with a circle of shaded chalk. Show how the light path would be refracted when the light slows down as it passes into Earth's atmosphere from space.

EXTENSION
For students who have mastered this section, use the **Reinforcement** and **Enrichment** masters or other OPTIONS provided.

3 CLOSE

▶ Have all students stand in the middle of the room. After discussing the benefits and drawbacks of operating the Hubble Space Telescope, designate one side of the room for those who take the position, "Yes, we should spend whatever is necessary to investigate these questions of our cosmos." Designate the other side to take the position, "No, we should first spend money to solve our problems on Earth." Have students show their feelings by standing on either end of the room or somewhere in-between. Ask some students to explain their point of view.

SECTION REVIEW ANSWERS
1. Telescopes on Earth form images distorted by Earth's atmosphere.
2. unsolved questions about the universe—such as how it began, or if there is life on other planets

YOU DECIDE!

SCIENCE & SOCIETY
Answers will vary. Make sure students can support their answers.

PREPARATION

SECTION BACKGROUND

▶ Lasers are available in a variety of colors; the wavelength and color of light emitted depends on the materials in the laser. The most common one is probably the helium-neon laser, which explains why so many people imagine lasers as a red beam of light.

▶ Laser stands for **L**ight **A**mplification by **S**timulated **E**mission of **R**adiation. In contrast with the spontaneous release of light during a flame test of an element, the electrons in a laser remain excited until struck by a photon of light emitted by another electron.

▶ Excited electrons emit light polarized in the direction they are vibrating. In most light sources, the electrons are vibrating in infinitely many directions and light is emitted in every imaginable plane. Use polarization to support the fact that light waves are transverse, not longitudinal like sound.

PREPLANNING

▶ If you don't have a laser, arrange to borrow one from a nearby high school, university, or business.

1 MOTIVATE

▶ Walk into class wearing a pair of sunglasses or 3-D glasses. Ask students why you might want to wear them. Note that polarized sunglasses are more expensive and far more effective at cutting glare. This is a good lead-in to a discussion of polarized light.

Science and WRITING

This is a good time to discuss advertising image versus reality as it relates to a wide variety of products. Science can make us better consumers also.

20-5 Applications of Light

New Science Words

polarized light
laser
coherent light
incoherent light
total internal reflection
optical fibers

Objectives

▶ Describe polarized light and the uses of polarizing lenses.
▶ Explain how a laser produces coherent light and how it differs from incoherent light.
▶ Apply the concept of total internal reflection to the uses of optical fibers.

Science and WRITING

Write an article for your school newspaper answering the question that's on everyone's mind—which sunglasses are best? Do a preference poll among your classmates. Check the claims in the ads and see what research magazines, such as *Consumer Reports*, have to say.

Figure 20-14. Very little light passes through two polarized filters that are aligned at right angles to each other (a). A polarizing filter is used in the left photo (b) to reduce glare.

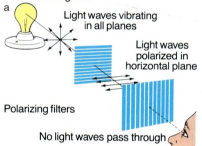

Light waves vibrating in all planes
Light waves polarized in horizontal plane
Polarizing filters
No light waves pass through

Polarized Light

Have you ever purchased a new pair of sunglasses? You may have tried on dozens of pairs of sunglasses before you found the pair you wanted. Did you notice that some of them had a sticker on them that said *polarized*? What makes them different from other kinds of sunglasses?

Recall modeling a transverse wave on a rope in Chapter 18. You could make the waves vibrate in any direction—horizontal, vertical, or anywhere in between. Most light sources, such as incandescent lamps and the sun, emit light that also vibrates in many directions. If this light passes through a special filter, called a polarizing filter, the light becomes polarized. **In polarized light, the transverse waves vibrate only on one plane. A polarizing filter consists of chains of long, thin molecules lined up in parallel rows. Only light waves vibrating in the same direction as these molecular chains are allowed to pass through** ❶

OPTIONS

Meeting Different Ability Levels

For Section 20-5, use the following **Teacher Resource Masters** depending upon individual students' needs.

◆ **Study Guide Master** for all students.
● **Reinforcement Master** for students of average and above average ability levels.
▲ **Enrichment Master** for above average students.

Additional Teacher Resource Package masters are listed in the OPTIONS box throughout the section. The additional masters are appropriate for all students.

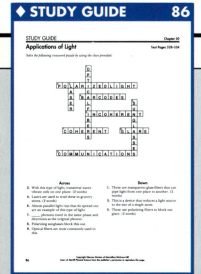

◆ STUDY GUIDE   86

STUDY GUIDE   Chapter 20
Applications of Light   Text Pages 528–534

Solve the following crossword puzzle by using the clues provided.

Across

2. With this type of light, transverse waves vibrate only on one plane. (2 words)
4. Lasers are used to read these in grocery stores. (2 words)
6. Almost parallel light rays that do spread out are an example of this type of light.
7. _____ photons travel in the same phase and directions as the original photon.
8. Polarizing sunglasses block this out.
9. Optical fibers are most commonly used in this.

Down

1. These are transparent glass fibers that can pipe light from one place to another. (2 words)
3. This is a device that reduces a light source to the size of a single atom.
5. These use polarizing filters to block out glare. (2 words)

them. If a second polarizing filter is aligned so its molecules are oriented at right angles to the first filter, very little light is passed through, as illustrated in Figure 20-14(a).

Light that is reflected from horizontal surfaces, such as a lake or a car's hood, is partially polarized horizontally. This annoying reflection is called glare. Polarizing sunglasses are made with vertically polarizing filters. They block out most of the glare while allowing vertically polarized light through. In addition, the lenses are darkly colored to absorb even more light. Polarizing filters can also be placed over camera lenses to reduce the glare when taking pictures.

Have you ever watched a 3-D movie? Did you wear special glasses to see the effects? The characters seemed like they were right in front of you, didn't they? In three dimensional (3-D) glasses, one filter is aligned vertically and one filter is aligned horizontally. The movie is shown through two projectors, one with a horizontally polarizing filter and the other with a vertically polarizing filter. As a result, your right eye sees a slightly different picture than your left eye. This creates the impression of depth, or three dimensions.

Next time you shop for sunglasses, you will know why some are polarized. They are designed to reduce glare, while sunglasses that aren't polarized don't reduce glare. What kind do you think you would prefer?

Figure 20-15. Polarizing filters are often used by photographers to reduce glare.

TYING TO PREVIOUS KNOWLEDGE: Recall from Chapter 19 that light can be modeled as a transverse wave. Ask students to show how they would model a transverse wave (a wave on a rope). This conceptual understanding is important to the three new applications of light in this section.

OBJECTIVES AND SCIENCE WORDS: Have students review the objectives and science words to become familiar with this section.

2 TEACH

Key Concepts are highlighted.

CONCEPT DEVELOPMENT

▶ Have a laser behind your desk. When you turn it on, tell students they must find the position of the laser beam. They will be disappointed to find only a small dot on the wall. How are laser beams visible in the pictures and laser shows students may have seen? Scatter some chalk dust in the air to make the laser light visible. Discuss how the laser light must be reflected off a particle into your eye for you to see the beam.

▶ Borrow an oven rack from the home-economics room. Use the grill to make vertical slits and thread a rope through two of them. Have one student hold the grill while another makes a vertical transverse wave while yet another student holds the other end. The rope should pass through the grill. Now have the student holding the grill slowly turn it until the slits are horizontal. Students should observe that the vertical wave is blocked, but a horizontal one could get through.

529

▶Use two Polaroid filters to illustrate Figures 20-14,15. Place one filter on the overhead projector and then slowly rotate the second one over it. Ask students to identify when the filters are parallel (when it is light) and when they are perpendicular (when it is dark).

▶Use the same setup as above, but put a piece of stretched plastic wrap or pieces of cut-up storage bags between the filters. Rotate the second filter over it again. You should see an array of continually changing colors and brightness. The chains of molecules in the plastic are rearranged when stretched, and this produces the polarization of light of different wavelengths.

▶After talking about the function of a laser and the coherent nature of laser light, give a small laser show of your own. Have a student clap erasers together to give you a continual source of particles in the air. Show diffraction through a thin slit, through a Fresnel lens, and take the opportunity to review refraction and reflection.

Science and READING

Each process utilizes different characteristics (power, directionality and monochromaticity) of the various light emitting mediums (ruby crystal, CO_2, HeNe, argon, yttrium, aluminum, or garnet).

Science and READING

How can a laser be used in such a wide range of activities as welding, performing surgery, transmitting communications signals, printing, etc.?

What is laser light?

Lasers

The narrow beams of light that zip across the stage and through the auditorium during a rock concert are produced by **lasers.** Beams of laser light do not spread out as does light from other light sources because laser light is coherent. **Coherent light** is electromagnetic energy of only one wavelength which travels with its crests and troughs aligned. The beam does not spread out because all the waves travel in the same direction. Light from an ordinary light bulb is incoherent because it lacks the characteristics of coherent light. **Incoherent light** may contain more than one color and its electromagnetic waves do not travel in the same direction, causing the beam to spread out.

Photons in a beam of coherent light are identical and travel in the same direction. Such photons can be produced by a laser. A laser's light begins when a photon is spontaneously emitted from an atom. This photon is reflected back and forth between two facing mirrors at opposite ends of the laser. One mirror is partially coated to allow some light to leave that end of the laser. If the emitted photon travels perpendicular to one of the mirrors it will be reflected between them many times. As it moves back and forth, it can stimulate other atoms to emit identical photons as well. The continual production of photons travelling perpendicularly to the mirror by *other* photons produces a coherent beam of laser light.

Figure 20-16. A laser produces a coherent beam of visible light of the same wavelengths.

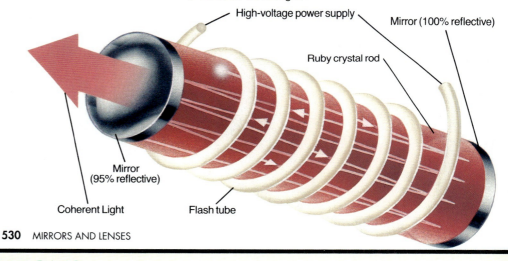

High-voltage power supply

Mirror (100% reflective)

Ruby crystal rod

Mirror (95% reflective)

Coherent Light

Flash tube

OPTIONS

INQUIRY QUESTIONS

▶**Does polarized light support the wave theory of light or the particle theory of light?** *the wave theory, because it is discussed as being transverse waves vibrating on only one plane*

▶**Would laser light support the wave theory of light or the particle theory of light?** *the particle theory, because laser light is described in terms of photons*

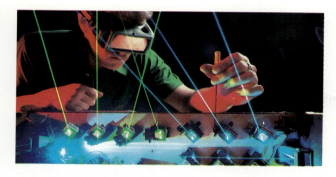

Figure 20-17. There are many practical uses for laser light.

Lasers can be made with many different materials, including gases, liquids, and solids. One of the most common lasers is the helium-neon laser, which produces a beam of red light. As the name implies, a mixture of helium and neon gases is sealed in a tube with mirrors at both ends. An electric spark is used to excite the atoms in the gases.

❷ Laser light has many applications. Perhaps you have seen lasers used in grocery stores to read the bar codes on packages. One reason that compact discs maintain high sound quality is that the laser used to read the disc doesn't scratch the disc's surface. Surgeons can use lasers in place of a scalpel to cut cleanly through body tissues. The energy from the laser can seal off some blood vessels in the incision to reduce bleeding. Lasers are routinely used to remove cataracts and repair the retina in the eye. Powerful lasers are used for cutting and welding materials in industry. Surveyors and builders use lasers for measuring and leveling. Lasers beamed at the moon allow us to measure the moon's orbit with great accuracy. The beam is reflected from mirrors placed on the moon by astronauts. Lasers also provide a coherent light source for fiber-optic communications.

What materials can lasers be made from?

Optical Fibers

Did you ever dangle your legs from the side of a swimming pool and watch your feet disappear as you raised them in the water? The disappearance of your feet is an example of total internal reflection. **Total internal reflection** occurs when light striking a surface between two transparent materials reflects totally from that surface, back into the first material. As you know, to see your feet in

Figure 20-18. Total internal reflection causes gems to sparkle.

20-5 APPLICATIONS OF LIGHT **531**

TEACHER F.Y.I.

▶ The stimulated emissions that produce laser light are similar to the phenomenon that produces flame tests. As a result, the color of laser light depends on the nature of the materials used to produce it.

CONCEPT DEVELOPMENT

▶ Be sure to show the class what a simple optical fiber looks like. Small desktop decorations made of optical fibers are relatively inexpensive. Emphasize that just one optical fiber can carry thousands of telephone conversations efficiently.

▶ Demonstrate total internal reflection by shining a laser at a large angle at a prism or another object that usually transmits light. Since diamonds have a very high index of refraction and a lot of facets, total internal reflection allows light to exit only at certain points. As a result, we say that diamonds "sparkle."

REVEALING MISCONCEPTIONS

▶ The laser is often thought of as a very powerful and efficient energy source. The typical classroom laser will not burn a hole through your skin, as some students may believe. The laser beam should not be directed into anyone's eyes, however. Classroom lasers are a very inefficient light source; they are often less than 1 percent efficient!

INQUIRY QUESTIONS

▶ **Laser light can be in many colors, not just red. Would you expect red laser light to have more energy than blue laser light? Explain your answer.** *no, because blue light has more energy than red light*

▶ **Why can't we measure the moon's orbit with a beam of incoherent light instead of laser light?** *The rays would diverge over such a great distance.*

PROGRAM RESOURCES

From the **Teacher Resource Package** use: **Technology,** pages 17-18, Compact Discs.

CROSS CURRICULUM

▶ **Communications:** Have students investigate how optical fibers are used to send telephone conversations, television programs, and computer information. How does this information become light?

CHECK FOR UNDERSTANDING

Use the Mini Quiz to check for understanding.

MINI QUIZ

Use the Mini Quiz to check students' recall of chapter content.

1 **How does polarized light differ from ordinary light?** *The waves all vibrate in one plane.*

2 **List three applications of lasers.** *read grocery bar codes, compact disc players, surgery, cutting and welding, fiber optic communications*

3 **A(n) _____ is a transparent glass fiber that pipes light from one place to another.** *optical fiber*

RETEACH

To reinforce the idea of coherent light, first have everyone in the class clap their own individual rhythm. It sounds scattered and jumbled. Now have everyone clap on the number as you count "one and two and three and...." The sound is "coherent" or together and more intense.

EXTENSION

For students who have mastered this section, use the **Reinforcement** and **Enrichment** masters or other OPTIONS provided.

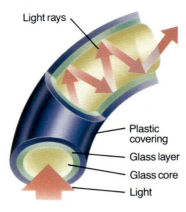

Figure 20-19. An optical fiber is designed to reflect light so that it is piped through the fiber without leaving it, except at the ends.

Light rays
Plastic covering
Glass layer
Glass core
Light

Figure 20-20. Just one of these optical fibers can carry thousands of phone conversations at the same time.

the pool, light must reflect from your feet to your eyes. As you raise your feet in the pool, the light reflecting from your feet strikes the surface between the water and the air and reflects back into the water. Your feet seem to disappear because light reflecting from your feet never reaches your eyes. Total internal refelection depends on the speed of light in the two materials and the angle at which the light strikes the surface. The speed of light in the first materials must be less than it is in the second. Also, the angle at which the light strikes the surface of the first material must be large.

Total internal reflection makes light transmission in optical fibers possible. **Optical fibers** are transparent glass fibers that can pipe light from one place to another. As shown in Figure 20-19, light entering one end of the fiber is continuously reflected from the sides of the fiber until it emerges from the other end. Very little light is lost or absorbed in optical fibers.

Optical fibers are most comonly used in communications. Telephone conversations, television programs, and computer information can be used to modulate light beams into optical signals. The signals are transmitted by a laser through the optical fibers with far less loss of signal than if similar electric signals were transmitted though copper wires. Because of total internal reflection, signals can't leak from one fiber to another and interfere with other messages. As a result, the signal is clearly transmitted. One optical fiber can carry thousands of phone conversations at one time because the signals can be produced quite rapidly and travel at high speeds through the fiber.

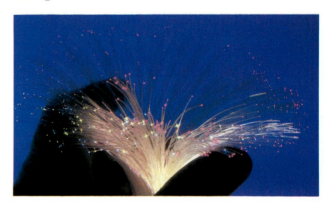

OPTIONS

ENRICHMENT

▶ Have students investigate the use of polarized optical fibers in communications.

▶ Have students find out how law enforcement agencies are using lasers and fiber optics to detect the smuggling of illegal drugs.

TECHNOLOGY

The Light Scalpel

Optical fibers piping laser energy deep inside the human body may replace some conventional surgical procedures. The effect of the laser on human tissue depends on wavelength and intensity of the laser light, and the color of the body tissue. As a result of varying wavelength and intensity of a laser, it can target a particular kind of tissue for surgery.

Low-power lasers are used to seal soft tissue, and to treat ulcers in the stomach, intestine, and colon. Many other surgical applications, however, require high-power lasers. One of the most exciting applications of a high-power laser and optical fiber system would be in the treatment of cardiovascular diseases. An optical fiber-conducted laser may be used to treat a patient with a blocked artery. The optical fiber would be used to deliver pulses of high-powered laser light to blast the artery clear.

Think Critically: What problems might arise in using a high-power laser to blast an artery clear of an obstruction?

SECTION REVIEW

1. What is polarized light?
2. Distinguish between coherent and incoherent light.
3. Explain how an optical fiber transmits light.
4. **Apply:** Which of the following materials could possibly be substituted for the glass in an optical fiber: clear plastic, wood, or water? Explain your answer.

☒ Sequencing

Sequence the events that occur in a laser in order to produce coherent light. Begin with the emission of a photon from an atom. If you need help, refer to Sequencing in the **Skill Handbook** on page 676.

Skill Builder

Skill Builder

1. emission of a photon from an atom
2. bounces back and forth between two mirrors
3. stimulates other atoms to emit photons which must move in the same phase and direction as the original photon
4. Coherent photons of light escape from the mirror at the end of the laser.
5. Coherent light travels with very little spreading out.

---

3 CLOSE

▶ Discuss the medical applications of lasers and optical fibers. Lasers are used for precise cutting and cauterization of blood vessels. Optical fibers are inserted into small incisions inside the body. Light travels down one set of fibers, is reflected, and returns up another set of fibers to produce an image on a computer screen. Together, they revolutionize many kinds of surgery because the required incision is so small.

▶ Have the students make a card file of the various types of lasers. This file should include the wavelength of light produced by the laser and its current applications. Relate the wavelength of light to energy.

▶ If the technology is accessible, put this information into a database. Use the database to arrange the lasers from the most powerful to the least powerful.

▶ Ask questions 1-3 and the **Apply** Question in the Section Review.

TECHNOLOGY

▶ **Reference:** Katzir, Abraham. "Optical Fibers in Medicine." *Scientific American.* May 1989, pp. 120-125.
Think Critically: The wall of the artery might absorb enough energy to be damaged.

SECTION REVIEW ANSWERS

1. All light waves vibrate in the same plane.
2. Coherent, or laser light has a single wavelength and travels with its crests and troughs aligned. This means in phase. Most light contains many wavelengths and is incoherent.
3. The light undergoes total internal reflection as it strikes the inside of the glass tube.
4. **Apply:** Plastic would work because it is transparent. Water is also transparent, and would work, but is impractical to use because it is a liquid. Wood is opaque and wouldn't transmit light.

ACTIVITY 20-2
20 minutes

OBJECTIVE: Investigate practical applications of polarized light.

PROCESS SKILLS applied in this activity:
▶**Observing** in Steps 1-4 and Conclude and Apply Question 4.
▶**Inferring** in Analyze Question 2 and Conclude and Apply Questions 4, 5, and 6.

👥 COOPERATIVE LEARNING
The class can share one source of bright light. Each problem solving team can share a pair of filters.

TEACHING THE ACTIVITY
▶Polarized light filters can be cut into small pieces, but keep edges in line with direction of polarization.
▶Lenses of polarizing sunglasses make good polarizing filters.
Troubleshooting: Use blocks of polished or painted wood or plastic. Do not use either dull or mirrored surfaces.
▶Take apart an inexpensive calculator or digital watch and remove the polar filter. The colors reverse when the filter is turned.

PROGRAM RESOURCES
From the **Teacher Resource Package** use:

Activity Worksheets, pages 160-161, Activity 20-2: Polarized Light.

ACTIVITY 20-2
Polarized Light

Problem: *How can polarized light be identified?*

Materials
- two polarizing filters
- light source
- objects with flat, hard surfaces

Procedure
1. Turn one filter against the other while looking through them. When the maximum light can be seen, mark the edges of the filters "X" and "Y" as shown.
2. Hold an object with its flat surface horizontal. Reflect light from its surface. Look at the reflection through one filter and turn it until the glare disappears.
3. Turn the object so that light reflects from a vertical surface and repeat Step 2.
4. Light from the sky which is 90° from the sun is polarized. Look through the filter at this part of the sky and rotate the filter to make the sky darken.

Analyze
1. How many degrees must you turn one filter from the other to change the light from brightest to darkest?
2. When the light glare from the horizontal surface disappears, which filter edge is up, "X" or "Y"? Is this also true for glare from the vertical surface?
3. If there are clouds in the sky, how do they appear as the filter darkens the sky?

Conclude and Apply
4. LCD or digital calculators and watches are polarized. Why does it matter which way a digital watch's polarizing filter is oriented?
5. Would your polarizing sunglasses work as well if you turned them sideways?
6. Photographs look best if taken in polarized light. What is the best time of day to take pictures?

534 MIRRORS AND LENSES

ANSWERS TO QUESTIONS
1. The filter must be turned 90 degrees.
2. If *X* is the answer to part one, then *Y* is the answer to part two.
3. Clouds do not darken as the filter is turned.
4. The polarizing filter must be oriented so people wearing polarized glasses can see the time.
5. Since most glare is horizontal, the glasses won't work as well.
6. Take pictures in the morning and afternoon when overhead light is polarized.

SUMMARY

20-1: The Optics of Mirrors

1. Plane mirrors and convex mirrors produce virtual images. Concave mirrors produce real images.

2. A concave mirror is like the inside of a shiny spoon, and a convex mirror is like the outside of a shiny spoon.

20-2: The Optics of Lenses

1. Convex lenses form real images; concave lenses form virtual images.

2. Convex lenses converge light rays and can form images on a screen. Concave lenses diverge light rays and are used in combination with other lenses to extend the focal length.

3. Corrective lenses can be used in combination with the lens in your eye to focus images on the retina. Farsighted people must wear convex lenses, and nearsighted persons must wear concave lenses.

20-3: Optical Instruments

1. A refracting telescope uses convex lenses to magnify distant objects; a reflecting telescope uses concave and plane mirrors, and a convex lens to magnify distant objects.

2. Light passing through the lens of a camera is focused on photographic film inside the camera. The image on the film is real, inverted, and smaller than the object being photographed.

20-4: Science and Society: The Hubble Space Telescope

1. The Hubble Space Telescope produces sharper images than telescopes on Earth; in addition, it can detect infrared and ultraviolet radiation.

2. Scientists hope space telescopes will provide information that will answer our questions about the universe.

20-5: Applications of Light

1. Polarized light consists of transverse waves that only vibrate along one plane. Polarized lenses act as filters to block light waves that aren't polarized in the same plane as the filter.

2. A laser produces coherent light by emitting a beam of photons that travel in the same phase and direction. Light that spreads out from its source is incoherent.

3. Optical fibers can "pipe" light rays because the fibers are made of a material that allows the light rays to reflect totally inside the fibers.

KEY SCIENCE WORDS

a. coherent light
b. concave lenses
c. concave mirror
d. convex lenses
e. convex mirror
f. focal length
g. focal point
h. incoherent light
i. laser
j. microscope
k. optical fibers
l. plane mirror
m. polarized light
n. real image
o. reflecting telescope
p. refracting telescope
q. telephoto lenses
r. total internal reflection
s. virtual image
t. wide-angle lenses

UNDERSTANDING VOCABULARY

Match each phrase with the correct term from the list of Key Science Words.

1. mirror with a flat surface
2. image that cannot be projected onto a screen
3. image formed where light rays actually meet
4. curved mirror that diverges reflected light
5. lenses that converge light at their focal point
6. a telescope that uses two convex lenses
7. an instrument used to study very small objects
8. light waves that vibrate in only one plane
9. light produced by lasers
10. often used to transmit telephone signals

MIRRORS AND LENSES **535**

CHAPTER
REVIEW

SUMMARY

Have students read the Summary statements to review the major concepts of the chapter.

UNDERSTANDING VOCABULARY

1. l	**6.** p
2. s	**7.** j
3. n	**8.** m
4. e	**9.** a
5. d	**10.** k

OPTIONS

ASSESSMENT

To assess student understanding of the material in this chapter, use the resources listed.

COOPERATIVE LEARNING

Consider using Cooperative Learning in the THINK AND WRITE CRITICALLY, APPLY, and MORE SKILL BUILDERS sections of the Chapter Review.

PROGRAM RESOURCES

From the **Teacher Resource Package** use:

Chapter Review, pages 43-44.

Chapter and Unit Tests, pages 130-133, Chapter Test.

Chapter and Unit Tests, pages 134-135, Unit Test.

CHECKING CONCEPTS

1. c	**6.** d
2. b	**7.** b
3. c	**8.** d
4. c	**9.** d
5. b	**10.** d

UNDERSTANDING CONCEPTS

11. five
12. convex
13. wide-angle
14. total internal reflection
15. atmosphere

THINK AND WRITE CRITICALLY

16. Light rays are reflected through the mirror's focal point. Light rays approaching a concave mirror are reflected parallel to the optical axis.

17. To give us more information and to answer some unsolved questions about the universe.

18. In convex lenses, light is refracted towards the center of the lens and converges at the focal point of the lens, hence, the name converging lens. In contrast, light is refracted towards the edges of concave lenses therefore it diverges away from the lens' focal point. Concave lenses are thus called diverging lenses.

19. Both are used to magnify objects. However, telescopes are used to magnify very large objects that are quite far away, while microscopes magnify very small objects that are close at hand. The refracting telescope is built according to the same principles as the microscope.

20. A photon is emitted from an atom and reflected between two mirrors at the ends of the laser. This photon excites other atoms within the laser and they emit photons, as well. Some of the photons penetrate one of the mirrors and leave the end of the laser in a fine stream of coherent light.

CHAPTER
REVIEW

CHECKING CONCEPTS

Choose the word or phrase that completes the sentence.

1. Images formed by plane mirrors are not _____.
a. upright
b. reversed
c. enlarged
d. virtual

2. An object that reflects light and curves inward is called a _____.
a. plane mirror
b. concave mirror
c. convex mirror
d. concave lens

3. Mirrors that can magnify a reflection are _____.
a. convex
b. plane
c. concave
d. all of these

4. The light bulb in a headlight, flashlight, or spotlight is placed at the focal point of a _____.
a. concave lens
b. convex lens
c. concave mirror
d. convex mirror

5. Lenses form images by _____.
a. reflecting light
b. refracting light
c. diffracting light
d. interfering with light

6. A concave lens bends light towards its _____.
a. focal point
b. optical axis
c. center
d. edges

7. Farsighted people must wear _____.
a. flat lenses
b. convex lenses
c. concave lenses
d. unevenly curved lenses

8. Reflecting telescopes don't contain a _____.
a. plane mirror
b. concave mirror
c. convex lens
d. concave lens

9. Sunglasses and 3-D glasses use _____.
a. concave lenses
b. convex lenses
c. telephoto lenses
d. polarizing lenses

10. Lasers are often used in _____.
a. cutting and welding
b. reading bar codes
c. surgery
d. all of these

UNDERSTANDING CONCEPTS

Complete each sentence.

11. The image of a girl five meters in front of a plane mirror appears to be _____ meters behind the mirror.

12. Images formed by _____ mirrors are virtual, small, and upright.

13. Camera lenses with short focal lengths that include much of the surroundings in their images are _____ lenses.

14. Optical fibers can transmit light around corners because light undergoes _____ within the fiber.

15. The Hubble Space Telescope can detect infrared and ultraviolet radiation that is usually blocked out by Earth's _____.

THINK AND WRITE CRITICALLY

16. Describe how a concave mirror reflects light rays that approach it parallel to its optical axis. How does such a mirror reflect approaching light rays that pass through its focal point?

17. Why was the Hubble Space Telescope built?

18. Convex lenses are often called converging lenses while concave lenses are often called diverging lenses. Explain these different names by describing how each type of lens refracts light.

19. Compare and contrast the uses of telescopes and microscopes. Which type of telescope is built most like a microscope?

20. Explain how a laser produces coherent light.

APPLY

21. If the object the audience was looking at were really an image in a concave mirror, the magician could make this image disappear by moving the object to the focal point of the mirror where no image is formed.

22. It will produce an enlarged, upright, virtual image that can't be projected onto a screen.

23. a convex lens

24. No. The convex mirror would produce a virtual image that cannot be magnified by the eyepiece.

25. A zoom lens. Since zoom lenses have adjustable focal lengths, they can be used for normal, wide-angle, and telephoto applications.

APPLY

21. Magicians often make objects disappear by using "trick" mirrors. How might a magician seem to make an object disappear by using a concave mirror?

22. What would happen if a movie projector's lens was less than one focal length from the film?

23. If you were an optician, what type of lens would you prescribe for a patient who can't focus clearly on close objects?

24. Would a reflecting telescope work properly if its concave mirror were replaced by a convex mirror? Explain.

25. You only have enough money to buy one lens for your camera. What type of lens would be most useful? Explain.

MORE SKILL BUILDERS

If you need help, refer to the Skill Handbook.

1. Outlining: Summarize in an outline the different types of images formed by plane, concave, and convex mirrors.

2. Observing and Inferring: Infer the effects of a hard, rigid eye lens on human vision. Would this make the eye more or less like a simple camera?

3. Recognizing Cause and Effect: Distinguish between and describe the causes and effects of the following vision problems: nearsightedness, farsightedness, and an astigmatism.

4. Hypothesizing: Rough, uncut diamonds lack the sparkle of diamonds that have been cut by a gem cutter. Propose a hypothesis to explain this observation.

5. Concept Mapping: Below is a concept map summarizing characteristics of coherent and incoherent light. Use the following terms to complete the map (terms may be used more than once): wavelength(s), frequency(ies), color(s), sun, lasers, coherent light, incoherent light.

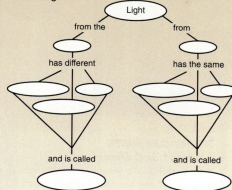

PROJECTS

1. Write a report tracing the development of the telescope from the time of Galileo to the Hubble Space Telescope.

2. Investigate the types of mirrors used in funhouses. Explain how these mirrors give distorted images and report your findings to the class.

4. Hypothesizing: One possible hypothesis might be: Cutting diamonds in specific ways gives them inner surfaces that refracted light can strike at angles large enough to produce total internal reflection and thus the diamond sparkles.

5. Concept Mapping: Student maps will vary.

1. Outlining: *Mirror Images*
  I. Plane mirrors (for all object distances)
      A. virtual
      B. upright
      C. same size as object
      D. reversed
      E. image distance equals object distance
  II. Concave Mirrors
      A. Object distance: less than one focal length
          1. virtual
          2. upright
          3. larger than object
      B. Object distance: focal length
          1. no image
      C. Object distance: more than one focal length but less than two focal lengths
          1. real
          2. inverted
          3. larger
      D. Object distance: at two times the focal length
          1. real
          2. inverted
          3. same size
      E. Object distance: more than two focal lengths
          1. real
          2. inverted
          3. smaller than the object
  III. Convex Mirrors
      A. virtual
      B. upright
      C. smaller than object

2. Observing and Inferring: A hard, rigid eye lens would have a fixed focal length. This means that the image of an object could only be focused on the retina when the object is a specific distance from the eye. Such an eye would be more like a simple camera which has a lens of fixed focal length.

3. Recognizing Cause and Effect: *Nearsightedness—cause:* an abnormally long eyeball or bulging cornea. *effect:* light from a distant object is focused in front of the retina. *Farsightedness—cause:* abnormally short eyeball or flattened cornea. *effect:* light from nearby objects is focused behind the retina. *Astigmatism—cause:* unevenly curved cornea. *effect:* all light is poorly focused on the retina.

Objective

In this unit-ending feature, the unit topic, "Waves, Light, and Sound," is extended into other disciplines. Students will see how waves, light, and sound affect events around the planet.

Motivate

Cooperative Learning: Assign one Connection to each group of students. Using the Expert Teams strategy, have each group research to find out more about the geographic location of the Connection—its climate, culture, flora and fauna, and ecological issues.

Teaching Tips

▶ Tell students to keep in mind the connection between waves and each event described in this feature.

▶ Ask students to explain any differences in the kinds of waves involved in the different Connections.

Wrap-Up

Conclude this lesson by having students predict how new knowledge about waves, light, and sound might affect their future lives.

GEOLOGY

Background: The October 17th earthquake registered 7.1 on the Richter scale and was felt across a million square kilometers. Structures built on mud, sand, or fill collapsed as seismic waves burned the soil and groundwater into a quicksand-like "soup."

Discussion: Discuss the accuracy of earthquake predictions. Ask students to discuss the benefits of being able to accurately predict where and when earthquakes will happen.

Answer to Question: Earthquake waves were amplified by the soft fill material where the Marina district had expanded into San Francisco Bay. L-waves travel along Earth's surface and cause the most damage.

Extension: Have students research the 1988 Armenian and 1985 Mexico City earthquakes.

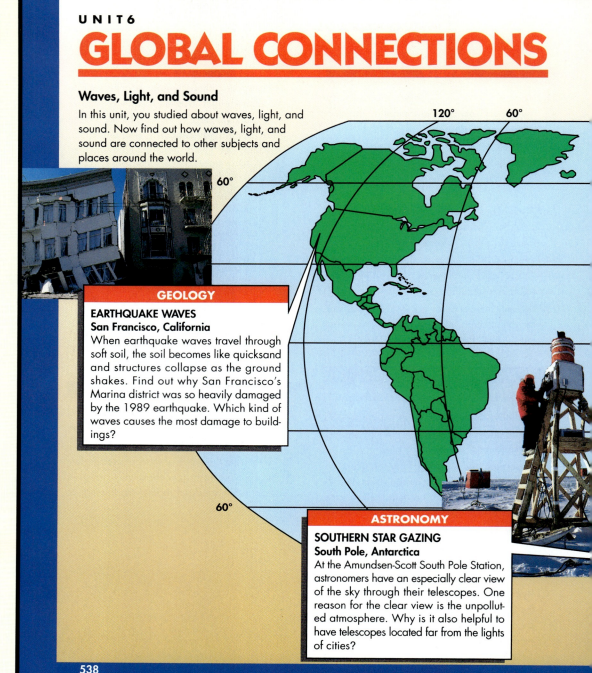

Waves, Light, and Sound

In this unit, you studied about waves, light, and sound. Now find out how waves, light, and sound are connected to other subjects and places around the world.

GEOLOGY

EARTHQUAKE WAVES
San Francisco, California
When earthquake waves travel through soft soil, the soil becomes like quicksand and structures collapse as the ground shakes. Find out why San Francisco's Marina district was so heavily damaged by the 1989 earthquake. Which kind of waves causes the most damage to buildings?

ASTRONOMY

SOUTHERN STAR GAZING
South Pole, Antarctica
At the Amundsen-Scott South Pole Station, astronomers have an especially clear view of the sky through their telescopes. One reason for the clear view is the unpolluted atmosphere. Why is it also helpful to have telescopes located far from the lights of cities?

538

ASTRONOMY

Background: The moving layers of Earth's atmosphere interfere with astronomers' views of celestial objects. For this reason, telescopes are usually located where the atmosphere is the least dense.

Discussion: Discuss with students why many telescopes are located high on mountains where the air is less dense. Ask students to describe how the view from the South Pole telescope would differ from the view from those in the United States.

Answer to Question: Lights from cities make it more difficult to see faint objects in the sky.

Extension: Have students find out why astronomers were so anxious to have the Hubble Space Telescope launched.

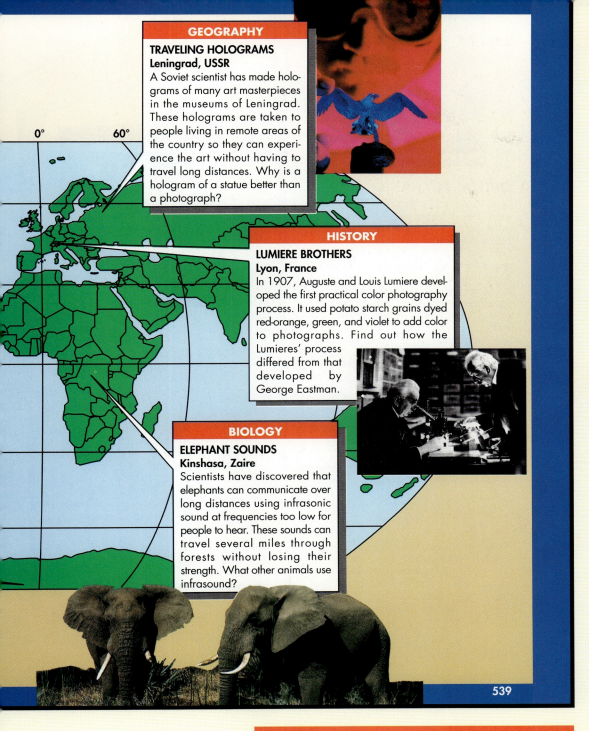

GEOGRAPHY

TRAVELING HOLOGRAMS
Leningrad, USSR

A Soviet scientist has made holograms of many art masterpieces in the museums of Leningrad. These holograms are taken to people living in remote areas of the country so they can experience the art without having to travel long distances. Why is a hologram of a statue better than a photograph?

HISTORY

LUMIERE BROTHERS
Lyon, France

In 1907, Auguste and Louis Lumiere developed the first practical color photography process. It used potato starch grains dyed red-orange, green, and violet to add color to photographs. Find out how the Lumieres' process differed from that developed by George Eastman.

BIOLOGY

ELEPHANT SOUNDS
Kinshasa, Zaire

Scientists have discovered that elephants can communicate over long distances using infrasonic sound at frequencies too low for people to hear. These sounds can travel several miles through forests without losing their strength. What other animals use infrasound?

539

BIOLOGY

Background: An elephant makes infrasonic sounds by vibrating a spot on its forehead. The spot, near the nasal openings, flutters at frequencies between 14 and 24 hertz. Infrasonic sounds travel much farther than high-frequency sounds.

Discussion: Discuss with students how using infrasonic calls would help keep a group of elephants together while traveling through a dense forest.

Answer to Question: Some types of birds, including pigeons, can hear infrasonic waves. Fin whales also produce infrasonic calls.

Extension: Have students research how different species of bats use ultrasonic sounds.

HISTORY

Background: The Lumieres' starch grains were coated with light-sensitive chemicals, which filtered colors as light passed through. The developed plate produced a negative which was exposed to light and redeveloped. The result was a transparency with specks of color that formed a full-color image.

Discussion: Discuss with students how the development of color photography might have changed people's ideas about the world around them.

Answer to Question: Kodachrome film, from George Eastman's Kodak labs, uses dyes of cyan, magenta, and yellow which were introduced layer by layer during processing.

Extension: Have students research information on color blindness.

GEOGRAPHY

Background: Holograms are 3-dimensional pictures that are produced by the use of laser light. However, lasers are not needed to view all holograms.

Discussion: Discuss with students how holograms differ from photographs. Ask them if they have seen holograms on credit cards, magazine covers, or cereal boxes.

Answer to Question: Because a statue is a 3-dimensional object, a hologram shows it better than a photograph.

Extension: Have students examine with a hand lens the holograms on the March 1984, November 1985, or December 1988 covers of *National Geographic*.

OPTICAL MECHANIC

Background: Optical mechanics may work in factories where cameras and binoculars are manufactured or in centers where eyeglasses and contact lenses are made.

Related Career	Education
Optician	technical school
Optometrist	college degree
Ophthalmologist	medical school
Laser technician	college degree

Career Issue: Recently people have become concerned about problems with extended-wear contact lenses. Some ophthalmologists and optometrists are advising patients against these products because of potential eye damage.

What do you think? Lead students in a discussion of their own attitudes about contact lenses, particularly the extended-wear type. What are the advantages and disadvantages for wearers?

PHOTOGRAPHER

Background: Many photographers are self-employed. Some specialize in portrait photography; others specialize in advertising photography or nature photography. Some photographers work for newspapers and magazines.

Related Career	Education
Film technician	high school
Retouch artist	technical school
Food stylist	technical school
Cinematographer	college degree

Career Issue: Computer technology now allows photographic images to be manipulated to add or delete items or people from pictures, or to combine images from several photographs. Some people are concerned about the ethics of altering photographs, particularly if it occurs in newspapers or news magazines.

What do you think? Lead students in a discussion of how they feel about alteration of photographs. Can they always believe what they see in a photograph?

OPTICAL MECHANIC

An *optical mechanic* uses special equipment to grind and polish lenses. Some optical mechanics make lenses for cameras and binoculars, while others make lenses for eyeglasses. Each pair of eyeglass lenses is made according to a prescription written by an optometrist or ophthalmologist. The optical mechanic makes sure each lens is correctly ground and then fits them into the eyeglass frames.

Most optical mechanics receive on-the-job training for about three years. If you're interested in becoming an optical mechanic, you should take courses in biology and physics.

For Additional Information

Contact the Optical Laboratories Association, 6935 Wisconsin Avenue, Suite 200, Chevy Chase, Maryland 20816.

PHOTOGRAPHER

A *photographer* uses light meters, lights, and cameras to take photographs. Some photographers work in commercial studios, photographing products or people. Others work for magazines or newspapers. Many photographers are self-employed.

A person interested in photography should have good color vision and artistic skills. High school classes in art, chemistry, and physics are helpful. If you're interested in becoming a photographer, there are several options for training. He or she can work as an assistant and receive on-the-job training for two or three years, or attend an art school or college that offers special programs in photography. A photographer who wants to specialize in medical or scientific subjects needs additional college classes in science.

For Additional Information

Contact the Professional Photographers of America, Inc., 1090 Executive Way, Des Plaines, Illinois 60018.

UNIT READINGS

▶ Heckman, Philip. *The Magic of Holography.* New York: Atheneum, 1986.
▶ Ward, Alan. *Experimenting With Light and Illusions.* London, England: Batsford, 1985.
▶ Wolkomir, Richard and Joyce. "When Animals Sound Off." *National Wildlife,* April - May, 1990, pp. 48-50.

540

UNIT READINGS

Background

▶ *The Magic of Holography* describes how holography is used today and how it might be used in the future.
▶ *Experimenting with Light and Illusions* contains experiments that illustrate the nature of light and illusions.
▶ "When Animals Sound Off" describes the various ways different animals use sound.

More Readings

1. Filson, Brent. *Exploring with Lasers.* New York, NY: Messner, 1984. This book describes how lasers operate and how they are used.
2. Proujan, C. "Looking Through 'Walls.'" *Scholastic Science World.* October 5, 1984, p. 11. A brief look at X rays.

Alma Woodsey Thomas — Color Field Painter

Alma Thomas was a black artist who achieved prominence in the mainstream art community. She worked in the modern tradition of Color Field painting.

She was born in 1892 in Columbus, Georgia. Because her aunts were teachers, she decided at an early age that teaching could be her way to a better life, too. Her family moved to Washington, D.C., in 1907. In 1924, she was the first graduate of the new art department at Howard University.

She taught art in the Washington schools for 35 years. During that time, she earned an M.A. at Teachers College of Columbia University. During her teaching years, she exhibited realistic paintings in shows of Afro-American artists. But in the 1950s, she took painting classes at American University and became interested in color and abstract art.

By 1959, her paintings had become abstract. By 1964, she had discovered a way to create an image through small dabs of paint laid edge to edge across the painting's surface. In *Iris, Tulips, Jonquils, and Crocuses*, the color bands move vertically and horizontally across the canvas to represent a breeze moving over a sunlit spring garden. In *Autumn Leaves Fluttering in the Wind*, rust-colored patches move in patterns like those of swirling autumn leaves. The spaces between show glimpses of blue, yellow, and green, representing the sky and the land.

Thomas's paintings are mosaics of patches of color that she said, "represent my communion with nature." She wrote, "Color is life. Light reveals to us the spirit and living soul of the world through colors."

In Your Own Words
▶ Alma Thomas wrote that she was "intrigued with the changing colors of nature as the seasons progress." Describe how you would paint a natural scene using the Color Field painting style.

541

Biography: Alma Woodsey Thomas (1892-1978) was the first black woman to have a solo exhibition at the Whitney Museum of American Art (1972). During her years of teaching she was an important force in the Washington arts scene. She organized clubs and art lectures for her students, established art galleries in the public schools, and helped found the Barnett-Aden Gallery, one of the first galleries in Washington devoted to modern art.

TEACHING STRATEGY
Have students read through the passage about Alma Thomas. Then have them respond to the discussion questions below.

Discussion Questions
1. **From the information in the article on Alma Thomas, how do you think she felt about the use of color in paintings?** *She used mosaics of color patches to convey abstract images of nature. She said that color is life and the spirit of the world is revealed in colors.*
2. **Compare the technique used by Alma Thomas to the technique used by artists who work with stained glass. How are they alike and how do they differ?** *Both Thomas and stained-glass artists use small areas of color to create a larger image. The colors seen in a painting are seen by light reflected from the canvas and the colors seen in stained-glass art are seen as light is transmitted through the glass.*

Other Works
▶ Other Color Field works by Alma Thomas include *Wind and Crepe Myrtle Concerto* (1973), *New Galaxy* (1970), and *Flowers at Jefferson Memorial* (1970).

Classics
▶ Bob Thomas, ed. *Directors in Action.* New York, NY: Bobbs-Merrill Company, Inc., 1973. Describes the work of a variety of film directors who translate movie scripts into films.

In Unit 7, students are first introduced to electricity and magnetism and how they are related. The world of micro-electronics is then discussed. Radio-activity is introduced with emphasis given to its application. The unit ends with a discussion of energy consumption, alternative energy sources, and the role of energy conservation.

CONTENTS

ADVANCE PREPARATION

Audiovisuals
▶ Show the film *Electrostatic Charges and Forces,* Coronet.
▶ Show the video *Learning About Magnetism,* EBEC.

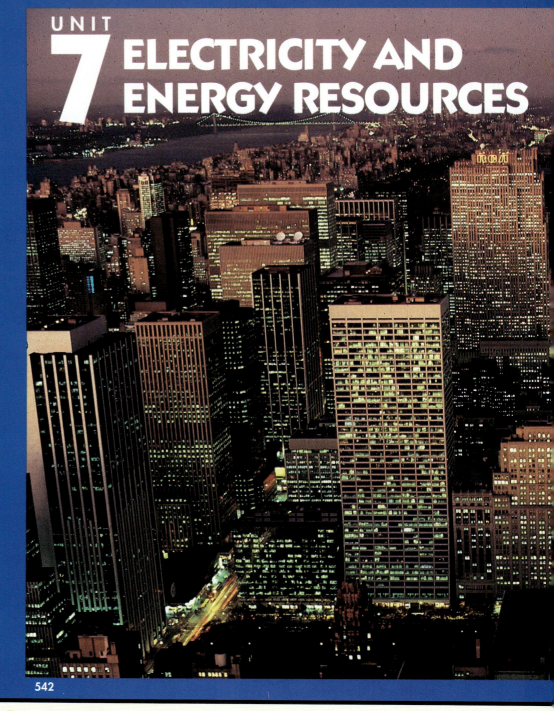

542

OPTIONS

Cross Curriculum
Have students keep logs of the ways that electrical energy is used in their classes. At the end of the unit, have students volunteer suggestions that might be used to conserve electrical energy.

Science at Home
Cooperative Learning: Have groups of students monitor TV and newspapers for coverage of problems concerning the processing and storing of radioactive wastes.
▶ Have students keep daily logs of their electrical energy uses. Have them note the device or appliance used, its function, if it is battery-operated or not, and how long it was used. Have them calculate or approximate their personal electrical energy consumption by using tables of appliance power-rating supplied by most utility companies.

What's Happening Here?

When the sun goes down, New York City's lights go on. New York City generates electricity for lighting by burning fossil fuels, harnessing water power, and controlling nuclear reactions. What does it mean to "generate" electricity? How do solar collectors like the ones shown below generate electricity? Why is it important to develop alternatives to fossil fuels? In this power-packed unit, you'll learn the answers to these questions. You'll also learn about magnetism, nuclear reactions, and computers.

UNIT CONTENTS

543

Multicultural Awareness

Have interested students research how peoples of various cultures have adapted their lifestyles to the consumption of limited sources of fossil fuels or the exploitation of alternative energy sources.

Inquiry Questions

Use the following questions to focus a discussion of electricity and its uses.

▶ **What is the most apparent way that electricity is being used in this picture?** lighting
▶ **How else do you suppose electricity is being used in these buildings?** *Accept all reasonable answers. heating, cooling, office cleaning equipment, elevators, computers, movie projectors*
▶ **Would these uses change during the year?** *Accept all reasonable answers. Air conditioning would be heavier during the summer.*

INTRODUCING THE CHAPTER

What's Happening Here?

▶ Have students look at the photos and read the text. Ask them to tell you what's happening here. Point out to students that in this unit they will learn what electrical energy is; how it is converted to light, heat, and other forms of energy; and how other forms of energy are converted into electrical energy.
▶ **Background:** About 70% of the electricity produced in the United States is produced by the burning of fossil fuels, 20% from nuclear fission, and 10% from moving water. Lighting accounts for the smallest fraction of electricity's use. Most electricity is used for heating, cooling, and operating industrial machinery. In most cases, electricity is produced by generators that convert mechanical energy into electrical energy. However, in solar cells, electricity is produced by silicon wafers that convert radiant energy into electrical energy.

Previewing the Chapters

▶ Have students use the photographs in the unit to identify a household device that (1) uses both electrical energy and nuclear energy; *smoke detector, Figure 24-12, page 620,* (2) converts electrical energy into radiant energy; *light bulb or electric heater, Figure 21-6, page 555,* (3) converts electrical energy into sound; *radio, page 599,* (4) converts electrical energy into mechanical energy; *drill, Figure 22-8, page 580.*

Tying to Previous Knowledge

▶ Have students brainstorm lists of electrical appliances and devices. Then have them categorize the appliance or device as to its major function, such as heating, cooling, lighting, motion, etc. Have them conjecture which category probably accounts for their greatest personal use of electrical energy.
▶ Have students discuss energy uses and energy sources that they are now familiar with. Ask them to discuss what they perceive as energy conservation and how it can be accomplished.
▶ Use the **inquiry questions** in the OPTIONS box below to focus on the topic of electricity.

21 Electricity

CHAPTER SECTION	OBJECTIVES	ACTIVITIES
21-1 Electric Charge (1 day)	1. **Describe** the effects of static electricity. 2. **Distinguish** between conductors and insulators. 3. **Recognize** the presence of charge in an electroscope.	**MINI-Lab:** *Can static charge move things?* p. 548
21-2 Lightning—Its Causes and Effects *Science & Society* (1 day)	1. **Explain** the occurrence of lightning in terms of induction and static discharge. 2. **Evaluate** the positive and negative aspects of lightning-induced forest fires.	
21-3 Electric Current (2 days)	1. **Describe** how potential energy of an electron changes as it moves through a simple circuit. 2. **Explain** how a dry cell is a source of electricity. 3. **Conceptually** and **mathematically relate** potential difference, resistance, and current.	**Activity 21-1:** *A Model of Ohm's Law,* p. 559
21-4 Electrical Circuits (2 days)	1. **Sketch** a series and a parallel circuit, and **list** applications of each type of circuit. 2. **Recognize** the function of circuit breakers and fuses.	**Activity 21-2:** *Electric Circuits,* p. 564
21-5 Electrical Power and Energy (2 days)	1. **Explain** and **calculate** electric power. 2. **Calculate** the amount of electrical energy in kilowatt-hours.	**MINI-Lab:** *How much power operates an electric toy?* p. 567
Chapter Review		

ACTIVITY MATERIALS

FIND OUT	ACTIVITIES		MINI-LABS	
Page 545 tissue paper plastic rulers	**21-1 A Model of Ohm's Law, p. 559** plastic funnel ring stand with ring 1 m rubber tubing meterstick 2 250-mL beakers stopwatch or clock	**21-2 Electric Circuits, p. 564** aluminum foil cellophane tape scissors 3 lights with sockets 6 paper clips battery (6 or 9 volt)	**Can static charge move things? p. 548** plastic food wrap cotton cloth paper hole punch aluminum foil	**How much power operates an electric toy? p. 567** milliammeter 3 wires with small alligator clips strips of aluminum foil electric toy with battery tape or rubber bands

CHAPTER FEATURES	TEACHER RESOURCE PACKAGE	OTHER RESOURCES
Problem Solving: *How Can Birds Perch on Power Lines?* p. 548 **Skill Builder:** *Observing and Inferring,* p. 549	**Ability Level Worksheets** ◆ **Study Guide,** p. 87 ● **Reinforcement,** p. 87 ▲ **Enrichment,** p. 87 **MINI-Lab Worksheet,** p. 173	
You Decide! p. 551	**Ability Level Worksheets** ◆ **Study Guide,** p. 88 ● **Reinforcement,** p. 88 ▲ **Enrichment,** p. 88 **Concept Mapping,** pp. 47, 48	
Technology: *Shake and Bake Superconductors,* p. 556 **Skill Builder:** *Making and Using Tables,* p. 558	**Ability Level Worksheets** ◆ **Study Guide,** p. 89 ● **Reinforcement,** p. 89 ▲ **Enrichment,** p. 89 **Activity Worksheet,** pp. 167, 168 **Critical Thinking/Problem Solving,** p. 27 **Science and Society,** p. 25	**Lab Manual 43,** Wet Cell Battery
Skill Builder: *Hypothesizing,* p. 563	**Ability Level Worksheets** ◆ **Study Guide,** p. 90 ● **Reinforcement,** p. 90 ▲ **Enrichment,** p. 90 **Activity Worksheet,** pp. 169, 170 **Transparency Masters,** pp. 83-86	**Color Transparency 42,** Series & Parallel Circuits **Color Transparency 43,** Household Circuits **Lab Manual 44,** Simple Circuits
	Ability Level Worksheets ◆ **Study Guide,** p. 91 ● **Reinforcement,** p. 91 ▲ **Enrichment,** p. 91 **MINI-Lab Worksheet,** p. 174 **Cross-Curricular Connections,** p. 27	
Summary Think & Write Critically Key Science Words Apply Understanding Vocabulary More Skill Builders Checking Concepts Projects Understanding Concepts	**Chapter Review,** pp. 45, 46 **Chapter Test,** pp. 143-146	**Chapter Review Software** **Test Bank**

◆ **Basic**   ● **Average**   ▲ **Advanced**

ADDITIONAL MATERIALS

SOFTWARE	AUDIOVISUAL	BOOKS/MAGAZINES
Current, Voltage, and Power, Bergwall Educational Software. *Electricity,* Focus. *Electrical Charge and Direct Current,* Queue. *Investigating Electric Fields,* IBM. *Electric Circuits,* William K. Bradford Publishing Co.	*Electricity at Work,* filmstrips/cassettes, SVE. *Electrostatic Series,* EBEC. *Electrostatic Charges and Forces,* Coronet/MTL. *Experimenting with Electricity,* filmstrip, EBEC.	Baker, Glenn and Leonard R. Crow. *Electricity Fundamentals.* New York: Macmillan, 1971. Blumenthal, Howard. *The Electronic Home Advisor.* Kansas City, MO: Universal Press, 1988. Grob, Bernard. *Basic Electronics.* New York: McGraw-Hill, 1988.

THEME DEVELOPMENT: This chapter introduces the basic science and applications of electricity. Energy is developed as a major theme of this chapter. Emphasize conservation of energy; electricity is a convenient way to deliver energy, but it is often changed to other forms such as light and mechanical energy as we use it.

CHAPTER OVERVIEW

▶ **Section 21-1:** This section investigates the causes and effects of static electricity, the behavior of conductors and insulators, and the use of an electroscope.

▶ **Section 21-2: Science and Society:** The science behind lightning is explained, followed by a discussion of lightning-induced forest fires. The You Decide question asks whether natural fires should be allowed to burn.

▶ **Section 21-3:** Electric currents are introduced and explained. Resistance, current, and potential difference are related conceptually and mathematically.

▶ **Section 21-4:** This section illustrates series, parallel, and complex circuits through diagrams and examples.

▶ **Section 21-5:** Electrical power and energy are distinguished, and calculations of power and energy are included.

CHAPTER VOCABULARY

static	dry cell
electricity	wet cell
electric field	resistance
conductor	Ohm's law
insulator	series circuits
electroscope	parallel
lightning rod	circuits
potential difference	electrical
circuit	power
current	kilowatt-hour

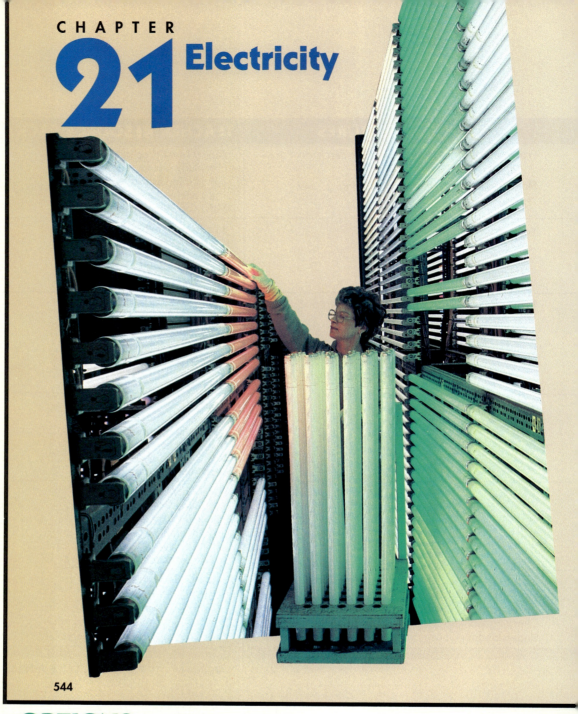

CHAPTER

21 Electricity

544

OPTIONS

For Your Gifted Students

Have students investigate conductors and insulators. First, they can brainstorm ways to test a list of objects and predict the results. Students should design and make a circuit tester to test the objects. They can make a chart to show which items are conductors and which are insulators.

Throughout the day you see examples of electricity and its uses. All of us have come to depend on electricity on a daily basis. Electricity provides us with entertainment, transportation, and convenience. So where does electricity come from? What is it? How does it affect matter?

FIND OUT!

Do this simple activity to find out how matter can be affected by electric charges.

Get a thin plastic ruler. Tear some tissue paper into tiny pieces less than 1 cm² and scatter them on your desk top. Rub the plastic ruler briskly across your hair several times and slowly lower it near the paper. What happens? Touch the ruler with your other hand and lower it to the paper again. What happens now?

Gearing Up
Previewing the Chapter
Use this outline to help you focus on important ideas in this chapter.

Previewing Science Skills
▶ In the **Skill Builders,** you will observe and infer, hypothesize, and make a concept map.
▶ In the **Activities,** you will measure in SI, predict, and formulate models.
▶ In the **MINI-Labs,** you will observe, hypothesize, and interpret data.

What's next?

Now you may wonder what electric charges are and where they come from? As you read on, you will find out more about electric charges and electricity.

545

INTRODUCING THE CHAPTER
Use the Find Out activity to introduce the effects of electric charges to students. Tell them they will be investigating what causes these attractions and how they can be used.

FIND OUT!
Preparation: Obtain at least one plastic ruler for every two students. Hand out only enough tissue paper to do the experiment.

Materials: tissue paper, plastic rulers

Cooperative Learning: Use the Paired Partners strategy for this activity. One student can tear up the tissue paper while the other charges the ruler.

Teaching Tips
▶ Ask students to try to explain their observations. It is likely they will know the words *static electricity* from taking clothes out of the dryer. Note that this is the same phenomenon. Ask why the paper and ruler do not stay charged after they touch the ruler.

Gearing Up
Have students study the Gearing Up section to familiarize themselves with the chapter. Discuss the relationships of the topics in the outline.

What's Next?
Before beginning the first section, make sure students understand the connection between the Find Out activity and the topics to follow.

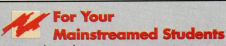
For Your Mainstreamed Students
Kinesthetic learners can investigate materials to determine which ones produce an electrical charge. Have students place several pieces of newspaper on a wooden board. They can take various objects (plastic wrap, wool, foil, and so on) and then rub over the paper. They should then lift the sheet of newspaper from the wood. If an electrical charge was produced, the paper will be attracted to the wood.

21-1 Electric Charge

PREPARATION

SECTION BACKGROUND

▶ Benjamin Franklin arbitrarily named the two types of electric charge *positive* and *negative*. Actually, Franklin thought of electricity as a type of fluid; whatever excess charge was given to one object in a system, the other object had a deficiency of an equal amount of charge. This is consistent with the law of conservation of electric charge.

▶ Electrical forces between charged objects are many, many times stronger than gravitational attraction. The positively charged protons and negatively charged electrons in the nuclei of atoms are responsible for electric forces.

PREPLANNING

▶ Try to obtain access to a Van de Graaff generator and several electroscopes for demonstration purposes.

1 MOTIVATE

▶ Obtain a copy of the 1990 hit song "Opposites Attract" by Paula Abdul. To pique students' curiosity, have it playing when they come into the room. Ask them what the main phrase of the song means and how it might apply to this chapter.

TYING TO PREVIOUS KNOWLEDGE: Ask students what sometimes happens when they take clothes out of the dryer to fold. They will likely mention "static cling" and may mention they can hear it crackle. Explain that this is caused by static discharge of electricity, the topic of this section.

OBJECTIVES AND SCIENCE WORDS: Have students review the objectives and science words to become familiar with this section.

21-1 Electric Charge

New Science Words

static electricity
electric field
conductor
insulator
electroscope

Objectives

▶ Describe the effects of static electricity.
▶ Distinguish between conductors and insulators.
▶ Recognize the presence of charge in an electroscope.

Static Electricity

Have you ever walked across a carpeted floor and were stung by a spark as you reached out to touch something? If you immediately touched the object a second time, you might have felt a very small spark, or none at all. If you shuffled your feet on the carpet again, you might've felt a larger spark again. What caused this startling and sometimes painful phenomenon?

When your feet rubbed on the carpet, some of the atoms in the carpet were disturbed. Recall from Chapter 10 that atoms contain protons, neutrons, and electrons. Neutrons have no charge, protons are positively charged, and electrons are negatively charged. An atom is electrically neutral if it has an equal number of protons and electrons. Sometimes electrons are not held tightly in the atom. For example, as you walked on the carpet some electrons that were loosely held by the atoms rubbed from the carpet onto your shoes. As a result, your shoes gained electrons, and they were no longer neutral, but instead had a negative charge. The carpet lost electrons, leaving it positively charged. The excess electrons, stored in your body, gave you an overall negative electric charge. This is an example of static electricity. **Static electricity** is the accumulation of electric charges on an object. Can you think of any other examples of static electricity?

Have you noticed how a sock will cling to your shirt when you remove them from the dryer? Electrons can be rubbed off some clothes while they are tumbling around inside the dryer. Clothes that gain electrons become negatively charged, whereas those that lose electrons become positively charged. Clothes with opposite charges cling together, but clothes with the same charge

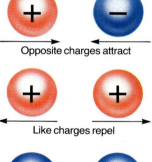
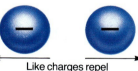

Figure 21-1. When charges are brought together, opposite charges attract and like charges repel.

Opposite charges attract

Like charges repel

Like charges repel

546 ELECTRICITY

OPTIONS

Meeting Different Ability Levels

For Section 21-1, use the following **Teacher Resource Masters** depending upon individual students' needs.

◆ **Study Guide Master** for all students.

● **Reinforcement Master** for students of average and above average ability levels.

▲ **Enrichment Master** for above average students.

Additional Teacher Resource Package masters are listed in the OPTIONS box throughout the section. The additional masters are appropriate for all students.

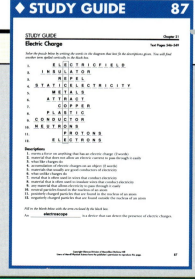

repel each other. Electrically charged objects obey the following rule: opposite charges attract, and like charges repel.

Charged objects can cause electrons to rearrange their position on a neutral object. For example, suppose you charge a balloon by rubbing it with a cloth. If you bring the negatively charged balloon near your sleeve, the extra electrons on the balloon will repel the electrons in the sleeve. The electrons near the surface will move away from the balloon, leaving a positively charged area on the surface of the sleeve. As a result, the negatively charged balloon will attract the positively charged area of the sleeve. The rearrangement of electrons on a neutral object caused by a charged object is called charging by induction.

How can an electron exert a force on a particle that is some distance away? It does this by setting up an **electric field** in space. This electric field exerts a force on anything that has an electric charge. The electric field is strongest near the electron and becomes weaker as distance from the electron increases.

Conductors and Insulators

You now know you can build up a negative charge by walking across a carpet. Suppose you then could touch either a wooden door or a metal doorknob. Which one would you prefer to touch? If your choice was the metal doorknob, be prepared to feel a spark.

When you put your finger near the doorknob, the electric field between your finger and the knob became so strong that it pulled electrons out of molecules in the air. These molecules became positively charged ions. Movement of these ions and the electrons created the spark that you saw and felt.

The electrons can move through your body to the metal doorknob because both your body and the metal are conductors. A **conductor** is a material that allows electrons to move easily through it. Metals such as copper and silver are made of atoms that don't hold their electrons tightly, so electrons can move easily through materials made up of these kinds of atoms. For this reason, electric wires are usually made of copper, a good conductor. Silver wire also conducts electricity very well, but silver is much more costly to use than copper.

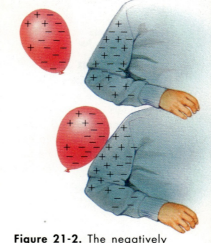

Figure 21-2. The negatively charged balloon induces a positive charge in the sleeve by repelling its electrons.

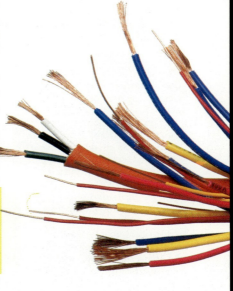

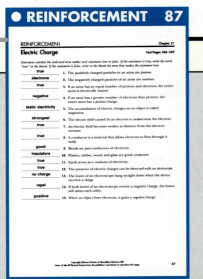

● **REINFORCEMENT** 87

▲ **ENRICHMENT** 87

547

PROBLEM SOLVING

▶The chimpanzee was injured when the electric current passed from the wire through his body and the aluminum ladder to the ground.
Think Critically: The sparrows are not injured sitting on the power lines because they are too small to touch two wires, or one wire and the ground at the same time. In other words, they are not grounded.

STUDENT TEXT QUESTION

▶ Page 548, paragraph 1: **Would you expect static discharge to occur if you touched the wooden door instead of the metal doorknob?** *no*

 **MINI-Lab**

Materials: plastic wrap, cotton cloth, paper punch, aluminum foil
Teaching Tips
▶ Pull back the plastic wrap *slowly*.
▶ Overhead projector film can be used in place of food wrap.
▶ **Answers:** No response is seen from the chips until the plastic is separated from the table because charging the plastic by rubbing induces an opposite charge in the tabletop. Pieces that fly off the plastic have received the plastic's charge by *conduction*. Those that stick have an opposite charge by *induction*.
▶ Chips tend to repel each other because most of them have the same charge.
▶ Paper chips would respond in the same way.
▶ Like charges repel and unlike charges attract.

CHECK FOR UNDERSTANDING

▶ Instruct the class to watch while you touch a charged electroscope with your finger. The leaves fall to neutral position. Your finger and body act as a ground to absorb or donate electrons to remove the charge in the electroscope. Have students write a short explanation of this at their desks and ask for volunteers to share their ideas.
▶ Ask questions 1-2 and the **Apply**

 P R O B L E M   S O L V I N G

How Can Birds Perch on Power Lines?

As Maria was watching television one evening, she saw an advertisement on the dangers of electric power lines. The advertisement showed a man climbing an aluminum ladder to saw off some tree branches near some power lines. Near the top of the ladder, he reached for the branches and the ladder began to wobble. Unbalanced, he reached out toward the power lines for support

Just before he grasped the power lines, the man turned into a chimpanzee and the television screen went blank. A message then appeared on the screen warning people not to monkey around power lines.

The next day, Maria noticed several sparrows perching on a high voltage power line. She thought about the advertisement she had seen on television and wondered how the birds could safely perch on a power line. Explain how the advertisement inferred that the chimpanzee was injured by electric current when he grabbed the power lines.
Think Critically: How could the sparrows perch on the power line without getting injured?

 **MINI-Lab**

Can static charge move things?
Get a piece of plastic food wrap, about 30 cm by 30 cm. Lay it on a table top and smooth it down flat with a cotton cloth. Use a paper punch to make round chips of aluminum foil. Put the foil chips in a pile in the center of the plastic wrap. Lift the plastic wrap slowly from the table and observe the response of the aluminum. How do the aluminum chips react to the plastic? How do they react to each other? Would paper chips respond the same way? How would you summarize the behavior of electrically charged objects?

What covers the metal wires in cords attached to telephones and other household appliances? They are usually coated with some type of plastic, an insulating material. An **insulator** is a material that doesn't allow electrons to move through it easily. In addition to plastic, wood, rubber, and glass are good insulators. Would you expect static discharge to occur if you touched the wooden door instead of the metal doorknob?

The largest object you touch is Earth. Earth contains a large supply of electrons and functions as a conductor of electricity. It is sometimes desirable to provide a path for the static discharge to reach Earth. An object connected to Earth, or the ground, by a good conductor is said to be grounded. Look around you. Do you see anything that might act as a path to the ground? Plumbing fixtures, such as metal faucets, sinks, and pipes, often provide a convenient ground connection.

OPTIONS

Question in the Section Review.

INQUIRY QUESTIONS

▶ **If electric charges cause the attraction between socks in your dryer, do you think this electricity could be used to run your portable tape player? Why or why not?** *No. The movement, or discharge, of electricity happens rapidly and does not continue. It could not be used as a continuous supply of energy.*
▶ **Can an electric field exert a force on an**

The Electroscope

The presence of electric charges can be detected by an **electroscope.** An electroscope is made of two thin metal leaves attached to a metal rod with a knob at the top. The leaves are allowed to swing freely from the metal rod. When the device is not charged, the leaves hang straight down.

Suppose a negatively charged balloon touches the knob. Because the metal is a good conductor, electrons travel down the rod into the leaves. Both leaves become negatively charged as they gain electrons. Because the leaves have similar charges, they repel each other.

If a glass rod is rubbed with silk, electrons leave the glass rod and build up on the silk. The glass rod becomes positively charged. When the positively charged glass rod is touched to the metal knob, electrons are conducted out of the metal leaves and onto the rod. The leaves repel each other because each leaf becomes positively charged as it loses electrons.

Can you think of any other effects of static electricity you have seen? Can you explain them in terms of like or opposite charges. How do objects become charged, and what happens when they discharge? In Section 21-3, you will find out how electrons can move continuously to keep a light bulb glowing or make a tape player play music.

Knob

Metal rod

Metal leaves

a

Electrons move toward knob

Electrons move away from knob

Figure 21-3. Notice the position of the leaves on the electroscope when they are uncharged (a), positively charged (b), and negatively charged (c).

SECTION REVIEW

1. What is static electricity?
2. Distinguish between electrical conductors and insulators and give an example of each.
3. **Apply:** Assume you have already charged an electroscope with a positively charged glass rod. Hypothesize what would happen if you touched the knob again with another positively charged object.

☒ Observing and Inferring

Suppose that you observe the individual hairs on your arm rise up when a balloon is placed near them. Using the concept of induction and the rules of electricity, what could you infer about the cause of this phenomenon? If you need help, refer to Observing and Inferring in the **Skill Handbook** on page 678.

Skill Builder

21-1 ELECTRIC CHARGE **549**

RETEACH

Carefully demonstrate the function of the electroscope again, using a diagram to show positive and negative areas. Have a student rub a glass rod with silk, so the electrons leave the glass rod and build up on the silk. Touch the electroscope with the glass rod. **Why do the leaves split apart?** *Electrons flow from the leaves into the glass rod. The leaves are positive and repel each other.*

EXTENSION

For students who have mastered this section, use the **Reinforcement** and **Enrichment** masters or other OPTIONS provided.

3 CLOSE

▶ Charge up a Van de Graaff generator. Slowly approach the dome with a lit match. The match will go out. Have students work in pairs to offer an explanation for this phenomenon. The negative charges ionize the oxygen so it cannot be used for combustion of the match.

SECTION REVIEW ANSWERS

1. the accumulation of electric charges on an object; socks clinging together when they come out of the dryer
2. A conductor is a material that allows electrons to move easily through it; copper and silver are conductors. An insulator is a material that doesn't allow electrons to pass easily through it; plastic, wood, rubber, and glass are good insulators.
3. **Apply:** The leaves might spread farther apart.

Skill Builder

The attraction between the balloon and the hairs on your arm was probably caused by opposite charges. The negatively charged balloon repelled the electrons near the surface of your arm, leaving a positive surface for the balloon to be attracted to.

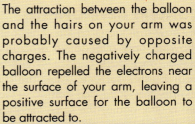

ENRICHMENT

▶ Have interested students investigate Coulomb's law, the relationship between the electric force, charge, and distance between two charged objects. Coulomb's law is an inverse square law similar to Newton's law of gravitation.

PREPARATION

SECTION BACKGROUND

▶ A bolt of lightning is so high in energy and happens so fast that it can have 3 750 000 000 kW of power. The surrounding air temperature can rise by 30 000°C.

1 MOTIVATE

▶ Ask students how they think most forest fires are started. They will say careless campers, smokers, and perhaps lightning. Ask them to think of a good reason why a park ranger might decide to let a lightning-induced fire burn.

TYING TO PREVIOUS
KNOWLEDGE: Ask students if they have ever tried to measure the distance to a lightning bolt by counting the time between the flash of light and the crack of thunder. Ask them what produces the light and sound. In this section, the process and effects of lightning will be discussed.

OBJECTIVES AND
SCIENCE WORDS: Have students review the objectives and science words to become familiar with this section.

2 TEACH

Key Concepts are highlighted.

CONCEPT DEVELOPMENT

▶ Draw a diagram on the chalkboard showing how a negative area in a cloud can induce a positive charge near Earth's surface. After the discharge, the cloud and Earth's surface are neutral again. The same thing can be shown between clouds.

 **21-2**

Lightning—Its Causes and Effects

New Science Words

lightning rod

Objectives

▶ Explain the occurrence of lightning in terms of induction and static discharge.
▶ Evaluate the positive and negative aspects of lightning-induced forest fires.

Should Lightning-induced Forest Fires Be Left to Burn?

Have you ever seen lightning strike Earth? Lightning is actually a very large discharge of static electricity. The moving air currents in a storm cause charged particles to move about. Sometimes the charged particles become separated to form areas of positive and negative charge within a cloud. If the bottom portion of a cloud has a negative charge, it can induce a positive charge on Earth's surface. As the difference in charge increases, electrons may be attracted toward the positively charged ground. A lightning bolt occurs when many electrons are transferred at the same time. Each lightning bolt that strikes Earth may carry several billion billion electrons!

Much of the lightning you see doesn't strike Earth's surface. Electrons can also move through lightning bolts from the negative area of one cloud to the positive area of another cloud. The electrical energy in a lightning bolt produces great amounts of heat. The heat causes the air in the clouds to expand very rapidly, producing thunder. Have you ever tried to time the difference between the flash of light and the loud crack of lightning in a thunderstorm? Because sound travels much slower than light, you see the lightning flash before you hear the crack or rumble of the thunder.

The sudden discharge of so much electricity can be quite dangerous. Lightning strikes Earth many times

---

OPTIONS

Meeting Different Ability Levels

For Section 21-2, use the following **Teacher Resource Masters** depending upon individual students' needs.

◆ **Study Guide Master** for all students.
● **Reinforcement Master** for students of average and above average ability levels.
▲ **Enrichment Master** for above average students.

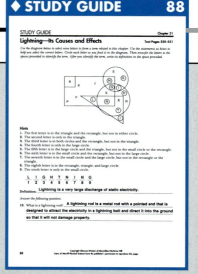

each day. If it strikes a populated area, it can cause power outages, fires, or even injury or loss of life. One way to prevent lightning damage is to provide a path for the electrons to travel to the ground. Many buildings have lightning rods. A **lightning rod** is a pointed metal rod that extends above the highest part of a structure with a cable that connects the rod to the ground. Electric charges leak from the clouds to the lightning rod, which carries them safely into the ground.

Lightning is also responsible for an important cycle in Earth's forests. You have probably seen news reports about huge forest fires burning out of control in dry regions. Many of these fires were started by lightning. Often, the flames creep along the ground and don't destroy large healthy trees. In order to protect the beauty of our national parks and wilderness areas, these fires usually were promptly extinguished. However, it became evident to ecologists that nature's cycle of growth and renewal might not be consistent with the human version of natural beauty. Therefore, laws were passed in the 1970s to allow fires started by lightning to burn naturally unless they threaten people or property.

Many people were upset in 1989 when one-third of Yellowstone National Park was burned. Suppressing fires can allow dead debris to accumulate in the forest, and increase the risk of a rapidly spreading natural fire. In addition, when the ground is covered with debris, fires don't burn holes in the shade covering of the forest, so the plant life changes. Perhaps protecting the forest by putting out fires from lightning doesn't preserve a forest as well as allowing nature to take its course.

SECTION REVIEW

1. How are lightning and thunder produced?
2. What is the purpose of a lightning rod?

You Decide!

Suppose a lightning storm has started a large fire in Yosemite National Park in California. Should it be allowed to burn along its natural course, or should it be put out to preserve areas for human and wildlife use? Would your decision be different if the fire was caused by careless campers?

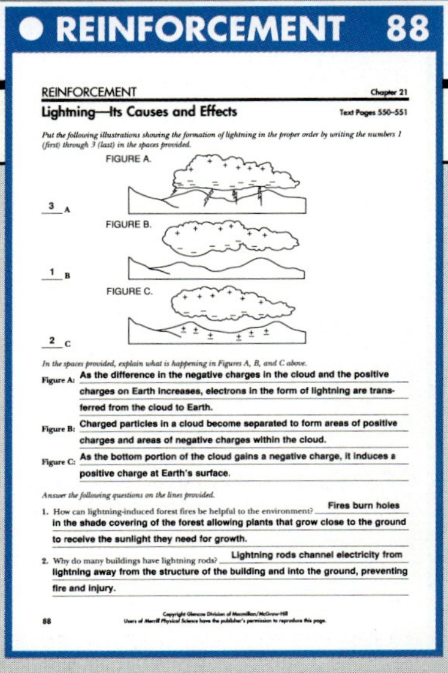

SCIENCE & SOCIETY

● **REINFORCEMENT** 88   ▲ **ENRICHMENT** 88   551

REINFORCEMENT   Chapter 21
Lightning—Its Causes and Effects   Text Pages 550-551

Put the following illustrations showing the formation of lightning in the proper order by writing the numbers 1 (first) through 3 (last) in the spaces provided.

FIGURE A.

FIGURE B.

FIGURE C.

In the spaces provided, explain what is happening in Figures A, B, and C above.

Figure A: As the difference in the negative charges in the cloud and the positive charges on Earth increases, electrons in the form of lightning are transferred from the cloud to Earth.

Figure B: Charged particles in a cloud become separated to form areas of positive charges and areas of negative charges within the cloud.

Figure C: As the bottom portion of the cloud gains a negative charge, it induces a positive charge at Earth's surface.

Answer the following questions on the lines provided.

1. How can lightning-induced forest fires be helpful to the environment? Fires burn holes in the shade covering of the forest allowing plants that grow close to the ground to receive the sunlight they need for growth.

2. Why do many buildings have lightning rods? Lightning rods channel electricity from lightning away from the structure of the building and into the ground, preventing fire and injury.

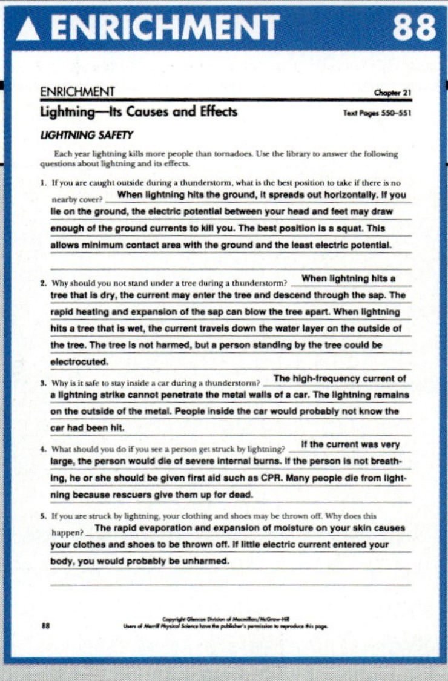

ENRICHMENT   Chapter 21
Lightning—Its Causes and Effects   Text Pages 550-551

LIGHTNING SAFETY

Each year lightning kills more people than tornadoes. Use the library to answer the following questions about lightning and its effects.

1. If you are caught outside during a thunderstorm, what is the best position to take if there is no nearby cover? When lightning hits the ground, it spreads out horizontally. If you lie on the ground, the electric potential between your head and feet may draw enough of the ground currents to kill you. The best position is a squat. This allows minimum contact area with the ground and the least electric potential.

2. Why should you not stand under a tree during a thunderstorm? When lightning hits a tree that is dry, the current may enter the tree and descend through the sap. The rapid heating and expansion of the sap can blow the tree apart. When lightning hits a tree that is wet, the current travels down the water layer on the outside of the tree. The tree is not harmed, but a person standing by the tree could be electrocuted.

3. Why is it safe to stay inside a car during a thunderstorm? The high-frequency current of a lightning strike cannot penetrate the metal walls of a car. The lightning remains on the outside of the metal. People inside the car would probably not know the car had been hit.

4. What should you do if you see a person get struck by lightning? If the current was very large, the person would die of severe internal burns. If the person is not breathing, he or she should be given first aid such as CPR. Many people die from lightning because rescuers give them up for dead.

5. If you are struck by lightning, your clothing and shoes may be thrown off. Why does this happen? The rapid evaporation and expansion of moisture on your skin causes your clothes and shoes to be thrown off. If little electric current entered your body, you would probably be unharmed.

CHECK FOR UNDERSTANDING

Ask students to diagram how an ordinary car antenna might function as a lightning rod to prevent lightning from discharging to your car. Charges accumulate and leak off to the surroundings from the tip at the end of the antenna. Or if lightning does strike, it would be drawn through the antenna and to the ground.

RETEACH

Use a Wimshurst machine to show how charge leaks off a metal point to avoid a large discharge of electricity. Small spheres can hold only small amounts of charge before discharging, so a large charge cannot build up. This is the reason lightning rods and antennas have small metal spheres on their tips.

EXTENSION

For students who have mastered this section, use the **Reinforcement** and **Enrichment** masters or other OPTIONS provided.

3 CLOSE

▶ Ask questions 1-2 in the Section Review.
▶ Use the You Decide question to analyze the controversial question of natural forest fires.

SECTION REVIEW ANSWERS

1. Lightning is a static discharge between negative areas and positive areas. Thunder is produced by the rapid expansion of air due to the heat of the discharge.
2. A lightning rod acts as a ground.

YOU DECIDE!

Answers will vary. You might divide the class into groups to debate this issue.

PROGRAM RESOURCES

From the **Teacher Resource Package** use:

Concept Mapping, pages 47-48.

PREPARATION

SECTION BACKGROUND

▶ In 1800, an Italian physicist named Alessandro Volta observed that two metals connected by a conducting liquid produced a continuous transfer of electrons. This phenomenon was different from the rapid static discharge observed by Ben Franklin. This moving electric charge was later called an electric current.

1 MOTIVATE

▶ Obtain a fresh lemon, new penny, and a silver dime (before 1965). Attach an alligator clip to each coin and insert the coins about 2 cm apart into the lemon. Use the leads from the coins to connect a piezoelectric buzzer to complete the circuit. Ask students what makes the buzzer go off.

New Science Words

potential difference
circuit
current
dry cell
wet cell
resistance
Ohm's law

Objectives

▶ Describe how the potential energy of an electron changes as it moves through a simple circuit.
▶ Explain how a dry cell is a source of electricity.
▶ Conceptually and mathematically relate potential difference, resistance, and current.

Flowing Electrons

You read in Section 21-1 that if you touch a conductor after building up a negative charge in your body, electrons will move from you to the conductor. Could you light a lamp in this manner? Probably not, because the static discharge occurs for an instant and then stops. The lamp needs a continuous flow of electrons to stay lit. Why does the static discharge stop so suddenly?

Recall from Chapter 5 that heat flows from objects with higher temperatures to objects with lower temperatures. Heat ceases to flow when the temperatures of the objects become the same. Similarly, a negatively charged object has electrons with more potential energy to move and do work with than those of an uncharged object. This difference in potential energy causes the electrons to flow from places of higher potential energy to those with lower potential energy. In a static discharge, the potentials quickly become equal and electron flow stops.

The potential energy difference per unit of charge is called the electrical potential. The difference in potential between two different places is the **potential difference.** Potential difference is measured in volts, (V). Potential difference, often called voltage, is measured by a voltmeter. The voltage doesn't depend on the number of electrons flowing, but on a comparison of the energy carried by electrons at different points.

How can you get electrons to flow through a lamp continuously? You must connect it in an electric circuit. A **circuit** is a closed path through which electrons can flow. Because the lamp is part of a circuit, there is a potential

How does the electric potential energy of a negatively charged object compare to that of an uncharged object?

OPTIONS

Meeting Different Ability Levels

For Section 21-3, use the following **Teacher Resource Masters** depending upon individual students' needs.

◆ **Study Guide Master** for all students.

● **Reinforcement Master** for students of average and above average ability levels.

▲ **Enrichment Master** for above average students.

Additional Teacher Resource Package masters are listed in the OPTIONS box throughout the section. The additional masters are appropriate for all students.

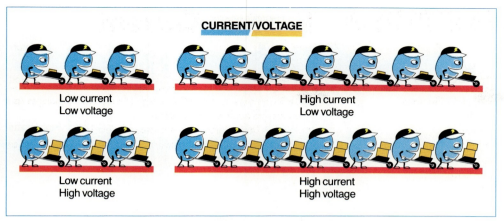

TYING TO PREVIOUS KNOWLEDGE: Ask students if they have ever tried to play a tape in a portable tape player only to find the sound slow and sluggish. They will say the problem was dead batteries, but what is the real problem when the battery "dies"? It stops producing an adequate electric current to operate the tape player. In this section, students will learn what an electric current is and how it is produced.

difference across it. If the lamp is turned on, electrons will move through it causing it to produce light. The electrons will continue to flow in the circuit as long as there is a potential difference and the path of the flowing electrons is unbroken.

The flow of electrons through a wire or any conductor is called **current.** The amount of electric current depends on the number of electrons passing a point in a given time. The rate of flow of electrons in a circuit is measured in amperes (A). One ampere is one coulomb of charge flowing past a point in one second. One coulomb is the charge carried by 6.24 billion billion electrons. Current is measured with an ammeter.

In order to keep the current moving through a circuit, there must be a device that maintains a potential difference. One common source of potential difference is a battery. Unlike a static discharge from your finger to a doorknob, a battery can light a lamp by maintaining a potential difference in the circuit.

Batteries

Have you ever noticed how a tape begins to drag in a portable tape player after using it for several hours? Perhaps you decided the batteries were dead and replaced them. Do you know why batteries are required to operate your tape player?

You probably have the option of plugging your tape player into a wall outlet, or using batteries to supply the

Figure 21-4. The amount of energy delivered each second in a circuit, or the rate of electron flow, depends on the number of electrons and how much energy each electron carries.

What is current?

What keeps current moving through a circuit?

OBJECTIVES AND SCIENCE WORDS: Have students review the objectives and science words to become familiar with this section.

2 TEACH

Key Concepts are highlighted.

CONCEPT DEVELOPMENT

▶ Have a stereo music box in front of the room. Ask students what you need to make the stereo work. They will say plug it in or use batteries. **What do batteries and the wall outlet have in common?** *They both supply electric current to the stereo.*

▶ Use Figure 21-4 to explain potential difference and current in a way that is easier for the students to understand. Have them brainstorm some analogies that could represent the same idea.

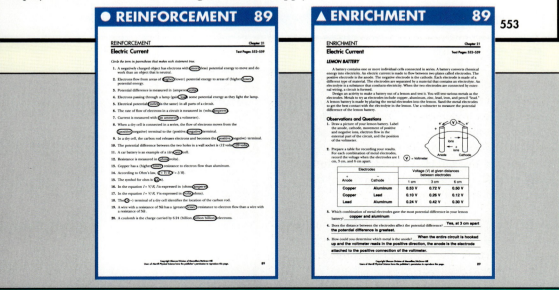

CONCEPT DEVELOPMENT

▶ Obtain a flashlight battery and take it to the shop room. Have it cut lengthwise to reveal the carbon rod, zinc case, and electrolyte paste inside. Some of these chemicals are corrosive, so seal the two halves in a plastic bag to pass around to the class.

REVEALING MISCONCEPTIONS

▶ People commonly refer to single dry cells as batteries. According to physics definitions, a battery is actually more than one dry cell or wet cell connected in series. Most devices use more than one cell to supply electric power, so "battery-operated" is a correct term.

Science and READING

Accidents involving car batteries have become more frequent and serious in recent years. Point out the precautions and the steps to be followed in jump starting a car with a dead battery. These should be listed in the owner's manual.

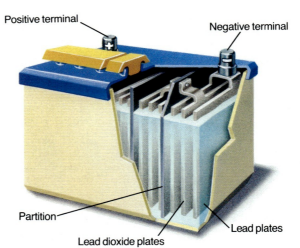

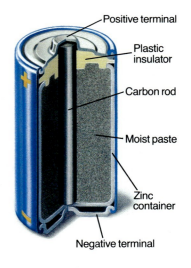

Figure 21-5. The car battery on the left is a series of wet cells, and the dry cell on the right can be connected in series with other dry cells to form a battery.

Science and READING

Read an automobile owner's manual to see if it explains how to "jump start" a car with a discharged battery. Explain this process to your classmates.

energy it needs to operate. If you want to take the tape player outside, you will have to use batteries, or dry cells. Look at the dry cell shown in Figure 21-5. Can you locate the positive and negative terminals of the dry cell in the diagram? They are located at opposite ends. Notice that the zinc container of the dry cell contains a moist chemical paste with a solid carbon rod suspended in the middle. The carbon rod forms the positive terminal of the dry cell, and the zinc can forms the negative terminal. A **dry cell** can act as an electron pump because it has a potential difference between the positive and negative terminals. Batteries are usually combinations of dry cells.

When the two terminals of the battery are connected in a circuit, electrons are released from the carbon rod as a chemical reaction occurs between the zinc and the chemical paste. The carbon rod becomes positive, forming the positive (+) terminal of the battery. Extra electrons accumulate on the zinc cell, making it negative. The potential difference between these two terminals causes current to flow through the closed circuit. As long as the chemical reaction continues, electrons are pumped from the negative to positive terminals of the dry cell. Two or more cells can be connected together to produce a higher voltage. How many dry cells does your tape player or camera require?

Another way to operate your tape player is by plugging it into a wall socket. The potential difference between

❷

OPTIONS

INQUIRY QUESTIONS

▶ **Why is it technically incorrect to say, "I use four batteries to operate my tape player"?** *A battery is actually a combination of dry cells, so it requires only one battery to operate.*

▶ **How is a dry cell (or battery) similar to a wall socket?** *They both provide potential difference to cause a current.*

two holes in a wall socket is 120 V. The electricity coming out of the wall socket is provided by an electric generator, instead of a battery.

Batteries can also be made up of a series of wet cells. A **wet cell** contains two connected plates made of different metals or metallic compounds in an electrolyte solution. One of the most common wet cell batteries is a car battery. Most car batteries contain wet cells made up of lead and lead dioxide plates in a sulfuric acid solution, as shown in Figure 21-5. As a chemical reaction occurs between lead and sulfuric acid inside the battery, electrons move from the lead plates through the conductor to the lead dioxide plates. As a result, a negative terminal with an excess of electrons and a positive terminal with a shortage of electrons form. This potential difference produces a current in the circuit between the battery and various parts of the car. Can you think of any other situations where wet cell batteries are used?

Resistance

One function of the car battery mentioned earlier is to light various light bulbs in the car's electric circuits. Do you know what makes a light bulb glow? Look at the light bulb in Figure 21-6. Part of the circuit through the bulb contains a filament. As a current flows through the filament, electrical energy is converted by the filament into light and heat. The current loses electrical energy as it moves through the filament because the filament, as do most materials, resists the flow of electrons through it.

③ **Resistance** is the tendency for a material to oppose the flow of electrons. With the exception of a few substances called superconductors, all conductors have some resistance. The amount of resistance varies with each conductor. Resistance is measured in ohms (Ω).

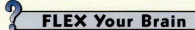
How does a car battery maintain a potential difference in a circuit?

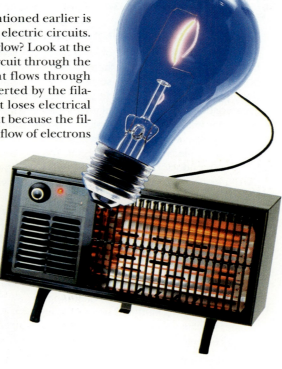

Figure 21-6. The light bulb and the heater glow and give off heat as current moves through them because they each have a high resistance to the flow of electrons.

CONCEPT DEVELOPMENT

▶ Usually, the resistance of conductors increases with increasing temperature because the atoms are moving more. In carbon, however, the electrons are separated from their atoms at high temperature. As a result, electric current is increased and resistance is decreased.

▶ Wet appliances are a hazard because ions in normal tap water make the electrical resistance lower. If your hand contacts the appliance near a wet switch, the low resistance allows a high current to pass through your body.

STUDENT TEXT QUESTION

▶ Page 555, paragraph 2: **Can you think of any other situations where wet cell batteries are used?** *boats*

❓ FLEX Your Brain

Use the Flex Your Brain activity to have students explore BATTERIES.

ENRICHMENT

▶ Have students research and make a scientific diagram to illustrate how a Van de Graaff generator works.

PROGRAM RESOURCES

From the **Teacher Resource Package** use:

Critical Thinking/Problem Solving, page 27, Are Electrical Cars Practical?

Science and Society, page 25, Electricity and Safety.

Activity Worksheets, page 5, Flex Your Brain.

Use **Laboratory Manual,** Wet Cell Battery.

▶ Demonstration: Set up a wet cell and show that it produces a current by connecting it to an ammeter. There are a number of wet cells possible; a simple one consists of copper metal in copper sulfate solution connected to zinc in zinc chloride solution. Connect the two electrodes through an ammeter and place a salt bridge between the beakers of the two solutions.

▶ Purchase a two-potato clock from Edmund Scientific Co. You can power a digital clock from two potatoes.

CROSS CURRICULUM

▶ Biology: Have students find out why *Torpedo nobiliana* is commonly called the electric eel. **How does it produce its electrical current?** *Because its numerous cell membranes are connected in parallel, it can produce a 1-A current at 600 V.*

TECHNOLOGY

To find out more about shake and bake superconductors, see Maranto, Gina. "Superconductivity: Hype Vs. Reality." *Discover.* August 1987, pp 22-32.

Think Critically: The superconductors require low temperatures, and the power used for refrigeration would count toward the total power loss.

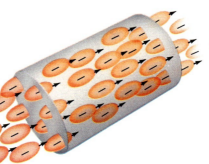

Copper is an excellent conductor; it has low resistance to the flow of electrons. Copper is used in household wiring because very little electrical energy is converted to thermal energy as current passes through the wires. In contrast, tungsten wire glows white-hot as current passes through it. Tungsten's high resistance to current makes it very suitable for use as filaments in light bulbs.

Figure 21-7. A short, thick piece of wire has less resistance than a long, thin piece of wire.

The size of wires also affects their resistance. Figure 21-7 illustrates how electrons have more room to travel through thick wires than thin wires. In wires of the same

TECHNOLOGY

Shake and Bake Superconductors

Mix together some oxides of lanthanum, barium, and copper, grind them up, and bake them in a furnace with some oxygen and, presto, you have made your own superconductor. After you cool your superconductor to its critical temperature, it will offer very little resistance and produce very little heat as electrons flow through it. The first superconductors were cooled to temperatures near absolute zero (273°C) to achieve these results. However, your "shake and bake" compound will become superconductive at a comparatively warm 178°C. In other words, your superconductor can be cooled easier and with less expense than the first superconductors.

The future of these new superconductive materials is promising and challenging. First, however, we must find ways to fashion these brittle superconducting materials into wires and thin films. The rewards of

solving these problems are tremendous. For example, high powered electric cars, magnetically levitated trains, super fast computers, and extremely efficient power transmission might become realities.

Think Critically: Even though superconductive materials lose very little energy as heat, a power transmission system using these new superconductors would not be energy-loss free. Where would these energy losses occur?

OPTIONS

ENRICHMENT

▶ Have students find out why it is desirable to have resistors in some circuits, even though they don't appear to do any work (light a bulb, turn a motor, and so on).

Figure 21-8. As the height of the hose increases, the potential difference increases and water flows at a faster rate. Electrons also flow at a faster rate when the potential difference in a circuit is increased.

length and material, thinner wires have greater resistance to electron flow. Likewise, if the diameters of two wires of the same material are the same, the longer wire offers a greater resistance. In most conductors, the resistance also increases as the temperature increases.

Ohm's Law

When you try to understand the relationship between voltage, current, and resistance, it is helpful to think of the way water behaves in a pipe. If one end of the pipe is higher than the other, there is a difference in the potential energy of the water due to gravity. This causes a stream, or current, of water to flow. If the height difference increases, the current increases. In a similar way, a greater potential difference in a circuit also causes the electric current to increase. Also, just as the walls and any obstructions in the pipe resist the flow of water, so do atoms in a wire resist the flow of electricity. As a result, the current in a circuit depends on both the voltage and the resistance.

This relationship is expressed mathematically in Ohm's law. **Ohm's law** states that the current is equal to the potential difference divided by the resistance.

$$\text{current (amperes)} = \frac{\text{potential difference (volts)}}{\text{resistance (ohms)}}$$

$$I = V/R$$

Did You Know?

The highest synthetic potential difference ever achieved was more than 30 million volts.

4

INQUIRY QUESTIONS

▶ **Form a hypothesis to explain why the resistance of a conductor usually increases with temperature.** *Atoms have more kinetic energy at higher temperatures, and this motion creates more resistance to the flow of the charge.*

CONCEPT DEVELOPMENT

▶ When discussing the relationship between the variables in Ohm's law, expand on the analogy relating water traveling through a pipe to current through a wire. Water is like the current, pressure is like the potential difference, and the size and roughness of the pipe are like the electrical resistance.

▶ Punch three holes in a vertical line in the side of a coffee can, evenly spaced from the bottom to the top. Fill it with water and observe how the water comes out of the holes. The bottom hole shoots water the farthest, since it is under the most pressure. Draw an analogy between this and the fact that when the potential difference is large (electrical pressure), the current is also large (assuming resistance is the same).

MINI QUIZ

Use the Mini Quiz to check students' recall of chapter content.

1. **The electric _____ is determined by the number of electrons passing a point in a given time.** *current*
2. **What are batteries?** *combinations of dry or wet cells that have a potential difference between positive and negative terminals*
3. **The tendency for a material to oppose the flow of electrons is _____ .** *resistance*
4. **What three quantities are related by Ohm's law?** *voltage, current, resistance*

CHECK FOR UNDERSTANDING

▶ To check the students' understanding of the relationships in Ohm's law, ask them the following question: **If the resistance of a circuit is doubled and the potential difference remains the same, what will happen to the current?** *The current will be half of what it was before.*

▶ Ask questions 1-3 and the **Apply** Question in the Section Review.

RETEACH

Students often have trouble rearranging the equation for Ohm's law. Show them the following diagram to go with the expression $V = IR$. When the desired variable is covered, the other two variables are in appropriate mathematical order.

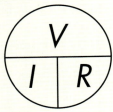

EXTENSION

For students who have mastered this section, use the **Reinforcement** and **Enrichment** masters or other OPTIONS provided.

PRACTICE PROBLEM ANSWERS

1. $I = \dfrac{V}{R} = \dfrac{120 \text{ V}}{20 \text{ }\Omega} = 0.6 \text{ A}$

$I = \dfrac{6 \text{ V}}{20 \text{ }\Omega} = \dfrac{0.3 \text{ A}}{20}$

2. $R = \dfrac{V}{I} = \dfrac{120 \text{ V}}{1.5 \text{ A}} = 80 \text{ }\Omega$

3 CLOSE

▶ Set up a simple circuit by connecting a dry cell (or power source), a variable resistor, and a small light bulb. Have students explain what happens to the current and potential difference as you vary the resistance.

▶ Explain that there are two main ways parts of a circuit can be connected, and these will be discussed in the next section.

SECTION REVIEW ANSWERS

1. A circuit has continuous current provided by a voltage source. A static discharge happens very rapidly. Both are caused by potential difference.

2. A chemical reaction causes a negative charge on the zinc terminal and a positive charge on the carbon rod. This creates a potential difference and causes a current.

3. $V = IR = (0.3\text{A})(25 \text{ }\Omega) = 7.5 \text{ V}$

4. Apply: The current is halved. It has no effect on the current.

EXAMPLE PROBLEM: Calculating Current

Problem Statement:
Strategy Hint: Make sure the decimal is correctly placed.

A light bulb with a resistance of 160 Ω is plugged into a 120-V outlet. What is the current flowing through the bulb?

Known Information:
resistance, $R = 160 \text{ }\Omega$
voltage, $V = 120 \text{ V}$

Unknown Information:
current (I)

Equation to Use:
$I = V/R$

Solution:
$I = V/R = 120 \text{ V}/160 \text{ }\Omega = 0.75 \text{ A}$

PRACTICE PROBLEMS

Strategy Hint: Your answer will be in amperes.

Strategy Hint: Your answer will be in ohms. Use $R = V/I$.

1. Find the current flowing through a wire if its resistance is 20 Ω and it is connected to a 12-V battery. What if it was connected to a 6-V battery?
2. The current flowing through a lamp is 1.5 A. It is plugged into a 120-V outlet. What is the resistance of the lamp?

SECTION REVIEW

1. How does a current traveling through a circuit differ from the static discharge that may occur when you touch a metal doorknob?
2. Briefly describe how a carbon-zinc dry cell supplies electricity for your tape player.
3. Calculate the potential difference across a 25-Ω resistor if a 0.3-A current is flowing through it.
4. **Apply:** How is the current in a circuit affected if the resistance is doubled? What if both the voltage and resistance are doubled?

Skill Builder — ☑ Making and Using Tables

Suppose you individually connect three copper wires of unequal length to a 1.5-V dry cell and an ammeter. The following currents were obtained: wire #1, 1.2 A; wire #2, 1.4 A; wire #3, 1.1 A. Make a table showing current (given) and resistance (use Ohm's law). If you need help, refer to Making and Using Tables in the **Skill Handbook** on page 686.

Skill Builder

Students should use Ohm's Law, $R = V/I$, to calculate the resistance needed to complete the table for each of the three wires.

Wire	Current (A)	Resistance (Ω)
1	1.2A	1.3 Ω
2	1.4A	1.1 Ω
3	1.1A	1.4 Ω

ACTIVITY 21-1
A Model of Ohm's Law

Problem: *How is flowing water like flowing electrons?*

Materials
- plastic funnel
- ring stand with ring
- rubber tubing (1 m)
- meterstick
- 2 beakers (250 mL)
- stopwatch or clock

Procedure
1. Copy the data table below.
2. Assemble the apparatus as shown. Place the funnel as high as possible.
3. Measure the height from the top of the funnel to the outlet end of the rubber tubing, in meters. Record your data on the table.
4. Pour 200 mL water into the funnel fast enough to keep it full, but not overflowing.
5. Measure the time for 0.10 L water to flow into the lower beaker, and record it on the table.
6. Repeat Steps 2 through 4 at least three more times, lowering the funnel for each trial.

Data and Observations   Sample Data

Trial	Height (m)	Time (s)	Rate (L/s)
1	0.60	10	0.010
2	0.50	12	0.0083
3	0.40	15	0.0067

Analyze
1. Gravity causing water to move can be compared to voltage causing electrons to move. Which trial can represent a circuit with the highest voltage?
2. The rate (L/sec) of flow of water from the tubing can be compared to current. Which trial can represent the highest current?
3. If voltage is increased, what happens to current?

Conclude and Apply
4. According to Ohm's law, what should happen to the current if the voltage stays the same but the resistance is reduced?
5. If a long tube has more resistance, what should happen to rate of flow of water if the tube is shorter?

21-3   ELECTRIC CURRENT   **559**

OBJECTIVE: Produce and operate a water analogy of an electric circuit.

PROCESS SKILLS applied in this activity:
▶ **Measuring** in Procedure Steps 3-6.
▶ **Predicting** in Conclude and Apply Questions 4 and 5.
▶ **Experimenting** in Conclude and Apply Question 5.
▶ **Formulating Models** in Analyze Questions 1 and 2.

👥 COOPERATIVE LEARNING
Three to four students can be assigned to each Science Investigation group. Assign individual tasks such as timer, pourer, recorder, and measurer.

TEACHING THE ACTIVITY
▶ The water should be poured fast enough to keep the funnel full. The timer should measure the flow into the lower beaker.
▶ The tube outlet should be kept at a constant height for all trials.
▶ A second tube with a length of 0.5 m can be provided for further experimentation.
▶ Students may need help calculating rate.
▶ The actual rates of flow depend on the diameter of the tubing.

ANSWERS TO QUESTIONS
1. The highest funnel position represents the greatest voltage. (The most *work* done on a quantity of water is similar to the most work done on a quantity of electrons.)
2. The greatest amount of water flowing per second occurs when the funnel is at its highest position. The quantity of water flowing per second compares to the quantity of electrons flowing per second (current).

3. A greater voltage in a circuit produces a greater current.
4. According to Ohm's law, if the voltage remains the same, the current will increase as the resistance is decreased.
5. A shorter tube offers less resistance, resulting in higher rate of water flow.

PREPARATION

SECTION BACKGROUND

▶ In studying and teaching circuits, use the steady state approach. According to this idea, you assume that the resistance, potential, and current in a given circuit are constant. If you change one or more of these, you can assume that the other measurements will adjust accordingly.

PREPLANNING

▶ Gather the materials needed for Activity 21-2 and the Motivate Demonstration below.

1 MOTIVATE

▶ **Demonstration:** Try to have several small objects with electrical circuits, partially taken apart, in the room for students to examine. You might display a small radio, a flashlight, and/or a telephone.

STUDENT TEXT QUESTION

▶ Page 560, paragraph 2: **When this happens, does the dryer still operate?** *no*

Science and WRITING

Any home safety manual should have a list of problems caused by these electrical circuits.

21-4 Electrical Circuits

New Science Words

series circuit
parallel circuits

Objectives

▶ Sketch a series and a parallel circuit, and list applications of each type of circuit.
▶ Recognize the function of circuit breakers and fuses.

Series Circuits

Look around you. How many electrical devices, such as lights, alarm clocks, stereos, and televisions, do you see that are plugged into wall outlets? These devices all rely on circuits to supply electricity where it is needed. Most circuits include a voltage source, a conductor, and one or more devices that use the electricity to do work.

Consider, for example, a circuit that includes an electric hair dryer. The dryer must be plugged into a wall outlet to receive current. The dryer and the circuit in the house both contain conducting wires to carry the current. A generator at a power plant probably produces a potential difference in the circuit, causing the electrons to move. The hair dryer turns the electricity into thermal and mechanical energy to do work. When you unplug the hair dryer, or turn off its switch, you are opening the circuit and breaking the path of the current. When this happens, does the dryer still operate?

Science and WRITING

With two other students, brainstorm a list of possible home safety problems caused by faulty or improperly used electrical circuits.

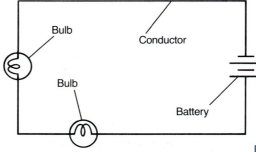

Figure 21-9. There is only one path for electrons to follow in a series circuit.

Bulb
Conductor
Bulb
Battery

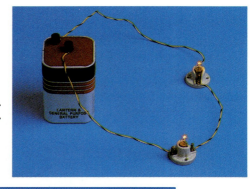

◆ **STUDY GUIDE** 90

STUDY GUIDE   Chapter 21
Electrical Circuits   Text Pages 560-564

Use the clues below to identify the term described by each statement. Write the term in the blank to the left. Then, find and circle each term in the hidden word puzzle. Terms can go across, up and down, backward, or diagonally.

series circuit	1. circuit that has only one path
parallel circuit	2. circuit that has more than one path
wire	3. In a circuit diagram, the symbol ─●──●─ means ____.
switch	4. In a circuit diagram, the symbol ─o── means ____.
light bulb	5. In a circuit diagram, the symbol means ____.
voltage	6. Another term for potential difference is ____.
ohm	7. The symbol Ω stands for ____.
dry cell	8. A flashlight battery is an example of a ____.
voltmeter	9. Potential difference can be measured with a ____.
resistance	10. tendency for a material to oppose the flow of electrons
coulomb	11. unit that means 6.24 billion billion electrons
ampere	12. units used to measure the rate of electron flow

OPTIONS

Meeting Different Ability Levels

For Section 21-4, use the following **Teacher Resource Masters** depending upon individual students' needs.

◆ **Study Guide Master** for all students.
● **Reinforcement Master** for students of average and above average ability levels.
▲ **Enrichment Master** for above average students.

Additional Teacher Resource Package masters are listed in the OPTIONS box throughout the section. The additional masters are appropriate for all students.

There are several kinds of circuits. One kind of circuit is called a series circuit. Some holiday lights are wired together in a series circuit. **In a series circuit, the current has only one path it can travel along.** Look at the diagram of the series circuit in Figure 21-9. If you have ever decorated a window or a tree with a string of lights, you may have had the frustrating experience of trying to find one burned out bulb. How can one faulty bulb cause the whole string to be out? Because the parts of a series circuit are wired one after another, the amount of current is the same through every part. **When any part of a series circuit is disconnected, no current can flow through the circuit. This is called an "open" circuit. The electrons require a closed path or they won't move at all.** Does this explain how a broken bulb can ruin a whole string of lights?

Figure 21-10 shows the symbols used in diagramming electric circuits. Notice how the switch must be closed for the circuit to be continuous.

Parallel Circuits

What would happen if your home was wired in series and you turned off a light? All other lights and appliances in your home would go out too! Fortunately, houses, and some holiday lights, are wired in parallel. **Parallel circuits contain separate branches for current to move through.** Look at the parallel circuit in Figure 21-11. The current splits up to flow through the different branches. **More current flows through the paths of lowest resistance.** Because all branches connect the same two points

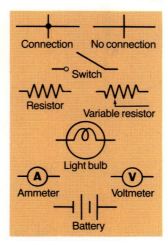

Figure 21-10. A circuit diagram is very easy to draw when you use these symbols.

Figure 21-11. There is more than one path for current to follow in a parallel circuit; the current can follow any of the branches.

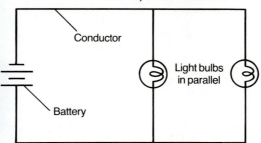

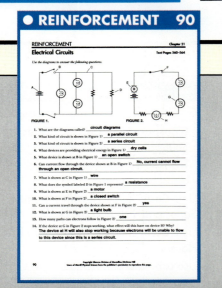

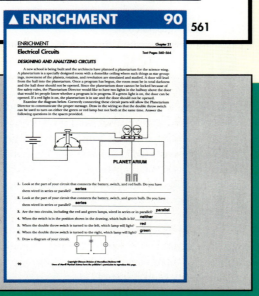

OBJECTIVES AND SCIENCE WORDS:
Have students review the objectives and science words to become familiar with this section.

TEACHER F.Y.I.

▶ In a series circuit, the total resistance is equal to the sum of the individual resistances. $R(\text{total}) = R(1) + R(2) + ...$ The potential difference across any resistance is equal to the current times that specific resistance.

▶ In a parallel circuit, the total resistance can be calculated by the following equation. $1/R(\text{total}) = 1/R(1) + 1/R(2) + ...$ The total resistance is less than any single resistance in a parallel circuit.

2 TEACH

Key Concepts are highlighted.

CONCEPT DEVELOPMENT

▶ Emphasize that electrons move in all parts of a circuit simultaneously. Electrons in the circuit outside the battery lose energy as they move through devices in the circuit that convert electrical energy into other forms of energy, such as light, heat, and mechanical energy. Within the battery, electrons gain energy produced by chemical reactions. The battery converts chemical energy to electrical energy.

561

What will happen when one lamp in a simple series circuit is disconnected? *Current ceases in the entire circuit.* **What will happen when one lamp on a parallel branch of a circuit is disconnected?** *Current stops in the broken branch, but continues in other parts of the circuit.*

RETEACH

Demonstration: Set up a simple series circuit with a battery and a couple of small light bulbs. You might want to connect ammeters in two different places to show that the current is the same everywhere in the circuit. Now disconnect one lamp to show that the entire circuit is broken. Do the same for a parallel circuit, showing that the current is not the same everywhere in a parallel circuit. Disconnect a lamp to show only that branch is affected. The broken branch no longer carries current, thus altering the current elsewhere in the parallel circuit.

EXTENSION

For students who have mastered this section, use the **Reinforcement** and **Enrichment** masters or other OPTIONS provided.

STUDENT TEXT QUESTION

▶ Page 562, paragraph 2: **Would you expect it to be part of a series or parallel circuit?** *parallel*

CROSS CURRICULUM

▶ **Electrical Engineering:** Contact a local building contractor to find out how the wiring on new buildings is done. Try to obtain a blueprint of the electrical plan and try to identify the major parts.

CONCEPT DEVELOPMENT

▶ **Demonstration:** Obtain a fuse and a circuit breaker from an electrical or hardware store. Let students examine each device. Then set up a demonstration circuit you can use to first blow a fuse, and then cause the circuit breaker to open.

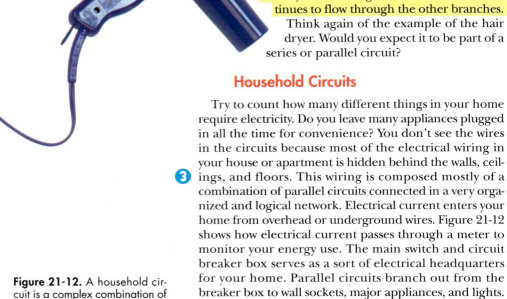

of the circuit, the potential difference is the same in each branch.

Parallel circuits have the advantage that when one branch of the circuit is opened, such as when you turn a light off, the current continues to flow through the other branches.

Think again of the example of the hair dryer. Would you expect it to be part of a series or parallel circuit?

Household Circuits

Try to count how many different things in your home require electricity. Do you leave many appliances plugged in all the time for convenience? You don't see the wires in the circuits because most of the electrical wiring in your house or apartment is hidden behind the walls, ceilings, and floors. This wiring is composed mostly of a combination of parallel circuits connected in a very organized and logical network. Electrical current enters your home from overhead or underground wires. Figure 21-12 shows how electrical current passes through a meter to monitor your energy use. The main switch and circuit breaker box serves as a sort of electrical headquarters for your home. Parallel circuits branch out from the breaker box to wall sockets, major appliances, and lights.

Figure 21-12. A household circuit is a complex combination of parallel circuits.

Light circuit   Stove circuit

Meter

Light switch

Ground

Wall socket

OPTIONS

INQUIRY QUESTIONS

▶ Imagine a circuit containing two lamps connected in series. What would happen to the brightness of each lamp if two more lamps were added? *The resistance would increase, and the current would decrease. The intensity, or brightness, of the lamps would decrease.*

▶ Why does the entire light bulb fail to light if a part of the filament is broken? *There is only one path for the current to follow. Breaking the filament is like opening a switch; there is no current in the bulb.*

PROGRAM RESOURCES

From the **Teacher Resource Package** use:

Transparency Masters, pages 83-84, Series and Parallel Circuits.

Transparency Masters, pages 85-86, Household Circuits.

Use **Color Transparency** number 42, Series and Parallel Circuits.

Use **Color Transparency** number 43, Household Circuits.

Use **Laboratory Manual,** Simple Circuits.

Many appliances can draw current from the same circuit, so protection against overheating must be built in. If a great amount of current is drawn through the wires, the wires can actually become hot enough to start a fire. Either a fuse or a circuit breaker is wired between every parallel circuit and the main switch box as a safety device.

What does it mean to say somebody has "blown a fuse"? Usually it refers to somebody losing his or her temper. This expression comes from the function of an electrical fuse. A fuse contains a small piece of metal that melts if the current causes the circuit wire to heat up too much. When it melts, it causes a break in the circuit and prevents more current from flowing through the overloaded circuit. To complete the circuit, you must replace the damaged fuse with a new one.

A circuit breaker is another guard against overheating a wire. A circuit breaker contains a piece of metal that bends when it gets hot. The bending causes a switch to open the circuit, preventing the flow of more current. Circuit breakers can usually be reset by flipping the switch. Before you reset a circuit breaker or replace a blown fuse, you should unplug some of the appliances from the overloaded circuit.

Figure 21-13. The circuit breaker (above) and fuses (below) prevent circuits from overheating.

SECTION REVIEW

1. Use symbols to draw a series circuit containing a battery, an open switch, a resistor, and a light bulb.
2. Use symbols to draw a parallel circuit with a battery and two resistors wired in parallel.
3. Compare and contrast fuses and circuit breakers. Which is easier to use?
4. **Apply:** Explain why buildings are wired in parallel instead of series circuits.

ENRICHMENT

▶ Have students investigate other electrical components commonly found in electrical circuits (see Chapter 23). Resistors, capacitors, and diodes have unique appearances and functions.

3 CLOSE

▶ Ask questions 1-3 and the **Apply** Question in the Section Review.

SECTION REVIEW ANSWERS

1.
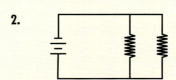

2.
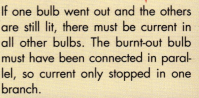

3. Both break overloaded circuits. Fuses melt and must be replaced. Circuit breakers bend to flip a switch which can be easily reset. Circuit breakers are easier to use.
4. Apply: Buildings are wired in parallel so the voltage is the same everywhere in the circuit and opening one part of the circuit does not affect the other parts.

ACTIVITY 21-2
1 class period

OBJECTIVE: Construct, test, and **compare** working examples of some electric circuits.

PROCESS SKILLS applied in this activity:
▶ **Communicating** in Procedure Steps 1 and 6 and Analyze Questions 3 and 4.
▶ **Experimenting** in Procedure Step 5, Analyze Question 1, and Conclude and Apply Question 7.
▶ **Formulating Models** in Conclude and Apply Questions 5 and 6.

⬛ COOPERATIVE LEARNING
Divide the class into Science Investigation teams of four. One student pair can build a series circuit while the other pair builds the parallel circuit. Final testing and observations of both circuits can be done by the entire team.

TEACHING THE ACTIVITY
▶ Cut apart a string of mini-lights for Christmas trees. A string of 50 or more provides low-voltage lights, sockets, and hook-up wire at low cost.
▶ Tape on aluminum provides strength and reduces conductivity. Some students may forget that one side is an insulator.
▶ Wires from lights are twisted onto small paper clips to make connectors.
Troubleshooting: Less than 6 volts makes lights in series too dim.
CAUTION: *Do not use a car battery. It delivers too much current to a short circuit.*

PROGRAM RESOURCES
From the **Teacher Resource Package** use:
Activity Worksheets, pages 169-170, Activity 21-2: Electric Circuits.

ACTIVITY 21-2
Electric Circuits

Problem: How do parallel and series circuits work?

Materials
- aluminum foil
- cellophane tape
- scissors
- 3 lights with sockets
- 6 paper clips
- battery (6 or 9 volt)

Procedure
1. On a sheet of paper, draw a series circuit of three lights and a battery as shown.
2. Make conductors by taping a 30-cm piece of cellophane tape to a sheet of aluminum foil. Use scissors to cut this into three narrow strips.
3. Tape the conductor strips over the conductor lines on your drawing. Leave loose ends of about 3 cm at the lights and battery.
4. Connect the lights to the circuit with the paper clips.
5. Test the circuit by touching the remaining two conductor ends to the poles of the battery.
6. Draw a three-light parallel circuit on another sheet of paper and repeat the procedure.

Analyze
1. If one light is removed from the series circuit, will the other lights still work? Is this also true of the parallel circuit?
2. In which kind of circuit do the lights shine the brightest?
3. Mark your circuit diagram with (+) and (−) to identify the battery poles.
4. Mark your circuit diagram with arrows to show the flow of electrons through the circuit.

Conclude and Apply
5. Where in the parallel circuit would you place a switch to control all three lights? Where would a switch be placed to control only one light?
6. How do you know that your house lights are connected in parallel to each other?
7. How can you make a switch that will work in your circuit?

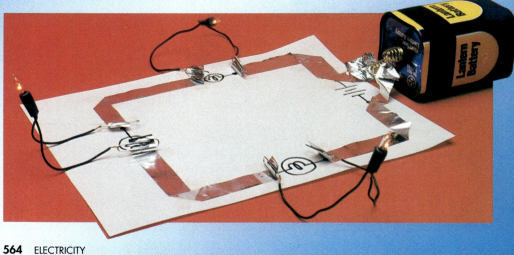

564 ELECTRICITY

ANSWERS TO QUESTIONS
1. All lights in series must be connected for any of them to work. Lights in parallel can work independently.
2. Lights in parallel shine the brightest.
3. Answers will vary.
4. Arrows should show electrons moving away from the (–) pole and toward the (+) pole.

5. A switch next to the battery will turn out all lights. A switch next to a light will turn out only that light.
6. If a light burns out or is removed, the other lights still work.
7. You can make a switch in the circuit by opening and closing one of the connections.

Electrical Power and Energy

21-5

Objectives

▶ Explain and calculate electric power.
▶ Calculate the amount of electrical energy in kilowatt-hours.

New Science Words

electrical power
kilowatt-hour

Electrical Power

What do you think of when you hear the word *power*? The word *power* has many different meanings. Earlier, in Chapter 7, you read that power is the rate at which work is done. Electricity can do work for us. Electrical energy is easily converted to other types of energy to do work. For example, the blades of a fan can rotate and cool you as electrical energy is changed into mechanical energy. An iron changes electrical energy into heat. **Electrical power is the rate at which electrical energy is converted to another form of energy.** **①**

How does electrical energy do work?

Table 21-1

ENERGY USED BY HOME APPLIANCES			
Appliance	Time of Usage (hours/day)	Power Usage (watts)	Energy Usage (kWh/day)
Hair dryer, blower	0.25	1000	0.25
Microwave oven	0.5	1450	0.73
Radio/record player	2.5	109	0.27
Range (oven)	1	2600	2.60
Refrigerator/freezer (15 cu ft, frostless)	24	615	14.76
Television (color)	3.25	200	0.65
Electric toothbrush	0.08	7	0.0006
100-watt light bulb	6	100	0.60
40-watt fluorescent light bulb	1	40	0.04

CONCEPT DEVELOPMENT

▶ Bring in some advertisements for microwave ovens, hair dryers, and stereos, as well as some light bulb boxes. Find the rate at which each appliance uses energy in watts. Have students make a list of these ranging from high to low users of electric power.

▶ Using the list suggested above, estimate the usage time of each appliance in an average day. Ask which appliances now seem to be the largest users of electrical power.

PRACTICE PROBLEM ANSWERS

1. $P = IV = (0.625\ A)(120\ V)$
   $P = 75\ W$

2. $P = IV$, so $I = I = \dfrac{P}{V}$

   $I = \dfrac{1000\ W}{120\ V} = 8.3\ A$

REVEALING MISCONCEPTIONS

▶ Plants that generate electricity are commonly called power plants. This leads to the misconception that you buy power. It is electrical energy, not electrical power, you pay for each month.

EcoTip

Remove dust from light bulbs regularly, and you might be able to user lower wattage bulbs and save energy.

The rate at which different appliances use energy varies. Appliances are often advertised with their power rating, which depends on the amount of electrical energy each appliance needs to operate. Table 21-1 shows the power requirements of some appliances.

Electrical power is expressed in watts (W), or kilowatts, (kW). The amount of power used by an appliance can be calculated by multiplying the potential difference by the current.

$$power = current \times voltage$$
$$watts = amperes \times volts$$
$$P = I \times V$$

One watt of power is produced when one ampere of current flows through a circuit with a potential difference of one volt. Look again at Table 21-1. Which appliance requires the most electrical power to operate? You can tell by looking at the number of watts listed for that appliance under the power usage column. Now see which appliance requires the least amount of electrical power to operate. The example problem below shows you how to calculate the electrical power usage for an appliance. This can be easily done as long as you know the values of the current and voltage.

EXAMPLE PROBLEM: Calculating Power

Problem Statement:	A calculator has a 0.1-A current flowing through it. It operates with a potential difference of 9 V. How much power does it use?
Known Information: Strategy Hint: Remember that electrical power is measured in watts.	current, $I = 0.1$ A potential difference, $V = 9$ V
Unknown Information:	power (P)
Equation to Use:	$P = I \times V$
Solution:	$P = I \times V = (0.1\ A)(9\ V) = 0.9\ W$

PRACTICE PROBLEMS

Strategy Hint: Be sure your decimal is correctly placed after you multiply.

Strategy Hint: Your answer should be in amperes.

1. A lamp operates with a current of 0.625 A and a potential difference of 120 V. How much power does the lamp use?

2. A microwave oven uses 1000 W of power. The voltage source is 120 V. What is the current flowing through the microwave?

OPTIONS

Meeting Different Ability Levels

For Section 21-5, use the following **Teacher Resource Masters** depending upon individual students' needs.

◆ **Study Guide Master** for all students.

● **Reinforcement Master** for students of average and above average ability levels.

▲ **Enrichment Master** for above average students.

Additional Teacher Resource Package masters are listed in the OPTIONS box throughout the section. The additional masters are appropriate for all students.

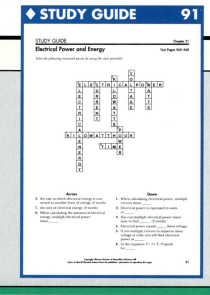

Electrical Energy

Why is it important that you not waste electricity? Most electrical energy is produced from natural resources, which are limited in supply. Electrical energy also costs you money. All the electricity you use in your home is measured by a device called an electrical meter. You have probably noticed that the meter for your home has a wheel that spins quickly when you are using a great deal of electricity and is stopped when no electricity is being used. ==The amount of electrical energy you use depends on the power required by appliances in your home and how long they are used.== For example, you can calculate the amount of energy a refrigerator uses in a day by multiplying the power required by the amount of time it uses that power.

$$\text{energy} = \text{power} \times \text{time}$$
$$\text{kWh} = \text{kW} \times 0$$
$$E = P \times t$$

==The unit of electrical energy is the **kilowatt-hour** (kWh). One kilowatt-hour is 1000 watts of power used for one hour.== The electric utility company charges you periodically for each kilowatt-hour you use. You can figure your electric bill by multiplying the energy used by the cost per kilowatt-hour. Table 21-2 shows some sample costs of running electrical appliances.

Table 21-2

MONTHLY COSTS OF USING APPLIANCES

	APPLIANCE		
	Hair dryer	Stereo	Color television
Average power in watts	600	109	200
Hours used daily	.25	3.0	2.5
Hours used monthly	7.5	90.0	75.0
Monthly watt hours	4500	9810	15 000
kWh used a month	4.5	9.81	15.000
Rate charged	$0.09	$0.09	$0.09
Monthly cost	$0.41	$0.88	$1.35

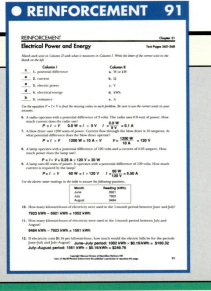
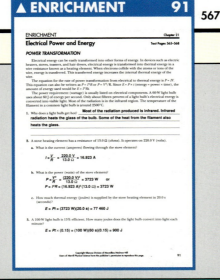
567

EXAMPLE PROBLEM: Calculating Electrical Energy

Problem Statement: A refrigerator is one of the major users of electrical power in your home. If it uses 700 W and runs 24 hours each day, how much energy (in kWh) is used in one day?

Known Information: power, $P = 700$ W
Strategy Hint: Convert W to kW before you multiply.
time, $t = 24$ h

Unknown Information: energy (E)

Equation to Use: $E = P \times t$

Solution: Convert W to kW, 700 W/1000 W/kW = 0.7 kW
$E = P \times t = (0.7 \text{ kW})(24 \text{ h}) = 16.8 \text{ kWh}$

PRACTICE PROBLEMS

Strategy Hint: Remember to convert watts to kilowatts.

Strategy Hint: Use the equation $P = E/t$; convert minutes to hours.

1. A 100-W light bulb is left on for 5.5 hours. How many kilowatt-hours of energy is used?
2. How much power is used by an electric hair dryer that uses 0.15 kWh of energy during 6 minutes of use?

To get an idea of energy costs in your home, you can make a list of all the appliances you use and add together their monthly energy costs. How do you think this value would compare to your electric bill?

SECTION REVIEW

1. What is electrical power?
2. A television uses a current of 1.5 A at 120 V. The television is used for 2 hours. Calculate the power used in kW and the energy used in kWh.
3. **Apply:** Assume your 110-W stereo is used 3 hours each day. If electricity costs 9 cents per kilowatt-hour, find the cost of listening to your stereo for one day.

Skill Builder ☑ **Concept Mapping**

Prepare a concept map that shows the steps in calculating the energy used in operating an electrical device with known voltage and current for a known amount of time. If you need help, refer to Concept Mapping in the **Skill Handbook** on pages 684 and 685.

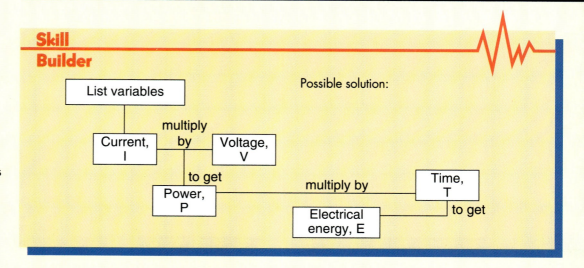

Skill Builder

List variables — Current, I — multiply by — Voltage, V — to get — Power, P — multiply by — Time, T — to get — Electrical energy, E

Possible solution:

CHAPTER REVIEW

SUMMARY

21-1: Electric Charge

1. Static electricity is the accumulation of electric charges on an object.

2. An electrical conductor is a material that allows electrons to move through it easily. An electrical insulator is a material that doesn't allow electrons to move through it easily.

3. An electroscope contains two suspended metal leaves in a jar that move apart when induced with an electrical charge.

21-2: Science and Society: Lightning—Its Causes and Effects

1. Clouds often contain areas of positively and negatively charged particles and can cause nearby objects to become charged by induction. A static discharge, lightning, occurs when excess electrons flow between the cloud and the charged object.

2. Some lightning-caused forest fires are allowed to burn as part of the natural processes in the forest.

21-3: Electric Current

1. The potential energy stored in an electron decreases as it moves through a circuit.

2. A dry cell creates a potential difference in a circuit, causing the electrons to flow.

3. Ohm's law states that the current in a circuit is equal to the potential difference divided by the resistance.

21-4: Electrical Circuits

1. Current only has one path along which it can travel in a series circuit. Parallel circuits provide more than one path for current to follow.

2. Circuit breakers and fuses are safety devices that open a circuit if the current becomes too great.

21-5: Electrical Power and Energy

1. Electrical power is the rate at which electrical energy can be transformed into other kinds of energy.

2. A kilowatt-hour is a thousand watts of power used for one hour.

KEY SCIENCE WORDS

a. circuit
b. conductor
c. current
d. dry cell
e. electrical power
f. electric field
g. electroscope
h. insulator
i. kilowatt-hour
j. lightning rod
k. Ohm's law
l. parallel circuits
m. potential difference
n. resistance
o. series circuit
p. static electricity
q. wet cell

UNDERSTANDING VOCABULARY

Match each phrase with the correct term from the list of Key Science Words.

1. buildup of electric charges on an object
2. exerts a force on an electric charge
3. a material through which electrons can move
4. a device that is used to detect electric charges
5. closed path through which electrons flow
6. composed of two connected plates made of different metals or metallic compounds in an electrolyte solution
7. opposes the flow of electrons in a conductor
8. electric current has at least two separate paths
9. the rate at which electrical energy is converted to a different form of energy
10. relates voltage and resistance to current

CHAPTER REVIEW

SUMMARY

Have students read the summary statements to review the major concepts of the chapter.

UNDERSTANDING VOCABULARY

1. p	**6.** q
2. f	**7.** n
3. b	**8.** l
4. g	**9.** e
5. a	**10.** k

OPTIONS

ASSESSMENT

To assess student understanding of material in this chapter, use the resources listed.

COOPERATIVE LEARNING

Consider using cooperative learning in the THINK AND WRITE CRITICALLY, APPLY, and MORE SKILL BUILDERS sections of the Chapter Review.

PROGRAM RESOURCES

From the **Teacher Resource Package** use:

Chapter Review, pages 45-46.

Chapter and Unit Tests, pages 143-146, Chapter Test.

CHECKING CONCEPTS

1. a	**6.** d
2. a	**7.** a
3. d	**8.** c
4. c	**9.** d
5. b	**10.** d

UNDERSTANDING CONCEPTS

11. electrons
12. Induction
13. chemical
14. series
15. Fuses or Breakers

THINK AND WRITE CRITICALLY

16. Both involve charged particles. In static electricity, these charges are stationary, whereas in current electricity these charges are continually flowing.

17. In the atoms of conductors, electrons are loosely held by the nucleus and are therefore free to move. In insulators, electrons are tightly bound by atomic nuclei and are not free to move.

18. Electrons flow in a circuit because of a difference in electrical potential between two points in the circuit. Electrons flow from the point of highest potential energy (negative electrode) to the point of lowest potential energy (positive electrode). When electrons move through an appliance, they do work on the appliance, and some of their potential energy is converted to some other form of energy that operates the appliance.

19. Lightning occurs when opposite charges build up in a cloud and Earth's surface. Lightning is actually a large static discharge.

20. According to Ohm's law, resistance and current are inversely related: as resistance increases, current decreases; as resistance decreases, current increases. Potential difference and current are directly related: as the potential difference increases, current increases, and as the potential difference decreases, the current decreases.

CHAPTER
REVIEW

CHECKING CONCEPTS

Choose the word or phrase that completes the sentence or answers the question.

1. An object becomes positively charged when it _____.
a. loses electrons   **c.** gains electrons
b. loses protons   **d.** none of these

2. When two negative charges are brought close together, they will _____.
a. repel   **c.** neither attract nor repel
b. attract   **d.** ground

3. As the distance from a charged particle increases, the strength of the electric field ____.
a. varies   **c.** increases
b. remains the same   **d.** decreases

4. An example of a good insulator is _____.
a. copper   **c.** wood
b. silver   **d.** salt water

5. Connecting a charged object to Earth in order to discharge the object into Earth is called _____.
a. charging   **c.** conduction
b. grounding   **d.** induction

6. The difference in potential energy per unit charge between two electrodes is measured in _____.
a. amperes   **c.** ohms
b. coulombs   **d.** volts

7. The difference in energy carried by electrons at different points in a circuit will determine the _____.
a. voltage   **c.** current
b. resistance   **d.** power

8. Resistance in an electrical wire causes electrical energy to be converted to _____.
a. chemical energy   **c.** heat
b. nuclear energy   **d.** sound

9. Which of the following wires would tend to have the least amount of electrical resistance?
a. long   **c.** hot
b. fiberglass   **d.** thick

10. Electrical energy is measured in _____.
a. volts   **c.** kilowatts
b. newtons   **d.** kilowatt-hours

UNDERSTANDING CONCEPTS

Complete each sentence.

11. The number of protons is equal to the number of _____ in an electrically neutral atom.

12. _____ occurs when a charged object causes electrons on a second object to rearrange without touching it.

13. In a battery, _____ energy is converted into electrical energy.

14. When any part of a _____ circuit is disconnected, no current can flow.

15. _____ open a circuit when too much current flows through it.

THINK AND WRITE CRITICALLY

16. Compare and contrast static electricity and current electricity.

17. How are the atoms of conductors different from the atoms of insulators?

18. What causes electrons to move through a circuit? What happens to the electrons' potential energy as they pass through an electrical appliance?

19. How does lightning occur?

20. How are resistance and potential difference related to the amount of current flowing through a circuit?

APPLY

21. Because they are higher than the roof of a building, they are struck first. They discharge the electric charges of a lightning strike into Earth.

22. To detect a negatively charged object, place a positive charge on an electroscope. Observe the electroscope's leaves as you bring the positively charged electroscope close to the object. If the object is negatively charged, the leaves will move closer together because the electrons on the object will repel electrons from the knob into the leaves, making the leaves less repulsive.

23. Given: $I = 1.5A$; $R = 2 \, \Omega$
Unknown: $V = ?$
Equation: $I = V/R$ or $V = I \times R$
Solution: $V = (1.5A)(2 \, \Omega) = 3 \, V$

24. Given: $V = 120 \, V$; $I = 2 \, A$; $t = 4 \, h$
Unknowns = P, E
Equations: $P = V \times I$; $E = P \times t$
Solutions: (1) $P = V \times I = (120 \, V)(2 \, A)$
$P = 240 \, W = 0.240 \, kW$
(2) $E = P \times t$
$= (0.240 \, W)(4 \, h)$
$E = 0.96 \, kWh$

21. Lightning rods are conductors on roofs of buildings that are grounded. How do they protect buildings from lightning?
22. Explain how an electroscope could be used to detect a negatively charged object.
23. A toy car has a 1.5-A current and its internal resistance is 2 ohms. How much voltage does the car require?
24. The current flowing through an appliance connected to a 120-V electron source is 2 A. How many kilowatt-hours of electrical energy does the appliance use in 4 hours?
25. You are asked to connect a stereo, a television, a VCR, and a lamp in a single, complex circuit. Would you connect these appliances in parallel or in series? How would you prevent an electrical fire? Explain your answers.

MORE SKILL BUILDERS

If you need help, refer to the Skill Handbook.

1. **Making and Using Graphs:** The resistance in a 1-cm length copper wire at different temperatures is shown below.

Resistance in Microohms	Temperature in °C
2	50
3	200
5	475

Construct a line graph for the above data. Is copper a better conductor on a cold day or a hot day?

2. **Interpreting Data:** Look at the power usage of the appliances in Table 21-1 and calculate the current each appliance pulls from a 120-V electron source. Which appliance draws the most current?

3. **Concept Mapping:** List the events that occur when an electroscope is brought near a positively charged object and a negatively charged object. Be sure to indicate which way electrons flow and the charge and responses of the leaves.

4. **Using Variables, Constants, and Controls:** Design an experiment to test the effect on current and voltage in a circuit when two batteries of equal voltage are connected in parallel and in series. What is your hypothesis? What are the variables and control?

PROJECTS

1. Research the origin and history of lightning rods. Relate your findings in a written report.
2. Obtain information from your electric company about safety rules of using electricity and make a poster to display.

---

25. The appliance should be connected in parallel, because then if one appliance went out the others would still work. Either a fuse or a circuit breaker could be used to protect the circuit from excess current and therefore an electrical fire.

MORE SKILL BUILDERS

1. Making and Using Graphs: According to the graph, copper would be a better conductor on a cold day because its resistance decreases with temperature.

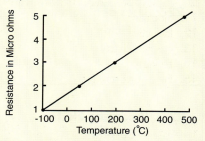

2. Interpreting Data: The current drawn by each appliance can be solved as follows:

$$I = \frac{P \text{ as given in table}}{120 \text{ V}}$$

The appliance drawing the highest current must have the highest power. The range oven has the highest current.

3. Concept Mapping:

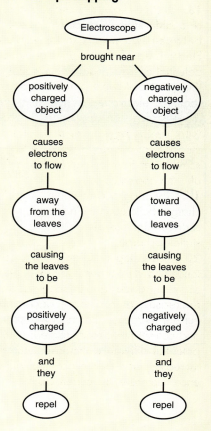

4. Using Variables, Constants, and Controls: Answers will vary somewhat, but the conclusions of the experiment should be that connecting two batteries of equal voltage in parallel increases the current without affecting the voltage, whereas connecting them in series increases the voltage without affecting the current.

CHAPTER 22

Magnetism and Its Uses

CHAPTER SECTION	OBJECTIVES	ACTIVITIES
22-1 Characteristics of Magnets (1 day)	1. **Explain** the properties of magnets. 2. **Define** the region of force around a magnet. 3. **Model** magnetic behavior using domains.	**MINI-Lab:** *What's "invisible" to a magnetic field?* p. 577
22-2 Uses of Magnetic Fields (2 days)	1. **Explain** how a coil carrying electric current can induce a magnetic field. 2. **Compare** and contrast ammeters and voltmeters. 3. **Describe** the function of an electric motor.	**Activity 22-1:** *Electric Motors,* p. 582
22-3 Producing Electric Current (2 days)	1. **Describe** how a generator produces an electric current using electromagnetic induction. 2. **Distinguish** between alternating current and direct current. 3. **Explain** how a transformer can step up or step down the voltage of an alternating current.	
22-4 Superconductivity Science & Society (1 day)	1. **Describe** the characteristics of superconductors. 2. **Consider** various applications of superconductivity.	**Activity 22-2:** *Transformers,* p. 590
Chapter Review		

ACTIVITY MATERIALS

FIND OUT	ACTIVITIES		MINI-LABS
Page 573 pencil paper	**22-1 Electric Motors, p. 582** paper cup nail magnet wire, 22 ga. magnet wire, 32 ga. bare copper wire, 16 ga. soda straw tape 2 6-volt batteries sandpaper magnetic compass	**22-2 Transformers, p. 590** 6-volt battery AC power supply, low voltage light, low voltage insulated wire, 32 ga. soda straw, cut to length of nail large nail knife paper clip	**What's "invisible" to a magnetic field? p. 577** ring stand utility clamp needle thread (1 meter) tape magnet selection of solids which includes iron and pure nickel

CHAPTER FEATURES	TEACHER RESOURCE PACKAGE	OTHER RESOURCES
Problem Solving: *A Magnetic Puzzle,* p. 576 **Skill Builder:** *Hypothesizing,* p. 577	**Ability Level Worksheets** ◆ *Study Guide,* p. 92 ● *Reinforcement,* p. 92 ▲ *Enrichment,* p. 92 **MINI-Lab Worksheet,** p. 182 **Technology,** pp. 19, 20	**Lab Manual 45,** Magnets
Technology: *Flying Trains,* p. 579 **Skill Builder:** *Comparing and Contrasting,* p. 581	**Ability Level Worksheets** ◆ *Study Guide,* p. 93 ● *Reinforcement,* p. 93 ▲ *Enrichment,* p. 93 **Activity Worksheet,** pp. 176, 177 **Concept Mapping,** pp. 49, 50 **Cross-Curricular Connections,** p. 28 **Transparency Masters,** pp. 87, 88	**Color Transparency 44,** Electric Motor-DC Generator **Lab Manual 46,** Electromagnets
Skill Builder: *Concept Mapping,* p. 587	**Ability Level Worksheets** ◆ *Study Guide,* p. 94 ● *Reinforcement,* p. 94 ▲ *Enrichment,* p. 94 **Critical Thinking/Problem Solving,** p. 28 **Science and Society,** p. 26 **Transparency Master,** pp. 89, 90	**Color Transparency 45,** Transformers
You Decide! p. 589	**Ability Level Worksheets** ◆ *Study Guide,* p. 95 ● *Reinforcement,* p. 95 ▲ *Enrichment,* p. 95 **Activity Worksheet,** pp. 178, 179	
Summary · Think & Write Critically Key Science Words · Apply Understanding Vocabulary · More Skill Builders Checking Concepts · Projects Understanding Concepts	**Chapter Review,** pp. 47, 48 **Chapter Test,** pp. 147-150	**Chapter Review Software** **Test Bank**

◆ **Basic**　　● **Average**　　▲ **Advanced**

ADDITIONAL MATERIALS

SOFTWARE	AUDIOVISUAL	BOOKS/MAGAZINES
Electricity and Magnetism, Focus. *Magnets and Electromagnetism,* Queue.	*Learning About Magnetism,* 2nd ed., film, EBEC. *Mr. Wizard's World: Current Electricity,* video, Macmillan/McGraw-Hill School Division. *Electromagnets and Their Uses,* film, Coronet/MTI. *Electricity and Magnetism,* filmstrips, EBEC.	Chikazumi, Sushin and Stanley H. Charap. *Physics of Magnetism,* Melbourne, FL: Robert E. Kreiger Publishing Co., Inc., 1978. Kalvius, G.M. and Robert S. Tebble. *Experimental Magnetism,* Vol. 1, Ann Arbor, MI: Books on Demand. Dean, Roger and Marilyn Dean. *Magnetic Storm.* NY: Crown Publishing, Inc., 1985.

THEME DEVELOPMENT: This chapter introduces the concept of magnetism, illustrated by several everyday applications. A theme that should be developed in this chapter is the pattern of change occurring in magnetic materials. The relationship between electricity and magnetism should be emphasized.

CHAPTER OVERVIEW

▶ **Section 22-1:** Magnetism as a property of certain materials is introduced, citing common applications of magnets. The domain model is developed to suggest a way to visualize magnetic behavior.

▶ **Section 22-2:** The formation of electromagnets by electric currents is discussed, followed by an illustration of how electromagnets are used in meters and electric motors.

▶ **Section 22-3:** Electromagnetic induction is introduced, with a focus on generators. Direct and alternating currents are contrasted. The functions of step-up and step-down transformers are also explained.

▶ **Section 22-4: Science and Society:** Finally, electricity and magnetism are tied together with a discussion of the science and applications of superconductors. The You Decide question deals with the development of superconducting trains as an alternative source of transportation.

CHAPTER VOCABULARY

magnetism	electromagnetic
magnetic poles	induction
magnetic field	generator
magnetic	direct
domains	current (DC)
electromagnet	alternating
ammeters	current (AC)
voltmeters	transformers
commutator	superconductors

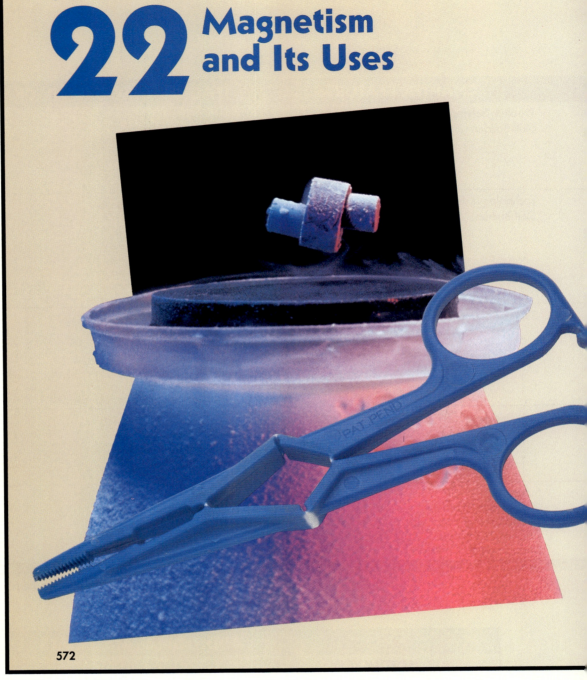

CHAPTER

22 Magnetism and Its Uses

572

OPTIONS

For Your Gifted Students

Students can make a magnetic field picture. Using a hot plate, have them melt candle wax or paraffin in an aluminum pan. They should dip sheets of paper into the liquid and then allow the sheets to cool. The coated, cooled paper should be placed on a piece of cardboard. Next, students add iron filings and design a picture using a magnet. The cardboard and paper should be placed on a *warmed* hot plate until the wax softens, allowing the filings to sink and become permanent.

Did you ever get lost on your first day in a new school? Perhaps your homeroom teacher gave you a map of the building, or you had to ask an older student to help you find your way.

How do you think sailors found their way across the ocean hundreds of years ago? Maybe they had maps, but they couldn't stop for directions. They used a compass to show them which way was north.

FIND OUT!

Make and use a compass in this simple activity.

Magnetize a sewing needle by stroking it in one direction with a magnet. Then tie a piece of thread around the needle and let it hang. It will line up in a north-south direction. Which end points north? Use your needle compass to make a map from your science classroom to the library. Let a friend use your map and compass to find the library.

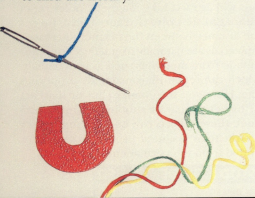

Gearing Up
Previewing the Chapter

Use this outline to help you focus on important ideas in this chapter.

Section 22-1   Characteristics of Magnets
▶ Magnets
▶ Magnetic Fields
▶ A Model for Magnetism
Section 22-2   Uses of Magnetic Fields
▶ Electromagnets
▶ Meters
▶ Electric Motors
Section 22-3   Producing Electric Current
▶ Generators
▶ Direct and Alternating Currents
▶ Transformers
Section 22-4   Science and Society
Superconductivity
▶ Are Superconductors Important?

Previewing Science Skills
▶ In the Skill Builders, you will hypothesize, compare and contrast, and make a concept map.
▶ In the Activities, you will observe, predict, interpret, and formulate models.
▶ In the MINI-Lab, you will hypothesize, observe, and interpret data.

What's next?

You have already discovered one important use of magnets. Technology has advanced by leaps and bounds since the first compass was used. We have learned how magnets work, and we have found many applications for them. As you read this chapter, think about all the ways you use magnets.

573

PREPARATION

SECTION BACKGROUND

▶ Demonstration magnets, such as the ones you may have in your classroom, are often made of alloys of magnetic substances. ALNICO is a common commercial magnetic material, made from *aluminum*, *nickel*, *cobalt*, and *iron*.

▶ The strength of a magnetic field can be measured in terms of the magnetic flux per unit area. Magnetic flux is the number of magnetic field lines in any given region. It is strongest around the poles.

PREPLANNING

▶ Round up a selection of magnets in different sizes, shapes, and strengths to use in demonstrations. Paper clips, wire, and meters are also suggested.

1 MOTIVATE

▶ **Demonstration:** Anchor a tall pencil in some clay, or hold it. Obtain two or more ring magnets, with holes in the center. Stack them with opposite poles facing each other; they will levitate. Ask students what causes this phenomenon. This is similar to the principle that is used to operate fast trains on magnetic repulsion systems.

TYING TO PREVIOUS
KNOWLEDGE: Ask students what kinds of attractions and repulsions they have studied this year. They should at least recall gravitation and the interaction between opposite electrical charges. If they need a hint, look at the ground and jump up and down or drop something. Note that magnetic forces are related to electrical forces.

OBJECTIVES AND
SCIENCE WORDS: Have students review the objectives and science words to become familiar with this section.

22-1 Characteristics of Magnets

New Science Words

magnetism
magnetic poles
magnetic field
magnetic domains

Objectives

▶ Explain the properties of magnets.
▶ Define the region of force around a magnet.
▶ Model magnetic behavior using domains.

Magnets

Have you ever stuck two magnets together? The Greeks were experimenting with magnetic materials more than 2000 years ago. They found a mineral that pulled iron objects toward it. If this mineral dangled freely on a string, it always pointed north. They described this mineral as being magnetic. Today we know that magnetism is related to electricity. Together, magnetic and electric forces can generate electricity and operate electric motors.

Magnetism is a property of matter in which there is a force of repulsion or attraction between like or unlike poles. Bring two magnets close together and they will either attract or repel. The magnetic forces are strongest near the ends, or **magnetic poles**, of the magnets. All magnets have two magnetically opposite poles, north (N), and south (S). If a bar magnet is suspended so it turns freely, the north end will point north.

When you bring the north ends of two magnets close together, they repel. However, the north and south ends of two magnets will attract. Like magnetic poles repel and opposite magnetic poles attract. These forces decrease as the distance between the magnets increases. ②

Only a few materials are naturally magnetic. Permanent magnets are made from materials such as iron, cobalt, and nickel, which can retain their magnetic properties for a long time. Have you seen paper clips or nails act like magnets? By being near or rubbing against a permanent magnet, these objects can become temporary magnets. They lose their magnetic properties soon after they are separated from the permanent magnet.

What is magnetism?

Figure 22-1. Magnetite is a mineral with natural magnetic properties.

OPTIONS

Meeting Different Ability Levels

For Section 22-1, use the following **Teacher Resource Masters** depending upon individual students' needs.

◆ **Study Guide Master** for all students.
● **Reinforcement Master** for students of average and above average ability levels.
▲ **Enrichment Master** for above average students.

Additional Teacher Resource Package masters are listed in the OPTIONS box throughout the section. The additional masters are appropriate for all students.

◆ STUDY GUIDE 92

STUDY GUIDE   Chapter 22
Characteristics of Magnets   Text Pages 574–577

Use the words in the box to fill in the blanks.

magnetic field	magnetism	cobalt	attraction
permanent	nickel	repulsion	metals
magnetic domains	magnetic poles	iron	electrons

Magnetism is a property of matter in which there is a force of __attraction__ or __repulsion__ between like or unlike __magnetic poles__. __Permanent__ magnets are made from materials which retain their magnetic properties for a long time. __Iron__, __cobalt__, and __nickel__ are examples of such materials. These three elements are also classified as __metals__. Each atom of these elements acts like a very small magnet because of unpaired __electrons__. The __magnetic field__ created by each atom exerts a force on the other atoms. The like poles of the atoms line up and face the same direction forming groups of aligned atoms called __magnetic domains__.

In each of the following sets of words, circle the word that does NOT belong with the others. Then explain how the remaining terms are related.

1. magnet, current, pole, north-seeking   All of the remaining terms are associated with magnets.

2. iron, cobalt, silver, nickel   All of these metals can be made into magnets.

3. gravitational, magnetic, electrical, chemical   All are force fields.

4. compass, Earth, horseshoe magnet, north   A compass can be used to find northern directions on Earth.

5. atoms, domains, random arrangement, like poles   In a magnet, the atoms with like poles line up to form magnetic domains.

6. north, south, repel, attract   Opposite poles of a magnet attract each other.

92

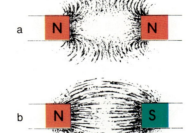

Magnetic Fields

Hold one bar magnet still and move another magnet slowly around it. What happens? Depending on the positions of the magnets, you may feel attractive or repulsive forces, or no force at all. The magnetic strength varies at different places on a magnet. **The magnetic field is the area around the magnet where magnetic forces act.** Figure 22-2 shows how you can model the magnetic field lines by sprinkling iron filings around a bar magnet. The filings line up along the magnetic field lines of the magnet. Notice that these magnetic lines of force are most dense around the poles of the magnet. Figure 22-3 shows how magnetic field lines differ when two poles repel or attract.

Have you used a compass to find out which way was north? A compass contains a magnetic needle that freely rotates in a circle and always points north. This happens because Earth is like a giant magnet surrounded by a magnetic field that extends beyond the atmosphere. The compass aligns with Earth's magnetic lines of force.

A Model for Magnetism

Many magnets are made of iron. What happens if you hold an iron nail close to a refrigerator door and let go? It falls to the floor. Why doesn't it stick to the refrigerator? Why is it that many substances can't become magnets? Because you can't see magnetism, a model or mental picture will help you answer these questions.

Electrons in most atoms exist in pairs, with each electron spinning in an opposite direction. Each moving electron causes a magnetic field to form around it. In most materials, the magnetic field of one electron is can-

Figure 22-2. The magnetic lines of force around this bar magnet can be modeled with iron filings.

Figure 22-3. Notice the magnetic lines of force when like poles repel (a) and unlike poles attract (b).

a

N   N

b

N   S

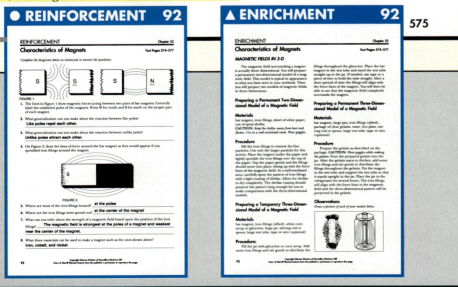
575

2 TEACH

Key Concepts are highlighted.

CONCEPT DEVELOPMENT

▶ Begin teaching magnetism by letting students feel the phenomenon and experiment with it a bit. You might set up informal investigation stations around the room and give groups of three students several minutes at each station. Include ring magnets on a pencil, a horseshoe magnet and some paper clips and nails, and a bar magnet with selected coins. (Canadian nickels are pure nickel and will be attracted by a magnet.)

▶ **Demonstration:** Show the arrangement of the areas of intensity around the ends of bar magnets by scattering iron filings around a bar magnet on an overhead projector. By convention, magnetic field lines are said to go from north to the south pole of the magnet. Be sure to put an acetate under the filings to avoid messes.

TEACHER F.Y.I.

▶ The SI unit for magnetic field strength is the tesla (T). Earth's magnetic field intensity at the surface is 10^{-4} T. Magnetic fields generated in the lab commonly reach 10 T and can be up to 100 T for a short time interval.

CROSS CURRICULUM

▶ **Language Arts:** Have students research the origin of the word *magnet*. They should find that it comes from the Greek word meaning "the stone of magnesia." This stone was lodestone, a metallic rock that possibly led humans to first observe magnetism.

PROGRAM RESOURCES

From the **Teacher Resource Package** use:

Technology, pages 19-20, Magnetic Resonance Imaging.

PROBLEM SOLVING

A Magnetic Puzzle

When Shantelle came to physical science class today, Mrs. Kline placed the students in groups. She gave each group three magnets and a long piece of string. Mrs. Kline then told the students to work with the other members of their group to determine the polarity of the three magnets.

Shantelle suggested, "Since Earth is magnetic, we can hang one of the magnets from a string to make a compass. The north pole of the magnet will swing to point to the North Pole."

The group tried Shantelle's suggestion with a red and silver magnet. As a result of their findings, they labeled the red end North and the silver end South. Next, they determined the polarity of a green and yellow magnet. The green end of the magnet pushed the red end away, and yellow end attracted the red end.

They tested a blue and pink magnet last. The blue end was attracted to the red end of the hanging magnet. They were surprised when the pink end was also attracted to the red end.

How did Shantelle's group label the green and yellow magnet?

Think Critically: What should Shantelle's group infer from the results of testing the blue and pink magnet?

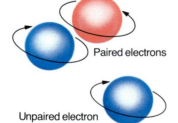

Figure 22-4. Elements with paired electrons aren't magnetic, but those elements with unpaired electrons are magnetic.

Paired electrons

Unpaired electron

celled by an opposite magnetic field produced by the other electron in the pair. The atoms in materials such as iron, cobalt, and nickel have unpaired electrons, so they don't cancel the electrons' magnetic fields. As a result, each atom of these elements acts like a very small magnet.

The magnetic field created by each iron atom exerts force on the other atoms, causing groups of atoms to align their magnetic poles so that all like poles are facing the same direction. These groups of atoms are called **magnetic domains.** Figure 22-5b shows how the domains are randomly arranged in an ordinary, unmagnetized nail. If a permanent magnet strokes the nail or comes near it, the domains rearrange to orient themselves in the direction of the nearby magnetic field, as in Figure 22-5a. The nail now acts as a magnet itself. When the strong magnet is removed, the magnetic domains in the nail soon return to their random arrangement. For this reason, the nail is a temporary magnet. Even permanent magnets can lose some of their magnetic properties if they are dropped or heated. Their magnetic domains would be rattled or melted out of alignment.

What happens when a magnet is broken in two? Would you expect one piece to be a north pole and one piece to be a south pole? Look again at the domain model in Figure 22-5. Because each magnet is actually made of many aligned smaller magnets, even the smallest pieces of a magnet have both a north and south pole.

Although people have been observing magnets since the Greeks first discovered them, and the magnetic domain model explains many observations about magnets, some questions about magnets and magnetic fields are still unanswered. For example, one of the most puzzling questions involves Earth's own magnetic field. We know Earth's magnetic poles have reversed, or flip-flopped north and south, more than 170 times during Earth's history. Scientists are unable to explain why the magnetic field reverses. They have, however, found many uses and applications for magnetism. As you read the next section, you will find out more about these applications.

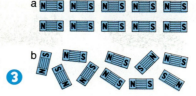

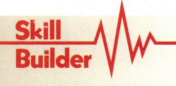

Figure 22-5. Magnetic domains are magnetized (a) and unmagnetized (b).

MINI-Lab

What's "invisible" to a magnetic field?

Clamp a magnet to a ring stand. Thread a needle. Stick the needle on the magnet and tape the thread to the table and pull the thread until the needle is suspended below the magnet. Slip some paper between the needle and magnet. The needle doesn't fall; therefore, the paper is "invisible." Repeat the experiment with aluminum foil, coins, and other solids. If the needle falls, the substance is "seen" by the field.

SECTION REVIEW

1. Describe what happens when you bring two magnetic poles together.
2. What is a magnetic field and where is it strongest?
3. **Apply:** You have a bar magnet dangling horizontally from a string. Explain two ways you could use another magnet to rotate the suspended magnet without touching it.

Hypothesizing — Skill Builder

Suppose you had a strong bar magnet and allowed your younger brother or sister to play with it. When you got the magnet back, it was barely magnetic. Write a hypothesis to explain what might have happened to your magnet. How could you fix it? If you need help, refer to Hypothesizing in the **Skill Handbook** on page 682.

MINI QUIZ

Use the Mini Quiz to check students' recall of chapter content.

1. **The area around a magnet where magnetic forces act is the ____ .** *magnetic field*
2. **What will happen if you bring two north poles of magnets together?** *They will repel each other.*
3. **Why might magnets lose their magnetic properties if they are dropped or heated?** *Their domains become scattered, physically jarred, and randomized.*

3 CLOSE

▶ Ask questions 1-2 and the **Apply** Questions in the Section Review.

MINI-Lab

CAUTION: *The needle is a sharp object.*

▶**Materials:** ring stand, utility clamp, needle, thread (one meter), tape, magnet, selection of solids which includes iron and pure nickel

▶The thread can be used to pull the needle about in the field. If the field is very strong, the needle will tend to follow the direction of the field.

SECTION REVIEW ANSWERS

1. Like poles repel and unlike poles attract.

2. a space around a magnet where magnetic forces act; at the poles

3. Apply: Pull the magnet in a circle by bringing opposite poles near each other, or push the magnet around by bringing like poles together.

Skill Builder

A reasonable hypothesis might be that your sibling dropped or heated the magnet. This could scatter the domains and reduce the magnetic properties. To fix it, you could try bringing a strong magnet near it to help realign the domains.

ENRICHMENT

▶ Give a short lesson in using compasses in orienteering. Have students learn to orient themselves and find hidden markers using only a compass. In nice weather, this makes a good outside activity.

▶ Have students find out what ferromagnetic, paramagnetic, and diamagnetic substances are. They can give oral presentations of their findings.

PROGRAM RESOURCES

From the **Teacher Resource Package** use:

Activity Worksheets, page 182, Mini-Lab: What's invisible to a magnetic field?

Use **Laboratory Manual,** Magnets.

SECTION BACKGROUND

▶ It is very interesting to note that Oersted's discovery that an electric current can produce a magnetic field was accidental, as many discoveries are. While doing a demonstration, he observed that moving a current through a wire produced a response in a nearby compass. Also, Oersted was a high school teacher!

PREPLANNING

▶ Try to gather some examples of electromagnets, meters, and electric motors for students to experiment with.

1 MOTIVATE

▶ **Demonstration:** Begin with Oersted's experiment. Loop a wire to the positive and negative ends of a battery and set it near a compass. Then reverse the connections—show how the magnetic field reverses.
▶ Have a fan blowing toward the class when they come in. Ask them what makes the blades of the fan rotate. Note that electrical energy is changed to mechanical energy. See page 580 for an explanation.

TYING TO PREVIOUS
KNOWLEDGE: Tell students that whenever they ring a doorbell, listen to music from loudspeakers, or use an electric motor, they are making use of a connection between electricity and magnetism. This connection will be explored in this section.

OBJECTIVES AND
SCIENCE WORDS: Have students review the objectives and science words to become familiar with this section.

New Science Words

electromagnet
ammeters
voltmeters
commutator

Objectives

▶ Explain how a coil carrying electric current can induce a magnetic field.
▶ Compare and contrast ammeters and voltmeters.
▶ Describe the function of an electric motor.

Electromagnets

In 1820, Hans Christian Oersted, a Danish physics teacher, observed that a current moving through a wire moved the needle on a nearby compass. When the current was reversed, the compass needle was deflected in the opposite direction. These magnetic effects ceased when the current in the wire stopped. Therefore, Oersted hypothesized, the electric current must produce a magnetic field around the wire, causing the direction of the field to change with the direction of the current.

Figure 22-6a shows magnetic field lines going around a straight wire with current in it. Figure 22-6b shows how the magnetic field lines bunch up when the wire is looped. Even more loops can be bent in the wire to form a coil, Figure 22-6c. Adding turns of the wire to the coil causes more overlapping of the magnetic field lines, and, as a result, the magnetic field grows stronger. When a current is passed through such a coil, a strong temporary magnet called an **electromagnet** is formed. One end of the coil acts as the north pole and the other end as the south pole of the electromagnet. The strength of the magnetic field can be increased by adding more turns to the wire coil and by increasing the amount of current passing through the wire. The electromagnet can also be made stronger by inserting an iron core inside the coil of wire. The iron core becomes a magnet and its magnetic field is aligned with that of the electromagnet.

Electromagnets operate doorbells and loudspeakers and lift large metal objects in construction machines.

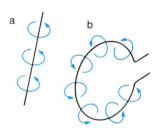

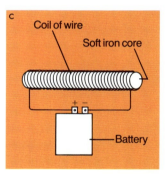

Figure 22-6. Magnetic fields form around any wire that is conducting current (a) (b); that is, the principle behind the electromagnet (c).

OPTIONS

Meeting Different Ability Levels

For Section 22-2, use the following **Teacher Resource Masters** depending upon individual students' needs.
◆ **Study Guide Master** for all students.
● **Reinforcement Master** for students of average and above average ability levels.
▲ **Enrichment Master** for above average students.
Additional Teacher Resource Package masters are listed in the OPTIONS box throughout the section. The additional masters are appropriate for all students.

Flying Trains

Can you imagine flying over the ground at speeds of more than 500 kilometers per hour without an airplane? German and Japanese firms are currently developing high-speed trains that ride on magnets instead of rails.

One such magnetically levitated train, called a maglev, is being built by a German company. This train will run from the airport to downtown in Las Vegas, Nevada. The undercarriage of this train is lined with strong permanent magnets. These magnets are attracted to steel guide tracks above them, thus providing lift. Electric current is delivered at just the right time to devices mounted on the guide track so they will produce magnetic fields that pull and push the train along at speeds up to 90 km/h.

A high-speed prototype in Japan uses superconductive magnets mounted on the underside of the vehicle. These magnets interact with nonelectric coils in the guide track to produce lift and with electric coils in the guide track to produce the push and pull. This maglev will travel between cities at speeds of 500 km/h.

Think Critically: Compare the advantages and disadvantages of magnetically levitated trains versus standard rail transportation.

They change electrical energy to mechanical energy to do work. Another important feature of electromagnets is that they can be turned on and off by controlling the flow of current through the coil. What would happen if the magnetic field in the doorbell was permanent?

Meters

The sensitivity of electromagnets to electrical currents makes them useful in detecting electric current. An instrument used to detect currents is called a galvanometer. It is made of a coil of wire connected to a circuit and suspended so it can rotate in the magnetic field of a permanent magnet. When current flows through the coil, the magnetic force causes the coil to rotate against a spring. A needle is attached to the coil and turns with it to provide a reading on a scale.

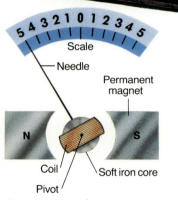

Figure 22-7. A galvanometer uses an electromagnet to detect electric currents.

● REINFORCEMENT 93

▲ ENRICHMENT 93

579

▶ Use a "perpetual motion" toy (often found in museum stores) to demonstrate how a magnetic field and an electric coil interact to produce motion.

▶ To find out more about maglevs, refer to "310-mph Flying Trains—in the '90s—in the U.S." by David Scott and John Free, *Popular Science,* May 1989, pp. 132-135.

▶ **Think Critically:** Magnetically levitated trains would be quieter and cheaper to operate because of the reduced friction. Maglev trains would be faster, but this might increase the accident potential. The magnetic fields produced by maglev trains may pose health hazards.

2 TEACH

Key Concepts are highlighted.

CONCEPT DEVELOPMENT

▶ The right-hand rule can be used to determine the direction of the magnetic field and current. Place the right thumb in the direction of the current through the wire. The fingers of the right hand then curl in the direction of the magnetic field.

▶ A coil of wire with many turns placed close together is called a solenoid.

Cooperative Learning: Divide the class into Science Investigation teams. Have each team build an electromagnet by winding wire into a coil around a large iron nail. Then have them select items they would like to try to pick up (paper clips, staples, etc.).

▶ There are situations where a magnetic field around a wire is not desired. Ask students if they have any idea how this problem could be avoided. An insulated wire with current traveling in the opposite direction can be placed beside the original wire or wrapped around it. This causes the total current and the total magnetic field to be zero.

▶ **Music/Acoustics:** Have students research the function of an electromagnet in a loudspeaker. Have them write a clear explanation and draw a scientific diagram to illustrate how it works. If possible, take a real speaker apart and identify the parts.

TEACHER F.Y.I.

▶ The resistance of an ammeter must be very low compared to the total resistance in the circuit. This prevents the meter from interfering with the current it is measuring. A voltmeter should have a huge resistance so that little current passes through it.

CONCEPT DEVELOPMENT

▶ Reinforce the idea that a galvanometer can be calibrated to measure both current (as an ammeter) and potential difference (as a voltmeter).

▶ If available, use a demonstration motor and have students guide you in identifying the major parts discussed in the section on electric motors. If one is not available, be sure to go over the parts labeled in the illustrations.

CHECK FOR UNDERSTANDING

Use the Mini Quiz to check for understanding.

MINI QUIZ

Use the Mini Quiz to check students' recall of chapter content.

1 **How is an electromagnet formed?** *by passing a current through a coil, usually with an iron core through the center*

2 **Who discovered that a current moving through a wire makes a compass respond?** *Hans Christian Oersted*

3 **An instrument that can be used to detect current or potential difference is a(n) _____ .** *galvanometer*

4 **A(n) _____ is a reversing switch that rotates with the electromagnet.** *commutator*

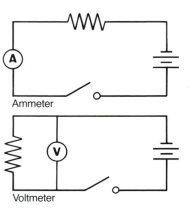

Ammeter

Voltmeter

EcoTip

Use a magnet to separate aluminum and tin cans for recycling.

Galvanometers can be calibrated to measure current or electrical potential depending on whether they are contained within an ammeter or a voltmeter. **Ammeters measure the electrical current of a circuit in amperes. An ammeter should be connected in series with a circuit to measure the current passing through it.**

Voltmeters measure the potential difference of a circuit in volts. Unlike ammeters, voltmeters should be placed in parallel across a part of a circuit. The readings in volts depend on the amount of current passing through the voltmeters. The higher the current in the voltmeter, the larger the potential difference across that part of the circuit.

Electric Motors

Do you ever use a fan to keep cool during periods of hot weather? Your fan has an electric motor in it that changes electric energy into mechanical energy, which then turns the blades of your fan. The turning blades push air toward you so your skin feels cooler.

Like a galvanometer, the electric motor in your fan contains an electromagnet that is free to rotate. It rotates between opposite poles of a permanent, fixed magnet. When a current flows through the moveable electromagnet, a magnetic field is induced. This causes enough attraction and repulsion with the permanent magnet to force the coil to turn. But the rotation would stop when opposite poles of the magnet were near each other. How could you make the coil turn again?

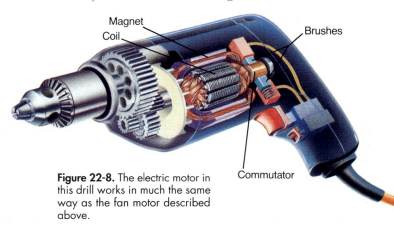

Figure 22-8. The electric motor in this drill works in much the same way as the fan motor described above.

Magnet
Coil
Brushes
Commutator

OPTIONS

INQUIRY QUESTIONS

▶ **What part of a galvanometer is actually an electromagnet?** *the coil of wire that is connected to the circuit and suspended in the magnetic field*

▶ **Why does the coil in a galvanometer rotate when current passes through it?** *It becomes an electromagnet, and since it is suspended in the magnetic field of a permanent magnet, it will rotate so the magnetic fields are aligned.*

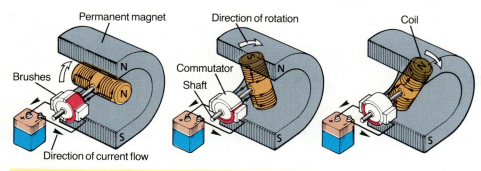

Permanent magnet   Direction of rotation   Coil

Brushes

Commutator
Shaft

Direction of current flow

To make the coil in the fan motor spin steadily, the direction of the current through the coil must be reversed after each half revolution. This causes the poles of the rotating electromagnet to switch and turn toward the opposite pole of the permanent magnet. A fan's electric motor operating on direct current must have a device to change the direction of the current. A **commutator** is a reversing switch that rotates with the electromagnet. Electric current reaches the commutator through fixed electrical contacts called brushes. The continual rotation of the electromagnet in your fan's motor keeps the fan's blades turning.

Figure 22-9. The commutator in a motor switches the direction of the current so the coil will turn continuously.

Did You Know?

Lightning can magnetize objects so strongly that they are capable of lifting objects as much as three times their own weight.

SECTION REVIEW

1. Does a straight wire or a looped wire have a stronger magnetic field when both carry the same amount of current? Explain your answer.
2. What is a galvanometer?
3. Why is it important that the current in an electric motor change its direction frequently?
4. **Apply:** Why does the magnetic field inside a current-carrying coil increase if a piece of iron is placed in the coil?

☑ Comparing and Contrasting

Compare and contrast ammeters and voltmeters. Discuss what they measure, how they are connected, and the relative resistance each meter has. If you need help, refer to Comparing and Contrasting in the **Skill Handbook** on page 679.

Skill Builder

22-2   USES OF MAGNETIC FIELDS   **581**

OBJECTIVE: Construct and **test** a working example of an electric motor.

PROCESS SKILLS applied in this activity:
▶ **Observing** in Procedure Step 3.
▶ **Formulating Models** in Procedure Steps 1, 4, and 6.
▶ **Predicting** in Conclude and Apply Questions 4 and 5.

COOPERATIVE LEARNING
Arrange the students in Expert Teams of four. Two students can build the field, and two students can build the armature.

TEACHING THE ACTIVITY
Troubleshooting: Build a working model to determine the lengths of wire needed.
▶ Make available a pair of wire cutters or strong scissors.
▶ Procedure Step 5 is critical. About 180 degrees around the wire must be scraped to allow current to flow long enough during a revolution of the armature. The *same* side of both ends must be scraped. See diagram below.
▶ Put your working model on display for student reference.
▶ Use the trial and error of this activity as an opportunity for students to devise solutions through careful observation and analysis.

PROGRAM RESOURCES
From the **Teacher Resource Package** use:

Activity Worksheets, pages 176-177, Activity 22-1: Electric Motors.

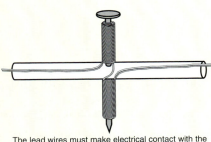

The lead wires must make electrical contact with the metal support for half a revolution, going on and off twice per revolution.

ACTIVITY 22-1
Electric Motors

Problem: *How does an electric motor work?*

Materials
- paper cup or beaker
- nail
- magnet wire, 22 ga
- magnet wire, 32 ga
- bare copper wire, 16 ga
- soda straw
- tape
- 6-volt batteries (2)
- sandpaper
- magnetic compass

Procedure
1. Construct the field as shown by wrapping wire around the top of the plastic cup.
2. Sandpaper the coating from 3 cm of each end of the wire.
3. Test the field coil by holding the compass inside the coil and connecting its wires to a battery. The compass should respond.
4. Construct the armature as shown. Make the direction of wrap of wire the same on both sides of the armature.
5. Scrape the coating from one side of the ends of the armature wire which extend from each end of the straw.
6. Assemble as shown. Attach the batteries and start the motor.

Analyze
1. When testing the field coil, what does the movement of the compass tell you about the field?
2. The armature is designed to turn on and off as it spins. What test could you use to see if it is working?
3. As the armature spins, what is the best position for it to turn on? At what position should it turn off?

Conclude and Apply
4. Would the motor work if the field coil were replaced by a permanent magnet?
5. Why would the motor not work if the armature were replaced by a permanent magnet?

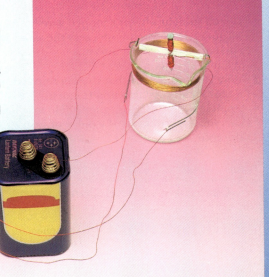

ANSWERS TO QUESTIONS
1. The response of the compass shows that the field is magnetic and that its poles are at the open ends of the coil.
2. With the field current turned off, hold a compass near the armature as it is turned by hand. Or, a light connected in series with the armature as it is turned by hand should go on and off.
3. The armature should be on when horizontal and go off when vertical.
4. Yes. The field remains constant.
5. The shape of a permanent magnet cannot be easily changed, and the field cannot be strengthened to get the motor to function.

Producing Electric Current   22-3

Objectives

▶ Describe how a generator produces an electric current using electromagnetic induction.
▶ Distinguish between alternating current and direct current.
▶ Explain how a transformer can step up or step down the voltage of an alternating current.

New Science Words

electromagnetic induction
generator
direct current (DC)
alternating current (AC)
transformer

Generators

After Oersted discovered that magnetism could be produced from electric currents, scientists tried to produce an electric current using magnets. Working independently in 1831, a British scientist, Michael Faraday, and an American scientist, Joseph Henry, found that moving a wire through a magnetic field induced an electric current in that wire. **Electromagnetic induction** is the process in which the motion of a wire through a magnetic field produces a current. Moving a magnet in and out of a coil of wire also produces a current. This important discovery led to numerous applications. Most of the electrical energy you use has been converted to useful electricity by electromagnetic induction.

Have you wondered what produces the electricity that comes to your home and school? Most of the electricity you use each day was electromagnetically induced in generators. A **generator** produces electric current by rotating a loop of wire in a magnetic field. The wire loop is connected to a source of mechanical energy and placed between the poles of a magnet, as shown in Figure 22-10. The design of the generator is very much like that of an electric

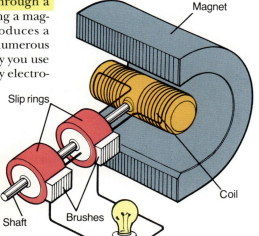

Figure 22-10. Electric current is produced in a generator when a loop of wire is rotated in a magnetic field.

Magnet

Slip rings

Coil

Shaft

Brushes

PREPARATION

SECTION BACKGROUND

▶ Michael Faraday made many discoveries in the areas of chemistry and physics. Apprenticed to a bookseller at the age of 14, his scientific background was largely self-taught, as he had almost no formal education. He also hypothesized that light consisted of vibrations of electric and magnetic field lines, an idea later expressed in mathematical form by Maxwell.

▶ Some records indicate that Joseph Henry discovered electromagnetic induction in the United States in the same year of Faraday's work (1831).

PREPLANNING

▶ Obtain a strong magnet and a TV monitor for the demonstration below.
▶ Obtain a hand-crank generator and a small light bulb for the demonstration on page 584.

1 MOTIVATE

▶ **Demonstration:** Bring a strong magnet near a television screen that is turned on to show what happens. Magnetic fields around a television picture tube are used to direct the beam of electrons from the back of the tube to strike the screen at the front of the tube and produce an image. When a bar magnet is brought close to the face of the tube, it changes the magnetic field around the tube, and the image is distorted. The distortion is evidence that moving electrons are affected by magnetic fields. **CAUTION:** Not suggested for home trials. This can damage the picture tube.

TYING TO PREVIOUS KNOWLEDGE:
Ask students to recall from the last section Oersted's discovery that an electric current produces a magnetic field. Explain that they will now learn how a changing magnetic field can produce a current in a coil.

OPTIONS

ENRICHMENT

▶ Have students work in groups to build a simple generator and then have them demonstrate how their generator works for the other students in the class.

▶ Have students find out the difference between AC (alternating current) and DC (direct current) generators. Have them draw a diagram of each, label the parts, and list the function of each part.

2 TEACH

Key Concepts are highlighted.

CONCEPT DEVELOPMENT

▶ Emphasize that the electromagnetic induction process occurs only when the magnetic field is changing or the wire loop is moving. When both are stationary, no current is produced.

▶ Ask students where they have heard the word *generator* before. Some will probably mention the connection between electric plants and generators. **But where does the electrical energy come from?** *Mechanical energy is converted to electrical energy.*

▶ **Demonstration:** Use a hand-crank generator to produce enough electricity to light a small bulb. What happens when you turn it faster? The bulb burns more brightly. The mechanical work is converted to electrical energy. Now disconnect the bulb and turn the crank. It is easier to turn because there is no load.

CROSS CURRICULUM

▶ **Earth Science:** Have students research the Van Allen radiation belts, composed of charged particles captured by Earth's magnetic field. Have interested students explain the Aurora Borealis (the northern lights).

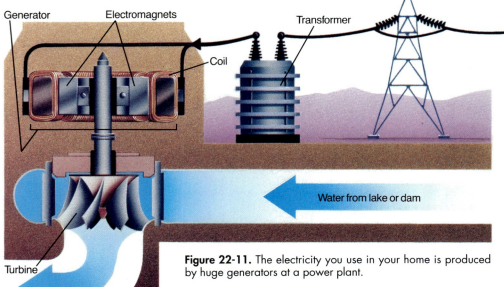

Figure 22-11. The electricity you use in your home is produced by huge generators at a power plant.

What is a turbine?

motor. The wire loop, however, is made to rotate by externally supplied forces. When it rotates, an electric current is produced. This is the opposite of how a motor acts. In a generator, the wire crosses through the magnetic lines of force as it rotates, causing electrons to move along the wire in one direction. After one-half revolution of the wire loop, the current changes direction. As a result, the direction of the current changes twice with each revolution. The rotation speed of generators is regulated so the current always changes direction with the same frequency.

Do you have a generator in your home that supplies all the electricity you need to watch television or wash your clothes? Probably not! You get your electricity from huge generators at a local power plant. These generators are more complex than the ones discussed here. The electromagnets in these generators are made of many loops of wire wrapped around iron cores. A source of mechanical energy is needed to rotate the loop in the generator. One such source, a turbine, is a large wheel that rotates when pushed by water, wind, or steam. Potential energy released by the burning of fossil fuels or from nuclear reactions can heat water to produce steam. The thermal energy of the steam changes to ② mechanical energy in the turbine. The generator then changes this mechanical energy into an electric current that is easily conducted to your home.

584 MAGNETISM AND ITS USES

◆ **STUDY GUIDE** 94

STUDY GUIDE — Chapter 22
Producing Electric Current — Text Pages 583-587

Direct and Alternating Currents

Do you have a tape player that operates on batteries or the electric current in your home? Is the electric current you use in your home that's been produced by a generator the same as the current produced by a dry cell? Both devices cause the electrons to move through a wire and to operate appliances. However, the currents produced by these electric sources are not the same.

==When you use a dry cell or battery to run your tape player, you are using direct current. **Direct current (DC)** flows only in one direction through a wire. Electrons always move out of the negative terminal toward the positive terminal. Whenever direct current flows, it always flows in the same direction.==

3 ==When you plug your tape player into the wall outlet, you are using alternating current. **Alternating current (AC)** reverses its direction in a regular pattern.== In North America, generators produce alternating current at a frequency of 60 cycles per second (60 Hz). ==Because current in a generator changes direction twice during each rotation of the shaft, 60-Hz alternating current changes direction 120 times each second.==

Are electric currents produced by a dry cell and a generator the same?

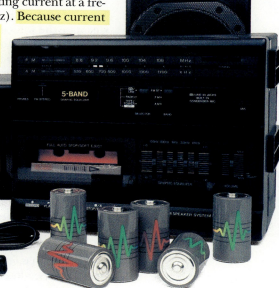

Figure 22-12. Some electrical devices, such as the tape player shown, are designed to operate on AC or DC.

Transformers

The alternating current traveling through power lines is at an extremely high voltage. Before alternating current from the power plant can enter your home, its voltage must be decreased. The current must flow

TEACHER F.Y.I.
▶ Although you plug most appliances into an AC wall outlet, they actually require DC to operate. Computers, stereos, and televisions are examples of appliances that must first convert, or rectify, the AC to DC before use.

CHECK FOR UNDERSTANDING
Ask students to contrast AC and DC and give examples of their sources. In AC, the electrons are moved first in one direction and then reversed. It is supplied from wall outlets. Electrons in DC always move in the same direction. It is supplied by batteries.

RETEACH
To help students visualize the difference between AC and DC, sketch a straight line on the chalkboard to represent DC. Below the DC line, sketch a transverse wave to represent AC. The crests and troughs represent the changing voltage. Emphasize that in many appliances, the incoming AC is converted to DC before use.

EXTENSION
For students who have mastered this section, use the **Reinforcement** and **Enrichment** masters or other OPTIONS provided.

585

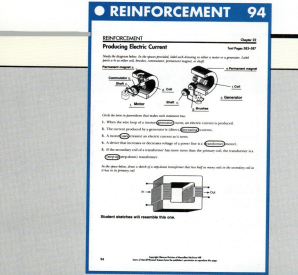
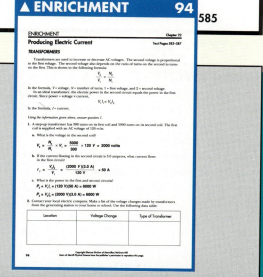

▶ Emphasize that transformers are only effective at stepping up or stepping down alternating currents. The current must alternate to change direction of the magnetic field. If the magnetic field did not change, no current would be induced in the secondary coil.

▶ Because energy is conserved, the power produced in the primary coil of a transformer can be considered equal to that produced in the secondary coil. That is,

$$P_{primary} = P_{secondary}$$
$$(V \times I)_{primary} = (V \times I)_{secondary}$$

In a step-up transformer, the voltage of the alternating current produced in the secondary coil is much greater than that of the AC supplied to the primary coil. Thus, the magnitude of the alternating current produced in the secondary coil is much less than that of the AC supplied to the primary coil.

▶ It is advantageous to use large step-up transformers to transmit alternating current through power lines at high voltage and low current. The rate at which heat is dissipated from a resistor as a current passes through it is given by the relationship $P = I^2R$. Therefore, transmitting AC at low current values reduces the energy lost as heat in the transmission lines.

REVEALING MISCONCEPTIONS

▶ On the surface it seems that a step-up transformer gives you "free electricity." Review the law of conservation of energy, the fact that you can't get something for nothing. The same energy is transferred from the primary to the secondary coil, with no gain in energy. In fact, some energy may be lost as low-temperature thermal energy to the iron core of the transformer.

Science and WRITING

Results will vary; each method has advantages and disadvantages. Students should identify these. It's good for students to realize that there is a connection between their own use of electricity and various environmental problems.

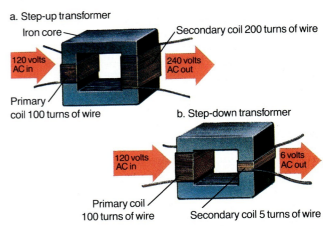

Figure 22-13. A step-up transformer increases voltage (a), and a step-down transformer decreases voltage (b).

What is a transformer?

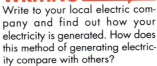

Science and WRITING

Write to your local electric company and find out how your electricity is generated. How does this method of generating electricity compare with others?

What kind of transformer decreases voltage?

through a device called a transformer so the voltage is lowered to a useful level. A **transformer** can increase or decrease the voltage of an alternating current. The operation of a transformer involves principles of both electromagnetism and electromagnetic induction.

A simple transformer is made of two coils of wire called the primary and secondary coils. These coils are wrapped around an iron core, as shown in Figure 22-13. As an alternating current passes through the primary coil, the iron core becomes an electromagnet with its own magnetic field. Because the current varies in direction, the magnetic field also changes its direction. The changing magnetic field electromagnetically induces an alternating current in the secondary coil. The number of turns of wire on the secondary coil in the transformer can determine if it is a step-up transformer or a step-down transformer. If the secondary coil has more turns of wire than the primary coil, then it increases voltage. If the secondary coil has fewer turns of wire than the primary coil, it decreases voltage.

Transformers are used to reduce the voltage of the alternating current entering your home from several thousand volts to 120 volts. A transformer that reduces voltage is called a step-down transformer. Figure 22-13 shows how the output voltage of a transformer will be decreased if the number of turns in the secondary coil is less than the number of turns in the primary coil.

4

OPTIONS

ENRICHMENT

▶ Have students call the local electric company and find out what a typical voltage of the power lines in your neighborhood would be. They may be able to provide diagrams or pictures of the transformers they use. Locate where the transformers around you are.

PROGRAM RESOURCES

From the **Teacher Resource Package** use:

Transparency Masters, pages 85-86, Transformers.

Science and Society, page 26, High-Voltage Power Lines.

Critical Thinking/Problem Solving, page 28, Making Electric Power Decisions.

Use **Color Transparency** number 45, Transformers.

Suppose the secondary coil of a transformer has half as many turns as the primary coil. If the input voltage is 120 V, the output voltage will be half the input voltage, or 60 V. Step-down transformers allow you to operate devices such as tape players, model trains, and doorbells with 120-V household current.

Power plants commonly produce alternating current because its voltage can be increased or decreased with transformers. To transmit alternating current efficiently over long distances, power plants increase their voltages to very high values. In a step-up transformer the output voltage is greater than the input voltage because the secondary coil has more turns than the primary coil. For example, the secondary coil of a step-up transformer at a generating plant may have 100 times the number of turns as the primary coil. That means that an input voltage of 2000 V would increase to 200 000 V—high voltage indeed!

Think back over this section. Could you describe how electromagnetic induction, generators, alternating current, and transformers all affect your tape player? See if you can recall the series of steps in which AC current is produced, transported, and delivered to your home in a form that you can safely use.

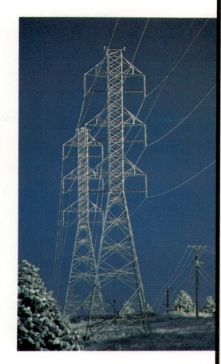

SECTION REVIEW

1. How does a generator use electromagnetic induction to produce a current?
2. A transformer in a neon sign contains 20 turns in the primary coil and 80 turns in the secondary coil. Will the output voltage be greater or less than the input voltage?
3. Compare and contrast alternating current and direct current.
4. **Apply:** Explain why a transformer can't be used to step up the voltage in a direct current.

☑ Concept Mapping

Skill Builder

Prepare an events chain concept map to show how electricity is produced by a generator, as discussed on pages 583 aand 584. If you need help, refer to Concept Mapping in the **Skill Handbook** on pages 684 and 685.

Skill Builder

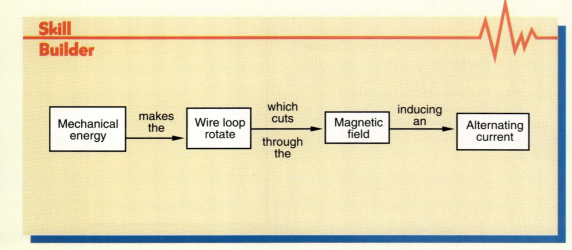

Use the Mini Quiz to check students' recall of chapter content.

1. **What is the process in which a current can be produced by the motion of a wire through a magnetic field?** *electromagnetic induction*
2. **A generator operates by changing _____ energy into _____ energy.** *mechanical; electrical*
3. **Which kind of current reverses its direction in a regular pattern?** *alternating current*
4. **A device that can decrease the voltage of electricity before it enters your home is called a(n) _____ .** *step-down transformer*

3 CLOSE

▶ Do the Skill Builder activity in class to show how electricity is produced by a generator.

❓ FLEX Your Brain

Use the Flex Your Brain activity to have students explore USES OF ALTERNATING AND DIRECT CURRENT.

▶ Ask questions 1-3 and the **Apply** Question in the Section Review.

SECTION REVIEW ANSWERS

1. A loop of wire is turned in a magnetic field and the magnetic force induces a current to flow in the loop.
2. It will be greater.
3. Alternating current reverses its polarity at regular intervals and is produced by a generator. Direct current travels only in one direction and is produced by systems such as dry cells.
4. **Apply:** The current in the secondary coil in a transformer is induced by the fluctuating magnetic field. DC would not cause the magnetic field to move; a changing magnetic field is required for electromagnetic induction.

PROGRAM RESOURCES

From the **Teacher Resource Package** use:

Activity Worksheets, page 5, Flex Your Brain.

PREPARATION

SECTION BACKGROUND

▶ The levitation of a magnet over a superconductor can be explained by a theory called the Meissner effect. The current carried by a superconductor must move on the surface.

1 MOTIVATE

▶ Show a superconductor levitating a magnet. Demonstration kits can be purchased relatively inexpensively, or you might be able to borrow one from a nearby college.

TYING TO PREVIOUS
KNOWLEDGE: Previously, students learned that incandescent bulbs produce light as a result of passing current through a filament, which would produce heat and light because of electrical resistance. A superconductor is a material that loses all electrical resistance, so a current can actually move without energy loss for years.

OBJECTIVES AND
SCIENCE WORDS: Have students review the objectives and science words to become familiar with this section.

2 TEACH

Key Concepts are highlighted.

CONCEPT DEVELOPMENT

▶ Use an analogy to explain the advantage of superconductors. Imagine yourself on a bumpy road on roller skates. Once you set your body in motion, you will lose energy due to friction with the ground. But if you were on frictionless ice, you literally could not stop. A current in a normal conductor experiences some resistance as it moves, but it can move without resistance in a superconductor.

 **22-4 Superconductivity**

New Science Words

superconductors

Objectives

▶ Describe the characteristics of superconductors.
▶ Consider various applications of superconductivity.

Are Superconductors Important?

What do you think about the idea of having train systems that would be levitated, or suspended over magnets, instead of running on rails? Is this a realistic idea? How is this possible?

Recall that conducting materials all have some resistance to electron flow. Some of the electricity moving through the conductor is lost as heat due to this resistance. Likewise, as the temperature of a material increases, the resistance of the material also increases. Ideally, the most efficient transfer of electricity would occur if conducting materials had no electrical resistance.

Superconductors are materials that have no electrical resistance. In 1911, a Dutch physicist, Heike Kamerlingh Onnes, discovered that some materials lose all electrical resistance when cooled to temperatures near absolute zero (0 K), −273°C. The temperature at which a material becomes superconducting is called the critical temperature.

One way to cool a material to superconducting temperatures is to submerge it in liquid helium. Helium is

normally a gas, but it liquefies at 4.2 K. In 1986, Bednorz and Muller received a Nobel prize for making a ceramic material that became a superconductor at 30 K. This opened a new field of research to find "high temperature" superconductors. New materials have been developed that are superconducting at more than 120 K.

Because superconductors have no electrical resistance, a current can flow indefinitely through them without losing energy. In one experiment, a current traveled through a superconducting loop for more than two years without losing ener-

OPTIONS

Meeting Different Ability Levels

For Section 22-4, use the following **Teacher Resource Masters** depending upon individual students' needs.

◆ **Study Guide Master** for all students.
● **Reinforcement Master** for students of average and above average ability levels.
▲ **Enrichment Master** for above average students.

◆ STUDY GUIDE 95

STUDY GUIDE   Chapter 22
Superconductivity   Text Pages 588-590

Determine whether each statement agrees with what was said in your textbook. If the statement agrees, write "agree" in the space provided. If the statement does not agree, rewrite the statement to make it agree.

1. Conducting materials have some resistance to electron flow.   **agree**

2. Some electricity moving through a conductor is lost as friction.   **Some electricity moving through a conductor is lost as heat.**

3. Materials that have no electrical resistance are called insulators.   **Materials that have no electrical resistance are called superconductors.**

4. Some materials lose all electrical resistance when cooled to temperatures near absolute zero.   **agree**

5. Absolute zero is −273 K.   **Absolute zero is 0 K.**

6. One way to cool a material to superconducting temperatures is to submerge it in helium gas.   **One way to cool a material to superconducting temperatures is to submerge it in liquid helium.**

7. The temperature at which a material becomes a superconductor is called the critical temperature.   **agree**

8. Superconductors could make electric motors, generators, and computer parts more efficient.   **agree**

9. A current that flows through a superconductor can flow indefinitely, but it loses some energy.   **A current that flows through a superconductor can flow indefinitely without losing energy.**

10. A magnet moving away from a conductor induces a current in the conductor.   **A magnet moving toward a conductor induces a current in the conductor.**

Copyright Glencoe Division of Macmillan/McGraw-Hill
Users of Merrill Physical Science have the publisher's permission to reproduce this page.   95

gy. This characteristic of superconductors gives them potential for many different uses.

The use of superconductors could eliminate much of the electrical energy waste that we experience today. Ten percent of the energy transmitted through electrical power lines is lost as heat. For similar reasons, superconductors could make electric motors, generators, and computer parts more efficient as well. One problem to be resolved is that superconducting materials are often brittle, and therefore hard to shape into wires.

The picture at the right shows the spectacular levitation effects of magnets over superconductors. Recall that a magnet moving toward a conductor induces a current in the conductor. The current, in turn, produces a magnetic field around the conductor. If the conductor is a superconductor cooled to its critical temperature, the current will move continuously through it. The magnetic forces of these currents moving through the superconductor repel the magnet. This repulsion causes the magnet to float, or levitate, above the superconductor. This is the principle behind levitated trains. If a train had a powerful magnet beneath it and the rails were made of a superconducting material, the train would move on a pocket of air above the rails without friction. It would not lose energy to the environment and would not give off pollutants. What do you think it would be like to ride on a superconducting train?

SECTION REVIEW

1. How do superconductors differ from ordinary conductors?
2. Explain how a magnet can be levitated over a superconductor.

You Decide!

What would be the advantages and disadvantages of developing superconducting trains? Use information in this section to determine what the difficulties of perfecting this system might be. Do you think superconducting trains would be one part of the solution to energy shortages?

SCIENCE & SOCIETY

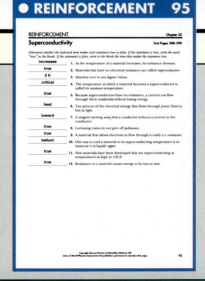

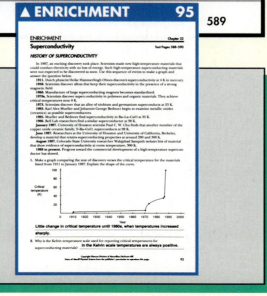

589

Ask students why people are so anxious to find materials that will be superconducting at higher temperatures. Ask them how they would build a train system if the superconductors had to be continually cooled with liquid helium or nitrogen.

RETEACH

Have the students calculate how cold the "high temperature" superconductors must actually be. Convert 120 K to °C. 120 – 273 = –153°C. That is far below the freezing point of water! This should help students realize how inconvenient it would be to keep superconductors cool.

EXTENSION

For students who have mastered this section, use the **Reinforcement** and **Enrichment** masters or other OPTIONS provided.

3 CLOSE

▶ Ask questions 1 and 2 in the Section Review.

Cooperative Learning: Have students work in groups of four to answer the You Decide activity. Then compile a class list of advantages and disadvantages. Analyze the ways in which this would help relieve the energy crisis and environmental harm caused by burning fossil fuels.

SECTION REVIEW ANSWERS

1. Superconductors have no resistance to electrical currents.
2. A magnet moving toward a wire loop induces a current in the loop. The magnetic force caused by these currents repels the magnets.

YOU DECIDE!
SCIENCE & SOCIETY

Answers will vary. Make sure students can support their answers. Also see Technology on p. 579 for more information.

ACTIVITY 22-2
one class period

OBJECTIVE: Compare the energy-carrying abilities of AC and DC magnetic fields.

PROCESS SKILLS applied in this activity:
▶ **Observing** in Procedure Steps 4, 5 and 6.
▶ **Interpreting** in Conclude and Apply Questions 5 and 6.

👥 COOPERATIVE LEARNING
Transformers should be built by teams of two or three. If the class suggests variations, different types can be built by different teams.

TEACHING THE ACTIVITY
Troubleshooting: For safety, the output voltage of the AC supply should not exceed 7 volts.
▶ A 117- to 6.5-volt transformer such as is used for doorbells can be used for an AC source. Be sure students are shielded from the high voltage side of the AC source.
▶ Coat the coils with glue and cut the straw to separate them. They can be used in various combinations for other experiments.
Alternate Materials: Mini-lights from a string of holiday lights will work, but bulbs rated for 1.5 V will be brighter.
▶ Purchase several small rolls of magnet wire rather than one big one.

PROGRAM RESOURCES
From the **Teacher Resource Package** use:

Activity Worksheets, pages 178-179, Activity 22-2: Transformers.

ACTIVITY 22-2
Transformers

Problem: *Can electricity move between unconnected wires?*

Materials
- battery, 6 V
- AC power supply, low voltage
- light, low voltage
- insulated wire, 32 ga
- soda straw, cut to length of nail
- large nail
- knife
- paper clip

Procedure
1. Construct a transformer as shown.
2. Insert nail in straw. Wrap 300 turns of the insulated wire in a tight coil at one end of the straw. Make an identical coil at the other end.
3. Scrape the insulation off the wire ends with the knife.
4. Connect the battery to one coil and the light to the other coil. Gently touch the nail with a paper clip.
5. Connect the AC source in place of the battery. Observe the light and notice the reaction of the paper clip.
6. Observe the light as you slide the nail out of the straw.

Analyze
1. Does the battery produce a magnetic field in the nail? Does its energy reach the light?
2. Does an AC current produce a magnetic field in the nail? Does its energy reach the light?
3. How does the battery magnetism differ from the AC magnetism?
4. What happens when the nail is removed?

Conclude and Apply
5. What kind of current transfers energy by magnetic fields?
6. How is a transformer like a DC generator?
7. What is the purpose of the nail?

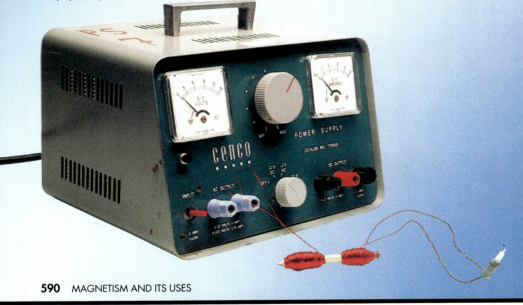

ANSWERS TO QUESTIONS
1. The field is produced but does not transfer energy to the light.
2. The field is produced and transfers energy to the light.
3. The DC current from the battery produces a steady magnetic force. The AC field changes.
4. The magnetic field disappears and the bulb does not light.
5. A field produced by AC electricity can transfer energy.
6. Both contain magnetic fields. In a transformer, the changing magnetic field of the primary coil induces an alternating current in the secondary coil. In a generator, a coil of wire rotating in a magnetic field has an alternating current induced in it.
7. It acts as the iron core, which intensifies the magnetic field, of the transformer which becomes an electromagnet when AC passes through the primary coil.

CHAPTER
REVIEW

CHAPTER
REVIEW

SUMMARY

22-1: Characteristics of Magnets

1. Opposite poles of magnets attract; like poles repel.

2. The magnetic field is the area around the magnet where magnetic forces act.

3. Groups of atoms with aligned magnetic poles are called magnetic domains.

22-2: Uses of Magnetic Fields

1. An electric current passing through a coil of wire can produce a magnetic field around the wire. The coil becomes an electromagnet; one end of the coil forms the magnet's north pole, and the other end forms the south pole.

2. Ammeters measure electrical current in amperes and should be connected in series. Voltmeters measure the potential difference in volts and should be connected parallel.

3. An electric motor contains a rotating electromagnet that converts electrical energy to mechanical energy.

22-3: Producing Electric Current

1. A generator produces electric current by rotating a loop of wire in a magnetic field.

2. Direct current flows in one direction through a wire; alternating current reverses its direction in a regular pattern.

3. The number of turns of wire in the primary and secondary coils of a transformer determine whether it increases or decreases voltage.

22-4: Science and Society: Superconductivity

1. Superconductors are materials that have no electrical resistance.

2. The use of superconductors can eliminate electrical energy waste in the form of heat. Magnets used with superconductors could provide alternatives to current transportation methods.

KEY SCIENCE WORDS

a. **alternating current (AC)**
b. **ammeters**
c. **commutator**
d. **direct current (DC)**
e. **electromagnet**
f. **electromagnetic induction**
g. **generator**
h. **magnetic domains**
i. **magnetic field**
j. **magnetic poles**
k. **magnetism**
l. **superconductors**
m. **transformer**
n. **voltmeters**

UNDERSTANDING VOCABULARY

Match each phrase with the correct term from the list of Key Science Words.

1. area around a magnet in which a magnetic force acts

2. a property of matter in which there is a force of repulsion or attraction between like or unlike poles

3. a temporary magnet made of a wire coil through which an electric current passes

4. measure electric current

5. a device that reverses the direction of a direct current in an electric motor

6. the production of an electric current by moving a wire through a magnetic field

7. current that flows in only one direction

8. a device that changes the voltage of an alternating current

9. materials with no electrical resistance

10. regions of magnets where magnetic lines of force are most dense

MAGNETISM AND ITS USES **591**

SUMMARY

Have students read the summary statements to review the major concepts of the chapter.

UNDERSTANDING VOCABULARY

1. i
2. k
3. e
4. b
5. c
6. f
7. d
8. m
9. l
10. j

OPTIONS

ASSESSMENT

To assess student understanding of material in this chapter, use the resources listed.

COOPERATIVE LEARNING

Consider using cooperative learning in the THINK AND WRITE CRITICALLY, APPLY, and MORE SKILL BUILDERS sections of the Chapter Review.

PROGRAM RESOURCES

From the **Teacher Resource Package** use:
Chapter Review, pages 47-48.
Chapter and Unit Tests, pages 147-150, Chapter Test.

CHAPTER
REVIEW

CHECKING CONCEPTS

1. a
2. c
3. d
4. b
5. d
6. d
7. c
8. b
9. b
10. a

UNDERSTANDING CONCEPTS

11. Unlike
12. a magnetic domain
13. direction of the current
14. generator
15. more

THINK AND WRITE CRITICALLY

16. Spinning electrons create small magnetic fields. Paired electrons spin in opposite directions and cancel one another. The magnetic fields of unpaired electrons are not cancelled and, if aligned in a substance, make it magnetic.

17. Both have a coil of wire through which an electric current passes as it is suspended between two magnets. The coil rotates in the field produced by the fixed magnets. For the coil to keep rotating, an electric motor must also have a commutator that reverses the direction of the current in the coil.

18. A wire coil is made to rotate in a magnetic field. If a conducting loop cuts across the magnetic field, electrons in the wire loop move and produce a current.

19. It contains two coils of wire wrapped around an iron core. An alternating current passes through the first coil and produces a changing magnetic field, which induces current in the second coil. If the second coil has more turns than the primary coil, the voltage of the alternating current in the second coil is greater. This type of transformer is a step-up transformer. In a step-down transformer, the secondary coil has fewer turns than the primary coil and the voltage of the current is reduced.

20. Superconducting power lines would conduct electricity with no energy loss due to electrical resistance. Superconductors could replace fuels used for mass transit.

CHAPTER
REVIEW

CHECKING CONCEPTS

Choose the word or phrase that completes the sentence or answers the question.

1. A magnet's force is strongest at its _____.
   a. north and south poles c. north pole
   b. south pole d. center

2. As the distance between two magnetic poles decreases, the magnetic force _____.
   a. remains constant c. increases
   b. changes unpredictably d. decreases

3. Atoms at the north pole of a bar magnet have _____.
   a. north magnetic poles only
   b. south magnetic poles only
   c. no magnetic poles
   d. both north and south magnetic poles

4. Which of the following would not change the strength of an electromagnet?
   a. increasing the amount of current
   b. changing the current's direction
   c. inserting an iron core inside the loop
   d. increasing the number of loops

5. Ammeters should be _____.
   a. designed to have high resistance
   b. designed without magnets
   c. connected in parallel
   d. calibrated in amperes

6. A device containing a wire coil suspended in a magnetic field that measures potential difference is called a(n) _____.
   a. transformer c. ammeter
   b. electromagnet d. voltmeter

7. The direction of the electric current in an AC circuit _____.
   a. remains constant c. changes regularly
   b. is direct d. changes irregularly

8. Before current in power lines can enter your home, it must pass through a _____.
   a. step-up transformer c. commutator
   b. step-down transformer d. voltmeter

9. Some materials lose all electrical resistance when they are _____.
   a. at room temperature
   b. at their critical temperatures
   c. below absolute zero
   d. heated

10. Superconductors can levitate magnets because the continuous electric current through the superconductor produces _____.
    a. a repulsive magnetic force
    b. an attractive magnetic force
    c. an anti-gravity force
    d. a mechanical force

UNDERSTANDING CONCEPTS

Complete each sentence.

11. _____ magnetic poles attract one another.
12. When the poles of atoms containing unpaired electrons are aligned, _____ is produced.
13. The direction of the magnetic field produced by an electric current will change when the _____ changes.
14. In a(n) _____, a loop of wire is mechanically rotated in a magnetic field in order to produce a current.
15. In order for a transformer to increase voltage, its secondary coil must have _____ turns than its primary coil.

APPLY

21. The magnetic pole at Earth's north pole must actually be a south magnetic pole, since it attracts north magnetic pole of a compass needle.

22. Magnetic domains are formed when atoms having unpaired electrons are lined up. When a magnet is dropped or heated, its atoms are forced out of position and the alignment of magnetic domains is destroyed.

23. An ammeter is connected in series to measure the total current of the circuit. A voltmeter is connected in parallel because the voltage is the same across all parallel branches.

24. 120 V is ten times less than 1200 V. Therefore, the number of turns in the secondary coil is ten times less than 100, or ten.

25. You must find a substance that is not too brittle and exhibits superconductivity at normal temperatures. Current superconductors only work at very low temperatures and are too brittle.

THINK AND WRITE CRITICALLY

16. Describe the magnetic domain model.
17. Describe the basic device used in both galvanometers and electric motors. What additional device does an electric motor have? Why is this device necessary?
18. Explain how a generator produces an electric current.
19. Explain how a transformer works. How do step-up and step-down transformers differ?
20. How might superconductors help conserve energy resources?

APPLY

21. If a magnetic compass needle points north, what is the actual polarity of Earth's northern magnetic pole? Explain.
22. Explain why dropping or heating a permanent magnet causes its magnetic domains to shift out of alignment.
23. Why must an ammeter be connected in series with a circuit? Why must a voltmeter be connected in parallel across a circuit?
24. A step-down transformer reduces a 1200 V current to 120 V. If the primary coil has 100 turns, how many must its secondary coil have?
25. You are developing a superconducting train. On what two problems will you concentrate your research? Why?

MORE SKILL BUILDERS

If you need help, refer to the Skill Handbook.

1. **Comparing and Contrasting:** Compare and contrast electric and magnetic forces.
2. **Comparing and Contrasting:** Compare and contrast AC generators and DC motors.

3. **Recognizing Cause and Effect:** Earth's magnetic field has reversed itself many times in the past. What would be the likely effect of this switching of Earth's magnetic poles on the alignment of magnetic minerals deposited in Earth?
4. **Hypothesizing:** Some metals are strongly attracted by a magnetic field; others such as zinc are not. Propose a hypothesis about the arrangement of electrons in zinc.
5. **Concept Mapping:** Complete the following events chain map by supplying the name and function of devices used to convert the mechanical energy of a turbine at an electrical power plant into the mechanical energy of an electric fan in your home.

Initiating Step

Final Outcome

PROJECTS

1. Research the most recent developments in superconductors. Write a brief paper stating whether or not the government should spend more money on superconductor research. Give reasons supporting your position.
2. Invent a new device that uses an electric motor. Make a poster diagram of the device.

MAGNETISM AND ITS USES **593**

MORE SKILL BUILDERS

1. **Comparing and Contrasting:** Both electric and magnetic forces are produced by electrons. Charged objects produce electric fields, and the charge itself is produced by too few or too many electrons. Magnetic fields are produced by the motion of electrons. Both types of forces become weaker as the distance from the source of the force is increased. Both forces are attractive when unlike charges or poles are brought together and repulsive when like charges or poles are brought together.
2. **Comparing and Contrasting:** Both have wire coils suspended between two fixed magnets. In a generator, the coil mechanically rotates in the magnetic field. This induces an electric current in the coil. In an electric motor, a current passes through the coil and makes it an electromagnet that rotates in the field of the fixed magnets. If an electric motor is battery-powered, then it runs off a direct current. A generator, on the other hand, always produces an alternating current.
3. **Recognizing Cause and Effect:** If Earth's magnetic field reversed its direction many times in the past, then the orientation of magnetic mineral deposits would be reversed as many times. Some layers in Earth would have magnetic minerals aligned ("pointing") to the north, whereas other layers would have minerals aligned to the south. Such alternating layers have, in fact, been found and are themselves strong evidence that Earth's magnetic field has often reversed its polarity.
4. **Hypothesizing:** Iron is attracted by a magnetic field because it has magnetic domains, aligned atoms with unpaired electrons. A reasonable hypothesis for why zinc is repelled might therefore be: Because electrons in zinc atoms are paired, zinc is unaffected by a magnetic field.
5. **Concept Mapping:**
See the map at the left.

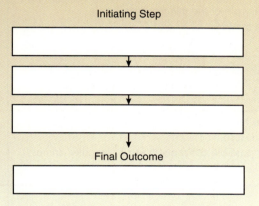

Initiating Step

Generator: converts mechanical energy of turbine into electrical current

Step-up transformer: raises voltage of current to minimize energy loss in power lines

Step-down transformer: lowers voltage to standard 120 V

Final Outcome

Electric Motor: turns fan blades by converting electrical energy back to mechanical energy

CHAPTER 23 Electronics and Computers

CHAPTER SECTION	OBJECTIVES	ACTIVITIES
23-1 Semiconductor Devices (2 days)	1. **Describe** how the two types of doped semiconductors conduct a current. 2. **Explain** the device that changes AC into DC. 3. **Realize** the practical benefits of an integrated circuit.	**Activity 23-1:** *Semiconductors,* p. 598
23-2 Radio and Television (1 day)	1. **Describe** how radio and television programs are transmitted. 2. **Explain** the operation of a cathode-ray tube.	**MINI-Lab:** *How do electrons make a TV picture?* p. 605
23-3 Microcomputers (2 days)	1. **Identify** the basic parts of a microcomputer. 2. **Describe** the role of the microprocessor. 3. **Distinguish** between RAM and ROM.	**MINI-Lab:** *What makes a calculator "user friendly"?* p. 609
23-4 Computer Crimes Science & Society (1 day)	1. **Discuss** the types of crimes that can be committed by computer misuse. 2. **Predict** the possible consequences of computer crimes.	**Activity 23-2:** *Information Storage,* p. 614
Chapter Review		

ACTIVITY MATERIALS

FIND OUT	ACTIVITIES		MINI-LABS	
Page 595 a musical greeting card	**23-1 Semiconductors, p. 598** diode 2 LEDs, different colors hook-up wire 1000 ohm resistor 6 volt battery AC power supply, 6 volts	**23-2 Information Storage, p. 614** 12 disk magnets 2 sheets and a thin strip of card stock paper transparent tape metric ruler	**How do electrons make a TV picture? p. 605** CRT a small magnet	**What makes a calculator "user friendly"? p. 609** a pocket-sized calculator

CHAPTER FEATURES	TEACHER RESOURCE PACKAGE	OTHER RESOURCES
Skill Builder: *Interpreting Scientific Illustrations,* p. 601	**Ability Level Worksheets** ♦ *Study Guide,* p. 96 ● *Reinforcement,* p. 96 ▲ *Enrichment,* p. 196 **Activity Worksheet,** pp. 184, 185 **Transparency Masters,** pp. 91, 92	**Color Transparency 46,** Semiconductors
Technology: *HDTV,* p. 604 **Skill Builder:** *Concept Mapping,* p. 605	**Ability Level Worksheets** ♦ *Study Guide,* p. 97 ● *Reinforcement,* p. 97 ▲ *Enrichment,* p. 97 **MINI-Lab Worksheet,** p. 190	
Problem Solving: *Computer Art,* p. 610 **Skill Builder:** *Comparing and Contrasting,* p. 611	**Ability Level Worksheets** ♦ *Study Guide,* p. 98 ● *Reinforcement,* p. 98 ▲ *Enrichment,* p. 98 **MINI-Lab Worksheet,** p. 191 **Critical Thinking/Problem Solving,** p. 29 **Concept Mapping,** pp. 51, 52 **Cross-Curricular Connections,** p. 29 **Science and Society,** p. 27	
You Decide! p. 613	**Ability Level Worksheets** ♦ *Study Guide,* p. 99 ● *Reinforcement,* p. 99 ▲ *Enrichment,* p. 99 **Activity Worksheet,** pp. 186, 187	
Summary Think & Write Critically Key Science Words Apply Understanding Vocabulary More Skill Builders Checking Concepts Projects Understanding Concepts	**Chapter Review,** pp. 49, 50 **Chapter Test,** pp. 151-154	**Chapter Review Software** **Test Bank**

♦ **Basic**　　● **Average**　　▲ **Advanced**

ADDITIONAL MATERIALS

SOFTWARE	AUDIOVISUAL	BOOKS/MAGAZINES
Introduction to Computer Electronics, Merlan Scientific Ltd.	*Computer Hardware: What It Is and How It Works,* filmstrips, The Center for Humanities. *Computers in Our Society,* filmstrips, EBEC. *Miniature Miracle: The Computer Chip,* laserdisc, Image Entertainment.	Billings, Charlene W. *Microchip: Small Wonder.* NY: Putnam Publishing Group, 1984. Dertouzos, Michal L. and J. Moses, eds. *The Computer Age: A Twenty-Year View.* Cambridge, MA: MIT Press, 1979. Lauenbruch, David. *Television.* Milwaukee, WI: Raintree Publishing, Inc, 1984.

THEME DEVELOPMENT: A major theme that should be emphasized in this chapter is how electronic and magnetic systems interact to help us create useful devices. The connection between electricity and magnetism was discussed in the previous chapter. It will be illustrated here with numerous applications.

CHAPTER OVERVIEW

▶ **Section 23-1:** The theory of semiconductors is introduced in this section. Semiconductor applications including diodes, transistors, amplification, and integrated circuits are illustrated.

▶ **Section 23-2:** This section presents a discussion of radio and television transmission. A cathode-ray tube is illustrated to explain how a picture tube produces an image on the screen.

▶ **Section 23-3:** The components of a microcomputer are identified, and the microprocessor is discussed specifically. The function of computer memory and methods of data storage are also presented.

▶ **Section 23-4: Science and Society:** This section features a discussion of computer crimes, including viruses and hacking. The You Decide question asks students to evaluate how computer crimes should be treated by our legal system.

CHAPTER VOCABULARY

semiconductors	cathode-ray tube
rectifier	microprocessor
diode	RAM
transistor	ROM
amplification	computer virus
integrated circuit	

CHAPTER

23 Electronics and Computers

594

OPTIONS

For Your Gifted Students

Students can test the effectiveness of various radio antennas that they design and make. Students can make antennas from different materials, vary the size and shape, or connect the antenna to available items such as pipes, phone lines, and so on. They will test the antenna's effectiveness by recording how many radio stations can be received. Predictions and results should be charted and shared.

Have you ever received a greeting card from a friend that made you feel especially happy? Did you ever get a card that played a song when you opened it? How can a greeting card play music? A small electronic device located inside the card actually plays the song you hear.

FIND OUT!

Observe a simple application of electronics as you do this activity.

Get a musical greeting card and examine the electronic device inside. Notice that the music plays only when the card is opened. Do you see the tiny metal disc inside the card? The disc is a type of electronic device containing a small speaker. The music is created from electric signals within the disc that are amplified and turned into sound waves within the tiny speaker. Carefully examine the parts inside the disc with a powerful hand lens. What do you see?

Previewing Science Skills
▶ In the **Skill Builders,** you will interpret scientific illustrations, make a concept map, and compare and contrast.
▶ In the **Activities,** you will observe, infer, classify, and communicate.
▶ In the **MINI-Labs,** you will observe, infer, and interpret.

What's next?

You've examined one type of simple electronic device. Read on to find out how this and other electronic devices are actually applications of the principles of electricity and magnetism you studied in Chapters 21 and 22.

595

INTRODUCING THE CHAPTER
Use the Find Out activity to help students notice the parts and details of electronic devices. Explain that they will be learning the functions of some of the parts they see in the device.

FIND OUT!
Preparation: Obtain several musical greeting cards from card shops.
Materials: musical greeting cards
Cooperative Learning: Form Science Investigation teams of four to share a musical card and discuss the questions you ask together.
Teaching Tips
▶ Have students try to draw the parts of the electronic device and label them descriptively. Have them speculate where the music originates and where the sound comes out. Tell them they will be learning about some of the parts used in electronic devices.

Gearing Up
Have students study the Gearing Up feature to familiarize themselves with the chapter. Discuss the relationships of the topics in the outline.

What's Next?
Before beginning the first section, make sure students understand the connection between the Find Out activity and the topics to follow.

For Your Mainstreamed Students
▶ Students can brainstorm a list of the careers that are associated with the field of electronics. For a firsthand look at a career option, have them visit a television or radio station to observe the electronic broadcasting equipment.
▶ Invite a computer expert to visit the class to display a computer circuit board, explain recent technological advances in computers, or discuss predictions for electronics in the next decade.

Semiconductor Devices

PREPARATION

SECTION BACKGROUND

▶ The science behind semiconductors is included in the vast field of solid-state physics, which is the study of the structure of solids. An explanation of the properties and behavior of semiconductors at the atomic level can be found in electron band theory, based on quantum mechanics.

▶ Pure, undoped semiconductors are said to be intrinsic.

PREPLANNING

▶ Obtain examples of transistors, diodes, resistors, and microchips from a local electronics store. They may even have some spare parts they would be willing to donate to your school.

1 MOTIVATE

▶ If possible, bring a transparent phone to class. The wiring in a phone appears complex, but is actually made of just a few kinds of electrical devices. Ask students if they can identify any of the parts.

New Science Words

rectifier
diode
transistor
amplification
integrated circuit

Objectives

▶ Describe how the two types of doped semiconductors conduct a current.
▶ Explain the device that changes AC into DC.
▶ Realize the practical benefits of an integrated circuit.

Semiconductors

Do you use a calculator when you do your homework, average your grades, or add up the amount of money you've saved? You probably use a calculator to work a math problem every day. Your calculator is only one of thousands of complex electronic devices made possible by advances in the applications of electricity and magnetism. If you carefully removed the front of your calculator, you would see tiny circuits with all sorts of unusual parts inside. You might see several kinds of semiconductor devices: a diode, a rectifier, and a transistor.

To understand what a semiconductor is, and how it works, you must first think about the periodic table you studied in Chapter 10. Recall that the elements on the left side and center of the table are metals. These metals are conductors of electricity. Nonmetals—poor conductors of electricity—are found on the right side of the table. They are electrical insulators. How would you classify the elements found along the staircase-shaped border between the metals and nonmetals? Would you call these conductors or insulators?

Figure 23-1. A calculator contains several different types of semiconductor devices.

OPTIONS

Meeting Different Ability Levels

For Section 23-1, use the following **Teacher Resource Masters** depending upon individual students' needs.

◆ **Study Guide Master** for all students.

● **Reinforcement Master** for students of average and above average ability levels.

▲ **Enrichment Master** for above average students.

Additional Teacher Resource Package masters are listed in the OPTIONS box throughout the section. The additional masters are appropriate for all students.

◆ **STUDY GUIDE** 96

STUDY GUIDE   Chapter 23
Semiconductor Devices   Text Pages 596–601

The information in two of the phrases following each term is true for that term. The information in the other statement is not true for that term. Place a check mark (✓) beside the two statements that are true.

1. Semiconductors
   ✓ a. are less conductive than metals.
   b. cause an appliance to use more current.
   ✓ c. are more conductive than nonmetal insulators.

2. A rectifier
   a. changes direct current to alternating current.
   ✓ b. changes alternating current to direct current.
   ✓ c. is used as an adapter.

3. A diode
   ✓ a. allows current to flow in only one direction.
   ✓ b. is a type of semiconductor device.
   c. allows current to flow in two directions.

4. A transistor
   a. can only be made from 1 n-type with 2 p-type semiconductors.
   ✓ b. can be made by doping both sides of a p-type semiconductor with arsenic.
   ✓ c. amplifies an electric signal.

5. Amplification
   ✓ a. is a process of increasing the strength of an electric current.
   ✓ b. uses transistors.
   c. changes the direction of a current.

6. An integrated circuit
   ✓ a. can contain thousands of semiconductor devices on a thin slice of silicon.
   ✓ b. is sometimes called a chip.
   c. can handle large currents.

96

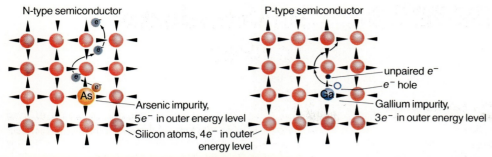

N-type semiconductor

P-type semiconductor

unpaired e^-

e^- hole

Gallium impurity,
$3e^-$ in outer energy level

Arsenic impurity,
$5e^-$ in outer energy level

Silicon atoms, $4e^-$ in outer
energy level

Figure 23-2. Doping semiconductor crystals with impurities can change their resistance and conductivity.

The elements located between the metals and nonmetals on the periodic table are metalloids. Some metalloids, such as silicon and germanium, are semiconductors. Semiconductors are less conductive than metals, but more conductive than nonmetal insulators. Your calculator and other electronic devices in your home that use semiconductors use less current to operate than similar devices that don't use semiconductors.

The conductivity of semiconductor crystals can be increased by adding impurities. This process is called doping. Doped silicon is a commonly used semiconductor. Silicon atoms have four electrons in their outer energy level. If small amounts of another element with more than four electrons in its outer energy level are added, the semiconducting crystal will have a few additional electrons. These extra electrons can move easily through the crystal to increase its conductivity. For this reason, silicon is often doped with arsenic as shown in Figure 23-2a. Notice that arsenic has five electrons in its outer energy level. Arsenic-doped silicon has more negative electrons and is called an *n*-type (negative-type) semiconductor.

Silicon semiconductors can also be doped with a material, such as gallium, that has fewer than four electrons in its outer energy level. Because gallium-doped silicon has fewer electrons in its crystal than does pure silicon, the doping creates "holes" in the electron structure of the silicon crystal. You can picture these holes as imaginary positive charges throughout the silicon crystal. Gallium-doped silicon is an example of a *p*-type semiconductor. When a potential difference is applied across a *p*-type semiconductor, electrons move to fill the holes as if they were attracted to the imaginary positive charges. Figure 23-2b illustrates how moving electrons create more holes in the crystal. The process produces a current in the semiconductor.

What is doping?

What is an *n*-type semiconductor?

What is a *p*-type semiconductor?

597

TYING TO PREVIOUS KNOWLEDGE: Ask students to distinguish between a conductor and an insulator. Explain that a semiconductor, as the prefix *semi-* implies, is in-between a conductor and an insulator. Tell them they will be finding out how semiconductors are used in common electrical devices.

OBJECTIVES AND SCIENCE WORDS: Have students review the objectives and science words to become familiar with this section.

2 TEACH

Key Concepts are highlighted.

CONCEPT DEVELOPMENT

▶ You will need to help students conceptualize the idea behind *p*- and *n*-type semiconductors. Use Figure 23-2 to help illustrate why having either additional electrons or a deficit of electrons will ease the flow of electric current.

CROSS CURRICULUM

▶ **Chemistry:** Have students research how pure semiconductors, such as silicon or germanium, are obtained. Pure silicon crystals often have less than 1 part in 1 billion as impurities.

PROGRAM RESOURCES

From the **Teacher Resource Package** use:

Transparency Masters, pages 91-92, Semiconductors.

Use **Color Transparency** number 46, Semiconductors.

ACTIVITY 23-1
45 minutes

OBJECTIVE: Apply observations of current flow to understanding of the operation of a diode.

PROCESS SKILLS applied in this activity:
▶ **Experimenting** in Procedure Steps 1-8.
▶ **Observing** in Procedure Steps 5-8.
▶ **Inferring** in Analyze Questions 1-4.
▶ **Interpreting** in Conclude and Apply Questions 5 and 6.

★★ COOPERATIVE LEARNING
Divide the class into Science Investigation teams of three or four students.

TEACHING THE ACTIVITY
Troubleshooting: The resistor should be about 1000 Ω. The LEDs will burn out if a resistor is not in series with them.
▶ A 120 VAC – 6.5 VAC transformer with a 1000-Ω, 10-W resistor in series to restrict current output can provide a reasonably safe AC source.
▶ Hook-up wire can be twisted together, but alligator clips are more convenient.
▶ A demonstration of AC, DC, and pulsating DC is provided by attaching the operating LED assembly by long wires and whirling it about in a circle. In a darkened room, AC will show alternating streaks of color. DC will be a continuous streak of one color. Rectified AC will show as pulses of one color.

PROGRAM RESOURCES
From the **Teacher Resource Package** use:

Activity Worksheets, pages 184-185, Activity 23-1: Semiconductors.

ACTIVITY 23-1
Semiconductors

Problem: *How can diodes be used to change AC to DC?*

Materials
- diode
- two LEDs, different colors
- hook-up wire
- resistor, 1000 ohms
- battery, 6 volt
- AC power supply, 6 volts

Procedure
1. Attach the resistor to one of the LEDs before connecting it to the battery. Reverse battery connections until the LED lights.
2. Mark the positive side of the LED.
3. Repeat Steps 1 and 2 with the second LED.
4. Twist the positive wire of one LED with the negative wire of the other. Attach the resistor to the other two wires.
5. Connect the assembly to the poles of the battery and notice which LED light works. Reverse the connections and observe.
6. Connect the assembly to 6 volts AC and observe.
7. Attach the diode in series with the assembly and connect it to 6 volts AC.
8. Reverse the direction of the diode and reconnect to the AC current. Notice the response of the LEDs.

Analyze
1. A battery sends current in one direction. How does the LED assembly show this?
2. How does the LED assembly detect an alternating current?
3. What does the addition of a diode do to an alternating current?
4. What does reversing the direction of the diode accomplish?

Conclude and Apply
5. In an AC circuit, are the LEDs "on" all the time? How about in the DC circuit?
6. The resistance of a diode is very high in one direction and low in the other. How did this experiment show that to be true?

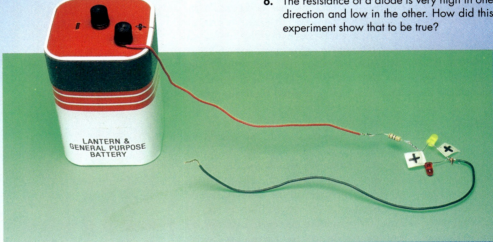

ANSWERS TO QUESTIONS
1. Only one LED at a time will light.
2. Both LEDs show light.
3. Only one LED shows light the same as DC.
4. The other LED shows light demonstrating that current has reversed.
5. An AC current reverses direction, so the LEDs must be going on and off. They would be on all the time in pure DC.
6. Current flows through diodes in one direction but is blocked if the diode is turned around.

Diodes

Have you noticed that some portable radios have adapters that plug into wall sockets? Why do they need an adapter? Radios operate on low-voltage direct current. For the radio to operate with household alternating current, the voltage of the current must be lowered and the current must be changed to flow in one direction. A radio adapter contains a transformer, which reduces the voltage, and a rectifier. A **rectifier** is a device that changes alternating current into direct current.

Many household devices are built to operate on direct current. Some, such as smoke detectors and clocks, can easily be supplied with current from batteries. Other appliances that use large amounts of electricity, such as your television or computer, would not be practical to operate with batteries. Therefore, transformers and rectifiers are wired into the circuits inside of radios, televisions, computers, and other appliances to supply them with low-voltage direct current from a source of alternating current.

A diode is one type of rectifier. A **diode** allows current to flow only in one direction. A diode can be made by doping the ends of a crystal with different elements to make one end a *p*-type semiconductor and the other end an *n*-type semiconductor. Electrons can easily flow from the *n*-type end to fill the electron holes in the *p*-type end, but it is more difficult to make them flow in the other direction. This device is called a *pn*-diode. Your radio's adapter plug probably contains a *pn*-diode rectifier.

Transistors and Amplification

Have you wondered why some radios are called transistor radios? They contain electrical devices called transistors. A **transistor** is a semiconductor that amplifies an electric signal. The signal in an electronic device is the varying electric current that represents a sound, picture, or some other piece of information. Transistors can be made by doping both sides of a thin *p*-type semiconductor with arsenic. This process sandwiches a *p*-type semiconductor between the two *n*-type semiconductors

Figure 23-3. Diodes and rectifiers change alternating current into direct current.

What is a transistor?

TEACHER F.Y.I.

▶ A zener [zā-ner] diode is a diode used to create a steady voltage in a circuit over a range of currents.

CONCEPT DEVELOPMENT

▶ A graph of current versus voltage for resistors in a circuit produces a straight line. However, a graph of current versus voltage for diodes and transistors in a circuit does not produce a straight line; they are nonlinear devices.

▶ Ask students if they own transistor radios. They probably are not transistor radios, as these have been replaced by radios with more compact and efficient wiring systems.

▶ Introduce diodes as a type of valve or gate that allows current to move in only one direction. This analogy may help students understand how a rectifier can be used to convert AC to DC.

OPTIONS

INQUIRY QUESTIONS

▶ **Use the periodic table to determine whether a semiconductor is more or less conductive than iron and sulfur.** *A semiconductor would be less conductive than iron, a metal, and more conductive than sulfur, a nonmetal.*

▶ **Would doping silicon with carbon be likely to increase its conductivity? Explain.** *Like silicon, carbon also has four electrons in its outer energy level. This would create neither* a surplus of electrons nor "holes" to increase its conductivity.

▶ **What type (*n*- or *p*-type) of semiconductor would be produced by doping antimony with tin? Explain.** *Tin has fewer electrons (4) in its outer energy level than antimony (5). A deficiency of electrons in the structure results in a p-type (positive) semiconductor.*

▶ Explaining how a transistor can amplify an electrical signal can be confusing. Emphasize that the small current received as an input signal controls the large current from the power source.

CHECK FOR UNDERSTANDING

Use the Mini Quiz to check for understanding.

MINI QUIZ

Use the Mini Quiz to check students' recall of chapter content.

1 _____ are less conductive than metals, but more conductive than insulators. *Semiconductors*

2 A common method of increasing the conductivity of a superconductor is the process of _____ . *doping*

3 An adapter in a toaster which changes AC into DC probably contains a(n) _____ . *rectifier*

4 What is the main purpose of using transistors? *to amplify an electrical signal*

RETEACH

Have students interpret and explain the diagram in Figure 23-2 on page 597. Have them explain why some semiconductors are doped.

EXTENSION

For students who have mastered this section, use the **Reinforcement** and **Enrichment** masters or other OPTIONS provided.

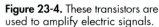

Figure 23-4. These transistors are used to amplify electric signals.

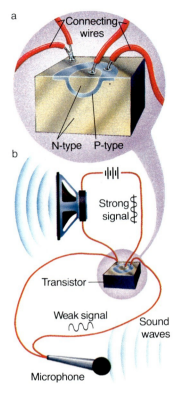

Figure 23-5. The *npn*-transistor shown above uses a weak input current to control the flow of a much larger current.

producing an *npn*-transistor. An *npn*-transistor can amplify a weak electric signal. **Amplification** is the process of increasing the strength of an electric signal.

Another type of transistor can be made by placing a thin *n*-type semiconductor between two *p*-type semiconductors, forming a *pnp*-transistor. They differ slightly in operation, but both types of transistors can be used to amplify an input signal or current. Like diodes, these electronic components are very small and lightweight.

The signal that travels many kilometers from a broadcast station to your stereo and television receivers is too weak to reproduce the information it carries into picture or sound. In other words, the signal produced by the radio waves received by your stereo does not have a large enough amplitude to vibrate the loudspeaker and create sound that can be heard. An *npn*-transistor in the electric circuit of the stereo uses a small current from a weak incoming signal to control a large current provided by a power source. The varying current produced by the radio signals flows between the center *p*-type area to an *n*-type area of the transistor This produces a large varying current through the two *n*-type areas of the transistor which are connected in series with a speaker to a power source. Thus, the small input signal supplied to the transistor results in a large, varying output current which can vibrate the speaker.

Your school PA (public address) system contains several transistors. When someone speaks over the system, the sound wave is converted to an electrical signal by a microphone and amplified by transistors within the circuit of the system. The amplified signal is then changed back into sound waves by a speaker. Transistors and their ability to amplify signals make it possible for you to use tape players, bullhorns, hearing aids, and televisions. They are also used in medical diagnoses to amplify tiny electrical signals given off by the heart and brain so these signals can be detected. None of these electronic devices or their applications would be possible without the transistor. It is considered the most fundamental part of an electronic circuit.

600 ELECTRONICS AND COMPUTERS

OPTIONS

INQUIRY QUESTIONS

▶ **Why do *pn*-diodes only allow current to flow in one direction?** *The n-type semiconductor has extra electrons in its structure and the p-type semiconductor has a deficiency in electron distribution. The electrons move in from the n- to p-type direction to fill the holes, but there is not a surplus of electrons to move the other direction.*

▶ **What combination of devices might you use if you wanted to use a wall socket to provide electricity for a radio and you needed to amplify the signal before it reached the loud-** speaker? *Use a rectifier or diode, followed by a transistor.*

▶ **Why does a radio have to be plugged in or have batteries if there is an incoming signal (from the radio waves)?** *A power source must supply the large current which is modified by the signal when it passes through a transistor.*

▶ **Why are transistors very important medical detection devices?** *They can amplify small electrical signals given off during body functions of organs such as the heart and brain.*

Integrated Circuits

Before transistors were invented, devices called vacuum tubes were used to amplify electric signals. These low-pressure glass or metal tubes regulated the electron flow of a circuit's current as it went through each tube. Your grandparents probably owned a television or radio that used these tubes to amplify signals. Televisions and radios today have semiconductor components instead of vacuum tubes. After the development of the transistor, integrated circuits became a reality. As a result of this electronics breakthrough, today's televisions and radios are much smaller than the older ones.

An **integrated circuit** can contain thousands of resistors, diodes, and transistors on a thin slice of silicon. These thin silicon slices, called chips, can be smaller than 1 cm on a side. The miniature circuit components in an integrated circuit are made by doping the silicon chip with small amounts of impurities. The conductors between the components are made by painting tiny aluminum wires on the silicon chip. Having circuit components so close together reduces the time required for a current to travel through a circuit. As a result, the integrated circuit is a very effective design for rapid information processing, which is essential in devices such as microcomputers.

Figure 23-6. Vacuum tubes, such as the one above, were used to amplify electric signals in early electronic devices.

Did You Know?

The integrated circuit concept was developed in 1952, but the actual product was not produced for 20 more years.

SECTION REVIEW

1. Describe two ways the conductivity of a semiconductor can be improved.
2. What device can you use to change AC to DC? How does it work?
3. How are integrated circuits made?
4. **Apply:** Would carbon atoms be useful in doping a silicon semiconductor? Explain.

☑ Interpreting Scientific Illustrations

Skill Builder

Look at the periodic table of the elements on pages 258 and 259. List the metals, nonmetals, and metalloids. Classify each of these as a conductor, an insulator, or a semiconductor. If you need help, refer to Interpreting Scientific Illustrations in the **Skill Handbook** on page 689.

ENRICHMENT

▶Have students investigate how integrated circuits are constructed in such miniature size. Note that radios will now even fit in a wristwatch. They used to be the size of modern televisions. This decrease in size is the result of integrated circuits.

CONCEPT DEVELOPMENT

▶ Have some microchips with integrated circuits on them available for students to observe. Examine one through a microscope. Give students a rough idea of how many of each kind of electrical device were included in the vacuum tube. They should realize how tiny the components can be and still be effective. You might want to bring in an old calculator to show them the difference in size and price between early and modern calculators.

3 CLOSE

▶ Ask questions 1-3 and the **Apply** Question in the Section Review.
▶ Bring in an electrical device you have not previously discussed and expose the circuitry. Have students identify the parts discussed in this section by name and function.

SECTION REVIEW ANSWERS

1. by doping it with gallium or arsenic
2. a rectifier; It may be a doped semiconductor that allows electrons to flow in only one direction.
3. Integrated circuits are made by doping silicon chips with impurities and painting thin aluminum wires on the chips.
4. Apply: No, carbon atoms would not have extra or too few electrons. They have the same number of electrons in their outer energy level as silicon.

Skill Builder

The elements listed for metals should come from the left side and center of the periodic table; nonmetals are on the right side; and metalloids are in-between the metals and non-metals. The metals should be listed as conductors, the nonmetals as insulators, and the metalloids as semiconductors.

PREPARATION

SECTION BACKGROUND

▶ Recall that electromagnetic waves were first used to transmit messages over long distances after the invention of the wireless telegraph in the late 1800s.

▶ The electrical signal carrying sound information is called an AF, or audio frequency, signal. The frequencies correspond to the range of hearing (20 to 20 000 Hz). The carrier waves are called RF, or radio frequency, waves. They have much higher frequencies.

1 MOTIVATE

▶ Have a television or radio on when students come into the room. Then ask them where the picture or sound comes from. They will probably say from the TV or radio station. Explain that in this section, they will study the transmission of signals and the formation of sounds and images from those signals.

▶ Bring a tape recorder to class and let each student quickly say something into it. Then play it back. Ask them how this sound differs from radio music. This helps increase their curiosity about how radio signals become audible music.

TYING TO PREVIOUS KNOWLEDGE:

Ask students what radio waves are. Remind them that radio waves make up the longest wavelengths in the electromagnetic spectrum. They can be reflected and are hitting each student right now. Students will find out what it takes to change these silent, invisible waves to sounds they can hear and images they can see.

OBJECTIVES AND SCIENCE WORDS:

Have students review the objectives and science word to become familiar with this section.

New Science Words

cathode-ray tube (CRT)

Objectives

▶ Describe how radio and television programs are transmitted.
▶ Explain the operation of a cathode-ray tube.

Radio Transmission

Now that you've studied sound, electromagnetic waves, and electricity, you should be comfortable with the concepts that explain how a radio works. Radios operate by changing transverse radio waves into vibrations that produce compressional sound waves. Recall that radio waves are the kind of electromagnetic radiation with the longest wavelength and shortest frequency. Radio waves travel at the speed of light, like all electromagnetic radiation. However, the conversion to sound waves is not possible without first converting the radio waves to electrical signals.

At the radio station, a microphone collects the compressional waves created by musical sounds. The microphone changes the sound waves into electrical signals. The electric current vibrations vary according to the sound vibrations. These signals are then amplified and passed through the modulator. Modulation was discussed in Chapter 19. The type of modulation varies in AM and FM radio stations. When the electrical signals are used to produce variations in the amplitude of the radio waves, they are called amplitude-modulated, or AM, waves. When the electrical signals are used to produce

OPTIONS

Meeting Different Ability Levels

For Section 23-2, use the following **Teacher Resource Masters** depending upon individual students' needs.

◆ **Study Guide Master** for all students.
● **Reinforcement Master** for students of average and above average ability levels.
▲ **Enrichment Master** for above average students.

Additional Teacher Resource Package masters are listed in the OPTIONS box throughout the section. The additional masters are appropriate for all students.

◆ **STUDY GUIDE** 97

variations in the frequency of the radio waves, they are called frequency-modulated, or FM, waves. The electric currents are amplified and sent to an antenna, where they are transformed into radio waves.

Your receiving radio has an antenna that collects these radio waves and transforms them into electric currents. If the radio is tuned to the same frequency as the radio waves, the waves will be amplified again. The carrier wave—the wave of the frequency to which the radio is tuned—is removed. This leaves only the waves that correspond to the original sound waves. The radio's loudspeaker vibrates to cause sound waves like those of the original music to leave the radio. As a result, you hear music!

Look at the radio dial pictured below. Notice that a set of numbers on the top of the dial corresponds to the FM range and a separate set of numbers on the bottom corresponds to the AM range. Every radio station, AM or FM, operates at a specific frequency and wavelength. FM stations broadcast at carrier frequencies ranging from 88 to 108 megahertz. AM stations broadcast at carrier frequencies between 540 and 1600 kilohertz. Do AM stations operate at a higher frequency than FM stations?

Television Transmission

What do radios have in common with television sets? Both have tuners that tune the circuits to the frequency of the radio waves. Both have a loudspeaker to vibrate and produce sound and an antenna to collect radio signals. The antennas on modern radios and television sets are often hidden in the circuits of these devices. Televisions not only turn the radio waves into sound, but they also use these signals to create a visual image. Television is like a radio with pictures.

EcoTip

Save energy by turning off radios and televisions when you are not using them.

603

---

2 TEACH

Key Concepts are highlighted.

CONCEPT DEVELOPMENT

▶ After introducing radio transmission, but before discussing television, have students make a list of the similarities and differences between radios and television sets. This will help them think of the common parts, such as channel tuners, antennas, volume control, and loudspeakers.

▶ Discuss the function of antennas. Common antennas are made of metal rods. The radio waves produce an electric field which causes the electrons in the conductor to vibrate at the frequencies of the incoming waves.

CROSS CURRICULUM

▶ **Communications:** Occasionally students may be changing stations on their radios and pick up a signal from a station in a different part of the country. Have the students do library research to find out what makes this possible. They should find that layers of the atmosphere, especially the ionosphere, reflect radio waves back to Earth.

MINI-Lab

Materials: a CRT, a small magnet
Teaching Tips
▶ Any small magnet will work. A stronger magnet will produce a stronger image distortion. It's best not to use too strong a magnet.
▶ A still pattern may be easier to analyze than a moving picture.
Answers
▶ The region above the magnet will show distortion downward or upward depending on the pole used.
▶ Color TVs will show a region of color change above or below the magnet.

STUDENT TEXT QUESTION

Page 603, paragraph 3: **Do AM stations operate at a higher frequency than FM stations?** *No, FM stations operate at the higher frequency.*

MINI QUIZ

Use the Mini Quiz to check students' recall of chapter content.

1 **What are the two ways radio waves can be modulated?** *amplitude-modulated, frequency-modulated*

2 **What is the role of the loudspeaker in a radio?** *to vibrate in response to an electrical signal, producing sound waves*

3 **What kind of signal transmits TV video images?** *amplitude-modulated*

RETEACH

Bring a radio or television into your classroom. Have students demonstrate the use of each device with proper physics explanations. They should include explanations such as how the radio waves are picked up and transformed to sound, and what is happening when you change the channel.

EXTENSION

For students who have mastered this section, use the **Reinforcement** and **Enrichment** masters or other OPTIONS provided.

TECHNOLOGY

For more information about HDTV, see Cook, William J. "Making a Leap in TV Technology." *U.S. News and World Report,* January 23, 1989, pages 48-49.

Think Critically: Television signals are broadcast on AM and FM radio waves. Answers will vary, but make sure students can support their ideas.

---

3 The audio, or sound, signal for television programs is sent and received like an FM radio signal. The video images are sent by AM carrier waves. Just as a microphone is used to change sound waves into varying electric currents, a television camera is used to change light into electric currents that represent the images. This electric video signal then amplitude-modulates a carrier wave. A television station simultaneously transmits the audio and video signals from its antenna.

Tuning into a television station is much like tuning a radio. When you select a channel, only a certain carrier frequency is picked up and amplified within the set. The audio portion of the television program is changed to sound by a loudspeaker. The picture you see on the screen is created by a more complex process. You may have heard that if the picture tube inside your television goes

TECHNOLOGY

HDTV

Would you like to have a large-screen TV with pictures as clear as a 35-millimeter photograph and the sound quality of a compact disc? This is the pledge of a new generation of television referred to as "high-definition television" (HDTV). HDTV sets will provide images by constructing a picture from 1 125 individual horizontal lines rather than the 525 horizontal lines you have on your current TV set. This means that you can see a clear picture even if you are close to an HDTV screen that is four or five feet across.

The technology for the design and construction of the new TV sets is relatively simple to achieve. Problems arise, however, in trying to move from the United States' current broadcast system to the new broadcast system without making TV sets that aren't HDTV obsolete. Because the HDTV signals encode much more information than conventional TV signals, broadcasting HDTV

signals could interfere with conventional TV broadcasts. Japan, the United States, and some European countries are competing to set the standard for these new HDTV signals. This competition could result in the development of other forms of delivering HDTV signals such as direct broadcast satellites or fiber-optic cables.

Think Critically: How are TV signals currently broadcast? What form of broadcasting do you think would be best for HDTV signals that would not interfere with other TV signals?

OPTIONS

INQUIRY QUESTIONS

▶ **Distinguish between radio waves and sound waves. Why are radio waves, not sound waves, used to send music or voices over long distances?** *Radio waves are electromagnetic waves, which are transverse and travel very rapidly. Sound waves are compressional waves and travel much more slowly through air. Radio waves are faster and more efficient. If sound waves were used, we would hear all stations at the same time.*

▶ **What type of modulation would exist in a radio wave with a frequency of 101.3 MHz?** *FM, or frequency-modulated*

▶ **If video signals are carried by AM carrier waves and audio signals are carried by FM carrier waves in television transmission, why do the waves arrive in your home at the same time?** *AM and FM waves are both radio waves, and all electromagnetic radiation travels at the same speed.*

out, you are faced with a major repair bill or should probably buy a new television. That's because this picture tube is the most expensive component in your TV set. The picture tube is a type of cathode-ray tube. A **cathode-ray tube (CRT)** uses electrons and fluorescent materials to produce images on a screen.

Look at the CRT in the television set at the right. A CRT is a sealed glass vacuum tube. When power is applied to the components in the tube, electrons come off a negative cathode and are focused into a beam. They move toward the screen, which is coated on the inside with materials that glow when struck by the electrons. The direction of the beam is changed by electromagnets outside of the CRT. This allows the beam of electrons to sweep the surface of the screen many times each second.

The cathode-ray tube of a color TV contains a screen lined with different materials that give off light in one of the three primary colors: red, blue, or green. The radio waves that carry the picture signal are changed into electrical signals in the television. These electrical signals control the intensity and position of the electron beams, which determine the colors and patterns of the image that forms on the screen. If you look closely at your television screen, you can see the tiny dots of red, blue, and green that make up each image. How is this process similar to the way your eye forms color images?

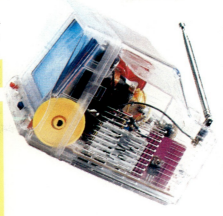

Figure 23-7. A television set contains a CRT.

MINI-Lab
How do electrons make a TV picture?
Electrons are guided to the screen of a CRT by electrical and magnetic fields. A chemical inside the screen reacts to the electrons by flashing a color of the light. Place a small magnet on the glass surface of an operating CRT and observe the response. Do both poles of the magnet produce the same reaction? What happens to the colors on the screen?

SECTION REVIEW

1. Explain what happens inside your radio when you tune in to a particular radio station.
2. How does a cathode-ray tube produce an image?
3. **Apply:** How might a cathode-ray tube that produces a color image differ from one with a black and white image?

☑ Concept Mapping

Make a concept map that shows the steps involved in radio broadcasts. Begin with the voice at the microphone and end with the radio waves leaving the transmitter. If you need help, refer to Concept Mapping in the **Skill Handbook** on pages 684 and 685.

Skill Builder

Skill Builder

| Voice or music causes compressional waves | → | Microphone changes sound waves to electric current | → | Vibrations in current are amplified | → | Modulator creates AM or FM radio waves | → | Radio waves sent out from antenna |

▶ If possible, have a cathode-ray tube available to show your students. Television or electronics dealers may have picture tubes available for demonstration purposes. Point out the major parts and their functions.

3 CLOSE

▶ Ask questions 1 and 2 and the **Apply** Question in the Section Review.
▶ Have students write a paragraph explaining the similarities to the way an eye and a CRT produce color images. Review the discussion of vision processes in Chapter 19.

STUDENT TEXT QUESTION

▶ Page 605, paragraph 3: **How is this process similar to the way your eye forms color images?** *Both the picture tube and the retina are sensitive to red, green, and blue. With the eye, there are red, blue, and green sensitive cones. With the TV there are red, blue, and green fluorescing materials.*

SECTION REVIEW ANSWERS

1. The radio picks up and amplifies radio waves of the frequency to which the receiver is tuned.
2. Electron beams cause specific materials on the screen of the tube to fluoresce. The intensity and pattern of the beams determine the image.
3. Apply: The fluorescent materials in a color picture tube will give off red, blue, or green light. Combinations of these colors can form all other colors. But, a black and white picture tube forms images when electron beams strike a flourescent material that glows white.

PROGRAM RESOURCES

From the **Teacher Resource Package** use:

Activity Worksheets, page 190, Mini-Lab: How do electrons make a TV picture?

PREPARATION

SECTION BACKGROUND

▶ Information can be stored on magnetic floppy disks because ferromagnetic materials have the property called hysteresis. Hysteresis is the lagging behind of magnetization on a disk.

▶ Magnetic disks are made by coating the disk with a thin liquid suspension of tiny magnetized iron oxide particles. These permanent magnets are aligned by a strong magnetic field as the liquid is dried, making them resistant to reasonably rough treatment.

PREPLANNING

▶ Make sure you have at least one computer available for demonstration purposes to use with instruction in this section.

1 MOTIVATE

▶ Ask students to try to come to an agreement about whether or not computers can think. **What does a computer need to solve problems for you?** *It needs a program or set of instructions.* **How does a computer's problem solving process differ from your own?** *A computer can only perform operations that it has been programmed to do.*

New Science Words

microprocessor
RAM
ROM

Objectives

▶ Identify the basic parts of a microcomputer.
▶ Describe the role of the microprocessor.
▶ Distinguish between RAM and ROM.

Microcomputer Components

How often do you use microcomputers? You may use them to play computer games, practice math problems, or locate a book in the library. A computer is a device you can program to carry out calculations and make logical decisions. How many simple addition problems can you do in ten seconds? Computers can store large amounts of information and perform up to several million calculations in each second. This ability makes them very efficient at processing and storing large amounts of information.

What are the three main capabilities of microcomputers?

Microcomputers must have three main capabilities. First, they must be capable of storing the data or information needed to solve a problem. Next, microcomputers must be able to follow instructions to perform tasks in a logical way. Finally, microcomputers must communicate their information to the outside world. These requirements can be fulfilled with a combination of hardware and software components.

Computer hardware refers to the major permanent components of the microcomputer. When you think of a computer

OPTIONS

Meeting Different Ability Levels

For Section 23-3, use the following **Teacher Resource Masters** depending upon individual students' needs.

◆ **Study Guide Master** for all students.
● **Reinforcement Master** for students of average and above average ability levels.
▲ **Enrichment Master** for above average students.

Additional Teacher Resource Package masters are listed in the OPTIONS box throughout the section. The additional masters are appropriate for all students.

you probably think of the input and output devices. Output devices usually include a screen, part of the video display terminal, and a printer. The video screen in most computers is a cathode-ray tube similar to the one in your television set. Input devices allow you to communicate your ideas to the computer. Keyboards, joysticks, and mouses are common input devices. Disk drives can both input and output information. The main circuit board inside the computer holds the central processing unit (CPU) and the main memory.

Name three output devices.

Microprocessors

The first computers were very large and slow compared to the computers you are familiar with. The United States built several of the first computers shortly after World War II, between 1946 and 1951. These early computers operated on complex circuits composed of thousands of vacuum tubes. They used a lot of energy and were large enough to fill entire rooms. The

Figure 23-8. The computerized video game on the opposite page can hold more memory and perform more operations than this early computer.

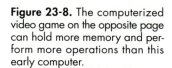

607

▶ To help distinguish between RAM and ROM, emphasize that RAM is temporary memory because information is stored electronically. Information stored in RAM can be very rapidly recalled for use. Information in ROM is retained even when the power is shut off because it is magnetically stored.

▶ Use the information found in Revealing Misconceptions below to generate a discussion about the prefix *kilo-* as used by computer designers.

REVEALING MISCONCEPTIONS

▶ Students are probably familiar with the metric prefix *kilo-*, which means one thousandth of the base unit. The term has a slightly different meaning as a unit of computer memory size. One K, or a computer kilo, actually represents 1024 bytes rather than 1000 bytes.

Science and WRITING

Students have a way of simplifying things that can teach all of us something. The novice is bombarded with strange terms from the time he or she begins shopping for a computer. If a student does a particularly good job, he or she might be able to use the information in a brochure or news article.

STUDENT TEXT QUESTION

▶ Page 608, paragraph 2: **How many bytes of information can be stored in 30 kilobytes of memory?**

$$30 \text{ kilobytes} \times \frac{1024 \text{ bytes}}{\text{kilobytes}}$$

$$= 30\ 720 \text{ bytes}$$

Science and WRITING

If you are "computer wise" you may be able to help novices by developing a dictionary of computer terms. Start with the terms in computer ads.

Table 23-1

BINARY CODE		
Number	Binary	Switch
0	0	○
1	1	●
2	10	● ○
3	11	● ●
4	100	● ○ ○
5	101	● ○ ●
6	110	● ● ○
7	111	● ● ●
8	1000	● ○ ○ ○
9	1001	● ○ ○ ●
10	1010	● ○ ● ○

invention of the integrated circuit rapidly improved the efficiency of computers.

A **microprocessor** serves as the brain of the computer. A microprocessor is an integrated circuit on the main circuit board. It receives electrical input from the user and tells other parts of the computer how to respond, just as your brain tells your hand to move when you touch a hot pan. It might store information using a disk drive, change a video display, or make a sound. The microprocessor contains the CPU, which is the circuitry that actually carries out the arithmetic and logical operations. CPUs are different among various kinds of microcomputers. The details of the CPU in the microprocessor determine how "user friendly" a computer is.

Computer Memory

Information is collected and stored in the memory of the computer. The memory contains thousands of tiny circuits which have switches with two positions: open (off) or closed (on). Recall that a switch must be closed for current to flow. All computer information is processed with combinations of just two numbers, zero and one, to represent these situations. This is called a binary number system. Each 0 (off) or 1 (on) represents one binary digit and is called a bit. Numbers, letters, and symbols are grouped in your computer in arrangements of eight bits called bytes. Often computer memory is expressed in terms of larger units, such as kilobytes and megabytes. How many bytes of information can be stored in 30 kilobytes of memory?

There are several kinds of memory in a microcomputer. Temporary memory stores documents and data while they are being used. The computer can send information to the memory by turning certain bits on or off. Similarly, the computer can read information from the memory by determining whether certain bits are on or off. This temporary memory is called random-access memory, or **RAM,** because any bit can be used in storing information. Because information is electronically stored in RAM, the information is lost when the computer is turned off. However, using information stored in RAM is much faster than pulling it from mechanical disk drives.

When you purchase a computer, it comes with some information already stored in permanent memory. This

OPTIONS

INQUIRY QUESTIONS

▶ Which part of the computer would store the information that allows certain commands to the computer to be meaningful? *the microprocessor, or CPU*

▶ Why is the memory system in a computer called a binary system? *There are only two possible numbers, 0 or 1, that give the computer information. The prefix bi- means two.*

information contains instructions required by the micro-processor to operate the computer. The computer can read this memory, but information can't be added to it. For this reason, it is called read-only memory, or **ROM**. Information in ROM is permanently stored inside the computer and, therefore, isn't lost when the computer is turned off. Neither RAM nor ROM is useful in helping you store your work between uses.

Data Storage

One of the main advantages of using computers is that you can save information and then come back later to make changes to it. Because RAM is lost when you turn off the computer, and you can't save information in ROM, the information must be stored in another way. Disk drives are used to record information magnetically. This process is similar to the way music is recorded on cassette tapes, but much more information can be stored on for-matted computer disks. There are two main kinds of disks used for data storage.

Most computers have at least one disk drive for stor-ing information on a "floppy" disk. A floppy disk is a thin, round, plastic disk coated with a magnetic material, such as iron oxide. The disk is encased in a thicker plastic case for protection. Information can be saved on the disk, and the disk can be removed from the disk drive for storage. Floppy disks can be used in different computers if they have compatible systems. Floppy disks can be used to transfer data or programs from one computer to anoth-er computer.

Hard disk drives are found inside the main part of some computers. Hard disks are rigid metal disks that stay inside the computer. The disks spin continuously when the computer is on. Hard drives are useful because they hold many times more informa-tion than do floppy disks. They also retrieve information much faster. A hard drive is a costly, but help-ful, addition to a computer system.

Figure 23-9. A hard disk, like the one at the far right, is a perma-nent part of some computers. It is used to store data.

PROBLEM SOLVING

He would lose the design if he hadn't saved it on a hard or floppy disk.
Think Critically: He could save the design on floppy disk to use later.

Science and READING

Ask students who have created something original for sale how they would feel if it were copied and they were deprived of the income. The issue often centers on whether it is okay to steal from a large corporation, which can be compared to such crimes as shoplifting or cheating on taxes.

CHECK FOR UNDERSTANDING

Use the Mini Quiz to check for understanding.

MINI QUIZ

Use the Mini Quiz to check students' recall of chapter content.

1 **What does CPU stand for? What does the CPU do?** *Central processing unit; it is the circuitry that performs arithmetic and logical operations.*

2 **Which kind of memory can be readily accessed and used to store temporary information?** *RAM*

3 **Which holds more information, hard disks or floppy disks?** *hard disks*

4 **A(n) _____ is a set of instructions that tells a computer what to do.** *program*

RETEACH

Draw an analogy between taking an open-note exam and the RAM/ROM difference. The material you do not know is written in front of you in the notes (RAM). If you take the notes away, the information is gone. Some answers are stored permanently in your brain (ROM).

EXTENSION

For students who have mastered this section, use the **Reinforcement** and **Enrichment** masters or other OPTIONS provided.

PROBLEM SOLVING

Computer Art

Emilio spent most of his spare time drawing and painting. His teachers and friends liked his artwork and they thought it was very creative.

Emilio used the family computer to write reports for school, but he really wanted to use the computer to create artwork. He visited a computer store at the mall to see what hardware was available that he could use for this purpose.

He found a graphic tablet and a light pen that allowed him to draw on the CRT screen. First, he tried the graphic tablet. He drew on a special pad with a stylus, and his design appeared on the computer screen. To use the light pen, he drew directly on the CRT. Because the graphic tablet was less expensive and easier to use, he decided to buy it. If Emilio was creating a design and the power went off, what would happen to the design?

Think Critically: How could Emilio save a design he was working on to finish at some other time?

Uses for Computers

Computers can't complete a task without guidelines for carrying out a series of operations. **4** A program is a group of instructions that tells a computer what to do. Programs are sometimes referred to as software. Computer programmers use special languages that convert your language into instructions the CPU can understand. BASIC, Pascal, and Fortran are examples of computer languages. Whenever you play a computer game, use a word processor, or solve mathematical problems, a computer program is instructing the computer to perform in a certain way.

Microcomputers are becoming useful in more and more applications. You often use them in situations where a computer screen is not visible. For example, computers are regularly used to regulate mechanical processes in cars, to monitor heating and cooling systems in build-

What is a program?

OPTIONS

PROGRAM RESOURCES

From the **Teacher Resource Package** use:

Cross-Curricular Connections, page 29, Using a Spreadsheet to Analyze Lab Data.

Science and Society, page 27, Junk Mail.

ings, and to enter inventory bar codes in grocery stores. Many calculators can now be programmed as well. Even some kitchen appliances contain simple small computers to enhance their operations. Microcomputers wouldn't exist without advances in electronics, such as the transistor and the integrated circuit. Can you imagine going through one week without using a microcomputer of some sort? How do you think we'll use microcomputers of the future?

Figure 23-10. Look closely at the computer screen above and you will see this two-page spread. Computers are commonly used for desktop publishing.

SECTION REVIEW

1. What are three main functions of a computer?
2. Describe the function of a microprocessor.
3. What is the difference between RAM and ROM?
4. **Apply:** If you wanted to transfer a computer program from your computer to a friend's computer, how would you do it?

☑ Comparing and Contrasting

Compare and contrast the advantages and disadvantages of floppy disk drives and hard disk drives. If you need help, refer to Comparing and Contrasting in the **Skill Handbook** on page 679.

Skill Builder

23-3 MICROCOMPUTERS **611**

---

3 CLOSE

▶ Ask questions 1-2 and the **Apply** Question in the Section Review.

Cooperative Learning: Arrange students into Problem Solving teams. Assign each group one of the aspects of computer function discussed in this chapter. Give them about 15 minutes to come up with a short presentation about their topic. Each group should share their topic with the class, ensuring that all major parts of the computer have been covered.

❓ FLEX Your Brain

Use the Flex Your Brain activity to bridge to the Science and Society topic of computer crimes by having students explore WAYS COMPUTERS MIGHT BE MISUSED.

SECTION REVIEW ANSWERS

1. They must store data, decide what operations to perform next, and communicate with the outside world.
2. A microprocessor receives an electrical input from the user and then instructs other parts of the computer what to do.
3. Information can be added to RAM by the user and read by the computer. Information is temporarily stored in RAM and is lost when the computer is turned off. ROM is permanent memory that the computer can only read, giving it instructions for operating the microprocessor.
4. Apply: Transfer the program to a floppy disk. Move the floppy disk to the other computer and load the program into the RAM or hard disk drive.

Skill Builder

Floppy disk drives are useful because floppy disks can be used to transport information from one computer to another and are relatively inexpensive. However, hard disks drives can store much more information and can rapidly process information. The main disadvantage of hard disk drives is that they are very expensive.

Computer Crimes

PREPARATION

SECTION BACKGROUND

▶ A distinction is sometimes made between a computer virus and a worm program. A virus replicates itself and attaches itself to other programs to produce sometimes bizarre effects. A worm loads a system with information that replicates itself and fills the memory and files in the computer. This slows or stops the computer from functioning.

1 MOTIVATE

▶ Ask students if they think breaking into a government office to find classified information is a crime. Then ask if sitting in your own home reading classified government files on a computer screen seems just as wrong.

TYING TO PREVIOUS KNOWLEDGE:
In this chapter, you have studied microcomputers. With modems it is possible for computer systems in different places to communicate with each other through phone lines. Explain that we will learn how this is a possible problem, as it provides a door which can be broken into.

OBJECTIVES AND SCIENCE WORDS:
Have students review the objectives and science words to become familiar with this section.

2 TEACH

Key Concepts are highlighted.

CONCEPT DEVELOPMENT

▶ Photocopy or make an overhead of a software copyright agreement. Discuss how easy it is to copy software, even with the copyright.

New Science Words

computer virus

Objectives

▶ Discuss the types of crimes that can be committed by computer misuse.
▶ Predict the possible consequences of computer crimes.

How Serious Are Computer Crimes?

What do you think of when you hear the word *crime*? You probably think of stealing, vandalism, or violence. Would you believe an increasingly common type of crime is being committed by the misuse of computers?

You may have copied a friend's cassette tape onto a blank tape for your own personal use. Computer programs can also be copied from one floppy disk to another. When you purchase a program, the software company usually intends for you to make one backup copy in case the original one becomes damaged. The companies don't intend for you to copy the program to give to your friends. These programs are protected by copyright laws. However, some programs are free and can be copied legally for distribution. ==Sharing of illegal copies of software is probably the most common of computer crimes, as well as the most difficult computer crime to safeguard against.==

In recent years, computer viruses have become a problem. Some computer viruses can be deliberately planted in a computer. ==A **computer virus** is a type of program that can multiply inside a computer and use so much memory that it harms the system.== Like a virus in your body, it can remain inactive in the computer until something causes it to spread. As a result of the virus attack, data in memory might be lost, and a strange message might appear on the screen. The infected computer might even just stop functioning. Viruses can be sent through phone lines linking computers, or can spread from infected software shared between computers. Sometimes antivirus programs can find and destroy viruses before they spread, or even fix the damage already done. Do you think it is a crime to purposefully spread a computer virus?

OPTIONS

Meeting Different Ability Levels

For Section 23-4, use the following **Teacher Resource Masters** depending upon individual students' needs.
◆ **Study Guide Master** for all students.
● **Reinforcement Master** for students of average and above average ability levels.
▲ **Enrichment Master** for above average students.

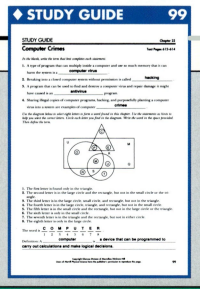

◆ **STUDY GUIDE** 99

Perhaps the most controversial computer crime is "hacking." People who break into closed computer systems without permission are called hackers. They may have several motives. Some hackers may just find hacking challenging, but others are looking for specific restricted information.

Hacking is an invasion of privacy. For example, a hacker might be able to find out about your parents' financial history without permission. A hacker could break into your school's computer to alter his or her grades. Do you think this is the same type of crime as breaking into someone's house?

We are very dependent on computers. Make a list of the activities in your life that involve computers. How do computer crimes affect these activities? Stealing software can cause the price of software programs to go up. If a virus were to shut down a major computer system, such as the system at your bank, how would you be affected?

SECTION REVIEW

1. How does a computer virus interfere with a computer?
2. What is computer hacking?

You Decide!

Suppose a computer hacker broke into a secret government computer system. Should this be considered a criminal offense, such as treason, or should it be considered a misdemeanor crime, such as breaking and entering? Do you think the hacker should be punished in the same manner as someone who broke into a building and took secret files? Explain your point of view.

REINFORCEMENT 99

ENRICHMENT 99

613

TEACHER F.Y.I.
▶ Programmers have now developed "disinfectant programs" which can be run on a hard drive or floppy disk to scan for signs of a viral infection.

CHECK FOR UNDERSTANDING
▶ Ask questions 1 and 2 in the Section Review.
▶ Ask students if they can be sure their computer or a classroom computer is free of viruses. Note that the virus may be hiding in the computer waiting for a date or other signal to activate it.

RETEACH
For students who have had life science, you could draw a useful analogy between viruses that cause human diseases and computer viruses. For example, the virus that causes AIDS can be inactive for years before it spreads and attacks the body.

EXTENSION
For students who have mastered this section, use the **Reinforcement** and **Enrichment** masters or other OPTIONS provided.

CROSS CURRICULUM
▶ **Criminal Justice:** Find the legal definition of the terms *felony* and *misdemeanor*. Make a list of crimes that fall into these categories. Identify the typical punishments for these crimes.

3 CLOSE
▶ Use the You Decide activity to encourage students to evaluate their own point of view on computer crimes.

SECTION REVIEW ANSWERS
1. A virus multiplies and expands to fill the memory of a computer. It may cause lost data or prevent the computer from functioning.
2. Hacking is breaking into a computer system to gain information without permission.

YOU DECIDE!

Answers will vary. Have students justify their choices.

ACTIVITY 23-2
one class period

OBJECTIVE: Invent a system of communication which stores information in magnetic fields.

PROCESS SKILLS applied in this activity:
▶ **Classifying** in Procedure Steps 1-3.
▶ **Communicating** in Procedure Steps 4-8.
▶ **Defining** in Procedure Step 8 and Conclude and Apply Questions 4 and 5.

👥 COOPERATIVE LEARNING

Divide the class into teams of three or four. The purpose of trading magnetic "words" is to get feedback for improvement. Follow up with a second trial.

TEACHING THE ACTIVITY

▶ Provide each team two sheets 8"×10" cardstock and at least 12 ceramic magnets. Shaped magnets with poles on faces will work, but magnets should be of equal strength.
▶ Encourage creativity in inventing the binary code for letters and the way the message sheet is structured. Students must adequately describe their own operating rules in order for the other team to read what is written.
▶ Follow-up discussion can further develop the lab analogy to the writing and reading of information on the magnetic material of a computer disk.

PROGRAM RESOURCES

From the **Teacher Resource Package** use:

Activity Worksheets, pages 186-187, Activity 23-2: Information Storage.

ACTIVITY 23-2
Information Storage

Problem: Can you store information in a magnetic field?

Materials
- disk magnets, 12
- cardstock paper, 2 sheets and a thin strip
- transparent tape
- metric ruler

Procedure
1. Divide one sheet of the cardstock into four rows of squares as shown.
2. Put all the magnets in a single stack. Mark the top side of each magnet with the number 1 and the bottom with number 0.
3. Invent a code using only the numbers 1 and 0 to represent the letters of the alphabet. Make a code table as shown.
4. Choose a three or four letter word to "write" with eleven magnets.
5. Tape the magnets, code number side up, to the "message sheet" made in Step 1. Tape one magnet to a square so that each row shows the code of a particular letter.
6. Cover the magnets with a second sheet marked with the location of squares on the message sheet.
7. Tape a magnet to the end of a strip of cardstock. Holding the other end of the strip, slide the magnet over the top sheet and "read" its response to the message magnets.
8. Write down the operating rules for "reading" your word. Trade your rules and magnetic message with another team.

Analyze
1. How do you know what kind of letter is underneath the "reading" message.
2. How many letters can be made with two magnets each?
3. How much of the alphabet can be made if no letter can have more than four magnets?

Conclude and Apply
4. Why are the operating rules for reading as important as knowing the code number?
5. Why are there only two numbers in the code?

LETTER CODES	
A — 0	F — 11
B — 1	G — 000
C — 00	H — 001
D — 01	I — 011
E — 10	J — 111

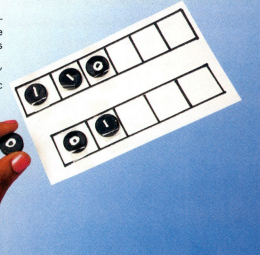

ANSWERS TO QUESTIONS

1. The reading magnet will be either attracted or repelled depending on which pole of the message magnet is up.
2. 00, 01, 10, and 11 (4 letters)
3. all of it
4. The reader must know which way to scan; right to left, left to right, top to bottom, and so on. The reader must know if attraction means 1 or 0.
5. The magnet has only two poles. Only attraction and repulsion are possible.

REVIEW

SUMMARY

23-1: Semiconductor Devices

1. The conductivity of semiconductors can be increased by adding impurities to them.
2. A rectifier changes alternating current into direct current.
3. Electronic devices containing integrated circuits are much smaller than those that don't contain these circuits.

23-2: Radio and Television

1. Radio and television signals are transmitted by changing electrical signals into electromagnetic radiation.
2. A cathode-ray tube uses electrons and fluorescent materials to produce pictures on a television screen.

23-3: Microcomputers

1. The basic parts of a microcomputer include the input devices, the output devices, disk drives, and the main circuit board.
2. The microprocessor receives input and tells the computer how to respond.
3. RAM is the temporary memory in a computer. ROM is memory that is permanently stored inside the computer.

23-4: Science and Society: Computer Crimes

1. Computer crimes include illegally copying software, planting computer viruses, and hacking.
2. Some computer crimes can involve stealing restricted information or altering records.

KEY SCIENCE WORDS

a. **amplification**
b. **cathode-ray tube (CRT)**
c. **computer virus**
d. **diode**
e. **integrated circuit**
f. **microprocessor**
g. **RAM**
h. **rectifier**
i. **ROM**
j. **transistor**

UNDERSTANDING VOCABULARY

Match each phrase with the correct term from the list of Key Science Words.

1. miniature components on a slice of silicon
2. converts AC to DC
3. amplifies an electric signal
4. the process of making an electric current stronger
5. a TV picture tube
6. transfers a user's commands to other parts of the computer
7. a computer's temporary memory
8. a computer program that multiplies and causes a computer's memory to be lost
9. contains stored information needed by a microprocessor to operate a computer
10. a type of rectifier

SUMMARY

Have students read the summary statements to review the major concepts of the chapter.

UNDERSTANDING VOCABULARY

1. e	**6.** f
2. h	**7.** g
3. j	**8.** c
4. a	**9.** i
5. b	**10.** d

OPTIONS

ASSESSMENT

To assess student understanding of material in this chapter, use the resources listed.

👥 COOPERATIVE LEARNING

Consider using cooperative learning in the THINK AND WRITE CRITICALLY, APPLY, and MORE SKILL BUILDERS sections of the Chapter Review.

PROGRAM RESOURCES

From the **Teacher Resource Package** use:
Chapter Review, pages 49-50.
Chapter and Unit Tests, pages 151-154, Chapter Test.

CHECKING CONCEPTS

1. a	6. d
2. a	7. b
3. d	8. b
4. a	9. a
5. b	10. c

UNDERSTANDING CONCEPTS

11. diodes
12. transistor
13. Transistors
14. electron beams, fluorescent materials, and electromagnets
15. program

THINK AND WRITE CRITICALLY

16. In diodes, semiconductors are used to convert an alternating current into a direct current by placing an *n*-type semiconductor at one end of the diode and a *p*-type at the other so current can only flow in one direction. In transistors, semiconductors are used to amplify current.

17. The advantages of integrated circuits are that they have little electrical resistance and minimize energy loss, and a current can travel faster through the circuit. Integrated circuits cannot handle large currents, and they are too small to be easily manipulated.

18. Computers must be able to store data, perform tasks, and have some way to communicate with the outside world.

19. Computer crime includes copying and distributing copyrighted computer software, sending a computer virus to grow and wipe out a computer's memory, and breaking into closed program systems. Answers will vary, but students should support their answers.

20. Answers to this question will vary but may include such activities as playing computer games, writing papers on word processors, buying groceries, and driving a car.

CHECKING CONCEPTS

Choose the word or phrase that completes the sentence.

1. Elements that are semiconductors are located on the periodic table _____.
   a. between metals and nonmetals
   b. on the right side
   c. at the bottom
   d. on the left side

2. Solid-state electronic devices use _____.
   a. low current   c. no current
   b. high current   d. vacuum tubes

3. Rectifiers are used in _____.
   a. adapter plugs   c. computers
   b. televisions   d. all of these

4. The signal in an electronic device that represents sound and images is a _____.
   a. varying current   c. radio wave
   b. constant current d. sound wave

5. Transistors are used in all of the following except _____.
   a. medical diagnoses   c. hearing aids
   b. TV vacuum tubes   d. tape players

6. Integrated circuits consist of _____.
   a. silicon chips with painted aluminum wires
   b. transistors
   c. resistors
   d. all of these

7. The video images for a television program are transmitted to your home as _____.
   a. frequency-modulated radio waves
   b. amplitude-modulated radio waves
   c. cathode rays
   d. electric current

8. Computer hardware consists of all of the following except _____.
   a. video display terminal   c. disk drives
   b. programs   d. keyboards

9. A computer represents information using _____.
   a. a binary number system
   b. sequences of numbers
   c. arrangements of 4 bits
   d. the numbers 1 through 10

10. Computer data and programs both can be stored permanently and transferred to other computers using _____.
    a. RAM   c. floppy disks
    b. ROM   d. hard disks

UNDERSTANDING CONCEPTS

Complete each sentence.

11. Both *p*-type and *n*-type semiconductors are used in the construction of _____.

12. An electric signal is amplified by a sandwich of three alternating semiconductors in a(n) _____.

13. _____ are the most fundamental components of modern electronic circuits.

14. Cathode-ray tubes use _____ to produce images on their screens.

15. A computer _____ is a group of instructions that tells a computer what to do.

THINK AND WRITE CRITICALLY

16. How are semiconductors used in diodes and transistors?

17. Describe the advantages and disadvantages of integrated circuits.

18. Identify three functions of a microcomputer.

19. Describe three types of computer crime. Which do you think is the most serious? Why?

20. Describe how computers affect you in everyday life.

APPLY

21. Diodes convert alternating current because electrons must flow from an area where there is an excess of electrons (the end with an *n*-type semiconductor) to an area where there is a deficiency of electrons (the end with a *p*-type semiconductor). If a diode had only one or the other type of semiconductor, electrons could still move but not in one direction only.

22. It is not necessary to take the CD player back because the only problem is that an amplifier was never hooked up to the player. The CD player's signal is too weak to vibrate the speakers and requires a larger outside current provided by the amplifier current.

21. Could a diode work properly if *both* of its ends were either *p*-type or *n*-type semiconductors? Explain your answer.

22. You have connected your new compact disc player directly to your stereo speakers, but when you turn on the CD, you hear nothing. Should you return the CD player to the store? Why or why not?

23. Which would do more harm to the operation of a computer, the loss of its random-access memory or the loss of its read-only memory? Explain your answer.

24. You need to store information on your computer that you can retrieve rapidly whenever you use your computer. What is the best way to store this information?

25. Why might your school keep written records even when it has computers that can store these records much more efficiently?

MORE SKILL BUILDERS

If you need help, refer to the Skill Handbook.

1. **Recognizing Cause and Effect:** Complete the following table by identifying either the cause or effect of problems associated with cathode-ray tubes.

Cause	Effect
1. Inside of tube coated with a non-fluorescent material.	1.
2.	2. Electron beam doesn't sweep the entire screen.
3. Incoming electrical signals are garbled.	3.

2. **Comparing and Contrasting:** Compare and contrast *n*-type and *p*-type semiconductors. Discuss the purpose of each semiconductor, how each functions, and what elements each uses and why.

3. **Making and Using Tables:** Construct a table to organize what you know about the parts of the microcomputer and the function of each part.

4. **Interpreting Scientific Illustrations:** Look at the two diagrams of doped silicon crystals in Figure 23-2 on page 597. Read the statements below and separate them into two columns. Label these columns N-type Semiconductor and P-type Semiconductor. Be sure to place the statements in each column in the correct order. Some statements can be used twice.
   a. Electrons move to fill holes, creating more holes in the crystal.
   b. Current flows through the doped crystal.
   c. The extra electrons move through the crystal.
   d. A silicon crystal is doped with gallium.
   e. A silicon crystal is doped with arsenic.
   f. Voltage is applied across the crystal.
   g. An electron hole is near each gallium atom in the crystal.
   h. The crystal has extra electrons that are free to move.

PROJECTS

1. Find out how microphones convert sound and turntable needles convert mechanical vibrations into electrical signals. Make a poster illustrating how each works.

2. Learn one of the basic computer languages and write a simple program.

Component	Function
Input devices (keyboards, etc.)	Allow the user to communicate with the computer
Output devices (screen, etc.)	Allow computer to communicate with the user
Microprocessor	Carries out the computer's operations; receives and translates the users commands to the computer
RAM	Temporarily stores information while the computer is being used
ROM	Stores the information needed by the microprocessor
Floppy disk	Contains information and programs to be stored and transferred to other computers
Hard disk	Contains information and programs to be stored permanently in the computer

23. The loss of read-only memory would be much more serious because the information stored here is absolutely necessary for the operation of the computer by the microprocessor. A computer could still be used without RAM; you simply could not store information while using it without transferring it either to a hard or floppy disk.

24. The best way to store such information would be to store it on the computer's hard disk because this disk can hold much more information and can be retrieved much more rapidly than from a floppy disk.

25. Because of problems such as user error and computer viruses, computer records could be irretrievably lost. Written records are necessary for these reasons, as well as in case a hacker invades the school's computer system and changes grades.

MORE SKILL BUILDERS

1. Recognizing Cause and Effect:
Effect: 1. Fluorescent light is not produced. No picture.
Cause: 2. Electromagnets outside the CRT fail to function properly.
Effect: 3. Patterns and colors of image are garbled.

2. Comparing and Contrasting: Both types of semiconductors have been doped to increase their conductivity, and are used in devices such as diodes and transistors. They differ, however, in terms of how they allow more electrons to flow. An *n*-type semiconductor is doped with an element that has more electrons in the outer energy level than does the semiconductor. A *p*-type semiconductor is said to be a positive semiconductor because it is doped with an element that has fewer electrons in the outer electron level than does the semiconductor. The lack of electrons can be thought of as "holes" in the crystal structure of the semiconductor. When a potential difference is applied across a semiconductor, electrons are conducted through it, producing a current.

3. Making and Using Tables: See table at left.

4. Interpreting Scientific Illustrations:
N-type Semiconductor
b, c, e, f, h
P-type Semiconductor
a, b, d, f

24 Radioactivity and Nuclear Reactions

CHAPTER SECTION	OBJECTIVES	ACTIVITIES
24-1 Radioactivity (1 day)	1. **Discuss** the discovery of radioactivity. 2. **Contrast** properties of radioactive versus stable nuclides.	**MINI-Lab:** *Does radiation change film?* p. 621
24-2 Nuclear Decay (2 days)	1. **Distinguish** among alpha, beta, and gamma radiation. 2. **Calculate** the amount of radioactive substance remaining after a time based on its half-life. 3. **Relate** half-life to the process of radioactive dating.	**Activity 24-1:** *Half-life,* p. 629
24-3 Detecting Radioactivity (1 day)	1. **Describe** how radioactivity can be detected. 2. **Explain** how a Geiger counter can determine the quantity of radiation present.	**MINI-Lab:** *What senses atomic radiation?* p. 631
24-4 Nuclear Reactions (1 day)	1. **Distinguish** between nuclear fission and fusion. 2. **Explain** how nuclear fission can begin a chain reaction. 3. **Discuss** how nuclear fusion occurs in the sun.	
24-5 Nuclear Medicine Science & Society (1 day)	1. **Describe** how radioactive tracers can be used to diagnose medical problems. 2. **Discuss** how radioactive isotopes can aid in the treatment of cancers.	**Activity 24-2:** *Nuclear Fusion,* p. 638
Chapter Review		

ACTIVITY MATERIALS

FIND OUT	ACTIVITIES		MINI-LABS	
Page 619 jar or cup marbles or other small, uniformly shaped objects	**24-1 Half-life, p. 629** rubber stoppers graph paper	**24-2 Nuclear Fusion, p. 638** 6 balls of green clay 6 smaller balls of white clay	**Does radiation change film? p. 621** photographic film badge or some undeveloped film a weak radioactive source, such as a small sample of uranium or pitchblende	**What senses atomic radiation? p. 631** dosimeter match source of beta radiation

CHAPTER FEATURES	TEACHER RESOURCE PACKAGE	OTHER RESOURCES
Technology: *Super Atom Smasher,* p. 622 **Skill Builder:** *Comparing and Contrasting,* p. 623	**Ability Level Worksheets** ◆ *Study Guide,* p. 100 ● *Reinforcement,* p. 100 ▲ *Enrichment,* p. 100 **MINI-Lab Worksheet,** p. 199	**Lab Manual 47,** The Effects of Radiation on Seeds
Problem Solving: *The Radioactive Clock,* p. 626 **Skill Builder:** *Interpreting Scientific Illustrations,* p. 628	**Ability Level Worksheets** ◆ *Study Guide,* p. 101 ● *Reinforcement,* p. 101 ▲ *Enrichment,* p. 101 **Activity Worksheet,** pp. 193, 194 **Concept Mapping,** pp. 53, 54 **Science and Society,** p. 28 **Transparency Masters,** pp. 93, 94	**Color Transparency 47,** Types of Radiation **Lab Manual 48,** Radioactive Decay—A Simulation
Skill Builder: *Observing and Inferring,* p. 632	**Ability Level Worksheets** ◆ *Study Guide,* p. 102 ● *Reinforcement,* p. 102 ▲ *Enrichment,* p. 102 **MINI-Lab Worksheet,** p. 200 **Critical Thinking/Problem Solving,** p. 30	
Skill Builder: *Concept Mapping,* p. 635	**Ability Level Worksheets** ◆ *Study Guide,* p. 103 ● *Reinforcement,* p. 103 ▲ *Enrichment,* p. 103 **Cross-Curricular Connections,** p. 30 **Transparency Master,** pp. 95, 96	**Color Transparency 48,** Nuclear Chain Reaction
You Decide! p. 637	**Ability Level Worksheets** ◆ *Study Guide,* p. 104 ● *Reinforcement,* p. 104 ▲ *Enrichment,* p. 104 **Activity Worksheet,** pp. 195, 196	
Summary Think & Write Critically Key Science Words Apply Understanding Vocabulary More Skill Builders Checking Concepts Projects Understanding Concepts	**Chapter Review,** pp. 51, 52 **Chapter Test,** pp. 155-158	**Chapter Review Software Test Bank**

◆ **Basic**   ● **Average**   ▲ **Advanced**

ADDITIONAL MATERIALS

SOFTWARE	AUDIOVISUAL	BOOKS/MAGAZINES
Radioactivity, J&S Software.	*A is for Atom, B is for Bomb,* video, NOVA (PBS). *Fusion: The Energy Promise,* video, NOVA (PBS). *The Bomb's Lethal Legacy,* video, NOVA (PBS). *The Nuclear Nightmare,* video, Focus. *Cold Fusion,* video, NOVA (PBS).	Condon, E.U. and H. Odabasi. *Atomic Structure.* NY: Cambridge University Press, 1980. Killingray, David. Ed. by Malcolm Yapp et al. *Atom Bomb.* San Diego, CA: Greenhaven Press, 1980.

THEME DEVELOPMENT: Patterns of change is a theme developed in this chapter. Throughout this book, the nucleus of the atom is modeled as essentially stable. In this chapter, students learn that the nucleus can undergo patterns of change and transformation. The identity of atoms can change when a nucleus undergoes radioactive decay. Since fission and fusion processes release tremendous amounts of energy, energy can also be brought out as a theme.

CHAPTER OVERVIEW

▶**Section 24-1:** The nature of radioactive elements is discussed through the discovery and current applications of radioactivity. Characteristics of radioactive nuclides are distinguished from those of stable nuclides.

▶**Section 24-2:** The three types of radioactive decay are introduced. Nuclear half-life is presented as a useful tool for helping us date samples of once-living tissue.

▶**Section 24-3:** Methods of detecting and counting radiation are illustrated, including cloud chambers, bubble chambers, and Geiger counters.

▶**Section 24-4:** Processes and applications of nuclear fission and chain reactions are presented. They are then compared to those of nuclear fusion, using the fusion in the sun as an illustration.

▶**Section 24-5: Science and Society:** This section features a discussion of the use of radioisotopes in medicine. The You Decide question asks students to evaluate whether the benefits of nuclear medicine outweigh the possible risks.

CHAPTER

24 Radioactivity and Nuclear Reactions

618

OPTIONS

For Your Gifted Students

▶Students can discuss what they know about radiation given off by the sun. Have them research the positive and negative aspects of the sun's rays upon humans and write a report. They may have to contact a local doctor for help.

▶Have students survey local tanning salons for information regarding the types of rays emitted from their tanning beds. Have them compare the effect of sun versus tanning bed and make recommendations for safety.

Have you ever watched a news report about the disposal of radioactive materials? Have you wondered how long these materials remain radioactive? Why are so many problems associated with radioactive materials?

FIND OUT!

Do the following activity to find out how radioactive materials decay into nonradioactive materials.

Put 32 marbles in a jar. Let these marbles represent radioactive atoms that will decay into nonradioactive atoms. Use a stopwatch or a second hand to time one-minute intervals. During the first minute, take half of the 32 marbles out of the jar and put them aside. These marbles represent atoms that have decayed into another element. During the second and third minutes, remove half of the remaining marbles from the jar. What happens to the radioactive atoms during each one-minute interval? What's the rate of decay of this radioactive element? Predict how many minutes it would take for all of the radioactive sample to decay.

Gearing Up
Previewing the Chapter
Use this outline to help you focus on important ideas in this chapter.

Section 24-1   Radioactivity
► Radioactive Elements
► Nuclides

Section 24-2   Nuclear Decay
► Nuclear Radiation
► Half-life
► Radioactive Dating

Section 24-3   Detecting Radioactivity
► Radiation Detectors
► Counting Radioactivity

Section 24-4   Nuclear Reactions
► Nuclear Fission
► Nuclear Fusion

Section 24-5   Science and Society
Nuclear Medicine
► Are Radioactive Isotopes Useful in Medicine?

Previewing Science Skills
► In the **Skill Builders,** you will compare and contrast, interpret scientific illustrations, observe and infer, and make a concept map.
► In the **Activities,** you will predict, interpret, and formulate models.
► In the **MINI-Labs,** you will observe and infer.

What's next?

If you predicted it would take about six minutes for the radioactive atoms in the Find Out activity to decay, you were correct. Some radioactive elements decay in less than one second; others take thousands of years. As you read this chapter, you will learn more about the many radioactive elements and how they decay.

619

CHAPTER VOCABULARY

radioactivity	cloud chamber
nuclide	bubble chamber
alpha particles	nuclear fission
transmutation	chain reaction
beta particle	nuclear fusion
gamma rays	tracers
half-life	

INTRODUCING THE CHAPTER

Use the Find Out activity to help students realize that not all nuclei are stable and that some decay into other elements. Explain that we will be learning more about how this happens, as well as studying applications of radioactive decay.

FIND OUT!

Preparation: Obtain jars and place 32 marbles (paper clips, pebbles, M&M's, etc.) into each one.
Materials: jar or cup; marbles or other small, uniformly shaped objects

Cooperative Learning: Have students work in Science Investigation groups of three. One student should time; one should count marbles; and one should record the answers to the questions presented.
Teaching Tips
► Emphasize that the marbles taken out decay but do not disappear; they change into a stable nucleus.

Gearing Up

Have students study the Gearing Up feature to familiarize themselves with the chapter. Discuss the relationships of the topics in the outline.

What's Next?

Before beginning the first section, make sure students understand the connection between the Find Out activity and the topics to follow.

For Your Mainstreamed Students

►Students can make a time line of the important discoveries and events in the area of nuclear power beginning with Henri Bequerel's discovery.
►Have the students hypothesize the future of nuclear power.

PREPARATION

SECTION BACKGROUND
▶ The elements 93 and beyond can only be produced synthetically. Glen T. Seaborg's work led to the discovery of several transuranium elements. He actually received patents for these elements and turned the rights over to the U.S. Government.

PREPLANNING
▶ To prepare for the Mini-Lab on page 621, gather some photographic film badges or some undeveloped Polaroid film and a weak source of radiation.

1 MOTIVATE

▶ Ask students to write some of the first things they think of when they hear the word *radiation*. Make a master list on the chalkboard and mention that you will explore most of the applications of radiation listed. How many of them had negative connotations?

▶ Tell students they are being exposed to radiation. See how many possible sources they can list. Radiation sources may include cosmic radiation (esp. while flying on airplanes), smoke detectors, radiation from soil, impurities in the brick or wood their houses are made of, radon gas in their basements, and medical/dental X rays.

TYING TO PREVIOUS
KNOWLEDGE: Remind students of their study of atomic structure. They learned that chemical reactions depend mostly on electron structures. In this chapter, the nucleus, which consists of protons and neutrons, determines the nuclear reactions.

OBJECTIVES AND
SCIENCE WORDS: Have students review the objectives and science words to become familiar with this section.

24-1 Radioactivity

New Science Words
radioactivity
nuclide

Objectives
▶ Discuss the discovery of radioactivity.
▶ Contrast properties of radioactive versus stable nuclides.

Radioactive Elements

Do you have a smoke detector in your home to alert you if there's a fire? If it is an ionizing smoke detector, it probably contains a small amount of a radioactive element called americium-241. How do you feel about having a radioactive element in your home?

The discovery of radioactivity about 100 years ago has led to major advances in medical diagnoses and treatments, the use of nuclear energy, and the designing of nuclear weapons. Do you consider radioactivity to be helpful or harmful? It's certainly easy to see why some uses of radiation and nuclear energy are so controversial. Look around the room. Can you detect any evidence of radioactivity? Did you know there are small amounts of radioactivity all around you? You can't see, hear, taste, touch, or smell it. You even have small amounts of radioactivity inside your body.

You may wonder how radiation was first discovered if it can't be detected by your senses. Henri Bequerel accidentally discovered radioactivity in 1896 when he left some uranium salt in a desk drawer with a photographic plate. When he later removed the plate and developed it, he found an outline of the uranium salt. He hypothesized that the uranium had given off some invisible energy and exposed the film. This process is called radiation, and the particles given off by the uranium are sometimes referred to as "radiation." Marie Curie and her husband Pierre took interest in Bequerel's discovery. They began looking for other radioactive elements in a uranium ore called pitchblende. Two years after

Figure 24-1. Many smoke detectors, such as this one, contain a small amount of a radioactive element.

OPTIONS

Meeting Different Ability Levels
For Section 24-1, use the following **Teacher Resource Masters** depending upon individual students' needs.

◆ **Study Guide Master** for all students.

● **Reinforcement Master** for students of average and above average ability levels.

▲ **Enrichment Master** for above average students.

Additional Teacher Resource Package masters are listed in the OPTIONS box throughout the section. The additional masters are appropriate for all students.

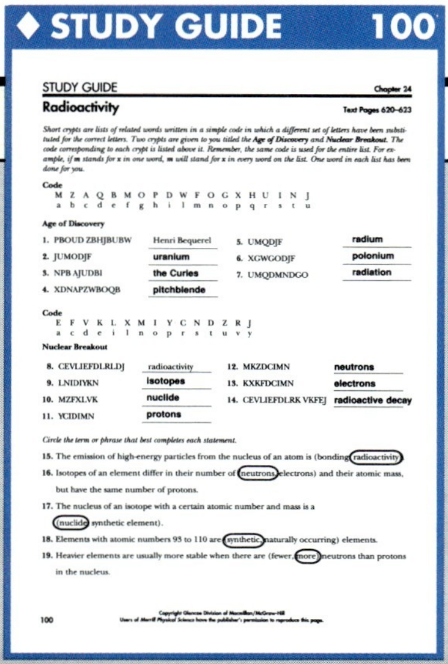

◆ STUDY GUIDE 100

STUDY GUIDE   Chapter 24
Radioactivity   Text Pages 620-623

Short crypts are lists of related words written in a simple code in which a different set of letters have been substituted for the correct letters. Two crypts are given to you titled the Age of Discovery and Nuclear Breakout. The code corresponding to each crypt is listed above it. Remember, the same code is used for the entire list. For example, if m stands for x in one word, m will stand for x in every word on the list. One word in each list has been done for you.

Code
M Z A Q B M O P D W F O G X H U I N J
a b c d e f g h i l m n o p q r s t u

Age of Discovery
1. PBOUD ZBHJBUBW   Henri Bequerel   5. UMQDJF   **radium**
2. JUMODJF   **uranium**   6. XGWGODJF   **polonium**
3. NPB AJUDBI   the Curies   7. UMQDMNDGO   **radiation**
4. XDNAPZWBOQB   pitchblende

Code
E F V K L X M I Y C N D Z R J
a c d e i l n o p r s t u v y

Nuclear Breakout
8. CEVLIEFDLRLDJ   radioactivity   12. MKZDCIMN   **neutrons**
9. LNIDYKN   **isotopes**   13. KXKFDCIMN   **electrons**
10. MZFXLVK   **nuclide**   14. CEVLIEFDLRK VKFEJ   radioactive decay
11. YCJDIMN   **protons**

Circle the term or phrase that best completes each statement.
15. The emission of high-energy particles from the nucleus of an atom is (bonding, radioactivity)
16. Isotopes of an element differ in their number of (neutrons, electrons) and their atomic mass, but have the same number of protons.
17. The nucleus of an isotope with a certain atomic number and mass is a (nuclide, synthetic element).
18. Elements with atomic numbers 95 to 110 are (synthetic, naturally occurring) elements.
19. Heavier elements are usually more stable when there are (fewer, more) neutrons than protons in the nucleus.

Copyright Glencoe Division of Macmillan/McGraw-Hill
Users of Merrill Physical Science have the publisher's permission to reproduce this page.
100

Bequerel's discovery, they discovered the elements polonium and radium. These elements are even more radioactive than uranium.

Notice where these three elements are found on the periodic table. These elements all have high atomic numbers and therefore are located near the bottom of the chart. All elements that have an atomic number greater than 83 are radioactive. Some other elements are also radioactive.

You know that all elements are made of atoms, and that atoms are made up of protons, neutrons, and electrons. The protons and neutrons are held together in the nucleus by what scientists call the strong force. This force is strong enough to prevent the positive protons from pushing each other out of the nucleus of the atom; however, this force is very short range and only acts across very small distances. As a result, those elements with high atomic numbers—many protons and neutrons—are held together less securely than, say, an oxygen atom. Particles or energy can escape from all nuclei with atomic numbers of 84 or higher. This process is called radioactive decay. These nuclei are considered to be unstable. **Radioactivity,** therefore, is the emission of high energy radiation or particles from the nucleus of a radioactive atom.

Find the elements with atomic numbers 93 to 110 on the periodic table. Elements with these atomic numbers don't exist naturally on Earth. They have been produced in labs and are called synthetic elements. All these synthetic elements are very unstable. Why might these elements be difficult to study?

Nuclides

Recall that most elements have isotopes. Isotopes of an element differ in their number of neutrons and in their atomic mass, but they have the same number of protons. Some isotopes are radioactive and others are not. Why is this so? The nucleus of an isotope with a certain atomic number and mass is called a **nuclide.** In many nuclides, the strong force is enough to keep the nucleus permanently together, creating a stable nuclide. However, the strong force is not sufficient to hold unstable nuclides together permanently. These unstable nuclides are radioactive because they decay to give off matter and energy.

24-1 RADIOACTIVITY 621

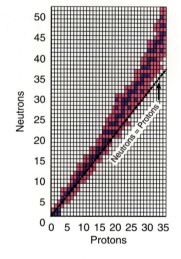

Figure 24-2. Elements with low atomic numbers have stable nuclides when the numbers of protons and neutrons are close.

— stable nuclides

— unstable nuclides

MINI-Lab
Does radiation change film?
Radiation was discovered as a result of placing a radioactive source near a photographic plate. Today, some workers that are in danger of being exposed to radiation wear photographic film badges. Obtain one of these badges or some undeveloped film and a weak source of radiation. Place the source near the film or badge for ten minutes and observe the film. Describe the changes you observed.

TEACHER F.Y.I.
► X rays were actually discovered by Wilhelm Roentgen several months before the phenomenon of radioactivity was discovered in 1896 by Henri Bequerel.

MINI-Lab
Materials: a photographic film badge or some undeveloped film; a weak radioactive source, such as a small sample of uranium ore or pitchblende
Teaching Tips
Depending on the strength of the source, it may be necessary to leave the sample in contact with the film for several hours.
Answers: The appearance of the film should change with exposure to radiation. If the source is placed directly on top of the film, its image should be detectable in the film.

2 TEACH

Key Concepts are highlighted.

CONCEPT DEVELOPMENT
► Be sure students can identify the portion of the periodic table where the synthetic elements are found. They should see the tendency for larger nuclei to be less stable.

REVEALING MISCONCEPTIONS
► Many people have been given the impression (in movies, especially) that radioactive materials glow. Energy is given off, but not in the form of visible light. Radiation can, however, induce fluorescence in some materials. Radioactive material is not distinguishable by its appearance.

STUDENT TEXT QUESTION
► Page 621, paragraph 4: **Why might synthetic elements be difficult to study?** *Their nuclei decay, and they change into different elements rapidly.*

PROGRAM RESOURCES
From the **Teacher Resource Package** use:
Activity Worksheets, page 199, Mini-Lab: Does radiation change film?

▶To find out more about super atom smashers, see "The World's Biggest Machine" by Arthur Fisher, *Popular Science*, June 1987, pp. 56-57.

Think Critically: The force is needed to overcome the strong force in the atomic nucleus, so it will split. It will help us to learn more about the particles and forces in nature.

CONCEPT DEVELOPMENT

▶ Emphasize that isotopes differ in atomic mass and nuclear stability, but not in nuclear charge. Ask students why the atomic masses listed on the periodic table are not whole numbers. They may remember that the mass listed is the average of all isotopes and their respective amounts.

CHECK FOR UNDERSTANDING

Place the following representations of nuclides on the chalkboard. Have students list the separate elements present and specify which ones are isotopes.

$^{234}_{91}Pa$ $^{214}_{82}Pb$ $^{214}_{83}Bi$ $^{214}_{84}Po$ $^{210}_{82}Pb$

$^{210}_{83}Bi$ $^{206}_{82}Pb$ $^{210}_{84}Po$ $^{218}_{85}At$

RETEACH

Write each of the above nuclides on a piece of paper and have a student hold each one. Instruct them to find other nuclides that have the same atomic number. Some may be left alone. Emphasize that the groups represent different isotopes of the same element.

EXTENSION

For students who have mastered this section, use the **Reinforcement** and **Enrichment** masters or other OPTIONS provided.

CROSS CURRICULUM

▶ **Geography:** U-235 is used as the energy resource in nuclear fission reactors. Research the locations in the world which have rich reserves of uranium, especially this U-235 isotope.

Super Atom Smasher

Probing the structure of the nucleus is a difficult task. As a result, construction of the largest and most expensive scientific instrument ever produced is under way. This instrument, called the superconducting super collider—or SSC—will improve our understanding of nuclear structure. The SSC is a particle accelerator that is designed to smash atomic particles together to produce a shower of basic particles that will provide clues to nuclear structure.

The SSC will be able to smash particles together in a way that is 20 times more powerful than any existing accelerator. Two beams of protons will accelerate in opposite directions around a 53-mile racetrack-shaped vacuum chamber. The proton beams will be guided by 10 000 superconducting magnets. As the beams approach the speed of light, they will smash together, creating new particles.

The SSC may help scientists answer questions about the structure of matter that are so fundamental that many other fields will benefit. A totally new and unexpected understanding of the laws of nature may emerge from the knowledge gained from the SSC.

Think Critically: Why do you think the proton beams need to be smashed with such great force? How will this help us learn more about matter?

What isotopes are unstable?

Isotopes of elements differ in the ratio of neutrons to protons. This ratio affects the stability of the nucleus. An isotope of a less massive element is stable if the ratio is about 1 to 1. An isotope of a heavier element is stable when the ratio of neutrons to protons is about 3 to 2. However, the nuclei of isotopes of both lighter and heavier elements that differ much from these ratios are unstable. That is, nuclei with too many or too few neutrons are radioactive.

How can you distinguish one isotope from another of the same element? A nuclide can be represented by a symbol that gives the atomic number, mass number, and element symbol. You know the atomic number is the same as the number of protons in the element, and the mass

OPTIONS

INQUIRY QUESTIONS

▶ Nucleons are particles found in the nucleus of an atom. Which of the following particles would be considered nucleons—protons, electrons, neutrons? *protons and neutrons*

▶ What makes the unstable synthetic elements difficult to study? *Many isotopes of the synthetic elements have very short half-lives, making it difficult to run any tests before they decay. They are artificially made, so it is hard to make more than a tiny sample.*

PROGRAM RESOURCES

Use **Laboratory Manual,** The Effect of Radiation on Seeds.

Table 24-1

RADIOACTIVE NUCLIDES OF SOME ELEMENTS				
Element	Nuclide	Atomic mass number	Protons	Neutrons
Hydrogen	^3_1H	3	1	2
Helium	^5_2He	5	2	3
Lithium	^8_3Li	8	3	5
Carbon	$^{14}_6C$	14	6	8
Nitrogen	$^{16}_7N$	16	7	9
Potassium	$^{40}_{19}K$	40	19	21

number is the total number of protons and neutrons in the nucleus. The nucleus of the stable isotope of potassium is shown below.

$$\text{mass number} \rightarrow \quad {}^{39}_{19}K \leftarrow \text{element symbol}$$
$$\text{atomic number} \rightarrow$$

Now compare the stable isotope of potassium to the radioactive isotope below.

$$\text{mass number} \rightarrow \quad {}^{40}_{19}K \leftarrow \text{element symbol}$$
$$\text{atomic number} \rightarrow$$

The stable isotope is called potassium-39. This isotope has 19 protons and 20 neutrons. The radioactive isotope is potassium-40. How many neutrons does potassium-40 have?

SECTION REVIEW

1. Identify the contributions of the three scientists who discovered the first radioactive elements.
2. What is the range of atomic numbers in which all isotopes are radioactive? Which of these are synthetic?
3. **Apply:** What is the ratio of protons to neutrons in lead-214? Explain whether you would expect this isotope to be radioactive or stable.

☑ Comparing and Contrasting

Skill Builder

Compare and contrast stable and unstable isotopes of potassium. What do they have in common? How do they differ? If you need help, refer to Comparing and Contrasting in the **Skill Handbook** on page 679.

EcoTip

Radon is an odorless, colorless, radioactive gas that comes from underground rocks. Keep radon out of your house by sealing cracks in the basement floor and walls, and spaces around water pipes and drains.

▶Page 623, paragraph 3:

STUDENT TEXT QUESTION

▶Page 623, paragraph 3: **How many neutrons does potassium-40 have?** *21*

MINI QUIZ

Use the Mini Quiz to check students' recall of chapter content.

1. All elements that have atomic numbers greater than _____ are radioactive. *83*
2. **What is radioactivity?** *the emission of high energy radiation or particles from the nucleus of a radioactive atom*
3. **When are isotopes of heavier elements most stable?** *when they have a neutron to proton ratio of about 3 to 2*

3 CLOSE

▶Ask questions 1-2 and the **Apply** Question in the Section Review.
▶Have students list as many applications of nuclear physics, beneficial or destructive, that they can think of. Mention that they will be discussing many of these ideas throughout this chapter.

SECTION REVIEW ANSWERS

1. Bequerel found radioactivity was given off by uranium salt. Marie and Pierre Curie isolated polonium and radium from pitchblende.
2. Elements 84-110 are radioactive. Elements 93-110 are synthetic.
3. **Apply:** 82/132 = 0.62 It is likely to be radioactive because it has many more neutrons than protons. The ratio of protons to neutrons differs much from the 2 to 3 stable ratio for heavy elements.

Skill Builder

The stable and unstable isotopes of potassium listed above have the same number of protons and the same number of electrons. However, the unstable isotope of potassium has a higher mass number because it has one more neutron than the stable nuclide.

INQUIRY QUESTIONS

▶**One isotope of uranium, U-238, has a half-life of 4.5 billion years. Use a periodic chart to find the atomic number and calculate how many neutrons the isotope has.** *238 – 92 protons = 146 neutrons*
▶**Explain the structural similarities and differences between U-238 and U-235.** *They are both isotopes of uranium and each has 92 protons in the nucleus. U-238 has three more neutrons than U-235.*

PREPARATION

SECTION BACKGROUND
▶ Both alpha and beta particles cause transmutation because the nucleus loses or gains protons, causing a change in atomic number. Emitting gamma radiation does not change the identity of a nuclide.

PREPLANNING
▶ Obtain stoppers and graph paper for Activity 24-1.

1 MOTIVATE

▶ Have an expedition to prospect for "uranium ore." Conceal a radioactive source inside a glass container somewhere in the classroom. Have teams of students use a Geiger counter to track down the location of the sample. Change the hiding place for each team. **CAUTION:** *Do not allow students to touch the radioactive source. Handle all radioactive materials with care. Note the precautions on the manufacturers label. Demonstrate proper safety techniques for students even if the source is weak.*

TYING TO PREVIOUS
KNOWLEDGE: Ask the students to recall their study of electromagnetic radiation. What were the most energetic kinds of electromagnetic radiation? Gamma radiation has the highest frequency and shortest wavelength. Explain that this is one kind of radiation emitted during radioactive decay.

OBJECTIVES AND
SCIENCE WORDS: Have students review the objectives and science words to become familiar with this section.

24-2 Nuclear Decay

New Science Words
alpha particles
transmutation
beta particle
gamma rays
half-life

Objectives
▶ Distinguish between alpha, beta, and gamma radiation.
▶ Calculate the amount of a radioactive substance remaining after a time based on its half-life.
▶ Relate half-life to the process of radioactive dating.

Nuclear Radiation

You've heard the terms *radiation* and *radioactive* ever since you were a young child. Maybe you didn't know what these words meant then, but now you know they refer to unstable, radioactive nuclei that emit radiation composed of small particles or energy. There are three main types of nuclear radiation—alpha, beta, and gamma radiation. Figure 24-3 shows the path that each type of nuclear radiation follows as it moves through a magnetic field. As you can see, each type of radiation is affected differently. Which type of radiation is most affected by a magnetic field?

Radiation in the form of **alpha particles** is given off when a nucleus releases two protons and two neutrons. Notice that the alpha particle is the same as a helium nucleus, as shown in Table 24-2. An alpha particle has a charge of +2 and an atomic mass of 4. It is the largest and slowest form of radiation, so it is also the least penetrat-

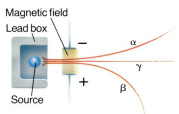

Figure 24-3. Notice how alpha and beta particles are deflected by a magnetic field.

Table 24-2

THREE TYPES OF NUCLEAR RADIATION				
Type	Symbol	Charge	Mass	Can be stopped by
alpha	He	+2	4	Paper
beta	e	–1	0	Aluminum
gamma	none	none	0	Lead or concrete

OPTIONS

Meeting Different Ability Levels
For Section 24-2, use the following **Teacher Resource Masters** depending upon individual students' needs.
◆ **Study Guide Master** for all students.
● **Reinforcement Master** for students of average and above average ability levels.
▲ **Enrichment Master** for above average students.
Additional Teacher Resource Package masters are listed in the OPTIONS box throughout the section. The additional masters are appropriate for all students.

◆ **STUDY GUIDE** 101

STUDY GUIDE   Chapter 24
Nuclear Decay   Text Pages 624–629

Use the clues and the letters in the boxes to identify the term that best fits each description. Write one letter in each space.

1. G A M M A R A Y S
2. H E L I U M
3. B E T A P A R T I C L E
4. T R A N S M U T A T I O N
5. H A L F - L I F E
6. P O S I T R O N

Clues
1. radiation in the form of electromagnetic waves (2 words)
2. An alpha particle is the same as the nucleus of this element.
3. negative electron emitted from the nucleus of an atom at a high speed (2 words)
4. process of changing one element to another through nuclear decay
5. time it takes for half the nuclides in a radioactive sample to decay
6. positively charged electron that is also a beta particle

ing. Alpha particles can be stopped by a sheet of paper, but they can be deadly if they are released by atoms inside your body.

The smoke detector mentioned earlier in this chapter gives off alpha particles that ionize the surrounding air. An electric current flows through the ionized air, but the circuit is broken when smoke particles enter the ionized air. When the circuit is broken, the alarm is set off.

3 Isotopes that give off alpha or beta particles undergo transmutation. **Transmutation** is the process of changing one element to another through nuclear decay. The nuclear equation below shows a nuclear transmutation. Because two protons are lost from the nucleus in alpha decay, the new element formed has an atomic number two less than that of the original element. The atomic mass number of the new element is four less than the original element. In a transmutation, the atomic mass number of the decayed nuclide equals the sum of the mass numbers of the newly formed nuclide and the emitted particle.

$$^{218}_{84}\text{Po} \longrightarrow {}^{214}_{82}\text{Pb} + {}^{4}_{2}\text{He}$$

2 Sometimes a neutron inside a nucleus decays spontaneously into a proton and an electron. The electron is emitted from the nucleus at very high speed and is called a **beta particle**. The proton formed by the decaying neutron stays in the nucleus, forming an element with an atomic number one greater than the original element. Because the beta particle has such a tiny mass, the atomic mass number of the new element is the same as that of the original element. A proton can also decay into a neutron and a positron. A positron is similar to an electron, but has a positive charge. Positrons are also considered to be beta particles. In a transmutation, the charge of the original nuclide equals the sum of the charges of the nuclide and particle formed, as shown in the equation below.

$$^{214}_{82}\text{Pb} \longrightarrow {}^{214}_{83}\text{Bi} + {}^{0}_{-1}\text{e}$$

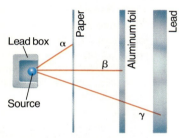

Figure 24-4. Alpha particles can be stopped by paper, beta particles by aluminum foil, and gamma rays by lead.

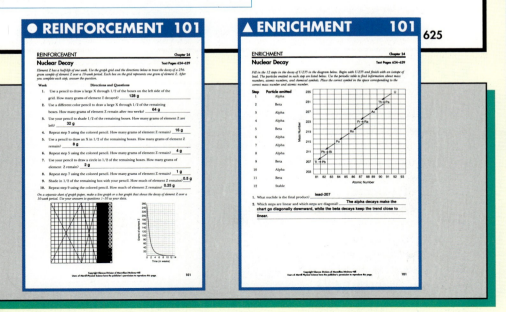

CONCEPT DEVELOPMENT

▶ In class discussions, use the Greek letters as symbols for alpha (α), beta (β), and gamma (γ) radiation.

CHECK FOR UNDERSTANDING

Ask students why fallout shelters would be needed following a nuclear attack. Ask what type of radiation would pose the greatest risk to people who stayed in their own houses. Most alpha and beta particles would be stopped by the materials used to build a typical house, but gamma radiation requires a thick slab of material such as lead or concrete to stop penetration.

RETEACH

Emphasize that the relatively big size and double positive charge of alpha particles makes them easily captured by other atoms or molecules. Beta particles, or electrons, are many times smaller, but they still have a charge. This charge causes attractions and repulsions with other particles. Gamma radiation has no mass or charge, so it is difficult to interact with and slow down.

EXTENSION

For students who have mastered this section, use the **Reinforcement** and **Enrichment** masters or other OPTIONS provided.

Science and MATH

One percent is 0.01 or 1/100. The easiest approach is to have students write the series 1, 1/2, 1/4, 1/8, 1/16, 1/32, 1/64, 1/128 and count the number of half-lives that have passed when the fraction becomes less than 1/100. One half life passes in the interval between fractions. Students should count 7 half-lives, 196 years.

PROBLEM SOLVING

▶The radioactive decay of the radium releases energy, causing the phosphors to emit tiny flashes of light that make the hands of the clock appear to glow.
Think Critically: As the radium decays, it releases less energy to excite the phosphor.

 Beta particles are much faster and more penetrating than alpha particles. However, they can be stopped by a sheet of aluminum foil.

The most penetrating and potentially dangerous form of radiation is not made of particles at all. **Gamma rays** are electromagnetic waves with very high frequency and energy. They have no mass, no charge, and they travel at the speed of light. They are usually released along with alpha or beta particles. Gamma rays are the most penetrating form of radiation, and thick blocks of materials with dense nuclei are required to stop them. Lead and concrete are commonly used barriers for gamma rays. Compare the symbols and the relative penetrating powers of the three kinds of radiation shown in Table 24-2.

Science and MATH

How long does it take for strontium-90, with a half-life of 28 years, to be reduced to less than one percent of its rate of decay?

Half-life

Safe disposal of a some radioisotopes is not a problem because their nuclides decay to stable nuclides in less than a second. However, nuclides of other radioactive isotopes may require millions of years to decay. A mea-

PROBLEM SOLVING

The Radioactive Clock

Kristine had a difficult time waking up for school. Her mother had to call to her to wake her up several times each morning.

Kristine found an old alarm clock in the attic. Now she can wake up without her mother calling her.

During the night Kristine awoke. She was startled by a greenish-white glow next to her bed. Then she realized that the glow was coming from the hands of the alarm clock. She wondered what caused the hands to glow.

The next day, she did some research in the school library and found that the hands of the clock were coated with a paint containing radium and zinc sulfide. The zinc sulfide emits little flashes of light when excited by radiation. These tiny flashes of light make the hands of the clock appear to glow. Why does the zinc sulfide in the paint appear to glow?

Think Critically: Explain why the glow of the hands will become dimmer over time.

OPTIONS

INQUIRY QUESTIONS

▶**When thorium-230 undergoes alpha decay, what nuclide is formed?** *radium-226, which has two fewer protons and two fewer neutrons than Th-230*

▶**When lead-210 undergoes beta decay, what nuclide is formed?** *bismuth-210, which has one more proton and one fewer neutron after the first emission of an electron from the nucleus*

▶**If a beta particle is actually a particle, why does the mass number stay the same after beta decay?** *The mass of the electron given off is very small compared to the mass of protons and neutrons, so the mass change can be considered insignificant.*

sure of the time required by the nuclides of an isotope to decay is called half-life. The **half-life** of an isotope is the amount of time it takes for half the nuclides in a sample of a given radioactive isotope to decay. Half-lives vary widely among the radioactive isotopes. For example, polonium-214 has a half-life of about a thousandth of a second; but uranium-238 has a half-life of 4.5 billion years.

You can determine the amount of a radioactive sample that will remain after a given amount of time if you know the half-life of the sample. The half-lives of some radioactive elements are listed in Table 24-3. Look at the problem below to see how to calculate the amount of remaining sodium-24, which has a half-life of 15 hours.

Table 24-3

SAMPLE HALF-LIVES	
Isotope	Half-life
$^{3}_{1}H$	12.3 years
$^{14}_{6}C$	5730 years
$^{131}_{53}I$	8.07 days
$^{212}_{82}Pb$	10.6 hours
$^{194}_{84}Po$	0.7 second
$^{235}_{92}U$	7.1×10^{8} years

EXAMPLE PROBLEM: Calculating the Quantity of a Radioactive Element

Problem Statement: How much of a 20-g sample of sodium-24 would remain after decaying for 15 hours?

Known Information:
Strategy Hint: Find the half-life of sodium-24 above.

Amount of original sample of sodium-24 = 20 g
Time elapsed = 15 hours
Half-life of sodium-24 = 15 hours

Unknown Information: amount of remaining sodium-24

Equation to Use:

$$\text{amount remaining} = \frac{\text{amount of original sample}}{2^{n}}$$

n = number of half-lives elapsed

Solution:

$$\frac{20 \text{ g}}{2^{1}} = \frac{20 \text{ g}}{2} = 10 \text{ g}$$

PRACTICE PROBLEM

Strategy Hint: Determine how many half-lives of sodium-24 elapse in 45 hours.

1. How much of a 20-g sample of sodium-24 would remain after 45 hours?

Radioactive Dating

It was mentioned earlier that you have some radioactive materials inside your body. One of these is a radioactive isotope of carbon, carbon-14. This isotope is in some of the carbon dioxide molecules plants take in as they respire. As a result, you have carbon-14 inside of you from the plants and animals you eat. Carbon-14 emits a beta particle and decays into nitrogen.

TEACHER F.Y.I.

▶Note that the rate of radioactive decay is nearly impossible to change. Attempts to change this rate by altering temperature and pressure conditions, other chemical reactions, or exposure to electric and magnetic fields have been unsuccessful.

CONCEPT DEVELOPMENT

▶Give each person in the class a penny. Have students all toss their coins once, representing one half-life. Announce that all who had tails have now decayed and must move to the back of the room. Count the remaining students (about half) and record it on the chalkboard. Repeat this process until no students remain. Note that this is a random process, because you cannot tell when a specific student will decay. The same is true for atoms. The results can be graphed to show the exponential nuclear decay.
▶The mathematical relationship that involves half-life patterns can be used to determine the half-life by measuring the change in radioactive sample size over an known time interval.

TEACHER F.Y.I.

▶Radiocarbon dating was developed in the 1940s by Willard Libby. Cosmic rays from space interact with atoms in Earth's atmosphere and liberate neutrons. The presence of carbon-14 in our atmosphere results from neutron bombardment of nitrogen, which causes a proton to be emitted:

$$^{1}_{0}n + {}^{14}_{7}N \rightarrow {}^{14}_{6}C + {}^{1}_{1}H$$

PRACTICE PROBLEM ANSWER

1. Amount of original sample = 20 g
   Time Elapsed = 45 hours
   Half-life of sodium 24 = 15 hours
   n = number of half-lives elapsed
   n = 3
   Equation: Amount Remaining =
   $$\frac{\text{Amount of Original}}{2^{n}}$$
   Amount Remaining = $\frac{20 \text{ g}}{2^{3}}$
   = 2.5 g

INQUIRY QUESTIONS

▶The half-life of Ra-226 is 1620 years. Predict how much of a 10 g sample will be left after 1620 years. After 3240 years. *5 g; 2.5 g*
▶How can we know the half-life of U-238 if it has a half-life of 4.5 billion years? That is the approximate age of Earth, and humans have only existed a small fraction of that time. *By looking at decay rates during known amounts of time, mathematical relationships allow us to calculate the actual half-life.*

▶**Archaeology:** Have students do research to learn how radioactive dating has been used to determine the ages of artifacts found in archeological digs.

Use the Mini Quiz to check students' recall of chapter content.

❶ **What kind of radiation is identical to a helium nucleus?** *alpha particles*

❷ **Arrange three kinds of nuclear radiation in order of increasing penetrating power.** *alpha particles, beta particles, gamma rays*

❸ **What is transmutation?** *the process by which one element changes to another by nuclear decay involving alpha or beta particles*

❹ **What isotope is used in radioactive dating?** *carbon-14*

3 CLOSE

▶Ask questions 1-3 and the **Apply** Question in the Section Review.

SECTION REVIEW ANSWERS

1. Alpha particles, helium nuclei, are the least penetrating, and can be stopped by paper. Beta particles are electrons, and can be stopped by aluminum foil. Gamma rays are the most penetrating kind of neclear radiation, and are stopped by lead or concrete.

2. $^{222}_{86}Rn \rightarrow {}^{218}_{84}Po + {}^{4}_{2}He$; polonium

3. 20 g; 10 g; 5 g

4. Apply: Yes. In beta decay, a neutron decays into an electron and a proton. The new proton increases the atomic number of the element by one.

Skill Builder

The gamma ray has no charge and will not be affected by the magnetic field. The oppositely charged alpha and beta particles will be deflected in opposite directions.

All living things contain a somewhat constant amount of carbon-14. Decaying carbon-14 is constantly replaced by new carbon-14 in a living organism, but when the organism dies, its carbon-14 decays without replacement. The half-life of carbon-14 is 5730 years. ==By measuring the amount of carbon-14 remaining in a fossil or skeleton, scientists can determine the approximate age of the material. This process is called carbon-14 dating.==

How does the age of a rock compare with fossils in it?

Do you think carbon-14 dating could be used to determine the age of a dinosaur skeleton? No, it wouldn't work, because the last dinosaur species died out well over 50 million years ago. Only remains of plants and animals that lived within the last 50 000 years contain enough carbon-14 to measure.

You may wonder how the ages of fossils more than 50 000 years old and rocks can be determined. If the rock contains some amount of a radioactive element, such as uranium-238 with a half-life of 4.5 billion years, the time of the rock's formation can be determined. If the rock contains fossils, it is assumed that the age of the fossils is the same as that of the rock.

SECTION REVIEW

1. Describe each of the three types of radiation and compare their penetrating power.
2. Write a nuclear equation to show how radon-222 decays to give off an alpha particle and another element. What is the other element?
3. The half-life of iodine-131 is about eight days. How much of a 40-g sample will be left after eight days? After 16 days? After 32 days?
4. **Apply:** Is it possible for an isotope to decay to an element with a higher atomic number? Explain.

Skill Builder ☑ Interpreting Scientific Illustrations

Use Figure 24-3 on page 624 to explain why the alpha particle appears to curve up, the beta particle curves down, and the gamma particle travels straight through the magnet. If you need help, refer to Interpreting Scientific Illustrations in the **Skill Handbook** on page 689.

628 RADIOACTIVITY AND NUCLEAR REACTIONS

OPTIONS

INQUIRY QUESTIONS

▶**A new bone sample contains more C-14 than an old bone sample of the same size. Explain this pattern.** *Since C-14 is radioactive, some of the C-14 in the old bone sample will already have decayed. This makes the level less in the old bone than in the new bone.*

▶**Could the carbon dating method be useful in dating old iron utensils? Explain why or why not.** *No. The iron utensils do not contain C-14.*

PROGRAM RESOURCES

Use **Laboratory Manual,** Radioactive Decay—A Simulation.

ACTIVITY 24-1
Half-life

Problem: *What is a half-life?*

Materials
- rubber stopper
- graph paper

Procedure
1. Copy the data table.
2. Hold a rubber stopper and stand an equal distance from nearby classmates.
3. When the teacher says "go," *gently* toss your stopper to a nearby student and catch the stopper tossed to you.
4. If you drop the stopper, *don't* pick it up.
5. If you catch the stopper, immediately toss it to someone other than the person who threw it to you.
6. When the teacher says "stop," hold your stopper up. Count the stoppers that are held up and record the number on your data table.
7. Repeat Steps 3 through 6 for three more time intervals.
8. Plot the data from the table on a graph. Connect the points with a smooth curve.

Data and Observations Sample Data

Interval	Total Time	Atoms Remaining
0	0 sec	32
1	5 sec	12
2	10 sec	5
3	15 sec	3
4	20 sec	2

Analyze
1. Assume each stopper is an atom of a radioactive element. The stoppers that hit the floor represent atoms that have changed into another element. During which time interval were most of the "atoms" changed?
2. Were all the "atoms" changed during the experiment? If not, how long do you think it would take for all of them to change?
3. According to your graph, how long did it take for half the atoms to change? How many atoms changed in twice that amount of time?

Conclude and Apply
4. According to your graph, if 20 stoppers are still "unchanged," how many seconds ago did the class start throwing stoppers?
5. What would the half-life curve look like for a class of 40 students if the half-life time was the same as for your class?

24-2 NUCLEAR DECAY **629**

ACTIVITY 24-1
20 minutes

OBJECTIVE: **Construct a graph** from half-life data and use it to **describe** the event.

PROCESS SKILLS applied in this activity:
▶ **Predicting** in Conclude and Apply Question 5.
▶ **Interpreting** in Analyze Questions 1-3.
▶ **Formulating Models** in Procedure Steps 1-8.

COOPERATIVE LEARNING
Use Problem Solving Teams to graph and interpret data.

TEACHING THE ACTIVITY
Alternate Materials: Any kind of small, soft, unbreakable objects could be used. Each student should have one object.

Troubleshooting: Over half the stoppers will most likely be dropped in the first five seconds. After 15 seconds, individual student skill begins to override random dropping and the half-life model is less representative.
▶ Emphasize that students should try to help others catch the stopper, not make them miss.
▶ Time intervals of 5 seconds work well, but other intervals could be used. Adjust the time according to the ability level of students.
▶ Emphasize that a student who drops a stopper is not "out" and can still be thrown to.

PROGRAM RESOURCES
From the **Teacher Resource Package** use:

Activity Worksheets, pages 193-194, Activity 24-1: Half-life.

ANSWERS TO QUESTIONS
The following answers are based on sample data. Answers from your class will vary according to results.
1. Most atoms changed during the first time interval.
2. Not all atoms changed. It is not possible to predict the change of the last atom.
3. Half the atoms changed in about four seconds. Eight atoms would remain after two half-lives.
4. The throwing between two and 3 seconds ago.

5. The curve would have the same shape but the data points would have higher values.

PREPARATION

SECTION BACKGROUND

►There are several units for measuring radiation. Some are based on the number of disintegrations per second, such as the curie and the bequerel (the SI unit). Others, such as the roentgen, the rad, and the gray (SI unit), measure the effect the radiation has on the absorbing material. Biological damage is most effectively measured by a unit called a rem.

1 MOTIVATE

►Bring in a smoke detector that uses americium-241. Light some flash paper, a candle, or other smoke-producing material to produce a controlled amount of smoke. Direct the smoke toward the smoke detector to make it go off. Explain that the radioactive material present ionizes the air around it permitting an electric current to travel through the air. The smoke interrupts this path and triggers the alarm.

TYING TO PREVIOUS
KNOWLEDGE: Point out that moving charged particles can ionize nearby neutral particles. This is what makes radiation so dangerous. This fact also makes it possible for us to detect radiation.

OBJECTIVES AND
SCIENCE WORDS: Have students review the objectives and science words to become familiar with this section.

PROGRAM RESOURCES

From the **Teacher Resource Package** use:

Activity Worksheets, page 200, Mini-Lab: What senses atomic radiation?

Critical Thinking/Problem Solving, page 30, Radon.

▌24-3 Detecting Radioactivity

New Science Words

cloud chamber
bubble chamber

Objectives

► Describe how radioactivity can be detected.
► Explain how a Geiger counter can determine the quantity of nuclear radiation present.

Radiation Detectors

Because you can't feel a single proton or gamma ray, you must use instruments to detect their presence. Methods of detecting radioactivity depend on radiation forming ions by removing electrons from matter it passes through. The newly formed ions can be detected in several ways.

Have you ever seen clouds formed in a cloud chamber? **A cloud chamber can be used to detect charged nuclear particles as they leave cloud tracks.** It contains supersaturated water or ethanol vapor. When a charged particle from a radioactive sample moves through the chamber, it leaves a path of ions behind as it knocks electrons off the atoms in the air. The vapor condenses around these ions to provide a visible path of droplets along the track of the particle. Do you think the trail of a beta particle might differ from the trail of an alpha particle? Beta particles leave long, thin trails, and alpha particles leave shorter and thicker trails.

How does a cloud chamber detect nuclear particles?

Figure 24-5. A cloud chamber is a device used to detect particles of nuclear radiation.

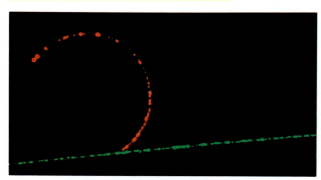

OPTIONS

Meeting Different Ability Levels

For Section 24-3, use the following **Teacher Resource Masters** depending upon individual students' needs.

◆ **Study Guide Master** for all students.

● **Reinforcement Master** for students of average and above average ability levels.

▲ **Enrichment Master** for above average students.

Additional Teacher Resource Package masters are listed in the OPTIONS box throughout the section. The additional masters are appropriate for all students.

◆ **STUDY GUIDE** 102

STUDY GUIDE   Chapter 24
Detecting Radioactivity   Text Pages 630-632

Use the clues given below to identify terms related to radioactivity detection. Write each term in the space provided. Then, find and circle each term in the hidden word puzzle. The term may be written up, down, forward, backward, or diagonal.

	Clues
bubble chamber	1. uses lines of bubbles in a superheated liquid to track particles
cloud chamber	2. detects charged particles by the cloud tracks they leave
electroscope	3. device that detects electric charges
Geiger counter	4. device that produces clicking sounds or flashing light by amplifying an electric current formed when radiation is present
gamma ray	5. radiation that travels as waves
beta particle	6. a particle which leaves a long, thin trail in a cloud chamber
alpha particle	7. a particle which leaves a short, thick trail in a cloud chamber
radioactivity	8. emission of high-energy radiation or particles from the nucleus of a radioactive atom
nuclide	9. nucleus of an isotope with a certain atomic mass and number

102

Copyright Glencoe Division of Macmillan/McGraw-Hill
Users of Merrill Physical Science have the publisher's permission to reproduce this page.

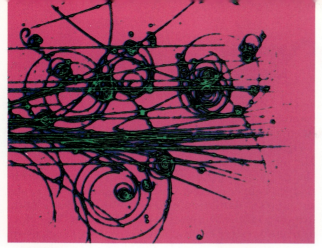

Figure 24-6. Particles of nuclear radiation can be detected as they leave trails of bubbles in a bubble chamber.

Another way to detect and monitor the paths of nuclear particles is by using a bubble chamber. A **bubble chamber** holds a superheated liquid, which doesn't boil even though it's hot enough. When a moving particle leaves ions behind, the liquid boils along the trail. The path shows up as tracks of bubbles.

Do you remember how an electroscope was used to detect electric charges in Chapter 21? When an electroscope is given a negative charge, the leaves repel each other and spread apart. They will remain apart until the extra electrons have somewhere to go and discharge the electroscope. A nuclear particle moving through the air will remove electrons from air molecules, leaving them positively charged. When this occurs near an electroscope, the positively charged air molecules will attract the electrons from the leaves. As these negatively charged leaves lose their charges, they no longer repel and move together again.

Counting Radioactivity

You constantly receive small doses of radiation from your environment. It is not known whether this radiation is harmful to your body tissues. Larger doses of radiation, however, can be harmful to living tissue. If you worked or lived in an environment that could result in exposure to high levels of radiation—a nuclear testing facility, for example—you might want to know exactly how much radiation you were being exposed to. The simplest

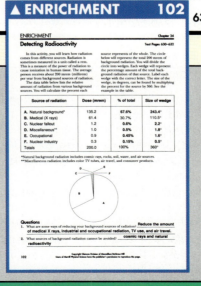

RETEACH

Review the reasons that an electroscope discharges and that a Geiger counter activates in the presence of radioactivity. Have students explain the operation of a Geiger counter by interpreting the diagram in Figure 24-7.

EXTENSION

For students who have mastered this section, use the **Reinforcement** and **Enrichment** masters or other OPTIONS provided.

CROSS CURRICULUM

▶**Occupational Safety:** Geiger counters are used at job sites to determine radiation levels. Find out how much additional radiation workers in a hospital radioassay lab or nuclear power plant would be exposed to.

3 CLOSE

▶Ask questions 1-2 and the **Apply** Question in the Section Review.

SECTION REVIEW ANSWERS

1. Geiger counter, cloud chamber, bubble chamber, electroscope, and photographic film
2. Radiation enters the tube, causing electrons to move from the gaseous atoms to the wire. This current is amplified and causes a speaker to click to count the radiation intensity.
3. Apply: A Geiger counter if it is small and portable; it can precisely measure the intensity of the radiation. A film badge would be more useful if the radiation level varied.

Skill Builder

Since alpha particles have a higher charge and lower penetrating power, they would most likely produce the shortest trails. Beta particles are much smaller and have higher penetrating ability, so they probably produced the long, thin trails.

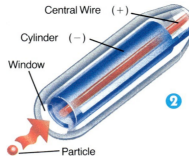

Central Wire (+)
Cylinder (−)
Window
Particle
Power supply
Capacitor
Resistor
Amplifier/Counter

Figure 24-7. A Geiger counter can be used to measure the intensity of nuclear radiation.

② method of counting radioactivity is to use a Geiger counter. A Geiger counter is a device that produces an electric current when radiation is present.

Figure 24-7 illustrates the parts of a Geiger counter. The tube is filled with gas at a low pressure. A positively charged wire runs through the center of a negatively charged copper cylinder. These are connected to a voltage source. Radiation enters the tube at one end, stripping electrons from the gaseous atoms. The electrons are attracted to the positive wire. They knock more electrons off the atoms in the gas and an "electron avalanche" is produced. A large number of electrons reach the wire, producing a short, intense current in the wire. This current is amplified to produce a clicking sound or flashing light. The intensity of radiation present is determined by the number of clicks in each second.

Geiger counters can be made very small and portable. They are often used to test the radioactivity at job sites where workers can be exposed to radioactive materials. For example, workers in a hospital radiation lab or at a nuclear power plant could actually wear small Geiger counters to monitor their exposures.

SECTION REVIEW

1. What are four ways radioactivity can be detected?
2. Explain the basic function of a Geiger counter.
3. **Apply:** Suppose you needed to check the level of radioactivity in the laboratory of a hospital. Which method would you use? Explain your choice.

Skill Builder   ☑ **Observing and Inferring**

Suppose that you are observing the presence of nuclear radiation with a bubble chamber. You see two kinds of trails. Some trails are short and others are long and thin. What type of nuclear radiation might have caused each trail? If you need help, refer to Observing and Inferring in the **Skill Handbook** on page 678.

OPTIONS

INQUIRY QUESTIONS

▶**Why can't a Geiger counter detect microwaves?** *A Geiger counter relies on incoming radiation to ionize the gaseous atoms present inside. Microwaves have relatively low energy and do not produce ionization.*

▶**If you were carrying a Geiger counter down the hall and suddenly heard more clicks, what would you suspect?** *You would suspect a source of radioactivity, perhaps in a room you walked by.*

▶**After U-235 undergoes nuclear fission, the mass of the products is less than the mass of the U-235 nucleus and bombarding neutron. Does this violate the law of conservation of mass? Explain.** *Yes. However, Einstein established the theory that the total amount of mass and energy in the universe was constant. This is stated as the law of conservation of mass-energy. In fission, a small amount of mass can be changed into a huge amount of energy.*

Nuclear Reactions 24-4

Objectives

▶ Distinguish between nuclear fission and fusion.
▶ Explain how nuclear fission can begin a chain reaction.
▶ Discuss how nuclear fusion occurs in the sun.

New Science Words

nuclear fission
chain reaction
nuclear fusion

Nuclear Fission

Have you ever played a game of pool? What happens when you shoot the cue ball into an area of densely packed balls? They split apart, or "break" the pack. In 1938, physicists Otto Hahn and Fritz Strassmann found that a similar result occurs when a neutron is shot into the large nucleus of a U-235 atom. Earlier, another physicist, Enrico Fermi, had tried to bombard large nuclei with neutrons in an effort to make larger nuclei than uranium. Splitting an atomic nucleus wasn't the expected outcome of this process.

Lise Meitner was the first to offer a theory to explain this process. She concluded that the neutron fired into the nucleus disturbs the already unstable nucleus and causes it to split into two nuclei of nearly equal mass. The process of splitting a nucleus into two nuclei with smaller masses is called **nuclear fission.** You may have heard of the fission that occurs in cells, or of fissures in the Earth's surface. In all of these cases, fission means to divide. Typically, large nuclei with atomic numbers above 90 can undergo nuclear fission.

In addition to splitting into two new nuclei, a fission reaction usually emits two or three individual neutrons as well. For example, the U-235 nucleus is easily split by bombarding it with a neutron. It forms a barium-141 nucleus and a krypton-92 nucleus and releases three neutrons.

$$^{1}_{0}n + ^{235}_{92}U \longrightarrow ^{141}_{56}Ba + ^{92}_{36}Kr + 3^{1}_{0}n$$

24-4 NUCLEAR REACTIONS **633**

Did You Know?

An estimated one million gallons of radioactive liquid will need to be disposed of daily by the year 2000.

①

What is nuclear fission?

Skill Builder

Answer to Skill Builder on page 635.

SECTION 24-4

PREPARATION

SECTION BACKGROUND

▶ Nuclear fission is often understood by modeling a nucleus such as U-235 as a liquid drop. When a neutron is absorbed into the nucleus the added internal energy causes it to take on an elongated form. The strong nuclear force is weakened over this increased distance, and the repulsive electric forces dominate. When this occurs, the nucleus splits into two fission fragments and several neutrons. The fission fragments are usually close, but not equal, in mass.

1 MOTIVATE

▶**Demonstration:** Model a chain reaction by setting up a fan of dominoes so that each domino will hit two others as it falls over. Or, fan out the matches from a fresh book of matches. Hold the matches vertically with metal tongs and ignite the match in the lower corner using another match.

TYING TO PREVIOUS KNOWLEDGE: To introduce this section, tie nuclear science to students' previous knowledge of the use of nuclear energy, especially in generating electricity and in nuclear bombs. Both processes give a hint about the tremendous amounts of energy involved in nuclear reactions.

OBJECTIVES AND SCIENCE WORDS: Have students review the objectives and science words to become familiar with this section.

Key Concepts are highlighted.

CONCEPT DEVELOPMENT

▶ Discuss the relationship between the principles of conservation of mass and conservation of energy for the students. Recall that Einstein said that mass and energy are interchangeable, and that the total amount of mass + energy in the universe is constant. Discuss the equation $E = mc^2$.

CROSS CURRICULUM

▶ **History:** Use resources of scientific history to make a time line of the discoveries and events that marked the beginning of the "nuclear age." Begin with the discovery of nuclear fission in 1938. Progress through the development of the atomic bomb and hydrogen bomb. Continue with the planning and construction of nuclear power plants.

PROGRAM RESOURCES

From the **Teacher Resource Package** use:

Cross-Curricular Connections, page 30, Survey on Nuclear Issues.

Transparency Masters, pages 95-96, Nuclear Chain Reaction.

Use **Color Transparency** 48, Nuclear Chain Reaction.

CHECK FOR UNDERSTANDING

Use the Mini Quiz to check for understanding.

MINI QUIZ

Use the Mini Quiz to check students' recall of chapter content.

❶ In nuclear reactors, the process used to release nuclear energy by splitting a U-235 nucleus into smaller fragments is called _____ . *nuclear fission*

❷ What occurs when the neutrons released in a fission reaction cause other nuclei to split? *a chain reaction*

❸ Describe the process that produces helium in the sun. *Hydrogen nuclei fuse to become a helium nucleus by the process of thermonuclear fusion.*

The total mass of the products is somewhat less than the mass of the U-235 nucleus and the neutron. This reaction releases a tremendous amount of energy because some of the mass has been converted to energy.

Do you think the energy released in the fission of a single nucleus would be dangerous? Probably not by itself. However, the three neutrons produced in the fission reaction can bombard other nuclei in the sample to split three more nuclei. These reactions will each release more neutrons, and so on. If there is not some stable material present to absorb these neutrons, a chain reaction may result. **A chain reaction is an ongoing series of fission reactions. This can cause billions of reactions to occur in each second, resulting in the release of tremendous amounts of energy.** In the next chapter, you will read about ways scientists control nuclear fission and use the energy to produce electricity.

What is a chain reaction?

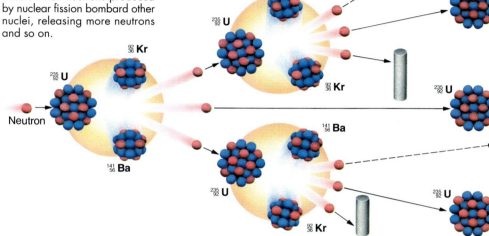

Figure 24-8. A chain reaction occurs when neutrons produced by nuclear fission bombard other nuclei, releasing more neutrons and so on.

Nuclear Fusion

You read in the last section how tremendous amounts of energy can be released in nuclear fission. In fact, splitting one U-235 nucleus produces several million times more energy than exploding one molecule of dynamite. Even more energy can be released in another type of nuclear reaction. This process is caused by the fusing together of nuclei, so it is the opposite of fission. **Nuclear fusion is the combining of two nuclei with low masses to**

OPTIONS

Meeting Different Ability Levels

For Section 24-4, use the following **Teacher Resource Masters** depending upon individual students' needs.

◆ **Study Guide Master** for all students.

● **Reinforcement Master** for students of average and above average ability levels.

▲ **Enrichment Master** for above average students.

Additional Teacher Resource Package masters are listed in the OPTIONS box throughout the section. The additional masters are appropriate for all students.

◆ **STUDY GUIDE** 103

STUDY GUIDE   Chapter 24
Nuclear Reactions   Text Pages 633-635

Match the terms in Column II with the definitions in Column I. Write the number of the correct term in the correct box in the grid. If you correctly complete the grid, the sum of numbers in each horizontal and vertical row will be the same. The first one is done for you.

Column I	Column II
___ A. emission of high-energy particles from the nucleus of a radioactive atom	1. isotope
___ B. ongoing series of fission reactions	2. uranium
___ C. amount of time it takes for 1/2 the amount in a radio-active atom to decay	3. alpha particle
___ D. uses tracks of bubbles to detect radiation	4. nuclide
___ E. combines two light nuclei to make an atom with a heavier nucleus	5. half-life
___ F. nucleus of an isotope with a certain atomic mass and number	6. electroscope
___ G. positively charged electron	7. transmutation
___ H. process of changing one element to another through nuclear decay	8. pitchblende
___ I. device that produces an electric current when radiation is present	9. beta particle
___ J. high-speed electron emitted from a nucleus	10. radioactivity
___ K. used to detect charged nuclear particles as they leave cloud tracks	11. cloud chamber
___ L. device used to detect electrical charges	12. bubble chamber
___ M. two protons and two neutrons	13. nuclear fission
___ N. process of splitting a nucleus into two nuclei with smaller masses	14. nuclear fusion
___ O. uranium ore	15. radium
___ P. electromagnetic waves with high-frequency energy	16. chain reaction
	17. Geiger counter
	18. gamma rays
	19. positron
	20. polonium

A	10	B	16	C	5	D	12	43
E	13	F	4	G	19	H	7	43
I	17	J	9	K	11	L	6	43
M	3	N	14	O	8	P	18	43
	43		43		43		43	

103

form one nucleus of larger mass. Nuclear fusion is difficult to induce in a controlled situation because extremely high temperatures are required for this process to occur.

These extremely high temperatures do exist in the stars, including the sun. The sun is a star of medium internal temperature, averaging about 20 million degrees Celsius. At these high temperatures, the atoms have so much kinetic energy that positive nuclei and electrons exist separately. Matter in this state is called plasma. This kind of fusion is called thermonuclear fusion, because such tremendous thermal conditions must exist.

When the sun first formed, most of its nuclei were hydrogen nuclei. As thermonuclear fusion occurs, four hydrogen nuclei are fused to become a helium nucleus. This process is still occurring, and about one percent of the mass of the sun's original nuclei is changed to energy and released in the form of electromagnetic radiation. As the star ages, the percentage of helium nuclei gradually increases and the amount of hydrogen nuclei decreases until there is no more for the reaction to occur. Scientists estimate that the sun has enough hydrogen to keep this reaction going for another five billion years.

As you will read in Chapter 25, scientists are searching for a way to induce and control nuclear fusion in the laboratory. If they achieve this goal in the future, many of our current energy problems will be solved. Can you think of other applications of nuclear fusion?

Science and READING

Find out what happens to the byproducts of fission-produced electricity.

 ③

SECTION REVIEW

1. Compare and contrast nuclear fission and fusion.
2. Why does a chain reaction often occur when a U-235 nucleus is split?
3. **Apply:** Account for the mass of the four hydrogen nuclei that undergo fusion to form a helium nucleus within the sun.

☑ Concept Mapping

Make a concept map to show how a chain reaction occurs when U-235 is bombarded with a neutron. Show how each of the three neutrons given as products begins another fission reaction. If you need help, refer to Concept Mapping in the **Skill Handbook** on pages 684 and 685.

Skill Builder

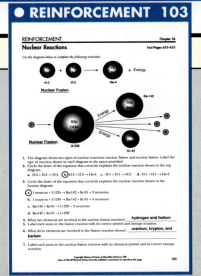

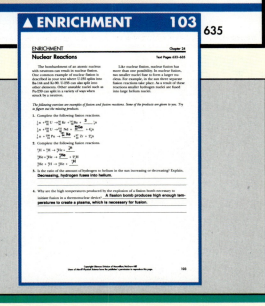

635

RETEACH
Cooperative Learning: Group students into Paired Partners for this activity. Contrast nuclear fusion and nuclear fission by using balls of clay as models. Give each pair a chunk of modeling clay. Have one student tell the other how to model fission with the clay and have him or her do it. For fission, bring a tiny piece of clay (neutron) into a large ball of clay. The student should split the ball of clay when the neutron strikes. Switch roles. For fusion, show how two small balls of clay can fuse to become a larger nucleus.

EXTENSION
For students who have mastered this section, use the **Reinforcement** and **Enrichment** masters or other OPTIONS provided.

Science and READING

Radioactive byproducts are used in medicine, food preservation, and industry. At present, we can use only a small fraction of the by-products. The remainder must be disposed of safely. This disposal is a problem.

3 CLOSE
▶Ask questions 1-2 and the **Apply** Question in the Section Review.

SECTION REVIEW ANSWERS
1. Fission is the splitting of large nuclei, and fusion is the joining of small nuclei. Both processes produce large amounts of energy.
2. It produces 3 neutrons, which can bombard and cause fission in other U-235 nuclei.
3. Apply: Most of the mass of the hydrogen nuclei forms the helium nucleus, however a small amount is converted to energy.

Skill Builder
Answered on page 633.

SCIENCE & SOCIETY

24-5 Nuclear Medicine

PREPARATION

SECTION BACKGROUND

▶ Cells that are immature or rapidly dividing are most susceptible to damage by radiation. For this reason, cancer cells can often be destroyed with radiotherapy. Infants and fetuses are more sensitive to ionizing radiation, as are reproductive organs where cells divide rapidly.

1 MOTIVATE

▶ Take a poll. How many students in your class remember having an X ray at the dentist or doctor's office? Explain that they will learn how radiation can help diagnose medical problems in the body and even cure some cancers.

TYING TO PREVIOUS KNOWLEDGE:
Remind students that a radioactive isotope decays at a constant rate. This is important in the use of radioactive isotopes for medical purposes. Different isotopes can be selected for long-term or short-term treatment depending on their half-lives.

OBJECTIVES AND SCIENCE WORDS:
Have students review the objectives and science word to become familiar with this section.

CONCEPT DEVELOPMENT

▶ Ask students why a tracer with a half-life of several hours would be very useful. Tracers should have relatively short half-lives (several hours) so they continually emit an amount of radiation that can be detected in a short time interval. The half-life is short enough so the nuclides lose their radioactive properties rapidly.

▶ Emphasize that tracers eliminate the need for much exploratory surgery by providing a way to monitor internal body processes. Surgery and being under anesthesia always pose a health risk. There are also risks associated with ingesting radioisotopes.

New Science Words

tracers

Objectives

▶ Describe how radioactive tracers can be used to diagnose medical problems.
▶ Discuss how radioactive isotopes can aid in the treatment of cancers.

Are Radioactive Isotopes Useful in Medicine?

Did you know that radioactive isotopes can help locate and even kill cancerous tumors in the body? The rapidly growing field of nuclear medicine involves the use of radioactive isotopes in the diagnosis and treatment of many medical problems.

Just as wildlife conservationists tag animals to make them easy to follow, scientists can tag molecules with radioactive isotopes. Within the body, these radioactive isotopes behave like any other atom of the same element. However, they emit radiation as they move and can be followed with a radiation detector. Radioisotopes that are put in the body to monitor a bodily process are called **tracers.** Tracers typically have a relatively short half-life so they are constantly emitting a fair amount of radiation.

Certain parts of your body need specific elements, so the tracer is attached to a particular element that will travel to a desired location. For example, your thyroid gland, which regulates body growth and other processes, requires a certain amount of iodine to function normally. A doctor can examine the way the thyroid uses iodine by having the person drink a solution containing a radioactive isotope of iodine called I-131. The amount of this isotope in the thyroid can be determined by a detector. A thyroid problem is detected if the rate at which iodine is used in the gland is abnormal.

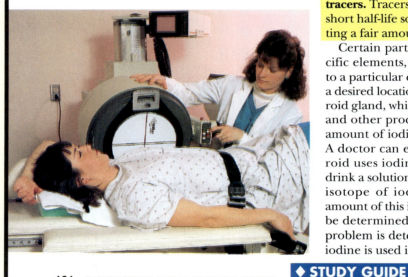

636 RADIOACTIVITY AND NUCLEAR REACTIONS

OPTIONS

Meeting Different Ability Levels

For Section 24-5, use the following **Teacher Resource Masters** depending upon individual students' needs.

◆ **Study Guide Master** for all students.
● **Reinforcement Master** for students of average and above average ability levels.
▲ **Enrichment Master** for above average students.

◆ STUDY GUIDE   104

STUDY GUIDE   Chapter 24
Nuclear Medicine   Text Pages 636–638

Match each term in Column II with its description in Column I. Write the letter of the correct term in the space provided.

	Column I		Column II
g	1. uses radioactive isotopes in the diagnosis and treatment of illnesses		a. cobalt-60
b	2. an isotope of an element that is radioactive		b. radioisotope
d	3. radioisotope used to diagnose a thyroid problem		c. side effect
d	4. any radioisotope used to monitor bodily processes		d. iodine-131
f	5. radioisotope used to detect brain tumors		e. tracer
a	6. radioisotope used as an external source of ionizing radiation		f. technetium-99
c	7. unwanted effect such as hair loss caused by medical treatment		g. nuclear medicine

Determine whether the italicized term makes each statement true or false. If the statement is true, write the word "true" in the blank. If the statement is false, write in the blank the term that makes the statement true.

true	8. Radioisotopes in the body *act the same* as any other atoms of the same element.
technetium-99	9. Brain tumors can be detected by the use of *iodine-131.*
true	10. Iodine-131 is often used *internally.*
true	11. Cancerous cells in the body reproduce *rapidly.*
external	12. Cobalt-60 is used as an *internal* source of ionizing radiation.
true	13. Nausea, hair loss, and *fatigue* are side effects of cobalt-60 treatments.
the thyroid gland	14. Body growth is regulated by *cancer cells.*

Copyright Glencoe Division of Macmillan/McGraw-Hill
Users of Merrill Physical Science have the publisher's permission to reproduce this page.

104

Tumors can also be found with radioactive isotopes. Cancerous cells reproduce very rapidly, so more of the radioactive isotope gathers in these cells than in those of healthy tissues. For example, technetium-99 is one element that is rapidly absorbed in brain tumors. The exact location of the tumor can be determined by using tracers, thus eliminating the need for risky exploratory surgery.

Tracing techniques are helpful in diagnosing cancer, but the problem of treating the cancer remains. There are many kinds of cancer treatment. One treatment, therapy with ionizing radiation, often complements or replaces surgery. This radiation can be given either internally or externally. I-131 is sometimes given internally to treat thyroid cancer. Cobalt-60 is often used as an external source of ionizing radiation. A beam of this radiation is aimed at the cancerous spot to destroy the cancerous cells. This treatment can shrink, and even eliminate, some cancerous tumors. Unfortunately, healthy tissue can also be damaged by radiation therapy. This treatment may produce unpleasant side effects, such as hair loss, fatigue, and nausea.

Although the use of radiation in medicine does have some risks associated with it, the risks are often smaller than the possible complications of surgery or even medication. The decision to take any kind of medical treatment involves a certain amount of risk. Nuclear medicine is responsible for saving many lives. Do you know anyone who has had medical testing or treatment with radioactive isotopes?

SECTION REVIEW

1. How does a radioactive tracer work?
2. Describe two ways radioactive isotopes can be used in the treatment of cancerous tumors.

You Decide!

Radioactive isotopes used in medicine produce radioactive wastes that are potentially hazardous to people and the environment for many years. Should radioactive isotopes continue to be used in medical treatments? Explain your position.

SCIENCE & SOCIETY

● REINFORCEMENT 104

▲ ENRICHMENT 104

637

2 TEACH

Key Concepts are highlighted.

CROSS CURRICULUM

▶ **Medicine:** A common use of X rays in hospitals now is the CAT scan, which stands for computer-assisted tomography or computerized axial tomography. Find out how CAT scans are used in medical diagnosis.

CHECK FOR UNDERSTANDING

Ask students how I-131 might be useful in treating a tumor without damaging other body tissue. Because the thyroid uses iodine, most of the iodine travels to the thyroid gland.

RETEACH

Most students will have seen wildlife shows on TV. Ask how the use of radioactive tracers in the body is similar to the use of radio collars to track wild animals. Point out that, after being collared, the animal does not have to be caught to be detected.

EXTENSION

For students who have mastered this section, use the **Reinforcement** and **Enrichment** masters or other OPTIONS provided.

3 CLOSE

▶ Ask questions 1-2 in the Section Review.

SECTION REVIEW ANSWERS

1. A tracer acts like any atom of the same element and travels through the body. The movement of the tracer is followed with a radiation detector.

2. They can be given internally, or radiation can be projected to the site through a beam from an external radioactive sample.

SCIENCE & SOCIETY

YOU DECIDE!

Have students debate the You Decide topic in teams. Be sure that all points of view are considered.

ACTIVITY 24-2
30 minutes

OBJECTIVE: **Illustrate** the hydrogen fusion process through the use of physical models.

PROCESS SKILLS applied in this activity:
▶ **Formulating Models** in Procedure Steps 1-4.
▶ **Interpreting** in Analyze Questions 1-3.
▶ **Inferring** in Conclude and Apply Questions 4 and 5.

COOPERATIVE LEARNING

Divide the class into Science Investigation groups of three to six students. Provide each team with materials for making six protons. Teams can interact using the leftover protons for a second cycle of fusion.

TEACHING THE ACTIVITY

Alternate Materials: Any combination of large and small objects can be used to represent neutrons and positrons. Clay requires no pins to hold parts together but has the disadvantage of sometimes ending up on the ceiling.

Troubleshooting: Be sure students construct the correct nuclei at each step. If they do not, they will not be able to draw a correct conclusion.

▶ The proton model shown here is useful for this activity but otherwise not representative. The released positron is a short-lived particle that reacts with an electron to become gamma radiation.

PROGRAM RESOURCES

From the **Teacher Resource Package** use:

Activity Worksheets, pages 195-196, Activity 24-2: Nuclear Fusion.

ACTIVITY 24-2
Nuclear Fusion

Problem: *Can you simulate thermonuclear fusion?*

Materials
- 6 balls of green clay
- 6 smaller balls of white clay

Procedure
1. Make six hydrogen nuclei (protons) by sticking one small white positron to each large green neutron.
2. Refer to Step 1 of the table and make two particles of $^2_1$H.
3. Refer to Step 2 of the table and make two particles of $^3_2$He.
4. Refer to Step 3 of the table and make one particle of $^4_2$He.

	FUSION REACTIONS
Step 1	$^1_1$H + $^1_1$H → $^2_1$H + positron
Step 2	$^1_1$H + $^2_1$H → $^3_2$He
Step 3	$^3_2$He + $^3_2$He → $^4_2$He + 2$^1_1$H

Analyze
1. Describe the steps necessary to change $^1_1$H into $^4_2$He.
2. In this process, what is lost and what is left over?
3. How many atoms of hydrogen does it take to make one atom of helium?

Conclude and Apply
4. What can the leftover hydrogen be used for?
5. Refer to the periodic table on pages 258-259. Compare the mass of one helium atom to the mass of four hydrogen atoms. If leftover mass changes to energy, where does the energy of the sun come from?

ANSWERS TO QUESTIONS

1. Two protons fuse as a positron is released, and a proton changes to a neutron. Then a normal hydrogen nucleus fuses with hydrogen-2 to make helium-3. Finally, two helium-3 nuclei fuse to make one helium-4 and two normal hydrogens.

2. Two positrons are lost. Two protons are left over.

3. It takes six hydrogen-1 to make one helium-4 nucleus. However, two hydrogen are regained in the process. Therefore, the net usage is four hydrogen-1.

4. Hydrogen that is produced in the fusion reaction can be used for the next cycle of fusion.

5. He = 4.002 602 u   4H = (4)(1.007 94 u)
= 4.031 76 u

mass loss = 4.031 76 u − 4.002 602 u
= 0.029 16 u

This mass is converted to energy in the fusion process. The energy of the sun comes from the conversion of mass during fusion according to the relationship $E = mc^2$.

CHAPTER REVIEW

SUMMARY

24-1: Radioactivity
1. Radioactivity was accidentally discovered by Henri Bequerel about 100 years ago.
2. Radioactive nuclides are unstable and therefore decay. Stable nuclides don't decay.

24-2: Nuclear Decay
1. The three types of radiation that can be emitted from a decaying nucleus are alpha particles, beta particles, and gamma rays.
2. The amount of a remaining radioactive substance can be determined if you know the amount of the original sample and the number of half-lives that have elapsed.
3. The ages of rocks and fossils can be determined by a process called radioactive dating.

24-3: Detecting Radioactivity
1. Radioactivity can be detected with a cloud chamber, a bubble chamber, an electroscope, or a Geiger counter.

2. A Geiger counter can indicate the intensity of radiation present by producing a clicking sound or a flashing light that increases in frequency as more radiation is present.

24-4: Nuclear Reactions
1. Atomic nuclei are split during fission and combined during fusion.
2. Subatomic particles released from a nucleus during fission can split other nuclei.
3. Hydrogen atoms in the sun undergo fusion, and as a result, form helium atoms and electromagnetic radiation.

24-5: Science and Society: Nuclear Medicine
1. Radioactive tracers can go to certain areas of the body to indicate abnormalities.
2. Some radioactive isotopes can kill cancer cells.

KEY SCIENCE WORDS

a. alpha particles
b. beta particle
c. bubble chamber
d. chain reaction
e. cloud chamber
f. gamma rays
g. half-life
h. nuclear fission
i. nuclear fusion
j. nuclide
k. radioactivity
l. tracers
m. transmutation

UNDERSTANDING VOCABULARY

Match each phrase with the correct term from the list of Key Science Words.

1. emission of high-energy particles from an unstable nucleus
2. a particle of nuclear radiation with a charge of +2 and an atomic mass of 4
3. nuclear decay that results in the formation of a new element
4. the time for one-half of a sample of a radioactive isotope to decay
5. detects nuclear particles as they leave a trail of condensed water or ethanol vapor
6. splitting a nucleus into two smaller masses
7. radioactive isotopes that are used to monitor human body functions
8. the nucleus of a specific isotope
9. radiation in the form of electromagnetic waves
10. two nuclei combining into a larger nucleus

RADIOACTIVITY AND NUCLEAR REACTIONS **639**

SUMMARY

Have students read the summary statements to review the major concepts of the chapter.

UNDERSTANDING VOCABULARY

1. k	**6.** h
2. a	**7.** l
3. m	**8.** j
4. g	**9.** f
5. e	**10.** i

OPTIONS

ASSESSMENT
To assess student understanding of material in this chapter, use the resources listed.

COOPERATIVE LEARNING
Consider using cooperative learning in the THINK AND WRITE CRITICALLY, APPLY, and MORE SKILL BUILDERS sections of the Chapter Review.

PROGRAM RESOURCES
From the **Teacher Resource Package** use:
Chapter Review, pages 51-52.
Chapter and Unit Tests, pages 155-158, Chapter Test.

CHAPTER
REVIEW

CHECKING CONCEPTS

1. a		**6.** b	
2. a		**7.** a	
3. b		**8.** c	
4. a		**9.** a	
5. d		**10.** d	

UNDERSTANDING CONCEPTS

11. strong force
12. bubble chamber
13. energy
14. chain reaction
15. more

THINK AND WRITE CRITICALLY

16. Radioactivity was discovered by Henri Bequerel in 1896. Marie and Pierre Curie later discovered the radioactive elements polonium and radium. Nuclear fission was produced in 1938 by Otto Hahn and Fritz Strassman and explained by Lise Meitner.

17. The strong nuclear force is weakened when the ratio of protons to neutrons in the nucleus is not 1-to-1.

18. In all living organisms there is a fixed percentage of carbon-14 while the organism is still alive. Once the organism dies, the carbon-14 that decays is not replaced. By measuring the percentage of carbon-14 in a sample of once-living material and comparing this to the percentage of carbon-14 in a living sample, scientists can determine the age of the sample.

19. In a cloud chamber, the ions produced by the radiation cause supersaturated vapor to condense. This results in a cloud trail. In a bubble chamber, ionized atoms of a superheated liquid boil leaving a trail of bubbles. In an electroscope, radiation strips electrons from the air molecules, giving them a positive charge. These ions cause the electroscope to discharge.

20. Because cancer cells have accelerated physiological processes, they take up a radioactive tracer much more rapidly than healthy cells. Thus, most of the tracer will accumulate at the tumor and the tumor can be detected.

CHECKING CONCEPTS

Choose the word or phrase that completes the sentence.

1. Radioactivity can be _____.
   a. found in your classroom   c. seen
   b. found with a tracer   d. smelled

2. Elements that have been produced artificially through nuclear reactions have atomic numbers _____.
   a. greater than 92   c. between 83 and 92
   b. greater than 83   d. none of these

3. When a neutron decays by turning into a proton and an electron, it emits _____.
   a. an alpha particle   c. gamma radiation
   b. a beta particle   d. both a and c

4. The time for half the nuclides in a sample of a radioactive isotope to decay _____.
   a. is constant   c. increases with time
   b. varies   d. decreases with time

5. Carbon-14 dating could be used to date _____.
   a. an ancient Roman scroll
   b. an ancient marble column
   c. dinosaur fossils
   d. Earth's oldest rocks

6. Radiation in a nuclear laboratory could best be measured with _____.
   a. a cloud chamber   c. an electroscope
   b. a Geiger counter   d. a bubble chamber

7. A _____ is an ongoing series of fission reactions.
   a. chain reaction
   b. decay reaction
   c. transmutation reaction
   d. fusion reaction

8. The sun is powered by _____.
   a. nuclear decay   c. thermonuclear fusion
   b. nuclear fission d. combustion

9. A radioisotope that acts as an external source of ionizing radiation in the treatment of cancer is _____.
   a. cobalt-60   c. iodine-131
   b. carbon-14   d. technetium-99

10. Disadvantages of using radiation to treat cancer include _____.
    a. hair loss   c. fatigue
    b. nausea   d. all of these

UNDERSTANDING CONCEPTS

Complete each sentence.

11. The _____ in an atom's nucleus weakens across small distances and prevents protons from repelling one another.

12. As nuclear particles move through the superheated liquid in a(n) _____, they ionize the liquid in their path and cause it to boil.

13. Some mass is converted to _____ in both nuclear fission and nuclear fusion.

14. The splitting of one heavy nucleus can result in a(n) _____ if individual neutrons are released and split nearby nuclei.

15. Nuclear fusion releases _____ energy than nuclear fission.

THINK AND WRITE CRITICALLY

16. Briefly discuss the history of nuclear science.
17. Explain why certain nuclides decay.
18. Describe the basic principles of carbon-14 dating.
19. Discuss the similarities and differences in the devices that detect radioactivity.
20. Discuss the use of radioactive tracers. How do they detect cancer cells?

640   RADIOACTIVITY AND NUCLEAR REACTIONS

APPLY

21. Yes. The process depends only on electron structure. Other than being radioactive, the salt would be chemically the same as normal salt.

22. $^{66}_{29}Cu \rightarrow ^{66}_{30}Zn + ^{0}_{-1}e$

    $^{226}_{88}Ra \rightarrow ^{222}_{86}Rn + ^{4}_{2}He$

23. Four half-lives elapse in 40 minutes. Therefore:
    remaining mass = 320 g/2^4
    = 320 g/16
    = 20 grams

24. The temperatures and pressures in the interior of a star are sufficiently high for atoms in the plasma state to undergo thermonuclear fusion and form successively heavier atoms as lighter nuclei collide.

25. Ionizing radiation can kill cells. Therefore, radiation can be used to kill bacteria in food and thus give it longer shelf-life. As for the study of plant physiology, radioisotopes such as K-40 can be placed in the soil of lab plants. Using radiation detectors, scientists can monitor how they are taken up by the plant.

APPLY

21. Can a radioactive isotope of sodium combine with chlorine to form table salt? If so, would its chemical and physical properties be the same as ordinary table salt? Explain your answer.
22. Copper-66 releases a beta particle as it decays, and radium-226 releases an alpha particle. Write a nuclear equation for each of these transmutations.
23. Nitrogen-13 has a half-life of about 10 minutes. How much of a 320-g sample of nitrogen-13 would remain after decaying for 40 minutes?
24. Explain the presence of heavy elements such as carbon, oxygen, magnesium, and iron in stars.
25. Explain how radioisotopes are used to preserve foods and to study how plants take up nutrients from the soil.

MORE SKILL BUILDERS

If you need help, refer to the Skill Handbook.

1. **Concept Mapping:** Complete the following concept map summarizing how a Geiger counter works.

Initiating Event

Final Outcome

2. **Making and Using Tables:** Construct a table summarizing the characteristics of each of the three types of radiation.
3. **Observing and Inferring:** Another type of particle of nuclear radiation is a positron which has a charge of +1 and essentially no mass. This particle is given off when a proton spontaneously changes into a neutron. Infer what type of radiation will be emitted from each of the following radioisotopes:
   a. Boron-8 which is unstable due to an extra proton.
   b. Thorium-232 which is unstable due to its large nucleus containing too many protons and neutrons.
   c. Potassium-40 which is unstable due to an extra neutron.
4. **Making and Using Graphs:** Using the data below, construct a graph plotting the mass numbers vs. the half-lives of radioisotopes. Plot mass numbers to the nearest ten. Is it possible to use your graph to predict the half-life of a radioisotope given its mass number?

Radio Isotope	Mass Number	Half-life
Radium	222	4 days
Thorium	234	25 days
Iodine	131	8 days
Bismuth	210	5 days
Polonium	210	138 days

PROJECTS

1. Write a biography of a person who made an important contribution to nuclear science.
2. Research the causes and effects of radon pollution in the home. Report your findings to the class.

Type of Radiation	Charge	Mass	Rel. Speed	Penetrating Power	Symbol
Alpha	+2	4	Slow	Low; Stopped by paper	$^4_2 He$
Beta	−1	0	Fast	Moderate; Stopped by aluminum foil	$^0_{-1} e$
Gamma	0	0	Speed of light	Great; Stopped by thick lead or concrete	γ

MORE SKILL BUILDERS

1. **Concept Mapping:**

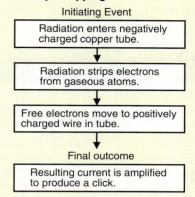

2. **Making and Using Tables:** See below, left.
3. **Observing and Inferring:** To make the proper inferences, students must consider what is causing the nuclide's instability and then think of the type of radiation that will remedy the destabilizing condition. Therefore:
   a) emission of positron (extra proton is changed into neutron)
   b) emission of alpha particle (removes both neutrons and protons in very heavy nuclides)
   c) emission of beta particle (extra neutron is changed into proton)
4. **Making and Using Graphs:** Students should construct a bar graph, *not a line graph*, because the data is for discrete entities, not a continuum.

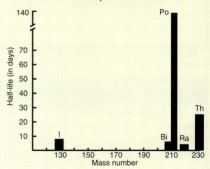

It is not possible to predict the half-life of a radioisotope given its mass number. The graph shows no correlation between mass number and greatly differing half-lives.

CHAPTER
25 Energy Sources

CHAPTER SECTION	OBJECTIVES	ACTIVITIES
25-1 Fossil Fuels (1 day)	**1. Discuss** the origin and characteristics of the three main types of fossil fuels. **2. Describe** the need and methods for energy conservation.	**MINI-Lab:** *Can efficient use conserve fuel?* p. 646
25-2 Nuclear Energy (2 days)	**1. Outline** the operation of a nuclear reactor. **2. Describe** the problems and methods associated with nuclear waste disposal. **3. Discuss** nuclear fusion as a possible energy source.	**Activity 25-1:** *Nuclear Waste Disposal,* p. 653
25-3 Breeder Reactors Science & Society (1 day)	**1. Distinguish** between breeder reactors and normal nuclear fission reactors. **2. Assess** the advantages and disadvantages of operating breeder reactors.	
25-4 Alternate Energy Sources (2 days)	**1. Analyze** the need for alternative energy sources. **2. Discuss** the methods of generating electricity with several energy sources. **3. Describe** the advantages and disadvantages of several alternative energy sources.	**Activity 25-2:** *Energy Alternatives,* p. 662
Chapter Review		

ACTIVITY MATERIALS

FIND OUT	ACTIVITIES		MINI-LABS
Page 643 microscope slides petroleum jelly microscope tong car	**25-1 Nuclear Waste Disposal, p. 653** 4 pellets sodium hydroxide 4 100-mL beakers phenolphthalein solution plastic food wrap aluminum foil 3 rubber bands 2 twist ties modeling clay forceps goggles	**25-2 Energy Alternatives, p. 662** large sheet of poster paper set of colored flow pens miscellaneous construction supplies	**Can efficient use conserve fuel? p. 646** candle water aluminum foil 100-mL beaker thermometer cardboard ring stand balance graduated cylinder

CHAPTER FEATURES	TEACHER RESOURCE PACKAGE	OTHER RESOURCES
Technology: *Gas Instead of Gasoline,* p. 646 **Skill Builder:** *Comparing and Contrasting,* p. 647	**Ability Level Worksheets** ◆ *Study Guide,* p. 105 ● *Reinforcement,* p. 105 ▲ *Enrichment,* p. 105 **MINI-Lab Worksheet,** p. 208 **Transparency Masters,** pp. 97, 98	**Color Transparency 49,** Petroleum Distillation **Lab Manual 49,** Solar Cells
Skill Builder: *Concept Mapping,* p. 652	**Ability Level Worksheets** ◆ *Study Guide,* p. 106 ● *Reinforcement,* p. 106 ▲ *Enrichment,* p. 106 **Activity Worksheet,** pp. 202, 203 **Critical Thinking/Problem Solving,** p. 31 **Transparency Masters,** pp. 99, 100	**Color Transparency 50,** Nuclear Power Plant
You Decide! p. 655	**Ability Level Worksheets** ◆ *Study Guide,* p. 107 ● *Reinforcement,* p. 107 ▲ *Enrichment,* p. 107	
Problem Solving: *Renewable Energy Sources for Beachtown,* p. 661 **Skill Builder:** *Outlining,* p. 661	**Ability Level Worksheets** ◆ *Study Guide,* p. 108 ● *Reinforcement,* p. 108 ▲ *Enrichment,* p. 108 **Activity Worksheet,** pp. 204, 205 **Concept Mapping,** pp. 55, 56 **Cross-Curricular Connections,** p. 31 **Science and Society,** p. 29	**Lab Manual 50,** Using the Sun's Energy
Summary Think & Write Critically Key Science Words Apply Understanding Vocabulary More Skill Builders Checking Concepts Projects Understanding Concepts	**Chapter Review,** pp. 53, 54 **Chapter Test,** pp. 159-162 **Unit Test,** pp. 163, 164	**Chapter Review Software** **Test Bank**

◆ Basic   ● Average   ▲ Advanced

ADDITIONAL MATERIALS

SOFTWARE	AUDIOVISUAL	BOOKS/MAGAZINES
Seatter, CONDUIT. *Three Mile Island,* Muse Software. *Power Grid,* Queue.	*Energy: The Ultimate Problem,* film, Coronet/MTI. *Energy Sources for the Future,* film, ORM/McGraw-Hill Films. *Solar Energy,* filmstrips, Learning Arts. *Energy for Societies,* video, AIT. *Back to Chernobyl,* (NOVA), laserdisc, Image Entertainment.	Manassah, Jamal T. *Alternative Energy Sources.* San Diego, CA: Academic Press, Inc., 1981. Sayigh, A.A. *Solar Energy Application in Buildings.* San Diego, CA: Academic Press, Inc., 1979.

THEME DEVELOPMENT: Energy is an obvious theme throughout this chapter. The sections compare the use of fossil fuels, nuclear energy, solar energy, and other alternative energy sources as methods of supplying useful energy to large communities. The environmental effects of generating usable energy should also be discussed.

CHAPTER OVERVIEW

▶ **Section 25-1:** This section focuses on methods of using fossil fuels as our most common energy resource. Fossil fuels are discussed as a non-renewable resource.

▶ **Section 25-2:** The process of using nuclear reactors to generate electricity is illustrated. Nuclear waste disposal is discussed. The challenges of developing fusion power are also presented.

▶ **Section 25-3: Science and Society:** This section provides a description of the function of breeder reactors.

▶ **Section 25-4:** Alternate energy sources are compared. These include biomass, solar energy, hydroelectricity, tidal energy, wind energy, and geothermal energy.

CHAPTER VOCABULARY

petroleum	breeder reactor
fractional	photovoltaic cell
distillation	hydroelectricity
nonrenewable	tidal energy
resources	geothermal
nuclear reactor	energy
nuclear wastes	

C H A P T E R

25 Energy Sources

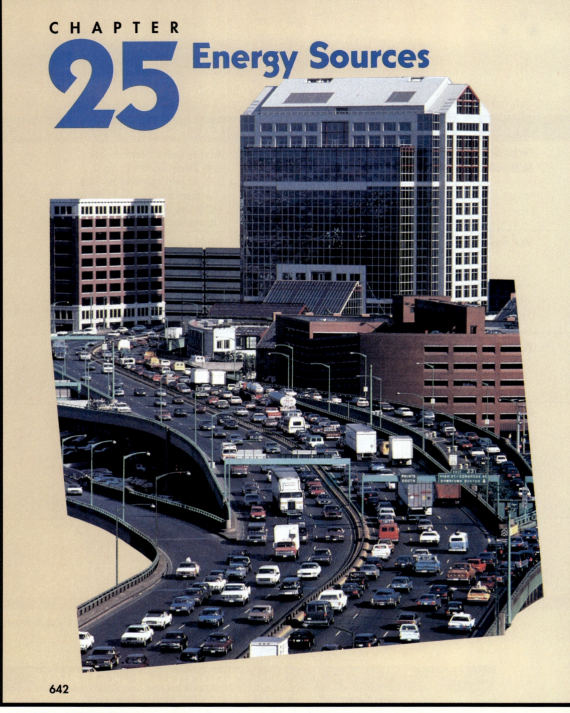

642

OPTIONS

For Your Gifted Students

▶ Have students design and build a solar oven. They can try out their models by trying to warm a pastry or cook a hot dog.

▶ Students can write a story about how they survived an imaginary week-long loss of energy sources (electric and fossil fuel). Have them describe what they imagine their daily routine would be. They should try to come up with ideas for an alternate energy source.

▶ Have students brainstorm ways energy is wasted and then ways to turn the waste to conservation. They can design buttons or bumper stickers to advertise their conservation ideas.

How many times do you ride in a car or bus in one week? Is that car or bus powered by a gasoline engine? It probably is, because most automobiles are fueled by gasoline. If you live in a large city, you may often see a layer of smog all around you. Smog is a type of pollution that forms from the exhausts of thousands of cars.

FIND OUT!

Do the following activity to find out about automobile emissions.

Have an adult help you with this activity. Hold a microscope slide, on which you have smeared a thin layer of petroleum jelly, near the opening of an automobile's exhaust pipe. Have the adult start the car and let it idle IN PARK. Be careful not to touch the exhaust pipe or breathe the vapors. Remove the slide after two minutes and observe it under a microscope or with a powerful hand lens. What do you see?

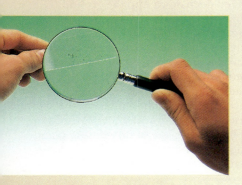

Gearing Up

Previewing the Chapter

Use this outline to help you focus on important ideas in the chapter.

Section 25-1   Fossil Fuels
▶ Petroleum
▶ Other Fossil Fuels
▶ Fuel Conservation

Section 25-2   Nuclear Energy
▶ Nuclear Reactors
▶ Nuclear Generation of Electricity
▶ Nuclear Waste Disposal
▶ Fusion Power

Section 25-3   Science and Society
Breeder Reactors
▶ Are Breeder Reactors Really Such a Good Idea?

Section 25-4   Alternative Energy Sources
▶ The Need for Alternatives
▶ Solar Energy
▶ Hydroelectricity
▶ Tidal Energy
▶ Wind Energy
▶ Geothermal Energy

Previewing Science Skills

▶ In the **Skill Builders,** you will compare and contrast, make a concept map, and outline.
▶ In the **Activities,** you will formulate models, hypothesize, and make observations.
▶ In the **MINI-Lab,** you will measure, observe, and make conclusions.

What's next?

Did you observe some dark particles on the slide in the Find Out activity? Tons of particles like these are released into the atmosphere daily when gasoline and other fossil fuels are burned for energy. Consider some of the energy alternatives mentioned as you read this chapter.

643

INTRODUCING THE CHAPTER

Use the Find Out activity to help students think about the nature of our energy resources. Point out that alternatives to fossil fuels are necessary to fulfill the energy demands of society and that they will be studying some of these options.

FIND OUT!

Preparation: You may want to make several slides ahead of time if doing it in class is not practical. Have students hold slides with tongs.

Materials: microscope slides, petroleum jelly, microscopes, tongs, a car

Teaching Tips

▶ If time is limited, make enough slides to have one slide for every two people. Have students make suggestions about the nature of the particles given off in the exhaust.

▶ If the car is cold, allow it to run until the exhaust system heats up. A cold exhaust puts out too much condensed water vapor.

Gearing Up

Have students study the Gearing Up feature to familiarize themselves with the chapter. Discuss the relationships of the topics in the outline.

What's Next?

Before beginning the first section, make sure students understand the connection between the Find Out activity and the topics to follow.

For Your Mainstreamed Students

▶Students can create mobiles illustrating different energy sources, conservation models, and examples of waste. They can make drawings or find them in other media. Illustrations should be labeled and grouped according to category.

▶Have students develop an energy scrapbook to keep track of related articles that appear in newspapers or magazines. They should classify the articles by energy source, conservation effort, or example of waste.

PREPARATION

SECTION BACKGROUND

▶ Over 50 percent of the world's oil reserves are located in the Persian Gulf region, so we depend heavily on this region for imported oil. Political strife in the region and its effect on importing oil have encouraged the U.S. to seek new energy sources.

▶ The first oil well in the U.S. was drilled by Edwin Drake in Titusville, Pennsylvania, in 1859. The refineries produced mostly kerosene and heating oil until the development of gasoline powered transportation in the 1890s.

PREPLANNING

▶ Posters on coal mining and petroleum processing are sometimes available from state and federal departments of energy or from petroleum and coal companies.

1 MOTIVATE

▶ Have students list the ways in which they have encountered products made from petroleum. They may think of gasoline, petroleum jelly, baby oil, kerosene, or motor oil. Point out that many plastics, cosmetics, and detergents are also derived from oil.

TYING TO PREVIOUS KNOWLEDGE:
Students have studied hydrocarbons—compounds made of hydrogen and carbon—in Chapter 13. Petroleum and natural gas, both fossil fuels, are made of hydrocarbon molecules.

OBJECTIVES AND SCIENCE WORDS:
Have students review the objectives and science words to become familiar with this section.

25-1 Fossil Fuels

New Science Words

petroleum
fractional distillation
nonrenewable resources

Objectives

▶ Discuss the origin and characteristics of the three main types of fossil fuels.
▶ Describe the need and methods for energy conservation.

Petroleum

Do you own a sweater made of synthetic fibers such as polyester, rayon, or nylon? If so, are you aware that your sweater has something in common with the gasoline used for fuel in cars and buses? Synthetic fibers are made with chemicals that come from crude oil, and gasoline is refined from crude oil.

Crude oil, or **petroleum,** is a liquid source of energy made from the remains of plants and animals that lived several hundred million years ago. Petroleum, along with natural gas and coal, is called a fossil fuel. When ancient plants and animals died, they were covered with layers of sand, mud, volcanic ash, and other matter that collected on the surface of Earth over many years. Great pressure, heat, and bacterial action acted on these buried organisms, forming fossil fuels. Petroleum and natural gas are probably made from this process acting on the remains of sea organisms.

Have you ever seen oil wells pumping in a field as you rode along a highway? Petroleum is pumped to the surface from wells drilled deep down into the ground. The crude oil that comes from these wells contains a variety of different chemicals that originated in plants and animals. Because plants and animals contain large amounts of hydrogen and carbon, petroleum is composed mostly of compounds containing these elements. As a result, petroleum compounds are called hydrocarbons.

These various hydrocarbon compounds must be separated to make use of the chemical energy stored in petroleum. If you have ever seen an oil refining plant, you may have noticed several tall towers. These towers are called fractionating towers. Fractionating towers use

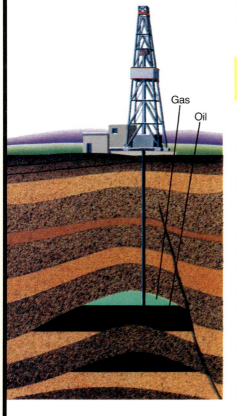

Gas
Oil

644 ENERGY SOURCES

OPTIONS

Meeting Different Ability Levels

For Section 25-1, use the following **Teacher Resource Masters** depending upon individual students' needs.

◆ **Study Guide Master** for all students.
● **Reinforcement Master** for students of average and above average ability levels.
▲ **Enrichment Master** for above average students.

Additional Teacher Resource Package masters are listed in the OPTIONS box throughout the section. The additional masters are appropriate for all students.

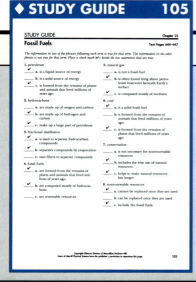

a process called **fractional distillation** to separate hydrocarbon compounds. First, crude oil is pumped into the bottom of the tower and heated. The chemical compounds in the crude oil, called fractions, boil and evaporate according to their individual boiling points. Those materials with the lowest boiling points rise to the top of the column as vapor and are separated and collected. When the vapor cools below its boiling point, it again turns to a liquid. Hydrocarbons with very high boiling points may remain as liquid and be drained off through the bottom of the tower. Notice all the different products made from petroleum fractions that are shown in Figure 25-1.

Oil can be carried through pipelines, such as the Alaskan pipeline, or it can be carried in fuel tankers. You use petroleum every day for electricity and transportation. You probably know that burning petroleum has serious side effects on the environment. When petroleum is burned in cars and at electric power plants, it gives off smoke as well as carbon monoxide and other chemical compounds. These particles and compounds affect the quality of the air you breathe.

Other Fossil Fuels

Do you cook on a gas stove at home? If so, you burn natural gas to get energy to cook your food. Natural gas, like petroleum, is a fossil fuel. Natural gas most likely originated from plants and animals that lived in Earth's oceans. It is often found lying above liquid petroleum reservoirs below Earth's surface; it is extracted with the petroleum.

Natural gas is composed mostly of methane, CH_4, but it also contains smaller amounts of hydrocarbon gases such as propane, C_3H_8 and butane, C_4H_{10}. When natural gas or petroleum is burned, it combines with oxygen, and heat is given off. During this process, carbon dioxide and water are formed as chemical by-products. This is a combustion reaction. Natural gas is burned to provide energy for cooking, heating, and manufacturing.

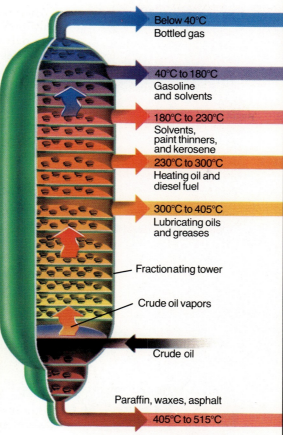

Below 40°C
Bottled gas

40°C to 180°C
Gasoline and solvents

180°C to 230°C
Solvents, paint thinners, and kerosene

230°C to 300°C
Heating oil and diesel fuel

300°C to 405°C
Lubricating oils and greases

Fractionating tower

Crude oil vapors

Crude oil

Paraffin, waxes, asphalt
405°C to 515°C

Figure 25-1. Fractional distillation is used to separate the hydrocarbon components in petroleum.

Did You Know?

Energy consumption per household decreased in the United States by more than 25 percent between 1978 and 1987.

2 TEACH

Key Concepts are highlighted.

CONCEPT DEVELOPMENT

▶Most fossil fuels are easily combustible, so this is a good time to caution your students about some possible dangers. Gasoline should not be used in lanterns or heaters because it is more volatile and flammable than kerosene.

▶Many of your students may have outdoor grills or camping stoves that use propane gas. Propane is a by-product of both natural gas and petroleum processing. It is also used in transportation, especially in vehicles that run indoors, because it burns much more cleanly than other fossil fuels.

TEACHER F.Y.I.

▶At times, the U.S. imports over 4 million barrels of oil daily. One barrel contains 42 gallons of oil.

CROSS CURRICULUM

▶**History:** Investigate the political situation that led to the oil embargo in 1973. Another oil shortage also occurred in the late 1970s. How did these shortages affect consumers and our approach to energy resources?

REVEALING MISCONCEPTIONS

▶Ask students in your class how many of them have a gas stove. Turn on a gas jet in your room for a few moments and let students smell the characteristic odor. Contrary to popular belief, this odor is not the odor of methane or propane. Natural gas is odorless, colorless, and tasteless. Gas companies add the odorant to the gas for safety reasons so gas leaks can be detected.

PROGRAM RESOURCES

From the **Teacher Resource Package** use:

Transparency Masters, pages 97-98, Petroleum Distillation.

Use **Color Transparency** 49, Petroleum Distillation.

● REINFORCEMENT 105

REINFORCEMENT   Chapter 25
Fossil Fuels   Text Pages 644-647

Complete the table below by placing a check mark (✓) beneath the headings of the substances that have each characteristic described in the first column.

Characteristic	Petroleum	Natural Gas	Coal
1. Is a fossil fuel	✓	✓	✓
2. Forms from plants and animals	✓	✓	
3. Forms only from plants			✓
4. Is a solid			✓
5. Is a liquid	✓		
6. Is a gas		✓	
7. Is made up of hydrocarbons	✓	✓	✓
8. Is a source of energy	✓	✓	✓
9. Is nonrenewable resource	✓	✓	✓
10. Is pumped from wells	✓	✓	
11. Is separated using fractional distillation	✓		
12. Is also called crude oil	✓		
13. Is transported long distances through pipes	✓	✓	
14. Is mined from Earth			✓
15. Produces polluting substances when burned	✓	✓	✓
16. Produces thermal energy when burned	✓	✓	✓
17. Can be used to produce electricity	✓	✓	✓
18. Is the least polluting fossil fuel		✓	

Copyright Glencoe Division of Macmillan/McGraw-Hill
Users of Merrill Physical Science have the publisher's permission to reproduce this page.
105

▲ ENRICHMENT 105

ENRICHMENT   Chapter 25
Fossil Fuels   Text Pages 644-647

OIL FROM THE ARCTIC

Oil is the leading source of energy in the United States. It supplies more than 40 percent of our total energy needs. One of our largest domestic sources of crude oil comes from the icy, frigid area of Alaska called the North Slope. Under the North Slope's frozen ground, called permafrost, lies the Prudhoe Bay Oil Field. It is the largest oil deposit ever discovered on the North American continent. It holds over 22 billion barrels of oil. About half of this oil is expected to be recovered by current methods of production.

The Alaskan Pipeline was built to carry the oil from Prudhoe Bay to the port of Valdez, Alaska. The pipeline was completed in 1977, cost $8 billion, and took three years to build. The 1300-kilometer pipeline is 1.25 meters in diameter. It has 1.25-centimeter thick walls designed to withstand the extreme Alaskan environments. The pipe is insulated with 10 centimeters of fiberglass and jacketed with galvanized steel. It carries 1.6 million barrels of oil per day, about 15 percent of the total United States production.

On its way from Prudhoe Bay and Valdez, the pipeline crosses three mountain ranges and hundreds of rivers and streams. Only half of it is buried. The above-ground portion snakes along on supports 3 to 4.5 meters above the ground. Each support consists of steel posts with a crossbeam between them. The reinforced pipeline rests on the supports with room to sway from side to side in the event of earthquakes or expansions or contractions caused by temperature changes.

The pipeline wasn't placed above ground just because it was easier to build that way. The reasons for this related mainly to environmental and safety concerns. Oil travels through the pipeline at about 60°C. In order to prevent the permafrost from thawing, which would make the pipeline unstable, the pipeline was elevated. At points where caribou migration routes would have crossed the elevated pipeline, it has been buried and refrigerated to leave these routes undisturbed. A series of safety valves provides further protection to the environment. These valves close automatically if the oil flow stops or reverses on uphill stretches. It is also possible to shut off whole sections of the line if leaks or spills should occur.

Questions

1. Look at a map of Alaska. Find Prudhoe Bay and Valdez. What type of terrain does the Alaskan Pipeline travel through? **three mountain ranges, many rivers, permafrost**

2. Many people feared that the Alaskan pipeline would damage the environment that it passed through. What precautions have been taken to protect the environment along its route? **It is elevated to protect the permafrost. Safety valves are used in case of spills or leaks. Caribou trails are maintained.**

3. Do you think that all of the planning, work, and cost of building the Alaskan pipeline was worth the final product, domestic oil? **Yes—the importance of having domestic oil far outweighs any cost of procuring that oil. No—there are other oil reserves on Earth; the luxury of domestic oil is excessive.**

Copyright Glencoe Division of Macmillan/McGraw-Hill
Users of Merrill Physical Science have the publisher's permission to reproduce this page.
105

When natural gas is used properly, it doesn't pollute the environment with the compounds that result from burning petroleum. However, the carbon dioxide that it produces can cause Earth's atmospheric temperature to rise. Natural gas is like petroleum, in that it can be transported long distances by large underground pipelines.

Coal is a solid fossil fuel made from the remains of plants. About one-fourth of the world's supply of coal is in the United States. It is sometimes mined near the surface, but is more commonly mined several hundred feet underground. The quality of a coal sample depends on its age and on the type of plant life from which it formed.

When used as a fuel, coal must be cleaned to remove sulfur and other impurities that would be released into the air when the coal is burned. Sulfur compounds can be removed from unburned coal or from the smoke from burning coal to prevent the formation of compounds in the air that cause acid rain. Harmful nitrogen oxides often form when coal is burned at high temperatures. Therefore, it is desirable to find ways to burn coal at lower temperatures.

Because coal is mined from Earth, digging coal mines can disturb the natural environment. Today, laws exist to require that the environment is returned to something close to its original state when a coal mine is closed.

TECHNOLOGY

Gas Instead of Gasoline

One fuel that is an alternative to gasoline is natural gas. Cars, buses, and other vehicles that currently run on gasoline can be modified to use natural gas instead. Natural gas vehicles (NGVs) appear to contribute less than gasoline to the problems of pollution and global warming. That's because NGVs don't release as much carbon monoxide, carbon dioxide, and other pollutants as gasoline. It is estimated that 30 000 NGVs are already in use on our nation's highways.

Think Critically: The cost of converting a vehicle that runs on gasoline to an NGV can be offset by fuel cost savings. What other problems might NGV owners encounter?

Fuel Conservation

Think of how many times you ride in a car, turn on a light, or use an electric appliance. Each time you do one of these things, you probably use some type of fossil fuel as a source of energy. We depend on fossil fuels to meet a large percentage of our energy needs. Fossil fuel reserves are decreasing as our population and industrial energy demands are increasing. At our current rate of consumption, the United States may be out of oil in less than 80 years. Coal is more plentiful, but like petroleum, it is a nonrenewable resource. All fossil fuels are **nonrenewable resources**—they cannot be replaced after they are used.

We must conserve nonrenewable energy resources that we do have. Conservation can be as simple as turning off a light when you leave a room, avoiding unnecessary speeding when driving a car, or riding a bike instead of driving the car at all. Insulating your home and using energy-efficient appliances can conserve energy within your home. Trees around your home can keep it cooler in summer and reduce the use of air conditioning. We need to develop some alternative energy sources to help us conserve now and to prepare for the time when fossil fuels may not be readily available.

SECTION REVIEW

1. Describe the three main types of fossil fuels.
2. Which type of fossil fuel is the most abundant in the United States? What are the advantages and disadvantages of using this fuel?
3. **Apply:** As the plants and animals living on Earth today die, they will decay and be buried to form the fossils of tomorrow. If the formation of fossil fuels is a continuous cycle, why are they considered to be *nonrenewable* resources?

☑ Comparing and Contrasting

Compare and contrast the different fossil fuels. Include the advantages and disadvantages of using each as a source of energy. If you need help, refer to Comparing and Contrasting in the **Skill Handbook** on page 679.

Skill Builder

Many of our energy conservation techniques refer to what we can do in the home, but most of us spend at least half of our waking hours outside of the home. What can you do to conserve energy at school?

Figure 25-2. Find ways to conserve energy at home, such as caulking around windows.

EXTENSION

For students who have mastered this section, use the **Reinforcement** and **Enrichment** masters or other OPTIONS provided.

Science and WRITING

Some students may get involved enough to want to form an energy conservation club at school. The utility companies and national conservation organizations can provide good information to help them get started. Perhaps students could get information from your school administration on energy usage and costs.

3 CLOSE

▶Ask questions 1-2 and the **Apply** Question in the Section Review.
▶Put the following list on the chalkboard and ask students to identify what the items have in common. They will be surprised that all of these are actually derived from fossil fuels: gasoline, paint solvents, synthetic fabrics, plastics, photographic film, shoe polish, candles, pesticides, some drugs, detergents, and waxed paper.

SECTION REVIEW ANSWERS

1. Petroleum is a liquid composed mostly of hydrocarbons. Natural gas is composed mostly of methane. Coal is a solid fossil fuel.

2. Coal—it has the advantage of being the most abundant fossil fuel and it gives off large amounts of energy. Burning impure coal pollutes the air; mining deforms natural environments; it is a nonrenewable resource.

3. Apply: We use up fossil fuels faster than they are replaced. Therefore, they are nonrenewable, for all practical purposes.

Skill Builder

Students should compare coal, petroleum, and natural gas based on the points discussed in this section.

ENRICHMENT

▶Have students report on the reasons that petroleum and natural gas are considered more desirable than coal to use as fuel. They should take into account ease of obtaining fuel, transporting the fuel, and environmental factors involved in the use of coal.

▶Have students do research to make a map showing where the largest reserves of petroleum, natural gas, and coal are found in the world. They should find out why other parts of the world might have a keen interest in politics in the Middle East. Students should consider the effects of the invasion of Kuwait by Iraq in August, 1990, the burning of Kuwaiti oil fields, and the aftermath of the Persian Gulf War.

PREPARATION

SECTION BACKGROUND

▶ Compared to fossil fuels, nuclear energy has only recently been developed as an energy resource. The atom was first split in 1939.

▶ Countries differ widely in their opinion on the use of nuclear energy. France is aiming to eventually produce up to 90 percent of its electricity from nuclear energy, while Sweden and some other nations have decided to decrease or omit reliance on nuclear energy.

PREPLANNING

▶ A number of items are needed for Activity 25-1 on page 653. Begin assembling these materials.

1 MOTIVATE

▶ Take a secret vote (to avoid peer pressure) in your class before beginning this section. Write the following question on the chalkboard: "If this community were facing an energy shortage, would you want to have a nuclear power plant supply electricity?" Those who say no should suggest ways that the community can provide energy or reduce consumption. Those who say yes should suggest how nuclear waste should be disposed of.

TYING TO PREVIOUS
KNOWLEDGE: In the last chapter students learned that nuclear fission and fusion release huge amounts of energy. In this section, they will study how this energy can be used to generate electricity.

OBJECTIVES AND
SCIENCE WORDS: Have students review the objectives and science words to become familiar with this section.

New Science Words

nuclear reactor
nuclear wastes

Objectives

▶ Outline the operation of a nuclear reactor.
▶ Describe the problems and methods associated with nuclear waste disposal.
▶ Discuss nuclear fusion as a possible energy source.

Nuclear Reactors

In the last chapter you learned that nuclear fission chain reactions give off a great deal of energy. **A nuclear reactor uses the energy from a controlled nuclear fission chain reaction to generate electricity.** Nuclear reactors can vary in design. Most fission reactors have several parts in common, including fuel, control rods, and cooling systems. The actual fission of the radioactive fuel occurs in a relatively small part of the reactor, the core.

Once the core of the reactor contains fuel, uranium oxide, a chain reaction starts from a single uranium atom that spontaneously splits into two parts, releasing two or more neutrons. If two of these neutrons reached U-235 atoms and made them split, releasing two neutrons each, there would now be four neutrons. These four could produce eight, then sixteen. This happens so fast that in one millisecond there could be 1000 neutrons. Each of those would produce 1000 more in the next millisecond, make one thousand thousand (or one million neutrons) in two milliseconds, then one thousand million (one billion) in three milliseconds. The reactor would be out of control.

To control the reaction, rods containing boron or cadmium are used to absorb some of the neutrons. Moving these control rods deeper into the reactor allows them to capture more neutrons and slow down the chain reaction. Eventually only one neutron per fission is able to react with a U-235 atom to produce another fission, and energy is released at a constant rate.

The nuclear fission reaction inside the core generates tremendous amounts of thermal energy. The core is surrounded by water that cools it. The water also carries

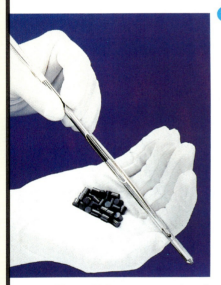

Figure 25-3. Uranium oxide pellets are used to fuel nuclear reactors.

648 ENERGY SOURCES

OPTIONS

Meeting Different Ability Levels

For Section 25-2, use the following **Teacher Resource Masters** depending upon individual students' needs.

◆ **Study Guide Master** for all students.
● **Reinforcement Master** for students of average and above average ability levels.
▲ **Enrichment Master** for above average students.

Additional Teacher Resource Package masters are listed in the OPTIONS box throughout the section. The additional masters are appropriate for all students.

thermal energy away from the core. The superheated water is pumped through a heat exchanger, where the thermal energy released boils a separate system of water to produce steam. The core and cooling system are surrounded by a barrier of thick concrete. The entire building is also built with steel-lined concrete to prevent the escape of radiation from the reactor.

Nuclear Generation of Electricity

Nuclear fission reactors currently supply over 20 percent of our nation's electricity. One advantage of using nuclear energy is that it's less harmful to the environment than the use of fossil fuels. The fission process produces no air pollution, whereas the burning of coal and petroleum creates nearly 20 000 metric tons of pollutants each day. Nuclear fission doesn't produce carbon dioxide that will escape into the atmosphere and contribute to the problem of global warming. On the other hand, the mining of uranium and extraction of U-235 does cause environmental damage.

How much of our nation's energy is supplied by fission reactors?

Using nuclear fission to generate electricity also has other disadvantages. The water that circulates around the core of the reactor must cool before it goes back into streams and rivers. If it is released into those waterways while still warm, the excess heat could harm fish and other plants and animals in the water. The most serious risk of nuclear fission is the escape of harmful radiation from the power plant. There is an elaborate system of safeguards in nuclear reactors to ensure that this doesn't happen. Strict safety precautions and highly trained workers can prevent most accidents.

After the chain reaction has occurred, however, the fuel rods contain fission products that are highly radioactive. These products must be contained in insulated surroundings while they decay so no

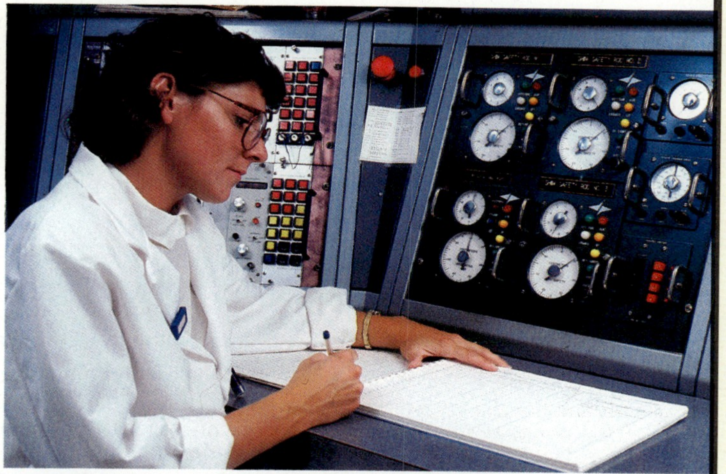

Figure 25-4. Many safeguards are taken to prevent accidents in nuclear fission reactors.

2 TEACH

Key Concepts are highlighted.

CONCEPT DEVELOPMENT

▶Students may be familiar with nuclear accidents that have occurred, especially at the Three Mile Island plant in 1979 in Pennsylvania and the Soviet Chernobyl accident in 1986. The background of these should be discussed.

▶In the Three Mile Island plant, a hydrogen bubble developed above the core and was in danger of exploding. Workers accidentally turned off several safeguards against a meltdown, so the building was flooded with water to avoid a total meltdown and the bubble was slowly released into the atmosphere. The containment building was sealed off, but steam carried low-level radiation into the environment. The long-term effects of this accident are still being studied.

▶The Chernobyl accident was much more severe. The water coolant was lost and the core melted. The graphite moderators burned, allowing clouds of radioactive smoke to escape into the atmosphere. More than 30 people had died after a few months and many more suffer long-term effects. Most U.S. reactors use water as a moderator.

TEACHER F.Y.I.

▶Some sources estimate that accessible uranium reserves will last around 500 years. The fissionable U-235 isotope makes up less than one percent of uranium ore. Uranium must be enriched so that fuel pellets contain about three percent U-235 to sustain a chain reaction.

● REINFORCEMENT 106

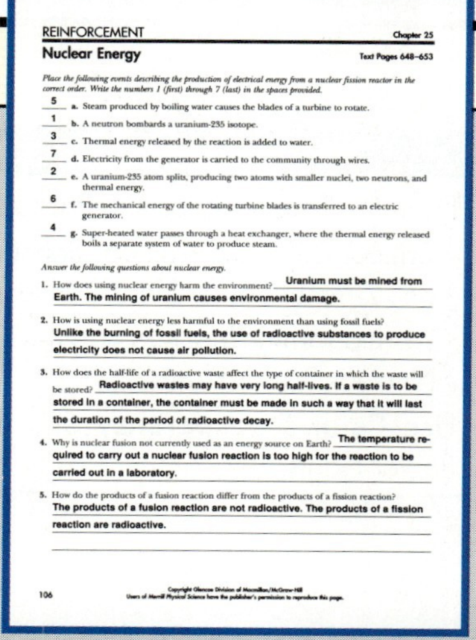

REINFORCEMENT — Chapter 25

Nuclear Energy — Text Pages 648–653

Place the following events describing the production of electrical energy from a nuclear fission reactor in the correct order. Write the numbers 1 (first) through 7 (last) in the spaces provided.

5 a. Steam produced by boiling water causes the blades of a turbine to rotate.

1 b. A neutron bombards a uranium-235 isotope.

3 c. Thermal energy released by the reaction is added to water.

7 d. Electricity from the generator is carried to the community through wires.

2 e. A uranium-235 atom splits, producing two atoms with smaller nuclei, two neutrons, and thermal energy.

6 f. The mechanical energy of the rotating turbine blades is transferred to an electric generator.

4 g. Super-heated water passes through a heat exchanger, where the thermal energy released boils a separate system of water to produce steam.

Answer the following questions about nuclear energy.

1. How does using nuclear energy harm the environment? **Uranium must be mined from Earth. The mining of uranium causes environmental damage.**
2. How is using nuclear energy less harmful to the environment than using fossil fuels? **Unlike the burning of fossil fuels, the use of radioactive substances to produce electricity does not cause air pollution.**
3. How does the half-life of a radioactive waste affect the type of container in which the waste will be stored? **Radioactive wastes may have very long half-lives. If a waste is to be stored in a container, the container must be made in such a way that it will last the duration of the period of radioactive decay.**
4. Why is nuclear fusion not currently used as an energy source on Earth? **The temperature required to carry out a nuclear fusion reaction is too high for the reaction to be carried out in a laboratory.**
5. How do the products of a fusion reaction differ from the products of a fission reaction? **The products of a fusion reaction are not radioactive. The products of a fission reaction are radioactive.**

106

▲ ENRICHMENT 106

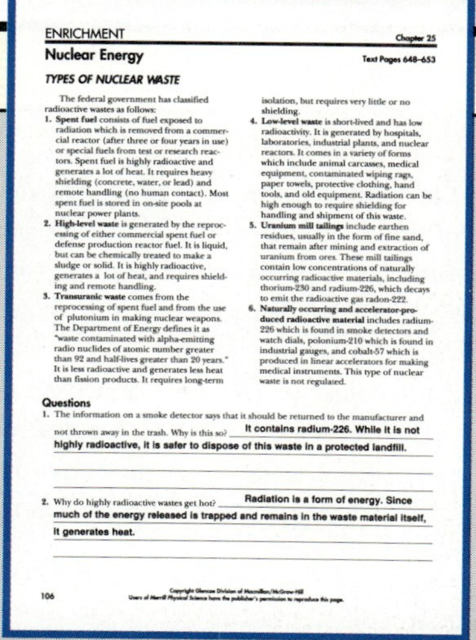

ENRICHMENT — Chapter 25

Nuclear Energy — Text Pages 648–653

TYPES OF NUCLEAR WASTE

The federal government has classified radioactive wastes as follows:

1. **Spent fuel** consists of fuel exposed to radiation which is removed from a commercial reactor (after three or four years in use) or special fuels from test or research reactors. Spent fuel is highly radioactive and generates a lot of heat. It requires heavy shielding (concrete, water, or lead) and remote handling (no human contact). Most spent fuel is stored in on-site pools at nuclear power plants.
2. **High-level waste** is generated by the reprocessing of either commercial spent fuel or defense production reactor fuel. It is liquid, but can be chemically treated to make a sludge or solid. It is highly radioactive, generates a lot of heat, and requires shielding and remote handling.
3. **Transuranic waste** comes from the reprocessing of spent fuel and from the use of plutonium in making nuclear weapons. The Department of Energy defines it as "waste contaminated with alpha-emitting radio nuclides of atomic number greater than 92 and half-lives greater than 20 years." It is less radioactive and generates less heat than fission products. It requires long-term isolation, but requires very little or no shielding.
4. **Low-level waste** is short-lived and has low radioactivity. It is generated by hospitals, laboratories, industrial plants, and nuclear reactors. It comes in a variety of forms which include animal carcasses, medical equipment, contaminated wiping rags, paper towels, protective clothing, hand tools, and old equipment. Radiation can be high enough to require shielding for handling and shipment of this waste.
5. **Uranium mill tailings** include earthen residues, usually in the form of fine sand, that remain after mining and extraction of uranium from ores. These mill tailings contain low concentrations of naturally occurring radioactive materials, including thorium-230 and radium-226, which decays to emit the radioactive gas radon-222.
6. **Naturally occurring and accelerator-produced radioactive material** includes radium-226 which is found in smoke detectors and watch dials, polonium-210 which is found in industrial gauges, and cobalt-57 which is produced in linear accelerators for making medical instruments. This type of nuclear waste is not regulated.

Questions

1. The information on a smoke detector says that it should be returned to the manufacturer and not thrown away in the trash. Why is this so? **It contains radium-226. While it is not highly radioactive, it is safer to dispose of this waste in a protected landfill.**
2. Why do highly radioactive wastes get hot? **Radiation is a form of energy. Since much of the energy released is trapped and remains in the waste material itself, it generates heat.**

106

CONCEPT DEVELOPMENT

▶To convey the idea of how mass-efficient nuclear energy is, tell students that in an average person's lifetime, over 1.5 million kilograms of coal versus 2.5 uranium fuel pellets will be needed to supply the person's energy needs.

▶In addition to being an important scientific issue, the use of nuclear energy is a subject of political debate because it affects public safety.

▶Have interested students compose a clearly written formal letter to the congressional representatives of their choice giving informed views on the use of nuclear energy. Students should consider not only the problems of nuclear energy use but also the problems of burning fossil fuels to generate energy and the decreased standard of living that would result from energy shortage.

▶You might provide them with a list of names and addresses of senators and representatives.

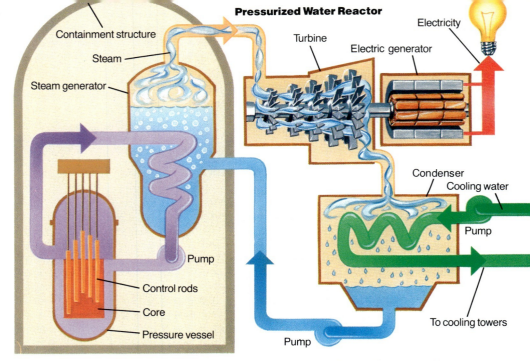

Figure 25-5. The coolant water and the water used to produce the steam that turns the turbines are not the same in a water-cooled nuclear power plant.

radiation will escape into the environment. Because these fission products have long half-lives, they must be stored in containers that will last the duration of the period of radioactive decay, which can be as long as tens of thousands of years.

Another problem is the disposal of the reactor itself when it no longer runs as it should. Every nuclear reactor has a limited useful life span of a few decades. After that time the reactor's efficiency is severely reduced by the presence of large amounts of fission products that can't be cleaned up. The reactor is then shut down or "decommissioned."

Nuclear Waste Disposal

Has your watch ever run down because the battery was too old? The battery wasn't able to produce enough energy to allow your watch to keep correct time. Once you replaced the battery, your watch worked. A similar thing happens to the fuel source in a nuclear reactor. After about three years, there is not enough fissionable U-235 left in the fuel pellets to sustain the chain reaction. These

OPTIONS

INQUIRY QUESTIONS

▶**Why is decommissioning a nuclear reactor not an easy task?** *Many parts of the reactor are contaminated with low-level radioactive waste and must be cared for as nuclear waste.*

▶**If spent fuel contains reduced amounts of fissionable U-235, why must it be treated as radioactive waste?** *It contains radioactive fission products, as well as remaining uranium.*

PROGRAM RESOURCES

From the **Teacher Resource Package** use:

Critical Thinking/Problem Solving, page 31, Zimmer Power Plant Conversion.

Transparency Masters, pages 99-100, Nuclear Power Plants.

Use **Color Transparency** 50, Nuclear Power Plants.

used fuel pellets are called "spent" fuel. The spent fuel contains the radioactive fission products in addition to the remaining uranium. This is an example of nuclear waste. **Nuclear wastes** are radioactive by-products that result when radioactive materials are used. They are usually classified as high-level and low-level wastes for disposal.

Radiation is around you all the time. Low-level nuclear waste usually contains a small amount of radioactive material diluted by a large amount of nonradioactive material. Products of some medical and industrial processes are low-level wastes. They may include items used in handling radioactive materials such as protective gloves. These low-level wastes are usually buried in sealed containers in locations licensed by the federal government. When dilute enough, they are sometimes released into the air or water.

High-level nuclear waste is generated in nuclear power plants and by defense research. After spent fuel is removed from a reactor, it is stored in a deep, heavily insulated pool of water. Many of the radioactive materials in high-level nuclear waste have short half-lives. Almost half of the radiation will have been emitted in several months. But the spent fuel also contains materials that will continue to decay for thousands of years. For this reason, the waste must be disposed of in extremely durable and stable containers.

Fusion Power

Imagine the amount of energy the sun must give off to heat Earth 93 million miles away. In Chapter 24, thermonuclear fusion was explained as the process that releases this energy. Recall that thermonuclear fusion is the joining together of small nuclei at high temperatures. Fusing the nuclei in one gram of heavy hydrogen gives off about the same amount of energy as burning more than eight million grams of coal. If we could make thermonuclear fusion happen in a laboratory, we would likely have the answer to Earth's energy problems.

Figure 25-6. A solid capsule of nuclear waste, can be made by mixing the wastes with molten glass. These capsules are buried in sealed containers.

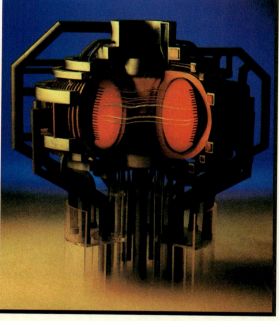

Figure 25-7. Two nuclei fuse to form a larger nucleus in this experimental fusion reactor.

CONCEPT DEVELOPMENT
▶ Ask students to generate their own lists of ideas for nuclear waste disposal. Have them share their ideas in a small group, and arrive at a class consensus about what disposal methods seem the most feasible.

CROSS CURRICULUM
▶ **Geology:** In 1987, Congress voted to build the first national permanent nuclear repository site at Yucca Mountain, Nevada. Burial of waste is scheduled to start in 2003, although this date has been set back several times. Find out what kind of geological features this location has that make it suitable for a nuclear repository.

CHECK FOR UNDERSTANDING
Use the Mini Quiz to check for understanding.

MINI QUIZ

Use the Mini Quiz to check students' recall of chapter content.

1 **What type of nuclear reaction is used to generate electricity in a nuclear reactor?** *nuclear fission*
2 **Which isotope of uranium is used as the fuel in a fission reactor?** *U-235*
3 **What is "spent fuel"?** *used fuel pellets that do not contain enough U-235 to sustain a chain reaction*

RETEACH
Refer to Investigate 24-1 on page 629. Make an analogy between spent fuel and rubber stoppers dropped.

EXTENSION
For students who have mastered this section, use the **Reinforcement** and **Enrichment** masters or other OPTIONS provided.

CONCEPT DEVELOPMENT

▶ Help students recall that a magnet can exert a force on moving charged particles. If designed correctly, this magnetic force could contain plasma while it undergoes fusion at very high temperatures. Stress that fusion is a possible and desirable future energy source because it is plentiful and clean.

Science and READING

The technology to turn sunlight into usable energy is inefficient and expensive at the present time.

3 CLOSE

▶ Ask questions 1-3 and the **Apply** Question in the Section Review.

▶ This is a good place to emphasize the difference between science and technology. Knowing how to split an atom is not harmful, but humans can choose to create harmful devices with it.

▶ Have students write a short essay explaining and commenting on the following quote by Albert Einstein. Write the quote on the chalkboard or put it on the overhead. "The discovery of the nuclear chain reaction need not bring about the destruction of mankind any more than did the discovery of matches."

SECTION REVIEW ANSWERS

1. Control rods are inserted among the fuel rods to absorb excess neutrons. The circulating water also slows the neutrons.

2. Both processes are used to release thermal energy to boil water and produce steam. The generation process is the same after the steam is produced.

3. It is difficult to maintain the high temperatures required for nuclear fusion. At these temperatures, materials cannot be used to contain the fusion.

4. Apply: This is a sample of high-level nuclear waste. It should initially be allowed to cool and decay in water. Then it should be sealed in an insulated container and buried deep in the ground in a repository.

Science and READING

The energy that reaches us from the sun is 50 000 times as much as the whole world uses. In light of this fact, why do you think we continually have energy shortages?

What is the source of energy for nuclear fusion?

The challenge lies in creating and containing nuclear fusion. The temperature needed to carry out a nuclear fusion reaction is over one million degrees Celsius. The plasma containing the hydrogen nuclei can't be contained by any material at this temperature. However, it can be contained for a short time in a "magnetic bottle" which uses a magnetic field to keep the particles in a small volume. Unfortunately, the energy required to maintain the high temperatures needed for the fusion reaction is greater than the energy output from the fusion of the nuclei.

Let's examine the benefits of nuclear fusion as a source of energy. Hydrogen nuclei, such as those found in water, are the source of energy for nuclear fusion. Hydrogen is the most abundant element in the universe. Unlike those in nuclear fission, the products of nuclear fusion are not radioactive. Some neutrons released by the fusion reactions, however, can react with the walls of a fusion reactor to make the walls radioactive. Helium, the gas commonly used to fill balloons, is the main product of hydrogen fusion. Someday nuclear fusion may provide a permanent and economical way to generate electricity.

SECTION REVIEW

1. How is the rate of fission in a nuclear reactor controlled?
2. What do the nuclear generation of electricity and the burning of fossil fuels to generate electricity have in common?
3. Explain the major obstacles in controlling nuclear fusion.
4. **Apply:** Suppose that in a research project, you have generated a 10-gram sample of nuclear waste. Some of the materials have a fast half-life and some will decay for thousands of years. How would you classify it and how will it likely be disposed of?

Skill Builder

☑ Concept Mapping

Design an events chain concept map for the generation of electricity in a nuclear fission reactor. Begin with the bombarding neutron and end with electricity in overhead lines. If you need help, refer to Concept Mapping in the **Skill Handbook** on pages 684 and 685.

Skill Builder

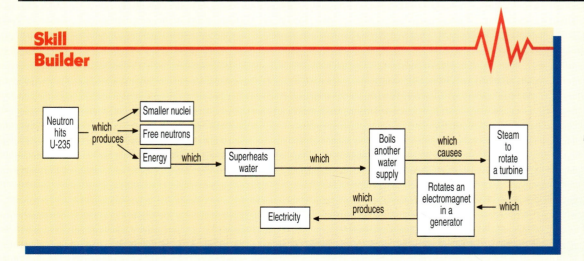

ACTIVITY 25-1
Nuclear Waste Disposal

Problem: *Can you design a safe storage method?*

Materials

- sodium hydroxide pellets (4)
- 100 mL beakers (4)
- phenolphthalein solution
- plastic food wrap
- aluminum foil
- rubber bands (3)
- twist ties (2)
- modeling clay
- forceps
- goggles

Procedure

1. Copy the data table.
2. Let the sodium hydroxide pellets represent pellets of nuclear waste. Your job is to test materials that may be able to keep unwanted chemicals from leaking into the environment.
3. **CAUTION:** *Do not touch the sodium hydroxide pellets or solution with your hands. Always wear goggles when handling sodium hydroxide. Wipe up all spills.*
4. Fill all four beakers with water and add 3 or 4 drops of phenolphthalein to each.
5. Using the forceps, place one pellet in one of the beakers. Record your observations.
6. Wrap each of the remaining pellets; one in aluminum foil, one in plastic wrap, and one in clay. Secure the plastic with twist ties.
7. Drop the wrapped pellets into the remaining three beakers and cover them with food wrap.
8. Make observations each day for three days to determine if there is leakage from the containers. Record your observations in the data table.
9. After the last observations, pour the solutions into a container provided by your teacher.

Data and Observations Sample Data

Beaker Containing Pellets	Observations		
	Day 1	Day 2	Day 3
Unwrapped	Red color	indicates	leakage
Wrapped in aluminum foil	Leakage	Leakage	Leakage
Wrapped in plastic wrap	No leakage	Leakage	Leakage
Embedded in clay	No leakage	No leakage	No leakage

Analyze

1. Was red color seen in any of the beakers after the first day?
2. After three days, which, if any, of the beakers show no red color?

Conclude and Apply

3. What kind of wrapping appears to be the most leak proof?
4. Why do you think storing and disposing nuclear wastes is a major concern of society?

ANSWERS TO QUESTIONS

1. All of the beakers containing aluminum samples will corrode, leak, and turn red. Some of the plastic containers may show leakage and turn red.
2. Clay, if properly applied, will continue to contain the chemical and the solution will remain clear.
3. the clay
4. Nuclear generation of electricity is a reliable energy source if plant safety can be maintained and a secure method of disposal can be found. Some nuclear waste will be radioactive for thousands of years.

PROGRAM RESOURCES

From the **Teacher Resource Package** use:
Activity Worksheets, pages 202-203, Activity 25-1: Nuclear Waste Disposal.

ACTIVITY 25-1
3 days, 20 min/day

OBJECTIVE: Simulate the problems of nuclear waste disposal.

PROCESS SKILLS applied in this activity:
▶**Observing** in Procedure Steps 5 and 8.
▶**Formulating Models** in Procedure Step 2.

COOPERATIVE LEARNING
Form Science Investigation teams of three to six students. Have only one person on each team manipulate the pellets.

TEACHING THE ACTIVITY
Troubleshooting: When students seal the pellet in clay, have them start with a patty of clay about 0.5 cm thick, pull the clay up around the pellet, seal very well, and roll the material *gently* into a smooth ball.
▶**CAUTION:** *Sodium hydroxide is very caustic. It must not come in contact with skin or other tissues. Do not attempt this activity unless you emphasize safety at every step. Eye safety is essential and goggles must be worn. Make eye wash equipment available. Keep track of every pellet. Sodium hydroxide can absorb water from the air until it becomes a puddle of caustic solution. Wipe up all spills. Skin will feel slippery if contaminated. Have students wash their hands if they come in contact with the pellets and before they leave the lab.*
▶The need for following strict handling precautions helps make the point of the activity.
▶Discuss the idea that each pellet represents a pellet of radioactive waste and that good containment must resist environmental contamination.
▶Provide small squares (5 cm × 5 cm) of aluminum foil and plastic. Provide enough modeling clay to enclose a pellet.
▶Before disposing of solutions, neutralize them by adding just enough dilute hydrochloric acid to make the red color disappear.

PREPARATION

SECTION BACKGROUND

▶ Natural uranium is only 0.7 percent fissionable U-235. Breeder reactors can multiply the amount of fissionable fuel available.

1 MOTIVATE

▶ Table tennis balls and spring mousetraps can be used to demonstrate breeder reactors. Imagine that among the "fissionable" mousetraps there are mixed in several that were almost set, but needed the spring compressed only one more millimeter. Now suppose a way could be found to harness a portion of the energy of the snapping traps to complete arming of these other traps. This is comparable to what takes place in a breeder reactor.

TYING TO PREVIOUS KNOWLEDGE:
Ask students if they think it is possible to use energy and, at the same time, produce more energy than you started with. It is not possible because of the law of conservation of energy. Remind them that energy does not disappear, it simply changes to less useful forms.

OBJECTIVES AND SCIENCE WORDS:
Have students review the objectives and science words to become familiar with this section.

2 TEACH

Key Concepts are highlighted.

CONCEPT DEVELOPMENT

▶ Share this idea with your students. Imagine that by using lights in your home you could actually send out more electricity than you started with. Of course this is not possible, but it may help students understand the advantage of a breeder reactor.

New Science Words

breeder reactor

Objectives

▶ Distinguish between breeder reactors and normal nuclear fission reactors.
▶ Assess the advantages and disadvantages of operating breeder reactors.

Are Breeder Reactors Really Such a Good Idea?

You read about using nuclear fission as a way of generating electricity in the last section. Do you remember the isotope that is commonly used as a fuel source in a fission reactor? The fuel rods are made of a small amount of U-235 in a larger sample of unfissionable U-238. The fissionable U-235 isotope is not plentiful in nature. It is a nonrenewable resource that may be depleted in less than 100 years. If nuclear energy is to be a long-lasting energy source, other nuclear fuels must be developed.

A **breeder reactor** is a nuclear reactor that produces, or "breeds," new fuel as it operates. In a breeder reactor, some of the neutrons produced by the fission of U-235 are absorbed by the U-238 nuclei while other neutrons cause fission of U-235. This requires that more neutrons be captured in the fuel rods, and it leads to difficulties in the reactor design. The new U-239 nuclei decays in several days to form Pu-239, as illustrated in the picture equation shown below.

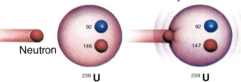

Neutron   238 U

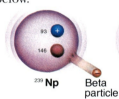

239 U

239 Np   Beta particle   239 Pu

This isotope of plutonium is fissionable. Thus, a large supply of new Pu-239 fuel can be produced from the otherwise useless U-238 nuclei. Three new plutonium atoms are formed for every two plutonium atoms that under-

OPTIONS

Meeting Different Ability Levels

For Section 25-3, use the following **Teacher Resource Masters** depending upon individual students' needs.

◆ **Study Guide Master** for all students.
● **Reinforcement Master** for students of average and above average ability levels.
▲ **Enrichment Master** for above average students.

CROSS CURRICULUM
▶ History: Research the Manhattan Project, which led to the making of the nuclear bombs.

CHECK FOR UNDERSTANDING
Ask questions 1-2 in the Section Review.

RETEACH
Place 99 colored marbles in a jar to represent U-238. Place one marble of a different color in the jar to represent fissionable U-235. Explain that breeder reactors can turn the other U-238 atoms into fissionable plutonium.

EXTENSION
For students who have mastered this section, use the **Reinforcement** and **Enrichment** masters or other OPTIONS provided.

go fission. As a result, more fuel is present after fission has occurred in the reactor than was present before the fission occurred. After operating for several years, a breeder reactor can produce twice as much fissionable fuel as it started with.

Breeder reactors have obvious efficiency advantages. The Pu-239 can be chemically separated from the remaining uranium and used in another reactor. So, breeder reactors can prolong the life of nuclear energy as an energy resource. This process decreases our burning of fossil fuels and the resulting pollution.

Breeder reactors can cause several hazards for society. As with nuclear fission reactors, safe radioactive waste disposal is still a problem. There is a risk of releasing low-level radioactive materials into the air and water. The plutonium fuel produced in a breeder reactor has a half-life of 24 000 years. Elemental plutonium is chemically poisonous in addition to being radioactive, but it usually combines with oxygen to form inert compounds.

SECTION REVIEW

1. How does a breeder reactor differ from a nuclear fission reactor?
2. List the advantages and disadvantages of using breeder reactors.

You Decide!

Breeder reactors produce Pu-239. This is an important component of nuclear fission weapons. How do you think breeder reactors should be regulated? Explain your point of view.

3 CLOSE

▶ Use the You Decide question to facilitate discussion of the advantages and disadvantages of breeder reactors. Point out that one of the dangers is that breeder reactors produce relatively concentrated plutonium that would allow cheap nuclear weapons to be produced. If not properly regulated, terrorists could possibly even acquire plutonium by theft.

SECTION REVIEW ANSWERS

1. A breeder reactor produces more fissionable material as it operates; a fission reactor produces spent fuel.
2. They procure Pu-239, which is chemically toxic, has a long half-life, and remains radioactive for many years. It can be used to make nuclear weapons.

YOU DECIDE!

Discussions should reflect both the advantages and disadvantages of breeder reactors. You may want to guide students to discuss the depletion of uranium by ordinary reactors as well as the safety and security problems with breeder reactors.

● REINFORCEMENT 107

REINFORCEMENT   Chapter 25
Breeder Reactors   Text Pages 654–655

Circle the term or phrase in the parenthesis that makes each statement true.

1. Most nuclear reactors use (uranium-235) uranium-238) as a fuel.
2. Uranium-235 is a (renewable, (nonrenewable) resource.
3. The fissionable uranium-235 isotope of uranium (is, (is not) plentiful in nature.
4. A nuclear reactor that produces new fuel as it operates is a (breeder) fission) reactor.
5. U-239 nuclei produced in a breeder reactor decay in a few days to form (U-238, (Pu-239)).
6. Plutonium-239 is formed from the decay of ((U-239), U-238) nuclei.
7. After several years, a breeder reactor produces ((twice), one-half) as much fuel as it started with.
8. Elemental plutonium is both radioactive and ((poisonous) nontoxic).
9. Plutonium-239 isotope (is, (is not) fissionable.
10. Nuclear energy (does, (does not) cause air pollution.
11. Plutonium has a half-life of 24 000 (days, (years)).
12. When plutonium combines with oxygen, it forms ((inert), poisonous) compounds.

In the space provided, list three advantages and three disadvantages of using breeder reactors to produce electricity. **Answers will vary. All logical responses should be accepted.**

13. Advantages
   • **The use of breeder reactors does not cause air pollution.**
   • **The use of breeder reactors decreases the amount of fossil fuels used to produce electricity.**
   • **The use of breeder reactors prolongs the life of nuclear energy as an energy source because it makes additional fuel.**

14. Disadvantages
   • **Plutonium produced in breeder reactors is both radioactive and very toxic.**
   • **Safe disposal of radioactive wastes is a problem because of their long half-lives.**
   • **Radioactive materials that are released into air and water supplies are harmful to living things.**

Copyright Glencoe Division of Macmillan/McGraw-Hill
Users of *Merrill Physical Science* have the publisher's permission to reproduce this page.   107

▲ ENRICHMENT 107

ENRICHMENT   Chapter 25
Breeder Reactors   Text Pages 654–655

A NEW TYPE OF NUCLEAR REACTOR

The concern over global warming has led to renewed research in the use of nuclear energy. A new type of breeder reactor, called the Integral Fast Reactor (IFR), is being developed by Argonne National Laboratory. This type of reactor may be able to overcome the roadblocks to the use of nuclear energy posed by public safety concerns.

The IFR can process its own fuel. It does not need backup systems or human intervention. It will not produce waste that needs to be disposed of in some distant site. It consists of a core, fuel, and a reprocessing facility. It is a pool-type, sodium-cooled reactor. The major components sit in a pool of thousands of gallons of molten sodium. The pool prevents overheating in case of accidents.

The IFR uses a metal-alloy fuel made up of uranium, plutonium, and zirconium. The metal-alloy transmits heat quickly, thus limiting heat buildup in the core and enhancing core cooling. The metal fuel is easily reprocessed and recast into new fuel.

IFR fuel reprocessing takes place entirely by remote control in a facility attached to the plant. After loading the core the first time, the facility creates and processes all fuel. This eliminates the need to transport radioactive material to or from the site during the reactor's lifetime.

Existing nuclear power plants use about one percent of the energy contained in an enriched and fissionable uranium-235. The rest is unused waste. The IFR uses a process that converts 100% of natural uranium into plutonium. The plutonium and by-products of the nuclear reaction are recycled into the core. These wastes are then destroyed in the core. In time, the amount of waste being destroyed equals the amount of material being created by the breeder reactor. This limits the amount of material that must be stored for long periods of time.

Tests of meltdown accidents similar to those occurring at Chernobyl (when coolant stopped flowing) and Three Mile Island (when the reactor lost its ability to transfer heat to components that produce steam and generate electricity) were conducted. In both cases, the small IFR-like reactor simply shut itself down without human intervention or backup safety systems taking action.

Questions
1. How can the IFR breeder reactor provide a long-term solution to global warming and dependence on foreign oil? **It does not produce carbon dioxide which contributes to global warming. It provides a safe alternative to crude oil.**

2. What are the advantages and disadvantages of IFR technology over present nuclear reactors? **Advantages: It is more efficient and produces less waste. Disadvantages: It produces plutonium which could be stolen to make nuclear weapons.**

Copyright Glencoe Division of Macmillan/McGraw-Hill
Users of *Merrill Physical Science* have the publisher's permission to reproduce this page.   107

PREPARATION

SECTION BACKGROUND

▶ During the Arab Oil Embargo of 1973, President Nixon declared that the U.S. would meet its own energy needs by the end of the decade. His program was called Project Independence. Years later, we still rely on imported energy to meet much of our energy needs.

▶ Biomass is waste material that can be burned to produce steam. In Hawaii, the sugar industry produces a lot of bagasse, dry fiber similar to wood. Over one-third of the energy needed on two Hawaiian islands is supplied by this biomass.

▶ Solar energy actually originates in thermonuclear fusion of hydrogen to helium in the sun. It travels to Earth as electromagnetic radiation.

PREPLANNING

▶ Gather materials needed for Activity 25-2. The earlier students begin to prepare for this activity, the better.

1 MOTIVATE

▶ Have the following items displayed on a table: a toy windmill or pinwheel, a beaker of water, a pan of wood scraps or other organic waste, and a photovoltaic cell. Have students tell how each of the items could be used to do work. Mention that these are small scale versions of the energy sources discussed in this chapter.

TYING TO PREVIOUS
KNOWLEDGE: Mention that students have learned about fossil fuels and nuclear fission, which supply the majority of our energy requirements. But those are nonrenewable resources and they will run out.

25-4 Alternative Energy Sources

New Science Words

photovoltaic cell
hydroelectricity
tidal energy
geothermal energy

Objectives

▶ Analyze the need for alternative energy sources.
▶ Discuss the methods of generating electricity with several energy sources.
▶ Describe the advantages and disadvantages of several alternative energy sources.

EcoTip

Keep the outside of your family car clean and waxed. Also make sure the tires are properly inflated. These measures will increase gas mileage and help to conserve gasoline.

The Need for Alternatives

Can you name any sources of energy other than fossil fuels and nuclear energy? Although we have enough of these energy sources to fill our energy demands today, there is a great need to develop alternative sources of energy for the future. As you have already discovered, using fossil fuels and nuclear fission for our energy needs has many disadvantages.

Nuclear fission and the burning of fossil fuels are both processes used to boil water to produce steam. Other materials can be burned to give off energy as well. Biomass is renewable organic matter, such as wood, sugar cane fibers, rice hulls, and animal manure. It can be burned in the presence of oxygen to convert the stored chemical energy to thermal energy. Biomass burning is probably the oldest use of natural resources for human needs.

Have you ever seen gasohol advertised at a gas station? How does this fuel differ from normal gasoline? Corn and other plant fibers can be fermented to produce alcohol, another combustible fuel source. In fermentation, yeast converts the sugar and starch in the grain to ethanol. The ethanol is combined with fossil fuels in gasoline. This product, commonly called gasohol, is combusted inside your car engine.

Biomass and gasohol are just two examples of many energy alternatives that reduce our consumption of fossil fuels. The energy alternatives discussed in this section

OPTIONS

Meeting Different Ability Levels

For Section 25-4, use the following **Teacher Resource Masters** depending upon individual students' needs.

◆ **Study Guide Master** for all students.

● **Reinforcement Master** for students of average and above average ability levels.

▲ **Enrichment Master** for above average students.

Additional Teacher Resource Package masters are listed in the OPTIONS box throughout the section. The additional masters are appropriate for all students.

◆ STUDY GUIDE 108

STUDY GUIDE   Chapter 25
Alternative Energy Sources   Text Pages 656–662

1. energy produced from the movement of ocean waters (2 words)
2. fuel made from petroleum and alcohol
3. type of alcohol used in gasohol
4. energy produced from radioactive materials (2 words)
5. energy produced from thermal energy deep inside Earth (2 words)
6. moving air
7. energy from the sun (2 words)
8. electricity produced by harnessing the kinetic energy in moving water
9. device that produces electricity from moving air
10. device that converts solar energy into electricity; _____ cell
11. country where all power plants use geothermal energy
12. type of fuel produced from renewable organic materials

make use of processes that occur naturally on Earth. What natural processes do you see around you which could be used to generate electricity or provide heat?

Solar Energy

The sun is Earth's only source of new energy. Have you ever seen an automobile powered by sunlight? The solar panels on the car collect and use solar energy to power the car. Methods of collecting and using solar energy are usually divided into two categories, passive and active solar energy.

Passive solar heating is the direct use of the sun's energy in maintaining comfortable indoor temperatures. Passive solar heating was used centuries ago by the Romans to heat their bath houses. Efforts in energy conservation have renewed interest in this method of heating. Buildings constructed with strategically-placed windows can be heated by the sun. On warm days, these windows can be covered with blinds to prevent excessive heating.

In active solar heating, solar panels collect and store solar energy. Solar panels are made of large, darkly colored trays covered with transparent glass or plastic. Large mirrors are sometimes used to focus the sun's radiation into these solar collectors. The panels absorb the sun's energy and use it to heat water. The heated water can be used directly, or it can be stored to give off thermal energy. Solar energy can even be used to drive electric power generators in solar thermal power plants.

A device used to convert solar energy into electricity is the **photovoltaic cell,** also called the solar cell. Do you own a solar-powered calculator? It contains a solar cell. Photovoltaic cells are made of a semiconductor lined on both surfaces with a conducting metal. As light strikes the surface of the cell, electrons flow between the two metal layers. If these metal layers are connected into a circuit, an electric current moves through the solar cell. Many cells connected in a circuit can provide significant amounts of electricity.

What is passive solar heating?

Figure 25-8. Solar cells can be used to supply the electricity to operate an automobile.

657

▶ Water wheels probably first provided mechanical energy around 200 B.C. They have been used to turn levers and run machines, such as sawmills and grain grinders. Falling water was first harnessed for the purpose of providing electricity at Niagara Falls in 1879.

CONCEPT DEVELOPMENT

▶ U.S. electric utility companies have also devised ways of storing hydropower to meet times of emergency or peak demand. An upper and lower reservoir are constructed near a power plant. When extra electricity is needed, water is allowed to flow from the upper to the lower reservoir. During off-peak times, electricity is used to pump water back to the upper reservoir.

▶ Water is a free and renewable resource. Ask your students why hydroelectricity does not supply more of our energy needs. Point out that most sites suitable for developing hydroelectric power are already in use. Many locations do not have the required water resources. Also, hydroelectric plants cannot be built in many locations because they disrupt the natural ecosystem.

This method of producing electricity is more expensive on a large scale than the use of fossil fuels, but it can be less expensive in isolated areas, when the cost of building transmission lines to those areas is considered. Solar energy is a pollution-free resource that is becoming more economical as our solar technology develops.

Hydroelectricity

One way to produce electricity is with water. Water flowing in rivers carries tremendous amounts of kinetic and potential energy. Dams are built to store vast amounts of

water. Right behind a dam, the water is very deep. Near the base of a hydroelectric dam, water is allowed to rush out through tunnels. The rushing water spins a turbine. The turbine rotates the shaft of an electric generator, which produces electricity.

Hydroelectricity is electricity produced by the energy of moving water. Hydroelectric power plants are a very efficient way to produce electricity. They produce almost no pollution. The bodies of water held back by dams can provide lakes for recreational uses and irrigation. The ongoing natural water cycle makes hydroelectric power a permanent resource. After the initial cost of building a dam and power plant, the electricity is relatively cheap. However, artificial dams can disturb the balance of natural ecosystems.

Tidal Energy

The gravitational forces of the moon and the sun cause bulges in Earth's oceans. As Earth rotates, the two bulges of ocean water move westward. Each day the level of the ocean on a coast rises and falls continually. A kind of hydroelectric power can be generated by these ocean tides. The moving water can be trapped by building a dam at the opening of a river or bay. The flowing water spins a turbine, which operates an electric generator. Energy generated by tidal motion is called **tidal energy.**

OPTIONS

ENRICHMENT

▶ Research the possible ecological hazards of building tidal power facilities. Some shallow-water organisms depend on unrestricted cycles of tides to bring food and remove waste.

▶ Have interested students research wave power, a form of hydroelectric power which uses the kinetic energy of waves and converts it to electricity.

PROGRAM RESOURCES

From the **Teacher Resource Package** use:
Science and Society, page 29, Hydroelectric Power: Past or Future?
Use **Laboratory Manual,** Using the Sun's Energy.

Like producing hydroelectric power, generating electricity from tidal motion is nearly pollution-free. But, there are only a few places on Earth where the difference between high and low tide is large enough to be an efficient source of energy. In the United States the use of tidal energy is being explored in the Cook Inlet in Alaska and Passamaquoddy Bay in Maine. The ocean environment will possibly make construction and maintenance of these plants difficult. Salt water corrodes metals, so corrosion-resistant building materials will have to be used. Ocean storms can also be violent and damaging. Tidal energy probably will be a limited source of energy in the future.

Wind Energy

You may have seen a windmill on a farm. Or, in a windy region you may have seen several hundred windmills. A windmill is a turbine that is turned by the wind instead of steam or water. The windmill spins and rotates an electric generator to produce electricity. Obviously, electricity cannot be produced when there is very little wind.

Only a few places on Earth consistently have enough wind to rely on wind power to meet energy needs. Improved design of wind generators can increase their efficiency, so new methods of using the wind's energy are being researched. Wind generators do not actually use up any resources. They do not pollute the atmosphere or water. However, they do change the appearance of a landscape.

25-4 ALTERNATIVE ENERGY SOURCES 659

Use the Mini Quiz to check for understanding.

MINI QUIZ

Use the Mini Quiz to check students' recall of chapter content.

1 A device that is used to convert solar energy into electricity is called a(n) _____ . *photovoltaic cell*

2 Renewable organic matter that can be used as an energy resource is called _____ . *biomass*

3 How do windmills produce electricity? *They spin and rotate an electric generator.*

4 Where does geothermal energy come from? *the hot gases and molten rock beneath the surface of Earth*

RETEACH

Ask students to list the six energy sources discussed in this section. These are biomass, solar, hydroelectricity, tidal, wind, and geothermal. Once you have established that students have a complete list, ask them to write a sentence describing how we can obtain usable energy from each source.

EXTENSION

For students who have mastered this section, use the **Reinforcement** and **Enrichment** masters or other OPTIONS provided.

Geothermal Energy

Look down at the ground. What do you see and feel underneath your feet? Although you may think of the Earth as a solid sphere, hot gases and molten rock lie far beneath the surface. **4** The inner parts of Earth contain a great deal of thermal energy, called **geothermal energy.** You do not usually notice this energy because most of it is far below Earth's crust.

In some places, Earth's crust has cracks or thin spots in it. These areas allow some of the geothermal energy to rise up near the surface of Earth. Active volcanoes permit hot gases and molten lava from deep within Earth to escape. Perhaps you have seen a geyser shoot steam and hot water from Earth. Have you ever visited or seen pictures of the famous geyser, Old Faithful, in Yellowstone National Park? This water was heated by hot rocks in contact with geothermal energy. Wells can be drilled deep within Earth to pump out this hot water. The temperature of this water and steam ranges from 150°C to 350°C, and the steam can be used to rotate turbines and turn electric generators. Use of geothermal energy can release some sulfur compounds from gases within Earth. This pollution can be controlled by pumping the water and steam back into Earth.

As with wind and tidal energy, there are only certain places on Earth where geothermal energy is accessible as an economical energy resource. For example, in Iceland, all power plants are run by geothermal energy.

What similarities can you identify between all of the alternative energy sources discussed in this chapter? Which ones do you think would be the most useful in your area?

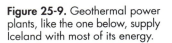
Where is most of Earth's geothermal energy found?

Figure 25-9. Geothermal power plants, like the one below, supply Iceland with most of its energy.

OPTIONS

ENRICHMENT

▶ Have students find out what natural resources are used to provide energy in your community. Have them determine if there are any other sources available that are not being used.

▶ Have students locate on a United States map the areas that use nuclear, tidal, solar, wind, hydroelectric, geothermal, and fossil fuels as sources of energy.

PROBLEM SOLVING

Renewable Energy Sources for Beachtown

Rosa and her family live on the coast in Beachtown. Rosa enjoys the recreation opportunities offered by living on an ocean coast. During the hot, sunny summer, Rosa enjoys cool swims in the ocean and the strong breezes blowing on the beach. She also enjoys fishing at an inlet close to her house.

Like Rosa, many other people think Beachtown is a great place to live and are moving there. Lots of new businesses are being built all over town. The mayor and city council are concerned because the growth of the city is exceeding the production capability of the old fossil-fueled power plant.

Think Critically: What alternative energy sources could the power company consider when planning to increase its output? How do these renewable resources compare with using fossil fuels for energy?

Think Critically: Solar, wind, and tidal energy are renewable and do not pollute the air. Fossil fuels cannot be replaced and cause air pollution. The renewable energy sources are expensive to use and provide limited amounts of energy. Fossil fuels are less expensive and produce more energy when burned.

3 CLOSE

▶Ask questions 1-4 and the **Apply** Question in the Section Review.
▶Have students evaluate what alternative energy sources might be available in your geographical area. What advantages and disadvantages do you see in developing these sources?

SECTION REVIEW

1. Why is there a need for developing and using alternative energy sources?
2. Describe three main ways to use direct solar energy.
3. Identify some advantages and limitations of using hydroelectric and tidal energy.
4. Explain how geothermal energy is used to generate electricity.
5. **Apply:** What single resource do most of the energy alternatives discussed in this section either directly or indirectly depend on?

SECTION REVIEW ANSWERS

1. Fossil fuels and fissionable materials are both nonrenewable resources. Fossil fuels especially are in limited supply. Burning of fossil fuels causes pollution, and nuclear waste disposal is an unsolved problem.
2. Passive solar heating: Put windows and buildings in places where the sun warms and lights the rooms. Active solar heating: Use solar panels and mirrors to focus the sun's energy for heating water or air. Photovoltaic cells: Produce an electric current from the sun's energy.
3. Both hydroelectric and tidal energy use the natural motion of water, are inexpensive, and are relatively nonpolluting. Only certain locations have the resource of moving water, and artificial dams can damage the balance of an ecosystem.
4. Hot water, heated by geothermal energy, is obtained from geysers or deep wells. This steam and hot water is used to operate a turbine generator.
5. Apply: the sun

☑ Outlining

Make an outline of the energy alternatives discussed in this section. List at least one advantage and one disadvantage of each. If you need help, refer to Outlining in the **Skill Handbook** on page 677.

Skill Builder

Skill Builder

Answers will vary; they should be similar to the outline below.

I. Biomass
   A. Uses waste as an energy source.
   B. Produces air pollution.
II. Solar Energy
   A. Causes no pollution.
   B. Initial building is costly.
III. Hydroelectricity
   A. Inexpensive, almost no pollution.
   B. Damages the ecosystem.
C. Useful only in limited areas.
IV. Tidal Energy
   A. Almost pollution free.
   B. Only a few places are suitable.
V. Wind Energy
   A. Almost pollution free.
   B. The wind is not consistent.
VI. Geothermal
   A. The water and steam can be returned to their environment.
   B. It is not feasible in many places.

ACTIVITY 25-2
3 class periods

OBJECTIVE: **Develop** and **present** arguments for decision making regarding the use of various sources of energy.

PROCESS SKILLS applied in this activity:
▶**Communicating** in Procedure Steps 1-3.
▶**Formulating Models** in Procedure Step 4.
▶**Predicting** in Analyze Questions 1-3.

👥 COOPERATIVE LEARNING
Divide the class into Problem Solving Teams, one for each energy source. Students will serve dual roles—as members of study committees and as members of the State Legislature.

TEACHING THE ACTIVITY

Troubleshooting: If a team wishes to take the position that no plant is necessary, they must provide ways of reducing energy needs and defend the possibility of a reduced standard of living.
▶You may want to allow more than two days for this activity.
▶Assign each study team an energy source—coal, petroleum, nuclear, solar, wind, hydro, tidal, or geothermal. Note that not all of these energy sources are appropriate for some states.
▶Provide large sheets of butcher paper, cardboard, tape, scissors, and other items that can be used to make posters and construct models. Encourage students to bring things from home.
▶Allow one period for planning and poster making, one day for model making and report preparation, and one day for reporting and voting.
▶Limit committee reports to five minutes each. Use the remainder of the period for discussion and voting.

PROGRAM RESOURCES
From the **Teacher Resource Package** use:

Activity Worksheets, pages 204-205, Activity 25-2: Energy Alternatives.

ACTIVITY 25-2
Energy Alternatives

Problem: **What kind of energy is practical?**

Materials
- large sheet of poster paper
- set of colored flow pens
- miscellaneous construction supplies

Procedure
1. Your team has been appointed by the state legislature to prepare a recommendation for the construction of a new power plant. You will research the problem and prepare an illustrated oral report on the energy source assigned to you by the governor.
2. Your report must describe the energy source. How does it work? What is it best suited for? What are its limitations?
3. Your report must include an illustration or diagram showing at least one important idea about the construction or operation of the power plant.
4. You must construct a model which can be used to demonstrate how some important part of the power plant works.
5. When all reports have been heard, the legislature will vote on the type of power plant to be constructed.

Analyze
1. Listen to the points being made in each report. Consider the appropriateness of the power source for your state. Does your state have enough sunshine for solar, or enough water for hydro?
2. Are the environmental issues acceptable? Are pollution problems involved? Is there suitable space for construction?
3. Will the power plant provide enough power to meet the need? Is it to be a primary power source for an expanding population or a supplementary source for an existing population?

Conclude and Apply
4. Acting as a member of the legislature, determine how you can best serve the present energy needs of the state and preserve the state's environmental qualities.
5. Acting as a member of the study committee, should you try to influence the legislature to vote in favor of your project?

662   ENERGY SOURCES

ANSWERS TO QUESTIONS
1. Students should consider both climate and terrain.
2. Environmental issues may be ignored in the report. If time permits, encourage the Legislator to ask questions.
3. The energy need may be specified prior to the study or determined after the study is complete. Unless your area has exceptional resources, wind and solar might better be considered as supplements.
4. Questions of this type usually involve trade offs. Lead students to see the need for compromise in both directions.
5. This question can lead to discussion of the role of the scientist in political decision making.

SUMMARY

25-1: Fossil Fuels

1. The three types of fossil fuels are petroleum, natural gas, and coal. They formed from the buried remains of ancient plants and animals.
2. All fossil fuels are nonrenewable energy resources. Supplies will run out soon if they aren't used wisely.

25-2: Nuclear Energy

1. A nuclear reactor uses the energy from a controlled nuclear chain fission reaction to generate electricity.
2. Nuclear wastes must be carefully contained and disposed of so radiation from nuclear decay will not leak into the environment.
3. Nuclear fusion releases greater amounts of energy than nuclear fission, but fusion must occur at temperatures that are too high to be contained in a laboratory.

25-3: Science and Society: Breeder Reactors

1. Breeder reactors make a continuous source of nuclear fuel as a by-product of the chain reaction.
2. Breeder reactors produce plutonium, a fissionable fuel that can be used in nuclear fission reactors or to make nuclear weapons.

25-4: Alternative Energy Sources

1. Alternate energy resources are needed to supplement or replace nonrenewable energy resources.
2. Other sources of energy include hydroelectricity, and solar, wind, tidal, and geothermal energy.
3. Although some alternative energy sources don't pollute the environment and are renewable, their use is often limited to certain regions, as well as being expensive.

KEY SCIENCE WORDS

a. **breeder reactor**
b. **fractional distillation**
c. **geothermal energy**
d. **hydroelectricity**
e. **nonrenewable resources**
f. **nuclear reactor**
g. **nuclear wastes**
h. **petroleum**
i. **photovoltaic cell**
j. **tidal energy**

UNDERSTANDING VOCABULARY

Match each phrase with the correct term from the list of Key Science Words.

1. separates the hydrocarbons in crude oil
2. liquid remains of dead organisms
3. generates electricity from a controlled fission reaction
4. thermal energy inside Earth
5. sources of energy that can't be replaced
6. converts solar energy directly into electricity
7. electricity produced by the energy of moving water
8. energy produced by the rise and fall of ocean levels
9. a fission reactor that produces new reactor fuel
10. by-product of fission reactions

CHAPTER

REVIEW

SUMMARY

Have students read the summary statements to review the major concepts of the chapter.

UNDERSTANDING VOCABULARY

1. b	**6.** i
2. h	**7.** d
3. f	**8.** j
4. c	**9.** a
5. e	**10.** g

OPTIONS

ASSESSMENT

To assess student understanding of material in this chapter, use the resources listed.

COOPERATIVE LEARNING

Consider using cooperative learning in the THINK AND WRITE CRITICALLY, APPLY, and MORE SKILL BUILDERS sections of the Chapter Review.

PROGRAM RESOURCES

From the **Teacher Resource Package** use:
Chapter Review, pages 53-54.
Chapter and Unit Tests, pages 159-162, Chapter Test.
Chapter and Unit Tests, pages 163-164, Unit Test.

CHAPTER
REVIEW

CHECKING CONCEPTS

1.	d	**6.**	d
2.	c	**7.**	b
3.	a	**8.**	b
4.	a	**9.**	c
5.	c	**10.**	d

UNDERSTANDING CONCEPTS

11. core
12. absorbing extra neutrons
13. active solar heating
14. neutrons
15. breeder reactors

THINK AND WRITE CRITICALLY

16. Fossil fuels and biomass are burned to boil water and produce steam. Steam is produced naturally by geothermal energy. Nuclear reactors produce steam with heat from fission reactions. The steam produced by these sources turns a turbine. Hydroelectric and tidal energy use moving water to turn a turbine. Wind turns a turbine-like device. Turbines turn generators, which produce electricity.

17. Our current major energy resource—fossil fuels—is nonrenewable and will soon be depleted. Energy is conserved by turning off lights, adjusting the thermostat, and so on.

18. It is not possible because the concentration of fissionable U-235 in the reactor fuel rods is far below that needed for a nuclear explosion.

19. We do not possess the technology to build fusion reactors that can maintain the high temperatures required.

20. It has been created by the problems of our current primary energy resources. Fossil fuels are nonrenewable and produce pollutants. Nuclear reactors produce radioactive wastes that aren't easily disposed of. Alternative energy resources are not used because the necessary technology does not yet exist, is too expensive, or has limited applicability.

CHECKING CONCEPTS

Choose the word or phrase that completes the sentence.

1. Plant and animal remains that are buried under sediments and acted upon by _____ form fossil fuels.
   a. bacteria   **c.** heat
   b. pressure   **d.** all of these

2. Hydrocarbons react with _____ during the combustion of fossil fuels.
   a. carbon dioxide   **c.** oxygen
   b. carbon monoxide   **d.** water

3. Fossil fuels are becoming more scarce as industrial demands increase and _____.
   a. the population increases
   b. the population decreases
   c. the number of nuclear reactors increases
   d. fewer plants and animals die

4. Both burning fossil fuels and nuclear fission must first be used to produce _____ in order to produce electricity.
   a. steam
   b. carbon dioxide
   c. plutonium
   d. water

5. A major advantage of using nuclear fusion reactors is that they _____.
   a. use hydrogen from air as fuel
   b. produce no radioactivity.
   c. produce only helium as a product
   d. produce no air pollutants

6. Nuclear wastes include _____.
   a. products of fission reactors
   b. materials with very short half-lives
   c. products from medical and industrial processes
   d. all of these

7. High-level nuclear wastes are currently disposed of by _____.
   a. releasing them into water
   b. storing them in a deep, insulated pool of water
   c. burying them in unstable areas
   d. releasing them into the air

8. All of Earth's energy resources can ultimately be traced back to _____.
   a. plants   **c.** geothermal resources
   b. the sun   **d.** fossil fuels

9. Photovoltaic cells must be made _____ before they can be more widely used to produce electricity.
   a. pollution-free   **c.** less expensive
   b. nonrenewable   **d.** all of these

10. _____ is an alternate source of energy that uses water heated naturally by Earth's internal heat.
   a. Hydroelectricity **c.** Tidal energy
   b. Nuclear fission   **d.** Geothermal energy

UNDERSTANDING CONCEPTS

Complete each sentence.

11. The actual fission of uranium occurs in the _____ of a nuclear reactor.

12. Control rods slow the rate of fission in a nuclear reactor by _____.

13. In _____, energy from the sun is collected and stored in solar panels.

14. The major difference between breeder reactors and other fission reactors is that in breeder reactors U-238 nuclei absorb _____ to produce Pu-239.

15. A major disadvantage of _____ is that they make plutonium, which has a very long half-life.

THINK AND WRITE CRITICALLY

16. Most of the energy resources discussed in this chapter produce electricity by means of an electric generator. Briefly discuss how each resource is used to do this.

17. Why is energy conservation important? What are some ways to conserve energy?

18. How great is the possibility of a nuclear explosion in a nuclear reactor?

19. Why isn't fusion being used today as a source of energy?

20. What specific problems have created the need for alternative energy resources? Why aren't these resources more widely used today?

APPLY

21. Which fossil fuel do you think we should use to generate electricity? What are the pros and cons of using this fossil fuel?

22. Match each of the energy resources described in the chapter with the proper type of energy conversion listed below:
    a. kinetic energy to electricity
    b. thermal energy to electricity
    c. nuclear energy to electricity
    d. chemical energy to electricity
    e. light energy to electricity

23. Evaluate the following disposal methods of high-level nuclear wastes:
    a. Bury the wastes in an area of high earthquake and volcanic activity.
    b. Place the wastes on the ocean floor.
    c. Rocket the wastes into space.

24. Classify the energy resources discussed in this chapter as renewable or nonrenewable.

25. Suppose that new reserves of petroleum were discovered and that a non-polluting way to burn them for energy were found. Why would it still be a good idea to decrease our use of petroleum as a source of energy? (HINT: Consider fractional distillation.)

MORE SKILL BUILDERS

If you need help, refer to the Skill Handbook.

1. **Sequencing:** The ultimate source of energy for cooking food on an electric stove is the sun. List in order the steps that must occur before you can use the sun's energy in this way.

2. **Recognizing Cause and Effect:** Complete the following table which describes changes in the normal operation of a nuclear reactor and the possible effects of these changes.

Cause	Effect
1. Uranium oxide pellets containing only U-238	1.
2. Control rods are removed	2.
3.	3. Reactor core overheats; "meltdown"

3. **Making and Using Tables:** Construct a table to summarize the advantages and disadvantages of each of the energy resources discussed in this chapter.

PROJECTS

1. Research the ways in which scientists are currently trying to contain and control a fusion reaction. Write a report and present it to your classmates.

2. Design a campaign to raise public awareness of current energy problems. Point out possible solutions.

APPLY

21. Answers will vary; however, coal might be a logical choice since its supplies are still relatively abundant, but sulfur and nitrogen oxide impurities must be removed from it.

22. (a) wind energy, hydroelectricity, tidal energy; (b) geothermal energy; (c) nuclear fission and fusion; (d) fossil fuels, biomass; (e) photovoltaic cells

23. (a) Not a good way since containment canisters might rupture in geologically unstable areas and release radiation. (b) This removes wastes from human populations; but corrosion by ocean water, pressure, and geological activity could result in leakage. (c) The possibility of an accidental rocket explosion should be considered.

24. renewable: solar energy, hydroelectricity, tidal energy, geothermal energy, wind energy, nonrenewable: fossil fuels, nuclear fusion, fission reactors.

25. The burning of oil as a source of energy should be curtailed so that more of it could be used to produce important chemicals, plastics, and medicines.

MORE SKILL BUILDERS

1. **Sequencing:** Solar energy is: (1) stored as chemical energy in the molecules of plants and animals; (2) released as thermal energy when organic remains (fossil fuels) are combusted; (3) converted to the kinetic energy of steam in a conventional power plant; (4) converted to the mechanical energy of a turbine; (5) converted to electricity by a generator; (6) converted to thermal energy for cooking by a stove.

2. **Recognizing Cause and Effect:** (1) The reaction will not occur since only U-235 is fissionable. (2) The reaction will continue on, uncontrolled and will overheat the reactor core. (3) The reactor's cooling system fails or the control rods fail.

3. **Making and Using Tables:** See left.

RESOURCE	ADVANTAGES	DISADVANTAGES
Fossil fuels	Easily transported	Nonrenewable, cause air pollution
Nuclear fission	Nonpolluting, much energy from little fuel	Produce dangerous nuclear wastes
Nuclear fusion	Nonpolluting, no radioactive wastes	Needed technology does not yet exist
Biomass	Cheap, renewable	CO_2 contributes to global warming
Photovoltaic cells	Clean, inexhaustible	Too expensive
Hydroelectricity, tidal energy, wind energy, geothermal	Clean, renewable	Limited applicability

GLOBAL CONNECTIONS

Objective

In this unit-ending feature, the unit topic, "Electricity and Energy Resources," is extended to other disciplines. Students will see how electricity and energy sources are related to events occurring around the planet.

Motivate

Cooperative Learning: Assign one Connection to each group of students. Using the Expert Teams strategy, have each group find out more about the geographic location of the Connection—its climate, culture, flora and fauna, and ecological issues.

Teaching Tips

▶ Tell students to keep in mind the connection between energy resources and the technology described in each area as they are reading this feature.

▶ Ask students to predict how each technology could be used elsewhere in the world.

Wrap-Up

Conclude this lesson by having students explain how each of the Connections relates back to the unit.

HISTORY

Background: During World War I, radio communication had been restricted to use by the military. The call letters, KDKA, were assigned from a roster of letters that had previously been assigned only to ships and marine stations.

Discussion: Discuss the importance of commercial radio. Ask students to discuss how the instant communication of radio changed people's lives.

Answer to Question: It is an AM station because it broadcasts between 540 and 1600 kilohertz.

Extension: Have students interview older adults about their memories of early radio. Let students share the information with the class.

UNIT7
GLOBAL CONNECTIONS

Electricity and Energy Resources

In this unit, you studied about electricity, magnetism, and energy resources. Now find out how these subjects are connected to other subjects and places around the world.

120°   60°

BIOLOGY

MANURE POWER
Imperial Valley, California
A power plant fired by cow manure generates enough electricity for 20 000 homes. Besides saving about 300 barrels of oil a day, the plant has solved the problem of what to do with the manure from 400 000 cattle in nearby feedlots. What type of alternative energy source does this plant use?

HISTORY

RADIO BROADCASTING
Pittsburgh, Pennsylvania
On the evening of November 2, 1920, the first commercial radio station, KDKA, began broadcasting. The first broadcast was of the Harding-Cox presidential election returns. Hundreds of people, from as far away as Kentucky, heard the broadcast. KDKA operates at 1020 kilohertz. Is it an AM or an FM station?

ASTRONOMY

SPACE TECHNOLOGY ON EARTH
Cape Kennedy, Florida
Cordless power tools are now common around many houses. The first cordless power tools were developed for and used on NASA expeditions to the moon. A cordless drill allowed astronauts to take core samples of the moon. Find out how cordless power tools work.

666

BIOLOGY

Background: The Mesquite Lake Resource Recovery Project burns about 900 tons of manure each day. Ash from the plant is sold as a concrete additive and as an absorbent for toxic wastes.

Discussion: Discuss other possible sources of biomass that could be used to generate electricity in areas that might not have access to cow manure.

Answers to Question: Cow manure is classified as biomass because it is renewable organic matter.

Extension: Have students research heating stoves and furnaces for homes that burn corn as fuel. What are their advantages and disadvantages.

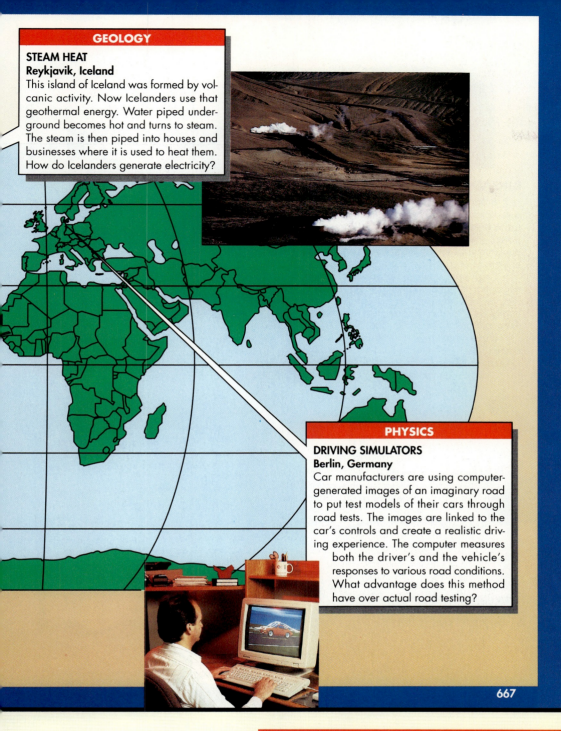

STEAM HEAT
Reykjavik, Iceland
This island of Iceland was formed by volcanic activity. Now Icelanders use that geothermal energy. Water piped underground becomes hot and turns to steam. The steam is then piped into houses and businesses where it is used to heat them. How do Icelanders generate electricity?

PHYSICS

DRIVING SIMULATORS
Berlin, Germany
Car manufacturers are using computer-generated images of an imaginary road to put test models of their cars through road tests. The images are linked to the car's controls and create a realistic driving experience. The computer measures both the driver's and the vehicle's responses to various road conditions. What advantage does this method have over actual road testing?

667

ASTRONOMY

Background: In addition to being used for jobs around the house, cordless power tools are also used in industry and medicine.
Discussion: Discuss the reason cordless power tools were needed on lunar expeditions. Ask students to cite examples of where they might use cordless power tools.
Answer to Question: Cordless power tools contain rechargeable batteries. They must be plugged into an outlet periodically to recharge the battery. After the battery is recharged, they can be used for several hours.
Extension: Have students research the kinds of batteries that are used in cordless power tools.

GEOLOGY

Background: Iceland is located near the Arctic Circle in the cold waters of the North Atlantic. In Iceland, active volcanoes are common. The island was formed by volcanoes along the Mid-Atlantic Ridge. Along the ridge, lava seeps up through deep rifts in the ocean floor.
Discussion: Discuss the advantages and disadvantages of living in an area rich in geothermal energy. Point out to students that steam-heated greenhouses also provide Icelanders with fresh produce all year long.
Answer to Question: They use the steam to rotate turbines, which then turn electric generators.
Extension: Have students research other locations where geothermal energy is used.

PHYSICS

Background: Computer programs used in airplane flight simulators are so realistic that experienced copilots can be certified by the FAA as pilots based only on simulator training and testing.
Discussion: Discuss other uses for this kind of computer program. Ask students if they think it might be useful in driver education classes.
Answer to Question: The car can be tested in situations and conditions that would be dangerous in real circumstances, such as testing the response of the car's brakes on icy roads.
Extension: Have students research how computers are used in both automobile design (CAD) and manufacturing (CAM).

BROADCAST ENGINEER

Background: Generally, the larger the station, the more specialized the job a broadcast engineer has. They often work odd hours and on weekends and holidays.

Related Career	Education
Field technician	technical school
Transmitter technician	technical school
Set decorator	college degree
Copywriter	college degree

Career Issue: On live call-in radio broadcasts, engineers set up a time delay so that "offensive" language can be "bleeped" and not broadcast.

What do you think? Lead students in a discussion about their own attitudes toward "bleeping." Do they think this practice should be stopped or continued?

COMPUTER PROGRAMMER

Background: Programmers may work in such business applications as accounting or inventory control, or in such scientific applications as research and development. Some programmers work for computer manufacturers or system software developers.

Related Career	Education
Hardware specialist	college degree
Systems analyst	college degree
Data entry operator	high school
Computer maintenance technician	technical school

Career Issue: Some people feel that we are too computerized and that too much personal information is available to too many people because of computer access.

What do you think? Lead students in a discussion of their own attitudes toward computerization. Can computers be used to invade people's privacy?

BROADCAST ENGINEER

Broadcast engineers are responsible for a wide variety of electronic equipment used in radio or television transmission. In small stations, they usually set up and operate equipment, as well as keep it working. In larger stations, the jobs are more specialized.

Engineers operate equipment such as microphones, lights, recording equipment, projectors, and cameras. In the control room, engineers also run the equipment that controls the quality of sound and pictures.

If you're interested in becoming a broadcast engineer, you must be flexible and be able to keep a cool head under pressure. High school classes in math and science are helpful. Broadcast engineers must have a license issued by the Federal Communications Commission. Technical schools offer course work designed specifically for preparing you to pass the tests for FCC licensing.

For Additional Information
Contact the Federal Communications Commission, Washington, DC 20036.

COMPUTER PROGRAMMER

A *computer programmer* writes programs that enable a computer to perform particular tasks or functions. The programmer takes a specific problem, studies and analyzes various ways to solve it, then devises a step-by-step procedure in terms that a computer can understand.

Programmers must be problem solvers who have the ability to think logically, yet creatively. They must also learn to use new programming languages as they are needed.

If you're interested in becoming a computer programmer you should take classes in science, mathematics, and computer science. Most computer programmers have college degrees in computer science or mathematics.

For Additional Information
Contact the Electronics Industries Association, 2001 I Street NW, Washington, DC 20006.

UNIT READINGS

▶McGowen, Tom. *Radioactivity: From the Curies to the Atomic Age.* Danbury, CT: Watts, 1986.
▶Vogt, Gregory. *Electricity and Magnetism.* Danbury, CT: Watts, 1985.

668

UNIT READINGS

Background
▶ *Computers in Entertainment and the Arts* tells how computers are used in writing, graphic arts, music, and special effects.
▶ *Oceans of Energy* discusses the possibilities of generating electricity from the oceans and extracting natural gas from kelp farms.
▶ *Radioactivity: From the Curies to the Atomic Age* traces the history of radioactivity.
▶ *Electricity and Magnetism* tells how one scientist uses the discoveries of others in the understanding of electricity and magnetism.

More Readings
1. Satry, Laurence. *Magnets.* Mahwah, NJ: Troll, 1985. Discusses the history of discoveries about magnetism.
2. Markle, Sandra. *Power Up: Experiments, Puzzles, and Games Exploring Electricity.* New York, NY: Atheneum, 1989. A fresh approach to understanding how electricity works.

Earthships: Environmental Architecture

The passage that follows describes a house design that solves a number of environmental problems.

Architecture is the art and profession of designing buildings. Architecture is one of the oldest art forms and dates from prehistoric times. It has been said that a society's architecture reflects the values and ideals of its people.

In that context, environmental architecture reflects the growing concern of people for the future of planet Earth with its fragile ecology and disappearing resources. Architect Michael Reynolds' concern for the environment led him to design houses he calls "Earthships."

Reynolds' earthships help solve a number of environmental problems simultaneously. First, they use discarded tires as building materials. The Environmental Protection Agency says that tires are discarded at a rate of 240 million per year in the United States. The interior and exterior walls of the earthships are constructed of tires filled with dirt and laid like concrete blocks. The walls are then covered with a coat of plaster or adobe.

Using tires provides a house with walls that are about one meter thick and gives it a very large mass. Because of this "thermal mass," the house utilizes little or no energy for cooling and heating. The base of the house is built below the frost line, meaning that the temperature of the walls will stay at approximately the temperature of Earth below that point — about 15°C. If a house gets no sun at all, but has this amount of mass, it will never get below 15°C.

Earthships in the Southwest have been built in the mountains where temperatures reach −34° in winter and +38° in summer. These houses are able to maintain a temperature that varies only a few degrees year round with no energy used for heating or cooling. Asked if earthships would work anywhere in the country, Reynolds said yes—even if you put them where there is no sun and you are heating with gas, you will reduce your heating costs by 90 percent.

Some earthships also generate their own electricity with solar panels mounted on the roof. They also are able to grow food year round in the greenhouse that Reynolds incorporated in the earthship design. Even the design of the plumbing system was given environmental consideration. "Black water" from toilets goes into a septic system, but "gray water" from sinks, bathtubs, and the washing machine goes into holding tanks to be used in greenhouse irrigation.

Reynolds stresses that earthships are easy and comparatively inexpensive to build. But more importantly, he said, these are buildings that take care of people. That is why he calls them earthships.

In Your Own Words

▶ Would you like to live in an earthship? Write an essay explaining why or why not.

669

Classics

▶ Clark, Wilson. *Energy for Survival.* New York, NY: Anchor Books, 1974. Explores the energy basis of our civilization and the energy alternatives for the future.

Other Works

▶ Other articles on energy conservation and environmental concerns include: Lewis, Thomas A. "The Heat Is On!" *National Wildlife.* April-May, 1990, pp. 38-41. Matthews, Samuel W. "Under the Sun." *National Geographic.* Oct. 1990, pp. 66-99.

Biography: Michael Reynolds currently operates Solar Survival Architecture in Taos, New Mexico. His inspiration for environmental architecture came in the early 1970s during an evening news program. Three separate reports on litter, forest depletion, and a shortage of affordable housing gave him an idea. He first constructed several houses with walls constructed from aluminum cans. Later, discarded tires became his material of choice, although cans are still incorporated into parts of his earthships.

TEACHING STRATEGY

Have students read through the article on earthships. Then have them respond to the discussion questions below.

Discussion Questions

1. **Does Michael Reynolds' architecture reflect the values and ideals of our society? Explain your answer.** *More people are becoming environmentally aware. They realize that Earth has limited resources and steps must be taken to protect what they value. In this context, Reynolds' architecture does reflect newer values of society.*

2. **What environmental problems does Reynolds' earthship design address?** *The design of earthships helps to recycle discarded tires, thus reducing the problem of what to do with them. It also reduces the use of gas, oil, or electricity for heating and cooling houses. It recycles some of the water used in the houses for greenhouse irrigation, while enabling people to grow more of their own food. And in some cases, it allows homes to generate their own electricity with solar panels.*

▶ Students can obtain more information on earthships by writing to Michael Reynolds, c/o Solar Survival Architecture, Box 1041, Taos, New Mexico 87511.

APPENDIX A

SI Units of Measurement

Table A-1

SI BASE UNITS					
Measurement	**Unit**	**Symbol**	**Measurement**	**Unit**	**Symbol**
length	meter	m	temperature	kelvin	K
mass	kilogram	kg	amount of substance	mole	mol
time	second	s	intensity of light	candela	cd
electric current	ampere	A			

Table A-2

UNITS DERIVED FROM SI BASE UNITS			
Measurement	**Unit**	**Symbol**	**Expressed in Base Units**
energy	joule	J	$kg \cdot m^2/s^2$
force	newton	N	$kg \cdot m/s^2$
frequency	hertz	Hz	$1/s$
potential difference	volt	V	$kg \cdot m^2/(A \cdot s^3)$ or (W/A)
power	watt	W	$kg \cdot m^2/s^3$ or (J/s)
pressure	pascal	Pa	$kg/(m^2 \cdot s^2)$ or (N/m^2)
quality of electric charge	coulomb	C	$A \cdot s$

Table A-3

COMMON SI PREFIXES					
Prefix	**Symbol**	**Multiplier**	**Prefix**	**Symbol**	**Multiplier**
Greater than 1			Less than 1		
mega-	M	1 000 000	deci-	d	0.1
kilo-	k	1 000	centi-	c	0.01
hecto-	h	100	milli-	m	0.001
deka-	da	10	micro-	µ	0.000 000 1

Table A-4

SI/METRIC TO ENGLISH CONVERSIONS			
	When you want to convert:	**Multiply by:**	**To find:**
Length	inches	2.54	centimeters
	centimeters	0.394	inches
	feet	0.305	meters
	meters	3.28	feet
	yards	0.914	meters
	meters	1.09	yards
	miles	1.61	kilometers
	kilometers	0.621	miles
* Mass and Weight	ounces	28.35	grams
	grams	0.0353	ounces
	pounds	0.454	kilograms
	kilograms	2.205	pounds
	tons	0.9072	tonnes (metric tons)
	tonnes (metric tons)	1.102	tons
	pounds	4.448	newtons
	newtons	0.225	pounds
Volume	cubic inches	16.38	cubic centimeters
	cubic centimeters	0.0610	cubic inches
	cubic feet	0.0283	cubic meters
	cubic meters	35.3	cubic feet
	liters	1.06	quarts
	liters	0.264	gallons
	gallons	3.78	liters
Area	square inches	6.45	square centimeters
	square centimeters	0.115	square inches
	square feet	0.0929	square meters
	square meters	10.76	square feet
	square miles	2.59	square kilometers
	square kilometers	0.386	square miles

*Weight as measured in standard Earth gravity

SI/Temperature Scale Conversions

Table A-5

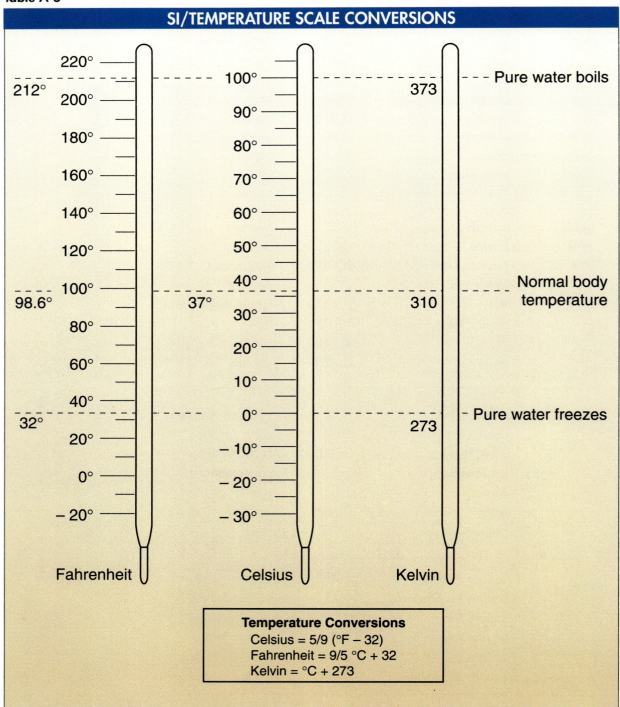

SI/TEMPERATURE SCALE CONVERSIONS

Fahrenheit scale: 220°, 212°, 200°, 180°, 160°, 140°, 120°, 100°, 98.6°, 80°, 60°, 40°, 32°, 20°, 0°, –20°

Celsius scale: 100°, 90°, 80°, 70°, 60°, 50°, 40°, 37°, 30°, 20°, 10°, 0°, –10°, –20°, –30°

Kelvin scale: 373, 310, 273

Fahrenheit — Celsius — Kelvin

Pure water boils
Normal body temperature
Pure water freezes

Temperature Conversions
Celsius = 5/9 (°F − 32)
Fahrenheit = 9/5 °C + 32
Kelvin = °C + 273

672

APPENDIX B

Safety in the Classroom

1. Always obtain your teacher's permission to begin an investigation.
2. Study the procedure. If you have questions, ask your teacher. Be sure you understand any safety symbols shown on the page.
3. Use the safety equipment provided for you. Goggles and a safety apron should be worn when any investigation calls for using chemicals.
4. Always slant test tubes away from yourself and others when heating them.
5. Never eat or drink in the lab, and never use lab glassware as food or drink containers. Never inhale chemicals. Do not taste any substances or draw any material into a tube with your mouth.
6. If you spill any chemical, wash it off immediately with water. Report the spill immediately to your teacher.
7. Know the location and proper use of the fire extinguisher, safety shower, fire blanket, first aid kit, and fire alarm.
8. Keep all materials away from open flames. Tie back long hair and loose clothing.
9. If a fire should break out in the classroom, or if your clothing should catch fire, smother it with the fire blanket or a coat, or get under a safety shower. NEVER RUN.
10. Report any accident or injury, no matter how small, to your teacher.

Follow these procedures as you clean up your work area.

1. Turn off the water and gas. Disconnect electrical devices.
2. Return all materials to their proper places.
3. Dispose of chemicals and other materials as directed by your teacher. Place broken glass and solid substances in the proper containers. Never discard materials in the sink.
4. Clean your work area.
5. Wash your hands thoroughly after working in the laboratory.

Table B-1

FIRST AID	
Injury	**Safe response**
Burns	Apply cold water. Call your teacher immediately.
Cuts and bruises	Stop any bleeding by applying direct pressure. Cover cuts with a clean dressing. Apply cold compresses to bruises. Call your teacher immediately.
Fainting	Leave the person lying down. Loosen any tight clothing and keep crowds away. Call your teacher immediately.
Foreign matter in eye	Flush with plenty of water. Use eyewash bottle or fountain.
Poisoning	Note the suspected poisoning agent and call your teacher immediately.
Any spills on skin	Flush with large amounts of water or use safety shower. Call your teacher immediately.

Safety Symbols

This textbook uses the safety symbols in Table B-2 below to alert you to possible laboratory dangers.

Table B-2

SAFETY SYMBOLS

DISPOSAL ALERT This symbol appears when care must be taken to dispose of materials properly.		**ANIMAL SAFETY** This symbol appears whenever live animals are studied and the safety of the animals and the students must be ensured.	
BIOLOGICAL HAZARD This symbol appears when there is danger involving bacteria, fungi, or protists.		**RADIOACTIVE SAFETY** This symbol appears when radioactive materials are used.	
OPEN FLAME ALERT This symbol appears when use of an open flame could cause a fire or an explosion.		**CLOTHING PROTECTION SAFETY** This symbol appears when substances used could stain or burn clothing.	
THERMAL SAFETY This symbol appears as a reminder to use caution when handling hot objects.		**FIRE SAFETY** This symbol appears when care should be taken around open flames.	
SHARP OBJECT SAFETY This symbol appears when a danger of cuts or punctures caused by the use of sharp objects exists.		**EXPLOSION SAFETY** This symbol appears when the misuse of chemicals could cause an explosion.	
FUME SAFETY This symbol appears when chemicals or chemical reactions could cause dangerous fumes.		**EYE SAFETY** This symbol appears when a danger to the eyes exists. Safety goggles should be worn when this symbol appears.	
ELECTRICAL SAFETY This symbol appears when care should be taken when using electrical equipment.		**POISON SAFETY** This symbol appears when poisonous substances are used.	
PLANT SAFETY This symbol appears when poisonous plants or plants with thorns are handled.		**CHEMICAL SAFETY** This symbol appears when chemicals used can cause burns or are poisonous if absorbed through the skin.	

674

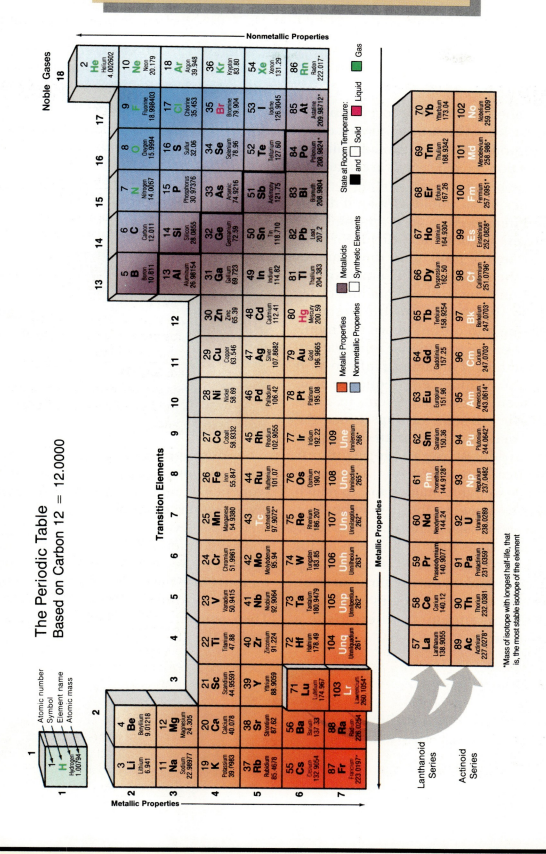

The Periodic Table
Based on Carbon 12 = 12.0000

Organizing Information

Sequencing

Think about going to a grocery store to purchase a loaf of bread. As you walk down the aisles, you notice that canned fruits are in one section, boxed cereals are in another, and the bread you are looking for is in yet another. What would happen if different food items were placed randomly on the shelves? It would be difficult for people to locate the food items they wanted. Just like the grocery store, much of the world around you has been put into order to make it easier to understand. Sequencing and outlining are two methods scientists use to organize information.

One method of organizing information is to create a sequence. A sequence is an arrangement of things or events in a particular order. In some of your classes, the students may have been seated in alphabetical order. By organizing students alphabetically, teachers find it easier to remember students' names and to match papers with names in their grade books.

Think about baking chocolate chip cookies. Certain steps have to be followed for the cookies to taste good. If you skip a step in order, the cookies will not turn out right. Baking chocolate chip cookies is an example of the arrangement of events in a particular order.

When you are asked to sequence things or events, you must first identify what comes first. You then decide what should come second. Continue to choose things or events until they are all accounted for and in order. Then, go back over the sequence to make sure each thing or event logically leads to the next.

Suppose you wanted to watch a movie that just came out on videotape. What sequence of events would you have to follow to watch the movie? You would first turn the television set to channel 3 or 4. You would then turn the videotape player on, insert the tape, and press the "play" button. Once the tape had started playing, you would adjust the sound and picture. Then, when the movie was over, you would rewind the tape.

recipe CHOCOLATE CHIP COOKIES serves 4-5 DOZ.
1/3 cup soft shortening   1 egg
1/3 cup butter   1/2 cup brown sugar
1/2 cup granulated sugar   1 teaspoon vanilla
Mix ingredients thoroughly in bowl.   Stir in
                            1/2 teaspoon soda
1-1/2 cups flour
1/2 teaspoon salt
Work in 1/2 cup chopped walnuts, 1 cup chocolate chips. Bake 8 to 10 minutes on ungreased baking sheet.

676

Outlining

Have you ever wondered why teachers ask students to outline what they read? The purpose of outlining is to show the relationships between main ideas and information about the main ideas. Outlining can help you organize, remember, and review written material.

When you are asked to outline, you must first find a group of words that summarizes the main idea. This group of words corresponds to the Roman numerals in an outline. Next, determine what is said about the main idea. Ideas of equal importance are grouped together and are given capital letters. Ideas of equal importance are further broken down and given numbers and letters.

To get an idea how to outline, compare the following outline with Chapter 20 of your textbook.

Plane mirror

Chapter 20 Mirrors and Lenses
I. The Optics of Mirrors
 A. Plane Mirrors
  1. has flat surface
  2. reflection of
   a. left and right sides of image appear reversed
   b. image upright
   c. image same size
  3. results in virtual image
   a. light rays don't form image in front of mirror
   b. light rays meet to form image that appears like object but reversed
 B. Concave Mirrors
  1. surface curved inward
  2. reflection depends on distance of image from mirror

II. The Optics of Lenses
 A. Convex Lenses

Notice that the outline shows the pattern of organization of the written material. The boldface title is the main idea and corresponds with Roman numerals I and II. The capital letters and numbers and letters that follow divide the rest of the text into supporting ideas.

Concave mirror

Thinking Critically

Observing and Inferring

Imagine that you have just finished a volleyball game with your friends. You hurry home to get a cold drink. Opening the refrigerator, you see a jug of orange juice at the back of the top shelf. The jug feels cold as you grasp it. "Ah, just what I need," you think. You hear the tone rise as you pour the juice into a tall glass. When you quickly down the drink, you smell the oranges and enjoy the tart taste in your mouth.

As you imagined yourself in the story, you used your senses to make observations. The basis of all scientific investigation is observation. Scientists are careful to make their observations accurate. When possible they use instruments, like microscopes or telescopes, to extend their senses.

Often they use instruments to make measurements. When observations involve measurements, they are called quantitative observations. Because measurements are easy to communicate and provide a concrete means of comparing collected data, scientists use them whenever possible.

When you make observations in science, you may find it helpful to first examine the entire object or situation. Then, look carefully for details using your sense of sight. Write down everything you see before using another sense to make additional observations. Continue until you have used all five senses.

Scientists often use their observations to make inferences. An inference is an attempt to explain or interpret observations or to determine what caused what you observed. For example, if you observed a CLOSED sign in a store window around noon, you might infer the owner is taking a lunch break. But, perhaps the owner has a doctor's appointment or has taken the day off to go fishing. The only way to be sure your inference is correct is to investigate further.

When making an inference, be certain to make accurate observations and to record them carefully. Then, based on everything you know, try to explain or interpret what you observed. If possible, investigate further to determine if your inference is correct.

678

Comparing and Contrasting

Observations can be analyzed and then organized by noting the similarities and differences between two or more objects or situations. When you examine objects or situations to determine similarities, you are comparing. Contrasting is looking at similar objects or situations for differences.

Suppose you were asked to compare and contrast transverse and compressional waves. You start by examining your observations. You then divide a piece of paper into two columns, listing ways the waves are similar in one column and ways they are different in the other column. After completing your lists, you report your findings in a table or in a paragraph.

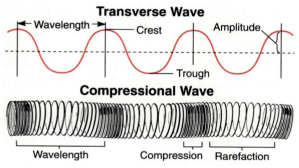

Transverse Wave

Wavelength — Crest — Amplitude — Trough

Compressional Wave

Wavelength — Compression — Rarefaction

A similarity you would point out is that both transverse and compressional waves carry energy through matter and space. A difference you might list is that matter in transverse waves moves at right angles to the direction the wave travels, but matter in compressional waves moves parallel to the direction the wave travels.

Recognizing Cause and Effect

Have you ever observed something happen and then tried to figure out why or how it might have happened? If so, you have observed an event and have inferred a reason for the event. The event or result of action is the effect, and the reason for the event is the cause.

Suppose that you had a clothesline outside your bedroom window. You look out your window every morning to determine what kind of weather the day will bring forth. You notice one warm fall day that the clothesline is sagging and make a mental note to help pull the line tighter. Another morning upon looking outside, you find the weather is quite cold, and notice the clothesline is no longer sagging. Instead, the line is taut and almost parallel to the ground.

What is the effect and what would you infer to be the cause? The effect is the change of position of the clothesline from sagging to taut. You might infer the cause to be the drop in temperature. In trying to determine cause and effect, you have made a logical inference based on observations.

Perhaps, someone in the family tightened the line while you were at school. When scientists are unsure of the cause for a certain event, they often design controlled experiments to determine what caused their observations. How could you determine what caused the tautness of the clothesline?

Experimentation Skills

Measuring in SI

You are probably familiar with the metric system of measurement. The metric system is a uniform system of measurement developed in 1795 by a group of scientists. The development of the metric system helped scientists avoid problems with different units of measurement by providing an international standard of comparison for measurements. A modern form of the metric system called the International System, or SI, was adopted for worldwide use in 1960.

You will find that your text uses metric units in almost all its measurements. In the activities you will be doing, you'll use the metric system of measurement.

The metric system is easy to use because it has a system for naming of units and a decimal base. For example, meter is the base unit for measuring length, gram for measuring mass, and liter for measuring volume. Unit sizes vary by multiples of ten. When changing from smaller units to larger, you divide by ten. When changing from larger units to smaller, you multiply by ten. Prefixes are used to name larger and smaller units. Look at the following table for some common metric prefixes and their meanings.

METRIC PREFIXES			
Prefix	Symbol	Meaning	
kilo-	k	1000	thousand
hecto-	h	100	hundred
deka	da	10	ten
deci-	d	0.1	tenth
centi	c	0.01	hundredth
milli-	m	0.001	thousandth

Do you see how the prefix *kilo-* attached to the unit *gram* is *kilogram*, or 1000 grams, or how the prefix *deci-* attached to the unit *meter* is *decimeter*, or one tenth (0.1) of a meter?

You have probably measured distance many times. The meter is the SI unit used to measure distance. To visualize the length of a meter, think of a baseball bat. A baseball bat is about one meter long. When measuring smaller distances, the meter is divided into smaller units called centimeters and millimeters. A centimeter is one hundredth (0.01) of a meter, which is about the size of the width of the fingernail on your little finger. A millimeter is one thousandth of a meter (0.001), about the thickness of a dime.

Most metersticks and metric rulers have lines indicating centimeters and millimeters. Look at the illustration. The centimeter lines are the longer numbered lines, and the shorter lines between the centimeter lines are millimeter lines.

When using a metric ruler, you must first decide on a unit of measurement. You then line up the 0 centimeter mark with the end of the object being measured and read the number of the unit where the object ends.

Units of length are also used to measure the surface area. The standard unit of area is the square meter (m^2), or a square one meter long on each side. Similarly, a square centimeter (cm^2) is a square one centimeter long on each side. Surface area is determined by multiplying the number of units in length times the number of units in width.

The volume of rectangular solids is also calculated using units of length. The cubic meter (m^3) is the standard SI unit of volume. A cubic meter is a cube one meter on a side. You can determine the volume of rectangular solids by multiplying length times width times height.

Liquid volume is measured using a unit called a liter. You are probably familiar with a two-liter soft drink bottle. One liter is about one half of the two-liter bottle. A liter has the volume of 1000 cubic centimeters. Because the prefix *milli-* means thousandth (0.001), a milliliter would equal one cubic centimeter. One milliliter of liquid would completely fill a cube measuring one centimeter on each side.

During science activities, you will measure liquids using beakers marked in milliliters and graduated cylinders. A graduated cylinder is a tall cylindrical container marked with lines from bottom to top. Each graduation represents one milliliter.

Scientists use a balance to find the mass of an object in grams. In science class, you will likely use a beam balance similar to the one illustrated. Notice that on one side of the beam balance is a pan and on the other side is a set of beams. Each beam has an object of a known mass called a rider that slides on the beam.

You must be careful when using a balance. When carrying the balance, hold the beam support with one hand and place the other hand under the balance. Also, be careful about what you place on the pan. Never place a hot object on the pan or pour chemicals directly on it. Mass a suitable container and place dry or liquid chemicals into the container to mass.

Before you find the mass of an object, you must set the balance to zero by sliding all the riders back to the zero point. Check the pointer to make sure it swings an equal distance above and below the zero point on the scale. If the swing is unequal, find and turn the adjusting screw until you have an equal swing.

You are now ready to use the balance to mass the object. Place the object on the pan. Slide the rider with the largest mass along the beam until the pointer drops below the zero point. Then move it back one notch. Repeat the process on each beam until the pointer swings an equal distance above and below the zero point. Read the masses indicated on the beams. The sum of the masses will be the mass of the object.

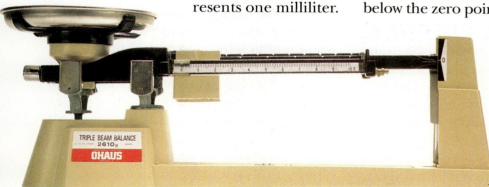

Hypothesizing

What would you do if the combination lock on your locker didn't work? Would you try the combination again? Would you check to make sure you had the right locker? You would likely try several possible solutions until you managed to open the locker.

Scientists generally use experiments to solve problems and answer questions. An experiment is a method of solving a problem in which scientists use an organized process to attempt to answer a question.

Experimentation involves defining a problem and formulating and testing a hypothesis, or testable prediction about how to solve a problem. Each prediction is tested during an experiment, which includes making careful observations and collecting data. After analysis of the collected data, a conclusion is formed and compared to the hypothesis.

Imagine it's after school, and you are changing clothes. You notice a brownish-black spot on a favorite shirt. Your problem is how to remove the stain from the shirt without damaging the shirt. You think that soap and water will remove the stain. You have made a hypothesis regarding the solution to the problem. But, making a hypothesis is not enough—the hypothesis must be tested. You try soap and water, but the stain doesn't budge.

You then observe the stain more carefully and decide that you will need to use a solvent. You have revised your hypothesis based on your observations. The new hypothesis is still only a testable prediction until you test it and examine the results. If the test removes the stain, the hypothesis is accepted. But, if the test doesn't remove the stain, you will have to revise and refine the hypothesis.

Using Variables, Constants, and Controls

When scientists do experiments, they are careful to manipulate or change only one condition and keep all other conditions in the experiment the same. The condition that is manipulated is called the independent variable. The conditions that are kept the same during an experiment are called constants. The dependent variable is any change that results from manipulating the independent variable.

Scientists can know that the independent variable caused the change in the dependent variable only if they keep all other factors constant in the experiment. Scientists also use controls to be certain that the observed changes were a result of manipulation of the independent variable. A control is a sample that is treated exactly like the experimental group except that the independent variable is not applied to the control. After the experiment, the change in the dependent variable of the control sample is compared to the change observed in the experimental group to see the effect of the application of the independent variable.

Suppose you were asked to bring your portable compact disc player on a weekend camping trip. You put in fresh dry cell batteries so that you and your friends can play CDs all weekend. But, the player loses volume about midday Sunday and soon won't play at all. You expected the dry cell batteries to last all weekend. You played the CDs louder than you do at home, so you wonder if the volume of the player affects how long the batteries last and decide to design an experiment to find out. What would be the independent and dependent variables, the constants, and the control in your experiment?

682

This is how you might set up your experiment. You decide to compare the amount of time the player will operate at different volume settings. You purchase enough fresh dry cell batteries to operate the player at number 6, your normal listening volume, and at lower and higher volume settings. You first set the volume at number 6 and operate the player until you can no longer hear the music. You then repeat the experiment two more times using volume settings of 3 and 9. You record the amount of time the player operates at each volume setting in a data table. Your data table might look like this:

DURATION MUSIC IS HEARD	
Volume	Amount of Time
3	23 h, 46 min
6	18 h, 13 min
9	14 h, 53 min

What are the independent and dependent variables in the experiment? Because you are changing the volume setting of the compact disc player, the independent variable is the volume setting. The dependent variable is any change that results from the independent variable, so the dependent variable is the number of hours and minutes music is heard on the player.

What factors are constants in the experiment? The constants are using identical dry cell batteries, playing the same compact disc, and keeping the compact disc player in the same environment for each test. What was the purpose of playing the compact disc player at your normal setting? The normal setting of the player is the control. The duration that music is heard at the normal volume setting will be used to compare the durations at lower and higher volume settings.

Interpreting Data

After doing a controlled experiment, you must analyze and interpret the collected data, form a conclusion, and compare the conclusion to your hypothesis. Analyze and interpret the data in the table. On which volume setting did the dry cell batteries last the longest? The batteries lasted the longest on number 3, the lowest setting. On which volume setting did the dry cell batteries last the shortest duration? The batteries lasted the shortest duration on volume setting number 9. What conclusion did you form? The data indicate that as the volume increases, the dry cell batteries last for a shorter duration. How does the conclusion compare with your hypothesis for this experiment? Was it supported by the experiment or not?

683

Graphics Organizers

Concept Mapping

If you were taking an automobile trip, you would likely take along a road map. The road map shows your location, your destination, and other places along the way. By examining the map, you can understand where you are in relation to other locations on the map.

A concept map is similar to a road map. But, a concept map shows the relationships among ideas (or concepts) rather than places. A concept map is a diagram that visually shows how concepts are related. Because the concept map shows the relationships among ideas, it can clarify the meanings of ideas and terms and help you to understand what you are studying.

Look at the construction of a concept map called a **network tree.** Notice how some words are circled and others are written on connecting lines. The circled words are science concepts. The lines in the map show relationships between concepts, and the words written on them describe relationships between the concepts.

A network tree can also show more complex relationships between the concepts. For example, a line labeled "affected by" could be drawn from *plants* and *animals* to *chemistry,* because chemical processes occur in plants and animals. Another example of a relationship that crosses branches would be a line labeled "caused by interactions of" connecting *Earth changes* with *matter and energy.* Earth changes are caused by interactions of matter and energy.

When you are asked to construct a network tree, state the topic and select the major concepts. Find related concepts and put them in order from general to specific. Branch the related concepts from the major concept and describe the relationships on the lines. Continue to write the more specific concepts. Write the relationships between the concepts on the lines until all concepts are mapped. Examine the concept map for relationships that cross branches and add them to the concept map.

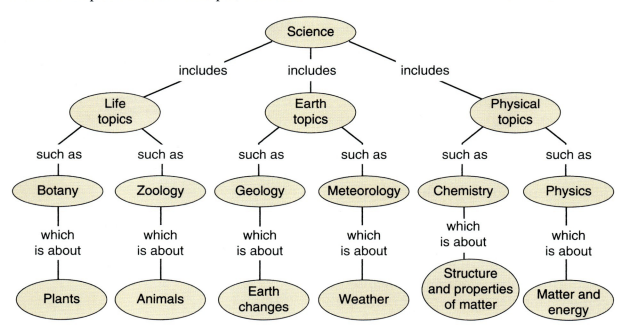

An **events chain** is another type of concept map. An events chain map is used to describe ideas in order. In science, an events chain can be used to describe a sequence of events, the steps in a procedure, or the stages of a process.

When making an events chain, you first must find the one event that starts the chain. This event is called the initiating event. You then find the next event in the chain and continue until you reach an outcome. Suppose your mother asked you to wash the dinner dishes. An events chain map might look like the one below. Notice that connecting words may not be necessary.

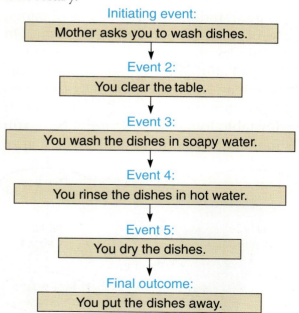

Initiating event:
Mother asks you to wash dishes.

Event 2:
You clear the table.

Event 3:
You wash the dishes in soapy water.

Event 4:
You rinse the dishes in hot water.

Event 5:
You dry the dishes.

Final outcome:
You put the dishes away.

A **cycle concept map** is a special type of events chain map. In a cycle concept map, the series of events do not produce a final outcome. The last event in the chain relates back to the initiating event.

As in the events chain map, you first decide on an initiating event and then list each important event in order. Because there is no outcome and the last event relates back to the initiating event, the cycle repeats itself. Look at the cycle map of physical changes of water:

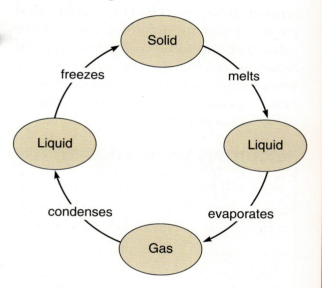

There is usually more than one correct way to create a concept map. As you are constructing a map, you may discover other ways to construct the map that show the relationships between concepts better. If you do discover what you think is a better way to create a concept map, do not hesitate to change it.

Concept maps are useful in understanding the ideas you have read about. As you construct a map, you are constructing knowledge and learning. Once concept maps are constructed, you can use them again to review and study and to test your knowledge.

Making and Using Tables

Browse through your textbook, and you will notice many tables both in the text and in the activities. The tables in the text arrange information in such a way that it is easier for you to understand. Also, many activities in your text have tables to complete as you do the activity. Activity tables will help you organize the data you collect during the activity so that they can be interpreted easily.

Most tables have a title telling you what is being presented. The table itself is divided into columns and rows. The column titles list items to be compared. The row headings list the specific characteristics being compared. Within the grid of the table, the collected data are recorded. Look at the following table:

COMMON BASES AND THEIR USES

Name of base	Formula	Uses
Sodium hydroxide	NaOH	Drain cleaner, Soap making
Aluminum hydroxide	$Al(OH)_3$	Antacid, Deodorant
Magnesium hydroxide	$Mg(OH)_2$	Laxative, Antacid
Ammonium hydroxide	NH_4OH	Cleaner

What is the title of this table? The title is "Common Bases and Their Uses." What items are being compared? The uses of common bases are being compared.

What is the use of ammonium hydroxide? To find the answer, you must locate the column labeled *Uses* and the row labeled *ammonium hydroxide*. The information contained in the box where the column and row intersect is the answer. Did you answer "cleaner"? What is the formula for sodium hydroxide? The answer is NaOH. Which two bases are commonly used as antacids? If you answered aluminum hydroxide and magnesium hydroxide, you have an understanding of how to use a table.

RECYCLED MATERIALS

Day of Week	Paper (kg)	Aluminum (kg)	Plastic (kg)
Mon.	4	2	0.5
Wed.	3.5	1.5	0.5
Fri.	3	1	1.5

To make a table, you simply list the items compared in columns and the characteristics compared in rows. Make a table and record the data comparing the masses of recycled materials collected by a class. On Monday, students turned in 4 kg of paper, 2 kg of aluminum, and 0.5 kg of plastic. On Wednesday, they turned in 3.5 kg of paper, 1.5 kg of aluminum, and 0.5 kg of plastic. On Friday, the totals were 3 kg of paper, 1 kg of aluminum, and 1.5 kg of plastic. If your table looks like the one shown, you should be able to make tables to organize data.

WE RECYCLE

Making and Using Graphs

After scientists organize data in tables, they often display the data in graphs. A graph is a diagram that shows a comparison between variables. Because graphs show a picture of collected data, they make interpretation and analysis of the data easier. The three basic types of graphs used in science are the line graph, bar graph, and pie graph.

A line graph is used to show the relationship between two variables. The variables being compared go on the two axes of the graph. The independent variable always goes on the horizontal axis, called the *x*-axis. The dependent variable always goes on the vertical axis, or *y*-axis.

Suppose a school started a peer study program with a class of students to see how it affected their science grades.

| AVERAGE GRADES OF STUDENTS IN STUDY PROGRAM ||
Grading Period	Average Science Grade
First	81
Second	85
Third	86
Fourth	89

You could make a graph of the grades of students in the program over a period of time. The grading period is the independent variable and should be placed on the *x*-axis of your graph. The average grade of a student in the program is the dependent variable and would go on the *y*-axis.

After drawing your axes, you would label each axis with a scale. The *x*-axis simply lists the grading periods. To make a scale of grades on the *y*-axis, you must look at the data values. Because the lowest grade was 81 and the highest was 89, you know that you will have to start numbering at least at 81 and go through 89. You decide to start numbering at 80 and number by twos through 90.

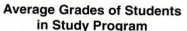
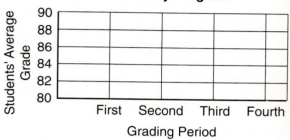

Next you must plot the data points. The first pair of data you want to plot is the first grading period and 81. Locate "First" on the *x*-axis and 81 on the *y*-axis. Where an imaginary vertical line from the *x*-axis and an imaginary horizontal line from the *y*-axis would meet, place the first data point. Place the other data points the same way. After all the points are plotted, connect them with a smooth line.

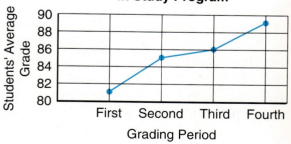

What if you wanted to compare the average grades of the class in the study group with the grades of another science class? The data of the other class can be plotted on the same graph to make the comparison. You must include a key with two different lines, each indicating a different set of data. Also change the title of the new graph to represent the data you are comparing.

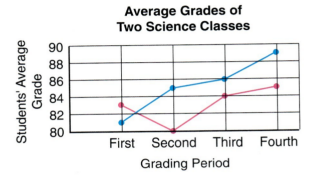

**Average Grades of
Two Science Classes**

KEY Class or study students ————

Regular class ————

Bar graphs are similar to line graphs, except they are used to compare or display data that do not continuously change. In a bar graph, thick bars show the relationships among data rather than data points.

To make a bar graph, set up the *x*-axis and *y*-axis as you did for the line graph. The data is plotted by drawing thick bars from the *x*-axis up to an imaginary point where the *y*-axis would intersect the bar if it was extended.

Look at the bar graph comparing the masses lifted by an electromagnet with different numbers of dry cell batteries. The independent variable is the number of dry cell batteries, and the dependent variable is the mass lifted. The lifting power of the electromagnet as it changed with different numbers of dry cell batteries is being compared.

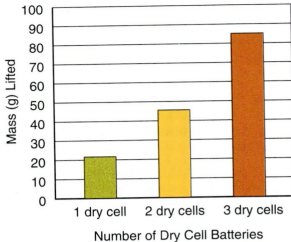

Mass Lifted by Electromagnets

A pie graph uses a circle divided into sections to display data. Each section represents part of the whole. When all the sections are placed together, they equal 100 percent of the whole.

Suppose you wanted to make a pie graph of the periodic table to show how many elements have nonmetallic properties, how many are metalloids, and how many have metallic properties. You would have to determine the total number of elements and the number of elements of each type. Because there are 109 elements, the whole pie will represent this amount.

You count the number of elements of each type and find out there are 17 elements with nonmetallic properties, 8 metalloids, and 84 elements with metallic properties.

To find out how much of the pie each section should take, you must divide the number of elements in each group by the total number of elements. You then multiply your answer by 360, the number of degrees in a circle. Round your answer to the nearest whole number. The percentage of elements with nonmetallic properties would be determined as follows:

$$\frac{17}{109} \times 360 = 56.1, \text{ or about 56 degrees}$$

Use the formula to compute how much of the circle metalloids and elements with metallic properties would fill. Metalloids would take up 26 degrees, and metallic elements would take up 278 degrees.

To plot the groups on the pie graph, you need a compass and protractor. Use the compass to draw a circle. Then draw a straight line from the center to the edge of the circle. Place your protractor on this line and use it to mark a point on the edge of the circle at 56 degrees. Connect this point to the center of the circle with a straight line. This is the part of the circle representing elements with nonmetallic properties. Place your protractor on the line you just made and use it to mark a point on the edge of the circle at 26 degrees. Again draw a straight line from this point to the center of the circle. This part represents the metalloids. The remaining part of the circle represents the percentage of metallic elements. Complete the graph by labeling the sections of your graph and giving the graph a title.

Nonmetals, Metalloids, and Metals in the Periodic Table

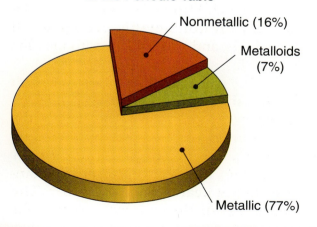

Nonmetallic (16%)

Metalloids (7%)

Metallic (77%)

Interpreting Scientific Illustrations

Your science textbook contains many scientific illustrations to help you understand, interpret, and remember what you read. When you are reading the text and encounter an illustration, examine it carefully and relate it to the text you have just read. Also read the caption for the illustration. The caption is a brief comment that explains or identifies the illustration.

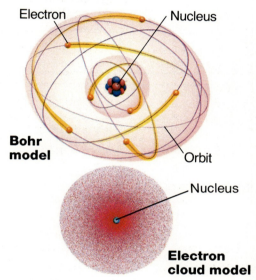

Electron   Nucleus

Bohr model

Orbit

Nucleus

Electron cloud model

Figure 10-2. The top illustration is an early model of an atom with defined paths for electrons. The lower illustration is a later model showing a region where electrons are likely to be.

Some illustrations are designed to show you how the internal parts of a structure are arranged. Look at the illustrations of atoms. The illustrations are models that with the text will help you understand an atom's internal parts. Notice that a caption briefly describes each illustration. Also, note that the illustrations include labels to help you understand the locations of the internal parts of an atom.

Other illustrations will help you understand how something works. The illustration of the circulation of air in a room of a house shows how a furnace works and how hot and cool air circulate within the room. The arrows indicate the flow of air within the heating system and the room to help you understand the text.

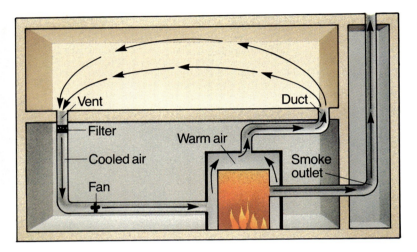

Vent
Filter
Cooled air
Fan
Warm air
Duct
Smoke outlet

Figure 6-9. In a forced-air heating system, air heated by the furnace is used to heat the rooms of the house.

The illustrations of the house and heating system show what is called a cross section. A cross section is a section that is formed by cutting through an object. The illustration of the cross section is formed by cutting at right angles to the horizontal axis of the house and heating system.

Scientific illustrations similar to that of the heating system of a house are two-dimensional. A two-dimensional illustration has height and width. However, many of the illustrations in this text, such as the model of atoms, are three-dimensional. Three-dimensional illustrations have not only height and width but also depth. An illustration in three dimensions is similar to the way you see the world, so it is even more useful in helping you understand the science ideas you are reading about.

GLOSSARY

This glossary defines each key term that appears in **bold type** in the text. It also shows the page number where you can find the word used. Some other terms that you may need to look up are included, too. We also show how to pronounce some of the words. A key to pronunciation is in the table below.

A

acceleration: the rate of change in velocity (speed and/or direction). (66)

acid: a substance that produces hydrogen ions (H^+) when dissolved in water; this lowers the solution's pH below 7. (426)

acid rain: rain that is more acidic than normal because it contains dilute sulfuric acid (from coal-burning power plants) and dilute nitric acid (from car exhausts). (438)

acoustics: the study of sound. (478)

actinoid: any of the 14 radioactive elements having atomic numbers 89-102; used in nuclear power generation and nuclear weapons.

active solar heating: collecting the sun's energy with solar panels, heating water with that energy, and storing the heated water to use the energy later.

aerosol: a liquid sprayed from a pressurized container; for example, a can of insect spray.

air resistance: the frictional force air exerts on a moving object, opposite in direction to the object's motion. (88)

alchemist: a medieval version of the modern chemist; a practitioner blended primitive chemistry with magic, seeking to turn ordinary metals into gold.

alcohol: a substituted hydrocarbon in which one or more hydrogen atoms have been replaced by an –OH group; for example, ethanol. (335)

allotropes: different molecular structures of the same element; for example, some carbon molecules form soft graphite whereas others form hard diamonds. (317)

alloy: a solid solution of a metal with other metals or nonmetals; for example, brass or steel. (352)

alpha particle: a low-energy particle given off by a radioactive atomic nucleus; it is a helium nucleus (two protons and two neutrons with a positive charge). (624)

alternating current (AC): electrical current that reverses its direction many times each second; the AC in our homes reverses direction 60 times each second. (585)

amalgam: an alloy containing the element mercury; for example, dental fillings are amalgams. (355)

ammeter: a galvanometer that measures the electrical current flowing in a circuit, in amperes. (580)

amorphous: something that has no specific shape; for example, a liquid or gas.

ampere: the unit for measuring the rate of flow of electrons in a circuit; abbreviated *A*; 1 ampere = 1 coulomb of charge flowing past a point in 1 second.

amplification: the process of increasing the strength of an electric current. (600)

amplitude: in a wave, the distance from the resting position to either the crest or trough (they are the same distance). (459)

691

amplitude-modulated (AM) waves: radio waves whose amplitude is varied with voice, music, video, or data for transmission over long distances.

angle of incidence: in waves, the angle formed by the incident wave and the normal (perpendicular); labeled *i*.

angle of reflection: in waves, the angle formed by the reflected wave and the normal (perpendicular); labeled *r*.

anhydrous: a chemical compound that normally has water molecules attached to its ions, but from which the water has been removed.

antacid: an "anti-acid," or a chemical that changes an acid substance to a neutral substance.

antifreeze: a solute added to a solvent to lower the temperature at which the solvent will freeze; for example, the antifreeze added to water in a car's cooling system.

aqueous: describes a solution made with water; for example, ammonia water is an aqueous solution of ammonia gas.

Archimedes' principle: the Greek mathematician Archimedes stated that the buoyant force that pushes up on an object in a fluid is equal to the weight of the fluid displaced by the object. (210)

aromatic compounds: chemical compounds that contain the benzene ring structure; most have distinctive aromas. (334)

astigmatism: an uneven curvature of the eye's cornea, causing blurry vision.

atomic number: the number of protons in an atom's nucleus; each element has a unique number (hydrogen = 1, helium = 2, and so on). (243)

average atomic mass: the average mass of all isotopes of an element; used as a convenience, because most elements have more than one isotope and therefore more than one mass number. (253)

average speed: a rate of motion determined by dividing the distance traveled by travel time. (61)

B

balance: a device used in laboratories to measure mass; it works by balancing an "unknown" (material whose mass is to be determined) with a standard mass that is known.

balanced chemical equation: a chemical equation that has the same number of atoms of each element on both sides of the equation. (410)

balanced forces: forces that are equal in size and opposite in direction. (70)

bar graph: a type of graph used to show information collected by counting; uses vertical or horizontal bars of different lengths to help people compare quantities.

base: a substance that produces hydroxide ions (OH⁻) when dissolved in water; this raises the solution's pH above 7. (430)

Bernoulli's principle: the Swiss mathematician Daniel Bernoulli stated that, as the velocity of a fluid increases, the pressure exerted by the fluid decreases. (212)

beta particle: a high-energy particle given off by a radioactive atomic nucleus; it is a negatively charged electron. (625)

BHA: a food preservative; it is a chemical inhibitor that slows the chemical reactions that spoil food (*B*utylated *H*ydroxy*a*nisole).

BHT: a food preservative; it is a chemical inhibitor that slows the chemical reactions that spoil food (*B*utylated *H*ydroxy*t*oluene).

binary compound: a chemical compound composed of two elements; for example, sodium chloride. (283)

biodegradable: describes a material that can be decomposed into a harmless form by the biological action of organisms such as bacteria.

biogas: gas (mostly methane) produced by plant and animal wastes that rot in the absence of air. (338)

biomass: all plant and animal material, both dead and alive; sometimes used as fuel. (338)

boiling point: the temperature at which vapor bubbles form in a liquid and rise to the surface, increasing evaporation.

Boyle's law: English physicist Robert Boyle stated that, if a container of gas is made smaller, the pressure throughout the gas increases (if the temperature stays the same). (205)

breeder reactor: a type of nuclear reactor that breeds new fuel as it operates. (654)

brittleness: a characteristic of certain materials that makes them break easily when stressed.

bubble chamber: a chamber filled with a superheated liquid; used to detect charged nuclear particles, which leave a trail of bubbles as they pass through. (631)

buoyant force: the upward force exerted on an object when it is completely immersed in a fluid. (209)

butane: a flammable gas (C₄H₁₀); a part of natural gas.

byte: a basic unit of computer memory that represents a character (number, symbol, or alphabet letter); consists of 8 bits.

C

calorimeter: an instrument used to measure changes in thermal energy.

carbohydrate: an organic compound characteristically having twice as many hydrogen atoms as oxygen atoms; for example, glucose = C₆H₁₂O₆. (343)

carbon-14 dating: age-determining method for carbon-containing objects up to 50 000 years old; works by calculating the half-life of the radioactive carbon-14 remaining in the object.

catalyst: a substance that speeds a chemical reaction without itself being changed. (418)

cathode-ray tube (CRT): a picture tube with an internal electron gun that fires a stream of electrons (cathode rays) at a fluorescent screen to produce pictures. (605)

central processing unit (CPU): the main circuit board inside a computer that performs the calculating and holds the main memory.

centripetal (sen TRIHP uh tuhl) acceleration: acceleration (change in speed and/or direction) toward the center of a curve. (92)

centripetal force: the force that causes an object to move toward the center of a curve. (92)

ceramic: a material made from clay or sand, usually baked at a high temperature. (357)

cermet: a synthetic material made to have the properties of both a ceramic and an alloy; for example, some magnets use cermet material (*cer*amic + *met*al). (358)

chain reaction: a continuing series of fission reactions in which neutrons from fissioning nuclei cause other nuclei to split, releasing more neutrons which split more nuclei, and so on. (634)

Charles's law: French scientist Jacques-Alexandre Charles stated that the volume of a gas increases when temperature increases (if the pressure stays the same). (205)

chemical bond: the force that holds together the atoms in a compound. (271)

chemical change: the change of one substance to another substance by changing the elements in it, or by changing their proportions. (232)

chemical formula: a precise statement of the elements in a compound and their ratio; for example, H_2O, CO_2, or $C_{12}H_{22}O_{11}$. (269)

chemically stable: describes an atom whose outermost energy level is filled with electrons, so that it does not form compounds under normal conditions; for example: helium, neon. (270)

chemically unstable: describes an atom whose outermost energy level is not filled with electrons, so it seeks electrons from other atoms and thus forms compounds; for example: sodium, chlorine.

chemical property: a characteristic of a substance that indicates whether it can undergo a certain chemical change. (233)

chemical reaction: a change in which substances are converted to different substances that have different properties. (404)

chemical symbol: a shorthand way to write the name of an element; for example: *O* for oxygen, *Fe* for iron. (242)

chloro- prefix meaning chlorine, as in tetra-chloroethylene or chlorofluorocarbon.

chlorofluorocarbon (CFC): a group of chemicals compounded of chlorine, fluorine, and carbon; used as refrigerants and spray propellants; damaging to the atmosphere's ozone layer. (409)

circuit: a closed path through which electrons (electricity) can flow. (552)

circuit breaker: a device that protects an electrical circuit. If too much current flows, the circuit breaker switches off the current flow.

cloud chamber: a chamber filled with water-saturated air; used to detect charged nuclear particles, which leave a vapor trail as they pass through. (630)

coal: a rock formed of ancient decayed plants; burned as a fossil fuel.

coefficient: in a chemical equation, a number to the left of each reactant and product that shows the relative amount of each substance involved in the reaction; for example, the *3* in $3H_2O$. (406)

coherent light: a beam of light in which all rays travel parallel to one another, so that the beam spreads out very little even over thousands of kilometers. (530)

colloid: a heterogeneous mixture containing tiny particles that do not settle; for example, milk and gelatin. (223)

combustion: rapid oxidation, or burning. (148)

commutator: a reversing switch in a direct-current electric motor that changes the polarity of the current with each half-revolution. (581)

composite: a material made by mixing other materials to combine the desirable properties of each. (367)

compound: matter that is a combination of atoms of two or more elements. (220)

compound machine: a combination of two or more simple machines. (174)

compression: in compressional waves, the dense area of the wave.

compressional wave: a wave that vibrates in the same direction in which the wave is traveling. (464)

computer: a device you can program to do calculations, make logical decisions, and manipulate data.

computer virus: a computer program designed to infect a computer and make it "sick"; it can erase data, scramble other programs, or fill up memory so the system won't work right. (612)

concave lens: a lens that is thinner in the middle and thicker at the edges and thus curves inward. (519)

concave mirror: a mirror whose surface curves inward, producing a reflected image that is enlarged. (513)

concentrated solution: a solution in which the amount of solute is near the maximum that the solvent can hold.

concentration: generally, the proportion of a solute dissolved in a solvent; specifically, the milliliters of solute, plus enough solvent to total 100 mL of solution.

condensation: the change of a substance from a gaseous state to a liquid state; for example, water vapor condensing on a cold surface. (201)

693

condense: to go from the gas state to the liquid state, due to a loss of heat.

conduction: the transfer of energy through matter by direct contact of particles; the movement of heat or electricity through a substance. (134)

conductor: a material that allows heat or electrons to move easily through it. (547)

constant: in an experiment, a factor that cannot change. (21)

constant speed: a rate of motion that does not vary, such as Earth's speed in orbit. (61)

contract: movement of molecules toward one another, so that they occupy a smaller space.

control: in an experiment, the standard for comparison. (20)

convection: the transfer of energy through matter by movement of the matter itself, as in air or water currents. (135)

convex lens: a lens that is thicker in the middle than at the edges and thus curves outward. (518)

convex mirror: a mirror with a surface that curves outward. (515)

cooling tower: a tower-shaped device in which water is cooled by fans or evaporation; used in factories and power plants. (147)

corrosive: describes any substance that attacks and alters metals, human tissue, or other materials; for example, battery acid, bleach, and cleaners for ovens, toilets, and drains. (274)

coulomb: the charge carried by 6.24 billion billion electrons.

covalent bond: A type of chemical bond formed by atoms when they share electrons; this force holds together molecules in gases like oxygen (O_2) and nitrogen (N_2), and in compounds like water (H_2O). (278)

crest: in waves, the highest point of a wave. (459)

critical temperature: in superconductors, the very low temperature at which a material ceases to have any electrical resistance.

critical thinking: the process of using thinking skills to solve problems. (14)

crystal: a solid having a distinctive shape because its atoms are arranged in repeating geometric patterns. (191)

current: the flow of electrons through a conductor, measured in amperes with an ammeter. (553)

deceleration: the rate of change in velocity (speed and/or direction) when velocity is decreasing; also called negative acceleration.

decibel: the unit of measure for sound intensity, abbreviated *dB*. The faintest sound most people can hear = 0 dB.

decomposition reaction: a chemical reaction in which a substance breaks down (decomposes) into two or more simpler substances. (414)

dehydrating agent: a substance that removes water from materials; for example, sulfuric acid. (428)

density: how tightly packed a substance's molecules are; expressed as the mass of a substance divided by its volume, in g/cm^3. (39)

dependent variable: in an experiment, the factor that is forced to change because the independent variable is changed. (21)

derived unit: a unit of measurement formed by combining other units of measurement; for example, density is a derived unit formed by dividing an object's mass by its volume. (38)

desalination: removing dissolved salts from seawater to produce fresh, drinkable water. (386)

desalination plant: facility for removing dissolved salts from seawater to produce fresh, drinkable water.

detergent: an organic salt similar to soap, except that detergents do not form "soap scum" in hard water. (444)

diatomic molecule: a molecule made up of two atoms of the same element; for example, hydrogen (H_2) or oxygen (O_2). (311)

diesel engine: an internal combustion engine that compresses a fuel-air mixture so much that it ignites from the heat of compression, without a spark.

diffraction: the bending of waves around a barrier. (503)

diffraction grating: a piece of glass or plastic with many parallel slits that acts like a prism, causing white light that passes through it to separate into its component colors (the spectrum). (505)

dilute solution: a solution in which the amount of solute is much less than the maximum the solvent can hold.

diode: a type of rectifier that allows electric current to flow only in one direction. (599)

direct current (DC): electrical current that flows in only one direction; thus direct current cells (batteries) are labeled + and − so you can install them the right way. (585)

disinfectant: a chemical that kills bacteria, such as alcohol.

dissociation: the breaking apart of an ionic compound (like salt) into positive and negative ions when dissolved in water. (396)

distillation: a water-purifying process in which water is evaporated from a solution, and the vapor is cooled to condense it to a pure liquid. (387)

DNA: *deoxyribonucleic acid*, an acid in the nuclei of cells that codes and stores genetic information.

doping: adding an impurity to a semiconductor to increase its electrical conductivity.

Doppler effect: an increase or decrease in wave frequency, caused by motion of the source and/or motion of the observer; applies to all waves (including light, heat, sound, and so on).

694

dot diagram: a diagram of an atom, using the element symbol with dots to show the electrons in the outer energy level. (257)

double displacement reaction: a chemical reaction in which the positive ions in two or more substances trade places. (415)

dry cell: a power source that generates electric current by a chemical reaction; "dry" because it uses a thick, pasty electrolyte in a sealed container instead of a liquid electrolyte as in a car battery. (554)

ductile: describes metals that can be pulled into thin strands (wire). (300)

E

efficiency: the amount of work put into a machine compared to how much useful work is put out by the machine; always between 0 percent and 100 percent. (175)

effort arm: the part of a lever to which the effort force (F_e) is applied. (163)

effort force (F_e): the force applied to a machine. (159)

electrical power: the rate at which electrical energy is converted to another form of energy, such as heat; measured in kilowatt-hours. (565)

electric field: a force surrounding an electron that affects anything nearby that has an electric charge; is strongest near the electron and weakens with distance. (547)

electric motor: a device that changes electric energy into mechanical energy; for example, the motor in an electric fan.

electrolyte: a substance that forms ions in a water solution, making the water an electrical conductor; for example, sodium chloride and hydrogen chloride. (396)

electromagnet: a temporary magnet formed when an electric current is passed through a wire coil that surrounds an iron core. (578)

electromagnetic induction: electrical current induced in a wire when it is moved through a magnetic field. (583)

electromagnetic radiation: transverse energy waves that radiate in all directions from their source; vary in length from very long radio waves to extremely short X rays and gamma rays.

electromagnetic spectrum: the classification of electromagnetic waves, either by wavelength or frequency. (484)

electron: a negatively charged particle that orbits around the nucleus of an atom. (243)

electron arrangement: in an atom, how the electrons are distributed in the atom's various energy levels.

electron cloud: actually not a cloud, but the space where electrons most probably exist around the nucleus of an atom. (244)

electroscope: a device used to detect the presence of electric charges. (549)

element: matter in which all the atoms are alike; for example, zinc, chlorine, and aluminum. (220)

endothermic reaction: a chemical reaction that requires the addition of heat energy to proceed; thus the reaction absorbs heat from its surroundings. (417)

energy: the ability to cause change. (110)

energy farming: the growing of plants for use as fuel. (338)

energy transfer: the movement of energy from one object to another; for example, thermal energy flowing as heat from a stove to a skillet.

ester: a chemical compound formed by reacting an organic acid with an alcohol; some provide the scents in flowers, fruits, and candy. (444)

evaporation: the change of a substance from a liquid state to a gaseous state. (200)

exothermic reaction: a chemical reaction that releases heat energy. (418)

expand: outward movement of molecules away from one another, so that they occupy a larger space.

experiment: a controlled procedure for testing a hypothesis. (20)

external combustion engine: an engine in which the fuel is burned outside the engine, and energy from it is used to operate the engine; for example, an old-fashioned steam engine. (150)

F

factor: a condition that affects the outcome of an event.

farsighted: describes a person who sees faraway things clearly, but has trouble focusing on nearby objects.

fiberglass: hairlike strands of glass that make a good insulator when arranged in puffy layers.

filter: in working with light, a device that allows one or more colors to be transmitted while others are absorbed.

flame test: a laboratory test to identify elements by heating a substance in a flame and observing the flame color.

flammable: a chemical characteristic of a substance that allows it to oxidize rapidly; also called burnable.

flash distillation: a desalination process where seawater is pumped into a vacuum chamber so it boils quickly and at a lower temperature (because the normal air pressure is absent).

fluid: any material that can flow, such as air, water, or molten metal. (135)

fluorescence: occurs when a material absorbs ultraviolet radiation, which stimulates it to radiate visible light.

fluorescent light: light produced by phosphors when they are stimulated by ultraviolet light, as in a fluorescent light bulb. (498)

focal length: the distance from the center of a lens or mirror to its focal point. (513)

focal point: a point on the optical axis of a concave mirror or convex lens where the light rays come together. (513)

force: a push or a pull exerted by one body on another. (70)

fractional distillation: a process used in oil refineries to separate petroleum into gasoline, kerosene, and other products. (645)

fractionating towers: towers at oil refineries used for fractional distillation of petroleum.

free-fall: how an object moves in space when it is influenced only by gravity.

freeze distillation: a desalination process in which seawater is frozen to form salt-free ice.

freon: a refrigerant gas used in refrigerators and air conditioners.

frequency: the number of waves that pass a point during one second, expressed as hertz; for example, 60 waves per second = 60 hertz. (459)

frequency-modulated (FM) waves: radio waves whose frequency is varied with voice, music, video, or data for transmission over long distances.

friction: the force that resists motion between two surfaces that are touching each other. (73)

fuel rod: a metal rod filled with uranium pellets, used as the fuel in a nuclear reactor.

fulcrum (FUL krum): the fixed point around which a lever pivots. (163)

fuse: a device that protects an electrical circuit. If too much current flows, the fuse melts, breaking the circuit to stop current flow.

galvanometer: an instrument (meter) used to detect electric currents; most electrical meters are galvanometers.

gamma rays: electromagnetic waves given off by a radioactive atomic nucleus; they have very short wavelength (high frequency), high energy, and are very penetrating. (490, 626)

gaseous solution: a homogeneous gas that is composed of two or more gases.

gasohol: a biomass fuel that is about 90 percent gasoline and 10 percent alcohol (ethanol); used in cars and trucks. (339)

gear: a wheel with teeth around its edge, designed to mesh with teeth on another gear, so as to transfer force and motion.

gelatin: a substance obtained by boiling animal bones; used in glues and foods.

generator: a device that uses electromagnetic induction to induce electrical current by rotating loops of wire through a magnetic field. (583)

geothermal energy: thermal energy from the magma underneath volcanoes. (660)

glass: a solid ceramic mixture lacking a crystal structure. (358)

graduated cylinder: a cylinder marked with a volume scale, used in laboratories for measuring liquid volumes.

granite: an igneous rock that is a mixture of crystals of several different compounds.

graph: a visual display of information or data, organized to help people interpret, understand, or quickly find information. (42)

graphite: a mineral made of carbon atoms arranged in layers that easily slide past one another, forming a dry lubricant.

gravity: the attracting force exerted by every object on every other object. The amount of force depends on the masses of the objects and their distance apart. (75)

greenhouse effect: the process by which heat radiated from Earth's surface is trapped and reflected back to Earth by carbon dioxide in the atmosphere. (18)

grounded: electrically connected to Earth (the ground), either directly or through a wire or other metal object.

groundwater: water in the ground that comes from rain and melting snow. Although often pure enough to drink, it is easily polluted by dumps, sewers, and chemical spills.

group: one of the 18 vertical columns in the periodic table. All elements in a group have similar properties. (257)

hacker: a person who uses a computer to break into other computer systems without permission.

half-life: the time required for half of the atoms in a radioactive substance to decay. (627)

halogens: highly active elements in periodic table Group 17 (fluorine, chlorine, bromine, iodine, astatine); halogens have seven electrons in their outer shells and readily combine with Group 1 elements such as sodium.

heat: the type of energy that moves from anything having a higher temperature to anything having a lower temperature. (121)

heat engine: a device that converts thermal energy into mechanical energy; for example, an automobile engine. (148)

heat mover: a device that removes thermal energy from one location and transfers it to another location having a different temperature; for example, a refrigerator, air conditioner, or heat pump. (151)

heat of fusion: the amount of energy needed to change a material from the solid state to the liquid state. (201)

heat of vaporization: the amount of energy needed to change a material from the liquid state to the gaseous (vapor) state. (202)

696

heat pump: a two-way heat mover that pumps heat out of a building in warm weather and into a building in cold weather. (151)

herbicide: a chemical poison that kills undesirable plants.

hertz: the unit of measure for frequency, abbreviated Hz; for example, 440 waves per second = 440 Hz.

heterogeneous mixture: a mixture in which different materials are distributed unevenly, so at any place in the mixture different combinations of materials occur. (222)

high-speed photography: a photographic method that takes clear (not blurred) pictures of fast-moving objects.

homogeneous mixture: a mixture in which different materials are blended evenly, so that the mixture is the same throughout; also called a solution. (222)

horizontal: a direction parallel to Earth's surface.

hydrate: a compound that has water molecules chemically attached to its ions. (287)

hydraulic: describes a system operated by applying pressure to a liquid.

hydrocarbon: a chemical compound containing only carbon and hydrogen atoms; for example, methane gas (CH_4). (329)

hydroelectricity: electricity produced by the energy of moving water. (658)

hydronium ion: the ion (H_3O^+) that makes a solution acidic; formed by the bonding of a hydrogen ion (H^+) to a water molecule (H_2O). (432)

hypothesis: a proposed solution to a problem or explanation of how something works; a hypothesis can be tested to see if it is correct. (16)

ideal machine: a machine in which work input equals work output; such a machine would be frictionless and 100 percent efficient. (160)

incandescent light: light produced by heat, as from a hot filament in an incandescent light bulb. (498)

inclined plane: a simple machine consisting of a sloping surface (ramp) used to raise objects; it changes the amount of force. (169)

incoherent light: light rays that are nearly parallel, but spread out. (530)

independent variable: in an experiment, the factor changed to see what effect it will have on the dependent variable. (21)

indicator: an organic compound that changes color when in an acid solution or a basic solution; for example, phenolphthalein. (426)

induction: electrically charging an object or creating an electrical current in it, without physically touching it.

inertia (ihn UR shuh): the tendency of an object to resist any change in motion; if motionless, it remains still; if moving, it keeps moving. (71)

infrared radiation: electromagnetic waves that have a wavelength slightly longer (lower frequency) than visible light; commonly known as heat; abbreviated *IR*. (487)

infrasonic waves: waves at frequencies below the limit of human hearing (below 20 Hz).

inhibitor: a substance that slows a chemical reaction. (418)

instantaneous speed: the rate of motion at any given instant, such as that given on a speedometer. (60)

insulator: a material through which heat or electricity cannot move easily. (137, 548)

integrated circuit: a thin slice of silicon, often less than 1 cm on a side, which may contain thousands of resistors, diodes, and transistors, and can perform several electronic functions at once; used in computers and electronic equipment; also called a chip. (601)

intensity: in sound waves, the amount of energy in each wave. (468)

interference: the mixing of two or more waves, which combine to form a new wave. (476)

internal combustion engine: an engine in which fuel is burned inside chambers (cylinders); for example, an automobile engine. (148)

ion: an atom having an electrical charge, either positive or negative; for example, Na^+, Cl^-. (277)

ionic bond: A type of chemical bond that holds together compounds of oppositely charged ions; for example, ionic bonding holds together Na^+ and Cl^- to make salt, NaCl. (277)

ionization: the breaking apart of a molecular polar substance (such as hydrogen chloride) to form ions when dissolved in water. (396)

isomers: compounds that have identical chemical formulas but different molecular structures and shapes. (333)

isometric exercise: exercise in which muscles push against other muscles, instead of pushing or pulling against gravity. (97)

isotopes: atoms of the same element that have different numbers of neutrons; for example, uranium-235 and uranium-238. (251)

joule (JEWL): the basic unit of energy and work, named for English scientist James Prescott Joule; 1 joule (J) = a force of 1 newton moving through 1 meter.

kelvin: the SI unit of temperature; 0 K = absolute zero (the coldest possible temperature) = −273°C. (41)

kilogram: the SI unit of mass; 1000 grams. (39)

kilowatt-hour: the unit of electrical power; 1 kilowatt-hour = 1000 watts of power used for 1 hour. (567)

kinetic energy: energy that causes change in the form of motion, as in a rolling ball. (111)

kinetic theory of matter: the theory that all matter is made up of tiny particles that are in constant motion. (191)

lanthanoid: any of the 14 metallic elements having atomic numbers 57-70; used in magnets, ceramics, and television picture tubes.

laser: a device that generates a beam of coherent light. (530)

law of conservation of energy: a law stating that energy can change form (for example, from potential to kinetic), but it cannot be created or destroyed under ordinary conditions. (115)

law of conservation of mass: a law stating that the mass of all substances involved in a chemical change will be the same after the change; matter is neither created nor destroyed during a chemical change. (234)

law of conservation of momentum: a law stating that the total momentum of a group of objects does not change unless outside forces act on the objects. (102)

lever: a simple machine consisting of a bar that is free to pivot (rotate) around a fixed point (fulcrum); it changes the direction or amount of force. (163)

lightning rod: a metal rod mounted atop a structure and connected to Earth (grounded) to leak off electric charges between the clouds and Earth before they grow strong enough to cause lightning. (551)

line graph: a type of graph used to show trends or continuous change by drawing a line that connects data points.

lipid: an organic compound containing more hydrogen atoms and fewer oxygen atoms than carbohydrates; for example, fats and oils. (344)

liquid solution: a liquid solvent that has dissolved in it a gas, liquid, or solid.

liter: the unit of liquid volume (L). (38)

loudness: the human perception of sound intensity. (468)

lubricant: a substance used to reduce the friction between two surfaces that move together; for example, oil, grease, or graphite.

machine: a device that makes work easier by changing the speed, direction, or amount of a force. (158)

magma (MAG muh): hot melted rock originating beneath Earth's surface; it is a potential source of energy for heating and generating electricity. (122)

magnetic: a physical property of matter that causes it to be attracted to a magnet.

magnetic bottle: a powerful magnetic field that creates a container ("bottle") to hold the hydrogen plasma needed for a nuclear fusion reaction.

magnetic domain: a group of aligned atoms in a magnetic material such as iron, caused by the magnetic field around each atom exerting a force on nearby atoms. (576)

magnetic field: the area of magnetic force around a magnet. (575)

magnetic poles: the two ends of a piece of magnetic material where the magnetic forces are strongest, labeled north pole (N) and south pole (S). (574)

magnetism: a property of matter that creates forces of attraction and repulsion between certain substances. (574)

magnifier: a device that makes things appear larger so that more detail can be seen; for example, a magnifying glass or microscope.

malleable: describes metals that can be hammered or rolled into thin sheets, like foil. (300)

mass: the amount of matter in an object; its SI unit is the kilogram (kg). (39)

mass number: total particles in an atom's nucleus; mass number = protons + neutrons; also called atomic mass. (251)

mechanical advantage (MA): the number of times a machine multiplies the effort force (the force applied to it). (160)

mechanical energy: the total kinetic energy and potential energy in a system. (115)

medium: a material (solid, liquid, or gas) through which a mechanical wave can transfer energy. (458)

melt: the changing of a substance from a solid state to a liquid state when heated above the substance's freezing/melting point.

melting point: the temperature at which a solid changes to a liquid.

metal: an element usually having these characteristics: shiny, ductile (can be drawn into wire), and a good conductor of heat and electricity. (260)

metallic bonding: the type of chemical bond that holds metals together; loose electrons and metal ions attract one another, holding the metal atoms together. (301)

metalloid: an element having some properties of both a metal and a nonmetal; for example, boron and silicon. (262)

meter: the SI unit of length (m). (34)

methane: a flammable gas (CH_4); the main gas in natural gas.

microprocessor: an integrated circuit on the main circuit board of a computer; the computer's "brain." (608)

microscope: an optical instrument that uses two convex lenses with relatively short focal lengths to magnify objects that are very small and up close. (524)

microwaves: electromagnetic waves that are very short (very high frequency) and have high energy. (486)

mixture: a substance made of elements or compounds stirred together but not combined chemically.

model: a representation of an idea or process to make it understandable, using a diagram, formula, or physical structure; for example, Ping-Pong balls to model a molecule or a mathematical formula to model a river's flow. (12)

modulation: the process of adding voice, music, video, or other data to radio waves, by varying either their amplitude or frequency. (486)

momentum: a property of any moving object; equals the object's mass times its velocity. (100)

monomers: organic molecules that are strung together to form polymers.

music: sound created using specific pitches, sound quality, and patterns. (474)

nearsighted: describes a person who sees nearby things clearly, but has trouble focusing on distant objects.

net force: the resulting velocity of an object when multiple forces are applied to it. (71)

neutral: (1) electrically neutral: a compound having no overall electrical charge because the total positive charge equals the total negative charge; (2) chemically neutral: a solution that is neither acidic nor basic.

neutralization: a chemical reaction between an acid and a base; the acid's hydronium ions (H_3O^+) combine with the base's hydroxide ions (OH^-) to produce water (H_2O), and the acid's negative ions combine with the base's positive ions to produce a salt. (440)

neutralize: to change an acidic solution or a basic solution so that it is neutral.

neutron: one of the two types of particles (protons and neutrons) that occur in an atom's nucleus; a neutron is neutral and has no electrical charge (neither negative nor positive). (243)

Newton's first law: English physicist Sir Isaac Newton stated that an object moving at a constant velocity keeps moving at that velocity unless a net force acts on it. (72)

Newton's second law of motion: English physicist Sir Isaac Newton stated that an object accelerates in the direction of the net force applied to it. (85)

Newton's third law of motion: English physicist Sir Isaac Newton stated that for every action, there is an equal and opposite reaction. (98)

noise: sound that has no pattern or definite pitch. (474)

noise pollution: sound that is loud, annoying, or harmful to the ear. (472)

nonelectrolyte: a substance that does not form ions in a water solution, so the water does not become an electrical conductor; for example, sugar or alcohol. (396)

nonmetal: an element that usually lacks the characteristics of a metal (shiny, can be drawn into wire, and a good conductor of heat and electricity). (261)

nonpolar molecule: a molecule in which the atoms have an equal attraction for electrons, so the molecule is not polarized into positive and negative ends. (280)

nonrenewable resources: resources such as coal, oil, and natural gas that we are using up faster than natural processes can replace. (647)

normal: in the study of light, an imaginary line drawn perpendicular to a reflecting surface or perpendicular to a medium that light is entering.

nuclear fission: the splitting of an atom's nucleus into two nuclei having smaller masses, with a simultaneous release of particles and energy. (633)

nuclear fusion: the fusing together of two atomic nuclei into a single nucleus of larger mass. (634)

nuclear reactor: a device in which uranium atoms fission to release energy; the energy is used to generate electricity. (648)

nuclear waste: waste products from nuclear power generation, nuclear weapons manufacture, nuclear medicine, and industrial use of radioactive materials. (651)

nucleic acid: an organic polymer that controls the activities and reproduction of cells. (342)

nucleus: the positively charged center of an atom. (243)

nuclide: an isotope having a specific atomic number and atomic mass. (621)

observation: using your senses to gather information; in science we use instruments to help our senses make more accurate and more detailed observations. (16)

ohm: the unit for measuring resistance; symbol Ω.

Ohm's law: German physicist Georg Ohm stated that electric current (I) equals the potential difference or voltage (V) divided by the resistance to current flow (R). (557)

opaque materials: materials you can't see through because they absorb or reflect nearly all light. (492)

optical axis: a line perpendicular to the center of a mirror or lens.

optical fibers: transparent glass fibers that can pipe light from one place to another. (532)

ore: a mineral or rock containing a useful substance that can be mined at a profit; for example, iron ore or silver ore. (356)

organic compound: a chemical compound containing the element carbon; about 90 percent of all compounds are organic. (328)

oxidation number: a positive or negative number that indicates an element's ability to form a compound. (283)

ozone layer: a layer of Earth's atmosphere that contains plentiful ozone, which absorbs ultraviolet radiation from the sun. (18)

parallel circuit: an electrical circuit where the current flows in several separate branches. If one branch is interrupted, current still flows through the other branches. (561)

pascal: the international unit of pressure; 1 pascal = 1 newton/square meter. (204)

Pascal's principle: French scientist Blaise Pascal stated that pressure applied to a fluid is transmitted equally throughout the fluid. (211)

passive solar heating: direct use of the sun's energy to heat something, without storing the energy.

petroleum: crude oil, formed by decay of ancient plants and animals; a fossil fuel that is burned and used to make lubricants and plastics. (644)

period: a horizontal row of elements in the periodic table; increasing from left to right is the number of electrons in the atoms' outer shells. (260)

periodic table: a table of the elements, in order by increasing atomic mass, arranged in rows and columns to show their repeated (periodic) properties. (255)

pH: a measure of hydronium ion (H_3O^+) concentration in a water solution, expressed on the pH scale from 0 to 14. From 7 down to 0, a solution is increasingly acidic; at 7 it is neutral (pure water); from 7 up to 14, a solution is increasingly basic. (pH = *p*otential of *H*ydrogen) (435)

phenolphthalein (feen ul THAYL een): a chemical used as a color indicator in titration; colorless in an acidic solution, but turns pink in a basic solution.

photon: a particle of light. (485)

photovoltaic cell: a solar cell; a semiconductor that converts light energy into electrical energy. (657)

physical change: a change in a substance's size, shape, color, or state (solid, liquid, gas). (230)

physical property: any characteristic of a material that you can observe, such as state, shape, size, or color. (228)

physical science: the study of matter and energy. (7)

pickling: a process that removes oxides and other impurities from steel and other metal surfaces by dipping them in hydrochloric acid. (429)

pitch: the highness or lowness of a sound, which is determined by the frequency (wavelength) of the sound. (466)

plane mirror: a mirror with a flat surface. (512)

plankton: tiny plants and animals that live in water and are food for small fish; they are easily killed by acid rain. (439)

plasma: a gaslike mixture of positively and negatively charged particles; it is the commonest state of matter in the universe. (194)

plastic: a material made from synthetic organic polymers that can be easily molded; nylon and polyethylene are examples. (362)

polarized light: light in which the waves vibrate only in one plane. (528)

polarizing filter: a filter made of chains of molecules in parallel rows that will transmit only light waves vibrating in the same direction as the molecular chains.

polar molecule: a molecule in which one atom has a stronger attraction for electrons than the other, giving the molecule a positive end and a negative end. (278)

polluted water: water that is contaminated with substances that may be harmful to living things. (199)

polyatomic ion: a group of covalently bonded atoms in which the whole group has a positive or negative charge, like NH_4^+ or CO_3^{2-} (286)

polymer: a huge molecule made of many smaller organic molecules (monomers) linked together; examples are proteins and plastics. (340)

positron: a positively charged electron.

potential difference: the difference in electric potential energy between two different points. (552)

potential energy: energy that is not causing change right now but is stored for potential use, as in a battery or a wound-up spring. (111)

power: the rate at which work is done; power = work ÷ time. (177)

precipitate: an insoluble solid that settles out of a chemical reaction occurring in a liquid. (414)

pressure: the amount of force exerted per unit of area; pressure = force ÷ area. (204)

principle: a basic rule or law describing how something always works in the natural world; for example, "gravity always pulls objects toward each other."

products: in a chemical reaction, the substances formed by the reaction. (404)

projectile: any object shot or thrown through the air. (90)

propane: a flammable gas (C_3H_8); a part of natural gas.

protein: an organic polymer formed from amino acids; various proteins make up many body tissues. (340)

proton: one of the two types of particles (protons and neutrons) that occur in the nucleus of an atom; a proton has a positive charge. (243)

pulley: a simple machine consisting of a grooved wheel with a rope or a chain running along the groove; it changes the direction and/or amount of force. (166)

700

quality: in sound, the differences among sounds that have the same pitch and loudness. (475)

quark: a very small particle of matter that makes up protons and neutrons; five or six different quark types may exist. (248)

radiation: the transfer of energy through matter or space by electromagnetic waves such as heat, light, radio waves, X rays and gamma rays. (136, 484)

radiator: a device with a large surface area that transfers heat to surrounding air by conduction. (142)

radioactive element: an unstable element (like uranium) that naturally decays to form other elements by radiation (expelling an alpha particle, beta particle, or gamma ray from the atom's nucleus). (302)

radioactivity: the emission of particles or gamma rays from the nucleus of an atom that is unstable and radioactive. (621)

radio waves: electromagnetic waves that have long wavelengths (low frequencies). (485)

radius: the distance from the center of a circle to its circumference.

RAM: *r*andom-*a*ccess *m*emory in a computer; the temporary electronic memory in a chip that "forgets" as soon as the power is turned off. (608)

rarefaction: in compressional waves, the less dense area of the wave.

reactants: in a chemical reaction, the substances you start with before the reaction. (404)

real image: an image produced where light rays converge, as with a concave mirror or convex lens; a real image can be projected on a screen. (514)

rectifier: a device that changes alternating current into direct current. (599)

recycling: reprocessing of waste products into new products; for example, aluminum cans are recycled to make other aluminum cans or foil. (360)

reflecting telescope: an optical instrument that uses a concave mirror and a convex lens to magnify distant objects. (523)

reflection: bouncing of a wave off an object; this includes all types of waves—light, sound, radio, ocean, and so on. (500)

refraction: the bending of waves, caused by changing their speed. (501)

resistance: the opposition to the flow of electrons through a conductor, measured in ohms with an ohmmeter. (555)

resistance arm: the part of a lever that exerts the resistance force (F_r). (163)

resistance force (F_r): the force exerted by a machine to overcome resistance to gravity or friction. (159)

resonance: the tendency of an object to vibrate at the same frequency as a sound source. (475)

reverberation: the echoing effect produced by multiple reflections of sound. (477)

RNA: *r*ibo*n*ucleic *a*cid, a nucleic acid that controls production of proteins that make new cells.

ROM: *r*ead-*o*nly *m*emory in a computer; it is permanent memory stored inside the computer, even when the power is turned off. (609)

salt: a compound containing negative ions from an acid combined with positive ions from a base; forms during a neutralization reaction. (440)

saponification: the process of making soap. (443)

saturated hydrocarbon: a hydrocarbon compound in which each carbon atom is joined to four other atoms by single covalent bonds; an example is methane gas (CH_4). (331)

saturated solution: a solution that has dissolved all the solute it can hold at a specific temperature. (390)

scientific law: a rule that describes a pattern in nature and predicts what will happen under specific conditions. (16)

screw: a simple machine consisting of an inclined plane wrapped in a spiral around a cylindrical post; it changes the amount of force. (169)

second: the SI unit of time. (40)

semiconductor: an element that conducts electricity under certain conditions; in the periodic table, semiconductors are between metals and nonmetals. (317)

series circuit: an electrical circuit where the current flows only in one path. If the path is interrupted at any point, it stops current flow in the entire circuit. (561)

SI: International System of Units, the standard worldwide system of measurement used by all scientists; a modern version of the metric system. (31)

simple machine: a device that performs work with only one movement. Simple machines include the lever, pulley, wheel and axle, inclined plane, screw, and wedge. (158)

single displacement reaction: a chemical reaction in which one element replaces another element in a compound. (414)

smog: a form of air pollution; a colloid in which invisible solid particles mix with the air gases that we breathe. (226)

soap: an organic salt made by reacting fats or oils with a strong base such as sodium hydroxide. (443)

solar collector: a device that absorbs radiant energy from the sun. (144)

solar energy: energy from the sun, which includes heat, light, radio, ultraviolet, gamma, and other waves. (144)

701

solubility: the amount of a substance (solute) that will dissolve in a solvent; scientifically it is how many grams of solute will dissolve in 100 g of a solvent, at a specific temperature. (388)

solute: the substance being dissolved in a solvent; for example, in a sweet drink sugar is the solute and water is the solvent. (381)

solution: a homogeneous mixture containing tiny particles that don't settle and don't scatter light. (222)

solvent: the substance that dissolves a solute; for example, in a sweet drink sugar is the solute and water is the solvent. (381)

specific heat: the amount of energy needed to raise the temperature of 1 kilogram of a material 1 degree Celsius. (124)

speed: the rate of motion, or the rate of change in position. (60)

standard: in measurement, an exact quantity that everyone agrees to use for comparison; for example, a meter, kilogram, liter, kelvin, joule, and so on. (30)

state of matter: any of the four conditions in which matter can exist: solid, liquid, gas, or plasma. (190)

static electricity: the accumulation of electric charges on an object. No current flows because the electricity is static (motionless). (546)

step-down transformer: an electrical transformer that decreases (steps down) the voltage of a power line.

step-up transformer: an electrical transformer that increases (steps up) the voltage of a power line.

strong acid: an acid that ionizes almost completely in water solution, thus containing large numbers of hydronium ions (H_3O^+); for example, hydrochloric acid. (434)

strong base: a base that dissociates almost completely in water solution, thus containing a large number of hydroxide ions (OH^-); for example, sodium hydroxide. (435)

sublimation: a type of evaporation in which a solid changes directly to a gas without going through a liquid state. (313)

submerge: to fully immerse (completely cover) something in a fluid.

substance: matter that is an element or a compound. (221)

substituted hydrocarbon: a hydrocarbon in which one or more hydrogen atoms have been replaced by atoms of other elements. (335)

supercollider: a device to make protons collide at high speed so they break apart into quarks.

superconductor: a supercooled material that has no electrical resistance and so is a "super" conductor of electricity. (588)

supersaturated solution: an unstable solution that contains more solute than the solvent can dissolve at a specific temperature. (392)

suspension: a heterogeneous mixture containing larger particles that eventually settle out. (224)

synthesis reaction: a chemical reaction in which two or more substances combine to form a different substance. (413)

synthetic fiber: a strand of a synthetic polymer; examples are nylon, rayon, and Kevlar fibers. (365)

technology: the application of scientific knowledge to improve the quality of human life. (7)

telephoto lens: a lens having a long focal length and producing an enlarged, closeup image of an object. (525)

temperature: a measure of the average kinetic energy of the particles in matter; expressed in degrees kelvin or Celsius. (118)

terminal velocity: the greatest velocity reached by a falling object. (89)

theory: a solution to a problem; a former hypothesis that has been tested with repeated experiments and observations and found always to work. (16)

thermal energy: the total energy of particles in a material, including both kinetic and potential energy. (119)

thermal expansion: a characteristic of matter causing it to expand when heated and contract when cooled. (195)

thermal pollution: pollution caused when waste thermal energy raises the temperature of the environment. (146)

thermonuclear fusion: nuclear fusion that occurs under conditions of enormous heat (millions of degrees), as in a star or our sun.

tidal energy: electricity generated by the ocean tides. (658)

time: the interval between two events; the SI unit is the second. (40)

titration: a method for finding the concentration of an acidic or basic solution, using a solution of known concentration. (442)

total internal reflection: occurs when all the light entering an object is reflected internally, maintaining the intensity of the light. (531)

toxic: describes any substance that can injure living tissue; a poison. (274)

tracer: a radioactive isotope used for medical diagnosis; it allows a doctor to trace the location of tumors and fluid movements in the body.

transformer: a device that transforms electrical current to a higher voltage or a lower voltage. (586)

transistor: a semiconductor that amplifies an electrical signal. (599)

transition element: an element in Groups 3-12 of the periodic table; each is metallic, with one or two electrons in its outer energy level. (304)

translucent materials: materials that can be partially seen through because they allow some light to pass, but not enough for a clear image. (492)

702

transmutation: changing one element to another through radioactive decay; for example, uranium-238 is transmuted into lead-206 after enough particles and rays have been emitted from its nucleus. (625)

transparent materials: materials that can be seen through because they allow nearly all light to pass through them. (492)

transuranium element: any element beyond uranium in the periodic table (having a higher atomic number than 92); these radioactive synthetic elements are made in laboratories or nuclear reactors. (309)

transverse wave: a wave that vibrates at right angles to the direction the wave is traveling. (458)

trough: in waves, the lowest point of a wave. (459)

Tyndall effect: the scattering of light by particles in a mixture, as occurs with a flashlight beam in the night sky. (226)

ultraviolet radiation: electromagnetic waves that have a wavelength slightly shorter (higher frequency) than visible light; abbreviated *UV*. (489)

unsaturated hydrocarbon: a hydrocarbon compound in which each carbon atom is joined to other atoms by double or triple covalent bonds; an example is acetylene. (331)

unsaturated solution: a solution that is capable of dissolving more solute at a specific temperature. (391)

velocity: the rate of motion in a specific direction. (65)

virtual image: an image formed of diverging light rays, as in a flat or convex mirror, or seen through a concave lens. A virtual image isn't "real" and can't be projected. (513)

visible radiation: electromagnetic waves in the only part of the electromagnetic spectrum we can see—light. (488)

volt: the unit for measuring electrical potential energy, abbreviated *V*.

voltage: a difference in electrical potential, measured in volts with a voltmeter.

voltmeter: a galvanometer that measures electrical potential differences in a circuit, in volts. (580)

volume: the amount of space occupied by an object; its SI unit is the cubic meter (m^3). (37)

Watt (W): the unit of power, one joule per second. (177)

wave: a rhythmic disturbance that carries energy through matter or space. Mechanical waves require a medium to travel in; electromagnetic waves can travel either through a medium or space. (458)

wavelength: the distance between a point on one wave and the identical point on the next wave; for example, the distance between two crests or two troughs. (459)

weak acid: an acid that ionizes only partially in water solution, thus creating a small number of hydronium ions (H_3O^+); for example, acetic acid. (434)

weak base: a base that dissociates only partially in water solution, thus creating a small number of hydroxide ions (OH^-); for example, magnesium hydroxide. (435)

wedge: a simple machine consisting of an inclined plane with one or two sloping sides; examples are a chisel, knife, and axe. It changes the amount of force. (170)

weight: the measure of the force of gravity on an object, usually the force between Earth and an object at its surface. (76)

wet cell: a power source that generates electric current by a chemical reaction; "wet" because it uses a liquid electrolyte, as in an automobile battery. (555)

wheel and axle: a simple machine consisting of two wheels of different sizes that are connected so they rotate together, such as a doorknob or wheel-handled faucet; it changes the amount of force. (167)

wide-angle lens: a lens having a short focal length and producing a relatively small image of an object, but including much of the object's surroundings. (525)

work: the transfer of energy through motion; work = force × distance. (112)

X rays: electromagnetic waves having a wavelength shorter (higher frequency) than ultraviolet radiation; often used in medical photography because they can penetrate human tissue. (490)

INDEX

The Index for *Merrill Physical Science* will help you locate major topics in the book quickly and easily. Each entry in the Index is followed by the numbers of the pages on which the entry is discussed. A page number given in **boldface type** indicates the page on which that entry is defined. A page number given in *italic type* indicates a page on which the entry is used in an illustration or photograph. The abbreviation *act.* indicates a page on which the entry is used in an activity.

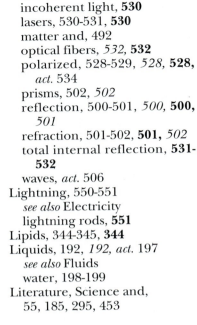

PHOTO CREDITS

(r)StudiOhio; **304,** Doug Martin; **305,** (t)Doug Martin, (b)NASA; **306,** (l)Ken Frick, (r)Doug Martin; **307,** Doug Martin; **308,** Ken Frick; **309,** Martin Bond/Photo Researchers; **311,** Annie Griffiths/Westlight; **312,** (t)Ken Frick, (b)Doug Martin; **313,** (t)Ken Frick, (b)Ben Simmons/The Stock Market; **314,** Dan McCoy/Rainbow; **315,** Doug Martin; **317,** (t)StudiOhio, (c)(r)Doug Martin; **318,** Ken Frick; **319,** Doug Martin; **320,** Manfred Kage/Peter Arnold Inc.; **321,** Ken Frick; **322,** Doug Martin; **324,** Ken Frick; **326,327,328,** Doug Martin; **329,** (t)R. Krubner/H. Armstrong Roberts, (c)Phil Degginger, (b)Doug Martin; **330,** Ken Frick; **331,** (t)Doug Martin, (b)Steve Strickland/Westlight; **332,** (t)StudiOhio, (b)Ken Frick; **334,** (l)Skinnet-Veron/Fig. Mag/Gamma Liaison, (r)Ken Frick; **335,** (t)Ken Frick, (b)Doug Martin; **337,** Doug Martin; **338,** Mark N. Boulton/Photo Researchers; **339,** Bruce Sampsel; **340,** (t)Ken Frick, (l)CNRI/Science Photo Library/Photo Researchers, (r)Lab. of Molecular Biology, MCR/Science Photo Library/Photo Researchers; **341,** (t)Elaine Comer-Shay, (b)Doug Martin; **342,** Nelson Max/CCNL/Photo Researchers; **343,** Ken Frick; **344,** (t)Courtesy of the Simplesse Company, (b)Ken Frick; **345,** Ken Frick; **346,** Doug Martin; **348,** Ken Frick; **350,** ©Terry O'Neill/Woodfin Camp & Associates, (l&r)Ken Frick; **351,** StudiOhio; **352,** FPG International; **353,** Ken Frick; **354,** (t)Ed Degginger, (tr)(c)(br)Doug Martin; **355,** (t)Tim Courlas, (b)Mike Devlin/Science Photo Library/Photo Researchers; **356,** Bill Tronca/Tom Stack & Assoc.; **357,** (t)The Smithsonian Institution, (bl)(br)Ken Frick, (c)BLT Productions; **358,359,** Doug Martin; **360,** William E. Ferguson; **361,** Randall L. Schieber; **362,** Ken Frick; **365,** (t)StereoLithography is a proprietary product of 3D Systems, Inc., (b)Doug Martin; **366,** Doug Martin; **367,** (l)Dan McCoy, (r)Ken Frick; **368,369,** Doug Martin; **370,** Ken Frick; **372,** (t)Michael Doolittle/Rainbow, (b)Carl Frank/Photo Researchers; **373,** (t)Blaine Harrington III/The Stock Market, (c)Courtesy of General Motors, (b)The Bettmann Archive; **374,** (tl)Doug Martin, (tr)Bill Weems/Woodfin Camp & Associates, (bl)Aaron Haupt, (br)Pictures Unlimited; **375,** Photo from the Collection of Michele Tofoya; **376-377,** Hans Pfletschinger/Peter Arnold Inc.; **377,** Jeffrey M. Spielman/Stockphotos; **378,** Steven Burr Williams/The Image Bank; **379,** StudiOhio; **380,** Ken Frick; **381,** (t)Doug Martin, (tc)Ken Frick, (b)Doug Martin; **384,** Bud Fowle; **385,** Ken Frick; **386,** Bill Ross/Westlight; **388,** Doug Martin; **389,** Latent Images; **392,393,394,** Doug Martin; **395,** Ken Frick; **398,399,** Doug Martin; **401,** Bud Fowle; **402,** Guido Alberto Rossi/The Image Bank; **403,** Ken Frick; **404,** Culver Pictures; **405,** Doug Martin; **407,** ZEFZ-U.K./H. Armstrong Roberts; **408,** NASA; **409,** StudiOhio; **412,** Doug Martin; **414,** (t)Ken Frick, (b)Doug Martin; **416,** Doug Martin; **417,** Lawrence Hughes/The Image Bank; **418,** (t)Tim Courlas, (b)Grant Heilman; **420,** Doug Martin; **422,** Ted Rice; **424,** Ron Watts/Westlight; **425,** Doug Martin; **426,** (t)StudiOhio, (b)Doug Martin; **428,** Doug Martin; **429,** (t)First Image, (b)Aaron Haupt; **430,431,** Ken Frick; **434,435,437,** Doug Martin; **438,** Tom McHugh/Photo Researchers; **439,** Runk/Schoenberger from Grant Heilman; **441,** Doug Martin; **442,** (t)Tim Courlas, (b)Doug Martin; **446,** Doug Martin; **448,** Tim Courlas; **449,** Panographics/L. S. Stepanowicz; **450,** (t)Tom Bean/The Stock Market, (b)Phil Degginger; **451,** (t)The Bettman Archive, (c)Culver Pictures, (b)Francis Current/Photo Researchers; **452,** (tl)Doug Martin, (tr)Roger Tully/TSW, (bl)Doug Martin, (br)Steve Weber/TSW; **453,** The Salt Institute; **454-455,** Courtesy of Dr. Otis Brown, Rosentiel School of Marine and Atmospheric Science, University of Miami; **455,** NASA; **456,** Doug Martin; **457,** StudiOhio; **458,** Steve Lissau; **463,** StudiOhio; **465,** Ed Degginger; **467,** Burton McNeely/The Image Bank; **469,** Doug Martin; **471,472,473,** StudiOhio; **475,478**(t), Doug Martin; **478**(inset),**480,** StudiOhio; **482,** Pete Saloutos/The Stock Market; **483,** Shay/Gerard; **484,** File Photo; **486,** (tl)StudiOhio, (r)Tim Courlas, (b)StudiOhio; **487,** (l)Dan McCoy/Rainbow, (r)© Howard Sochurek/The Stock Market; **488,** Bud Fowle; **489,** StudiOhio; **490,** Science Photo Library/Photo Researchers; **491,** Doug Martin; **492,493,494,** StudiOhio; **497,** Doug Martin; **498,499,500,** StudiOhio; **501,** Pictures Unlimited; **502,** (l)Ed Degginger, (r)Kodak; **503,** Vance A. Tucker; **504,505,** Dan McCoy/Rainbow; **506,** Doug Martin; **508,** Allen Zak; **510,** Cobalt Productions; **511,513,** StudiOhio; **514,** (t)Aaron Haupt, (b)Latent Images; **515,516,517,** Doug Martin; **522,** (l)Kurt Thorson, (r)Johnny Johnson; **525,** Doug Martin; **526,** NASA; **528,** Cobalt Productions; **529,** (t)StudiOhio, (b)Doug Martin; **531,** (t)Lou Jones/The Image Bank, (b)Doug Martin; **532,** John Feingersh 1988/The Stock Market; **533,** Tom Tracy Photography; **534,** Doug Martin; **536,** StudiOhio; **538,** (t)Garry Gay/The Image Bank, (b)Michael Parfit; **539,** (t)Chuck O'Rear/Westlight, (c)The Bettmann Archive, (b)William E. Ferguson; **540,** (tl)Ted Kawalerski/The Image Bank, (cl)Ken Frick, (tr)StudiOhio, (br)Ken Frick; **541,** Art Resource; **542-543,** D. W. Hamilton/The Image Bank; **543,** Jean Marc Giboux/Gamma Liaison; **544,** Hank Morgan/Rainbow; **545,547,** StudiOhio; **548,** Steven Burr Williams/The Image Bank; **550,** © Thomas Ives/The Stock Market; **551,** 1986 © Mark Gibson/The Stock Market; **555,** (t)T. J. Florian/Rainbow, (b)StudiOhio; **556,** Sheffield University/Science Photo Library/Photo Researchers; **557,** StudiOhio; **559,** Doug Martin; **560,561,** Tim Courlas; **562,** StudiOhio; **563,** (t)Elaine Comer-Shay, (b)Doug Martin; **564,** Doug Martin; **567,** Mark Burnett; **570,** Ken Frick; **572,** Larry Hamill; **572(inset),** Doug Martin; **573,** Ken Frick; **574,575,576,** Doug Martin; **579,** P&G Bowater/The Image Bank; **582,** Doug Martin; **585,** Ken Frick; **587,** Joe Bator/The Stock Market; **588,** Lou Jones/The Image Bank; **589,** © 1989 Makoto Iwafuji/The Stock Market; **590,** Doug Martin; **592,** StudiOhio; **594,595,** StudiOhio; **596,** StudiOhio; **598,** Doug Martin; **599,** (t)Ken Frick, (b)Doug Martin; **600,** Doug Martin; **601,** StudiOhio; **604,** Hank Morgan/Rainbow; **605,606,** StudiOhio; **607,** The Bettmann Archive; **609,** Hickson & Associates; **610,611,** Doug Martin; **612,** Hickson & Associates; **613,614,** Doug Martin; **615,** StudiOhio; **618,** TSW; **619,** Ken Frick; **620,** Doug Martin; **622,** Hank Morgan/Photo Researchers; **626,** Ken Frick; **628,** Ed Degginger; **629,** Doug Martin; **630,** Science Photo Library/Photo Researchers; **631,** Patrice Loiez, CERN/Science Photo Library/Photo Researchers; **636,637,638,** Doug Martin; **642,** Steve Dunwell/The Image Bank; **643,** Doug Martin; **646,** Randall L. Schieber; **647,** Doug Martin; **648,** D.O.E./Science Source/Photo Researchers; **649,** Light Source; **651,** (t)Y. Arthus-Bertrand/Peter Arnold Inc., (b)Gordon Gahar/Lawrence Livermore Laboratory; **653,** Doug Martin; **654,** Dan McCoy/Rainbow; **655,** Ed Degginger; **657,** Mike Brown/Gamma Liaison; **658,** Coco McCoy/Rainbow; **659,** (b)Spencer Swanger/Tom Stack & Assoc., (r)Ed Degginger; **660,** Barry Griffiths/Photo Researchers; **661,** David W. Hamilton/The Image Bank; **662,664,** Doug Martin; **666,** (tl)David Sailors/The Stock Market, (bl)Courtesy of Westinghouse Electric Corporation, (r)Hickson & Associates; **667,** (t)Blaine Harrington/The Stock Market, (b)First Image; **668,** (tl)Doug Martin, (tr)(br)Hickson & Associates, (bl)Doug Martin; **669,** Coco McCoy/Rainbow.

713